PHARMACOGRAPHIA

PHARMACOGRAPHIA

A HISTORY

OF

THE PRINCIPAL DRUGS

OF VEGETABLE ORIGIN,

MET WITH IN

GREAT BRITAIN AND BRITISH INDIA

FRIEDRICH A. FLUCKIGER,

DANIEL HANBURY, F.R.S.

GYAN

Published by

Gyan Publishing House
5, Ansari Road
Daryaganj, New Delhi-110002
Phone: 011-47034999, 9811692060
E-mail: books@gyanbooks.com

Distribution Network
gyanbooks.com
India, USA, Canada, UK, Australia, France

ISBN : 978-81-212-9452-2 (PB)
First Published, 1879

2nd Impression 2023

Printed at: Gyan Press, Delhi.

PHARMACOGRAPHIA
Author: FRIEDRICH A. FLUCKIGER , DANIEL HANBURY

PHARMACOGRAPHIA.

PHARMACOGRAPHIA.

A HISTORY

OF

THE PRINCIPAL DRUGS

OF VEGETABLE ORIGIN,

MET WITH IN

GREAT BRITAIN AND BRITISH INDIA.

BY

FRIEDRICH A. FLUCKIGER,

PHIL. DR., PROFESSOR IN THE UNIVERSITY OF STRASSBURG,

AND

DANIEL HANBURY, F.R.S.,

FELLOW OF THE LINNEAN AND CHEMICAL SOCIETIES OF LONDON.

SECOND EDITION

London:

MACMILLAN AND CO.

1879.

PHARMACOGRAPHIA.

PREFACE.

PHARMACOGRAPHIA, the word which gives the title to this book, indicates the nature of the work to which it has been prefixed. The term means simply a *writing about drugs;* and it has been selected not without due consideration, as in itself distinctive, easily quoted, and intelligible in many languages.

Pharmacographia, in its widest sense, embodies and expresses the joint intention of the authors. It was their desire, not only to write upon the general subject, and to utilize the thoughts of others; but that the book which they decided to produce together should contain observations that no one else had written down. It is in fact a record of personal researches on the principal drugs derived from the vegetable kingdom, together with such results of an important character as have been obtained by the numerous workers on Materia Medica in Europe, India, and America.

Unlike most of their predecessors in Great Britain during this century, the authors have not included in their programme either Pharmacy or Therapeutics; nor have they attempted to give their work that diversity of scope which would render it independent of collateral publications on Botany and Chemistry.

While thus restricting the field of their inquiry, the authors have endeavoured to discuss with fuller detail many points of interest which are embraced in the special studies of the pharmacist; and at the same time have occasionally indicated the direction in which further investigations are desirable. A few remarks on the heads under which each particular article is treated, will explain more precisely their design.

The drugs included in the present work are chiefly those which are commonly kept in store by pharmacists, or are known in the drug and spice market of London. The work likewise contains a small number which belong to the *Pharmacopœia of India:* the appearance of this volume seemed to present a favourable opportunity for giving some more copious notice of the latter than has hitherto been attempted.

Supplementary to these two groups must be placed a few substances which possess little more than historical interest, and have been introduced rather in obedience to custom, and for the sake of completeness, than on account of their intrinsic value.

Each drug is headed by the Latin name, followed by such few synonyms as may suffice for perfect identification, together in most cases with the English, French, and German designation.

In the next section, the *Botanical Origin* of the substance is discussed, and the area of its growth, or locality of its production is stated. Except in a few instances, no attempt has been made to furnish botanical descriptions of the plants to which reference is made. Such information may readily be obtained from original and special sources, of which we have quoted some of the most important.

Under the head of *History*, the authors have endeavoured to trace the introduction of each substance into medicine, and to bring forward other points in connection therewith, which have not hitherto been much noticed in any recent work. This has involved researches which have been carried on for several years, and has necessitated the consultation of many works of general literature. The exact titles of these works have been scrupulously preserved, in order to enable the reader to verify the statements made, and to prosecute further historical inquiries. In this portion of their task, the authors have to acknowledge the assistance kindly given them by Professors Heyd[1] of Stuttgart, Winkelmann of Heidelberg, Monier Williams of Oxford, Dümichen of Strassburg; and on subjects connected with China, by Mr. A. Wylie and Dr. Bretschneider. The co-operation in various directions of many other friends has been acknowledged in the text itself.

In some instances the *Formation, Secretion*, or *Method of Collection* of a drug, has been next detailed: in others, the section *History* has been immediately followed by the *Description*, succeeded by one in which the more salient features of *Microscopic Structure* have been set forth. The authors have not thought it desirable to amplify the last-named section, as the subject deserves to be treated in a special work, and to be illustrated by engravings. Written descriptions of micro-

[1] The admirable work of this author—*Geschichte des Levantehandels im Mittelalter*, 2 vols., Stuttgart, 1879—appeared when the second edition of our Pharmacographia was already in the press.

scopic structure are tedious and uninteresting, and however carefully drawn up, must often fail to convey the true meaning which would be easily made evident by the pencil. The reader who wishes for illustrations of the minute structure of drugs may consult the works named in the foot-note.[1]

The next division includes the important subject of *Chemical Composition*, in which the authors have striven to point out to the reader familiar with chemistry what are the constituents of greatest interest in each particular drug—what the characters of the less common of those constituents—and by whom and at what date the chief investigations have been made. A knowledge of the name and date provides a clue to the original memoir, which may usually be found, either *in extenso* or in abstract, in more than one periodical. It has been no part of the authors' plan to supersede reference to standard works on chemistry, or to describe the chemical character of substances[2] which may be easily ascertained from those sources of information which should be within the reach of every pharmaceutical inquirer.

In the section devoted to *Production and Commerce*, the authors have given such statistics and other trade information as they could obtain from reliable sources; but they regret that this section is of very unequal value. Duties have been abolished, and a general and continuous simplification of tariffs and trade regulations has ensued. The details, therefore, that used to be observed regarding the commerce in drugs, exists no longer in anything like their former state of completeness: hence the fragmentary nature of much of the information recorded under this head.

The medicinal uses of each particular drug are only slightly mentioned, it being felt that the science of therapeutics lies within the province of the physician, and may be wisely relinquished to his care. At the same time it may be remarked that the authors would have rejoiced had they been able to give more definite information as to the technical or economic uses of some of the substances they have described.

[1] Berg, *Anatomischer Atlas zur pharmazeutischen Waarenkunde*, Berlin, 1865. 4to., with 50 plates.

Flückiger, *Grundlagen der pharmaceutischen Waarenkunde, Einleitung in das Studium der Pharmacognosie*, Berlin, 1873.

Planchon, *Traité pratique de la détermination des drogues simples d'origine végétale*, Paris, 1874.

Luerssen, *Medicinisch-Pharmaceutische Botanik*, Leipzig (in progress).

[2] For further information, see Flückiger, *Pharmaceutische Chemie*, Berlin, 1879.

What has been written under the head of *Adulteration* is chiefly the result of actual observation, or might otherwise have been much extended. The authors would rather rely on the characters laid down in preceding sections than upon empirical methods for the determination of purity. The heading of *Substitutes* has been adopted for certain drugs, more or less related to those described in special articles, yet not actually used by way of adulteration.

A work professing to bring together the latest researches in any subject will naturally be thought to contain needless innovations. Whilst deprecating the inconvenience of changes of nomenclature, the authors have had no alternative but to adopt the views sanctioned by the leaders of chemical and botanical science, and which the progress of knowledge has required. The common designations of drugs may indeed remain unchanged:—hellebore, aconite, colchicum, anise, and caraway, need no modernizing touch. But when we attempt to combine with these simple names, words to indicate the organ of the plant of which they are constituted, questions arise as to the strict application of such terms as root, rhizome, tuber, corm, about which a diversity of opinion may be entertained.

It has been the authors' aim to investigate anew the field of Vegetable Materia Medica, in order as far as possible to clear up doubtful points, and to remove some at least of the uncertainties by which the subject is surrounded. In furtherance of this plan they have availed themselves of the resources offered by Ancient and Modern History; nor have they hesitated to lay under contribution either the teaching of men eminent in science, or the labours of those who follow the paths of general literature. How far they have accomplished their desire remains for the public to decide.

CORRIGENDA.

Page 57, foot-note 4; *for* qui produit, *read* qui a produit.
,, 86, 13th line from bottom; *for* Bauchin, *read* Bauhin.
,, 128, foot-note 3; *read* Adversariorum, *for* Adersariorum.
,, 161, line from top; *read* southern and south-western part, *for* northern part.
,, 265, foot-note 2, *for* 4794 grammes, *read* 4·794 grammes.
,, 271, line 5 from bottom; *read* στύραξ ὑγρὸς *for* πύρα ξυγρὸς.
,, 368, line 12 from bottom; *read* Flora, *for* Floræ.
,, ,, ,, 20 ,, ,, mossing, *for* motsing.
,, 369, ,, 17 from top; *read* José, *for* Jose.
,, 404, ,, 2 from bottom; *read* Xarnauz, *for* Xarnaux.
,, ,, foot-note 7; *read* por, *for* par.
,, ,, line 12 from bottom; *read* Barbarigo, *for* Barberigo.
,, 407, ,, 5 ,, ,, benzoic, *for* benzoin.
,, 469, lines 21 and 24 from top; with reference to *Nicotiana rustica* and *N. repanda*, see *Pharm. Journ.* ix. (1878) 710.
,, 558, foot-note 3; *read* 562, *for* 652.
,, 559, line 24 from top; *read* 1849, *for* 1749.

PREFACE TO THE SECOND EDITION.

THE premature death—March 24, 1875—of my lamented friend Daniel Hanbury, having deprived me of his invaluable assistance, I have attempted to prepare the new edition of our work with adherence to the same principles by which we were guided from the beginning.

I desire to acknowledge my obligations for great and valuable assistance to my friend Thomas Hanbury, Esq., F.L.S., who has also honoured the memory of his late brother by causing the scientific researches of the latter to be collected and republished in the handsome volume entitled, "Science Papers, chiefly Pharmacological and Botanical, by Daniel Hanbury, edited, with memoir, by Joseph Ince," London. 1876. To Dr. Charles Rice of New York, editor of "New Remedies," I am indebted for much kindly extended and valuable information, and to whose intimate acquaintance with oriental literature, both ancient and modern, many of the following pages bear ample testimony. I am likewise indebted for similar assistance to my friends Professors Goldschmidt and Nöldeke, Strassburg. Information of various kinds, as well as valuable specimens of drugs, have also been courteously supplied to me by the following gentlemen, viz.:—Cesar Chantre, Esq., F.L.S., London; Prof. Dymock, Bombay; H. Fritzsche, Esq. (Schimmel & Co., Leipzig); E. M. Holmes, Esq., F.L.S., &c., London; J. E. Howard, Esq., F.R.S., &c., London; David Howard, Esq., F.C.S., &c.; Wm. Dillworth Howard, F.I.C., London; Capt. F. M. Hunter, F.G.S., &c., Assistant Resident, Aden; A. Oberdörffer, Esq., Hamburg; Prof. Edward Schär, Zürich; Dr. J. E. de Vry, the Hague, &c.

On mature consideration, it was deemed expedient to omit in the new edition a large number of references relating more especially to chemical facts. Yet, in most instances, not only the author but also the year has been stated in which the respective observation or discovery was made, or at least the year in which it was published or recorded. Every such fact of any importance may thus, by means of those short references, be readily traced and consulted, if wished for, either in the original sources, in abstracts therefrom, or in the periodical reports. Opportunities of the latter kind are abundantly afforded by the German *Jahresbericht der Pharmacie*, &c., published at Göttingen since 1844, successively by Martius, Wiggers, Husemann, and at the present time by Dragendorff. The same may be said, since 1857, of the *Report on the Progress of Pharmacy*, as contained annually in the Proceedings of the American Pharmaceutical Association, and likewise, since 1870, of the *Yearbook of Pharmacy*, for which the profession is indebted to the British Pharmaceutical Conference.

PROF. FLÜCKIGER.

STRASSBURG, GERMANY, *October*, 1879.

EXPLANATIONS.

Polarization.—Most essential oils, and the solutions of several substances described in this book are capable of effecting the deviation of a ray of polarized light. The amount of this rotatory power cannot be regarded as constant in essential oils, and is greatly influenced by various causes. As to alkaloids and other organic compounds, the deviation frequently depends upon the nature and quantity of the solvent. The authors have thought it needful to record in numerous cases the results of such optical investigations, as determined by means of the *Polaristrobometer* invented by Wild, and described in Poggendorff's *Annalen der Physik und Chemie*, vol. 122 (1864) p. 626; or more completely in the *Bulletin de l'Académie impériale des Sciences de St. Pétersbourg*, tome viii. (1869) p. 33.

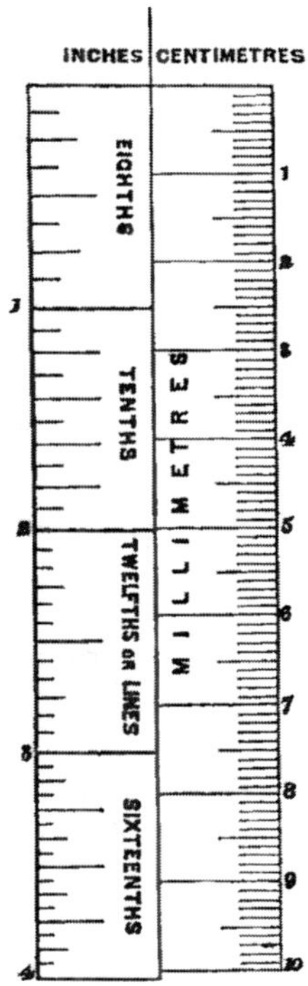

Measurements and Weights.—The authors regret to have been unable to adopt one standard system of stating measurements. They have mostly employed the English inch: the accompanying woodcut will facilitate its comparison with the French decimal scale. The word *millimetre* is indicated in the text by the contraction *mm.*; *micromillimetre*, signifying the thousandth part of a millimetre, and only used in reference to the microscope, is abbreviated thus, *mkm.*

1 inch	=	25·399 millimetres.		
1 gallon	=	4·543 litres.		
1 ounce (oz.) avdp.	=	28·34 grammes.		
1 lb. avoirdupois	=	453·59 „		
1 cwt.	=	112 lb.	=	50·8 kilogrammes.
1 ton	=	2240 „	=	1016 „
1 kilogramme	=	2·204 lb. avoirdupois.		
1 pecul	=	133·33 lb.	=	60·479 kilogrammes.

Thermometer.—The *Centigrade Thermometer* has been alone adopted. The following table is given *for comparing the degrees of the Centigrade or Celsius Thermometer with those of Fahrenheit's Scale.*

THERMOMETRIC TABLE.

CENT.	FAHR.	CENT.	FAHR.	CENT.	FAHR.	CENT.	FAHR.
— 29°	— 20·2°	+ 41°	+ 105·8°	+ 111	+ 231·8	+ 181	+ 357·8
28	18·4	42	107·6	112	233·6	182	359·6
27	16·6	43	109·4	113	235·4	183	361·4
26	14·8	44	111·2	114	237·2	184	363·2
25	13·0	45	113·0	115	239·0	185	365·0
24	11·2	46	114·8	116	240·8	186	366·8
23	9·4	47	116·6	117	242·6	187	368·6
22	7·6	48	118·4	118	244·4	188	370·4
21	5·8	49	120·2	119	246·2	189	372·2
20	4·0	50	122·0	120	248·0	190	374·0
19	2·2	51	123·8	121	249·8	191	375·8
18	— 0·4	52	125·6	122	251·6	192	377·6
17	+ 1·4	53	127·4	123	253·4	193	379·4
16	3·2	54	129·2	124	255·2	194	381·2
15	5·0	55	131·0	125	257·0	195	383·0
14	6·8	56	132·8	126	258·8	196	384·8
13	8.6	57	134·6	127	260·6	197	386·6
12	10·4	58	136·4	128	262·4	198	388·4
11	12·2	59	138·2	129	264·2	199	390·2
10	14·0	60	140·0	130	266·0	200	392·0
9	15·8	61	141·8	131	267·8	201	393·8
8	17·6	62	143·6	132	269·6	202	395·6
7	19·4	63	145·4	133	271·4	203	397·4
6	21·2	64	147·2	134	273·2	204	399·2
5	23·0	65	149·0	135	275·0	205	401·0
4	24·8	66	150·8	136	276·8	206	402·8
3	26·6	67	152·6	137	278·6	207	404·6
2	28·4	68	154·4	138	280·4	208	406·4
— 1	30·2	69	156·2	139	282·2	209	408·2
0	32·0	70	158·0	140	284·0	210	410·0
+ 1	33·8	71	159·8	141	285·8	211	411·8
2	35·6	72	161·6	142	287·6	212	413·6
3	37·4	73	163·4	143	289·4	213	415·4
4	39·2	74	165·2	144	291·2	214	417·2
5	41·0	75	167·0	145	293·0	215	419·0
6	42·8	76	168·8	146	294·8	216	420·8
7	44·6	77	170·6	147	296·6	217	422·6
8	46·4	78	172·4	148	298·4	218	424·4
9	48·2	79	174·2	149	300·2	219	426·2
10	50·0	80	176·0	150	302·0	220	428·0
11	51·8	81	177·8	151	303·8	221	429·8
12	53·6	82	179·6	152	305·6	222	431·6
13	55·4	83	181·4	153	307·4	223	433·4
14	57·2	84	183·2	154	309·2	224	435·2
15	59·0	85	185·0	155	311·0	225	437·0
16	60·8	86	186·8	156	312·8	226	438·8
17	62·6	87	188·6	157	314·6	227	440·6
18	64·4	88	190·4	158	316·4	228	442·4
19	66·2	89	192·2	159	318·2	229	444·2
20	68·0	90	194·0	160	320·0	230	446·0
21	69·8	91	195·8	161	321·8	231	447·8
22	71·6	92	197·6	162	323·6	232	449·6
23	73·4	93	199·4	163	325·4	233	451·4
24	75·2	94	201·2	164	327·2	334	453·2
25	77·0	95	203·0	165	329·0	235	455·0
26	78·8	96	204·8	166	330·8	236	456·8
27	80·6	97	206·6	167	332·6	237	458·6
28	82·4	98	208·4	168	334·4	238	460·4
29	84·2	99	210·2	169	336·3	239	462·2
30	86·0	100	212·0	170	338·0	240	464·0
31	87·8	101	213·8	171	339·8	241	465·8
32	89·6	102	215·6	172	341·6	242	467·6
33	91·4	103	217·4	173	343·4	243	469·4
34	93·2	104	219·2	174	345·2	244	471·2
35	95·0	105	221·0	175	347·0	245	473·0
36	96·8	106	222·8	176	348·8	246	474·8
37	98·6	107	224·6	177	350·6	247	476·6
38	100·4	108	226·4	178	352·4	248	478·4
39	102·2	109	228·2	179	354·2	249	480·2
40	104·0	110	230·0	180	356·0	250	482·0

CONTENTS.

I.—PHÆNOGAMOUS OR FLOWERING PLANTS.

Dicotyledons and Gymnosperms.

CONTENTS.

Gymnosperms.

Monocotyledons.

II.—CRYPTOGAMOUS OR FLOWERLESS PLANTS.

Vascular Cryptogams.

Thallogens.

APPENDIX.

PHARMACOGRAPHIA.

I.—PHÆNOGAMOUS OR FLOWERING PLANTS.

Dicotyledons and Gymnosperms.

RANUNCULACEÆ.

RADIX HELLEBORI NIGRI.

Radix Ellebori nigri, Radix Melampodii; Black Hellebore Root;
F. *Racine d'Ellebore noir;* G. *Schwarze Nieswurzel.*

Botanical Origin—*Helleborus niger* L., a low perennial herb, native of sub-alpine woods in Southern and Eastern Europe. It is found in Provence, Northern Italy, Salzburg, Bavaria, Austria, Bohemia, and Silesia, as well as, according to Boissier,[1] in Continental Greece.

Under the name of *Christmas Rose*, it is often grown in English gardens on account of its handsome white flowers, which are put forth in mid-winter.

History—The story of the daughters of Prœtus, king of Argos, being cured of madness by the soothsayer and physician Melampus, who administered to them hellebore, has imparted great celebrity to the plant under notice.[2]

But admitting that the medicine of Melampus was really the root of a species of *Helleborus*, its identity with that of the present plant is extremely improbable. Several other species grow in Greece and Asia Minor, and Schroff[3] has endeavoured to show that of these, *H. orientalis* Lam. possesses medicinal powers agreeing better with the ancient accounts than those of *H. niger* L. He has also pointed out that the ancients employed not the entire root but only the bark separated from the woody column; and that in *H. niger* and *H. viridis* the peeling of the rhizome is impossible, but that in *H. orientalis* it may be easily effected.

[1] *Flora Orientalis*, i. (1867) 61.

[2] See the list of theses and memoirs on Hellebore given by Mérat and De Lens, *Dict.* iii. (1831) 472, 473.

[3] *Zeitschr. d. Gesellsch. d. Aerzte zu Wien.* 1860, No. 25; Canstatt's *Jahresbericht* for 1859. i. 47. 1860. i. 55.

According to the same authority the hellebores differ extremely in their medicinal activity. The most potent is *H. orientalis* Lam.; then follow *H. viridis* L. and *H. fœtidus* L. (natives of Britain), and *H. purpurascens* Waldst. et Kit., a Hungarian species, while *H. niger* is the weakest of all.[1]

Description—Black Hellebore produces a knotty, fleshy, brittle rhizome which creeps and branches slowly, forming in the course of years an intangled, interlacing mass, throwing out an abundance of stout, straight roots. Both rhizome and roots are of a blackish brown, but the younger roots are of lighter tint and are covered with a short woolly tomentum.

In commerce the rhizome is found with the roots more or less broken off and detached. It is in very knotty irregular pieces, 1 to 2 or 3 inches long and about $\frac{2}{10}$ to $\frac{3}{10}$ of an inch in diameter, internally whitish and of a horny texture. If cut transversely (especially after maceration), it shows a circle of white woody wedges, 8 to 12 in number, surrounded by a thick bark. The roots are unbranched, scarcely $\frac{1}{10}$ of an inch in diameter. The younger, when broken across, exhibit a thick bark encircling a simple woody cord; in the older this cord tends to divide into converging wedges which present a stellate appearance, though not so distinctly as in *Actæa*. The drug when cut or broken has a slight odour like that of senega. Its taste is bitterish and slightly acrid.

Microscopic Structure—The cortical part both of the rhizome and the rootlets exhibits no distinct medullary rays. In the rootlets the woody centre is comparatively small and enclosed by a narrow zone somewhat as in sarsaparilla. A distinct pith occurs in the rhizome but not always in the rootlets, their woody column forming one solid bundle or being divided into several. The tissue contains small starch granules and drops of fatty oil.

Chemical Composition—The earlier investigations of Black Hellebore by Gmelin, and Feneulle and Capron, and of Riegel indicated only the presence of the more usual constituents of plants.

Bastick, on the other hand, in 1852 obtained from the root a peculiar, non-volatile, crystalline, chemically-indifferent substance which he named *Helleborin*. It is stated to have a bitter taste and to produce in addition a tingling sensation on the tongue; to be slightly soluble in water, more so in ether, and to dissolve freely in alcohol.

Marmé and A. Husemann extracted helleborin (1864) by treating with hot water the green fatty matter which is dissolved out of the root by boiling alcohol. After recrystallization from alcohol, it is obtainable in shining, colourless needles, having the composition $C^{36}H^{42}O^{6}$. It is stated to be highly narcotic. Helleborin appears to be more abundant in *H. viridis* (especially in the older roots) than in *H. niger*, and yet to be obtainable only to the extent of 0·4 per mille. When it is boiled with dilute sulphuric acid, or still better with solution of zinc chloride, it is converted into sugar and *Helleboresin*, $C^{30}H^{38}O^{4}$.

Marmé and Husemann succeeded in isolating other crystallized principles from the leaves and roots of *H. niger* and *H. viridis*, by precipitation with phospho-molybdic acid. They obtained firstly a

[1] Between *purpurascens* and *niger*, Schroff places *L. ponticus* A. Br., a plant which Boissier holds to be simply *H. orientalis* Lam.

slightly acid glucoside which they named *Helleboreïn*. It occurs only in very small proportion, but is rather more abundant in *H. niger* than in *H. viridis*. When boiled with a dilute acid, helleboreïn, $C^{26}H^{44}O^{15}$, is resolved into *Helleboretin*, $C^{14}H^{20}O^{3}$, of a fine violet colour, and sugar, $C^{12}H^{24}O^{12}$. It is remarkable that helleboretin has no physiological action, though helleboreïn is stated to be poisonous.

An organic acid accompanying helleborin was regarded by Bastick as probably aconitic (equisetic) acid. There is no tannin in hellebore.

Uses—Black Hellebore is reputed to be a drastic purgative. In British medicine its employment is nearly obsolete, but the drug is still imported from Germany and sold for the use of domestic animals.

Adulteration—Black Hellebore root as found in the market is not always to be relied on, and without good engravings it is not easy to point out characters by which its genuineness can be made certain. In fact to ensure its recognition, some pharmacopœias required that it should be supplied with leaves attached.

The roots with which it is chiefly liable to be confounded are the following:—

1. *Helleborus viridis* L.—Although a careful comparison of authenticated specimens reveals certain small differences between the roots and rhizomes of this species and of *H. niger*, there are no striking characters by which they can be discriminated. The root of *H. viridis* is far more bitter and acrid than that of *H. niger*, and it exhibits more numerous drops of fatty oil. In German trade the two drugs are supplied separately, both being in use; but as *H. viridis* is apparently the rarer plant and its root is valued at 3 to 5 times the price of that of *H. niger*, it is not likely to be used for sophisticating the latter.

2. *Actæa spicata* L.—In this plant the rhizome is much thicker; the rootlets broken transversely display a cross or star, as figured in Flückiger's "Grundlagen" (see p. vii.), fig. 64, p. 76. The drug has but little odour; as it contains tannin its infusion is blackened by a persalt of iron, which is not the case with an infusion of Black Hellebore.

RHIZOMA COPTIDIS.

Radix Coptidis; Coptis Root, Mishmi Bitter, Mishmi Tita.

Botanical Origin—*Coptis Teeta* Wallich, a small herbaceous plant, still but imperfectly known, indigenous to the Mishmi mountains, eastward of Assam. It was first described in 1836 by Wallich.[1]

History—This drug under the name of *Mahmira* is used in Sind for inflammation of the eyes, a circumstance which enabled Pereira[2] to identify it with a substance bearing a nearly similar designation, mentioned by the early writers on medicine, and previously regarded as the root of *Chelidonium majus* L.

Thus we find that Paulus Ægineta in the 7th century was acquainted with a knotty root named Μαμιρὰς.[3] Rhazes, who according to

[1] *Trans. of Med. and Phys. Soc. of Calcutta*, viii. (1836) 85. Reprinted in *Pereira's* Materia Medica, vol. ii. part 2 (1857), 699.

[2] *Pharm. Journ.* xi. (1852) 204; also *Mat. Med. l.c.*

[3] See also Meyer, *Geschichte der Botanik*, ii. (1855) 419.

Choulant died in A.D. 923 or 932, mentions *Mamiran*, and it is also noticed by Avicenna a little later as a drug useful in diseases of the eye. *Μαμηρά* likewise occurs in exactly the same way in the writings of *Leo*, "Philosophus et Medicus."[1] Ibn Baytar called the drug *Mamiran* and *Uruk*, and described it as a small yellow root like turmeric, coming from China. Other writers of the middle ages allude to it under the name of *Memeren*.

Hajji Mahomed, in the account of Cathay which he gave to Ramusio (*circa* A.D. 1550) says that the *Mambroni chini*, by which we understand the root in question, is found in the mountains of Succuir (Suh-cheu) where rhubarb grows, and that it is a wonderful remedy for diseases of the eye.[2] In an official report published at Lahore in 1862,[3] *Mamiran-i-chini* is said to be brought from China to Yarkand.

The rhizome of *Coptis* is used by the Chinese under the names *Hwang-lien* and *Chuen-lien*.[4] It is enumerated by Cleyer[5] (1682) as "*radix pretiosa amara*," and was described in 1778 by Bergius[6] who received it from Canton.

More recently it was the subject of an interesting notice by Guibourt[7] who thought it to be derived from *Ophioxylon serpentinum* L., an apocyneous plant widely removed from *Coptis*. Its root was recommended in India by MacIsaac[8] in 1827 and has been subsequently employed with success by many practitioners.

There is a rude figure of the plant in the Chinese herbal *Pun-tsao*.

Description—*Tita*, as the drug is called in the Mishmi country, whence it is sent by way of Sudiya on the Bramaputra to Bengal, is a rhizome about the thickness of a quill occurring in pieces an inch or two in length. It often branches at the crown into two or three heads, and bears the remains of leafstalks and thin wiry rootlets, the stumps of which latter give it a rough and spiny appearance. It is nearly cylindrical, often contorted, and of a yellowish brown colour. The fracture is short, exhibiting a loose structure, with large bright yellow radiating woody bundles. The rhizome is intensely bitter,[9] but not aromatic even when fresh.

It is found in the Indian bazaars in neat little open-work bags formed of narrow strips of rattan, each containing about half an ounce. We have once seen it in bulk in the London market.[10]

Microscopic Structure—Cut transversely the rhizome exhibits an inner cortical tissue, through which sclerenchymatous groups of cells are scattered. The latter are most obvious on account of their bright yellow colour. In the woody central column a somewhat concentric

[1] *F. Z. Ermerins*, Anecdota medica Graeca, e codicibus MSS. expromsit. Lugd. Bat. 1840. Leonis Philosophi et Medici conspectus medicinae, lib. iii. cap. I. (Κεφ. ά. Περὶ ὀφθαλμῶν. . . . . σαρκοκόλλης, κρόκου, γλαυκίῳ, μαμηρᾷ καὶ καμφορᾷ).

[2] Yule, *Cathay and the way thither*, (Hakluyt Society) i. (1866) p. ccxvi.

[3] Davies, *Report on the trade of the countries on the N. W. boundary of India*, Lahore, 1862.

[4] Otherwise written *Honglane*, *Choulin*, *Chynlen*, *Chouline*, *Souline*, &c.

[5] *Specimen Medicinæ Sinicæ*, Med. Simp. No. 27.

[6] *Mat. Med.* ii. (1778) 908.

[7] *Hist. des Drog.* ii. (1849) 526.

[8] *Trans. of Med. and Phys. Soc. of Calcutta*, iii. (1827) 432.

[9] Teeta is the Hindustani tītā, from the Sanskrit tikta, "bitter." (Dr. Rice.)

[10] Two cases were offered for sale as *Olen* or *Mishmee* by Messrs. Gray and Clark, drug-brokers, 22th Nov. 1858.

arrangement is found, corresponding to two or three periods of annual growth. The pith, not the medullary rays, begins to be obliterated at an early period. The structure of the drug is, on the whole, very irregular, on account of the branches and numerous rootlets arising from it.

The medullary rays contain small starch granules, while the bark, as well as the pith, are richer in albuminous or mucilaginous matters.

Chemical Composition—The colouring matter in which the rhizome of *Coptis* abounds, is quickly dissolved by water. If the yellow solution obtained by macerating it in water is duly concentrated, nitric acid will produce an abundant heavy precipitate of minute yellow crystals, which if redissolved in a little boiling water will separate again in stellate groups. Solution of iodine also precipitates a cold infusion of the root.

These reactions as well as the bitterness of the drug are due to a large proportion of *Berberine*, as proved by J. D. Perrins.[1] The rhizome yielded not less than 8½ per cent., which is more than has been met with in any other of the numerous plants containing that alkaloid.

As pure berberine is scarcely dissolved by water, it must be combined in *Coptis* with an acid forming a soluble salt. Further researches are requisite to determine the nature of this acid. In some plants berberine is accompanied by a second basic principle: whether in the present instance such is the case, has not been ascertained.

Uses—The drug has been introduced into the *Pharmacopœia of India* as a pure, bitter tonic.

Substitutes—*Thalictrum foliolosum* DC., a tall plant common at Mussooree and throughout the temperate Himalaya at 5000—8000 feet, as well as on the Khasia Hills, affords a yellow root which is exported from Kumaon under the name *Momiri*. From the description in the *Pharmacopœia of India*, it would appear to much resemble the *Mishmi Tita*, and it is not impossible that some of the observations made under the head *History* (p. 3) may apply to *Thalictrum* as well as to *Coptis*.

In the United States the rhizome of *Coptis trifolia* Salisb., a small herb indigenous to the United States and Arctic America, and also found in European and Asiatic Russia, is employed for the same purposes as the Indian drug. It contains berberine and another crystalline principle.[2]

SEMEN STAPHISAGRIÆ.

Stavesacre; F. *Staphisaigre*; G. *Stephanskörner, Läusesamen.*

Botanical Origin—*Delphinium Staphisagria* L., a stout, erect, biennial herb growing 3 to 4 feet high, with palmate, 5- to 9-lobed leaves, which as well as the rest of the plant are softly pubescent.

It is a native of Italy, Greece, the Greek Islands and Asia Minor, growing in waste and shady places; it is now also found throughout

[1] *Journ. of Chem. Soc.* xv. (1862) 339.

[2] Gross in *Am. Journ. of Pharm.* May 1873. 193.

the greater part of the Mediterranean regions and in the Canary Islands, but whether in all instances truly indigenous is questionable. It is cultivated to some extent in Puglia, very little now near Montpellier.

History—Stavesacre was well known to the ancients. It is the *ἀγροτέρη σταφὶς* of Nicander,[1] the *σταφὶς ἀγρία* of Dioscorides,[2] and Alexander Trallianus,[3] the *Staphisagria* or *Herba pedicularia* of Scribonius Largus,[4] the *Astaphis agria* or *Staphis* of Pliny.[5] The last-named author mentions the use of the powdered seeds for destroying vermin on the head and other parts of the body.

The drug continued in use during the middle ages. Pietro Crescenzio,[6] who lived in the 13th century, mentions the collection of the seeds in Italy; and Simon Januensis,[7] physician to Pope Nicolas IV. (A.D. 1288—1292), describes them—"*propter excellentem operationem in caputpurgio.*"

Description—The fruit consists of three downy follicles, in each of which about 12 seeds are closely packed in two rows. The seeds (which alone are found in commerce) are about 3 lines in length and rather less in width; they have the form of a very irregular 4-sided pyramid, of which one side, much broader than the others, is distinctly vaulted. They are sharp-angled, a little flattened, and very rough, the testa being both wrinkled and deeply pitted. The latter is blackish-brown, dull and earthy-looking, rather brittle, yet not hard. It encloses a soft, whitish, oily albumen with a minute embryo at its sharper end.

The seeds have a bitter taste and occasion a tingling sensation when chewed. Ten of them weigh about 6 grains.

Microscopic Structure—The epidermis of the seed consists of one layer of large cells, either nearly cubical or longitudinally extended: hence the wrinkles of the surface. The brown walls of these cells are moderately thickened by secondary deposits, which may be made very obvious by macerating thin sections in a solution of chromic acid, 1 p. in 100 p. of water. By this treatment numerous crystals after a short time make their appearance,—without doubt the chromate of one of the alkaloids of staphisagria.

The outer layer of the testa is made up of thin-walled narrow cells, which become larger near the edges of the seed and in the superficial wrinkles. They contain a small number of minute starch granules and are not altered on addition of a salt of iron. The interior layer exhibits a single row of small, densely-packed cells. The albumen is composed of the usual tissue loaded with granules of albuminoid matter and drops of fatty oil.

Chemical Composition—Brandes (1819) and Lassaigne and Feneulle (1819) have shown this drug to contain a basic principle. Erdmann in 1864 assigned it the formula $C^{24}H^{35}NO^{2}$; he obtained it to the extent of 1 per mille in crystals, soluble in ether, alcohol,

[1] O. Schneider, *Nicandrea*, Lips. 1856. 271.

[2] *De Mat. Med.* lib. iv. c. 153.

[3] Puschmann's edition (quoted in the Appendix) i. 450.

[4] *De Compositione Medicamentorum*, c. 165.

[5] Lib. xxiii. c. 13.

[6] *Libro della Agricultura*, Venet. (1511) lib. vi. c. 108.

[7] *Clavis Sanationis*, Venet. 1510.

chloroform, or benzol. The alkaloid has an extremely burning and acrid taste, and is highly poisonous.

Couerbe[1] in 1833 pointed out the presence in stavesacre of a second alkaloid separable from delphinine by ether in which it is insoluble.

The treatment of the shell of the seed with chromic acid, detailed above, shows that this part of the drug is the principal seat of the alkaloids; and the albumen indeed furnishes no crystals of any chromate. In confirmation of this view we exhausted about 400 grammes of the *entire seeds* with warm spirit of wine acidulated with a little acetic acid. The liquid was allowed to evaporate and the residue mixed with warm water. The solution thus obtained, separated from the resin, yielded on addition of chromic acid an abundant precipitate of chromate. The same solution likewise furnished copious precipitates when bichloride of platinum,[2] iodohydrargyrate of potassium, or bichromate of potassium were added. By repeating the above treatment on a larger scale we obtained crystals of delphinine of considerable size, and also a second alkaloid not soluble in ether.

In the laboratory of Dragendorff, Marquis in 1877 succeeded in isolating the following alkaloids:—1. *Delphinine*, $C^{22}H^{35}NO^{6}$, yielding crystals one inch in length, belonging to the rhombic system. They are soluble in 11 parts of ether, 15 parts of chloroform, and 20 of absolute alcohol. 2. *Staphisagrine*, $C^{22}H^{33}NO^{5}$, is amorphous, soluble in less than 1 part of ether, also in 200 parts of water at 150°. This alkaloid, although it would appear to be the anhydride of the former, is in every respect widely different from delphinine. 3. *Delphinoidine* (formula not quite settled), amorphous, soluble in three parts of ether, more abundantly occurring in the seed than the two former alkaloids. In its physiological action delphinoidine agrees with delphinine, not with staphisagrine. 4. *Delphisine* (formula doubtful) forms crystalline tufts, occurs in but small amount, is sparingly soluble in alcohol, chloroform, or ether.—The total amount of alkaloids afforded by stavesacre is about 1 per cent.

By exhausting the seeds with boiling ether, we get 27 per cent. of a greenish, fatty oil, which continued fluid even at −5° C. It concreted by means of hyponitric acid, and is therefore to be reckoned among the non-drying oils; it contained a large part of the alkaloids.

The drug air-dry contains 8 per cent. of hygroscopic water. Dried at 100° C. and incinerated it left 8·7 per cent. of ash.

Nothing exact is known of the *Delphinic acid* of Hofschläger (about 1820) said to be crystalline and volatile.

Commerce—The seeds are imported from Trieste and from the south of France, especially from Nismes, near which city as well as in Italy (Puglia) the plant is cultivated.

Uses—Stavesacre seeds are still employed as in old times for the destruction of *pediculi* in the human subject, for which purpose they are reduced to powder which is dusted among the hair. Dr. Balmanno Squire[3] having ascertained that *prurigo senilis* is dependent on the presence of *pediculus*, has recommended an ointment of which the

[1] *Ann. de Chimie et de Phys.* lii. (1833) 352.

[2] The platinic compound is in fine microscopic crystals.

[3] *Pharm. Journ.* vi. (1865) 405, and vii. (1877) 1043.

essential ingredients is the fatty oil of stavesacre seeds extracted by ether. It is plain that such a preparation would contain delphinine. Delphinine itself has been used externally in neuralgic affections. Stavesacre seeds are largely consumed for destroying the pediculi that infest cattle.

RADIX ACONITI.

Tuber Aconiti; Aconite Root[1]; F. *Racine d'Aconit*; G. *Eisenhutknollen, Sturmhutknollen.*

Botanical Origin—*Aconitum Napellus* L.—This widely-diffused and most variable species grows chiefly in the mountainous districts of the temperate parts of the northern hemisphere.

It is of frequent occurrence throughout the chain of the Alps up to more than 6500 feet, the Pyrenees, the mountains of Germany and Austria, and is also found in Denmark and Sweden. It has become naturalized in a few spots in the west of England and in South Wales. Eastward it grows throughout the whole of Siberia, extending to the mountain ranges of the Pacific coast of North America. It occurs in company with other species on the Himalaya at 10,000 to 16,000 feet above the sea-level.

The plant is cultivated for medicinal use, and also for ornament. The Abbé Armand David[2] saw in northern Sz-chuen (Setchuan) fields planted with Aconite (A. Napellus ?).

History—The 'Ακόνιτον of the Greeks and the *Aconitum* of the Romans are held to refer to the genus under notice, if not precisely to *A. Napellus.* The ancients were well aware of the poisonous properties of the aconites, though the plants were not more exactly distinguished until the close of the middle ages. The Greek name is supposed to refer to the same source as that of Conium. (See article on Fructus Conii.)

Aconite has been widely employed as an arrow-poison. It was used by the ancient Chinese,[3] and is still in requisition among the less civilized of the hill tribes of India. Something of the same kind was in vogue among the aborigines of ancient Gaul.[4] Aconite was pointed out in the thirteenth century, in "*The Physicians of Myddvai,*"[5] as one of the plants which every physician is to grow.

Störck of Vienna introduced aconite into regular practice about the year 1762[6]; the root and the herb occur in the German pharmaceutical tariff of the seventeenth century.

Description—The herbaceous annual stem of aconite starts from an elongated conical tuberous root 2 to 4 inches long and sometimes as much as an inch in thickness. This root tapers off in a long tail, while numerous branching rootlets spring from its sides. If dug up in the summer it will be found that a second and younger root (occasionally a third) is attached to it near its summit by a very short branch

[1] We use the word *root* as most in accordance with the teaching of English botanists.

[2] *Journal de mon troisième voyage en Chine*, i. (Paris 1875) 367.

[3] F. Porter Smith, *Mat. Med. and Nat. Hist of China*, Shanghai, 1871. 2, 3.

[4] Pliny, lib. xxvii. c. 76, also xxv. 25.

[5] *The Physicians of Myddvai; Meddygon Myddfai.* Published for the Welsh MSS. Society. Llandovery, 1861. 282, 457.

[6] *De Stramonio, Hyoscyamo et Aconito*, Vindob. 1762.

and is growing out of it on one side. This second root has a bud at the top which is destined to produce the stem of the next season. It attains its maximum development at the latter part of the year, the parent root meanwhile becoming shrivelled and decayed. This form of growth is therefore analogous to that of an orchis.

The dried root is more or less conical or tapering, enlarged and knotty at the summit which is crowned with the base of the stem. It is from 2 to 3 or 4 inches long and at the top from ½ to 1 inch thick. The tuber-like portion of the root is more slender, much shrivelled longitudinally, and beset with the prominent bases of rootlets. The drug is of a dark brown; when dry it breaks with a short fracture exhibiting a white and farinaceous, or brownish, or grey inner substance sometimes hollow in the centre. A transverse section of a sound root shows a pure white central portion (pith) which is many-sided and has at each of its projecting angles a thin fibro-vascular bundle.

In the fresh state the root of aconite has a sharp odour of radish which disappears on drying. Its taste which is at first sweetish soon becomes alarmingly acrid, accompanied with sensations of tingling and numbness.

Microscopic Structure—The tuberous root as seen in a transverse section, consists of a central part enclosed by a delicate cambial zone. The outer part of this central portion exhibits a thin brownish layer made up of a single row of cells (*Kernscheide* of the Germans). This is more distinctly obvious in the rootlets, which also show numerous, scattered, thick-walled cells of a yellow colour.

The fibro-vascular bundles of aconite root are devoid of true ligneous cells; its tissue is for the largest part built up of uniform parenchymatous cells loaded with starch granules.

Chemical Composition—Aconite contains chemical principles which are of great interest on account of their virulent effects on the animal economy.

The first to be mentioned is *Aconitine*, a highly active crystallizable alkaloid, furnishing readily crystallizable salts. It is accompanied by another active alkaloid, *Pseudaconitine*, which is crystallizable, but yields mostly amorphous salts. According to the admirable researches of Wright and Luff,[1] aconitine may be decomposed according to the following equation:—

$$\underset{\text{Aconitine.}}{C^{33}H^{43}NO^{12}} \;.\; OH^{2} = \underset{\text{Benzoic acid.}}{C^{7}H^{6}O^{2}} \;.\; \underset{\text{Aconine.}}{C^{26}H^{39}NO^{11}},$$

and pseudaconitine breaks up in accordance with the equation:

$$\underset{\text{Pseudaconitine.}}{C^{36}H^{49}NO^{11}} \;.\; OH^{2} = \underset{\text{Dimethyl-protocatechuic acid.}}{C^{9}H^{10}O^{4}} \;.\; \underset{\text{Pseudaconine.}}{C^{27}H^{41}NO^{8}}$$

The decomposition of aconitine, as well as of pseudaconitine, may be performed by means of mineral acids, alkaline solutions, or also by heating the bases with water in sealed tubes. The two alkaloids, *Aconine* and *Pseudaconine*, appear to be present already in the roots of Aconitum; they, moreover, contain two other alkaloids of less

[1] *Pharm. Journ.* 1875 to 1878, also *Yearbook of Pharmacy*, the results being summarized in the *Yearbook* for 1877, 466.—Comparative qualitative reactions of Aconitine, Aconine, Pseudaconitine, and Pseudaconine, see *Yearbook* (1877) 459.

physiological potency. One of them, *Picraconitine*, $C^{31}H^{45}NO^{10}$, is merely bitter, producing no lip-tingling; it gives well crystallized salts, although it is itself amorphous. Commercial aconitine is a mixture of the above alkaloids. The total yield of basic substances afforded by aconite root is not more than about 0·07 per cent.

The other constituents of aconite root are but imperfectly known. In the preparation of the alkaloids, a dark green mixture of resin and fat is obtained; it is much more abundant in European than in Nepal aconite (Groves). The root contains *Mannite*, as proved by T. and H. Smith (1850), together with cane sugar, and another sugar which reduces cupric oxide even in the cold. Tannin is absent, or is limited to the corky coat. The absence of a volatile alkaloid in the root was proved by Groves in 1866.

Uses—Prescribed in the form of tincture as an anodyne liniment; occasionally given internally in rheumatism.

Adulteration and Substitution—Aconite root, though offered in abundance in the market, is by no means always obtained of good quality. Collected in the mountainous parts of Europe by peasants occupied in the pasturing of sheep and cattle, it is often dug up without due regard to the proper season or even to the proper species,—a carelessness not surprising when regard is had to the miserable price which the drug realizes in the market.[1]

One of the species not unfrequent in the Alps, of which the roots are doubtless sometimes collected, is *A. Störckeanum* Reichenb. In this plant the tuberous roots are developed to the number of three or four, and have an anatomical structure slightly different from that of *A. Napellus*.[2] *A. variegatum* L., *A. Cammarum* Jacq., and *A. paniculatum* Lam. are blue-flowered species having tuberous roots resembling those of *A. Napellus*, but according to Schroff somewhat less active.

The yellow-flowered *A. Anthora* L. and *A. Lycoctonum* L. produce roots which cannot be confounded with those of *A. Napellus* L.

The root of *A. japonicum* Thunb. has been noticed in Europe by Christison as early as 1859[3]; it is now imported occasionally from the East. It forms grey or almost blackish tubers from $\frac{6}{10}$ of an inch to upwards of 1 inch in length, and from $\frac{2}{10}$ to $\frac{4}{10}$ of an inch in diameter, oblong or ovoid, either tapering or rounded at their extremities. They are of plump, scarcely shrivelled appearance.[4]

Japanese aconite afforded to Wright and Luff a crystallized active alkaloid different from both aconitine and pseudaconitine.

Holmes[5] states that the *aromatic* roots of *Imperatoria Ostruthium* L. have been found mixed with aconite.

[1] Thus the continental druggists are able to offer it in quantity as low as 4*d*. to 5*d*. per lb., and a pound, we find, contains fully 150 roots!

[2] See figure in Berg's *Atlas zur pharm. Waarenkunde* (1865) fig. 24.

[3] Hanbury, *Science Papers* (1876) 258, with figure. See also *Pharm. Journ.* ix. (1879) 615, where the drug is derived from Aconitum Fischeri.

[4] Their microscopic structure is figured in the paper of Dr. Dunin (quoted farther on, in our article on Aconitum heterophyllum at p. 14) 217-225.

[5] *Pharm. Journ.* vii. (1877) 749.

FOLIA ACONITI.

Herba Aconita; Aconite Leaves; F. *Feuilles d'Aconit;* G., *Eisenhutkraut, Sturmhutkraut.*

Botanical Origin—*Aconitum Napellus* L., see preceding article.

History—Aconite herb was introduced into medicine in 1762 by Störck of Vienna; and was admitted into the London Pharmacopœia in 1788.

Description—The plant produces a stiff, upright, herbaceous, simple stem, 3 to 4 feet high, clothed as to its upper half with spreading, dark green leaves, which are paler on their under side. The leaves are from 3 to 5 or more inches in length, nearly half consisting of the channelled petiole. The blade, which has a roundish outline, is divided down to the petiole into three principal segments, of which the lateral are subdivided into two or even three, the lowest being smaller and less regular than the others. The segments, which are trifid, are finally cut into 2 to 5 strap-shaped pointed lobes. The leaves are usually glabrous, and are deeply impressed on their upper side by veins which run with but few branchings to the tip of every lobe. The uppermost leaves are more simple than the lower, and gradually pass into the bracts of the beautiful raceme of dull-blue helmet-shaped flowers which crowns the stem.

The leaves have when bruised a herby smell; their taste is at first mawkish but afterwards persistently burning.

Chemical Composition—The leaves contain aconitine in small proportion and also aconitic acid,—the latter in combination with lime.

Aconitic Acid, $C^6H^6O^6$, discovered by Peschier in 1820 in somewhat considerable quantity in the leaves of aconite, occurs also in those of larkspur, and is identical with the *Equisetic Acid* of Braconnot and the *Citridic Acid* of Baup.[1] It has been stated to be present likewise in Adonis vernalis L. (Linderos, 1876,—10 per cent. of dried leaves!) and in the sugar cane (Behr, 1877).

Schoonbroodt[2] (1867) on treating the extract with a mixture of alcohol and ether, obtained acicular crystals, which he thought were the so-called *Aconella* of Smith. He further found that the distillate of the plant was devoid of odour, but was acid, and had a burning taste. By saturation with an alkali he obtained from it a crystalline substance, soluble in water, and having a very acrid taste. Experiments made about the same time by Groves,[3] a careful observer, led to opposite results. He distilled on different occasions both fresh herb and fresh roots, and obtained a *neutral* distillate, smelling and tasting strongly of the plant, but entirely devoid of acridity. Hence he concluded that *A. Napellus* contains no volatile acrid principle.

In an extract of aconite that has been long kept, the microscope reveals crystals of aconitate of calcium, as well as of sal-ammoniac.

The leaves contain a small proportion of sugar, and a tannin striking

[1] Gmelin, *Chemistry*, xi. (1857) 402.

[2] Wittstein's *Vierteljahresschrift*, xviii. (1869) 82, also *Jahresbericht* of Wiggers and Husemann (1869) 12.

[3] *Pharm. Journ.* viii. (1867) 118.

green with iron. When dried they yield on incineration 16·6 per cent. of ash.

Uses—In Britain the leaves and small shoots are only used in the fresh state, the flowering herb being purchased by the druggist in order to prepare an inspissated juice,—*Extractum Aconiti*. This preparation, which is considered rather uncertain in its action, is occasionally prescribed for the relief of rheumatism, inflammatory and febrile affections, neuralgia, and heart diseases.

RADIX ACONITI INDICA.

Bish, Bis or Bikh, Indian Aconite Root, Nepal Aconite.

Botanical Origin—The poisonous root known in India as *Bish, Bis,* or *Bikh*[1] is chiefly derived from *Aconitum ferox* Wallich, a plant growing 3 to 6 feet high and bearing large, dull-blue flowers, native of the temperate and sub-alpine regions of the Himalaya at an elevation of 10,000 to 14,000 feet in Garwhal, Kumaon, Nepal and Sikkim.[2] In the greater part of these districts, other closely allied and equally poisonous species occur, viz. *A. uncinatum* L., *A. luridum* H. f. et Th., *A. palmatum* Don, and also abundantly *A. Napellus* L., which last, as already mentioned, grows throughout Europe as well as in Northern Asia and America. The roots of these plants are collected indiscriminately according to Hooker and Thomson[3] under the name of *Bish* or *Bikh.*

History—The Sanskrit name of this potent drug, *Visha*, signifies simply *poison*, and *Ativisha*, a name which it also bears, is equivalent to "*summum venenum.*" *Bish* is mentioned by the Persian physician Alhervi[4] in the 10th century as well as by Avicenna[5] and many other Arabian writers on medicine,—one of whom, Isa Ben Ali, calls it the most rapid of deadly poisons, and describes the symptoms it produces with tolerable correctness.[6]

Upon the extinction of the Arabian school of medicine this virulent drug seems to have fallen into oblivion. It is just named by Acosta (1578) as one of the ingredients of a pill which the Brahmin physicians give in fever and dysentery.[7] There is also a very strange reference to it as "*Bisch*" in the Persian Pharmacopœia of Father Ange, where it is stated[8] that the root, though most poisonous when fresh, is perfectly innocuous when dried, and that it is imported into Persia from India, and *mixed with food and condiments as a restorative!* Ange was aware that it was the root of an aconite.

[1] The Arabic name *Bish* or Persian *Bis* is stated by Moodeen Sheriff in his *Supplement to the Pharmacopœia of India* (p. 265) to be a more correct designation than *Bikh*, which seems to be a corruption of doubtful origin. We find that the Arabian writer Ibn Baytar gives the word as *Bish* (not *Bikh*).

[2] Figured in Bentley and Trimen, *Med. Plants* (1877) pt. 27.

[3] *Flor. Ind.* i. (1855) 54, 57; and Introd. Essay, 3.

[4] Abu Mansur Mowafik ben Ali Alherui, *Liber Fundamentorum Pharmacologiæ*, i. (Vindob. 1830) 47. Seligmann's edition.

[5] Valgrisi edition, 1564, lib. ii. tract. 2. it. N. (p. 347).

[6] Ibn Baytar, Sontheimer's transl. i. (1840) 199.

[7] Clusius, *Exotica*, 289.

[8] *Pharm. Persica*, 1681, p. 17, 319, 358. The word *bisch* is correctly given in Arabic characters, so that of its identity there can be no dispute. (*Pharm. persica*, see appendix: Angelus.)

The poisonous properties of *Bish* were particularly noticed by Hamilton (late Buchanan)[1] who passed several months in Nepal in 1802-3: but nothing was known of the plant until it was gathered by Wallich and a description of it as *A. ferox* communicated by Seringe to the Société de physique de Genève in 1822.[2] Wallich himself afterwards gave a lengthened account of it in his *Plantæ Asiaticæ Rariores* (1830).[3]

Description—Balfour, who also figures *A. ferox*,[4] describes the plant from a specimen that flowered in the Botanical Garden of Edinburgh as—"having 2—3 fasciculated, fusiform, attenuated tubers, some of the recent ones being nearly 5 inches long, and 1½ inches in circumference, dark brown externally, white within, sending off sparse, longish branching fibres."

Aconite root has of late been imported into London from India in considerable quantity, and been offered by the wholesale druggists as *Nepal Aconite*.[5] It is of very uniform appearance, and seems derived from a single species, which we suppose to be *A. ferox*. The drug consists of simple tuberous roots of an elongated conical form, 3 to 4 inches long, and ½ to 1¾ inches in greatest diameter. Very often the roots have been broken in being dug up and are wanting in the lower extremity: some are nearly as broad at one end as at the other. They are mostly flattened and not quite cylindrical, often arched, much shrivelled chiefly in a longitudinal direction, and marked rather sparsely with the scars of rootlets. The aerial stem has been closely cut away, and is represented only by a few short scaly rudiments.[6]

The roots are of a blackish brown, the prominent portions being often whitened by friction. In their normal state they are white and farinaceous within, but as they are dried by fire-heat and often even scorched, their interior is generally horny, translucent, and extremely compact and hard. The largest root we have met with weighed 555 grains.

In the Indian Bazaars, *Bish* is found in another form, the tuberous roots having been steeped in cow's urine to preserve them from insects.[7] These roots which in our specimen[8] are mostly plump and cylindrical, are flexible and moist when fresh, but become hard and brittle by keeping. They are externally of very dark colour, black and horny within, with an offensive odour resembling that of hyraceum or castor. Immersed in water, though only for a few moments, they afford a deep brown solution. Such a drug is wholly unfit for use in medicine, though not unsuitable, perhaps, for the poisoning of wild beasts, a purpose to which it is often applied in India.[9]

[1] *Account of the Kingdom of Nepal*, Edin. 1819, 98.

[2] *Musée Helvétique d'Hist. Nat.* Berne, i. (1823) 160.

[3] Yet strange to say confused the plant with *A. Napellus*, an Indian form of which he figured as *A. ferox!*

[4] *Edinb. New Phil. Journ.* xlvii. (1849) 366, pl. 5.

[5] The first importation was in 1869, when ten bags containing 1,000 lbs., said to be part of a much larger quantity actually in London, were offered for sale by a drug-broker.

[6] There is a rude woodcut of the root in *Pharm. Journ.* i. (1871) 434.

[7] A specimen of ordinary *Bish* in my possession for two or three years became much infested by a minute and active insect of the genus *Psocus*.—D. H.

[8] Obligingly sent to me in 1867 by Messrs. Rogers & Co. of Bombay, who say it is the only kind there procurable.—D. H.

[9] According to Moodeen Sheriff (*Supple-*

Microscopic Structure—Most of the roots fail to display any characteristic structure by reason of the heat to which they have been subjected. A living root sent to us from the Botanical Garden of Edinburgh exhibited the thin brownish layer which encloses the central part in *A. Napellus*, replaced by a zone of stone cells,—a feature discernible in the imported root.

Chemical Composition—According to Wright and Luff (see previous article) the roots of *Aconitum ferox* contain comparatively large quantities of pseudaconitine with a little aconitine and an alkaloid, apparently non-crystalline, which would appear not to agree with the analogous body from *A. Napellus*.

Uses—The drug has been imported and used as a source of aconitine. It is commonly believed to be much more potent than the aconite root of Europe.

RADIX ACONITI HETEROPHYLLI.

Atís or Atees.

Botanical Origin—*Aconitum heterophyllum* Wallich, a plant of 1 to 3 feet high with a raceme of large flowers of a dull yellow veined with purple, or altogether blue, and reniform or cordate, obscurely 5-lobed, radical leaves.[1] It grows at elevations of 8000 to 13,000 feet in the temperate regions of the Western Himalaya, as in Simla, Kumaon and Kashmír.

History—We have not met with any ancient account of this drug, which however is stated by O'Shaughnessy[2] to have been long celebrated in Indian medicine as a tonic and aphrodisiac. It has recently attracted some attention on account of its powers as an antiperiodic in fevers, and has been extensively prescribed by European physicians in India.

Description—The tuberous roots of *A. heterophyllum* are ovoid, oblong, and downward-tapering or obconical; they vary in length from $\frac{1}{2}$ to $1\frac{1}{2}$ inches and in diameter from $\frac{3}{10}$ to $\frac{6}{10}$ of an inch, and weigh from 5 to 45 grains. They are of a light ash colour, wrinkled and marked with scars of rootlets, and have scaly rudiments of leaves at the summit. Internally they are pure white and farinaceous. A transverse section shows a homogeneous tissue with 4 to 7 yellowish vascular bundles. In a longitudinal section these bundles are seen to traverse the root from the scar of the stem to the opposite pointed end, here and there giving off a rootlet. The taste of the root is simply bitter with no acridity.

ment to Pharm. of India, pp. 25-32, 265) there are several kinds of aconite root found in the Indian bazaars, some of them highly poisonous, others innocuous. The first or poisonous aconites he groups under the head *Aconitum ferox*, while the second, of which there are three varieties mostly known by the Arabic name *Jadwár* (Persian *Zadwár*), he refers to undetermined species of *Aconitum*.

The surest and safest names in most parts of India for the poisonous aconite roots are *Bish* (Arabic); *Bis* (Persian); *Singyā-bis*, *Mīthā-zahar*, *Bachhnāg* (Hindustani); *Vasha-nāvi* (Tamil); *Vasa-nābhi* (Malyalim).

[1] Beautifully figured in Royle's *Illustrations of the Botany of the Himalayan mountains*, &c., 1839, tab. 13; also in Bentley and Trimen's *Medicinal Plants*, Part 27 (1877).

[2] *Bengal Dispensatory*, 1842. 167.

Microscopic Structure—The tissue is formed of large angular thin-walled cells loaded with starch which is either in the form of isolated or compound granules. The vascular bundles contain numerous spiroid vessels which seen in transverse section appear arranged so as to form about four rays. The outer coat of the root is made up of about six rows of compressed, tabular cells with faintly brownish walls.

Chemical Composition—The root contains *Atisine*, an amorphous alkaloid of intensely bitter taste discovered by Broughton,[1] who assigns to it the formula $C^{46}H^{74}N^2O^5$, obtained from concurrent analysis of a platinum salt. The alkaloid is readily soluble in bisulphide of carbon or in benzol, also to some extent in water. It is of decidedly alkaline reaction, devoid of any acridity. Atisine has also been prepared (1877) by Dunin[2] from the root in the laboratory of one of us. We have before us its hydroiodate, forming colourless crystallized scales, which we find to be very sparingly soluble in cold alcohol or water. At boiling temperature the hydroiodate of atisine is readily dissolved; the aqueous solution on cooling yields beautiful crystals. They agree, according to Dunin, with the formula $C^{46}H^{74}N^2O^4 . HI + OH^2$; this chemist has also shown atisine not to be poisonous. The absence in the drug of aconitine is proved by medical experience,[3] and fully confirmed by the absence of any acridity in the root.

Uses—The drug is stated to have proved a valuable remedy in intermittent and other paroxysmal fevers. In ordinary intermittents it may be given in powder in 20-grain doses. As a simple tonic the dose is 5 to 10 grains thrice a day.

Substitutes—The native name *Atís* is applied in India to several other drugs, one of which is an inert tasteless root commonly referred to *Asparagus sarmentosus* L. In Kunawar the tubers of *Aconitum Napellus* L. are dug up and eaten as a tonic, the name *atís* being applied to them as well as to those of *A. heterophyllum*.[4]

RADIX CIMICIFUGÆ.

Radix Actææ racemosæ; Black Snake-root, Black Cohosh, Bugbane.

Botanical Origin—*Cimicifuga racemosa* Elliott (*Actæa racemosa* L.), a perennial herb 3 to 8 feet high, abundant in rich woods in Canada and the United States, extending southward to Florida.[5] It much resembles *Actæa spicata* L., a plant widely spread over the northern parts of Europe, Asia, and America, occurring also in Britain; but it differs in having an elongated raceme of 3 to 8 inches in length and dry dehiscent capsules. *A. spicata* has a short raceme and juicy berries, usually red.

[1] *Pharm. Journ.* vi. (1875) 189; also Blue Book, East India Chinchona Cultivation, 1877. 133.

[2] Dr. M. Dunin von Wasowicz has devoted to the drug under notice an elaborate paper in the *Archiv der Pharmacie*, 214 (1879) 193-216, including its structure, which he illustrates by engravings.

[3] *Pharm. of India*, 1868. 4. 434.

[4] Hooker and Thomson (on the authority of Munro) *Flor. Ind.* 1855. 58.

[5] For figure, see Bentley and Trimen, *Med. Plants*, Part 23 (1877).

History—The plant was first made known by Plukenet in 1696 as *Christophoriana Canadensis racemosa.* It was recommended in 1743 by Colden[1] and named in 1749 by Linnæus in his *Materia Medica* as *Actæa racemis longissimis.* In 1823 it was introduced into medical practice in America by Garden; it began to be used in England about the year 1860.[2]

Description—The drug consists of a very short, knotty, branching rhizome, ½ an inch or more thick, having, in one direction, the remains of several stout aerial stems, and in the other, numerous brittle, wiry roots, $\frac{1}{20}$ to $\frac{1}{10}$ of an inch in diameter, emitting rootlets still smaller. The rhizome is of somewhat flattened cylindrical form, distinctly marked at intervals with the scars of fallen leaves. A transverse section exhibits in the centre a horny whitish pith, round which are a number of rather coarse, irregular woody rays, and outside them a hard, thickish bark. The larger roots when broken display a thick cortical layer, the space within which contains converging wedges of open woody tissue 3 to 5 in number forming a star or cross,—a beautiful and characteristic structure easily observed with a lens. The drug is of a dark blackish brown; it has a bitter, rather acrid and astringent taste, and a heavy narcotic smell.

Microscopic Structure—The most striking character is afforded by the rootlets, which on a transverse section display a central woody column, traversed usually by 4 wide medullary rays and often enclosing a pith. The woody column is surrounded by a parenchymatous layer separated from the cortical portion by one row of densely packed small cells constituting a boundary analogous to the nucleus-sheath (*Kernscheide*) met with in many roots of monocotyledons, as for instance in sarsaparilla. The parenchyme of cimicifuga root contains small starch granules. The structure of the drug is, on the whole, the same as that of the closely allied European *Actæa spicata* L.

Chemical Composition—Tilghmann[3] in 1834 analysed the drug, obtaining from it gum, sugar, resin, starch and tannic acid, but no peculiar principal.

Conard[4] extracted from it a neutral crystalline substance of intensely acrid taste, soluble in dilute alcohol, chloroform, or ether, but not in benzol, oil of turpentine, or bisulphide of carbon. The composition of this body has not been ascertained. The same chemist showed the drug not to afford a volatile principle, even in its fresh state.

The American practitioners called *Eclectics* prepare with *Black Snake-root* in the same manner as they prepare podophyllin, an impure resin which they term *Cimicifugin* or *Macrotin.* The drug yields, according to Parrish, 3¾ per cent. of this substance, which is sold in the form of scales or as a dark brown powder.

Uses—Cimicifuga usually prescribed in the form of tincture (called *Tinctura Actææ racemosæ*) has been employed chiefly in rheumatic affections. It is also used in dropsy, the early stages of phthisis, and in chronic bronchial disease. A strong tincture has been lately recom-

[1] *Acta Soc. Reg. Scient. Upsal.* 1743. 131.
[2] Bentley, *Pharm. Journ.* ii. (1861) 460.
[3] Quoted by Bentley.
[4] *Am. Journ. of Pharm.* xliii. (1871) 151; *Pharm. Journ.* April 29, 1871. 866.

mended in America as an external application for reducing inflammation.[1]

MAGNOLIACEÆ.

CORTEX WINTERANUS.

Cortex Winteri, Cortex Magellanicus; Winter's Bark, Winter's Cinnamon; F. *Ecorce de Winter*; G. *Wintersrinde, Magellanischer Zimmt.*

Botanical Origin—*Drimys*[2] *Winteri* Forster, a tree distributed throughout the American continent from Mexico to Cape Horn. It presents considerable variation in form and size of leaf and flower in the different countries in which it occurs, on which account it has received from botanists several distinct specific names. Hooker[3] has reduced these species to a single type, a course in which he has been followed by Eichler in his monograph of the small order *Winteraceæ*[4].—In April, 1877, the tree was blossoming in the open air in the botanic garden at Dublin.

History—In 1577 Captain Drake, afterwards better known as Sir Francis Drake, having obtained from Queen Elizabeth a commission to conduct a squadron to the South Seas, set sail from Plymouth with five ships; and having abandoned two of his smaller vessels, passed into the Pacific Ocean by the Straits of Magellan in the autumn of the following year. But on the 7th September, 1578, there arose a dreadful storm, which dispersed the little fleet. Drake's ship, the *Pelican*, was driven southward, the *Elizabeth*, under the command of Captain Winter, repassed the Straits and returned to England, while the third vessel, the *Marigold*, was heard of no more.

Winter remained three weeks in the Straits of Magellan to recover the health of his crew, during which period, according to Clusius (the fact is not mentioned in Hakluyt's account of the voyage), he collected a certain aromatic bark, of which, having removed the acridity by steeping it in honey, he made use as a spice and medicine for scurvy during his voyage to England, where he arrived in 1579.

A specimen of this bark having been presented to Clusius, he gave it the name of *Cortex Winteranus*, and figured and described it in his pamphlet: "Aliquot notæ in Garciæ aromatum historiam," Antverpiæ, 1582, p. 30, and also in the *Libri Exoticorum*, published in 1605. He afterwards received a specimen with wood attached, which had been collected by the Dutch navigator Sebald de Weerdt.

Van Noort, another well-known Dutch navigator, who visited the Straits of Magellan in 1600, mentions cutting wood at Port Famine to make a boat, and that the bark of the trees was hot and biting like pepper. It is stated by Murray that he also brought the bark to Europe.

[1] *Yearbook of Pharmacy*, 1872. 385.

[2] From δριμύς, *acrid, biting*.

[3] *Flora Antarctica*, ii. (1847) 229.

[4] Martius, *Flor. Bras.* fasc. 38 (1864) 134. Eichler however admits five principal varieties, viz. α. *Magellanica*; β. *Chilensis*; γ. *Granatensis*; δ. *revoluta*; ε. *angustifolia*.

But although the straits of Magellan were several times visited about this period, it is certain that no regular communication between that remote region and Europe existed either then or subsequently; and we may reasonably conclude that Winter's Bark became a drug of great rarity, and known to but few persons. It thus happened that, notwithstanding most obvious differences, the Canella alba of the West Indies, and another bark of which we shall speak further on, having been found to possess the pungency of Winter's Bark, were (owing to the scarcity of the latter) substituted for it, until at length the peculiar characters of the original drug came to be entirely forgotten.

The tree was figured by Sloane in 1693, from a specimen (still extant in the British Museum) brought from Magellan's Straits by Handisyd, a ship's surgeon, who had experienced its utility in treating scurvy.

Feuillée,[1] a French botanist, found the Winter's Bark-tree in Chili (1709–11), and figured it as *Boigue cinnamomifera*. It was, however, Forster,[2] the botanist of Cook's second expedition round the world, who first described the tree accurately, and named it *Drimys Winteri*. He met with it in 1773 in Magellan's Straits, and on the eastern coasts of Tierra del Fuego, where it grows abundantly, forming an evergreen tree of 40 feet, while on the western shores it is but a shrub of 10 feet high. Specimens have been collected in these and adjacent localities by many subsequent botanists, among others by Dr. J. D. Hooker, who states that about Cape Horn the tree occurs from the sea-level to an elevation of 1000 feet.

Although the bark of *Drimys* was never imported as an article of trade from Magellan's Straits, it has in recent times been occasionally brought into the market from other parts of South America, where it is in very general use. Yet so little are drug dealers acquainted with it, that its true name and origin have seldom been recognized.[3]

Description—We have examined specimens of true Winter's Bark from the Straits of Magellan, Chili, Peru, New Granada, and Mexico, and find in each the same general characters. The bark is in quills or channelled pieces, often crooked, twisted or bent backwards, generally only a few inches in length. It is most extremely thick ($\frac{1}{10}$ to $\frac{3}{10}$ of an inch) and appears to have shrunk very much in drying, bark a quarter of an inch thick having sometimes rolled itself into a tube only three times as much in external diameter. Young pieces have an ashy-grey suberous coat beset with lichens. In older bark, the outer coat is sometimes whitish and silvery, but more often of a dark rusty brown, which is the colour of the internal substance, as well as of the surface next the wood. The inner side of the bark is strongly characterized by very rough striæ, or, as seen under a lens, by small short and sharp longitudinal ridges, with occasional fissures indicative of great contraction of the inner layer in drying. In a piece broken or cut transversely, it is easy to perceive that the ridges in question are the ends of rays of white liber which diverge towards the circumference in radiate

[1] *Journ. des observations physiques*, &c. iv. 1714. 10, pl. 6.

[2] *Characteres Generum Plantarum*, 1775. 42.

[3] We have seen it offered in a drug sale at one time as "*Pepper Bark*," at another as "*Cinchona*." Even Mutis thought it a Cinchona, and called it "*Kinkina urens*"!

order, a dark rusty parenchyme intervening between them. No such feature is ever observable in either *Canella* or *Cinnamodendron*.

Winter's Bark has a short, almost earthy fracture, an intolerably pungent burning taste, and an odour which can only be described as terebinthinous. When fresh its smell may be more agreeable. The descriptions of Clusius, as alluded to above, are perfectly agreeing and even his figures as nearly as might be expected.

Microscopic Structure—In full-grown specimens the most striking fact is the predominance of sclerenchymatous cells. The tissue moreover contains numerous large oil-ducts, chiefly in the inner portion of the large medullary rays. A fibrous structure of the inner part of the bark is observable only in the youngest specimens.[1] Very small starch granules are met with in the drug, yet less numerous than in canella. The tissue of the former assumes a blackish blue colour on addition of perchloride of iron.

The wood of *Drimys* consists of dotted prosenchyme, traversed by medullary rays, the cells of which are punctuated and considerably larger than in *Coniferæ*.

Chemical Composition—No satisfactory chemical examination has been made of true Winter's Bark. Its chief constituents, as already pointed out, are tannic matters and essential oil, probably also a resin. In a cold aqueous infusion, a considerable amount of mucilage is indicated by neutral acetate of lead. On addition of potash it yields a dark somewhat violet liquid. Canella alba is but little altered by the same treatment. By reason of its astringency the bark is used in Chili for tanning.[2]

Uses—Winter's Bark is a stimulating tonic and antiscorbutic, now almost obsolete in Europe. It is much used in Brazil and other parts of South America as a remedy in diarrhœa and gastric debility.

Substitute—*False Winter's Bark*—We have shown that the bark of *Drimys* or True Winter's Bark has been confounded with the pungent bark of *Canella alba* L., and with an allied bark, also the produce of Jamaica. The latter is that of *Cinnamodendron corticosum* Miers,[3] a tree growing in the higher mountain woods of St. Thomas-in-the-Vale and St. John, but not observed in any other of the West Indian islands than Jamaica. It was probably vaguely known to Sloane when he described the "*Wild Cinamon tree, commonly, but falsely, called* Cortex Winteranus," which, he says, has leaves resembling those of *Lauro-cerasus*; though the tree he figures is certainly *Canella alba*.[4] Long[5] in 1774, speaks of *Wild Cinamon, Canella alba,* or *Bastard Cortex Winteranus*, saying that it is used by most apothecaries instead of the true *Cortex Winteranus*.

It is probable that both writers really had in view *Cinnamodendron*, the bark of which has been known and used as *Winter's Bark*, both in England and on the continent from an early period up to the present

[1] The structure of Winter's Bark is beautifully figured by Eichler, *loc. cit.* tab. 32.

[2] Perez-Rosales, *Essai sur le Chili*, 1857. 113.

[3] *Annals of Nat. Hist.*, May 1858; also Miers' *Contributions to Botany*, i. 121, pl. 24, *Bot. Magaz.*, Sept. 1874, vol. xxx. pl. 6121, and Bentley and Trimens' *Medicinal Plants*, part 10.

[4] *Phil. Trans.* xvii. for 1693. 465.

[5] *Hist. of Jamaica*. London, iii. (1774) 705 —also i. 495.

time.[1] It is the bark figured as *Cortex Winteranus* by Goebel and Kunze[2] and described by Mérat and De Lens,[3] Pereira, and other writers of repute. Guibourt indeed pointed out in 1850 its great dissimilarity to the bark of *Drimys* and questioned if it could be derived from that genus.

It is a strange fact that the tree should have been confounded with *Canella alba* L., differing from it as it does in the most obvious manner, not only in form of leaf, but in having the flowers *axillary*, whereas those of *C. alba* are *terminal*. Although *Cinnamodendron corticosum* is a tree sometimes as much as 90 feet high[4] and must have been well known in Jamaica for more than a century, yet it had no botanical name until 1858 when it was described by Miers[5] and referred to the small genus *Cinnamodendron* which is closely allied to *Canella*.

The bark of *Cinnamodendron* has the general structure of Canella alba. There is the same thin corky outer coat (which is *not* removed) dotted with round scars, the same form of quills and fracture. But the tint is different, being more or less of a ferruginous brown. The inner surface which is a little more fibrous than in canella, varies in colour, being yellowish, brown, or of a deep chocolate. The bark is violently pungent but not bitter, and has a very agreeable cinnamon-like odour.

In *microscopic structure* it approaches very close to canella; yet the thick-walled cells of the latter exist to a much larger extent and are here seen to belong to the suberous tissue. The medullary rays are loaded with oxalate of calcium.

Cinnamodendron bark has not been analysed. Its decoction is blackened by a persalt of iron whereby it may be distinguished from Canella alba; and is coloured intense purplish brown by iodine, which is not the case with a decoction of true Winter's Bark.

FRUCTUS ANISI STELLATI.

Semen Badianæ[6]; *Star-Anise*; F. *Badiane, Anis étoilé*; G. *Sternanis*.

Botanical Origin—*Illicium anisatum* Loureiro (*I. religiosum* Sieb.). A small tree, 20 to 25 feet high, native of the south-western provinces of China; introduced at an early period into Japan by the Buddhists and planted about their temples.

Kämpfer in his travels in Japan, in 1690—1692, discovered and figured a tree called *Somo* or *Skimmi*[7] which subsequent authors assumed to be the source of the drug Star-anise. The tree was also found in Japan by Thunberg[8] who remarked that its capsules are not so aromatic as those found in trade. Von Siebold in 1825 noticed the

[1] It is so labelled in the Museum of the Pharmaceutical Society, 28th April, 1873.

[2] *Pharm. Waarenkunde*, 1827-29. i. Taf. 3. fig. 7.

[3] As shown by De Lens' own specimen kindly given to us by Dr. J. Léon Soubeiran. There are specimens of the same bark about a century old marked *Cortex Winteranus verus* in Dr. Burges's cabinet of drugs belonging to the Royal College of Physicians.

[4] Griesbach calls it a low shrubby tree, 10—15 feet high. Mr. N. Wilson, late of the Bath Botanic Garden, Jamaica, has informed me it grows to be 40—45 in height, but that he has seen a specimen 90 feet high. (Letter 22 May 1862.)—D. H.

[5] *Loc. cit.*

[6] From the Arabic *Bádiyán fennel*.

[7] *Amœnitates*, 1712. 880.

[8] *Flora Japonica*, 1784. 235.

same fact, in consequence of which he regarded the tree as distinct from that of Loureiro, naming it *Illicium Japonicum*, a name he changed in 1837 to *I. religiosum*. Baillon,[1] while admitting certain differences between the fruits of the Chinese and Japanese trees, holds them to constitute but one species, and the same view is taken by Miquel.[2]

The star-anise of commerce is produced in altitudes of 2500 metres in the north-western parts of the province of Yunnan in South-western China where the tree, which attains a height of 12 to 15 feet, grows in abundance.[3] The fruits of the Japanese variety of the tree are not collected, and the Chinese drug alone is in use even in Japan.

History—Notwithstanding its striking appearance, there is no evidence that star-anise found its way to Europe like other Eastern spices during the middle ages. Concerning its ancient use in China, the only fact we have found recorded is, that during the Sung dynasty, A.D. 970—1127, star-anise was levied as tribute in the southern part of Kien-chow, now Yen-ping-fu, in Fokien.[4]

Star-anise was brought to England from the Philippines by the voyager Candish, about A.D. 1588. Clusius obtained it in London from the apothecary Morgan and the druggist Garet, and described it in 1601.[5] The drug appears to have been rare in the time of Pomet, who states (1694) that the Dutch use it to flavour their beverages of tea and "sorbec."[6] In those times it was brought to Europe by way of Russia, and was thence called *Cardamomum Siberiense*, or *Annis de Sibérie*.

Description—The fruit of *Illicium anisatum* is formed of 8 one-seeded carpels, originally upright, but afterwards spread into a radiate whorl and united in a single row round a short central column which proceeds from an oblique pedicel. When ripe they are woody and split longitudinally at the upturned ventral suture, so that the shining seed becomes visible. This seed, which is elliptical and somewhat flattened, stands erect in the carpel; it is truncated on the side adjoining the central column, and is there attached by an obliquely-rising funicle. The upper edge of the seed is keeled, the lower rounded. The boat-shaped carpels, to the number of 8, are attached to the column through their whole height, but adhere to each other only slightly at the base; the upper or split side of each carpel occupies a nearly horizontal position. The carpels are irregularly wrinkled, especially below, and are more or less beaked at the apex; their colour is a rusty brown. Internally they are of a brighter colour, smooth, and with a cavity in the lower half corresponding to the shape of the seed. The cavity is formed of a separate wall, ½ millim. thick, which, as well as the testa of the seed, distinctly exhibits a radiate structure. The small embryo lies next the hilum in the soft albumen, which is covered by a dark

[1] *Adansonia*, viii. 9; *Hist. des Plantes, Magnoliacées*, 1868. 154.

[2] *Ann. Mus. Bot.* Lugdun. Batav. ii. (1865—1866). 257.

[3] Thorel, *Notes Médicales du voyage d'exploration du Mékong et de Cochinchine*, Paris, 1870. 31.—Garnier, *Voyage d'exploration en Indo-Chine II.* (Paris, 1873) 439.—Rondot, *Etude pratique du commerce d'exportation de la Chine*, 1848. 11.

[4] Bretschneider in [Foochow] *Chinese Recorder*, Jan., 1871, 220, reprinted in his "Study and Value of Chinese Botanical Works," Foochow, 1872, 13.—See also Hirth du Frênes, in *New Remedies*, New York, 1877, 181.

[5] *Rarior. Plant. Hist.* 202.

[6] *Hist. des Drog.* pt. i. liv. i. 43.

brown endopleura. The seed, which is not much aromatic, amounts to about one-fifth of the entire weight of the fruit.

Star-anise has an agreeable aromatic taste and smell, more resembling fennel than anise, on which account it was at first designated *Fœniculum Sinense*.[1] When pulverised, it has a sub-acid after-taste.

Microscopic Structure—The carpels consist of an external, loose, dark-brown layer and a thick inner wall, separated by fibro-vascular bundles. The outer layer exhibits numerous large cells, containing pale yellow volatile oil. The inner wall of the carpels consists of woody prosenchyme in those parts which are exterior to the seed cavity, and especially in the shining walls laid bare by the splitting of the ventral suture. The inner surface of the carpel is entirely composed of sclerenchyme. A totally different structure is exhibited by this stony shell where it lines the cavity occupied by the seed. Here it is composed of a single row of cells, consisting of straight tubes exactly parallel to one another, more than 500 mkm. long, and 70 mkm. in diameter, placed vertically to the seed cavity; their porous walls, marked with fine spiral striations, display splendid colours in polarized light. The seed contains albumen and drops of fat. Starch is wanting in star-anise, except a little in the fruit-stalk.

Chemical Composition—The volatile oil amounts to four or five per cent. Its composition is that of the oils of fennel or anise. We observed that oil of star-anise, as distilled by one of us, continued fluid below 8° C. It solidified at that temperature as soon as a crystal of anethol (see our article on Fructus Anisi) was brought in contact with the oil. The crystallized mass began to melt again at 16° C. The oils of anise and star-anise possess no striking optical differences, both deviating very little to the left. We are unable to give any chemical characters by which they can be discriminated, although they are distinguished by dealers; the oil of star-anise imparts a somewhat different flavour, for instance, to drinks than that produced by anise oil.

Star-anise is rich in sugar, which seems to be cane-sugar inasmuch as it does not reduce alkaline cupric tartrate. An aqueous extract of the fruit assumes, on addition of alcohol, the form of a clear mucilaginous jelly, of which pectin is probably a constituent. The seeds contain a large quantity of fixed oil.

Commerce—Star-anise is shipped to Europe and India from China. In 1872 Shanghai imported, mostly by way of Hong-Kong 5273 peculs (703,066 lb.), a large proportion of which was re-shipped to other ports of China.[2] According to Rondot (*l. c.*) the best is first brought by junks from Fokien to Canton, being exported from Tsiouen-tchou-fou. A little is also collected in Kiang-si and Kuang-tung. The same drug, under the name of *Bādiyāne-khatāi* (i.e. *Chinese fennel*), is carried by inland trade from China to Yarkand and thence to India, where it is much esteemed.

Uses—Star-anise is employed to flavour spirits, the principal consumption being in Germany, France, and Italy. It is not used in medicine at least in England, except in the form of essential oil, which is often sold for oil of aniseed.

[1] Redi, *Experimenta*, Amstelod. 1675, p. 172.

[2] *Returns of Trade at the Treaty Ports in China for* 1872, 4—8.

MENISPERMACEÆ.

RADIX CALUMBÆ.

Radix Columba; Calumba or Colombo Root; F. *Racine de Colombo;* G. *Kalumbawurzel, Columbowurzel.*

Botanical Origin—*Jateorhiza palmata* Miers[1] a diœcious perennial plant, with large fleshy roots and herbaceous annual stems, climbing over bushes and to the tops of lofty trees. The leaves are of large size and on long stalks, palmate-lobed and membranous. The male flowers are in racemose panicles a foot or more in length, setose-hispid at least in their lower part, or nearly glabrous. The whole part is more or less hispid with spreading setæ and glandular hairs.

It is indigenous to the forests of Eastern Africa between Ibo or Oibo, the most northerly of the Portuguese settlements (lat. 12° 28′ S.), and the banks of the Zambesi, a strip of coast which includes the towns of Mozambique and Quilimane. Kirk found it (1860) in abundance at Shupanga, among the hills near Morambala, at Kebrabasa and near Senna, localities all in the region of the Zambesi. Peters[2] states that on the islands of Ibo and Mozambique the plant is cultivated. In the Kew Herbarium is a specimen from the interior of Madagascar.

The plant was introduced into Mauritius a century ago in the time of the French governor Le Poivre, but seems to have been lost, for after many attempts it was again introduced in 1825 by living specimens procured from Ibo by Captain Owen.[3] It still thrives there in the Botanical Garden of Pamplemousses.

It was taken from Mozambique to India in 1805 and afterwards cultivated by Roxburgh in the Calcutta Garden, where however it has long ceased to exist.

History—The root is held in high esteem among the natives of

[1] Synonyms — *Menispermum palmatum* Lamarck, *Cocculus palmatus* DC, *Menispermum Columba* Roxb., *Jateorhiza Calumba* Miers, *J. Miersii* Oliv., *Chasmanthera Columba* Baillon. As we thus suppress a species admitted in recent works, it is necessary to give the following explanation. *Menispermum palmatum* of Lamarck, first described in the *Encyclopédie méthodique* in 1797 (iv. 99), was divided by Miers into two species, *Jateorhiza palmata* and *J. Calumba*. Oliver in his *Flora of Tropical Africa*, i. (1868) 42, accepted the view taken by Miers, but to avoid confusion abolished the specific name *palmata*, substituting for it that of *Miersii*. At the same time he noticed the close relationship of the two species, and suggested that further investigation might warrant their union. The characters supposed to distinguish them *inter se* are briefly these :— In *J. palmata*, the lobes at the base of the leaf *overlap*, and the male inflorescence is nearly glabrous; while in *J. Calumba*, the basal lobes are rounded, but *do not overlap*, and the male inflorescence is setose-hispid ("*sparsely pilose*" Miers). On careful examination of a large number of specimens, including those of Berry from Calcutta, and others from Mauritius, Madagascar, and the Zambesi, together with the drawings of Telfair and Roxburgh, and the published figures and descriptions, I am convinced that the characters in question are unimportant and do not warrant the establishment of two species. In this view I have the support of Mr. Horne of Mauritius, who at my request has made careful observations on the living plant and found that both forms of leaf occur on the same stem.—D. H.

[2] *Reise nach Mossambique*, Botanik i. (1862) 172.

[3] Hooker, *Bot. Mag.* lvii. (1830) tabb. 2970-71.

Eastern Africa who call it *Kalumb*, and use it for the cure of dysentery and as a general remedy for almost any disorder.

It was brought to Europe by the Portuguese in the 17th century, and is first noticed briefly in 1671 by Francesco Redi, who speaks of it[1] as an antidote to poison deserving trial.

No further attention was paid to the drug for nearly a century, when Percival[2] in 1773 re-introduced it as "*a medicine of considerable efficacy . . . not so generally known in practice as it deserves to be.*" From this period it began to come into general use. J. Gurney Bevan, a London druggist, writing to a correspondent in 1777 alludes to it as—"an article not yet much dealt in and subject to great fluctuation." It was in fact at this period extremely dear, and in Mr. Bevan's stock-books is valued in 1776 and 1777 at 30*s.* per lb., in 1780 at 28s., 1781 at 64*s.*, 1782 at 15*s.*, 1783 at 6*s.* Calumba was admitted to the *London Pharmacopœia* in 1788.

Collection—As to the collection and preparation of the drug for the market, the only account we possess is that obtained by Dr. Berry,[3] which states that the roots are dug up in the month of March, which is the dry season, cut into slices and dried in the shade.

Description—The calumba plant produces great fusiform fleshy roots growing several together from a short head. Some fresh specimens sent to one of us (H.) from the Botanic Garden, Mauritius, in 1866, and others from that of Trinidad in 1868, were portions of cylindrical roots, 3 to 4 inches in diameter, externally rough and brown and internally firm, fleshy, and of a brilliant yellow. When sliced transversely, and dried by a gentle heat, these roots exactly resemble imported calumba except for being much fresher and brighter.

The calumba of commerce consists of irregular flattish pieces of a circular or oval outline, 1 to 2 inches or more in diameter, and $\frac{1}{8}$ to $\frac{1}{2}$ an inch thick. In drying, the central portion contracts more than the exterior: hence the pieces are thinnest in the middle. The outer edge is invested with a brown wrinkled layer which covers a corky bark about $\frac{3}{8}$ of an inch thick, surrounding a pithless internal substance, from which it is separated by a fine dark shaded line. The pieces are light and of a corky texture, easily breaking with a mealy fracture. Their colour is a dull greenish yellow, brighter when the outer surface is shaved off with a knife.[4] The drug has a weak musty odour and a rather nauseous bitter taste. It often arrives much perforated by insects, but seems not liable to such depredations here.

Microscopic Structure—On a transverse section the root exhibits a circle of radiate vascular bundles only in the layer immediately connected with the cambial zone; they project much less distinctly into the cortical part. The tissue of the whole root, except the cork and vascular bundles, is made up of large parenchymatous cells. In the outer part of the bark, some of them have their yellow walls thickened and are

[1] "Sono ancora da farsi nuove esperienze intorno alla *radice di Calumbe*, creduta un grandissimo alessifarmaco."—*Esperienze*, p. 125. (See Appendix, R.)

[2] *Essays Medical and Experimental*, Lond. ii. (1773) 3.

[3] *Asiatick Researches*, x. (1808) 385; Ainslie, *Mat. Med. of Hindoostan*, 298.

[4] Wholesale druggists sometimes *wash* the drug to improve its colour.

loaded with fine crystals of oxalate of calcium, whilst all the other cells contain very large starch granules, attaining as much as 90 mkm. The short fracture of the root is due to the absence of a proper ligneous or liber tissue.

Chemical Composition—The bitter taste of calumba, and probably likewise its medicinal properties, are due to three distinct substances, *Columbin*, *Berberine*, and *Columbic Acid*.

Columbin or *Columba-Bitter* was discovered by Wittstock in 1830. It is a neutral bitter principle, crystallizing in colourless rhombic prisms, slightly soluble in cold alcohol or ether, but dissolving more freely in those liquids when boiling. It is soluble in aqueous alkalis and in acetic acid.

The presence of *Berberine* in calumba was ascertained in 1848 by Bödeker, who showed that the yellow cell-walls of the root owe their colour to it and (as we may add) to *Columbic Acid*, another substance discovered by the same chemist in the following year. Columbic Acid is yellow, amorphous, nearly insoluble in cold water, but dissolving in alcohol and in alkaline solutions. It tastes somewhat less bitter than columbin. Bödeker surmises that it may exist in combination with the berberine.

Bödeker has pointed out a connection between the three bitter principles of calumba. If we suppose a molecule of ammonia, NH^3, to be added to columbin $C^{42}H^{44}O^{14}$, the complex molecule thence resulting will contain the elements of berberine $C^{20}H^{17}NO^4$, columbic acid $C^{22}H^{24}O^7$, and water $3H^2O$.

Among the more usual constituents of plants, calumba contains (in addition to starch) pectin, gum, and nitrate of potassium, but no tannic acid. It yields when incinerated 6 per cent. of ash.

Commerce—Calumba root is shipped to Europe and India from Mozambique and Zanzibar, and exported from Bombay and other Indian ports.

Uses—It is much employed as a mild tonic, chiefly in the form of tincture or of aqueous infusion.

PAREIRA BRAVA.

Radix Pareiræ; *Pareira Brava*[1]; F. *Racine de Butua ou de Pareira-Brava*; G. *Grieswurzel*.

Botanical Origin—*Chondodendron tomentosum* Ruiz et Pav. (non Eichler) (*Cocculus Chondodendron* DC., *Botryopsis platyphylla* Miers[2]).—It is a lofty climbing shrub with long woody stems, and leaves as much as a foot in length. The latter are of variable form, but mostly broadly ovate, rounded or pointed at the extremity, slightly cordate at the base, and having long petioles. They are smooth on the upper side; on the under covered between the veins with a fine close tomentum of

[1] From the Portuguese *parreira*, signifying a vine that grows against a wall (in French *treille*), and *brava*, wild.

[2] For a figure see Bentley and Trimen, *Medic. Plants*, Part 5 (1876); also Eichler in Martius' *Flor. Bras.* fasc. 38. tab. 48. The *Cissampelos Abutua* of Vellozo's *Flora Fluminensis*, tom. x. tab. 140 appears to us the same plant.

an ashy hue. The flowers are unisexual, racemose, minute, produced either from the young shoots or from the woody stems. The fruits are ¾ of an inch long, oval, black and much resembling grapes in form and arrangement.[1]

The plant grows in Peru and Brazil,—in the latter country in the neighbourhood of Rio de Janeiro, where it occurs in some abundance on the range of hills separating the Copacabana from the basin of the Rio de Janeiro. It is also found about San Sebastian further south.

History—The Portuguese missionaries who visited Brazil in the 17th century became acquainted with a root known to the natives as *Abutua* or *Butua*, which was regarded as possessing great virtues. As the plant affording it was a tall climbing shrub with large, simple, long-stalked leaves, and bore bunches of oval berries resembling grapes, the Portuguese gave it the name of *Parreira brava* or Wild Vine.

The root was brought to Lisbon where its reputed medicinal powers attracted the notice of many persons, and among others of Michel Amelot, ambassador of Louis XIV., who took back some of it when he returned to Paris in 1688. Specimens of the drug also reached the botanist Tournefort, and one presented by him to Pomet was figured and described by the latter in 1694.[2] The drug was again brought to Paris by Louis-Raulin Rouillé, the successor to Amelot at Lisbon, together with a memoir detailing its numerous virtues.

Specimens obtained in Brazil by a naval officer named De la Mare in the early part of the last century, were laid before the French Academy, which body requested a report upon them from Geoffroy, professor of medicine and pharmacy in the College of France, who was already somewhat acquainted with the new medicine. He reported many favourable trials in cases of inflammations of the bladder and suppression of urine.[3] The drug was a favourite remedy of Helvetius,[4] physician to Louis XIV. and Louis XV., who administered it for years with great success.

Both Geoffroy and Helvetius were in frequent correspondence with Sloane[5] who received from the former as well as from other sources specimens of Pareira Brava, which are still in the British Museum and have enabled us fully to identify the drug as the root of *Chondodendron tomentosum*.

Several other plants of the order *Menispermaceæ* have stems or roots employed in South America in the same manner as *Chondodendron*. Pomet had heard of two varieties of Pareira Brava, and two were known to Geoffroy.[6] Lochner of Nürnberg who published a treatise on Pareira Brava in 1719[7] brought forward a plant of Eastern Africa figured in 1675 by Zanoni,[8] and supposed to be the mother-plant of the

[1] See *Pharm. Journ.* Aug. 2, 1873. 83; *Yearbook,* 1873. 28; *Am. Journ. of Pharm.* Oct. 1, 1873. fig. 3; *Hanbury Science Papers.* 382.

[2] *Hist. des Drog.* Paris, 1694. part i. livre 2. cap. 14.

[3] *Hist. de l'Acad. roy. des Sciences,* anneé 1710. 56.

[4] *Traité des maladies les plus fréquentes et des remèdes spécifiques pour les guérir,* Paris, 1703. 98.

[5] In the volumes of Sloane MSS. No. 4045 and 3322 contained in the British Museum, are a great many letters to Sloane from Etienne-François Geoffroy and from his younger brother Claude-Joseph, dating 1699 to 1744.

[6] *Tract. de Mat. Med.* ii. (1741) 21—25.

[7] *Schediasma de Parreira Brava,* 1719. (ed. 2. auctior.)

[8] *Istoria Botanica,* 1675. 59. fig. 22.

drug. A species of *Cissampelos* called by the Portuguese in Brazil *Caapeba*, *Cipó de Cobras* or *Herva de Nossa Senhora* described by Piso in 1648,[1] afterwards became associated with Pareira Brava on account of similarity of properties.

Thus was introduced a confusion which we may say was *consolidated* when Linnæus in 1753,[2] founded a species as *Cissampelos Pareira*, citing it as the source of Pareira Brava,—a confusion which has lasted for more than a hundred years. This plant is very distinct from that yielding true Pareira Brava, and though its roots and stems are used medicinally in the West Indies,[3] there is nothing to prove that they were ever an object of export to Europe.

As Pareira Brava failed to realise the extravagant pretensions claimed for it, it gradually fell out of use,[4] and the characters of the true drug became forgotten. This at least seems to be the explanation of the fact that for many years past the Pareira Brava found in the shops and supposed to be genuine is a substance very diverse from the original drug,—albeit not devoid of medicinal properties. More recently even this has become scarce, and an inert Pareira Brava has been almost the sole kind obtainable. The true drug has however still at times appeared in the European market, and attention having been directed to it,[5] we may hope that it will arrive in a regular manner.

The re-introduction of Pareira Brava into medical practice is due (so far as Great Britain is concerned) to Brodie[6] who recommended it in 1828 for inflammation of the bladder.

Description—True Pareira Brava as derived from *Chondodendron tomentosum* is a long, branching, woody root, attaining 2 inches or more in diameter, but usually met with much smaller and dividing into rootlets no thicker than a quill or even than a horse-hair. It is remarkably tortuous or serpentine and marked with transverse ridges as well as with constrictions and cracks more or less conspicuous; besides which the surface is strongly wrinkled longitudinally. The bark is of a dark blackish brown or even quite black when free from earth, and disposed to exfoliate. The root breaks with a coarse fibrous fracture; the inner substance is of a light yellowish brown,—sometimes of a dull greenish brown.

Roots of about an inch in diameter cut transversely exhibit a central column 0·2 to 0·4 of an inch in diameter composed of 10 to 20 converging wedges of large-pored woody tissue with 3 or 4 zones divided from each other by a wavy light-coloured line. Crossing these zones are wedge-shaped woody rays, often rather sparsely and irregularly distributed. The interradial substance has a close, resinous, waxy appearance.

The root though hard is easily shaved with a knife, some pieces giving the impression when cut of a waxy, rather than of a woody and

[1] *Medicina Brasiliensis*, 1648. 94.

[2] *Species Plantarum*, Holmiæ, 1753; see also *Mat. Med.* 1749. No. 459.

[3] Lunan, *Hort. Jamaic.* ii. (1814) 254; Descourtilz, *Flor. méd. des Antilles*, iii. (1827) 231.

[4] Thus it was omitted from the London pharmacopœias of 1809 and 1824, and from many editions of the *Edinburgh Dispensatory*.

[5] Hanbury in *Pharm. Journ.* Aug. 2—9, 1873, pp. 81 and 102.

[6] *Lond. Med. Gazette*, Feb. 16, 1828; Brodie, *Lectures on Diseases of the Urinary Organs*, ed. 3. 1842. 108, 138.

fibrous substance. The taste is bitter, well marked but not persistent. The drug has no particular odour. Its aqueous decoction is turned inky bluish-black by tincture of iodine.

The aerial stems especially differ by enclosing a small but well-defined pith.

Microscopic Structure—The most interesting character consists in the arrangement rather than in the peculiarity of the tissues composing this drug. The wavy light-coloured lines already mentioned are built up partly of sclerenchymatous cells. The other portions of the parenchyme are loaded with large starch granules, which are much less abundant in the stem.

Chemical Composition—From the examination of this drug made by one of us in 1869,[1] it was shown that the bitter principle is the same as that discovered in 1839 by Wiggers in the drug hereafter described as *Common False Pareira Brava*, and named by him *Pelosine*. It was further pointed out that this body possesses the chemical properties of the *Bibirine* of Greenheart bark and of the *Buxine* obtained by Walz from the bark of *Buxus sempervirens* L. It was also obtained on the same occasion (1869) from the stems and roots of *Cissampelos Pareira* L. collected in Jamaica; but from both drugs in the very small proportion of about ½ per cent.

Whether to *Buxine* (for by this name rather than *Pelosine* it should be designated) is due the medicinal power of the drug may well be doubted. No further chemical examination of true Pareira Brava has been made.

Uses—The medicine is prescribed in chronic catarrhal affections of the bladder and in calculus. From its extensive use in Brazil[2] it seems deserving of trial in other complaints. Helvetius used to give it in substance, which in 5-grain doses was taken in infusion made with boiling water from the powdered root and not strained.

Substitutes—We have already pointed out how the name *Pareira Brava* has been applied to several other drugs than that described in the foregoing pages. We shall now briefly notice the more important.

1. *Stems and roots of Cissampelos Pareira* L.—Owing to the difficulty of obtaining good Pareira Brava in the London market, although this plant is very widely diffused over all the tropical regions of both hemispheres, the firm of which one of us was formerly a member (Messrs. Allen and Hanburys, Plough Court, Lombard Street) caused to be collected in Jamaica, under the superintendence of Mr. N. Wilson, of the Bath Botanical Gardens, the stems and root of *Cissampelos Pareira* L., of which it imported in 1866–67–68 about 300 lb. It was found impracticable to obtain the root *per se;* and the greater bulk of the drug consisted of long cylindrical stems,[3] many of which had been decumbent and had thrown out rootlets at the joints. They had very

[1] *Neues Jahrb. f. Pharm.* xxxi. (1869) 257; *Pharm. Journ.* xi. (1870) 192.

[2] "Presentamente [Abutua] é reputada diaphoretica, diuretica e emenagoga, e usada interiormente na dóse de duas a quatro oitavas para uma libra de infusão ou cozimento, nas febres intermittentes, hydropisias, e suspensão de lochios."—Langgaard, *Diccionario de Medicina domestica e popular*, Rio de Janeiro, i. (1865) 17.

[3] Figured, together with the plant, in Bentley and Trimen, *Medic. Plants*, part 9 (1876).

much the aspect of the climbing stems of *Clematis vitalba* L., and varied from the thickness of a quill to that of the forefinger, seldom attaining the diameter of an inch. The stems have a light brown bark marked longitudinally with shallow furrows and wrinkles, which sometimes take a spiral direction. Knots one to three feet apart, sometimes throwing out a branch, also occur. The root is rather darker in colour, but not very different in structure from the stem.

The fracture of the stem is coarse and fibrous. The transverse section, whether of stem or root, shows a thickish, corky bark surrounding a light brown wood composed of a number of converging wedges (10 to 20) of very porous structure, separated by narrow medullary rays. There are *no concentric layers* of wood,[1] nor is the arrangement of the wedges oblique as in many other stems of the order. The drug is inodorous, but has a very bitter taste without sweetness or astringency.

2. ***Common False Pareira Brava***—Under this name we designate the drug which for many years past has been the ordinary Pareira Brava of the shops, and regarded until lately as derived from *Cissampelos Pareira* L. We have long endeavoured to ascertain, through correspondents in Brazil, from what plant it is derived, but without success. We only know that it belongs to the order *Menispermaceæ*.

The drug consists of a ponderous, woody, tortuous stem and root, occurring in pieces from a few inches to a foot or more in length, and from 1 to 4 inches in thickness, coated with a thin, hard, dark brown bark. The pieces are cylindrical, four-sided, or more or less flattened—sometimes even to the extent of becoming ribbon-like. In transverse section, their structure appears very remarkable. Supposing the piece to be *stem*, a well-defined pith will be found to occupy the centre of the first-formed wood, which is a column about $\frac{1}{4}$ of an inch in diameter. This is succeeded by 10 to 15 or more concentric or oftener eccentric zones, $\frac{1}{10}$ to $\frac{2}{10}$ of an inch wide, each separated from its neighbour by a layer of parenchyme, the outermost being coated with a true bark. In pieces of *true root*, the pith is reduced to a mere point.

Sometimes the development of the zones has been so irregular that they have formed themselves entirely on one side of the primitive column, the other being coated with bark. The zones, including the layer, around the pith (if pith is present), are crossed by numerous small medullary rays. These do not run from the centre to the circumference, but traverse only their respective zones, on the outside of which they are arched together.

The drug, when of good quality, has its wood firm, compact, and of a dusky yellowish brown hue, and a well-marked bitter taste. It exhibits under the knife nothing of the close waxy texture seen in the root of *Chondodendron*, but cuts as a tough, fibrous wood. Its decoction is not tinged blue by iodine. It was in this drug that Wiggers in 1839 discovered *pelosine*.

The drug just described, which is by no means devoid of medicinal power, has of late years been almost entirely supplanted in the market

[1] It is therefore entirely different to the wood figured as that of *C. Pareira* by Eichler in Martius' *Flor. Bras.* xiii. pars. i. tab. 50. fig. 7.

by another sort consisting exclusively of stems which are devoid of bitterness and appear to be wholly inert. They are in the form of sticks or truncheons, mostly cylindrical. Cut traversely, they display the same structure as the sort last described, with a well-defined pith. The wood is light in weight, of a dull tint, and disposed to split. The bark, which consists of two layers, is easily detached.

3. *Stems of Chondodendron tomentosum* R. et P.—These have been recently imported from Brazil, and sold as *Pareira Brava.*[1] The drug consists of truncheons about 1½ feet in length, of a rather rough and knotty stem, from 1 to 4 inches thick.[2] The larger pieces, which are sometimes hollow with age, display, when cut traversely, a small number (5—9) nearly concentric woody zones. The youngest pieces have the bark dotted over with small dark warts.

The wood is inodorous, but has a bitterish taste like the root, of which it is probably an efficient representative. Some pieces have portions of root springing from them, and detached roots occur here and there among the bits of stem. The structure and development of the latter has been elaborately examined and figured by Moss,[3] and also by Lanessan,[4] in the French translation of our book.

4. *White Pareira Brava*—Stems and roots of *Abuta rufescens* Aublet.—Mr. J. Correa de Méllo of Campinas has been good enough to send to one of us (H.) a specimen of the root and leaves[5] of this plant, marked *Parreira Brava grande.* The former we have identified with a drug received from Rio de Janeiro as *Abutua Unha de Vaca,* i.e. *Cow-hoof Abutua,* and also with a similar drug found in the London market. Aublet[6] states that the root of *Abuta rufescens* was, in the time of his visit to French Guiana, shipped from that colony to Europe as *Pareira Brava Blanc* (White Pareira Brava).

This name is well applicable to the drug before us, which consists of short pieces of a root, ½ an inch to 3 inches thick, covered with a rough blackish bark, and also of bits of stem having a pale, striated, corky bark. Cut transversely, the root displays a series of concentric zones of white amylaceous cellular tissue, each beautifully marked with narrow wedge-shaped medullary rays of dark, porous tissue. The wood of the stem is harder than that of the root, the medullary rays are closer together and broader, and there is a distinct pith.

The wood, neither of root nor stem, has any taste or smell. A decoction of the root is turned bright blue by iodine.

5. *Yellow Pareira Brava*—This drug, of which a quantity was in the hands of a London drug-broker in 1873, is, we presume, the *Pareira Brava jaune* of Aublet—the bitter tasting stem of his "*Abuta amara* folio levi cordiformi ligno flavescente,"—a plant of Guiana unknown to recent botanists. That which we have seen consists of portions of a hard woody stem, from 1 to 5 or 6 inches in diameter, covered with a

[1] 45 packages containing about 20 cwt. were offered for sale by Messrs. Lewis and Peat, drug-brokers, 11 Sept. 1873, but there had been earlier importations.

[2] From these knots, which are at regular intervals, and sometimes very protuberant, it would appear that the panicles of flower arise year after year.

[3] *Pharm. Journ.* vi. (1876) 702.

[4] *Histoire des Drogues d'origine végétale,* i. (Paris, 1878) 72.

[5] I have compared these leaves with Aublet's own specimen in the British Museum.—D. H.

[6] *Hist. des Plantes de la Guiane Françoise,* i. (1775) 618. tab. 250.

whitish bark. Internally it is marked by numerous regular concentric zones, is of a bright yellow colour and of a bitter taste. It contains berberine. The same drug, apparently, was exhibited in the Paris exposition of 1878 as "Liane amère" from French Guiana.

COCCULUS INDICUS.

Fructus Cocculi; Cocculus Indicus; F. *Coque du Levant;* G. *Kokkelskörner.*

Botanical Origin—*Anamirta paniculata* Colebrooke, 1822 (*Menispermum Cocculus* L.; *Anamirta Cocculus* Wight et Arnott, 1834), a strong climbing shrub found in the eastern parts of the Indian peninsula from Concan and Orissa to Malabar and Ceylon, in Eastern Bengal, Khasia and Assam, and in the Malayan Islands.

History—It is commonly asserted that *Cocculus Indicus* was introduced into Europe through the Arabs, but the fact is difficult of proof; for though Avicenna [1] and other early writers mention a drug having the power of poisoning fish, they describe it as a *bark*, and make no allusion to it as a production of India. Even Ibn Baytar [2] in the 13th century professed his inability to discover what substance the older Arabian authors had in view.

Cocculus Indicus is not named by the writers of the School of Salerno. The first mention of it we have met with is by Ruellius,[3] who, alluding to the property possessed by the roots of *Aristolochia* and *Cyclamen* of attracting fishes, states that the same power exists in the little berries found in the shops under the name of *Cocci Orientis*, which when scattered on water stupify the fishes, so that they may be captured by the hand.

Valerius Cordus [4] thought the drug which he calls *Cuculi de Levante* to be the fruit of a *Solanum* growing in Egypt.

Dalechamps [5] repeated this statement in 1586, at which period and for long afterwards, Cocculus Indicus used to reach Europe from Alexandria and other parts of the Levant. Gerarde,[6] who gives a very good figure of it, says it is well known in England (1597) as *Cocculus Indicus*, otherwise *Cocci* vel *Cocculæ Orientales*, and that it is used for destroying vermin and poisoning fish. In 1635 it was subject to an import duty of 2*s*. per lb., as *Cocculus Indiæ*.[7]

The use of Cocculus Indicus in medicine was advocated by Battista Codronchi, a celebrated Italian physician of the 16th century, in a tractate entitled *De Baccis Orientalibus*.[8] In the "Pinax" Caspar Bauhin (about 1660) states that *Cocculæ officinarum* "saepe racematim pediculis hærentes, hederæ corymborum modo, ex Alexandria adferuntur."

The word *Cocculus* is derived from the Italian *coccola*, signifying a

[1] Valgrisi edition, 1564. lib. ii. tract. 2. cap. 488.

[2] Sontheimer's transl. ii. 460.

[3] *De Natura Stirpium*, Paris, 1536. lib. iii. c. 4.

[4] *Adnotationes*, 1549. cap. 63 (p. 509).

[5] *Hist. Gen. Plant.* 1586. 1722.

[6] *Herball*, Lond. 1636. 1548—49.

[7] *The Rates of Marchandizes*, Lond. 1635.

[8] It forms part of his work *De Christiana ac tuta medendi ratione*, Ferrariæ, 1591.

small, berry-like fruit.[1] Mattioli remarks that as the berries when first brought from the East to Italy had no special name, they got to be called *Coccole di Levante.*[2]

Description—The female flower of *Anamirta* has normally 5 ovaries placed on a short gynophore. The latter, as it grows, becomes raised into a stalk about $\frac{1}{2}$ an inch long, articulated at the summit with shorter stalks, each supporting a drupe, which is a matured ovary. The purple drupes thus produced are 1 to 3 in number, of gibbous ovoid form, with the persistent stigma on the straight side, and in a line with the shorter stalk or carpodium. They grow in a pendulous panicle, a foot or more in length.

These fruits removed from their stalks and dried have the aspect of little round berries, and constitute the Cocculus Indicus of commerce. As met with in the market they are shortly ovoid or subreniform, $\frac{4}{10}$ to $\frac{5}{10}$ of an inch long, with a blackish, wrinkled surface, and an obscure ridge running round the back. The shorter stalk, when present, supports the fruit very obliquely. The pericarp, consisting of a wrinkled skin covering a thin woody endocarp, encloses a single reniform seed, into which the endocarp deeply intrudes. In transverse section the seed has a horse-shoe form; it consists chiefly of albumen, enclosing a pair of large, diverging lanceolate cotyledons, with a short terete radicle.[3]

The seed is bitter and oily, the pericarp tasteless. The drug is preferred when of dark colour, free from stalks, and fresh, with the seeds well preserved.

Microscopic Structure—The woody endocarp is built up of a peculiar sclerenchymatous tissue, consisting of branched, somewhat elongated cells. They are densely packed, and run in various directions, showing but small cavities. The parenchyme of the seed is loaded with crystallized fatty matter.

Chemical Composition—*Picrotoxin*, a crystallizable substance occurring in the seed to the extent of $\frac{3}{4}$ to 1 per cent., was observed by Boullay, as early as 1812, and is the source of the poisonous property of the drug. Picrotoxin does not neutralize acids. It dissolves in water and in alkalis; the solution in the latter reduces cupric or bismutic oxide like the sugars, but to a much smaller extent than glucose. The alcoholic solutions deviate the ray of polarized light to the left. The aqueous solution of picrotoxin is not altered by any metallic salt, or by tannin, iodic acid, iodohydrargyrate or bichromate of potassium —in fact by none of the reagents which affect the alkaloids. It may thus be easily distinguished from the bitter poisonous alkaloids, although in its behaviour with concentrated sulphuric acid and bichromate of potassium it somewhat resembles strychnine, as shown in 1867 by Köhler.

Picrotoxin melts at 200° C.; its composition, $C^9H^{10}O^4$, as ascertained in 1877 by Paternò and Oglialoro, is the same as that of everninic,

[1] Frutto d'alcuni alberi, e d'alcune piante, o erbe salvatiche, come cipresso, ginepro, alloro, pugnitopo, e lentischio, e simili.—Lat. *bacca*; Gr. *ἀκρόδρυα*.—*Vocabolario degli Accademici della Crusca.*

[2] Quoted by J. J. von Tschudi, *Die Kokkelskörner und das Pikrotoxin*, St. Gallen, 1847.

[3] The fruit should be macerated in order to examine its structure.

hydrocoffeïc, umbellic and veratric (or dimethylprotocatechuic acid—see Semen Sabadillæ) acids.

Pelletier and Couerbe (1833) obtained from the pericarp of Cocculus Indicus two crystallizable, tasteless, non-poisonous substances, having the same composition, and termed respectively *Menispermine* and *Paramenispermine*. These bodies, as well as the very doubtful amorphous *Hypopicrotoxic Acid* of the same chemists, require re-examination.

The fat of the seed, which amounts to about half its weight, is used in India for industrial purposes. Its acid constituent, formerly regarded as a peculiar substance under the name of *Stearophanic* or *Anamirtic Acid*, was found by Heintz to be identical with stearic acid.

Commerce—Cocculus Indicus is imported from Bombay and Madras, but we have no statistics showing to what extent. The stock in the dock warehouses of London on 1st of December, 1873, was 1168 packages, against 2010 packages on the same day of the previous year. The drug is mostly shipped to the Continent, the consumption in Great Britain being very small.

Uses—In British medicine Cocculus Indicus is only employed as an ingredient of an ointment for the destruction of *pediculi*. It has been discarded from the *British Pharmacopœia*, but has a place in that of India.

GULANCHA.

Caulis et radix Tinosporæ.

Botanical Origin—*Tinospora cordifolia* Miers (*Cocculus cordifolius* DC.), a lofty climbing shrub found throughout tropical India from Kumaon to Assam and Burma, and from Concan to Ceylon and the Carnatic.[1] It is called in Hindustani *Gulancha*; in Bombay the drug is known under the name of *Goolwail*.

History—The virtues of this plant which appear to have been long familiar to the Hindu physicians, attracted the attention of Europeans in India at the early part of the present century.[2] According to a paper published at Calcutta in 1827,[3] the parts used are the stem, leaves, and root, which are given in decoction, infusion, or a sort of extract called *pálo*, in a variety of diseases attended with slight febrile symptoms.

O'Shaughnessy declares the plant to be one of the most valuable in India, and that it has proved a very useful tonic. Similar favourable testimony is borne by Waring. Gulancha was admitted to the *Bengal Pharmacopœia* of 1844, and to the *Pharmacopœia of India* of 1868.

Description—The stems are perennial, twining and succulent, running over the highest trees and throwing out roots many yards in length which descend like slender cords to the earth. They have a thick corky bark marked with little prominent tubercles.

[1] Fig. in Bentley and Trimen, *Med. Plants*, part 13.

[2] Fleming, *Catal. of Indian Med. Plants and Drugs*, Calcutta, 1810. 27.

[3] On the native drug called *Gulancha* by Ram Comol Shen.—*Trans. of Med. and Phys. Soc. of Calcutta*, iii. (1827) 295.

As found in the bazaars the drug occurs as short transverse segments of a cylindrical woody stem from ¼ of an inch up to 2 inches in diameter. They exhibit a shrunken appearance, especially those derived from the younger stems, and are covered with a smooth, translucent, shrivelled bark which becomes dull and rugose with age. Many of the pieces are marked with warty prominences and the scars of adventitious roots. The outer layer which is easily detached covers a shrunken parenchyme. The transverse section of the stem shows it to be divided by about 12 to 14 meduallry rays into the same number of wedge-shaped woody bundles having very large vessels, but no concentric structure. The drug is inodorous but has a very bitter taste. The root is stated by O'Shaughnessy[1] to be large, soft, and spongy.

Microscopic Structure—The suberous coat consists of alternating layers of flat corky cells and sclerenchyme, sometimes of a yellow colour. The structure of the central part reminds one of that of *Cissampelos Pareira* (p. 28), like which it is not divided into concentric zones. The woody rays which are sometimes intersected by parenchyme, are surrounded by a loose circle of arched bundles of liber tissue.

Chemical Composition—No analysis worthy of the name has been made of this drug, and the nature of its bitter principle is wholly unknown. We have had no material at our disposal sufficient for chemical examination.

Uses—Gulancha is reputed to be tonic, antiperiodic and diuretic. According to Waring[2] it is useful in mild forms of intermittent fever, in debility after fevers and other exhausting diseases, in secondary syphilitic affections and chronic rheumatism.

Substitute—*Tinospora crispa* Miers, an allied species occurring in Silhet, Pegu, Java, Sumatra, and the Phillipines, possesses similar properties, and is highly esteemed in the Indian Archipelago as a febrifuge.

BERBERIDEÆ.

CORTEX BERBERIDIS INDICUS.

Indian Barberry Bark.

Botanical Origin—This drug is allowed in the *Pharmacopœia of India* to be taken indifferently from three Indian species of *Berberis*[3] which are the following:—

1. *Berberis aristata* DC., a variable species occurring in the temperate regions of the Himalaya at 6000 to 10,000 feet elevation, also found in the Nilghiri mountains and Ceylon.[4]

2. *B. Lycium* Royle, an erect, rigid shrub found in dry, hot situations of the western part of the Himalaya range at 3000 to 9000 feet above the sea-level.

[1] *Bengal Dispensatory*, 1842. 198.

[2] *Pharm. of India*, 1868. 9.

[3] For remarks on the Indian species of *Berberis*, see Hooker and Thomson's *Flora Indica* (1855), also Hooker's *Flora of British India*, i. (1872) 108.

[4] Fig. in Bentley and Trimen, *Med. Plants*, part 25.

3. *B. asiatica* Roxb.—This species has a wider distribution than the last, being found in the dry valleys of Bhotan and Nepal whence it stretches westward along the Himalaya to Garwhal, and occurs again in Affghanistan.

History—The medical practitioners of ancient Greece and Italy made use of a substance called *Lycium* (λύκιον) of which the best kind was brought from India. It was regarded as a remedy of great value in restraining inflammatory and other discharges; but of all the uses to which it was applied the most important was the treatment of various forms of ophthalmic inflammation.

Lycium is mentioned by Dioscorides, Pliny, Celsus, Galen, and Scribonius Largus; by such later Greek writers as Paulus Ægineta, Ætius, and Oribasius, as well as by the Arabian physicians.

The author of the Periplus of the Erythrean Sea who probably lived in the 1st century, enumerates λύκιον as one of the exports of Barbarike at the mouth of the Indus, and also names it along with Bdellium and Costus among the commodities brought to Barygaza:—and further, lycium is mentioned among the Indian drugs on which duty was levied at the Roman custom house of Alexandria about A.D. 176—180.[1]

An interesting proof of the esteem in which it was held is afforded by some singular little vases or jars of which a few specimens are preserved in collections of Greek antiquities.[2] These vases were made to contain lycium, and in them it was probably sold; for an inscription on the vessel not only gives the name of the drug but also that of a person who, we may presume, was either the seller or the inventor of the composition. Thus we have the *Lycium of Jason*, of *Musæus*, and of *Heracleus*. The vases bearing the name of Jason were found at Tarentum, and there is reason to believe that that marked *Heracleus* was from the same locality. Whether it was so or not, we know that a certain Heraclides of Tarentum is mentioned by Celsus[3] on account of his method of treating certain diseases of the eye; and that Galen gives formulæ for ophthalmic medicines[4] on the authority of the same person.

Innumerable conjectures were put forth during at least three centuries as to the origin and nature of lycium, and especially of that highly esteemed kind that was brought from India.

In the year 1833, Royle[5] communicated to the Linnean Society of London a paper proving that the Indian Lycium of the ancients was identical with an extract prepared from the wood or root of several species of *Berberis* growing in Northern India, and that this extract, well known in the bazaars as *Rusot* or *Rasot*, was in common use among the natives in various forms of eye disease.[6] This substance attracted

[1] Vincent, *Commerce and Navigation of the Ancients in the Indian Ocean*, ii. (1807) 390, 410, 734.

[2] Figures of these vessels were published by Dr. J. Y. Simpson in an interesting paper entitled *Notes on some ancient Greek medical vases for containing Lycium*, of which we have made free use.—See (*Edinb.*) *Monthly Journal of Med. Science*, xvi. (1853) 24, also *Pharm. Journ.* xiii. (1854) 413.

[3] Lib. vii. c. 7.—See also Cælius Aurelianus, *De morbis chronicis* (Haller's ed.) lib. i. c. 4, lib. iii. c. 8.

[4] Cataplasmata lippientium quibus usus est Heraclides Tarentinus—Galen, *De Comp. Med. sec. locos*, lib. iv. (p. 153 in Venice edit. of 1625).

[5] On the *Lycium* of Dioscorides.—*Linn. Trans.* xvii. (1837) 83.

[6] It is interesting to find that two of the

considerable notice in India, and though its efficacy *per se*[1] seemed questionable, it was administered with benefit as a tonic and febrifuge.[2] But the *rusot* of the natives being often badly prepared or adulterated, the bark of the root has of late been used in its place, and in consequence of its acknowledged efficacy has been admitted to the *Pharmacopœia of India.*

Description.—In *B. asiatica* (the only species we have examined) the roots which are thick and woody, and internally of a bright yellow, are covered with a thin, brittle bark. The bark has a light-brown corky layer, beneath which it appears of a darker and greenish-yellow hue, and composed of coarse fibres running longitudinally. The inner surface has a glistening appearance by reason of fine longitudinal striæ. The bark is inodorous and very bitter.

Chemical Composition.—Solly[3] pointed out in 1843 that the root-bark of the Ceylon barberry [*B. aristata*] contains the same yellow colouring matter as the barberry of Europe. L. W. Stewart[4] extracted *Berberine* in abundance from the barberry of the Nilkhiri Hills and Northern India, and presented specimens of it to one of us in 1865.

The root-bark of *Berberis vulgaris* L. was found by Polex (1836) to contain another alkaloid named *Oxyacanthine*, which forms with acids colourless crystallizable salts of bitter taste.[5]

Uses.—The root-bark of the Indian barberries administered as a tincture has been found extremely useful in India in the treatment of fevers of all types. It has also been given with advantage in diarrhœa and dyspepsia, and as a tonic for general debility. In the collection of the Chinese customs at Paris, in 1878, the root-barks of *Berberis Lycium* and *B. chinensis*, from the province of Shen-si, were likewise exhibited (No. 1,823) as a tonic.

RHIZOMA PODOPHYLLI.

Radix podophylli; Podophyllum Root.

Botanical Origin—*Podophyllum peltatum* L., a perennial herb growing in moist shady situations throughout the eastern side of the North American continent from Hudson's Bay to New Orleans and Florida.

The stem about a foot high, bears a large, solitary, white flower, rising from between two leaves of the size of the hand composed of 5 to 7 wedge-shaped divisions, somewhat lobed and toothed at the apex. The yellowish pulpy fruit of the size of a pigeon's egg is slightly acid and is sometimes eaten under the name of *May Apple*. The leaves partake of the active properties of the root.

History—The virtues of the rhizome as an anthelminthic and emetic

names for *lycium* given by Ibn Baytar in the 13th century are precisely those under which *rusot* is met with in the Indian bazaars at the present day.

[1] The natives apply it in combination with alum and opium.

[2] O'Shaughnessy, *Bengal Dispensatory* (1842) 203—205.

[3] *Journ. of R. Asiat. Soc.* vii. (1843) 74.

[4] *Pharm. Journ.* vii. (1866) 303.

[5] Gmelin, *Chemistry*, xvii. (1866) 197.

have been long known to the Indians of North America. The plant was figured in 1731 by Catesby[1] who remarks that its root is an excellent emetic. Its cathartic properties were noticed by Schöpf[2] and Barton[3] and have been commented upon by many subsequent writers. In 1820, podophyllum was introduced into the *United States Pharmacopœia*, and in 1864 into the *British Pharmacopœia*. Hodgson published in 1832 in the *Journal of the Philadelphia College of Pharmacy*[4] the first attempt of a chemical examination of the rhizome, which now furnishes one of the most popular purgatives, the so-called *Podophyllin*, manufactured on a large scale at Cincinnati and in other places in America, as well as in England.

Description—The drug consists of the rhizome and rootlets. The former creeps to a length of several feet, but as imported is mostly in somewhat flattened pieces of 1 to 8 inches in length and 2 to 4 lines in longest diameter: it is marked by knotty joints showing a depressed scar at intervals of a few inches which marks the place of a fallen stem. Each joint is in fact the growth of one year, the terminal bud being enclosed in papery brownish sheaths. Sometimes the knots produce one, two, or even three lateral buds and the rhozime is bi- or tri-furcate. The reddish-brown or grey surface is obscurely marked at intervals by oblique wrinkles indicating the former attachment of rudimentary leaves. The rootlets are about ½ a line thick and arise from below the knots and adjacent parts of the rhizome, the internodal space being bare. They are brittle, easily detached, and commonly of a paler colour. The rhizome is mostly smooth, but some of the branched pieces are deeply furrowed. Both rootstock and rootlets have a short, smooth, mealy fracture; the transverse section is white, exhibiting only an extremely small corky layer and a thin simple circle of about 20 to 40 yellow, vascular bundles, enclosing a central pith which in the larger pieces is often 2 lines in diameter.

The drug has a heavy narcotic, disagreeable odour, and a bitter, acrid, nauseous taste.

Microscopic Structure—The vascular bundles are composed of spiral and scalariform vessels intermixed with cambial tissue. From each bundle a narrow-tissued, wedge- or crescent-shaped liber-bundle projects a little into the cortical layer. This, as well as the pith, exhibits large thin-walled cells. The rootlets are as usual of a different structure, their central part consisting of one group of vascular bundles more or less scattered.[5] The parenchymatous cells of the drug are loaded with starch granules; some also contain stellate tufts of oxalate of calcium.

Chemical Composition—The active principles of podophyllum exist in the resin, which according to Squibb[6] is best prepared by the process termed *re-percolation*. The powdered drug is exhausted by alcohol which is made to percolate through successive portions. The

[1] *Nat. Hist. of Carolina*, i. tab. 24.

[2] *Materia Med. Americ.* Erlangæ, 1787, p. 86. Schöpf was physician to German troops fighting in the War of Independence.

[3] *Collections for an Essay on Mat. Med. of U.S.* Philad. 1798, 31.

[4] Vol. iii. 273.

[5] Figured by Power, *Proc. American Phar. Assoc.*, 1877. 420—433.

[6] *American Journ. of Pharm.* xvi. (1868) 1—10.

strong tincture thus obtained is slowly poured into a large quantity of water acidulated with hydrochloric acid (one measure of acid to 70 of water), and the precipitated resin dried at a temperature not exceeding 32° C. The acid is used to facilitate the subsidence of the pulverulent resin which according to Maisch settles down but very slowly if precipitated by cold water simply, and if thrown down by hot water fuses into a dark brown cake. The resin re-dissolved in alcohol and again precipitated by acidulated water, after thorough washing with distilled water and finally drying over sulphuric acid, amounts to about 2 per cent.

Resin of podophyllum is a light, brownish-yellow powder with a tinge of green, devoid of crystalline appearance, becoming darker if exposed to a heat above 32° C., and having an acrid, bitter taste; it is very incorrectly called *Podophyllin.* The product is the same whether the rhizome or the rootlets are exclusively employed.[1] It is soluble in caustic, less freely in carbonated alkalis, even in ammonia, and is precipitated, apparently without alteration, on addition of an acid. Ether separates it into two nearly equal portions, the one soluble in the menstruum, the other not, but both energetically purgative. From the statements of Credner[2] it appears that if caustic lye is shaken with the ethereal solution, about half the resin combines with the potash, while the other half remains dissolved in the ether. If an acid is added to the potassic solution a red-brown precipitate is produced which is no longer soluble in ether nor possessed of purgative power. According to Credner, the body of greatest purgative activity was precipitated by ether from an alcoholic solution of crude podophyllin.

By exhausting the resin with boiling water, Power found that finally not more than 20 per cent. of the resin remained undissolved. By melting the crude resin with caustic soda, a little protocatechuic acid was obtained.

F. F. Mayer[3] of New York stated podophyllum to contain, beside the resin already mentioned, a large proportion of *Berberine,* a colourless alkaloid, an odoriferous principle which might be obtained by sublimation in colourless scales, and finally *Saponin.* From all these bodies the resin as prepared by Power,[4] was ascertained by him to be destitute; he especially proved the absence of berberine in Podophyllum.

Uses—Podophyllum is only employed for the preparation of the resin (*Resina Podophylli*) which is now much prescribed as a purgative.

[1] Saunders in *Am. Journ. of Pharm.* xvi. 75.

[2] *Ueber Podophyllin* (*Dissertation*), Giessen, 1869.

[3] *Am. Journ. of Pharmacy,* xxxv. (1863) 97.

[4] L. cit., also *Am. Journ. of Pharm.* (1878) 370.

PAPAVERACEÆ.

PETALA RHŒADOS.

Flores Rhœados; Red Poppy Petals; F. *Fleurs de Coquelicot;* G. *Klatschrosen.*

Botanical Origin—*Papaver Rhœas* L.—The common Red Poppy or Corn Rose is an annual herb found in fields throughout the greater part of Europe often in extreme abundance. It almost always occurs as an accompaniment of cereal crops, frequently disappearing when this cultivation is given up. It is plentiful in England and Ireland, but less so in Scotland; is found abundantly in Central and Southern Europe and in Asia Minor, whence it extends as far as Abyssinia, Palestine, and the banks of the Euphrates. But it does not occur in India or in North America.

From the evidence adduced by De Candolle[1] it would appear that the plant is strictly indigenous to Sicily, Greece, Dalmatia, and possibly the Caucasus.

History—*Papaver Rhœas* was known to the ancients, though doubtless it was often confounded with *P. dubium* L. the flowers of which are rather smaller and paler. The petals were used in pharmacy in Germany in the 15th century.[2]

Description—The branches of the stem are upright, each terminating in a conspicuous long-stalked flower, from which as it opens the two sepals fall off. The delicate scarlet petals are four in number, transversely elliptical and attached below the ovary by very short, dark-violet claws. As they are broader than long, their edges overlap in the expanded flower. In the bud they are irregularly crumpled, but when unfolded are smooth, lustrous, and unctuous to the touch. They fall off very quickly, shrink up in drying, and assume a brownish-violet tint even when dried with the utmost care. Although they do not contain a milky juice like the green parts of the plant, they have while fresh a strong narcotic odour and a faintly bitter taste.

Chemical Composition—The most important constituent of the petals is the colouring matter, still but very imperfectly known. According to L. Meier (1846) it consists of two acids, neither of which could be obtained other than in an amorphous state. The colouring matter is abundantly taken up by water or spirit of wine but not by ether. The aqueous infusion is not precipitated by alum, but yields a dingy violet precipitate with acetate of lead, and is coloured blackish-brown by ferric salts or by alkalis.

The alkaloids of opium cannot be detected in the petals. Attfield in particular has examined the latter (1873) for morphine but without obtaining a trace of that body.

[1] *Géogr. botanique,* ii. (1855) 649.

[2] Flores Papaveris rubri—in the list of the pharmaceutical shop of the town of Nördlingen. See Flückiger, in the *Archiv der Pharm.* 211 (1877) 97, No. 62.

The milky juice of the herb and capsules has a narcotic odour, and appears to exert a distinctly sedative action. Hesse obtained from them (1865) a colourless crystallizable substance, *Rhœadine*, $C^{21}H^{21}NO^{6}$, of weak alkaline reaction. It is tasteless, not poisonous, nearly insoluble in water, alcohol, ether, chloroform, benzol, or aqueous ammonia, but dissolves in weak acids. Its solution in dilute sulphuric or hydrochloric acid acquires after a time a splendid red colour, destroyed by an alkali but reappearing on addition of an acid. Hesse further believes (1877) the milky juice to contain meconic acid.

Uses—Red Poppy petals are employed in pharmacy only for the sake of their fine colouring matter. They should be preferred in the fresh state.

CAPSULÆ PAPAVERIS.

Fructus Papaveris; Poppy Capsules, Poppy Heads; F. *Capsules ou Têtes de Pavot;* G. *Mohnkapseln.*

Botanical Origin—*Papaver somniferum* L. Independently of the garden-forms of this universally known annual plant, we may, following Boissier,[1] distinguish three principal varieties, viz.:—

α. setigerum (*P. setigerum* DC.), occurring in the Peloponnesus, Cyprus, Corsica and the islands of Hières, the truly wild form of the plant with acutely toothed leaves, the lobes sharp-pointed, and each terminating in a bristle. The leaves, peduncles, and sepals are covered with scattered bristly hairs, and the stigmata are 7 or 8 in number.

β. glabrum—Capsule subglobular, stigmata 10 to 12. Chiefly cultivated in Asia Minor and Egypt.

γ. album (*P. officinale* Gmelin)—has the capsule more or less egg-shaped and devoid of apertures. It is cultivated in Persia.

Besides the differences indicated above, the petals vary from white to red or violet, with usually a dark purplish spot at the base of each.[2] The seeds also vary from white to slate-coloured.

History—The poppy has been known from a remote period throughout the eastern countries of the Mediterranean, Asia Minor, and Central Asia, in all which regions its cultivation is of very ancient date.[3]

Syrup of poppies, a medicine still in daily use, is recommended as a sedative in catarrh and cough in the writings of the younger Mesue (*ob.* A.D. 1015) who studied at Bagdad, and subsequently resided at Cairo as physician to the Caliph of Egypt. Their medicinal use seems to have reached Europe at an early period, for the Welsh "Physicians of Myddvai" in the 13th century already stated:[4] "Poppy heads bruised in wine will induce a man to sleep soundly." They even prepared pills with the juice of poppy, which they called *opium*. In the *Ricettario Fiorentino* (see Appendix R) a formula is given for the syrup

[1] *Flora Orientalis*, i. (1867) 116.

[2] English growers prefer a *white-flowered* poppy.

[3] For further particulars consult Ritter, *Erdkunde von Asien*, vi. (1843) 773, etc.; Unger, *Botanische Streifzüge auf dem Gebiete der Culturgeschichte*, ii. (1857) 46.

[4] *Meddygon Myddfai*, Llandovery, 1861, 50. 216. 400.

as *Syroppo di Papaveri semplici di Mesue*; in the first pharmacopœia of the London College (1618), the medicine is prescribed as *Syrupus de Meconio Mesuæ*.

Description—The fruit is formed by the union of 8 to 20 carpels, the edges of which are turned inwards and project like partitions towards the interior, yet without reaching the centre, so that the fruit is really one-celled. In the unripe fruit, the sutures of the carpels are distinctly visible externally as shallow longitudinal stripes.

The fruit is crowned with a circular disc, deeply cut into angular ridge-like stigmas in number equal to the carpels, projecting in a stellate manner with short obtuse lobes. Each carpel opens immediately below the disc by a pore, out of which the seeds may be shaken; but in some varieties of poppy the carpel presents no aperture even when fully ripe. The fruit is globular, sometimes flattened below, or it is ovoid; it is contracted beneath into a sort of neck immediately above a tumid ring at its point of attachment with the stalk. Grown in rich moist ground in England, it often attains a diameter of three inches, which is twice that of the capsules of the opium poppy of Asia Minor or India. While growing it is of a pale glaucous green, but at maturity becomes yellowish brown, often marked with black spots. The outer wall of the pericarp is smooth and hard; the rest is of a loose texture, and while green exudes on the slightest puncture an abundance of bitter milky juice. The interior surface of the pericarp is rugose, and minutely and beautifully striated transversely. From its sutures spring thin and brittle placentæ directed towards the centre and bearing on their perpendicular faces and edges a vast number of minute reniform seeds.

The unripe fruit has a narcotic odour which is destroyed by drying; and its bitter taste is but partially retained.

Microscopic Structure—The outer layer consists of a thin cuticle exhibiting a large number of stomata; the epidermis is formed of a row of small thick-walled cells. Fragments of these two layers, which on the whole exhibit no striking peculiarity, are always found in the residue of opium after it has been exhausted by water.

The most interesting part of the constituent tissues of the fruit is the system of laticiferous vessels, which is of an extremely complicated nature inasmuch as it is composed of various kinds of cells intimately interlaced so as to form considerable bundles.[1] The cells containing the milky juice are larger but not so much branched as in many other plants.

Chemical Composition—The analyses of poppy heads present discrepant results with regard to morphine. Merck and Winckler detected it in the ripe fruit to the extent of 2 per cent., and it has also been found by Groves (1854) and by Deschamps d'Avallon (1864). Other chemists have been unable to find it.

In recent pharmacopœias poppy heads are directed to be taken previous to complete maturity, and both Meurein and Aubergier have shown that in this state they are richer in morphine than when more advanced. Deschamps d'Avallon found them sometimes to contain

[1] For particulars see Trécul, *Ann. des Sciences Nat.* v. (1866) 49; also Flückiger, *Grundlagen der Pharmaceutischen Waarenkunde*, 1873. 45.

narcotine. He also obtained mucilage perceptible by neutral acetate of lead, ammonium salts, meconic, tartaric, and citric acid, the ordinary mineral acids, wax, and lastly two new crystalline bodies, *Papaverin*, and *Papaverosine*. The former is not identical with Merck's alkaloid of the same name; although nitrogenous and bitter, it has an acid reaction (?), yet does not combine with bases. It yields a blue precipitate with a solution of iodine in iodide of potassium.

Papaverosine on the other hand is a base to which sulphuric acid imparts a violet colour, changing to dark yellowish-red on addition of nitric acid.

In ripe poppy heads, Hesse (1866) found *Rhœadine*. Groves in 1854 somewhat doubtfully announced the presence of *Codeine*. Fricker[1] stated to have obtained from the capsules 0·10 per cent. of alkaloid, and Krause[2] was able to prove the presence of traces of morphine, narcotine, and meconic acid. Ripe poppy capsules (seeds removed) dried at 100° C. afforded us 14·28 per cent. of ash, consisting chiefly of alkaline chlorides and sulphates, with but a small quantity of phosphate.

Production—Poppies are grown for medicinal uses in many parts of England, mostly on a small scale. The large and fine fruits (poppy heads) are usually sold entire; the smaller and less slightly are broken and the seeds having been removed are supplied to the druggist for pharmaceutical preparations. The directions of the pharmacopœia as to the fruit being gathered when "nearly ripe" does not appear to be much regarded.

Uses—In the form of syrup and extract, poppy heads are in common use as a sedative. A hot decoction is often externally applied as an anodyne.

In upper India an intoxicating liquor is prepared by heating the capsules of the poppy with jagghery and water.[3]

OPIUM.

Botanical Origin—*Papaver somniferum* L., see preceding article.

History[4]—The medicinal properties of the milky juice of the poppy have been known from a remote period. Theophrastus who lived in the beginning of the 3rd century B.C. was acquainted with the substance in question, under the name of Μηκώνιον. The investigations of Unger (1857; see *Capsulæ Papaveris*,) have failed to trace any acquaintance of ancient Egypt with opium.

Scribonius Largus in his *Compositiones Medicamentorum*[5] (*circa* A.D. 40) notices the method of procuring opium, and points out that the true drug is derived from the capsules, and not from the foliage of the plant.

[1] Dragendorff's *Jahresbericht*, 1874. 148.

[2] *Archiv der Pharm.* 204 (1874) 507.

[3] *Catal. Ind. Departm. Internat. Exhibition.* 1862. No. 742.

[4] For more particulars see Dr. Rice's learned notes in *New Remedies*, New York, 1876, 229, reprinted in *Pharm. Journ.* vii. (2 Dec. 1876; 23 June 1877), pp. 452 and 1041.

[5] Ed. Bernhold, Argent. 1786, c. iii. sect. 22.

About the year 77 of the same century, Dioscorides[1] plainly distinguished the juice of the capsules under the name of ὀπός from an extract of the entire plant, μηκώνειον, which he regarded as much less active. He described exactly how the capsules should be incised, the performing of which operation he designated by the verb ὀπίζειν. We may infer from these statements of Dioscorides that the collection of opium was at that early period a branch of industry in Asia Minor. The same authority alludes to the adulteration of the drug with the milky juices of *Glaucium* and *Lactuca*, and with gum.

Pliny[2] devotes some space to an account of *Opion*, of which he describes the medicinal use. The drug is repeatedly mentioned as *Lacrima papaveris* by Celsus in the 1st century, and more or less particularly by numerous later Latin authors. During the classical period of the Roman Empire as well as in the early middle ages, the only sort of opium known was that of Asia Minor.

The use of the drug was transmitted by the Arabs to the nations of the East, and in the first instance to the Persians. From the Greek word ὀπός, *juice*, was formed the Arabic word *Afyun*, which has found its way into many Asiatic languages.[3]

The introduction of opium into India seems to have been connected with the spread of Islamism, and may have been favoured by the Mahommedan prohibition of wine. The earliest mention of it as a production of that country occurs in the travels of Barbosa[4] who visited Calicut on the Malabar coast in 1511. Among the more valuable drugs the prices of which he quotes, opium occupies a prominent place. It was either imported from Aden or Cambay, that from the latter place being the cheaper, yet worth three or four times as much as camphor or benzoin.

Pyres[5] in his letter about Indian drugs to Manuel, king of Portugal, written from Cochin in 1516, speaks of the opium of Egypt, that of Cambay and of the kingdom of Coûs (Kus Bahár, S.W. of Bhotan) in Bengal. He adds that it is a great article of merchandize in these parts and fetches a good price;—that the kings and lords eat of it, and even the common people, though not so much because it costs dear.

Garçia d'Orta[6] informs us that the opium of Cambay in the middle of the 16th century was chiefly collected in Malwa, and that it is soft and yellowish. That from Aden and other places near the Erythrean Sea is black and hard. A superior kind was imported from Cairo, agreeing as Garçia supposed with the opium of the ancient Thebaïd, a district of Upper Egypt near the modern Karnak and Luksor.

In India the Mogul Government uniformly sold the opium monopoly,

[1] Lib. iv. c. 65.

[2] Lib. xx. c. 76.

[3] There are no ancient Chinese or Sanskrit names for opium. In the former language the drug is called *O-fu-yung* from the Arabic. Two other names *Ya-pien* and *O-pien* are adaptations to the Chinese idiom of our word *opium*. There are several other designations which may be translated *Smoking dirt*, *Foreign poison*, *Black commodity*, &c.

[4] *Coasts of East Africa and Malabar* (Hakluyt Soc.), Lond. 1866. 206, 223.

[5] *Journ. de Soc. Pharm. Lusit.* ii. (1838) 36. Pires, or Pyres, was the first ambassador from Europe to China: Abel Rémusat, *Nouv. mélanges asiatiques*, ii. (1829) 203. See also Pedro José da Silva, *Elogio historico e noticia completa de Thomé Pires, pharmaceutico e primeiro naturalista da India*, Lisboa, 1866 (Library of the Pharm. Soc., London, Pamphlets, No. 30).

[6] *Aromatum . . . Historia*, edit Clusius, Antv. 1574. lib. i. c. 4.

and the East India Company followed their example, reserving to itself the sole right of cultivating the poppy and selling the opium.

Opium thebaïcum was mentioned by Simon Januensis,[1] physician to Pope Nicolas IV. (A.D. 1288-92), who also alludes to *meconium* as the dried juice of the pounded capsules and leaves. Prosper Alpinus,[2] who visited Egypt in 1580-83, states that opium or meconium was in his time prepared in the Thebaïd from the expressed juice of poppy heads.

The German traveller Kämpfer, who visited Persia in 1685, describes the various kinds of opium prepared in that country. The best sorts were flavoured with nutmeg, cardamom, cinnamon and mace, or simply with saffron and ambergris. Such compositions were called *Theriaka*, and were held in great estimation during the middle ages, and probably supplied to a large extent the place of pure opium. It was not uncommon for the sultans of Egypt of the 15th century to send presents of *Theriaka* to the doges of Venice and the sovereigns of Cyprus.[3]

In Europe opium seems in later times not to have been reckoned among the more costly drugs; in the 16th century we find it quoted at the same price as benzoin, and much cheaper than camphor, rhubarb, or manna.[4]

With regard to China it is supposed that opium was first brought thither by the Arabians, who are known to have traded with the southern ports of the empire as early as the 9th century. More recently, at least until the 18th century, the Chinese imported the drug in their junks as a return cargo from India. At this period it was used almost exclusively as a remedy for dysentery, and the whole quantity imported was very small. It was not until 1767 that the importation reached 1,000 chests, at which rate it continued for some years, most of the trade being in the hands of the Portuguese. The East India Company made a small adventure in 1773; and seven years later an opium depôt of two small vessels was established by the English in Lark's Bay, south of Macao.

The Chinese authorities began to complain of these two ships in 1793, but the traffic still increased, and without serious interruption until 1820, when an edict was issued forbidding any vessel having opium on board to enter the Canton river. This led to a system of contraband trade with the connivance of the Chinese officials, which towards the expiration of the East India Company's charter in 1834 had assumed a regular character. The political difficulties between England and China that ensued shortly after this event, and the so-called Opium War, culminated in the Treaty of Nanking (1842), by which five ports of China were opened to foreign trade, and opium was in 1858 admitted as a legal article of commerce.[5]

The vice of opium-smoking began to prevail in China in the second

[1] *Clavis Sanationis*, Venet. 1510. 46.

[2] *De Medicina Ægyptiorum*, Lugd. Bat. 1719. 261.

[3] De Mas Latrie, *Hist. de Chypre*, iii. 406. 483; Muratori, *Rerum Italic. Scriptores*, xxii. 1170; Amari, *I diplomi Arabi del archivio Fiorentino*, Firenze, 1863. 358.

[4] Fontanon, *Edicts et ordonnances des roys de France*, ii. (1585) 347.

[5] For more ample particulars on these momentous events, see S. Wells Williams's *Middle Kingdom*, vol. ii. (1848); *British Almanac Companion* for 1844, p. 77.

half of the 17th century,[1] and in another hundred years had spread like a plague over the gigantic empire. The first edict against the practice was issued in 1796, since which there have been innumerable enactments and memorials,[2] but all powerless to arrest the evil which is still increasing in an alarming ratio. Mr. Hughes, Commissioner of Customs at Amoy, thus wrote on this subject in his official *Trade Report*[3] for the year 1870:—"Opium-smoking appears here as elsewhere in China to be becoming yearly a more recognized habit,—almost a necessity of the people. Those who use the drug now do so openly, and native public opinion attaches no odium to its use, so long as it is not carried to excess. . . . In the city of Amoy, and in adjacent cities and towns, the proportion of opium-smokers is estimated to be from 15 to 20 per cent. of the adult population. . . . In the country the proportion is stated to be from 5 to 10 per cent. . . ."

Production—The poppy in whatever region it may grow always contains a milky juice possessing the same properties; and the collection of opium is *possible* in all temperate and sub-tropical countries where the rainfall is not excessive. But the production of the drug is limited by other conditions than soil and climate, among which the value of land and labour stands pre-eminent.

At the present day opium is produced on an important scale in Asia Minor, Persia, India, and China; to a small extent in Egypt. The drug has also been collected in Europe, Algeria,[4] North America,[5] and Australia,[6] but more for the sake of experiment than as an object of commerce.

We shall describe the production of the different kinds under their several names.

1. *Opium of Asia Minor; Turkey, Smyrna, or Constantinople Opium*[7]—The poppy from which this most important kind of opium is obtained is *Papaver somniferum*, var. *β. glabrum* Boissier. The flowers are commonly purplish, but sometimes white, and the seeds vary from white to dark violet.

The cultivation is carried on throughout Asia Minor, both on the more elevated and the lower lands, the cultivators being mostly small peasant proprietors. The plant requires a naturally rich and moist soil, further improved by manure, not to mention much care and attention on the part of the grower. Spring frosts, drought, or locusts sometimes effect its complete destruction. The sowing takes place at intervals from November to March, partly to insure against risk of total failure, and partly in order that the plants may not all come to perfection at the same time.

The plants flower between May and July according to the elevation of the land. A few days after the fall of the petals the poppy head

[1] Bretschneider, *Study of Chinese Bot. Works*, 1870. 48.

[2] *Chinese Repository*, vol. v. (1837) vi. &c.

[3] Addressed to the Inspector-General of Customs, Pekin, and published at Shanghai, 1871.

[4] *Pharm. Journ.* xv. (1856) 348.

[5] *Am. Journ. of Phar.* xviii. (1870) 124; *Journ. of Soc. of Arts*, Dec. 1, 1871.

[6] *Pharm. Journ.* Oct. 1, 1870. 272.

[7] Much information under this head has been derived from a paper *On the production of Opium in Asia Minor* by S. H. Maltass (*Pharm. Journ.* xiv. 1855. 395), and one *On the Culture and Commerce in Opium in Asia Minor*, by E. R. Heffler, of Smyrna (*Pharm. Journ.* x. 1869. 434).

being about an inch and a half in diameter is ready for incision. The incision is made with a knife transversely, about half-way up the capsule, and extends over about two-thirds the circumference, or is carried spirally to beyond its starting point. Great nicety is required not to cut too deep so as to penetrate the capsule, as in that case some of the juice would flow inside and be lost. The incisions are generally made in the afternoon and the next morning are found covered with exuded juice. This is scraped off with a knife, the gatherer transferring it to a poppy leaf which he holds in his left hand. At every alternate scraping, the knife is wetted with saliva by drawing it through the mouth, the object being to prevent the adhesion of the juice to the blade. Each poppy-head is, as a rule, cut only once; but as a plant produces several heads all of which are not of proper age at the same time, the operation of incising and gathering has to be gone over two or three times on the same plot of ground.

As soon as a sufficient quantity of the half-dried juice has been collected to form a cake or lump, it is wrapped in poppy leaves and put for a short time to dry in the shade. There is no given size for cakes of opium, and they vary in weight from a few ounces to more than two pounds. In some villages it is the practice to make the masses larger than in others. Before the opium is ready for the market, a meeting of buyers and sellers is held in each district, at which the price to be asked is discussed and settled,—the peasants being most of them in debt to the buyers or merchants.

To the latter the opium is sold in a very soft but natural state. These dealers sometimes manipulate the soft drug with a wooden pestle into larger masses which they envelope in poppy leaves and pack in cotton bags sealed at the mouth for transport to Smyrna. According to another account, the opium as obtained from the grower is at once packed in bags together with a quantity of the little chaffy fruits of a dock (*Rumex* sp.) to prevent the lumps from sticking together, and so brought in baskets to Smyrna, or ports farther north.

The opium remains in the baskets (placed in cool warehouses to avoid loss of weight) till sold, and it is only on reaching the buyer's warehouse that the seals are broken and the contents of the bags exposed. This is done in the presence of the buyer, seller, and a public examiner, the last of whom goes through the process of inspecting the drug piece by piece, throwing aside any of suspicious quality. Heffler of Smyrna asserts that the drug is divided into three qualities, viz.—the *prime*, which is not so much a selected quality as the opium of some esteemed districts,—the *current*, which is the mercantile quality and constitutes the great bulk of the crop,—and lastly the inferior or *chiqinti*.[1] The opium of very bad quality or wholly spurious he would place in a fourth category. Maltass applies the name *chiqinti* (or *chicantee*) to opium of every degree of badness.

The examination of opium by the official expert is not conducted in any scientific method. His opinion of the drug is based on colour, odour, appearance and weight, and appears to be generally very correct. Fayk Bey (1867) has recommended the Turkish government to adopt the more certain method of assaying opium by chemical means.

In Asia Minor the largest quantities of opium are now produced in

[1] Probably signifying *refuse*,—*that which comes out.*

the north-western districts of Karahissar Sahib, Balahissar, Kutaya, and Kiwa (or Geiveh), the last on the river Sakariyeh which runs into the Black Sea. These centres of large production of opium send a superior quality of the drug to Constantinople by way of Izmid; the best apparently from Bogaditch and Balikesri, near the Susurlu river. Angora and Amasia are other places in the north of Asia Minor whence opium is obtained.

In the centre of the peninsula Afium Karahissar (literally *opium-black-castle*) and Ushak are important localities for opium, which is also the case with Isbarta, Buldur and Hamid farther south. The product of these districts finds its way to Smyrna, in the immediate neighbourhood of which but little opium is produced. The export from Smyrna in 1871, in which year the crop was very large, was 5650 cases, valued at £784,500.[1]

Turkey Opium, as it is generally called in English trade, occurs in the form of rounded masses which according to their softness become more or less flattened or many-sided, or irregular by mutual pressure in the cases in which they are packed. There appears to be no rule as to their weight[2] which varies from an ounce up to more than 6 ℔.; from ½ ℔. to 2 ℔. is however the most usual. The exterior is covered with the remains of poppy leaves strewn over with the *Rumex* chaff before alluded to, which together make the lumps sufficiently dry to be easily handled. The consistence is such that the drug can be readily cut with a knife, or moulded between the fingers. The interior is moist and coarsely granular, varying in tint from a light chestnut to a blackish brown. Fine shreds of the epidermis of the poppy capsule are perceptible even to the naked eye, but are still more evident if the residue of opium washed with water, is moistened with dilute chromic acid (1 to 100). The odour of Turkey opium is peculiar, and though commonly described as narcotic and unpleasant, is to many persons far from disagreeable. The taste is bitter.

The substances alleged to be used for adulterating Turkey opium are sand, pounded poppy capsules, pulp of apricots or figs, gum tragacanth or even turpentine. Bits of lead are sometimes found in the lumps, also stones and masses of clay.

2. *Egyptian Opium*—though not abundant little as formerly is still met with in European commerce. It usually occurs in hard, flattish cakes about 4 inches in diameter covered with the remnants of a poppy leaf, but not strewn over with rumex-fruits. We have also seen it (1873) as freshly imported, in a soft and plastic state The fractured surface of this opium (when hard) is finely porous, of a dark liver-colour, shining here and there from imbedded particles of quartz or gum, and reddish-yellow points (of resin ?). Under the microscope an abundance of starch granules is sometimes visible. The morphine in a sample from Merck amounted to 6 per cent.

According to Von Kremer who wrote in 1863,[3] there were then in

[1] Consul Cumberbatch, *Trade Report for* 1871, presented to Parliament.

[2] The largest lump I have seen weighed 6 ℔. 6 oz., being part of 65 packages which I examined 2nd July, 1873.—D. H.

[3] *Aegypten, Forschungen über Land und Volk während eines 10 jährigen Aufenthaltes*, Leipzig, 1863.

Upper Egypt near Esneh, Kenneh, and Siout, as much as 10,000 *feddan* (equal to about the same number of English acres) of land cultivated with the poppy from which opium was obtained in March, and seed in April. Hartmann[1] states that the cultivation is carried on by the government, and solely for the requirement of the sanitary establishments.

S. Stafford Allen in 1861 witnessed the collection of opium at Kenneh in Upper Egypt,[2] from a white-flowered poppy. An incision is made in the capsule by running a knife twice round it transversely, and the juice scraped off the following day with a sort of scoop-knife. The gatherings are collected on a leaf and placed in the sun to harden. The produce appeared extremely small and was said to be wholly used in the country

Gastinel, director of the Experimental Garden at Cairo, and government inspector of pharmaceutical stores, has shown (1865) that the poppy in Egypt might yield a very good product containing 10 to 12 per cent. of morphine, and that the present bad quality of Egyptian opium is due to an over-moist soil, and a too early scarification of the capsule, whereby (not to mention wilful adulteration) the proportion of morphine is reduced to 3 or 4 per cent.

In 1872, 9636 lb. of opium, value £5023, were imported into the United Kingdom from Egypt.

3. *Persian Opium.*—Persia, probably the original home of the baneful practice of opium-eating, cultivates the drug chiefly in the central provinces where, according to Boissier, the plant grown to furnish it is *Papaver somniferum*, var. γ *album* (*P. officinale* Gm.) having ovate roundish capsules. Poppy heads from Persia which we saw at the Paris Exhibition in 1867, had vertical incisions and contained white seeds.

The strongest opium called in Persia *Teriak-e-Arabistani* is obtained in the neighbourhood of Dizful and Shuster, east of the Lower Tigris. Good opium is likewise produced about Sari and Balfarush in the province of Mazanderan, and in the southern province of Kerman. The lowest quality which is mixed with starch and other matters, is sold in light brown sticks; it is made at Shahabdulazim, Kashan, and Kum.[3] A large quantity of opium appears to be produced in Khokan and Turkestan.

Persian opium is carried overland to China through Bokhara, Khokan and Kashgar;[4] but since 1864 it has also been extensively conveyed thither by sea, and it is now quoted in trade reports like that of Malwa, Patna, and Benares.[5] It is exported by way of Trebizond to Constantinople where it used to be worked up to imitate the opium

[1] *Naturgeschichtl. medicin. Skizze der Nilländer*, Berlin, 1866. 353.
[2] *Pharm. Journ.* iv. (1863) 199.
[3] Polak, *Persien*, ii. (1865) 248, &c.
[4] Powell, *Economic Products of the Punjab*, i. (1868) 294.
[5] Thus in the *Trade Report* for Foochow, for 1870, addressed to Mr. Hart, Inspector-General of Customs, Pekin, is the following table :

		Malwa.	Patna.	Benares.	Persian.
Imports of Opium in 1867 . .	chests	2327	1673	724	300
,, ,, 1868 . .	,,	2460	1257	377	544
,, ,, 1869 . .	,,	2201	1340	410	493
,, ,, 1870 . .	,,	1849	1283	245	630

of Asior Minor, and at the same time adulterated.[1] Since 1870, Persian opium which was previously rarely seen as such in Europe, has been imported in considerable quantity, being shipped now from Bushire and Bunder Abbas, in the Persian Gulf, to London or to the Straits Settlements and China. It occurs in various forms, the most typical being a short rounded cone weighing 6 to 10 ounces. We have also seen it in flat circular cakes, 1¼ lb. in weight. In both forms the drug was of firm consistence, a good opium-smell, and internally brown of a comparatively light tint. The surface was strewn over with remnants of stalks and leaves. Some of it had been collected with the use of oil as in Malwa (see p. 51), which was apparent from the greasiness of the cone, and the globules of oil visible when the drug was cut. The best samples of this drug as recently imported, have yielded 8 to 10·75 per cent. of morphine, reckoned on the opium in its moist state.[2]

Carles,[3] from a specimen which seems to have been adulterated with sugar, obtained 8·40 per cent. of morphine, and 3·60 of narcotine, the drug not having been previously dried.

Inferior qualities of Persian opium have also been imported. Some that was soft black and extractiform afforded *undried* only 3 to ½ per cent. of morphine (Howard); while some of very pale hue in small sticks, each wrapped in paper, yielded no more than 0·2 per cent.! (Howard). For further details, see p. 61.

In Turkestan an aqueous extract of poppy heads collected before maturity is prepared; it seems to be rich in alkaloids.[4]

4. *European Opium*—From numerous experiments made during the present century in Greece, Italy, France, Switzerland, Germany, England, and even in Sweden, it has been shown that in all these countries a very rich opium, not inferior to that of the East, can be produced.

The most numerous attempts at opium-growing in Europe have been made in France. But although the cultivation was recommended in the strongest terms by Guibourt,[5] who found in French opium the highest percentage of morphine yet observed (22·8 per cent.), it has never become a serious branch of industry.

Aubergier of Clermont-Ferrand has carried on the cultivation with great perseverance since 1844, and has succeeded in producing a very pure inspissated juice which he calls *Affium*, and which is said to contain uniformly[6] 10 per cent. of morphine. It is made up in cakes of 50 grammes, but is scarcely an article of wholesale commerce.[7]

Some careful and interesting scientific investigations relating to the production of opium in the neighbourhood of Amiens, were made by Decharme in 1855 to 1862.[8] He found 14,725 capsules incised within

[1] Letter from Mr. Merck to Dr. F. 1863.

[2] Information kindly given us (9th June, 1873) by Mr. W. Dillworth Howard, of the firm of Howard and Sons, Stratford. A morphine manufacturer has no particular interest in ascertaining the amount of water in the opium he purchases. All he requires to know is the percentage of morphine which the drug contains. It is otherwise with the pharmaceutist, whose preparations have to be made with *dried opium*.

[3] *Journ de Pharm.* xvii. (1873) 427.

[4] Fedschenko's Catalogue of the Moscow Exhibition, Turkestan department, in Buchner's *Repertorium für Pharmacie*, xxii. (1873) 221.

[5] *Journ. de Pharm.* xli. (1862) 184, 201.

[6] How this uniformity is insured we know not.

[7] Dorvault, *Officine*, éd. 8. 1872. 648.

[8] They are recorded in several pamphlets, for which we are indebted to the author, reprinted from the *Mém. de l'Acad. du dé.*

6 days to afford 431 grammes of milky juice, yielding 205 grammes (= 47·6 per cent.) of dry opium containing 16 per cent. of morphine. Another sample of dried opium afforded 20 per cent. of morphine. Decharme observed that the amount of morphine diminished when the juice is very slowly dried,—a point of great importance deserving attention in India. The peculiar odour of opium as observable in the oriental drug, is developed, according to the same authority, by a kind of fermentation.[1] Adrian even suggests that morphine is formed only by a similar process, inasmuch as he could obtain none by exhausting fresh poppy capsules with acidulated alcohol, while capsules of the same crop yielded an opium rich in morphine.

5. *East Indian Opium*—The principal region of British India distinguished for the production of opium is the central tract of the Ganges, comprising an area of about 600 miles in length, by 200 miles in width. It reaches from Dinajpur in the east, to Hazaribagh in the south, and Gorakhpur in the north, and extends westward to Agra, thus including the flat and thickly-populated districts of Behar and Benares. The amount of land here actually under poppy cultivation was estimated in 1871-72 as 560,000 acres.

The region second in importance for the culture of opium consists of the broad table-lands of Malwa, and the slopes of the Vindhya Hills, in the dominions of the Holkar.

Beyond these vast districts, the area under poppy cultivation is comparatively small,[2] yet it appears to be on the increase. Stewart[3] reports (1869) that the plant is grown (principally for opium) throughout the plains of the Punjab, but less commonly in the north-west. In the valley of the Biās, east of Lahore, it is cultivated up to nearly 7500 feet above the sea-level.

The manufacture of opium in these parts of India is not under any restriction as in Hindustan. Most districts, says Powell (1868),[4] cultivate the poppy to a certain extent, and produce a small quantity of indifferent opium for local consumption. The drug, however, is prepared in the Hill States, and the opium of Kūlū (E. of Lahore), is of excellent quality, and forms a staple article of trade in that region. Opium is also produced in Nepal, Basāhīr and Rāmpūr, and at Doda Kashtwar in the Jammū territory.[5] It is exported from these districts to Yarkand, Khutan, Aksu, and other Chinese provinces,—to the extent in 1862 of 210 *maunds* (= 16,800 lb.). The Madras Presidency exports no opium at all.

The opium districts of Bengal[6] are divided into two agencies, those of Behar and Benares, which are under the control of officials residing respectively at Patna and Ghazipur. The opium is a government monopoly—that is to say, the cultivators are under an obligation to sell their produce to the government at a price agreed on beforehand; at the

partement de la Somme and the *Mém. de l'Académie Stanislas.*

[1] *Journ. de Pharm.* vi. (1867) 222.

[2] So we may infer from the fact that of the 39,225 chests which paid duty to Government at Bombay in 1872, 37,979 were Malwa opium, the remaining 1,246 being reckoned as from Guzerat.—*Statement of the Trade and Nav. of Bombay for* 1871-72, p. xv.

[3] *Punjab Plants*, Lahore, 1869. 10.

[4] *Op. cit.* i. 294.

[5] At the base of the Himalaya, S. and S.E. of Kashmir.

[6] Much of what follows respecting Bengal opium is derived from a paper by Eatwell, formerly First Assistant and Opium Examiner in the Government Factory at Ghazipur.—*Pharm. Journ.* xi. (1852) 269, &c.

same time it is wholly optional with them, whether to enter on the cultivation or not.

The variety of poppy cultivated is the same as in Persia, namely, *P. somniferum*, var. γ *album*. As in Asia Minor, a moist and fertile soil is indispensable.[1] The plant is liable to injury by insects, excessive rain, hail, or the growth on its roots of a species of *Orobanche*.

In Behar the sowing takes place at the beginning of November, and the capsules are sacrificed in February or March (March or April in Malwa). This operation is performed with a peculiar instrument, called a *nushtur*, having three or four two-pointed blades, bound together with cotton thread.[2] In using the *nushtur*, only one set of points is brought into use at a time, the capsule being scarified vertically from base to summit. This scarification is repeated on different sides of the capsule at intervals of a few days, from two to six times. In many districts of Bengal, transverse cuts are made in the poppy-head as in Asia Minor.

The milky juice is scraped off early on the following morning with an iron scoop, which as it becomes filled is emptied into an earthen pot carried by the collector's side. In Malwa a flat scraper is used which, as well as the fingers of the gatherer, is wetted from time to time with linseed oil to prevent the adhesion of the glutinous juice. All accounts represent the juice to be in a very moist state by reason of dew, which sometimes even washes it away; but so little is this moisture of the juice thought detrimental that, as Butter states,[3] the collectors in some places actually wash their scrapers in water, and add the washings to the collection of the morning!

The juice when brought home is a wet granular mass of pinkish colour; and in the bottom of the vessel in which it is contained, there collects a dark fluid resembling infusion of coffee, which is called *pasēwā*. The recent juice strongly reddens litmus, and blackens metallic iron. It is placed in a shallow earthen vessel, which is tilted in such a manner that the *pasēwā* may drain off as long as there is any of it to be separated. This liquor is set aside in a covered vessel. The residual mass is now exposed to the air, though never to the sun, and turned over every few days to promote its attaining the proper degree of dryness, which according to the Benares regulations, allows of 30 per cent. of moisture. This drying operation occupies three or four weeks.

The drug is then taken to the Government factory for sale; previous to being sold it is examined for adulteration by a native expert, and its proportion of water is also carefully determined. Having been received into stock, it undergoes but little treatment beyond a thorough mixing, until it is required to be formed into globular cakes. This is effected in a somewhat complicated manner, the opium being strictly of standard consistence. First the quantity of opium is weighed out, and having been formed into a ball is enveloped in a crust of dried poppy petals, skilfully agglutinated one over the other by means of a liquid called *lēwā*. This consists partly of good opium, partly of *pasēwā*, and partly of opium of inferior quality, all being mixed with the washings of the various pots and vessels which have contained opium, and then

[1] It is said (1873) that the ground devoted to poppy-culture in Bengal is becoming impoverished, and that the plant no longer attains its usual dimensions.

[2] For figures of the instrument, see *Pharm. Journ.* xi. (1862) 207.

[3] *Pharm Journ.* xi. (1852) 209.

evaporated to a thick fluid, 100 grains of which should afford 53 of dry residue. These various things are used to form a ball of opium in the following proportions :—

	seers.	chittaks.
Opium of standard consistence	1	7·50
,, contained in *lewa*		3·75
Poppy petals		5·43
Fine *trash*		0·50
	2	1·18= { about 4 lb. 3¼ oz avoirdupois.

The finished balls usually termed *cakes*, which are quite spherical and have a diameter of 6 inches, are rolled in *poppy trash* which is the name given to the coarsely powdered stalks, capsules and leaves of the plant; they are then placed in small dishes and exposed to the direct influence of the sun. Should any become distended, it is at once opened, the gas allowed to escape, and the cake made up again. After three days the cakes are placed, by the end of July, in frames in the factory where the air is allowed to circulate. They still however require constant watching and turning, as they are liable to contract mildew which has to be removed by rubbing in *poppy trash*. By October the cakes have become perfectly dry externally and quite hard, and are in condition to be packed in cases (40 cakes in each) for the China market which consumes the great bulk of the manufacture.

For consumption in India the drug is prepared in a different shape. It is inspissated by solar heat till it contains only 10 per cent. of moisture, in which state it is formed into square cages of 2 lb. each which are wrapped in oil paper, or it is made into flat square tablets. Such a drug is known as *Abkāri Opium*.

The Government opium factories in Bengal are conducted on the most orderly system. The care bestowed in selecting the drug, and in excluding any that is damaged or adulterated is such that the merchants who purchase the commodity rarely require to examine it, although permission is freely accorded to open at each sale any number of chests or cakes they may desire. In the year 1871-72 the number of chests sold was 49,695, the price being £139 per chest, which is £26 higher than the average of the preceding year. The net profit on each chest was £90.[1]

In Malwa the manufacture of opium is left entirely to private enterprise, the profit to Government being derived from an export duty of 600 rupees (£60) per chest.[2] As may readily be supposed, the drug is of much less uniform quality than that which has passed through the Bengal agencies, and having no guarantee as to purity it commands less confidence.

Malwa opium is not made into balls, but into rectangular masses, or bricks which are not cased in poppy petals; it contains as much as 95 per cent. of dry opium. Some opium sold in London as *Malwa Opium* in 1870 had the form of rounded masses covered with vegetable remains. It was of firm consistence, dark colour, and rather smoky odour. W. D. Howard obtained from it (*undried*) 9 per cent. of morphine. Other

[1] *Statement exhibiting the moral and material progress and condition of India during the year* 1871-72,—Blue Book ordered to be printed 29th July, 1873. p. 10.

[2] The revenue by this duty upon opium exported from Bombay in the year 1871-72, was £2,353,500.

importations afforded the same chemist 4·8 and 6 per cent. respectively.

The chests of Patna opium hold 120 catties or 160 ℔. Those of Malwa opium 1 pecul or 133⅓ ℔.

The quantity of opium produced in India cannot be ascertained, but the amount exported[1] is accurately known. Thus from British India the exports in the year ending March 31, 1872, were 93,364 chests valued at £13,365,228. Of this quantity Bengal furnished 49,455 chests, Bombay 43,909 chests: they were exported thus:—

To China	85,470 chests.
The Straits Settlements	7,845 ,,
Ceylon, Java, Mauritius and Bourbon	38 ,,
The United Kingdom	4 ,,
Other countries	7 ,,
Total	93,364 ,,

The net revenue to the Government of India from opium in the year 1871-72 was £7,657,213.

6. *Chinese Opium*—China consumes not only nine-tenths of the opium exported from India, and a considerable quantity of that produced in Asia Minor, but the whole of what is raised in her own provinces. How large is this last quantity we shall endeavour to show.

The drug is mentioned as a production of Yunnan in a history of that province, of which the latest edition appeared in 1736. But it is only very recently that its cultivation in China has assumed such large proportions as to threaten serious competition with that in India.[2]

In a *Report upon the Trade of Hankow* for 1869, addressed to Mr. Hart, Inspector-General of Customs, Pekin, we find *Notes of a journey through the opium districts of Szechuen*, undertaken for the special purpose of obtaining information about the drug.[3] From these notes it appears that the estimated crop of the province for 1869 was 4235 peculs (=564,666 ℔.). This was considered *small*, and the Szechuen opium merchants asserted that 6000 peculs was a fair average. The same authorities estimated the annual yield of the province of Kweichow at 15,000, and of Yunnan at 20,000 peculs, making a total of 41,000 peculs or 5,466,666 ℔. In 1869 also, Sir R. Alcock reported that about two-thirds of the province of Szechuen and one-third of that of Yunnan were devoted to opium.[4]

Mr. Consul Markham states[5] that the province of Shensi likewise

[1] *Annual Statement of the Trade and Navigation of British India with foreign countries*, published by order of the Governor-General, Calcutta, 1872. 52.

[2] In the *Report on the Trade of Hankow for* 1869 addressed to Mr. Hart, Inspector-General of Customs, Pekin, it is stated—"The importation of opium is considerably short for the last two seasons, but this is not to be wondered at now that each opium-shopkeeper in this and the surrounding districts advertises native drug for sale."

W. H. Medhurst, British Consul at Shanghai, says—"The drug is now being so extensively produced by the Chinese upon their own soil as sensibly to affect the demand for the India-grown commodity."—*Foreigner in Far Cathay*, Lond. 1872. 20.

The quantity of opium exported from Bombay in 1871-72 was less by 1719 chests than that exported in 1870-71, the decrease being attributed to the present large cultivation in China.—*Statement of the Trade and Nav. of Bombay for* 1871-72, pp. xii. xvi.

[3] According to the French missionaries, the cultivation of the poppy in the great province of Szechuen was hardly known even so recently as 1840.

[4] *Calcutta Blue Book*, p. 205.

[5] *Journ. of Soc. of Arts*, Sept. (1872) 6, p. 338.

furnishes important supplies. Mr. Edkins the well-known missionary has lately pointed out from personal observation[1] the extensive cultivation of the poppy in the north-eastern province of Shantung.

Opium of very fair quality is now produced about Ninguta (lat. 44°) in north-eastern Manchuria, a region having a rigorous winter climate. Consul Adkins of Newchwang who visited this district in 1871, reports that the opium is inspissated in the sun until hard enough to be wrapped in poppy leaves, and that its price on the spot is equal to about 1s. per ounce.[2]

Shensi opium is said to be the best, then that of Yunnan. But Chinese consumers mostly regard home-grown opium as inferior in strength and flavour, and only fit for use when mixed with the Indian drug.[2]

It must not be supposed that the growing of opium in China has passed unnoticed by the Chinese Government. Whatever may be the nature of the sanction now accorded to this branch of industry, it was "rigorously" prohibited, at least in some provinces, about ten years ago, the effect of the prohibition being to stimulate the foreign importations. Thus at Shanghai in 1865, the importation of Benares opium was 2637 peculs,[3] being more than double that of the previous year, and Persian opium, very rarely seen before, was imported to the extent of 533 peculs, besides about 70 peculs of Turkish.[4]

Of the growth of the trade in opium between India and China, the following figures[5] will give some idea; value of exports in

1852–53 — £6,470,915. 1861–62 — £9,704,972. 1871–72 — £11,605,577.

and[6]

In	1872	1873	1874	1875	1876
Chests opium, .	93,364	82,908	88,727	94,746	88,350
Value, . .	£13,365,228	11,426,280	11,341,857	11,956,972	11,148,426

In 1877 the imports of opium in Hong Kong were stated to consist of 6818 peculs, valued at 2,380,665 taels, coming from Patna (2158 peculs), Benares (3596 peculs), Persia (1041 peculs), Malwa (10 peculs), Turkey (3½ peculs). In the same year 4043 peculs of opium were imported in Amoy.

Poppy cultivation in the south-west of China has been briefly described by Thorel,[7] from whose remarks it would appear to be exactly like that of India. The poppy is white-flowered; the head is wounded with a three-bladed knife, in a series of 3 to 5 vertical incisions, and the exuded juice is scraped off and transferred to a small pot suspended at the waist. How the drug is finished off we know not. A Chinese account states simply that the best opium is sun-dried. But little is known of its physical and chemical properties. Thorel speaks of it as a soft substance resembling an extract. Dr. R. A. Jamieson[8] describes

[1] *North China Herald*, June 28, 1873.

[2] *Reports of H. M. Consuls in China*, 1871 (No. 3, 1872), 1874 (No. 5, 1875), p. 4, 23.

[3] One pecul = 133⅓ lb.

[4] *Reports on the Trade at the Treaty Ports in China for* 1865. 125.

[5] Taken from the *Annual Statement of the Trade and Navigation of British India with foreign countries*, published by order of the Governor-General, Calcutta, 1872—199.

[6] *Statistical Abstract relating to British India from* 1866-67 to 1875-76. London, 1877, pp. 51, 53.

[7] *Notes médicales du voyage d'exploration du Mékong et de Cochinchine*, Paris, 1870. 23.

[8] *Report on the Trade of Hankow*, before quoted.

a sample submitted to him as a flat cake enveloped in the sheathing petiole of bamboo; externally it was a blackish-brown, glutinous substance, dry and brittle on the outside. It lost by drying 18 per cent. of water, and afforded upon incineration 7·5 per cent. of ash. In 100 grains of the (undried) drug, there were found 5·9 of morphine, and 7·5 of narcotine. (See also p. 62.)

The Chinese who prepare opium for use by converting it into an aqueous extract which they smoke, do not estimate the value of the drug according to its richness in morphine, but by peculiarities of aroma and degree of solubility. In China the preparation of opium for smoking is a special business, not beneath the notice even of Europeans.[1]

7. ***Zambezi*** or ***Mozambik Opium***—From a notice in Pharm. Journal viii. (1878) 1007, it would appear that the Portuguese have formed in 1877 a large company called the "Mozambique Opium Cultivating and Trading Company."

Description—The leading characteristics of each kind of opium have been already noticed. The following remarks bear chiefly on the microscopic appearances of the drug.

As will be presently shown, a more or less considerable part of the drug consists of peculiar substances which are mostly crystallizable and are many of them present in a crystalline state in the drug itself. All kinds of opium appear more or less crystalline when a little in a dry state is triturated with benzol and examined under the microscope. The forms are various: opium from Asia Minor exhibits needles and short imperfect crystals usually not in large quantity, whereas Indian and still more Persian opium is not only highly crystalline but shows a variety of forms which become beautifully evident when seen by polarized light. In several kinds large crystals occur which are doubtless sugar, either intentionally mixed or naturally present. The crystals seen in opium are not however sufficiently developed to warrant positive conclusions as to their nature, besides which the opium constituents when pure are capable under slightly varied circumstances of assuming very different forms. Hence the attempt to obtain from solutions crystals which shall be comparable with those of the same substances in a state of purity often fails. Some interesting observations in this direction were made by Deane and Brady in 1864-5.[2]

All opium has a peculiar narcotic odour and a sharp bitter taste.

Chemical Composition—Poppy-juice like analogous vegetable fluids is a mixture of several substances in variable proportion. With the commoner substances which constitute the great bulk of the drug we are not yet sufficiently acquainted.

[1] In 1870, a British firm at Amoy opened an establishment for preparing opium for the supply of the Chinese in California and Australia.—*Pall Mall Gazette*, Nov. 7th, 1878, p. 7, announces: "The monopoly of preparing and selling opium in the 14 districts of Kwang-chow-fu, has been leased to a Hong at Canton for 3 years, . . . innovation on former practice. . . . . Opium shops are henceforth to be licensed, and the Exchequer will receive the yearly sum of 140,000 dollars—a welcome addition to the revenue."

[2] *Pharm. Journ.* vi. 234; vii. 183. with 4 beautiful plates representing the crystallizations from extract and tincture of opium as well as from the pure opium constituents. When the juice of the poppy is prevented from rapid drying by the addition of a little glycerin, crystals are developed in it.

In the first place (independently of water) there is found mucilage distinct from that of gum arabic, also pectic matter,[1] and albumin. These bodies, together with unavoidable fragments of the poppy-capsules, probably amount on an average to more than half the weight of the opium.[2]

In addition to these substances, the juice also contains sugar in solution,—in French opium to the extent of 6½ to 8 per cent.: according to Decharme it is uncrystallizable. Sugar also exists in other opium, but whether always naturally has not been determined.

Fresh poppy-juice contains in the form of emulsion, wax, pectin, albumin and insoluble calcareous salts. When good Turkey opium is treated with water these substances remain in the residue to the extent of 6 to 10 per cent.

Hesse (1870) has isolated the *wax* by exhausting the refuse of opium with boiling alcohol and a little lime. He thus obtained a crystalline mass from which he separated by chloroform *Palmitate* and *Cerotate of Cerotyl*, the former in the larger proportion.

The presence of *Caoutchouc* has also been pointed out; Procter[3] found opium produced in Vermont to contain about 11 per cent. of that substance, together with a little fatty matter and resin.

Respecting the colouring matter and an extremely small quantity of a volatile body with pepper-like odour, we know but little. After the colouring matter has been precipitated from an aqueous solution of opium by lead acetate, the liquid becomes again coloured by exposure to the air. As to the volatile body, it may be removed by acetone or benzol, but has not yet been isolated.

The salts of inorganic bases, chiefly of calcium, magnesium and potassium, contain partly the ordinary acids such as phosphoric and sulphuric, and partly an acid peculiar to the poppy.

Good opium of Asia Minor dried at 100° C. yields 4 to 8 per cent. of ash.

Poppy-juice contains neither starch nor tannic acid, the absence of which easily-detected substances affords one criterion for judging of the purity of the drug.

The proportion of water in opium is very variable. In drying Turkey opium previous to pulverization and for other pharmaceutical purposes, the average loss is about 12½ per cent.[4] Bengal opium, which resembles a soft black extract, is manufactured so as to contain 30 per cent. of water.

As the active constituents of opium, or at all events the morphine, can be completely extracted by cold water, the proportion of soluble matter is of practical importance. In good opium of Asia Minor previously dried, the extract (dried at 100° C.) always amounts to between 55 and 66 per cent.,—generally to more than 60,—thus affording in many instances a test of the pureness of the drug. Dried

[1] We had the opportunity of examining very good specimens of pectic matter and caoutchouc from opium, with which we were presented (1879) by Messrs. J. F. Macfarlane & Co., of London and Edinburgh.

[2] Flückiger, in *Pharm. Journ.* x. (1869) 208.

[3] *American Journ. of Pharm.*, 1870. 124.

[4] From the laboratory accounts of Messrs. Allen and Hanburys, London, by which it appears that 200 ℔. of Turkey opium dried at various times in the course of 10 years lost in weight 25¼ ℔.

Indian opium yields from 60 to 68 per cent. of matter soluble in cold water.[1]

The peculiar constituents of opium are of basic, acid, or neutral nature. Some of these substances were observed in opium as early as the 17th and 18th century, and designated *Magisterium Opii*. Bucholz in 1802 vainly endeavoured to obtain a salt from the extract by crystallization. In 1803, however, Charles Derosne, an apothecary of Paris, in diluting a syrupy aqueous extract of opium, observed crystals of the substance now called *Narcotine*, which he prepared pure. He believed that the same body was obtained by precipitating the mother liquor with an alkali, but what he so got was morphine. It is needless to pursue the further researches of Derosne. Ingenious as they were, it was reserved for Friedrich Wilhelm Adam Sertürner, apothecary of Eimbeck in Hanover (*nat.* 1783, *ob.* 1841) to discover their true interpretation.

Sertürner had been engaged since 1805 with the chemical investigation of opium, and in 1816 he summarized his results in the statement that he had enriched science (we now translate his own words[2]) —"not only with the knowledge of a remarkable new vegetable acid [*Mekonsäure* (meconic acid) which he had made known as *Opiumsäure* in 1806], but also with the discovery of a new alkaline salifiable base, *Morphium*, one of the most remarkable substances, and apparently related to ammonia." Sertürner in fact distinctly recognised the basic nature and the organic constitution of morphium (now called *Morphine*, *Morphia*, or *Morphinum*), and prepared a number of its crystalline salts. He likewise demonstrated the poisonous nature of these substances by experiments on himself and others. Lastly, he pointed out, though very incorrectly, the difference between morphine and the so-called *Opium-salt* (Narcotine) of Derosne. It is possible that this latter chemist may have had morphine in his hands at the same time as Sertürner, or even earlier. This honour is also due to Séguin, whose paper "*Sur l'Opium*," read at the Institute, December 24, 1804, was, strange to say, not published till 1814.[3] To Sertürner, however, undoubtedly belongs the merit of first making known the existence of organic alkalis in the vegetable kingdom,[4]—a series of bodies practically interminable. As to opium, it still remains after nearly seventy years a *nidus* of new substances.

Solutions of morphine in acids or in alkalis rotate the plane of polarization to the left.

The morphine in opium is combined with meconic acid, and is therefore easily soluble in water.[5] The *Narcotine* is present in the free state, and can be extracted by chloroform, boiling alcohol, benzol, ether, or volatile oils,[6] but not by water. It dissolves in 3 parts of chloroform, in 20 of boiling alcohol, in 21 of benzol, in 40 of boiling ether. Its alkaline properties are very weak, and it does not affect

[1] Calculated from official statements given by Eatwell in the paper quoted at p. 50.

[2] Gilbert's *Annalen der Physik*, lv. (1817) 57.

[3] *Annales de Chimie*, xcii. (1814) 225.

[4] The Institut de France on the 27th June, 1831, awarded to Sertürner a prize of 2000 francs—"pour avoir reconnu la nature alcaline de la morphine, et avoir ainsi ouvert une voie qui produit de grandes découvertes médicales."

[5] There are exceptional cases in which it is asserted that water does *not* take up the whole amount of morphine.

[6] In large crystals by means of oil of turpentine.

vegetable colours. If we examine opium by the microscope we cannot at once detect the presence of narcotine, but if first moistened with glycerin, numerous large crystals may generally be found after the lapse of some days. If the opium has been previously exhausted with benzol or ether, in order to remove the narcotine, no such crystals will be formed. Hence it follows that narcotine pre-exists in an amorphous state.

By decomposition with sulphuric acid, narcotine yields *Cotarnine*, an undoubted base, together with *Opianic Acid*, and certain derivatives of the latter.

The discovery of another base, *Codeine*, was made in 1832 by Robiquet. It dissolves in 17 parts of boiling water, forming a highly alkaline solution which perfectly saturates acids, and exhibits in polarized light a levogyre power. Codeine is also readily soluble at ordinary temperatures in 7 parts amylic alcohol, and in 11 of benzol.

The codeine of commerce is in very large crystals containing 2 atoms = 5·66 per cent. of water. By crystallization from ether the alkaloid may be obtained in small anhydrous crystals.

Since 1832 other alkaloids have been found in opium, as may be seen in the following table, which includes all the 17 now known.[1]

A very large number of derivatives of several among them have been prepared, of which we point out a few in smaller type. The molecular constitution of these opium alkaloids being not yet thoroughly settled, we add only their empirical formulæ, which however exhibit unmistakeable connections.

Papaverosine discovered by Deschamps in poppy-heads (p. 42) can hardly be absent from opium. In some points it appears to resemble cryptopine.

Among the peculiar non-basic constituents of opium, the first to call for notice is *Meconic Acid*, $C^7H^4O^7$, discovered, as already observed, by Sertürner in 1805. It is distinguished by the red colour which it produces with ferric salts, the same as that of ferric sulphocyanate; but the latter only dissolves in ether. Meconic acid is soluble in 4 parts of boiling water, but immediately gives off CO^2, and the remaining solution instead of depositing micaceous crystalline scales of meconic acid, yields on cooling (but best after boiling with hydrochloric acid) hard granular crystals of *Comenic Acid*, $C^6H^4O^5$.

Lactic Acid was discovered by T. and H. Smith in the opium-liquors produced in the manufacture of morphine. These chemists regarded it as a peculiar body, and under the name of *Thebolactic Acid*, exhibited it together with its copper and morphine salts at the London International Exhibition of 1862. Its identity with ordinary lactic acid was ascertained by Stenhouse (whose experiments have not been published) and also by J. Y. Buchanan.[2] T. and H. Smith consider it to be a regular constituent of Turkey opium; they obtained it as a calcium-salt to the amount of about 2 per cent., and have prepared it in this form and in a pure state to the extent of over 100 ℔. In our opinion it is not an original constituent of poppy-juice.

[1] In 1851 Hinterberger described as a peculiar alkaloid, *Opianine*; Dr. Hesse has examined Hinterberger's specimen of this body, and found (1875) it to consist of impure narcotine.

[2] *Berichte d. Deutsch. Chem. Gesellsch. zu Berlin*, iii. (1870) 182.

NATURAL ALKALOIDS OF OPIUM

and a few of their Artificial Derivatives.

DISCOVERED BY		C	H	N	O
Wöhler, 1844	.. .. .. COTARNINE .. .. Formed by oxidizing narcotine; soluble in water.	12	13	1	3
Hesse, 1871	.. .. 1. **HYDROCOTARNINE** .. .. Crystallizable, alkaline, volatile at 100°.	12	15	1	3
Matthiessen and Wright, 1869 ..	.. .. .. APOMORPHINE .. .. .. From morphine, by hydrochloric acid. Colourless, amorphous, turning green by exposure to air; emetic.	17	17	1	2
Wright, 1871	.. .. .. DESOXYMORPHINE	17	19	1	2
Sertürner, 1816 ..	.. .. .. 2. **MORPHINE** .. .. .. Crystallizable, alkaline, levogyre.	17	19	1	3
Pelletier and Thiboumèry, 1835 ..	.. 3. **PSEUDOMORPHINE** .. .. Crystallizes with H^2O; does not unite even with acetic acid.	17	19	1	4
Matthiessen and Burnside, 1871 ..	.. .. .. APOCODEINE .. .. .. From codeine by chloride of zinc; amorphous, emetic.	18	19	1	2
Wright, 1871	.. .. .. DESOXYCODEINE	18	21	1	2
Robiquet, 1832 ..	.. .. .. 4. **CODEINE** .. .. .. Crystallizable, alkaline, soluble in water.	18	21	1	3
Matthiessen and Foster, 1868 ..	.. .. .. NORNARCOTINE	19	17	1	7
Thiboumèry, 1835 ..	.. .. .. 5. **THEBAINE** .. .. .. Crystallizable, alkaline, isomeric with buxine.	19	21	1	3
Hesse, 1870	.. .. .. THEBENINE	19	21	1	3
Hesse, 1870	.. .. .. THEBAICINE .. .. .. From thebaine or thebenine by hydrochloric acid.	19	21	1	3
Hesse, 1871	.. .. .. 6. **PROTOPINE** .. .. . Crystallizable, alkaline.	20	19	1	5
Matthiessen and Foster, 1868 ..	.. .. .. METHYLNORNARCOTINE	20	19	1	7
Hesse, 1871	.. .. .. DEUTEROPINE .. .. .. Not yet isolated.	20	21	1	5
Hesse, 1870	.. .. .. 7. **LAUDANINE** .. .. .. An alkaloid which, as well as its salts, forms large crystals; turns orange by hydrochloric acid.	20	25	1	4
Hesse, 1878	.. .. .. 8. **CODAMINE** .. .. .. Crystallizable, alkaline; can be sublimed; becomes green by nitric acid.	20	25	1	4
Merck, 1848	.. .. .. 9. **PAPAVERINE** .. .. .. Crystallizable, also its hydrochlorate; sulphate in sulphuric acid precipitated by water.	21	21	1	4
Hesse, 1865	.. .. 10. **RHŒADINE** .. .. .. Crystallizable, not distinctly alkaline; can be sublimed; occurs also in *Papaver Rhœas*.	21	21	1	6
Hesse, 1865	.. .. .. RHŒAGENINE .. .. .. From rhœadine; crystallizable, alkaline.	21	21	1	6
Armstrong, 1871 ..	.. .. DIMETHYLNORNARCOTINE	21	21	1	7
Hesse, 1870	.. .. 11. **MECONIDINE** .. .. Amorphous, alkaline, melts at 58°, not stable, the salts also easily altered.	21	23	1	4
T. & H. Smith, 1864 ..	.. .. 12. **CRYPTOPINE** .. .. Crystallizable, alkaline; salts tend to gelatinize; hydrochlorate crystallizes in tufts.	21	23	1	5
Hesse, 1871	.. .. 13. **LAUDANOSINE** .. .. Crystallizable, alkaline.	21	27	1	4
Derosne, 1803	.. .. .. 14. **NARCOTINE** .. .. Crystallizable, not alkaline; salts not stable.	22	23	1	7
Hesse, 1870	.. .. 15. **LANTHOPINE** .. .. Microscopic crystals not alkaline, sparingly soluble in hot or cold spirit of wine, ether or benzol.	23	25	1	4
Pelletier, 1832 ..	.. .. .. 16. **NARCEINE** .. .. .. Crystallizable (as a hydrate), readily soluble in boiling water or in alkalis, levogyre.	23	29	1	9
T. & H. Smith, 1878 ..	.. .. 17. **GNOSCOPINE** .. .. Crystallizable, melts at 233°, soluble in chloroform and bisulphide of carbon, slightly so in benzol, not in ether. The salts have an acid reaction.	34	36	2	11

In the year 1826, Dublanc[1] observed in opium a peculiar substance having neither basic nor acid properties which was afterwards (1832) prepared in a state of purity by Couerbe. It has been called *Opianyl* or (by Couerbe) *Meconine.* It has the composition $C^{10}H^{10}O^4 = C^6H^2.CH^2.O.CO(OCH^3)^2$. Meconin forms prisms which fuse under water at 77° C. or *per se* at 110°, and distil at 155°; it dissolves in about 20 parts of boiling water, from which it may be readily crystallized. Meconin may be formed by heating narcotine with nitric acid.

An analogous substance *Meconoiosin* $C^8H^{10}O^3 = C^6H^2.(OH)^2.(CH^3)^2$, has been discovered in 1878 by T. and H. Smith. Meconoiosin is readily soluble in 27 parts of cold water, and melts at 88° C. When heated with slightly diluted sulphuric acid, and when the evaporation has reached a certain point, meconoiosin produces a deep red; with meconin the coloration is a beautiful green.

Proportion of peculiar constituents—The substances described in the foregoing section exist in opium in very variable proportion; and as it is on their presence, but especially that of morphine, that the value of the drug depends, the importance of exact estimation is evident.

Opium whether required for analysis or for pharmaceutical preparations has to be taken *exclusively in the dry state.* The amount of water it contains is so uncertain that the drug must be reduced to a fixed standard by complete desiccation at 100° C., before any given weight is taken.

Morphine—Guibourt[2] who analysed a large number of samples of opium, and whose skill and care in such research are not disputed, obtained from a sample of French opium produced near Amiens, 22·88 per cent. of morphine crystallized from spirit of wine. This percentage has not to our knowledge been ever exceeded. From another specimen produced in the same district he got 21·23 per cent., from a third 20·67. The lowest percentage from a French opium was 14·96, —in each case reckoned on material previously dried.

Chevallier extracted from opium grown by Aubergier at Clermont in the centre of France, 17·50 per cent. of morphine. Decharmes from a French opium obtained 17·6 per cent., and Biltz from a German opium 20 per cent. Opium produced in Würtemberg sent to the Vienna Exhibition of 1873 afforded Hesse 12 to 15 per cent. of morphine; and opium from Silesia 9 to 10 per cent.[3]

A pure American opium collected in the State of Vermont yielded Proctor 15·75 per cent. of morphine and 2 per cent of narcotine.[4]

The opium of Asia Minor furnishes very nearly the same proportions of morphine as that of Europe. The maximum recorded by Guibourt is 21·46 per cent. obtained from a Smyrna opium sold in Paris. The mean yield of 8 samples of opium sent by Della Sudda of Constantinople to the Paris Exhibition of 1855 was 14·78 per cent. The mean percentage of morphine afforded by 12 other samples of Turkey opium obtained from various sources was 14·66.

[1] *Annales de Chimie et de Physique,* xlix. (1832) 5—20.—The paper was read before the Acad. de Méd., 13th May, 1826.

[2] *Mémoire sur le dosage de l'Opium et sur la quantité de morphine que l'opium doit contenir,* Paris, 1862.

[3] Schroff, *Ausstellungsbericht, Arzneiwaaren,* p. 31.

[4] *Am. Journ. of Pharm.* xviii. (1870) 124.

Chevallier[1] states that Smyrna opium, of which several cases were received by Merck of Darmstadt in 1845, afforded 12 to 13 per cent. of pure morphine reckoned upon the drug in its *fresh and moist state.*

Fayk Bey[2] analysed 92 samples of opium of Asia Minor, and found that half the number yielded more than 10 per cent. of morphine. The richest afforded 17·2 per cent.

From the foregoing statements we are warranted in assuming that *good* Smyrna opium deprived of water ought to afford 12 to 15 per cent. of morphine, and that if the percentage is less than 10, adulteration may be suspected.

Egyptian opium has usually been found very much weaker in morphine than that of Asia Minor. A sample sent to the Paris Exhibition of 1865 and presented to one of us by Figari Bey of Cairo, afforded us 5·8 per cent. of morphine and 8·7 of narcotine.

Persian opium appears extremely variable, probably in consequence of the practice of combining it with sugar and other substances. It is however sometimes very good. Séput[3] obtained from four samples the respective percentages of 13·47, 11·52, 10·12, 10·08 of morphine, the opium being free from water. Mr. Howard as already stated (p. 49) extracted from Persian opium, not previously dried, from 8 to 10·75 per cent. of morphine.

East Indian opium is remarkable for its low percentage of morphine, a circumstance which we think is attributable in part to climate and in part to a method of collection radically defective. It is scarcely conceivable that the long period during which the juice remains in a wet state,—always three to four weeks,—does not exercise a destructive action on its constituents.

According to Eatwell[4] the percentage of morphine in the samples of Benares opium officially submitted for analysis gave the following averages.—

1845–46	1846–47	1847–48	1848–49
2·48	2·38	2·20	3·21

The same observer has recorded the results of the examination of freshly collected poppy-juice, which in three instances afforded respectively 1·4, 3·06, and 2·89 per cent. of morphine, reckoned on the material deprived of water; but the conditions under which the experiments were made appear open to great objection.[5]

Such very low results are not always obtained from East Indian opium. In a sample from Khandesh furnished by the Indian Museum, we found 6·07 of morphine. Solly from the same kind obtained about 7 per cent.

Patna Garden Opium which is the sort prepared exclusively for medicinal use, afforded us 8·6 per cent. of purified morphine and 4 per cent. of narcotine.[6] Guibourt obtained from such an opium 7·72

[1] *Notice historique sur l'opium indigène,* Paris, 1852.

[2] *Monographie des Opiums de l'Empire Ottoman envoyés à l'Exposition de Paris,* 1867.

[3] *Journ. de Pharm.* xxxix. (1861) 163.

[4] *Pharm. Journ.* xi. (1852) 361.

[5] In one case the juice was allowed to stand in a basin from 23rd Feb. to 7th May, being "occasionally stirred"!

[6] This drug made in 1838 came from the Apothecary-General, Calcutta, and was presented by Christison to the Kew Museum. It is in rectangular tablets 2¼ inches square and ¾ of an inch thick, cased in wax.

per cent. Christison from a sample sent to Duncan of Edinburgh in 1830,[1] 9·50 per cent. of hydrochlorate of morphine.

Samples from the Indian Museum placed at our disposal by Dr. J. Forbes Watson gave[2] us the following percentages of morphine:—*Medical (Indian) Opium*, 1852-53, portion of a square brick, 4·3; *Garden Behar Opium*, 4·6; *Abkāri Provision Opium, Patna*, No. 5380, 3·5; *Sind Opium*, No. 28, 3·8; *Opium, Hyderabad, Sind*, 3·2 (and 5·4 of narcotine); *Malwa Opium*, 6·1.

With regard to the percentage of morphine in *Chinese Opium*, the following data have been obligingly furnished to us by Mr. T. W. Sheppard, F.C.S., Opium Examiner to the Benares Opium Agency, of analyses made by himself from samples of the drug procured in China by Sir R. Alcock:—Szechuen opium, 2·2; Kweichow, 2·5; Yunnan, 4·1; Kansu, 5·1 per cent. Mr. S. informs us that Dr. Eatwell obtained in 1852 from Szechuen opium 3·3, and from Kweichow opium 6·1[3] per cent.—the opium in all instances being reckoned as *dry*. The samples examined by Mr. S. contained 86 to 95 per cent of dry opium, and yielded (undried) 36 to 53 per cent. of extract soluble in cold water. The proportion of morphine in the sample of Chinese opium analysed by Dr. Jamieson (p. 55) was nearly 7·2 per cent. calculated on the dry drug.

Pseudomorphine—occurs only in very small quantities. Hesse found it in some sorts of opium to the extent of 0·02 per cent,—in others still less.

Codeine—has been found in Smyrna, French and Indian opium, but only to the extent of ¼ to ⅛ per cent. T. and H. Smith give the proportion in Turkey opium as 0·3 per cent.[4]

Thebaine—which has likewise been obtained from French opium, amounts in Turkey opium according to Merck to about 1 per cent. In the latter sort T. and H. Smith found only about 8·15 per cent., but of

Papaverine—in the same drug, 1 per cent.

Narcotine—exists in opium in widely different proportions and often in considerable abundance. Thus Schindler obtained in 1834 from a Smyrna opium yielding 10·30 per cent. of morphine, 1·30 per cent. of narcotine. Biltz (1831) analysed an oriental opium which afforded 9·25 per cent. of morphine and 7·50 of narcotine. Reveil (1860) obtained from Persian opium not rich in morphine, from half as much to twice as much narcotine as morphine. The utmost of narcotine was 9·90 per cent. We have found in German opium of undubitable purity[5] 10·9 per cent. of narcotine.

East Indian opium was found by Eatwell (1850) always to afford more narcotine than morphine,—frequently twice as much. The sample from Khandesh referred to on the opposite page, afforded us 7·7 per cent. of pure narcotine.

French opium collected from the *Pavot œillet* sometimes affords neither narcotine, thebaine, nor narceine.[6]

[1] The actual specimen is in the Kew Museum.

[2] *Pharm Journ.* v. (1875) 845.

[3] This sample, the richest of all in morphine, is noted as of "*2nd quality.*"

[4] *Pharm. Journ.* vii. (1866) 183.

[5] Collected in 1829 by Biltz and obligingly placed in 1867 at my disposal by his son.—F. A. F.

[6] The statement of Biltz (1831) that an opium collected by himself from poppies grown in 1829 at Erfurt afforded 33 per

Narceine—Of this substance Couerbe found in opium 0·1 per cent.; T. and H. Smith 0·02 and Schindler 0·71.

Cryptopine—exists in opium in very small proportion. T. and H. Smith state that since the alkaloid first came under their notice, they have collected of it altogether about 5 ounces in the form of hydrochlorate, and this small quantity in operating on many thousands of pounds of opium. But they by no means assert that the whole of the cryptopine was obtained.

Rhœadine—is also found only in exceedingly minute quantity.

Meconic Acid—If the average amount of morphine in opium be estimated at 15 per cent., and the alkaloid be supposed to exist as a tribasic meconate, it would require for saturation 3·4 per cent. of meconic acid. Wittstein obtained rather more than 3 per cent., T. and H. Smith 4 per cent., and Decharmes 4·33. Opium produced in Vermont yielded, according to Proctor (1870) 5·25 per cent. of meconic acid. The quantity of acid required to unite with the other bases assuming them to exist as salts can be but extremely small.

Estimation of Morphine in Opium—The practical valuation of opium turns in the first instance upon the estimation of the water present in the drug, and in the second upon the proportion which the latter contains of morphine.[1]

The first question is determined by exposing a known quantity of the drug divided into small slices or fragments to the heat of a water-bath until it cease to lose weight.

For the estimation of the morphine many processes have been devised, but none is perfectly satisfactory.[2] That which we recommend is thus performed:—Take of opium previously dried at 100° C., as above stated, and powdered, 10 grammes; shake it with 100 grammes alcohol 0·950 sp. gr., and filter after a day or two. The weight of the liquid should be made equal to 100 grammes. Add to it 50 grammes of ether and 2 grammes of ammonia water 0·960 sp. gr.; collect the crystals of opium which separate slowly, after a day or two, dry them at 100°C., and weigh them.—On applying this method to Indian opium, we were but little satisfied with it.

Commerce—By official statistics it appears that the quantity of opium imported into the United Kingdom in 1872 was 356,211 ℔., valued at £361,503. The imports from Asiatic and European Turkey are stated in the same tables thus:—

1868	1870	1872	1874
317,133 lb.	276,691 lb.	325,572 lb.	514,000 lb.

It is thus evident that the drug used in Great Britain is chiefly Turkish. The import of opium from Persia has been very irregular. In 1871, 21,894 ℔. are reported as received from that country; in 1872, none.

cent. of narcotine is contrary to the experience of all other chemists. The same must be said of Mulder's assertion respecting an opium giving 6 to 13 per cent. of narceine.

[1] In selecting a sample for analysis, care should be taken that it fairly represents the bulk of the drug. We prefer to take a little piece from each of several lumps, mix them in a mortar, and weigh from the mixed sample the required quantity.

[2] See also Proctor, *Pharm. Journ.* vii. (1876) 244, and *Yearbook of Pharm.* 1877. 528.

Except that a little Malwa opium has occasionally been imported, it may be asserted the opium of India is entirely unknown in the English market, and that none of it is to be found even in London in the warehouse of any druggist.

As to other countries, we may point out that in 1876 the import of opium (prepared) into the colony of Victoria was valued at £104,557.

Uses—Opium possesses sedative powers which are universally known. In the words of Pereira, it is the most important and valuable medicine of the whole Materia Medica; and we may add, the source by its judicious employment of more happiness and by its abuse of more misery [1] than any other drug employed by mankind.

Adulteration—The manifold falsifications of opium have been already noticed, and the method by which its more important alkaloid may be estimated has been pointed out. Moreover as already stated, neither tannic acid nor starch ever occur in genuine opium; and the proportion of ash left upon the incineration of a good opium does not exceed 4 to 8 per cent. of the dried drug. Another criterion is afforded by the amount soluble in cold water which ought to exceed 55 per cent. reckoned on dry opium. Finally, if we are correct, the gum contained in pure opium is distinct from gum arabic, being precipitable by neutral acetate of lead. If we exhaust with water opium falsified with gum arabic, the mucilage peculiar to opium will be precipitated by neutral acetate of lead, the liquid separated from the precipitate will still contain the gum arabic which may be thrown down by alcohol. If gum is present to some extent, an abundant precipitate is produced.

CRUCIFERÆ.

SEMEN SINAPIS NIGRÆ.

Black, Brown or Red Mustard; F. *Moutarde noire ou grise;* G. *Schwarzer Senf.*

Botanical Origin—*Brassica nigra* Koch (*Sinapis nigra* L.). Black Mustard is found wild over the whole of Europe excepting the extreme north. It also occurs in Northern Africa, Asia Minor, Mesopotamia, the Caucasian region, Western India, as well as in Southern Siberia and China. By cultivation, which is conducted on a large scale in many countries (as Alsace, Bohemia, Holland, England and Italy), it has doubtless been diffused through regions where it did not anciently exist. It has now become naturalized both in North and South America.

History—Mustard was well known to the ancients. Theophrastus mentions it as Νάπυ,—Dioscorides as Νάπυ or Σίνηπι. Pliny notices three kinds which have been referred by Fée [2] to *Brassica nigra* Koch,

[1] See Tingling, J. F. B., *The poppy-plague and England's crime*, London, 1876 (192 p.); Turner, F. S. (Secretary of the Anglo-Oriental Society for the Suppression of the Opium Trade), *British Opium Policy and its results to India and China.* London, 1876 (308 pages); Sir Edw. Fry, *England, China, and Opium*, 1878 (61 p.).

[2] *Botanique et Matière Méd. de Pline*, ii. (1833) 446.

B. alba Hook. f. et Th., and to a South European species, *Diplotaxis erucoides* DC. (*Sinapis erucoides* L.). The use of mustard seems up to this period to have been more medicinal than dietetic. But from an edict of Diocletian, A.D. 301 [1] in which it is mentioned along with alimentary substances, we must suppose it was then regarded as a condiment at least in the eastern parts of the Roman Empire.

In Europe during the middle ages mustard was a valued accompaniment to food, especially to the salted meat which constituted a large portion of the diet of our ancestors during the winter.[2] In the Welsh "Meddygon Myddvai," of the 13th century, a paragraph is devoted to the "Virtues of Mustard." In household accounts of the 13th and 14th centuries, mustard under the name of *Senapium* is of constant occurrence.

Mustard was then cultivated in England, but not as it would seem very extensively. The price of the seed between A.D. 1285 and 1395 varied from 1*s*. 3*d*. to 6*s*. 8*d*. per quarter, but in 1347 and 1376 it was as high as 15*s*. and 16*s*.[3] In the accounts of the abbey of St. Germain-des-Prés in Paris, commencing A.D. 800, mustard is specifically mentioned as a regular part of the revenue of the convent lands.[4]

The essential oil of mustard was, apparently, noticed about the year 1660 by Nicolas Le Febvre (see in the article Rad. Inulae), more distinctly in 1732 by Boerhaave. Its acridity and high specific gravity were pointed out by Murray.[5] Thibierge in 1819 observed that sulphur was one of the constituents of the oil, and Guibourt[6] stated that it is not pre-existing in the seed.

Production—Mustard is grown in England only on the richest alluvial soils, and chiefly in the counties of Lincolnshire and Yorkshire. Very good seed is produced in Holland.

Description—The pod of *Brassica nigra* is smooth, erect, and closely pressed against the axis of the long slender raceme. It has a strong nerve on each of its two valves and contains in each cell from 4 to 6 spherical or slightly oval seeds. The seeds are about $\frac{1}{25}$ of an inch in diameter and $\frac{1}{10}$ of a grain in weight; they are of a dark reddish-brown. The surface is reticulated with minute pits, and often more or less covered with a whitish pellicle which gives to some seeds a grey colour.[7] The testa which is thin, brittle and translucent encloses an exalbuminous embryo having two short cotyledons folded together longitudinally and forming a sort of trough in which the radicle lies bent up. The embryo thus coiled into a ball completely fills the testa; the outer cotyledon is thicker than the inner, which viewed in transverse section seems to hold the radicle as a pair of forceps. The seeds when pul-

[1] Mommsen in *Berichte der sächs. Gesellsch. der Wissenschaften zu Leipzig*, 1851. 1—80.

[2] Enclosed pasture land in England was rare, and there was but scanty provision for preserving stock through the winter, root crops being unknown. Hence in November there was a general slaughtering of sheep and oxen, the flesh of which was salted for winter use.—See also *Pharm. Journ.* viii. (1876, April 27) 852.

[3] Rogers, *Hist. of Agriculture and Prices in England*, i. (1866) 223.

[4] Guérard, *Polyptique de l'Abbé Irminon*, Paris, i. (1844) 715.

[5] *Apparatus medicaminum*, ii. (1794) 399.

[6] *Journ. de Pharm.* xvii. (1831) 360.

[7] The grey colour of the seed, which is attributed to rain during the ripening, is very detrimental to its value. The great aim of the grower is to produce seed of a bright reddish brown, with no grey seed intermixed.

verized have a greenish yellow hue. Masticated they have for an instant a bitterish taste which however quickly becomes pungent. When triturated with water they afford a yellowish emulsion emitting a pungent acrid vapour which affects the eyes, and has a strong acid reaction. The seeds powdered dry have no such pungency. When the seeds are triturated with solution of potash, the pungent odour is not evolved; nor when they are boiled in water. Neither is the acridity developed on triturating them with alcohol, dilute mineral acids, or solution of tannin, or even with water when they have been kept in powder for a long time.

Microscopic Structure—The whitish pellicle already mentioned, which covers the seed, is made up of hexagonal tabular cells. The epidermis consists of one row of densely packed brown cells, radially elongated and having strong lateral and inner walls. Their outer walls on the other hand are thin and not coloured; they are not clearly obvious when seen under oil, but swell up very considerably in presence of water, emitting mucilage.[1] Seeds immersed in water become therefore covered with a glossy envelope, levelling down the superficial inequalities, so that the wet seed appears smooth. The tissue of the cotyledons exhibits large drops of fatty oil and granules of albumin.

Chemical Composition—By distilling brown mustard with water, the seed having been previously macerated, the pungent principle, *Essential Oil of Mustard*, is obtained.

The oil, which has the composition $SCN(C^3H^5)$, (allyl isosulphocyanate), boils at 148° C.; it has a sp. gr. of 1·017, no rotatory power, and is soluble without coloration or turbidity in three times its weight or more of cold strong sulphuric acid. To this oil is due the pungent smell and taste of mustard and its inflammatory action on the skin. As already pointed out, mustard oil is not present in the dry seeds, but is produced only after they have been comminuted and mixed with water, the temperature of which should not exceed 50° C.

The remarkable reaction which gives rise to the formation of mustard oil was explained by Will and Körner in 1863. They obtained from mustard a crystallizable substance, then termed *Myronate of potassium*, now called *Sinigrin*, It is to be regarded, according to the admirable investigations of these chemists, as a compound of

Isosulphocyanate of allyl or mustard oil .	C^4	H^5	NS	
Bisulphate of potassium		H	KS	O^4
Sugar (dextroglucose)	C^6	H^{12}		O^6
so that the formula	C^{10}	H^{18}	KNS^2	O^{10}

is that of sinigrin. It does in fact split into the above-mentioned three substances when dissolved in water and brought into contact with *Myrosin*.

This albuminous body discovered by Bussy in 1839, but the composition of which has not been made out, likewise undergoes a certain decomposition under these circumstances. Sinigrin may likewise be decomposed by alkalis and, according to Ludwig and Lange, by silver

[1] Most minutely described and figured by F. von Höhnel, in Haberlandt's *Untersuchungen auf dem Gebiete des Pflanzenbaues*, i. (Vienna, 1875) 171—202.

nitrate. These chemists obtained sinigrin from the seeds in the proportion of 0·5 per cent.; Will and Körner got 0·5 to 0·6 per cent. The extraction of the substance is therefore attended with great loss, as the minimum yield of volatile oil, 0·42 per cent. indicates 2·36 of potassium myronate.

The aqueous solution of myrosin coagulates at 60° C. and then becomes inactive: hence mustard seed which has been heated to 100° C. or has been roasted yields no volatile oil, nor does it yield any if powdered and introduced at once into boiling water. The proportion of myrosin in mustard has not been exactly determined. The total amount of nitrogen in the seed is 2·9 per cent. (Hoffmann) which would correspond to 18 per cent. of myrosin, supposing the proportion of nitrogen in that substance to be the same as in albumin, and the total quantity of nitrogen to belong to it. Sometimes black mustard contains so little of it, that an emulsion of white mustard requires to be added in order to develop all the volatile oil it is capable of yielding.

An emulsion of mustard or a solution of pure sinigrin brought into contact with myrosin, frequently deposits sulphur by decomposition of the allyl sulphocyanide, hence crude oil of mustard sometimes contains a considerable proportion (even half) of *Allyl cyanide*, C^4H^5N, distinguished by its lower sp. gr. (0·839) and lower boiling point (118° C.).

The seeds, roots, or herbaceous part of many other plants of the order *Cruciferæ* yield a volatile oil composed in part of mustard oil and in part of allyl sulphide $C^6H^{10}S = \left.\begin{matrix} C^3H^5 \\ C^3H^5 \end{matrix}\right\} S$, which latter is likewise obtainable from the bulbs of garlic. Many *Cruciferæ* afford from their roots or seeds chiefly or solely oil of mustard, and from their leaves oil of garlic. As to other plants, the roots of *Reseda lutea* L. and *R. luteola* L. have been shown by Volhard (1871) to afford oil of mustard.[1] The strong smell given off by the crushed seeds or roots of several Mimoseæ, as for instance, *Albizzia lophantha* Benth. (*Acacia* Willd.) is perhaps due to some allied compound.

The artificial preparation of mustard oil was discovered in 1855 by Zinin, and at the same time also by Berthelot and De Luca. It may be obtained in decomposing bromide of allyl by means of sulphocyanate of ammonium:—

$$C^3H^5Br \;.\; SCN(NH^4) = NH^4Br \;.\; C^3H^5SCN.$$

The liquid C^3H^5SCN, boiling at 161°, is sulphocyanate of allyl; if it is gently warmed with a little alcoholic potash, and then acidulated, the red coloration of ferric sulphocyanate is produced on addition of perchloride of iron, but by submitting the sulphocyanate of allyl to distillation it is at once transformed in the isosulphocyanate, *i.e.* in mustard oil; the latter is not coloured by ferric salts, but it would appear that in the cold emulsion of mustard, even at 0°, a little sulphocyanate makes also its appearance.

Mustard submitted to pressure affords about 23 per cent.[2] of a mild-tasting, inodorous, non-drying oil, solidifying when cooled to − 17·5° C., and consisting of the glycerin compounds of stearic, oleic and *Erucic* or *Brassic Acid*. The last-named acid, $C^{22}H^{42}O^2$, occurs also in the fixed

[1] See also *Radix Armoraciæ*, p. 68.

[2] I have obtained as much as 33·8 per cent. by means of boiling ether.—F. A. F.

oil of white mustard and of rape, and is homologous with oleic acid. Darby (1849) has pointed out the existence of another body, *Sinapoleic Acid*, $C^{20}H^{38}O^{2}$, which occurs in the fixed oil of both black and white mustard. Goldschmiedt, in 1874, ascertained the presence also of *Behenic Acid*, $C^{22}H^{44}O^{2}$ in black mustard. Sinigrin being not altered by the extraction of the fatty oil, either by pressure or by means of bisulphide of carbon, the powdered seed, deprived of fatty oil, still yields the whole amount of the irritating "essential" oil. This important fact has been ingeniously used by Rigollot[1] for the preparation of his mustard paper.

Mustard seed when ripe is devoid of starch; the mucilage which its epidermis affords amounts to 19 per cent. of the seed (Hoffmann). The ash-constituents amounting to 4 per cent. consist chiefly of the phosphates of calcium, magnesium, and potassium.

Uses—Black mustard is employed in the form of poultice as a powerful external stimulant; but it is rarely used in its pure state, as the *Flour of Mustard* prepared for the table, which contains in addition white mustard, answers perfectly well and is at hand in every house.[2]

The essential oil of mustard dissolved in spirit of wine is occasionally prescribed as a liniment.

Substitute—*Brassica juncea* Hook. f. et Th. (*Sinapis juncea* L.) is extensively cultivated throughout India (where *B. nigra* is rarely grown), Central Africa, and generally in warm countries where it replaces *B. nigra* and is applied to the same uses. Its seeds constitute a portion of the mustard of Europe, as we may infer from the fact that British India exported in the year 1871-72, of "*Mustard seed*," 1418 tons, of which 790 tons were shipped to the United Kingdom, and 516 tons to France.[3] *B. juncea* is largely grown in the south of Russia and in the steppes north-east of the Caspian where it appears to flourish particularly well in the saline soil. At Sarepta in the Government of Saratov, an establishment has existed since the beginning of the present century where this sort of mustard is prepared for use to the extent of 800 tons of seed annually. The seeds make a fine yellow powder employed both for culinary and medicinal purposes. By pressure they yield more than 20 per cent. of fixed oil which is used in Russia like the best olive oil. The seeds closely resemble those of *B. nigra* and afford when distilled the same essential oil; it is largely made at Kiew.

SEMEN SINAPIS ALBÆ.

White Mustard; F. *Moutarde blanche ou Anglaise*; G. *Weisser Senf.*

Botanical Origin—*Brassica alba* Hook. f. et Th. (*Sinapis alba* L.) This plant appears to belong to the more southern countries of Europe and Western Asia. According to Chinese authors[4] it was introduced

[1] *Journ. de Pharm.* vi. (1867) 269.

[2] The best *Flour of Mustard* such as is made by the large manufacturers, contains nothing but brown and white mustard seeds. But the lower and cheaper qualities made by the same firms contain flour, turmeric, and capsicum. Unmixed flour of Black Mustard is however kept for those who care to purchase it.

[3] *Annual Statement of the Trade and Navigation of British India*, Calcutta, 1872. 62.

[4] Bretschneider, *Study of Chinese Botan. Works*, 1870. 17.

into China from the latter region. Its cultivation in England is of recent introduction, but is rapidly extending.[1] The plant is not uncommon as a weed on cultivated land.

History—White mustard was used in former times indiscriminately with the brown. In the materia medica of the *London Pharmacopœia* of 1720 the two sorts are separately prescribed. The important chemical distinction between them was first made known in 1831 by Boutron-Charlard and Robiquet.[2]

Production—White mustard is grown as an agricultural crop in Essex and Cambridgeshire.

Description—*Brassica alba* differs from *B. nigra* in having the pods bristly and spreading. They are about an inch long, half the length being occupied by a flat veiny beak. Each pod contains 4 to 6 yellowish seeds about $\frac{1}{12}$ of an inch in diameter and $\frac{1}{10}$ of a grain in weight. The brittle, nearly transparent and colourless testa encloses an embryo of a bright pure yellow and of the same structure as that of black mustard. The surface of the testa is likewise pitted in a reticulate manner, but so finely that it appears smooth except under a high magnifying power.

When triturated with water the seeds form a yellowish emulsion of very pungent taste, but it is inodorous and does not under any circumstances yield a volatile oil. The powdered seeds made into a paste with cold water act as a highly stimulating cataplasm. The entire seeds yield to cold water an abundance of mucilage.

Microscopic Structure—The epidermal cells of white mustard afford a good illustration of a mucilage-yielding layer such as is met with, under many variations, in the seeds of numerous plants. The cuticle consists of large vaulted cells, exhibiting very regular hexagonal outlines when cut across.[3] The inner layer of the epidermis is made up of thin-walled cells, which when moistened swell and give off the mucilage. In the dry state or seen under oil, the outlines of the single cells of this layer are not distinguishable. The tissue of the cotyledons is loaded with drops of fatty oil and with granular albuminoid matter; starch which is present in the seed while young, is altogether absent when the latter reaches maturity.

Chemical Composition—White mustard deprived of fatty oil yields to boiling alcohol colourless crystals of *Sinalbin*, an indifferent substance, readily soluble in cold water, but sparingly in cold alcohol. From the able investigations of Will (1870) it follows, that it is to be regarded as composed of three bodies, namely:

Sulphocyanate of Acrinyl	C^8	H^7	N	S	O
Sulphate of Sinapine	C^{16}	H^{25}	N	S	O^9
Sugar	C^6	H^{12}			O^6
so that the formula	C^{30}	H^{44}	N^2	S^2	O^{16}

represents according to Will the composition of sinalbin. It is actually resolved into these three substances when placed at ordinary tempera-

[1] Morton's *Cycloped. of Agriculture*, ii. (1855) 440.

[2] *Journ. de Pharm.* xvii. (1831) 279.

[3] An interesting object for the polarizing microscope.

tures, in contact with water and *Myrosin*, the latter of which is a constituent of white mustard as well as of brown (p. 66). The liquid becomes turbid, the first of the above-named substances separates (together with coagulated albumin) as an oily liquid, not soluble in water, but dissolving in alcohol or ether. This *Sulphocyanate of Acrinyl* is the rubefacient and vesicating principle of white mustard. It does not pre-exist, as shown by Will, in the seed, and cannot be obtained by distillation. By treating it with a salt of silver, Will obtained crystals of cyanide of acrinyl, C^8H^7NO: by warming it (or sinalbin itself, or an alcoholic extract of the seed) with caustic potash, sulphocyanide of potassium is produced. The presence of the latter may be indicated by adding a drop of perchloride of iron, when a blood-red coloration will be produced.[1]

Sulphate of Sinapine imparts to the emulsion of white mustard, in which it is formed, an acid reaction. Sinapine is itself an alkaloid, which has not yet been isolated, as it is very liable to change. Thus its solution on addition of a trace of alkali immediately assumes a bright yellow colour indicating decomposition, and a similar colour is produced in an aqueous extract of the seed.

The above statements show, that the chemical properties of sinalbin and its derivatives correspond closely with those of sinigrin (p. 66) and the substances which make their appearance in an emulsion of black mustard.

The other constituents of white mustard seed are nearly the same as those of black. The fat oil appears to yield in addition to the acids mentioned at p. 67, *Benic* or *Behenic Acid*, $C^{22}H^{44}O^2$. White mustard is said to be richer than black in myrosin, so that, as explained in the previous article, the pungency of the latter may be often increased by an addition of white mustard. By burning white mustard dried at 100° C., with soda-lime, we obtained from 4·20 to 4·30 per cent. of nitrogen, answering to about 28 per cent. of protein substances.[2] The fixed oil of the seed amounts to 22 per cent. The mucilage as yielded by the epidermis is precipitable by alcohol, neutral lead acetate, or ferric chloride, and is soluble in water after drying.

Erucin and *Sinapic Acid*, mentioned by Simon (1838)[3] as peculiar constituents of white mustard, are altogether doubtful, yet may deserve further investigation. The sinapic acid of Von Babo and Hirschbrunn[4] (1852) is a product of the decomposition of sinapine.

Uses—White Mustard seed reduced to powder and made into a paste with cold water act as a powerful stimulant when applied to the skin, notwithstanding that such paste is entirely wanting in essential oil. But for sinapisms they are actually used only in the form of the *Flour of Mustard* which is prepared for the table and which contains also Brown Mustard seed.

[1] The red compound thus formed with sulphocyanide is readily soluble in ether, yet in the case of white mustard we find it *not* to be so.

[2] Experiments performed by Mr. Weppen in my laboratory, 1869.—F. A. F.

[3] Gmelin, *Chemistry*, xiv. (1860) 521 and 529.

[4] Ibid. 521.

RADIX ARMORACIÆ.

Horse-radish ; F. *Raifort* (*i.e. racine forte*), *Cran de Bretagne ;* G. *Meerrettig.*

Botanical Origin—*Cochlearia Armoracia* L., a common perennial with a stout tapering root, large coarse oblong leaves with long stalks, and erect flowering racemes 2 to 3 feet high. It is indigenous to the eastern parts of Europe, from the Caspian through Russia and Poland to Finland. In Britain and in other parts of Europe from Sicily to the polar circle, it occurs cultivated or semi-wild; in the opinion of Schübeler[1] it is not truly indigenous to Norway.

History—The vernacular name *Armon* is stated by Pliny[2] to be used in the Pontic regions to designate the *Armoracia* of the Romans, the Wild Radish (ῥαφανὶς ἀγρία) of the Greeks, a plant which cannot be positively identified with that under notice.

Horse-radish is called in the Russian language *Chren*, in Lithuanian *Krenai*, in Illyrian *Kren*, a name which has passed into several German dialects, and as *Cran* or *Cranson* into French.

From these and similar facts, De Candolle[3] has drawn the conclusion that the propagation of the plant has travelled from Eastern to Western Europe.

Both the root and leaves of horse-radish were used as a medicine and also eaten with food in Germany and Denmark during the middle ages.[4] But the use of the former was not common in England until a much later period. The plant is mentioned in the *Meddygon Myddfai* and was known in England as *Red-cole* in the time of Turner, 1568, but is not quoted by him[5] as used in food, nor is it noticed by Boorde,[6] 1542, in his chapter on edible roots. Gerarde[7] at the end of the 16th century remarks that horse-radish—"is commonly used among the Germans for sauce to eat fish with, and such like meats, as we do mustard." Half a century later the taste for horse-radish had begun to prevail in England. Coles[8] (1657) states that the root sliced thin and mixed with vinegar is eaten as a sauce with meat as among the Germans. That the use of horse-radish in France had the same origin is proved by its old French name *Moutarde des Allemands.*

The root to which certain medicinal properties had always been assigned, was included in the materia medica of the London Pharmacopœias of the last century under the name of *Raphanus rusticanus.*

Description—The root which in good ground often attains a length of 3 feet and nearly an inch in diameter, is enlarged in its upper part into a crown, usually dividing into a few short branches each surmounted by a tuft of leaves, and annulated by the scars of fallen foliage; below the crown it tapers slightly, and then for some distance is

[1] *Pflanzenwelt Norwegens* (1873) 296.
[2] Lib. xix. c. 26 (Littré's translation).
[3] *Géographie Botanique*, ii. (1855) 655.
[4] Meyer, *Geschichte der Botanik*, iii. (1856) 531 ; also Schübeler *l.c.* ; Pfeiffer, *Buch der Natur von Konrad von Megenberg*, Stuttgart, 1861. 418.
[5] *Herball*, part 2. (1568) 111.
[6] *Dyetary of Helth*, Early English Text Society, 1870. 278.
[7] *Herball*, edited by Johnson, 1636, 240.
[8] *Adam in Eden, or Nature's Paradise*, Lond. 1657. chap. 256.

often almost cylindrical, throwing off here and there filiform and long slender cylindrical roots, and finally dividing into two or three branches. The root is of a light yellowish brown; internally it is fleshy and perfectly white, and has a short non-fibrous fracture. Before it is broken it is inodorous, but when comminuted it immediately exhales its characteristic pungent smell. Its well-known pungent taste is not lost in the root carefully dried and not kept too long.

A transverse section of the fresh root displays a large central column with a radiate and concentric arrangement of its tissues, which are separated by a small greyish circle from the bark, whose breadth is from ½ to 2 lines. In the root branches there is neither a well-defined liber nor a true pith. The short leaf-bearing branches include a large pith surrounded by a circle of woody bundles. The bark adheres strongly to the central portion, in which zones of annual growth are easily perceptible, at least in older specimens.

Microscopic Structure—The corky layer is made up of small tabular cells as usual in suberous coats. In the succeeding zone of the middle bark, thick-walled yellow cells are scattered through the parenchyme, chiefly at the boundary line of the corky layer. In the root the cellular envelope is not strikingly separated from the liber, whilst in its leafy branches this separation is well marked by wedge-shaped liber bundles, which are accompanied by a group of the yellow longitudinally-elongated stone cells. The woody bundles contain a few short yellow vessels, accompanied by bundles of prosenchymatous, not properly woody cells. The centre, in the root, shows these woody bundles to be separated by the medullary parenchyma; in the branches the central column consists of an uniform pith without woody bundles, the latter forming a circle close to the cambium. The parenchyma of the whole root collected in spring is loaded with small starch granules.

Chemical Composition—Among the constituents of horse-radish root (the chemical history of which is however far from perfect) the volatile oil is the most interesting. The fresh root submitted to distillation with water in a glass retort, yields about ½ per mille of oil which is identical with that of Black Mustard as proved in 1843 by Hubatka. He combined it with ammonia and obtained crystals of thiosinammine, the composition of which agreed with the thiosinammine from mustard oil.

An alcoholic extract of the root is devoid of the odour of the oil, but this is quickly evolved on addition of an emulsion of *White* Mustard. The essential oil does not therefore pre-exist, but only sinigrin (myronate of potassium) and an albuminoid matter (myrosin) by whose mutual reaction in the presence of water it is formed (p. 66). This process does not go on in the growing root, perhaps because the two principles in question are not contained in the same cells, or else exist together in some condition that does not allow of their acting on each other,—a state of things analogous to that occurring in the leaves of *Laurocerasus*.

By exhausting the root with water either cold or hot, the sinigrin is decomposed and a considerable proportion of bisulphate is found in the concentrated decoction. Alcohol removes from the root some fatty matter and sugar (Winckler 1849). Salts of iron do not alter thin slices of it, tannic matters being absent. The presence of myrosin, which at present has been inferred rather than proved, ought to be further investigated. The root dried at 100° afforded 11·15 per cent. of ash to Mutschler (1878).

Uses—An infusion or a distilled spirit of horse-radish is reputed stimulant, diaphoretic, and diuretic, but is not often employed.

Substitute—In India the root of *Moringa pterygosperma* Gärtn. is considered a substitute for horse-radish. It yields by distillation an essential oil of disgusting odour which Broughton, who obtained it in minute quantity, has assured us is not identical with that of mustard or of garlic.

CANELLACEÆ.

CORTEX CANELLÆ ALBÆ.

Canella Bark, Canella Alba Bark; F. *Canelle blanche;* G. *Canella-Rinde.*

Botanical Origin—*Canella alba* Murray,[1] a tree, 20 to 30 or even 50 feet in height, found in the south of Florida, the Bahama Islands (whence alone its bark is exported), Cuba, Jamaica, Ste. Broix, Guadaloupe, Martinique, Barbadoes and Trinidad.

History—The drug was first mentioned in 1605 by Clusius,[2] who remarks that it had been then newly brought to Europe and had received the name of *Canella alba* (White Cinnamon). It was afterwards known as *Costus Corticosus, Costus dulcis, Cassia alba, Cassia lignea Jamaicensis* or *Jamaica Winter's Bark.* Dale[3] writing in 1693 notices it as not unfrequently sold for Winter's Bark. Pomet[4] (1694) describes it as synonymous with Winter's Bark, and observes that it is common, yet but little employed.

The drug is mentioned by most subsequent writers, some of whom like Pomet probably confounded it with the bark of *Cinnamodendron* (p. 19). It is usually described as produced in Jamaica or Guadaloupe, from which islands no Canella alba is now exported. On the other hand, New Providence, one of the Bahamas whence the Canella alba of the present day is shipped, is not named. Nor do we find any allusion to the drug in the records of the Company (1630-50) which was formed for the colonization of New Providence and the other islands of the group, though their staple productions are frequently enumerated.[5]

Canella alba Murr. was described and figured by Sloane (1707) and still better by Patrick Brown in 1789, and Olaf Swartz in 1791.[6]

Collection—In the Bahamas, where the drug is known as *White Wood Bark* or *Cinnamon Bark,* it is collected thus:—preparatory to

[1] Fig. in Bentley and Trimen, *Medic. Plants,* part 6 (1876).

[2] *Exotica,* 78.

[3] *Pharmacologia,* 432.

[4] *Hist. des Drog.* part i. 130.

[5] *Calendar of State Papers, Colonial Series,* 1584—1660, Lond. 1860.

[6] O. Swartz, Trans. of the Linnean Soc., i. 96. See also Bonnet, *Monographie des Canellées,* 1876.

being stripped from the wood, the bark is gently beaten with a stick, which removes the suberous layer. By a further beating, the remaining bark is separated, and having been peeled off and dried, is exported without further preparation.[1]

Description—Canella bark occurs in the form of quills, more or less crooked and irregular, or in channelled pieces from 2 or 3 up to 6, 8, or more inches in length, ½ an inch to 1 or 2 inches in width, and a line or two in thickness. The suberous layer which here and there has escaped removal is silvery grey, and dotted with minute lichens. Commonly, the external surface consists of inner cellular layers (*mesophlœum*) of a bright buff, or light orange-brown tint, often a little wrinkled transversely, and dotted (but not always) with round scars. The inner surface is whitish or cinnamon-coloured, either smooth or with slight longitudinal striæ. Some parcels of canella show the bark much bruised and longitudinally fissured by the abovementioned process of beating. The bark breaks transversely with a short granular fracture, which distinctly shows the three, or in uncoated specimens the two, cortical layers, that of the liber being the largest, and projecting by undulated rays or bundles into the middle layer, which presents numerous large and unevenly scattered oil-cells of a yellow colour.

Canella has an agreeable cinnamon-like odour, and a bitter, pungent acrid taste.[2] Even the corky coat is somewhat aromatic.

Microscopical Structure—The spongy suberous coat consists of very numerous layers of large cells with thin walls, showing an undulated rather than rectangular outline. The next small zone is constituted of sclerenchymatous cells in a single, double, or triple row, or forming dense but not very extensive groups. This tissue is sometimes (in unpeeled specimens) a continuous envelope, marking the boundary between the corky layer and the middle portion of the cellular layer; but an interruption in this thick-walled tissue often takes place when portions of it are enveloped and separated by the suberous layer.

The proper cellular envelope shows a narrow tissue with numerous very large cells filled with yellow essential oil. The liber forming the chief portion of the whole bark, exhibits thin prosenchymatous cells, which on traverse section form small bands of a peculiar horny or cartilaginous appearance, on which account they have been distinguished as *horny liber* (*Hornbast* of German writers).[3] The liber-fibres show reticulated marks due to the peculiar character of the secondary deposits on their cell walls. The oil-cells in the liber are less numerous and smaller; the medullary rays are not very obvious unless on account of the crystalline tufts of oxalate of calcium deposited in the latter. This crystalline oxalate retains air obstinately, and has a striking dark appearance.

[1] Information communicated to me by the Hon. J. C. Lees, Chief-Justice of the Bahamas. The second beating would seem to be not always required.—D. H.

[2] A specimen in Sloane's collection in the British Museum labelled "*Cortex Winteranus of the Isles*," but under the microscope seen to be absolutely identical with canella alba, still retains its proper fragrance after nearly two centuries.—F. A. F.

[3] First figured and described by Oudemans,—*Aanteekeningen op het . . . . Gedeelte der Pharm. Neerlandica*, 1854-56. 467.

Chemical Composition—The most interesting body in canella is the volatile oil, examined in 1843 under Wöhler's direction by Meyer and Von Reiche, who obtained it in the proportion of 0·94 from 100 parts of bark. They found it to consist of four different oils, the first being identical with the *Eugenol* or *Eugenic Acid* of oil of cloves; the second is closely allied to the chief constituent of cajuput oil. The other oils require further examination.[1]

The bark, of which we distilled 20 lb., afforded 0·74 per cent. of oil. This when distilled with caustic potash in excess was found to be composed of 2 parts of the acid portion and 1 part of the neutral hydrocarbon; the latter has an odour suggesting a mixture of peppermint and cajaput.

Meyer and Von Reiche evaporated the aqueous decoction of canella, and removed from the bitter extract by alcohol 8 per cent. of mannite, which they ascertained to be the so-called *Canellin* described in 1822 by Petroz and Robinet.

The bark yielded the German chemists 6 per cent. of ash, chiefly carbonate of calcium. The bitter principle has not yet been isolated. An aqueous infusion is not blackened by a persalt of iron.

Commerce—Canella alba is collected in the Bahama Islands and shipped to Europe from Nassau in New Providence, the chief seat of trade in the group. In 1876 the export of the bark amounted to 125 cwt.

Uses—The bark is an aromatic stimulant, now but seldom employed. It is used by the West Indian negroes as a condiment.

BIXINEÆ.

SEMEN GYNOCARDIÆ.

Chaulmugra Seed.

Botanical Origin—*Gynocardia odorata* R. Br. (*Chaulmoogra* Roxb., *Hydnocarpus* Lindl.), a large tree[2] with a globular fruit of the size of a shaddock, containing numerous seeds immersed in pulp. It grows in the forests of the Malayan peninsula and Eastern India as far north as Assam, extending thence along the base of the Himalaya westward to Sikkim.

History—The inhabitants of the south-eastern countries of Asia have long been acquainted with the seeds of certain trees of the tribe *Pangieæ* (ord. *Bixineæ*) as a remedy for maladies of the skin. In China a seed called *Ta-fung-tsze* is imported from Siam[3] where it is

[1] Gmelin, *Chemistry*, xiv. (1860) 210.

[2] Fig. in Bentley and Trimen, *Medic. Plants*, part. 26 (1877). Also in Christy, *New Commercial Plants*, No. 2 (1878).

[3] The *Commercial Report from H.M. Consul-General in Siam for the year* 1871, presented to Parliament, Aug. 1872, states that 48 peculs (6400 lb.) of *Lukrabow seeds* were exported from Bangkok to China in 1871. Sir Joseph Hooker (*Report on the Royal Gardens at Kew*, 1877, p. 33) has been informed by Mr. Pierre, the director of the Botanic Garden at Saigon, Cochin-china, that the seeds have proved to derive from a Hydnocarpus (Gynocardia).—See also our article Semen Ignatii and *Science Papers*, p. 235.

known as *Lukrabo* and used in a variety of cutaneous complaints. The tree affording it, which is figured in the *Pun-tasao* (*circa* A.D. 1596) has not been recognised by botanists, but from the structure of the seed it is obviously closely related to *Gynocardia*.[1]

The properties of *G. odorata* were known to Roxburgh who, Latinizing the Indian name of the tree, called it (1814) *Chaulmoogra odorata*. Of late years the seeds have attracted the notice of Europeans in India, and having been found useful in certain skin diseases, they have been admitted a place in the *Pharmacopœia of India*.

Description—The seeds, 1 to $1\frac{1}{4}$ inches long and about half as much in diameter, are of irregular ovoid form, and more or less angular or flattened by mutual pressure; they weigh on an average about 35 grains each. The testa is thin (about $\frac{1}{80}$ of an inch), brittle, smooth, dull grey; within there is a brown oily kernel, marked with a darker colour at its basal end. The weight of the kernel is, on an average, twice that of the testa. The former encloses in its copious, soft albumen a pair of large, plain, leafy, heart-shaped cotyledons with a stout radicle. The taste of the kernel is simply oily.

Microscopic Structure—The testa is chiefly formed of cylindrical thick-walled cells. The albumen exhibits large angular cells containing fatty oil, masses of albuminous matter and tufted crystals of calcium oxalate. Starch is not present.

Chemical Composition—The kernels afforded us by means of ether 51·5 per cent. of fatty oil, which is almost colourless or somewhat brownish if the seeds are not fresh. Either extracted or expressed it is of no peculiar taste. The pressed oil concretes at 17° C.; that extracted by ether or bisulphate of carbon requires for solidification a lower temperature. The expressed oil is slightly fluorescent, less so that extracted by means of bisulphide of carbon. If the oil, either pressed or extracted, is diluted with the bisulphide, and then concentrated sulphuric or nitric acid is added, no peculiar coloration is produced.

From the powdered kernels deprived of oil, water removes the usual constituents, glucose, mucilage and albumin.

Uses—The seeds are said to have been advantageously used as an alternative tonic in scrofula, skin diseases and rheumatism. They should be freed from the testa, powdered, and given in the dose of 6 grains gradually increased. Reduced to a paste and mixed with Simple Ointment, they constitute the *Unguentum Gynocardiæ* of the *Indian Pharmacopœia*, which, as well as an expressed oil of the seeds may be employed externally in herpes, tinea, &c.[2]

Substitute—It has been suggested that the seeds of *Hydnocarpus Wightiana* Bl., a tree of Western India, and of *H. venenata* Gärtn., native of Ceylon, might be tried where those of *Gynocardia* are not procurable. The seeds of both species of *Hydnocarpus* (formerly con-

[1] Hanbury, *Notes on Chinese Mat. Med.* (1862) 23.—*Science Papers*, 244. Dr. Porter Smith assumes the Chinese drug to be derived from *G. odorata*, but as I have pointed out, the seeds have a much stronger testa than those of that tree.—D.H.

[2] For particulars see Christy's pamphlet alluded to above, p. 75.

founded together as *H. inebrians* Vahl) afford a fatty oil which the natives use in cutaneous diseases.[1]

POLYGALEÆ.

RADIX SENEGÆ.

Radix Senekæ; Senega or Seneka Root; F. *Racine de Polygala de Virginie;* G. *Senegawurzel.*

Botanical Origin—*Polygala Senega* L., a perennial plant with slender ascending stems 6 to 12 inches high, and spikes of dull white flowers resembling in form those of the Common Milkwort of Britain. It is found in British America as far north as the river Saskatchewan, and in the United States from New England to Wisconsin, Kentucky, Tennessee, Virginia and the upper parts of North Carolina, as well as in Georgia and Texas, not in the Rocky Mountains.

The plant, which frequents rocky open woods and plains, has become somewhat scarce in the Atlantic states, and as a drug is now chiefly collected in the west, the plant growing profusely in Iowa and Minnesota, west of New York.

History—The employment of this root among the Seneca Indians as a remedy for the bite of the rattle-snake attracted the notice of Tennent, a Scotch physician in Virginia; and from the good effects he witnessed he concluded that it might be administered with advantage in pleurisy and peripneumonia. The result of numerous trials made in the years 1734 and 1735 proved the utility of the drug in these complaints, and Tennent communicated his observations to the celebrated Dr. Mead of London in the form of an epistle, afterwards published together with an engraving of the plant, then called the *Seneca Rattlesnake Root.*[2] Tennent's practice was to administer the root in powder or as a strong decoction, or more often infused in wine. The new drug was favourably received in Europe, and its virtues discussed in numerous theses and dissertations, one written in 1749 being by Linnæus.[3]

Description—Senega root is developed at its upper end into a knotty crown, in old roots as much as an inch in diameter, from which spring the numerous wiry aerial stems, beset at the base with scaly rudimentary leaves often of a purplish hue. Below the crown is a simple tap-root $\frac{2}{10}$ to $\frac{3}{10}$ of an inch thick, of contorted or somewhat spiral form, which usually soon divides into 2 or 3 spreading branches and smaller filiform rootlets.

The bark is light yellowish-grey, translucent, horny, shrivelled, knotted and partially annulated. Very frequently a keel-shaped ridge occurs, running like a shrunken sinew through the principal root; it has no connexion with the wood, but originates in a one-sided development of the liber-tissue. The bark encloses a pure, white woody column

[1] Waring, *Pharm. of India*, 1868. 27.

[2] Tennent (John), *Epistle to Dr. Richard Mead concerning the epidemical diseases of Virginia*, &c., Edinb. 1738.

[3] *Amœnitates Academicæ*, ii. 126.

about as thick as itself. After the root has been macerated in water the bark is easily peeled off, and the peculiar structure of the wood can then be studied. The latter immediately below the crown is a cylindrical cord, cleft however by numerous, fine, longitudinal fissures. Lower down these fissures increase in an irregular manner, causing a very abnormal development of the wood. Transverse sections of a root therefore differ greatly, the circular woody portion being either penetrated by clefts or wide notches, or one-half or even more is altogether wanting, the space where wood should exist being in each case filled up by uniform parenchymatous tissue.

Senega root has a short brittle fracture, a peculiar rancid odour, and a very acrid and sourish taste. When handled it disperses in irritating dust.

Microscopic Structure—The woody part is built up of dotted vessels surrounded by short porous ligneous cells; the medullary rays consist of one or two rows of the usual small cells. There is no pith in the centre of the root. The clefts and notches are filled up with an uniform tissue passing into the primary cortical tissue without a distinct liber; the large cells of this tissue are spirally striated. In the keel-shaped rider the proper liber rays may be distinguished from the medullary rays. The former are made up of a soft tissue, hence the cortical part of the root breaks short together with the wood.

Neither starch granules nor crystals of oxalate of calcium are present in this root; the chief contents of its tissue are albuminoid granules and drops of fatty oil.

Chemical Composition—The substance to which the drug owes its irritating taste was distinguished by the name of *Senegin* by Gehlen as early as 1804, and is probably the same as the *Polygalic Acid* of Quevenne (1836) and of Procter (1859). Christophsohn (1874) extracted it by means of boiling water, evaporated the solution and exhausted the residue with boiling alcohol (0·853 sp. gr.). The liquid after a day or two, deposits the crude senegin, which is to be washed with alcohol (0·813 sp. gr.), and again dissolved in water, from which it is precipitated by a large excess of hydrate of baryum. The barytic compound, dissolved in water, is decomposed by carbonic acid, by which carbonate of baryum is separated, senegin remaining in solution. It is lastly to be precipitated by alcohol. It is amorphous, insoluble in ether and in cold water; it forms with boiling water a frothing solution. Like saponin, to which it is very closely allied, it excites violent sneezing.

Dilute inorganic acids added to a warm solution of senegin throw down a flocculent jelly of *Sapogenin*, the liquid retaining in solution uncrystallizable sugar. Alkalis give rise to the same decomposition; but it is difficult to split up the senegin completely, and hence the formulas given for this process are doubtful. Even the formula of senegin itself is not definitely settled. According to Christophsohn, the root yields about 2 per cent. of this substance; according to earlier authorities, who doubtless had it less pure, a much larger proportion. From Schneider's investigations (1875) it would appear that the rootlets are richest in senegin.

Senega root contains a little volatile oil, traces of resin, also gum, salts of malic acid, yellow colouring matter, and sugar (7 per cent. according to Rebling, 1855). The *Virginic Acid* said by Quevenne to be contained in it, and the bitter substance *Isolusin* mentioned by Peschier, are doubtful bodies.

Uses—Senega is prescribed as a stimulating expectorant and diuretic, useful in pneumonia, asthma and rheumatism. It is much esteemed in America.

Adulteration—The drug is not liable to be wilfully falsified, but through careless collecting there is occasionally a slight admixture of other roots. One of these is American Ginseng (*Panax quinquefolium* L.) a spindle-shaped root which may be found here and there both in senega and serpentaria. The rhizome of *Cypripedium pubescens* Willd. has also been noticed; it cannot be confounded with that of *Polygala Senega*. The same may be said with regard to the rhizome of *Cynanchum Vincetoxicum* R. Brown (*Asclepias* L., *Vincetoxicum officinale* Mönch).

RADIX KRAMERIÆ.

Radix Ratanhiæ, Rhatanhiæ v. Rathaniæ; Rhatany or Rhatania Root, Peruvian or Payta Rhatany; F. *Racine de Ratanhia;* G. *Ratanhiawurzel.*[1]

Botanical Origin—*Krameriæ triandra* Ruiz et Pav., a small woody shrub with an upright stem scarcely a foot high and thick decumbent branches 2 to 3 feet long.[2] It delights in the barren sandy declivities of the Bolivian and Peruvian Cordilleras at 3000 to 8000 feet above the sea-level, often occurring in great abundance and adorning the ground with its red starlike flowers and silver-grey foliage.

The root is gathered chiefly to the north, north-east, and east of Lima, as at Caxatambo, Huanuco, Tarma, Jauja, Huarochiri and Canta; occasionally on the high lands about lake Titicaca. It appears likewise to be collected in the northern part of Peru, since the drug is now frequently shipped from Payta.

History—Hipolito Ruiz,[3] the Spanish botanist, observed in 1784 that the women of Huanuco and Lima were in the habit of using for the preservation of their teeth a root which he recognized as that of *Krameria triandra*, a plant discovered by himself in 1779. On his return to Europe he obtained admission for this root into Spain in 1796, whence it was gradually introduced into other countries of Europe.

The first supplies which reached England formed part of the cargo of a Spanish prize, and were sold in the London drug sales at the commencement of the present century. Some fell into the hands of Dr. Reece who recommended it to the profession.[4]

About 20 years ago there appeared in the European market some

[1] Ruiz and Pavon state that the root is called at Huanuco *ratanhia*. The derivation of the word which is of the Quichua language is obscure.

[2] Fig. in Bentley and Trimen, *Medicinal Plants*, part 30 (1876).

[3] *Mem. de la R. Acad. med. de Madrid*, i. (1797) 349—366.

[4] *Medicinal and Chirurgical Review*, Lond., xiii. (1806) ccxlvi.; also Reece, *Dict. of Domest. Med.*, 1808.

other kinds of rhatany previously unknown: of these the more important are noticed at pp. 81, 82.

Description—The root which attains a considerable size in proportion to the aerial part of the shrub, consists of a short thick crown, sometimes much knotted and as large as a man's fist. This ramifies beneath the soil even more than above, throwing out an abundance of branching, woody roots (frequently horizontal) some feet long and $\frac{1}{4}$ to $\frac{1}{2}$ an inch thick. These long roots used formerly to be found in commerce; but of late years rhatany has consisted in large proportion of the more woody central part of the root with short stumpy branches, which from their broken and bruised appearance have evidently been extracted with difficulty from a hard soil.

The bark which is scaly and rugged, and $\frac{1}{10}$ to $\frac{1}{20}$ of an inch in thickness, is of a dark reddish brown. It consists of a loose cracked cork-layer, mostly smooth in the smaller roots, covering a bright brown-red inner bark, which adheres though not very firmly to a brownish yellow wood. The bark is rather tough, breaking with a fibrous fracture. The wood is dense, without pith, but marked with thin vessels arranged in concentric rings, and with still thinner, dark medullary rays. The taste of the bark is purely astringent; the wood is almost tasteless; neither possesses any distinctive odour.

Kr. cistoidea Hook, a plant scarcely to be distinguished from *Kr. triandra*, affords in Chili a rhatany very much like that of Peru. Its root was contributed to the Paris Exhibition of 1867.

Microscopic Structure—The chief portion of the bark is formed of liber, which in transverse section exhibits numerous bundles of yellow fibres separated by parenchymatous tissue and traversed by narrow brown medullary rays. The small layer of the primary bark is made up of large cells, the surface of the root of large suberous cells imbued with red matter. The latter also occurs in the inner cortical tissue, and ought to be removed by means of ammonia in order to get a clear idea of the structure. Many of the parenchymatous cells are loaded with starch granules; oxalate of calcium occurs in the neighbourhood of the liber bundles. The woody portion exhibits no structure of particular interest.

Chemical Composition—Wittstein (1854) found in the bark of rhatany (the only part of the drug having active properties) about 20 per cent. of a form of tannin called *Ratanhia-tannic Acid*, closely related to catechu-tannic acid. It is an amorphous powder, the solution of which is not affected by emetic tartar, but yields with ferric chloride a dark greenish precipitate. By distillation Eissfeldt (1854) obtained pyrocatechin as a product of the decomposition of ratanhia-tannic acid. The latter is also decomposed by dilute acids which convert it into crystallizable sugar and *Ratanhia-red*, a substance nearly insoluble in water, also occurring in abundance ready formed in the bark.

Grabowski (1867) showed that by fusing ratanhia-red with caustic potash, protocatechuic acid and phloroglucin[1] are obtained. Ratanhia-red has the composition $C^{26}H^{22}O^{11}$, the same, according to Grabowski, as an analogous product of the decomposition of the peculiar tannic acid occurring (as shown by Rochleder in 1866) in the horse-chestnut.

[1] See art. Kino.

The same red substance may also be obtained, as stated by Rembold (1868), from the tannic acid of the root of tormentil (*Potentilla Tormentilla* L.).

As to rhatany root, Wittstein also found it to contain wax, gum and uncrystallizable sugar (even in the wood! according to Cotton[1]). Cotton further pointed out the presence in very minute quantity of an odorous, volatile, solid body, obtainable by means of ether or bisulphide of carbon; it occurs in a somewhat more considerable amount in the other sorts of rhatany. The root contains no gallic acid.

A dry extract of rhatany resembling kino used formerly to be imported from South America, but how and where manufactured we know not. It is however of some interest as containing a crystalline body which Wittstein who discovered it (1854) regards as *Tyrosin*, $C^9H^{11}NO^3$, previously supposed to be exclusively of animal origin.[2] Städeler and Ruge (1862) assigned to it a slightly different composition, $C^{10}H^{13}NO^3$, and gave it the name of *Ratanhin*. It dissolves in hot water which is acidulated by a little nitric acid; the solution on boiling turns red, blue, and lastly green, and becomes at the same time fluorescent. Kreitmair (1875) extracted 0·7 per cent. of ratanhin from an old specimen of commercial extract of rhatany; but he did not succeed in obtaining it from other specimens. He also showed that ratanhin is *not* a constituent of the roots of Krameria. The same substance has been abundantly found by Gintl (1868) in the natural exudation called *Resina d'Angelim pedra*[3] which is met with in the alburnum of *Ferreirea spectabilis* Allem., a large Brazilian tree of the order *Leguminosæ* (tribe *Sophoreæ*). Peckolt, who first extracted it, named it *Angelin*; it forms colourless, neutral crystals yielding compounds both with alkalis and acids, which have been investigated by Gintl in 1869 and 1870.

Uses—Rhatany is a valuable astringent, but is not much employed in Great Britain.

Other sorts of Rhatany—Of the 20 to 25 other species of *Krameria*, all of them belonging to America, several have astringent roots which have been collected and used in the place of the rhatany of Peru. The most important of these drugs is that known as—

Para Rhatany,—so called from having been shipped from Pará in Brazil. Berg who described it in 1865 termed it *Brazilian Rhatany*, Cotton in 1868, *Ratanhia des Antilles*. It is a drug nearly resembling the following, but of a darker and less purple hue; it is also in longer sticks which are remarkably flexible, and covered with a thick bark having numerous transverse cracks.[4] It is apparently derived from the *Krameria argentea* of Martius,[5] the root of which is collected in the dry districts of the provinces of Bahia and Minas Geraes, that plant growing throughout north-eastern Brazil. It is also called *Rhatany from Ceará*.

[1] *Etudes sur le Genre Krameria* (thèse), Paris, 1868. 83.

[2] Gmelin, *Chemistry*, xiii. (1859) 358.

[3] See Vogl's Paper on it in Pringsheim, *Jahrbücher für wissenschaftliche Botanik*, ix. (1874) 277—285.

[4] For further particulars, see Flückiger, *Pharm. Journ.*, July 30, 1870. 84.

[5] *Syst. Mat. Med. Bras.*, 1843. 51; Langgaard, *Diccionario de Medicina*, Rio de Janeiro, iii. (1865) 384.—Krameria argentea is figured in *Flora Brasiliensis*, Fascicul. 63 (1874, pg. 71) tab. 28.

Savanilla or New Granada Rhatany. The plant yielding it is *Krameria tomentosa* St. Hil. (*Kr. Ixina* var. β *granatensis* Triana, *Kr. grandifolia* Berg), a shrub 4 to 6 feet high covering large arid tracts in the valley of Jiron between Pamplona and the Magdalena in New Granada, in which locality the collection of the root was observed by Weir in 1864.[1] According to Triana it also grows at Socorro, south of Jiron. The same plant is found near Santa Marta and Rio Hacha in north-eastern New Granada, in British Guiana, and in the Brazilian provinces of Pernambuco and Goyaz.

The stem or root-crown of Savanilla rhatany is never so knotty and irregular as that of the Peruvian drug, nor are the roots so long or so thick. Separate pieces of root of sinuous form, 4 to 6 inches long and $\frac{2}{10}$ to $\frac{3}{10}$ of an inch thick are most frequent. The drug is moreover well distinguished by its dull purplish brown colour, its thick smooth bark marked with longitudinal furrows, and here and there with deep transverse cracks, and by the bark not easily splitting off as it does in common rhatany.

The anatomical difference depends chiefly upon the more abundant development of the bark which in thickness is $\frac{1}{3}$ to $\frac{1}{4}$ the diameter of the wood. In Peruvian rhatany the cortical layer attains only $\frac{1}{6}$ to $\frac{1}{8}$ of the diameter of the woody column. The greater firmness of the suberous coat in Savanilla rhatany is due to its cells being densely filled with colouring matter.

Savanilla rhatany differs from the Peruvian root in its tannic matter. This becomes evident by shaking the powdered root (or bark) with water and iron reduced by hydrogen. The liquid filtered from the Savanilla sort and diluted with distilled water exhibits an intense violet colour, that from Peruvian rhatany a dingy brown; the latter turns light red by alkalis. Thin sections of the Peruvian root assume a greyish hue when moistened with a ferrous salt; Savanilla root by a similar treatment displays the above violet colour. The Savanilla root is richer in soluble matter and from the greater development of its bark may deserve to be preferred for medicinal use.

In the English market, Savanilla root is of less frequent occurrence than that of Pará.

A kind of rhatany attributed to *Krameria secundiflora* DC., a herbaceous plant of Mexico, Texas and Arkansas, was furnished to Berg in 1854, but has not been in commerce. Its anatomical structure has been described by Berg.[2]

[1] Hanbury, *Origin of Savanilla Rhatany*, in *Pharm. Journ.* vi. (1865) 460.—Also *Science Papers*, 333.—In that paper I referred the drug to a variety of *Kr. Ixina* which M. Cotton has shown to differ in no respect from St. Hilaire's *Kr. tomentosa*, a conclusion in which, after careful re-examination of specimens, I fully agree.—D. H.

Fig. of *Kr. Ixina* in Bentley and Trimen, *Med. Pl.* part 10.

[2] *Bot. Zeitung*, 14th Nov. 1856. 797

GUTTIFERÆ.

CAMBOGIA.

Gummi Gambogia, Gummi Gutti; Gamboge; F. *Gomme Gutte;* G. *Gutti, Gummigutt.*

Botanical Origin—*Garcinia Morella* Desrousseaux, var. *β. pedicellata*, a diœcious tree,[1] with handsome laurel-like folliage and small yellow flowers, found in Camboja, Siam (province of Chantibun and the islands on the east coast of the gulf of Siam), and in the southern parts of Cochin China. It was introduced about thirty years ago into Singapore where several specimens are still thriving (1873) on the estate of Dr. Jamie. The finest is now a tree of 20 feet high, with a trunk a foot in diameter, and a thick, spreading head of foliage.

G. Morella Desr.—The typical form of this tree having *sessile* male flowers grows in moist forests of Southern India and Ceylon, and is capable of affording good gamboge.

G. pictoria Roxb., a large tree of Southern India, produces a sort of gamboge found by Christian (1846) essentially the same as that of Siam. It has been examined more recently by Broughton (1871) who states it to be quite equal to that of *G. Morella*. We have also been unable to find any difference between the product of *G. pictoria* as sent from Ceylon and common gamboge. *Garcinia pictoria* moreover is thought by Sir Jos. Hooker to agree with *G. Morella*.

History—The Chinese had intercourse with Camboja as early as the time of the Sung dynasty (A.D. 970—1127); and a Chinese traveller who visited the latter country in 1295-97, describes gamboge and the method of obtaining it by incisions in the stem of the tree.[2] The celebrated Chinese herbal *Pun-tsao*, written towards the close of the 16th century, mentions gamboge *(Tang-hwang)* and gives a rude figure of the tree. The drug is regarded by the Chinese as poisonous, and is scarcely employed except as a pigment.

The first notice of the occurrence of gamboge in Europe is in the writings of Clusius[3] who describes a specimen brought from China by the Dutch Admiral, Jacob van Neck, and given to him in 1603, under the name of *Ghittaiemou.*[4] It appears that shortly after this time it began to be employed in medicine in Europe, for in 1611, Michael Reuden, a physician of Bamberg, made use of it as he stated in 1613.[5] He termed the drug a "novum gummi purgans," or also, Gummi de

[1] It has been named *Garcinia Hanburyi* by Sir Joseph Hooker (*Journ. of the Linnean Soc.* xiv., 1873, 435), but I presume my lamented friend Daniel Hanbury would not have considered the plant under notice as a distinct species. Consult also Bentley and Trimen, *Med. Plants*, part 30.—F.A.F.

[2] *Description de Camboge* in Abel-Remusat's *Nouv. Mélanges asiatiques*, i. (1829) 134.—The Chinese traveller calls the exudation *Kiang-hwang* which is the name for *turmeric*, but his description is unmistakeable.

[3] *Exotica* (1605) 82.

[4] Dr. R. Rost is of opinion that this word is derived from the Malay *gătăh*, gum, and the Javanese *jamŭ* signifying medicinal, such mixing of the two languages being of common occurrence.

[5] *De nova gummi purgante*, Lipsiæ, 1614. We have only seen the second edition published at Leiden in 1625, its preface dating from 1613.

Peru, the latter strange name no doubt being a corruption of the above mentioned Ghitta-iemou. The appellation "gummi de Peru" is met with in pharmaceutical tariffs during the 17th and 18th centuries.

Gamboge is one of the articles of the tariff of the pharmaceutical shops of the City of Frankfort in 1612: "Gutta gemou, a strong purgative dried juice, coming from the Kingdom of *Patana* in the East Indies." Patana or Patani is the most populous province of the east coast of the peninsula of Malacca. The Dutch established there a factory in 1602, and were followed in 1612 by the English. The settlement was abandoned in 1700; gamboge was probably brought there from the opposite shore of the gulf of Siam.[1]

In 1615, a considerable quantity of gamboge was offered for sale in London by the East Indian Company. The entry respecting it in the Court Minute Books of the company under date October 13, 1615, is to this effect:—Three chests, one rundlet, and a basket, containing 13, 14, or 15 hundredweights, more or less, of *Cambogium "a drugge unknown here,"*—the use of which was much commended as a "*a gentle purge,*" were offered for sale at 5s. per ℔., but met with no purchaser.

Jacob Bontius,[2] a Dutch physician, resident, towards 1629, in Batavia, stated that "gutta Cambodja," as he termed the drug, came from the country of the same name; he supposed it to be derived from an Euphorbiaceous plant.

Parkinson,[3] who was an apothecary of London and wrote in 1640, speaks of this "*Cambugio,*" called by some *Catharticum aureum*, as a drug of recent importation which arrived in the form of "*wreathes or roules*" yellow within and without.

In the *London Pharmacopœia* of 1650, gamboge is called *Gutta Gamba*[4] or *Ghitta jemou.*

The mother plant of the drug was not fully examined and figured until 1864; yet in 1677 already, Hermann, a German physician residing in Ceylon, had pointed out that it was a Garcinia.[5]

Secretion—We have examined a portion of a branch two inches in diameter of the gamboge-tree,[6] and have found the yellow gum-resin to be contained chiefly in the middle layer of the bark in numerous ducts like those occurring in the roots of *Inula Helenium* and other roots of the same natural order. A little is also secreted in the dotted vessels of the outermost layer of the wood, and in the pith. The wood, which is white, acquires a bright yellow tint when exposed to the vapour of ammonia or to alkaline solutions.

Production—At the commencement of the rainy season the gamboge-collectors start for the forest in search of the trees which in some localities are plentiful. Having found one of the full size they make a spiral incision in the bark round half the circumference of the trunk, and place a joint of bamboo to receive the sap which slowly exudes for

[1] Flückiger, *Documente zur Geschichte der Pharmacie*, 1876. 41.

[2] *De Medicina Indorum*, lib. iv. Lugduni Batav. (1642) 119. 150.

[3] *Theatrum Botanicum* (1640) 1575.

[4] This name is the Hindustani *Gótá-gambá*, signifying according to Moodeen Sheriff (*Suppl. to Pharm. of India*, 83) *juice or extract of rhubarb.* It is still applied to gamboge.

[5] Hanbury in *Trans. of Linn. Soc.* xxiv. (1864) 487. tab. 50; also *Science Papers*, 1876. 326.

[6] Obligingly sent to us by Dr. Jamie of Singapore.

several months. When it first issues from the tree, it is a yellowish fluid, which after passing through a viscid state hardens into the gamboge of commerce.

The trees grow both in the valleys and on the mountains and will yield on an average in one season enough to fill three joints of bamboo 20 inches in length by 1½ inches in diameter. The tree appears to suffer no injury provided the tapping is not more frequent than every other year.[1]

According to Dr. Jamie of Singapore, the gamboge-tree grows most luxuriantly in the dense jungles. The best time for collecting is from February to March or April. The trees, the larger the better, are wounded by a parang or chopping-knife, in various parts of the trunk and large branches, when prepared bamboos are inserted between the root and the bark of the trees. The bamboo cylinders being tied or inserted, are examined daily till filled, which generally takes from 15 to 30 days. Then the bamboos are taken to a fire, over which they are gradually rotated till the water in the gum-resin is evaporated and it gets sufficiently hard to allow of the bamboo being torn off.[2]

Description—The drug arrives in the form of sticks or cylinders 1 to 2½ inches in diameter, and 4 to 8 inches in length, striated lengthwise with impressions from the inside of the bamboo. Often the sticks are agglutinated, or folded, or the drug is in compressed or in shapeless masses. It is when good of a rich brownish orange tint, dense and homogeneous, breaking easily with a conchoidal fracture, scarcely translucent even in thin splinters. Touched with water it instantly forms a yellow emulsion. Triturated in a mortar it affords a brilliant yellow powder, slightly odorous. Gamboge has a disagreeable acrid taste.

Much of the gamboge shipped to Europe is of inferior quality, being of a brownish hue or exhibiting when broken a rough, granular, bubbly surface. Sometimes it arrives imperfectly dried and still soft.

Chemical Composition—Gamboge consists of a mixture of resin with 15 to 20 per cent. of gum. The resin dissolves easily in alcohol, forming a clear liquid of fine yellowish-red hue, and not decidedly acid reaction. It forms darker-coloured solutions with ammonia or the fixed alkalis, and a copious precipitate with basic acetate of lead. Perchloride of iron colours a solution of the resin deep blackish brown.

By fusing purified gamboge resin with potash, Hlasiwetz and Barth (1866) obtained acetic acid and other acids of the same series, together with *phloroglucin*, $C^6H^3(OH)^3$, *pyrotartaric* acid, $C^5H^8O^4$, and *isuvitinic* acid, $C^6H^3CH^3(COOH)^2$.

The gum which we obtained to the extent of 15·8 per cent. by completely exhausting gamboge with alcohol and ether, was found readily soluble in water. The solution does not redden litmus, and is not precipitated by neutral acetate of lead, nor by perchloride of iron, nor by silicate or biborate of sodium. It is therefore not identical with gum arabic.

Commerce—The drug finds its way to Europe from Camboja by Singapore, Bangkok, or Saigon. In 1877 the first place exported 240

[1] Spenser St. John, *Life in the Forests of the Far East*, Lond. 1862. ii. 272.

[2] *Pharm. Journ.* iv. (1874) 803.

peculs, Bangkok in 1875 no less than 346 peculs, value 48,835 dollars; from Saigon there have of late been shipped from 30 to 40 peculs annually (one pecul = 133·3 lbs. = 60·479 kilogrammes).[1]

Uses—Gamboge is a drastic purgative, seldom administered except in combination with other substances.

Adulteration—The Cambojans adulterate gamboge with rice flour, sand, or the pulverized bark of the tree,[2] which substances may be easily detected in the residue left after exhausting the drug successively by spirit of wine and cold water.

Other Sources of Gamboge—Although the gamboge of European commerce appears to be exclusively derived from the form of the plant named at the head of this article, *Garcinia travancorica* Beddome, is capable of yielding a similar drug which may be collected to some small extent for local use, but not for exportation. It is a beautiful tree of the southern forests of Travancore and the Tinnevelly Ghats (3,000 to 4,500 feet). According to its discoverer Lieut. Beddome,[3] it yields an abundance of bright yellow gamboge.

OLEUM GARCINIÆ.

Concrete Oil of Mangosteen, Kokum Butter.

Botanical Origin.—*Garcinia indica* Choisy (*G. purpurea* Roxb. *Brindonia indica* Dup. Th.), an elegant tree with drooping branches and dark green leaves.[4] It bears a smooth round fruit the size of a small apple, containing an acid purple pulp in which are lodged as many as 8 seeds. The tree is a native of the coast region of Western India known as the Concan, lying between Daman and Goa.

History—The fruit is mentioned by Garcia d'Orta (1563) as known to the Portuguese of Goa by the name of *Brindones*. He states that it has a pleasant taste though very sour, and that it is used in dyeing; and further that the peel serves to make a sort of vinegar. Several succeeding authors (as Bauchin and Ray) have contented themselves with repeating this account.

As to the fruit yielding a fatty oil, we find no reference to such fact till about the year 1830, when it was stated in an Indian newspaper[5] that an oil of the seeds is well known at Goa and often used to adulterate ghee (liquid butter). It was afterwards pointed out as the result of some experiments that the oil was of an agreeable bland taste and well adapted for use in pharmacy. A short article on Kokum Butter was published by Pereira[6] in 1851. With the view of bringing the substance into use for pharmaceutical preparations in India, it has been introduced into the *Pharmacopœia of India* of 1868.

Preparation—The seeds are reniform, somewhat crescent-shaped or oblong, laterally compressed and wrinkled, $\frac{6}{10}$ to $\frac{8}{10}$ of an inch long

[1] *Report from H.M. Consul-General in Siam for* 1875. 9.

[2] Spenser St. John, *op. cit.*

[3] *Flora Sylvatica*, Madras, part xv. (1872) tab. 173.

[4] Fig. Bentley and Trimen, *Medic. Plants*, part 31 (1878).

[5] Quoted by Graham, *Catal. of Bombay Plants*, 1839. 25.

[6] *Pharm. Journ.* xi. (1852) 65.

by about $\frac{1}{10}$ broad. Each seed weighs on an average about eight grains. The thick cotyledons, which are inseparable,[1] have a mild oily taste. Examination under the microscope shows them to be built up of large reticulated cells containing a considerable proportion of crystalline fat readily soluble in benzol. In addition globular masses of albuminous matter occur which with iodine assume a brownish yellow hue. With perchloride of iron the walls strike a greenish-black.

The process followed by the natives of India (by whom alone the oil is prepared) has been thus described:—The seeds having been dried by exposure for some days to the sun are bruised, and boiled in water. The oil collects on the surface, and concretes when cool into a cake which requires to be purified by melting and straining.

Description—Kokum Butter is found in the Indian bazaars in the form of egg-shaped or oblong lumps about 4 inches long by 2 inches in diameter, and weighing about a quarter of a pound. It is a whitish substance, at ordinary temperatures, firm, dry, and friable, yet greasy to the touch. Scrapings (which are even pulverulent) when examined in glycerin under the microscope show it to be thoroughly crystalline. They have a mild oily taste, yet redden litmus if moistened with alcohol.

By filtration in a steam-bath, kokum butter is obtained perfectly transparent and of a light straw-colour, concentrating again at 27·5° C. into a white crystalline mass: some crystals appear even at 30°. Melted in a narrow tube, cooled and then warmed in a water bath, the fat begins to melt at 42·5° C., and fuses entirely at 45°. The residue left after filtration of the crude fat is inconsiderable, and consists chiefly of brown tannic matters soluble in spirit of wine.

When kokum butter is long kept it acquires an unpleasant rancid smell and brownish hue, and an efflorescence of shining tufted crystals appears on the surface of the mass.

Chemical Composition—Purified kokum butter boiled with caustic soda yields a fine hard soap which, when decomposed with sulphuric acid, affords a crystalline cake of fatty acids weighing as much as the original fat. The acids were again combined with soda and the soap having been decomposed, they were dissolved in alcohol of about 94 per cent. By slow cooling and evaporation crystals were first formed which, when perfectly dried, melted at 69·5° C.: they are consequently *Stearic Acid*. A less considerable amount of crystals which separated subsequently had a fusing point of 55°, and may be referred to *Myristic Acid*.

A portion of the crude fat was heated with oxide of lead and water, and the plumbic compound dried and exhausted with ether, which after evaporation left a very small amount of liquid oil, which we refer to *Oleic Acid*.

Finally the sulphuric acid used at the outset of the experiments was saturated and examined in the usual manner for volatile fatty acids (butyric, valerianic, &c.) but with negative results.

[1] The embryo, according to Bentley and Trimen (*l. c.*) consists chiefly of the *thickened* radicle, and is almost devoid of cotyledons.

The fat of the seeds of *G. indica* was extracted by ether and examined chemically in 1857 by J. Bouis and d'Oliveira Pimentel.[1] It was obtained to the extent of 30 per cent., was found to fuse at 40° C. and to consist chiefly of stearin (tristearin). The seeds yielded 1·72 per cent. of nitrogen. Their residue after exhaustion by ether afforded to alkaline solutions or alcohol a fine red colour.

Uses—The results of the experiments above-noted show that kokum butter is well suited for some pharmaceutical preparations. It might also be advantageously employed in candle-making, as it yields stearic acid more easily and in a purer state than tallow and most other fats. But that it is possible to obtain it in quantities sufficiently large for important industrial uses, appears to us very problematical.

DIPTEROCARPEÆ.

BALSAMUM DIPTEROCARPI.

Balsamun Gurjunæ; Gurjun Balsam, Wood Oil.

Botanical Origin—This drug is yielded by several trees of the genus *Dipterocarpus*, namely—

D. turbinatus Gärtn. f. (*D. lævis* Ham., *D. indicus* Bedd), a native of Eastern Bengal, Chittagong and Pegu to Singapore, and French Cochin China.

D. incanus Roxb., a tree of Chittagong and Pegu.

D. alatus Roxb., growing in Chittagong, Burma, Tenasserim, the Andaman Islands, Siam, and French Cochin China.

D. zeylanicus Thw. and *D. hispidus* Thw., indigenous to Ceylon.

D. crispalatus . . . . . abounding, together with *D. turbinatus* and *D. alatus*, in French Cochin China.

D. trinervis Bl., a native of Java and the Philippines, and *D. gracilis* Bl., *D. littoralis* Bl., *D. retusus* Bl. (*D. Spanoghei* Bl.), trees of Java supply a similar useful product which as yet appears to be of less commercial importance.[2]

The Gurjun trees are said by Hooker[3] to be among the most magnificent of the forests of Chittagong. They are conspicuous for their gigantic size, and for the straightness and graceful form of their tall unbranched trunk, and small symmetrical crown of broad glossy leaves. Many individuals are upwards of 200 feet high and 15 feet in girth.

History—Gurjun balsam was enumerated as one of the productions of Ava by Francklin[4] in 1811, and in 1813 it was briefly noticed by Ainslie.[5] Its botanical origin was first made known by Roxburgh, who also described the method by which it is extracted.

[1] *Comptes Rendus*, xliv. (1857) 1355.

[2] That of *D. trinervis* is especially used in Java. Filet, *Plantkundig Woordenboek voor Nederlandsch Indië*, Leiden, 1876, No. 6157.

[3] *Himalayan Journal*, ed. 2, ii. (1855) 332.

[4] *Tracts on the Dominions of Ava*, Lond. 1811. 26.

[5] In the *Catalogue des Produits des*

The medicinal properties of Gurjun balsam were pointed out by O'Shaughnessy[1] as entirely analogous to those of copaiba; and his observations were confirmed by many practitioners in India. This has obtained for the drug a place in the *Pharmacopœia of India* (1868).

Extraction—A recent account of the production of this drug is found in the *Reports of the Jury of the Madras Exhibition of 1855.* It is there stated that *Wood Oil*, as the balsam is commonly called, is obtained for the most part from the coast of Burma and the Straits, and is procured by tapping the trees about the end of the dry season. Several deep incisions are made with an axe into the trunk of the tree and a good-sized cavity scooped out. In this, fire is placed, and kept burning until the wood is somewhat scorched, when the balsam begins to exude, and is then led away into a vessel of bamboo. It is afterwards allowed to settle, when a clear liquid separates from a thick portion called the "*guad.*" The oil is extracted year after year, and sometimes there are two or three holes in the same tree. It is produced in extraordinary abundance; from 30 to 40 gallons according to Roxburgh may sometimes be obtained from a single tree in the course of a season, during which it is necessary to remove from time to time the old charred surface of the wood and burn afresh.

If a growing tree is felled and cut into piece, the oleo-resin exudes and concretes on the wood, very much, it is said, *resembling camphor* (?) and having an aromatic smell.

Description—As Gurjun balsam is the produce of different trees as well as of different countries, it is not surprising to find that it varies considerably in its properties.

The following observations refer to a balsam of which 400 ℔. were recently imported from Moulmein for a London drug firm. It is a thick and viscid fluid, exhibiting a remarkable fluorescence, so that when seen by reflected light it appears opaque and of dingy greenish grey; yet when placed between the observer and strong daylight it is seen to be perfectly transparent and of a dark-reddish brown.[2] It has a weak aromatic copaiba-like odour and a bitterish aromatic taste without the persistent acridity of copaiba. Its sp. gr. at 16·9° C. is 0·964.

With the following liquids Gurjun affords perfectly clear solutions which are more or less fluorescent, namely pure benzol (from benzoate of calcium), cumol, chloroform, sulphide of carbon, essential oils. On the other hand, it is not entirely soluble in methylic, ethylic, or amylic alcohol; in ether, acetic ether, glacial acetic acid, acetone, phenol (carbolic acid), or in caustic potash dissolved in absolute alcohol. Many samples of commercial benzin also are not capable of dissolving the oleo-resin perfectly, but we have not ascertained on what constituent of such benzin this depends. We have further noticed that that portion of petroleum which is known as *Petroleum Ether*, containing the most volatile hydrocarbons, does not wholly dissolve the oleo-resin. One hundred parts of the balsam warmed and shaken with 1000

Colonies françaises, Exposition Universelle de 1878, p. 175, it is stated that the balsam of *D. alatus* in French Cochin China is preferred, being a "*huile blanche.*"

[1] *Mat. Med. of Hindoostan*, Madras, 1813. 186.

[2] *Bengal Dispensatory*, 1842. 22.

parts of absolute alcohol yielded on cooling a precipitate of resin amounting when dried to 18·5 parts. All concentrated solutions of the balsam are precipitated by amylic alcohol.

If the balsam is kept for a long time in a stoppered vessel at 100° C. it simply becomes a little turbid; but about 130° C. it is transformed into a jelly, and on cooling does not resume its former fluidity. Balsam of copaiba heated in a closed glass tube to 220° C. does not at all lose its fluidity, whereas Gurjun balsam becomes an almost solid mass.

Chemical Composition—Of the balsam 6·99 grammes dissolved in benzol and kept in a water bath until the residue ceased to lose weight, yielded 3·80 grammes of a dry, transparent, semi-fluid resin, corresponding to 54·44 per cent., and 45·56 of volatile matters expelled by evaporation. But another sample afforded us much less residue. By submitting larger quantities of the above balsam to the usual process of distillation with water in a large copper still, 37 per cent. of volatile oil were easily obtained. The water passing over at the same time did not redden litmus paper. A dark, viscid, liquid resin remained in the still.

The essential oil is of a pale straw-colour and less odorous than most other volatile oils. Treated with chloride of calcium and again distilled, it begins to boil at 210° C. and passes over at 255°—260° C., acquiring a somewhat empyreumatic smell and light yellowish tint. The purified oil has a sp. gr. of 0·915;[1] it is but sparingly soluble in absolute alcohol or glacial acetic acid, but mixes readily with amylic alcohol.

According to Werner (1862) this oil has the composition $C^{20}H^{32}$ like that of copaiba. He says it deviates the ray of polarized light to the left, but that prepared by one of us deviated strongly to the *right*, the residual resin dissolved in benzol being wholly inactive. The oil does not form a crystalline compound with dry hydrochloric acid, which colours it of a beautiful blue.[2] De Vry[3] states that the essential oil after this treatment deviates the ray to the right.

The resin contains, like that of copaiba, a small proportion of a crystallizable acid which may be removed by warming it with ammonia in weak alcohol. That part of the resin which is insoluble even in absolute alcohol,[4] we found to be uncrystallizable. The *Gurgunic Acid*, as the crystallized resinous acid is called by Werner,[5] but which it is more correct to write *Gurjunic*, may consequently be prepared by extracting the resin with alcohol (·838) and mixing the solution with ammonia. From the ammoniacal solution gurjunic acid is precipitated on addition of a mineral acid, and if it is again dissolved in ether and alcohol it may be procured in the form of small crystalline crusts. From the specimen under examination we were not successful in obtaining indubitable crystals.

Gurjunic acid, $C^{44}H^{68}O^{8}$ according to Werner, melts at 220° C., and concretes again at 180° C.; it begins to boil at 260° C., yet at the same time decomposition takes place. By assigning to this acid the formula $C^{44}H^{64}O^{5}+3H^{2}O$, which agrees well with Werner's analytical results, we

[1] 0·944 according to Werner; 0·931 O'Shaughnessy; 0·928 De Vry (1857).

[2] This magnificent colouring matter is not dissolved by ether.

[3] *Pharm. Journ.* xvi. (1857) 374.

[4] The sample of gurjun balsam examined by Werner as well as the resin it contained were entirely soluble in boiling potash lye.

[5] Gmelin, *Chemistry*, xvii. 545.

may regard it as a hydrate of abietinic acid, the chemical behaviour of which is perfectly analogous. Gurjunic acid is soluble in alcohol 0·838, but not in weak alcohol; it is dissolved also by ether, benzol, or sulphide of carbon (Werner).

In copaiba from Maracaibo, Strauss (1865) discovered *Metacopaivic Acid* which is probably identical with gurjunic; the former, however, fuses at 206° C.

The amorphous resin forming the chief bulk of the residue of the distillation of the balsam, has not yet been submitted to exact analysis. We find that after complete desiccation it is not soluble in absolute alcohol. A crystallized constituent of Gurjun, which we obtained from a balsam of unknown origin, has been shown[1] to answer to the formula $C^{28}H^{46}O^{2}$. Its crystals, belonging to the asymmetric system, melt at 126°—130°C.; they are entirely devoid of acid character. A comparative examination of the product of each of the above named species of Dipterocarpus would be highly desirable.

Commerce—Gurjun balsam is exported from Singapore, Moulmein, Akyab and the Malayan Peninsula, and is a common article of trade in Siam. It is likewise produced in Canara in Southern India. It is occasionally shipped to Europe. More than 2000 ℔. were offered for sale in London under the name of *East India Balsam Capivi*, 4th October 1855; and in October 1858, a no less quantity than 45 casks appeared in the catalogue of a London drug-broker. It is now not unfrequent in the London drug sales.

Uses—In medicine it has hitherto been employed only as a substitute for copaiba, and chiefly in the hospitals of India.

In the East its great use is as a natural varnish, either alone or combined with pigments; and also as a substitute for tar as an application to the seams of boats, and for preserving timber from the attacks of the white ant. To the first application it is often made better appropriated[2] by boiling it, so that the essential oil is evaporated.

Wood Oil of China—The oleo-resin of Dipterocarpus must not be confounded with the so-called *Wood Oil* of China, which is of a totally different nature. The latter is a fatty oil expressed from the seeds of *Aleurites cordata* Müll. Arg. (*Dryandra cordata* Thunb. *Elaeococca Vernicia* Sprgl. Prodromus xv. part 2, p. 724), the well-known *Tung* tree of the Chinese. It is a large tree of the order *Euphorbiaceæ*, found in China and Japan. The oil is an article of enormous consumption among the Chinese, who use it in the caulking and painting of junks and boats, for preserving woodwork, varnishing furniture, and also in medicine. In the commercial reports of H.M. Consuls in China (No. 5, 1875, p. 3, 26) we find that this oil is largely exported from Hankow: 199·654 peculs in 1874, and forms an article of import at Ningpo: 15·123 peculs in 1874 (pecul=133·33 ℔. avoirdupois). It is, however, not shipped to foreign countries. The oil of the Tung tree is also extremely remarkable on account of its chemical properties as shown by Cloëz (1875—1877).

[1] Flückiger, *Pharm. Journ.* (1878) 725, with fig.

[2] *Catalogue of the French Colonies, Paris Exhibition*, 1878, 101, quoted above.

MALVACEÆ.

RADIX ALTHÆÆ

Marshmallow Root; F. Racine de Guimauve; G. Ebischwurzel.

Botanical Origin—*Althæa officinalis* L., the marshmallow, grows in moist places throughout Europe, Asia Minor, and the temperate parts of Western and Northern Asia, but is by no means universally distributed. It prefers saline localities such as in Spain the salt marshes of Saragossa, the low-lying southern coasts of France near Montpellier, Southern Russia, and the neighbourhood of salt-springs in Central Europe. In southern Siberia Althæa has been met with by Semenoff (1857) ascending as high as 3,000 feet in the Alatau mountains, south of the Balkash Lake.

In Britain it occurs in the low grounds bordering the Thames below London, and here and there in many other spots in the south of England and of Ireland.

The cultivated marshmallow thrives as far north as Throndhjem in Norway, and has been naturalized in North America (salt marshes of New England and New York) and Australia. It is largely cultivated in Bavaria and Würtemberg.

History—Marshmallow had many uses in ancient medicine, and is described by Dioscorides as *'Αλθαία*, a name derived from the Greek verb *ἀλθειν, to heal.*

The diffusion of the plant in Europe during the middle ages was promoted by Charlemagne who enjoined[1] its culture (A.D. 812) under the name of "*Mismalvas*, id est alteas quod dicitur ibischa."

Description—The plant has a perennial root attaining about a foot in length and an inch in diameter. For medicinal use the biennial roots of the cultivated plant are chiefly employed. When fresh they are externally yellowish and wrinkled, white within and of tender fleshy texture. Previous to drying, the thin outer and a portion of the middle bark are scraped off, and the small root filaments are removed. The drug thus prepared and dried consists of simple whitish sticks 6 to 8 inches long, of the thickness of the little finger to that of a quill, deeply furrowed longitudinally and marked with brownish scars. Its central portion, which is pure white, breaks with a short fracture, but the bark is tough and fibrous. The dried root is rather flexible and easily cut. Its transverse section shows the central woody column of undulating outline separated from the thick bark by a fine dark outline shaded off outwards.

The root has a peculiar though very faint odour, and is of rather mawkish and insipid taste, and very slimy when chewed.

Microscopic Structure—The greater part of the bark consists of liber, abounding in long soft fibres, to which the toughness of the cortical tissue is due. They are branched and form bundles, each con-

[1] Pertz, *Monumenta Germaniæ historica*, Legum tom. i. (1835) 181.—*Ibischa* from the Greek *ἰβίσκος*.

taining from 3 to 30 fibres separated by parenchymatous tissue. Of the cortical parenchyme many cells are loaded with starch granules, others contain stellate groups of oxalate of calcium, and a considerable number of somewhat larger cells are filled with mucilage. The last-named on addition of alcohol is seen to consist of different layers.

The woody part is made up of pitted or scalariform vessels, accompanied by a few ligneous cells and separated by a parenchymatous tissue, agreeing with that of the bark. On addition of an alkali, sections of the root assume a bright yellow hue.

Chemical Composition—The mucilage in the dry root amounts to about 25 per cent. and the starch to as much more. The former appears from the not very accordant analysis of Schmidt and of Mulder to agree with the formula $C^{12}H^{20}O^{10}$, thus differing from the mucilage of gum arabic by one molecule less of water. It likewise differs in being precipitable by neutral acetate of lead. At the same time it does not show the behaviour of cellulose, as it does not turn blue by iodine when moistened with sulphuric acid, and it is not soluble in ammoniacal solution of oxide of copper.

The root also contains pectin and sugar (cane-sugar according to Wittstock), and a trace of fatty oil. Tannin is found in very small quantity in the outer bark alone.

In 1826 Bacon, a pharmacien of Caen, obtained from althæa root crystals of a substance at first regarded as peculiar, but subsequently identified with *Asparagin*, $C^4H^8N^2O^3, H^2O$. It had been previously prepared (1805) by Vauquelin and Robiquet from Asparagus, and is now known to be a widely-diffused constituent of plants.[1] Marshmallow root does not yield more than 0·8 to 2·0 per cent. Asparagin crystallizes in large prisms or octohedra of the rhombic system; it is nearly tasteless, and appears destitute of physiological action. Its relation to succinic acid may be thus represented:—

$$\text{Succinic acid: } C^2H^4\begin{cases}COOH\\COOH\end{cases};\quad \text{Asparagin: } C^2H^3(NH^2)\begin{cases}CONH^2\\COOH\end{cases}.$$

Asparagin is quite permanent whether in the solid state or dissolved, but it is easily decomposed if the solution contains the albuminoid constituents of the root, which act as a ferment. Leguminous seeds, yeast or decayed cheese induce the same change, the final product of which is succinate of ammonium, the asparagin taking the elements of water and hydrogen set free by the fermentation, thus—

$$\underset{\text{Asparagin.}}{C^4H^8N^2O^3} + H^2O + 2H = \underset{\text{Succinate of Ammonium.}}{2NH^4,C^4H^4O^4}$$

Under the influence of acids or bases, or even by the prolonged boiling of its aqueous solution, asparagin is converted into *Aspartate of Ammonium*, $C^4H^6(NH^4)NO^4$, of which the hydrated asparagin contains the elements.

These transformations, especially the former, are undergone by the asparagin in the root, if the latter has been imperfectly dried, or has

[1] It plays an interesting part in the germination of the seeds of papilionaceous and other plants. It is abundant in the young plants, but in most it speedily disappears. Its presence can be proved in the juice by means of the microscope and absolute alcohol, in which latter asparagin is insoluble. See Pfeffer in Pringsheim's *Jahrb. f. wiss. Bot.* 1872. 533—564.—Borodin in *Bot. Zeitung*, 1878. 801 and seq.

been kept long, or not very dry. Under such conditions, the asparagin gradually disappears, and the root then yields a brownish decoction, sometimes having a disagreeable odour of butyric acid. There is no doubt that a protein-substance here acts as a ferment. The sections of the root when touched with ammonia or caustic lye should display a bright yellow, not a dingy brown, colour.

The peeled root dried at 100° C. and incinerated afforded us 4·88 of ash, rich in phosphates.

Uses—Althæa is taken as a demulcent; it is sometimes also applied as an emollient poultice. It is far more largely used on the continent than in England

FRUCTUS HIBISCI ESCULENTI.

Capsulae Hibisci esculenti; Uĕhka, Okro, Okra, Bendi-kai[1]; F. *Gombo* (in the French Colonies).

Botanical Origin—*Hibiscus esculentus* L. (*Abelmoschus esculentus Guill. et Perr.*) an herbaceous annual plant 2 to 3 or even 10 feet high, indigenous to the Old World.[2] It has been found growing abundantly wild on the White Nile by Schweinfurth, and also in 1861 by Col. Grant in Unyoro, 2° N. lat., near the lake Victoria Nyanza, where it is known to the natives as Bameea.

The plant is now largely cultivated in several varieties in all tropical countries.

History—The Spanish Moors appear to have been well acquainted with *Hibiscus esculentus*, which was known to them by the same name that it has in Persian at the present day—*Bámiyah*. Abul-Abbas el-Nebáti, a native of Seville learned in plants, who visited Egypt in A.D. 1216, describes[3] in unmistakeable terms the form of the plant, its seeds and fruit, which last he remarks is eaten when young and tender with meat by the Egyptians. The plant was figured among Egytian plants in 1592 by Prosper Alpinus,[4] who mentions its uses as an external emollient.

The powdered fruits as imported from Arabia Felix were known for some time (about the year 1848) in Europe as *Nafé of the Arabs*. They are noticed in the present work from the circumstance that they have a place in the *Pharmacopœia of India*.

Description—The fruit is a thin capsule, 4 to 6 or more inches long and about an inch in diameter, oblong, pointed, with 5 to 7 ridges corresponding to the valves and cells, each of which latter contains a single row of round seeds. It is covered with rough hairs and is green or purplish when fresh; it has a slightly sweet mucilaginous taste and a weak herbaceous odour. Like many other plants of the order, *Hibiscus esculentus* abounds in all its parts with insipid mucilage.

[1] Uĕhka in Arabic, according to Schweinfurth. *Okro* or *Okra* are common names for the plant in the East and West Indies. *Bendikai*, a Canarese and Tamil word, is used by Europeans in the South of India. *Gigambo* in Curaçao.

[2] Fig. Bentley and Trimen, *Med. Plants*, part 35 (1878).

[3] Ibn Baytar, Sontheimer's translation, i. 118; Wüstenfeld, *Geschichte der Arab. Aerzte* etc. 1840. 118.

[4] *De plant. Ægypt.*, Venet. 1592. cap. 27.

Microscopic Structure—A characteristic part for microscopic examination are the hairs of the fruit. They exhibit at the base one large cell, but their elongated and often slightly curved end is built up at a considerable number of small cells, without any solid contents. The middle and outer zone of the pericarp shows enormous holes filled up with colourless mucilage. In polarized light it is easily seen to be composed of successive layers.

Chemical Composition—It is probable that the fruits contain the same mucilage as *Althæa*, but we have had no opportunity of investigating the fact. Landrin[1] says it turns violet with iodine and yields no mucic acid when treated with nitric acid. Popp, who examined the green fruits in Egypt, states[2] that they abound in pectin, starch and mucilage. He found that when dried they afforded 2 to 2·4 per cent. of nitrogen, and an ash rich in salts of lime, potash and magnesia. The ripe seeds gave 2·4—2·5 per cent. of nitrogen ; their ash 24 per cent. of phosphoric acid.

Uses—The fresh or dried, unripe fruits are used in tropical countries as a demulcent like marshmallow, or as an emollient poultice, for which latter purpose the leaves may also be employed. They are more important from an economic point of view, being much employed for thickening soups or eaten boiled as a vegetable. The root has been recommended as a substitute for that of *Althæa*.[3] The stems of the plant yield a good fibre.

STERCULIACEÆ.

OLEUM CACAO.

Butyrum Cacao, Oleum Theobromatis ; Cacao Butter, Oil of Theobroma ; F. *Beurre de Cacao ;* G. *Cacaobutter, Cacaotalg.*

Botanical Origin—Cacao seeds (from which Cacao Butter is extracted) are furnished by *Theobroma Cacao* L., and apparently also by *Th. leiocarpum* Bernoulli, *Th. pentagonum* Bern., and *Th. Salzmannianum* Bern.[4] These trees are found in the northern parts of South America and in Central America as far as Mexico, both in a wild state and in cultivation.

History—Cacao seeds were first noticed by Capitan Gonzalo Fernandez de Oviedo y Valdés (1514-1523), who stated[5] that they had been met with by Columbus, being used among the inhabitants of Yucatan instead of money. They were likewise pointed out to Charles V., by Cortes in one of his letters to the Emperor, dated Temixtitan,

[1] *Journ. de Pharm.* 22 (1875) 278.

[2] *Archiv der Pharmacie*, cxcv. (1871) 142.

[3] Della Sudda, *Rép. de Pharm.*, Janvier, 1860. 229.

[4] Bernoulli, *Uebersicht der bis jetzt bekannten Arten von Theobroma.*—Reprinted from *Denkschriften der Schweizerischen Gesellschaft für Naturwissenschaften*, xxiv. (Zürich, 1869) 4°. 376.

[5] *Historia general y natural de las Indias islas y tierra firme del mar oceano*, iii. (Madrid, 1853) 253.

Sept. 3rd 1526.[1] The tree as well as the seeds and their uses, were at length described by Benzoni,[2] who lived in the new world from 1541 to 1555. Clusius figured the seeds in his "Notæ in Garciæ Aromatum historiam," Antwerpiæ, 1582.

Cacao butter was prepared and described by Homberg[3] as early as 1695, at which time it appears to have had no particular application, but in 1719 it was recommended by D. de Quelus[4] both for ointments and as an aliment.

An essay published at Tübingen in 1735[5] called attention to it as "*novum atque commendatissimum medicamentum.*" A little later it is mentioned by Geoffroy[6] who says that it is obtained either by boiling or by expressing the seeds, that it is recommended as the basis of cosmetic pomades and as an application to chapped lips and nipples, and to hæmorrhoids.

Production—Cacao butter is procured for use in pharmacy from the manufacturers of chocolate, who obtain it by pressing the warmed seeds. These in the shelled state yield from 45 to 50 per cent. of oil. The natural seeds consist of about 12 per cent. of shell (testa) and 88 of kernels (cotyledons).

Description—At ordinary temperatures cacao butter is a light yellowish, opaque, dry substance, usually supplied in the form of oblong tablets having somewhat the aspect of white Windsor soap. Though unctuous to touch, it is brittle enough to break into fragments when struck, exhibiting a dull waxy fracture. It has a pleasant odour of chocolate, and melts in the mouth with a bland agreeable taste. Its sp. gr. is 0·961 ; its fusing point 20° to 30° C.

Examined under the microscope by polarized light, cacao butter is seen to consist of minute crystals. It is dissolved by 20 parts of boiling absolute alcohol, but on cooling separates to such an extent that the liquid retains not more than 1 per cent. in solution. The fat separated after refrigeration is found to have lost most of its chocolate flavour. Litmus is not altered by the hot alcoholic solution.

Cacao butter in small fragments is slowly dissolved by double its weight of benzol in the cold (10° C.), but by keeping partially separates in crystalline warts.

Chemical Composition—The fat under notice is composed, in common with others, of several bodies which by saponification furnish glycerin and fatty acids. Among the latter occurs also oleic acid,[7] contained in that part of the cacao butter which remains dissolved in cold alcohol as above stated. In fact by evaporating that solution a soft fat is obtained. But the chief constituents of cacao butter appear to be stearin, palmitin, and another compound of glycerin containing

[1] Vedia, *Cartas de relacion enviadas al emperador Carlos V. desde Nueva España.* Madrid, 1852. T. 1.

[2] Chavveton (Urbain) *Hist. nouv. du Nouveau Monde . . . . extraite del' italien de M. Hierosme Benzoni Milanais.* 1579. p. 504.

[3] *Hist. d. l'Acad. Roy. des Sciences*, tome ii. depuis 1686 jusqu'à 1699, Paris, 1733. p. 248.

[4] *Hist. nat. du Cacao et du Sucre*, Paris, 1719. (According to Haller, *Bibl. Bot.* ii. 158.)

[5] B. D. Mauchart præside—dissertatio : *Butyrum Cacao.* Resp. Theoph. Hoffmann.

[6] *Tract. de Mat. Med.* ii. (1741) 409.

[7] See article *Amygdalæ dulces.*

probably an acid of the same series richer in carbon,—perhaps arachic acid, $C^{20}H^{40}O^{2}$, or "*theobromic acid,*" $C^{64}H^{128}O^{2}$, as suggested in 1877 by Kingzett.

Uses—Cacao butter, which is remarkable for having but little tendency to rancidity, has long been used in continental pharmacy; it was introduced into England a few years ago as a convenient basis for suppositories and pessaries.

Adulteration—The description given of the drug sufficiently indicates the means of ascertaining its purity.

LINEÆ.

SEMEN LINI.

Linseed, Flax Seed; F. *Semence de Lin;* G. *Leinsamen, Flachssamen.*

Botanical Origin—*Linum usitatissimum* L., Common Flax, is an annual plant, native of the Old World, where it has been cultivated from the remotest times. It sows itself as a weed in tilled ground, and is now found in all temperate and tropical regions of the globe. Heer regards it as a variety evolved by cultivation from the perennial *L. angustifolium* Huds.

History—The history of flax, its textile fibre and seed, is intimately connected with that of human civilization. The whole process of converting the plant into a fibre fit for weaving into cloth is frequently depicted on the wall-paintings of the Egyptian tombs.[1] The grave-clothes of the old Egyptians were made of flax, and the use of the fibre in Egypt may be traced back, according to Unger,[2] as far as the 23rd century B.C. The old literature of the Hebrews[3] and Greeks contains frequent reference to tissues of flax; and fabrics woven of flax have actually been discovered together with fruits and seeds of the plant in the remains of the ancient pile-dwellings bordering the lakes of Switzerland.[4]

The seed in ancient times played an important part in the alimentation of man. Among the Greeks, Alcman in the 7th century B.C., and the historian Thucydides, and among the Romans Pliny, mention linseed as employed for human food. The roasted seed is still eaten by the Abyssinians.[5]

Theophrastus expressly alludes to the mucilaginous and oily properties of the seed. Pliny and Dioscorides were acquainted with its medical application both external and internal. The latter, as well as Columella, exhaustively describes flax under its agricultural aspect. In an edict of the Emperor Diocletian *De pretiis rerum venalium*[6] dating A.D. 301, linseed is quoted 150 *denarii;* sesamé seed 200,

[1] Wilkinson, *Ancient Egyptians*, iii. (1837) 138, &c.

[2] *Sitzungsberichte der Wiener Akademie*, Juni 1866.

[3] Exod. ix. 31; Lev. xiii. 47, 48; Isaiah xix. 9.

[4] Heer in Trimen's *Journ. of Bot.* i. (1872) 87.

[5] A. de Candolle, *Géogr. Botanique*, 835.—A. Braun, *Flora*, 1848. 94.

[6] See p. 65, note 1.

hemp seed 80, and poppy seed 150, the *modius castrensis*, equal to about 880 cubic inches.[1] The propagation of flax in Northern Europe as of so many other useful plants was promoted by Charlemagne.[2] It seems to have reached Sweden and Norway before the 12th century.[3]

Description— The capsule which is globose splits into 5 carpels, each containing two seeds separated by a partition. The seeds are of flattened, elongated ovoid form with an acute edge, and a slightly oblique point blunt at one end. They have a brown, glossy, polished surface which under a lens is seen to be marked with extremely fine pits. The hilum occupies a slight hollow in the edge just below the apex. The testa which is not very hard encloses a thin layer of albumen surrounding a pair of large cotyledons having at their pointed extremity a straight embryo. The seeds of different countries vary from $\frac{1}{4}$ to $\frac{1}{6}$ of an inch in length, those produced in warm regions being larger than those grown in cold. We find that 6 seeds of Sicilian linseed, 13 of Black Sea and 17 of Archangel linseed weigh respectively *one grain*.

When immersed in water, the seeds become surrounded by a thin, slippery, colourless, mucous envelope, which quickly dissolves as a neutral jelly, while the seed slightly swells and loses its polish. The seed when masticated has a mucilaginous oily taste.

Microscopic Structure—On examining the testa under almond oil or oil of turpentine, the outlines of the epidermal cells are not distinctly visible. But under dilute glycerin or in water the epidermis quickly swells up to 3 or 4 times its original thickness; on warming, the entire epidermis is resolved into mucilage, except a thin skeleton of cell-walls, which withstands even the action of caustic lye. The formation of the mucilage may be conveniently studied by the use of a solution of ferrous sulphate, with which thin sections of the testa should be moistened. Other structural peculiarities may be seen if they are imbued with concentrated sulphuric acid, washed and then moistened with a solution of iodine. The application of polarized light is also useful. By the latter means crystalloid granules of albuminoid matter become visible if the sections are examined under oil. The tissue of the albumen and the cotyledons abounds in drops of fatty oil.

Chemical Composition—The constituent of chief importance is the fixed oil which the seed contains to about $\frac{1}{3}$ of its weight. The proportion obtained by pressure on a large scale is 20 to 30 per cent. varying with the quality of the seed. The oil when pressed without heat and when fresh has but little colour, is without unpleasant taste, and does not solidify till cooled to $-20°$ C. The commercial oil however is dark yellow, and has a sharp repulsive taste and odour. On exposure to the air, especially after having been heated with oxide of lead, it quickly dries up to a transparent varnish consisting chiefly of *Linoxyn*, $C^{32}H^{54}O^{11}$. The crude oil increases in weight

[1] The English *imperial gallon* = 277·27 cubic inches.

[2] For further historical information on flax in ancient times, we may refer to Hehn, *Kulturpflanzen und Hausthiere* . . . Berlin, 1870. 97, 430.

[3] Schübeler, *Die Pflanzenwelt Norwegens*, Christiania, 1873—1875. p. 332.

11 to 12 per cent., although at the same time its glycerin is destroyed by oxidation.

By saponification, linseed oil yields glycerin, and 95 per cent. of fatty acids, consisting chiefly of *Linoleic Acid*, $C^{16}H^{28}O^2$, accompanied by some oleic, palmitic, and myristic acid. The action of the air transforms linoleic acid into the resinoid *Oxylinoleic Acid*, $C^{16}H^{28}O^5$. Linoleic acid appears to be contained in all drying oils, notably in that of poppy seed. It is not homologous either with ordinary fatty acids or with the oleic acid of oil of almonds, $C^{18}H^{34}O^2$. The chemistry of the drying oils, especially those of linseed and poppy, has been particularly investigated by Mulder.[1]

The viscid mucilage of linseed cannot be filtered till it has been boiled. It contains in the dry state more than 10 per cent. of mineral substances, when freed from which and dried at 110° C. it corresponds, like althæa-mucilage, to the formula $C^{12}H^{20}O^{10}$. The seeds by exhaustion with cold or warm water afford of it about 15 per cent. By boiling nitric acid it yields crystals of mucic acid; by dilute mineral acids it is broken up into dextrogyre gum and sugar and cellulose.[2]

Linseed contains about 4 per cent. of nitrogen corresponding to about 25 per cent. of protein-substances. After expression of the oil these substances remain in the cake so completely that the latter contains 5 per cent. of nitrogen, and constitutes a very important article for feeding cattle.

In the ripe state linseed is altogether destitute of starch, though this substance is found in the immature seed in the very cells which subsequently yield the mucilage. The latter may be regarded as in analogous cases to be a product of the transformation of starch.

The amount of water retained by the air-dry seed is about 9 per cent.

The mineral constituents of linseed, chiefly phosphates of potassium, magnesium, and calcium, amount on an average to 3 per cent., and pass into the mucilage. By treating thin slices of the testa and its adhering inner membrane with ferrous sulphate, it is seen that this integument is the seat of a small amount of tannin.

Production and Commerce—Flax is cultivated on the largest scale in Russia, from which country there was imported into the United Kingdom in 1872 linseed to the value of 3 millions sterling. The shipments were made in about equal proportion from the northern and the southern ports of Russia.

The imports from India in the same year amounted in value to £1,144,942, and from Germany and Holland to £144,108. The total import in 1872 was 1,514,947 quarters, value £4,513,842.

The cultivation of flax in Great Britain appears to be declining. The area under this crop in 1870 was 23,957 acres; in 1871, 17,366 acres; in 1872, 15,357 acres; and in 1873, 14,683 acres. The last-named area reckoning the yield at 2 to 2½ quarters of seed per acre would represent a production of about 30,000 to 38,000 quarters.

[1] His numerous investigations on this subject have been published in a separate pamphlet, of which we have before us a German translation: G. J. Mulder, *Die Chemie der austrocknenden Oele* . . Berlin, 1867, pp. 255.

[2] Kirchner and Tollens, *Annalen der Chemie*, 175 (1874) 215.

In English price-currents, eight sorts of linseed are enumerated, namely, English, Calcutta, Bombay, Egyptian, Black Sea and Azof, Petersburg, Riga, Archangel. The first three appear to fetch the highest prices.

Uses—In medicine, linseed is chiefly used in the form of poultice which may be made either of the seed simply ground or of the pulverized cake. In either case the powder should not be long stored, as the oil in the comminuted seed is rapidly oxidized and fatty acids produced. An infusion of the seeds called *Linseed Tea* is a common popular demulcent remedy.

Adulteration—Linseed is very liable to adulteration with other seeds, especially when the commodity is scarce. The admixture in question is due in part to careless harvesting and in part to intentional additions. In 1864 the impure condition of the linseed shipped to the English market had become so detrimental to the trade that the importers and crushers founded an association called *The Linseed Association of London*, by which they bound themselves to refuse all linseed containing more than 4 per cent. of foreign seeds, and this step very rapidly improved the quality of the article.[1]

As the druggist has to *purchase* linseed meal, he must of necessity rely to some extent on the character of the oil-presser from whom he derives his supplies. The presence of the seeds of *Cruciferæ* (as rape and mustard) which is common, may be recognized by the pungent odour of the essential oil which they develope in contact with water. The introduction of cereals would also be easily discovered by iodine, which strikes no blue colour in a decoction of linseed. The microscope will also afford important aid in the examination of linseed cake or meal.

ZYGOPHYLLEÆ.

LIGNUM GUAIACI.

Lignum sanctum; Guaiacum Wood, Lignum Vitæ; F. *Bois de Gaïac;* G. *Guaiakholz, Pockholz.*

Botanical Origin—This wood is furnished by two West Indian species of *Guaiacum*, namely:—

1. *G. officinale* L., a middle-sized or low evergreen tree, with light blue flowers, paripinate leaves having ovate, very obtuse leaflets in 2, less often in 3 pairs, and 2-celled fruits. It grows in Cuba, Jamaica (abundantly on the arid plains of the south side of the island), Les Gonaives in the N.W. of Hayti (plentiful), St. Domingo, Martinique, St. Lucia, St. Vincent, Trinidad, and the northern coast of the South American continent. This tree affords the Lignum Vitæ of Jamaica (of which very little is imported), a portion of that shipped from the ports of Hayti, and probably the small quantity exported by the United States of Colombia.

2. *G. sanctum* L., a tree much resembling the preceding, but distinguishable by its leaves having 3 to 4 pairs of leaflets which are very

[1] Greenish in *Yearbook of Pharmacy*, 1871. 590; *Pharm. Journ.* Sept. 9, 1871. 211.

obliquely obovate or oblong, passing into rhomboid-ovate, and mucronulate; and a 5-celled fruit. It is found in Southern Florida, the Bahama Islands, Key West, Cuba, St. Domingo (including the part called Hayti) and Puerto Rico, and is certainly the source of the small but excellent Lignum Vitæ exported from the Bahamas as well as of some of that shipped from Hayti.

History—There can be no doubt but that the earliest importations of Lignum Vitæ were obtained from St. Domingo, of which island, Oviedo[1] who landed in America in 1514 mentions the tree, under the name of *Guayacan*, as a native. He points out its fruits as yellow and resembling two joined lupines, which could only be said with reference to *G. officinale*, and would not apply to the ovoid five-cornered fruits of *G. sanctum*. Oviedo appears however to have been aware of two species, one of which he found in Española (St. Domingo) as well as in Nagrando (Nicaragua) and the other in the island of St. John (Puerto Rico), whence it was called *Lignum sanctum*.

The first edition of Oviedo was printed in 1526; but some years before this the wood must have been known in Germany, as is evident by the treatises written in 1517, 1518, and 1519 by Nicolaus Poll,[2] Leonard Schmaus[3] and Ulrich von Hutten.[4] The last which gives a tolerable description of the tree, its wood, bark, and medicinal properties, was translated into English in 1533 by Thomas Paynel, canon of Merton Abbey, and published in London in 1536 under the title—"*Of the wood called Guaiacum that healeth the Frenche Pockes and also helpeth the gout in the feete, the stoone, the palsey, lepree, dropsy, fallynge euyll, and other dyseases.*" It was several times reprinted.

In the old pharmacy the products of destructive distillation of guaiacum wood were known as *Oleum ligni sancti*. It must have consisted of the substances which we mention further on in the following article.

Description—The wood (always known in commerce as *Lignum Vitæ*) as imported consists of pieces of the stem and thick branches, usually stripped of bark, and often weighing a hundredweight each. It is remarkably heavy and compact. Its sp. gr. which exceeds that of most woods is about 1·3.

Lignum Vitæ is mostly imported for turnery,[5] and the chips, raspings and shavings are the only form in which it is commonly seen in pharmacy. A stem 7 to 8 inches in diameter cut transversely exhibits a light-yellowish zone of sapwood about an inch wide, enclosing a sharply defined heartwood of a dark greenish brown. Both display alternate lighter and darker layers, which especially in the sapwood are further distinguished by groups of vessels. In this manner are formed a large

[1] *Natural Hystoria de las Indias*, Toledo, 1526. fol. xxxvii.

[2] *De cura Morbi Gallici per Lignum Guayacanum libellus*, printed in 1535 but dated 19 Dec. 1517, 8 pages 8°.

[3] *De Morbo Gallico tractatus*, Salisburgi, November 1518,—reprinted in the *Aphrodisiacus* of Luisinus, Lugd. Bat. 1728. 383.—We have only seen the latter.

[4] *Ulrichi de Hutten equitis de Guaiaci medicina et morbo gallico liber unus*, 4°. (26 chapters) Moguntiæ, 1519.

[5] It is much used for the wheels (technically "*sheaves*") of ships' blocks (pulleys), the circumference of which ought to consist of the white sapwood. It is also required for caulking mallets, skittle balls and for the large balls used in American bowling alleys, for which purposes it should be as sound and homogeneous as possible.

number of circles resembling annual rings, the general form of which is evident, though the individual rings are by no means well defined. More than 20 such rings may be counted in the sapwood of a log such as we have mentioned, and more than 30 in the heartwood. The pithless centre is usually out of the axis. The medullary rays are not visible to the naked eye, but may be seen by a lens to be very numerous and equidistant. The pores of the heartwood may be distinguished as containing a brownish resin, while those of the outermost layer of sapwood are empty.

In the thickest pieces sapwood is wanting, and even in stems of about a foot in diameter it is reduced to $\frac{1}{8}$ of an inch. It is of looser texture than the heartwood and floats on water, whereas the latter sinks. Both sapwood and heartwood owe their tenacity to an extremely peculiar zigzag arrangement[1] of the woody bundles. The sapwood is tastless. The heartwood has a faintly aromatic and slightly irritating taste, and when heated or rubbed emits a weak agreeable odour.

The bark which was formerly officinal but is now almost obsolete, is very rich in oxalate of calcium and affords upon incineration not less than 23 per cent. of ash. It contains a resin distinct from that of the wood, and also a bitter acrid principle.[2]

The Lignum Vitæ of Jamaica (*G. officinale*) and that of the Bahamas (*G. sanctum*), of which authentic specimens have been kindly placed at our disposal by Mr. G. Shadbolt, display the same appearance as well as microscopic structure.[3]

Microscopic Structure—The wood cousists for the most part of pointed, not very long, ligneous cells (libriform), traversed by one-celled rows of medullary rays. There are also thin layers of parenchymatous tissue, to which the zones apparent in a transverse section of the drug are due. The pitted vessels are comparatively large but not very numerous. The structure of the sapwood is the same as that of the heartwood, but in the latter the ligneous cells are filled with resin. The parenchymatous cells contain crystals of oxalate of calcium.

Chemical Composition—The only constituent of any interest is the resin which the heartwood contains to the extent of about a fourth of its weight. The sapwood afforded us 0·91 and the heartwood 0·60 per cent. of ash.

Commerce—Lignum Vitæ varies much in estimation, according to size, soundness, and the cylindrical form of the logs. The best is exported from the city of Santo Domingo, whither it is brought from the interior of the island. The quantity shipped from this port during 1871 was 1494 tons;[4] 220 tons were exported in 1877 from Puerto Plata on

[1] It has been remarkably well pointed out already by Valerius Cordus (*obiit* 1544). See Gesner's edition of his *Hist. Stirpium Argentorat.*, 1561. 191.

[2] See also Oberlin et Schlagdenhauffen, *Journ. de Pharm.* 28 (1878) 246 and plate vi.

[3] That of *Guaiacum arboreum* DC. is apparently very different. This tree, occurring in New Granada, has already been noticed (1571—1577) by Francisco Hernandez (*Nova plantarum, animal. et mineral. mexicanor. hist.*, Romae 1651, fol. 63) under the name of *Guayacan*. He mentions its large umbels with yellow flowers, those of Guaiacum officinale, the "*Hoaxacan*" or Lignum sanctum, being blue. In the *Prodromus Floræ Neo-Granatentis* (*Ann. Scienc. nat.* xv., 1872. p. 361) J. E. Planchon also describes Guaiacum arboreum, known there as *Guayacan polvillo*; its wood is of an almost pulverulent fracture.

[4] *Consular Reports* presented to Parliament, Aug. 1872.

the northern coast of the island. The wood obtained from the Haytian ports (of the western part of the same island) is much less esteemed in the London market.

Some small wood of good quality comes from the Bahamas, and an ordinary quality, also small, from Jamaica. From the latter island, the quantity exported in 1871 was only 14 tons;[1] from the Bahamas in the same year 199 tons.[2] Lignum Vitæ was shipped from Santa Marta in 1872 to the extent of 115 tons.[3]

Hamburg is also an important place for the wood under notice; in 1877 there were imported 22,404 centners from S. Domingo and 3551 centners from Venezuela.

Uses—Guaiacum wood is only retained in the pharmacopœia as an ingredient of the Compound Decoction of Sarsaparilla. It is probably inert, at least in the manner in which it is now administered.[4]

Adulteration—In purchasing guaiacum chips it is necessary to observe that the non-resinous sapwood is absent, and still more that there is no admixture of any other wood. A spurious form of the drug seems to be by no means rare in the United States.[5]

RESINA GUAIACI.

Guaiacum Resin; F. Résine de Gaïac; G. Guaiakharz.

Botanical Origin—*Guaiacum officinale* L., see preceding article.

History—Hutten[6] in 1510 stated that guaiacum wood when set on fire exudes a blackish resin which quickly hardens, but of which he knew no use. The resin was in fact introduced into medicine much later than the wood. The first edition of the *London Pharmacopœia* in which we find the former named is that of 1677.

Production[7]—In the island of St. Domingo, whence the supplies of guaiacum resin are chiefly derived, the latter is collected from the stems of the trees, in part as a natural exudation, and in part as the result of incisions made in the bark. In some districts as in the island of Gonave near Port-au-Prince, another method of obtaining it is adopted. A log of the wood is supported in a horizontal position above the ground by two upright bars. Each end of the log is then set on fire, and a large incision having been previously made in the middle, the melted resin runs out therefrom in considerable abundance. 36,350 lbs. of it have been exported in 1875 from Port-au-Prince.

The resin is collected chiefly from *G. officinale*, which affords it in greater plenty than *G. sanctum*.

[1] Blue Book—Island of Jamaica for 1871.

[2] Blue Book for Colony of Bahamas for 1871.

[3] *Consular Reports*, Aug. 1873. 746.

[4] The ancient treatment of syphilis by guaiacum which gained for the drug such immense reputation, consisted in the administration of vast quantities of the decoction, the patient being shut up in a warm room and kept in bed.—See Hutten's pamphlet quoted before, and its numerous reprints and translations.

[5] Schulz, in the (Chicago) *Pharmacist*, Sept. 1873.

[6] *Op. cit.* at p. 101.

[7] We have to thank Mr. Eugène Nau of Port-au-Prince for the information given under this head, as well as for some interesting specimens.

Description—The resin occurs in globular tears ½ an inch to 1 inch in diameter, but much more commonly in the form of large compact masses, containing fragments of wood and bark. The resin is brittle, breaking with a clean, glassy fracture; in thin pieces it is transparent and appears of a greenish brown hue. The powder when fresh is grey, but becomes green by exposure to light and air. It has a slight balsamic odour and but little taste, yet leaves an irritating sensation in the throat.

The resin has a sp. gr. of about 1·2. It fuses at 85° C., emitting a peculiar odour somewhat like that of benzoin. It is easily soluble in acetone, ether, alcohol, amylic alcohol, chloroform, creasote, caustic alkaline solutions, and oil of cloves; but is not dissolved or only partially by other volatile oils, benzol or bisulphide of carbon. By oxidizing agents it acquires a fine blue colour, well shown when a fresh alcoholic solution is allowed to dry up in a very thin layer and this is then sprinkled with a dilute alcoholic solution of ferric chloride. Reducing agents of all kinds, and heat produce decoloration. An alcoholic solution may be thus blued and decolorized several times in succession, but it loses at length its susceptibility. This remarkable property of guaiacum was utilized by Schönbein in his well-known researches on ozone.

Chemical Composition—The composition of guaiacum resin was ascertained by Hadelich (1862) to be as follows:—

Guaiaconic Acid,	70·3	per cent.
Guaiaretic Acid,	10·5	,,
Guaiac Beta-resin,	9·8	,,
Gum,	3·7	,,
Ash constituents,	0·8	,,
Guaiacic Acid, colouring matter (Guaiac yellow), and impurities,	4·9	,,

If the mother liquor obtained in the preparation of the potassium salt of guaiaretic acid (*vide infra*) is decomposed by hydrochloric acid, and the precipitate washed with water, ether will extract from the mass *Guaiaconic Acid,* a compound discovered by Hadelich, having the formula $C^{38}H^{40}O^{10}$. It is a light brown, amorphous substance, fusing at 100° C. It is without acid reaction but decomposes alkaline carbonates, forming uncrystallizable salts easily soluble in water or alcohol. It is insoluble in water, benzol, or bisulphide of carbon, but dissolves in ether, chloroform, acetic acid or alcohol. With oxidizing agents it acquires a transient blue tint.

Guaiaretic Acid, $C^{20}H^{26}O^{4}$, discovered by Hlasiwetz in 1859, may be extracted from the crude resin by alcoholic potash or by quicklime. With the former it produces a crystalline salt; with the latter an amorphous compound: from either the liquid, which contains chiefly a salt of guaiaconic acid, may be easily decanted. Guaiaretic acid is obtained by decomposing one of the salts referred to with hydrochloric acid, and crystallizing from alcohol. The crystals, which are soluble also in ether, benzol, chloroform, carbon bisulphide or acetic acid, but neither in ammonia nor in water, melt below 80° C., and may be volatilized without decomposition. The acid is not coloured blue by oxidizing agents.

By exhausting guaiacum resin with boiling bisulphide of carbon a slightly yellowish solution is obtained (containing chiefly guaiaretic acid ?), which, on addition of concentrated sulphuric acid, turns beautifully red.

After the extraction of the guaiaconic acid there remains a substance insoluble in ether to which the name *Guaiac Beta-resin* has been applied. It dissolves in alcohol, acetic acid or alkalis, and is precipitated by ether, benzol, chloroform or carbon bisulphide in brown flocks, the composition of which appears not greatly to differ from that of guaiaconic acid.

Guaiacic Acid, $C^{12}H^{16}O^{6}$, obtained in 1841 by Thierry from guaiacum wood or from the resin, crystallizes in colourless needles. Hadelich was not able to obtain more than one part from 20,000 of guaiacum resin.

Hadelich's *Guaiac-yellow*, the colouring matter of guaiacum resin, first observed by Pelletier, crystallizes in pale yellow quadratic octohedra, having a bitter taste. Like the other constituents of the resin, it is not a glucoside.

The decomposition-products of guaiacum are of peculiar interest. On subjecting the resin to dry distillation in an iron retort and rectifying the distillate, *Guaiacene* (*Guajol* of Völckel), $C^{5}H^{8}O$, passes over at 118° C. as a colourless neutral liquid having a burning aromatic taste.

At 205°—210° C., there pass over other products, *Guaiacol*, $C^{6}H^{4}.OCH^{3}.OH$, (methylic ether of pyrocatechin), and *Kreosol* $C^{6}H^{3}.OH(CH^{3})^{2}$. Both are thickish, aromatic, colourless liquids, which become green by caustic alkalis, blue by alkaline earths, and are similar in their chemical relations to eugenic acid. Guaiacol has been prepared synthetically by Gorup-Besanez (1868) by combining iodide of methyl, $CH^{3}I$, with pyrocatechin, $C^{6}H^{4}(OH)^{2}$.

After the removal by distillation of the liquids just described, there sublime upon the further application of heat pearly crystals of *Pyroguaiacin*, $C^{38}H^{44}O^{6}$, an inodorous substance melting at 180° C. The same compound is obtained together with guaiacol by the dry distillation of guaiaretic acid. Pyroguaiacin is coloured green by ferric chloride, and blue by warm sulphuric acid. The similar reactions of the crude resin are probably due to this substance (Hlasiwetz).

Beautiful coloured reactions are likewise exhibited by two new acids which Hlasiwetz and Barth obtained (1864) in small quantity together with traces of fatty volatile acids, by melting purified resin of guaiacum with potassium hydrate. One of them is isomeric with pyrocatechuic acid.

Uses—Guaiacum resin is reputed diaphoretic and alterative. It is frequently prescribed in cases of gout and rheumatism.

Adulteration—The drug is sometimes imported in a very foul condition and largely contaminated with impurities arising from a careless method of collection.

RUTACEÆ.

CORTEX ANGOSTURÆ.

Cortex Cuspariæ; Angostura Bark, Cusparia Bark, Carony Bark; F. *Ecorce d'Angusture de Colombie;* G. *Angostura-Rinde.*

Botanical Origin—*Galipea Cusparia* St. Hilaire (*G. officinalis* Hancock, *Bonplandia trifoliata* Willd., *Cusparia trifoliata* Engler 1874, *Flora Brasil.* 113), a small tree, 12 to 15 feet high, with a trunk 3 to 5 inches in diameter, growing in abundance on the mountains of San Joaquin de Caroni in Venezuela, between 7° and 8° N. lat., also according to Bonpland[1] near Cumana. According to Hancock,[2] who was well acquainted with the tree, it is also found in the Missions of Tumeremo, Uri, Alta Gracia, and Cupapui, districts lying eastward of the Caroni and near its junction with the Orinoko. The bark is brought into commerce by way of Trinidad.

History—Angostura Bark is said to have been used in Madrid by Mutis as early as 1759[3] (the year before he left Spain for South America,) but it was certainly unknown to the rest of Europe until much later. Its real introducer was Brande, apothecary to Queen Charlotte, and father of the distinguished chemist of the same name, who drew attention to some parcels of the bark imported into England in 1788.[4] In the same year a quantity was sent to a London drug firm by Dr. Ewer of Trinidad, who describes it[5] as brought to that island from Angostura by the Spaniards. The drug continued to arrive in Europe either by way of Spain or England, and its use was gradually diffused. In South America it is known as *Quina de Caroni* and *Cascarilla del Angostura.*

Description—The bark occurs in flattish or channelled pieces, or in quills rarely as much as 6 inches in length and mostly shorter. The flatter pieces are an inch or more in width and ⅛ of an inch in thickness. The outer side of the bark is coated with a yellowish-grey corky layer, often soft enough to be removeable with the nail, and then displaying a dark brown, resinous under surface. The inner side is light brown with a rough, slightly exfoliating surface indicating close adhesion to the wood, strips of which are occasionally found attached to it; the obliquely cut edge also shows that it is not very easily detached.

[1] Humboldt, *Reise in die Aequinoctial-gegenden des neuen Continents,* iv. (Stuttgart, 1860), 252.—Humboldt and Bonpland in 1804 obtaining, from the Caroni river, flowering branches of the "*Cuspa*" (*l.c.* I. 300) or "*Cuspare,*" as it is called by the Indians, believed it to constitute a new genus. In 1824 St. Hilaire ascertained it to belong to the genus Galipea.

The tree is figured in Bentley and Trimen, *Med. Plants,* part 26 (1877).

[2] *Observations on the Orayuri or Angustura Bark Tree,—Trans. of Medico-Botanical Society,* 1827-29.—Hancock endeavoured to prove his tree distinct from *G. Cusparia* St. Hil., but Farre and Don who subsequently examined his specimens decided that the two were the same. With the assistance of Prof. Oliver, I also have examined (1871) Hancock's plant, comparing it with his figure and other specimens, and have arrived at the conclusion that it is untenable as a distinct species. —D. H.

[3] Martiny, *Encyklopädie,* i. (1843) 242.

[4] Brande, *Experiments and Observations on the Angustura Bark.* 1791. 2nd ed. 1793.

[5] *London Med. Journ.* x. (1789) 154.

The bark has a short, resinous fracture, and displays on its transverse edge sharply defined white points, due to deposits of oxalate of calcium. It has a bitter taste and a nauseous musty odour.

Microscopic Structure—The most striking peculiarity is the great number of oil-cells scattered through the tissue of the bark. They are not much larger than the neighbouring parenchymatous cells, and are loaded with yellowish essential oil or small granules of resin. Numerous other cells contain bundles of needle-shaped crystals of oxalate of calcium or small starch granules. The liber exhibits bundles of yellow fibres, to which the foliaceous fracture of the inner bark is due. The structure of the bark under notice has been very minutely described and figured by Oberlin and Schlagdenhauffen.[1]

Chemical Composition—Angostura bark owes its peculiar odour to an essential oil which it was found by Herzog[2] to yield to the extent of $\frac{3}{4}$ per cent. It is probably a mixture of a hydrocarbon ($C^{10}H^{16}$) with an oxygenated oil. Its boiling point is 266° C. Oberlin and Schlagdenhauffen obtained 0·19 per cent. of the oil, and found it to be slightly dextrogyre; it assumes a fine red colour when shaken with aqueous ferric chloride, and turns yellow with concentrated sulphuric acid.

The bitter taste of the bark is attributed to a substance pointed out in 1833 by Saladin and named *Cusparin*. It is said to be crystalline, neutral, melting at 45° C., soluble in alcohol, sparingly in water, precipitable by tannic acid. The bark is stated to yield it to the extent of 1·3 per cent. Herzog endeavoured to prepare it but without success, nor have Oberlin and Schlagdenhauffen met with it. The latter chemists, on the other hand, isolated an alkaloid *Angosturine* $C^{10}H^{40}NO^{14}$. It is in thin prisms, melting at 85° and yielding a crystallized chlorhydrate or sulphate. Angosturine turns red when touched with concentrated sulphuric acid, or green if nitric acid or iodic acid, or other oxydizing substances, have been previously mixed with the sulphuric acid. The alcoholic solution of the alkaloid is of decidedly alkaline reaction. A cold aqueous infusion of angostura bark yields an abundant red-brown precipitate with ferric chloride. Thin slices of the bark are not coloured by solution of ferrous sulphate, so that tannin appears to be absent.

Uses—Angostura bark is a valuable tonic in dyspepsia, dysentery and chronic diarrhœa, but is falling into disuse.

Adulteration—About the year 1804, a quantity of a bark which proved to be that of *Strychnos Nux Vomica* reached Europe from India, and was mistaken for Cusparia. The error occasioned great alarm and some accidents, and the use of angostura was in some countries even prohibited. The means of distinguishing the two barks (which are not likely to be again confounded) are amply contained in the above-given descriptions and tests, and at length pointed out by Oberlin and Schlagdenhauffen. They also described the bark of *Esenbeckia febrifuga* Martius (*Evodia febrifuga* Saint Hilaire), a

[1] *Journ. de Pharm. et de Chimie*, 28 (1877), 226; plates I., II., III. The bark is also figured by Berg, *Anatomischer Atlas*, Tab. 37.

[2] *Archiv d. Pharm.* xcii. (1858) 146.

Brazilian tree belonging to the same natural order. Maisch[1] was the first to draw attention to this "*new false Angostura bark.*" It is at once distinguished by being devoid of aromatic properties; its taste is purely bitter.

FOLIA BUCHU.

Folia Buceo; Buchu, Bucchu, Bucha or Buku Leaves; F. *Feuilles de Bucco;* G. *Bukublätter.*

Botanical Origin—The Buchu leaves are afforded by three species of *Barosma.*[2] The latter are erect shrubs some feet in height, with glabrous rod-like branches, opposite leaves furnished with conspicuous oil-cells on the toothed margin as well as generally on the under surface. The younger twigs and several parts of the flower are also provided with oil-cells. The white flowers with 5-partite calyx, and the fruit formed of five erect carpels, are often found, together with small leafy twigs, in the drug of commerce.

The leaves of the three species referred to may be thus distinguished:—

1. *Barosma crenulata* Hook. (*B. crenata* Kunze).—Oblong, oval, or obovate, obtuse, narrowed towards the base into a distinct petiole; margin serrulate or crenulate; dimensions, $\frac{3}{4}$ to $1\frac{1}{2}$ inches long, $\frac{3}{10}$ to $\frac{4}{10}$ of an inch wide.

2. *B. serratifolia* Willd.—Linear-lanceolate, equally narrowed towards either end, three-nerved, apex truncate always furnished with an oil-cell; margin sharply serrulate; 1—$1\frac{1}{2}$ inches long by about $\frac{2}{10}$ of an inch wide.

3. *B. betulina* Bartling.—Cuneate-obovate, apex recurved; margin sharply denticulate, teeth spreading; $\frac{1}{2}$ to $\frac{3}{4}$ of an inch long by $\frac{3}{10}$ to $\frac{5}{10}$ wide. Substance of the leaf more harsh and rigid than in the preceding.

B. crenulata and *B. betulina* grow in the Divisions of Clanwilliam and Worcester, north and north-east of Cape Town, and the former even on Table Mountain close to the capital; *B. serratifolia* is found in the Division of Swellendam farther south.

History—The use of Buchu leaves was learnt from the Hottentots by the colonists of the Cape of Good Hope. The first importations of the drug were consigned to the house of Reece & Co., of London, who introduced it to the medical profession in 1821.[3] The species appears to have been *B. crenulata.*

Description—In addition to the characters already pointed out, we may observe that buchu leaves of either of the kinds mentioned are smooth and glabrous, of a dull yellowish-green hue, somewhat paler on the under side, on which oil-cells in considerable number are perceptible.

The leaves of *B. crenulata* vary in shape and size in different parcels, in some the leaves being larger and more elongated than in others, probably according to the luxuriance of the bushes in particular localities.

[1] *Am. Journ. of Pharm.* 1874. 50; also *Yearbook of Pharm.* 1874. 91.

[2] From βαρύς, *heavy*, and ὀσμή, *odour*.

[3] R. Reece, *Monthly Gazette of Health* for Feb. 1821. 799.

Those of *B. serratifolia* and *B. betulina* present but little variation. Each kind is always imported by itself. Those of *B. betulina* are the least esteemed, and fetch a lower price than the others, yet appear to be quite as rich in essential oil.

Buchu leaves have a penetrating peculiar odour and a strongly aromatic taste.

Microscopic Structure—The essential oil is contained in large cells close beneath the epidermis of the under side of the leaf. The oil-cells are circular and surrounded by a thin layer of smaller cells; they consequently partake of the character of the oil-ducts in the aromatic roots of *Umbelliferæ* and *Compositæ*. The latter, however, are elongated.

The upper side of the leaf of *Barosma* exhibits an extremely interesting peculiarity.[1] There is a colourless layer of cells separating the epidermis from the green inner tissue (mesophyllum). If the leaves are examined under alcohol or almond-oil the colourless layer is seen to be very narrow, and the thin walls of its cells shrunken and not clearly distinguishable. If the transverse sections are examined under water, these cells immediately swell up, and become strongly distended, giving off an abundance of mucilage, the latter being afforded by the solution of the very cell-walls. The mucilage of buchu leaves thus originates in the same way as in flax seed or quince seed, but in the former the epidermis is thrown off without alteration. We are not aware that other mucilaginous leaves possess a similar structure, at least not those of *Althæa officinalis* and of *Sesamum* which we examined.[2]

Chemical Composition—The leaves of *B. betulina* afforded us by distillation 1·56 per cent. of volatile oil,[3] which has the odour rather of peppermint than of buchu, and deviates the ray of polarized light considerably to the left. On exposure to cold it furnishes a camphor which, after re-solution in spirit of wine, crystallizes in needle-shaped forms. After repeated purification in this manner, the crystals of *Barosma Camphor* have an almost pure peppermint odour; they fuse at 85° C., and begin to sublime at 110° C. After fusion they again solidify only at 50° C. Submitted to elementary analysis, the crystals yielded us 74·08 per cent. of carbon and from 9 to 10 per cent. of hydrogen.[4] Barosma camphor is abundantly soluble in bisulphide of carbon.

The crude oil from which the camphor has been separated has a boiling point of about 200° C., quickly rising to 210° or even higher. That which distilled between these temperatures was treated with sodium, rectified in a current of common coal gas and submitted to elementary analysis, afforded us 77·86 per cent. of carbon and 10·58 of hydrogen. The formula $C^{10}H^{16}O$ would require 78·94 of carbon and 10·53 of hydrogen.

Wayne's experiments[5] appear to indicate that the oil also contains

[1] Flückiger in *Schweiz. Wochenschrift für Pharm.* Dec. 1873, with plate.

[2] See also Radlkofer, *Monographie der Sapindaceen-Gattung Serjania*, München, 1875, p. 100–105.

[3] Messrs. Allen and Hanburys operating on larger quantities obtained 1·63 per cent. —*Barosma serratifolia* appears to be less rich, according to Bedford (1863).

[4] Our supply of the substance having been exhausted by two analyses we cannot regard the above figures as sufficient for the calculation of a formula.

[5] *Am. Journ. of Pharm.* 1876. 19.

a substance capable of being converted into *salicylic acid*. An aqueous infusion of buchu leaves turns beautifully yellow if it is mixed with alkali.

On addition of perchloride of iron the infusion assumes a dingy brownish-green colour changing to red by an alkali. The infusion added to a concentrated solution of acetate of copper causes a yellow precipitate[1] which dissolves in caustic potash, affording a green solution. This may be due to the presence of a substance of the quercitrin or rutin class.

When the leaves are infused in warm water, the mucilage noticed under the microscope may easily be pressed out. It requires for precipitation a large amount of alcohol, being readily miscible with dilute alcohol. Neutral acetate of lead produces a yellow precipitate in an infusion of the leaves; the liquid affords a precipitate by a subsequent addition of *basic* acetate of lead. The latter precipitate is (probably) due to the mucilage, that afforded by neutral acetate partly to mucilage and partly, we suppose, to rutin or an allied substance. Yet the mucilage of buchu leaves is of the class which is not properly dissolved by water, but only swells up like tragacanth.

The leaves of *B. crenulata* afforded us upon incineration 4·7 per cent. of ash. Jones (1879) obtained on an average 4·54 per cent. from the same species; 5·27 from *B. serratifolia;* and 4·49 from *B. betulina*. He pointed out the presence of manganate in this ash.

The *Diosmin* of Landerer[2] is entirely unknown to us.

Commerce—The export of buchu from the Cape Colony in 1872 was 379,125 ℔., about one-sixth of which quantity was shipped direct to the United States.[3]

Uses—Buchu is principally administered in disorders of the urino-genital organs. It is reputed diuretic and diaphoretic. In the Cape Colony the leaves are much employed as a popular stimulant and stomachic, infused in water, sherry, or brandy. They are also extensively used in the United States, both in regular medicine and by the vendors of secret remedies.

Substitutes—The leaves of *Empleurum serrulatum* Ait., a small shrub of the same order as *Barosma* and growing in the same localities, have been imported rather frequently of late and sold as *Buchu*. They have the same structure as regards mucilage, and nearly the same form as those of *B. serratifolia*, but are easily distinguished. They are still narrower, and often longer than those of *B. serratifolia*, devoid of lateral veins, and terminate in an *acute* point *without an oil-duct*. They have a bitterish taste and a less powerful odour than those of Barosma, even in fresh leaves as imported in London. The odour of *Empleurum* is moreover distinctly different from that of the leaves of Barosma. The flowers of *Empleurum* are still more distinct, for they are apetalous and reddish brown. The fruit consisting of a single, compressed, oblong carpel, terminated by a flat-shaped horn, is quite unlike that of buchu.

The leaves of *Barosma Eckloniana* Berg (regarded by Sonder[4] as

[1] It seems *green* as long as it is in the blue cupric liquid.

[2] Gmelin's *Chemistry*, xviii. 194.

[3] *Blue Book* published at Cape Town, 1873.

[4] Harvey and Sonder, *Flora Capensis*, i. (1859-60) 393.

a form of *B. crenulata*) have to our knowledge been imported on one occasion (1873). They are nearly an inch long, oval, *rounded at the base*, strongly crenate, and grow from *pubescent* shoots.

We have seen other leaves which had been imported from South Africa and offered as buchu; but though probably derived from allied genera they were not to be mistaken for the genuine drug.

RADIX TODDALIÆ.

Botanical Origin—*Toddalia aculeata* Pers., a ramous prickly bush,[1] often climbing over the highest trees, common in the southern parts of the Indian Peninsula as the Coromandel Coast, South Concans, and Canara, also found in Ceylon, Mauritius, the Indian Archipelago and Southern China.

History—The pungent aromatic properties which pervade the plant, but especially the fresh root-bark, are well known to the natives of India and have been utilized in their medical practice. They have also attracted the attention of Europeans, and the root of the plant is now recognized in the *Pharmacopœia of India*.

It is from this and other species of *Toddalia*, or from the allied genus *Zanthoxylum*,[2] that a drug is derived which under the name of *Lopez Root* had once some celebrity in Europe. This drug which was more precisely termed *Radix Indica Lopeziana* or *Root of Juan Lopez Pigneiro*, was first made known by the Italian physician Redi;[3] who described it in 1671 from specimens obtained by Pigneiro at the mouth of the river Zambesi in Eastern Africa,—the very locality in which in our times *Toddalia lanceolata* Lam. has been collected by Dr. Kirk.[4] It was actually introduced into European medicine by Gaubius[5] in 1771 as a remedy for diarrhœa, and acquired so much reputation that it was admitted to the Edinburgh Pharmacopœia of 1792. The root appears to have been sometimes imported from Goa, but its place of growth and botanical origin were entirely unknown, and it was always extremely rare and costly.[6] It has long been obsolete in all countries except Holland, where until recently it was to be met with in the shops. The *Pharmacopœia Neerlandica* of 1851 says of it "*Origo botanica perquam dubia—Patria Malacca ?*"

Description—The specimen of the root of *Toddalia aculeata* which we have examined was collected for us by Dr. G. Bidie of Madras whose statements regarding the stimulant and tonic action of the drug may be found in the *Pharmacopœia of India*, p. 442. It is a dense woody root in cylindrical, flexuous pieces, which have evidently been of considerable length and are from ½ to 1½ inches in diameter, covered

[1] Fig. in Bentley and Trimen, part 18.

[2] The root of a *Zanthoxylum* sent to us from Java by Mr. Binnendyk of the Buitenzorg Botanical Garden has exactly the aspect of that of *Toddalia*. The root of *Z. Bungei* which we have examined in the fresh state is also completely similar. It is covered with a soft, corky, yellow bark having a very bitter taste with a strong pungency like that of pellitory.

[3] *Esperienze intorno a diverse cose naturali*, Firenze, 1671. 121.

[4] Oliver, *Flor. of Trop. Africa*, i. (1868) 307.

[5] *Adversaria*, Leidae, p. 78.

[6] Our friend Dr. de Vry informs us that he remembers the price in Holland in 1828 being equivalent to about 24*s*. the ounce!

with bark $\frac{1}{10}$ to $\frac{1}{12}$ of an inch in thickness. The bark has a soft, dull yellowish, suberous coat, wrinkled longitudinally, beneath which is a very thin layer of a bright yellow colour, and still lower and constituting two-thirds or more of the whole, is the firm, brown middle cortical layer and liber, which is the part chiefly possessing the characteristic pungency and bitterness of the drug. The yellow corky coat is however not devoid of bitterness. The wood is hard, of a pale yellow, and without taste and smell. The pores of the wood, which are rather large, are arranged in concentric order and traversed by numerous narrow medullary rays.

In a letter which Frappier[1] wrote to Guibourt from the island of Réunion where *Toddalia aculeata* is very common, he states that the roots of the plant are of enormous length (*longueur incroyable*) and rather difficult to get out of the basaltic rock into the fissures of which they penetrate. Mr. J. Horne of the Botanical Garden, Mauritius, has sent us a specimen of the root of this plant, the bark of which is of a dusky brown, with the suberous layer but little developed.

Microscopic Structure—We have examined the root for which we are indebted to Dr. Bidie, and may state that its cortical tissue is remarkable by the number of large cells filled with resin and essential oil; they are scattered through the whole tissue, the cork excepted. The parenchymatous cells are loaded with small starch granules or with crystals of oxalate of calcium. The vessels of younger roots abound in yellow resin.

Chemical Composition—None of the constituents of the Toddalia root of India have yet been satisfactorily examined. The bark contains an essential oil, which would be better extracted from fresh than from dry material. The tissue of the bark is but little coloured by salts of iron. In the aqueous infusion, tannic acid produces an abundant precipitate, probably of an indifferent bitter principle rather than of an alkaloid. We have been unable to detect the presence in the bark of berberine.

Lopez root was examined in Wittstein's laboratory by Schnitzer[2] who found that the bark contains in addition to the usual substances a large proportion of resin,—a mixture probably of two or three different bodies. The essential oil afforded by the bark had an odour resembling cinnamon and melissa.

Uses—The drug has been introduced into the *Pharmacopœia of India* chiefly upon the recommendation of Dr. Bidie of Madras, who considers it of great value as a stimulating tonic. The bark rasped or shaved from the woody root is the only part that should be used.

[1] *Journ. de Phar.* v. (1867) 403.

[2] Wittstein's *Vierteljahresschrift für prakt. Pharm.* xi. (1862) i.—The drug examined was the Lopez root sold at that period at Amsterdam.

FOLIA PILOCARPI.

Folia Jaborandi.

Botanical Origin—*Pilocarpus pennatifolius*[1] Lemaire, a slightly branched shrub, attaining about 10 feet in height. It is distributed through the eastern provinces of Brazil.

Pilocarpus Selloanus[2] Engler, occurring in Southern Brazil and Paraguay, appears to be not considerably different from *P. pennatifolius.*

History—Piso[3] recommended an infusion made with Ipecacuanha and Jaborandi. Plumier,[4] who also mentioned this, figured under the name of Jaborandi two plants of the order Piperaceæ. The introduction of the leaves of *Pilocarpus pennatifolius* into medical use is due to Dr. Coutinho of Pernambuco, 1874. The plant has been cultivated in European greenhouses since about the year 1847; we have repeatedly seen it flowering at Strassburg. Baillon in 1875 showed the fragments of Jaborandi as supplied by Coutinho to belong to *P. pennatifolius,* which had been described in 1852 by Lemaire. Holmes (1875) in examining the drug as imported from Pernambuco came to the same conclusion.

Description—The leaves of the species under examination are long-stalked, imparipennate, the opposite leaflets in 2 to 5, in cultivated plants most commonly in 2 pairs, the terminal one longer stalked, while the others are provided with a petiole attaining 1½ inch in length or remaining much shorter. The whole leaf is frequently 1½ feet long, the leaflets being often as much as 5 inches long by 2 inches wide. The latter are entire oblong, tapering or rounded at the base, tapering or obtuse or even emarginate at the apex. The leaflets are coriaceous, with a slightly revolute margin and a prominent midrib below. In transmitted light they show very numerous pellucid oil glands.

The taste of the leaves of Pilocarpus is at first bitterish and aromatic; they subsequently produce a tingling sensation in the mouth and an abundant flow of saliva.

Microscopic Structure[5]—The oil glands consist of large cells of the same structure as those occurring generally in the leaves of Rutaceæ, Aurantiaceæ, Myrtaceæ. In Pilocarpus they are largely distributed in the tissue covered on both sides of the leaf by the epidermis; the oil cells are also abundantly met with in the petiole and in the bark of the stems and branches.

Chemical Composition—The active principle of Jaborandi is the alkaloid *Pilocarpine,* $C^{22}H^{34}N^4O^4 + 4OH^2$, discovered in 1875 by Hardy. It is an amorphous soft mass, but yielding crystallized salts, among which the hydrochlorate and the nitrate are now more frequently

[1] Fig. in Bentley and Trimen, *Med. Plants,* part 32 (1878).

[2] Fig. by Engler in *Flora Brasil.* fasc. 65 (1874) tab. 30. *Pilocarpus pauciflorus* St. Hilaire (*Flora Brasiliæ meridionalis,* i. 1824. tab. 17) appears also to be very similar.

[3] Lib. iv. cap. 57, 59, and v. cap. 19, p. 310, of the work quoted in the appendix.

[4] *Description des Plantes de l'Amérique,* 1693. 58. Pl. lxxv. and lxxvi.

[5] Stiles, *Pharm. J.* vii. (1877) 629; also Lanessan's French translation of the *Pharmacographia,* i. (1878) 253.

used than the drug itself. The leaves afford about ½ per cent. of the nitrate.

The occurrence of another peculiar alkaloid in Pilocarpus has been asserted, but not ultimately proved.

The leaves contain about ½ per cent. of essential oil, the prevailing constituent of it being a dextrogyrate terpene, $C^{10}H^{16}$, boiling at 178°, which forms a crystallized compound $C^{10}H^{16} + 2HCl$ melting at 49°·5 C.

Uses—Pilocarpine being a powerful diaphoretic and sialagogue, the leaves of Jaborandi are used to some extent in pharmaceutical preparations.

Other Kinds of Jaborandi—This name, as above stated, has originally been given to plants of the order Piperaceae, some of which are still known in Brazil under the name Jaborandi. The following may be quoted as being used at least in that country: *Serronia Jaborandi*[1] Gaudichaud, *Piper reticulatum* L. (*Enckea* Miquel), *Piper citrifolium* Lamarck (*Steffensia* Kunth), *Piper nodulosum* Link, *Artanthe mollicoma* Miq.

Aubletia trifolia[2] Richard (*Monniera* L.) and *Xanthoxylum elegans* Engler, belonging to the same order as Pilocarpus itself, are also sometimes called Jaborandi.

We are not aware that other leaves than those of Pilocarpus are imported to some extent in Europe under the name of Jaborandi.

AURANTIACEÆ.

FRUCTUS LIMONIS.

Lemon; F. Citron, Limon; G. Citrone, Limone.

Botanical Origin—*Citrus Limonum* Risso (*C. Medica* var. β Linn.), a small tree 10 to 15 feet in height, planted here and there in gardens in many sub-tropical countries, but cultivated as an object of industry on the Mediterranean coast between Nice and Genoa, in Calabria, Sicily, Spain, and Portugal.

The tree which is supposed to represent the wild state of the lemon and lime, and as it seems to us after the examination of numerous specimens in the herbarium of Kew, of the citron (*Citrus Medica* Risso) also, is a native of the forests of Northern India, where it occurs in the valleys of Kumaon and Sikkim.

The cultivated lemon-tree is of rather irregular growth, with foliage somewhat pallid, sparse, and uneven, not forming the fine, close head of deep green that is so striking in the orange-tree. The young shoots are of a dull purple; the flowers, which are produced all the year except during the winter, and are in part hermaphrodite and in part unisexual, have the corolla externally purplish, internally white, and a delicate aroma distinct from that of orange blossom. The fruit is pale yellow, ovoid, usually crowned by a nipple.

[1] Already known to Piso.

[2] The original Jaborandi of Piso, according to Peckolt. Dragendorff's *Jahresbericht*, 1875. 163.

History—The name of the lemon in Sanskrit is *Nimbuka;* in Hindustani, *Limbu, Limu,* or *Ninbu.* It is probably originally a Cashmere word, which was transferred to the Sanskrit in comparatively modern times, not in the antiquity.[1] From these sounds the Arabians formed the word *Limun,* which has passed into the languages of Europe.

The lemon was unknown to the inhabitants of ancient Greece and Rome; but it is mentioned in the Book of Nabathæan Agriculture,[2] which is supposed to date from the 3rd or 4th century of our era. The introduction of the tree to Europe is due to the Arabians, yet at what precise period is somewhat doubtful. *Arance* and *Limone* are mentioned by an Arabic poet living in the 11th century, in Sicily, quoted by Falcando.[3] The geographer Edrisi,[4] who resided at the court of Roger II., king of Sicily, in the middle of the 12th century, mentions the lemon (*limouna*) as a very sour fruit of the size of an apple which was one of the productions of Mansouria on the Mahrân or Indus; and he speaks of it in a manner that leads one to infer it was not then known in Europe. This is the more probable from the fact that there is no mention either of lemon or orange in a letter written A.D. 1239 concerning the cultivation of the lands of the Emperor Frederick II. at Palermo,[5] a locality in which these fruits are now produced in large quantity.

On the other hand the lemon is noticed at great length by Ibn Baytar of Malaga, who flourished in the first half of the 13th century, but of its cultivation in Spain at that period there is no actual mention.[6] In 1369 at least citron trees, "arbores citronorum," were planted in Genoa,[7] and there is evidence that also the lemon-tree was grown on the Riviera di Ponente about the middle of the 15th century, since *Limones* and also *Citri* are mentioned in the manuscript *Livre d'Administration* of the city of Savona, under date 1486.[8] The lemon was cultivated as early as 1494 in the Azores, whence the fruit used to be largely shipped to England; but since the year 1838 the exportation has totally ceased.[9]

Description—The fruit of *Citrus Limonum* as found in the shops[10] is from about 2 to 4 inches in length, egg-shaped with a nipple more or less prominent at the apex; its surface, of a pale yellow, is even or rugged, covered with a polished epidermis. The parenchyme within the latter abounds in large cells filled with fragrant essential oil. The roughness of the surface of the rind is due to the oil-cells. The peel, which varies considerably in thickness but is never so thick as that of the citron, is internally white and fibrous, and is adherent to the pale-yellow pulp. The latter is divided into 10 or 12 segments each contain-

[1] Dr. Rice in *New Remedies,* 1878, 263; also private information.

[2] Meyer, *Geschichte der Botanik,* iii. (1856) 68.

[3] Amari, *Storia dei Musulmani di Sicilia,* ii. (1858) 444.

[4] *Géographie d'Edrisi,* traduite par Jaubert, i. (1836) 162.

[5] Huillard-Bréholles, *Historia diplomatica Friderici secundi,* Paris, v. (1857) 571.

[6] *Heil- und Nahrungsmittel von Ebn Baithar,* übersetzt von Sontheimer, ii. (1842) 452.

[7] Belgrano, *Vita privata dei Genovesi,* Genova (1875) 158.

[8] Gallesio, *Traité du Citrus* (1811) 89, 103.

[9] Consul Smallwood, in *Consular Reports,* Aug. 1873. 986.

[10] There are many kinds of lemon as well as of orange which are never seen in commerce. Risso and Poiteau enumerate 25 varieties of the former and 30 of the latter. See also Alfonso, *Coltivazione degli Agrumi,* Palermo, 2nd edition, 1875.

ing 2 or 3 seeds. It abounds in a pale-yellow acid juice having a pleasant sour taste and a slight peculiar odour quite distinct from that of the peel. When removed from the pulp by pressure, the juice appears as a rather turbid yellowish fluid having a sp. gr. which varies from 1·040 to 1·045, and containing in each fluid ounce from 40 to 46 grains of citric acid, or about 9½ per cent.[1] In Italy all the fine and perfect fruit is exported; the windfalls and the damaged fruit are used for the production of the essential oil and the juice. About 13,000 lemons of this kind yield one pipe (108 gallons) of raw juice. Sicilian juice in November will contain about 9 ounces of citric acid per gallon, but 6 ounces when afforded by the fruit collected in April. The juice is boiled down in copper vessels, over an open fire, till its specific gravity is about 1·239.[2] Lemon juice (*Succus limonis*) for administration as a medicine should be pressed as wanted from the recent fruit whenever the latter is obtainable.

The peel (*Cortex limonis*) cut in somewhat thin ribbons from the fresh fruit is used in pharmacy, and is far preferable to that sold in a dried state.

Microscopic Structure of the Peel.—The epidermis exhibits numerous stomata; the parenchyme of the pericarp encloses large oil-cells, surrounded by small tabular cells. The inner spongy tissue is built up of very remarkable branched cells, separated by large intercellular spaces. A solution of iodine in iodide of potassium imparts to the cell-walls a transient blue coloration. The outer layers of the parenchymatous tissue contain numerous yellowish lumps of a substance which assumes a brownish hue by iodine, and yields a yellow solution if potash be added. Alkaline tartrate of copper is reduced by this substance, which probably consists of hesperidin. There also occur large crystals of oxalate of calcium, belonging to the monoclinic system. The interior tissue is irregularly traversed by small vascular bundles.

Chemical Composition—The peel of the lemon abounds in essential oil, which is a distinct article of commerce, and will be described hereafter.

Lemons, as well as other fruits of the genus *Citrus*, contain a bitter principle, *Hesperidin*, of which E. Hoffmann[3] obtained 5 to 8 per cent. from unripe bitter oranges. He extracted them with dilute alcohol, after they had previously been exhausted by cold water. The alcohol should contain about 1 per cent. of caustic potash; the liquid on cooling is acidulated with hydrochloric acid, when it yields a yellowish crystalline deposit of hesperidin, which may be obtained colourless and tasteless by recrystallization from boiling alcohol. By dilute sulphuric acid (1 per cent.) hesperidin is broken up as follows:—

$$\underset{\text{Hesperidin.}}{C^{22}H^{26}O^{12}} = \underset{\text{Hesperetin.}}{C^{16}H^{14}O^{6}} \;.\; \underset{\text{Glucose.}}{C^{6}H^{12}O^{6}}.$$

Hesperidin is very little soluble even in boiling water or in ether, but dissolves readily in hot acetic acid, also in alkaline solutions, the latter then turning soon yellow and reddish. Pure hesperidin, as presented

[1] Stoddart, in *Pharm. Journ.* x. (1869) 203.

[2] R. Warington, *Pharm. Journ.* v. (1875) 385.

[3] *Berichte der Deutschen Chemischen Gesellschaft* (1876) 26, 685, 693.

to one of us by Hoffmann, darkens when it is shaken with alcoholic perchloride of iron, and turns dingy blackish brown when gently warmed with the latter.

Hesperetin forms crystals melting at 223° C., soluble both in alcohol or ether, not in water; they taste sweet. They are split up by potash in Phloroglucin and *Hesperetic acid*, $C^{10}H^{10}O^{4}$.

On addition of ferric chloride, thin slices of the peel are darkened, owing probably to some derivative of hesperidin, or to hesperidin itself.

The name hesperidin had also been applied to *yellow* crystals extracted from the shaddock, *Citrus decumana* L., the dried flowers of which afford about 2 per cent. of that substance. It is, as shown in 1879 by E. Hoffmann, quite different from hesperidin as described above; he calls it *Naringin* and assigns to it the formula $C^{23}H^{26}O^{12}+4OH^{2}$. Naringin is readily soluble in hot water or in alcohol, not in ether or chloroform. Its solutions turn brown red on addition of ferric chloride.

Lemon juice, some of the characters of which have been already noticed, is an important article in a dietetic point of view, being largely consumed on shipboard for the prevention of scurvy. In addition to citric acid it contains 3 to 4 per cent. of gum and sugar, and 2·28 per cent. of inorganic salts, of which according to Stoddart only a minute proportion is potash. Cossa[1] on the other hand, who has recently studied the products of the lemon tree with much care, has found that the ash of dried lemon juice contains 54 per cent. of potash, besides 15 per cent. of phosphoric acid.

Stoddart has pointed out the remarkable tendency of citric acid to undergo decomposition,[2] and has proved that in lemons kept from February to July this acid generally decreases in quantity, at first slowly, but afterwards rapidly, until at the end of the period it entirely ceases to exist, having been all split up into glucose and carbonic acid. At the same time the sp. gr. of the juice was found to have undergone but slight diminution:—thus it was 1·044 in February, 1·041 in May, and 1·027 in July, and the fruit had hardly altered in appearance. Lemon juice may with some precautions be kept unimpaired for months or even years. Yet it is capable of undergoing fermentation by reason of the sugar, gum, and albuminoid matters which it contains.

Commerce—Lemons are chiefly imported from Sicily, to a smaller extent from the Riviera of Genoa and from Spain. From the published statistics of trade, in which lemons are classed together with oranges under one head, it appears that these fruits are being imported in increasing quantities. The value of the shipments to the United Kingdom in 1872 (largely exceeding those of any previous year) was £1,154,270. Of this sum, £986,796 represents the value of the oranges and lemons imported from Spain, Portugal, the Canary Islands and Azores; £155,330 the shipments of the same fruit from Italy; and £3,825 those from Malta.

Of concentrated *lemon juice* there were exported in 1877 from Messina 1,631,332 kilogrammes, valued at 2,446,996 lire. The value of

[1] *Gazetta Chimica Italiana*, ii. (1872) 385; *Journ. of Chem. Soc.* xi. (1873) 402.

[2] Stoddart's statement that if potash be added to lemon juice, *oxalic acid* may be detected in the mixture after a few days, is not supported by our observations.

concentrated *lime juice* exported in 1874 from Montserrat was £3,390. From Dominica, 11,285 gallons, value £1,825, were shipped in 1875.

Uses—Lemon peel is used in medicine solely as a flavouring ingredient. Freshly prepared lemon juice is often administered with an alkaline bicarbonate in the form of an effervescing draught, or in a free state.

Concentrated *lemon juice* is imported for the purpose of making citric acid; it is derived not only from the lemon, but also, to a smaller extent, from the lime and bergamot. *Lime juice* of the West Indies is chiefly used as a beverage; small quantities of it are also exported for the manufacture of citric acid. The culture of *Citrus Limetta* Risso, the *lime*, was introduced in Montserrat in 1852.

OLEUM LIMONIS.

Oleum Limonum; Essential Oil or Essence of Lemon; F. *Essence de Citron;* G. *Citronenöl.*

Botanical Origin—*Citrus Limonum* Risso (see p. 114).

History—The chemists of the 16th century were well acquainted with the method of extracting essential oils by distillation. Besson in his work *L'art et moyen parfaict de tirer huyles et eaux de tous medicaments simples et oleogineux*, published at Paris in 1571, mentions *lemon-* (citron) and orange-peel among the substances subjected to this process. Giovanni Battista Porta,[1] a learned Neapolitan writer, describes the method of preparing *Oleum ex corticibus Citri* to consist in removing the peel of the fruit with a rasp and distilling it so comminuted with water; and adds that the oils of lemon and orange may be obtained in the same manner. Essence of lemon of two kinds, namely *expressed* and *distilled*, was sold in Paris in the time of Pomet, 1692.

Production—Essential oil of lemon is manufactured in Sicily, at Reggio in Calabria, and at Mentone and Nice in France.

The lemons are used while still rather green and unripe, as being richer in oil than when quite mature. Only the small and irregular fruit, such as is not worth exporting, is employed for affording the essence.

The process followed in Sicily and Calabria may be thus described;[2] it is performed in the months of November and December.

The workman first cuts off the peel in *three* thick longitudinal slices, leaving the central pulp of a three-cornered shape with a little peel at either end. This central pulp he cuts transversely in the middle, throwing it on one side and the pieces of peel on the other. The latter are allowed to remain till the next day and are then treated thus:—the workman seated holds in the palm of his left hand a flattish piece of

[1] *Magiæ Naturalis libri xx.* Neapoli. 1589. 188.

[2] Through the kindness of Signor Mallandrino of Giampilieri near Messina, I had the pleasure of seeing how the essence is made. Though the time of my visit (13 May 1872) was not that of the manufacture, Signor M. sent for one of his workmen, and having procured a few lemons, set him to work on them in order that I might have ocular demonstration of the process.—D. H.

sponge, wrapping it round his fore-finger. With the other he places on the sponge one of the slices of peel, the outer surface downwards, and then presses the zest-side (which is uppermost) so as to give it for the moment a convex instead of a concave form. The vesicles are thus ruptured, and the oil which issues from them is received in the sponge with which they are in contact. Four or five squeezes are all the workman gives to each slice of peel, which done he throws it aside. Though each bit of peel has attached to it a small portion of pulp, the workman contrives to avoid pressing the latter. As the sponge gets saturated the workman wrings it forcibly, receiving its contents in a coarse earthen bowl provided with a spout; in this rude vessel, which is capable of holding at least three pints, the oil separates from the watery liquid which accompanies it and is then decanted.

The yield is stated to be very variable, 400 fruits affording 9 to 14 ounces of essence. The prisms of pulp and the exhausted pieces of peel are submitted to pressure in order to extract from them lemon juice, and are said to be also subjected to distillation. The foregoing is termed the *sponge-process;* it is also applied to the orange. It appears rude and wasteful, but when honestly performed it yields an excellent product.

Essence of lemon is prepared at Mentone and Nice by a different method. The object being to set free and to collect the oil contained in the vesicles of the peel, an apparatus is employed, which may be thus described:—a stout saucer or shallow basin of pewter, about 8½ inches in diameter with a lip on one side for convenience of pouring. Fixed in the bottom of this saucer are a number of stout, sharp, brass pins, standing up about half an inch; the centre of the bottom is deepened into a tube about an inch in diameter and five inches in length, closed at its lower end. This vessel, which is called an *écuelle à piquer*, has therefore some resemblance to a shallow, dish-shaped funnel, the tube of which is closed below.

The workman takes a lemon in the hand, and rubs it over the sharp pins, turning it round so that the oil-vessels of the entire surface may be punctured. The essential oil which is thus liberated is received in the saucer whence it flows down into the tube; and as this latter becomes filled, it is poured into another vessel that it may separate from the turbid aqueous liquid that accompanies it. It is finally filtered and is then known as *Essence de Citron au zeste*. A small additional produce is sometimes obtained by immersing the scarified lemons in warm water and separating the oil which floats off.

A second kind of essence termed *Essence de Citron distillée* is obtained by rubbing the surface of fresh lemons, or of those which have been submitted to the process just described, on a coarse grater of tinned iron, by which the portion of peel richest in essential oil is removed. This grated peel is subjected to distillation with water, and yields a colourless essence of very inferior fragrance, which is sold at a low price.

Description[1]—The oil obtained by the sponge process and that of

[1] For specimens of the *Essence au zeste* and of the *Essence distillée* of guaranteed purity we have to thank M. Médecin, distiller of essences, Mentone; and Messrs. G. Pannucio e figli, for an authentic sample of the essence made by the sponge process in

the *écuelle à piquer* are mobile liquids of a faint yellow colour, of exquisite fragrance and bitterish aromatic taste.

The different specimens which we have examined are readily miscible with bisulphide of carbon, but dissolve sparingly in spirit of wine (0·830). An equal weight of the oil and of spirit of wine forms a turbid mixture. No peculiar coloration is produced by mixture with perchloride of iron.

The oils are dextrogyre, but differ in their rotatory power, as may be illustrated by the following results, which we obtained by examining them in a column 50 millimetres long in the polaristrobometer of Wild. The oil of Signori Panuccio, due to the sponge-process (p. 118, note 2), deviated 20·9°, that of Monsieur Médecin (*Essence de Citron au zeste*) obtained by the *écuelle à piquer* deviated 33·4° and his distilled oil 28·3°.

Chemical Composition—The prevailing portion of most essential oils of the *Aurantiaceæ* agrees with the formula $C^{10}H^{16}$; the differences which they exhibit chiefly concern their optical properties, odour, and colour. The boiling point mostly varies from about 170° to 180° C., the sp. gr. between 0·83 and 0·88. These oils are a mixture of isomeric hydrocarbons, and also contain a small amount of cymene, $C^{10}H^{14}$, and of oxygenated oils, not yet well known; of these we may infer the presence either from analytical results or simply from the fact that the crude oils are altered by metallic sodium. If they are purified by repeated rectification over that metal, they are finally no longer altered by it. Oils thus purified cease to possess their original fragrance, and often resemble oil of turpentine, with which they agree in composition and general chemical behaviour.

As to essential oil of lemons, its chief constituent is the terpene, $C^{10}H^{16}$, which, like oil of turpentine, easily yields crystals of terpin, $C^{10}H^{16}3OH^2$. There is further present, according to Tilden (1879) another hydrocarbon, $C^{10}H^{16}$, which already boils at 160° C., whereas the foregoing boils at 176° C. Lastly a small amount of cymene and of a compound acetic ether, $C^2H^3O(C^{10}H^{17}O)$, would appear to occur also in oil of lemons. The crude oil of lemons already yields the crystalline compound $C^{10}H^{16} + 2HCl$, when saturated with anhydrous hydrochloric gas, whereas by the same treatment oil of turpentine affords the solid compound $C^{10}H^{16} + HCl$.

Essential oil of lemons (not the distilled) when long kept deposits a greasy mass, from which we have obtained small crystals apparently of *Bergaptene* (p. 123).

Commerce—Essence of lemons is shipped chiefly from Messina and Palermo, packed in copper bottles called in Italian *ramiere* and by English druggists "*jars*," holding 25 to 50 kilo. or more; sometimes in tin bottles of smaller size. The quantity of essences of lemon, orange and bergamot exported from Sicily in 1871 was 368,800 lb., valued at £144,520, of which about two-thirds were shipped to England.[1] In

their establishment at Reggio. We have also had a small quantity prepared by the *écuelle* by one of ourselves near Mentone, 15th June 1872.—D. H.

[1] Consul Dennis, *On the Commerce, &c. of Sicily in* 1869, 1870, 1871. (*Reports from H.M. Consuls.* No. 4. 1873.

1877 the export of these essential oils from Messina amounted to 306,948 kilogrammes, valued at 6,130,960 lire.

Uses—Essence of lemon is used in perfumery, and as a flavouring ingredient; and though much sold by druggists is scarcely employed in medicine.

Adulteration—Few drugs are more rarely to be found in a state of purity than essence of lemon. In fact it is stated that almost all that comes into the market is more or less diluted with oil of turpentine or with the cheaper *distilled* oil of lemons. Manufacturers of the essence complain that the demand for a cheap article forces them to this falsification of their product.

OLEUM BERGAMOTTÆ.

Oleum Bergamii; Essence or Essential Oil of Bergamot; F. *Essence de Bergamotte;* G. *Bergamottöl.*

Botanical Origin—*Citrus Bergamia* var. *vulgaris* Risso et Poiteau,[1] a small tree closely resembling in flowers and foliage the Bitter Orange. Its fruit is 2½ to 3 inches in diameter, nearly spherical, or slightly pear-shaped, frequently crowned by the persistent style; it is of a pale golden yellow like a lemon,[2] with the peel smooth and thin, abounding in essential oil of a peculiar fragrance; the pulp is pale yellowish green, of a bitterish taste, and far less acid than that of the lemon.

The tree is cultivated at Reggio in Calabria, and is unknown in a wild state.

History—The bergamot is one of the cultivated forms which abound in the genus *Citrus*, and which constitute the innumerable varieties of the orange, lemon and citron. Whether it is most nearly related to the lemon or to the orange is a point discussed as early as the beginning of the last century. Gallesio[3] remarks that it so evidently combines the characters of the two that it should be regarded as a hybrid between them. The bergamot first appeared in the latter part of the 17th century. It is not mentioned in the grand work on orange trees of Ferrari,[4] published at Rome in 1646, nor in the treatise of Commelyn[5] (1676), nor in the writings of Lanzoni (1690),[6] or La Quintinie (1692).[7] So far as we know, it is first noticed in a little book called *Le Parfumeur François*, printed at Lyons in 1693. The author who calls himself *Le Sieur Barbe, parfumeur*, says that the *Essence de Cedra ou Berga-motte* is obtained from the fruits of a lemon-tree which has been grafted on the stem of a bergamot

[1] *Histoire naturelle des Orangers*, Paris, 1818. p. 111. tab. 53, or the same work, new edition, by Dubreuil, 1873, p. 82. We accept the name given by these authors for the sake of convenience and definiteness, and not because we concur in their opinion that the Bergamot deserves to be ranked as a distinct botanical species.

[2] Fig. in Bentley and Trimen, *Med. Plants*, part 31.

[3] *Traité du Citrus*, 1811. 118.

[4] *Hesperides, seu de malorum, aureorum cultura et usu.*

[5] *Nederlantze Hesperides*, Amsterd. 1676. fol. (an English translation in 1683).

[6] *Citrologia*, Ferrariæ, 1690.

[7] *Instruction pour les Jardins fruitiers... avec un traité des Orangers*, ed. 2, 1692.

pear; he adds that it is got by squeezing small bits of the peel with the fingers in a bottle or globe large enough to allow the hand to enter.

Volkamer of Nuremberg, who produced a fine work on the Citron tribe in 1708, has a chapter on the *Limon Bergamotta*, which he describes as *gloria limonum et fructus inter omnes nobilissimus*. He states that the Italians prepare from it the finest essences, which are sold at a high price.[1]

But, as shown by one of us,[2] the essential oil of bergamot had already, in 1688, a place among the stores of an apothecary of the German town of Giessen.

The name Bergamotta was originally applied to a large kind of pear, called in Turkish "beg-ârmûdî," *i.e.* prince's pear.[3]

Production—The bergamot is cultivated at Reggio, on low ground near the sea, and in the adjacent villages. The trees are often intermixed with lemon and orange trees, and the soil is well irrigated and cropped with vegetables.

The essential oil (*Oleum Bergamottæ*) is obtained from the full-grown but still unripe and more or less green fruits, gathered in the months of November and December. They are richer in oil than any one of the allied fruits. It was formerly made like that of lemon by the sponge-process, but during the last 20 years this method has been generally superseded by the introduction of a special machine for the extraction of the essential oil. In this machine the fruits are placed in a strong, saucer-like, metallic dish, about 10 inches in diameter, having in the centre a raised opening which with the outer edge forms a broad groove or channel; the dish is fitted with a cover of similar form. The inner surface both of the dish and cover is rendered rough by a series of narrow, radiating metal ridges of blades which are about ¼ of an inch high and resemble the backs of knifes. The dish is also furnished with some small openings to allow of the outflow of essential oil; and both dish and cover are arranged in a metallic cylinder, placed over a vessel to receive the oil. By a simple arrangement of cog-wheels moved by a handle, the cover, which is very heavy, is made to revolve rapidly over the dish, and the fruit lying in the groove between the two is carried round, and at the same time is subjected to the action of the sharp ridges, which, rupturing the oil-vessels, cause the essence to escape, and set it free to flow out by the small openings in the bottom of the dish. The fruits are placed in the machine, 6, 8, or more at a time, according to their size, and subjected to the rotatory action above described for about half a minute, when the machine is stopped, they are removed, and fresh ones substituted. About 7,000 fruits can thus be worked in one of these machines in a day. The yield of oil is said to be similar to that of lemon, namely 2½ to 3 ounces from 100 fruits.

Essence of bergamot made by the machine is of a greener tint than that obtained by the old sponge-process. During some weeks after

[1] *Hesperides Norimbergenses*, 1713. lib. 3. cap. 26. and p. 156 b. (We quote from the Latin edition.)

[2] Flückiger, *Documente zur Geschichte der Pharmacie*, Halle, 1876. 72.

[3] Information, for which I am indebted to Dr. Rice.—The name has no reference to the town of Bergamo, where bergamota cannot succeed.—F.A.F.

extraction it gradually deposits a quantity of white greasy matter (bergaptene), which, after having been exhausted as much as possible by pressure, is finally subjected to distillation with water in order to separate the essential oil it still contains.

The fruits from which the essence has been extracted are submitted to pressure, and the juice, which is much inferior in acidity to lemon juice, is concentrated and sold for the manufacture of citric acid. Finally, the residue from which both essence and juice have been removed, is consumed as food by oxen.

Description[1]—Essential oil of bergamot is a thin and mobile fluid of peculiar and very fragnant odour, bitterish taste, and slightly acid reaction. It has a pale greenish yellow tint, due to traces of chlorophyll, as may be shown by the spectroscope. Its sp. gr. is 0·86 to 0·88; its boiling point varies from 183° to 195° C.

The oil is miscible with spirit of wine (0·83 sp. gr.), absolute alcohol, as well as with crystallizable acetic acid. Four parts dissolve clearly one part of bisulphide of carbon, but the solution becomes turbid if a larger proportion of the latter is added. Bisulphide of carbon itself is incapable of dissolving clearly any appreciable quantity of the oil. A mixture of 10 drops of the oil, 50 drops of bisulphide of carbon and one of strong sulphuric acid has an intense yellow hue. Perchloride of iron imparts to bergamot oil dissolved in alcohol a dingy brown colour.

Panuccio's oil of bergamot examined in the same way as that of lemon (p. 120) deviates 7° to the right, and has therefore a dextrogyre power very inferior to that of other oils of the same class.[2] But it probably varies in this respect, for commercial specimens which we judged to be of good quality deviated from 6·8° to 10·4° to the right.

Chemical Composition—If essential oil of bergamot is submitted to rectification, the portions that successively distill over do not accord in rotatory power or in boiling point, a fact which proves it to be a mixture of several oils, as is further confirmed by analysis. It appears to consist of hydrocarbons, $C^{10}H^{16}$, and their hydrates, neither of which have as yet been satisfactorily isolated. Oil of bergamot, like that of turpentine, yields crystals of the composition $C^{10}H^{16} + 3H^2O$, if 8 parts are allowed to stand some weeks with 1 part of spirit of wine, 2 of nitric acid (sp. gr. 1·2) and 10 of water, the mixture being frequently shaken. No solid compound is produced by saturating the oil with anhydrous hydrochloric gas.

The greasy matter that is deposited from oil of bergamot soon after its extraction, and in small quantity is often noticeable in that of commerce, is called *Bergaptene* or *Bergamot Camphor*. We have obtained it in fine, white, acicular crystals, neutral and inodorous, by repeated solution in spirit of wine. Its composition according to the analysis of Mulder (1837) and of Ohme (1839) answers to the formula $C^6H^6O^3$, which in our opinion requires further investigation. Crystallized bergaptene is abundantly soluble in chloroform, ether, or

[1] The characters are taken from some Essence of Bergamot presented to one of us (15 May 1872) as a type-sample by Messrs. G. Panuccio e figli, manufacturers of essences at Reggio and also large cultivators of the bergamot orange.

[2] See however *Oleum Neroli*, p. 127.

bisulphide of carbon; the alcoholic solution is not altered by ferric salts.

Commerce—Essence of bergamot, as it is always termed in trade, is chiefly shipped from Messina and Palermo in the same kind of bottles as are used for essence of lemon.

Uses—Much employed in perfumery, but in medicine only occasionally for the sake of imparting an agreeable odour to ointments.

Adulteration—Essence of bergamot, like that of lemon, is extensively and systematically adulterated, and very little is sent into the market entirely pure. It is often mixed with oil of turpentine, but a finer adulteration is to dilute it with essential oil of the leaves or with that obtained by distillation of the peel or of the residual fruits. Some has of late been adulterated with petroleum.

The optical properties, as already mentioned, may afford some assistance in detecting fraudulent admixtures, though as regards oil of turpentine it must be borne in mind that there are *levogyre* as well as *dextrogyre* varieties. This latter oil and likewise that of lemon is less soluble in spirit of wine than that of bergamot.

CORTEX AURANTII.

Bitter Orange Peel; F. Ecorce ou Zestes d'Oranges amères; G. Pomeranzenschale.

Botanical Origin—*Citrus vulgaris* Risso (*C. Aurantium* var. *α amara* Linn., *C. Bigaradia* Duhamel).

The Bitter or Seville or Bigarade Orange, *Bigaradier*[1] of the French, is a small tree extensively cultivated in the warmer parts of the Mediterranean region, especially in Spain, and existing under many varieties.

Northern India is the native country of the orange tree. In Gurhwal, Sikkim, and Khasia there occurs a wild orange which is the supposed parent of the cultivated orange, whether Sweet or Bitter.

The Bitter Orange reproduces itself from seed, and is regarded, at least by cultivators, as quite distinct from the Sweet Orange, from which however it cannot be distinguished by any important botanical characters. Generally speaking, it differs from the latter in having the fruit rugged on the surface, of a more deep or reddish-orange hue, with the pulp very sour and bitter. The peel, as well as the flowers and leaves, are more aromatic than the corresponding parts of the Sweet Orange, and the petiole is more broadly winged.

History—The orange was unknown to the ancient Greeks and Romans; and its introduction to Europe is due to the Arabs, who, according to Gallesio,[2] appear to have established the tree first in Eastern Africa, Arabia, and Syria, whence it was gradually conveyed to Italy, Sicily, and Spain. In the opinion of the writer just quoted, the bitter orange was certainly known at the commencement of the 10th century

[1] From the Basque "bizarra" = beard (Rice, *New Remedies*, 1878. 231), or from the Sanskrit Bijouri (?).

[2] *Traité du Citrus*, Paris, 1811. 222.

to the Arabian physicians, one of whom, Avicenna,[1] employed its juice in medicine.

There is strong evidence to show that the orange first cultivated in Europe was the *Bitter Orange* or *Bigarade*. The orange tree at Rome, said to have been planted by St. Dominic about A.D. 1200, and which still exists at the monastery of St. Sabina, bears a *bitter* fruit; and the ancient trees standing in the garden of the Alcazar at Seville are also of this variety. Finally, the oranges of Syria (*ab indigenis* Orenges *nuncupati*) described by Jacques de Vitri, Bishop of Acon (*ob.* A.D. 1214) were *acidi seu pontici saporis*.[2]

The Sweet Orange began to be cultivated about the middle of the 15th century, having been introduced from the East by the Portuguese. It has probably long existed in Southern China, and may have been taken thence to India. In the latter country there are but few districts in which its cultivation is successful, and the Bitter Orange is hardly known at all. The name it has long borne of *China*[3] or *Portugal Orange* indicates what has been the usual opinion as to its origin. It probably alludes more exactly to a superior variety brought about 1630 from China to Portugal.[4]

One of the first importations of oranges into England occurred in A.D. 1290, in which year a Spanish ship came to Portsmouth, of the cargo of which the queen of Edward I. bought one frail of Seville figs, one of rasins or grapes, one bale of dates, 230 pomegranates, 15 citrons, and 7 *oranges* ("*poma de orenge*").[5]

Description—The Bitter Orange known in London as the *Seville Orange* is a globular fruit, resembling in size, form, and structure the common Sweet Orange, but having the peel much rougher, and when mature of a somewhat deeper hue. The pulp of the fruit is filled with an acid bitter juice. The ripe fruit is imported into London; the peel is removed from it with a sharp knife in one long spiral strip, and quickly dried, or it is sold in the fresh state. It is the more esteemed when cut thin, so as to include as little as possible of the white inner layer.

Well-dried orange peel should be externally of a bright tint and white on its inner surface; it should have a grateful aromatic smell and bitter taste. The peel is also largely imported into London ready dried, especially from Malta. We have observed it from this latter place of three qualities, namely in elliptic pieces or quarters, in broad curled strips, and lastly a very superior kind, almost wholly free from white zest, in strips less than $\frac{1}{8}$ of an inch in width, cut apparently by a machine. Such needless subdivision as this last has undergone must greatly favour an alteration and waste of the essential oil. Foreign-dried orange peel fetches a lower price than that dried in England.

Microscopic Structure—There is no difference between the tissues of this drug and those of lemon peel.

[1] *Opera*, ed. Valgrisi 1564. lib. v. sum. 1. tract. 9. p. 289.—The passage, which is the following, seems rather inconclusive :—". . succi acetositatis citri et succi acetositatis citranguli."

[2] Vitriaco, *Hist. orient. et occident.* 1597. cap. 86.

[3] Hence the Dutch *Sinaasappel* or *Appelsina* and the German *Apfelsine*.

[4] Goeze, *Beitrag zur Kenntniss der Orangengewächse*, Hamburg, 1874. 29.

[5] *Manners and Household Expenses of England in the 13th and 15th centuries*, Lond. (Roxburghe Club) 1841. xlviij.

Chemical Composition—The essential oil to which the peel of the orange owes its fragrant odour, is a distinct article of commerce, and will be noticed hereafter under a separate head. The other constituents of the peel probably agree with those of lemon peel. The substance mentioned under the name of *Hesperidin* (p. 116) particularly abounds in unripe bitter oranges.

Uses—Bitter orange peel is much used in medicine as an aromatic tonic.

OLEUM NEROLI,

Oleum Aurantii florum ; Oil or Essence of Neroli ; F. *Essence de Néroli ;* G. *Neroliöl.*

Botanical Origin—*Citrus vulgaris* Risso. (See page 124.)

History—Porta, the Italian philosopher of the 16th century referred to (p. 118), was acquainted with the volatile oil of the flowers of the citron tribe ("*Oleum ex citriorum floribus*"), which he obtained by the usual process of distillation, and describes as possessing the most exquisite fragrance. That distilled from orange flowers acquired a century later (1675-1685) the name of *Essence of Neroli* from Anne-Marie de la Trémoille-Noirmoutier, second wife of Flavio Orsini, duke of Bracciano and prince of Nerola or Neroli. This lady employed it for the perfuming of gloves, hence called in Italy *Guanti di Neroli.*[1] It was known in Paris to Pomet, who says[2] the perfumers have given it the name of *Neroli*, and that it is made in Rome and in Provence.

Production—Oil of Neroli is prepared from the fresh flowers of the Bigarade or Bitter Orange by the ordinary process of distillation with water, conducted in small copper stills. The flowers of all the allied plants are far less aromatic. The water which distills over with the oil constitutes, after the removal of the latter from its surface, the *Orange Flower Water* (*Aqua aurantii florum vel Aqua Naphæ*)[3] of commerce. The manufacture is carried on chiefly in the south of France at Grasse, Cannes, and Nice. The yield is about 0·6 to 0·7 per cent. of oil from fresh flowers, as stated by Poiteau et Risso.[4] The flowers of the sweet orange afford but half that amount of oil.

Description and Chemical Composition—Oil of Neroli as found in commerce is seldom pure, for it generally contains an admixture of the essential oil of orange-leaf called *Essence of Petit Grain.*

By the kind assistance of Mr. F. G. Warrick of Nice, we have obtained a sample of Bigarade Neroli of guaranteed purity, to which the following observations relate. It is of a brownish hue, most fragrant odour, bitterish aromatic taste, and is neutral to test-paper. Its sp. gr. at 11° C. is 0·889. When mixed with alcohol, it displays a bright violet fluorescence, quite distinct from the blue fluorescence of a

[1] Menagio, *Origini della Lingua Italiana*, 1685 ; *Dict. de Trévoux*, Paris, vi. (1771) 178.—The town of Nerola is about 16 miles north of Tivoli.

[2] *Histoire des Drogues*, 1694. 234. ii.

[3] Naphé or Naphore — according to Poiteau et Risso, *Hist. Nat. des Orangers* 1873. 211, these names perhaps originated in Languedoc.

[4] *L.c.* 211.

solution of quinine. In oil of Neroli the phenomenon may be shown most distinctly by pouring a little spirit of wine on to the surface of the essential oil, and causing the liquid to gently undulate. The oil is but turbidly miscible with bisulphide of carbon. It assumes a very pure, intense, and permanent crimson hue if shaken with a saturated solution of bisulphide of sodium. Examined in a column of 100 mm. we observed the oil to deviate the ray of polarized light 6° to the right.

Subjected to distillation, the larger part of the oil passes over at 185°–195° C.; we found this portion to be colourless, yet to display in a marked manner the violet fluorescence and also to retain the odour of the original oil. The portion remaining in the retort was mixed with about the same volume of alcohol (90 per cent.) and some drops of water added, yet not sufficient to occasion turbidity. A very small amount of the crystalline *Neroli Camphor* then made its appearance, floating on the surface of the liquid; by re-solution in boiling alcohol it was obtained in crystals of rather indistinct form. The re-distilled oil gave no camphor whatever.

Neroli Camphor was first noticed by Boullay in 1828. According to our observations it is a neutral, inodorous, tasteless substance, fusible at 55° C., and forming on cooling a crystalline mass. The crystallization should be effected by cooling the hot alcoholic solution, no good crystals being obtainable by slow evaporation or by sublimation. The produce was extremely small, about 60 grammes of oil having yielded not more than 0·1 gramme. Perhaps this scantiness of produce was due to the oil being a year and a half old, for according to Plisson[1] the camphor diminishes the longer the oil is kept.[2] We were unable to obtain any similar substance from the oils of bergamot, petit grain, or orange peel.

Orange Flower Water is a considerable article of manufacture among the distillers of essential oils in the south of Europe, and is imported thence for use in pharmacy. According to Boullay[3] it is frequently acid to litmus when first made,—is better if distilled in small than in large quantities, and if made from the petals *per se*, rather than from the entire flowers. He also states that only 2 lb. of water should be drawn from 1 lb. of flowers, or 3 lb. if petals alone are placed in the still. As met with in commerce, orange flower water is colourless or of a faintly greenish yellow tinge, almost perfectly transparent, with a delicious odour and a bitter taste. Acidulated with nitric acid, it acquires a pinkish hue more or less intense, which disappears on saturation by an alkali.

Uses—Oil of Neroli is consumed almost exclusively in perfumery. Orange flower water is frequently used in medicine to give a pleasant odour to mixtures and lotions.

Adulteration—The large variation in value of oil of Neroli as shown by price-currents[4] indicates a great diversity of quality. Besides being very commonly mixed, as already stated, with the distilled oil of

[1] *Journ. de Pharm.* xv. (1829) 152.

[2] Yet we extracted it from an old sample labelled "*Essence de Néroli Portugal—Méro.*"

[3] *Bulletin de Pharm*, i. (1809) 337-341.

[4] Thus in the price-list of a firm at Grasse, Neroli is quoted as of *four* qualities, the lowest or "commercial" being less than half the price of the finest.

the leaves (*Essence de Petit Grain*),[1] it is sometimes reduced by addition of the less fragrant oil obtained from the flowers of the Portugal or Sweet Orange. In some of these adulterations we must conclude that orange flower water participate: metallic contamination of the latter is not unknown.

Other Products of the genus Citrus.

Essence or Essential Oil of Petit Grain—was originally obtained by subjecting little immature oranges to distillation (Pomet—1692); but it is now produced, and to a large extent, by distillation of the leaves and shoots either of the Bigarade or Bitter Orange, or of the Portugal or Sweet Orange. The essence of the former is by far the more fragrant, and commands double the price. Poiteau and Risso[2] state that the leaves of the Brigaradier with bitter fruit are by far the richest in essential oil among all the allied leaves; they are obtained in the lemon-growing districts of the Mediterranean where the essence is manufactured. Lemon-trees being mostly grafted on orange-stocks, the latter during the summer put forth shoots, which are allowed to grow till they are often some feet in length. The cultivator then cuts them off, binds them in bundles, and conveys them to the distiller of *Petit Grain*. The strongest shoots are frequently reserved for walking-sticks. The leaves of the two sorts of orange are easily distinguished by their smell when crushed. Essence of Petit Grain, which in odour has a certain resemblance to Neroli, is used in perfumery and especially in the manufacture of Eau de Cologne.

According to Gladstone (1864) it consists mainly of a hydrocarbon probably identical with that from oil of Neroli.

Essential Oil of Orange Peel—is largely made at Messina and also in the south of France. It is extracted by the sponge-, or by the *écuelle*-process, and partly from the Bigarade and partly from the Sweet or Portugal Orange, the scarcely ripe fruit being in either case employed. The oil made from the former is much more valuable than that obtained from the latter, and the two are distinguished in price-currents as *Essence de Bigarade* and *Essence de Portugal*.

These essences are but little consumed in England, in liqueur-making and in perfumery. For what is known of their chemical nature, the reader can consult the works named at foot.[3]

Essence of Cedrat—The true Citron or Cedrat tree is *Citrus medica* Risso, and is of interest as being the only member of the Orange tribe the fruit of which was known in ancient Rome. The tree itself, which appears to have been cultivated in Palestine in the time of Josephus, was introduced into Italy in about the 3rd century.

[1] We have been informed on good authority that the Neroli commonly sold contains $\frac{3}{8}$ of Essence of Petit Grain, and $\frac{1}{8}$ of Essence of Bergamot, the remaining $\frac{1}{2}$ being true Neroli.

[2] *Loc. c.*, edition of 1873. 211.

[3] Gmelin, *Chemistry*, xiv. (1860) 305. 306: Gladstone, *Journ. of Chem. Soc.* xvii. (1864) 1: Wright (and Piesse) in *Year-book of Pharmacy*, 1871. 546; 1873. 518; *Journ. of Chem. Soc.* xi. (1873) 552, &c. We may moreover point out the existence of a crystallized constituent of the oil of orange peel from the island of Curaçao. It was noticed as long ago as the year 1771 by Gaubius: "Sal aromaticus, nativus, ex oleo corticum mali aurei Curassavici," in his book, "Adersariorum varii argumenti, lib. unus." Leidae, 1771. 27.

In A.D. 1003 it was much grown at Salerno near Naples, whence its fruits were sent as presents to the Norman princes.[1]

At the present day, the citron appears to be nowhere cultivated extensively, the more prolific lemon tree having generally taken its place. It is however scattered along the Western Riviera, and is also grown on a small scale about Pizzo and Paola on the western coast of Calabria, in Sicily, Corsica, and Azores. Its fruits, which often weigh several pounds, are chiefly sold for being candied. For this purpose the peel, which is excessively thick, is salted and in that state shipped to England and Holland. The fruit has a very scanty pulp.[2]

Essence of Cedrat which is quoted in some price-lists may be prepared from the scarcely ripe fruit by the sponge-process; but as it is more profitable to export the fruit salted, it is very rarely manufactured, and that which bears its name is for the most part fictitious.

FRUCTUS BELÆ.

Bela; Bael Fruit, Indian Bael, Bengal Quince.

Botanical Origin—*Ægle Marmelos*[3] Correa (*Cratæva Marmelos* L.), a tree found in most parts of the Indian peninsula, which is often planted in the neighbourhood of temples, being esteemed sacred by the Hindus. It is truly wild in the forests of the Coromandel Ghâts and of the Western Himalaya, ascending often to 4,000 feet and growing gregarious when wild.

It attains a height of 30–40 feet, is usually armed with strong sharp thorns and has trifid leaves, the central leaflet being petiolate and larger than the lateral. The fruit is a large berry, 2 to 4 inches in diameter, variable in shape, being spherical or somewhat flattened like an orange, ovoid, or pyriform,[4] having a smooth hard shell; the interior divided into 10–15 cells each containing several woolly seeds, consists of a mucilaginous pulp, which becomes very hard in drying. In the fresh state the fruit is very aromatic, and the juicy pulp which it contains has an agreeable flavour, so that when mixed with water and sweetened, it forms a palatable refrigerant drink. The fruit is never eaten as dessert, though its pulp is sometimes made into a preserve with sugar.

The fruit of the wild tree is described as small, hard, and flavourless, remaining long on the tree. The bark of the stem and root, the flowers and the expressed juice of the leaves are used in medicine by the natives of India.

History—The tree under the name of *Bilva*[5] is constantly alluded to as an emblem of increase and fertility in ancient Sanskrit poems,

[1] Gallesio, *Traité du Citrus*, 1811. 222.

[2] Oribasius accurately describes the citron as a fruit consisting of three parts, namely a central acid pulp, a thick and fleshy zest and an aromatic outer coat.—*Medicinalia collecta*, lib. i. c. 64.

[3] *Ægle*, one of the Hesperides.—*Marmelos* from the Portuguese *marmelo*, a quince.—Fig. in Bentley and Trimen, part 11.

[4] In the Botanical Garden of Buitenzorg in Java, three varieties are grown, namely—*fructibus oblongis, fructibus subglobosis*, and *macrocarpa*.

[5] We are indebted to Professor Monier Williams of Oxford for pointing out to us many references to *Bilva* in the Sanskrit writings.

some of which as the Yajar Veda are supposed to have been written not later than 1000 B.C.—Constantinus Africanus was acquainted with the fruit under notice.

Garcia de Orta, who resided in India as physician to the Portuguese viceroy at Goa in the 16th century, wrote an account of the fruit under the name of *Marmelos de Benguala* (Bengal Quince) *Cirifole* or *Beli*,[1] describing its use in dysentery.

In the following century it was noticed by Bontius, in whose writings edited by Piso[2] there is a bad figure of the tree as *Malum Cydonium*. It was also figured by Rheede,[3] and subsequently under the designation of *Bilack* or *Bilack tellor* by Rumphius.[4] The latter states that it is indigenous to Gujarat, the eastern parts of Java, Sumbawa and Celebes, and that it has been introduced into Amboina.

But although *Ægle Marmelos* has thus been long known and appreciated in India, the use of its fruit as a medicine attracted no attention in Europe till about the year 1850. The dried fruit which has a place in the *British Pharmacopœia* is now not unfrequently imported.

Description—We have already described the form and structure of the fruit, which for medicinal use should be dried when in a half ripe state. It is found in commerce in dried slices having on the outer side a smooth greyish shell enclosing a hard, orange or red, gummy pulp in which are some of the 10 to 15 cells existing in the entire fruit. Each cell includes 6 to 10 compressed oblong seeds nearly 3 lines in length, covered with whitish woolly hairs. When broken the pulp is seen to be nearly colourless internally, the outside alone having assumed an orange tint. The dried pulp has a mucilaginous, slightly acid taste, without aroma, astringency, or sweetness.

There is also imported Bael fruit which has been collected when ripe, as shown by the well-formed seeds. Such fruits arrive broken irregularly and dried, or sawn into transverse slices and then dried, or lastly entire, in which case they retain some of their original fragrance resembling that of elemi.

Microscopic Structure—The rind of the fruit is covered with a strong cuticle, and further shows two layers, the one exhibiting not very numerous oil-cells, and the other an inner made up of sclerenchyme. The tissue of the pulp, which, treated with water, swells into an elastic mass, consists of large cells with considerable cavities between them. The seeds when moistened yield an abundance of mucilage nearly in the same way as White Mustard or Linseed. In the epidermis of the seeds certain groups of cells are excessively lengthened, and thus constitute the curious woolly hairs already noticed. They likewise afford mucilage in the same way as the seed itself.

Chemical Composition—We are unable to confirm the remarkable analyses of the drug alluded to in the *Pharmacopœia of India*;[5] nor can we explain by any chemical examination upon what constituent the alleged medicinal efficacy of bael depends.

The pulp moistened with cold water yields a red liquid containing

[1] *Siri-phal* and *Bel* are Hindustani names.—See also Flückiger, *Documente*, 29.

[2] *De Indiæ re nat. et med.* 1658, lib. vi. c. 8.

[3] *Hort. Malab.* iii. (1682) tab. 37 (*Covalam*).

[4] *Herb. Amb.* i. tab. 81.

[5] Edition 1868, pp. 46 and 441.

chiefly mucilage, and (probably) pectin which separates if the liquid is concentrated by evaporation. The mucilage may be precipitated by neutral acetate of lead or by alcohol, but is not coloured by iodine. It may be separated by a filter into a portion truly soluble (as proved by the addition of alcohol or acetate of lead), and another, comprehending the larger bulk, which is only swollen like tragacanth, but is far more glutinous and completely transparent.

Neither a per- nor a proto-salt of iron shows the infusion to contain any appreciable quantity of tannin,[1] nor is the drug in any sense possessed of astringent properties.

Uses—Bael is held in high repute in India as a remedy for dysentery and diarrhœa; at the same time it is said to act as a laxative where constipation exists.

Adulteration—The fruit of *Feronia Elephantum* Correa, which has a considerable external resemblance to that of *Ægle Marmelos* and is called by Europeans *Wood Apple*, is sometimes supplied in India for bael. It may be easily distinguished: it is *one-celled* with a large five-lobed cavity (instead of 10 to 15 cells) filled with numerous seeds. The tree has pinnate leaves with 2 or 3 pairs of leaflets. We have seen *Pomegranate Peel* offered as *Indian Bael*.[2]

SIMARUBEÆ.

LIGNUM QUASSIÆ.

Quassia, Quassia Wood, Bitter Wood; F. *Bois de Quassia de la Jamaïque, Bois amer; Jamaica Quassiaholz.*

Botanical Origin—*Picræna excelsa* Lindl. (*Quassia excelsa* Swartz, *Simaruba excelsa* DC., *Picrasma excelsa* Planchon), a tree 50 to 60 feet in height, somewhat resembling an ash and having inconspicuous greenish flowers and black shining drupes the size of a pea. It is common on the plains and lower mountains of Jamaica, and is also found in the islands of Antigua and St. Vincent. It is called in the West Indies *Bitter Wood* or *Bitter Ash*.

History—Quassia wood was introduced into Europe about the middle of the last century. It was derived from *Quassia amara* L., a shrub or small tree with handsome crimson flowers, belonging to the same order, native of Panama, Venezuela, Guiana, and Northern Brazil. It was subsequently found that the *Bitter Wood* of Jamaica which Swartz and other botanists referred to the same genus, possessed similar properties, and as it was obtainable of much larger size, it has since the end of the last century been generally preferred. The wood of *Q. amara*, called *Surinam Quassia*, is however still used in France and Germany.[3]

[1] We are thus at variance with Collas of Pondichéry, who attributes to the ripe fruit 5 *per cent. of tannin.*—*Hist. nat. etc. du Bel ou Vilva* in *Revue Coloniale*, xvi. (1856) 220-238.

[2] 40 bags in a drug sale, 8th May, 1873.

[3] The *Pharmacopœa Germanica* of 1872 expressly forbids the use of the wood of *Picræna* in place of *Quassia*.

The first to give a good account of Jamaica quassia was John Lindsay,[1] a medical practitioner of the island, who writing in 1791 described the tree as long known not only for its excellent timber, but also as a useful medicine in putrid fevers and fluxes. He adds that the *bark* is exported to England in considerable quantity—"for the purposes of the brewers of ale and porter."

Quassia, defined as the wood, bark, and root of *Q. amara* L., was introduced into the London Pharmacopœia of 1788; in the edition of 1809, it was superseded by the wood of *Picræna excelsa*. In the stock-book of a London druggist (J. Gurney Bevan, of Plough Court, Lombard Street) we find it first noticed in 1781 (as *rasuræ*), when it was reckoned as having cost 4*s*. 2*d*. per lb.

Description—The quassia wood of commerce consists of pieces of the stem and larger branches, some feet in length, and often as thick as a man's thigh. It is covered with bark externally of a dusky grey or blackish hue, white and fibrous within, which it is customary to strip off and reject. The wood, which is of a very light yellowish tint, is tough and strong, but splits easily. In transverse section it exhibits numerous fine close medullary rays, which intersect the rather obscure and irregular rings resembling those of annual growth of our indigenous woody stems. The centre is occupied by a cylinder of pith of minute size. In a longitudinal section, whether tangential or radial, the wood appears transversely striated by reason of the small vertical height of the medullary rays.

The wood often exhibits certain blackish markings due to the mycelium of a fungus; they have sometimes the aspect of delicate patterns, and at others appear as large dark patches.

Quassia has a strong, pure bitter taste, but is devoid of odour. It is always supplied to the retail druggist in the form of turnings or raspings, the former being obtained in the manufacture of the *Bitter Cups*, now often seen in the shops.

Microscopic Structure—The wood consists for the most part of elongated pointed cells (libriform), traversed by medullary rays, each of the latter being built up of about 15 vertical layers of cells. The single layers contain from one to three rows of cells. The ligneous rays thus enclosed by medullary parenchyme, are intersected by groups of tissue constituting the above-mentioned irregular rings. On a longitudinal section this parenchyme exhibits numerous crystals of oxalate of calcium, and sometimes deposits of yellow resin. The latter is more abundant in the large vessels of the wood. Oxalate and resin are the only solid matters perceptible in the tissues of this drug.

Chemical Composition—The bitter taste of quassia is due to *Quassiin*, which was first obtained, no doubt, from the wood of *Quassia amara*, by Winckler in 1835. It was analysed by Wiggers,[2] who assigned it the formula $C^{10}H^{12}O^{3}$, now regarded as doubtful. According to the latter, quassiin is an irresolvable, neutral substance, crystallizable from dilute alcohol or from chloroform. It requires for solution about 200 parts of water, but is not soluble in ether; it forms an insoluble compound with tannic acid. Quassia wood is said to yield about $\frac{1}{10}$

[1] *Trans. Roy. Soc. Edinburgh*, iii. (1794) 205. tab. 6.

[2] Liebig's *Annalen der Pharm.* xxi. (1837) 40.

per cent. of quassiin. A watery infusion of quassia, especially if a little caustic lime has been added to the drug, displays a slight fluorescence, due apparently to quassiin. Goldschmiedt and Weidel (1877) failed in obtaining quassiin. They isolated the yellow resin which we mentioned above, and stated that it yields protocatechuic acid when melted with potash. Quassia wood dried at 100° C. yielded us 7·8 per cent. of ash.

Commerce—The quantity of Bitter Wood shipped from Jamaica in 1871 was 56 tons.[1]

Uses—The drug is employed as a stomachic and tonic. It is poisonous to flies, and is not without narcotic properties in respect to the higher animals.

Substitutes—The wood of *Quassia amara* L., the *Bitter Wood of Surinam*, bears a close resemblance, both external and structural, to the drug just noticed; but its stems never exceed four inches in diameter and are commonly still thinner. Their thin, brittle bark is of a greyish yellow, and separates easily from the wood. The latter is somewhat denser than the quassia of Jamaica, from which it may be distinguished by its medullary rays being composed of a single or less frequently of a double row of cells, whereas in the wood of *Picræna excelsa*, they consist of two or three rows, less frequently of only one.

Surinam Quassia Wood is exported from the Dutch colony of Surinam. The quantity shipped thence during the nine months ending 30th Sept., 1872, was 264,675 lb.[2]

The bark of *Samadera indica* Gärtn., a tree of the same natural order, owes its bitterness to a principle[3] which agrees perhaps with quassiin. The aqueous infusion of the bark is abundantly precipitated by tannic acid, a compound of quassiin probably being formed. A similar treatment applied to quassia would possibly easier afford quassiin than the extraction of the wood by means of alcohol, as performed by Wiggers.

BURSERACEÆ.

OLIBANUM.

Gummi-resina Olibanum, Thus masculum[4]; *Olibanum, Frankincense*; F. *Encens*; G. *Weihrauch.*

Botanical Origin—Olibanum is obtained from the stem of several species of *Boswellia*, inhabiting the hot and arid regions of Eastern

[1] *Blue Book*, Island of Jamaica, for 1871.

[2] *Consular Reports*, No. 3, presented to Parliament, July 1873.

[3] Rost van Tonningen, *Jahresbericht* of Wiggers (Canstatt) for 1858. 75; *Pharm. Journ.* ii. (1872) 644. 654.

[4] The λίβανος of the Greeks, the Latin *Olibanum*, as well as the Arabic *Lubân*, and the analogous sounds in other languages, are all derived from the Hebrew *Lebonah*, signifying *milk*: and modern travellers who have seen the frankincense trees state that the fresh juice is *milky*, and hardens when exposed to the air. The word *Thus*, on the other hand, seems to be derived from the verb θύω, *to sacrifice*.

Africa, near Cape Gardafui and of the southern coast of Arabia. Notwithstanding the recent elaborate and valuable researches of Birdwood,[1] the olibanum trees are still but imperfectly known, as will be evident in the following enumeration :—

1. *Boswellia Carterii* Birdw.—This includes the three following forms, which may be varieties of a single species, or may belong to two or more species,—a point impossible to settle until more perfect materials shall have been obtained.

a. *Boswellia* No. 5, Oliver, *Flora of Tropical Africa*, I. (1868) 324, *Mohr meddu* or *Mohr madow* of the natives ; *meddu*, according to Playfair and Hildebrandt, means black. The leaflets are crenate, undulate, and pubescent on both sides.

This tree is found in the Somali Country, growing a little inland in the valleys and on the lower part of the hills, never on the range close to the sea. It yields the olibanum called *Lubân Bedowi* or *Lubân Sheheri* (Playfair).

Hildebrandt describes the Mohr meddu as a tree 12 to 15 feet high, with a few branches, indigenous to the limestone range of Ahl or Serrut, in the northern part of the Somali Country, where it occurs in elevations of from 3000 to 5000 feet. To this tree belongs the figure 58 in Bentley and Trimen's *Medicinal Plants* (Part 20, 1877).

b. *Boswellia* No. 6, Oliver, *op. cit.*, Birdwood, *Linn. Trans.* xxvii., tab. 29.—Sent by Playfair among the specimens of the preceding, and with the same indications and native name. This form, the "Mohr meddu" of the Somalis, has obscurely serrulate or almost entire leaflets, velvety and paler below, glabrous above. The figure (which is not given in the reprint) is very much the same as that of the following.

c. *Maghrayt d'sheehaz* of the Maharas, Birdwood, *l. c.* tab. 30, reprinted in Cooke's report, plate I ; Carter, *Journ. of Bombay Branch of R. Asiat. Soc.* ii., tab. 23 ; *B. sacra* Flückiger, *Lehrbuch der Pharmakognosie des Pflanzenreiches*, 1867. 31.—Ras Fartak, S.E. coast of Arabia, growing in the detritus of limestone cliffs and close to the shore,[2] also near the village of Merbat (Carter, 1844–1846).

Birdwood's figure refers to a specimen propagated in the Victoria Gardens, Bombay, from cuttings sent there from the Somali country by Playfair.

2. *B. Bhau-Dajiana* Birdw. *l. c.* tab. 31, or plate III. of the reprint. —Somali Country (Playfair) ; cultivated in Victoria Gardens, Bombay, where it flowered in 1868. The differences between this species and B. Carterii are not very obvious.

[1] *On the Genus* Boswellia, *with descriptions and figures of three new species.—Linn. Trans.* xxvii. (1870) 111. 148. This paper is reprinted as an appendix to Cooke's "Report on the gums, resins, ... of the Indian Museum," Lond. 1874.—The original plates are much superior and more complete than the reprints.—The materials on which Dr. Birdwood's observations have been chiefly founded, and to which we also have had access, are,—1. Specimens collected during an expedition to the Somali Coast made by Col. Playfair in 1862.—2. Growing Plants at Bombay and Aden, raised from cuttings sent by Playfair.—3. A specimen obtained by H. J. Carter in 1846, near Ras Fartak, on the south-east coast of Arabia, and still growing in Victoria Gardens, Bombay ; and figured by Carter in *Journ. of Bombay Branch of R. Asiatic Soc.* ii. (1848) 380, tab. 23.

[2] In the λιβανωτοφόρος χώρα of the antiquity, the hill region (where Mohr meddu is growing) used to be contrasted with the coast region, the Sabil. See Sprenger (quoted further on, page 136, foot-note 3), page 90.

3. *Boswellia* No. 4, Oliver, *op. cit.*—Bunder Murayah, Somali Country (Playfair). Grows out of the rock, but sometimes in the detritus of limestone; never found on the hills close to the sea, but further inland and on the highest ground. Yields *Lubân Bedowi* and *L. Sheheri;* was received at Kew as *Mohr add*, a name applied by Birdwood also to *B. Bhau-Dajiana.*

From the informations due to Captains Miles[1] and Hunter and to Haggenmacher[2] it would appear that the *Beyo* or *Beyu* of the Somalis (Boido, Capt. Hunter) is agreeing with this tree.

4. *Boswellia neglecta*, S. Le M. Moore, in *Journ. of Botany*, xv. (1877) 67 and tab. 185. This tree has been collected by Hildebrandt in the limestone range, Ahl or Serrut, in the northern part of the Somali Country. It occurs in elevations of 1000 to 1800 metres, and attains a height of 5 to 6 metres. Its exudation, according to Hildebrandt, is collected in but small quantity and mixed with the other kinds of olibanum. Moore gives *Murlo* as the vernacular name of this tree, Hildebrandt calls it *Mohr add.*

In addition to the foregoing, from which the olibanum of commerce is collected, it may be convenient to mention also the following:—

1. *Boswellia Frereana* Birdw., a well-marked and very distinct species of the Somali Country, which the natives call *Yegaar*. It abounds in a highly fragrant resin collected and sold as *Lubân Meyeti* or *Lubân Mati*, which we regard to be the substance originally known as *Elemi* (see this article).

2. *B. papyrifera* Richard (*Plösslea floribunda* Endl.), the "Makar" of Sennaar and the mountainous region ascending to 4000 feet above the level of the sea on the Abyssinian rivers Takazze and Mareb. It appears not to grow in the outer parts of north-eastern Africa. Its resin is not collected, and stated by Richard[3] to be transparent; it consists no doubt merely of resin (and essential oil ?) without gum.[4]

3. *B. thurifera* Colebr. (*B. glabra* et *B. serrata* Roxb.), the *Salai* tree of India, produces a soft odoriferous resin which is used in the country as incense but is not the olibanum of commerce. The tree is particularly abundant on the trap hills of the Dekhan and Satpura range. Berg, in "Offizinelle Gewächse," xiv. c. gives a good figure of this species.

History—The use of olibanum goes back to a period of extreme antiquity, as proved by the numerous references[5] in the writings of the Bible to *incense*, of which it was an essential ingredient. It is moreover well known that many centuries before Christ, the drug was one of the most important objects of the traffic which the Phœnicians[6] and Egyptians carried on with Arabia.

Professor Dümichen[7] of Strassburg has discovered at the temple of

[1] See his picturesque description of the tree, *Journ. R. Geograph. Soc.* 22 (1872) 64.

[2] Flückiger, *Pharm. Journ.* viii. (1878) 805.

[3] *Tent. Floræ Abyssinicae*, i. (1847) 248; figure of the tree tab. xxxiii.

[4] See the paper quoted in note 2.

[5] As for instance, Exod. xxx. 34; 1 Chron. x. 29; Matth. ii. 11.

[6] Movers, *Das phönizische Alterthum*, iii. (1856) 99. 299.—Sprenger, *l.c.* p. 299, also points out the importance of the olibanum with regard to the commercial relations of those early periods.

[7] Dümichen (Joannes), *The fleet of an*

Dayr el Báhri in Upper Egypt, paintings illustrating the traffic carried on between Egypt and a distant country called Punt or Pount as early as the 17th century B.C. In these paintings there are representations not only of bags of olibanum, but also of olibanum trees planted in tubs or boxes, being conveyed by ship from Arabia to Egypt. Inscriptions on the same building, deciphered by Professor D., describe with the utmost admiration the shipments of precious woods, heaps of incense, verdant incense trees,[1] ivory, gold, stimmi (sulphide of antimony), silver, apes, besides other productions not yet identified. The country Pount was first thought to be southern Arabia, but is now considered to comprehend the Somali coast, together with a portion of the opposite Arabian coast. Punt possibly refers to "Opone," an old name for Hafoon, a place south of Cape Gardafui.

A detailed account of frankincense is given by Theophrastus[2] (B.C. 370–285) who relates that the commodity is produced in the country of the Sabæans, one of the most active trading nations of antiquity, occupying the southern shores of Arabia. It appears from Diodorus that the Sabæans sold their frankincense to the Arabs, through whose hands it passed to the Phœnicians who disseminated the use of it in the temples throughout their possessions, as well as among the nations with whom they traded. The route of the caravans from south-eastern Arabia to Gaza in Palestine, has recently (1866) been pointed out by Professor Sprenger. Plutarch relates that when Alexander the Great captured Gaza, 500 talents of olibanum and 100 talents of myrrh were taken, and sent thence to Macedonia.

The *libanotophorous region* of the old Sabæans is in fact the very country visited by Carter in 1844 and 1846, and lying as he states on the south coast of Arabia between long. 52° 47′ and 52° 23′ east.[3] It was also known to the ancients, at least to Strabo and Arrian, that the opposite African coast likewise produced olibanum,[4] as it is now doing almost exclusively; and the latter states that the drug is shipped partly to Egypt and partly to Barbaricon at the mouth of the Indus.

As exemplifying the great esteem in which frankincense was held by the ancients, the memorable gifts presented by the Magi to the infant Saviour will occur to every mind. A few other instances may be mentioned: Herodotus[5] relates that the Arabians paid to Darius, king of Persia, an annual tribute of 1000 talents of frankincense.

A remarkable Greek inscription, brought to light in modern times[6] on the ruins of the temple of Apollo at Miletus, records the gifts made to the shrine by Seleucus II., king of Syria (B.C. 246–227), and his brother Antiochus Hierax, king of Cilicia, which included in addition

Egyptian Queen from the 17th century before our era, and ancient Egyptian military parade, represented on a monument of the same age . . . . after a copy taken from the terrace of the temple of Dêr-el-Baheri, translated from the German by Anna Dümichen, Leipzig, 1868.—See also Mariette-Bey, *Deir-el-Bahari*, Leipzig, 1877, Pl. 6, 7, 8.

[1] In one of the inscriptions they are referred to in terms which Professor D. has thus rendered :—"Thirty-one verdant incense-trees brought among the precious things from the land of Punt for the majesty of this god Amon, the lord of the terrestrial thrones. Never has anything similar been seen since the foundation of the world."

[2] *Hist. Plant.* lib. iv. c. 7.—See also Sprenger, *l.c.* 219.

[3] See also Sprenger, *Die alte Geographie Arabiens.* Bern, 1875. 296, 302, also 244.

[4] "Thus transfretanum," Sprenger, 299.

[5] Rawlinson's *Herodotus*, ii. (1858) 488. —Sprenger, *l.c.* 300, alludes to olibanum being exported to Babylonia and Persia.

[6] Chishull, *Antiquitates Asiaticæ*, Lond. 1758. 65–72.

two vessels of gold and silver, ten talents of frankincense (λιβανωτὸς) and one of myrrh.

The emperor Constantine made numerous offerings to the church under St. Silvester, bishop of Rome A.D. 314–335, of costly vessels and fragrant drugs and spices,[1] among which mention is made in several instances of *Aromata* and *Aromata in incensum*, terms under which olibanum is to be understood.[2]

With regard to the consumption of olibanum in other countries, it is an interesting fact that the Arabs in their intercourse with the Chinese, which is known to have existed as early as the 10th century, carried with them *olibanum*, myrrh, dragon's blood, and liquid storax,[3] drugs which are still imported from the west into China. The first-named is called *Ju-siang*, i.e. *milk perfume*, a curious allusion to its Arabic name *Lubân* signifying *milk*. In the year 1872, Shanghai imported[4] of this drug no less than 1,360 peculs (181,333 lb.).

Collection—The fragrant gum resin is distributed through the leaves and bark of the trees, and even exudes as a milky juice also from the flowers; its fragrance is stated to be already appreciable in a certain distance. Cruttenden,[5] who visited the Somali Country in 1843, thus describes the collecting of olibanum by the Mijjertheyn tribe, whose chief port is Bunder Murayah (lat. 11° 43′ N.)[6]:—

"During the hot season the men and boys are daily employed in collecting gums, which process is carried on as follows:—About the end of February or beginning of March, the Bedouins visit all the trees in succession and make a deep incision in each, peeling off a narrow strip of bark for about 5 inches below the wound. This is left for a month when a fresh incision is made in the same place, but deeper. A third month elapses and the operation is again repeated, after which the gum is supposed to have attained a proper degree of consistency. The mountain-sides are immediately covered with parties of men and boys, who scrape off the large clear globules into a basket, whilst the inferior quality that has run down the tree is packed separately. The gum when first taken from the tree is very soft, but hardens quickly. . . . . Every fortnight the mountains are visited in this manner, the trees producing larger quantities as the season advances, until the middle of September, when the first shower of rain puts a close to the gathering that year."

The informations due to J. M. Hildebrandt, who visited the Somali in 1875, are in accordance with Cruttenden's statements. The former says, that the latest crops are greatly injured by the rains, the drug being partly dissolved by the water.

Carter[7] describing the collection of the drug in southern Arabia,

[1] These remarkable gifts are enumerated by Vignoli in his *Liber Pontificalis*, Rome, 1724-55, and include beside Olibanum, *Oleum nardinum*, *Oleum Cyprium*, *Balsam*, *Storax Isaurica*, *Stacte*, *Aromata cassiæ*, *Saffron* and *Pepper*.

[2] The ancient name of Cape Gardafui was *Promontorium Aromatum*.

[3] Bretschneider, *Ancient Chinese*, &c. Lond. 1871. 19.

[4] *Returns of Trade at the Treaty Ports in China for* 1872, p. 4.

[5] *Trans. Bombay Geograph. Soc.* vii. (1846) 121.

[6] See sketch of the Somali coast. *Pharm. Journ.* viii. (13 Apr. 1878) 806.

[7] See my paper on Luban Mati and Olibanum, *Pharm. Journ.* viii. (1878) 805, also Hildebrandt's note in the "Sitzungs-Bericht der Gesellschaft naturforschender Freunde zu Berlin," 19th Nov. 1878, 195.—F.A.F.

writes thus:—"The gum is procured by making longitudinal incisions through the bark in the months of May and December, when the cuticle glistens with intumescence from the distended state of the parts beneath; the operation is simple, and requires no skill on the part of the operator. On its first appearance the gum comes forth white as milk, and according to its degree of fluidity, finds its way to the ground, or concretes on the branch near the place from which it first issued, from whence it is collected by men and boys employed to look after the trees by the different families who possess the land in which they grow." According to Captain Miles,[1] the drug is not collected by the people of the country, but by Somalis who cross in numbers from the opposite coast, paying the Arab tribes for the privilege. The Arabian *Lubân*, he says, is considered inferior to the African.

It would even appear that the collection of the drug has ceased in Arabia, and that the names of Luban Maheri or Mascati or Sheehaz, referring to the coast of Arabia between Ras Fartak (52° 10′ E.) and Ras Morbas (54° 34′) are now applied to the olibanum brought there from the opposite African coast.[2] Hildebrandt informed one of us (letter dated 26th Dec., 1878) that he has ascertained at Aden, that all the frankincense imported in Aden comes from Africa.

Description—Olibanum as found in commerce varies rather considerably in quality and appearance. It may in general terms be described as a dry gum-resin, consisting of detached tears up to an inch in length, of globular, pear-shaped, clavate, or stalactitic form, mixed with more or less irregular lumps of the same size. Some of the longer tears are slightly agglutinated, but most are distinct. The predominant forms are rounded,—angular fragments being less frequent, though the tears are not seldom fissured. Small pieces of the translucent brown papery bark are often found adhering to the flat pieces. The "Luban Fasous Bedow" as exported from the Mijjertheyn district, in the eastern part of the Somali Country, is in very fine large tears.

The colour of the drug is pale yellowish or brownish, but the finer qualities consist of tears which are nearly colourless or have a greenish hue. The smallest grains only are transparent, the rest are translucent and somewhat milky, and not transparent even after the removal of the white dust with which they are always covered. But if heated to about 94° C., they become almost transparent. When broken they exhibit a rather dull and waxy surface. Examined under the polarizing microscope no trace of crystallization is observable.

Olibanum softens in the mouth; its taste is terebinthinous and slightly bitter, but by no means disagreeable. Its odour is pleasantly aromatic, but is only fully developed when the gum-resin is exposed to an elevated temperature. At 100° C. the latter softens without actually fusing, and if the heat be further raised decomposition begins.

Chemical Composition—Cold water quickly changes olibanum into a soft whitish pulp, which when rubbed down in a mortar forms an emulsion. Immersed in spirit of wine, a tear of olibanum is not

[1] *Loc. cit.*

[2] *On the neighbourhood of Bunder-Murayah*, in *Journ. of R. Geograph Society*, xxii. (1872) 65.

altered much in form, but it becomes of an almost pure opaque white. In the first case the water dissolves the gum, while in the second the alcohol removes the resin. We find that pure olibanum treated with spirit of wine leaves 27 to 35 of gum,[1] which forms a thick mucilage with three parts of water. Dissolved in 5 parts of water it yields a neutral solution, which is precipitated by perchloride of iron as well as by silicate of sodium, but not by neutral acetate of lead. It is consequently a gum of the same class as gum arabic, if not identical with it. Its solution contains the same amount of lime as gum arabic affords.

The resin of olibanum has been examined by Hlasiwetz (1867), according to whom it is a uniform substance having the composition $C^{20}H^{30}O^{3}$. We find that it is not soluble in alkalis, nor have we succeeded in converting it into a crystalline body by the action of dilute alcohol. It is not uniformly distributed throughout the tears; if they are broken after having been acted upon by dilute alcohol, it now and then happens that a clear stratification is perceptible, showing a concentric arrangement.

Olibanum contains an essential oil, of which Braconnot (1808) obtained 5 per cent., Stenhouse (1840) 4 per cent., and Kurbatow (1871-1874) 7 per cent. According to Stenhouse it has a sp. gr. of 0·866, a boiling point of 179·4° C., and an odour resembling that of turpentine but more agreeable. Kurbatow separated this oil into two portions, the one of which has the formula $C^{10}H^{16}$, boils at 158° C., and combines with HCl to form crystals; the other contains oxygen. The bitter principle of olibanum forms an amorphous brown mass.

The resin of olibanum submitted to destructive distillation affords no umbelliferone. Heated with strong nitric acid it develops no peculiar colour, but at length camphretic acid (see Camphor) is formed, which may be also obtained from many resins and essential oils if submitted to the same oxidizing agent.

Commerce—The olibanum of Arabia is shipped from several small places along the coast between Damkote and Al Kammar, but the quantity produced in this district is much below that furnished by the Somali Country in Eastern Africa. The latter is brought to Zeyla, Berbera, Bunder Murayah, and many smaller ports, whence it is shipped to Aden or direct to Bombay. The trade is chiefly in the hands of Banians, and the great emporium for the drug is Bombay. A certain portion is shipped through the straits of Bab-el-Mandeb to Jidda,—Von Kremer[2] says to the value of £12,000 annually. The quantity exported from Bombay in the year 1872–73 was 25,100 cwt., of which 17,446 cwt. were shipped to the United Kingdom, and 6,184 cwt. to China.[3]

Uses—As a medicine olibanum is nearly obsolete, at least in Britain. The great consumption of the drug is for the incense used in the Roman Catholic and Greek Churches.

[1] I obtained 32·14 per cent. from the finest tears of the kind called Fasous Bedowi, with which I was presented by Capt. Hunter of Aden.—F.A.F.

[2] *Aegypten, Forschungen über Land und Volk*, Leipzig, 1863.

[3] *Statement of the Trade and Navigation of the Presidency of Bombay for* 1872-73, pt. ii. 78.

MYRRHA.

Gummi-resina Myrrha; Myrrh; F. *Myrrhe;* G. *Myrrhe.*

Botanical Origin—Ehrenberg who visited Egypt, Nubia, Abyssinia, and Arabia in the years 1820–26, brought home with him specimens of the myrrh trees found at Ghizan (Gison or Dhizân), a town on the strip of coast-region called Tihâma, opposite the islands of Farsan Kebir and Farsan Seghir, and a little to the north of Lohaia, on the eastern side of the Red Sea, in latitude 16° 40′, and also on the neighbouring mountains of Djara (or Shahra) and Kara. Here the myrrh trees form the underwood of the forests of *Acacia, Moringa,* and *Euphorbia.* Nees von Esenbeck who examined these specimens, drew up from them a description of what he called *Balsamodendron Myrrha,* which he figured in 1828.[1]

After Ehrenberg's herbarium had been incorporated in the Royal Herbarium of Berlin, Berg examined these specimens, and came to the conclusion that they consist of *two species,* namely that described and figured by Nees, and a second to which was attached (*correctly* we must hope) two memoranda bearing the following words:—"*Ipsa Myrrhæ arbor ad Gison,—Martio,*" and "*Ex huic simillima arbore ad Gison ipse Myrrham effluentem legi.*[2] *Hæc specimina lecta sunt in montibus Djara et Kara Februario.*" This plant Berg named *B. Ehrenbergianum.*[3] Oliver in his *Flora of Tropical Africa* (1868)[4] is disposed to consider Berg's plant the same as *B. Opobalsamun* Kth., a tree or shrub yielding myrrh, found by Schweinfurth on the Bisharrin mountains in Abyssinia, not far from the coast between Suakin and Edineb. But Schweinfurth himself does not admit the identity of the two plants.[5] It is certain, however, that the myrrh of commerce is chiefly of African origin.

Captain F. M. Hunter, Assistant Resident of Aden, informed us[6] that the Arabian myrrh tree, the *Didthin,* is found not only in the southern provinces of Arabia, Yemen, and Hadramant, probably also in the southern part of Oman, but likewise on the range of hills which, on the African shore, runs parallel to the Somali coast. The Somalis who gather the myrrh in Arabia allege that the Arabian "Didthin" is identical with that of their own district. Its exudation is the true myrrh, "*Mulmul*" of the Somalis, the "*Mur*" of the Arabs, or "*Heerabole*"[7] of the Indians.

Another myrrh tree, according to Captain Hunter, is growing in Ogadain and the districts round Harrar, that is between the 7th and 10th parallels, N. lat., and 43° to 50° E. long. This is the "*Habaghadi*" of the Somalis, which is not found in Arabia, nor in the coast range of

[1] *Plantæ Medicinales,* Dusseldorf, ii. (1828) tab. 355.

[2] On applying in 1872 to Prof. Ehrenberg to know if it were possible that we could *see* this very specimen, we received the answer that it could not be found.

[3] Berg u. Schmidt, *Darstellung u. Beschreibung . . . offizin. Gewächse,* iv. (1863) tab. xxix. *d.;* also *Bot. Zeitung,* 16 Mai, 1862. 155.

[4] Vol. i. 326.

[5] Petermann, *Geogr. Mittheilungen,* 1868. 127.

[6] Letters addressed in 1877 to F.A.F.

[7] *Bola, Bal,* or *Bol* were names of the myrrh in the Egyptian antiquity.—Ehrenberg, *De Myrrhæ et Opocalpasi . . . . . . detectis plantis,* Berolini, 1841, fol.

the Somali country, but only at a considerable distance from the sea-shore. Its exudation is the coarse myrrh, habaghadi of the Somalis and Arabs and "*Baisabole*" of the Indians.

Hildebrandt has collected the didthin, or didin as he writes, in the coast range alluded to, that is in the Ahl or Serrut Mountains, where the tree is growing on sunny slopes in elevations of 500 to 1,500 metres. He has ascertained that it is identical with Ehrenberg's tree, *Balsamodendron Myrrha* Nees. It is a low tree of crippled appearance, attaining not more than 3 metres. This species must therefore be pointed out as the source of true myrrh of the European commerce.

History—(See also further on, Bissabol). Myrrh has been used from the earliest times together with olibanum as a constituent of incense,[1] perfumes, and unguents. It was an ingredient of the holy oil used in the Jewish ceremonial as laid down by Moses: and it was also one of the numerous components of the celebrated *Kyphi* of the Egyptians, a preparation used in fumigations, medicine, and the process of embalming, and of which there were several varieties.

In the previous article we have pointed out (p. 137) several early references to myrrh in connection with olibanum, in which it is observable that the myrrh (when weights are mentioned) is always in the smaller quantity. Of the use of the drug in mediæval Europe there are few notices, but they tend to show that the commodity was rare and precious. This myrrh is recommended in the Anglo-Saxon Leech-books[2] to be used with frankincense in the superstitious medical practice of the 11th century. In a manuscript of the Monastery of Rheinau, near Schaffhausen, Switzerland, we also find that, apparently in the 11th century, myrrh as well as olibanum were used in ordeals in the "judicium aquæ bullientis."[3] The drug was also used by the Welsh "Physicians of Myddfai" in the 13th century. In the Wardrobe accounts of Edward I. there is an entry under date 6th January, 1299, for gold, frankincense, and *myrrh*, offered by the king in his chapel on that day, it being the Feast of Epiphany.[4] Myrrh again figures in the accounts of Geoffroi de Fleuri,[5] master of the wardrobe (*argentier*) to Philippe le Long, king of France, where record is made of the purchase of—"4 onces d'estorat calmite" (see Styrax) "et *mierre* (myrrh) . . . . encenz et laudanon," (Ladanum, the resin of Cistus creticus L.)—for the funeral of John, posthumous son of Louis X., A.D. 1316.

Gold, silver, silk, precious stones, pearls, camphor, musk, *myrrh*, and spices are enumerated[6] as the presents which the Khan of Cathay sent to Pope Benedict XII. at Avignon about the year 1342. The myrrh destined for this circuitous route to Europe[7] was doubtless that of the

[1] Cantic. i. 13, iii. 6; Genes. xliii. 11; Exod. ii. 12, 30, xxiii. 34-36; John xix. 39; Mark xv. 23; Proverbs vii. 17.

[2] Cockayne, *Leechdoms &c. of Early England*, ii. (1865) 295, 297.

[3] Runge, *Adjurationen, Exorcismen, Benedictionen, &c., in Mittheilungen der antiquar. Gesellschaft in Zürich*, xii. (1859) 187.

[4] *Liber quotidianus Contrarotulatoris Garderobæ . . . . Edwardi I.*, Lond. 1787. pp. xxxii. and 27.—The custom is still observed by the sovereigns of England, and the Queen's oblation of gold, frankincense, and myrrh is still annually presented on the Feast of Epiphany in the Chapel Royal in London.

[5] Doüet d'Arcq, *Comptes de l'Argenterie des rois de France*, 1851. 19.

[6] Yule, *Cathay and the way thither*, ii. 357.

[7] For the costly presents in question *never reached their destination*, having been all plundered by the way!

Arabian traders, with whom the Chinese had constant intercourse during the middle ages. Myrrh in fact is still somewhat largely consumed in China.[1]

The name *Myrrh* is from the Hebrew and Arabic *Mur*, meaning bitter, whence also the Greek *σμύρνα*. The ancient Egyptian *Bola* or *Bal*, and the Sanskrit *Vola* are preserved in the Persian and Indian words *Bol*, *Bola*, and *Heera-bol*, well-known names for myrrh.

Stacte (*στακτὴ*), a substance often mentioned by the ancients, is said by Pliny to be a spontaneous liquid exudation of the myrrh tree, more váluable than myrrh itself. The author of the Periplus of the Erythrean Sea represents it as exported from Muza in Arabia[2] together with myrrh. Theophrastus[3] speaks of myrrh as of two kinds, solid and liquid. No drug of modern times has been identified with the *stacte* or *liquid myrrh* of the ancients: that it was a substance obtainable in quantity seems evident from the fact that 150 pounds of it, said to be the offering of an Egyptian city, were presented to St. Silvester at Rome, A.D. 314–335.[4]

The myrrh of the ancients was not always obtained from Arabia. The author of the Periplus,[5] who wrote about A.D. 64, records it to have been an export of Abalites, Malao, and Mosyllon (the last-named the modern Berbera), ancient ports of the African coast outside the straits of Bab-el-Mandeb; and he even mentions that it is conveyed by small vessels to the opposite shores of Arabia.

Secretion—Marchand[6] who examined and figured the sections of a branch of three years' growth of *B. Myrrha*, represents the gum-resin as chiefly deposited in the cortical layers, with a little in the medulla.

Collection—By the Somal tribe myrrh is largely collected as it flows out, incisions, according to Hildebrandt, being never practised. From the information given by Ehrenberg to Nees von Esenbeck,[7] it appears that myrrh when it first exudes is of an oily and then of a buttery appearance, yellowish white, gradually assuming a golden tint and becoming reddish as it hardens. It exudes from the bark like cherry-tree gum, and becomes dark and of inferior value by age. Although Ehrenberg says that the myrrh he saw was of fine quality, he does not mention it being gathered by the natives.

With regard to the localities[8] in which the drug is collected, Cruttenden,[9] who visited the Somali coast in 1843, says that myrrh is brought from the Wadi Nogâl, south west of Cape Gardafui, and from Murreyhan, Ogadain and Agahora; and that some few trees are found on the mountains behind Bunder Murayah. Major Harris[10] saw the myrrh tree in the Adel desert and in the jungle of the Háwash, on the way from Tajura to Shoa.

[1] Shanghai imported in 1872, 18,600 lbs. of myrrh.—*Reports of Trade at the Treaty Ports in China for* 1872, p. 4.

[2] Vincent, *Commerce of the Ancients*, ii. (1870) 316.—Muza or Moosa is supposed to be identical with a place still bearing that name lying about 20 miles east of Mokha.

[3] Lib. ix. c. 4.

[4] Vignolius, *Liber Pontificalis*, i. (1724) 95.

[5] Vincent, *op. cit.* ii. 127. 129, 135.

[6] *Recherches sur l'Organisation des Burseracées*, Paris, 1868, p. 42, pl. i.

[7] *Op. cit.* at p. 140, note 1.

[8] See paper with map in *Ocean Highways*, April, 1873, also *Pharm. Journ.* 19 April, 1873. 821, and Hanbury's *Science Papers*, 378.

[9] *Trans. Bombay Geogr. Soc.* vii. (1846) 123.

[10] *Highlands of Æthiopia* (1844) i. 426; ii. 414.

Vaughan [1] states that the Somali Country and the neighbourhood of Hurrur (or Harar or Adari, 9° 20′ N., 42° 17′ E.) south west of Zeila are the chief producing districts. It is generally brought to the great fair of Berbera held in November, December, and January, where it is purchased by the Banians of India, and shipped for Bombay.

It appears that all these informations rather refer to the Bisabol or Habaghadi variety of myrrh; only the first notice, due to Hildebrandt, applies to true myrrh.

Myrrh trees abound on the hills about Shugra and Sureea in the territory of the Fadhli or Fudthli tribe, lying to the eastward of Aden; myrrh is collected from them by Somalis who cross from the opposite coast for the purpose and pay a tribute for the privilege to the Arabs, who appear to be scarcely acquainted with this drug.[2] But a sample of it, received by one of us from Vaughan in 1852, and others we have since seen in London (and easily, recognized), proved it to be somewhat different from typical myrrh, and it is probably afforded by another species than Balsamodendron Myrrha.

It would thus appear that there are three different trees affording myrrh, namely that just alluded to, secondly the "Habaghadi," and thirdly that growing east of Aden.

Description—Myrrh consists of irregular roundish masses, varying in size from small grains up to pieces as large as an egg, and occasionally much larger. They are of an opaque reddish brown with dusty dull surface. When broken, they exhibit a rough or waxy fracture, having a moist and unctuous appearance, especially when pressed, and a rich brown hue. The fractured, translucent surface often displays characteristic whitish marks which the ancients compared to the light mark at the base of the finger-nails. Myrrh has a peculiar and agreeable fragrance with an aromatic, bitter, and acrid taste. It cannot be finely powdered until deprived by drying of some of its essential oil and water; nor when heated does it melt like colophony.

Water disintegrates myrrh, forming a light brown emulsion, which viewed under the microscope appears made up of colourless drops, among which are granules of yellow resin. Alcohol dissolves the resin of myrrh, leaving angular non-crystalline particles of gum [3] and fragments of bark.

Chemical Composition—Myrrh is a mixture, in very varying proportions, of resin, mucilaginous matters, and essential oil. A fine specimen of myrrh from the Somali coast, with which Captain Hunter, in 1877, kindly presented one of us, yielded 27 per cent. of resin. The undissolved portion is partly soluble in water.

The resin dissolves completely in chloroform or alcohol, and the colour of the latter solution is but slightly darkened by perchloride of iron. It is but partially soluble in alkalis or in bisulphide of carbon.

[1] *Pharm. Journ.* xii. (1853) 226.

[2] Capt. S. B. Miles, in *Journ. of R. Geograph. Soc.* xli. (1871) 236. The country visited by Miles and Munzinger is the "Smyrnifera regio exterior," the outer country producing myrrh of the ancients, about 14° 10′ N. lat. and 57° E. long. See also Sprenger, *Alte Geographie Arabiens*, 313.

[3] Druggists who prepare large quantities of Tincture of Myrrh may utilize this gum for making a common sort of mucilage.—*Pharm. Journ.* 10 June, 1871, 1001.

Brückner (1867) found this portion to yield 75·6 per cent. of carbon and 9·5 of hydrogen. The resin which the bisulphide refuses to dissolve, is freely soluble in ether. It contains only 57·4 per cent. of carbon. The resin of myrrh to which, when moistened with alcohol, a small quantity of concentrated nitric or hydrochloric acid is added, assumes a violet hue, but far less brilliant than that displayed by resin of galbanum when treated in a similar manner. But a most intensely violet liquid may be obtained by adding bromine to the resin dissolved in bisulphide of carbon. If the resin of myrrh as afforded by alcohol is warmed with petroleum (boiling at 70° C)., only a small amount of resin is dissolved. This liquid becomes turbid if vapours of bromine are added; a violet flocculent matter deposits, whereas the just above-mentioned solution in the bisulphide continues clear on addition of bromine.

The resin of myrrh is not capable of affording umbelliferone like that of galbanum. By melting it with potash, pyrocatechin and protocatechuic acid are produced in small amount.

Myrrh yields on distillation a volatile oil which in operating on 25 lb. of the drug, we obtained to the extent of ⅞ per cent.[1] It is a yellowish, rather viscid liquid, neutral to litmus, having a powerful odour of myrrh and sp. gr. 0·988 at 13° C.[2] In a column 50 mm. long, it deviates a ray of light 30·1° to the left. By submitting it to distillation, we obtained before the oil boiled, a few drops of a strongly acid liquid having the smell of formic acid. Neutralized with ammonia, this liquid produced in solution of mercurous nitrate a whitish precipitate which speedily darkened, thus indicating formic acid, which is developed in the oil. Old myrrh is in fact said to yield an acid distillate. The oil begins to boil at about 266° C., and chiefly distills over between 270° and 290°.

On combustion in the usual way it afforded carbon 84·70, hydrogen 9·98. Having been again rectified in a current of dry carbonic acid, it had a boiling point of 262–263° C., and now afforded[3] carbon 84·70, hydrogen 10·26, which would nearly answer to the formula $C^{22}H^{32}O$. The results of Ruickholdt's analysis (1845) of essential oil of myrrh assign it the formula $C^{10}H^{14}O$, which is widely different from that indicated by our experiments.

The oil which we rectified displays a faintly greenish hue; it is miscible in every proportion with bisulphide of carbon, the solution exhibiting at first no peculiar coloration when a drop of nitric or sulphuric acid is added. Yet the mixture to which nitric acid (1·20) has been added, assumes after an hour or two a fine violet hue which is very persistent, enduring even if the liquid is allowed to dry up in a large capsule. If to the crude oil dissolved in bisulphide of carbon bromine be added, a violet hue is produced; and if the solution is allowed to evaporate, and the residue diluted with spirit of wine, it assumes a fine blue which disappears on addition of an alkali. The

[1] Ruickholdt got 2·18 per cent.; Bley and Diesel (1845) from 1·6 to 3·4 per cent. of an acid oil. We are kindly informed by Mr. Fritzsche of Leipzig (Messrs. Schimmel & Co.) that good myrrh distilled on a large scale yields as much as 4·4 per cent. of oil. (Letter dated 13th June, 1878.)

[2] Gladstone (1863) found the oil a little *heavier* than water.

[3] Analyses performed in my laboratory by Dr. Buri, February, 1874. See also my paper on Carvol, *Pharm. Journ.* vii. (1876) 75, or *Yearbook of Pharmacy* (1877) 51—F.A.F.

oil is not much altered by boiling with alcoholic potash, nor does it combine with alkaline bisulphites.

The *Bitter principle* of myrrh is contained in the resin as extracted by alcohol. By exhausting the resin with warm water an acid brown solution is obtained, from which a dark, viscid, neutral mass separates if the liquid is concentrated; it is contaminated with a large amount of inorganic matter, from which it may be purified by means of ether. Yet the latter affords also but an amorphous, somewhat brittle brown substance, softening at 80°–90°C. This bitter principle reminds us of that mentioned in our article Elemi, page 151; it is but sparingly soluble in water; the yellowish solution is intensely bitter. The bitter principle of myrrh appears to be a glucoside. We have not succeeded in preparing it in a more satisfactory state.

Commerce—Myrrh is chiefly shipped by way of Berbera to Aden, and thence either to Europe or to Bombay. The exports of Aden in the fiscal year 1875 to 1876 were 1,439 cwt.; one half of which went to Bombay, one third to the United Kingdom.[1]

The bags or bales which contain the myrrh are opened in Bombay, and the drug is sorted. The better portion goes to Europe, the refuse to China, where it is probably used as an incense.[2]

Uses—Myrrh, though much used, does not appear to possess any very important medicinal powers, and is chiefly employed on account of its bitter, aromatic properties.

Other Varieties of Myrrh—Though the myrrh of commerce exhibits some diversity of appearance, the drug-brokers and druggists of London are not in the habit of applying any special designations to the different qualities. There are however two varieties which deserve notice.

1. *Bissa Bol* (*Bhesabol, Bysabole*), *Habaghadi* or *Hebbakhade* of the Somalis, formerly called *East India Myrrh.*[3]

This drug is of African origin, but of the plant which yields it nothing is known. Vaughan[4] who sent a sample from Aden to one of us in 1852, was told by the natives that the tree from which it is collected resembles that affording *Heera Ból* or true myrrh, but that it is nevertheless distinct. The drug is exported from the whole Somali coast to Mokha, Jidda, Aden, Makulla, the Persian Gulf, India and even China.[5] Bombay official returns show that the quantity imported thither in the year 1872-73, was 224 cwt., all shipped from Aden.

Some myrrh, no doubt that from the interior of north-eastern Africa, the Habaghadi or Baisabole, finds its way by the country of the Wagadain (Ugahden or Ogadain) to the small port of Brava (Barawa, Braoua), about 1° N. lat., and to Zanzibar.[6] This is, possibly,

[1] Information obligingly supplied by Captain Hunter, July 1877.

[2] Dymock, *Pharm. Journ.* vi. (1876) 661.

[3] *Myrrha indica*, Martiny, *Encyklop. der med-pharm. Rohwaarenkunde*, ii. (1854) 98, 101.

[4] *Pharm. Journ.* xii. (1853) 227.

[5] In 1865, 10 packages of this drug containing about 15 cwt. were consigned to me for sale in London by a friend in China, who had purchased the drug under the notion that it was *true myrrh*. The commodity was bad of its kind, and was sold with difficulty at 30*s*. per cwt.—D. H.

[6] Guillain, *Documents sur l'histoire, la géogr. et le commerce de l'Afrique orientale* iii. (1856) 350.

also the "*Mirra fina*," which is stated, about the year 1502, by Tomé Lopez to be collected (?) in the island of "Monzambiche."[1]

According to Vaughan, Bissa Bôl is mixed with the food given to milch cows and buffaloes in order to increase the quantity and improve the quality of their milk, and that it is also used as size to impart a bright gloss to whitewashed walls.

Miles mentions[2] that myrrh, called there *hodthai*, is only used in the Somali country, by men to whiten their shields (by means of an emulsion made with the drug), by women to cleanse their hair. Probably hodthai and habaghadi is one and the same thing.

Bissa Bôl differs from myrrh in its stronger, almost acrid *taste* and in *odour*, which, when once familiar is easily recognizable; fine specimens of the former have the outward characters of myrrh and perhaps are often passed off for it. A good sample of "coarse" habaghadi myrrh as sent in 1877 by Captain Hunter from Aden proved to contain but very little resin. This resin is manifestly different from that of myrrh as already shown by its paler, more reddish colour. The resin of Bissa Bôl moreover is but very sparingly soluble in bisulphide of carbon; this solution is *not altered* by bromine, that of true myrrh, as above stated, assuming a most intense violet colour on addition of bromine Nor is the resin of habaghadi soluble in petroleum ether. Of the gummy substance, which is by far the prevailing constituent of this drug, a small portion only is soluble in water. These extremely marked differences no doubt depend upon a widely discrepant composition of the resins of the two kinds of myrrh as well as upon a different proportion of gum and resin. The Bissa Bôl usually seen is an impure and foul substance, which is regarded by London druggists as well as by the Banian traders in India as a very inferior dark sort of myrrh.

2. ***Arabian Myrrh***—The drug we have mentioned at p. 143 as collected to the eastward of Aden, is of interest as substantiating the statement of Theophrastus that both olibanum and myrrh grow in Southern Arabia.

The drug, which is not distinguished by any special name in English trade, is in irregular masses seldom exceeding 1½ inches long, and having a somewhat gummy-looking exterior. The larger lumps seem formed by the cohesion of small, rounded, translucent, externally shining tears or drops. The fracture is like that of common myrrh; but less unctuous and wants the whitish markings. The odour and taste are those of the ordinary drug. Pieces of a semi-transparent papery bark are attached to some of the lumps. We extracted the resin of a sample of this myrrh from the territory of the Fadhli, as sent to us by Captain Hunter. Its solution in bisulphide of carbon or petroleum ether was coloured by bromine as stated above, (p. 144) with regard to typical myrrh (Heerabol) from the Somali Country. The name applies to myrrh from the vicinity of Ras Morbat in the same region. But the resin of another kind of Arabian myrrh, for which we are likewise indebted to Captain Hunter, is *not coloured* when treated in the same way. This is the myrrh "Hodaidia Jebeli" from north and northwestern Yenen.

[1] In Ramusio (see Appendix, R) 239.

[2] *Journ. of the R. Geogr. Soc.* 22 (1872) 64.

ELEMI.

Resina Elemi; Elemi; F. *Résine Elémi;* G. *Elemiharz.*

Botanical Origin—The resin known in pharmacy as *Elemi* is derived from a tree growing in the Philippines, which Blanco,[1] a botanist of Manila, described in 1845 under the name of *Icica Abilo,* but which is completely unknown to the botanists of Europe. Blanco's description is such that, if correct, the plant cannot be placed in either of the old genera *Icica* or *Elaphrium,* comprehended by Bentham and Hooker in that of *Bursera,* nor yet in the allied genus *Canarium;* in fact even the order to which it belongs is somewhat doubtful.[2]

The tree grows in the province of Batangas in the island of Luzon (south of Manila), where its name in the Tagala language is *ábilo;* the Spaniards call it *Arbol a brea,* i.e. *pitch-tree,* from the circumstance that its resin is used for the caulking of boats.

History—The explicit statements of Theophrastus in the 3rd century B.C. relative to olibanum have already been mentioned. The same writer narrates[3] that a little above Coptus on the Red Sea, no tree is found except the acacia (ἀκάνθη) of the desert . . . but that on the sea there grow laurel (δάφνη) and olive (ἐλαία), from the latter of which exudes a substance much valued to make a medicine for the staunching of blood.

This story appears again in Pliny[4] who says that in Arabia the olive tree exudes tears which are an ingredient of the medicine called by the Greeks *Enhæmon,* from its efficacy in healing wounds.

Dioscorides[5] briefly notices the *Gum of the Ethiopian olive,* which he likens to scammony; and the same substance is named by Scribonius Largus[6] who practised medicine at Rome during the 1st century.

The writers who have commented on Dioscorides have generally adopted the opinion that the exudation of the so-called olive-tree of Arabia and Ethiopia was none other than the substance known to them as *Elemi,* though, as remarked by Mattioli,[7] the oriental drug thus called by no means well accords with the description left by that author.

As to that name, the earliest mention of it appears in the middle of

[1] *Flora de Filipians,* segunda impression, Manila, 1845. 256.

[2] On consulting Mr. A. W. Bennett, who is now studying the *Burseraceæ* of India, as to the probable affinities of Blanco's plant, we received from him the following remarks: "I have little hesitation in pronouncing that from the description, *Icica Abilo* cannot be a *Canarium,* but what it is, is more difficult to say. The leaves having the lowest pair of leaflets smallest, seems at first sight very characteristic of *Canarium;* but the following considerations tend the other way. 1. The *opposite* leaves which occur nowhere in *Burseraceæ* except in *Amyris,* with which the plant does not agree in many ways. 2. The *stipellæ* which are not found anywhere in the order.—3. The *quinate* flowers. In all species of *Canarium* the parts of the flowers are in threes, including *C. commune,* which according to Miquel extends to the Philippines. The only exception is *C.* (*Scutinanthe* Thwaites) *brunneum,* with which it does not agree in other respects.

"The foregoing reasons almost equally exclude *Icica* (*Bursera*); yet the fruit of Blanco's plant seems so eminently that of a *Burseracea,* that I think it must belong to that order, but with some error in the description of the leaves."

[3] *Hist. Plant.* lib. iv. c. 7.

[4] Lib. xii. c. 38.

[5] Lib. i. c. 141.

[6] *Compositiones Medicament.* cap. 103.

[7] *Comm. in lib. i. Dioscoridis.*

the 15th century. Thus in a list of drugs sold at Frankfort about 1450, we find *Gommi Elempnij*.[1] Saladinus,[2] who lived about this period, enumerates *Gumi Elemi* among the drugs kept by the Italian apothecaries, but we have not met with the name in any other writer of the school of Salerno. The *Arbolayre*,[3] a herbal supposed to have been printed about 1485, gives some account of *Gomme Elempni*, stating that it is the gum of the lemon tree and not of fennel as some think,—that it resembles Male Incense,—and makes an excellent ointment for wounds.

The name *Enhæmon*[4] of Pliny, also written *Enhæmi*, is probably the original form of the word *Animi*, another designation for the same drug, though also applied as at the present day to a sort of copal. It is even possible that the word *Elemi* has the same origin.[5]

This primitive Elemi is in our opinion identical with a peculiar sort of olibanum known as *Luban Meyeti*, afforded by *Boswellia Frereana* Birdwood (p. 135). It has a remarkable resemblance both in external appearance and in odour to the substance in after-times imported from America, and which were likened to the elemi and animi of the Old World. The description of "gummi elemnia" given by Valerius Cordus,[6] the most careful observer of his period, could in our opinion well apply to *Luban Meyeti*. (See p. 153 further on.)

The first reference to Elemi as a production of America comes from the pen of Monardes[7] who has a chapter on *Animi and Copal*. He describes animi as of a more oily nature than copal, of a very agreeable odour, and in grains resembling olibanum but of larger size, and adds that it differs from the animi of the Old World in being less white and clear.

At a somewhat later period this resin and some similar substances began to be substituted for *Elemi* which had become scarce.[8] Pomet,[9] who as a dealer in drugs was a man of practical knowledge, laments that this American drug was being sold by some as Elemi, and by others as Animi or as Tacamaca. It was however introduced in great plenty, and at length took the place of the original elemi which became completely forgotten.

American Elemi was in turn discarded in favour of another sort imported from the Philippines. The first mention of this substance is to be found among the descriptions accompanied by drawings sent by Father Camellus to Petiver of London, of the shrubs and trees of Luzon,[10] in the year 1701. Camellus states that the tree, which from his drawing preserved in the British Museum appears to us to be a species of

[1] Flückiger, *Die Frankfurter Liste*, Halle, 1873. 7. 16.—"Gumi elemi" is also found in a similar list of the year 1480, compiled in the town of Nördlingen, Bavaria. See *Archiv der Pharm.* 211 (1877) 103.

[2] *Compendium Aromatariorum*, Bonon. 1488.

[3] This very rare volume is one of the treasures of the National Library of Paris.

[4] From the Greek ἔναιμον, signifying *blood-stopping*.

[5] Brassavola observes—"quandoque inclinavimus ut gummi oleæ Æthiopicæ esset gummi *elemi* dicti, quasi *enhæmi*."—*Examen simplicium*, Lugd. 1537. 386.

[6] *Hist. Stirp. libri iv.*, edition of Gesner, Argentorati, 1561. 209.

[7] *Libro de las cosas que se traen de nuestras Indias Occidentales*, Sevilla, 1565.

[8] Thus Piso in 1658 describes the resin of an *Icica* as exactly resembling *Elemi* and quite as good for wounds.—*Hist. nat. et med. Ind. Occ.* 122.

[9] *Histoire des Drogues*, 1694, 261.

[10] Ray, *Hist. Plant.* iii. (1704), appendix, p. 67. No. 13.—Compare also p. 60, No. 10.

Canarium, is very tall and large, that it is called by the Spaniards *Arbol de la brea*, and that it yields an abundance of odorous resin which is commonly used for pitching boats. Living specimens of the tree together with samples of the resin were brought to Paris from Manila by the traveller Perrottet about the year 1820. For the last twenty years the resin has been common, and is now imported in large quantities[1] for use in the arts, so displacing all other kinds. It has been adopted as the *Elemi* of the *British Pharmacopœia* (1867), and is in fact the only variety of elemi now found in English commerce.

Description—Manila elemi is a soft, resinous substance, of granular consistence not unlike old honey, and when recent and quite pure is colourless; more often it is found contaminated with carbonaceous matter which renders it grey or blackish, and it is besides mixed with chips and similar impurities. By exposure to the air it becomes harder and acquires a yellow tint. It has a strong and pleasant odour suggestive of fennel and lemon, yet withal somewhat terebinthinous. When moistened with spirit of wine, it disintegrates, and examined under the microscope is seen to consist partly of acicular crystals. At the heat of boiling water the hardened drug softens, and at a somewhat higher temperature fuses into a clear resin.

Chemical Composition—Manila elemi is rich in essential oil. On submitting 28 lb. of it to distillation with water, we obtained 2 lb. 13 oz. (equivalent to 10 per cent.) of a fragrant, colourless, neutral oil, of sp. gr. 0·861 at 15° C. Observed in Wild's polaristrobometer we found it to be strongly dextrogyre.[2] H. Sainte Claire Deville[3] on the other hand has examined an oil of elemi that was strongly levogyre. This discrepancy shows that there are among the oils of various kinds of elemi, differences similar to those existing in the oils of turpentine and copaiba. By the action of dry hydrochloric acid gas, Deville obtained from his oil of elemi a solid crystalline substance, $C^{10}H^{16} + 2\,HCl$. We failed to produce any such compound from the oil of Manila elemi. Our oil of elemi dissolves in bisulphide of carbon; when mixed with concentrated sulphuric acid, it becomes thick and assumes a deep orange colour.

By submitting the crude oil to fractional distillation, we separated it into six portions, of which the first five were dextrogyre in gradually diminishing degree, while the sixth displayed a weak deviation to the left.[4] The first portion having been dissolved in four times its weight of strong sulphuric acid, washed and again distilled, exhibit a deviation to the left.[5]

[1] Thus in a drug-sale, May 8, 1873, there were offered 275 cases,—equal to about 480 cwt.

[2] I observed the following deviations :—

In a column of 25 millimetres from 47°·5 to 70°·5 (deviation 23°).
,, ,, 50 ,, ,, 93°·6 (,, 46°·1).
,, ,, 100 ,, ,, 49°·6 (2·1 + 90=92°·1).—F.A.F.

[3] *Comptes Rendus*, xii. (1841) 184.

[4] The following deviations were observed, in a column of 25 millimetres :—

1.	Oil distilled at 172°—180° C.	from 47°·6 to	74°·5;	deviation	26°·9 to the *right*.
2.	,, 180°—183°	,,	71°·2	,,	23°·6 ,,
3.	,, 183°—184°·5	,,	68°·8	,,	21°·2 ,,
4.	,, 184°—195°	,,	65°·8	,,	18°·2 ,,
5.	,, 200°—230°	,,	61°·0	,,	13°·4 ,,
6.	Thickish yellow residue	,,	46°·2	,,	1°·4 to the *left*.

From 47°·6 to 46°.

If the essential oil of elemi (8 parts) is shaken with alcohol, 0·816 sp. gr. (2 parts), nitric acid, 1·2 sp. gr. (1 part) and water (5 parts), the mixture, on exposure to air in a shallow capsule soon yields large crystals, which were found to agree crystallographically[1] perfectly with terpin, $C^{10}H^{20}O^2 + OH^2$ from oil of turpentine.

Maujean,[2] a French pharmacien, examined Manila elemi as long ago as 1821 and proved it to contain two resins, the one soluble in cold, the other only in hot spirit of wine. The former, which appears to constitute by far the prevailing part of all varieties of elemi, has not yet been satisfactorily examined. Bonastre[3] a little latter made a more complete analysis, showing that the less soluble resin which he obtained to the extent of 25 per cent. is easily crystallizable, and apparently identical with a substance obtainable in a similar manner from what he regarded as true elemi, which the Manila resin was not then held to be. Baup (1851) gave it the name of *Amyrin.* According to our experiments, it is readily isolated to the extent of 20 per cent. when Manila elemi is treated with cold spirit of wine, in which the crystals of amyrin are but slightly soluble. If the elemi is pure, the amyrin may be thus obtained (by washing with spirit and pressure between bibulous paper) in a cake of snowy whiteness, which may be further purified by crystallization from boiling alcohol. The fusing point of the crystals is 177°C.; their composition has been ascertained by Buri[4] to agree with the formula $C^{25}H^{42}O$, which may be written thus: $(C^5H^8)^5\ OH^2$. Amyrin at 16° C. dissolves in 27·5 parts of alcohol 0·816 sp. gr., being readily soluble also in all the usual solvents for resins. The alcoholic solution is slightly dextrogyre. Amyrin is a neutral substance, and may be sublimed in small quantities by very carefully heating it.

By heating amyrin with zinc dust Ciamician[5] obtained chiefly toluol, methyl-ethyl-benzol and ethyl-naphtalin.

By allowing an alcoholic solution of the amorphous resin of Manila elemi[6] to evaporate, Baup obtained in very small quantity crystals of *Bréine,* a substance fusing at 187° C., which he considered to be distinct from amyrin. In our opinion it was impure amyrin; it is extremely difficult, or rather practically impossible to extract all the crystallizable resin from the amorphous. If the latter, perfectly transparent, is kept for several years, an elegant crystallization at last begins to make its appearance throughout the bulk of the resin.

Baup further extracted from Manila elemi a crystallizable substance soluble in water to which he gave the name of *Bryoidin,*[7] and in smaller quantity a second also soluble in water which he called *Bréidine.* From the experiments of Baup it appears that bryoidin is soluble in 360 parts of water at 10° C., and melts at 135° C.; whereas bréidine requires for solution 260 parts of water and fuses at a temperature not much over 100° C.

We have also obtained *Bryoidin*[8] by operating in the following

[1] Examined at my request by Prof. Groth. —F.A.F.

[2] *Journ. de Pharm.* ix. (1823) 45. 47.

[3] *Id.* x. (1824) 199.

[4] *Pharm. Journ.* vii. (1876) 157, also *Yearbook of Ph.* 1877. 21.

[5] *Berichte der deutschen chemischen Gesellschaft,* 1878. 1347.

[6] I am indebted for a specimen of the material that Baup worked upon and which he called *Resin of Arbol a brea,* to M. Roux, pharmacien of Nyon, Switzerland—F. A. F.

[7] From the Greek βρύον, in allusion to the moss-like aspect sometimes assumed by the crystals.

[8] Fluckiger, *Pharm. Journ.* v. (1874 142.

manner: the watery liquid left in the still after the distillation of 28 lb. of Manila elemi was poured off from the mass of hard resin, and having been duly concentrated, it deposited together with a dark extractiform matter, colourless acicular crystals of bryoidin. The deposit in question having been drained and allowed to dry, the bryoidin may be separated by boiling water or by cold ether. We found the latter the more convenient; it readily takes up the bryoidin contaminated only with a little resin. The ethereal solution should be allowed to evaporate and the residual crystalline mass boiled in water, when the solution (which is colourless), poured off from the resin, will deposit upon cooling brilliant tufts of acicular crystals of bryoidin. The boiling in water requires to be several times repeated before the whole of the bryoidin can be removed; the latter sometimes crystallizes as a mossy arborescent growth. Bryoidin is a neutral substance, of bitter taste, scarcely soluble in cold water, but dissolving easily in boiling water, or in alcohol or ether. When a little is placed in a watch-glass, covered with a plate of glass, and then gently heated over a lamp, it sublimes in delicate needles. To obtain it perfectly pure, it is best to sublime it in a current of dry carbonic acid. Thus purified its fusing point is 133·5 C.; after fusion it concretes as a transparent, amorphous mass, which if immersed in glycerin and raised to the temperature of 135° C., suddenly crystallizes.

We have observed that if the filtered mother-liquor of bryoidin after complete cooling and standing for a day or two is warmed, it becomes turbid and that in a few minutes there separate from it long white flocks like bits of paper or wool, which do not disappear either by warming or by cooling the liquid; under the microscope they are seen to consist partly of thread-like, partly of acicular crystals. It is possible this substance is Baup's *Bréidine;* we found it to fuse at 135° C., to be neutral, and to crystallize from weak alcohol exactly like bryoidin. Both it and bryoidin look very voluminous in water, but are extremely small in weight, and are present in the drug in but a very small amount. The composition of bryoidin agrees with the formula $C^{20}H^{38}O^{3}$, which might be written thus $(C^{5}H^{8})^{4}+3OH^{2}$. But it contains no water of crystallization. In the vapour of dry hydrochloric gas, bryoidin assumes a fine red colour, turning violet, then blue, and lastly green. This behaviour is not at all displayed by amyrin.

The liquids from which bryoidin is obtained contain an amorphous brown substance of intensely bitter taste, at the same time somewhat aromatic. It is decomposed by dilute mineral acids, evolving a very peculiar strong odour.

Buri[1] isolated from Manila Elemi an extremely small amount of *Elemic acid*, $C^{35}H^{56}O^{4}$. It is in very brilliant crystals, much larger than those of the other constituents of elemi. Although we have before us some prisms of the acids several millimetres long, it has been found impossible to ascertain their crystallographic character, each of the prisms being formed of very intimately aggregated crystals. Elemic acid melts at 215°C.; its alcoholic solution decidedly reddens litmus. Elemate of potassium is a crystalline salt.

[1] *Pharm. Journ.* viii. (1878) 601.

The relations of the substances hitherto isolated from elemi may perhaps be given thus:—

Essential oil, ...	C^5H^8.
Amyrin, ...	$(C^5H^8)^5 + OH^2$
Amorphous resin (?) . . .	$(C^5H^8)^5 + OH^2$
Bryoidin, ...	$(C^5H^8)^4 + 3OH^2$
Elemic acid, ...	$(C^5H^8)^7 + O^4$

Uses—Elemi is scarcely used in British medicine except in the form of an ointment, sometimes prescribed as a stimulating application to old wounds.

Other sorts of Elemi—1. ***Mexican Elemi, Vera Cruz Elemi***—This drug, which used to be imported into London about thirty years ago, but which has now disappeared from commerce, is the produce of a tree named by Royle *Amyris elemifera* growing at Oaxaca in Mexico.[1] It is a light yellow, or whitish, brittle resin occurring in semi-cylindrical scraped pieces, or in irregular fragments which are sometimes translucent but more often dull and opaque. It easily softens in the mouth so that it may be masticated, and has an agreeable terebinthinous odour. Treated with cold spirit of wine (·828), it breaks down into a white magma of acicular crystals (*Amyrin ?*).

2. *Brazilian Elemi*—Was described as long ago as 1658 by the traveller Piso, as a substance completely resembling the elemi of the Old World and applicable to the same purposes. It is the produce of several trees described as species of *Icica*, as *I. Icicariba* DC.,[2] *I. heterophylla* DC., *I. heptaphylla* Aublet, *I. guianensis* Aubl., *I. altissima* Aubl.—In New Granada a similar exudation[3] is furnished by *I. Caranna* H.B.K.

A specimen in our possession from Pernambuco[4] is a translucent, greenish-yellow, fragrant, terebinthinous resin, which by cold spirit of wine may be separated into two portions, the one soluble, the other a mass of colourless acicular crystals. The resin spontaneously exuded and collected from the trunks, is often opaque and white, grey, or yellowish, looking not unlike fragments of old mortar. The microscope shows it to be made up of minute acicular crystals.[5]

3. *Mauritius Elemi*—Fine specimens of this substance and of *Colophonia Mauritiana* DC. the tree affording it, were sent to one of us (H.) in 1855 by Mr. Emile Fleurot of Mauritius. The resin accords in its general characters with Manila elemi, like which it leaves after treatment with cold spirit of wine, an abundance of crystals resembling amyrin.

4. *Luban Meyeti*[6] or *Luban Mati*.—This substance, which we claim to be the *Oriental* or *African Elemi* of the older writers, and also one of

[1] Royle's very imperfect specimens of this plant are in the British Museum.

[2] Now *Protium Icicariba* Marchand, in *Flora Brasiliensis*, fascicul. 65 (1874) tab. liii.

[3] G. Planchon, *Bulletin de la Soc. Bot. de France*, xv. (1868) 16.

[4] Given me by Mr. Manley, late of Pernambuco. I have also an authentic specimen of the resin of *I. heterophylla* collected at Santarem, Pará, by Mr. H. W. Bates in 1853.—D. H.

[5] For some experiments on the resin of *Icica*, see Gmelin, *Chemistry*, xvi. (1866) 421.—Also Stenhouse and Groves, in Liebig's *Annalen der Chemie*, 180 (1876) 253, on resin and oil of *Icica heptaphylla*. The former would appear to agree with the formula $(C^6H^8)9\ OH^2$.

[6] *Lubân* is the general Arabic name for

the resins anciently designated *Animi*,[1] is the exudation of *Boswellia Frereana* Birdwood, a remarkable tree gregarious on the bare limestone hills near Bunder Murayah to the west of Cape Gardafui. The tree which is called *Yegaar* by the natives, is of small stature, and differs from the other species of *Boswellia* growing on the same coast in having glabrous, glaucous leaves with obtuse leaflets, crisped at the margin.[2] The bark is smooth, papery, and translucent, and easily stripped off in thin sheets which are used for writing on. Though growing wild, the trees are said by Capt. Miles[3] to be carefully watched and even sometimes propagated. The resin exudes after incision in great plenty, soon hardens, and is collected by the Somali tribes who dispose of it to traders for shipment to Jidda and ports of Yemen: occasionally a package reaches London among the shipments of olibanum. It is used in the East for chewing like mastich.

In modern times Luban Mati has been mentioned by Wellsted in his "Travels in Arabia" (1838).

Luban Meyeti occurs in the form of detached droppy tears and fragments, occasionally in stalactitic masses several ounces in weight. It breaks very easily with a brilliant conchoidal fracture, showing an internal substance of a pale amber yellow and perfectly transparent. Externally it is more or less coated with a thin opaque white crust, which seen under the microscope appears non-crystalline. Many of the tears have pieces of the thin, brown, papery bark adhering to them. The resin has an agreeable odour of lemon and turpentine, and a mild terebinthinous taste.

Treated with alcohol (·838) it is almost entirely dissolved; the very small undissolved portion is not crystalline. The former agrees with the formula $C^{30}H^{30}O^{2}$. 20 lb. of Luban Mati yielded us 10 ounces of a volatile oil (=3·1 per cent.) having a fragrant odour suggestive of elemi and sp. gr. 0·856 at 17° C. The oil examined in a column 50 millim. long, deviates the ray 2°·5 to the left. By fractional distillation we found it to consist of dextrogyre hydrocarbon, $C^{10}H^{16}$, mixed with an oxygenated oil which we did not succeed in isolating; the latter is evidently lævogyre, and exists in proportion more than sufficient to overcome the weak dextrogyre power of the hydrocarbon.

There is no gum in this exudation; it is therefore essentially different from olibanum, the product of closely allied species of *Boswellia*.[4]

olibanum: *meyeti* perhaps from Jebel Meyet, a mountain of 1200 feet on the Somali Coast in long. 47° 10′.

[1] By the assistance of Professor G. Planchon we have ascertained that it is identically the same substance as described by Guibourt under the name *Tacamaque jaune huileuse* A.—*Hist. des Drogues*, iii. (1850) 483.

[2] Figured in Birdwood's paper, *Trans. Linn. Soc.* xxvii. (1870) tab. 32; also, (reduced) in Cooke's report on the *Gums, Resins, etc., of the India Museum*, 1874, plate iv.

[3] *Journ. Geograph. Soc.* xlii. (1872) 61.

[4] Flückiger, on Luban Mati and Olibanum, *Pharm. Journ.* viii. (1878) 805, with sketch map of the Somali Coast.

MELIACEÆ.

CORTEX MARGOSÆ.

Cortex Azadirachtæ; Nim Bark, Margosa Bark.

Botanical Origin—*Melia indica* Brandis (*M. Azadirachta* L., *Azadirachta indica* Juss.), an ornamental tree, 40 to 50 feet high and attaining a considerable girth,[1] well known throughout India by its Hindustani name of *Nim*, or by its Portuguese appellation of *Margosa*.[2] It is much planted in avenues, but occurs wild in the forests of Southern India, Ceylon and the Malay Archipelago, as far as Java.[3]

The hard and heavy wood which is so bitter that no insect will attack it, the medicinal leaves and bark, the fruit which affords an acrid bitter oil used in medicine and for burning, the gum which exudes from the stem, and finally a sort of toddy obtained from young trees, cause the *Nim* to be regarded as one of the most useful trees of India.

M. indica is often confounded with *M. Azedarach* L., a native of China,[4] and probably of India, now widely distributed throughout the warmer regions of the globe, and not rare even in Sicily and other parts of the south of Europe. The former has an oval fruit (by abortion) one-celled and one-seeded, and leaves simply pinnate. The latter has the fruit five-celled, and leaves bi-pinnate.

History—The tree under the Sanskrit name of *Nimba* is mentioned in Susruta, one of the most ancient Hindu medical writings, composed perhaps about the 10th century of our era.

In common with many other productions of India, it attracted the notice of Garcia de Orta, physician to the Portuguese viceroy at Goa, and he published an account of it in his work on drugs in 1563.[5] Christoval Acosta[6] in 1578 supplied some further details and also a figure of the tree. The tonic properties of the bark, long recognized by the native physicians of India, were successively tested by Dr. D. White of Bombay in the beginning of the present century, and have since been generally admitted.[7] The drug has a place in the *Pharmacopœia of India*.

Description—The bark in our possession[8] is in coarse fibrous pieces about ⅛ of an inch thick and 2 to 3 inches wide, slightly channelled. The suberous coat is rough and cracked, and of a greyish rusty hue. The inner surface is of a bright buff and has a highly foliaceous structure. On making a transverse section three distinct layers may be observed—firstly the suberous coat exhibiting a large brown

[1] Fig. in Bentley and Trimen, *Medic. Plants*, part 27.

[2] From *amargoso*, bitter.

[3] C. De Candolle, in *Monogr. Phanerogamar.* i. (1878) 459.

[4] It is mentioned in Chinese writings dating long prior to the Christian era.—Bretschneider, *Chinese Botanical Works*, 1870. 12.

[5] *Colloquios dos Simples, &c.*, Goa, 1563 *Colloq.* xl. p. 153.

[6] *Tractado de las Drogas y Medicinas de las Indias Orientales*, Burgos, 1578, cap. 43.

[7] Waring, in *Pharmacopœia of India*, 1868. 443.

[8] We are indebted for it to Mr. Broughton of Ootacamund.

parenchyme interwoven with small bands of corky tissue,—secondly a dark cellular layer, and then the foliaceous liber. The dry bark is inodorous and has a slightly astringent bitter taste.

Microscopic Structure—The suberous coat consists of numerous layers of ordinary cork-cells, which cover a layer of nearly cubic sclerenchymatous cells. This latter however is not always met with, secondary bands of cork (*rhytidoma*) frequently taking its place. The liber is commonly built up of strong fibre-bundles traversed by narrow medullary rays, and transversely separated by bands of parenchymatous liber tissue. Crystals of oxalate of calcium occur in the parenchyme more frequently than the small globular starch grains. The structure of the bark varies considerably according to the gradual development of the secondary cork-bands.

Chemical Composition—Margosa bark was chemically examined in India by Cornish[1] (1856), who announced it as a source of a bitter alkaloid to which he gave the name of *Margosine*, but which he obtained only in minute quantity as a "*double salt of Margosine and Soda*," in long white needles.

From the bitter oil of the seeds he isolated a substance which he called *Margosic Acid*, and which he doubted to be capable of affording crystallizable salts. The composition neither of this acid nor of margosine is known, nor have the properties of either been investigated.

The small sample of the bark at our disposal only enables us to add that an infusion produced with perchloride of iron a blackish precipitate, and that an infusion is not altered by tannic acid or iodohydrargyrate of potassium. If the inner layers of the bark are alone exhausted with water, the liquid affords an abundant precipitate with tannic acid; but if the *entire* bark is boiled in water, the tannic matter which it contains will form an insoluble compound with the bitter principle, and prevent the latter being dissolved. It is thus evident that to isolate the bitter matter of the bark, it would be advisable to work on the liber or inner layers alone, which might readily be done, as they separate easily.

According to the recent researches of Broughton[2] the bitter principle is an amorphous resin soluble in the usual solvents and in boiling solutions of fixed alkalis. From the latter it is precipitated by acids, yet, probably, altered. Broughton ascribed the formula $C^{36}H^{50}O^{11}$ to this bitter resin purified by means of bisulphide of carbon, ether and absolute alcohol; it fused at 92° C. He obtained moreover a small quantity of a crystallized principle, which he believed to be a fatty body, yet its melting point of 175° C. is not in favour of this suggestion.

Uses—In India the bark is used as a tonic and antiperiodic, both by natives and Europeans. Dr. Pulney Andy of Madras has found the leaves beneficial in small-pox.

[1] *Indian Annals of Medical Science*, Calcutta, iv. (1857) 104.

[2] *Madras Monthly Journ. Med. Science*, quoted in *Pharm. Journ.* June 14, 1873, 992.

CORTEX SOYMIDA.

Cortex Swieteniæ; Rohun Bark.

Botanical Origin—*Soymida*[1] *febrifuga* Juss. (*Swietenia febrifuga* Willd.), a tree of considerable size not uncommon in the forests of Central and Southern India. The timber called by Europeans *Bastard Cedar* is very durable and strong, and much valued for building purposes.

History—The introduction of Rohun Bark into the medical practice of Europeans is due to Roxburgh[2] who recommended the drug as a substitute for Cinchona, after numerous trials made in India about the year 1791. At the same time he sent supplies to Edinburgh, where Duncan made it the subject of a thesis[3] which probably led to it being introduced into the materia medica of the Edinburgh Pharmacopœia of 1803, and of the Dublin Pharmacopœia of 1807.

Though thus officially recognized, it does not appear that the bark came much into use or by any other means fulfilled the expectations raised in its favour. At present it is regarded simply as a useful astringent tonic, and as such it has a place in the *Pharmacopœia of India* (1868).

Description—Our specimen of Rohun bark[4] which is from a young tree, is in straight or somewhat curved, half-tubular quills, an inch or more in diameter and about ⅛ of an inch in thickness. Externally it is of a rusty grey or brown, with a smoothish surface exhibiting no considerable furrows or cracks, but numerous small corky warts. These form little elliptic scars or rings, brown in the centre and but slightly raised from the surface. The inner side and edges of the quills are of a bright reddish colour.

A transverse section exhibits a thin outer layer coloured by chlorophyll, and a middle layer of a bright rusty hue, traversed by large medullary rays and darker wedge-shaped rays of liber. The latter has a fibrous fracture, that of the outer part of the bark being rather corky or foliaceous. The whole bark when comminuted is of a rusty colour, becoming reddish by exposure to air and moisture. It has a bitter astringent taste with no distinctive odour. The older bark frequently half an inch thick and fibrous, has a thick ragged corky layer of a rusty blackish-brown colour, deeply fissured longitudinally, and minutely cracked transversely. Old bark, according to Dymock (1877), is generally in half quills of a rich red-brown colour.

Microscopic Structure—The bark presents but few structural peculiarities. The ring of liber is made up of alternating prosenchymatous and parenchymatous tissue. In the latter the larger cells are filled with mucilage, the others with starch. The prosenchymatous groups of the liber exhibit that peculiar form we have already described as

[1] From *Sómida*, the Teluga name of the tree; *Róhan* is its name in Hindustani.—Fig. in Bentley and Trimen, *Med. Plants*, part 18 (1877).—See also C. De Candolle, in *Monogr. Phanerogamar.* i. (1878) 722.

[2] *Medical Facts and Observations*, Lond. vi. (1795) 127.

[3] *Tentamen inaugurale de Swieteniâ Soymidâ*, Edinb. 1794.

[4] Kindly sent us by Mr. Broughton of Ootacamund.

hornbast (p. 74); it chiefly contains the tannic matter, besides stellate crystals of oxalate of calcium which are distributed through the whole tissue of the bark. The medullary rays are of the usual form, and contain starch granules. The corky coat is built up of a smaller number of vaulted cells.

Chemical Composition[1]—The bitter principle of the bark has been ascertained by Broughton[2] to be a nearly colourless resinous substance, sparingly soluble in water but more so in alcohol, ether, or benzol. It does not appear to unite with acids or bases, and is less soluble in water containing them than in pure water. It has a very bitter taste, and refuses to crystallize either from benzol or ether. It contains no nitrogen. To this we may add that the bark is rich in tannic acid.

Uses—Rohun bark is administered in India as an astringent tonic and antiperiodic, and is reported useful in intermittent fevers and general debility, as well as in the advanced stages of dysentery and in diarrhœa.

RHAMNACEÆ.

FRUCTUS RHAMNI.

Baccæ Rhamni, Baccæ Spinæ cervinæ; Buckthorn Berries; F. Baies de Neprun; G. *Kreuzdornbeeren.*

Botanical Origin—*Rhamnus cathartica* L., a robust diœcious shrub with spreading branches, the smaller of which often terminate in a stout thorn. It is indigenous to Northern Africa, the greater part of Europe, and stretches eastward to the Caucasus and into Siberia. We have seen stems 50 years old, having a diameter of 8 inches, sent from the government of Cherson, Southern Russia. In England the buckthorn though generally distributed is abundant only in certain districts; in Scotland it occurs wild in but a single locality. Yet in Norway, Sweden, and Finland it grows much further north.

The fruit which ripens in the autumn is collected for use chiefly in the counties of Hertfordshire, Buckinghamshire, Oxfordshire, and also from Wiltshire. The collectors usually prefer to supply the juice as expressed by themselves.

History—The Buckthorn was well known to the Anglo-Saxons, and is mentioned as *Hartsthorn* or *Waythorn* in their medical writings and glossaries dating before the Norman conquest. The Welsh physicians of Myddfai ("Meddygon Myddvai") in the 13th century prescribed the juice of the fruit of buckthorn boiled with honey as an aperient drink.

As *Spina Cervina* the shrub is referred to by Piero de' Crescenzi of Bologna[3] about A.D. 1305.

The medicinal use of the berries was familiar to all the writers on

[1] The analysis alluded to in the *Pharm. of India* (p. 444) concerns *Khaya (Swietenia) senegalensis*, and not the present species, as my friend Dr. Overbeck has informed me.—F. A. F.

[2] Beddome, *Flora Sylvatica*, Madras, part i. (1869) 8,—also information communicated direct.

[3] *Trattato dall' Agricoltura*, Milano, 1805, 10. iii. c. 53.

botany and materia medica of the 16th century. Syrup of buckthorn first appeared in the London Pharmacopœia of 1650; it was aromatized by means of aniseed, cinnamon, mastich and nutmeg.

Description—The fruits, which are only used in the fresh state, are small, juicy, spherical drupes the size of a pea, black and shining, bearing on the summit the remnants of the style, and supported below by a slender stalk expanded into a disc-like receptacle. Before ripening the fruit is green and distinctly 4-lobed, afterwards smooth and plump. It contains 4 one-seeded nuts[1] meeting at right angles in the middle. The seed is erect with a broad furrow on the back: in transverse section the albumen and cotyledons are seen to be curved into a horse-shoe form with the ends directed outwards.

The fresh juice is green, has an acid reaction and a sweetish, afterwards disagreeably bitter taste, and repulsive odour. It is coloured dingy green by ferric chloride, yellow by alkalis, red by acids. According to Umney[2] it should have a sp. gr. of 1·070 to 1·075, but is seldom sold pure. By keeping the juice gradually turns red.

Microscopic Structure—The epidermis consists of small tabular cells, followed by a row of large cubic cells and then by several layers of tangentially-extended cells rich in chlorophyll. This thick epicarp passes into the loose thin-walled and large-celled sarocarp. Besides chlorophyll it exhibits numerous cells each containing a kind of sac, which may be squeezed out of the cell. These sacs are violet, turning blue with alkalis. Similar, yet much more conspicuous bodies occur also in the pulp of the Locust Bean (*Ceratonia Siliqua* L.).

Chemical Composition—The berries of buckthorn and other species of *Rhamnus* contain interesting colouring matters, which have been the subject of much chemical research and controversy. Winckler in 1849 extracted from the juice *Rhamnocathartin*, a yellowish uncrystallizable bitter substance, soluble in water but not in ether. Alkalis colour it golden yellow; perchloride of iron, dark greenish brown.

In 1840 Fleury, a pharmacien of Pontoise, discovered in buckthorn juice a yellow substance forming cauliflower-like crystals to which he gave the name of *Rhamnine*. This body has been recently studied by Lefort,[3] who identified it with the *Rhamnetine* of Galletly (1858) and the *Chrysorhamnine* of Schützenberger and Bertèche (1865). Though obtainable from the berries of all kinds of *Rhamnus* used in dyeing (including the common buckthorn), it is got most easily and abundantly from Persian Berries. When pure, and crystallized from absolute alcohol, it is described as forming minute yellow translucent tables. It is scarcely soluble in cold water, though colouring it pale yellow; is soluble in hot alcohol, insoluble in ether or bisulphide of carbon. It is very soluble in caustic alkalis, forming uncrystallizable reddish-yellow solutions. From alkaline solutions it is precipitated by a mineral acid in the form of a glutinous magma resembling hydrated silica. Lefort assigns to it the formula $C^{12}H^{12}O^{5} + 2H^{2}O$.

[1] In *Rh. Frangula* L., the other British species, the fruit has 2 nuts.

[2] *Pharm. Journ.* Nov. 23 (1872) 404, and July 11 (1874) 21.

[3] *Sur les graines des Nerpruns tinctoriaux.*—*Journ. de Pharm.* iv. (1866) 420.—See also the investigations of Liebermann and Hörmann, 1879.

This chemist has likewise found in the berries of *Rhamnus*, though not with certainty in those of *R. cathartica*, a neutral substance isomeric with rhamnine, to which he has given the name of *Rhamnegine*. Unlike rhamnine it is very soluble in cold water, but in all other respects it agrees with that body in chemical and physical properties. The two substances have the same taste, almost the same tint, the same crystalline form, and lastly they give rise to the same reactions with chemical agents.

The conclusions of Lefort have been contested by Stein (1868) and by Schützenberger (1868), the latter of whom succeeded in decomposing rhamnegine and proving it a glucoside having the formula $C^{24}H^{32}O^{14}$. Its decomposition gives rise to a body named *Rhamnetin*, $C^{12}H^{10}O^{5}$, and a crystallizable sugar isomeric with mannite. Schützenberger admits that the berries contain an isomeric modification of rhamnegine; but in addition another colouring matter insoluble in water, which appears to be the *Rhamnine* of Lefort, but to which he assigns a different formula, namely, $C^{18}H^{22}O^{10}$. This is also a glucoside capable of being split into rhamnetin and a sugar. There are thus, according to Schützenberger, two forms of rhamnegine which may be distinguished as α and β, and there is the substance insoluble in water, named by Lefort *Rhamnine*.

The question of the purgative principles of buckthorn, it will be observed, has not been touched by all these researches.

Uses—From the juice of the berries is prepared a syrup having strongly purgative properties, much more used as a medicine for animals than for man. The pigment *Sap Green* is also made from the juice.

AMPELIDEÆ.

UVÆ PASSÆ.

Passulæ majores; Raisins; F. *Raisins;* G. *Rosinen.*

Botanical Origin—*Vitis vinifera* L., the Common Grape-vine. It appears to be indigenous to the Caucasian provinces of Russia, that is to say, to the country lying between the eastern end of the Black Sea and the south-western shores of the Caspian; extending thence southward into Armenia. Under innumerable varieties, it is cultivated in most of the warmer and drier countries of the temperate regions of both the northern and southern hemispheres. Humboldt defines the area of the profitable culture of the vine as a zone lying between 36° and 40° of north latitude.

History—The vine is among the oldest of cultivated plants, and is mentioned in the earliest Mosaic writings. *Dried* grapes as distinguished from *fresh* were used by the ancient Hebrews, and in the Vulgate are translated *Uvæ passæ*.[1] During the middle ages, raisins were an article of luxury imported into England from Spain.

Description—The ovary of *Vitis vinifera* is 2-celled with 2 ovules in each cell; it developes into a succulent, pedicellate berry of spherical

[1] Numbers vi. 3; 1 Sam. xxv. 18, xxx. 12; 2 Sam. xvi. 1; 1 Chron. xii. 40.

or ovoid form, in which the cells are obliterated and some of the seeds generally abortive. As the fruit is not articulated with the rachis or the rachis with the branch, it does not drop at maturity but remains attached to the plant, on which, provided there is sufficient solar heat, it gradually withers and dries: such fruits are called *Raisins of the sun*. Various methods are adopted to facilitate the drying of the fruit, such as dipping the bunches in boiling water or in a lye of wood ashes, or twisting or partially severing the stalk,—the effect of each operation being to arrest or destroy the vitality of the tissues. The drying is performed by exposure to the sun, sometimes supplemented by artificial heat.

The raisins commonly found in the shops are the produce of Spain and Asia Minor, and are sold either in entire bunches or removed from the stalk. The former kind, known as *Muscatel Raisins* and imported from Malaga, are dried and packed with great care for use as a dessert fruit. The latter kind, which includes the *Valencia Raisins* of Spain, and the *Eleme*, *Chesme* and stoneless *Sultana Raisins* of Smyrna, are used for culinary purposes. For pharmacy, Valencia raisins are generally employed.

Microscopic Structure—The outer layer or skin of the berry is made up of small tabular cells loaded with a reddish granular matter, which on addition of an alcoholic solution of perchloride of iron assumes a dingy green hue. The interior parenchyme exhibits large, thin-walled, loose cells containing an abundance of crystals (bitartrate of potassium and sugar). There are also some fibro-vascular bundles traversing the tissue in no regular order.

Chemical Composition—The pulp abounds in grape sugar and cream of tartar, each of which in old raisins may be found crystallized in nodular masses; it also contains gum and malic acid. The seeds afford 15 to 18 per cent. of a bland fixed oil, which is occasionally extracted. Fitz[1] has shown that it consists of the glycerides of *Erucic Acid*, $C^{22}H^{42}O^2$, stearic acid, and palmitic acid, the first-named acid largely prevailing. The crystals of erucic acid melt at 34° C.; by means of fused potash they may be resolved into arachic acid, $C^{20}H^{40}O^2$, and acetic acid, $C^2H^4O^2$.

The seeds further contain 5 to 6 per cent. of tannic acid, which also exists in the skin of the fruit. The latter is likewise the seat of chlorophyll and other colouring matter.

Commerce—The consumption of raisins in Great Britain is very large and is increasing. The imports into the United Kingdom have been as follows:—

1870.	1871.	1872.	1876.
365,418	427,056	617,418	583,860 cwt.
val. £593,527,	val. £707,344.	val. £1,149,337.	val. £1,058,406.

Of the quantity mentioned for 1872 there were 400,570 cwt. shipped from Spain, 176,500 cwt. from Asiatic Turkey, and the remainder from other countries.[2] It is stated that Greece, in 1874, exported about $1\frac{1}{3}$

[1] *Berichte der deutsch. chem. Gesellsch. zu Berlin*, iv. (1871) 442.

[2] *Annual Statement of the Trade of the United Kingdom.*

millions of cwt., value £28,000,000; much of this was shipped to England.

Uses—Raisins are an ingredient of Compound Tincture of Cardamoms and of Tincture of Senna. They have no medicinal properties, and are only used for the sake of the saccharine matter they impart.[1]

ANACARDIACEÆ.

MASTICHE.

Mastix, Resina Mastiche; Mastich; F. *Mastic;* G. *Mastix.*

Botanical Origin—*Pistacia Lentiscus* L., the lentisk, is a diœcious evergreen, mostly found as a shrub a few feet high; but when allowed to attain its full growth, it slowly acquires the dimensions of a small tree having a dense head of foliage. It is a native of the Mediterranean shores from Syria to Spain, and is found in Portugal, Morocco and the Canaries. In some parts of Italy it is largely cut for fuel.

Mastich is collected in the northern part of the island of Scio, which was long regarded as the only region in the world capable of affording it. Experiments made in 1856 by Orphanides[2] have proved that excellent mastich might be easily obtained in other islands of the Archipelago, and probably also in Continental Greece. The same botanist remarks that the trees yielding mastich in Scio are exclusively *male*.

History—Mastich has been known from a very remote period, and is mentioned by Theophrastus,[3] who lived in the 4th century before the Christian era. Both Dioscorides and Pliny notice it as a production of the island of Chio, the modern Scio.

Avicenna[4] described (about the year 1000) two sorts of mastich, the white or Roman (i.e. *Mediterranean* or *Christian*), and the dark or Nabathæan,—the latter probably one of the Eastern forms of the drug mentioned at p. 165.

Benjamin of Tudela,[5] who visited the island of Scio when travelling to the East about A.D. 1160–1173, also refers to it yielding mastich, which in fact has always been one of its most important productions, and from the earliest times intimately connected with its history.

Mastich was prescribed in the 13th century by the Welsh "Meddygon Myddvai" as an ingredient of ointments.

In the middle ages the mastich of Scio was held as a monopoly by the Greek emperors, one of whom, Michael Paleologus in 1261, permitted the Genoese to settle in the island. His successor Andronicus II. conceded in 1304 the administration of the island to Benedetto Zaccaria, a rich patrician of Genoa and the proprietor of the alum works of Fokia

[1] The amount of this is very small. On macerating crushed raisins in proof spirit in the proportion of 2 oz. to a pint, we found each fluid ounce of the tincture so obtained to afford by evaporation to dryness 28 grains of a dark viscid sugary extract.

[2] Heldreich, *Nutzpflanzen Griechenlands*, Athen, 1862. 61.

[3] *Hist. Plant.* lib. ix. c. 1.

[4] Lib. ii. c. 462.

[5] Wright, *Early Travels in Palestine*, 1848. 77. (Bohn's series).

(the ancient Phocæa), north-west of Smyrna, for ten years, renouncing all tribute during that period. The concession was very lucrative, a large revenue being derived from the *Contrata del Mastico* or Mastich district: and the Zaccaria family, taking advantage of the weakness of the emperor, determined to hold it as long as possible. In fact they made themselves the real sovereigns of Scio and of some of the adjacent islands, and retained their position until expelled by Andronicus III. in 1329.[1]

The island was retaken by the Genoese under Simone Vignosi in 1346; and then by a remarkable series of events became the property of an association called the *Maona* (the Arabic word for subsidy or reinforcement). Many of the noblest families of Genoa enrolled themselves in this corporation and settled in the island of Scio; and in order to express the community of interest that governed their proceedings, some of them relinquished their family names and assumed the general name of *Giustiniani.*[2] This extraordinary society played a part exactly comparable to that of the late East India Company. In Genoa it had its "*Officium Chii*"; it had its own constitution and mint, and it engaged in wars with the emperors of Constantinople, the Venetians and the Turks, who in turn attacked and ravaged the mastich island and adjacent possessions.

The Giustinianis regulated very strictly the culture of the lentisk and the gathering and export of its produce, and cruelly punished all offenders. The annual export of the drug was 300 to 400 quintals,[3] which were immediately assigned to the four regions with which the Maona chiefly traded. These were *Romania* (*i.e.* Greece, Constantinople and the Crimea), *Occidente* (Italy, France, Spain and Germany), *Vera Turchia* (Asia Minor), and *Oriente* (Syria, Egypt, and Northern Africa). In 1364, a quintal was sold for 40 *lire;* in 1417, the price was fixed at 25 *lire.* In the 16th century, the whole income from the drug was 30,000 ducats (£13,750),[4] a large sum for that period.

In 1566, the Giustinianis definitively lost their beautiful island, the Turks under Piali Pasha taking it by force of arms under pretext that the customary tribute was not duly paid.[5] A few years before that event, it was visited by the French naturalist Belon [6] who testifies from

[1] Friar Jordanus who visited Scio *circa* 1330 (?) noticed the production of mastich, and also the loss of the island by Martino Zaccaria.—*Mirabilia descripta, or Wonders of the East,* edited by Col. Yule for the Hakluyt Society, 1863.

[2] Probably partly for the reason that a Palazzo Giustiniani in Genoa had become the property of the Society. In the little "Piazza Giustiniani," near the cathedral of San Lorenzo, that palace may still be seen, but there is only a large view of the island of Scio which would remind of the Maona. I was told in 1874 by Sig. Canale, the historian of Genoa, that he thought it doubtful that the *Officium Chii* had resided in the said palace.—F. A. F.

[3] An incidental notice showing the value of the trade occurs in the letter of Columbus (himself a Genoese) announcing the result of his first voyage to the Indies. In stating what may be obtained from the island of Hispaniola, he mentions—gold and spices . . and *mastich,* hitherto found only in Greece in the island of Scio, and which the Signoria sells at its own price, as much as their Highnesses [Ferdinand and Isabella] shall command to be shipped. The letter bears date 15 Feb. 1493.—*Letters of Christobal Columbus* (Hakluyt Society) 1870. p. 15.

[4] The ducat being reckoned at 9*s.* 2*d.*

[5] For further particulars respecting the history of Scio, the Maona, and the trade of the Genoese in the Levant, see Hopf in Ersch and Grubber's *Encyclopädie,* vol. 68 (Leipzig, 1859) art. *Giustiniani;* also Heyd *Colonie commerciali degli Italiani in Oriente* i. (1866).

[6] *Observations de plusieurs singularitez et choses mémorables trouveés en Grèce,* etc. Paris, 1554. liv. ii. ch. 8. p. 836.

personal observation to the great care with which the lentisk was cultivated by the inhabitants.

When Tournefort[1] was at Scio in 1701, all the lentisk trees on the island were held to be the property of the Grand Signor, and if any land was sold, the sale did not include the lentisks that might be growing on it. At that time the mastich villages, about twenty in number, were required to pay 286 chests of mastich annually to the Turkish officers appointed to receive the revenue.

In the beginning of the present century, when Olivier[2] paid a visit to the island of Chios, he found 50,000 occhе (one occa=2·82 lb. avdp. = 1·28 kilogrammes) or somewhat more to be the annual harvest of mastich.

The month of January, 1850, was memorable throughout Greece and the Archipelago for a frost of unparalleled severity which proved very destructive to the mastich trees of Scio, and occasioned a scarcity of the drug that lasted for many years.[3]

The foregoing statements show that for centuries past Scio or Chios was famed for this resin; there are however a few evidences proving that at least a little mastich used also to be collected in other islands. Amari[4] quoted an Arabic geographer of the 12th century speaking of "*il mastice di Pantellaria cavato da' lentischi e lo storace odorifero.*" Pantellaria, Kossura of the ancients, is the small volcanic island southwest of Sicily, not far from Tunis. In a list enumerating the drugs to be met with in 1582 in the fair of Frankfurt[5] we find even mastich of *Cyprus* quoted as superior to the common. Cyprian mastich again occurs in the pharmaceutical tariffs of 1612 and 1669 of the same city, and in many others of that time.[6]

The disuse into which mastich has fallen makes it difficult to understand its ancient importance; but a glance at the pharmacopœias of the 15th, 16th, and 17th centuries shows that it was an ingredient of a large number of compound medicines.[7]

Secretion—In the bark of the stems and branches of the mastich shrub, there are resin-ducts like those in the aromatic roots of *Umbelliferæ* or *Compositæ*. In *Pistacia* they may even be shown in the petioles. The wood is devoid of resin,[8] so that slight incisions are sufficient to provoke the resinous exudation, the bark being not very thick, and liable to scale off.

Collection—In Scio incisions are made about the middle of June in the bark of the stems and principal branches. From these incisions which are vertical and very close together, the resin speedily flows, and

[1] *Voyage into the Levant*, i. (1718) 285.

[2] *Voyage dans l'Empire Othoman et la Perse*, ii. (Paris, 1801) 132–136.

[3] At Athens the mercury was for a short time at —10° C. (14° F.) In Scio, where the frost was probably quite as severe, though we have no exact data, the mischief to the lentisks varied with the locality, trees exposed to the north or growing at considerable elevations, being killed down to the base of the trunk, while those in more favoured positions suffered destruction only in some of their branches.

[4] *Storia dei Musulmani di Sicilia*, iii. (1872) 787.

[5] Flückiger, *Documente zur Geschichte der Pharmacie*, Halle, 1876. 31.

[6] *Ibid.* 41. 65.

[7] Thus in the *London Pharmacopœia* of 1632, mastich enters into 24 of the 37 different kinds of pill, besides which it is prescribed in troches and ointments.

[8] See Unger and Kotschy, *Die Insel Cypern*, Wien, 1865. 424.

soon hardens and dries. After 15 to 20 days it is collected with much care in little baskets lined with white paper or clean cotton wool. The ground below the trees is kept hard and clean, and flat pieces of stone are often laid on it that the droppings of resin may be saved uninjured by dirt. There is also some spontaneous exudation from the small branches which is of very fine quality. The operations are carried on by women and children and last for a couple of months. A fine tree may yield as much as 8 to 10 pounds of mastich.

The dealers in Scio distinguish three or four qualities of the drug, of which the two finer are called *κυλιστὸ* and *φλισκάρι*, that collected from the ground *πῆττα*, and the worst of all *φλοῦδα*.[1]

Description—The best sort of mastich consists of roundish tears about the size of small peas, together with pieces of an oblong or pear-shaped form. They are of a pale yellow or slightly greenish tint darkening by age, dusty and slightly opaque on the surface but perfectly transparent within. The mastich of late imported has been washed; the tears are no longer dusty, but have a glassy transparent appearance. Mastich is brittle, has a conchoidal fracture, a slight terebinthinous balsamic odour. It speedily softens in the mouth, and may be easily masticated and kneaded between the teeth, in this respect differing from sandarac, a tear of which breaks to powder when bitten.

Inferior mastich is less transparent, and consists of masses of larger size and less regular shape, often contaminated with earthy and vegetable impurities.

The sp. gr. of selected tears of mastich is about 1·06. They soften at 99° C. but do not melt below 108°.

Mastich dissolves in half its weight of pure warm acetone and then deviates the ray of polarized light to the right. On cooling, the solution becomes turbid. It dissolves slowly in 5 parts of oil of cloves, forming even in the cold a clear solution; it is but little soluble in glacial acetic acid or in benzol.

Chemical Composition—Mastich is soluble to the extent of about 90 per cent in cold alcohol; the residue, which has been termed *Masticin* or *Beta-resin of Mastich*, is a translucent, colourless, tough substance, insoluble in boiling alcohol or in solution of caustic alkali, but dissolving in ether or oil of turpentine. According to Johnston, it is somewhat less rich in oxygen than the following.

The soluble portion of mastich, called *Alpha resin of Mastich*, possesses acid properties, and like many other resins has the formula $C^{20}H^{32}O^{2}$. Hartsen[2] asserts that it can be obtained in crystals. Its alcoholic solution is precipitated by an alcoholic solution of neutral acetate of lead. Mastich contains a very little volatile oil.

Commerce—Mastich still forms the principal revenue of Scio, from which island the export in 1871 was 28,000 lb. of *picked*, and 42,000 lb. of *common*. The market price of picked mastich was equal to 6*s.* 10*d.* per lb.—that of common 2*s.* 10*d.* The superior quality is sent to Turkey, especially Constantinople, also to Trieste, Vienna, and Mar-

[1] Heldreich (and Orphanides) *Nutzpflanzen Griechenlands*, Athen, 1862, 60.

[2] *Berichte der deutschen chem. Gesellsch.* 1876. 316.

seilles, and a small quantity to England. The common sort is employed in the East in the manufacture of *raki* and other cordials.[1]

Uses—Mastich is not now regarded as possessing any important therapeutic virtues, and as a medicine is becoming obsolete. Even in varnish making it is no longer employed as formerly, its place being well supplied by less costly resins, such for example as dammar.

Varieties—There is found in the Indian bazaars a kind of mastich which though called *Mustagi-rúmí* (Roman mastich), is not imported from Europe but from Kábul, and is the produce of *Pistacia Khinjuk* Stocks, and the so-called *P. cabulica* St. trees growing all over Sind, Belúchistan and Kabul.[2] This drug, of which the better qualities closely approximate to the mastich of Scio, sometimes appears in the European market under the name of *East Indian* or *Bombay Mastich*. We find that when dissolved in half its weight of acetone or benzol, it deviates the ray of light to the right.

The solid resin of the Algerian form of *P. Terebinthus* L., known as *P. atlantica* Desf., is collected and used as mastich by the Arab tribes of Northern Africa.[3]

TEREBINTHINA CHIA

Terebinthina Cypria; Chian or Cyprian Turpentine; F. *Térébenthine ou Baume de Chio ou de Chypres;* G. *Chios Terpenthin, Cyprischer Terpenthin.*

Botanical Origin—*Pistacia Terebinthus* L. (*P. atlantica* Desf., *P. palæstina* Boiss., *P. cabulica* Stocks), a tree 20 to 40 feet or more in height, in some countries only a shrub, common on the islands and shores of the Mediterranean as well as throughout Asia Minor, extending, as *P. palæstina*, to Syria and Palestine; and eastward, as *P. cabulica*, to Belúchistan and Afghanistan. It is found under the form called *P. atlantica* in Northern Africa, where it grows to a large size, and in the Canary Islands.

These several forms are mostly regarded as so many distinct species; but after due consideration and the examination of a large number of specimens both dried and living, we have arrived at the conclusion that they may fairly be united under a single specific name. The extreme varieties certainly present great differences of habit, as anyone would observe who had compared *Pistacia Terebinthus* as the straggling bush which it is in Languedoc and Provence, with the noble umbrageous tree it forms in the neighbourhood of Smyrna. But the different types are united by so many connecting links, that we have felt warranted in dissenting from the opinion usually held respecting them.

On the branches of Pistacia Terebinthus, a kind of galls is produced, which we shall briefly notice in our article Gallae halepenses.

[1] Consul Cumberbatch, *Report on Trade of Smyrna* for 1871.—*Raki*, derived from the Turkish word *sáqiz*, for mastich, which, strange to say, would appear to have its home on the Baltic. In the vocabularies of the Old-Prussian idiom "sachis" is found meaning resin.—Blau, *Zeitschrift der Deutschen Morgenl. Gesellsch*, xxix. 582.

[2] Powell, *Economic Products of the Punjab*, Roorkee, 1868. 411.

[3] Guibourt, *Hist. d. Drog.* iii. (1850) 458; Armieux, *Topographie médicale du Sahara*, Paris, 1866. 58.

History—The terebinth was well known to the ancients; it is the τέρμινθος of Theophrastus, τερέβινθος of other authors, and the *Alah* of the Old Testament.[1] Among its products, the kernels were regarded by Dioscorides as unwholesome, though agreeable in taste. By pressing them, the original *Oil of Turpentine*, τερεβίνθινον ἔλαιον, a mixture of essential and fat oil was obtained, as it is in the East to the present day. The resinous juice of the stem and branches, the true, primitive turpentine, ῥητίνη τερμινθίνη, was celebrated as the finest of all analogous products, and preferred both to mastich and the pinic resins. To the latter however the name of turpentine was finally applied.[2]

Collection—The resinous juice is secreted in the bark, according to Unger,[3] and Marchand,[4] in special cells precisely as mastich in *P. Lentiscus*. That found in commerce is collected in the island of Scio. To some extent it exudes spontaneously, yet in greater abundance after incisions made in the stems and branches. This is done in spring, and the resin continues to flow during the whole summer; but the quantity is so small that not more that 10 or 11 ounces are obtained from a large tree in the course of a year. The turpentine, hardened by the coolness of the night, is scraped from the stem down which it has flowed, or from flat stones placed at the foot of the tree to receive it. As it is, when thus collected, always mixed with foreign substances, it is purified to some extent by straining through small baskets, after having been liquefied by exposure to the sun.

When Tournefort[5] visited Scio in 1701, the island was said to produce scarcely 300 okes or ocche (one occa = 2·82 lb. avdp.); a century later Olivier[6] stated, that the turpentine was becoming very scarce, 200 ocche only, or even less, being the annual yield. It was then carefully collected by means of little earthen vessels tied to the incised stems. The trade is asserted to be now almost exclusively in the hands of the Jews, who dispose of the drug in the interior part of the Turkish Empire.[7]

Description—A specimen collected by Maltass near Smyrna in 1858 was, after ten years, of a light yellowish colour, scarcely fluid though perfectly transparent, nearly of the odour of melted colophony or mastich, and without much taste. We found it readily soluble in spirit of wine, amylic alcohol, glacial acetic acid, benzol, or acetone, the solution in each case being very slightly fluorescent. The alcoholic solution reddens litmus, and is neither bitter nor acrid. Two parts of this genuine turpentine dissolved in one of acetone deviate a ray of polarized light 7° to the right[8] in a column 50 mm. long.

Chian turpentine as found in commerce and believed to be genuine, is a soft solid, becoming brittle by exposure to the air; viewed in mass it appears opaque and of a dull brown hue. If pressed while warm

[1] Genesis xii. 6, where the word is rendered in our version *plain*.

[2] Further historical information on the Terebinth may be found in Hehn's *Kulturpflanzen und Hausthiere*, Berlin, 1877. 336.

[3] Unger u. Kotschy, *die Insel Cypern*, 1865. 361. 424.

[4] *Revision du groupe des Anacardiacées*. Paris, 1869. 150. Plate iii. shows the resiniferous ducts of a branch two years old.

[5] *Voyage into the Levant*, i. (1718) 287.

[6] *Voy. dans l'Empire Othoman*, etc., ii. (1801) 136.

[7] Maltass, *Pharm. Journ.* xvii. (1856) 540.

[8] A solution of mastich made in the same proportion deviates 3° to the right.

between two slips of glass, it is seen to be transparent, of a yellowish brown, and much contaminated by various impurities in a state of fine division. It has an agreeable, mild terebinthinous odour and very little taste. The whitish powder with which old Chian turpentine becomes covered, shows no trace of crystalline structure when examined under the microscope.

Chemical Composition—Chian turpentine consists of resin and essential oil. The former is probably identical with the *Alpha-resin* of mastich. The *Beta-resin* or *Masticin* appears to be absent, for we find that Chian turpentine deprived of its essential oil by a gentle heat, dissolves entirely (impurities excepted) in alcohol sp. gr. 0·815, which is by no means the case with mastich.

The essential oil which we obtained by distilling with water 64 ounces of Chian turpentine of authentic origin, amounted to nearly 14½ per cent. It has the odour of the drug; sp. gr. 0·869; boiling point 161° C.; it deviates the ray of polarized light 12·1° to the right. In common with turpentine oils of the *Coniferæ*, it contains a small amount of an oxygenated oil, and is therefore vividly attacked by sodium. When this reaction is over and the oil is again distilled, it boils at 157° C. and has a sp. gr. of 0·862. It has now a more agreeable odour, resembling a mixture of cajuput, mace, and camphor, and nearly the same rotatory power (11·5° to the right). By saturation with dry hydrochloric acid, it yields a solid compound after some weeks. After treatment with sodium and rectification, the oil was found[1] to consist of C 88·75, H 11·40 per cent., which is the composition of oil of turpentine.

Uses—Chian Turpentine appears to have exactly the properties of the pinic turpentines; in British medicine it is almost obsolete. In Greece it is sometimes added to wine or used to flavour cordials, in the same manner as turpentine of the pine, or mastich.

GALLÆ CHINENSES SEU JAPONICÆ.

Botanical Origin—The plant which bears this important kind of gall, is *Rhus semialata* Murray (*Rh. Bucki-amela* Roxb.), a tree attaining 30 to 40 feet, common in Northern India, China and Japan, ascending in the outer Himalaya and the Kasia hills to elevations of 2,500 to 6,000 feet.[2]

History—In China these galls are probably known and used both medicinally and in dyeing since very long; they are mentioned in the herbal Puntsaou, written in the middle of the 16th century. They also occur in Cleyer's "Specimen medicinæ sinicæ," Frankfort, 1682, No. 225, under the name *u poi çu*.[3] Kämpfer[4] also mentions a tree "Baibokf, vulgo Fusi," growing on the hills, the pinnate leaves of which he found often provided with an excrescence: "'Επίφυσι foliorum informi, tuberosa, multiplici, tenui, dura, cava, Gallæ nostratis usu praestante." No

[1] From analysis performed in my laboratory by Dr. Kraushaar.—F. A. F.

[2] Wight, *Icones Plantar. Indiæ orientalis*, ii. (Madras, 1843) tab. 561, gives a good figure.

[3] Hanbury, *Science Papers*, 266.

[4] *Amœnitates exoticæ*, 1712. 895.

doubt this refers to the galls under notice; they began to be imported into Europe about 1724, and are noticed by Geoffroy[1] as *Oreilles des Indes*, but they seem to have soon disappeared from the market. Pereira directed attention to them in 1844, since which time they have formed a regular and abundant article of import both from China and Japan.

Formation—Chinese galls are vesicular protuberances formed on the leafstalks and branches of the above-mentioned tree, by the puncture of an insect, identified and figured by Doubleday[2] as a species of *Aphis*, and subsequently named provisionally by Jacob Bell[3] *A. chinensis*. We have no account by any competent observer of their growth; and as to their development, we can only imagine it from the analogous productions seen in Europe. According to Doubleday, it is probable that the female aphis punctures the upper surface of a leaf (more probably *leafstalk*), the result of the wound being the growth of a hollow expansion in the vegetable tissue. Of this cavity the creature takes possession and brings forth a progeny which lives by puncturing the inner surface of their home, thus much increasing the tendency to a morbid expansion of the soft growing tissue in an outward direction. Meanwhile the neck of the sac-like gall thickens, the aperture contracts and finally closes, imprisoning all the inmates. Here they live and multiply until, as in the case of the pistacia gall of Europe, the sac ruptures and allows of their escape. This, we may imagine, takes place at the period when, after some generations all wingless and perhaps all female (for the female aphis produces for several generations without impregnation), a winged generation is brought forth of both sexes. These may then fly to other spots, and deposit eggs for a further propagation of their race.

The galls are collected when their green colour is changing into yellow; they are then scalded.[4]

Description—The galls are light and hollow, varying in length from 1 to 2½ inches, and of extremely diverse and irregular form. The simplest are somewhat egg-shaped, the smaller end being attached to the leafstalk; but the form is rarely so regular, and more often the body of the gall is distorted by numerous knobby or horn-like protuberances or branches; or the gall consists of several lobes uniting in their lower part and gradually attenuated to the point by which the excrescence is attached to the leaf.[5] But though the form is thus variable, the structure of these bodies is very characteristic. They are striated towards the base, and completely covered on other parts with a thick, velvety, grey down, which rubbed off on the prominences, displays the reddish-brown colour of the shell itself. The latter is

[1] *Mém. de l'Académie royale des Sciences*, Paris, 1724. 324.—Also Du Halde, *Description de l'Empire de la Chine*, iii. (La Haye, 1736) 615—625. "Des Ou Poey tsé." The author quotes numerous medicinal applications for these galls.

[2] *Pharm. Journ.* vii. (1848) 310.

[3] *Ibid.* x. (1851) 128.

[4] Stanisl. Julien et P. Champion, *Industries anc. et modernes de l'Empire chinois*, 1869. 95.

[5] We have once met with galls imported from Shanghai which differed from ordinary Chinese galls in not being horned, but all of an elongated ovoid form, often pointed at the upper end, and having moreover a strong *cheesy* smell. They may be derived from *Distylium racemosum* S. et Z., though they do not perfectly accord with the depressed pear-shaped forms figured by Siebold and Zuccarini (*Flora Japonica*, tab. 94).

$\frac{1}{10}$ to $\frac{1}{20}$ of an inch in thickness, translucent and horny, but brittle with a smooth and shining fracture. It is rather smoother on the inner surface and of lighter colour than on the outer.

The galls when broken are generally found to contain a white, downy-looking substance, together with the minute, dried-up bodies of the killed insect.[1]

The drug as imported from Japan is usually a little smaller and paler; it mostly fetches a better price in the market.

Microscopic Structure—The tissue of the galls is made up of thin-walled, large cells irregularly traversed by small vascular bundles and laticiferous vessels. The latter are mostly not branched. The parenchyme is loaded with lumps of tannic matter and starch, the latter having mostly lost by the treatment with boiling water its granular appearance. The epidermis of the galls is covered with little tapering hairs, consisting each of 1-5 cells, to which is due the velvety down of the drug.

Chemical Composition—Chinese or Japanese galls contain about 70 per cent. of a tannic acid, which has been first shown by Stein in 1849 to be identical with that derived from oak galls (see Gallæ halepenses), the so-called *gallotannic* or common tannic acid.[2] It is remarkable that this substance, which is by no means widely distributed, is also present in *Rhus coriaria*, a species indigenous in the Mediterranean region. Its leaves and shoots are the well-known dyeing and tanning material *Sumach*.

Stein, however, pointed out at the same time, that in Chinese galls gallotannic acid is accompanied by a small amount, about 4 per cent., of a different tannic matter.

Commerce—At present the supplies arrive chiefly from Hankow, from which great trading city the export, in 1872, was no less than 30,949 peculs, equal to 36,844 cwt.; 21,611 peculs, value 136,214 taels (one tael about 6s.) in 1874. In 1877 all China exported not more than 17,515 peculs. A little is also shipped from Canton and Ningpo.[3] The quantity imported from China into the United Kingdom in 1872 was 8621 cwts., valued at £20,098. In the China trade returns, the drug is always miscalled "Nut galls," or "gallnuts." Only those called "Wu-pei-tze" are the galls under examination. There are also oak-galls exported from China resembling those from Western Asia. Japanese galls, "Kifushi," are shipped in increasing quantities at Hiogo.[4]

Uses—The galls under notice are employed chiefly in Germany, for the manufacture of tannic acid, gallic acid, and pyrogallol.

[1] See also Schenk, in Buchner's *Repertorium für Pharm.* v. (1850) 26–27, or short abstract of that paper in the *Jahresbericht* of Wiggers, 1850. 48.

[2] See also Stenhouse, *Proceedings of the Royal Society* xi. (1862) 402.

[3] *Returns of Trade at the Treaty Ports of China*, for 1872. 154; for 1874.

[4] Matsugata, *Le Japon à l'Exposition universelle* (Paris, 1878) 116. 146.

LEGUMINOSÆ.

HERBA SCOPARII.

Cacumina vel Summitates Scoparii ; Broom Tops ; F. Genêt à balais; G. Besenginster, Pfriemenkraut.

Botanical Origin—*Cytisus Scoparius* Link (*Spartium Scoparium* L., *Sarothamnus vulgaris* Wimmer), the Common Broom, a woody shrub, 3 to 6 feet high, grows gregariously in sandy thickets and uncultivated places throughout Great Britain, and Western and temperate Northern Europe. In continental Europe it is plentiful in the valley of the Rhine up to the Swiss frontier, in Southern Germany and in Silesia, but does not ascend the Alps, and is absent from many parts of Central and Eastern Europe, Polonia for instance. According to Ledebour, it is found in Central and Southern Russia and on the eastern side of the Ural Mountains. In Southern Europe its place is supplied by other species.

History—From the fact that this plant is chiefly a native of Western, Northern and Central Europe, it is improbable that the classical authors were acquainted with it; and for the same reason the remarks of the early Italian writers may not always apply to the species under notice. With this reservation, we may state that broom under the name *Genista, Genesta*, or *Genestra* is mentioned in the earliest printed herbals, as that of Passau,[1] 1485, the *Hortus Sanitatis*, 1491, the *Great Herbal* printed at Southwark in 1526, and others. It is likewise the Genista as figured and described by the German botanists and pharmacologists of the 16th century, like Brunfels, Fuchs, Tragus, Valerius Cordus ("Genista angulosa") and others. Broom was used in ancient Anglo-Saxon medicine[2] as well as in the Welsh "Meddygon Myddvai." It had a place in the London Pharmacopœia of 1618, and has been included in nearly every subsequent edition. Hieronymus Brunschwyg gives[3] directions for distilling a water from the flowers, "*flores genestæ*"—a medicine which Gerarde relates was used by King Henry VIII. "against surfets and diseases thereof arising."

Broom was the emblem of those of the Norman sovereigns of England descended from Geoffry the "Handsome," or "*Plantagenet*," count of Anjou (*obiit* A.D. 1150), who was in the habit of wearing the common broom of his country, the "*planta genista*," in his helmet.

Description—The Common Broom has numerous straight ascending wiry branches, sharply 5-angled and devoid of spines. The leaves, of which the largest are barely an inch long, consist of 3 obovate leaflets on a petiole of their own length. Towards the extremities of the twigs, the leaves are much scattered and generally reduced to a single ovate leaflet, nearly sessile. The leaves when young are clothed on both sides with long reddish hairs; these under the microscope are seen each to

[1] *Herbarius, Patavie* 1485.
[2] Cockayne *Leechdoms*, &c., iii. (1866) 316.
[3] *De arte distillandi*, first edition 1500, Argentorati, cap. xv.

consist of a simple cylindrical thin-walled cell, the surface of which is beset with numerous extremely small protuberances.

The large, bright yellow, odorous flowers, which become brown in drying, are mostly solitary in the axils of the leaves; they have a persistent campanulate calyx divided into two lips minutely toothed, and a long subulate style, curved round on itself. The legume is oblong compressed, $1\frac{1}{2}$ to 2 inches long by about $\frac{1}{2}$ an inch wide, fringed with hairs along the edge. It contains 10 to 12 olive-coloured albuminous seeds, the funicle of which is expanded into a large fleshy strophiole. They have a bitterish taste, and are devoid of starch.

The portion of the plant used in pharmacy is the younger herbaceous branches, which are required both fresh and dried. In the former state they emit when bruised a peculiar odour which is lost in drying. They have a nauseous bitter taste.

Chemical Composition—Stenhouse[1] discovered in broom tops two interesting principles, *Scoparin*, $C^{21}H^{22}O^{10}$, an indifferent or somewhat acid body, and the alkaloid *Sparteine*, $C^{15}H^{26}N^{2}$, the first soluble in water or spirit and crystallizing in yellowish tufts, the second a colourless oily liquid heavier than water and sparingly soluble in it, boiling at 288° C.

To obtain scoparin, a watery decoction of the plant is concentrated so as to form a jelly after standing for a day or two. This is then washed with a small quantity of cold water, dissolved in hot water and again allowed to repose. By repeating this treatment with the addition of a little hydrochloric acid, the chlorophyll may at length be separated and the scoparin obtained as a gelatinous mass, which dries as an amorphous, brittle, pale yellow, neutral substance, devoid of taste and smell. Its solution in hot alcohol deposits it partly in crystals and partly as jelly, which after drying are alike in composition. Hlasiwetz showed (1866) that scoparin when melted with potash is resolved, like kino or quercetin, into *Phloroglucin*, $C^{6}H^{6}O^{3}$, and *Protocatechuic Acid*, $2\ C^{7}H^{6}O^{4}$.

The acid mother-liquors from which scoparin has been obtained when concentrated and distilled with soda, yield besides ammonia a very bitter oily liquid, *Sparteine*. To obtain it pure, it requires to be repeatedly rectified, dried by chloride of calcium, and distilled in a current of dry carbonic acid. It is colourless, but becomes brown by exposure to light; it has at first an odour of aniline, but this is altered by rectification. Sparteine has a decidedly alkaline reaction and readily neutralizes acids, forming crystallizable salts which are extremely bitter. Conine, nicotine, and sparteine are the only volatile alkaloids devoid of oxygen hitherto known to exist in the vegetable kingdom.

Mills[2] extracted sparteine simply by acidulated water which he concentrated and then distilled with soda. The distillate was then saturated with hydrochloric acid, evaporated to dryness, and submitted to distillation with potash. The oily sparteine thus obtained was dried by prolonged heating with sodium in a current of hydrogen, and finally rectified *per se*. Mills succeeded in replacing one or two equivalents of the hydrogen of sparteine by one or two of $C^{2}H^{5}$ (ethyl). From 150 lb.

1 *Phil. Trans.* 1851. 422–431.

2 *Journ. of Chem. Soc.* xv. (1862) 1.; Gmelin's *Chem.* xvi. (1864) 282.

of the (dried?) plant, he obtained 22 cubic centimetres (f℥vj.) of sparteine, which we may estimate as equivalent to about ½ per mille.

Stenhouse ascertained that the amount of sparteine and scoparin depends much on external conditions, broom grown in the shade yielding less than that produced in open sunny places. He states that shepherds are well aware of the shrub possessing narcotic properties, from having observed their sheep to become stupified and excited when occasionally compelled to eat it.

The experiments of Reinsch (1846) tend to show that broom contains a bitter crystallizible principle in addition to the foregoing. The seeds of the allied *Cytisus Laburnum* L. afford two highly poisonous alkaloids, *Cytisine* and *Laburnine*, discovered by A. Husemann and Marmé in 1865.

Uses—A decoction of broom tops, made from the dried herb, is used as a diuretic and purgative. The juice of the fresh plant, preserved by the addition of alcohol, is also administered and is regarded as a very efficient preparation.

SEMEN FŒNI GRÆCI.

Semen Fœnugræci; Fenugreek; F. *Semences de Fenugrec;* G. *Bockshornsamen.*

Botanical Origin—*Trigonella Fœnum græcum* L., an erect, subglabrous, annual plant, 1 to 2 feet high, with solitary, subsessile, whitish flowers; indigenous to the countries surrounding the Mediterranean, in which it has been long cultivated, and whence it appears to have spread to India.

History—In the old Egyptian preparation *Kyphi*, an ingredient "Sebes or Sebtu" is mentioned, which is thought by Ebers to mean fenugreek. This plant was well known to the Roman writers on husbandry, as Porcius Cato (B.C. 234–149) who calls it *Fœnum Græcum* and directs it to be sown as fodder for oxen. It is the τῆλις of Dioscorides and other Greek writers. Its mucilaginous seeds, "siliquæ" of the Roman peasants, were valued as an aliment and condiment for man, and as such are still largely consumed in the East. They were likewise supposed to possess many medicinal virtues, and had a place in the pharmacopœias of the last century.

The cultivation of fenugreek in Central Europe was encouraged by Charlemagne (A.D. 812), and the plant was grown in English gardens in the 16th century.

Description—The fenugreek plant has a sickle-shaped pod, 3 to 4 inches long, containing 10 to 20 hard, brownish-yellow seeds, having the smell and taste which is characteristic of peas and beans, with addition of a cumarin- or melilot-flavour.

The seeds are about ⅛ of an inch long, with a rhomboid outline, often shrivelled and distorted; they are somewhat compressed, with the hilum on the sharper edge, and a deep furrow running from it and almost dividing the seed into two unequal lobes. When the seed is macerated in warm water, its structure becomes easily visible. The testa bursts by the swelling of the internal membrane or endopleura, which like a thick gelatinous sac encloses the cotyledons and their very large hooked radicle.

Microscopic Structure—The most interesting structural peculiarity of this seed arises from the fact that the mucilage with which it abounds is not yielded by the cells of the epidermis, but by a loose tissue closely surrounding the embryo.[1]

Chemical Composition—The cells of the testa contain tannin; the cotyledons a yellow colouring matter, but no sugar. The air-dried seeds give off 10 per cent. of water at 100° C., and on subsequent incineration leave 7 per cent. of ash, of which nearly a fourth is phosphoric acid.

Ether extracts from the pulverized seeds 6 per cent. of a fœtid, fatty oil, having a bitter taste. Amylic alcohol removes in addition a small quantity of resin. Alcohol added to a concentrated aqueous extract, forms a precipitate of mucilage, amounting when dried to 28 per cent. Burnt with soda-lime, the seeds yielded to Jahns[2] 3·4 per cent. of nitrogen, equivalent to 22 per cent. of albumin. No researches have been yet made to determine the nature of the odorous principle.

Production and Commerce—Fenugreek is cultivated in Morocco, in the south of France near Montpellier, in a few places in Switzerland, in Alsace, and in some other provinces of the German and Austrian empires, as Thuringia and Moravia. It is produced on a far larger scale in Egypt, where it is known by the Arabic name *Hulba*, and whence it is exported to Europe and India. In 1873 it was stated that the profits of the European growers were much reduced by the seed being largely exported from Mogador and Bombay.

Under the Sanscrit name of *Methi*, which has passed, slightly modified, into several of the modern Indian languages, fenugreek is much grown in the plains of India during the cool season. In the year 1872-73, the quantity of seed exported from Sind to Bombay was 13,646 cwt., valued at £4,405.[3] From the port of Bombay there were shipped in the same year 9,655 cwt., of which only 100 cwt. are reported as for the United Kingdom.[4]

Uses—In Europe fenugreek as a medicine is obsolete, but the powdered seeds are still often sold by chemists for veterinary pharmacy and as an ingredient of curry powder. The chief consumption is, however, in the so-called *Cattle Foods*.

The fresh plant in India is commonly eaten as a green vegetable, while the seeds are extensively used by the natives in food and medicine.

[1] Figured by Lanessan in his French translation of the *Pharmacographia*, i. (1878) 345.

[2] Experiments performed in my laboratory in 1867.—F. A. F.

[3] *Annual Statement of the Trade and Navigation of Sind*, for the year 1872-73, printed at Karachi, 1873. p. 36.

[4] *Annual Statement*, etc., Bombay, 1873. 89.

TRAGACANTHA.

Gummi Tragacantha; Tragacanth, Gum Tragacanth; F. Gomme Adragante; G. Traganth.

Botanical Origin.—Tragacanth is the gummy exudation from the stem of several pieces of *Astragalus*, belonging to the sub-genus *Tragacantha*. The plants of this group are low perennial shrubs, remarkable for their leaves having a strong, persistent, spiny petiole. As the leaves and shoots are very numerous and regular, many of the species have the singular aspect of thorny hemispherical cushions, lying close on the ground; while others, which are those furnishing the gum, grow erect with a naked woody stem, and somewhat resemble furze bushes.

A few species occur in South-western Europe, others are found in Greece and Turkey; but the largest number are inhabitants of the mountainous regions of Asia Minor, Syria, Armenia, Kurdistan and Persia. The tragacanth of commerce is produced in the last-named countries, and chiefly, though not exclusively, by the following species[1]:—

1. *Astragalus adscendens* Boiss. et Hausskr., a shrub attaining 4 feet in height, native, of the mountains of South-western Persia at an altitude of 9,000 to 10,000 feet. According to Haussknecht, it affords an abundance of gum.

2. *A. leiocIados* Boiss.

3. *A. brachycalyx* Fisch., a shrub of 3 feet high, growing on the mountains of Persian Kurdistan, likewise affords tragacanth.

4. *A. gummifer* Labill., a small shrub of wide distribution occurring on the Lebanon and Mount Hermon in Syria, the Beryt Dagh in Cataonia, the Arjish Dagh (Mount Argæus) near Kaisariyeh in Central Asia Minor, and in Armenia and Northern Kurdistan.

5. *A. microcephalus* Willd., like the preceding a widely distributed species, extending from the south-west of Asia Minor to the north-east coast, and to Turkish and Russian Armenia. A specimen of this plant with incisions in the stem, was sent some years ago to the Pharmaceutical Society by Mr. Maltass of Smyrna. We received a large example of the same species, the stem of which is marked by old incisions, from the Rev. W. A. Farnsworth of Kaisariyeh, who states that tragacanth is collected from it on Mount Argæus.

6. *A. pycnocladus* Boiss. et Haussk., nearly related to *A. microcephalus*; it was discovered on the high mountains of Avroman and Shahu in Persia by Professor Haussknecht, who states that it exudes tragacanth in abundance.

7. *A. stromatodes* Bunge, growing at an elevation of 5,000 feet on the Akker Dagh range, near Marash in Northern Syria.

8. *A. kurdicus* Boiss., a shrub 3 to 4 feet high, native of the mountains of Cilicia and Cappadocia, extending thence to Kurdistan.

[1] As described in Boissier's *Flora Orientalis*, ii. (1872). We have to thank Professor Haussknecht of Weimar for revising our list of species, and for some valuable information as to the localities in which the drug is produced.

Haussknecht has informed us that from this and the last-named species, the so-called *Aintab Tragacanth* is chiefly obtained.

Probably the drug is also to some extent collected from

9. *A. verus* Olivier, in North-western Persia and Asia Minor.

Lastly as to Greece, tragacanth is also afforded by

10. *A. Parnassi* Boiss., var. *cyllenea*, a small shrub found in abundance on the northern mountains of the Morea, which is stated by Heldreich[1] to be the almost exclusive source of the tragacanth collected about Vostizza and Patras.

History—Tragacanth has been known from a very early period. Theophrastus in the 3rd century B.C. mentioned Crete, the Peloponnesus and Media as its native countries. Dioscorides, who as a native of South-eastern Asia Minor was probably familiar with the plant, describes it correctly as a low spiny bush. The drug is mentioned by the Greek physicians Oribasius, Aëtius, and Paulus Ægineta (4th to 7th cent.), and by many of the Arabian writers on medicine. The abbreviated form of its name "Dragantum" already occurs in the book "Artis veterinariæ, seu mulomedicinæ" of Vegetius Renatus, who lived about A.D. 400. During the middle ages the gum was imported into Europe through the trading cities of Italy, as shown in the statutes of Pisa,[2] A.D. 1305, where it is mentioned as liable to impost.

Pierre Belon, the celebrated French naturalist and traveller, saw and described, about 1550, the collecting of tragacanth in the northern part of Asia Minor; and Tournefort in 1700 observed on Mount Ida in Candia the singular manner in which the gum is exuded from the living plant.[3]

Secretion—It has been shown by H. von Mohl[4] and by Wigand[5] that tragacanth is produced by metamorphosis of the cell membrane, and that it is not simply the dried juice of the plant.

The stem of a gum-bearing *Astragalus* cut transversely, exhibits concentric annual layers which are extremely tough and fibrous, easily tearing lengthwise into thin filaments. These inclose a central column, radiating from which are numerous medullary rays, both of very singular structure, for instead of presenting a thin-walled parenchyme, they appear to the naked eye as a hard translucent gum-like mass, becoming gelatinous in water. Examined microscopically, this gummy substance is seen to consist not of dried mucilage, but of the very cells of the pith and medullary rays, in process of transformation into tragacanth. The transformed cells, if their transformation has not advanced too far, exhibit the angular form and close packing of parenchyme-cells, but their walls are much incrassated and evidently consist of numerous very thin strata.

That these cells are but ordinary parenchyme-cells in an altered state, is proved by the pith and medullary rays of the smaller branches which present no such unusual structure. Mohl was able to trace this change from the period in which the original cell-membrane could be still easily distinguished from its incrusting layers, to that in which

[1] *Nutzpflanzen Griechenlands*, Athen, 1862. 71.

[2] Bonaini, *Statuti inediti della città di Pisa dal xii. al xiv. secolo*, iii. (1857) 106. 114.

[3] *Voyage into the Levant*, Lond. (1718) 43.

[4] *Botanische Zeitung*, 1857. 33; *Pharm. Journ.* xviii. (1859) 370.

[5] Pringsheim's *Jahrbücher f. wissenschaftl. Botanik*, iii. (1861) 117.

the transformation had proceeded so far that it was impossible to perceive any defined cells, the whole substance being metamorphosed into a more or less uniform mucilaginous mass.

The tension under which this peculiar tissue is held in the interior of the stem is very remarkable in *Astragalus gummifer* which one of us had the opportunity of observing on the Lebanon in 1860.[1] On cutting off a branch of the thickness of the finger, there immediately exudes from the centre a stream of soft, solid tragacanth, pushing itself out like a worm, to the length of ¾ of an inch, sometimes in the course of half an hour; while much smaller streams (or none at all) are emitted from the medullary rays of the thick bark.

Production—The principal localities in Asia Minor in which tragacanth is collected are the district of Angora, the capital of the ancient Galatia; Isbarta, Buldur and Yalavatz,[2] north of the gulf of Adalia; the range of the Ali Dagh between Tarsous and Kaisariyeh, and the mountainous country eastward as far as the valley of the Euphrates. The drug is also gathered in Armenia on the elevated range of the Bingol Dagh south of Erzerum; throughout Kurdistan from Mush for 500 miles in a south-eastern direction as far as the province of Luristan in Persia, a region including the high lands south of lake Van, and west of lake Urumiah. It is likewise produced in Persia farther east, over an area 300 miles long by 100 to 150 miles broad, between Gilpaigon and Kashan, southward to the Mahomed Senna range north-east of Shiraz, thus including the lofty Bakhtiyari mountains.

As to the way in which the gum is obtained, it appears from the statements of Maltass, that in July and August the peasants clear away the earth from around the stem of the shrub, and then make in the bark several incisions, from which during the following 3 or 4 days the gum exudes and dries in flakes. In some localities they also puncture the bark with the point of a knife. Whilst engaged in these operations, they pick from the shrubs whatever gum they find exuded naturally.

Hamilton,[3] who saw the shrub in 1836 on the hills about Buldur, says "the gum is obtained by making an incision in the stem near the root, and cutting through the pith, when the sap exudes in a day or two and hardens."

Formerly the peasants were content to collect the naturally exuded gum, no pains being taken to make incisions, whereby alone white flaky gum is obtained. We have in fact heard an old druggist state, that he remembered the first appearance of this fine kind of tragacanth in the London market. According to Professor Haussknecht, whose observations relate chiefly to Kurdistan and Persia, the tragacanth collected in these regions is mostly a spontaneous exudation.

Tragacanth is brought to Smyrna, which is a principal market for it, from the interior, in bags containing about 2 quintals each, by native dealers who purchase it of the peasants. In this state it is a very crude article, consisting of all the gatherings mixed together. To fit it for the European markets, some of which have their special requirements, it has to be sorted into different qualities, as *Flaky or Leaf Gum*,

[1] Hanbury, *Science Papers*, 29.
[2] *Pharm. Journ.* xv. (1856) 18.
[3] *Researches in Asia Minor, Pontus and Armenia*, i. (1842) 492.

Vermicelli and *Common* or *Sorts*; this sorting is performed almost exclusively by Spanish Jews.

Description—The peculiar conditions under which tragacanth exudes, arising from the pressure of the surrounding tissues and the power of solidifying a large amount of water, will account to some extent for the strange forms in which this exudation occurs.

The spontaneously exuded gum is mostly in mammiform or botryoidal masses from the size of a pea upwards, of a dull waxy lustre, and brownish or yellowish hue. It also occurs in vermiform pieces more or less contorted and very variable in thickness; some of them may have exuded as the result of artificial punctures. It is this form that bears the trade name of *Vermicelli.* The most valued sort is however the *Flake Tragacanth*, which consists of thin flattish pieces or flakes, 1, 2, 3 or more inches in length, by $\frac{1}{2}$ to 1 in width.[1] They are marked on the surface by wavy lines and bands, or by a series of concentric wave-marks, as if the soft gum had been forced out by successive efforts. The pieces are contorted and altogether very variable in form and size. The gum is valued in proportion to its purity and whiteness. The best, whether vermiform or flaky, is dull-white, translucent, devoid of lustre, somewhat flexible and horny, firm, and not easily broken, inodorous and with scarcely any or only a slight bitterish taste.

The tragacanth of Kurdistan and Persia shipped from Bagdad, which sometimes appears in the London drug sales under the incorrect name of *Syrian Tragacanth*, is in very fine and large pieces which are rather more translucent and ribbon-like than the selected tragacanth imported from Smyrna: in fact, the two varieties when seen in bulk are easily distinguishable.

The inferior kinds of tragacanth have more or less of colour, and are contaminated with bark, earth and other foreign substances. They used formerly to be much imported into Europe, and were frequently mentioned during the past centuries as *black tragacanth.*

Microscopic Structure—The transformation of the cells into tragacanth is usually not so complete, that every trace of the original tissue or its contents has disappeared. In the ordinary drug, the remains of cell-walls as well as starch granules may be seen, especially if thin slices are examined under oil or any other liquid not acting on the gum. Polarized light will then distinctly show the starch and the cell-walls. If a thin section is imbued with a solution of iodine in iodide of potassium and then moistened with concentrated sulphuric acid, the cell-walls will assume a blue colour as well as the starch.

Chemical Composition—When tragacanth is immersed in water

[1] In the Museum of the Pharmaceutical Society in London, there is some Flake Tragacanth remarkable for its enormous size, but in other respects precisely like the ordinary kind. The ribbon-like strips are as much as 2 inches wide and $\frac{3}{16}$ of an inch thick, and the largest which is several inches long weighs $2\frac{3}{4}$ ounces. Professor Haussknecht has informed us that he has seen in Luristan stems of *Astragalus eriostylus* Boiss. et Haussk. more than 6 feet in height and 5 inches in diameter, and bearing tragacanth. It is probable that the specimen of gum we have described was produced by some species attaining these extraordinary dimensions. Among the Kurdistan tragacanth, there occur curious cylindrical vermiform pieces, about $\frac{1}{4}$ of an inch in diameter, coated with a net-work of woody fibre. We are told by Professor H. that they are picked out of the centre of cut-off pieces of stem, split open by rapid drying in the sun.

it swells, and in the course of some hours disintegrates so that it can be diffused through the liquid. So great is its power of absorbing water that even with 50 times its weight, it forms a thick mucilage. If one part of tragacanth is shaken with 100 parts of water and the liquid filtered, a neutral solution may be obtained which yields an abundant precipitate with acetate of lead, and mixes clearly with a concentrated solution of ferric chloride or of borax,—in these respects differing from a solution of gum arabic. On the other hand, it agrees with the latter in that it is thrown down as a transparent jelly by alcohol, and rendered turbid by oxalate of ammonium. The residue on the filter is a slightly turbid, slimy, non-adhesive mucilage, which when dried forms a very coherent mass. It has received the name of *Bassorin, Traganthin* or *Adraganthin*, and agrees with the formula $C^{12}H^{20}O^{10}$.

Tragacanth is readily soluble in alkaline liquids, even in ammonia water and at the same time assumes a yellow colour; heated with ammonia in a sealed tube at 90° C. it blackens.

The drug loses by drying about 14 per cent. of water, which it absorbs again on exposure to the air. Pure flake tragacanth incinerated leaves 3 per cent. of ash.

Commerce—Tragacanth is shipped from Constantinople, Smyrna and the Persian Gulf. The annual export of the gum from Smyrna has been recently stated[1] to be 4,500 quintals, value 675,000 Austrian florins (£67,500); and the demand to be always increasing.

Uses—Though tragacanth is devoid of active properties, it is a very useful addition to many medicines. Diffused in water it acts as a demulcent, and is also convenient for the suspension of a heavy powder in a mixture. It is an important ingredient for imparting firmness to lozenges and pill masses.

Adulteration—The fine quantities consisting of large distinct pieces are not liable to adulteration, but the small and the inferior kinds are often sophisticated. At Smyrna, tragacanth is mixed with gums termed respectively *Mosul* and *Caramania Gum*. The former appears to be simply very inferior tragacanth; the latter which is sometimes called in the London market *Hog Gum Tragacanth* or *Bassora Gum*,[2] is said to be the exudation of almond and plum trees. It occurs in nodular masses of a waxy lustre and dull brown hue, which immersed in water gradually swells into a voluminous white mass. To render this gum available for adulteration, the lumps are broken into small angular fragments, the size of which is adjusted to the sort of tragacanth with which they are to be mixed. As the Caramania Gum is somewhat dark, it is usual to whiten it by *white lead*, previous to mixing it with *Small Leaf* or *Flake*, or with the *Vermicelli* gum.

By careful examination the fraud is easily detected, angular fragments not being proper to any true tragacanth. The presence of lead may be readily proved by shaking suspected fragments for a moment with dilute nitric acid, which will dissolve any carbonate present, and afford a solution which may be tested by the ordinary reagents.

[1] C. von Scherzer, *Smyrna*, Wien, 1873. 143.

[2] It is sometimes shipped from Bussorah.

RADIX GLYCYRRHIZÆ.

Radix Liquiritiæ; Liquorice Root; F. *Réglisse;* G. *Süssholz, Lakrizwurzel.*

Botanical Origin—*Glycyrrhiza glabra* L., a plant which under several well marked varieties[1] is found over an immense extent of the warmer regions of Europe, spreading thence eastward into Central Asia. The root used in medicine is derived from two principal varieties, namely:—

a. typica—Nearly glabrous, leaves glutinous beneath, divisions of the calyx linear-lanceolate often a little longer than the tube, corolla purplish blue, legume glabrous, 3–6 seeded. It is indigenous to Portugal, Spain, Southern Italy, Sicily, Greece, Crimea, the Caucasian Provinces and Northern Persia; and is cultivated in England, France and Germany.

γ. glandulifera (*G. glandulifera* W.K.)—Stems more or less pubescent or roughly glandular, leaves often glandular beneath, legume sparsely or densely echinate-glandular, many-seeded, or short and 2–3 seeded. It occurs in Hungary, Galicia, Central and Southern Russia, Crimea, Asia Minor, Armenia, Siberia, Persia, Turkestan and Afghanistan.

G. glabra L. has long, stout, perennial roots, and erect, herbaceous annual stems. In var. *a.*, the plant throws out long stolons which run horizontally at some distance below the surface of the ground.

History—Theophrastus[2] in commenting on the taste of different roots (3rd cent. B.C.) instances the sweet Scythian root which grows in the neighbourhood of the lake Mæotis (Sea of Azov), and is good for asthma, dry cough and all pectoral diseases,—an allusion unquestionably to liquorice. Dioscorides,[3] who calls the plant γλυκιρρίζη, notices its glutinous leaves and purplish flowers, but as he describes the pods to be in balls resembling those of the plane, and the roots to be subaustere (ὑποστρυφνοι) as well as sweet, it is possible he had in view *Glycyrrhiza echinata* L. as well as *G. glabra.*

Roman writers, as Celsus and Scribonius Largus, mention liquorice as *Radix dulcis.* Pliny, who describes it as a native of Cilicia and Pontus, makes no allusion to it growing in Italy.

The cultivation of liquorice in Europe does not date from a very remote period, as we conclude from the absence of the name in early mediæval lists of plants. It is, for instance, not enumerated among the plants which Charlemagne ordered (A.D. 812) to be introduced from Italy into Central Europe;[4] nor among the herbs of the convent gardens as described by Walafridus Strabus,[5] abbot of Reichenau, lake of Constance, in the 9th century; nor yet in the copious list of herbs contained in the vocabulary of Alfric, archbishop of Canterbury in the 10th century.[6]

On the other hand, liquorice is described as being cultivated in Italy

[1] We accept those adopted by Boissier in his *Flora Orientalis*, ii. (1872) 202.

[2] *Hist. Plant.* lib. ix. c. 13.

[3] Lib. iii. c. 5.

[4] Pertz, *Monumenta Germaniæ historica, Legum*, i. (1835) 186.

[5] Migne, *Patrologiæ Cursus*, cxiv. 1122.

[6] Wright, *Volume of Vocabularies*, 1857. 30. This work contains several other early lists of plants.

by Piero de' Crescenzi[1] of Bologna, who lived in the 13th century. The cultivation of the plant in the north of England existed at the close of the 16th century, but how much earlier we have not been able to trace.

As a medicine the drug was well known in Germany in the 11th century, and an extensive cultivation of the plant was carried on near Bamberg, Bavaria, in the 16th century, so that in many of the numerous pharmaceutical tariffs of those times in Germany not only Glycyrrhizæ succus creticus, seu candiacus, seu venetus is quoted, but also expressly that of Bamberg.[2]

The word *Liquiritia*, whence is derived the English name *Liquorice* (*Lycorys* in the 13th century), is a corruption of *Glycyrrhiza*, as shown in the transitional mediæval form *Gliquiricia*. The Italian *Regolizia*, the German *Lacrisse* or *Lakriz*, the Welsh *Lacris*,[3] and the French *Réglisse* (anciently *Requelice* or *Recolice*) have the same origin.

Cultivation, and habit of growth—The liquorice plant is cultivated in England at Mitcham and in Yorkshire, but not on a very extensive scale. The plants, which require a good deep soil, well enriched by manure, are set in rows, attain a height of 4 to 5 feet and produce flowers but not seeds. The root is dug up at the beginning of winter, when the plant is at least 3 or 4 years old. The latter has then a crown dividing into several aerial stems. Below the crown is a principal root about 6 inches in length, which divides into several (3 to 5) rather straight roots, running without much branching, though beset with slender wiry rootlets, to a depth of 3, 4 or more feet.[4] Besides these downward-running roots, the principal roots emit horizontal runners or stolons, which grow at some distance below the surface and attain a length of many feet. These runners are furnished with leaf buds and throw up stems in their second year.

Every portion of the subterraneous part of the plant is carefully saved; the roots proper are washed, trimmed, and assorted, and either sold fresh in their entire state, or cut into short lengths and dried, the cortical layer being sometimes first scraped off. The older runners distinguished at Mitcham as "*hard*," are sorted out and sold separately; the young, called "*soft*," are reserved for propagation.

In Calabria, the singular practice prevails of growing the liquorice among the wheat in the cornfields.

Description—Fresh liquorice (English) when washed is externally of a bright yellowish brown. It is very flexible, easily cut with a knife, exhibiting a light yellow, juicy, internal substance which consists of a thick bark surrounding a woody column. Both bark and wood are extremely tough, readily tearing into long, fibrous strips. The root has a peculiar earthy odour, and a strong and characteristic sweet taste.

[1] *Libro della Agricoltura*, Venet. 1511. lib. vi. c. 62.

[2] Gesner, *Valerii Cordi Hist. stirp.* Argentorati, 1561. 164.—Flückiger, *Documente zur Geschichte der Pharmacie*, Halle, 1876. 39. 46.

[3] In the "Meddygon Myddvai" of the 13th century, Llandovery, 1861, p. 159. 355 (it is written there Licras).

[4] This form of root, which reminds one of a whip with three or four lashes and a very short handle, is probably due to the method of propagating adopted at Mitcham, where a short stick or *runner* is planted upright in the ground.

Dried liquorice root is supplied in commerce either with or without the thin brown coat. In the latter state it is known as *peeled* or *decorticated*. The English root, of which the supply is very limited, is usually offered cut into pieces 3 or 4 inches long, and of the thickness of the little finger.

Spanish Liquorice Root, also known as *Tortosa* or *Alicante Liquorice*, is imported in bundles several feet in length, consisting of straight unpeeled roots and runners, varying in thickness from ¼ to 1 inch. The root is tolerably smooth or somewhat transversely cracked and longitudinally wrinkled; that from Tortosa is usually of a good external appearance, that from Alicante sometimes untrimmed, dirty, of very unequal size, showing frequently the knobby crowns of the root. Alicante liquorice root is sometimes shipped in bags or loose.

Russian Liquorice Root, which is much used in England, is we presume derived from *G. glabra* var. *glandulifera*. It is imported from Hamburg in large bales, and is met with both peeled and unpeeled. The pieces are 12 to 18 inches long, with a diameter of ¼ of an inch to 1 or even 2 inches. Sometimes very old roots, split down the centre and forming channelled pieces as much as 3½ inches wide at the crown end, are to be met with. This liquorice in addition to being sweet has a certain amount of bitterness.

Microscopic Structure—The root exhibits well-marked structural peculiarities. The corky layer is made up of the usual tabular cells; the primary cortical tissue of a few rows of cells. The chief portion of the bark consists of liber or endophlœum, and is built up for the most part of parenchymatous tissue accompanied by elongated fibres of two kinds, partly united into true liber-bundles and partly forming a kind of network, the smaller threads of which deviate considerably from the straight line. Solution of iodine imparts an orange hue to both kinds of bast-bundles, and well displays the structural features of the bark.

The woody column of the root exhibits three distinct forms of cell, namely ligneous cells (libriform) with oblique ends; parenchymatous, almost cubic cells; and large pitted vessels. In the Russian root, the size of all the cells is much more considerable than in the Spanish.

Chemical Composition—The root of liquorice contains, in addition to sugar and albuminous matter, a peculiar sweet substance named *Glycyrrhizin*, which is precipitated from a strong decoction upon addition of an acid or solution of cream of tartar, or neutral or basic acetate of lead. When washed with dilute alcohol and dried, it is an amorphous yellow powder, having a strong bitter-sweet taste and an acid reaction. It forms with hot water a solution which gelatinizes on cooling, does not reduce alkaline tartrate of copper, is not fermentable, and does not rotate the plane of polarization. From the analysis and experiments of Rösch, performed in the laboratory of Gorup-Besanez at Erlangen, in 1876, the formula $C^{16}H^{24}O^{6}$ was derived for glycyrrhizin. By boiling it with dilute hydrochloric or sulphuric acid it is resolved into a resinous amorphous bitter substance named *Glycyrretin*, and an uncrystallizable sugar having the characters of glucose. The formula of glycyrretin has not yet been settled. Weselsky and Benedikt, in 1876, showed that 65 per cent. of it may be obtained from glycyrrhizin.

By melting glycyrretin with about 5 parts of caustic potash paraoxybenzoïc acid is produced.

Alkalis easily dissolve glycyrrhizin with a brown colour and emission of a peculiar odour. In the root it perhaps exists combined with ammonia, inasmuch as the aqueous extract evolves that alkali when warmed with potash (Roussin, 1875). According to Sestini (1878) glycyrrhizin is present in the root combined with calcium; he obtained 6·3 per cent. of glycyrrhizin from the root previously dried at 110°. By exhausting glycyrrhizin with glacial acetic acid Habermann in 1876 succeeded in isolating almost *colourless* crystals having the sweet taste of the root. They yield, by boiling them with dilute acids, a yellow substance which would appear to agree with glycyrretin. The deep yellow walls of the vessels and prosenchymatous cells appear to be the chief seat of the glycyrrhizin.

The sugar of liquorice root has not yet been isolated; the aqueous infusion of the *dried* root separates protoxide of copper from an alkaline solution of cupric tartrate. Yet the sugar as extracted from the *fresh* root by cold water does not precipitate alkaline cupric tartrate at all in the cold, and not abundantly even on prolonged boiling.

Asparagin was obtained from the root by Robiquet (1809) and by Plisson (1827). Sestini (1878) isolated 2–4 parts of asparagin from 100 parts of the root dried at 110° C. Robiquet also found the root to contain malic acid. The presence of starch in abundance is shown by the microscope as well as by testing a decoction of the root with iodine. The outer bark of the root contains a small quantity of tannin.

Commerce—Liquorice root is imported into Great Britain from Germany, Russia and Spain, but there are no data for showing to what extent. France imported in 1872 no less than 4,348,789 kilogrammes (4282 tons), which was more than double the quantity imported the previous year.[1]

Liquorice root is much used in China, and is largely produced in some of the northern provinces. In 1870, 1,304 peculs were shipped from Ningpo,[2] and 7,147 peculs in 1877 from Cheefu (one pecul = 133·33 lb. avdp.).

Uses.—Liquorice root is employed for making extract of liquorice and in some other pharmaceutical preparations. The powdered root is used to impart stiffness to pill masses and to prevent the adhesion of pills. Liquorice has a remarkable power of covering the flavour of nauseous medicines. As a domestic medicine, liquorice root is far more largely used on the Continent than in Great Britain.

[1] *Documents statistiques réunis par l'administration des Douanes sur le commerce de la France*, année 1872, Paris, 1873.

[2] *Reports on Trade at the Treaty Ports in China for* 1870, Shanghai, 1871. 13. 62.

SUCCUS GLYCYRRHIZÆ.

Succus Liquiritiæ, Extractum Glycyrrhizæ Italicum ; Italian Extract of Liquorice, Spanish Liquorice, Spanish Juice ; F. *Jus ou Suc de Réglisse ;* G. *Süssholzsaft, Lakriz.*

Botanical Origin—*Glycyrrhiza glabra* L., see preceding article, p. 179.

History—Inspissated liquorice juice was known in the time of Dioscorides, and may be traced in the writings of Oribasius and Marcellus Empiricus in the latter half of the 4th century, and in those of Paulus Ægineta in the 7th. It appears to have been in common use in Europe during the middle ages. In A.D. 1264, "*Liquorice*" is charged in the Wardrobe Accounts of Henry III.;[1] and as the article cost 3*d.* per lb., or the same price as grains of paradise and one-third that of cinnamon, we are warranted in supposing the *extract* and not the mere *root* is intended. Again, in the Patent of Pontage granted by Edward I., A.D. 1305, to aid in repairing the London Bridge, permission is given to lay toll on various foreign commodities including *Liquorice*.[2] A political song written in 1436[3] makes mention of *Liquorice* as a production of Spain, but the plant is not named as an object of cultivation by Herrera, the author of a work on Spanish agriculture in 1513.

Saladinus,[4] who wrote about the middle of the 15th century, names it among the wares kept by the Italian apothecaries ; and it is enumerated in a list of drugs of the city of Frankfort written about the year 1450.[5]

Dorsten,[6] in the first half of the 16th century, mentions the liquorice plant as abundant in many parts of Italy, and describes the method of making the *Succus* by crushing and boiling the fresh root. Mattioli[7] states that the juice made into *pastilli* was brought every year from Apulia, and especially from the neighbourhood of Monte Gargano. Extract of liquorice was made at Bamberg in Germany, where the plant is still largely cultivated, as early as 1560.[8]

Manufacture—This is conducted on a large scale in Spain, Southern France, Sicily, Calabria, Austria, Southern Russia (Astracan and Kasan), Greece (Patras) and Asia Minor (Sokia and Nazli, near Smyrna); but the extract with which England is supplied is almost exclusively the produce of Calabria, Sicily and Spain.

The process of manufacture varies only by reason of the amount of intelligence with which it is performed, and the greater or less perfection of the apparatus employed. As witnessed by one of us (H.) at Rossano in Calabria in May, 1872, it may be thus described from notes made at the time. The factory employs about 60 persons, male and female. The root having been taken from the ground the previous

[1] Rogers, *Hist. of Agriculture and Prices*, ii. (1866) 543.
[2] *Chronicles of London Bridge*, 1827. 155.
[3] Wright, *Political Poems and Songs* (Master of the Rolls series), ii. (1861) 160.
[4] *Compendium Aromatariorum*, Bonon. 1488.
[5] Flückiger. *Die Frankfurter Liste*, Halle, 1873, page 10, No. 204.
[6] *Botanicon*, Francof. 1540. 175.
[7] *Comm. in lib. Diosc.*, Basil. 1574. 485.
[8] Gesner, *Horti Germanici*, Argent. 1561. 257, b.

winter, is stacked in the yard around the factory; it is mostly of the thickness of the fingers, with here and there a piece of larger size up to a diameter of nearly 2 inches; some of it sprouting.

As required, the root is taken within the building and crushed under a heavy millstone to a pulp, water-power being employed. It is then transferred to boilers and boiled with water over a naked fire. The decoction is run off and the residual root pressed in circular bags like those used in the olive-mills. The liquor which is received into cisterns below the floor is then pumped up into copper pans, in which the evaporation is conducted also over the naked fire—even to the very last, care being taken by constant stirring to avoid burning the extract. The extract or *pasta* is removed from the pan while warm, and taken in small quantities to an adjoining apartment where a number of women are employed in rolling it into sticks. It is first weighed into portions, each of which the woman seated at the end of a long table tears with her hand into about a dozen pieces. These are passed to the women sitting next who roll them with their hands into cylindrical sticks, the table on which the rolling is done being of wood, and the *pasta* moistened with oil to prevent its adhesion to the hands. Near the further end of the table are some frames made of marble or metal, clean and bright, so arranged as to bring the sticks when rolled in them to the proper length and thickness. When thus adjusted, they are carefully ranged on a board, and a woman then stamps them with the name of the manufacturer. Lastly the sticks laid on boards are stacked up in a room to dry.

In some establishments the vacuum pan has been introduced for the inspissation of the decoction. At the great manufactory of Mr. A. O. Clarke at Sokia near Smyrna, all the processes are performed by steam power.

Description—Liquorice juice of good quality is met with in cylindrical sticks stamped at one end with the maker's name or mark. They are of various sizes, but generally not larger than 6 to 7 inches long by about an inch in diameter. They are black, when new or warm slightly flexible, but breaking when struck, and then displaying a sharp-edged fracture, and shining conchoidal surface on which a few air-bubbles are perceptible; thin splinters are translucent. The extract has a special odour and dissolves in the mouth with a peculiar strong sweet taste. By complete drying, it loses from 11 to 17 per cent of water.

Several varieties of Stick Liquorice are met with in English commerce, and command widely different prices. The most famous is the *Solazzi Juice*, manufactured at Corigliano, a small town of Calabria in the gulf of Taranto, at an establishment belonging to the sons of Don Onorato Gaetani, duke of Laurenzano and prince of Piedimonte d'Alife, who inherited the manufacture from his father-in-law, the Cavaliere Domenico Solazzi Castriota. The Solazzi Juice destined for the English market is usually shipped at Naples; it has for many years been wholly consigned to two firms in London, and in quantity not always equal to the demand. Of the other varieties we may mention *Barracco*, manufactured at the establishment of Messieurs Barracco at Cotrone on the eastern coast of Calabria; *Corigliano*, produced at a factory at Corigliano, belonging to Baron Compagna. The sticks stamped *Pignatelli* are from the works of Vincenzo Pignatelli, prince of Strongoli, at Torre Cerchiora, where 300 to 400 workmen are employed.

The juice is also imported in a block form, having while warm and soft been allowed to run into the wooden case in which it is exported. This juice, which is known as *Liquorice Paste*, is largely imported from Spain and Asia Minor, but on account of a certain bitterness is unsuited for use as a sweetmeat.

Chemical Composition—Hard extract of liquorice, such as that just described, is essentially different in composition and properties from the Extract of Liquorice (*Extractum Glycyrrhizæ*) of the *British Pharmacopœia*.[1] The latter is a soft, hygroscopic substance, entirely soluble in cold water, whereas the so-called *Spanish Juice* when treated with cold water leaves a large residue undissolved.

It has been sometimes supposed that the presence of this residue indicates adulteration, but such is far from being the fact, as was conclusively shown by the researches of a French Commission appointed to investigate the process recommended by Delondre.[2] This commission subjected liquorice root to the successive action of cold water, boiling water, and lastly of steam. By the first menstruum 15 per cent., and by the second an additional 7½ per cent., were obtained of a hygroscopic extract much more soluble than commercial liquorice, and totally unsuitable for being moulded into sticks. The residue having been then exhausted by steam, 16 per cent. was obtained of an extract differing entirely from those of the previous operations. It was a dry friable substance, cracking and falling to pieces in the drying stove, having a sweet taste without acridity, not readily dissolving in the mouth, and very imperfectly soluble in cold water. This then was the substance required to give firmness to the more soluble matter, and to render possible the preparation of an extract possessing that degree of solubility and hardness which would render it an agreeable sweetmeat, as well as a permanent and stable commodity. In fact, by treating the root at once with steam according to Delondre's process, the experimenters obtained 42 to 45 per cent. of extract having all the qualities desired in good Italian or Spanish Juice.

When the latter substance is suspended in water undisturbed, the soluble matter may be dissolved out, the stick still retaining its original form. Glycyrrhizin, which is but slightly soluble in cold water, remains to some extent in the residue, and by an alkaline solution may be afterwards extracted together with colouring matter and probably also pectin. The proportion of soluble matter which the best varieties of liquorice juice yield to cold water varies from about 60 to 70 per cent. A sample of Solazzi Juice recently examined by one of us, lost 8·4 per cent. when dried at 100° C.; it was then exhausted by 60 times its weight of cold water used in successive quantities, by which means 66·8 per cent. of soluble matter were removed. The residue consisted of minute starch granules, fragments of the root, and colouring matter

[1] Made by treating the crushed root with cold water.

[2] *Journ. de Pharm.* xxx. (1856) 428; an abstract by Redwood in *Pharm. Journ.* xvi. (1857) 403.

partially soluble in ammonia. Small shreds of copper were also visible to the naked eye. The dried juice yielded 6·3 per cent. of ash.

Corigliano liquorice treated in the same manner gave 71·2 per cent. of extract soluble in cold water; Barracco liquorice 64·9.

The small liquorice lozenges known as *Pontefract Cakes* (Dunhill's), not previously dried, gave 71 per cent. of matter soluble in cold water.

Commerce—The value of the imports of Liquorice into the United Kingdom has been for the last five years as follows:—

1868	1869	1870	1871	1872
£89,482	£83,832	£70,165	£55,120	£75,991

The last-named sum represents a quantity of 28,000 cwt., of which 11,170 cwt. were furnished by Italy, and the remainder by Turkey, France, Spain and other countries.

The total exports of Liquorice Paste from Smyrna were estimated in 1872 as 1,200 to 1,400 tons (24,000 to 28,000 cwt.) per annum.

Uses—Stick liquorice is sucked as a remedy for coughs, and by children as a sweetmeat. It is also used in lozenges, and in some pharmacopœias is admitted as the raw material from which to prepare soft extract of liquorice.

The block liquorice, of which a large quantity is imported, is chiefly used in the manufacture of tobacco for smoking and chewing.

OLEUM ARACHIS.

Ground-nut oil, Earth-nut oil, Pea-nut oil, Arachis oil; F. *Huile d'Arachide ou de Pistache de terre;* G. *Erdnussöl.*

Botanical Origin—*Arachis hypogæa* L., a diffuse herbaceous annual plant, having stems a foot or two long, and solitary axillary flowers with an extremely long filiform calyx-tube. After the flower withers, the torus supporting the ovary becomes elongated as a rigid stalk, which bends down to the ground and forces into it the young pod, which matures its seeds some inches below the surface. The ripe pod is oblong, cylindrical, about an inch in length, indehiscent, reticulated, and contains one or two, or exceptionally even four irregularly ovoid seeds.

The plant is cultivated for the sake of its nutritious oily seeds in all tropical and subtropical countries, but especially on the west coast of Africa. It is unknown in the wild state. De Candolle[1] regards it as a native of Brazil, to which region the other species of the genus exclusively belong. But the opinion of one of us[2] is strongly in favour of the plant being indigenous to Tropical Africa, and so is that also of Schweinfurth. Arachis is one of the most universally cultivated plants throughout Tropical Africa, from Senegambia to lake Tanganyika. In Europe it has not proved remunerative.

History—The first writer to notice Ground Nut appears to be Fernandez de Oviedo y Valdes, who lived in Hayti from A.D. 1513 to 1525; he mentions in his *Cronica de las Indias*[3] that the Indians culti-

[1] *Géographie Botanique*, ii. (1855) 963.

[2] Flückiger, *Ueber die Erdnuss—Archiv der Pharmacie*, 190. (1869) 70–84, with figure.

[3] Lib. vii. cap. 5. Fol. 1074 f. (1547), as quoted by C. Ph. von Martius in *Gelehrte Anzeigen der bayerischen Akademie*, 1839. 969.

vated very much the fruit *Mani*, a name still used for Arachis in Cuba and in South America. A little later, Monardes,[1] described a nameless subterraneous fruit, found about the river Maranon and held in great esteem by both Indians and Spaniards. But before, the French colonists sent in 1555 by Admiral Coligny to the Brazilian coast had become acquainted with the "Mandobi," which Jean de Léry[2] described quite unmistakably. Good accounts and figures of it were given in the following century by Johannes de Laet (1625),[3] and by Marcgraf,[4] who calls it by its Brazilian name of *Mundubi*. It is enumerated by Stisser among the rare plants cultivated by him at Helmstedt (Brunswick), about the year 1697.[5]

It is only in very recent times that the value of the Ground Nut has been recognized in Europe. Jaubert, a French colonist at Gorée near Cape Verde, first suggested about 1840 its importation as an oil-seed into Marseilles, where it now constitutes one of the most important articles of trade.[6]

Description—The fat oil of *Arachis*, as obtained by pressure without heat, is almost colourless, of an agreeable faint odour and a bland taste resembling that of olive oil. An inferior oil is obtained by warming the seeds before pressing them. The best oil has a sp. gr. of about 0·918; it becomes turbid at 3° C., concretes at —3° to —4°, and hardens at —7°. On exposure to air it is but slowly altered, being one of the non-drying oils. At length it thickens considerably, and assumes even in closed vessels a disagreeable rancid smell and taste.

Chemical Composition—The oil consists of the glycerides of four different fatty acids. The common *Oleic Acid*, $C^{18}H^{34}O^2$, that is to say its glycerin compound, is the chief constituent of Arachis oil. *Hypogæic Acid*, $C^{16}H^{30}O^2$, has been pointed out by Gössmann and Scheven (1854) as a new acid, whereas it is thought by other chemists to agree with one of the fatty acids obtained from whale oil. The melting point of this acid from Arachis oil is 34–35° C. The third acid afforded by the oil is ordinary *Palmitic Acid*, $C^{16}H^{32}O^2$, with a fusing point of 62° C. *Arachic Acid*, $C^{20}H^{40}O^2$, the fourth constituent, has also been met with among the fatty acids of butter and olive oil, and, according to Oudemans (1866), in the tallow of *Nephelium lappaceum* L., an Indian plant of the order *Sapindaceæ*.

When ground-nut oil is treated with hyponitric acid, which may be most conveniently evolved by heating nitric acid with a little starch, a solid mass is obtained, which yields by crystallization from alcohol *Elaïdic and Gæidinic* acids, the former isomeric with oleic, the latter with hypogæic acid.

Production and Commerce—The pods are exported on an immense and ever increasing scale from the West Coast of Africa. From this region, not less than 66 millions of kilogrammes, value 26 millions of francs (£1,040,000), were imported in 1867, almost exclusively into

[1] *Las Cosas que se traen de nuestras Indias Occidentales*, Sevilla, 1569, part 2.

[2] *Histoire d'un voyage faict en la Terre du Bresil, autrement dite Amérique*, 1586. 204 (first edition *La Rochelle*, 1578).

[3] *Histoire du Nouveau Monde*, Leyde, 1640. 503.

[4] *Hist. Rerum Nat. Brasil.* 1648. 37.

[5] *Botanica curiosa*, Helmst. 1697. 38.

[6] Duval, *Colonies et politique coloniale de la France*, 1864. 101.—Mavidal, *Le Sénégal, son état présent, son avenir*, Paris, 1863. 171, —Carrère et Holle, *La Sénégambie Française*, 1855. 84.—Poiteau, in *Annales des Sciences nat., Botanique*, xix. (1853) 268.

Marseilles. From the French possessions on the Senegal, 24 millions of kilogr. were exported in 1876.

The oil is exported from India where the ground-nut is also cultivated, though not on so large a scale as in Western Africa. In Europe it is manufactured chiefly at Marseilles, London, Hamburg and Berlin. The yield of the seeds varies from 42 to nearly 50 per cent. The softness of the seeds greatly facilitates their exhaustion, whether by mechanical power or by the action of bisulphide of carbon or other solvent.

Uses—Good arachis oil may be employed in pharmacy in the same way as olive oil, for which it is a valuable substitute, though more prone to rancidity. It has been introduced into the *Pharmacopœia of India*, and is generally used instead of olive oil in the Indian Government establishments. Its largest application is for industrial purposes, especially in soap-making.

RADIX ABRI.

Indian Liquorice ; F. *Liane à réglisse, Réglisse d'Amérique.*

Botanical Origin—*Abrus precatorius* L., a twining woody shrub[1] indigenous to India, but now found in all tropical countries.

History—The plant is mentioned in the Sanskrit medical writings of Susruta, whence we may infer that it has long been employed in India. Its resemblance to liquorice was remarked by Sloane (1700), who called it *Phaseolus glycyrrhites*. As a substitute for liquorice, the root has been often employed by residents in the tropical countries of both hemispheres. It was introduced into the *Bengal Pharmacopœia* of 1844, and into the *Pharmacopœia of India* of 1868.

The seeds, of the size of a small pea, well known for their polish and beautiful black and red colours, have given their name of *Retti* to a weight (= $2\frac{3}{16}$ grains) used by Hindu jewellers and druggists.

Description—The root is long, woody, tortuous and branching. The stoutest piece in our possession is as thick as a man's finger, but most of it is much more slender. The cortical layer is extremely thin and of a light brown or almost reddish hue. The woody part breaks with a short fibrous fracture exhibiting a light yellow interior. The root has a peculiar, disagreeable odour, and a bitterish acrid flavour leaving a faintly sweet after-taste. When cut into short lengths it has a slight resemblance to liquorice, but may easily be distinguished by means of the microscope.

Mr. Moodeen Sheriff,[2] who says he has often examined the root of *Abrus* both fresh and dried, remarks that it is far from abounding in sugar as generally considered ;—that it does not possess any sweetness at all until it attains a certain size, and that even then its sweet taste is

[1] Fig. in Bentley and Trimen, *Medicinal Plants*, part 25 (1878).

[2] *Supplement to the Pharmacopœia of India*, Madras, 1869. 16.—The author has kindly sent us specimens of the root. We are also indebted for authentic samples to Mr. Thwaites of the Royal Botanical Garden, Ceylon, and to Mr. Prestoe of the Botanical Garden, Trinidad. The last named gentleman remarks—"I do not find any liquorice property in the root, even fresh, but it is very strong in the green leaves."

not always well marked. As it is often mixed in the Indian bazaars with true liquorice, he thinks the latter may have sometimes been mistaken for it.

Microscopic Structure—On a transverse section the bark exhibits some layers of cork cells, loaded with brown colouring matter, and then, within the middle zone of the bark, a comparatively thick layer of sclerenchymatous tissue. Strong liber fibres are scattered through the interior of the cortical tissue, but are not distributed so as to form wedge-shaped rays as met with in liquorice. In the latter the sclerenchyme (thick-walled cells) is wanting. These differences are sufficient to distinguish the two roots.

Chemical Composition—The concentrated aqueous infusion of the root of Abrus has a dark brown colour and a somewhat acrid taste accompanied by a faint sweetness. When it is mixed with an alkaline solution of tartrate of copper, red cuprous oxide is deposited after a short time: hence we may infer that the root contains sugar One drop of hydrochloric or other mineral acid mixed with the infusion produces a very abundant flocculent precipitate, which is soluble in alcohol. If the infusion of Abrus root is mixed with a very little acetic acid, an abundant precipitate is likewise obtained, but is dissolved by an excess. This behaviour is similar to that of glycyrrhizin (see p. 181).

Berzelius observed, so long ago as 1827, that the *leaves* of Abrus contain a sweet principle similar to that of liquorice.

Uses—The root has been used in the place of liquorice, for which it is in our opinion a very bad substitute.

SETÆ MUCUNÆ.

Dolichi pubes vel setæ; Cowhage, Cow-itch [1]; F. *Pois à gratter, Pois pouillieux*; G. *Juckborsten*.

Botanical Origin—*Mucuna pruriens* DC. (*Dolichos pruriens* L., *Stizolobium pruriens* Pers., *Mucuna prurita* Hook.), a lofty climbing plant [2] with large, dark purple papilionaceous flowers, and downy legumes in size and shape not unlike those of a sweet pea, common throughout the tropical regions of both Africa, India and America.

History—The earliest notice we have found of this plant is that of Parkinson, who in his *Theater of Plants*, published in 1640, names it "*Phaseolus siliquâ hirsutâ*, the Hairy Kidney-Beane called in Zurrate [Surat] where it groweth, *Couhage*." It was subsequently described by Ray (1686), who saw the plant raised from West Indian seeds, in the garden of the Hatton family in Holborn.[3] Rheede figured it in the *Hortus Malabaricus*,[4] and it was also known to Rumphius and the other older botanists. We find it even in the pharmaceutical tariff of the county of Nürnberg, A.D. 1714.[5]

[1] These names and the following are also applied to the entire pods, or even to the plant.

[2] Fig. in Bentley and Trimen, *Med. Plants*, part 13 (1876).

[3] *Hist. Plant.* i. 887.

[4] Tom. viii. (1700) tab. 35, sub nom. *Nāi Corana*.

[5] Flückiger, *Documente zur Geschichte der Pharmacie*, Halle, 1876. 84.

The employment of cowhage as a vermifuge originated in the West Indies, and is quite unknown in the East. In England the drug began to attract attention in the latter part of the last century, when it was strongly recommended by Bancroft in his *Natural History of Guiana* (1769), and by Chamberlaine, a surgeon of London, who published an essay[1] descriptive of its effects which went through many editions. It was introduced into the Edinburgh Pharmacopœia of 1783, and into the London Pharmacopœia of 1809. At the present day it has been almost discarded from European medicine, but has been allowed a place in the *Pharmacopœia of India* (1868).

The name *Cowhage* is Hindustani, and in the modern way is written *Kiwânch*, which is generally derived from the Sanskrit *Kapi-Kachchu*, monkey's itch (Dr. Rice); the corruption into *Cow-itch* is absurd. *Mucuna* is the Brazilian name of another species mentioned in 1648 by Marcgraf.[2]

Description—The pods are 2 to 4 inches long, about $\frac{4}{10}$ of an inch wide, and contain 4 to 6 seeds; they are slightly compressed and of a dark blackish brown. Each valve is furnished with a prominent ridge running from the apex nearly to the base, and is densely covered with rigid, pointed, brown hairs, measuring about $\frac{1}{10}$ of an inch in length. The hairs are perfectly straight and easily detached from the valves, out of the epidermis of which they rise. If incautiously touched, they enter the skin and occasion an intolerable itching.

Microscopic Structure—Under the microscope the hairs are seen to consist of a single, sharply pointed, conical cell, about $\frac{1}{40}$ of an inch in diameter at the base, with uniform brownish walls 5 mkm. thick, which towards the apex are slightly barbed. Occasionally a hair shows one or two transverse walls. Most of the hairs contain only air; others show a little granular matter which acquires a greenish hue on addition of alcoholic solution of perchloride of iron. If moistened with chromic acid, no structural peculiarity is revealed that calls for remark. The walls however are somewhat separated into indistinct layers, the presence of which is confirmed by the refractive power displayed by the hairs in polarized light.

Chemical Composition—The hairs when treated with sulphuric acid and iodine assume a dark brown colour. Boiling solution of potash does not considerably swell or alter them. They are completely decolorized by concentrated nitric acid.

Uses—Cowhage is administered for the expulsion of intestinal worms, especially *Ascaris lumbricoides* and *A. vermicularis*, which it effects by reason of its mechanical structure. It is given mixed with syrup or honey in the form of an electuary.

The root and seeds are reputed medicinal by the natives of some part of India. The pods when young and tender may be cooked and eaten.

[1] *On the efficacy of Stizolobium or Cowhage*, Lond. 2nd ed. 1784.

[2] *Hist. Nat. Brasil.* 18.

SEMEN PHYSOSTIGMATIS.

Faba Calabarica, Faba Physostigmatis; Calabar Bean, Ordeal Bean of Old Calabar, Eseré Nut, Chop-nut; F. *Fève de Calabar;* G. *Calabarbohne.*

Botanical Origin—*Physostigma venenosum* Balfour, a perennial plant resembling the common Scarlet Runner (*Phaseolus multiflorus* Lam.) of our gardens, but having a woody stem often an inch or two thick, climbing to a height of 50 feet or more. It grows near the mouths of the Niger and the Old Calabar River in the Gulf of Guinea.

The imported seeds germinate freely, but the plant, though it thrives vigorously in a hothouse, has not yet, we believe, flowered in Europe. It has already been introduced into India and Brazil. In the latter country Dr. Peckolt, late of Cantagallo, has raised plants which have blossomed abundantly, producing racemes of about 30 flowers each, pendent from the axils of the ternate leaves.

The flower, which is fully an inch across and of a purplish colour, has the form of *Phaseolus*, but is distinguished from that genus by two special characters, namely that it has the style developed beyond the stigma backwards as a broad, flat, hooked appendage,[1] and the seeds half surrounded by a deeply grooved hilum.

History—The pagan tribes of Tropical Western Africa compel persons accused of witchcraft to undergo the ordeal of swallowing some vegetable poison. One of the substances employed in this horrid custom is the seed under notice, which is administered in substance or in the form of emulsion, or even as a clyster. It was first made known in England by Dr. W. F. Daniell about the year 1840, and subsequently alluded to in a paper read by him before the Ethnological Society in 1846.[2] The highly poisonous effects of the bean were observed in 1855 by Christison[3] in his own person, and in 1858 by Sharpey, who administered it to frogs.

Before the seed became an object of commerce, it was regarded by the natives with some mystery and was reluctantly parted with to Europeans. It was moreover customary in Old Calabar to destroy the plant whenever found, a few only being reserved to supply seeds for judicial purposes, and of these seeds the store was kept in the custody of the native chief. In 1859, the Rev. W. C. Thomson, a missionary on the West Coast of Africa, forwarded the plant to Professor Balfour of Edinburgh, who figured and described it as a type of a new genus.[4]

Fraser of Edinburgh (about 1863 or earlier) discovered the specific power of the seed in contracting the pupil, when the alcoholic extract is applied to the eye. These myotic effects, counteracting those of atropine

[1] The name of the genus, from φῦσα, a bladder, was formed under the notion that this appendage is *hollow*, which is not the fact.—Mucuna cylindrosperma Welwitsch, from Angola, is probably the same plant. See Holmes, *Pharm. J.* ix. (1879) 913.

[2] *Edinb. New Phil. J.* xl. (1846) 313.

[3] *Edinb. Journ. of Medical Science*, xx. (1855) 193; *Pharm. Journ.* xiv. (1855) 470.

[4] *Trans. Roy. Soc. of Edinb.* xxii. (1861) 305. t. 16–17; see also Baillon, *Hist. des Plantes*, ii. 206. figg. 153–155, and Bentley and Trimen, *Med. Plants*, part 6 (1876).

and hyoscyamine, were further examined by many other experimenters on mammals or birds. The action of the poison when taken internally was found rapidly to affect the cardiac contractions and finally to paralyze the heart.

Description—The fruit of *Physostigma* is a dehiscent, oblong legume about 7 inches in length, containing 2 or 3 seeds. The latter, commonly known as *Calabar Beans*, are 1 to $1\frac{3}{8}$ inches long, about $\frac{6}{8}$ of an inch broad, and $\frac{4}{8}$ to $\frac{5}{8}$ of an inch in thickness, weighing on an average twenty seeds, 67 grains each.

They have an oblong, subreniform outline, one side being straight or but slightly incurved, the other boldly arched. The latter is marked by a broad furrow, $\frac{1}{8}$ of an inch wide, bordered with raised edges, and running from the micropyle, which is a small funnel-shaped depression, quite round the opposite end of the seed. In the middle of this remarkable furrow the raphe is seen as a long raised suture running from end to end. The surface of the seed is somewhat rough, but has a dull polish; it is of a deep chocolate brown, passing into a lighter tint on the ridges bordering the furrow. The latter is black, dull, and finely rugose.

When the seed is broken the cotyledons are found adherent to the testa, with a large cavity between them. The air thus included causes the seeds to float on water, but they sink immediately when broken. After digestion for some hours in warm water, the testa having been previously cracked, the whole seed softens and swells so that its structure may be easily studied. Each cotyledon is then seen to be marked on the hilum-side by a long shallow furrow, at one end of which, just below the micropyle, lies the plumule and radicle. A dark brown inner membrane, constituting part of the testa, surrounds the cotyledons.

The seeds have scarcely any taste, or not more than an ordinary bean; nor in the dry state have they any odour. After being boiled, or when their alcoholic tincture is evaporated, an odour suggesting cantharides is developed.

Microscopic Structure—The cotyledons are built up of large globular or ovoid cells, those of the outermost layer being smaller and of rather cubic form. This parenchyme is loaded with starch granules, frequently as much as 50 mkm. in diameter. Their interior part is less distinctly stratified than the outer; the hollow centre radiates in various directions around the axis of the ovate granule. Polarized light does not show a cross as in other more globular starch granules, but two elliptic curves approaching one another near the axis of the granule. Similar starch granules are commonly met with in the seeds of *Leguminosæ*.

In the Calabar seeds the starch is accompanied by numerous particles of albuminous matter becoming distinctly perceptible by addition of iodine, which imparts to them an orange colouration.

The shell of the seed is built up of four different layers; the prevailing layer consists of very long, simply cylindrical cells, densely packed so as to form only one radial row. Tison[1] has endeavoured to ascertain in what region of the seed the active principle

[1] *Histoire de la Fève de Calabar*, Paris, 1873. 38.

is lodged; and he has arrived at the conclusion that its seat is the granular protoplasmic particles, which alone acquire an orange tint by the action of weak caustic alkalis.

Chemical Composition—Jobst and Hesse[1] proved in 1863 that the poisonous nature of Calabar bean depends upon an alkaloid, to which they gave the name *Physostigmine*. It is obtained by the method generally adopted for extracting analogous substances, that is, by precipitating one of its salts from an aqueous solution by bicarbonate of sodium, and dissolving out the base with ether or benzol. As extracted by these chemists, physostigmine is an amorphous mass of decidedly alkaline reaction, soluble in much water and in acids. On exposure to the air the solution soon becomes red, or sometimes intensely blue, a partial decomposition of the alkaloid taking place. The red coloration may even be observed in the aqueous infusion of a few cotyledons. It disappears by sulphuretted hydrogen or sulphurous acid, but returns if these reducing agents are allowed to evaporate.

Hesse[2] ascertained (1867) that physostigmine consists of $C^{30}H^{21}N^{3}O^{4}$; he now obtained it perfectly colourless and tasteless, softening at 40° C., fusing at 45°, but not supporting a heat of 100° C., without decomposition, which is manifested by a red coloration.

In 1865 Vée and Leven,[3] by treating the powdered unpeeled seed in nearly the same way, prepared an alkaloid which they called *Eserine*. It differs from Hesse's physostigmine in that it forms colourless, rhomboidal, tabular crystals of a bitter taste, melting at 90° C. It dissolves easily in ether, alcohol, or chloroform, but very sparingly in water. The last named solution is alkaline, and reddens by exposure to the air.

It is assumed by some writers, as Tison,[4] that eserine is only the pure form of physostigmine; but at present we feel hardly warranted in admitting the identity of the two substances.

Harnack and Witkowski in 1876 ascertained the presence of another alkaloid in the seed, which they called *Calabarine*. It is nearly insoluble in ether and also very different from physostigmine in its physiological action, but somewhat similar to strychnine. Calabarine is consequently not to be found in those preparations of calabar bean which have been obtained or purified by means of ether.

Hesse (1878) exhausted the cotyledons of Physostigma with petroleum ether, and obtained crystals of a new indifferent substance $C^{26}H^{44}O + OH^2$, which he called *Phytosterin*. It is closely allied to Cholesterin, but, in its solution in chloroform, devoid of rotatory power and melting at 133°. Cholesterin melts at 145°, and deviates, in its ethereal solution, the ray of polarized light to the left. Phytosterin also occurs in peas; Hesse suggests that the crystallized appearance of alkaloids as prepared by former observers was perhaps due to phytosterin.

From the cotyledons *per se*, cold water extracts mucilage, precipitable by neutral acetate of lead. The watery infusion contains also albumin, which may be coagulated by heat or by alcohol. The infusion is colourless, does not redden litmus, nor does it contain sugar in ap-

[1] Liebig's *Annalen der Chem. u. Pharm.* 129 (1864) 115.

[2] *Ibid.* 141 (1867) 82; *Chem. News*, 22 March 1867, 149.

[3] *Comptes Rendus*, lx. (1865) 1194.

[4] *Op. cit.* chap. 2.

preciable proportion; a few drops of solution of potash cause it to assume an orange colour. An infusion of the shell of the seed is already of this colour, but the tint is intensified by caustic alkali.

The cotyledons yield to boiling ether $\frac{1}{2}$ to $\frac{1}{3}$ per cent. of fatty oil, and after exhaustion by ether and alcohol, afford to cold water 12 per cent. of albuminous and mucilaginous constituents. The proportion of starch according to Teich[1] amounts to 48 per cent., the albuminous matter to 23 per cent. The entire seed furnishes 3 per cent. of ash, chiefly phosphate of potash. These constituents do not widely differ in proportion from those found in the common bean, which yields 23 to 25 per cent. of albuminous matters, and 32 to 38 per cent. of starch, besides 1 to 3 per cent. of oil.

The shells of Calabar bean are stated by Fraser to be by no means devoid of active principle.

Vée asserts that if to a solution of eserine, a little potash, lime, or carbonate of sodium be added, there is developed a red colour which rapidly increases in intensity. This colour is transient, passing into yellow, green and blue. If chloroform is shaken with such coloured solution, it takes up the colour; ether on the other hand remains uncoloured.

Uses—Calabar has been hitherto chiefly employed as an ophthalmic medicine, for the purpose of contracting the pupil. It has however been occasionally administered in tetanus and in neuralgic, rheumatic, and other diseases.

Adulteration—Other seeds are sometimes fraudulently mixed with Calabar beans. We have noticed in particular those of a *Mucuna* and of the Oil Palm, *Elæis guineensis* Jacq. The slightest examination suffices for their detection.

KINO.

Kino, Gum Kino, East Indian Kino; F. and G. *Kino.*

Botanical Origin—*Pterocarpus Marsupium* Roxb., a handsome tree 40 to 80 feet high, frequent in the central and southern parts of the Indian Peninsula and also in Ceylon, and affording a valuable timber. In the Government forests of the Madras Presidency, it is one of the *reserved trees*, the felling of which is placed under restrictions.

Pt. indicus Willd., a tree of Southern India, the Malayan Peninsula and the Indian and Philippine Islands, is capable of yielding kino, and is the source of the small supplies of that drug that were formerly shipped from Moulmein.

Several other plants afford substances bearing the name of *Kino*, which will be noticed at the conclusion of the present article.

History—The introduction of kino into European medicine is due to Fothergill, an eminent physician and patron of economic botany of the last century. The drug which Fothergill examined was brought

[1] *Chemische Untersuchung der Calabarbohne.* — Inauguralschrift, St. Petersburg, 1867. We calculate the albuminous matters with reference to *Teich's* analysis, which proved the kernels to contain 3·65 per cent. of nitrogen.

from the river Gambia in West Africa as a rare sort of Dragon's Blood, and was described by him in 1757[1] under the name of *Gummi rubrum astringens Gambiense.* It had been noticed at least twenty years before as a production of the Gambia, by Moore, factor to the Royal African Company, who says that the tree yielding it is called in the Mandingo language *Kano.*[2] Specimens of this tree were sent to England in 1805 by the celebrated traveller Mungo Park, and recognized some years later as identical with the *Pterocarpus erinaceus* of Poiret.

It seems probable that African kino continued to reach England for some years, for we find "*Gummi rubrum astringens*" regularly valued in the stock of a London druggist[3] from 1776 to 1792.

Duncan in the *Edinburgh Dispensatory* of 1803, while asserting that "*kino is brought to us from Africa,*" admits that some, not distinguishable from it, is imported from Jamaica. In a later edition of the same work (1811), he says that the African drug is no longer to be met with, and alludes to its place being supplied by other kinds, as that of Jamaica, that imported by the East India Company, and that of New South Wales derived from *Eucalyptus resinifera* Sm. It will thus be seen that at the commencement of the present century several substances, produced in widely distant regions, bore the name of *Kino.* That however which was principally used in the place of the old African drug, was *East Indian* Kino, the botanical origin of which was shown by Wight and by Royle[4] (1844-46) to be *Pterocarpus Marsupium* Roxb.,—a tree which, curiously enough, is closely allied to the kino tree of Tropical Africa.

This is the drug which is recognized as legitimate kino in all the principal pharmacopœias of Europe. It appears to have been first prepared for the European market in the early part of the present century, on a plantation of the East India Company called Anjarakandy, a few miles from Tellicherry on the Malabar Coast; but as we learn from our friend Dr. Cleghorn, it was not grown there but on the ghats a short distance inland.

Extraction—Kino is the juice of the tree, dried without artificial heat.[5] As it exudes, it has the appearance of red currant jelly, but hardens in a few hours after exposure to the air. In the Government forests of the Malabar Coast whence the supplies are obtained, permission to collect the drug is granted on payment of a small fee, and on the understanding that the tapping is performed skilfully and without damage to the timber. The method pursued is this:—A perpendicular incision with lateral ones leading into it, is made in the trunk, at the foot of which is placed a vessel to receive the outflowing juice. This juice soon thickens, and when sufficiently dried by exposure to the sun and air, is packed into wooden boxes for exportation.

Description—Malabar kino[6] consists of dark, blackish-red, angular

[1] *Medical Observations and Inquiries,* i. (1757) 358.

[2] *Travels into the Inland Parts of Africa,* by Francis Moore, Lond. 1737. pp. 160. 209. 267.

[3] J. Gurney Bevan, Plough Court, Lombard Street.—The drug was priced in 1787 as having cost 16*s*., and in 1790–92, 21*s*. per lb.

[4] *Pharm. Journ.* v. (1846) 495.

[5] Cleghorn, *Forests and Gardens of South India,* 1861. 13.—Also from information communicated by him orally.

[6] Our sample obtained from *Pt. Marsupium* Roxb. on the Sigúr Ghat, Feb. 1868, was kindly submitted to us by Mr. McIvor of Ootacamund.—We find it to agree with commercial East Indian Kino.

fragments rarely larger than a pea, easily splitting into still smaller pieces, which are seen to be perfectly transparent, of a bright garnet hue, and amorphous under the microscope. In cold water they sink, but partially dissolve by agitation, forming a solution of very astringent taste, and a pale flocky residue. The latter is taken up when the liquid is made to boil, and deposited on cooling in a more voluminous form. Kino dissolves almost entirely in spirit of wine (·838), affording a dark reddish solution, acid to litmus paper, which by long keeping sometimes assumes a gelatinous condition. It is readily soluble in solution of caustic alkali, and to a large extent in a saturated solution of sugar.

Chemical Composition—Cold water forms with kino a reddish solution, which is at first not altered if a fragment of ferrous sulphate is added. But a violet colour is produced as soon as the liquid is cautiously neutralized. This can be done by diluting it with common water (containing bicarbonate of calcium) or by adding a drop of solution of acetate of potassium. Yet the fact of kino developing an intense violet colour in presence of a protosalt of iron, may most evidently be shown by shaking it with water, and iron reduced by hydrogen. The filtered liquid is of a brilliant violet, and may be evaporated at 100° without turning green; the dried residue even again forms a violet solution with water. By long keeping the violet liquid gelatinizes. It is decolorized by acids, and turns red on addition of an alkali, whether caustic or bicarbonated. Catechu, as well as crystallized catechin, show the same behaviour, but these solutions quickly turn green on exposure to air.

Solutions of acids, of metallic salts, or of chromates produce copious precipitates in an aqueous solution of kino. Ferric chloride forms a dirty green precipitate, and is at the same time reduced to a ferrous salt. Dilute mineral acids or alkalis do not occasion any decided change of colour, but the former give rise to light brownish-red precipitates of *Kino-tannic Acid.* By boiling for some time an aqueous solution of kinno-tannic acid, a red precipitate, *Kino-red,* is separated.

Kino in its general behaviour is closely allied to Pegu catechu, and yields by similar treatment the same products, that is to say, it affords *Pyrocatechin* when submitted to dry distillation, and *Protocatechuic Acid* together with *Phloroglucin* when melted with caustic soda or potash.

Yet in catechu the tannic acid is accompanied by a considerable amount of catechin, which may be removed directly by exhaustion with ether. Kino, on the other hand, yields to ether only a minute percentage of a substance, whose scaly crystals display under the microscope the character of *Pyrocatechin,* rather than that of catechin, which crystallizes in prisms. The crystals extracted from kino dissolve freely in cold water, which is not the case with catechin, and this solution assumes a fine green if a very dilute solution of ferric chloride is added, and turns red on addition of an alkali. This is the behaviour of catechin as well as of pyrocatechin; but the difference in solubility speaks in favour of the crystals afforded by kino being pyrocatechin rather than catechin.

We thought pyrocatechin must also occur in the mother-plant of kino, but this does not prove to be the case, no indication of its presence being perceptible either in the fresh bark or wood.[1]

Etti (1878) extracted from kino colourless prisms of *Kinoïn* by boiling the drug with twice its weight of hydrochloric acid, about 1·03 sp. gr. On cooling, kino-red separates, very little of it remaining in solution together with kinoïn. The latter is extracted by exhausting the liquid with ether, which by evaporation affords crystals of kinoïn. They should be re-crystallized from boiling water; they agree with the formula $C^{14}H^{12}O^{6}$, which is to be regarded as that of a methylated gallic ether of pyrocatechin, viz., $C^{6}H^{4}(OCH^{3})\,C^{7}H^{5}O^{5}$.

Kinoïn by heating it to 130° C. gives off water and turns red:

$$2\,C^{14}H^{12}O^{6} = OH^{2}\,.\,C^{28}H^{22}O^{11}.$$

The latter product is an amorphous mass agreeing with kino-red; by heating it at 160–170° it again loses water, thus affording another anhydride.

Etti succeeded in preparing methylic chloride, pyrocatechin $C^{6}H^{4}(OH)^{2}$, as well as gallic acid $C^{7}H^{6}O^{5}$, by decomposing kinoïn.

We have prepared kinoïn from *Australian kino* (see page 198), but failed in obtaining it from Malabar kino, which however Etti states to have used. Kino affords about 1½ per cent of kinoïn.

The solutions of kinoïn turn red on addition of ferric salts.

Commercial kino yielded us 1·3 per cent. of ash.

Commerce—The quantity of true kino collected in the Madras forests is comparatively small, probably not exceeding a ton or two annually. The drug is often shipped from Cochin.

Uses—Kino is administered as an astringent. It is said to be used in the manufacture of wines, and it might be employed if cheap enough in tanning and dyeing.

Other sorts of Kino.

1. ***Butea Kino, Butea Gum, Bengal Kino, Palas or Pulas Kino, Gum of the Palas or Dhak Tree.***

This is an exudation from *Butea frondosa* Roxb. (*Leguminosæ*), a tree of India and Burma, well known under the name of *Palas* or *Dhak*, and conspicuous for its splendid, large, orange, papilionaceous flowers.[2] According to Roxburgh it flows during the hot season from natural fissures or from wounds made in the bark, as a red juice which soon hardens into a ruby-coloured, brittle, astringent gum.

Authentic specimens of this kino have been placed at our disposal by Mr. Moodeen Sheriff of Madras and by Dr. J. Newton of Bellary. That received from the first-named gentleman consists of flattish, angular fragments (the largest about ½ an inch across) and small drops or tears of a very dark, ruby-coloured gum, which when held to the light is seen to be perfectly transparent. The flat pieces have been mostly dried on leaves, an impression of the veins of which they retain on one side,

[1] We have to thank Mr. Broughton, late of the Cinchona Plantations, Ootacamund, for determining this point. In the bark almost saturated with fresh liquid kino, he utterly failed to obtain any indication of pyrocatechin by the tests which he found to render it easily evident in dry kino.

[2] See Nees von Esenbeck, *Plantæ medicinales*, Düsseldorf, iii. (1833) tab. 79.

while the other is smooth and shining. The substance has a pure astringent taste, but no odour. It yielded us 1·8 per cent. of ash and contained 13·5 per cent. of water. Ether removes from it a small quantity of *pyrocatechin*. Boiling alcohol dissolves this kino to the extent of 46 per cent.; the solution which is but little coloured, produces an abundant greyish-green precipitate with perchloride of iron, and a white one with acetate of lead. It may be hence inferred that a tannic acid, probably kino-tannic acid, constitutes about half the weight of the drug, the remainder of which is formed of a soluble mucilaginous substance which we have not isolated in a state of purity. By submitting the Butea kino of Mr. Moodeen Sheriff to dry distillation we obtained pyrocatechin.

The sample from Dr. Newton is wholly in transparent drops and stalactitic pieces, considerably paler than that just described, but of the same beautiful ruby tint. The fragments dissolve freely and almost completely in cold water, the solution being neutral and exhibiting the same reactions as the former sample.

Butea kino, which in India is used in the place of Malabar kino, was long confounded with the latter by European pharmacologists, though the Indian names of the two substances are quite different. It is not obtained exclusively from *B. frondosa*, the allied *B. superba* Roxb. and *B. parviflora* Roxb. affording a similar exudation.

2. ***African or Gambia Kino***—Of this substance we have a specimen collected by Daniell[1] in the very locality whence it was obtained by Moore in 1733 (see p. 195), and by Park at the commencement of the present century. The tree yielding it, which still bears the Mandingo name *Kano*, and grows to a height of 40 to 50 feet, is *Pterocarpus erinaceus* Poiret, a native of Tropical Western Africa from Senegambia to Angola. The juices exude naturally from crevices in the bark, but much more plentifully by incisions; it soon coagulates, becoming deep blood-red and remarkably brittle. That in our possession is in very small, shining, angular fragments, which in a proper light appear transparent and of a deep ruby colour. In solubility and chemical characters, we can trace no difference between it and the kino of the allied *Pt. Marsupium* Roxb. This kino does not now find its way to England as a regular article of trade. From the statement of Welwitsch, it appears that the Portuguese of Angola employ it under the name of *Sangue de Drago*.[2]

3. ***Australian, Botany Bay, or Eucalyptus Kino***.—For some years past, the London drug market has been supplied with considerable quantities of kino from Australia; in fact at one period this kino was the only sort to be purchased.

As it is the produce of numerous species of *Eucalyptus*, it is not surprising that it presents considerable diversity of appearance. The better qualities closely agree with Pterocarpus kino. They are in dark reddish brown masses or grains, which when in thin fragments are seen to be transparent, of a garnet red hue and quite amorphous. The substance is mostly collected by the sawyers and wood-splitters. It is found within the trunks of trees of all sizes, in flattened cavities o

[1] See his paper *On the Kino Tree of West Africa, Pharm. Journ.* xiv. (1855) 55.

[2] *Madeiras e Drogas medicinaes de Angola* Lisboa, 1862, 37.

the otherwise solid wood which are often parallel to the annual rings. In such place the kino, which is at first a viscid liquid, becomes inspissated and subsequently hard and brittle. It may also be obtained in a liquid state by incisions in the stems of growing trees: such liquid kino has occasionally been brought into the London market; it is a viscid treacle-like fluid, yielding by evaporation about 35 per cent. of solid kino.[1]

Authentic specimens of the kino of 16 species of *Eucalyptus* sent from Australia by F. von Müller, have been examined by Wiesner of Vienna.[2] He found the drug to be in most cases readily soluble in water or in spirit of wine, the solution being of a very astringent taste. The solution gave with sulphuric acid a pale red, flocculent precipitate of *Kino-tannic Acid*; with perchloride of iron (as in common kino) a dusky greenish precipitate,—except in the case of the kino of *E. obliqua* L'Hér. (Stringy-bark Tree), the solution of which was coloured dark violet.

Wiesner further states, that Eucalyptus kino affords a little *Catechin*[3] and *Pyrocatechin*. It contains no pectinous matter, but in some varieties a gum like that of *Acacia*. In one sort, the kino of *E. gigantea* Hook.,[4] gum is so abundant that the drug is nearly insoluble in spirit of wine.

By Etti's process, as given at page 197, we obtained kinoïn from an Australian Kino, which contained numerous fragments of the wood. We noticed that both Australian and Malabar kino emitted a somewhat balsamic odour, when they were treated with hydrochloric acid.

From this examination, it is evident that the better varieties of Eucalyptus kino, such for instance as those derived from *E. rostrata* Schlecht. (*Red* or *White Gum*, or *Flooded Gum* of the colonists), *E. corymbosa* Sm. (*Blood-wood*) and *E. citriodora* Hook., possess the properties of Pterocarpus kino and might with no disadvantage be substituted for it.

LIGNUM PTEROCARPI.

Lignum Santalinum rubrum, Santalum rubrum; Red Sanders Wood, Ruby Wood; F. *Bois de Santal rouge*; G. *Rothes Sandelholz, Caliaturholz.*

Botanical Origin—*Pterocarpus santalinus* Linn. fil.—A small tree not often exceeding 3½ to 4 feet in girth, and 20 to 25 feet in height; it is closely related to *Pt. Marsupium* Roxb., from which it differs chiefly in having broader leaflets always in threes. It is a native of the southern part of the Indian Peninsula, as Canara, Mysore, Travancore and the Coromandel Coast, but also occurs in Mindanao, in the southern Philippines. In India the districts in which the wood is at present chiefly obtained are the forests of the southern portion of the

[1] Victoria Exhibition, 1861.—Jurors' Report on Class 3. p. 59.

[2] *Zeitschrift des österreich. Apotheker-Vereines* ix. (1871) 497; *Pharm. Journ.* Aug. 5, 1871. 102.

[3] In our opinion this is doubtful.

[4] Bentham unites this species to *E. obliqua* L'Hér (*Flor. Austr.* iii. 204).

Kurnool Hills, Cuddapah and North Arcot (W. and N.W. of Madras). The tree is now being raised in regular plantations.[1]

The wood is a staple article of produce, and the felling of the trees is strictly controlled by the forest inspectors. The fine trunk-wood is highly valued by the natives for pillars in their temples and other buildings, as well as for turnery. The stumps and roots are exported to Europe as a dye-stuff, mostly from Madras.

History—It is difficult to tell whether the appellation *Red* Sandal-wood used in connexion with *Yellow* and *White* Sandal-wood by some of the earlier writers on drugs, was intended to indicate the inodorous dye-wood under notice or the aromatic wood of a species of *Santalum*. Yet when Marco Polo[2] alludes to the sandal-wood imported into China, and to the *red* sandal ("*Cendal vermeil*") which grows in the island of Necuveran (Nicobar), it is impossible to doubt that he intended by this latter name some such substance as that under notice.

Garcia de Orta, who wrote at Goa in the middle of the 16th century, clearly distinguished the fragrant sandal of Timor from the red inodorous wood of Tenasserim and the Coromandel Coast. It is remarkable that the wood of *Pt. santalinus* is distinguished to the present day in all the languages of India by names signifying *red-coloured sandal-wood*, though it has none whatever of the peculiarities of the odorous wood of *Santalum*. Red Sanders Wood was formerly supposed to possess medicinal powers: these are now disregarded, and it is retained in use only as a colouring agent.

During the middle ages, it was used as well as alkanet for culinary purposes, such as the colouring of sauces and other articles of food. The price in England between 1326 and 1399 was very variable, but on an average exceeded 3*s*. per lb.[3] Many entries for the purchase of Red Sanders along with spices and groceries, occur in the accounts of the Monastery of Durham, A.D. 1530–34.[4]

Description—The wood found in English commerce is mostly that of the lower parts of the stem and that of the thickest roots. It appears in the market in ponderous, irregular logs, rarely exceeding the thickness of a man's thigh and commonly much smaller, 3, 4 or 5 feet in length; they are without bark or sapwood, and are externally of a dark colour. The internal wood is of a deep, rich, blood-red, exhibiting in transverse section zones of a lighter tint, and taking a fine polish.

At the present day, druggists generally buy the wood rasped into small chips, which are of a deep reddish brown hue, tasteless and nearly without odour.

Microscopic Structure—The wood is built up for the greater part of long pointed cells, having thick walls (libriform). Through this ligneous tissue, there are scattered small groups of very large vessels. In a direction parallel to the circumference of the stem, there are less

[1] [Beddome], *Report of the Conservator of Forests*, for 1869-70, Madras, 1870, pp. 3. 39. 123; for figure of the tree, see *Flora Sylvatica of Southern India* of the same author, tab. xxii.

[2] Pauthier, *Livre de Marco Polo*, 580—*Pt. indicus* Willd. grows in the adjacent Andaman Islands.

[3] Rogers, *Agriculture and Prices in England*, 1866, i. 631, ii. 545, &c.—The average price of a sheep during the same period was about 1*s*. 6*d*.

[4] *Durham Household Book*, Surtees Soc. 1844. 215; also Pegge, *Form of Cury*, Lond. 1780. p. xv.

coloured small parenchymatous layers, running from one vascular bundle to another. The whole tissue is finally traversed by very narrow medullary rays, which are scarcely perceptible to the unaided eye. The parenchymatous cells are each loaded with one crystal of oxalate of calcium, which are so large that, in a piece of the wood broken longitudinally, they may be distinguished without a lens. The colouring matter is contained especially in the walls of the vessels and the ligneous cells.

Chemical Composition—Cold water or fatty oil (almond or olive) abstracts scarcely anything from the wood, and hot water but very little. On the other hand, ether, spirit of wine, alkaline solutions, or concentrated acetic acid, readily dissolves out the colouring matter. Essential oils of bitter almond or clove take up a good deal of the red substance; that of turpentine none at all. This resinoid substance, termed *Santalic Acid* or *Santalin*,[1] is said to form microscopic prismatic crystals of a fine ruby colour, devoid of odour and taste, fusing at 104° C., insoluble in water but neutralizing alkalis and forming with them uncrystallizable salts.

Weidel (1870) exhausted the wood with boiling water, containing a little potash, and obtained by means of hydrochloric acid a red precipitate, which was redissolved in boiling alcohol and then furnished *colourless* crystals of *Santal*, $C^8H^6O^3$. They are devoid of odour or taste, not soluble in water, benzol, chloroform, bisulphide of carbon, and but sparingly in ether. Santal yields with potash a faintly yellow solution which soon turns red and green. The wood afforded Weidel not more than 3 per mille of santal.

Cazeneuve (1874)[2] mixed 4 parts of the wood with 1 part of slaked lime, and exhausted the dried powder with ether containing a little alcohol. After the evaporation of the ether, a small amount of colourless crystals of *Pterocarpin* was obtained, which were purified by recrystallization from boiling alcohol. They melt at 83° C., and are abundantly soluble in chloroform, in bisulphide of carbon, very little in cold alcohol, not at all in water. Pterocarpin agrees with the formula $C^{17}H^{16}O^5$. It yields a red solution with concentrated sulphuric acid, and a green with nitric acid 1·4 sp. gr. By submitting it to destructive distillation pyrocatechin appears to be formed.

Franchimont (1879) assigns the formula $C^{17}H^{16}O^6$ to another principle of Red Sanders Wood, which he isolated by means of alcohol. It is an amorphous substance, melting at 105°. By extracting the wood with a solution of carbonate of sodium, Hagenbach (1872) obtained a fluorescent solution. Red Sanders Wood yielded us of ash only 0·8 per cent.

Commerce—In the official year 1869-70, Red Sanders Wood produced to the Madras Government a revenue of 26,015 rupees (£2,601). The quantity taken from the forests was reported as 1,161,799 lb.

[1] Gmelin, *Chemistry*, xvi. (1864) 259; the formula assigned to santalic acid ($C^{15}H^{14}O^5$) appears to be doubtful. Weidel in proposing the formula $C^{14}H^{12}O^4$ points out that t may be allied to alizarin, $C^{14}H^8O^4$.

[2] See *Dictionnaire de Chimie*, art. *Santaline*, p. 1434, and for particulars: Cazeneuve, *Recherche et extraction des alcaloïdes*, etc. Paris, 1875. 66. It would appear that the author obtained about 4 per *mille* of pterocarpin from the wood.

Uses—Red Sanders Wood is scarcely employed in pharmacy except for colouring the Compound Tincture of Lavender; but it has numerous uses in the arts. The latter applies also to the wood of *Pterocarpus angolensis* DC., which is largely exported from the French colony of Gaboon; it is the "Santal rouge d'Afrique of the French," or Barwood of the English commerce.

BALSAMUM TOLUTANUM.

Balsam of Tolu; F. Baume de Tolu; G. Tolubalsam.

Botanical Origin—*Myroxylon Toluifera* H B K. (*Toluifera Balsamum* Miller, *Myrospermum toluiferum* A. Rich.),[1] an elegant and lofty evergreen tree with a straight stem, often as much as 40 to 60 feet from the ground to the first branch. It is a native of Venezuela and New Granada,—probably also of Ecuador and Brazil.

History—The first published account of Balsam of Tolu, is that of the Spanish physician Monardes, who in his treatise on the productions of the West Indies, which in its complete form first appeared at Seville in 1574,[2] relates how the early explorers of South America observed that the Indians collected this drug by making incisions in the trunk of the tree. Below the incisions they affixed shells of a peculiar black wax to receive the balsam, which being collected in a district near Cartagena called *Tolu*, took its name from that place. He adds that it is much esteemed both by Indians and Spaniards, that the latter buy it at a high price, and that they have lately brought it to Spain, where it is considered to be as good as the famous Balsam of Mecca.

Francisco Hernandez, who lived in 1561–1577 in Mexico, stated[3] that the balsam of the province of Tolu was thought to be quite as useful as, if not superior to, "balsamum indicum," *i.e.* peruvianum.

A specimen agreeing with this description was given to Clusius[4] in 1581 by Morgan, apothecary to Queen Elizabeth, but the drug was certainly not common till a much later period. In the price-list of drugs of the city of Frankfort of 1669, Balsam*us tolutanum* (sic) is expressly mentioned,[5] but there can be but little doubt that *Balsamum Americanum resinosum*[6] or *siccum* or *durum* as occurring in many other tariffs of the 17th century, printed in Germany, was also the balsam under notice;[7] in a similar list emanating from the city of Basle in 1646,[8] we noticed *B. indicum album*, *B. peruvianum* and

[1] Fig. in Bentley and Trimen, *Med. Plants*, part 23 (1877) under the name of *Toluifera Balsamum*. Though the change of names may be justified by the strict rules of priority, we are of opinion that at present it would be fraught with more of inconvenience than advantage.—*Myroxylon punctatum* Klotzsch, a tree stated to grow nearly all over the northern part of South America, is referred to the same species by Bentley and Trimen.

[2] *Historia de las cosas que se traen de nuestras Indias occidentales*, cap. del Balsamo de Tolu.

[3] *Nova Plantarum, animal. et mineral. mexicanorum. Historia*, Reccho's edition, Romæ, 1651. fol. 53.

[4] *Exoticor.* etc. 1605. lib. x. fol. 305.

[5] *Pharm. Journ.* vi. (1876) 102.

[6] Pharmaceutical tariff ("Taxa") of the city of Wittenberg 1632 (in the Hamburg library).

[7] Flückiger, *Documente zur Geschichte der Pharmacie*, Halle, 1876. 49. 50. 53.—Balsamum *Peruvianum* first occurs in the tariff of the city of Worms of 1609.—*Documente*, p. 39; *Pharm. Journ.* l. c.

[8] Contained in the *Medicine Tariffs*, in the library of the British Museum, bound together in one volume ($\frac{777.\ c.}{8}$). They include Schweinfurt 1614, Bremen 1644, Basle 1647, Rostock 1659, Quedlinburg 1665, Frankfort on Main 1669 (quoted above).

B. siccum,—the last with the explanatory words, "*trockner Balsam in der Kürbsen*" (*i.e.* in gourds), meaning probably balsam of Tolu.

As to the tree, of which Monardes figured a broken pod, leaflets of it, marked 1758, exist in Sloane's herbarium. Humboldt and Bonpland saw it in several places in New Granada during their travels (1799–1804), but succeeded only in gathering a few leaves. Among recent collectors, Warszewicz, Triana, Sutton Hayes, and Seemann were successful only in obtaining leaves. Weir in 1863 was more happy, for by causing a large tree of nearly 2 feet diameter to be felled, he procured good herbarium specimens including pods, but no flowers. Owing to this tree having been much wounded for balsam, its foliage and fruits were singularly small and stunted, and its branches overgrown with lichens.

That which botanists had failed to do, has been accomplished by an ornithologist, Mr. Anton Goering, who, travelling in Venezuela to collect birds and insects, made it a special object, at the urgent request of one of us (H.), to procure complete specimens of the Balsam of Tolu tree. By dint of much perseverance and by watching for the proper season, Mr. Goering obtained in December 1868 excellent flowering specimens and young fruits, and subsequently mature seeds from which plants have been raised in England, Ceylon and Java.

Extraction—The most authentic information we possess on this subject is derived from Mr. John Weir, plant collector to the Royal Horticultural Society of London, who when about to undertake a journey to New Granada in 1863, received instructions to visit the locality producing Balsam of Tolu. After encountering considerable difficulties, Mr. Weir succeeded in observing the manner of collecting the balsam in the forest near Plato, on the right bank of the Magdalena. Mr. Weir's information[1] may be thus summarized:—

The balsam tree has an average height of 70 feet with a straight trunk, generally rising to a height of 40 feet before it branches. The balsam is collected by cutting in the bark two deep sloping notches, meeting at their lower ends in a sharp angle. Below this V-shaped cut, the bark and wood is a little hollowed out, and a calabash of the size and shape of a deep tea-cup is fixed. This arrangement is repeated, so that as many as twenty calabashes may be seen on various parts of the same trunk. When the lower part has been too much wounded to give space for any fresh incisions, a rude scaffold is sometimes erected, and a new series of notches made higher up. The balsam-gatherer goes from time to time round the trees with a pair of bags of hide, slung over the back of a donkey, and empties into them the contents of the calabashes. In these bags the balsam is sent down to the ports where it is transferred to the cylindrical tins in which it reaches Europe. The bleeding of the trees goes on for at least eight months of the year, causing them ultimately to become much exhausted, and thin in foliage.

In some districts, as we learn from another traveller, it is customary to let the balsam flow down the trunk into a receptacle at its base, formed of the large leaf of a species of *Calathea*.

From the observations of Mr. Weir, it appears that the balsam tree

[1] *Journ. of the R. Hort. Soc.*, May 1864; *Pharm. Journ.* vi. (1865) 60.

is plentifully scattered throughout the Montaña around Plato and other small ports on the right bank of the Magdalena. He states that he saw at least 1,500 lb. of the drug on its way for exportation. From another source, we know that it is largely collected in the valley of the Sinu, and in the forests lying between that river and Cauca. None is collected in Venezuela.

Description—Balsam of Tolu freshly imported is a light brown, slow-flowing resin, soft enough to be impressible with the finger, but viscid on the surface.[1] By keeping, it gradually hardens so as to be brittle in cold weather, but it is easily softened by the warmth of the hand. Thin layers show it to be quite transparent and of a yellowish brown hue. It has a very agreeable and delicate odour, suggestive of benzoin or vanilla, especially perceptible when the resin is warmed, or when its solution in spirit is allowed to evaporate on paper. Its taste is slightly aromatic with a barely perceptible acidity, though its alcoholic solution decidedly reddens litmus.

In very old specimens, such as those which during the last century reached Europe in little calabashes[2] of the size and shape of an orange, the balsam is brittle and pulverulent, and exhibits when broken a sparkling, crystalline surface. This old balsam is of a fine deep amber tint and superior fragrance.

When Balsam of Tolu is pressed between two warmed plates of glass so as to obtain it in a thin even layer, and then examined with a lens, it exhibits an abundance of crystals of cinnamic acid. Balsam of Tolu dissolves easily and completely in glacial acetic acid, acetone, alcohol, chloroform or solution of caustic potash; it is less soluble in ether, scarcely at all in volatile oils, and not in benzol or bisulphide of carbon. The solution in acetone is devoid of rotatory power in polarized light.

Chemical Composition—The balsam consists partly of an *amorphous resin*, not soluble in bisulphide of carbon, which is supposed to be the same as the dark resin precipitated by the bisulphide from balsam of Peru. Scharling (1856) assigned the formula $C^{18}H^{20}O^{5}$ to that part of the balsam which is soluble in potash.

If Tolu balsam is boiled with water, it yields to it cinnamic and benzoic acid, which we have (1877) perfectly succeeded in separating by repeated recrystallization from water; we have before us good specimens of either, showing not only different melting points (133° C. and 121° C.), but as to our crystals of benzoïc acid, isolated from the balsam as stated above, we find that they also do *not* evolve bitter almond oil when mixed with sulphuric acid and chromate of potassium. The acids may also be removed by boiling bisulphide of carbon.

Busse[3] showed that *benzylic* ethers of both benzoic and cinnamic acid are also constituents of the balsam, the cinnamate of benzyl being present in larger quantity.

Upon distilling the balsam with water, it affords 1 per cent. of *Tolene*, $C^{10}H^{16}$, boiling at about 170° C. This liquid rapidly absorbs oxygen from the air. By destructive distillation, the balsam affords the

[1] I have seen it imported very fluid into London by way of New York.—Sept. 1878.—F. A. F.

[2] The gourds, "Kürbsen," of the list of Basle of 1647.

[3] *Berichte der Deutschen Chemischen Gesellschaft*, 1876. 833.

same substances as those obtainable from balsam of Peru, among which *Phenol* and *Styrol* have been observed.

Commerce—The balsam is exported from New Granada, packed in cylindrical tins holding about 10 lb. each. The quantity shipped from Santa Marta in 1870 was 2,002 lb.; in 1871, 2,183 lb.; in 1872, 1,206 lb. In 1876 from the port of Savanilla 27,180 kilogrammes are stated to have been exported.

Uses—Balsam of Tolu has no important medicinal properties. It is chiefly used as an ingredient in a pleasant-tasting syrup and in lozenges.

Adulteration—We have twice met with spurious Balsam of Tolu, but in neither instance did the fraudulent drug bear any great resemblance to the genuine.

Colophony, which might be mixed with the balsam, can be detected by warm bisulphide of carbon which dissolves it, but removes from the pure drug almost exclusively cinnamic and benzoic acid.

BALSAMUM PERUVIANUM.

Balsam umindicum nigrum; Balsam of Peru; F. *Baume de Pérou, Baume de San Salvador;* G. *Perubalsam.*

Botanical Origin—*Myroxylon Pereiræ* Klotzsch (*Myrospermum Pereiræ* Royle), a tree attaining a height of about 50 feet, and throwing out spreading, ascending branches at 6 to 10 feet from the ground.[1]

It is found in a small district of the State of Salvador in Central America (formerly part of Guatemala), lying between 13°·35 and 14°·10 N. lat., and 89° and 89°·40 W. long., and known as the *Costa del Balsamo* or Balsam Coast. The trees grow naturally in the dense forests; those from which the balsam is obtained are, if in groups, sometimes enclosed, in other cases only marked, but all have their distinct owners. They are occasionally rented for a term of years, or a contract is made for the produce of a certain number.

The principal towns and villages around which balsam is produced, are the following:—Juisnagua, Tepecoyo or Coyo, Tamanique, Chiltiuapan, Talnique, Jicalapa, Teotepeque, Comasagua and Jayaque. All the lands on the Balsam Coast are *Indian Reservation Lands.*

The Balsam of Peru tree was introduced in 1861 into Ceylon, where it flourishes with extraordinary vigour.

[1] We are not yet prepared to accept the opinion of Baillon, that *M. Pereiræ* is specifically identical with *M. Toluifera*, though we admit they are very closely related. According to our observations, the two trees exhibit the following differences:—

M. Toluifera.	*M. Pereiræ.*
Trunk tall and bare, branching at 40 to 60 feet from the ground, and forming a roundish crown of foliage.	Trunk throwing off ascending branches at 6 to 10 feet from the ground.
Calyx rather tubular.	Calyx widely cup-shaped, shallow.
Racemes dense, 3 to 4½ inches long.	Racemes loose, 6 to 7 inches long.
Legume scarcely narrowed towards the stalk-end.	Legume much narrowed towards the stalk-end.

See also Bentley and Trimen, *Medicinal Plants*, part 10 (1876), *Toluifera Pereiræ.*

History—As in the case of Balsam of Tolu, it is to Monardes of Seville that we are indebted for the earliest description of the drug under notice. In a chapter headed *Del Balsamo*,[1] he states that at the time he wrote (1565) the drug was not new, for that it had been received into medicine immediately after the discovery of New Spain. As the conquest of Guatemala took place about 1524, we may conclude that the balsam was introduced into Europe soon afterwards.

Monardes further adds, that the balsam was in such high estimation that it sold for 10 to 20 ducats (£4 10s. to £9) the ounce; and that when taken to Rome, it fetched even 100 ducats for the same quantity. The inducement of such enormous prices brought plenty of the drug to Europe, and its value, as well as its reputation, was speedily reduced.

The description given by Monardes of extracting the balsam by boiling the chopped wood of the trunk and branches, raises a doubt as to whether the drug he had in view was exactly that now known; but he never was in America, and may have been misinformed. Evidence that our drug was in use, is afforded by Diego Garcia de Palacio, who, in his capacity of Auditor of the Royal Audiencia of Guatemala, wrote an account to Philip II., king of Spain, describing the geography and productions of this portion of his majesty's dominions. In this interesting document, which bears date 1576 and has only recently been published,[2] Palacio tells the king of the great balsam trees of Guaymoco and of the coasts of Tonala,[3] and of the Indian method of promoting the exudation of the balsam by scorching the trunk of the tree. Prior to the conquest of the country by the Spaniards and for a short time after, balsam formed part of the tribute paid to the Indian chiefs of Cuscatlan, to whom it was presented in curiously ornamented earthen jars.

The idea of great virtues attaching to the balsam is shown by the fact that, in consequence of representations made by missionary priests in Central America, Pope Pius V. granted a faculty to the Bishops of the Indies, permitting the substitution of the balsam of Guatemala for that of Egypt, in the preparation of the chrism used in the Roman Catholic Church. This document, bearing date August 2, 1571, is still preserved in the archives of Guatemala.[4]

In the 16th century, the balsam tree grew in the warm regions of Panuco and Chiapan in Mexico, whence it was introduced into the famous gardens of Hoaxtepec near the city of Mexico, described by Cortes in his letter to Charles V. in 1552.[5]

A rude figure of the tree, certainly a *Myroxylon* and probably the species under notice, was published in the *Thesaurus Rerum Medicarum Novæ Hispaniæ* of Hernandez,[6] who also says that it had been trans-

[1] Occurring in the first book of the work quoted in the Appendix, which was published separately at Seville in 1565.

[2] Squier, *Documents and Relations concerning the Discovery and Conquest of America*, New York, 1859.—Frantzius, *San Salvador und Honduras im Jahre* 1576. Berlin, 1873.

[3] The ancient name of the Balsam Coast; Guaymoco is a village between Sonsonate and San Salvador. The pillars of wood of *Myroxylon* in the church are, perhaps, says Squier, the very same as those mentioned with admiration by Palacio.

[4] It may be found *in extenso* in the original Latin in *Pharm. Journ.* ii. (1861) 447 as well as in Hanbury's *Science Papers*, 1876. 294.

[5] Clavigero, *Hist. of Mexico*, English trans. i. (1787) pp. 32. 379.

[6] Rome, 1628; 2nd ed. 1651. fol. 51; the book written in the town of Mexico, bears at the same time also the title given in the Appendix.

ferred to the "Hoaxtepecences hortos" of the Mexican kings "delitiarum et magnificentiæ gratia."

Balsam of Peru was well known in German pharmacy in the beginning of the 17th century (see article *Balsamum Tolutanum*).

The exports of Guatemala being shipped chiefly at Acajutla, were formerly carried to Callao, the port of Lima, whence they were transmitted to Spain. This circumstance led to the balsam acquiring the misleading name of *Peru*, and in part to the notion that it was a production of South America.

The history of Balsam of Peru was much amplified by a communication of the late Dr. Charles Dorat, of Sonsonate, Salvador, in 1860 to the *American Journal of Pharmacy*, and by still further information accompanied by drawings and specimens, transmitted to one of us in 1863.[1] These statements have lastly been confirmed again on the spot by Mr. Theophilus Wyss, a Swiss apothecary, established in San Miguel la Union, San Salvador.[2]

Extraction of the Balsam—Early in November or December, or after the last rains, the stems of the balsam trees are beaten with the back of an axe, a hammer or other blunt instrument, on four sides, a similar extent of bark being left unbruised between the parts that are beaten. The bark thus injured soon cracks in long strips, and may be easily pulled off. It is sticky as well as the surface below it, and there is a slight exudation of fragrant resin, but not in sufficient quantity to be worth collecting. To promote an abundant flow, it is customary, five or six days after the beating, to apply lighted torches or bundles of burning wood to the injured bark, whereby the latter becomes charred. About a week later, the bark either drops or is taken off, and the stem commences to exude the balsam. This is collected by placing rags (of any kind or colour), so as entirely to cover the bare wood. As these rags in the course of some days become saturated with the exudation, they are collected, thrown into an earthen vessel of water, and gently boiled and stirred until they appear nearly clean, the balsam separating and sinking to the bottom. This process goes on for some hours, the exhausted rags being from time to time taken out, and fresh ones thrown in. As the rags are removed they are wrung out in a sort of rope bag, and the balsam so saved is added to the stock. When the boiler has cooled, the water is decanted, and the balsam is poured into *tecomates* or gourds, ready for the market.

The balsam prepared by means of rags is termed "balsamo de trapo;" a little balsam of inferior quality is also produced, according to Wyss, by boiling the bark with water. This method affords "Tacuasonte" or "balsamo de cascara," which is sometimes mixed with the balsamo de trapo. Tacuasonte means prepared without fire.

The Indians work a tree a second year, by bruising the bark that was left untouched the previous year. As the bark is said to be renewed in the short space of two years, it is possible to obtain from the same tree an annual yield of about 2 lb. of balsam for many years, provided

[1] Hanbury in *Pharm. Journ.* v. (1864) 241. 315; also *Science Papers*, 294-309.

[2] See my paper, with map, in *Schweizerische Wochenschrift für Pharmacie*, 1878. 219 (Library of the Pharm. Soc., London).—In the Catalogue of the contributions of San Salvador to the Paris exhibition, p. 33, Dr. D. J. Guzman gives: "Détails sur le moyen d'extraire et travailler le *Balsamo negro* du Salvador," which are far from satisfactory.—F. A. F.

a few years of rest be occasionally allowed. Clay or earth is sometimes smeared over the bare wood.

The trees sometimes exude spontaneously a greenish gum-resin of slightly bitter taste, but totally devoid of balsamic odour. It has been analyzed by Attfield (see opposite page).

Secretion of the Balsam—No observations have yet been made as to the secretion of the balsam in the wood, or the part that is played by the operation of scorching the bark. Neither the unscorched bark nor the wood, as we have received them, possess any aromatic odour.

The old accounts speak of a very fragrant resin, far more valuable than the ordinary balsam, obtained by incisions. We have made many inquiries for it, but without the least success. Such a resin is easily obtainable from the trunk of *M. Toluifera*.

Description—Balsam of Peru is a liquid having the appearance of molasses, but rather less viscid. In bulk it appears black, but when examined in a thin layer, it is seen to be of a deep orange brown and perfectly transparent. It has a balsamic, rather smoky odour, which is fragrant and agreeable when the liquid is smeared on paper and warmed. It does not much affect the palate, but leaves a disagreeable burning sensation in the fauces.

The balsam has a sp. gr. of 1·15 to 1·16. It may be exposed to the air for years without undergoing alteration or depositing crystals. It is not soluble in water, but yields to it a little cinnamic and traces of benzoic acid; from 6 to 8 parts of crystallized carbonate of sodium are required to neutralize 100 parts of the balsam. It is but partially and to a small extent dissolved by dilute alcohol, benzol, ether or essential or fatty oils, not at all by petroleum-ether. The balsam mixes readily with glacial acetic acid, anhydrous acetone, absolute alcohol or chloroform. Its rotatory power is very insignificant.

Chemical Composition—The peculiar process by which balsam of Peru is obtained, causes it to contain a variety of substances not found in the more natural resin of *Myroxylon Toluifera*; hence the two drugs, though derived from plants most closely allied, possess very different properties.

Three parts of the balsam mix readily with one part of bisulphide of carbon, yet a further addition of the latter will cause the separation of a brown flocculent resin. If the balsam be mixed with thrice its weight of bisulphide, a coherent mass of dark resin, sometimes amounting to about 38 per cent. of the balsam, is precipitated. The bisulphide of carbon forms then a perfectly transparent brown liquid. If this solution is shaken with water, the latter removes *Cinnamic* and *Benzoic* acids. To separate them, ammonia is cautiously added, yet not in excess.[1] The solution of cinnamate and benzoate thus obtained and duly concentrated, yields both these acids in white crystals on addition of acetic or hydrochloric acid.

The resin separated by means of bisulphide of carbon as above stated, is a black brittle amorphous mass, having no longer the specific odour of the balsam. It is soluble in caustic alkalis, also in alcohol; the solution

[1] By saturating the acid aqueous liquid with ammonia, it assumes a transient bright yellow hue; an excess of ammonia transforms the whole mixture into an emulsion, from which the cinnameïn again separates but imperfectly.

in the latter which may be considerably purified by charcoal, reddens litmus, and is abundantly precipitated by an alcoholic solution of neutral acetate of lead. Kachler (1869) by melting this resin with potash obtained about $\frac{3}{5}$ of its weight of proto-catechuic acid.[1] By destructive distillation, it furnishes benzoic acid, styrol, C^8H^8, and toluol, C^7H^8.

As to the solution obtained with bisulphide of carbon, it forms, after the bisulphide has evaporated, a brownish aromatic liquid of about 1·1 sp. gr., termed *Cinnameïn*. This substance may also be obtained by distillation, yet less easily, on account of its very high boiling point, about 300° C.

Cinnameïn, $C^{16}H^{14}O^2$, is resolved by concentrated caustic lye into benzylic alcohol, $C^7H^{14}O^2$, and cinnamic acid, $C^9H^8O^2$, whence it follows that cinnameïn is *Benzylic Cinnamate*. This is, according to Kraut (1858, 1869, 1870) and to Kachler (1869, 1870), the chief constituent of the balsam. The former chemist obtained from it nearly 60 per cent. cinnameïn. Kachler assigns to the balsam the following composition: 46 per cent. of cinnamic acid, 32 of resin, 20 of benzylic alcohol. These latter figures however are not quite consistent: 46 parts of cinnamic acid (molecular weight = 148) would answer to 73 parts of benzylic cinnamate; and 20 parts of benzylic alcohol require on the other hand only (mol. weight = 108) 27·4 parts of cinnamic acid in order to form benzylic cinnamate (mol. = 238).

Benzylic cinnamate, prepared as above stated, is a thick liquid, miscible both with ether or alcohol, not concreting at − 12° C., boiling at 305° C., yet under ordinary circumstances not without decomposition. By exposure to air, it slowly acquires an acid reaction; by prolonged action of potash, especially in an alcoholic solution, toluol is also formed. In this process, cinnamate of potassium finally forms a crystalline mass, while an oily mixture of benzylic alcohol and toluol, the so-called "*Peruvin*," constitutes the liquid part of the whole.

Grimaux (1868) has artificially prepared benzylic cinnamate by heating an alkaline cinnamate with benzylic chloride. Thus obtained, that substance forms crystals, which melt at 39° C., and boil at 225 to 235° C. They consequently differ much from cinnameïn.

Delafontaine (1868) is of the opinion, that cinnameïn contains besides benzylic cinnamate, cinnamylic cinnamate, $C^{36}H^{32}O^4$, the same substance as described under the name of styracin in the article *Styrax liquida*. He states that he obtained benzylic and cinnamylic alcohol when he decomposed cinnameïn by an alkali. The two alcohols however were separated only by fractional distillation.

From the preceding investigations it must be concluded, that the bark of the tree contains resin and probably benzylic cinnamate. The latter is no doubt altered by the process of collecting the balsam, which is followed on the Balsam Coast. To this are probably due the free acids in the balsam and its dark colour.

Another point of considerable interest is the fact, that the tree exudes a gum-resin, containing according to Attfield 77·4 per cent. of resin,[2] which is non-aromatic and devoid of cinnamic acid, and therefore entirely distinct from balsam of Peru. The leaves of the tree contain a fragrant oil.

[1] Numerous resins as benzoin, guaiacum, dragon's blood, myrrh, etc., and many other substances are capable of affording the same acid.

[2] *Pharm. Journ.* v. (1864) 248.

Commerce—The balsam is shipped chiefly at Acajutla. It used formerly to be packed in large earthenware jars, said to be Spanish wine-jars, which, wrapped in straw, were sewed up in raw hide. These packages have of late been superseded by metallic drums, which have the advantage of being much less liable to breakage. We have no exact statistics as to the quantity exported from Central America. In the catalogue of San Salvador (quoted above, page 207, note 2) p. 39, the value of the balsam exported in 1876 from that country is stated to have been 78,189 dollars. The value of tobacco amounted to 69,717 dollars, that of coffee to 1⅓ millions of dollars, indigo to 2¼ millions.

Uses—Occasionally prescribed in the form of ointment as a stimulating application to old sores, sometimes internally for the relief of asthma and chronic cough. It is said to be also employed for scenting soap.

Adulteration—We have before us a sample of an adulterated balsam, which, we are told, is largely prepared at Bremen. It is less aromatic, less rich in acids, and contains usually much less than 38 per cent. of resin separable, as above stated, by means of bisulphide of carbon. At first sight however the adulterated drug is not so easily recognized.

Other sorts of Balsam of Peru.

The value anciently set upon balsam for religious and medicinal uses, led to its being extracted from the pods and also from trees no longer employed for the purpose; and many of the products so obtained have attracted the attention of pharmacologists.[1] Parkinson writing in 1640 observes that—"there have been divers other sorts of liquours, called *Balsamum* for their excellent vertues, brought out of the West Indies, every one of which for a time after their first bringing was of great account with all men and bought at great prices, but as greater store was brought, so did the prices diminish and the use decay . . ."

In Salvador, the name *Balsamo blanco* (White Balsam) is applied to the soft resin contained in the large ducts of the legume of *Myroxylon Pereiræ*. This, when pressed out, forms a golden yellow, semi-fluid, granular, crystalline mass, hardening by age, having a rather unpleasant odour suggestive of melilot. Stenhouse (1850) obtained from it the neutral resin *Myroxocarpin*, $C^{24}H^{34}O^{3}$, in thin colourless prisms, an inch or more in length. We have succeeded in extracting it directly from the pods. This White Balsam, which is distinctly mentioned in the letter of Palacio in 1576 (see p. 206), is a scarce and valuable article, never prepared for the market. A large jar of it was sent to Pereira in 1850;[2] Guzman[3] and Wyss state that it is known in the country as "Balsamito," or "Balsamo *catolico* or Virgin Balsam."

A fragrant balsamic resin is collected, though in but very small quantity, from *Myroxylon peruiferum* Linn. f., a noble tree of New Granada, Ecuador, Peru, Bolivia, and Brazil. A fine sample of this substance, accompanied by herbarium and other specimens, was presented to one of us (H.) by Mr. J. Correa de Méllo of Campinas (Brazil);

[1] Guibourt, *Hist. des Drog.* iii. (1850) 440.

[2] *Pharm. Journ.* x. (1851) 286.

[3] In the Catalogue alluded to, page 207, note 2.

it is a resin having a general resemblance to Balsam of Tolu, but of somewhat deeper and redder tint, and greater hardness. Pressed between two slips of warmed glass, it does not exhibit any crystals.

In a treatise on Brazil written by a Portuguese friar about 1570-1600,[1] mention is made of the "*Cabueriba*" (*Cabure-iba*), from which a much-esteemed balsam was obtained by making incisions in the stem, and absorbing the exudation with cotton wool, somewhat in the same way as Balsam of Peru is now collected in Salvador. This tree is *Myrocarpus frondosus* Allem., now called *Cabriuva preta*. The genus is closely allied to *Myroxylon*.

Another fragrant oleo-resin, which has doubtless been confounded with that of a *Myroxylon*, is obtained in Central America from *Liquidambar styraciflua* L., either by incision or by boiling the bark.

SEMEN BONDUCELLÆ.

Semen Guilandinæ; Bonduc Seeds, Grey Nicker Seeds or Nuts; F. *Graines de Bonduc ou du Cniquier, Pois Quéniques, Pois Guénic.*

Botanical Origin—*Cæsalpinia Bonducella* Roxb. (*Guilandina Bonducella* L.), a prickly, pubescent, climbing shrub[2] of wide distribution, occurring in Tropical Asia, Africa and America, especially near the sea. The compressed, ovate, spiny legume is 2 to 3 inches long, and contains one or two, occasionally three or four, hard, grey, globular seeds.

The plant is often confounded with *C. Bonduc* Roxb., a nearly allied but much rarer species, distinguished by being nearly glabrous, having leaflets very unequal at the base, no stipules, erect bracts, and yellow seeds.

History—"*Pūti-Karanja*," stinking Karanja, in Susruta (I. 223, 1) is the plant under notice. The word *Bunduk*, occurring in the writings of the Arabian and Persian physicians, also in Constantinus Africanus, mostly signifies *hazel-nut*.[3] One of these authors, Ibn Baytar,[4] who flourished in the 13th century, further distinguished a drug called *Bunduk Hindi* (Indian hazel-nut), giving a description which indicates it plainly as the seed under notice. Both *Bunduk* and *Bunduk Hindi* are enumerated in the list of drugs of Noureddeen Mohammed Abdullah Shirazy,[5] physician to the Mogul emperor Shah Jehan, A.D. 1628-1661.

The pods of *C. Bonducella* were figured by Clusius in 1605, under the name of *Lobus echinodes*, and the plant both by Rheede[6] and Rumphius. Piso and Marcgraf (1648) noticed it in Brazil and gave some account of it with a bad woodcut, under the designation of *Inimbóy* (now *Inimboja*), or in Portuguese *Silva do Praya*.

In recent times, Bonduc seeds have been employed on account of their tonic and antiperiodic properties by numerous European practi-

[1] Purchas, *His Pilgrimes*, iv. (1625) 1308.

[2] Fig. in Bentley and Trimen, *Med. Plants*, part 24 (1877).

[3] The word also means *a little ball* or *a round stone*. Bunduk Hindi is frequently used by Arabic authors to denote also Areca-nut.

[4] Sontheimer's translation, i. 177.

[5] *Ulfaz Udwiyeh*, translated by Gladwin, 1793. No. 543. 551.

[6] *Hort. Malab.* ii. (1679) tab. 22, sub nom. *Caretti*.

tioners in the East, and have been included in the *Pharmacopœia of India*, 1868.

Description—The seeds are somewhat globular or ovoid, a little compressed, $\frac{4}{10}$ to $\frac{8}{10}$ of an inch in diameter and weighing 20 to 40 grains. They are of a bluish or greenish grey tint, smooth, yet marked by slightly elevated horizontal lines of a darker hue. The umbilicus is surrounded by a small, dark brown, semilunar blotch opposite the micropyle. The hard shell is from $\frac{1}{25}$ to $\frac{2}{25}$ of an inch thick, and contains a white kernel, representing from 40 to 50 per cent. of the weight of the seed. It separates easily from the shell, and consists of the two cotyledons and a stout radicle. When a seed is soaked for some hours in cold water, a very thin layer can be peeled from the surface of the testa. The kernel is bitter, but with the taste that is common to most seeds of the family *Leguminosæ*.

Microscopic Structure—The outer layer of the testa, the epidermis above alluded to, is composed of two zones of perpendicular, closely packed cells, the outer measuring about 130 mkm., the inner 100 mkm. in length and only 5 to 7 mkm. in diameter. The walls of these cylindrical cells are thickened by secondary deposits, which in transverse section show usually four or more channels running down nearly perpendicularly through the whole cell.

The spongy parenchyme, which is covered by this very distinct outer layer, is made up of irregular, ovate, subglobular or somewhat elongated cells with large spaces between them, loaded with brown masses of tannic matter, assuming a blackish hue when touched with perchloride of iron. The thick walls of these cells frequently exhibit, chiefly in the inner layers, undulated outlines. The tissue of the cotyledons is composed of very large cells, swelling considerably in water, and containing some mucilage (as may be ascertained when thin slices are examined in oil), small starch granules, fatty oil, and a little albuminous matter.

Chemical Composition—According to the medical reports alluded to in the *Pharmacopœia of India* (1868), Bonduc seeds, and still more the root of the plant, act as a powerful antiperiodic and tonic.

The active principle has not yet been adequately examined. It may perhaps occur in larger proportion in the bark of the root, which is said to be more efficacious than the seeds in the treatment of intermittent fever.[1]

In order to ascertain the chemical nature of the principle of the seeds, one ounce of the kernels[2] was powdered and exhausted with slightly acidulated alcohol. The solution after the evaporation of the alcohol was made alkaline with caustic potash, which did not produce a precipitate. Ether now shaken with the liquid, completely removed the bitter matter, and yielded it in the form of an amorphous white powder, devoid of alkaline properties. It is sparingly soluble in water, but readily in alcohol, forming intensely bitter solutions; an aqueous solution is not precipitated by tannic acid. It produces a yellowish or brownish solution with concentrated sulphuric

[1] Waring, *Bazaar Medicines*, Travancore, 1860. 18.

[2] Kindly furnished us by Dr. Waring.

acid, which acquires subsequently a violent hue. Nitric acid is without manifest influence. From these experiments, we may infer that the active principle of the Bonduc seed is a bitter substance not possessing basic properties.

Uses—The powdered kernels either *per se*, or mixed with black pepper (*Pulvis Bonducellæ compositus* Ph. Ind.), are employed in India against intermittent fevers and as a general tonic.

The fatty oil of the seeds is sometimes extracted and used in India; it was shown at the Madras Exhibitions of 1855 and 1857.

LIGNUM HÆMATOXYLI.

Lignum Campechianum v. Campescanum; Logwood, Peachwood; F. *Bois de Campèche, Bois d'Inde;* G. *Campecheholz, Blauholz.*

Botanical Origin—*Hæmatoxylon campechianum* L., a spreading tree[1] of moderate size, seldom exceeding 40 feet in height, native of the bay of Campeachy, Honduras and other parts of Central America. It was introduced into Jamaica by Dr. Barham[2] in 1715, and is now completely naturalized in that and other of the West Indian Islands.

History—Hernan Cortes in his letter to the Emperor Charles V., giving an account of his expedition to Honduras in 1525,[3] refers to the Indian towns of Xiculango and Tabasco as carrying on a trade in cacao, cotton cloth, and *colours for dyeing*,—in which last phrase there may be an allusion to logwood. We have sought for some more definite notice of the wood in the *Historia de las Indias* of Oviedo,[4] the first chronicler of America, but without much success.

Yet the wood must have been introduced into England in the latter half of the 16th century, for, in 1581, an Act of Parliament[5] was passed, abolishing its use and ordering that any found should be forfeited and burned. In this Act the obnoxious dye is described as "a certain kind of ware or stuff called *Logwood* alias *Blockwood* . . . of late years . . . . brought into this realm of England." The object of this measure was to protect the public against the bad work of the dyers, who, it seems, were unable at that period to obtain durable colours by the use of logwood. Eighty years later the art of dyeing had so far improved that logwood was again permitted,[6] the colours produced by it being declared as lasting and serviceable as those made by any other sort of dyewood whatsoever.

The wood is mentioned by De Laet (1633) as deriving its name from the town of Campeachy, whence, says he, it is brought in great plenty to Europe.[7]

As a medicine, logwood was not employed until shortly before the

[1] Fig. in Bentley and Trimen, *Med. Plants*, part 5 (1876).

[2] *Hortus Americanus*, Kingston, Jamaica, 1794. 91.

[3] *Fifth Letter of Hernan Cortes to the Emperor Charles V.*, Lond. (Hakluyt Society) 1868. 43.

[4] The first edition bears date 1535. We have used the modern one of Madrid, 1851-55, 4to., and may refer in particular to tom. i. lib. ix. c. 15, iii. lib. xxxi. c. 8 and c. 11.—See Appendix: Fernandez.

[5] 23 Eliz. c. 9.

[6] 13-14 Car. ii. c. 11. sect. 26 (A.D. 1662), by which the Act of Elizabeth was repealed.

[7] *Novus Orbis*, 1633. 274 and 265.

year 1746, when it was introduced into the London Pharmacopœia under the name of *Lignum tinctile Campechense*.

Description—The tree is fit to be felled when about ten years old; the dark bark and the yellowish sap-wood are chipped off, the stems cut into logs about three feet long, and the red heart-wood alone exported. By exposure to air and moisture, the wood acquires externally a blackish red colour; internally it remains brownish red. It splits well, although of a rather dense and tough texture.

The transverse section of a piece of logwood exhibits to the naked eye a series of very narrow concentric zones, formed by comparatively large pores, and of small parenchymatous circles separated by the larger and darker rings of the proper woody tissue. The numerous medullary rays are visible only by means of a lens. The wood has a pleasant odour.

For use in pharmacy, logwood is always purchased in the form of chips, which are produced by the aid of powerful machinery. The chips have a feeble, seaweed-like odour, and a slightly sweet, astringent taste, better perceived in a watery decoction than by chewing the dry wood, which however quickly imparts to the saliva its brilliant colour.

Microscopic Structure—Under a high magnifying power, the concentric zones are seen to run not quite regularly round the centre, but in a somewhat undulating manner, because they do not correspond, as in our indigenous woods, to regular periods of annual growth. The vascular bundles contain only a few vessels, and are transversely united by small lighter parenchymatous bands. The latter are made up of large, cubic, elongated or polygonal cells, each loaded with a crystal of oxalate of calcium. The large punctuated vessels having frequently 150 mkm. diameter, are surrounded by this woody parenchyme, while the prevailing tissue of the wood is composed of densely packed prosenchyme, consisting of long cylindrical cells (*libriform*) with thick, dark red-brown walls having small pores.

The medullary rays are of the usual structural character, running transversely in one to three straight rows; in a longitudinal section, the single rays show from 4 to 40 rows succeeding each other perpendicularly. No regular arrangement of the rays is obvious in a longitudinal section made in a tangential direction. The colouring matter is chiefly contained in the walls of the ligneous tissue and the vessels, and sometimes occurs in crystals of a greenish hue within the latter, or in clefts of the wood.

Chemical Composition—Logwood was submitted to analysis by Chevreul as early as the year 1810,[1] since which period all contributions to a knowledge of the drug refer exclusively to its colouring principle *Hæmatoxylin*, which Chevreul obtained in a crystallized state and called *Hématine*. The very interesting properties of this substance have been chiefly examined by Erdmann (1842) and by O. Hesse (1858-59).

Erdmann obtained from logwood 9 to 12 per cent. of crystallized hæmatoxylin, which he showed to have the formula $C^{16}H^{14}O^{6}$. In a pure state it is colourless, crystallizing with 1 or with 3 equivalents of water, and is readily soluble in hot water or in alcohol, but sparingly

[1] *Annales de Chimie*, lxxxi. (1812) 128.

in cold water or in ether. It has a persistent sweet taste like liquorice. The crystals of hæmatoxylin acquire a red colour by the action of sunlight, as likewise their aqueous solution. They are decomposed by ozone but not by pure and dry oxygen. In presence of alkalis, hæmatoxylin exposed to the air quickly yields dark purplish violet solutions, which soon acquire a yellowish or dingy brownish colour; hence in analytical chemistry hæmatoxylin is used as a test for alkalis.

By the combined action of ammonia and oxygen, dark violet crystalline scales of *Hæmateïn*, $C^{16}H^{14}O^{6} + 3\ OH^{2}$, are produced.[1] They show a fine green hue, which is also very commonly observable on the surface of the logwood chips of commerce. Hæmateïn may again be transformed into hæmatoxylin by means of hydrogen or of sulphurous acid.

Hæmatoxylin separates protoxide of copper from an alkaline solution of the tartrate, and deviates the ray of polarized light to the right hand. It is not decomposed by concentrated hydrochloric acid; by melting hæmatoxylin with potash, pyrogallol (pyrogallic acid, $C^{6}H^{6}O^{3}$) is obtained. Alum and the salts of lead throw down precipitates from solutions of hæmatoxylin, the latter being of a bluish-black colour. Logwood affords upon incineration 3·3 per cent. of ash.

The colouring matter being abundantly soluble in boiling water, an *Extract of Logwood* is also prepared on a large scale. It occurs in commerce in the form of a blackish brittle mass, taking the form of the wooden chest into which it is put while soft. The extract shares the chemical properties of hæmatoxylin and hæmateïn: whether it also contains gum requires investigation.

Production and Commerce—The felling and shipping of logwood in Central America have been described by Morelet,[2] who states that in the woods of Tabasco and Yucatan the trade is carried on in the most irrational and reckless manner. By advancing money to the natives, or by furnishing them with spirits, arms, or tools, the proprietors of the woods engage them to fell a number of trees in proportion to their debts. This is done in the dry season, the rainy period being taken for the shipment of the logs, which are conveyed chiefly to the island of Carmen in the Laguna de Terminos in South-western Yucatan, and to Frontera on the mouths of the Tabasco river, at which places European ships receive cargoes of the wood.

In 1877 the export of Laguna de Terminos amounted to 528,605 quintals (one quintal = 46 kilogrammes), that from Port-au-Prince, Hayti, in 1872, nearly to 90,000 tons.

Four sorts of logwood are found in the London market, namely *Campeachy*, quoted[3] at £8 10*s.* to £9 10*s.* per ton; *Honduras*, £6 10*s.* to £6 15*s.*; *St. Domingo*, £5 15*s.* to £6; *Jamaica*, £5 2*s.* 6*d.* to £5 10*s.* The imports into the United Kingdom were valued in 1872 at £233,035. The quantities imported during that and the previous three years were as follows:—

1869	1870	1871	1872
50,458 tons.	62,187 tons.	39,346 tons.	46,039 tons.

[1] Benedikt, in 1875, assigned them the formula $C^{48}H^{30}O^{18}N + 9\ OH^{2}$.

[2] *Voyage dans l'Amérique centrale, l'île de Cuba et le Yucatan*, Paris, 1857.

[3] *Public Ledger*, 28 Feb. 1874.

In 1876 the import was 64,215 tons, valued at £415,857. The largest quantity is supplied by the British West India Islands. Hamburg also imports annually about 20,000 tons of logwood.

Uses—Logwood in the form of decoction is occasionally administered in chronic diarrhœa, and especially in the diarrhœa of children. Cases have occurred in which its use has been followed by phlebitis. Its employment in the art of dyeing is far more important.

Adulteration—The woods of several species of *Cæsalpinia* imported under the name of *Brazil Wood* and used for dyeing red, bear an external resemblance to logwood, with which it is said they are sometimes mixed in the form of chips. They contain a crystallizable colouring principle called *Brasilin*, $C^{22}H^{20}O^7$, or, according to Liebermann and Burg (1876), $C^{16}H^{14}O^5$, which affords with alkalis *red* and not bluish or purplish solutions, and yields trinitrophenol, $C^6H^2(NO^2)^3OH$ (picric acid), when boiled with nitric acid, while hæmatoxylin yields oxalic acid only. The best source for brasilin is the wood of *Cæsalpinia Sappan* L., a tree of the East Indies, well known as *Bakam, Brazil Wood, Lignum Brasile, Verzino* of the Italians, an important object of commerce during the middle ages.[1]

FOLIA SENNÆ.

Sennæ Leaves; F. Feuilles de Séné; G. Sennesblätter.

Botanical Origin—The Senna Leaves of commerce are afforded by two species of *Cassia*[2] belonging to that section of the genus which is distinguished by having leaves without glands, axillary racemes elongating as inflorescence advances, membranaceous bracts which in the young raceme conceal the flower buds but drop off during flowering, and a short, broad, flat legume.

The senna plants are low perennial bushy shrubs, 2 to 4 feet high, having pari-pinnate leaves with leaflets unequal at the base, and yellow flowers. The pods contain 6 or more seeds in each, suspended on alternate valves by long capillary funicles. These run towards the pointed end of the seed, but are curved at their attachment to the hilum just below. The seeds are compressed and of an obovate-cuneate or oblong form, beaked at the narrower end.[3]

The species in question are the following:—

1. *Cassia acutifolia* Delile[4]—a shrub about 2 feet high, with pale subterate or obtusely angled, erect or ascending branches, occasionally slightly zigzag above, glabrous at least below. Leaves usually 4-5-jugate; leaflets oval or lanceolate, acute, mucronate, usually more or less distinctly

[1] See Yule, *Marco Polo*, ii. (1874). 369.

[2] Some writers have removed these plants from *Cassia* to a separate genus named *Senna*, but such subdivision is repudiated by the principal botanists. The intricate synonymy of the senna plants has been well worked out by J. B. Batka in his memoir entitled *Monographie der Cassien-Grappe Senna* (Prag, 1866), of which we have made free use. We have also had the advantage of the recent *Revision of the Genus Cassia* by Bentham (*Linn. Trans.*, xxvii. 1871. 503) and of the labours of Oliver on the same subject in his *Flora of Tropical Africa*, ii. (1871) 268-282.

[3] On the structure of the seed, see Batka, *Pharm. Journ.* ix. (1850) 30.

[4] *Synonyms*—*C. Senna β.* Linn.; *C. lanceolata* Nectoux; *C. lenitiva* Bisch.; *Senna acutifolia* Batka.

puberulous or at length glabrous, pale or subglaucous at least beneath, subsessile. Stipules subulate, spreading or reflexed, 1-2 lines long. Racemes axilliary, erect, rather laxly many-flowered, usually considerably exceeding the subtending leaf. Bracts membranous, ovate or obovate, caducous. Pedicels at length 2-3 lines. Sepals obtuse, membranous. Two of the anterior anthers much exceeding the rest of the fertile stamens. Legume flat, very broadly oblong, but slightly curved upwards, obliquely stipitate, broadly rounded at the extremity with a minute or obsolete mucro indicating the position of the style on the upper edge; 1½-2¼ inches long, ¾-1 inch broad; valves chartaceous, obsoletely or thinly puberulous, faintly transverse-veined, unappendaged. Seeds obovate-cuneate, compressed; cotyledons plane, extending the large diameter of the seed in transverse section.[1]

The plant is a native of many districts of Nubia (as Sukkot, Mahas, Dongola, Berber), Kordofan and Sennaar; grows also in Timbuktu and Sokoto, and is the source of *Alexandrian Senna*.

2. *C. augustifolia* Vahl[2]—This species is closely related to the preceding, the general description of which is applicable to it with the following exceptions. In the present plant the leaflets, which are usually 5-8-jugate, are narrower, being oval-lanceolate, tapering from the middle towards the apex; they are larger, being from one to nearly 2 inches long, and are either quite glabrous or furnished with a very scanty pubescence. The legume is narrower (7-8 lines broad), with the base of the style distinctly prominent on its upper edge.

The plant abounds in Yemen and Hadramaut in Southern Arabia; it is also found on the Somali coast, in Sind and the Punjab. In some parts of India it is now cultivated for medicinal use.

The uncultivated plant of Arabia supplies the so-called *Bombay Senna* of commerce, the true *Senna Mekki* of the East. The cultivated and more luxuriant plant, raised originally from Arabian seeds, furnishes the *Tinnevelly Senna* of the drug market.

History—According to the elaborate researches of Carl Martius,[3] a knowledge of senna cannot be traced back earlier than the time of the Elder Serapion, who flourished in the 9th or 10th century; and it is in fact to the Arabian physicians that the introduction of the drug to Western Europe is due. Isaac Judæus,[4] who wrote probably about A.D. 850-900 and who was a native of Egypt, mentions senna, the best kind of which he says is that brought from Mecca.

Senna (as *Ssinen* or *Ssenen*) is enumerated among the commodities liable to duty at Acre in Palestine at the close of the 12th century.[5] In France in 1542, a pound of senna was valued in an official tariff[6] at 15 sols, the same price as pepper or ginger.

The Arabian and the mediæval physicians of Europe used both the pods and leaves, preferring however the former. The pods (*Folliculi Sennæ*) are still employed in some countries.

[1] We borrow the above description from Prof. Oliver.

[2] *Synonyms*—*C. lanceolata* Roxb.; *C. elongata* Lem. Lis.; *Senna officinalis* Roxb.; *S. angustifolia* Batka.

[3] *Versuch einer Monographie der Sennesblätter*, Leipz. 1867.

[4] *Opera Omnia*, Lugd. 1515, lib. 2. Practices, c. 39,

[5] *Recueil des Historiens des Croisades, Lois*, ii. (1843) 177.

[6] Fontanon, *Edicts et Ordonnances des Roys de France*, éd. 2, ii. (1585) 349.

Cassia obovata Coll.[1] was the species first known to botanists, and it was even cultivated in Italy for medicinal use during the first half of the 16th century. Hence the term *Italian Senna* used by Gerarde and others. In the records of the "Cinque savii alla mercanzia" at Venice we found an order bearing date 1526 to the effect that Senna leaves of Tuscany were inadmissible; the same was applied in 1676 to the drug from Tripoli in Barbaria, that from Cairo being exclusively permitted.

Production—According to Nectoux,[2] whose observations relate to Nubia at the close of the last century, the peasants make two senna harvests annually, the first and more abundant being at the termination of the rains,—that is in September; while the other, which in dry seasons is almost *nil*, takes place in April.

The gathering consists in simply cutting down the shrubs, and exposing them on the rocks to the burning sun till completely dry. The drug is then packed in bags made of palm leaves holding about a quintal each, and conveyed by camels to Es-souan and Darao, whence it is transported by water to Cairo. By many travellers it is stated that *Senna jebeli*, i.e. *mountain senna* (*C. acutifolia*), finds its way to the ports of Massowhah and Suakin, and thence to Cairo and Alexandria.

Cassia obovata, which is called by the Arabs *Senna baladi*, i.e. *indigenous* or *wild senna*, grows in the fields of durra (*Sorghum*) at Karnak and Luxor, and in the time of Nectoux was held in such small esteem that it fetched but a quarter the price of the *Senna jebeli* brought by the caravans of Nubia and the Bisharrin Arabs. It is not now collected.

Description—Three kinds of senna are distinguished in English commerce:—

1. *Alexandrian Senna*—This is furnished by *Cassia acutifolia* and is imported in large bales. It used formerly always to arrive in a very mixed and dirty state, containing, in addition to leaflets of senna, a variable proportion of leafstalks and broken twigs, pods and flowers; besides which there was almost invariably an accompaniment of the leaves, flowers and fruits of *Solenostemma Argel* Hayne (p. 220), not to mention seeds, stones, dust and heterogeneous rubbish. Such a drug required sifting, fanning and picking, by which most of these impurities could be separated, leaving only the senna contaminated with leaves of argel. But Alexandrian Senna has of late been shipped of much better quality. Some we have recently seen (1872) was, as taken from the original package, wholly composed of leaflets of *C. acutifolia* in a well-preserved condition; and even the lower qualities of senna are never now contaminated with argel to the extent that was usual a few years ago.

The leaflets, the general form of which has already been described

[1] It is a glaucous shrub with obovate leaflets, broadly rounded and mucronulate, reniform legume terminated by persistent style, and marked along the middle of each valve by a series of crest-shaped ridges corresponding to the seeds. It is more widely distributed in the Nile region than the other species, and is also found in Sindh and Gujerat and (naturalized) in the West Indies. Its leaflets (also pods) may occasionally be picked out of Alexandrian Senna.

[2] *Voyage dans la Haute Egypte . . avec des observations sur les diverses espèces de Séné qui sont répandues dans le commerce*, Paris, 1808. fol.

(p. 216), are ¾ to 1¼ inches long, rather stiff and brittle, generally a little incurled at the edges, conspicuously veined, the midrib being often brown. They are covered with a very short and fine pubescence which is most dense on the midrib. The leaves have a peculiar opaque, light yellowish green hue, a somewhat agreeable tea-like odour, and a mucilaginous, not very marked taste, which however is sickly and nauseous in a watery infusion.

2. *Arabian Moka, Bombay or East Indian Senna*—This drug is derived from *Cassia augustifolia,* and is produced in Southern Arabia. It is shipped from Moka, Aden and other Red Sea ports to Bombay, and thence reaches Europe.

Arabian senna is usually collected and dried without care, and is mostly an inferior commodity, fetching in London sometimes as low a price as ½*d.* to ¼*d.* per ℔. Yet so far as we have observed, it is never adulterated, but consists wholly of senna leaflets, often brown and decayed, mixed with flowers, pods, and stalks. The leaflets have the form already described (p. 217); short adpressed hairs are often visible on their under surface.

3. *Tinnevelly Senna*—Derived from the same species as the last, but from the plant cultivated in India, and in a state of far greater luxuriance than it exhibits in the drier regions of Arabia where it grows wild. It is a very superior and carefully collected drug, consisting wholly of the leaflets. These are lanceolate, 1 to 2 inches in length, of a yellowish green on the upper side, of a duller tint on the under, glabrous or thinly pubescent on the under side with short adpressed hairs. The leaflets are less rigid in texture than those of Alexandrian senna, and have a tea-like, rather fragrant smell, with but little taste.

Tinnevelly senna has of late fallen off in size, and some importations in 1873 were not distinguishable from Arabian senna, except from having been more carefully prepared. The drug is generally shipped from Tuticorin in the extreme south of India.

Chemical Composition—The analysis of senna with a view to the isolation of its active principle has engaged the attention of numerous chemists, but as yet the results of their labours are not quite satisfactory.

Ludwig (1864) treated an alcoholic extract of senna with charcoal, and obtained from the latter by means of boiling alcohol two bitter principles, *Sennacrol,* soluble in ether, and *Sennapicrin,* not dissolved by ether.

Dragendorff and Kubly (1866) have shown the active substance of senna to be a colloid body, easily soluble in water but not in strong alcohol. When a syrupy aqueous extract of senna is mixed with an equal volume of alcohol, and the mucilage thus thrown down has been removed, the addition of a further quantity of alcohol occasions the fall of a dark brown, almost tasteless, easily alterable substance, which is indued with purgative properties. It was further shown that this precipitate was a mixture of calcium and magnesium salts of phosphoric acid and a peculiar acid. The last named, separated by hydrochloric acid, has been called *Cathartic Acid;* it is a black substance which in the mouth is at first insipid, but afterwards tastes acid and somewh astringent. In water or strong alcohol it is almost insoluble, and entirely so in ether or chloroform; but it dissolves in warm dilute alcohol. From this solution it is precipitable by many acids, but not by tannic.

Groves[1] in 1868, unaware of the researches of Dragendorff and Kubly, arrived at similar results as these chemists, and proved conclusively that a cathartate of ammonia possesses in a concentrated form the purgative activity of the original drug.

The exactness of the chief facts relative to the solubility in weak alcohol of the active principle of senna set forth by the said chemists, was also remarkably supported by the long practical experience of T. and H. Smith of Edinburgh.[2]

When cathartic acid is boiled with alcohol and hydrochloric acid, it is resolved into sugar and *Cathartogenic Acid*.

The alcoholic solution from which the cathartates have been separated contains a yellow colouring matter which was called *Chrysoretin* by Bley and Diesel (1849), but identified as *Chrysophan*[3] by Martius, Batka and others. Dragendorff and Kubly regard the identity of the two substances as doubtful.

The same alcoholic solution which contains the yellow colouring matter just described, also holds dissolved a sugar which has been named *Catharto-mannite*. It forms warty crystals, is not susceptible of alcoholic fermentation, and does not reduce alkaline cupric tartrate. The formula assigned to it is $C^{42}H^{44}O^{38}$.

Senna contains tartaric and oxalic acids with traces of malic acid. The large amount of ash, 9 to 12 per cent., consisting of earthy and alkaline carbonates, also indicates the presence of a considerable quantity of organic acids.

Commerce—Alexandrian Senna, the produce of Nubia and the regions further south, was formerly a monopoly of the Egyptian Government, the enjoyment of which was granted to individuals in return for a stipulated payment: hence it was known in continental trade as *Séné de la palte*, while the depots were termed *paltes* and those who farmed the monopoly *paltiers*.[4] All this has long been abolished, and the trade is now free, the drug being shipped from Alexandria.

Arabian senna is brought into commerce by way of Bombay. The quantity of senna imported thither from the Red Sea and Aden in the year 1871-72 was 4,195 cwt., and the quantity exported during the same period, 2,180 cwt.[5]

Uses—Senna leaves are extensively employed in medicine as a purgative.

Adulteration—The principal contamination to which senna is at present liable arises from the presence of the leaves of *Solenostemma Argel* Hayne, a plant of the order *Asclepiadeæ*, 2 to 3 feet high, growing in the arid valleys of Nubia. Whether these leaves are used for the direct purpose of adulteration, or under the notion of *improving* the drug, or in virtue of some custom or prejudice, is not very evident. It

[1] *Pharm. Journ.* x. (1869) 196.
[2] *Ibid.* 315.
[3] See Art. *Radix Rhei.*
[4] From Italian *appaltare*, to let or farm.
[5] *Statement of the Trade and Navigation of the Presidency of Bombay for* 1871-72, pt. ii. 21. 98.

is certain however that druggists have been found who *preferred* senna that contained a good percentage of argel.

Nectoux, to whom we owe the first exact account of the argel or hárgel plant,[1] describes it as never gathered with the senna by accident or carelessness, but always separately. In fact he saw, both at Esneh and Philæ, the original bales of argel as well as those of senna: and at Boulak near Cairo, at the beginning of the present century, the argel used to be regularly mixed with senna in the proportion of one to four.

The leaves of argel after a little practice are very easily recognized; but their complete separation from senna by hand-picking is a tedious operation. They are lanceolate, equal at the base, of the same size as senna leaflets but often larger, of a pallid, opaque, greyish-green, rigid, thick, rather crumpled, wrinkled and pubescent, not distinctly veined. They have an unmistakeably bitter taste. The small, white, star-like flowers, or more often the flower buds, in dense corymbs are found in plenty in the bales of Alexandrian senna. The slender, pear-shaped follicles, when mature 1½ inches long, with comose seeds are less frequent. It has been shown by Christison[2] that argel leaves administered *per se* have but a feeble purgative action, though they occasion griping. It is plain therefore that their admixture with senna should be deprecated.

The leaves or leaflets of several other plants were formerly mixed occasionally with senna, as those of the poisonous *Coriaria myrtifolia* L., a Mediterranean shrub, of *Colutea arborescens* L., a native of Central and Southern Europe, and of the Egyptian *Tephrosia Apollinea* Delile. We have never met with any of them.[3]

FRUCTUS CASSIÆ FISTULÆ.

Cassia Fistula; Purging Cassia; F. *Casse Canefice, Fruit du Caneficer;* G. *Röhrencassie.*

Botanical Origin—*Cassia Fistula* L. (*Cathartocarpus Fistula* Pers., *Bactyrilobium Fistula* Willd.) a tree indigenous to India, ascending to 4000 feet in the outer Himalaya, but now cultivated or subspontaneous in Egypt, Tropical Africa,[4] the West Indies and Brazil. It is from 20 to 30 feet high (in Jamaica even 50 feet) and bears long pendulous racemes of beautiful fragrant, yellow flowers. Some botanists have established for this tree and its near allies a separate genus, on account of its elongated, cylindrical indehiscent legume, but by most it is retained in the genus *Cassia*.

History—The name *Casia* or *Cassia* was originally applied exclusively to a bark related to cinnamon which, when rolled into a tube or pipe, was distinguished in Greek by the word σύριγξ, and in Latin by that of *fistula*. Thus Scribonius Largus,[5] a physician of Rome during

[1] *Op. cit.* (See p. 218).
[2] *Dispensatory*, ed. 2. 1848. 850.
[3] The reader will find figures of these leaves contrasted with Senna in Pereira's *Elem. of Mat. Med.* ii. part ii (1853) 1866.
[4] Schweinfurth found it in 6° N. lat. and 28-29° E. long., in the country of the Dor, where the tree may also be indigenous.
[5] *Compositiones Medicamentorum*, cap. 4. sec. 36.

the reigns of Tiberius and Claudius, with the latter of whom he is said to have visited Britain, A.D. 43, uses the expression "*Casiæ rufæ fistularum*" in the receipt for a collyrium. Galen[1] describing the different varieties of cassia, mentions that called *Gizi*[2] (γίζεις) as being quite like cinnamon or even better; and also names a well-known cheaper sort, having a strong taste and odour which is called *fistula*, because it is rolled up like a tube.

Oribasius, physician to the Emperor Julian in the latter half of the 4th and beginning of the 5th century, describes *Cassia fistula* as a *bark* of which there are several varieties, having pungent and astringent properties ("*omnes cassiæ fistulæ vires habent acriter exalfacientes et stringentes*"), and sometimes used in the place of cinnamon.[3]

It is doubtless the same drug which is spoken of by Alexander Trallianus[4] as Κασίας σῦριγξ (*casia fistula*) in connexion with costus, pepper and other aromatics; and named by other Greek writers as Κασία συριγγώδης (*casia fistularis*). Alexander still more distinctly calls it also Κασία αἰγυπτία.[5]

The tree under examination and its fruit were exactly described in the beginning of the 13th century by Abul Abbâs Annâbatî of Sevilla;[6] the fruit, the Cassia Fistula of modern medicine, is noticed by Joannes Actuarius, who flourished at Constantinople towards the close of the 13th century; and as he describes it with particular minuteness,[7] it is evident that he did not consider it well known. The drug is also mentioned by several writers of the school of Salernum. The tree would appear to have found at an early period its way to America, if we are correct in referring to it the Cassia Fistula enumerated by Petrus Martyr among the valuable products of the New World.[8] The drug was a familar remedy in England in the time of Turner, 1568.[9]

The tree was figured in 1553 by the celebrated traveller Belon who met with it in the gardens of Cairo, and in 1592 by Prosper Alpinus who also saw it in Egypt.

Description—The ovary of the flower is one-celled with numerous ovules, which as they advance towards maturity become separated by the growth of intervening septa. The ripe legume is cylindrical, dark chocolate-brown, 1½ to 2 feet long by ¾ to 1 inch in diameter, with a strong short woody stalk, and a blunt end suddenly contracted into a point. The fibro-vascular column of the stalk is divided into two broad parallel seams, the dorsal and ventral sutures, running down the whole length of the pod. The sutures are smooth, or slightly striated longitudinally; one of them is formed of two ligneous bundles coalescing

[1] *De Antidot.* i. c. 14.

[2] Noticed likewise among the commodities liable to duty at Alexandria in the 2nd century.—Vincent, *Commerce of the Ancients*, ii. 712.

[3] *Physica Hildegardis*, Argent. 1533. 227.

[4] Libri xii. J. Guinterio interprete, Basil., 1556. lib. vii. c. 8.

[5] Puschmann's edition (quoted in the appendix) i. 435.

[6] Meyer, *Geschichte der Botanik*, iii. (1856). 226.

[7] "Quemadmodum si ventrem mollire fuerit animus, pruna, et præcipué Damascena adjicimus, atque quippiam feré nigræ nominatæ casiæ. Est autem fructus ejus fistulus et oblongus, nigrum intus humorem concretum gestans, qui haudquaquam una continuitate coaluit, sed ex intervallo tenuibus lignosisque membranulis dirimitur. habens ad speciei propagationem, grana quædam seminalia, siliquæ illi quæ nobis innotuit, adsimilia."—*Methodus Medendi*, lib. v. c. 2.

[8] *De nuper sub D. Carolo repertis insulis*, Basil. 1521.

[9] *Herball*, part. 3. 20.

by a narrow line. If the legume is curved, the ventral suture commonly occupies its inner or concave side. The valves of the pods are marked by slight transverse depressions (more evident in small specimens) corresponding to the internal divisions, and also by inconspicuous transverse veins.

Each of the 25 to 100 seeds which a legume contains, is lodged in a cell formed by very thin woody dissepiments. The oval, flattish seed from $\frac{3}{10}$ to $\frac{4}{10}$ of an inch long, of a reddish-brown colour, contains a large embryo whose yellowish veined cotyledons cross diagonally, as seen on tranverse section, the horny white albumen. One side is marked by a dark line (the raphe). A very slender funicle attaches the seed to the ventral suture.

In addition to the seeds, the cells contain a soft saccharine pulp which in the recent state fills them up, but in the imported pods appears only as a thin layer, spread over the septum, of a dark viscid substance of mawkish sweet taste. It is this pulp which is made use of in pharmacy.

Microscopic Structure—The bands above described running along the whole pod, are made up of strong fibro-vascular bundles mixed with sclerenchymatous tissue. The valves consist of parenchymatous cells, and the whole pod is coated with an epidermis exhibiting small tabular cells, which are filled with dark granules of tannic matter. A few stomata are also met with. The thin brittle septa of the pod are composed of long ligneous cells, enclosing here and there crystals of oxalate of calcium.

The pulp itself, examined under water, is seen to consist of loose cells, not forming a coherent tissue. They enclose chiefly granules of albuminoid matters and stellate crystals of oxalate of calcium. The cell wall assumes, on addition of iodine, a blue hue if they have been previously washed by potash lye. The seeds are devoid of starch, but yield a copious amount of thick mucilage, which surrounds them like a halo if they are macerated in water.

Chemical Composition—No peculiar principle is known to exist either in the woody or the pulpy portion of cassia fistula. The pulp contains sugar in addition to the commonly occurring bodies noticed in the previous section.

Uses—The pulp separated from the woody part of the pods by crushing the latter, digesting them in hot water, and evaporating the strained liquor, is a mild laxative in common domestic use in the South of Europe,[1] but in England scarcely ever now administered except in the form of the well-known *Lenitive Electuary* (*Confectio sennæ*) of which it is an ingredient.

Commerce—Cassia fistula is shipped to England from the East and West Indies, but chiefly from the latter. The pulp *per se* has been occasionally imported, but it should never be employed when the legumes for preparing it can be obtained.

Substitutes—The pods of some other species of *Cassia* share the structure above described and have been sometimes imported.

[1] Thus there were imported into Leghorn in 1871, 103 tons of *Cassia Fistula* and Tamarinds.—*Consular Reports*, 1873, part i.

Those of *C. grandis* L. f. (*C. brasiliana* Lamarck), a tree of Central America and Brazil, are of much larger size, showing when broken transversely an elliptic outline, whose longer diameter exceeds an inch. The valves have very prominent sutures and transverse branching veins. The pulp is bitter and astringent.

The legumes of *Cassia moschata* H B K.,[1] a tree 30 to 40 feet high, growing in New Granada and known there as *Cañafistola de purgar*, bear a close resemblance to those of *Cassia Fistula* L., except that they are a little smaller and rather less regularly straight. They contain a sweetish astringent pulp of a bright brown hue. When crushed and exposed to the heat of a water-bath, they emit a pleasant odour like sandal-wood. The pulp is coloured dark blackish green by perchloride of iron.

TAMARINDI PULPA.

Tamarindus, Fructus Tamarindi; Tamarinds; F. *Tamarins;* G. *Tamarinden.*

Botanical Origin—*Tamarindus indica* L.—The tamarind is a large handsome tree, growing to a height of 60 to 80 feet, and having abruptly pinnate leaves of 10 to 20 pairs of small oblong leaflets, constituting an abundant and umbrageous foliage. Its purplish flower buds and fragrant, red-veined, white blossoms, ultimately assuming a yellowish tinge, contribute to its beautiful aspect and cause it to be generally cultivated in tropical countries.

T. indica appears to be truly indigenous to Tropical Africa between 12° N. and 18° S. lat. It grows not only in the Upper Nile regions (Sennaar, Kordofan, Abyssinia), but also in some of the remotest districts visited by Speke, Grant, Kirk, and Stanley, and as far south as the Zambesi. According to F. von Müller,[2] it occurs in Tropical Australia.

It is found throughout India, and as it has Sanskrit names it may even be really wild in at least the southern parts of the peninsula. It grows in the Indian islands, and Crawfurd[3] has adduced reasons to show that it is probably a true native of Java. The mediæval Arabian authors describe it as growing in Yemen, India, and Nigritia.

The tamarind has been naturalized in Brazil, Ecuador and Mexico. Hernandez,[4] who resided in the latter country from 1571 to 1575, speaks of it as "*nuper . . . ad eas oras translata.*" It abounds in the West Indies where it was also introduced together with ginger by the Spaniards at an early period. The tree found in these islands bears shorter and fewer-seeded pods than that of India, and hence was formerly regarded as a distinct species, *Tamarindus occidentalis* Gärtn.

History—The tamarind was unknown to the ancient Greeks and Romans; nor have we any evidence that the Egyptians were

[1] Hanbury in *Linn. Trans.* xxiv. 161. p. 26; *Pharm. Journ.* v. (1864) 348; *Science Papers*, p. 318.

[2] Exposition intercoloniale,—*Notes sur la Végétation de l'Australie*, Melb., 1866. 8.

[3] *Dict. of Indian Islands*, 1856. 425.

[4] *Nova plantarum, animalium et mineralium historia*, Romæ, 1651. 83.

acquainted with it,[1] which is the more surprising considering that the tree appears indigenous to the Upper Nile countries, and that its fruit is held in the greatest esteem in those regions.[2]

The earliest mention of tamarind occurs in the ancient Sanskrit writings where it is spoken of under several names.[3] From the Hindus, it would seem that the fruit became known to the Arabians, who called it *Tamare-hindi*, i.e. *Indian Date*. Under this name it was mentioned by Isaac Judæus,[4] Avicenna,[5] and the Younger Mesue,[6] and also by Alhervi,[7] a Persian physician of the 10th century who describes it as black, of the flavour of a Damascene plum, and containing fibres and stones.

It was doubtless from the Arabians that a knowledge of the tamarind, as of so many other eastern drugs, passed during the middle ages into Europe through the famous school of Salernum. *Oxyphœnica* ('Οξυφοίνικα) and *Dactyli acetosi* are names under which we meet with it in the writings of Matthæus Platearius and Saladinus, the latter of whom, as well as other authors of the period, considered tamarinds as the fruit of a wild palm growing in India.

The abundance of tamarinds in Malabar, Coromandel, and Java was reported to Manuel, king of Portugal, in the letter of the apothecary Pyres[8] on the drugs of India, written in Cochin, January 27th, 1516. A correct description of the tree was given by Garcia de Orta about fifty years later.

Preparation—Tamarinds undergo a certain preparation before being brought into commerce.

In the West Indies, the tree matures its fruit in June, July and August, and the pods are gathered when fully ripe, which is known by the fragility of the outer shell. This latter, which easily breaks between the finger and thumb, is then removed, and the pods deprived of shelly fragments are placed in layers in a cask, and boiling syrup is poured over them till the cask is filled. When cool, the cask is closed and is then ready for sale. Sometimes layers of sugar are placed between the fruits previous to the hot syrup being added.[9]

East Indian tamarinds are also sometimes preserved with sugar, but usually they are exported without such addition, the outer shell being removed and the fruits being pressed together into a mass.

In the Upper Nile regions (Darfur, Kordofan, Sennaar) and in Arabia, the softer part of tamarinds is, for the sake of greater permanence and convenience of transport, kneaded into flattened round cakes, 4 to 8 inches in diameter and an inch or two thick, which are dried in the sun. They are of firm consistence and quite black, externally

[1] Sir Gardner Wilkinson (*Ancient Egyptians*, i. 1841, 78) says that tamarind stones have been found in the tombs of Thebes; but on consulting Dr. Birch and the collections in the British Museum we have obtained no confirmation of the fact.

[2] Barth speaks of it as *an invaluable gift of Providence*: *Reisen und Entdeckungen in Nord- und Centralafrica*, Gotha, 1858. i. 614; iii. 334. 400; iv. 173.—The same says Rohlfs, *Reisen durch Nordafrica*, Gotha (1872) 23.

[3] *Susrutas Ayurvedas*, ed. Hessler, i. (1844) 141, iii. (1850) 171.

[4] *Opera Omnia*, Lugd. 1515, lib. ii. Practices, c. 41.

[5] *Opera*, Venet. 1564. ii. 339.

[6] *Opera*, Venet. 1561. 52.

[7] *Fundamenta Pharmacologiæ*, ed. Seligmann, Vindob. 1830, 49.

[8] *Journ. de Soc. Pharm. Lusit.* ii. (1838) 36.—See also Appendix.

[9] Lunan, *Hortus Jamaicensis*, ii. (1814) 224; Macfadyen, *Flora of Jamaica*, 1837. 335.

strewn with hair, sand, seeds and other impurities; they are largely consumed in Egypt and Central Africa, and sometimes find their way to the south of Europe as *Egyptian Tamarinds.*

Description—The fruit is an oblong, or linear oblong, strictly compressed, curved or nearly straight, pendulous legume, of the thickness of the finger and 3 to 6 inches in length, supported by a woody stalk. It has a thin but hard and brittle outer shell or epicarp, which does not split into valves or exhibit any very evident sutures. Within the epicarp is a firm, juicy pulp, on the surface of which and starting from the stalk are strong woody ramifying nerves; one of these extends along the dorsal (or concave) edge, two others on either side of the ventral (or convex) edge, while between these two there are usually 2, 3, or 4 less regular and more slender nerves,—all running towards the apex and throwing out branching filaments. The brownish or reddish pulp has usually an acid taste, though there are also sweetish varieties.

The seeds, 4 to 12 in number, are each of them enclosed in a tough, membraneous cell (endocarp), surrounded by the pulp (sarcocarp). They are flattened and of irregular outline, being roundish, ovate, or obtusely four-sided, about $\frac{6}{10}$ of an inch long by $\frac{3}{10}$ thick, with the edge broadly keeled or more often slightly furrowed. The testa is of a rich brown, marked on the flat sides of the seed by a large scar or oreole, of rather duller polish than the surrounding portion which is somewhat radially striated. The seed is exalbuminous, with thick hard cotyledons, a short straight included radicle, and a plumule in which the pinnation of the leaves is easily perceptible.

Tamarinds are usually distinguished in trade as *West Indian* and *East Indian,* the former being preserved with sugar, the latter without.

1. *West Indian Tamarinds, Brown or Red Tamarinds.*—A bright reddish brown, moist, saccharine mass consisting of the pulpy internal part of the fruit, usually unbroken, mixed with more or less of syrup. It has a very agreeable and refreshing taste, the natural acidity of the pulp being tempered by the sugar. It is this form of tamarinds that is usually found in the shops.

2. *East Indian Tamarinds, Black Tamarinds.*—These differ from the last described in that they are preserved without the use of sugar. They are found in the market in the form of a firm, clammy, black mass, consisting of the pulp mixed with the seeds, stringy fibres, and some remains of the outer shell. The pulp has a strong acid taste.

Notwithstanding the rather uninviting appearance of East Indian tamarinds, they afford a good pulp, which may be satisfactorily used in making the *Confectio Sennæ* of pharmacy. In fact, on the continent this sort of tamarind alone is employed for medicinal purposes.

Microscopic Structure—The soft part of tamarind consists of a tissue of thin-walled cells of considerable size, which is traversed by long fibro-vascular bundles. In the former a few very small starch-granules are met with, and more numerous crystals, which are probably bitartrate of potassium.

Chemical Composition—Water extracts from unsweetened tamarinds, sugar together with acetic, tartaric and citric acids, the acids being combined for the most part with potash. The neutralized solution reduces alkaline cupric tartrate after a while without heat, and therefore probably contains grape sugar. On evaporation, cream of tartar and sugar crystallize out. The volatile acids of the fatty series, the presence of which in the pulp has been pointed out by Gorup-Besanez, have not been met with by other chemists. Tannin is absent as well as oxalic acid. We have ascertained that in East Indian tamarinds, citric acid is present in but small quantity. No peculiar principle to which the laxative action of tamarinds can be attributed is known.

The fruit-pulp diffused in water forms a thick, tremulous, somewhat glutinous and turbid liquid. It was examined as early as the year 1790 by Vauquelin under the name of "*vegetable jelly*,"—the first described among the pectic class of bodies.

The hard *seeds* have a testa which abounds in tannin, and after long boiling is easily separated, leaving the cotyledons soft. These latter have a bland mucilaginous taste, and are consumed in India as food during times of scarcity.

Commerce—Tamarinds are shipped in comparatively small quantities from several of the West Indian islands, and also from Guayaquil.

The export from the Bombay Presidency in the year 1871-72 was 6286 cwt., which quantity was shipped chiefly to the Persian Gulf, Sind, and ports of the Red Sea.[1] 128,144 centners were re-exported in 1877 from Trieste.

Uses—In medicine, tamarinds are considered to be a mild laxative; they are sometimes used to make a refrigerant drink in fever. In hot countries, especially the interior of Africa, they are regarded as of the highest value for the preparation of refreshing beverages. The *Black Tamarinds* are said to be used in the manufacture of tobacco.

BALSAMUM COPAIBA.

Copaiba; Balsam of Copaiba or Copaiva, Balsam Capivi; F. *Baume ou Oléo-résine de Copahu;* G. *Copaivabalsam.*

Botanical Origin—The drug under notice is produced by trees belonging to the genus *Copaifera*, natives of the warmer countries of South America. Some are found in moist forests, others exclusively in dry and elevated situations. They vary in height and size, some being umbrageous forest trees, while others have only the dimension of shrubs; it is from the former alone that the oleo-resin is obtained.

The following are reputed to furnish the drug, but to what extent each contributes is not fully known.

1. *Copaifera officinalis* L. (*C. Jacquini* Desf.), a large tree of the hot coast region of New Granada as far north as Panama, of Venezuela and the island of Trinidad.

2. *C. guianensis* Desf., a tree of 30 to 40 feet high, very closely related to the preceding, native of Surinam, Cayenne, also of the Rio

[1] *Statement of the Trade and Navigation of the Presidency of Bombay*, 1871-72, pt. ii. 65.

Negro between Manaos and Barcellos (Spruce). According to Bentham it seems to be the same species as the *C. bijuga* of Hayne.[1]

3. *C. coriacea* Mart. (*C. cordifolia* Hayne), a large tree found in the *caatingas* or dry woods of the Brazilian provinces of Bahia and Piauhy.

4. *C. Langsdorffii* Desf.[2] (*C. nitida* Hayne, *C. Sellowii* Hayne, ? *C. Jussieui* Hayne), a polymorphous species, varying in the form and size of leaflets, and also in dimensions, being either a shrub, a small bushy tree, or a large tree of 60 feet high. Bentham admits, besides the type, three varieties :—β. *glabra* (*C. glabra* Vogel), γ. *grandifolia*, δ. *laxa* (*C. laxa* Hayne). The tree grows on dry *campos*, *caatingas* and other places in the provinces of S. Paulo, Minas Geraes, Goyaz, Mato Grosso, Bahia and Ceará; it is therefore distributed over a vast area. According to Gardner,[3] the Brazilian traveller, it yields an abundance of balsam.

In addition to these species, must be mentioned a tree described by Hayne and commonly cited under the name of *Copaifera multijuga*, as a special source of the drug shipped from Pará.[4] As its name implies, it is remarkable for the number of leaflets (6 to 10 pairs) on each leaf. But it is only known from some leaves in the herbarium of Martius which Bentham, who has examined them, informs us are unlike those of any *Copaifera* known to him, though certainly the leaflets are dotted with oil-vessels as in some species. In the absence of flowers and fruits, there is no sufficient evidence to prove that it belongs even to the genus *Copaifera*. It is not mentioned by Martius in his *Systema Materiæ Medicæ Brasiliensis* (1843) as a source of the drug.

History—Among the early notices of Brazil is a treatise by a Portuguese friar who had resided in that country from 1570 to 1600. The manuscript found its way to England, was translated, and was published by Purchas[5] in 1625. Its author notices many of the natural productions of the country, and among others *Cupayba* which he describes as a large tree from whose trunk, when wounded by a deep incision, there flows in abundance a clear oil much esteemed as a medicine.

Balsam. *Copæ. yvæ* is already enumerated in the 6th edition of the Pharmacopœa of Amsterdam, A.D. 1636.[6]

Father Cristoval d'Acuña,[7] who ascended the Amazon from Pará, arriving at Quito in 1638, mentions that the country affords very large Cassia fistula, excellent sarsaparilla, and the oils of Andirova (*Carapa guianensis* Aublet, *Meliaceæ*), and *Copaiba*, as good as balsam for curing wounds.

Piso and Marcgraf,[8] who in 1636 accompanied the Count of Nassau

[1] Hayne (1827) enumerated and figured 15 species, some of them founded on very imperfect materials. Bentham in the *Flora Brasiliana* of Martius and Endlicher (fasc. 50, *Leguminosæ*, ii. 1870. pp. 239–244) admits only 11, one of which is doubtful as to the genus.

[2] Fig. in Bentley and Trimen, *Med. Plants*, part 32 (1878); Langsdorffii, not Lansdorffii, is to be written; see *Pharm. Journ.* ix. (1879) 773.

[3] MS. attached to specimens in the Kew Herbarium.

[4] "Alle Arten geben mehr oder weniger Balsam, und den meisten giebt die in der Provinz Para vorkommende *Copaifera multijuga*."—Hayne, *Linnæa*, i. (1826) 429.

[5] *Pilgrimes and Pilgrimage*, Lond. iv. (1625) 1308.

[6] *Pharm. Journ.* vi. (1876) 1021.

[7] *Nuevo Descubrimiento del gran Rio de las Amazonas*, Madrid, 1641, No. 30.

[8] *Hist. Nat. Brasiliæ*, 1648, Piso, 56, Marcgraf, 130.

to the Dutch establishments in Brazil, each give an account of the *Copaiba* and the method of obtaining its oleo-resin. The former states that the tree grows in Pernambuco and the island of Maranhon, whence the balsam is conveyed in abundance to Europe.

The drug was formerly brought into European commerce by the Portuguese, and used to be packed in earthen pots pointed at the lower end; it often arrived in a very impure condition.[1] In the London Pharmacopœia of 1677, it was called *Balsamum Capivi*, which is still its most popular name.

Secretion—Karsten states that he observed resiniferous ducts, frequently more than an inch in diameter, running through the whole stem. He is of the opinion that the cell-walls of the neighbouring parenchyme are liquefied and transformed into the oleo-resin.[2] We are not able to offer any argument in favour of this opinion.

In the vessels already alluded to, the balsam sometimes collects in so large a quantity, that the trunk is unable to sustain the inward pressure, and *bursts*. This curious phenomenon is thus referred to in a letter addressed to one of us by Mr. Spruce:—"I have three or four times heard what the Indians assured me was the bursting of an old capivi-tree, distended with oil. It is one of the strange sounds that sometimes disturb the vast solitudes of a South American forest. It resembles the boom of a distant cannon, and is quite distinct from the crash of an old tree falling from decay which one hears not unfrequently."

A similar phenomenon is known in Borneo. The trunks of aged trees of *Dryobalanops aromatica* contain large quantities of oleo-resin or Camphor Oil,[3] which appears to be sometimes secreted under such pressure that the vast trunk gives way. "There is another sound," says Spenser St. John,[4] "only heard in the oldest forests, and that is as if a mighty tree were rent in twain. I often asked the cause, and was assured it was the camphor tree splitting asunder on account of the accumulation of camphor in some particular portion."

Extraction—Balsam Capivi is collected by the Indians on the banks of the Orinoco and its upper affluents, and carried to Ciudad Bolivar (Angostura); some of this balsam reaches Europe by way of Trinidad. But it is obtained much more largely on the tributaries of the Caisquiari and Rio Negro (the Siapa, Içanna, Uaupés, etc.) and is sent down to Pará. Most of the northern tributaries of the Amazon, as the Trombetas and Nhamundá, likewise furnish a supply. According to Spruce, in the Amazon valley it is the tall virgin forest, *Caaguaçú* of the Brazilians, *Monte Alto* of the Venezuelans, that yields most of the oils and gum-resins, and not the low, dry *caatingas*, or the riparial forests. The same observant traveller tells us that in Southern Venezuela, capivi is known only as *el Aceite de palo* (*wood-oil*), the name *Balsamo* being that of the so-called *Sassafras Oil*, obtained from a species of *Nectandra*.

Balsam Copaiba is also largely exported from Maracaibo where,

[1] Valmont de Bomare, *Dict. d'Hist. Nat.* i. (1775) 387.

[2] *Botanische Zeitung*, xv. (1857) 316.

[3] Motley in Hooker's *Journ. of Botany*, iv. (1852) 201.

[4] *Life in the Forests of the Far East*, ii. (1862) 152.

according to Engel,[1] it is produced by *C. officinalis*, the *Canime* of the natives.

The finest sort, called by the collectors white copaiba, is met with in the province of Pará, where Cross[2] saw a tree of a circumference of more than 7 feet at 3 feet from the ground. Its trunk was clear of branches to a height of at least 90 feet. The collector commenced the work by hewing out with his axe a hole or chamber in the trunk about a foot square, at a height of two feet from the ground. The base or floor of the chamber should be carefully and neatly cut with a gentle upward slope, and it should also decline to one side, so that the balsam on issuing may run in a body until it reaches the outer edge. Below the chamber a pointed piece of bark is cut and raised, which, enveloped with a leaf, serves as a spout for conveying the balsam from the tree to the tin.[3] The balsam, continues Cross, came flowing in a moderate sized cool current, full of air bubbles. At times the flow stopped for several minutes, when a singular gurgling noise was heard, after which followed a rush of balsam. When coming most abundantly a pint jug would have been filled in the space of one minute. The whole of the wood cut through by the axeman was bedewed with drops of balsam; the bark is apparently devoid of it. Trees of the largest size in good condition will sometimes yield four "potos," equal to 84 English imperial pints.

Description—Copaiba is more or less viscid fluid, varying in tint from a pale yellow to a light golden brown, of a peculiar aromatic, not unpleasant odour, and a persistent, acrid, bitterish taste. Pará copaiba newly imported is sometimes nearly colourless and almost as fluid as water.[4] The balsam is usually quite transparent, but there are varieties which remain always opalescent. Its sp. gr. varies from 0·940 to 0·993, according as the drug contains a greater or less proportion of volatile oil. Copaiba becomes more fluid by heat; if heated in a test-tube to 200° C. for some time, it does not lose its fluidity on cooling. It is sometimes slightly fluorescent. It dissolves in several times its weight of alcohol 0·830 sp. gr., and generally in all proportions in absolute alcohol,[5] acetone, or bisulphide of carbon, and is perfectly soluble in an equal volume of benzol. Glacial acetic acid readily dissolves the resin but not the essential oil.

Copaiba that is rich in resin of an acid character, unites with the oxides of baryum, calcium, or magnesium, to form a gradually hardening mass, provided a small proportion of water is present. Thus 8 to 16 parts of balsam will combine as a stiff compound when gently warmed with 1 part of moistened magnesia; and still more easily with lime or baryta.

Buignet has first shown (1861) that copaiba varies in its optical power. A sample from Trinidad examined by one of us was strongly

[1] *Zeitschrift der Gesellschaft für Erdkunde zu Berlin*, v. (1870) 435.

[2] Report to the Under Secretary of State for India, on the investigation and collecting of plants and seeds of the india-rubber trees of Pará and Ceara, and Balsam of Copaiba. March 1877,—8.

[3] See figure in the above Report.

[4] We saw such as this which had been imported into London in 1873; though regarded by the dealers with suspicion, we are not of opinion that it was sophisticated.

[5] Such is the case with some very authentic specimens collected for one of us in Central America by De Warszewicz, but other samples which we had no reason to suppose adulterated, left a certain amount of white residue when treated with *twice their weight* of alcohol sp. gr. 0·796.

dextrogyre, and also several samples imported in 1877 from Maturin (near Aragua, Venezuela), and Maracaibo into Hamburg, whereas we found Pará balsam to be levogyre.[1]

The Pará and Maranham balsams are regarded in wholesale trade as distinct sorts, and experienced druggists are able to distinguish them apart by odour and appearance, and especially by the greater consistence of the Maranham drug. Maracaibo balsam is reckoned as another variety, but is now rarely seen in the English market. West Indian copaiba is usually said to be of inferior quality, but except that it is generally opalescent, we know not on what precise grounds.

Chemical Composition—The balsam is a solution of resin in volatile oil; the latter constitutes about 40 to 60 per cent. of the balsam,[2] according to the age of the latter and its botanical origin. The oil has the composition $C^{15}H^{24}$; its boiling point is 245° C. or even higher. It smells and tastes like the balsam, and dissolves in from 8 to 30 parts of alcohol 0·830 sp. gr. The oil exhibits several modifications differing in optical as well as in other physical properties, but numerous samples of the drug, either *dextrogyre* or levogyre, invariably afforded us essential oils deviating to the left; their sp. gr. varies from about 0·88 to 0·91.

After the oil of copaiba has been removed by distillation, there remains a brittle amorphous resin of an acid character soluble both in benzol and amylic alcohol, and yielding only amorphous salts. Sometimes copaiba contains a small amount of crystallizable resin-acid, as first pointed out in 1829 by Schweitzer. By exposing a mixture of 9 parts of copaiba and two parts of aqueous ammonia (sp. gr. 0·95) to a temperature of — 10° C., Schweitzer obtained crystals of the acid resin termed *Copaivic Acid*. They were analysed in 1834 by H. Rose, and exactly measured and figured by G. Rose. Hess (1839) showed that Rose's and his own analyses assign to copaivic acid the formula $C^{20}H^{32}O^{2}$. It agrees with Maly's abietic acid from colophony in composition, but not in any other way. Copaivic acid is readily soluble in alcohol, and especially in warmed copaiba itself; much less in ether. We have before us crystals, no doubt of copaivic acid, which have been spontaneously deposited in an authentic specimen of the oleo-resin of *Copaifera officinalis* from Trinidad, which we have kept for many years. The crystals may be easily dissolved by warming the balsam; on cooling the liquid, they again make their appearance after the lapse of some weeks. After recrystallization from alcohol they fuse at 116–117 C°., forming an amorphous transparent mass which quickly crystallizes if touched with alcohol.

An analogous substance, *Oxycopaivic Acid*, $C^{20}H^{28}O^{3}$, was examined in 1841 by H. von Fehling, who met with it as a deposit in Pará Copaiba. And lastly Strauss (1865) extracted *Metacopaivic Acid*, $C^{22}H^{34}O^{4}$, from the balsam imported from Maracaibo. He boiled the latter with soda-lye, which separated the oil; the heavier adjacent liquid was then mixed with chloride of ammonium, which threw down the salts of the amorphous resin-acid, leaving in solution those of the metacopaivic acid. The latter acid was separated by hydrochloric acid and recrystallization from alcohol. We succeeded in obtaining metacopaivic acid by washing

[1] Flückiger in Wiggers and Husemann's *Jahresbericht* for 1867. 162, and for 1868. 140.

[2] Or 18 to 65 per cent., sp. gr. 0·915 to 0·995, according to Siebold (1877).

the balsam with a dilute solution of carbonate of ammonium, and precipitating by hydrochloric acid. The precipitate dissolved in dilute alcohol yields the acid in small crystals, but to the amount of only about one per cent.

These resin-acids have a bitterish taste and an acid reaction; their salts of lead and silver are crystalline but insoluble; metacopaivate of sodium may be crystallized from its watery solution.

Commerce—The balsam is imported in barrels direct from Pará and Maranham, sometimes from Rio de Janeiro, and less often from Demerara, Angostura, Trinidad, Maracaibo, Savanilla, and Cartagena. It often reaches England by way of Havre and New York. In 1875 there were exported 10,150 kilogrammes from Savanilla, 99,800 lb. from Ciudad Bolivar (Angostura), and 65,243 kilos. from Pará.

Uses—Copaiba is employed in medicine on account of its stimulant action on the mucous membranes, more especially those of the urino-genital organs.

Adulteration—Copaiba is not unfrequently fraudulently tampered with before it reaches the pharmaceutist; and owing to its naturally variable composition, arising in part from its diverse botanical origin, its purity is not always easily ascertained.

The oleo-resin usually dissolves in a small proportion of absolute alcohol: should it refuse to do so, the presence of some fatty oil other than castor oil may be surmised. To detect an admixture of this latter, one part of the balsam should be heated with four of spirit of wine (sp. gr. 0·838). On cooling, the mixture separates into two portions, the upper of which will contain any castor oil present, dissolved in alcohol and the essential oil. On evaporation of this upper layer, castor oil may be recognized by its odour; but still more positively by heating it with caustic soda and lime, when œnanthol will be formed, the presence of which may be ascertained by its peculiar smell. By the latter test an admixture of even one per cent. of castor oil can be proved.

The presence of fatty oil in any considerable quantity is likewise made evident by the greasiness of the residue, when the balsam is deprived of its essential oil by prolonged boiling with water.

The admixture of some volatile oil with copaiba can mostly be detected by the odour, especially when the balsam is dropped on a piece of warmed metal. Spirit of wine may also be advantageously tried for the same purpose. It dissolves but very sparingly the volatile oil of copaiba: the resins of the latter are also not abundantly soluble in it. Hence, if shaken with the balsam, it would remove at once the larger portion of any essential oil that might have been added. For the recognition of Wood Oil if mixed with copaiba, see page 233, note 1.

Substitutes—Under this head two drugs deserve mention, namely *Gurjun Balsam* or *Wood Oil*, described at p. 88, and

Oleo-resin of Hardwickia pinnata Roxb.—The tree, which is of a large size, belongs to the order *Leguminosæ* and is nearly related to *Copaifera*. According to Beddome,[1] it is very common in the dense moist forests of the South Travancore Ghats, and has also been found in

[1] *Flora Sylvatica for Southern India*, Madras, part 24 (1872), 255.

South Canara. The natives extract the oleo-resin in exactly the same method as that followed by the aborigines of Brazil in the case of copaiba,—that is to say, they make a deep notch reaching to the heart of the trunk, from which after a time it flows out.

This oleo-resin, which has the smell and taste of copaiba, but a much darker colour, was first examined by one of us in 1865, having been sent from the India Museum as a sample of Wood Oil; it was subquently forwarded to us in more ample quantity by Dr. Bidie of Madras. It is a thick, viscid fluid, which, owing to its intense tint, looks black when seen in bulk by reflected light; yet it is perfectly transparent. Viewed in a thin layer by transmitted light, it is light *yellowish-green*, in a thick layer *vinous-red*,—hence is dichromic. It is not fluorescent, nor is it gelatinized or rendered turbid by being heated to 130° C., thus differing from Wood Oil.[1] Broughton[2] obtained by prolonged distillation with water an essential oil to the extent of 25 per cent. from an old specimen, and of more than 40 per cent., from one recently collected. The oil was found to have the same composition as that of copaiba, to boil at 225° C., and to rotate the plane of polarization to the left. The resin[3] is probably of two kinds, of which one at least possesses acid properties. Broughton made many attempts, but without success, to obtain from the resin crystals of copaivic acid.

The balsam of *Hardwickia* has been used in India for gonorrhœa, and with as much success as copaiba.

GUMMI ACACIÆ.

Gummi Arabicum; Gum Arabic; F. *Gomme Arabique;* G. *Arabisches Gummi, Acacien-Gummi, Kordofan Gummi.*

Botanical Origin—Among the plants abounding in mucilage, numerous Acaciæ of various countries are in the first line. The species particularly known for affording the largest quantities of the finest gum arabic is *Acacia Senegal*[4] Willdenow (syn. *Mimosa Senegal* L., *A. Verek* Guillemin et Perrottet), a small tree not higher than 20 feet, growing abundantly on sandy soils in Western Africa, chiefly north of the river Senegal, where it constitutes extensive forests. It is called by the negroes *Verek*. The same tree is likewise found in Southern Nubia, Kordofan, and in the region of the Atbara in Eastern Africa, where it is known as *Hashab*. It has a greyish bark, the inner layers

[1] It may be further distinguished from Wood Oil as well as from copaiba, if tested in the following simple manner:—Put into a tube 19 drops of bisulphide of carbon and one drop of the oleo-resin, and shake them together. Then add one drop of a mixture of equal parts of strong sulphuric and nitric (1·42) acids. After a little agitation the appearance of the respective mixtures will be as follows:—

Copaiba—Colour faint reddish brown, with deposit of resin on sides of tube.

Wood Oil—Colour intense purplish-red, becoming violet after some minutes.

Oleo-resin of Hardwickia—No perceptible alteration; the mixture pale greenish yellow.

By this test the presence in copaiba of one-eighth of its volume of Wood Oil may be easily shown.

[2] Beddome, *op. cit.*

[3] See also Hazlett, *Madras Monthly Journ. of Med. Science*, June 1872.

[4] Figures in Guillemin and Perrottet *Floræ Senegamb. tent.* 1830, p. 246, tab. 56; also Bentley and Trimen, *Med. Plants*, part 17 (1877).

of which are strongly fibrous, small yellowish flowers densely arranged in spikes 2 to 3 inches long, and exceeding the bipinnate leaves, and a broad legume 3 to 4 inches in length containing 5 to 6 seeds.

According to Schweinfurth,[1] it is this tree exclusively that yields the fine white gum of the countries bordering the Upper Nile, and especially of Kordofan. He states that only brownish or reddish sorts of gum are produced by the Talch, Talha or Kakul, *Acacia stenocarpa* Hochstetter, by the Ssoffar, *A. fistula* Schweinf. (*A. Seyal* Delile, var. *Fistula*), as well as by the Ssant or Sont, *A. nilotica* Desfont (*A. arabica* Willd.). These trees grow in north-eastern Africa; the last-named is, moreover, widely distributed all over tropical Africa as far as Senegambia,[2] Mozambique and Natal, and also extends to Sindh, Gujarat[3] and Central India. We find even the first sort, "Karami," of gum exported from the Somali coast,[4] to be inferior to good common Arabic gum. Hildebrandt (1875) mentions that gum is there largely collected from *Acacia abyssinica* Hochst. and *A. glaucophylla* Steudel.

History—The history of this drug carries us back to a remote antiquity. The Egyptian fleets brought gum from the gulf of Aden as early as the 17th century B.C. Thus in the treasury of king Rhampsinit (Ramses III.) at Medinet Abu, there are representations of gum-trees, together with heaps of gum. The symbol used to signify *gum*, is read *Kami-en-punt*. i.e. *gum* from the country of Punt. This, in all probability, includes both the Somali coast as well as that of the opposite parts of Arabia (see article Olibanum, p. 136). Thus, gum is of frequent occurrence in Egyptian inscriptions; sometimes mention is made of gum from Canaan. The word *kami* is the original of the Greek κόμμι, whence through the Latin our own word *gum*.[5]

The Egyptians used gum largely in painting; an inscription exists which states that in one particular instance a solution of *Kami* (gum) was used to render adherent the mineral pigment called *chesteb*,[6] the name applied to lapis lazuli or to a glass coloured blue by cobalt.

Turning to the Greeks, we find that Theophrastus in the 3rd and 4th century B.C. mentioned Κόμμι as a product of the Egyptian Ἄκανθα, of which tree there was a forest in the Thebaïs of Upper Egypt. Strabo also, in describing the district of Arsinöe, the modern Fayûm, says that gum is got from the forest of the Thebaïc *Akanthe*.

Celsus in the 1st century mentions *Gummi acanthinum*; Dioscorides and Pliny also describe Egyptian gum, which the latter values at 3 *denarii* [2*s*.] per lb.

In those times gum no doubt used to be shipped from north-eastern Africa to Arabia; there is no evidence showing that Arabia itself had ever furnished the chief bulk of the drug. The designation gum *arabic*

[1] *Aufzählung und Beschreibung der Acacien-Artendes Nilgebiets*.—*Linnæa*, i. (1867) 308-376, with 21 plates. Schweinfurth's observations are strongly confirmed by an account of the commerce of Khartum in the *Zeitschrift für Erdkunde*, ii. (1867, Berlin) 474.

[2] The *A. Adansonii* Guill. et Perr. is the same tree.

[3] The "*Kikar*" of the Punjaub, or "*Babul*" or "*Babur*" of Central India.

[4] As presented to me by Capt. Hunter of Aden, July 1877.—F. A. F.

[5] We have to thank Professor Dümichen for most of the information relating to Egypt, which may be partly found in his own works, and partly in those of Brugsch, Ebers, and Lepsius.

[6] Lepsius, *Abhandl. der Akademie der Wissensch. zu Berlin* for 1871, p. 77. 126. Metalle in den Aegyptischen Inschriften.

occurs in Diodorus Siculus (2, 49) in the first century of our era, also in the list of goods of Alexandria mentioned in our article on Galbanum.

Gum was employed by the Arabian physicians and by those of the school of Salerno, yet its utility in medicine and the arts was but little appreciated in Europe until a much later period. For the latter purpose at least the gummy exudations of indigenous trees were occasionally resorted to, as distinctly pointed out about the beginning of the 12th century, by Theophilus or Rogker:[1] "gummi quot exit de arbore ceraso vel pruno."

During the middle ages, the small supplies that reached Europe were procured through the Italian traders from Egypt and Turkey. Thus Pegolotti,[2] who wrote a work on commerce about A.D. 1340, speaks of gum arabic as one of the drugs sold at Constantinople by the *pound* not by the *quintal*. Again, in a list of drugs liable to duty at Pisa in 1305,[3] and in a similar list relating to Paris in 1349,[4] we find mention of gum arabic. It is likewise named by Pasi,[5] in 1521, as an export from Venice to London.

Gum also reached Europe from Western Africa, with which region the Portuguese had a direct trade as early as 1449.

Production—Respecting the origin of gum in the tribe *Acaciæ*, no observations have been made similar to those of H. von Mohl on tragacanth.[6]

It appears that gum generally exudes from the trees spontaneously, in sufficient abundance to render wounding the bark superfluous. The Somali tribes of East Africa, however, are in the habit of promoting the outflow by making long incisions in the stem and branches of the tree.[7] In Kordofan the lumps of gum are broken off with an axe, and collected in baskets.

The most valued product, called *Hashabi* gum, from the province of Dejara in Kordofan, is sent northward from Bara and El Obeid to Dabbeh on the Nile, and thence down the river to Egypt; or it reaches the White Nile at Mandjara.

A less valuable gum, known as *Hashabi el Jesire*, comes from Sennaar on the Blue Nile; and a still worse from the barren table-land of Takka, lying between the eastern tributaries of the Blue Nile and the Atbara and Mareb; and from the highlands of the Bisharrin Arabs between Khartum and the Red Sea. This gum is transported by way of Khartum or El Mekheir (Berber), or by Suakin on the Red Sea. Hence, the worst kind of gum is known in Egypt as *Samagh Savakumi* (*Suakin Gum*).

According to Munzinger,[8] a better sort of gum is produced along the Samhara coast towards Berbera, and is shipped at Massowa. Some of it reaches Egypt by way of Jidda, which town being in the district of

[1] *Schedula diversarum artium*, Ilg's edition in Eitelberger's *Quellenschriften für Kunstgeschichte*, vii. (1874) 60.

[2] *Della Decima e di varie altre gravezze imposte dal commune di Firenze*, iii. (1766) 18.

[3] Bonaini, *Statuti inediti della città di Pisa*, Firenze, iii. (1857) 106. 114.

[4] *Ordonnances des Rois de France*, ii. (1729) 310.

[5] *Tariffa de pesi e misure*, Venet. 1521. 204. First edition, 1503.

[6] See, however, Möller, Academy of Vienna, *Sitzungsberichte*, June 1875.

[7] Vaughan (Drugs of Aden), *Pharm. Journ.* xii. (1853) 226.

[8] Private information to F.A.F.

Arabia called the Hejaz, the gum thence brought receives the name of *Samagh Hejazi*; it is also called *Jiddah* or *Gedda Gum*. The gums of Zeila, Berbera and the Somali country about Gardafui, are shipped to Aden, or direct to Bombay. A little gum is collected in Southern Arabia, but the quantity is said to be insignificant.[1]

In the French colony of Senegal, gum, which is one of its principal productions, is collected chiefly in the country lying north of the river, by the Moors who exchange it for European commodities. The gathering commences after the rainy season in November when the wind begins to set from the desert, and continues till the month of July. The gum is shipped for the most part to Bordeaux. The quantity annually imported into France since 1828 from Senegal is varying from between 1½ to 5 millions of kilogrammes.

Description—Gum arabic does not exhibit any very characteristic forms like those observable in gum tragacanth. The finest white gum of Kordofan, which is that most suitable for medicinal use, occurs in lumps of various sizes from that of a walnut downwards. They are mostly of ovoid or spherical form, rarely vermicular, with the surface in the unbroken masses, rounded,—in the fragments, angular. They are traversed by numerous fissures, and break easily and with a vitreous fracture. The interior is often less fissured than the outer portion. At 100° C. the cracks increase, and the gum becomes extremely friable. In moist air, it slowly absorbs about 6 per cent of water.

The finest gum arabic is perfectly clear and colourless; inferior kinds have a brownish, reddish or yellowish tint of greater or less intensity, and are more or less contaminated with accidental impurities such as bark. The finest white gum turns black and assumes an empyreumatic taste, when it is kept for months at a temperature of about 98° C., either in an open vessel, or enclosed in a glass tube, after having been previously dried over sulphuric acid or not.

An aqueous solution of gum deviates the plane of polarization 5° to the left in a column 50 mm. long; but after being long kept, it becomes strongly acid, the gum having been partly converted into sugar, and its optical properties are altered. An alkaline solution of cupric tartrate is not reduced by solution of gum even at a boiling heat, unless it contains a somewhat considerable proportion of sugar, extractable by alcohol, or a fraudulent admixture of dextrin.

We found the sp. gr. of the purest pieces of colourless gum dried in the air at 15° C., to be 1·487; but it increases to 1·525, if the gum is dried at 100°.

The foregoing remarks apply chiefly to the fine white gum of Kordofan, the *Picked Turkey Gum* or *White Sennaar Gum* of druggists. The other sorts which are met with in the London market are the following:—

1. *Senegal Gum*—As stated above, this gum is an important item of the French trade with Africa, but is not much used in England. Its colour is usually yellowish or somewhat reddish, and the lumps, which are of large size, are often elongated or vermicular. Moreover Senegal gum never exhibits the numerous fissures seen in Kordofan gum, so that the masses are much firmer and less easily broken. In

[1] Vaughan, *l.c.*

every other respect, whether chemical or optical, we find[1] Senegal gum and Kordofan gum to be identical; and the two, notwithstanding their different appearance, are produced by one and the same species of *Acacia*, namely *Acacia Senegal*.

2. ***Suakin Gum, Talca*** or ***Talha Gum***, yielded by *Acacia stenocarpa*, and by *A. Seyal* var. *Fistula*, is remarkable for its brittleness, which occasions much of it to arrive in the market in a semi-pulverulent state. It is a mixture of nearly colourless and of brownish gum, with here and there pieces of a deep reddish-brown. Large tears have a dull opaque look, by reason of the innumerable minute fissures which penetrate the rather bubbly mass. It is imported from Alexandria.

3. ***Morocco, Mogador*** or ***Brown Barbary Gum***—consists of tears of moderate size, often vermiform, and of a rather uniform, light, dusky brown tint. The tears which are internally glassy become cracked on the surface and brittle if kept in a warm room; they are perfectly soluble in water. The above mentioned *Acacia nilotica* is supposed to be the source of the gum exported from Morocco, and also from Fezzan.

Gums of various kinds, including the resin Sandrac, were exported from Morocco in the year 1872 to the extent of 5110 cwt., a quantity much below the average.[2]

4. ***Cape Gum***—This gum, which is uniformly of an amber brown, is produced in plenty in the Cape Colony, as a spontaneous exudation of *Acacia horrida* Willd. (*A. Karroo* Hayne, *A. capensis* Burch.), a large tree, the *Doornboom, Wittedoorn* or *Karródoorn* of the Cape colonists, the commonest tree of the lonely deserts of South Africa. The *Blue Book* of the Cape Colony, published in 1873, states the export of gum in 1872 as 101,241 lb.

5. ***East India Gum***—The best qualities consist of tears of various sizes, sometimes as large as an egg, internally transparent and vitreous, of a pale amber or pinkish hue, completely soluble in water. This gum is largely shipped from Bombay, but is almost wholly the produce of Africa; the imports into Bombay from the Red Sea ports, Aden and the African Coast in the year 1872-73, were 14,352 cwt. During the same year the shipments from Bombay to the United Kingdom amounted to 4,561 cwt.[3]

6. ***Australian Gum, Wattle Gum***—This occurs in large hard globular tears and lumps, occasionally of a pale yellow, yet more often of an amber or of a reddish-brown hue. It is transparent and entirely soluble in water; the mucilage is strongly adhesive, and said to be less liable to crack when dry than that of some other gums. The solution, especially that of the darker and inferior kinds, contains a little tannin, evidently derived from the very astringent bark which is often attached to the gum.

A. pycnantha Benth.; *A. decurrens* Willd. (*A. mollissima* Willd., *A. dealbata* Link), *Black* or *Green Wattle-tree* of the colonists, and *A. homalophylla* A. Cunn., are the trees which furnish the gum arabic of Australia.[4]

[1] Flückiger, in the *Jahresbericht* of Wiggers and Husemann, 1869. 149.

[2] *Consular Reports*, August, 1873. 917.

[3] *Statement of the Trade and Navigation of the Presidency of Bombay for* 1872-73, pt. ii. 34. 77.

[4] P. von Müller, *Select Plants for industrial culture in Victoria*. 1876; 2. 4.

Chemical Characters and Composition—At ordinary temperatures gum dissolves very slowly and without affecting the thermometer in an equal weight of water, forming a thick, glutinous, slightly opalescent liquid, having a mawkish taste and decidedly acid reaction. At higher temperatures the dissolution of gum is but slightly accelerated, and water does not take up a much larger quantity even at 100°. The finest gum dried at 100° C. forms with two parts of water a mucilage of sp. gr. 1·149 at 15° C.

This solution mixes with glycerine, and the mixture may be evaporated to the consistence of a jelly without any separation taking place. Solid gum in lumps, on the contrary, is but little affected by concentrated glycerine. In other liquids, gum is insoluble or only slightly soluble, unless there is a considerable quantity of water present. Thus 100 parts of spirit of wine containing 22 volumes per cent. of alcohol, dissolve 57 parts of gum; spirit containing 40 per cent. of alcohol takes up 10 parts, and spirit of 50 per cent. only 4 parts. Aqueous alcohol of 60 per cent. no longer dissolves gum, but extracts from it a small quantity ($\frac{1}{3}$ to $\frac{1}{2}$ per cent. according to the variety) of resin colouring matter, glucose, calcium chloride, and other salts.

Neutral acetate of lead does not precipitate gum arabic mucilage; but the basic acetate forms, even in a very dilute solution, a precipitate of definite constitution.

Soluble silicates, borates, and ferric salts render gum solution turbid, or thicken it to a jelly. It is not a compound of gum with any of these substances which is formed, but in the cases of the first, basic silicates separate. No alteration is produced by silver salts, mercuric chloride or iodine. Ammonium oxalate throws down the lime contained in a solution of gum. Gum dissolves in an ammoniacal solution of cupric oxide. Acted upon by nitric acid, mucic acid is produced.

Small, air-dried lumps of gum lose by desiccation over concentrated sulphuric acid (or by heating them in the water-bath) 12 to 16 per cent. of water. If gum independently of its amount of lime, be presented by the formula $C^{12}H^{22}O^{11} + 3\,H^2O$, the loss of 3 molecules of water will correspond to a decrease in weight of 13·6 per cent.; in carefully selected colourless pieces, we have found it to amount to 13·14 per cent. At a temperature of about 150° C., gum parts with another molecule of water, and partly loses its solubility and assumes a brownish hue and empyreumatic taste. Gum already by keeping it for a week at a temperature not exceeding 95° C. gradually acquires a decidedly empyreumatic taste. We have also observed, on the other hand, a fine white gum affording an imperfect solution which was *glairy*, like the mucilage of marsh-mallow, but in no other respect could we find that it differed from ordinary gum. On exposing it for some days to a temperature of 95° C., it afforded a solution of the usual character.

When gum arabic is dissolved in cold water and the solution is slightly acidulated with hydrochloric acid, alcohol produces it in a precipitate of *Arabin* or *Arabic Acid*. It may be also prepared by placing a solution of gum (1 gum + 5 water), acidulated with hydrochloric acid, on a dialyser, when the calcium salt will diffuse out, leaving behind a solution of arabin.

Solution of arabin differs from one of gum in not being precipitated by alcohol. Having been dried, it loses its solubility, merely swelling in water, but not dissolving even at a boiling heat. If an alkali is added, it forms a solution like ordinary gum. Neubauer who observed these facts (1854-57) showed that gum arabic is essentially an acid calcium salt of arabic acid.

Arabic Acid dried at 100° C. has the composition $C^{12}H^{22}O^{11}$, and gives up H^2O when it unites with bases. It has however a great tendency to form salts containing a large excess of acid. An acid calcium arabate of the composition $(C^{12}H^{21}O^{11})^2 Ca + 3 (C^{12}H^{22}O^{11} + 5 OH^2)$ would afford by incineration 4·95 per cent. of calcium carbonate. Nearly this amount of ash is in fact sometimes yielded by gum. The most carefully selected colourless pieces of it yield from 2·7 to 4 per cent. of ash, consisting mainly of calcium carbonate, but containing also carbonates of potassium and magnesium. Phosphoric acid appears never to occur in gums.

Natural gum may therefore be regarded as a salt of arabic acid having a large excess of acid, or perhaps as a mixture of such salts of calcium, potassium and magnesium. It is to the presence of these bases, which are doubtless derived from the cell-wall from which the gum exuded, that gum owes its solubility.

It still remains unexplained why certain gums, not unprovided with mineral constituents, merely swell up in water without dissolving, thus materially differing from gum arabic. There is also a marked difference between gum arabic and many other varieties of gum or mucilage, which immediately form a plumbic compound if treated with neutral acetate of lead. The type of the swelling, but not really soluble gums, is Tragacanth, but there are a great many other substances of the same class, some of them perfectly resembling gum arabic in external appearance. The name of *Bassora gum* has also been applied to the latter kinds.

Commerce—The imports of Gum Arabic into the United Kingdom have been as follows :—

1871	1872
76,136 cwt., value £250,088.	42,837 cwt., value £123,080.

The country whence by far the largest supplies are shipped, is Egypt.

Uses—Gum is employed in medicine rather as an adjuvant than as possessing any remedial powers of its own.

Substitutes—A great number of trees are capable of affording gums more or less similar to gum arabic. There is to be mentioned for instance *Prosopis glandulosa* Torrey, a tree growing from 30 to 40 feet in height, occurring very abundantly in Texas, and extending as far west as the Colorado and the gulf of California. It is universally known by its Mexican name *Mesquite.* It belongs to the same suborder of the Mimosæ like the Acaciæ tribe of the Adenanthereæ. *Mesquite gum* agrees not with the fine description, but with the inferior sorts of gum arabic, and is sometimes used in America,[1] since 1854, in the manufacture of confectionery and the arts.

Feronia Gum or *Wood Apple Gum.* This is the produce of *Feronia*

[1] *See Proceedings of Am. Pharm. Assoc.* 1875. 647; *Am. Journ. of Pharm.* 1878. 480.

Elephantum Correa, a spiny tree, 50 to 60 feet high, of the order of *Aurantiaceæ*, common throughout India from the hot valleys of the Himalaya to Ceylon, and also found in Java. There exudes from its bark abundance of gum, which appears not to be collected for exportation *per se*, but rather to be mixed indiscriminately with other gum, as that of *Acacia*.

Feronia gum sometimes forms small roundish transparent, almost colourless tears, more frequently stalactitic or knobby masses, of a brownish or reddish colour, more or less deep. In an authentic sample, for which we are indebted to Dr. Thwaites of Ceylon, horn-shaped pieces about ½ an inch thick and two inches long also occur.

Dissolved in two parts of water, it affords an almost tasteless mucilage, of much greater viscosity than that of gum arabic made in the same proportions. The solution reddens litmus, and is precipitated like gum arabic by alcohol, oxalate of ammonium, alkaline silicates, perchloride of iron, but not by borax. Moreover, the solution of Feronia gum is precipitated by neutral acetate of lead or caustic baryta, but not by potash. If the solution is completely precipitated by neutral acetate of lead, the residual liquid will be found to contain a small quantity of a different gum, identical apparently with gum arabic, inasmuch as it is not thrown down by acetate of lead. If the lime is precipitated from the Feronia mucilage by oxalate of potassium, the gum partially loses its solubility and forms a turbid liquid.

From the preceding experiments, it follows that a larger portion of Feronia gum is by no means identical with gum arabic. The former, when examined in a column of 50 mm. length, deviates the rays of polarized light 0°·4 to the right,—not to the *left* as gum arabic. This was, we believe, the first instance of a dextrogyre gum;[1] Scheibler has afterwards shown (1873) that there are also dextrogyre varieties among the African gum from Sennar. Gum arabic may be combined with oxide of lead; the compound (arabate of lead) contains 30·6 per cent. of oxide of lead, whereas the plumbic compound of Feronia gum, dried at 110° C., yielded us only 14·76 per cent. of PbO. The formula $(C^{12}H^{21}O^{11})^2Pb + 2(C^{12}H^{22}O^{11})$ supposes 14·2 per cent. of oxide of lead.

Feronia gum repeatedly treated with fuming nitric acid produces abundant crystals of mucic acid. We found our sample of the gum to yield 17 per cent. of water, when dried at 110° C. It left 3·55 per cent. of ash.

CATECHU.

Catechu nigrum; Black Catechu, Pegu Catechu, Cutch, Terra Japonica; F. *Cachou, Cachou brun ou noir;* G. *Catechu.*

Botanical Origin—The trees from which this drug is manufactured are of two species, namely:—

1. *Acacia Catechu* Willd. (*Mimosa Catechu* L. fil., *M. Sundra* Roxb.[2]), a tree 30 to 40 feet high, with a short, not very straight trunk

[1] Flückiger, *Pharm. Journ.* x. (1869). 641.

[2] Some Indian botanists, as Beddome, regard *Mimosa* (*Acacia*) *Sundra* as distinct from *A. Catechu*.—Fig. in Bentley and Trimen, part 17.

4 to 6 feet in girth, straggling thorny branches, light feathery foliage, and dark grey or brown bark, reddish and fibrous internally.

It is common in most parts of India and Burma, where it is highly valued for its wood, which is used for posts and for various domestic purposes, as well as for making catechu and charcoal, while the astringent bark serves for tanning. It also grows in the hotter and drier parts of Ceylon. *A. Catechu* abounds in the forests of Tropical Eastern Africa; it is found in the Soudan, Sennaar, Abyssinia, the Noer country, and Mozambique, but in none of these regions is any astringent extract manufactured from its wood.

2. *A. Suma* Kurz[1] (*Mimosa Suma* Roxb.), a large tree with a red heartwood, but a white bark, nearly related to the preceding but not having so extensive a geographical range. It grows in the South of India (Mysore), Bengal and Gujerat. The bark is used in tanning, and catechu is made from the heart-wood.

The extract of the wood of these two species of *Acacia* is *Catechu* in the true and original sense of the word, a substance not to be confounded with *Gambier*, which, though very similar in composition, is widely diverse in botanical origin, and always regarded in commerce as a distinct article.

History—Barbosa in his description of the East Indies in 1514[2] mentions a drug called *Cacho* as an article of export from Cambay to Malacca. This is the name for *Catechu* in some of the languages of Southern India.[3]

About fifty years later, Garcia de Orta gave a particular account of the same drug[4] under its Hindustani name of *Kat*, first describing the tree and then the method of preparing an extract from its wood. This latter substance was at that period made up with the flour of a cereal (*Eleusine coracana* Gärtn.) into tablets or lozenges, and apparently not sold in its simple state: compositions of this kind are still met with in India. In the time of Garcia de Orta the drug was an important article of traffic to Malacca and China, as well as to Arabia and Persia.

Notwithstanding these accounts, catechu remained unknown in Europe until the 17th century, when it began to be brought from Japan, or at least said to be exported from that country. It was known about 1641 to Johannes Schröder,[5] and is quoted at nearly the same time in several tariffs of German towns, being included in the simples of mineral origin.[6]

In 1671, catechu was noticed as a useful medicine by G. W. Wedel of Jena,[7] who also called attention to the diversity of opinion as to its

[1] Brandis, *Forest Flora of North-Western and Central India*, Lond. 1874. 187, from which excellent work we also borrow the description of *A. Catechu*.

[2] Published by the Hakluyt Society, Lond. 1866. p. 191.

[3] As Tamil and Canarese, in which according to modern spelling the word is written *Káshu* or *Káchu*. — Moodeen Sheriff, *Suppl. to Pharmacopœia of India*, 1879. 96.

[4] *Aromatum Historia*, ed. Clusius, 1574. 44.—He writes the word *Cate*.

[5] *Pharmacopœia medico-physica*, Ulmæ, 1649. lib. iii. 516. "Est et genus terræ exoticæ, colore purpureum, punctulis albis intertextum, ac si situm contraxisset, sapore austeriusculum, masticatum liquescens, subdulcemque post se relinquens saporem, *Catechu* vocant, seu *Terram japonicam*. . . Particulam hujus obtinui a Pharmacopœo nostrate curiosissimo Dn. Matthia Bansa." The preface is dated Frankfurt A.D. 1641.

[6] *Pharm. Journ.* vi. (1876) 1022.

[7] *Usus novus Catechu seu Terræ Japonicæ*, —*Ephemerides Nat. Cur.* Dec. i. ann. 2 (1671) 209.

mineral or vegetable nature. Schröck[1] in 1677 combated the notion of its mineral origin, and gave reasons for considering it a vegetable substance. A few years later, Cleyer,[2] who had a personal knowledge of China, pointed out the enormous consumption of catechu for mastication in the East,—that it is imported into Japan,—that the best comes from Pegu, but some also from Surat, Malabar, Bengal, and Ceylon.

Catechu was received into the London Pharmacopœia of 1721, but was even then placed among "*Terræ medicamentosæ.*"

The wholesale price in London in 1776 was £16 16*s.* per cwt.; in 1780 £20; in 1793 £14 14*s.*, from which it is easy to infer that the consumption could only have been very small.[3]

Manufacture—Cutch, commonly called in India *Kát* or *Kut*, is an aqueous extract made from the wood of the tree. The process for preparing it varies slightly in different districts.

The tree is reckoned to be of proper age when its trunk is about a foot in diameter. It is then cut down, and the whole of the woody part, with the exception of the smaller branches and the bark, is chopped into chips. Some accounts state that only the darker heartwood is thus used. The chips are then placed with water in earthen jars, a series of which is arranged over a mud-built fire-place, usually in the open air. Here the water is made to boil, the liquor as it becomes thick and strong being decanted into another vessel, in which the evaporation is continued until the extract is sufficiently inspissated, when it is poured into moulds made of clay, or of leaves pinned together in the shape of cups, or in some districts on to a mat covered with the ashes of cow-dung, the drying in each case being completed by exposure to the sun and air. The product is a dark brown extract, which is the usual form in which cutch is known in Europe.

In Kumaon in the north of India,[4] a slight modification of the process affords a drug of very different appearance. Instead of evaporating the decoction to the condition of an extract, the inspissation is stopped at a certain point and the liquor allowed to cool, "coagulate," and crystallize over twigs and leaves thrown into the pots for the purpose. How this drug is finished off we do not exactly know, but we are told that by this process there is obtained from each pot about 2 ℔. of "*Kath*" or catechu, of an ashy whitish appearance, which is quite in accordance with the specimens we have received and of which we shall speak further on.

In Burma the manufacture and export of cutch form, next to the sale of timber, the most important item of forest revenue. According to a report by the Commissioner of the Prome Division, the trade returns of 1869-70 show that the quantity of cutch exported from the province during the year was 10,782 tons, valued at £193,602, of which nearly one-half was the produce of manufactories situated in the British territory. Vast quantities of the wood are consumed as fuel, especially for the steamers on the Irrawadi.[5]

[1] *Ibid.* Dec. i. ann. 8 (1677) 88.

[2] *Ibid.* Dec. ii. ann. 4 (1685) 6.

[3] Pegu Cutch is quoted in a London price-current, March 1879, £1. 2*s.* per cwt.

[4] Madden in *Journ. of Asiat. Soc. of Bengal*, xvii. part i. (1848) 565; also private communication accompanied by specimens of tree, wood, and extract from Mr. F. E. G. Matthews, of the Kumaon Iron Works, Nynee Tal.

[5] Pearson (G. F.) *Report of the Administration of the Forest Department in the several provinces under the Government of India*, 1871-72, Calcutta, 1872, part 5. p. 22.

Description—Cutch is imported in mats, bags, or boxes. It is a dark brown, extractiform substance, hard and brittle on the surface of the mass, but soft and tenacious within, at least when newly imported. The large leaf of *Dipterocarpus tuberculatus* Roxb., the *Ein* or *Engben* of the Burmese, is often placed outside the blocks of extract.

Cutch when dry breaks easily, showing a shining but bubbly and slightly granular fracture. When it is soft and is pulled out into a thin film, it is seen to be translucent, granular and of a bright orange-brown. When further moistened and examined under the microscope, it exhibits an abundance of minute acicular crystals, precisely as seen in gambier. We have observed the same in numerous samples of the dry drug when rendered pulpy by the addition of water, or moistened with glycerin and viewed by polarized light.

The pale cutch referred to as manufactured in the north of India, is in the form of irregular fragments of a cake an inch or more thick, which has a laminated structure and appears to have been deposited in a round-bottomed vessel. It is a porous, opaque, earthly-looking substance of a pale pinkish brown, light, and easily broken. Under the microscope it is seen to be a mass of needle-shaped crystals exactly like gambier, with which in all essential points it corresponds. We have received from India the same kind of cutch made into little round cakes like lozenges, with apparently no addition. The taste of cutch is astringent, followed by a sensation of sweetness by no means disagreeable.

Chemical Composition—Extractiform cutch, such as that of Pegu, which is the only sort common in Europe, when immersed in cold water turns whitish, softens and disintegrates, a small proportion of it dissolving and forming a deep brown solution. The insoluble part is *Catechin* in minute acicular crystals. If a little of the thick chocolate-like liquid made by macerating cutch in water, is heated to the boiling point, it is rendered quite transparent (mechanical impurities being absent), but becomes turbid on cooling. Ferric chloride forms with this solution a dark green precipitate, immediately changing to purple if common water or a trace of free alkali be used.

Ether extracts from cutch, catechin. This substance has been investigated by many chemists, but as yet with discrepant results. It agrees, according to Etti (1877), with the formula $C^{19}H^{18}O^{8}$, when dried at 80° C. By gently heating catechin, *Catechutannic acid*, $C^{38}H^{34}O^{15}$, is produced:

$$2(C^{19}H^{18}O^{8}) - OH^{2} = C^{38}H^{34}O^{15}.$$

This is an undoubted acid, readily soluble in water, of decidedly tanning properties, precipitating also the alkaloids and albumin. Catechutannic acid being the first anhydride of catechin, there are several more substances of that class; one of them is called *Catechuretin*. This blackish brown almost insoluble substance is obtained by heating catechin with concentrated hydrochloric acid at 180°:

$$2(C^{19}H^{18}O^{8}) - 4\ OH^{2} = C^{38}H^{28}O^{12}.$$

Catechin, by melting it with caustic potash, affords Protocatechuic acid, $C^{6}H^{3}(OH)^{2}COOH$, and Phloroglucin, $C^{6}H^{3}(OH)^{3}$:

$$C^{19}H^{18}O^{8} + 2\ OH^{2} = 4\ H \cdot C^{7}H^{6}O^{4} \cdot 2\ C^{6}H^{6}O^{3}.$$

Gautier (1877) also obtained the two latter products, but he is of the opinion that they are due to a somewhat different reaction, the formula of catechin, as derived from his analyses, being $C^{20}H^{18}O^{8}$. He also asserts that the so-called catechin from Uncaria (see Gambier) is not identical with the substance under notice, nor with that found in the Mahogan wood, to which Gautier assigns the formula $C^{40}H^{34}O^{16}$.

Crystallized deposits of catechin are sometimes met with in fissures of the trunk of Acacia Catechu, and used medicinally in India under the name *Keersal.*[1]

Löwe (1873), by exhausting cutch with cold water and then agitating the solution with ether, obtained upon the evaporation of the latter a yellow crystalline substance which he ascertained to be *Quercetin*, $C^{27}H^{18}O^{12}$. Its solubility in water is probably favoured by the presence of catechin, water having but very little action upon pure quercetin. The amount of quercetin in cutch is exceedingly small.

When either cutch or gambier is subjected to dry distillation it yields, in common with many other substances, *Pyrocatechin*, $C^{6}H^{4}(OH)^{2}$.

Commerce—The importations of cutch into the United Kingdom from British India (excluding the Straits Settlements and Ceylon) were as under, almost the whole being from Bengal and Burma:—

1869	1870	1871	1872
2257 tons.	5252 tons.	4335 tons.	5240 tons.

The total value of the cutch imported in 1872 was estimated at £124,458.

Uses—Cutch under the name of *Catechu*, which name it shares with gambier, is employed in medicine as an astringent.

Analogous Products—See our articles Semen Arecæ and Gambier.

ROSACEÆ.

AMYGDALÆ DULCES.

Sweet Almonds; F. Amandes douces; G. Süsse Mandeln.

Botanical Origin—*Prunus Amygdalus* Baillon[2] var. *β. dulcis* (*Amygdalus communis* L. var. *β. dulcis* DC.)—The native country of the almond cannot be ascertained with precision. A. de Candolle,[3] after reviewing the statements of various authors concerning the occurrence of the tree in an apparently wild state, arrives at the conclusion that its original area possibly extended from Persia, westward to Asia Minor and Syria, and even to Algeria. The tree is found ascending to 4000 feet in the Antilebanon, to 3000 in Mesopotamia, and even to 9000 feet in the Avroman range, not far from Sulemãnia, Southern Kurdistan.[4]

At an early period the tree was spread throughout the entire Mediterranean region, and in favourable situations, far into the continent of Europe. It was apparently introduced into Italy from Greece, where

[1] Dymock, *Ph. Journ.* vii. (1876) 109.
[2] *Hist. des Plantes (Monogr. des Rosacées,* 1869) i. 415.
[3] *Géographie Botanique*, ii. (1855) 888.
[4] Boissier, *Flora Orientalis*, ii. (1872) 641.

according to Heldreich,[1] the bitter variety is truly wild. The almond-tree matures its fruit in the south of England, but is liable to destruction by frost in many parts of central Europe.

History—The earliest notice of the almond extant is that in the Book of Genesis,[2] where we read that the patriarch Israel commanded his sons to carry with them into Egypt a present consisting of the productions of Palestine, one of which is named as *almonds*.

From the copious references to the almond in the writings of Theophrastus, one cannot but conclude that in his day it was familiarly known.

In Italy, M. Porcius Cato[3] mentions towards the middle of the 2nd century B.C. *Avellanæ Græcæ* which we know from later authors signified *almonds*. Columella, who wrote about A.D. 60, calls them *Nuces Græcæ*. Bitter almonds ("*Amygdali amari*") are named about this latter period by Scribonius Largus.

As to more northern Europe, almonds are mentioned together with other groceries and spices as early as A.D. 716, in a charter granted by Chilperic II., King of France, to the monastery of Corbie in Normandy.[4] In 812 Charlemagne ordered the trees (*Amandalarii*) to be introduced on the imperial farms. In the later middle ages, the cultivation of the almond was carried on about Speier and in the Rhenish Palatinate. We learn from Marino Sanudo[5] that in the beginning of the 14th century, almonds had become an important item of the Venetian trade to Alexandria. They were doubtless in large part produced by the islands of the Greek Archipelago, then under Christian rule. In Cyprus for instance, the Knights Templar levied tithes in 1411 of *almonds*, honey, and sesamé seed.[6]

The consumption of almonds in mediæval cookery was enormous. An inventory made in 1372 of the effects of Jeanne d'Evreux, queen of France, enumerates only 20 lb. of sugar, but 500 lb. of almonds.[7]

In the *Form of Cury*, a manuscript written by the master cooks of King Richard II., A.D. 1390, are receipts for "*Creme of Almand, Grewel of Almand, Cawdel of Almand Mylke, Jowt of Almand Mylke*," &c.[8]

Almonds were sold in England by the "*hundred*," *i.e.* 108 lb. Rogers[9] gives the average price between 1259 and 1350 as 2d., and between 1351 and 1400 as 3⅛d. per lb.

Description—The fruit of the almond tree is a drupe, with a velvety sarcocarp which at maturity dries, splits, and drops off, leaving bare and still attached to the branch, an oblong, ovate pointed stone, pitted with irregular holes. The seed, about an inch in length, is ovate or oblong, more or less compressed, pointed at the upper, blunt at the lower end, coated with a scurfy, cinnamon-brown skin or testa. It is connected with the stone or putamen by a broad funicle, which runs

[1] *Nutzpflanzen Griechenlands*, Athen, 1862. 67.
[2] Ch. xliii. v. 11; Num. xvii. 8.
[3] *De Re Rustica*, cap. viii.
[4] Pardessus, *Diplomata Chartæ*, etc., Paris, 1849. ii. 309.
[5] *Liber Secretorum Fidelium*, ed. Bongars, 1611. 24.
[6] De Mas Latrie, *Hist. de l'île de Chypre*, ii. (1852) 500.
[7] Leber, *Appréciation de la fortune privée au moyen-âge*, éd. 2, Paris, 1847. 95.
[8] Published by Pegge, Lond. 1780.—Boorde in his *Dyetary of Helth*, 1542, mentions *Almon Mylke* and *Almon Butter*, the latter "*a commendable dysshe, specyallye in Lent.*"
[9] *Agriculture and Prices in England*, i. (1866) 641.

along its edge for more than a third of its length from the apex; hence the raphe passes downwards to the rounded end of the seed, where a scar marks the chalaza. From this, a dozen or more ramifying veins run up the brown skin towards the pointed end. After an almond has been macerated in warm water, the skin is easily removed, bringing with it the closely attached translucent inner membrane or endopleura. As the seed is without albumen, the whole mass within the testa consists of embryo. This is formed of a pair of plano-convex cotyledons, within which lie the flat leafy plumule and thick radicle, the latter slightly projecting from the pointed or basal end of the seed.

Almonds have a bland, sweet, nutty flavour. When triturated with water, they afford a pure white, milk-like emulsion of agreeable taste.

Varieties—The different sorts of almond vary in form and size, and more particularly in the firmness of the shell. This in some varieties is tender and easily broken in the hand, in others so hard as to require a hammer to fracture it. The form and size of the kernel likewise exhibit some variation. The most esteemed are those of Malaga, known in trade as *Jordan Almonds*. They are usually imported without the shell, and differ from all other sorts in their oblong form and large size. The other kinds of sweet almonds known in the London market are distinguished in the order of value as *Valencia*, *Sicily*, and *Barbary*.[1]

Microscopic Structure—Three different parts are to be distinguished in the brown coat of an almond. First, a layer of very large (as much as $\frac{1}{3}$ mm. in diameter) irregular cells, to which the scurfy surface is due. If these brittle cells are boiled with caustic soda, they make a brilliant object for microscopic examination in polarized light. The two inner layers of the skin are made up of much smaller cells, traversed by small fibro-vascular bundles. The brown coat assumes a bluish hue on addition of perchloride of iron, owing to the presence of tannic matter.

The cotyledons consist of thin-walled parenchyme, fibro-vascular bundles being not decidedly developed. This tissue is loaded with granular albuminous matter, some of which exhibits a crystalloid aspect, as may be ascertained in polarized light. Starch is altogether wanting in almonds.

Chemical Composition—The sweet almond contains fixed oil extractable by boiling ether to the extent of 50 to 55 per cent. A produce of 50 per cent. by the hydraulic press is by no means uncommon.

The oil (*Oleum Amygdalæ*) is a thin, light yellow fluid, of sp. gr. 0·92, which does not solidify till cooled to between −10 and −20° C. When fresh, it has a mild nutty taste, but soon becomes rancid by exposure to the air; it is not, however, one of the drying oils. It consists almost wholly of the glycerin compound of *Oleic Acid*, $C^{18}H^{34}O^{2}$.

Almonds easily yield to cold water a sugar tasting like honey, which reduces alkaline cupric tartrate even in the cold, and is therefore in part grape-sugar. Pelouze however (1855) obtained from almonds 10

[1] To be consulted for further information: Bianca, G. *Manuale della Cultivazione del Mandorlo in Sicilia*, Palermo, 1874 (444 pages).

per cent. of cane-sugar. The amount of gum appears to be very small; Fleury (1865) found that the *total amount* of sugar, dextrin and mucilage was altogether only 6·29 per cent.

If almonds are kept for several days in alcohol, crystals of asparagine (see article Rad. Althææ, p. 93) make their appearance, as shown by Henschen (1872), and by Portes (1876).

The almond yields 3·7 per cent. of nitrogen, corresponding to about 24 per cent. of albuminoid matters. These have been elaborately examined by Robiquet (1837-38), Ortloff (1846), Bull (1849), and Ritthausen (1872).[1] The experiments tend to show that there exist in the almond two different protein substances; Robiquet termed one of these bodies *Synaptase*, while others applied to it the name *Emulsin*.[2] Commaille (1866) named the second albuminous substance *Amandin*; it is the *Almond-legumin* of Gmelin's *Chemistry*, the *Conglutin* of Ritthausen. Emulsin has not yet been freed from earthly phosphates which, when it is precipitated by alcohol from any aqueous solution, often amount to a third of its weight. Amandin may be precipitated from its aqueous solution by acetic acid. According to Ritthausen, these bodies are to be regarded as modifications of one and the same substance, namely vegetable casein.

Blanched almonds comminuted yield, when slightly warmed with dilute potash, a small quantity of hydrocyanic acid and of ammonia; the former may be made manifest by means of Schönbein's test pointed out at p. 250.

The ash of almonds, amounting to from 3 to nearly 5 per cent., consists chiefly of phosphates of potassium, magnesium and calcium.

Production and Commerce—The quantity of almonds imported into the United Kingdom in 1872 was 70,270 cwt., valued at £204,592. Of this quantity, Morocco supplied 33,500 cwt., and Spain with the Canary Islands 22,000 cwt., the remainder being made up by Italy, Portugal, France, and other countries. The imports into the United Kingdom in 1876 were 77,169 cwt., valued at £244,078. Almonds are largely shipped from the Persian Gulf: in the year 1872-73, there were imported thence into Bombay, 15,878 cwt., besides 3,049 cwt. from other countries.[3]

Uses—Sweet almonds may be used for the extraction of almond oil, yet they are but rarely so employed (at least in England) on account of the inferior value of the residual cake. The only other use of the sweet almond in medicine is for making the emulsion called *Mistura Amygdalæ*.

AMYGDALÆ AMARÆ.

Bitter Almonds; F. *Amandes amères*; G. *Bittere Mandeln*.

Botanical Origin—*Prunus Amygdalus* Baillon var. *α. amara* (*Amygdalus communis* L. var. *α. amara* DC.). The Bitter Almond tree is not distinguished from the sweet by any permanent botanical character, and its area of growth appears to be the same (see p. 244).

[1] *Die Eiweisskörper der Getreidearten, Hülsenfrüchte und Oelsamen*, Bonn, 1872. 199.

[2] Gmelin, *Chemistry*, xviii. (1871) 452.

[3] *Statement of the Trade and Navigation of Bombay for* 1872-73, pt. ii. 31.

History—(See also preceding article.) Bitter almonds and their poisonous properties were well known in the antiquity, and used medicinally during the middle ages. Valerius Cordus prescribed them as an ingredient of trochisci.[1]

As early as the beginning of the present century, it was shown by the experiments of Bohm, a pharmaceutical assistant of Berlin, that the aqueous distillate of bitter almonds contains hydrocyanic acid and a peculiar oil which cannot be obtained from sweet almonds. It was then inferred that hydrocyanic acid itself might be poisonous, a fact which, strange to say, had not been noticed by Scheele, when he discovered that acid in 1782, as obtained by distilling potassium ferrocyanate with sulphuric acid. The dangerous action of hydrocyanic was then ascertained in 1802 and 1803 by Schaub and Schrader.[2]

Description—Bitter almonds agree in outward appearance, form, and structure with sweet almonds; they exist under several varieties, but there is none so far as we know that in size and form resembles the long sweet almond of Malaga.[3] In general, bitter almonds are of smaller size than sweet. Triturated with water, they afford the same white emulsion as sweet almonds, but it has a strong odour of hydrocyanic acid and a very bitter taste.

Varieties—These are distinguished in their order of goodness, as French, Sicilian, and Barbary.

Microscopic Structure—In this respect, no difference between sweet and bitter almonds can be pointed out. If thin slices of the latter are deprived of fat oil by means of benzol, and then kept for some years in glycerin, an abundance of crystals is slowly formed, of what we suppose to be amygdalin.

Chemical Composition—Bitter almonds, when comminuted and mixed with water, immediately evolve the odour of bitter almond oil. The more generally diffused substances are the same in both kinds of almond, and the fixed oil in particular of the bitter almond is identical with that of the sweet. Bitter almonds however contain on an average a somewhat lower proportion of oil than the sweet. In one instance that has come to our knowledge in which 28 cwt. of bitter almonds were submitted to pressure, the yield of oil was at the rate of 43·6 per cent. Mr. Umney, director of the laboratory of Messrs. Herrings and Co., where large quantities of bitter almonds are submitted to powerful hydraulic pressure, gives 44·2 as the average percentage of oil obtained during the years 1871-2.

Robiquet and Boutron-Charland in 1830 prepared from bitter almonds a crystalline substance, *Amygdalin*, and found that bitter almond oil and hydrocyanic acid can no longer be obtained from bitter almonds, the amygdalin of which has been removed by alcohol. Liebig and Wöhler in 1837 showed that it is solely the decomposition of this body (under conditions to be explained presently), that occasions the formation of

[1] *Dispensator.*, Paris, 1548. 336. 337. 343.

[2] J. B. Richter, *Neuere Gegenstände der Chymie*, Breslau, xi. (1802) 65. J. B. Trommsdorffs *Journ. d. Pharm.* xi (Leipzig, 1803) 262. Preyer, *Die Blausäure*, Bonn, 1870. 152.

[3] Hence to avoid bitter almonds being used instead of sweet, the *British Pharmacopœia* directs that *Jordan Almonds* alone shall be employed for Confection of Almonds.

the two compounds above named. Disregarding secondary products (ammonia and formic acid), the reaction takes place as represented in the following equation:

$$C^{20}H^{27}NO^{11} + 3\,OH^2 = OH^2 \cdot 2\,(C^6H^{12}O^6) \cdot NCH \cdot C^7H^6O.$$

Crystallized Amygdalin.	Anhydrous Dextro-glucose.	Hydro-cyanic Acid.	Bitter Almond Oil.

This memorable investigation first brought under notice a body of the glucoside class, now so numerous.

Amygdalin may be obtained crystallized when almonds deprived of their oil are boiled with alcohol of 84 to 94 per cent. The product amounts at most to 2½ or 3 per cent. Amygdalin *per se* dissolves in 15 parts of water at 8–12° C., forming a neutral, bitter, inodorous liquid, quite destitute of poisonous properties.

It would appear from the investigations of Portes (1877) that in young almonds, amygdalin is formed before the emulsin.

When bitter almonds have been freed from amygdalin and fixed oil, cold water extracts from the residue chiefly emulsin and another albuminoid matter separable by acetic acid. The emulsin upon addition of alcohol falls down in thick flocks, which, after draining, form with cold water a slightly opalescent solution. This liquid added to an aqueous solution of amygdalin, renders it turbid, and developes in it bitter almond oil. The reaction takes place in the same manner, if the emulsin has not been previously purified by acetic acid and alcohol, or if an emulsion of sweet almonds used. But after boiling, an emulsion of almonds is no longer capable of decomposing amygdalin.

What alteration the emulsin itself undergoes in this reaction, or whether it suffers any alteration at all, has not been clearly made out. The reaction does not appear to take place necessarily in atomic proportions; it does not cease until the emulsin has decomposed about three times its own weight of amygdalin, provided always that sufficient water is present to hold all the products in solution.

The leaves of *Prunus Lauro-cerasus* L., the bark of *P. Padus* L., and the organs of many allied plants, also contain emulsin or a substance analogous to it, not yet isolated. In the seeds of various plants belonging to natural orders not botanically allied to the almond, as for example in those of mustard, hemp, and poppy, and even in yolk of egg, albuminous substances occur which are capable of acting upon amygdalin in the same manner. Boiling dilute hydrochloric acid induces the same decomposition, with the simultaneous production of formic acid.

The distillation of bitter almonds is known to offer some difficulties on account of the large quantity present of albuminous substances, which give rise to bumping and frothing. Michael Pettenkofer (1861) has found that these inconveniences may be avoided by immersing 12 parts of powdered almonds in boiling water, whereby the albuminous matters are coagulated, whereas the amygdalin is dissolved. On then adding an emulsion of only 1 part of almonds (sweet or bitter), the emulsin contained in it will suffice to effect the required decomposition at a temperature not exceeding 40° C. In this manner, Pettenkofer obtained in some experiments performed with small quantities of almonds, as much as 0·9 per cent. of essential oil. In the case alluded to on the opposite page, in which 28 cwt. of almonds were treated, the yield of essential oil amounted to 0·87 per cent. From data obligingly furnished to us by Messrs. Herrings and Co. of London, who distill large quantities of almond cake, it appears that the yield of essential oil is very variable. The yearly averages as taken from the books of this firm, show that it may be as low as 0·74, or as high as 1·67 per cent., which, assuming 57 pounds of cake as equivalent to 100 pounds of almonds, would represent a percentage from the latter of 0·42 and 0·95 per cent. respectively. Mr. Umney explains this enormous variation as due in part to natural variableness in the different kinds of bitter almond, and in part to their admixture with sweet almonds. He also states that the action of the emulsin on the amygdalin when in contact with water, is extremely rapid, and that 200 pounds of almond marc are thoroughly exhausted by a distillation of only three hours.

In the distillation, the hydrocyanic acid and bitter almond oil unite into an unstable compound. From this, the acid is gradually set free, and partly converted into cyanide of ammonium and formic acid. Supposing bitter almonds to contain 3·3 per cent. of Amygdalin, they must yield 0·2 per cent. of hydrocyanic acid. Pettenkofer obtained by experiment as much as 0·25 per cent., Feldhaus (1863) 0·17 per cent.

Some manufacturers apply bitter almond oil deprived of hydrocyanic acid, but such purified oil is very prone to oxidation, unless carefully deprived of water by being shaken with fused chloride of calcium. The sp. gr. of the original oil is 1·061—1·065; that of the purified oil (according to Umney) 1·049. The purification by the action of ferrous sulphate and lime, and re-distillation, as recommended by Maclagan (1853), occasions, we are informed, a loss of about 10 per cent.

Bitter almond oil, $C^6H^5(COH)$, being the aldehyde of benzoic acid, $C^6H^5(COOH)$, is easily converted in that acid by spontaneous or artificial oxidation. The oil boils at 180° C. and is a little soluble in water; 300 parts of water dissolve one part of the oil.

There are a great number of plants which if crushed, moistened with water, and submitted to distillation, yield both bitter almond oil and hydrocyanic acid. In many instances the amount of hydrocyanic acid is so extremely small, that its presence can only be revealed by the most delicate test,—that of Schönbein.[1]

Among plants capable of emitting hydrocyanic acid, probably always accompanied with bitter almond oil, the tribes *Pruneæ* and *Pomeæ* of the rosaceous order may be particularly mentioned.

The farinaceous rootstocks of the Bitter Cassava, *Manihot utilissima*, Pohl, of the order *Euphorbiaceæ*, the source of tapioca in Brazil, have long been known to yield hydrocyanic acid.

A composite, *Chardinia xeranthemoides* Desf., growing in the Caspian regions, has been shown by W. Eichler also to emit hydrocyanic acid.[2] The same has been observed by the French in Gaboon[3] with regard to the fruits of *Ximenia americana* L. of the order *Olacineæ*, and the

[1] Applied in the following manner:—Let bibulous paper be imbued with a fresh tincture of the wood or resin of guaiacum, and after drying, let it be moistened with a solution composed of one part of sulphate of copper in 2000 of water. Such paper moistened with water will assume an intense blue coloration in the presence of hydrocyanic acid.

[2] *Bull. de la Soc. imp. des nat. de Moscou*, xxxv. (1862) ii. 444.

[3] Exposition Univers. de 1867.—*Produits des Colonies Françaises*, 92.

fact has been confirmed by Ernst of Caracas,[1] near which place the plant abounds. Mr. Prestoe of the Botanical Garden, Trinidad, informs us (1874) that in that island a convolvulaceous plant, *Ipomœa dissecta* Willd., contains a juice with a strong prussic acid odour. According to Lösecke, a common mushroom, *Agaricus oreades* Bolt., emits hydrocyanic acid.[2]

This acid is consequently widely diffused throughout the vegetable kingdom. Yet amygdalin has thus far only been isolated from a few plants belonging to the genus *Prunus* or its near allies.[3] In all other plants in which hydrocyanic acid has been met with, we know nothing as to its origin. Ritthausen and Kreusler (1871) have proved the *absence* of amygdalin in the seeds of a *Vicia*, which yield bitter almond oil and hydrocyanic acid. These chemists followed the process which in the case of bitter almonds easily affords amygdalin.

Commerce—See preceding article.

Uses—Bitter almonds are used almost exclusively for the manufacture of *Almond Oil*, while from the residual cake is distilled *Bitter Almond Oil*. An emulsion of bitter almonds is sometimes prescribed as a lotion.

Adulteration—The adulteration of bitter almonds with sweet is a frequent source of loss and annoyance to the pressers of almond oil, whose profit largely depends on the amount of volatile oil they are able to extract from the residual cake.

FRUCTUS PRUNI.

Prunes; F. *Pruneaux à médecine.*

Botanical Origin—*Prunus domestica* L., var. ξ. *Juliana* DC.—It is from this tree, which is known as *Prunier de St. Julien*,[4] that the true *Medicinal Prunes* of English pharmacy are derived. The tree is largely cultivated in the valley of the Loire in France, especially about Bourgueil, a small town lying between Tours and Angers.

History—The plum-tree (*P. domestica* L.) from which it is supposed the numerous cultivated varieties have descended, is believed to occur in a truly wild state in Greece, the south-eastern shores of the Black Sea (Lazistan), the Caucasus, and the Elburz range in Northern Persia, from some of which countries it was introduced into Europe long before the Christian era. In the days of Pliny, numerous species of plum were already in cultivation, one of which afforded a fruit having laxative properties.

Dried prunes, especially those taking their name from Damascus (*Pruna Damascena*), are frequently mentioned in the writings of the Greek physicians, by whom as well as at a later period by the practitioners of the Schola Salernitana, they were much employed.

In the older London pharmacopœias, many sorts of plum are

[1] *Archiv der Pharmacie*, 181 (1867) 222.

[2] *Jahresbericht* of Wiggers and Husemann for 1871. 11.

[3] Gmelin, *Chemistry*, vii. 389; xv. 422.

[4] Loiseleur-Deslongchamps et Michel, *Nouveau Duhamel, ou Traité des arbres et arbustes que l'on cultive en France*, v. (1812) 180. pl. 54. fig. 2, pl. 56. fig. 9.

enumerated, but in the reformed editions of 1746, 1788, and 1809, the French Prune (*Prunum Gallicum*) is specially ordered, its chief use being as an ingredient of the well-known *Lenitive Electuary;* and this fruit is still held by the grocers to be the legitimate *prune.* The same variety is regarded in France as the prune of medicine.

Description—The prune in its fresh state is an ovoid drupe of a deep purple hue, not depressed at the insertion of the stalk, and with a scarcely visible suture, and no furrow. The pulp is greenish and rather austere, unless the fruit is very ripe; it does not adhere to the stone. The stone is short ($\frac{7}{10}$ to $\frac{8}{10}$ of an inch long, $\frac{5}{10}$ to $\frac{6}{10}$ broad), broadly rounded at the upper end and slightly mucronulate, narrowed somewhat stalk-like at the lower, and truncate; the ventral suture is broader and thicker than the dorsal.

The fruit is dried partly by solar and partly by fire heat,—that is to say, it is exposed alternately to the heat of an oven and to the open air. Thus prepared, it is about $1\frac{1}{4}$ inches long, black and shrivelled, but recovers its original size and form by digestion in warm water. The dried pulp or sarcocarp is brown and tough, with an acidulous, saccharine, fruity taste.

Microscopic Structure—The skin of the prune is formed of small, densely packed cells, loaded with a dark solid substance; the pulp consists of larger shrunken cells, containing a brownish amorphous mass which is probably rich in sugar. This latter tissue is traversed by a few thin fibro-vascular bundles, and exhibits here and there crystals of oxalate of calcium. By perchloride of iron, the cell walls, as well as the contents of the cells, acquire a dingy greenish hue.

Chemical Composition—We are not aware of any analysis having been made of the particular sort of plum under notice, nor that any attempt has been made to discover the source of the medicinal property it is reputed to possess. Some nearly allied varieties have been submitted to analysis in the laboratory of Fresenius, and shown to contain saccharine matters to the extent of 17 to 35 per cent., besides malic acid, and albuminoid and pectic substances.[1]

Uses—The only pharmaceutical preparation of which the pulp of prunes is an ingredient, is *Confectio Sennæ*, the *Electuarium lenitivum* of the old pharmacopœias. The fruit stewed and sweetened is often used as a domestic laxative.

Substitute—When French prunes are scarce, a very similar fruit, known in Germany as *Zwetschen* or *Quetschen*, is imported as a substitute.[2] It is the produce of a tree which most botanists regard as a form of *Prunus domestica* L., termed by De Candolle var. *Pruneauliana.* K. Koch,[3] however, is decidedly of opinion that it is a distinct species, and as such he has revived for it Borkhausen's name of *Prunus œconomica.* The tree is widely cultivated in Germany for the sake of its fruit, which is used in the dried state as an article of food, but is not grown in England.

The dried fruit differs slightly from the ordinary prune in being

[1] Liebig's *Ann. der Chemie*, ci. (1857) 228.

[2] This was especially the case in the winter of 1873-74.

[3] *Dendrologie*, part i. (1869) 94.

rather larger and more elongated, and having a thicker skin; also in the stone being flatter, narrower, pointed at either end, with the ventral suture much more strongly curved than the dorsal. The fruits seem rather more prone to become covered with a saccharine efflorescence.

CORTEX PRUNI SEROTINÆ.

Cortex Pruni Virginianæ; Wild Black Cherry Bark.

Botanical Origin—*Prunus serotina* Ehrhart (*P. virginiana* Miller non Linn., *Cerasus serotina* DC.)—A shrub or tree, in favourable situations growing to a height of 60 feet, distributed over an immense extent of North America. It is found throughout Canada as far as 62° N. lat., and from Newfoundland and Hudson's Bay in the east, to the valleys west of the Rocky Mountains.[1] It is also common in the United States.

The tree is often confounded with *P. virginiana* L., from which, indeed, it seems to be separated by no fixed character, though American botanists hold the two plants as distinct. It is also nearly allied to the well-known *P. Padus* L. of Europe, the bark of which had formerly a place in the Materia Medica.

History—Experiments on the medicinal value of Wild Cherry Bark were made in America about the end of the last century, at which time the drug was supposed to be useful in intermittent fevers.[2] The bark was introduced into the *United States Pharmacopœia* in 1820. An elaborate article by Bentley[3] published in 1863 contributed to bring it into notice in this country, but it is still much more employed in America than with us.

Description—The inner bark of the root or branches is said to be the most suitable for medicinal use. That which we have seen is evidently from the latter; it is in flattish or channelled pieces, $\frac{1}{10}$ to $\frac{1}{20}$ of an inch in thickness, $\frac{1}{2}$ an inch to 2 inches broad, and seldom exceeding 5 inches in length. From many of the pieces, the outer suberous coat has been shaved off, in which case the whole bark is of a deep cinnamon brown; in others the corky layer remains, exhibiting a polished satiny surface, marked with long transverse scars. The inner surface is finely striated, or minutely fissured and reticulated. The bark breaks easily with a short granular fracture; it is nearly without smell, but if reduced to coarse powder and wetted with water it evolves a pleasant odour of bitter almonds. It has a decided but transient bitter taste.

The bark freshly cut from the stem is quite white, and has a strong odour of bitter almonds and hydrocyanic acid.

Microscopic Structure—The chief mass of the tissue is made up of hard, thick-walled, white cells, the groups of which are separated by a

[1] Hooker, *Flora Boreali-Americana*, i. (1833) 169.

[2] Schöpf, *Materia Medica Americana*, Erlangæ 1787; 77.—Also Barton, *Collections for Mat. Med. of U.S.*, Philad. 1798. 11.

[3] *Pharm. Journ.* v. (1864) 67. — Also Bentley and Trimen, *Med. Plants*, part 3: (1878).

brown fibrous prosenchyme. The liber is crossed in a radial direction by numerous broad medullary rays of the usual structure. The parenchymatous portion is loaded both with very large single crystals, and crystalline tufts of calcium oxalate. There is also an abundance of small starch granules, and brown particles of tannic matters. Thin slices of the bark moistened with perchloride of iron, assume a blackish coloration.

Chemical Composition—The bitterness and odour of the fresh bark depend no doubt on the presence of a substance analogous to amygdalin, which has not yet been examined. Hydrocyanic acid and essential oil are produced when the bark is distilled with water, and must be due to the mutual action of that substance alluded to, and some principle of the nature of emulsin. From the fact that an extract of the bark remained bitter although the whole of the essential oil and hydrocyanic acid had been removed, Proctor inferred the existence of another substance to which the tonic properties of the bark are perhaps due.

The fresh bark was found by Perot[1] to yield ½ per mille of hydrocyanic acid in April, 1 per mille in June, and 1·4 in October. The best time for collecting the bark is therefore the autumn.

Uses—In America, wild cherry bark is held in high estimation for its mildly tonic and sedative properties. It is administered most appropriately in the form of cold infusion or syrup, the latter being a strong cold infusion, sweetened; a fluid extract and a dry resinoid extract are also in use. The bark is said to deteriorate by keeping, and should be preferred when recently dried.

FOLIA LAURO-CERASI.

Common Laurel or Cherry-laurel Leaves; F. Feuilles de Laurier-cerise; G. Kirschlorbeerblätter.

Botanical Origin—*Prunus Lauro-cerasus* L., a handsome evergreen shrub, growing to the height of 18 or more feet, is a native of the Caucasian provinces of Russia (Mingrelia, Imeritia, Guriel), of the valleys of North-western Asia Minor, and Northern Persia. It has been introduced as a plant of ornament into all the more temperate regions of Europe, and flourishes well in England and other parts, where the winter is not severe and the summer not excessively hot and dry.

History—Pierre Belon, the French naturalist, who travelled in the East between 1546 and 1550, is stated by Clusius[2] to have discovered the cherry-laurel in the neighbourhood of Trebizond. Thirty years later, Clusius himself obtained the plant through the Imperial ambassador at Constantinople, and distributed it from Vienna to the gardens of Germany. Since it is mentioned by Gerarde[3] as a choice garden shrub, it must have been cultivated in England prior to 1597. Ray,[4] who like Gerarde calls the plant *Cherry-bay*, states that it is not known to possess medicinal properties.

In 1731, Madden of Dublin drew the attention of the Royal Society

[1] *Pharm. Journ.* xviii. (1852) 109.
[2] *Rariorum Plantarum Historia*, 1601. 4.
[3] *Herball* (1636) 1603.
[4] *Hist. Plant.* ii. (1693) 1549.

of London[1] to some cases of poisoning that had occurred by the use of a distilled water of the leaves. This water he states had been for many years in frequent use in Ireland among cooks, for flavouring puddings and creams, and also much in vogue with dram drinkers as an addition to brandy, without any ill effects from it having been noticed. The fatal cases thus brought forward occasioned much investigation, but the true nature of the poison was not understood till pointed out by Schrader in 1803 (see art. Amygdalæ amaræ, p. 248, note 2). Cherry-laurel water, though long used on the Continent, has never been much prescribed in Great Britain, and had no place in any British Pharmacopœia till 1839.

Description—The leaves are alternate, simple, of leathery texture and shining upper surface, 5 to 6 inches long by 1¾ to 2 inches wide, oblong or slightly obovate, attenuated towards either end. The thick leafstalk, scarcely half an inch in length, is prolonged as a stout midrib to the recurved apex. The margin, which is also recurved, is provided with sharp but very short serratures, and glandular teeth, which become more distant towards the base. The under side, which is of a paler colour and dull surface, is marked by 8 or 10 lateral veins, anastomosing towards the edge. Below the lower of these and close to the midrib, are from two to four shallow depressions or *glands*, which in spring exude a saccharine matter, and soon assume a brownish colour. By the glands with which the teeth of the serratures are provided, a rather resinous substance is secreted.[2]

The fresh leaves are inodorous until they are bruised or torn, when they instantly emit the smell of bitter almond oil and hydrocyanic acid. When chewed they taste rough, aromatic and bitter.

Microscopic Structure—The upper surface of the leaf is constituted of thin cuticle and the epidermis made up of large, nearly cubic cells. The middle layer of the interior tissue exhibits densely packed small cells, whereas the prevailing part of the whole tissue is formed of larger, loose cells. Most of them are loaded with chlorophyll; some enclose crystals of oxalate of calcium.

Chemical Composition—The leaves when cut to pieces and submitted to distillation with water, yield *Bitter Almond Oil* and *Hydrocyanic Acid*, produced by the decomposition of *Laurocerasin*. This is an amorphous yellowish substance isolated by Lehmann (1874) in Dragendorff's laboratory. He extracted the leaves with boiling alcohol, and purified the liquid by gently warming it with hydroxide of lead. From the liquid, crude laurocerasin was precipitated on addition of ether; it was again dissolved repeatedly in alcohol and precipitated by ether. The yield of the leaves is about 1⅓ per cent. Laurocerasin is readily soluble in water, the solution deviates the plan of polarization to the left, yet not to the same amount as amygdalin. The molecule of laurocerasin, $C^{40}H^{67}NO^{30}$, would appear to include those of amygdalin, $C^{20}H^{27}NO^{11}$, amygdalic acid, $C^{20}H^{28}O^{13}$ and 7 OH^2.

The proportion of hydrocyanic acid in the distilled water of the leaves has been the subject of many researches. Among the later are those of Broeker (1867), who distilled a given weight of the leaves

[1] *Phil. Trans.* xxxvii. (for 1731-32) 84.

[2] Reinke, in Pringsheim's *Jahrbücher für wissenschaftliche Botanik*, x. (1875) 129.

grown in Holland under precisely similar circumstances, in each month of the year. The results proved that the product obtained during the winter and early spring was weaker in the acid in the proportion of 17 to 24, 28, or 30, the strongest water being that distilled in July and August. This chemist found that a stronger product was got when the leaves were chopped fine, than when they were used whole. According to Christison,[1] the buds and very young leaves yield ten times as much essential oil as the leaves one year old. We have ascertained that leaves collected in January when they were thoroughly frozen yielded a distillate containing about ten times less of hydrocyanic acid than in summer. The product obtained from the leaves collected in January, but previously dried for several days at 100° C (212° F.), still proved to contain both essential oil and hydrocyanic acid.

The unwounded leaves of the cherry-laurel in vigorous vegetation have been shown by our friend Prof. Schaer, not to evolve naturally a trace of hydrocyanic acid, though they yield it on the slightest puncture. We are ignorant of the mode of distribution in the living tissue of the lauro-cerasin, and of the substances causing its decomposition, and how these two bodies are packed so as to prevent the slightest mutual reaction. The leaves may be even dried at 100° C. and powdered without the evolution of any odour of hydrocyanic acid, but the latter is at once developed by the addition of a little water; on distilling its presence is proved by means of all the usual tests in the first drops of the product.

Besides the substances concerned in the production of the essential oil, the leaves contain sugar which reduces cupric oxide in the cold, a small quantity of an iron-greening tannin, and a fatty or waxy substance.

Schoonbroodt (1868) treated the aqueous extract of the fresh leaves with alcoholic ether, which yielded ¼ per mille of bitter, acicular crystals; these quickly reduced cupric oxide, losing their bitterness.

Bougarel (1877) isolated from the leaves under notice and several others, *Phyllinic acid*, a crystalline powder melting at 170° C.

Uses—The leaves are only employed for making cherry-laurel water (*Aqua Lauro-cerasi*), the use of which in England is generally superseded by that of the more definite hydrocyanic acid.

FLORES KOSO.

Flores Brayeræ, Cusso, Kousso, Kosso.

Botanical Origin—*Hagenia abyssinica* Willd. (*Brayera anthelminthica* Kunth), a handsome tree growing to a height of 60 feet, found throughout the entire table-land of Abyssinia at an elevation of 3,000 to 8,000 feet above the sea-level.[2] We have never noticed it growing in any botanic garden. The tree[3] is remarkable for its abundant foliage and fine panicles of flowers, and is generally planted about the Abyssinian villages.

[1] *Dispensatory*, 1842. 592.

[2] The French section of the International African Association contributed Kousso from *Madagascar* to the Paris Exhibition of 1878.

[3] Fig. in Bentley and Trimen, *Med. Plants*, part 5 (1876).

History—The celebrated Bruce[1] during his journey to discover the source of the Nile, 1768-1773, found the koso tree in Abyssinia, observed the uses made of it by the natives, and published a figure of it in the narrative of his travels. It was also described in 1799 by Willdenow who called it *Hagenia* in honour of Dr. K. G. Hagen of Königsberg.

The anthelmintic virtues of koso were investigated by Brayer, a French physician of Constantinople, to which place parcels of the drug are occasionally brought by way of Egypt, and he published a small pamphlet on the subject.[2] Several scattered notices of koso appeared in 1839-41, but no supply of it reached Europe until about 1850, when a Frenchman who had been in Abyssinia obtained a large stock (1,400 lb., it was said), a portion of which he endeavoured to sell in London at 35*s. per ounce!* The absurd value set upon the drug produced the usual result: large quantities were imported, and the price gradually fell to 3*s*. or 4*s*. per lb. Koso was admitted a place in the British Pharmacopœia of 1864.

Description—The flowers grow in broad panicles, 10 to 12 inches in length. They are unisexual, but though male and female occur on the same tree, the latter are chiefly collected. The panicles are either loosely dried, often including a portion of stalk and sometimes a leaf, or they are made into cylindrical rolls, kept in form by transverse ligatures. Very often the panicles arrive quite broken up, and with the flowers in a very fragmentary state. They have a herby, somewhat tea-like smell, and a bitterish acrid taste.

The panicle consists of a zigzag stalk, which with its many branches is clothed with shaggy simple hairs, and also dotted over with minute stalked glands; it is provided at each ramification with a large sheathing bract. At the base of each flower are two or three rounded veiny membranous bracts, between which is the turbinate hairy calyx, having ten sepals arranged in a double series. In the male, the outer series consists of much smaller sepals than the inner; in the female, the outer in the ultimate development become enlarged, obovate and spreading, so that the whole flower measures fully ½ an inch across. In both, the sepals are veiny and leaflike. The petals are minute and linear, inserted with the stamens in the throat of the calyx. These latter are 10 to 25 in number, with anthers in the female flower, effete. The carpels are two, included in the calycinal tube; and each surmounted by a hairy style. The fruit is an obovate one-seeded nut.

Koso as seen in commerce has a light brown hue, with a reddish tinge in the case of the female flowers, so that panicles of the latter are sometimes distinguished as *Red Koso*.

Chemical Composition—Wittstein (1840) found in koso, together with the substances common to most vegetables (wax, sugar, and gum),

[1] Travels, v. (1790) 73.

[2] *Notice sur une nouvelle plante de la famille des Rosacées, employée contre le Tænia*, Paris, 1822. The reader should also consult the excellent notice by Pereira written when the drug was first offered for sale in London. *Pharm. Journ.* x. (1851) 15; reprinted in Pereira's *Elem. of Mat. Med.* ii. part 2 (1853) 1815.—Also Meyer-Ahrens, *Die Blüthen des Kossobaumes*, Zürich, 1851. 90 pp.

24 per cent. of tannin, and 6·25 of an acrid bitter resin, which was observed by Harms (1857) to possess acid properties.

The researches of Pavesi (1858), and still more those of Bedall[1] have made us acquainted with the active principle of the drug, which has been named *Koussin* or *Kosin*. It may be obtained by mixing the flowers with lime, exhausting them with alcohol and then with water; the solutions mixed, concentrated, and treated with acetic acid, deposit the kosin. We are indebted to Dr. Bedall for a specimen of it, which we find to consist chiefly of an amorphous, resinoid substance, from which we got a few yellow crystals by means of glacial acetic acid.

Mr. Merck favoured us with kosin prepared in his laboratory at Darmstadt. It is a tasteless substance of a yellow colour, forming fine crystals of the rhombic system,—readily soluble in benzol, bisulphide of carbon, chloroform or ether, less freely in glacial acetic acid, and insoluble in water. We found a solution of kosin in 20 parts of chloroform to be destitute of rotatory power. Of alcohol, sp. gr. 0·818, 1000 parts dissolve at 12° C. only 2·3 parts of this kosin. It is abundantly soluble in alkalis, caustic or carbonated, yet has nevertheless no acid reaction, and may be precipitated from these solutions by an acid without having undergone any alteration. It is then however a white amorphous mass, which yields the original yellow crystals by re-solution in boiling alcohol, in which it dissolves readily. The analysis which we have performed of kossin assigns it the formula $C^{31}H^{38}O^{10}$.

Kosin fuses at 142° C., and remains after cooling an amorphous, transparent yellow mass; but if touched with alcohol, it immediately assumes the form of stellate tufts of crystals. This may be repeated at pleasure, kosin not being altered by cautious fusion.

Kosin is not decomposed by boiling dilute acids. It dissolves in strong sulphuric acid, giving a yellow solution which becomes turbid by the addition of water, white amorphous kosin being thrown down. At the same time a well-marked odour exactly like that of Locust Beans, due to isobutyric acid, $CH^3.CH^3.CH.COOH$, is evolved. It would thus appear that in all probability kosin is a compound ether of that acid. It is very remarkable that the active principle of fern-root, the filicic acid (see Rhizoma Filicis), by decomposition yields butyric acid. If the sulphuric solution of kosin is allowed to stand for a week, it gradually assumes a fine red; and then yields, on addition of much water, an amorphous red mass which after drying is not soluble in bisulphide of carbon, and may thus be purified. We have not succeeded in obtaining this red derivative of kosin in a crystalline state.[2]

In its anthelmintic action, kosin is nearly allied with filicic acid.[3]

Distillation with water separates from the flowers of koso a stearoptene-like oil having the odour of koso, and traces of valerianic and acetic acid. No such body as the *Hagenic Acid* of Viale and Latini (1852) could be detected by Bedall.

Commerce—Koso is brought to England by way of Aden or Bombay; some appears also to reach Leghorn, probably carried thither direct from Egypt.

[1] Wittstein's *Vierteljahresschrift für prakt. Pharm.* viii. (1859) 481; xi. (1862) 207.

[2] Flückiger and Buri, *Yearbook of Ph.* 1875. 19.

[3] Buchheim, *Archiv der Pharmacie*, 208 (1876) 417.

Uses—The drug is employed solely as a vermifuge, and is effectual for the expulsion both of *Tœnia solium* and of *Bothriocephalus latus*. The Abyssinian practice is to administer the flowers in substance in a very ample dose, which is sometimes attended with alarming and even fatal results.

The notion that the action of the drug is partially mechanical and due to the hairs of the plant, prevails in England, and has led to the use of an *unstrained* infusion of the coarsely powdered flowers. This remedy, from the quantity of branny powder (2 to 4 drachms) that has to be swallowed, is far from agreeable; and as it occasions strong purgation and sometimes vomiting, it is not often prescribed.[1]

The fruit of the koso tree, a small indehiscent achene, is stated by M. Th. von Heuglin[2] to act even more powerful than the flowers; he calls it (or the seed ?) Kosála. It would appear that the fruits have been used as an anthelmintic two centuries ago in Abyssinia.[3] Dragendorff (1878) found them to be rich in fatty matters, but devoid of an alkaloid.

PETALA ROSÆ GALLICÆ.

Flores Rosœ rubrœ ; Red Rose Petals, Rose Leaves, True Provins Roses ; F. *Pétales de Roses rouges, Roses de Provins ;* G. *Essigrosenblätter.*

Botanical Origin—*Rosa gallica* L., a low-growing bush, with a creeping rhizome throwing up numerous stems. The wild form with single flowers occurs here and there in the warmer parts of Europe,[4] including Central and Southern Russia, and Greece; also in Asia Minor, Armenia, Kurdistan, and the Caucasus. But the plant passes into so many varieties, and has from a remote period been so widely cultivated, that its distribution cannot be ascertained with any exactness. As a garden plant it exists under a multitude of forms.

History—The use in medicine of the rose dates from a very remote period. Theophrastus[5] speaks of roses being of many kinds, including some with double flowers which were the most fragrant; and he also alludes to their use in the healing art. Succeeding writers of every age down to a recent period have discussed the virtues of the rose,[6] which however is scarcely now admitted to possess any special medicinal property.

One of the varieties of *R. gallica* is the *Provins Rose*, so called from having been long cultivated at Provins, a small town about 60 miles south-east of Paris, where it is said to have been introduced from the East by Thibaut VI., Count of Champagne, on his return from the Crusades, A.D. 1241. But it appears that he went then to Navarre and in later times never resided in the Champagne. Be this as it may, Provins became much celebrated not only for its dried rose-petals, but

[1] Johnston in his *Travels in Southern Abyssinia* (1844), speaking of koso, says its effects are "*dreadfully severe.*"—Even in Abyssinia, he adds, it is barely tolerated, and if any other remedy equally efficient for dislodging tapeworm were to be introduced, koso would be soon abandoned.

[2] *Reise nach Abessinien*, etc. Jena, 1868. 322.

[3] Jobi Ludolfi *Historia æthiopica*, Francofurti, 1681. lib. i. cap. ix.

[4] It has been found in *quasi*-wild state at Charlwood in Surrey.—*Seemann's Journ. of Bot.* ix. (1871) 273.

[5] *Hist. Plant.* lib. vi. c. 6.

[6] Consult in particular the learned essay of D'Orbessan contained in his *Mélanges historiques*, ii. (1768) 297–337.

also for the conserve, syrup and honey of roses made from them,—compositions which were regarded in the light of valuable medicines.[1]

It is recorded that when, in A.D. 1310, Philippe de Marigny, archbishop of Sens, made a solemn entry into Provins, he was presented by the notables of the town with wine, spices, and *Conserve of Roses*; and presents of dried roses and of the conserve were not considered beneath the notice of Catherine de Medicis, and of Henry IV.[2]

We find that Charles Estienne, in 1536, mentions both the *Rosæ purpureæ odoratissimæ*, which he says are called *Provinciales*, and those known to the druggists as *incarnatæ*,—the latter we presume a *pale* rose.[3] *Rosæ rubeæ* are named as an ingredient of various compound medicines by Valerius Cordus.[4]

Production—The flowers are gathered while in bud and just before expansion, and the petals are cut off near the base, leaving the paler claws attached to the calyx. They are then carefully and rapidly dried by the heat of a stove, and having been gently sifted to remove loose stamens, are ready for sale. In some districts the petals are dried entire, but the drug thus produced is not so nice.

In England, the Red Rose is cultivated at Mitcham, though now only to the extent of about 10 acres. It is also grown for druggists' use in Oxfordshire and Derbyshire. At Mitcham, it is now called *Damask Rose*, which is by no means a correct name. The English dried roses command a high price.

There is a much more extensive cultivation of this rose on the continent at Wassenaar and Noordwijk in Holland; in the vicinity of Hamburg and Nuremberg in Germany, and in the villages round Paris and Lyons. Roses are still, we believe, grown for medicinal use at Provins, but are no longer held in great esteem.

There appears to be a considerable production of dried roses in Persia, judging from the fact that in the year 1871-72, 1163 cwt. were exported from the Persian Gulf to Bombay.[5]

Description—The petals adhere together loosely in the form of little cones, or are more or less crumpled and separate. When well preserved, they are crisp and dry, with a velvety surface of an intense purplish crimson, a delicious rosy odour, and a mildly astringent taste. The white basal portion of the petals should be nearly absent. For making the confection, the petals are required in a fresh state.

Chemical Composition—Red rose petals impart to ether, without losing their colour, a soft yellow substance, which is a mixture of a solid fat and *Quercitrin*. Filhol has shown (1864) that it is the latter body, and not tannic acid, of which the petals contain but a trace, that produces the dark greenish precipitate with ferric salts. The same chemist found in the petals 20 per cent. (?) of glucose which, together with colouring matter and gallic acid, is extracted by alcohol after exhaustion

[1] Pomet, *Hist. des Drogues*, 1694, part i. 174–177, speaks of the roses of Provins being "hautes en couleur, c'est à dire d'un rouge noir, velouté . . . très astringentes."

[2] Assier, *Légendes, curiosités et traditions de la Champagne et de la Brie*, Paris, 1860. 191.

[3] Stephanus (Carolus), *De re hortens libellus*, Paris, 1536. 29 (in Brit. Mus.).

[4] *Dispensatorium*, 1548. 39. 52.

[5] *Statement of the Trade and Navigation of the Presidency of Bombay for* 1871–72, pt. ii. 43.

by ether. According to Rochleder (1867), the gallic acid in red roses is accompanied by quercitannic acid.

The colouring matter which is so striking a constituent of the petals, is according to Senier an acid, which appears to form crystallizable salts with potassium and sodium.[1] An infusion of the petals is pale red, but becomes immediately of a deep and brilliant crimson if we add to it an acid, such as sulphuric, hydrochloric, acetic, oxalic, or tartaric. An alkali changes the pale red, or the deep crimson in the case of the acidulated infusion, to bright green.

Uses—An infusion of red rose petals, acidulated with sulphuric acid and slightly sweetened, is a very common and agreeable vehicle for some other medicines. The confection made by beating up the petals with sugar, is also in use.

PETALA ROSÆ CENTIFOLIÆ.

Flores Rosæ pallidæ v. incarnatæ; Provence Rose, Cabbage Rose; F. *Pétales de Roses pâles;* G. *Centifolienrosen.*

Botanical Origin—*Rosa centifolia* L.—This rose grows in a wild state and with single flowers in the eastern part of the Caucasus.[2] Cultivated and with flowers more or less double, it is found under an infinity of varieties in all the temperate regions of the globe. The particular variety which is grown in England for medicinal use, is known in English gardens as the *Cabbage Rose,* but other varieties are cultivated for similar purposes on the Continent.

R. centifolia L. is very closely allied to *R. gallica* L.; though Boissier maintains the two species, there are other botanists who regard them as but one. The rose cultivated at Puteaux near Paris for druggists' use, and hence called *Rose de Puteaux,* is the *Rosa bifera* of Redouté, placed by De Candolle though doubtfully under *R. damascena.*

History—We are unable to trace the history of the particular variety of rose under notice. That it is not of recent origin, seems evident from its occurrence chiefly in old gardens. The *Rosa pallida* of the older English writers on drugs[3] was called *Damask Rose,* but that name is now applied at Mitcham to *Rosa gallica* L., which has very deep-coloured flowers.

Production—The Cabbage Rose is cultivated in England to a very small extent, rose water, which is made from its flowers, being procurable of better quality and at a lower cost in other countries, especially in the south of France. At Mitcham, whence the London druggists have long been supplied, there are now (1873) only about 8 acres planted with this rose, but a supply is also derived from the market gardens of Putney, Hammersmith and Fulham.

Description—The Cabbage Rose is supplied to the druggists in the fresh state, full blown, and picked off close below the calyx. A complete

[1] *Yearbook of Pharm.* 1877. 63; also Filhol in *Journ. de Pharm.* xxxviii. (1860) 21; Gmelin, *Chemistry,* xvi. (1864) 522.

[2] Boissier, *Flora Orientalis,* ii. (1872) 676.

[3] As Dale, *Pharmacologia,* 1693. 416.

description is scarcely required: we need only say that it is a large and very double rose, of a beautiful pink colour and of delicious odour. The calyx is covered with short setæ tipped with a fragrant, brown, viscid secretion. The petals are thin and delicate (not thick and leathery as in the Tea Roses), and turn brown on drying.

In making rose water, it is the custom in some laboratories to strip the petals from the calyx and to reject the latter; in others, the roses are distilled entire, and so far as we have observed, with equally good result.

Chemical Composition—In a chemical point of view, the petals of *R. centifolia* agree with those of *R. gallica*, even as to the colouring matter. Enz in 1867 obtained from the former, malic and tartaric acid, tannin, fat, resin, and sugar.

In the distillation of large quantities of the flowers, a little essential oil is obtained. It is a butyraceous substance, of weak rose-like, but not very agreeable odour. It contains a large proportion of inodorous stearoptene. For further particulars see remarks under the head *Attar of Rose.*

Uses—Cabbage roses are now scarcely employed in pharmacy for any other purpose than making rose water. A syrup used to be prepared from them, which was esteemed a mild laxative.

OLEUM ROSÆ.

Attar or Otto[1] *of Rose, Rose Oil;* F. *Essence de Roses;* G. *Rosenöl.*

Botanical Origin—*Rosa damascena* Miller, var.—This is the rose cultivated in Turkey for the production of attar of rose; it is a tall shrub with semi-double, light-red (rarely white) flowers, of moderate size, produced several on a branch, though not in clusters. Living specimens sent by Baur[2] which flowered at Tübingen, were examined by H. von Mohl and named as above.[3]

R. damascena is unknown in a wild state. Koch[4] asserts that it was brought in remote times to Southern Italy, whence it spread northward. In the opinion of Baker[5] Rosa damascena is to be referred to Rosa gallica (see p. 259 above); it must be granted that the Rose mentioned in foot-note 2, as grown with one of us, approaches very much to Rosa gallica.

History—Much as roses were prized by the ancients, no preparation such as rose water or attar of rose was obtained from them. The liquid that bore the name of *Rose Oil* (ῥόδινον ἔλαιον) is stated by Dioscorides[6] to be a fatty oil in which roses have been steeped. In Europe a similar preparation was in use down to the last century, *Oleum rosarum, rosatum* or *rosaceum*, signifying an infusion of roses in olive oil in the *London Pharmacopœia* of 1721.

[1] *Attar* or *Otto* is from the word *itr* signifying *perfume* or *odour*; the oil is called in Turkish *Itr-yàghi* i.e. *Perfume-oil*, and also *Ghyùl-yàghi* i.e. *Rose-oil.*

[2] A living plant followed by excellent herbarium specimens has been kindly given to me by Dr. Baur of Blaubeuren, the father of Dr. Baur of Constantinople—D. H.

[3] Wiggers u. Husemann, *Jahresbericht* for 1867. 350.

[4] *Dendrologie*, i. (1869) 250.

[5] *Journ. of Botany*, Jan. 1875. 8.

[6] Lib. i. c. 53.

The first allusion to the distillation of roses we have met with, is in the writings of Joannes Actuarius,[1] who was physician to the Greek emperors at Constantinople towards the close of the 13th century. Rose water was distilled at an early date in Persia; and Nisibin, a town north-west of Mosul, was famous for it in the 14th century.[2]

Kämpfer speaks[3] with admiration of the roses he saw at Shiraz (1683-4), and says that the water distilled from them is exported to other parts of Persia, as well as to all India; and he adds as a singular fact, that there separates from it a certain fat-like butter, called *Ættr gyl*, of the most exquisite odour, and more valuable even than gold. The commerce to India, though much declining, still exists; and in the year 1872-73, 20,100 gallons of rose water, valued at 35,178 rupees (£3,517), were imported into Bombay from the Persian Gulf.[4] Rose oil itself is no longer exported from Persia, as it still used to be from Shiraz in the time of Niebuhr (1778).

Rose water was much used in Europe during the middle ages, both in cookery and at the table. In some parts of France, vassals were compelled to furnish to their lords so many bushels of roses, which were consumed in the distillation of rose water.[5]

The fact that a butyraceous oil of delicious fragrance is separable from rose water, was noticed by Geronimo Rossi[6] of Ravenna in 1582 (or in 1574?) and by Giovanni Battista Porta[7] of Naples in 1589; the latter in his work on distillation says—"Omnium difficillime extractionis est rosarum oleum atque in minima quantitate sed suavissimi odoris."[8] The oil was also known to the apothecaries of Germany in the beginning of the 17th century, and is quoted in official drug-tariffs of that time.[9] Angelus Sala, about 1620, in describing the distillation of the oil speaks of it as being of ". . . . candicante pinguedine instar Spermatis Ceti." In Pomet's time (1694) it was sold in Paris, though, on account of its high price, only in very small quantity. The mention of it by Homberg[10] in 1700, and in a memoir by Aublet[11] (1775) respecting the distillation of roses in the Isle of France, shows that the French perfumers of the last century were not unacquainted with true rose oil, but that it was a rare and very costly article.

The history of the discovery of the essence in India, is the subject of an interesting and learned pamphlet by Langlès,[12] published in 1804. He tells us on the authority of oriental writers, how on the occasion of the marriage of the Mogul emperor Jehan Ghir with Nur-jehan, A.D. 1612, a canal in the garden of the palace was filled with rose water, and that the princess observing a certain scum on the surface, caused it to be collected and found it of admirable fragrance, on which account it received the name of *Atar-jehanghiri*, i.e. *perfume of Jehan Ghir*. In later

[1] ". . . . stillatitii rosarum liquoris libra una." *De Methodo Medendi*, lib. v. c. 4.

[2] *Voyage d'Ibn Batoutah*, trad. par Defrémery, ii. (1854) 140.

[3] *Amœnitates*, 1712. 373.

[4] *Statement of the Trade and Navigation of the Presidency of Bombay* for 1872-73, part ii. 52.

[5] Le Grand d'Aussy, *Hist. de la vie privée des François*, ii. (1815) 250.

[6] Hieronymi Rubei Rav. *De Destillatione*, Ravennæ, 1582. 102.

[7] *Magiæ Naturalis libri xx*, Neap. 1589. 188.

[8] *De Distillatione*, Romæ (1608) 75.

[9] Flückiger, *Documente zur Geschichte der Pharm.* Halle, 1876. 37. 38. 40.

[10] *Observations sur les huiles des plantes*—*Mém. de l'Acad. des Sciences*, 1700. 206.

[11] *Hist. des Plantes de la Guiane françoise*, ii. Mémoires, p. 125.

[12] *Recherches sur la découverte de l'Essence de Rose*, Paris, 1804.

times, Polier[1] has shown that rose oil is prepared in India by simple distillation of the flowers with water. But this Indian oil has never been imported into Europe as an article of trade.

As already stated, the supplies at present come from European Turkey; but at what period the cultivation of the rose and manufacture of its oil were then introduced, is a question on which we are quite in the dark. There is no mention of attar in the account given by Savary[2] in 1750 of the trade of Constantinople and Smyrna, but in the first years of the present century some rose oil was obtained in the Island of Chios as well as in Persia.[3]

In English commerce, attar of rose was scarcely known until the commencement of the present century. It was first included in the British tariff in 1809, when the duty levied on it was 10*s.* per ounce. In 1813 the duty was raised to 11*s.* 10½*d.*; in 1819 it was 6*s.*, and in 1828, 2*s.* per ounce. In 1832 it was lowered to 1*s.* 4*d.* per lb., in 1842 to 1*s.* and in 1860 it was altogether removed.[4]

On searching a file of the *London Price Current*, the first mention of "*Otto of Rose*" is in 1813, from which year it is regularly quoted. The price (in bond) from 1813 to 1815, varied from £3 to £5 5*s.* per ounce. The earliest notice of an importation is under date 1-8 July, 1813, when duty was paid on 232 ounces, shipped from Smyrna.

Production—The chief locality for attar of rose, and that by which European commerce is almost exclusively supplied, is a small tract of country on the southern side of the Balkan mountains, the "Tekne" of Kazanlik or Kisanlik, an undulated plain famous for its beauty, as picturesquely sketched by Kanitz[5] and many other travellers. The principal seat of the trade is the town of Kizanlik, in the valley of the Tunja. The other important districts are those of Philippopli, Eski Zaghra, Yeni Zaghra, Tchirpan, Giopca, Karadsuh-Dagh, Kojun-Tepe, Pazandsik. North of the Balkans, there is only Travina to be mentioned as likewise producing attar. All these places with Kizanlik were estimated in 1859 to include 140 villages, having 2,500 stills.

The rose is cultivated by peasants in gardens and open fields, in which it is planted in rows as hedges, 3 to 4 feet high. The best localities are those occupying southern or south-eastern slopes. Plantations in high mountainous situations generally yield less, and the oil is of a quality that easily congeals. The flowers attain perfection in April and May, and are gathered before sunrise; those not wanted for immediate use are spread out in cellars, but are always used for distilling the same day. The apparatus is a copper still of the simplest description, connected with a straight tin tube, cooled by being passed through a tub fed by a stream of water. The largest establishment, "Fabrika," at Kizanlik has 14 such stills. The charge for a still is 25 to 50 lb. of roses, from which the calyces are not removed. The first runnings are returned to the still; the second portion, which is received in glass flasks, is kept at a temperature not lower than 15° C.

[1] *Asiatick Researches*, i. (1788) 332.

[2] *Dict. de Commerce*, iv. 548.

[3] Oliver, *Voyage dans l'Empire Othoman*, etc. ii. (Paris, An 9) 139, v. (1807) 367.

[4] Information obligingly communicated by Mr. Seldon of the Statistical Office of the Custom House.

[5] *Donau-Bulgarien*, ii. (1877) 103–123.—A figure of a still is given, p. 123. A good map of the Tekne of Kizanlik and environs will be found in *Zeitschrift der Gesellschaft für Erdkunde zu Berlin*, xi. (1876) Taf. 2.

for a day or two, by which time most of the oil, bright and fluid, will have risen to the surface. From this, it is skimmed off by means of a small tin funnel having a fine orifice, and provided with a long handle. There are usually several stills together.

The produce is extremely variable. According to Baur,[1] whose interesting account of attar of rose is that of an eye witness, it may be said to average 0·04 per cent. Another authority estimates the average yield as 0·037 per cent.

The harvest during the five years 1867–71 was reckoned to average somewhat below 400,000 *meticals*,[2] or 4226 lb. avoirdupois; that of 1873, which was good, was estimated at 500,000 *meticals*, value about £70,000.[3]

Roses are cultivated to a considerable extent about Grasse, Cannes and Nice in the south of France; and besides much rose water, which is largely exported to England, a little oil is produced. The latter, which commands a high price, fuses less easily than the Turkish.

There is a large cultivation of the rose for the purpose of making rose water and attar, at Ghazipur on the Ganges, Lahore, Amritsar and other places in India, but the produce is wholly consumed in the country. The species thus cultivated is stated by Brandis[4] to be *R. damascena*. Medinet Fayum, south-west of Cairo, supplies the great demand of Egypt for rose vinegar and rose water.

Tunis has also some celebrity for similar products, which however do not reach Europe. A recent traveller[5] states that the rose grown there, and from which attar is obtained, is *Rosa canina* L., which is extremely fragrant; 30 lb. of the flowers afford about 1½ drachms, worth 15*s*. When at Genoa, in 1874, one of us (F.) had the opportunity of ascertaining that excellent oil of rose is occasionally imported there from Tunis.

The butyraceous oil which may be collected in distilling roses in England for rose water is of no value as a perfume.

Description—Oil of rose is a light-yellow liquid, of sp. gr. 0·87 to 0·89. By a reduction of temperature, it concretes owing to the separation of light, brilliant, platy crystals of a stearoptene, the proportion of which differs with the country in which the roses have been grown, the state of the weather during which the flowers were gathered, and other circumstances less well ascertained. The oil produced in the Balkans solidifies, according to Baur, at from 11 to 16° C. In some experiments made by one of us[6] in 1859, the *fusing* point of true Turkish attar was found to vary from 16 to 18°; that of a sample from India was 20° C.; of oil distilled in the south of France, 21 to 23°, of an oil produced in Paris, 29°; of oil obtained in distilling roses for rose water in London, 30 to 32° C.

From these data, it appears that a cool northern climate is not conducive to the production of a highly odorous oil; and even in

[1] *Pharm. Journ.* ix. (1868) 286.

[2] *Consular Reports presented to Parliament, May*, 1872.—The *metical*, *miskal* or *midkal* is equal to about 3 dwt. troy=4794 grammes.

[3] *Consular Reports presented to Parliament*, Aug. 1873. 1090.

[4] *Forest Flora of North-western and Central India*, 1874. 200.—D. Forbes Watson, Catal. of the Indian Department, Vienna exhibition, 1873. 98.

[5] Von Maltzan, *Reise in den Regentschaften Tunis und Tripolis*, Leipzig, 1870.

[6] Hanbury, *Pharm. Journ.* xviii. (1859). 504–509. *Science Papers*, 172.

Bulgaria experience shows that the oil of the mountain districts holds a larger proportion of stearoptene than that of the lowlands.

Turkish oil of rose is stated by Baur to deviate a ray of polarized light 4° to the right, when examined in a column of 100 mm. The oil from English roses which we examined exhibited no rotation.

Chemical Composition—Rose oil is a mixture of a liquid constituent containing oxygen, to which it owes its perfume, and the solid hydrocarbon or stearoptene already mentioned, which is entirely destitute of odour. The proportion which these bodies bear to each other is extremely variable. From the Turkish oil, it may be obtained to the extent of 18 per cent., and from French and English to 35, 42, 60 or even 68 per cent.

Though the stearoptene can be entirely freed from the oxygenated oil, no method is known for the complete isolation of the latter. As obtained by Gladstone,[1] it had a sp. gr. of 0·881 and a boiling point of 216° C.

With regard to the stearoptene of rose oil, the analyses of Théodore de Saussure (1820) and Blanchet (1833) long since showed its composition to accord with the formula C^nH^{2n}. The experiments of one of us [2] confirm this striking fact, which assigns to the stearoptene in question a very exceptional place among the hydrocarbons of volatile oils, all of which are less rich in hydrogen.

Rose stearoptene separates when attar of roses is mixed with alcohol. We have isolated it also from oil obtained from Mitcham roses, by diluting the oil with a little chloroform and precipitating with glacial acetic acid or spirit of wine, the process being several times repeated. The stearoptene was lastly maintained for some days at 100° C.; thus obtained, it is inodorous, but when heated evolves an offensive smell like that of heated wax or fat. At 32·5° it melts; at 150° vapour is evolved; at 272° C. it begins to boil, soon after which it turns brown and then blackish. Stains of the stearoptene on paper do not disappear by the heat of the waterbath and the relapse of some days.

If cautiously melted by the warmth of the sun, the stearoptene forms on cooling microscopic crystals of very peculiar shape. Most of them have the form of truncated hexahedral pyramids, not however belonging to the rhombohedric system, as the angles are evidently not equal; many of them are oddly curved, thus §. Examined under the polarizing microscope, these crystals from their refractive power make a brilliant object.

Rose stearoptene is a very stable body, yet by boiling it for some days with fuming nitric acid, it is slowly dissolved, and converted into various acids of the homologous series of fatty acids, and into oxalic acid. Among the former, we detected butyric and valerianic. The chief product is however succinic acid, which we obtained in pure crystals, showing all the well-known reactions.

The same products are obtained even much easier by treating paraffin with nitric acid; it yields however less of succinic acid. The general behaviour and appearance of paraffin is in fact nearly the same as that of rose stearoptene. But what is called *paraffin*, is a series of extremely similar hydrocarbons, answering to the general formula

[1] *Journ. of Chem. Soc.* x. (1872) 12.

[2] Flückiger, *Pharm. Journ.* x. (1869) 147.

C^nH^{2n+2} (*n* being equal to more than 16), the separation of which has not yet been thoroughly effected. The fusion point of the different kinds of paraffin generally ranges from 42 to 60° C., yet one sort from the bituminous shale of Autun, prepared and examined by Laurent,[1] melts at 33° C., and in this respect agrees with our stearoptene. It is therefore possible that the latter actually belongs to the paraffin series.

We have not ascertained the correctness of Baur's strange experiments (1872, *Jahresbericht der Pharm.* p. 460), by which he believes to have converted the liquid part of rose oil into the stearoptene by means of a current of hydrogen.

Commerce—Formerly attar of rose came into commerce by way of Austria; it is now shipped from Constantinople. From the interior, it is transported in flattened round tin bottles called *kunkumas*, holding from 1 to 10 lb., which are sewed up in white woollen cloth. These sometimes reach this country, but more commonly the attar is transferred at Constantinople to small white glass bottles, ornamented with gilding, imported from Germany.

Uses—Attar of rose is of no medicinal importance, but serves occasionally as a scent for ointments. Rose water is sometimes made with it, but is not so good as that distilled from the flowers. Attar is much used in perfumery, but still more in the scenting of snuff.

Adulteration—No drug is more subject than attar of rose to adulteration, which is principally effected by the addition of the volatile oil of an Indian grass, *Andropogon Schœnanthus* L. This oil, which is called in Turkish *Idris yàghi*, and also *Entershah*, and is more or less known to Europeans as *Geranium Oil*, is imported into Turkey for this express purpose, and even submitted to a sort of purification before being used.[2] It was formerly added to the attar only in Constantinople, but now the mixing takes place at the seat of the manufacture. It is said that in many places the roses are absolutely sprinkled with it before being placed in the still. As grass oil does not solidify by cold, its admixture with rose oil renders the latter less disposed to crystallize. Hence arises a preference among the dealers in Turkey for attar of the mountain districts, which, having a good proportion of stearoptene, will bear the larger dilution with grass oil without its tendency to crystallize becoming suspiciously small. Thus, in the circular of a commercial house in Constantinople, dated from Kizanlik, occur the phrases—"*Extra strong oil*,"—"*Good strong congealing oil*," —"*Strong good freezing oil;*"—while the 3rd quality of attar is spoken of as a "*not congealing oil*." The same circular states the belief of the writers, that in the season in which they wrote, "*not a single metical of unadulterated oil*" would be sent away.

The chief criteria, according to Baur, for the purity of rose oil are:—1. *Temperature at which crystallization takes place:* a good oil should congeal well in five minutes at a temperature of 12·5° C. 2. *Manner of crystallizing.*—The crystals should be light, feathery, shining plates, filling the whole liquid. Spermaceti, which has been sometimes used to replace the stearoptene, is liable to settle down in a *solid cake*, and is easily recognizable. Furthermore, it melts at 50° C.

[1] *Ann. de Chim. et de Phys.* liv. (1833) 394.

[2] For particulars, see Baur (p. 262, note 3).

and so do most varieties of paraffin. The microscopic crystals of the latter are somewhat similar to those of rose stearoptene, yet they may be distinguished by an attentive comparative examination.

FRUCTUS ROSÆ CANINÆ.

Cynosbata; Fruit of the Dog-rose, Hips; F. *Fruits de Cynorrhodon;* G. *Hagebutten.*

Botanical Origin—*Rosa canina* L., a bush often 10 to 12 feet high, found in hedges and thickets throughout Europe except Lapland and Finland, and reaching the Canary Islands, Northern Africa, Persia and Siberia; universally dispersed throughout the British Islands.[1]

History—The fruits of the wild rose, including other species besides *R. canina* L., have a scanty, orange, acid, edible pulp, on account of which they were collected in ancient times when garden fruits were few and scarce. Galen[2] mentions them as gathered by country people in his day, as they still are in Europe. Gerarde in the 16th century remarks that the fruit when ripe—"maketh most pleasant meats and banqueting dishes, as tarts and such like." Though the pulp of hips preserved with sugar which is here alluded to, is no longer brought to table, at least in this country,[3] it retains a place in pharmacy as a useful ingredient of pill-masses and electuaries.

Description—The fruit of a rose consists of the bottle-shaped calyx, become dilated and succulent by growth, and sometimes crowned with 5 leafy segments, enclosing numerous dry carpels or achenes, containing each one exalbuminous seed. The fruit of *R. canina* called a *hip*, is ovoid, about $\frac{3}{4}$ of an inch long, with a smooth, red, shining surface. It is of a dense, fleshy texture, becoming on maturity, especially after frost, soft and pulpy, the pulp within the shining skin being of an orange colour, and of an agreeable sweetish subacid taste. The large interior cavity contains numerous hard achenes, which, as well as the walls of the former, are covered with strong short hairs.

For medicinal use, the only part required is the soft orange pulp, which is separated by rubbing it through a hair sieve.

Microscopic Structure—The epidermis of the fruit is made up of tabular cells containing red granules, which are much more abundant in the pulp. The latter, as usual in many ripe fruits, consists of isolated cells no longer forming a coherent tissue. Besides these cells, there occur small fibro-vascular bundles. Some of the cells enclose tufted crystals or oxalate of calcium; most of them however are loaded with red granules, either globular or somewhat elongated. They assume a bluish hue on addition of perchloride of iron, and are turned blackish by iodine. The later colouration reminds one of that assumed by starch granules under similar circumstances; yet on addition of a very dilute solution of iodine, the granules always exhibit a *blackish*,

[1] Baker, *Journ. of Linn. Soc.* Bot. xi. (1869) 226.

[2] *De Alimentorum facultatibus*, ii. c. 14. In the Amur country a much larger and better fruit is afforded by *R. acicularis* Lindl. and *R. cinnamomea* L.—Maximowicz, *Primitiæ Floræ Amurensis*, 1859. 100. 453.

[3] In Switzerland and Alsace a very agreeable *confiture* of hips is still in use.

not a blue tint, so that they are not to be considered as starch granules. The hairs of the pulp are formed of a single, thick-walled cell, straight or sometimes a little crooked.

Chemical Composition—The pulp examined by Biltz (1824) was found to afford nearly 3 per cent. of citric acid, 7·7 of malic acid, besides citrates, malates and mineral salts, 25 per cent. of gum, and 30 of uncrystallizable sugar.

Uses—Hips are employed solely on account of their pulp, which mixed with twice its weight of sugar, constitutes the *Confectio Rosæ caninæ* of pharmacy.

SEMEN CYDONIÆ.

Quince Seeds, Quince Pips; F. *Semences ou Pepins de Coings;* G. *Quittensamen.*

Botanical Origin—*Pirus Cydonia* L. (*Cydonia vulgaris* Pers.), the quince tree, is supposed to be a true native of Western Asia, from the Caucasian provinces of Russia to the Hindu Kush range in Northern India. But it is now apparently wild also in many of the countries which surround the Mediterranean basin.

In a cultivated state, it flourishes throughout temperate Europe, but is far more productive in southern than in northern regions. Quinces ripen in the south of England, but not in Scotland, nor in St. Petersburg, or in Christiana.

History—The quince was held in high esteem by the ancients, who considered it an emblem of happiness and fertility; and, as such, it was dedicated to Venus, whose temples it was used to decorate. Some antiquarians maintain that quinces were the *Golden Apples* of the Hesperides. The name Cydonia alludes to the town of Kydon, now Canea, in Creta; in the Talmud quinces are called Cretan apples.

Porcius Cato in his graphic description of the management of a Roman farmhouse, alludes to the storing of quinces both cultivated and wild; and there is much other evidence to prove that from an early period the quince was abundantly grown throughout Italy. Charlemagne, A.D. 812, enjoined its cultivation in central Europe.[1] At what period it was introduced into Britain is not evident, but we have observed that *Baked Quinces* are mentioned among the viands served at the famous installation feast of Nevill, archbishop of York in 1466.[2]

The use of mucilage of quince seeds has come to us through the Arabians; it is still met with in Turkestan.

Description—The quince is a handsome fruit of a golden yellow, in shape and size resembling a pear. It has a very agreeable and powerful smell, but an austere, astringent taste, so that it is not eatable in the raw state. In structure, it differs from an apple or a pear in having many seeds in each cell, instead of only two.

The fruit is, like an apple, 5-celled, with each cell containing a

[1] Pertz, *Monumenta Germaniæ historica*, Legum, i. (1835) 187.

[2] Leland, *De rebus Britannicis Collectanea*, vi. (1774) 5.

double row of closely-packed seeds, 8 to 14 in number, cohering by a soft mucilaginous membrane with which each is surrounded. By drying, they become hard, but remain agglutinated as in the cell. The seeds have an ovoid or obconic form, rather flattened and 3-sided by mutual pressure. From the hilum at the lower pointed end, the raphe passes as a straight ridge to the opposite extremity, which is slightly beaked and marked with a scar indicating the chalaza. The edge opposite the raphe is more or less arched according to the position of the individual seed in the cell. The testa encloses two thick, veined cotyledons, having a straight radicle directed towards the hilum.

Quince seeds have a mahogany-brown colour, and when unbroken a simply mucilaginous taste. But the kernels have the odour and taste of bitter almonds, and evolve hydrocyanic acid when comminuted and mixed with water.

Microscopic Structure—The epidermis of the seed consists of one row of cylindrical cells, the walls of which swell up in the presence of water and are dissolved, so as to yield an abundance of mucilage. This process can easily be observed, if thin sections of the seed are examined under glycerine, which acts on them but slowly.

Chemical Composition—The mucilage of the epidermis is present in such quantity, that the seed easily coagulates forty times its weight of water. By complete exhaustion, the seeds afford about 20 per cent. of dry mucilage, containing considerable quantities of calcium salts and albuminous matter, of which it is not easily deprived. When treated with nitric acid, it yields oxalic acid. After a short treatment with strong sulphuric acid it is coloured blue by iodine. Tollens and Kirchner (1874) assign to it the formula $C^{18}H^{28}O^{14}$, regarding it as a compound of gum, $C^{12}H^{20}O^{10}$, and cellulose, $C^{6}H^{10}O^{5}$, less one molecule of water.

Quince mucilage has but little adhesive power, and is not thickened by borax. That portion of it which is really in a state of solution and which may be separated by filtration, is precipitable by metallic salts or by alcohol. The latter precipitate after it has been dried is no longer dissolved by water either cold or warm. Quince mucilage is, on the whole, to be regarded as a soluble modification of cellulose.

The seeds on distillation with water afford a little hydrocyanic acid, and, probably, bitter almond oil.

Commerce—Quince seeds reach England from Hamburg; and are frequently quoted in Hamburg price-currents as *Russian;* they are also brought from the south of France and from the Cape of Good Hope. They are largely imported into India from the Persian Gulf, and by land from Afghanistan.

Uses—A decoction of quince seeds is occasionally used as a demulcent external application in skin complaints. It is also sometimes added to eye-lotions. Quince seeds are in general use among the natives of India as a demulcent tonic and restorative. They have been found useful by Europeans in dysentery.

HAMAMELIDEÆ.

STYRAX LIQUIDUS.[1]

Balsamum Styracis; Liquid Storax; F. *Styrax liquide;* G. *Flüssiger Storax.*

Botanical Origin—*Liquidambar orientalis* Miller (*L. imberbe* Aiton, a handsome, umbrageous tree resembling a plane, growing to the height of 30 to 40 feet or more,[2] and forming forests in the extreme south-western part of Asia Minor. In this region the tree occurs in the district of Sighala near Melasso, about Budrum (the ancient Halicarnassus) and Moughla, also near Giova and Ullà in the Gulf of Giova, and lastly near Marmorizza and Isgengak opposite Rhodes. It also grows in the valley of the El-Asi (the ancient Orontes), as proved by a specimen in the Vienna herbarium, collected by Gödel, Austrian Consul at Alexandretta. In this locality it was seen by Kotschy in 1835, but mistaken for a plane. The same traveller informed one of us that he believed it to occur at Narkislik, a village near Alexandretta.

The tree is not known to grow in Cyprus, Candia, Rhodes, Kos, or indeed in any of the islands of the Mediterranean.[3]

History—Two substances of different origin have been known from a remote period under the name of *Styrax* or *Storax,* namely the resin of *Styrax officinalis* L. (see further on), and that of *Liquidambar orientalis* Miller, the latter commonly distinguished as *Liquid Storax.*

According to Krinos of Athens, who has carefully investigated the history of the drug,[4] the earliest allusions to Liquid Storax occur in the writings of Aëtius and of Paulus Ægineta,[5] who name both *Storax* and *Liquid Storax* (πύρα ζυγρὸς). Of these Greek physicians, who lived respectively in the 6th and 7th centuries, the second also mentions the resin of *Ζυγία,* which is regarded by Krinos as synonymous with the latter substance.[6]

We find in fact the term *Sigia* frequently mentioned by Rhazes (10th

[1] The feminine gender of Styrax has been in use for a long time. In Greek it denotes the tree, as also does sometimes the masculine gender, the *neutral* being reserved to the resin. In Latin the resin is masculini generis (Dr. Rice).

[2] For a good figure of *L. orientalis,* see Hooker's *Icones Plantarum* (3rd series, 1867) pl. 1019, or Hanbury, *Science Papers,* 1876. 140; also Bentley and Trimen, *Medicinal Plants,* part 27 (1877).

[3] The fine old trees existing at the convent of Antiphoniti on the north coast of Cyprus, and at that of Neophiti near Papho, specimens of which were distributed by Kotschy as *Liquidambar imberbis* Ait., agree in all points with the American *L. stryaciflua* L., and not with the Asiatic plant. Kotschy has told me that they have *certainly been planted,* and that no other examples exist in the island.—D. H. The same opinion is adopted by Boissier, *Flora Orientalis,* ii. (1872) 8319.

[4] Περὶ Στύρακος, διατριβὴ φαρμακογραφική, ἐν Ἀθῆναις, 1862.—This pamphlet is also the subject of a paper of Prof. Planchon, *Journ. de Pharm.* 24 (1876) 172. 243.

[5] *Medicæ Artis Principes post Hippocratem et Galenum,* Par. 1567.—Aëtii tetr. 4. serm. 4. c. 122; P. Ægineta, *De re med.* vii. 20.

[6] The foliage of the Liquidamabar much resembles that of the common maple (*Acer campestre* L.); hence the two trees as well as the plane (*Platanus orientalis* L.) are confounded under one name,—Ζυγὸς or Ζυγίᾳ. So *Styrax officinalis* L., from the resemblance of its leaves to those of *Pirus Cydonia* L., is known in Greece as Ἀγρία κυδωνέα, i.e. *wild quince.*

century) as signifying Liquid Storax. This and other Arabian physicians were also familiar with the same substance under the name of *Miha* (*may'a*), and also knew how and whence it was obtained.[1]

A curious account of the collecting of Liquid Storax from the tree *Zygia*, and from another tree called *Stourika*, is given in the travels through Asia Minor to Palestine of the Russian abbot of Tver in A.D. 1113-1115.[2]

The wide exportation and ancient use of Liquid Storax are very remarkable: even in the firstcentur y, as appears by the author of the Periplus of the Erythrean Sea, Storax, by which term there can be but little doubt *Liquid Storax* was intended, was exported by the Red Sea to India. Whether the *Storax* and *Storax Isaurica* offered to the Church of Rome under St. Silvester, A.D. 314-335, by the emperor Constantine,[3] was Liquid Storax or the more precious resin of *Styrax officinalis* L., is a point we cannot determine, That the Chinese used the drug was a fact known to Garcia de Orta (1535-63): Bretschneider[4] has shown from Chinese sources that, together with olibanum and myrrh, it was imported by the Arabs into China during the Ming dynasty, A.D. 1368-1628. This trade is still carried on: the drug is conveyed by way of the Red Sea to Bombay, and thence shipped to China. Official returns show that the quantity thus exported from Bombay in the year 1856-57 was 13,328 lb. In the time of Kämpfer (1690-92), Liquid Storax was one of the most profitable articles of shipment to Japan.[5]

Liquid Storax is known in the East, at least in the price-currents and trade statistics of Europeans, by the strange-sounding name of *Rose Malloes* (*Rosa Mallas, Rosum Alloes, Rosmal*), a designation for it in use in the time of Garcia de Orta. Clusius[6] considered it to be Arabic, which, however, the scholars whom we have consulted do not allow. Others identify it with *Rasamala*, the Malay name for *Altingia excelsa*. (See further on.)

The botanical origin of Liquid Storax was long a perplexing question to pharmacologists. It was correctly determined by Krinos, but his information on the subject published in a Greek newspaper in 1841, and repeated by Kosté in 1855,[7] attracted no attention in Western Europe. The question was also investigated by one of the authors of the present work, whose observations, together with a figure of *Liquidambar orientalis* Miller, were published in 1857.[8]

Method of Extraction—The extraction of Liquid Storax is carried on in the forests of the south-west of Asia Minor, chiefly by a tribe of wandering Turcomans called *Yuruks*. The process has been described on the authority of Maltass and McCraith of Smyrna, and of Campbell, British Consul at Rhodes.[9] The outer bark is said to be first removed from the trunk of the tree and rejected; the inner is then scraped off with a peculiar iron knife or scraper, and thrown into pits until a

[1] *Ibn Baytar*, Sontheimer's transl. ii. 539.

[2] Noroff, *Pèlerinage en Terre Sainte de l'Igoumène russe Daniel*, St. Péterab. 164. 4°.—The passage has been kindly abstracted for us by Prof. Heyd of Stuttgart.

[3] Vignolius, *Liber Pontificalis*, Romæ, i. (1724) 94.—The ancient Isauria was in Cilicia, the country of *Styrax officinalis* L.

[4] *On the knowledge possessed by the Chinese of the Arabs*, etc., Lond. 1871. 19.

[5] *Hist. of Japan*, ed. Scheuchzer, i. 353.

[6] *Exoticorum Libri*, 245.

[7] Ἐγχειρίδιον Φαρμακολογίας, ὑπὸ Ν. Κωστῆ, 1855. 356.

[8] Hanbury, *Pharm. Journ.* xvi. (1857) 417. 461, and iv. (1863) 436; *Science Papers*, 127-150.

[9] Hanbury, *l.c.*

sufficient quantity has been collected. It is then boiled with water in a large copper, by which process the resin is separated, so that it can be skimmed off. This seems to be performed with sea water; some chloride of sodium can therefore be extracted from the drug. The boiled bark is put into hair bags and squeezed under a rude lever, hot water being added to assist in the separation of the resin, or as it is termed *yagh*, i.e. *oil*. Maltass states that the bark is pressed in the first instance *per se*, and afterwards treated with hot water. In either case the products obtained are the opaque, grey, semi-fluid resin known as *Liquid Storax*, and the fragrant cakes of foliaceous, brown bark, once common [1] but now rare in European pharmacy, called *Cortex Thymiamatis*.

We are indebted to M. Felix Sahut of Montpellier for a specimen of the bark of *Liquidambar orientalis*, cut from the trunk of a fine tree on his property at the neighbouring village of Lattes. The bark which is covered with a very thick corky layer and soaked in its own fragrant resin, shows no tendency to exfoliate. The investigations of Unger [2] in Cyprus are consequently to us inexplicable; he asserts that the bark scales off, like that of the plane, by continued exfoliation, which is not the case with that of M. Sahut's tree.

Description—Liquid Storax is a soft viscid resin, usually of the consistence of honey, heavier than water, opaque and greyish brown. It always contains water, which by long standing rises to the surface. In one sample that had been kept more than 20 years, the resin at the bottom of the bottle formed a transparent layer of a pale golden brown. When liquid storax is heated, it becomes by the loss of water dark brown and transparent, the solid impurities settling to the bottom. Spread out in a very thin layer, it partially dries, but does not wholly lose its stickiness. When free from water (which reddens litmus) it dissolves in alcohol, spirit of wine, chloroform, ether, glacial acetic acid, bisulphide of carbon, and most of the essential oils, but not in the most volatile part of petroleum ("petroleum ether"). It has a pleasant balsamic smell, especially after it has been long kept; when recent, it is contaminated with an odour of bitumen or naphtalian that is far from agreeable. Its taste is sharply pungent, burning and aromatic.

When the opaque resin is subjected to microscopic examination, small brownish granules are observed in a viscid, colourless, transparent liquid, besides which large drops of a mobile watery liquid may be distinguished. In polarized light, numerous minute crystalline fragments with a few larger tabular crystals are obvious. But when thin layers of the resin are left on the object glass in a warm place, feathery or spicular crystals (styracin) shoot out on the edge of the clear liquid, while in the large, sharply-defined drops above mentioned, rectangular tables and short prisms (cinnamic acid) make their appearance. On applying more warmth after the water is evaporated, all the substances unite into a transparent, dark-brown, thick liquid, which exhibits no crystalline structure on cooling, or only after a very long time. Among the fragments of the bark occurring in the crude resin, liber fibres are frequently observable.

[1] It is no doubt the "*Cortex Olibani*" met with in the tariff of 1571, in Flückiger, *Documente zur Geschichte der Pharmacie*, 26.

[2] Unger u. Kotschy, *Die Insel Cypern*. Wien, 1865. 410.

Chemical Composition—The most abundant constituent of Styrax is probably the *Storesin*, $C^{36}H^{55}(OH)^3$, discovered in 1877 by W. von Miller, or rather cinnamic ethers of it and of an isomeric substance. Storesin is an amorphous substance melting at 168° C., readily soluble in petroleum ether. Several other compound ethers have also been observed in the drug, as for instance *cinnamic ether of phenylpropyl*, *cinnamic ether of ethyl*, cinnamic ether of benzyl, and especially cinnamate of cinnamyl, $C^9H^7O^2.C^9H^9$, the so-called *Styracin*. This substance, discovered by Bonastre in 1827, can be removed by ether, benzol or alcohol, after the separation from the resin of the cinnamic acid; it is insoluble in water, and volatile only in super-heated steam. It crystallizes in tufts of long rectangular prisms, which melt at 38° C., but it frequently does not solidify in a crystalline form, or only after a long time, or remains as an oily liquid. In its pure state it is inodorous and tasteless. By concentrated solution of potash, it is resolved into a cinnamate, and cinnamic alcohol (*Styrone*) $C^9H^{10}O$, which latter is not present in Liquid Storax. The *cinnamic acid* may be extracted to a small extent by boiling water, more completely by means of a boiling solution of carbonate of sodium, as it is present in the drug partly in the free state. Its compound ethers may be decomposed by caustic lye. The yield of cinnamic acid accordingly varies from 6 to 12 per cent.—or even, according to Löwe, as much as 23 per cent. of crystallized cinnamic acid can be obtained. The acid dissolves abundantly in ether, alcohol, or hot water, slightly in cold water; it is inodorous, but has an acrid taste. It fuses at 133° C., and boils at 290° C.; at a dull red heat it is resolved into carbonic acid and styrol, which latter is therefore related to it in the same manner as benzol (benzene) to benzoic acid. Liquid styrax is in fact the best source of cinnamic acid.

Another constituent of styrax is a fragrant substance, perhaps *ethylvanillin*, occurring in but small quantity.

Laubenheimer (1872) has shown that probably *Benzylic Alcohol*, C^7H^8O, boiling at 206° C., likewise occurs in Liquid Storax; it has not been found by Miller. The latter chemist also showed that water removes from the drug a little *benzoïc acid;* he observed moreover a substance similar to *caoutchouc* among the constituents of liquid styrax.

There is further to be mentioned as having been met with in Liquid Storax a hydrocarbon, C^8H^8, first prepared by Simon in 1839, which exists in the resin as a liquid, and also in a polymeric form as a solid. The former called *Styrol*, *Cinnamene*, or *Cinnamol*, has a sp. gr. of 0·924, and a boiling point of 146° C. It is a colourless, mobile liquid which may be obtained by distilling with water liquid storax, the odour and burning taste of which it possesses. When heated for a considerable time to 100°, or for a shorter period to 200° C., it is converted without change of composition into the colourless, transparent solid *Metastyrol*, which, unlike styrol, is not soluble in alcohol or ether. It has a sp. gr. of 1·054, and may be cut with a knife. By prolonged heating, it can be converted into its original liquid form.

Styrol is to be regarded as phenylated ethylene; it can be artificially obtained by shaking powdered cinnamic acid with saturated hydrobromic acid, when crystalline hydrobromated cinnamic acid, $C^6H^5.CH^2.CHBr.COOH$, is formed. One part of the latter, 10 parts of water, and a little more carbonate of sodium than the quantity required for saturation are mixed. The bromhydrocinnamate of sodium partly splits up immediately, even at 0°, according to the following equation

$$\underset{\text{Bromhydrocinnamate of sodium.}}{C^6H^5.CH^2.CHBr.COONa} = CO^2 + NaBr + \underset{\text{Styrol.}}{C^6H^5.CH.CH^2}.$$

24 parts of bromhydrocinnamic acid, recrystallized from boiling bisulphide of carbon, yield about 7 parts of styrol; no other method affords as much as this.

Styrol has been discovered in Styrax, but is not regularly, and at all events to a minute amount only, found in the drug of the present day. We have no explanation for the strange fact that it was apparently more abundantly met with in former times.

Lastly there has been found in Liquid Storax, by J. H. van t'Hoff (1876), about 0·4 per cent. of an *essential oil*, probably $C^{10}H^{16}O$; Miller also pointed out a compound ether of probably the same (alcoholic) substance as occurring in styrax.

By the action of oxidizing agents, as nitric or chromic acids, or peroxide of lead, the cinnamyl compounds are easily reduced, carbonic acid and water being evolved; and at the same time benzoic acid, bitter almond oil, and hydrocyanic acid are produced. These compounds are in fact abundantly evolved when 6 parts of Liquid Storax are gently warmed with 1 p. of caustic soda, and then mixed with 3 p. of permanganate of potassium dissolved in 20 p. of water.

We have examined several samples of Liquid Storax of average quality, and found by exposure of small quantities to the heat of the steam bath, that it lost from 10 to 20 per cent. of water. The remainder treated with alcohol yielded a residue amounting to 13 to 18 per cent., consisting chiefly of fragments of bark and inorganic impurities. The percentage of the drug soluble in alcohol, to which is due its therapeutic value, thus amounts to 56 to 72. This part, as may be inferred from the foregoing statements, consists chiefly of storesin, the various compound ethers above mentioned, of cinnamic acid and of styracin, no doubt in greatly varying proportions.

Commerce—The annual production of Liquid Storax was estimated by Campbell in 1855 as about 490 cwt. for the districts of Giova and Ullá, and 300 cwt. for those of Marmorizza and Isgengak. The drug is exported in barrels to Constantinople, Smyrna, Syra and Alexandria. Some is also packed with a certain proportion of water in goat-skins, and sent either by boats or overland to Smyrna, where it is transferred to barrels and shipped mostly to Trieste.

The chief consumption of Liquid Storax would appear to be in India and China. In the fiscal year 1866–67, Bombay imported 319 cwt. from the Red Sea. Liquid Storax is seldom seen in the London drug-sales.

Uses—Liquid Storax, which the *British Pharmacopœia* directs to be purified by solution in spirit of wine, is an ingredient in a few old-fashioned preparations but is hardly ever prescribed on its own account. It is stated to be expectorant and stimulant, and useful in chronic bronchial affections. It has been recommended by Pastau, Berlin (1865), as an external application for the cure of scabies, for which purpose it is mixed with linseed oil and now largely used.

Adulteration—The drug is occasionally mixed with sand, ashes, and other substances; these would be detected by solution in spirit of wine, as well as by the microscope.

Allied Substances.

Styrax Calamita (*Storax en pain* Guibourt)—The substance that now bears this name is by no means the *Styrax Calamita* of ancient times, but is an artificial compound made by mixing the residual Liquidambar bark called *Cortex Thymiamatis* (p. 273), coarsely powdered, with Liquid Storax in the proportions of 3 to 2. It is at first a clammy mass, acquiring after a few weeks an appearance of mouldiness, due to minute silky crystals of styracin. It is usually imported in wooden drums, and has a very sweet smell. When the bark is scarce, common sawdust is substituted for it, while qualities still inferior are made up with the help of olibanum, honey, and earthy substances. This drug is manufactured at Trieste, Venice and Marseilles.

Several other odoriferous compounds, of which Liquid Storax appears to be the chief ingredient, are made in the East and may still be found in old drug warehouses.[1]

Resin of Styrax officinalis L.; *True Storax*—This was a solid resin somewhat resembling benzoin, of fragrant, balsamic odour, held in great estimation from the time of Dioscorides and Pliny down to the close of the last century. It was perhaps the "storace odorifero" exported in the 12th century from Pantellaria[2] and Sicily. The drug was obtained from the stem of *Styrax officinalis* L. (*Styraceæ*), a native of Greece, Asia Minor and Syria, now found also in Italy and Southern France. This plant when permitted to grow freely for several years, forms a small tree, in which state alone it appears to be capable of affording a fragrant resin. But in most localities it has been reduced by ruthless lopping to a mere bush, the young stems of which yield not a trace of exudation. True storax has thus utterly disappeared.

Professor Krinos of Athens has informed us (1871) that about Adalia on the southern coast of Asia Minor, a sort of solid storax obtained from *S. officinalis* is still used as incense in the churches and mosques. The specimen of it which he has been good enough to send us, is not however resin, but *sawdust*; it is of a pale cinnamon-brown, and pleasant balsamic odour. By keeping, it emits an abundance of minute acicular crystals (styracin?). The substance is interesting in connection with the statement of Dioscorides, that the resin of *Styrax* is adulterated with the *sawdust of the tree itself*, and the fact that the region where this sawdust is still in use is one of the localities for the drug (Pisidia) which he mentions.

Resin of Liquidambar styraciflua L.—a large and beautiful tree, native of North America from Connecticut and Illinois southward to Mexico and Guatemala. In the United States, where it is called *Sweet Gum*, the tree yields from natural fissures or by incision, small quantities of a balsamic resin, which is occasionally used for chewing. We

[1] The *Storax noir* of Guibourt is one of these.

[2] Quoted before, p. 163, note 3; in the same book "*cotone storace e corallo*" occur as articles of export from Sicily.

have before us an excellent sample of it collected for Messrs. Wallace Brothers of Statesville, N. Carolina.[1]

In Central America this exudation is far more freely produced; an authentic specimen from Guatemala in our possession is a pale yellow, opaque resin of honey-like consistence, becoming transparent, amber-coloured and brittle by exposure to the air. It has a rather terebinthinous, balsamic odour. In the mouth it softens like benzoin or mastich, and has but little taste. Another specimen also from Guatemala, a thick, fluid oleo-resin, of a golden brown hue, was contributed to the Paris Exhibition in 1878.

The resin of *L. styraciflua* L. has been ascertained by Procter[2] to contain cinnamic, but not benzoic acid. Harrison[3] found it to contain styracin and essential oil (styrol ?).

Resin of Liquidambar formosana Hance—This tree, which we suppose may be the *Styrax liquida folio minore*, which Ray names[4] as occurring in a collection of plants from Amoy, is a native of Formosa and Southern China, where it affords a dry terebinthinous resin, of agreeable fragrance when heated. Of this resin, which is used by the Chinese, a specimen collected in Formosa by Mr. Swinhoe has been presented to us by Dr. Hooker. A tree figured under the name of *Fung-heang* in the *Pun-tsao*[5] is, we presume, this species.

Resin of Altingia excelsa Noronha (*Liquidambar Altingiana* Bl.) ***Rasamala*** of the Javanese and Malays—The *Rasamala* is a magnificent tree of the Indian Archipelago, Burma and Assam. In Java it yields by incisions in the trunk an odorous resin, yet only very slowly and in very small quantity; this resin is not, or at least not regularly, collected. In Burma, on the other hand, the tree affords a fragrant balsam, of which according to Waring[6] there are two varieties, the one pellucid and of a light yellowish colour, obtained by simple incision; the other thick, dark, opaque, and of terebinthinous odour, procured by boring the stem and applying fire around the trunk.

MYRTACEÆ.

OLEUM CAJUPUTI.

Oil of Cajuput, Kayu-puti Oil; F. *Essence de Cajuput*; G. *Cajeputöl.*

Botanical Origin—*Melaleuca Leucadendron* L., a tree often attaining a considerable size, with a thick spongy bark peeling off in layers, and slender, often pendulous branches. It is widely spread, and abundant in the Indian Archipelago and Malayan peninsula,

[1] Obligingly presented to me by our friend, Dr. Squibb, Brooklyn (1879). —F.A.F.

[2] *Proceedings of the Am. Pharm. Asso.* 1865. 160.

[3] *Am. Journ. of Pharm.* 1874. 161.—In the same periodical (1876, 335) 300 lbs. are stated to have been collected at Dyersburg, Tenn.

[4] *Hist. Plant.* iii. (1704), appendix p. 233.

[5] Chap. 34. sec. 5. § 1. *Aromatic Trees.* For a modern fig., see Hooker's *Icones Plant.* 3rd series, i. tab. 1020.

[6] *Pharm. of India*, 1868. 88.

and is also found in Northern Australia, Queensland, and New South Wales.

The tree, according to Bentham,[1] varies exceedingly in the size, shape, and texture of the leaves, in the young shoots being silky, and the spikes silky-villous or woolly, or the whole quite glabrous, in the short and dense, or long and interrupted spikes, in the size of the flower, and in the greenish-yellow, whitish, pink, or purple stamens, so that it is difficult to believe all can be forms of a single species. Yet upon examination, none of these variations are sufficiently constant or so combined, as to allow of the definition of distinct races.

The variety growing in Bouro, where the oil of cajuput has been distilled ever since the time of Rumphius, and known as *M. minor* Smith, is described by Lesson, who visited the island in 1823, as a tree resembling an aged olive, with flowers in little globose white heads, and a trunk the stout bark of which is composed of numerous satiny layers.

History—Rumphius, who passed nearly fifty years in the Dutch possessions in the East Indies and died at Amboyna in 1702, is the first to give an account of the oil under notice, and of the tree from which it is obtained.[2] From what he says, it appears that the aromatic properties of the tree are well known to the Malays and Javanese, who were in the habit of steeping its leaves in oil which they then impregnated with the smoke of benzoin and other aromatics, so obtaining an odorous liquid for anointing their heads. They likewise used cushions stuffed with the leaves, and also laid the latter in chests to keep away insects.

The fragrance of the foliage having thus attracted the attention of the Dutch, probably suggested submitting the leaves to distillation. Rumphius narrates how the oil was obtained in very small quantities, and was regarded as a powerful sudorific.

In Europe it appears to have been first noticed by J. M. Lochner,[3] of Nürnberg, physician to the German Emperor. About the same time (1717), a ship's surgeon, returning from the east, sold a provision of the oil to the distinguished apothecary Johann Heinrich Link at Leipzig, who published a notice on it and sold it.[4] It began then to be quoted in the tariffs of other German apothecaries,[5] although it was still reputed a very rare article in 1726.[6] Somewhat larger quantities appear to have been soon imported by Amsterdam druggists.[7] In Germany the oil took the name of *Oleum Wittnebianum*, from the recommendations bestowed on it by M. von Wittneben, of Wolfenbüttel, who was much engaged in natural sciences and long resident in Batavia.[8] In France and England, it was however scarcely known till the commencement of the present century, though it had a place in the Edinburgh Pharmacopœia of 1788. In the *London Price Current*, we do not find it

[1] *Flora Australiensis*, iii. (1866) 142.
[2] *Herb. Amboinense*, ii. (1741) cap. 26.
[3] *Acad. Nat. Curios. Ephemerid. Cent.* v. vi. (Nürnberget, 1717) 157.
[4] *Sammlung von Natur und Medicin. . . Geschichten*, Leipzig, 1719. 257.
[5] *Pharm. Journ.* vi. (1876) 1023.
[6] Vater, *Catalog. varior. exoticor. rarissimor.* . . . . Wittenbergæ, 1726.
[7] Schendus van der Beck, *De Indiæ rarioribus*, *Act. Nat. Cur.* i., appendix (1725) 123.
[8] Goetz, *Olei Caieput historia—Commercium Litterarium*, 1731. 3; Martini, *De Oleo Wittnebiano dissertatio*, 1751.

quoted earlier than 1813, when the price given is 3s. to 3*s*. 6d. per ounce, with a duty of 2*s*. 4½*d*. per ounce.

Manufacture—In the island of Bouro, in the Molucca Sea, the leaves of the *Kayu-puti* or Aij-puti, *i.e. White-wood* trees, are submitted to distillation with water, the operation being conducted in the most primitive manner, as already witnessed, about the year 1792, by Labillardière in his celebrated voyage with Lapérouse. Bickmore,[1] an American traveller who passed three months in the island in 1865, states that it produces about 8,000 bottles of the oil annually, and that this is almost its only export. The Trade Returns of the Straight Settlements published at Singapore, show that the largest quantity is shipped from Celebes, the great island lying west of Bouro.

Description—Oil of Cajuput is a transparent mobile fluid, of a light bluish-green hue, a fragrant camphoraceous odour, and bitterish aromatic taste. It has a sp. gr. of 0·926, and remains liquid even at (8°·6 F.) —13° C. It deviates the ray of polarized light to the left. On diluting it with bisulphide of carbon it becomes turbid.

Chemical Composition—The researches of Schmidl (1860) and of Gladstone (1872) have shown that cajuput oil consists chiefly of *Hydrate of Cajuputene* or *Cajuputol*, $C^{10}H^{16},H^2O$, which may be obtained from the crude oil by fractional distillation at 174° C. If it is repeatedly distilled from anhydrous phosphoric acid, *Cajuputene*, $C^{10}H^{16}$, passes over at 160–165° C.; it has an agreeable odour of hyacinths. After the cajuputene, *Isocajuputene* distils at 177°, and *Paracajuputene* at 310–316°, both agreeing in composition with cajuputene.

Like most essential oils having the formula $C^{10}H^{16}$, crude cajuput oil is capable of forming the crystallized compound $C^{10}H^{16}, 3OH^2$. This we have abundantly obtained by mixing 4 parts of the oil with 1 of alcohol 0·830 sp. gr., and one part of nitric acid 1·20 sp. gr.; the mixture should be allowed to stand in shallow dishes. By adding 1 vol. of absolute alcohol to 3 vol. of cajuput oil, and saturating it with anhydrous hydrochloric gas, crystals of the compound $C^{10}H^{16}(HCl)^2$ may be obtained. By vapour of bromine the oil acquires a beautiful green colour.

If 1 part of iodine be gradually dissolved in cajuput oil, the temperature being maintained at 50° C., fine green crystals of $(C^{10}H^{16}HI)^2OH^2$ are formed. They may be recrystallized from very little glacial acetic acid, but will not keep for more than a few weeks.

The green tint of the oil is due to copper, a minute proportion of which metal is usually present in all that is imported. It may be made evident by agitating the oil with water acidulated by a little hydrochloric acid. The compounds of copper with inorganic acids being comparatively of a fainter colour than the cupric salts of organic acids, the aqueous solution of chloride of copper now formed displays no longer the fine green tint. To the solution, after it has been put into a platinum capsule, a little zinc should be added, when the copper will be immediately deposited on the platinum. The liquid may be then poured off and the copper dissolved and tested. When the oil is rectified, it is obtained colourless, but it readily becomes green if in

[1] *Travels in the East Indian Archipelago*, Lond. 1868. 282.

contact for a short time with metallic copper. The presence of the metal in the oil may also be shown at once by a scrap of paper which has been impregnated with fresh tincture of guaiacum wood and dried. If it is then moistened with water containing 1 per cent. of sulphocyanate of potassium, the paper turns intensely blue by the contact with the oil provided the latter contains copper.

Guibourt[1] has however proved by experiment that the volatile oil obtained by the distillation of the leaves of several species of *Melaleuca*, *Metrosideros* and *Eucalyptus*, has naturally a fine green hue. It is not improbable that this hue is transient, and that the contamination with copper is intentional in order to obtain a permanent green.

Commerce—The oil is imported from Singapore and Batavia, packed in glass beer or wine bottles. From official statements[2] it appears that the imports into Singapore during 1871 were as under:—

From Java	445	gallons
„ Manilla	200	„
„ Celebes	3,895	„
„ other places	350	„
Total	4,890	„

Of this large quantity, the greater portion was re-shipped to Bombay, Calcutta, and Cochin China.

Uses—Cajuput oil is occasionally administered internally as a stimulant, antispasmodic and diaphoretic: externally as a rubefacient it is in frequent use.

Substitutes—The oil of *Eucalyptus oleosa* F. Muell. has, we find, the odour of cajuput; and according to Gladstone it agrees, as well as the oils of *Melaleuca ericifolia* Sm. and *M. linariifolia* Sm., almost entirely with cajuput oil, except in optical properties. The same is probably the case with the oil of *Eucalyptus globulus* Labill, which Cloez (1870) states to be dextrogyre. These oils are shipped to some extent from Australia to Europe, probably as adulterants of other essential oils.

CARYOPHYLLI.

Cloves; F. *Girofles, Clous de Girofles*; G. *Gewürznelken*.

Botanical Origin—*Eugenia caryophyllata* Thunberg (*Caryophyllus aromaticus* L.), a beautiful evergreen tree, 30 to 40 feet high, resembling a gigantic myrtle, bearing numerous flowers grouped in small terminal tricotomous cymes. The flower has an inferior ovary about ½ an inch long, cylindrical, of a crimson colour, dividing at the top into 4 sepals; and 4 round concave petals larger than the calyx, imbricated in the bud like a globe, but at length spreading and soon dropping off.

The clove-tree is said to be strictly indigenous only in the five small islands constituting the proper Moluccas, namely Tarnati, Tidor, Mortir, Makiyan and Bachian.[3] These form a chain on the west side of the

[1] *Hist. des Drog.* iii. (1869) 278.

[2] *Blue Book of the Colony of the Straits Settlements* for 1871, Singapore, 1872.

[3] Though these are the original Moluccas or Clove Islands, the name has been extended to all islands east of Celebes and west of New Guinea.

large island of Jilolo, where, strange to say, the tree appears not to exist in a wild state (Crawfurd). According to Rumphius, it was introduced into Amboyna before the arrival of the Portuguese, and is still cultivated there and in the neighbouring islands of Haruku, Saparua and Nusalaut, also in Sumatra and Penang. It is likewise now found in Malacca, the Mascarene Islands, the islands of Zanzibar and Pemba on the eastern coast of Africa, and the West Indies.

The tree which is grown for the spice appears to be a cultivated variety, of lower stature and more aromatic than the wild form.

History[1]—The Greek name Καρυόφυλλον is supposed to refer to the ball-like *petals* of the bud, which, as above described, might be compared to a small nut (κάρυον). But the name is very variably written, as γαροῦμφουλ, καρφούφουλ, γαρόφαλα,[2] whence it becomes probable that it is not really Greek, but an Asiatic word hellenized.

Cloves have been long known to the Chinese. Mr. Mayers, late Chinese Secretary to the British Legation at Pekin, has communicated to us the interesting fact that they are mentioned by several Chinese writers as in use under the Han dynasty, B.C. 266 to A.D. 220, during which period it was customary for the officers of the court to hold the spice in the mouth before addressing the sovereign, in order that their breath might have an agreeable odour.[3]

The Sanskrit name is "*Lavanga*," whence the vernacular Hindustani "*Laung*."

The first European author to mention *Caryophyllon* is Pliny, who describes it, after *pepper*, as a grain resembling that spice but longer and more brittle, produced in India, and imported for the sake of its odour. It is doubtful whether this description really refers to cloves.

By the 4th century, cloves must have become well known in Europe, if credence can be placed in a remarkable record preserved by Vignoli,[4] which states that the emperor Constantine presented to St. Silvester, bishop of Rome, A.D. 314–335, numerous vessels of gold and silver, incense and spices, among which last were 150 pounds of *Cloves*—a vast quantity for the period.

Kosmas Indicopleustes,[5] in his *Topographia Christiana* written about A.D. 547, states in the account of Taprobane (Ceylon) that silk, aloes [-wood], cloves (Καρυόφυλλον) and sandal wood, besides other productions, are imported thither from China, and other emporia, and transmitted to distant regions. Alexander Trallianus,[6] who was a friend of Kosmos and a pupil of his father, prescribed in several receipts 5 or 8 cloves, καρυοφύλλου κόκκους, from which fact it may be inferred that at his time (at Rome?) cloves were a very rare article. A century later, Paulus Ægineta[7] distinctly described cloves as *Caryophyllon—ex India, veluti flores cujusdam arboris . . odorati, acres. . .* and much used for a condiment and in medicine.

[1] For the history of the oil see our article Cortex Cinnamon, chemical composition.

[2] Langkavel, *Botanik der späteren Griechen*, Berlin, 1866. 19.

[3] At this period, the clove was called *Ki shêh hiang*, i.e. *fowl's tongue spice*. The modern name *Ting hiang*, i.e. *nail-scent* or *-spice*, was in use in the 5th or 6th century of our era.

[4] *Liber Pontificalis, seu de Gestis Romanorum Pontificum*, Romæ, i. (1724) 94.

[5] Migne, *Patrologiæ Cursus*, series Græca, lxxxviii. (1860) 446.

[6] Puschman's edition (quoted in the appendix) i. 435. 580. Alexander dedicated his work to his teacher, the father of Cosmas.

[7] *De re medica*, lib. vii. c. 3.

In the beginning of the 8th century, the same spice is noticed by Benedictus Crispus,[1] archbishop of Milan, who calls it *Cariophylus ater;* and in A.D. 716, it is enumerated with other commodities in the diploma granted by Chilperic II. to the monastery of Corbie in Normandy.[2]

We find cloves among the wares on which duty was levied at Acon (the modern Acre) in Palestine at the end of the 12th century, at which period that city was a great emporium of Mediterranean trade.[3] They are likewise enumerated in the tariff of Marseilles of A.D. 1228,[4] in that of Barcelona of 1252[5] and of Paris, 1296.[6]

These facts show that the spice was a regular object of commerce at this period. But it was very costly: the Household Book of the Countess of Leicester, A.D. 1265,[7] gives its price as 10*s*. to 12*s*. per lb., exactly the same as that of saffron. Several other examples of the high cost of the spice might be adduced.

Of the place of growth of cloves, the first distinct notice seems to be that of the Arabian geographer Ibn Khurdádbah,[8] A.D. 869–885, who names the spice, with cocoa-nuts, sugar, and sandal-wood as produced in Java. Doubtless he was misinformed, for the clove-tree had not come so far west at that period. Marco Polo[9] made the same mistake four centuries later: finding the spice in Java, he supposed it the growth of the island.

Nicolo Conti,[10] a Venetian merchant who lived from A.D. 1424 to 1448 in the Indian Archipelago, learned that cloves are brought to Java from the island of Banda, fifteen days' sail further east. With the arrival of the Portuguese at the commencement of the 16th century, more accurate accounts of the Spice Islands began to reach Europe; and Pigafetta,[11] the companion of Magellan, gave a very good description of the clove-tree as he observed it in 1521.

The Portuguese had the principal share in the clove trade for nearly a century. In 1605 they were expelled by the Dutch, who took exclusive possession of the Moluccas and adopted extraordinary measures for keeping the traffic in their own hands. Yet notwithstanding this, large supplies of cloves reached England direct. In 1609 a ship of the East India Company called the *Consent* arrived with 112,000 lb., the duty on which amounted to £1400 and the impost to as much more. The spice ungarbled was sold at 5*s*. 6*d*. and 5*s*. 9*d*. per lb.—of course, in bond.[12]

To effect their purpose, the Dutch endeavoured to extirpate the clove-tree from its native islands, and even instituted periodical

[1] *Poematium Medicum*—Migne, *Patrologiæ Cursus*, lxxxix. (1850) 374.

[2] Pardessus, *Diplomata, Chartæ*, etc., ii. (1849) 309.

[3] *Recueil des Historiens des Croisades, Lois*, (1843) 173.

[4] Méry et Guindon, *Hist. des Actes . . . de la municipalité de Marseille*, 1841. 373.

[5] Capmany, *Memorias sobre la marina etc. de Barcelona*, iii. 170.

[6] Douet d'Arcq, *Revue archéologique*, ix. (1852) 213.

[7] *Manners and Household Expenses in England* (Roxburgh Club), 1841. lii.

[8] *Le Livre des routes et des provinces*, traduit par C. Barbier de Meynard, *Journ. Asiat.* sér. 6. tome v. (1865) 227.

[9] Yule, *Marco Polo*, ii. (1871) 217.—It should however be borne in mind that the name Java was applied in a general sense by the Arab geographers to the islands of the Archipelago.

[10] Kunstmann, *Die Kenntniss Indiens im XVten Jahrhundert*, München, 1863. 46.

[11] Ramusio, *Delle navigationi et viaggi*, Venetia, 1554, fol. 404*b*.

[12] *Calendar of State Papers, Colonial series, East Indies*, 1862. 181.

expeditions for the purpose of destroying any young trees that might have accidentally sprung up. This policy, the object of which was to confine the growth of the spice to a group of small islands of which Amboyna is the largest, has but very recently been abandoned: though the cultivation of the spice was free in all other localities, the *clove parks* of the Amboyna islands remained the property of the Dutch Government. The original Moluccas or Clove Islands now produce no cloves at all.

The enterprise of Poivre, the French governor of Mauritius and Bourbon, so far eluded the vigilance of the Dutch, that both clove and nutmeg-trees were introduced into those islands in the year 1770.[1] The clove-tree was carried thence to Cayenne in 1793, and to Zanzibar about the end of the century.

Crawfurd,[2] in an excellent article of which we have made free use, aptly remarks that it is difficult to understand how the clove first came to the notice of foreign nations, considering the well-ascertained fact that it has never been used as a condiment or in any other way by the inhabitants of the islands of which it is a native. We may observe however that there were some singular superstitions among the islanders with regard to the so-called *Royal Clove* (p. 287), a tree of which on the island of Makiyan was long supposed to be unique.

Collection—The flower-buds of the clove-tree when young are nearly white, but afterwards become green and lastly bright red, when they must at once be gathered. This in Zanzibar is done by hand; each clove is picked singly, a moveable stage the height of the tree being used to enable the labourers to reach the upper branches. The buds are then simply dried in the sun, by which they acquire the familiar dark brown tint of the commercial article. The gathering takes place twice a year; in the Moluccas where the harvest occurs in June and December, the cloves are partly gathered by hand, and partly beaten off the tree by bamboos on to cloths spread beneath. The annual yield of a good tree is about 4½ pounds, but sometimes reaches double that quantity.

Description—Cloves are about $\frac{6}{10}$ of an inch in length, and consist of a long cylindrical calyx dividing above into 4 pointed spreading sepals which surround 4 petals, closely imbricated as a globular bud about $\frac{2}{10}$ of an inch in diameter.

The petals which are of lighter colour than the rest of the drug and somewhat translucent from numerous oil-cells, spring from the base of a 4-sided epigynous disc, the angles of which are directed towards the lobes of the calyx. The stamens which are very numerous, are inserted at the base of the petals and are arched over the style. The latter which is short and subulate, rises from a depression in the centre of the disc. Immediately below it and united with the upper portion of the calyx is the ovary, which is 2-celled and contains many ovules. The lower end of the calyx (*hypanthium*) has a compressed form; it is solid

[1] Tessier, *Sur l'importation du Girofier des Moluques aux Isles de France, de Bourbon et de Sechelles, et de ces isles à Cayenne.—Observations sur la physique*, Paris, Juillet, 1779.

[2] *Dictionary of the Indian Islands*, 1856, article *Clove*.

but has its internal tissue far more porous than the walls. The whole calyx is of a deep rich brown, has a dull wrinkled surface, a dense fleshy texture, and abounds in essential oil which exudes on simple pressure with the nail. Cloves have an agreeable spicy odour, and a strong biting aromatic taste.

The varieties of cloves occurring in commerce do not exhibit any structural differences. Inferior kinds are distinguished by being less plump, less bright in tint, and less rich in essential oil. In London price-currents, cloves are enumerated in the order of value thus: Penang, Bencoolen, Amboyna, Zanzibar.

Microscopic Structure—A transverse section of the lower part of a clove shows a dark rhomboid zone, the tissue on either side of which is of a lighter hue. The outer layer beneath the epidermis exhibits a large number of oil-cells, frequently as much as 300 mkm. in diameter. About 200 oil-cells may be counted in one transverse section, so that the large amount of essential oil in the drug is well shown by its microscopic characters. The above-mentioned zone is chiefly made up of about 30 fibro-vascular bundles, another stronger bundle traversing the centre of the clove. The fibro-vascular bundles, as well as the tissue bordering the oil-cells, assume a greenish black hue by alcoholic perchloride of iron. Oil-cells are also largely distributed in the leaves, petals and even the stamens of Eugenia.

Chemical Composition—Few plants possess any organ so rich in essential oil as the drug under consideration. The oil known in pharmacy as *Oleum Caryophylli*, which is the important constituent of cloves, is obtainable to the extent of 16 to 20 per cent. But to extract the whole, the distillation must be long continued, the water being returned to the same material.

The oil is a colourless or yellowish liquid with a powerful odour and taste of cloves, sp. gr. 1·046 to 1·058. It is a mixture of a hydrocarbon, and an oxygenated oil called *Eugenol*, in variable proportions. The former which is termed *light oil of cloves* and comes over in the first period of the distillation, has the composition $C^{15}H^{24}$, a sp. gr. of 0·918 and boils at 251° C. It deviates the plane of polarization slightly to the left, and is not coloured on addition of ferric chloride; it is of a rather terebinthinaceous odour.

Eugenol, sometimes called *Eugenic Acid*, has a sp. gr. of 1·087 at 0° C., and possesses the full taste and smell of cloves. Its boiling point is 247°·5. With alkalis, especially ammonia and baryta, it yields crystallizable salts. Eugenol may therefore be prepared by submitting the crude oil of cloves to distillation with caustic soda; the "light oil" distils then, the eugenol, being now combined with sodium, remains in the still. It will be obtained on addition of an acid and again distilling. Eugenol is devoid of rotatory power, whence the crude oil of cloves, of which eugenol is by far the prevailing constituent, is optically almost inactive. The constitution of eugenol is given by the formula $C^6H^3\begin{cases}OCH^3\\OH\\CH.CH.CH^3\end{cases}$. It belongs to the phenol class, and has also been met with in the fruits of Pimenta officinalis (see next article), in the Bay leaves, in Canella bark (see page 75), in the leaves and flower buds of Cinnamomum zeilanicum and in Brazilian clove-bark (*Dicypellium caryophyllatum* Nees).

Eugenol can be converted into *Vanillin* (see Fructus Vanillæ).

The water distilled from cloves is stated to contain, in addition to the essential oil, another body, *Eugenin*, which sometimes separates after a while in the form of tasteless, crystalline laminæ, having the same composition as eugenol.[1] We have never met with it.

According to Scheuch (1863), oil of cloves also (sometimes) contains a little *Salicylic acid*, $C^6H^4\left\{\begin{matrix}OH\\COOH\end{matrix}\right.$, which may be removed by shaking the oil with a solution of carbonate of ammonium.

Caryophyllin, $C^{20}H^{32}O$, is a neutral, tasteless, inodorous substance, crystallizing in needle-shaped prisms. We have obtained it in small quantity, by treating with boiling ether cloves, which we had previously deprived of most of their essential oil by small quantities of alcohol. E. Mylius (1873) obtained from it by nitric acid, crystals of *Caryophyllinic Acid*, $C^{20}H^{32}O^6$.

Carmufellic Acid obtained in colourless crystals, $C^{12}H^{20}O^{16}$, in 1851 by Muspratt and Danson after digesting an aqueous extract of cloves with nitric acid, is a product of this treatment and not a natural constituent of cloves.

Cloves contain a considerable proportion of gum; also a tannic acid not yet particularly examined.

Production and Commerce—Of late years the principal locality for the production of cloves has been the islands of Zanzibar and Pemba on the east coast of Africa, which until very recently were capable of producing a maximum crop of 10½ millions of pounds in a single season. On the 15th April 1872, Zanzibar was visited by a hurricane of extraordinary violence, by which about five-sixths of the clove-trees in the island were destroyed; and although the plantations are being renewed, many years must elapse before the crop can resume its former importance. Pemba, which is distant from Zanzibar 25 miles, and produced about half as much of the spice as that island, did not appreciably suffer from the storm.

The crop on these islands fluctuates, a good year alternating with a bad one. This is partly shown in the imports of Bombay, the great mart of Zanzibar produce, which have been as follows:—

1869-70	1870-71	1871-72	1872-73
45,642 cwt.	21,968 cwt.	43,891 cwt.	25,185 cwt.

The quantity of cloves shipped from Bombay to the United Kingdom is comparatively small, being in 1871-72, 3279 cwt.; in 1872-73, 3271 cwt.

The imports of cloves to the United Kingdom are from one million to four million pounds annually.

Cloves are also largely shipped direct from Zanzibar to the United States and Hamburg. A small amount is taken in native vessels to the Red Sea ports; these are packed in raw hides. Those for the European and American markets are shipped in mat bags made of split cocoa-nut leaf.

The clove trade of the Moluccas has been for many years in the

[1] Gmelin, *Chemistry*, xiv. (1860) 201.

hands of the Dutch Government, which, by its restrictive policy, assumed practically the position of growers, disposing of their produce through the Netherlands Trading Company at auctions held in Holland twice a year. This system having been abolished in 1872, has proved disastrous to the trade it was designed to protect, and to such a degree that the produce of cloves in the Moluccas is but a tenth of what it was in the early days of their intercourse with Europe. The crop of the four islands, Amboyna, Haruku, Saparua, and Nusalaut, the only Moluccas in which the tree is cultivated, was reckoned in 1854 as 510,912 lb.

The export of cloves from Java in 1871 was 1397 peculs[1] (186,226 lb.). The French island of Réunion which from 1825 to 1849 used to produce annually as much as 800,000 kilogrammes (1,764,571 lb.), now yields almost none, owing chiefly to the frequent hurricanes.

Uses—As a remedy, cloves are unimportant, though in the form of infusion or distilled water they are useful in combination with other medicines. The essential oil which sometimes relieves toothache is a frequent ingredient of pill-masses. The chief consumption of cloves is as a culinary spice.

Substitutes—1. *Clove Stalks*—*Festucœ vel Stipites Caryophylli*, in French *Griffes de Girofle*, in German *Nelkenstiele*, were an article of import into Europe during the middle ages, when they were chiefly known by their low Latin name of *fusti*, or the Italian *bastaroni*. Thus under the statutes of Pisa,[2] A.D. 1305, duty was levied not only on cloves (*garofali*), but also on *Folia et fusti garofalorum*. Pegolotti[3] a little later names both as being articles of trade at Constantinople. Clove *Leaves* are enumerated[4] as an import into Palestine in the 12th century; they are also mentioned in a list of the drugs sold at Frankfort[5] about the year 1450; we are not aware that they are used in modern times.

As to Clove Stalks, they are still a considerable object of trade, especially from Zanzibar, where they are called by the natives *Vikunia*. They taste tolerably aromatic, and yield 4 to 6·4 per cent. of volatile levogyre oil; they are used for adulterating the *Ground Cloves* sold by grocers. Such an admixture may be detected by the microscope, especially if the powder after treatment with potash be examined in glycerin. If clove stalks have been ground, thick-walled or stone-cells will be found in the powder; such cells do not occur in cloves. Powdered allspice is also an adulterant of powdered cloves; it also contains stone-cells, but in addition numerous starch-granules which are entirely wanting in cloves.

2. ***Mother Cloves, Anthophylli***—are the *fruits* of the clove-tree, and are ovate-oblong berries about an inch in length and much less rich in essential oil than cloves. Though occasionally seen in the London drug sales in some quantity, they are not an article of regular import.[6]

[1] *Consular Reports*, Aug. 1873. 952.

[2] Bonaini, *Statuti inediti della città di Pisa dal xii. al xiv. secolo*, iii. (1857) 106.

[3] See p. 235, note 2.

[4] *Recueil des Historiens des Croisades, Lois*, ii. (1843) 173.

[5] Flückiger, *Die Frankfurter Liste*, Halle, 1873. 11. 38.

[6] We find in the fortnightly price current of a London drug-broker under date

As they contain very large starch-granules, their presence as an adulteration of ground cloves would be revealed by the microscope.

3. *Royal Cloves*—Under this name or *Caryophyllum regium*, a curious monstrosity of the clove was formerly held in the highest reputation, on account of its rarity and the strange stories told respecting it.[1] Specimens in our possession show it to be a very small clove, distinguished by an abnormal number of sepals and large bracts at the base of the calyx-tube, the corolla and internal organs being imperfectly developed.

FRUCTUS PIMENTÆ.

Semen Amomi; Pimento, Allspice, Jamaica Pepper; F. *Poivre de la Jamaïque, Piment des Anglais, Toute-épice;* G. *Nelkenpfeffer, Nelkenköpfe, Neugewürz.*

Botanical Origin—*Pimenta officinalis* Lindley[2] (*Myrtus Pimenta* L., *Eugenia Pimenta* DC.), a beautiful evergreen tree, growing to about 30 feet in height, with a trunk 2 feet in circumference, common throughout the West India Islands. In Jamaica, it prefers limestone hills near the sea, and is especially plentiful on the north side of the island.

History—The high value placed on the spices of India sufficiently explains the interest with which aromatic and pungent plants were regarded by the early explorers of the New World; while the eager desire to obtain these lucrative commodities is shown by the names *Pepper*, *Cinnamon*, *Balsam*, *Melegueta*, *Amomum*, bestowed on productions totally distinct from those originally so designated.

Among the spices thus brought to the notice of Europe were the little dry berries of certain trees of the myrtle tribe, which had some resemblance in shape and flavour to peppercorns, and hence were named *Pimienta*,[3] corrupted to *Pimenta* or *Pimento*. It was doubtless a drug of this kind, if not our veritable allspice, that was given to Clusius in 1601 by Garret, a druggist of London, and described and figured by the former in his *Liber Exoticorum*.[4] A few years later it began to be imported into England, being, as Parkinson[5] says, "obtruded for *Amomum*" (*Round Cardamom*), so that "some more audacious than wise . . . put it in their compositions instead of the right." Francesco Redi mentioned the fruits as *Pimienta de Chapa*; Chiapas, now the south-eastern department of Mexico, bordering Guatemala. Redi states that the spice was also called *Pimienta de Tavasco* from the adjoining department of Tabasco. According to

Nov. 27, 1873, the announcement of the sale of 1,050 bags of Mother Cloves at 2*d*. to 3*d*. per lb., besides 4,200 packages of Clove Stalks at 3*d*. to 4*d*. per lb.

[1] Rumphius in his letter from Amboina, Sept. 20, 1696, to Dr. Schröck, in *Ephemerides Acad. Cæs. Leopold. Decur.* iii. Frankfurt and Leipzig. 1700. p. 308, with figure.—Also Rumphius, *Herb. Amb.* ii. (1742) 11. tab. 2.—See also Hasskarl, *Neuer Schlüssel zu Rumph's Herb. Amb.*, Halle, 1866; Berg, *Linnæa*, 1854. 137; Valmont de Bomare, *Dict. d'Hist. Nat.* iii. (1775) 70.

[2] Fig. in Bentley and Trimen, *Med. Plants*, part 20 (1877).

[3] *Pimienta*, the Spanish for *pepper*, is derived from *pigmentum*, a general name in mediæval Latin for *spicery*.—*Malaguetta* (see article Grana Paradisi) is also a name which has been transferred by the Spaniards and Portuguese to the drug under notice.

[4] Lib. i. c. 17.

[5] *Theatrum Botanicum* (1640) 1567.

Sloane[1] (1691) it was commonly sold by druggists for *Carpobalsamum*. Ray (1693) distinguished the spice as a production of Jamaica under the name of *Sweet-scented Jamaica Pepper* or *Allspice*, and states it to be abundantly imported into England, and in frequent use as a condiment, though not employed in medicine. The spice had a place in the London Pharmacopœia as early as 1721.

The consumption of Pimento has been enormous. In the year 1804-5, the quantity shipped from the British West Indies was 2,257,000 lb., producing on import duty a net revenue of £38,063.[2]

Production and Commerce—The spice found in commerce is furnished wholly by the island of Jamaica. A plantation, there called a *Pimento walk*, is a piece of natural woodland stocked with the trees, which require but little attention. The flowers appear in June, July, and August, and are quickly succeeded by the berries, which are gathered when of full size but still unripe. This is performed by breaking off the small twigs bearing the bunches. These are then spread out, and exposed to the sun and air for some days, after which the stalks are removed, and the berries are fit for being packed.

By an official document[3] it appears that, in the year 1871, the amount of land in Jamaica cropped with pimento was 7,178 acres. In that year the island exported of the spice 6,857,838 lb., value £28,574. Of this quantity Great Britain took 4,287,551 lb., and the United States 2,266,950 lb. In 1875 the export was 57,500 cwts., valued at £40,250, of which 10,894 cwts. only went to the United States.

Description—Allspice is a small, dry globular berry, rather variable in size, measuring $\frac{3}{10}$ to less than $\frac{2}{10}$ of an inch in diameter. It is crowned by a short style, seated in a depression, and surrounded by 4 short thick sepals; generally however the latter have been rubbed off, a scar-like raised ring marking their former position. The berry has a woody shell or pericarp, easily cut, of a dark ferruginous brown, and rugose by reason of minute tubercles filled with essential oil. It is two-celled, each cell containing a single, reniform, exalbuminous seed, having a large spirally curved embryo. The seed is aromatic, but less so than the pericarp.

Allspice has an agreeable, pungent, spicy flavour, much resembling that of cloves.

Microscopic Structure—The outer layer of the pericarp, immediately beneath the epidermis, contains numerous large cells filled with essential oil. The parenchyme further exhibits thick-walled cells loaded with resin, and smaller cells enclosing crystals of oxalate of calcium. The whole tissue is traversed by small fibro-vascular bundles. The seeds are also provided with a small number of oil-cells, and contain starch granules.

Chemical Composition—The composition of pimento resembles in many points that of cloves. The berries yield to the extent of 3 to 4½ per cent. a volatile oil, sp. gr. 1·037 (Gladstone), having the characteristic taste and odour of the spice, and known in the shops as *Oleum*

[1] *Description of the Pimienta or Jamaica Pepper-tree.—Phil. Trans.* xvii. No. 191.

[2] *Parliamentary Return*, March 1805, quoted in Young's *West-India Commonplace Book*, 1807. 79.

[3] *Blue Book* for Jamaica, printed 1872.

Pimentæ. We have found it to deviate the ray of polarized light 2° to the left, when examined in a column of 50 mm.

Oeser (1864), whose experiments have been confirmed by Gladstone (1872), has shown that oil of pimento has substantially the same composition as oil of cloves; salicylic acid has not been found. Pimento is rich in tannin, striking with a persalt of iron an inky black. Its decoction is coloured deep blue by iodine, showing the presence of starch. Dragendorff (1871) pointed out the existence in allspice of an extremely small quantity of an alkaloid, having somewhat the odour of coniine.

Uses—Employed as an aromatic clove; a distilled water (*Aqua Pimentæ*) is frequently prescribed. The chief use of pimento is as a culinary spice.

Substitute—The Mexican spice called *Pimienta de Tabasco* (*Piment Tabago* Guibourt) is somewhat larger and less aromatic than Jamaica allspice. Analogous products are afforded by *Pimenta acris* Wight[1] (*Myrcia acris* DC, *Amomis acris* Berg), the *Bay-berry* tree, and *P. Pimento* Griseb. The oil of bay-berry consists of eugenol and a hydrocarbon, possibly identical with the "light oil of cloves" (p. 284), but present in a larger amount. *Bay rum*, much used in the United States by the perfumers, is an alcoholic tincture flavoured with oil of bay-berry.

GRANATEÆ.

CORTEX GRANATI FRUCTUS.

Cortex Granati; Pomegranate Peel; F. *Ecorce de Grenades;* G. *Granatschalen.*

Botanical Origin—*Punica Granatum* L., a shrub or low tree, with small deciduous foliage and handsome scarlet flowers. It is indigenous to North-western India, and the counties south and south-west of the Caspian to the Persian Gulf and Palestine, and grows wild in the hills of Western Sindh in elevations of 4000 feet, in Balutchistan to 6000 feet, also in the east flank of Soliman range. The trunk is short, rarely over 20 feet high. The tree has long been cultivated, and is now found throughout the warm parts of Europe, and in the subtropical regions of both hemispheres.

History—The pomegranate has been highly prized by mankind from the remotest antiquity, as is shown by the references to it in the Scriptures,[2] and by the numerous representations of the fruit in the sculptures of Persepolis and Assyria,[3] and on the ancient monuments of Egypt.[4] It was probably introduced into the south of Italy by Greek colonists, and is named as a common fruit-tree by Porcius Cato[5] in the 3rd century B.C. The peel of the fruit was recognized as medicinal

[1] Figured in Bentley and Trimen, part 20.—The fruit of this species is easily distinguished, being crowned by 5-calyx lobes.

[2] *Exodus* xxviii. 33, 34; *Numbers* xx. 2; *Deut.* viii. 8; *Cant.* iv. 13; viii. 2.

[3] Layard, *Nineveh and its Remains*, ed. 5, ii. (1849) 296.

[4] Wilkinson, *Ancient Egyptians*, ii. (1837) 142.

[5] Nisard's edition, Paris, 1877, capp. 7. 127. 133.

by the ancients, and among the Romans was in common use for tanning leather,[1] as it still is in Tunis.

Description—The fruit of the pomegranate tree is a spherical, somewhat flattened and obscurely six-sided berry, the size of a common orange and often much larger, crowned by the thick, tubular, 5- to 9-toothed calyx. It has a smooth, hard, coriaceous skin, which when the fruit is ripe, is of a brownish yellow tint, often finely shaded with red. Membranous dissepiments, about 6 in number meeting in the axis of the fruit, divide the upper and larger portion into equal cells. Below these a confused conical diaphragm separates the lower and smaller half, which in its turn is divided into 4 or 5 irregular cells. Each cell is filled with a large number of grains, crowded on thick spongy placentæ, which in the upper cells are parietal but in the lower appear to be central. The grains, which are about ½ an inch in length, are oblong or obconical and many-sided, and consist of a thin transparent vesicle containing an acid, saccharine, red, juicy pulp, surrounding an elongated angular seed.

The only part of the fruit used medicinally is the peel, *Cortex Granati* of the druggists, which in the fresh state is leathery. When dry as imported, it is in irregular, more or less concave fragments, some of which have the toothed, tubular calyx still enclosing the stamens and style. It is $\frac{1}{16}$ to $\frac{1}{20}$ of an inch thick, easily breaking with a short corky fracture; externally it is rather rough, of a yellowish brown or reddish colour. Internally it is more or less brown or yellow, and honey-combed with depressions left by the seeds. It has hardly any odour, but has a strongly astringent taste.

Microscopic Structure—The middle layer of the peel consists of large thin-walled and elongated, sometimes even branched cells, among which occur thick-walled cells and fibro-vascular bundles. Both the outer and the inner surface are made up of smaller, nearly cubic and densely packed cells. Small starch granules occur sparingly throughout the tissue, as well as crystals of oxalate of calcium.

Chemical Composition—The chief constituent is tannin, which in an aqueous infusion of the dried peel produces with perchloride of iron an abundant dark blue precipitate. The peel also contains sugar and a little gum. Dried at 100° C. and incinerated, it yielded us 5·9 per cent. of ash.

Uses—Pomegranate peel is an excellent astringent, now almost obsolete in British medicine. Waring[2] asserts that when combined with opium and an aromatic, as cloves, it is a most useful remedy in the chronic dysentery of the natives of India, as well as in diarrhœa.

CORTEX GRANATI RADICIS.

Pomegranate-root Bark; F. *Ecorce de racine de Grenadier;* G. *Granatwurzelrinde.*

Botanical Origin— *unica Granatum* L., see page 289.

History—In addition to the particulars regarding the pomegranate

[1] See also Hehn, *Kulturpflanzen*, Berlin, 1877, 206.

[2] *Pharm. of India*, 1868. 93. 447.

tree given in the preceding article, the following which concern the drug under notice may be stated.

A decoction of the root of the pomegranate was recommended by Celsus,[1] Dioscorides,[2] and Pliny[3] for the expulsion of tape-worm; but the remedy had fallen into complete oblivion, until its use among the Hindus attracted the notice of Buchanan[4] at Calcutta about the year 1805. This physician pointed out the efficacy of the root-bark, which was further shown by Fleming and others. Pomegranate root is known to have been long used for a similar purpose by the Chinese.[5]

Though the medicine is admitted to be efficient, and is employed with advantage in India where it is easily procured both genuine and fresh, it is hardly ever administered in England, the extract of male-fern being generally preferred; but it has a place in several continental pharmacopœias.

Description—The bark occurs in rather thin quills or fragments, 3 to 4 inches long. Their outer surface is yellowish grey, sometimes marked with fine longitudinal striations or reticulated wrinkles, but more often furrowed by bands of cork, running together in the thickest pieces into broad flat conchoidal scales. The inner surface, which is smooth or marked with fine striæ and is of a greyish yellow, has often strips of the tough whitish wood attached to it. The bark breaks short and granular; it has a purely astringent taste, but scarcely any odour.

Microscopic Structure—On a transverse section, the liber is seen to be the prevailing part of the cortical tissue. The former consists of alternating layers of two kinds of cells—one of them loaded with tufted crystals of oxalate of calcium, the other filled with starch granules and tannic matter. The bark is traversed by narrow medullary rays, and very large sclerenchymatous cells are scattered through the liber. Touched with a dilute solution of a persalt of iron, the bark assumes a dark blackish blue tint.

Chemical Composition—The bark contains, according to Wackenroder (1824), more than 22 per cent. of tannic acid, which Rembold (1867) has ascertained to consist for the most part of a peculiar variety called *Punico-tannic Acid*, $C^{20}H^{16}O^{13}$; when boiled with dilute sulphuric acid, it is resolved into *Ellagic Acid*, $C^{14}H^{8}O^{9}$, and sugar. Punico-tannic acid is accompanied by common tannic acid, yielding, by means of sulphuric acid, gallic acid, which appears sometimes to pre-exist in the bark. If a decoction of pomegranate bark is precipitated by acetate of lead, and the lead is separated from the filtered liquid, the latter on evaporation yields a considerable amount of mannite. This is probably the *Punicin* or *Granatin* of former observers.

The tænicide power is due, according to Tanret (1878) to *Pelletierine*, $C^{8}H^{13}NO$, a liquid dextrogyre alkaloid, boiling at 180° to 185° C. It can be obtained colourless by evaporating its ethereal solution in a vacuum, but in the open air becomes yellow. Pelletierine, so called in

[1] *De Medicina*, lib. iv. c. 17.
[2] Lib. i. c. 153.
[3] Lib. xxiii. c. 60.
[4] *Edinb. Med. and Surg. Journ.*, iii. (1807) 22
[5] Debeaux, *Pharmacie et Mat. Méd. des Chinois*, 1865. 70.

honour of Pelletier, is readily soluble in water, alcohol or chloroform, and has a somewhat aromatic odour. Several of its salts are crystallizable, yet extremely hygroscopic. The yield of the root bark was about ½ per cent. of the alkaloid, or about 2 per cent. of crystallized sulphate from trees grown near Troyes, in the Champagne.

Uses—A decoction, followed by a purgative, is stated by Waring[1] and others to be most efficient for the expulsion of the tape-worm. The *fresh* bark is said to be preferable to the dried.

Adulterations—The commercial drug frequently consists partly or entirely of the bark of the stem or branches, characterized by its less abundant cork-formation, which exhibits longitudinal bands or ridges of light brownish cork, but not conchoidal exfoliations. The middle cortical layer is somewhat more developed, and contains in the outer cells deposits of chlorophyll. The cambial zone is not distinctly observable. Such bark is reputed to be less active than that of the root, but we are not aware that the fact has ever been proved.

The bark of *Buxus sempervirens* and of *Berberis vulgaris* are somewhat similar to the drug under notice, but their decoctions are not affected by salts of iron.

CUCURBITACEÆ.

FRUCTUS ECBALLII.

Fructus Elaterii; Elaterium Fruit, Squirting Cucumber, Wild Cucumber; F. *Concombre purgatif ou sauvage;* G. *Springgurke.*

Botanical Origin—*Ecballium*[2] *Elaterium* A. Richard (*Momordica Elaterium* L.), a coarse, hispid, fleshy, decumbent plant without tendrils, having a thick white perennial root. It is common throughout the Mediterranean region, extending eastward as far as Southern Russia and Persia, and westward to Portugal. It succeeds well in Central Europe, and is cultivated to a small extent for medicinal use at Mitcham and Hitchin in England.

History—Theophrastus mentions the plant under notice by the name of Σίκυος ἄγριος. It is also particularly noticed by Dioscorides, who explicitly describes the singular process for making elaterium (ἐλατήριον), which was almost exactly like that followed at the present day.

The Wild or Squirting Cucumber was well known and cultivated in gardens in England as early as the middle of the 16th century.[3]

Description—The fruit is ovoid-oblong, nodding, about 1½ inch long, hispid from numerous short fleshy prickles terminating in white elongated points. It is attached by a long scabrous peduncle, is fleshy and green while young, becoming slightly yellowish when mature; it is

[1] *Indian Annals of Med. Science*, vi. (1859); *Pharmacopœia of India*, 1868. 93.

[2] *Ecballium* from ἐκβάλλω, I expel, in allusion to the expulsion of the seeds: often erroneously written *Ecbalium*.

[3] Turner's *Herball*, 1568, part i. 190.

3-celled and contains numerous oblong seeds lodged in a very bitter succulent pulp. The fruit when ripe separates suddenly from the stalk, and at the same moment the seeds and juice are forcibly expelled from the aperture left by the detached peduncle. This interesting phenomenon[1] is due to the process of exosmosis, by which the juice of the outer part of the fruit gradually passes through the strong contractile tissue which lines the central cavity, until the pressure becomes so great that the cell gives way at its weakest point. This point is that at which the peduncle is articulated with the fruit; and it is the sudden and powerful contraction of the elastic tissue when relieved from pressure that occasions the violent expulsion of the contents of the central cavity.

For the preparation of the officinal elaterium, the fruit has to be employed while still somewhat immature, for the simple reason that it would be impossible to gather it so as to retain its all-important juice if left till quite ripe. When it is sliced longitudinally as in making elaterium, some of the juice is expelled by virtue of the endosmotic action already described, as can easily be seen on examining the contracted lining of the sliced fruit.

Pereira observes[2] that if the juice of a fruit is received on a plate of glass, it is seen to be nearly colourless and transparent. In a few minutes however, by exposure to the air, it becomes slightly turbid, and small white coagula are formed in it. By slow evaporation, minute rhomboidal crystals make their appearance: these are *elaterin*.

Hot, dry weather favours the development of the active principle of the drug.[3]

Microscopic Structure—The middle layer of the fruit is built up of large somewhat thick-walled cells, traversed by a few fibro-vascular bundles. The former abound in small starch grains, and also contain granules of albuminous matter.

Chemical Composition—The experiments of Clutterbuck (1819) proved that the active properties of the elaterium plant reside chiefly, though not exclusively, in the juice that surrounds the seeds; and it is to this juice and to the medicinal product which it yields, that the attention of chemists has been hitherto directed.

The juice obtained by lightly pressing the sliced fruits is at first greenish and slightly turbid. After having been set aside a few hours, it yields a deposit, which has to be collected on calico, rapidly drained with gentle pressure between layers of bibulous paper and porous bricks, and dried in a warm place. The substance thus obtained is the *Elaterium* of pharmacy.[4] The method recommended by Clutterbuck[5] involves no pressing. The juice of the sliced fruit is saved, and the pulp, scooped out by the thumb of the operator, is thrown on a sieve and slightly washed with pure water. From these liquors, elaterium is deposited.

[1] I have not yet seen Yule's paper on the dehiscence of this fruit in the *Journ. of Anat. and Physiology*, 1877. The structure of the testa of the seed is explained by Fickel, in the *Botanische Zeitung*, 1876. 774.—F.A.F.

[2] *Elem. of Mat. Med.* ii. (1853) 1745.

[3] Having had to procure elaterium fruits at Mitcham in the very fine summer of 1868, I was told that the people occupied in slicing the fruits had never suffered so severely from their work as in that year.—D. H.

[4] There is a genus of *Cucurbitaceæ* founded by Linnæus, also called *Elaterium*.

[5] *Lond. Med. Repository*, xii. (1820) 1.

Elaterium occurs in irregular cake-like fragments, light, friable, and opaque; when new, of a bright pale green, becoming by age greyish and exhibiting minute crystals on the surface. It has a herby tea-like odour and a very bitter taste. The produce is extremely small: 240 lb. of fruit gathered at Mitcham, 10th August 1868, yielded 4⅝ ounces of elaterium = 0·123 per cent.

Elaterium consists, according to Pereira, of *Elaterin*, to which the activity of the drug is due, contaminated with green colouring matter, cellular tissue, and starch, together with a little of the residue of the bitter liquor from which these substances were deposited. Yet, in our opinion, this description is not applicable to the best varieties of elaterium. We have examined elaterium carefully prepared in the laboratory of Messrs. Allen and Hanburys, London, and a fine specimen imported from Malta. Both are devoid of starch, as well as of cellular tissue, but were seen to be largely made up of crystals. The first sample contained 12 per cent. of water, and yielded after drying, 8·4 per cent. of ash.

The most interesting principle of elaterium is *Elaterin*, $C^{20}H^{28}O^{5}$, discovered about the year 1831 by Morries, and independently by Hennell. The best method of obtaining it, according to our experience, is to exhaust elaterium with chloroform. From this solution, a white crystalline deposit of elaterin is immediately separated by addition of ether. It should be washed with a little ether, and recrystallized from chloroform. We have thus obtained 33·6 per cent. of pure elaterin from the above-mentioned elaterium of London, and 27·6 per cent. from that of Malta. Elaterin crystallizes in hexagonal scales or prisms; it has an extremely bitter, somewhat acrid taste. It is readily soluble in boiling alcohol, amylic alcohol, bisulphide of carbon, or chloroform. Its alcoholic solutions are neutral and are not precipitated by tannin, nor by any metallic solution. It is but very little coloured by cold concentrated sulphuric acid.

Elaterin is the drastic principle of *Ecballium;* if to its boiling alcoholic solution, solid caustic potash is added, the liquid thus obtained is stated by Buchheim (1872) to be no longer precipitable by water. The elaterin is then in fact converted into an acid body, which may be separated by supersaturating the solution with a mineral acid. The principle thus obtained has been found by Buchheim to be devoid of drastic power.

The fresh juice of the fruits was found by Köhler (1869) to contain 95 per cent. of water, 3 to 3·5 of organic and 1 to 1·6 of inorganic constituents. The same chemist observed that the percentage of elaterin gradually diminished as the season advanced, until in the month of September he was unable to obtain any of it whatever.

Walz (1859) found in the juice of the fruits and herb of *Ecballium*, as well as in that of *Cucumis Prophetarum* L., a second crystallizable bitter principle, *Prophetin*, and the amorphous substances *Ecballin* or *Elateric Acid*, *Hydro-elaterin*, and *Elateride*, all of which require further examination.[1] Prophetin is a glucoside,—not so the other principles. The four together constitute, according to Walz, 8·7 per cent. of elaterium, which moreover contains about the same percentage of pectic matter.

[1] Gmelin's *Chemistry*, xvii. (1866) 335-367.

Uses—Squirting cucumbers are only employed for making elaterium, which is a very powerful hydragogue cathartic.[1] Elaterin is not employed in medicine, but seeing how much elaterium is liable to vary from climate or season, it might probably be introduced into use with advantage.

FRUCTUS COLOCYNTHIDIS.

Colocynth, Coloquintida, Bitter Apple; F. *Coloquinte;* G. *Coloquinthe.*

Botanical Origin—*Citrullus Colocynthis* Schrader (*Cucumis Colocynthis* L.)—The colocynth gourd is a slender scabrous plant with a perennial root, native of warm and dry regions in the Old World, over which it has an extensive area.

Commencing eastward, it occurs in abundance in the arid districts of the Punjab and Sind, in sandy places on the Coromandel coast, in Ceylon, Persia as far north as the Caspian, in Arabia (Aden), Syria, and in some of the Greek islands. It is found in immense quantities in Upper Egypt and Nubia, spreading itself over sand hillocks of the desert after each rainy season. It further extends throughout North Africa to Morocco and Senegambia, in the Cape de Verd Islands, and on maritime sands in the south-east of Spain and Portugal. Finally, it is said to have been collected in Japan.

History—Colocynth was familiar to the Greek and Roman, as well as to the Arabian physicians; it also occurs in Susruta ("Indravāruṇī"); and if we may judge by the mention of it in an Anglo-Saxon herbal of the 11th century,[2] was not then unknown in Britain. The drug was collected in Spain at an early period, as is evident from an Arabic calendar of A.D. 961.[3]

The plant has been long cultivated in Cyprus, and its fruit is mentioned in the 14th century as one of the more important products of the island.[4] Tragus (1552) figured the plant, and stated that the fruit is imported from Alexandria.

Description—The colocynth plant bears a gourd of the size and shape of an orange, having a smooth, marbled-green surface. It is sometimes imported simply dried, in which case it is of a brown colour; but far more usually it is found in the market peeled with a knife and dried. It then forms light, pithy, nearly white balls, which consist of the dried internal pulp of the fruit with the seeds imbedded in it. This pulp is nearly inodorous, but has an intensely bitter taste, perceptible by reason of its dust when the drug is slightly handled. The balls are generally more or less broken; when dried too slowly they have a light brown colour.

The seeds are disposed in vertical rows on 3 thick parietal placentæ, which project to the centre of the fruit, then divide and turn back, forming two branches directed towards one another. Owing to this structure, the fruit easily breaks up vertically into 3 wedges in each of which are lodged 2 rows of dark brown seeds. The seeds, of which a

[1] Clutterbuck says ⅛ of a grain purges violently.

[2] Cockayne, *Leechdoms*, etc., i. (1865) 325.

[3] *Le Calendrier de Cordoue*, publié par R. Dozy, Leyde, 1873. 92.

[4] De Mas Latrie, *Hist. de l'île de Chypre*, iii. (1852–61) 498.

fruit contains from 200 to 300, are of flattened ovoid form, $\frac{3}{10}$ of an inch long by $\frac{2}{10}$ broad, not bordered. The testa which is hard and thick, having its surface minutely granulated, is marked on each side of its more pointed end by two furrows directed towards the hilum. The seed, as in other *Cucurbitaceæ*, is exalbuminous, and has thick oily cotyledons, enclosing an embryo with short straight radicle directed towards the hilum.

Colocynth fruits are mostly supplied by wholesale druggists, broken up and having the seeds removed, the drug in such case being called *Colocynth Pulp* or *Pith.*

Microscopic Structure—The pulp is made up of large thin-walled parenchymatous cells, their outer layer consisting of rows of smaller cells more densely packed. The tissue is irregularly traversed by fibro-vascular bundles, and also exhibits numerous large intercellular spaces. The cells contain but an insignificant amount of minute granules, to which neither iodine nor a persalt of iron imparts any coloration. The tissue is not much swollen by water, although one part of the pulp easily retains from 10 to 12 parts of water like a sponge.

Chemical Composition—The bitter principle has been isolated in 1847 by Hübschmann.[1] He observed that alcohol removes from the fruit a large amount of *resin.* By submitting this solution to distillation, the bitter principle remains partly in the aqueous liquid, partly in the resin, from which the "*Colocynthin*" is to be extracted by boiling water. The whole solution was then concentrated and mixed with carbonate of potassium, when a thickish viscid liquid separated. Hübschmann dried it and redissolved it in a mixture of 1 part of strong alcohol and 8 parts of ether. After treatment with charcoal, the solvents were distilled and the remaining bitter principle removed by means of water. This on evaporating afforded 2 per cent. of the pulp of a yellow extremely bitter powder, readily soluble in water or alcohol, not in pure ether. Colocynthin is precipitated from its aqueous solution by carbonate of potassium. Colocynthin was further extracted by Lebourdais (1848) by evaporating the aqueous infusion of the fruit with charcoal, and exhausting the dried powder with boiling alcohol.

Again, another method was followed by Walz (1858). He treated alcoholic extract of colocynth with water, and mixed the solution firstly with neutral acetate of lead, and subsequently with basic acetate of lead. From the filtered liquid the lead was separated by means of sulphuretted hydrogen, and then tannic acid added to it. The latter caused the colocynthin to be precipitated; the precipitate washed and dried was decomposed by oxide of lead, and finally the colocynthin was dissolved out by ether.

Walz thus obtained about $\frac{1}{4}$ per cent. of a yellowish mass or tufts, which he considered as possessing crystalline structure and to which he gave the name *Colocynthin.* He assigns to it the formula $C^{56}H^{84}O^{23}$, which in our opinion requires further investigation. Colocynthin is a violent purgative; it is decomposed according to Walz by boiling dilute hydrochloric acid, and then yields *Colocynthein,* $C^{44}H^{64}O^{13}$, and grape sugar. The same chemist termed *Colocynthitin* that part of

[1] *Schweizerische Zeitschrift für Pharmacie,* 1858. 216.

the alcoholic extract of colocynth which is soluble in ether but not in water. Purified with boiling alcohol, colocynthitin forms a tasteless crystalline powder.

The pulp perfectly freed from seeds and dried at 100° C., afforded us 11 per cent of ash; the seeds alone yield only 2·7 per cent. They have, even when crushed, but a faint bitter taste, and contain 17 per cent. of fat oil.

The fresh leaves of the plant if rubbed emit a very unpleasant smell.

Commerce—The drug is imported from Mogador, Spain and Syria.

Uses—In the form of an extract made with weak alcohol, and combined with aloes and scammony, colocynth is much employed as a purgative. The seeds, roasted or boiled, are the miserable food of some of the poorest tribes of the Sahara.[1]

The people of the Berber upon the Nile make a curious application for the tar they obtain from the fruit. The latter is heated in an earthen vessel with a hole in it; the tar drips through to another vessel and is fit for smearing leather water-bags. The bad smell of the tar (and of the leaves) prevents the camels from cutting open the water-bags.[2]

Substitutes—*Cucumis trigonus* Roxb. (*C. Pseudo-colocynthis* Royle), a plant of the plains of Northern India, with spherical or elongated, sometimes obscurely trigonous, bitter fruits, prostate *rooting* stems, and deeply divided leaves, resembles the colocynth gourd and has been mistaken for it. Another species named by Royle *C. Hardwickii*, and known to the natives of India as *Hill Colocynth*, has oval oblong bitter fruits, but leaves entirely unlike those of the *Citrullus Colocynthis*.

UMBELLIFERÆ.

HERBA HYDROCOTYLES.

Indian Hydrocotyle, Indian Pennywort; F. *Bevilacqua.*

Botanical Origin—*Hydrocotyle asiatica* L., a small creeping herb,[3] with slender jointed stems, common in moist places throughout tropical Asia and Africa, ascending in Abyssinia to elevations of 6,000 feet. It also occurs in America from South Carolina to Valdivia, in the West Indies, the islands of the Pacific, New Zealand, and Australia.

History—Hydrocotyle is called in Sanskrit *mandūka-parnī*, in Hindi *khulakhudi*. The former name denotes various plants, but is thought to refer in Susruta to the plant under notice (Dr. Rice). It was known to Rheede[4] by its Malyalim name of *Codagam* (or *Kutakan*), and also to Rumphius.[5] It has been long used medicinally by the

[1] See my paper on *Cucumis Colocynthis* considered as a nutritive plant in the *Archiv der Pharmacie*, 201 (1872) 235.—F. A. F.

[2] Col. Grant, Botany of the Speke and Grant expedition, *Journ. Linn. Soc.* xxix. pt. 2 (1873) 77.

[3] Fig. in Bentley and Trimen, *Med. Plants*, pt. 24, 1877.

[4] *Hort. Mal.* x. tab. 46.

[5] *Herb. Amboin.* v. 169.

natives of Java and of the Coromandel coast. In 1852, Boileau, a French physician of Mauritius, pointed out its virtues in the treatment of leprosy,[1] for which disease it was largely tried in the hospitals of Madras by Hunter[2] in 1855. It has since been admitted to a place in the *Pharmacopœia of India.*

Description[3]—The peduncles and petioles are fasciculed; the latter are frequently 2½ inches long; the peduncles are shorter and bear a 3- or 4-flowered simple umbel with very short rays. The leaves are reniform, crenate, ½ to 2 inches in longest diameter, 7-nerved, glabrous, or when young somewhat hairy on the under side. The fruit is laterally compressed, orbicular, acute on the back; the mericarps reticulated, sometimes a little hairy, with 3 to 5 curved ribs; they are devoid of vittæ. The main root is an inch or two long, but roots are also thrown out by the procumbent stem.

When fresh, the herb is said to be aromatic and of a disagreeable bitter and pungent taste; but these qualities appear to be lost in drying.

Chemical Composition—An analysis of hydrocotyle has been made by Lépine, a pharmacien of Pondicherry,[4] who found it to yield a somewhat peculiar body which he called *Vellarin*, from *Valālrai*, the Tamil name of the plant, and regarded as its active principle. Vellarin, which is said to be obtainable from the dry plant to the extent of 0·8 to 1·0 per cent., is an oily, non-volatile liquid with the smell and taste of fresh hydrocotyle, soluble in spirit of wine, ether, caustic ammonia, and partially also in hydrochloric acid. These singular properties do not enable us to rank vellarin in any well-characterized class of organic compounds.

By exhausting 3 ounces of the dried herb with rectified spirit, we did not obtain anything like vellarin, but simply a green extract almost entirely soluble in warm water, and containing chiefly tannic acid, which produced an abundant green precipitate with salts of iron. With caustic potash, neither the herb nor its extract evolved any nauseous odour. The dried plant afforded Lépine 13 per cent. of ash.

Uses—As an alterative tonic, hydrocotyle is allowed to be of some utility, but the power claimed for it by Boileau of curing leprosy is generally denied. Dorvault[5] regards it as belonging to the class of narcotico-acrid poisons such as hemlock, but we see no evidence to warrant such an opinion. Besides being administered internally, it is sometimes locally applied in the form of a poultice. Boileau says that the entire plant is preferable to the leaves alone.[6]

Substitutes (?)—*H. rotundifolia* Roxb., another species common in India, may be known from *H. asiatica* by having 10 or more flowers in an umbel and much smaller fruits. The European *H. vulgaris* L., easily distinguishable from the allied tropical species just described, by having its leaves orbicular and peltate (not reniform), is said to possess deleterious properties.

[1] Bouton, *Med. Plants of Mauritius*, 1857. 73–83.
[2] *Medical Reports*, Madras, 1855. 356.
[3] Drawn up from Indian specimens.
[4] *Journ. de Pharm.* xxviii. (1855) 47.
[5] *L'Officine* (1872) 554.
[6] It is probably by oversight that the *leaves alone* are ordered in the *Pharmacopœia of India.*

FRUCTUS CONII.

Hemlock fruits; F. Fruits de Ciguë; G. Schierlingsfrucht.

Botanical Origin—*Conium maculatum* L., an erect biennial herbaceous plant, flourishing by the sides of fields and streams, and in neglected spots of cultivated ground, throughout temperate Europe and Asia. It occurs in Asia Minor and the Mediterranean islands, and has been naturalized in North and South America. But the plant is very unevenly distributed, and in many districts is entirely wanting. It is found in most parts of Britain from Kent and Cornwall to the Orkneys.

History—Κώνειον, occurring as early as the fourth or fifth century B.C. in the Greek literature, was the plant under notice, at least in most cases. The famous hemlock potion of the Greeks by which criminals were put to death[1] was essentially composed of the juice of this plant. The old Roman name of Conium was *Cicuta;* it prevails in the mediæval Latin literature, but was applied, about 1541, by Gesner (and probably before him by others) to *Cicuta virosa* L., another umbelliferous plant which is altogether wanting in Greece and in Southern Europe generally, and does not contain any poisonous alkaloid. To avoid the confusion arising from the same appellation given to these widely different and quite dissimilar plants, Linnæus, in 1737, restoring the classical Greek name, called it Conium maculatum.[2]

Hemlock was used in Anglo-Saxon medicine. It is mentioned as early as the 10th century in the vocabulary of Alfric, archbishop of Canterbury, as "*Cicuta*, hemlic,"[3] and also in the Meddygon Myddfai. Hemlock is derived from the Anglo-Saxon words "hem," border, shore, and "leác" leek. Its use in modern medicine is due chiefly to the recommendation of Störck of Vienna, since whose time (1760) the plant has been much employed. The extreme uncertainty and even inertness of its preparations, which had long been known to physicians and had caused its rejection by many, have been recently investigated by Harley.[4] The careful experiments of this physician show what are the real powers of the drug, and by what method its active properties may be utilized.

Description—The fruit has the structure usual to the order; it is broadly ovoid, somewhat compressed laterally, and constricted towards the commissure, attenuated towards the apex, which is crowned with a depressed stylopodium. As met with in the shops, it consists of the separated mericarps which are about ⅛ of an inch long. The dorsal surface of these has 5 prominent longitudinal ridges, the edges of which are marked with little protuberances giving them a jagged or crenate outline, which is most conspicuous before the fruits are fully ripe. The furrows are glabrous but slightly wrinkled longitudinally; they are

[1] See Imbert-Gourbeyre, *De la mort de Socrate par la Ciguë*, Paris, 1876.

[2] An extensive paper has been devoted by Albert Regel to the *History of Conium and Cicuta* in the *Bulletin de la Soc. imp. des Naturalistes de Moscou*, tome li. (1876, first part) 155-203 and lii. (1877) first part, 1-52.

[3] *Volume of Vocabularies*, edited by Wright, 1857. 31.

[4] *Pharm. Journ.* viii. (1867) 460-710; ix. (1868) 53.

devoid of vittæ. When a mericarp is cut transversely, the seed exhibits a reniform outline, due to a deep furrow in the albumen on the side of the commissure.

The fruits of hemlock are dull greenish grey, and have but little taste and smell; but when triturated with a solution of caustic alkali they evolve a strong and offensive odour.

Microscopic Structure—Hemlock fruits differ from other fruits of the order by the absence of vittæ.[1] In the endocarp, there is a peculiar layer of small nearly cubic cells surrounding the albumen. The cells of the endocarp are loaded with a brown liquid consisting chiefly of conine and essential oil.

Chemical Composition—The most important constituent of the fruits of hemlock *Conine* or *Conia*, $C^8H^{14}NH$, a limpid colourless oily fluid, 0·846 sp. gr. at 12°·5 C. It has a strong alkaline reaction, and boils at 170°C. in an atmosphere devoid of oxygen, without decomposition. It was first observed by Giseke at Eisleben, Saxony, in 1827, recognized as an alkaloid by Geiger in 1831, and more amply studied by Wertheim in 1856 and 1862. To obtain it, an alcoholic extract is submitted to distillation with a little slaked lime. The product should be neutralized with oxalic acid, and the oxalate of conine removed by absolute alcohol mixed with a little ether, oxalate of ammonium being insoluble. The oxalate of the alkaloid shaken with caustic lye and ether, affords the conine, on evaporating the solvent and distilling the alkaloid in a current of dry hydrogen. In the plant it is combined with an acid (malic?), and accompanied by ammonia, as well as by a second, less poisonous crystallizable base, called *Conhydrine*, $C^8H^{17}NO$, which may be converted into conine by abstraction of the elements of water. From these alkaloids a liquid non-poisonous hydrocarbon, *Conylene*, C^8H^{14}, has been separated by Wertheim. Even in nature one hydrogen atom of conine is frequently replaced by methyl, CH^3; and commercial conine commonly contains, as shown by A. von Planta and Kekulé, methyl-conine, $C^8H^{14}NCH^3$. Lastly there is present in hemlock fruits a third alkaloid having probably the composition $C^7H^{13}N$.

As to the yield of conine, it varies according to the development of the fruits, but it is at best only about $\frac{1}{5}$ per cent. According to Schroff (1870), the fruits are most active just before maturity, provided they are gathered from the biennial plant. At a later stage, conine is probably partly transformed into conhydrine, which however is present in but very small proportion,—about $1\frac{1}{4}$ per mille at most.

In its deleterious action, conine resembles nicotine, but is much less powerful.

Schiff (1871–1872) has artificially produced an alkaloid partaking of the general properties of conine, and having the same composition; but it is optically indifferent. Conine, on the other hand, we find turns the plane of polarization to the right.

The fruits of hemlock contain also a volatile oil which appears devoid of poisonous properties; it exists in but small quantity and has not yet been fully examined.

Uses—The fruits of hemlock are the only convenient source of the alkaloid conine. They were introduced into British medicine in 1864, as a

[1] See *Moynier de Villepoix*, *Annales des Sciences naturelles*, Botanique, v. (1878) 348.

substitute for the dried leaf in making the tincture. But it has been shown that a tincture, whether of leaf or fruit, is a preparation of very small value, and that it is far inferior to the preserved juice of the herb. It has however been pointed out by W. Manlius Smith,[1] and his observations have been confirmed by Harley,[2] that the *green unripe fruits* possess more than any other part the peculiar energies of the plant, and that they may even be dried without loss of activity. A medicinal fluid extract of considerable power has been made from them by Squibb of New York.

FOLIA CONII.

Hemlock Leaves ; F. *Feuilles de Ciguë ;* G. *Schierlingsblätter.*

Botanical Origin—*Conium maculatum* L., see p. 299.

History—See p. 299.

Description—Hemlock in its first year produces only a tuft of leaves ; but in its second a stout erect stem which often grows to the height of 5 or 9 feet, is much branched in its upper part, and terminates in small umbels, each having about 12 rays. The lower leaves, often a foot in length, have a triangular outline, and a hollow stalk as long as the lamina, clasping the stem at its base with a membranous sheath. Towards the upper portion of the plant, the leaves have shorter stalks, are less divided, and are opposite or in cohorts of 3 to 5. The involucral bracts are lanceolate, reflexed, and about a ¼ of an inch long. Those of the partial umbel are turned towards the outside, and are always 3 in number. The larger leaves are twice or thrice pinnate, the ultimate segments being ovate-oblong, acute, and deeply incised.

The stem is cylindrical and hollow, of a glaucous green, generally marked on its lower part with reddish-brown spots. The leaves are of a dull dark green, and like the rest of the plant quite glabrous. They have when bruised a disagreeable fœtid smell.

For medicinal purposes the plant should be taken when in full blossom.[3]

Chemical Composition—The leaves of hemlock contain, though in exceedingly small proportion, the same alkaloids as the fruits. Geiger obtained from the fresh herb not so much as one ten-thousandth part of conine. It is probable however that the active constituents vary in proportion considerably, and that a dry and sunny climate promotes their development.

The same observer, as well as Pereira, has pointed out that hemlock leaves when dried are very frequently almost devoid of conine, and the observation is supported by the more recent experiments of Harley (1867). It has also been shown by the last-named physician, that the inspissated juice known in pharmacy as *Extractum Conii* usually contains but a mere trace of alkaloid, the latter having in fact been dissipated by the heat

[1] *Trans. of the New York State Medical Society* for 1867.

[2] *The old Vegetable Neurotics*, Lond. 1869.

[3] The London herbalists often collect it while much of the inflorescence is still in bud, in which state it affords far more of leaf than when well matured ; but it is in the latter condition that the plant is to be preferred.

employed in reducing the juice to the required consistence. On the other hand, Harley has proved that the juice of fresh hemlock preserved by the addition of spirit of wine, as in the *Succus Conii* of the Pharmacopœia, possesses in an eminent degree the poisonous properties of the plant.

The entire amount of nitrogen in dried hemlock leaves was estimated by Wrightson (1845) at 6·8 per cent.; the ash at 12·8 per cent. The latter consists mainly of salts of potassium, sodium, and calcium, especially of sodium chloride and calcium phosphate.

A ferment-oil may be obtained from *Conium*; it is stated to have an odour unlike that of the plant and a burning taste, and not to be poisonous.[1]

Uses—Hemlock administered in the form of *Succus Conii*, has a peculiar sedative action on the motor nerves, on account of which it is occasionally prescribed. It was formerly much more employed than at present, although the preparations used were so defective that they could rarely have produced the specific action of the medicine.

Plants liable to be confounded with Hemlock—Several common plants of the order *Umbelliferæ* have a superficial resemblance to *Conium*, but can be discriminated by characters easy of observation. One of these is *Æthusa Cynapium* L. or *Fool's Parsley*, a common annual garden weed, of much smaller stature than hemlock. It may be known by its primary umbel having no involucre, and by its partial umbel having an involucel of 2 or 3 linear pendulous bracts. The ridges of its fruit moreover are not wavy or crenate as in hemlock, nor is its stem spotted.

Chærophyllum Anthriscus L. (*Anthriscus vulgaris* Pers.) and two or three other species of *Chærophyllum* have the lower leaves not unlike those of hemlock, but they are *pubescent* or *ciliated*. The fruits too are *linear-oblong*, and thus very dissimilar from those of *Conium*.

The latter plant is in fact clearly distinguished by its smooth spotted stem, the character of its involucral bracts and fruit, and finally by the circumstance that when triturated with a few drops of solution of caustic alkali, it evolves conine (and ammonia), easily observable as a white fume when a rod moistened with strong acetic acid is held over the mortar.

FRUCTUS AJOWAN.

Semen Ajavæ vel Ajouain; Ajowan, True Bishop's weed.

Botanical Origin—*Carum Ajowan* Bentham et Hooker (*Ammi copticum* L. *Ptychotis coptica* et *Pt. Ajowan* DC.)—an erect annual herb, cultivated in Egypt and Persia, and especially in India where it is well known as *Ajvan* or *Omam*.

History—The minute spicy fruits of the above-named plant have been used in India from a remote period, as we may infer from their being mentioned in Sanskrit writings, as, for instance, by the grammarian Pānini, in the third century B.C. (or later?), and in Susruta.

Owing to their having been confounded with some other very small umbelliferous fruits, it is difficult to trace them precisely in many of the

[1] Gmelin, *Chemistry*, xiv. 405.

older writers on materia medica. It is however probable that they are the *Ammi* which Anguillara[1] met with in 1549 at Venice, where it had then, exceptionally, been imported in small quantity from Alexandria. It is also, we suppose, the *Ammi perpusillum* of Lobel (1571), in whose time the drug was likewise imported from Egypt, as well as the *Ammi alterum parvum*, the seed of which Dodonæus (1583) mentions as being "minutissimum, acre et fervidum." Dale,[2] who says it is brought from Alexandria, reports it as very scarce in the London shops. Under the name of *Ajave Seeds*, the drug was again brought into notice in 1773 by Percival,[3] who received a small quantity of it from Malabar as a remedy for cholic; and still more recently, it has been favourably spoken of by Fleming, Ainslie, Roxburgh, O'Shaughnessy, Waring and other writers who have treated of Indian materia medica.

Description—Ajowan fruits, like those of other cultivated *Umbelliferæ*, vary somewhat in size and form. The largest kind much resemble those of parsley, being of about the same shape and weight. The length of the large fruits is about $\frac{1}{10}$, of the smaller form scarcely $\frac{1}{16}$ of an inch. The fruits are greyish brown, plump, very rough on the surface, owing to numerous minute tubercles (*fructus muriculatus*). Each mericarp has five prominent ridges, the intervening channels being dark brown, with a single vitta in each. The commissural side bears two vittæ. The fruits when rubbed exhale a strong odour of thyme (*Thymus vulgaris* L.), and have a biting aromatic taste.

Microscopic Structure—The oil-ducts of ajowan are very large, often attaining a diameter of 200 mkm. The ridges contain numerous spiral vessels; the blunt tubercles of the epidermis are of the same structure as those in anise, but comparatively larger and not pointed. The tissue of the albumen exhibits numerous crystalloid granules of albuminous matter (aleuron), distinctly observable in polarized light.

Chemical Composition—The fruits on an average afford from 4 to 4·5 per cent. of an agreeable aromatic, volatile oil; at the same time there often collects on the surface of the distilled water a crystalline substance, which is prepared at Oojein and elsewhere in Central India, by exposing the oil to spontaneous evaporation at a low temperature. This stearoptene, sold in the shops of Poona and other places of the Deccan, under the name of *Ajwain-ka-phul*, i.e. *flowers of ajwain*, was showed by Stenhouse (1855) and by Haines (1856) to be identical with

Thymol, $C^6H^3\begin{cases}OH\\CH^3\\C^3H^7\end{cases}$, as contained in *Thymus vulgaris*.

We obtained it by exposing oil of our own distillation, first rectified from chloride of calcium, to a temperature of 0° C., when the oil deposited 36 per cent. of thymol in superb tabular crystals, an inch or more in length. The liquid portion, even after long exposure to a cold some degrees below the freezing point, yielded no further crop. We found the thymol thus obtained began to melt at 44° C., yet using somewhat larger quantities, it appeared to require fully 51° C. for complete fusion. On cooling, it continues fluid for a long time, and only recrystallizes when a crystal of thymol is projected into it.

[1] *Semplici*, Vinegia, 1561. 130.
[2] *Pharmacologia*, 1693. 211.
[3] *Essays, Medical and Experimental*, ii. (1773) 226.

Thymol is more conveniently and completely extracted from the oil by shaking it repeatedly with caustic lye, and neutralizing the latter.

The oil of ajowan, from which the thymol has been removed, boils at about 172°, and contains cymene (or cymol), $C^{10}H^{14}$, which, with concentrated sulphuric acid, affords cymen-sulphonic acid, $C^{10}H^{13}SO^{2}OH$. The latter is not very readily crystallizable, but forms crystallized salts with baryum, calcium, zinc, lead, which are abundantly soluble in water. In the oil of ajowan no constituent of the formula $C^{10}H^{16}$ appears to be present; mixed with alcohol and nitric acid (see p. 279) it at least produces no crystals of terpin.

The residual portions of the oil, from which the cymene has been distilled, contains another substance of the phenol class different from thymol.

We have found that neither the thymol nor the liquid part of ajowan oil possesses any rotatory power.

Uses—Ajowan is much used by the natives of India as a condiment.[1] The distilled water which has been introduced into the *Pharmacopœia of India*, is reputed to be carminative, and a good vehicle for nauseous medicines. It has a powerful burning taste, and would seem to require dilution. The volatile oil may be used in the place of oil of thyme, which it closely resembles.

Ajowan seeds are largely imported into Europe since thymol has been universally introduced into medical practice (see Folia Thymi). They have proved much more remunerative for the manufacture of thymol than Thymus vulgaris. The largest quantities, we believe, of thymol have been made from ajowan at Leipzig.

Substitutes—Under the name *Semen Ammi*, the very small fruits of *Ammi majus* L. and of *Sison Amomum* L. have been often confounded with those of Ajowan; but the *absence of hairs* on the two former, not to mention some other differences, is sufficient to negative any supposition of identity.

The seeds of *Hyoscyamus niger* L. being called in India *Khorāsāni-ajwān*, a confusion might arise between them and true ajowan; though the slightest examination would suffice to show the difference.[2]

FRUCTUS CARUI.

Semen Carui vel Carvi; Caraway Fruits, Caraway Seeds, Caraways; F. *Fruits ou Semences de Carvi;* G. *Kümmel.*

Botanical Origin—*Carum Carvi* L., an erect annual or biennial plant not unlike a carrot, growing in meadows and moist grassy land over the northern and midland parts of Europe and Asia, but to what extent truly wild cannot be always ascertained.

It is much cultivated in Iceland, and is also apparently wild.[3] It grows throughout Scandinavia, in Finland, Arctic, Central, and

[1] Roxburgh, *Flor. Ind.* ii. (1832) 91.

[2] To such a mistake may probably be referred the statement of Irvine (*Account of the Mat. Med. of Patna*, 1848, p. 6) that the seeds of henbane are "used in food as carminative and stimulant"!

[3] Babington in *Journ. of Linn. Soc.*, Bot. xi. (1871) 310.

Southern Russia, Persia, and in Siberia. It appears as a wild plant in many parts of Britain (Lincolnshire and Yorkshire), but is also cultivated in fields, and may not be strictly indigenous. The caraway is found throughout the eastern part of France, in the Pyrenees, Spain, Central Europe, Armenia, and the Caucasian provinces; and it grows wild largely in the high alpine region of Lahul, in the Western Himalaya.[1]

But the most curious fact in the distribution of *Carum Carvi* is its occurrence in Morocco, where it is largely cultivated about El Araiche, and round the city of Morocco.[2] The plant differs somewhat from that of Europe; it is an annual with a single erect stem, 4 feet high. Its foliage is more divided, and its flowers larger, with shorter styles and on more spreading umbels than the common caraway, and its fruit is more elongated.[3]

History—The opinion that this plant is the Κάρος of Dioscorides, and that, as Pliny states, it derived its name from Caria (where it has never been met with in modern times) has very reasonably been doubted.[4]

Caraway fruits were known to the Arabians, who called them *Karawya*, a name they still bear in the East, and the original of our words *caraway* and *carui*, as well as of the Spanish *alcarahueya*. In the description of Morocco by Edrisi,[5] 12th century, it is stated that the inhabitants of Sidjilmâsa (the south-eastern province) cultivate cotton, *cumin*, *caraway*, henna (*Lawsonia alba* Lamarck). In the Arab writings quoted by Ibn Baytar,[6] himself a Mauro-Spaniard of the 13th century, caraway is compared to cumin and anise. The spice probably came into use about this period. It is not noticed by St. Isidore, archbishop of Seville in the 7th century, though he mentions fennel, dill, coriander, anise, and parsley; nor is it named by St. Hildegard in Germany in the 12th century. Neither have we found any reference to it in the Anglo-Saxon *Herbarium of Apuleius*, written *circa* A.D. 1050,[7] or in other works of the same period, though cumin, anise, fennel, and dill are all mentioned.

On the other hand, in two German medicine-books of the 12th and 13th centuries[8] there occurs the word *Cumich*, which is still the popular name of caraway, in Southern Germany; and *Cumin* is also mentioned. In the same period the seeds appear to have been used by the Welsh physicians of Myddvai.[9] Caraway was certainly in use in England at the close of the 14th century, as it figures with coriander, pepper and garlick in the *Form of Cury*, a roll of ancient English cookery compiled by the master-cooks of Richard II. about A.D. 1390.

The oriental names of caraway show that as a spice it is not a production of the East:—thus we find it termed *Roman* (i.e. *European*), *Armenian*, *mountain*, or *foreign Cumin*; *Persian* or *Andalusian*

[1] Aitchison in *Journ. of Linn. Soc.*, Bot., x. (1869) 76. 94.

[2] Leared in *Pharm. Journ.* Feb. 8, 1873. 623.

[3] I have cultivated the Morocco plant in 1872 and 1873 by the side of the common form.—D. H.

[4] Dierbach, *Flora Apiciana*, 1831. 53.

[5] *Description de l'Afrique et de l'Espagne trad. par Dozy et M. J. de Goeje*, Leyde, 1866, 75. 97. 150.

[6] Sontheimer's translation, ii. 368.

[7] *Leechdoms, etc. of Early England*, i. (1864).

[8] Pfeiffer, *Zwei deutsche Arzneibücher aus dem xii. und. xiii. Jahrhundert*, Wien 1863. 14.

[9] *Meddygon Myddfai*, 158. 354.

Caraway; or *foreign Anise.* And though it is now sold in the Indian bazaars, its name does not occur in the earlier lists of Indian spices.

Cultivation[1]—In England, the caraway is cultivated exclusively in Kent and Essex, on clay lands. It was formerly sown mixed with coriander and teazel seed, but now with the former only. The plant, which requires the most diligent and careful cultivation, yields in its second year a crop which is ready for harvesting in the beginning of July. It is cut with a hook at about a foot from the ground, and a few days afterwards may be thrashed. The produce is very variable, but may be stated at 4 to 8 cwt. per acre.

Description—The fruits, which in structure correspond to those of other plants of the order, are laterally compressed and ovate. The mericarps which hang loosely suspended from the arms of the carpophore, are in the English drug about $\frac{1}{8}$ of an inch in length and $\frac{1}{20}$ in diameter, subcylindrical, slightly arched, and tipped with the conical, shrivelled stylopodium. They are marked with five pale ridges, nearly half as broad as the shining, dark brown furrows, each of which is furnished with a conspicuous vitta; a pair of vittæ separated from each other by a comparatively thin fibro-vascular bundle, occurs on the commissure.

Caraways are somewhat horny and translucent; when bruised, they evolve an agreeable fragrance resembling that of dill, and they have a pleasant spicy taste. In the London market, they are distinguished as *English, Dutch, German,* and *Mogador,* the first sort fetching the highest price. The fruit varies in size, tint and flavour; the English is shorter and plumper than the others; the Mogador is paler, stalky, and elongated—often $\frac{3}{10}$ of an inch in length.

Microscopic Structure—Caraways are especially distinguished by their enormous vittæ, which in transverse section display a triangular outline, the largest diameter, *i.e.* the base of the triangle, often attaining as much as 300 mkm. Even those of the commissure are usually not smaller.

Chemical Composition—Caraways contain a volatile oil, which the Dutch drug affords to the extent of 5·5 per cent., that grown in Germany to the amount of 7 per cent.[2]; in Norway 5·8 per cent. have also been obtained from indigenous caraways.[3] The position and size of the vittæ account for the fact that comminution of the fruits previous to distillation, does not increase the yield of oil.

Vōlckel (1840) showed that the oil is a mixture of a hydrocarbon $C^{10}H^{16}$, and an oxygenated oil, $C^{10}H^{14}O$. Berzelius subsequently termed the former *Carvene* and the latter *Carvol.*

Carvene, constituting about one third of the crude oil, boils at 173° C., and forms with dry hydrochloric gas crystals of $C^{10}H^{16}+2HCl$. It has been ascertained by us that carvene, as well as carvol, has a dextrogyrate power, that of carvene being considerably the stronger; there are probably not many liquids exhibiting a stronger dextrogyrate rotation. Carvene is of a weaker odour than carvol, from which it has not yet been absolutely deprived; perfectly pure carvene would no doubt

[1] Morton, *Cyclop. of Agriculture,* i. (1855) 390.

[2] Information obligingly supplied by Messrs. Schimmel & Co., Leipzig.

[3] Schübeler, *Pflanzenwelt Norwegens.* Christiania, 1863–1875. 85.

prove no longer to possess the specific odour of the drug. By distilling it over sodium it acquires a rather pleasant odour; its spec. gr. at 15° C. is equal to 0·861.

Carvol at 20° C. has a sp. gr. of 0·953; it boils at 224° C.; the same oil appears to occur in dill (see Fructus Anethi), and an oil of the same percental constitution is yielded by the spearmint. The latter however deviates the plane of polarization to the left. If 4 parts of carvol, either from caraways, dill, or spearmint, are mixed with 1 part of alcohol, sp. gr. 0·830, and saturated with sulphuretted hydrogen, crystals of $(C^{10}H^{14}C)^2SH^2$ are at once formed as soon as a little ammonia is added.[1]

Oil of caraway of inferior quality is obtained from the refuse of the fruit; we find it less dextrogyrate than the oil from the fruits alone; this is due to the admixture of oil of turpentine before distilling.

If the carvol is distilled there remains in the still a thickish residue, from which a substance of the phenol class may be extracted by caustic lye.

Oil of caraway distilled in England from home-grown caraways is preferred in this country. On the Continent, that extracted from the caraways of Halle and Holland is considered to be of finer flavour than the oil obtained from those of Southern Germany.

The immature fruit of caraway is rich in tannic matter, striking blue with a salt of iron. It occurs abundantly in the tissue around the oil-ducts, where the presence of sugar may be also detected by alkaline tartrate of copper. Sugar occurs likewise in the embryo, but not in the albumen, in which latter protein substances predominate.

Production and Commerce—Caraways are exported from Finmark, the most northerly province of Norway; from Finland and Russia. In Germany, the cultivation, recommended by Gleditsch in 1776, is now largely carried on in Moravia, and in Prussia, especially in the neighbourhood of Halle. The districts of Erfurt and Merseburg, also in Prussia, are stated to yield annually about 30,000 cwt. Dutch caraways are produced in the provinces of North Holland, Gelderland and North Brabant, in the latter two from wild plants.[2] Caraways are frequently shipped from the ports of Morocco; the quantity exported thence in 1872 was 952 cwt. and 288 cwt. in 1875.[3]

The import of caraways into the United Kingdom in 1870 amounted to 19,160 cwt., almost all being from Holland.

The essential oil is manufactured on a large scale. According to a statement of the Chamber of Commerce of Leipzig,[4] four establishments of that district produced in 1872 no less a quantity than 30,955 kilo. (68,277 lb.), valued at £24,000.

Uses—Caraway in the form of essential oil or distilled water is used in medicine as an aromatic stimulant, or as a flavouring ingredient. But the consumption in Europe is far more important as a spice, in bread, cakes, cheese, pastry, confectionary, sauces, etc., or in the form of oil as an ingredient of alcoholic liquors. The oil is also used for the scenting of soap.

[1] *Pharm. Journ.* vii. (1876) 75.

[2] Oudemans, *Aanteekeningen*, etc., Rotterdam, 1854–1856. 351.

[3] *Consular Reports*, 1873 and 1876.

[4] *Pharmaceutische Zeitung*, 15th April 1874.

FRUCTUS FŒNICULI.

Fennel Fruits, Fennel Seeds; F. Fruits de Fenouil; G. Fenchel.

Botanical Origin—*Fœniculum vulgare* Gärtn. (*Anethum Fœniculum* L.), an erect, branching plant with an herbaceous stem and perennial rootstock, growing to the height of 3 or 4 feet, having leaves 3 or 3 times pinnate with narrow linear segments. In allusion to the latter the plant had also been named *Fœniculum capillaceum* by Gilibert.

It appears to be truly indigenous to the countries extending from the Caspian regions (or even China?) to the Mediterranean and the Greek Peninsula, but is a doubtful native in many parts of Central and Southern Russia. The plant on the other hand is also found apparently wild, over a large portion of Western Europe as far as the British Isles, especially in the vicinity of the sea.

Fennel is largely cultivated in the central parts of Europe, as Saxony, Franconia and Wurtemberg, also in the South of France about Nîmes, and in Italy. It is extensively grown in India and China. The Indian plant is an annual of somewhat low stature.[1]

The plant varies in stature, foliage, and in the size and form of its fruits; but all the forms belong apparently to a single species.

History—Fennel was used by the ancient Romans, as well for its aromatic fruits, as for its edible succulent shoots. It was also employed in Northern Europe at a remote period, as it is constantly mentioned in the Anglo-Saxon medical receipts, which date as early at least as the 11th century. The diffusion of the plant in Central Europe was stimulated by Charlemagne, who enjoined its cultivation on the imperial farms. Fennel shoots (*turiones fænuculi*), fennel water, and fennel seed, as well as anise, are all mentioned in an ancient record [2] of Spanish agriculture dating A.D. 961.

Description—The fennel fruits of commerce, commonly called *Fennel Seeds*, are of several kinds and of very different pecuniary value. The following are the principal sorts:—

1. *Sweet Fennel*,—known also as *Roman Fennel*, is cultivated in the neighbourhood of Nîmes in the south of France. The plant is a tall perennial with large umbels of 25 to 30 rays.[3] As the plants grow old, the fruits of each succeeding season gradually change in shape and diminish in size, till at the end of 4 or 5 years they are hardly to be distinguished from those of the wild fennel growing in the same district. This curious fact, remarked by Tabernæmontanus (1588), was experimentally proved by Guibourt.[4]

The fruits of Sweet Fennel as found in the shops are oblong, cylindrical, about $\frac{4}{10}$ of an inch in length by $\frac{1}{10}$ in diameter, more or less arched, terminating with the two-pointed base of the style, and smooth

[1] It is an annual even in England, ripening seeds in its first year, and then dying.

[2] *Le Calendrier de Cordoue de l'année*, 961, publié par R. Dozy, Leyde, 1873.

[3] The Nîmes fennel has been usually referred to *Fœniculum dulce* DC., but that plant has the stem compressed at the base, and only 6 to 8 rays in the umbel; and is the fennel which is eaten as a vegetable or as a salad.

[4] *Hist. des Drogues*, iii. (1869) 233.

on the surface. Each mericarp is marked by 5 prominent ridges, the lateral being thicker than the dorsal. Between the ridges lie vittæ, and there are two vittæ on the commissural surface,—all filled with dark oily matter. The fruits seen in bulk have a pale greenish hue; their odour is aromatic, and they have a pleasant, saccharine, spicy taste.

2. *German Fennel, Saxon Fennel,* produced especially near Weissenfels in the Prussian province of Saxony; the fruits are $\frac{2}{10}$ to $\frac{1}{4}$ of an inch long, ovoid-oblong, a little compressed laterally, slightly curved, terminating in a short conical stylopodium; they are glabrous, of a deep brown, each mericarp marked with 5 conspicuous pale ridges, of which the lateral are the largest. Seen in bulk, the fruits have a greenish brown hue; they have an aromatic saccharine taste, with the peculiar smell of fennel.

3. *Wild or Bitter Fennel (Fenouil amer),* collected in the south of France, where the plant grows without cultivation. They are smaller and broader than those of the German Fennel, being from $\frac{1}{5}$ to $\frac{1}{6}$ of an inch long by about $\frac{1}{15}$ of an inch wide. They have less prominent ridges and at maturity are a little scurfy in the furrows and on the commissure. Their taste is bitterish, spicy, and strongly fennel-like. The essential oil *(Essence de Fenouil amer)* is distilled from the entire herb.

4. *Indian Fennel.*—A sample in our possession from Bombay resembles Sweet Fennel, but the fruits are not so long, and are usually straight. The mother-plant of this drug is *F. Panmorium* DC., now regarded as a simple variety of *F. vulgare* Gärtn.

Microscopic Structure—The most marked peculiarity of fennel is exhibited by the vittæ, which are surrounded by a brown tissue. The latter is made up of cells resembling the usual form of cork-cells. In Sweet Fennel the vittæ are smaller than in the German fruit; in the transverse section of the latter, the largest diameter of these ducts is about 200 mkm.

Chemical Composition—The most important constituent of fennel fruits is the volatile oil, which is afforded both by the Sweet and the German fennel to the extent of about 3½ per cent.

Oil of fennel, from whatever variety of the drug obtained, consists of *Anethol* (or Anise-camphor) $C^6H^4\left\{\begin{array}{l}OCH^3\\CH.CH.CH^3\end{array}\right.$, and variable but less considerable proportions of an oil, isomeric with oil of turpentine. Anethol is obtainable from fennel in two forms, the solid and the liquid; crystals of the former are deposited when the oil is subjected to a somewhat low temperature; the liquid anethol may be got by collecting the portion of the crude oil passing over at 225° C. The crystals of anethol fuse between 16 and 20°; the liquid form of anethol remains fluid even at − 10° C. By long keeping, the crystals slowly become liquid and lose their power of reassuming a crystalline form.

Three varieties of oil of fennel are found in commerce, namely the oils of *Sweet Fennel* and *Bitter Fennel* offered by the drug-houses of the south of France; their money value is as 3 to 1, the oil of sweet fennel, which has a decidedly *sweet* taste, being by far the most esteemed. The third variety is obtained from Saxon fennel, especially by the manufacturers of Dresden and Leipzig.[1] We have been supplied with type-specimens of the first two oils by the distillers, Messrs. J. Sagnier, fils, & Cie., Nîmes; a specimen of the third has been distilled in the laboratory of one of ourselves.

Oil of fennel differs from that of anise by displaying a considerable rotatory power. We found the above-mentioned specimens, examined in a column 50 mm. long, to deviate the ray of polarized light to the right thus:—

Oil of Sweet Fennel	29°·8
„ Bitter „	4°·8
„ German „	9°·1

The rotatory power is due to the hydrocarbon contained in the oil; we ascertain that anethol from oil of anise is devoid of it.

Fennel fruits contain sugar, yet their sweetness or bitterness depends on the essential oil rather than on the presence of that body. The albumen of the seed contains fixed oil, which amounts to about 12 per cent. of the fruit.

Uses—Fennel fruits are used in medicine in the form of distilled water and volatile oil, but to no considerable extent. The chief consumption is in cattle medicines, and of the oil in the manufacture of cordials.

FRUCTUS ANISI.

Anise, Aniseed; F. Fruits d'Anis vert; G. Anis.

Botanical Origin—*Pimpinella Anisum* L., an annual plant, is indigenous to Asia Minor, the Greek Islands and Egypt, but nowhere to be met with undoubtedly growing wild. It is now also cultivated in many parts of Europe where the summer is hot enough for ripening its fruits, as well as in India and South America. It is not grown in Britain.

History—Anise, which the ancients obtained chiefly from Crete and Egypt, is among the oldest of medicines and spices.[2] It is mentioned by Theophrastus, by the later writers Dioscorides and Pliny, as well as by Edrisi,[3] who enumerates anise "sorte de graine douce" among the products of Tunisia. In Europe we find that Charlemagne (A.D. 812) commanded that anise should be cultivated on the imperial farms in Germany. The Anglo-Saxon writings contain frequent allusions to the use of dill and cumin, but we have failed to find in them any reference to anise, nor in the *Meddygon Myddfai*.

The Patent of Pontage granted by Edward I. in 1305 to raise funds for repairing the Bridge of London,[4] enumerates *Anise (anisium)* among the commodities liable to toll. There are entries for it under the name of *Annis vert* in the account of the expenses of John, king of France, during his abode in England, 1359-60;[5] and it is one of the spices of which the Grocers' Company of London had the weighing and oversight

[1] The Leipzig Chamber of Commerce reports the quantity made by four establishments in 1872, as 4350 kilo. (9594 lb.).

[2] On the *Anise* of the Bible, see note in our article Fructus Anethi.

[3] Page 150 of the "*Description*," etc., quoted in the article Fructus Carui, p. 305, note 5.

[4] [Thomson, R.], *Chronicles of London Bridge*, 1827. 156.

[5] Douet d'Arcq, *Comptes de l'Argenterie des Rois de France*, 1851. 206. 220.

from 1453.[1] By the *Wardrobe Accounts* of Edward IV., A.D. 1480,[2] it appears that the royal linen was perfumed by means of "lytill bagges of fustian stuffed with ireos and *anneys*."

Anise seems to have been grown in England as a potherb prior to 1542, for Boorde in his *Dyetary of Helth*, printed in that year,[3] says of it and fennel,—"these herbes be seldom vsed, but theyr seedes be greatly occupyde."

In common with all other foreign commodities, anise was enormously taxed during the reign of Charles I., the duties levied upon it amounting to 75s. per 112 ℔.[4]

Description—Anise fruits, which have the usual characters of the order, are about $\frac{3}{16}$ of an inch in length, mostly undivided and attached to a slender pedicel. They are of ovoid form, tapering towards the summit, which is crowned by a pair of short styles rising from a thick stylopode; they are nearly cylindrical, but a little constricted towards the commissure. Each fruit is marked by 10 light-coloured ridges which give it a prismatic form; these as well as the rest of the surface of the fruit, are clothed with short rough hairs. The drug has a greyish brown hue, a spicy saccharine taste, and an agreeable aromatic smell.

Microscopic Structure—The most striking peculiarity of anise fruit is the large number of oil-ducts or vittæ it contains; each half of the fruit exhibits in transverse section nearly 30 oil-ducts, of which the 4 to 6 in the commissure are by far the largest. The hairs display a simple structure, inasmuch as they are the elongated cells of the epidermis a little rounded at the end.

Chemical Composition—The only important constituent of anise is the essential oil *(Oleum Anisi)*, which the fruits afford to the extent of 3 per cent. from the best Moravian sort; Russian anise yields from 2·5 to 2·7 per cent., the German 2·3 per cent.[5] This oil is a colourless liquid, having an agreeable odour of anise and a sweetish aromatic taste; its sp. gr. varies from 0·977 to 0·983. At 10° to 15° C., it solidifies to a hard crystalline mass, which does not resume its fluidity till the temperature rises to about 17° C.

Oil of anise resembles the oils of fennel, star-anise, and tarragon, in that it consists almost wholly of *Anethol* or *Anise-camphor* described in the previous article (p. 309). This fact explains the rotatory power of oil of anise being inferior to that of fennel. Oil of German anise, distilled by one of us, examined under the conditions stated, page 310, deviated only 1°·7, but to the left. *Franck* (1868) found oil of Saxon anise deviating 1°·1 to the right.

Production and Commerce—Anise is produced in Malta, about Alicante in Spain, in Touraine and Guienne in France, in Puglia (Southern Italy), in several parts of Northern and Central Germany, Bohemia and Moravia. The Russian provinces of Orel, Tula and Woronesh, south of Moscow, also produce excellent anise, and in Southern Russia, Charkow is likewise known for the production of

[1] Herbert, *Hist. of the twelve Great Livery Companies of London*, 1834, 310.

[2] Edited by N. H. Nicolas, Lond. 1830. 131.

[3] Reprinted for the Early English Text Society, 1870. 281.

[4] *Rates of Marchandizes*, 1635.

[5] Laboratory notes obligingly furnished by Messrs. Schimmel & Co., Leipzig. (1878).

this drug. In Greece, anise is largely cultivated under the name of γλυκάνισον, and it is much grown in Northern India. Considerable quantities are also now imported from Chili. The drug is, on the whole, always of a remarkably uniform appearance.

Uses—Anise is an aromatic stimulant and carminative, usually administered in the form of essential oil as an adjunct to other medicines. It is also used as a cattle medicine. The essential oil is largely consumed in the manufacture of cordials, chiefly in France, Spain, Italy, and South America.

Adulteration—The fruits of anise are sometimes mixed with those of hemlock, but whether by design or by carelessness we know not. Careful inspection with a lens will reveal this dangerous adulteration. We have known *powdered* anise also to contain hemlock, and have detected it by trituration in a mortar with a few drops of solution of potash, a sample of pure anise for comparison being tried at the same time.

The essential oil of aniseed may readily be confounded with that of Star-anise, which is distilled from the fruits of the widely different *Illicium anisatum.* As stated at p. 22, these oils agree so closely in their chemical and optical properties, that no scientific means are known for distinguishing them.

RADIX SUMBUL.

Sumbul Root; F. *Racine de Sumbul, Sambola ou Sambula;* G. *Moschuswurzel.*

Botanical Origin—*Ferula Sumbul* Hooker fil. (*Euryangium Sumbul* Kauffmann[1]), a tall perennial plant discovered in 1869 by a Russian traveller, Fedschenko, in the mountains of Maghian near Pianjakent, in the northern part of the Khanat of Bukhara, nearly 40° N. lat., and 68° to 69° E. long. From Wittmann's statements (1876) it would appear that the Sumbul plant abounds far east from that country, in the coast province of the Amoor. A living plant transmitted from the former district to the Botanical Garden of Moscow flowered there in 1871, another in 1875 at Kew, where the plant died after flowering.

History—The word *sumbul*, which is Arabic and signifies *an ear* or *spike*, is used as the designation of various substances, but especially of *Indian Nard*, the rhizome of *Nardostachys Jatamansi* DC. Under what circumstances, or at what period, it came to be applied to the drug under notice, we know not. Nor are we better informed as to the history of sumbul root, which we have been unable to trace by means of any of the works at our disposal. All we can say is, that the drug was first introduced into Russia about the year 1835 as a substitute for musk, that it was then recommended as a remedy for cholera, and that it began to be known in Germany in 1840, and ten years afterwards in England. It was admitted into the *British Pharmacopœia* in 1867.

[1] *Nouv. Mém. de la Soc. imp. des Nat. de Moscou*, xii. (1871) 253. tabb. 24. 25.—Also figured in Bentley and Trimen, *Med. Plants*, part 20 (1877).

Description—The root as found in commerce consists of transverse slices, 1 to 2 inches, rarely as much as 5 inches in diameter, and an inch or more in thickness; the bristly crown, and tapering lower portions, often no thicker than a quill, are also met with. The outside is covered by a dark papery bark; the inner surface of the slices is of a dirty brown, marbled with white, showing when viewed with a lens an abundant resinous exudation, especially towards the circumference. The interior is a spongy, fibrous, farinaceous-looking substance, having a pleasant musky odour and a bitter aromatic taste.

Microscopic Structure—The interior tissue of sumbul root is very irregularly constructed of woody and medullary rays, while the cortical part exhibits a loose spongy parenchyme. The structural peculiarity of the root becomes obvious, if thin slices are moistened with solution of iodine, when the medullary rays assume by reason of the starch they contain an intense blue. The structure of the root differs from the usual arrangement by the formation of independent secondary cambial zones with fibro-vascular bundles within the original cambium. Similar peculiarities are also displayed by the roots of Myrrhis odorata, Convolvulus Scammonia, Ipomœa Turpethum and others.[1] Large balsam-ducts are also observable in Sumbul as well as in the roots of many other Umbelliferæ.[2]

Chemical Composition—Sumbul root yields about 9 per cent. of a soft balsamic resin soluble in ether, and ⅓ per cent. of a dingy bluish essential oil. The resin has a musky smell, not fully developed until after contact with water. According to Reinsch (1848), it dissolves in strong sulphuric acid with a fine blue colour, but in our experience with a crimson brown. The same chemist states that when subjected to dry distillation, it yields a blue oil.

Solution of potash is stated to convert the resin of sumbul into a crystalline potassium salt of *Sumbulamic Acid*, which latter was obtained in a crystalline state by Reinsch in 1843, but has not been further examined. Sumbulamic acid, which smells strongly of musk, appears to be a different substance from *Sumbulic* or *Sumbulolic Acid*, the potassium salt of which may be extracted by water from the above-mentioned alkaline solution. Ricker and Reinsch (1848), assert that the last-mentioned acid, of which the root contains about ¾ per cent., is none other than *Angelic Acid*, accompanied, as in angelica root, by a little valerianic acid. All these substances require further investigation, as well as the body called *Sumbulin*, which was prepared by Murawjeff (1853), and is said to form with acids, crystalline salts.

Sommer has shown (1859) that by dry distillation, sumbul resin yields *Umbelliferone*, which substance we shall further notice when describing the constituents of galbanum.

Uses—Prescribed in the form of tincture as a stimulating tonic.

Adulteration—*Bombay Sumbul*, or "*Boi*," is the root of Dorema Ammoniacum (see article Ammoniacum, p. 324), which is largely imported into Bombay, being used there in the Parsee fire temples as an

[1] See A. de Bary, *Anatomie*, 1877. 623.

[2] The structure and growth of Sumbul root have been elaborately studied by Tchistiakoff, of whose observations, first published in Russian in 1870, an Italian translation with two plates has appeared in the *Nuovo Giornale Botanico* for Oct. 1873. 298.

incense.[1] The largest roots, for which we are indebted to Professor Dymock, are three inches in diameter at the crown, by 8 inches in length. They are easily distinguished from the Sumbul by their decidedly yellowish hue as well as by the absence of any musky odour. We extracted by alcohol, from the root dried at 100° C., 26 per cent. of a resin identical with that afforded by commercial Ammoniacum.

Bombay Sumbul agrees with the *Indian Sumbul* as described by Pereira.[2]

ASAFŒTIDA.

Gummi-resina Asafœtida vel Assafœtida; Asafœtida; F. *Asafœtida;* G. *Asant, Stinkasant.*

Botanical Origin—Two perennial umbelliferous plants are now generally cited as the source of this drug; but though they are both capable of affording a gum-resin of strong alliaceous odour, it has not been proved that either of them furnishes the asafœtida of commerce. The plants in question are:—

1. *Ferula Narthex* Boiss. (*Narthex-Asafœtida* Falconer), a gigantic herbaceous plant, having a large root several inches in thickness, the crown of which is clothed with coarse bristly fibres; it has an erect stem attaining 10 feet in height, throwing out from near its base upwards a regular series of branches bearing compound umbels, each branch proceeding from the axil of a large sheathing inflated petiole, the upper of which are destitute of lamina. The radical leaves, 1½ feet long, are bipinnate with broadly ligulate obtuse lobes. It has a large flat fruit with winged margin. When wounded, the plant exudes a milky juice having a powerful smell of asafœtida. It commences to grow in early spring, rapidly throwing up its foliage, which dies away at the beginning of summer. It does not flower till the root has acquired a considerable size and is several years old.

F. Narthex, which now exists in several botanic gardens and has flowered twice in that of Edinburgh, was discovered by Falconer in 1838, in the valley of Astor or Hasora (35° N. lat., 74°·30 E. long, north of Kashmir.[3]

2. *Ferula Scorodosma* Bentham et Hooker (*Scorodosma fœtidum* Bunge; *Ferula Assa fœtida* L. in Boissier, Flora orientalis ii. 994)—In form of leaf, in the bristly summit of the root, and in general aspect, this plant resembles the preceding; but it has the stem (5 to 7 feet high) nearly naked, with the umbels, which are very numerous, collected at the summit; and the few stem-leaves have not the voluminous sheathing petioles that are so striking a feature in *Narthex.* In *Narthex,* the vittæ of the fruit are conspicuous,—in *Scorodosma* almost obsolete; but the development of these organs in feruloid plants varies considerably, and has been rejected by Bentham and Hooker as affording no important distinctive character. *Scorodosma* is apparently more pubescent than *Narthex.*

[1] *Pharm. Journ.* vi. (1875) 321.

[2] Elements of *Mat. Med.* ii. p. 2 (1857) 208; also Bentley, *Pharm. Journ.* ix. (1878) 479.

[3] We refrain from citing localities in Tibet, Beluchistan and Persia, where plants supposed to agree with that of Falconer have been found by other collectors.

F. Scorodosma was discovered by Lehmann in 1841, in the sandy deserts eastwards of the Sea of Aral, and also on the hills of the Karatagh range south of the river Zarafshan,—that is to say, south-east of Samarkand. In 1858-59, it was observed by Bunge about Herat. At nearly the same period, it was afresh collected between the Caspian and Sea of Aral, and in the country lying eastward of the latter, by Borszczow, a Russian botanist, who has made it the subject of an elaborate and valuable memoir.[1]

The most detailed account of the asafœtida plant we possess is that of the German traveller Engelbert Kämpfer, who in 1687 observed it in the Persian province of Laristán, between the river Shúr and the town of Kongún, also in the neighbourhood of the town of Dusgan or Disgun, in which latter locality[2] alone he saw the gum-resin collected. He states that he found the plant also growing near Herat. Kämpfer has given figures of his plant which he calls *Asa fœtida Disgunensis*, and his specimens consisting of remnants of leaves, a couple of mericarps (in a bad state) and a piece of the stem a few inches long, are still preserved in the British Museum.

These materials have been the subject of much study, in order to determine which of the asafœtida plants of modern botanists should be identified with that of Kämpfer. Falconer and Borszczow have arrived in turns at the conclusion that his own plant accords with Kämpfer's. But Kämpfer's figures agree well neither with *Narthex* nor with *Scorodosma*. The plant they represent does not form, it would seem, the branching pyramid of the *Narthex* (as it flowered at Edinburgh), nor has it the multitude of umbels seen in Borszczow's figure of *Scorodosma*.[3]

Whether Kämpfer's plant is really identical with either of those we have noticed, and whether the discrepancies observable are due to careless drawing, or to actual difference, are points that cannot be settled without the examination of more ample specimens.

Great allowance must be made for the period of growth at which these plants have been observed. Kämpfer saw his plant when quite mature, and not when its stem was young and flowering. *Narthex* is scarcely known except from specimens grown at Edinburgh, those obtained by Falconer in Tibet having been gathered when dry and withered. Even Borszczow's plant appears never to have been seen by any botanist while its flower-stem was in a growing state.

History—Whether the substance which the ancients called *Laser* was the same as the modern *Aasafœtida*, is a question that has been often discussed during the last three hundred years, and it is one upon which we shall attempt to offer no further evidence. Suffice it to say that *Laser* is mentioned along with products of India and Persia, among the articles on which duty was levied at the Roman custom house of Alexandria in the 2nd century.

"*Hingu*," doubtless meaning Asafœtida, occurs in many Sanskrit works, especially in epic poetry, but also in Susruta.

[1] *Die Pharmaceutisch-wichtigen Ferulaceen der Aralo-Caspischen Wüste*, St. Petersb. 1860, pp. 40, eight plates.—In the *Medicinal plants* of Bentley and Trimen, Narthex is figured in part 29 and Scorodosma in part 24.

[2] Which we cannot find on any map.

[3] Kämpfer figures his plant with about 6 umbels on a stalk, while *Scorodosma*, as represented by Borszczow, has at least 25.

Asafœtida was certainly known to the Arabian and Persian geographers and travellers of the middle ages. One of these, Ali Istakhri, a native of Istakir, the ancient Persepolis, who lived in the 10th century, states[1] that it produced abundantly in the desert between Sistan and Makran, and is much used by the people as a condiment. The region in question comprises a portion of Beluchistan.

The geographer Edrisi,[2] who wrote about the middle of the 12th century, asserts that asafœtida, called in Arabic *Hiltit*, is collected largely in a district of Afghanistan near Kaleh Bust, at the junction of the Helmand with the Arghundab, a locality still producing the drug. Other Arabian writers as quoted by Ibn Baytar,[3] describe asafœtida in terms which show it to have been well known and much valued.

Matthæus Platearius, who flourished in the second half of the 12th century, mentions asafœtida in his work on simple medicines, known as *Circa instans*, which was held in great esteem during the middle ages. It is also named a little later by Otho of Cremona,[4] who remarks that the more fœtid the drug, the better its quality. Like other productions of the East, asafœtida found its way in European commerce during the middle ages through the trading cities of Italy. It is worthy of remark that it is much less frequently mentioned by the older writers than galbanum, sagapenum and opopanax. In the 13th century, the "Physicians of Myddfai," in Wales,[5] considered asafœtida as one of the substances which every physician "ought to know and use."

Collection—The collecting of asafœtida on the mountains about Dusgun in Laristan in Persia, as described by Kämpfer,[6] is performed thus:—

The peasants repair to the localities where the plants abound, about the middle of April, at which time the latter have ceased growing, and their leaves begin to show signs of withering. The soil surrounding the plant is removed to the depth of a span, so as to bare a portion of the root. The leaves are then pulled off, the soil is replaced, and over it are laid the leaves and other herbage, with a stone to keep them in place, the whole being arranged in this way to prevent injury to the root by the heat of the sun.

About forty days later, that is towards the end of May, the people return, the men being armed with knives for cutting the root, and broad iron spatulas for collecting the exuded juice. Having first removed the leaves and earth, a thinnish slice is taken from the fibrous crown of the root, and two days later the juice is scraped from the flat cut surface. The root is again sheltered, care being taken that nothing rests on it. This operation is repeated twice in the course of the next few days, a very thin slice being removed from the root after each scraping. The product got during the first cutting is called *shīr*, i.e. *milk*, and is thinner and more milky and less esteemed than that obtained afterwards. It is not sold in its natural state, but is mixed with soft earth

[1] *Buch der Länder*, translated by Mordtmann, Hamburg, 1845. 111.

[2] *Géographie d'Edrisi*, traduite par Jaubert, i. (1836) 450.

[3] Sontheimer's transl. i. (1840) 84.

[4] Choulant, *Macer Floridus*, Lips. 1832. 159.

[5] *Meddygon Myddfai*. 282. 457 (see bibliographical notices at the end).

[6] *Amœnitates Exoticæ*, Lemgoviæ, 1712. 535-552.

(*terra limosa*) which is added to the extent of an equal, or even double, weight of the gum-resin, according to the softness of the latter.

After the last cutting, the roots are allowed to rest 8 or 10 days, when a thicker exudation called *pispaz*, more esteemed than the first, is obtained by a similar process carried on at intervals during June and July, or even latter, until the root is quite exhausted.

The only recent account of the production of asafœtida that we have met with, is that of Staff-surgeon H. W. Bellew, who witnessed the collection of the drug in 1857 in the neighbourhood of Kandahar.[1] The frail withered stem of the previous year with the cluster of newly-sprouted leaves, is cut away from the top of the root, around which a trench of 6 inches wide and as many deep, is dug in the earth. Several deep incisions are now made in the upper part of the root, and this operation is repeated every 3 or 4 days as the sap continues to exude, which goes on for a week or two according to the strength of the plant. The juice collects in tears about the top of the root, or when very abundant flows into the hollow around it. In all cases as soon as incisions are made, the root is covered with a bundle of loose twigs or herbs, or even with a heap of stones, to protect it from the drying effects of the sun. The quantity of gum-resin obtained is variable; some roots yield scarcely half an ounce, others as much as two pounds. Some of the roots are no larger than a carrot, others attain the thickness of a man's leg. The drug is said to be mostly adulterated before it leaves the country, by admixture of powdered gypsum or flour. The finest sort, which is generally sold pure, is obtained solely "from the node or leaf-bud in the centre of the root-head." At Kandahar, the price of this superior drug is equivalent to from 2*s*. 8*d*. to 4*s*. 8*d*. per ℔., while the ordinary sort is worth but from 1*s*. to 2*s*.

During a journey from North-western India to Teheran in Persia, through Beluchistan and Afghanistan, performed in the spring of 1872, the same traveller observed the asafœtida plant in great abundance on many of the elevated undulating pasture-covered plains and hills of Afghanistan, and of the Persian province of Khorassan. He states that the plant is of two kinds, the one called *Kamá-i-gawí* which is grazed by cattle and used as a potherb, and the other known as *Kamá-i-angúza* which affords the gum-resin of commerce. The collecting of this last is almost exclusively in the hands of the western people of the Kákarr tribe, one of the most numerous and powerful of the Afghan clans, who, when thus occupied, spread their camps over the plains of Kandahar to the confines of Herat.[2]

Wood, in his journey to the source of the Oxus, found asafœtida to be largely produced in a district to the north of this, namely the mountains around Saigan or Sykan (lat. 35° 10, long. 67° 40), where, says he, the land affording the plant is as regularly apportioned out and as carefully guarded as the cornfields on the plain.[3]

Description—The best asafœtida is that consisting chiefly of slightly or not agglutinated tears. This is the *Kandahari-Hing* of the

[1] *Journal of a Mission to Afghanistan*, Lond. 1862. 270

[2] Bellew, *From the Indus to the Tigris*, London. 1874. 101. 102. 286. 321. &c.

[3] Wood, *Journey to the Source of the River Oxus*, new ed. 1872, 131.

Bombay market, which is not always to be met with in Bombay, and even there is only used by wealthy people as a condiment. It is not exported to Europe. The best sort shipped to Europe is the *Anguzeh-i-Lari*, coming from Laristan by way of Afghanistan and the Bolan Pass to Bombay. It shows agglutinated tears, or when freshly imported, it forms a clammy yet hard yellowish-grey mass, in which opaque, white or yellowish milky tears, sometimes an inch or two long, are more or less abundant.

Sometimes asafœtida is imported as a fluid honey-like mass, apparently pure. We presume that such is that of the first gathering, which Kämpfer says is called *milk*. The drug is often adulterated with earthy matter which renders it very ponderous; it must be granted that an addition of such matters may often be necessary in order to enable the drug to be transported. This earthy or stony asafœtida constitutes at Bombay a distinct article of commerce under the name of *Hingra*.

By exposure to air, asafœtida acquires a bright pink and then a brown hue. The perfectly pure tears display when fractured a conchoidal surface, which changes from milky white to purplish pink in the course of some hours. If a tear is touched with nitric acid sp. gr. 1·2, it assumes for a short time a fine green colour.

When asafœtida is rubbed in a mortar with oil of vitriol, then diluted with water and neutralized, the slightly coloured solution exhibits a bluish fluorescence. The same will be observed, to some extent, if tears of the drug are immersed in water and a little ammonia is added. The tears of asafœtida when warmed become adhesive, but by cold are rendered so brittle that they may be powdered. With water they easily form a white emulsion.

The drug has a powerful and persistent alliaceous odour and a bitter acrid alliaceous taste.

Chemical Composition—Asafœtida consists of resin, gum and essential oil, in varying proportions, but the resin generally amounting to more than one half.

As to the oil, we have repeatedly obtained from 6 to 9 per cent. by distilling it from common copper stills. It is light yellow, has a repulsive, very pungent odour of asafœtida, tastes at first mild, then irritating, but does not stimulate like oil of mustard when applied to the skin. It is neutral, but after exposure to the air acquires an acid reaction and different odour; it evolves sulphuretted hydrogen. In the fresh state, the oil is free from oxygen; it begins to boil at 135° to 140° C., but with continued evolution of hydrogen sulphide, so that we did not succeed in preparing it of constant composition, the amount of sulphur varying from 20 to 25 per cent. We found it to have a sp. gr. of 0·951 at 25°, and a strong dextrogyrate power. If one drop of it is allowed to float on water it assumes a fine violet hue by vapours of bromine.

The essential oil of asafœtida submitted to fractional distillation yielded us, at 300°, a considerable proportion of a most *beautifully blue coloured* oil. By very cautiously oxidizing the crude oil, we obtained a small amount of extremely deliquescent crystals of a sulphonic acid. Sodium or potassium decomposes the oil with evolution of gas, forming potassium sulphide; the residual oil is found to have the odour of cinnamon.

The resin of asafœtida is not wholly soluble in ether or in chloroform, but dissolves with decomposition in warm concentrated nitric acid. It contains a little *Ferulaic Acid*, $C^6H^3\begin{pmatrix}OCH^3\\OH\end{pmatrix}CH.CH.COOH$, discovered by Hlasiwetz and Barth in 1866, crystallizing in iridescent needles soluble in boiling water; it is homologous with *Eugetic Acid*, $C^6H^2\begin{pmatrix}OCH^3\\OH\end{pmatrix}\begin{matrix}COOH\\CH.CH.CH^3\end{matrix}$, which is to be obtained by adding CO^2 to the molecule of eugenol (page. 284).

Ferulaic acid may be obtained from vanillin, $C^6H^3\begin{cases}OCH^3\\OH\\CHO\end{cases}$ (see article Vanilla).

Fused with potash, ferulaic acid yields oxalic and carbonic acids, several acids of the fatty series, and protocatechuic acid. The resin itself treated in like manner after it has been previously freed from gum, yields resorcin; and by dry distillation, oils of a green, blue, violet or red tint, besides about ½ per cent. of *Umbelliferone*, $C^9H^6O^3$.

The mucilaginous matter of asafœtida consists of a smaller part soluble in water and an insoluble portion. The former yields a neutral solution which is not precipitated by neutral acetate of lead. The insoluble part is readily dissolved by caustic lye and again separates on addition of acids.

Commerce—The drug is at the present day produced exclusively in Afghanistan. Much of it is shipped in the Persian Gulf for Bombay, whence it is conveyed to Europe; it is also brought into India by way of Peshawur, and by the Bolan pass in Beluchistan.

In the year 1872–73, there were imported into Bombay by sea, chiefly from the Persian Gulf, 3367 cwt. of asafœtida, and 4780 cwt. of the impure form of the drug called *Hingra*. The value of the latter is scarcely a fifth that of the genuine kind. The export of asafœtida from Bombay to Europe is very small in comparison with the shipments to other ports of India.

Uses—Asafœtida is reputed stimulant and antispasmodic. It is in great demand on the Continent, but is little employed in Great Britain. Among the Mahommedan as well as Hindu population of India, it is generally used as a condiment, and is eaten especially with the various pulses known as *dāl*. In regions where the plant grows, the fresh leaves are cooked as an article of diet.

Adulteration—The systematic adulteration, chiefly with earthy matter already pointed out, may be estimated by exhausting the drug with alcohol and incinerating the residue.

Allied Substances.

Hing from Abushahir, also in Bombay simply called *Hing*.

Among the natives of Bombay, a peculiar form of asafœtida is in use that commands a much higher price than those just described; it is also the only kind admitted there in the government sanitary establishments. This is the *Abushaheree Hing*, imported from Abushir (Bender Bushehr) and Bender Abassi on the Persian Gulf. It is the product of *Ferula alliacea* Boiss.[1] (*F. Asafœtida* Boiss. et Buhse, non Linn.) discovered in 1850 by Buhse, and observed in 1858–59 by Bunge in many places in Persia. This Hing is collected near Yezd in Khorassan, and also in the province of Kerman, the plant being known as *angúza*, the same name that is applied to *Scorodosma*.

Abushaheree Hing is never brought into European trade.[2] It forms an almost blackish brown, originally *translucent*, brittle mass, of extremely fœtid alliaceous odour, containing many pieces of the stem with no admixture of earth. Guibourt, by whom it was first noticed,[3] was convinced that it had not been obtained from the root, but had been *cut from the stem*. He remarks that Theophrastus alludes to asafœtida (as he terms the *Silphium*[4] of this author) as being of two kinds,—the one of the stem, the other of the root; and thinks the former may be the sort under notice. Vigier,[5] who calls it *Asafœtida nauséeux*, found it to contain in 100 parts, of resin and essential oil 37·5, and gum 23·7.

We find the odour of the Hing much more repulsive than that of common Asafœtida. The former yields an abundance of essential oil, which differs by its reddish hue from that of asafœtida. The oil of Hing, as distilled by one of us (1877) has also a higher specific gravity, namely, 1·02 at 25° C. We find also its rotatory power stronger; it deviated 38°·8 to the right, when examined in a column of 100 millimetres in length. The oil of common asafœtida deviated 13°·5 under the same conditions.

By gently warming the Abushaheree Hing with concentrated hydrochloric acid, about 1·12 sp. gr., it displays simply a dingy brown hue. By shaking it with water and a little ammonia no fluorescence is produced. In all these respects there is consequently a well-marked difference between the drug under examination and common asafœtida.

F. teterrima Kar. et Kir., a plant of Soungaria, is likewise remarkable for its intense alliaceous smell; but the plant is not known as the source of any commercial product.[6]

GALBANUM.

Gummi-resina Galbanum; Galbanum; F. *Galbanum;* G. *Mutterharz.*

Botanical Origin—The uncertainty that exists as to the plants which furnish asafœtida, hangs over those which produce the nearly allied drug *Galbanum*. Judging from the characters of the latter, it can scarcely be doubted that it is yielded by umbelliferous plants of at least two species, which are probably the following:[7]—

[1] *Flora Orientalis*, ii. (1872) 995.

[2] A large specimen of it was kindly presented to one of us (H.) by Mr. D. S. Kemp of Bombay. We have also examined the same drug in the Indian Museum, and further received good specimens by the kindness of Professor Dymock. See his notes *Pharm. Journ.* v. (1875) 103, and viii. (1877) 103.

[3] *Hist. des Drogues*, iii. (1850) 223.

[4] *Hist. Plantarum*, l. vi. c. 3.

[5] *Gommes-résines des Ombellifères* (thèse), Paris, 1869. 32.

[6] Borszczow, *op. cit.* 13-14.

[7] The following in addition have at various times been supposed to afford galbanum:—*Ferulago galbanifera* Koch, a native of the Mediterranean region and Southern Russia; *Opoidia galbanifera* Lindl., a Persian plant of doubtful genus; *Bubon Galbanum* L., a shrubby umbellifer of South Africa.

1. *Ferula galbaniflua* Boiss. et Buhse,[1]—a plant with a tall, solid stem, 4 to 5 feet high, greyish, tomentose leaves, and thin flat fruits, 5 to 6 lines long, 2 to 3 broad, discovered in 1848 at the foot of Demawend in Northern Persia, and on the slopes of the same mountain at 4,000 to 8,000 feet, also on the mountains near Kushkäk and Churchurä (Jajarúd?). Bunge collected the same plant at Subzawar. Buhse says that the inhabitants of the district of Demawend collect the gum resin of this plant which is *Galbanum*; the tears which exude spontaneously from the stem, especially on its lower part and about the bases of the leaves, are at first milk-white, but become yellow by exposure to light and air. It is not the practice, so far as he observed, to wound the plant for the purpose of causing the juice to exude more freely, nor is the gathering of the gum in this district any special object of industry.[2] The plant is called in Persian *Khassuih*, and the Mazanderan dialect *Boridsheh*.

2. *F. rubricaulis* Boiss.[3] (*F. erubescens* Boiss. ex parte, Aucher *exsicc.* n. 4614, Kotschy n. 666).—This plant was collected by Kotschy in gorges of the Kuh Dinar range in Southern Persia, and probably by Aucher-Eloy on the mountain of Dalmkuh in Northern Persia. Borszczow,[4] who regards it as the same as the preceding (though Boissier[5] places it in a different section of the genus), says, on the authority of Buhse, that it occurs locally throughout the whole of Northern Persia, is found in plenty on the slopes of Elwund near Hamadan, here and there on the edge of the great central salt-desert of Persia, on the mountains near Subzawar, between Ghurian and Kháf, west of Herat, and on the desert plateau west of Kháf. He states, though not from personal observation, that its gum-resin, which constitutes *Persian Galbanum*, is collected for commercial purposes around Hamadan. *F. rubricaulis* Boiss. has been beautifully figured by Berg[6] under the name of *F. erubescens*.

History—Galbanum, in Hebrew *Chelbenah*, was an ingredient of the incense used in the worship of the ancient Israelites,[7] and is mentioned by the earliest writers on medicine as Hippocrates and Theophrastus.[8] Dioscorides states it to be the juice of a *Narthex* growing in Syria, and describes its characters, and the method of purifying it by hot water exactly as followed in modern times. We find it mentioned in the 2nd century among the drugs on which duty was levied at the Roman custom house at Alexandria.[9] Under the name of *Kinnah* it was well known to the Arabians, and through them to the physicians of the school of Salerno.

In the journal of expenses of John, king of France, during his captivity in England, A.D. 1359-60, there is an entry for the purchase of 1 lb.

[1] *Aufzählung der in einer Reise durch Transkaukasien und Persien gesammelten Pflanzen.—Nouv. Mém. de la Soc. imp. des Nat. de Moscou*, xii. (1860) 99.—Fig. in Bentley and Trimen, *Med. Plants*, part 16.

[2] Buhse, *l.c.*; also *Bulletin de la Soc. imp. des Nat. de Moscou*, xxiii. (1850) 548.

[3] *Diagnoses Plantarum novarum præsertim orientalium*, ser. ii. fasc. 2 (1856) 92.

[4] *Op. cit.* 36 (see p. 315, note 1).

[5] *Flora Orientalis*, ii. (1872) 995.

[6] Berg u. Schmidt, *Offizinelle Gewächse*, iv. (1863) tab. 31 *b*.

[7] Exodus xxx. 34.—*Jes. Sirach* xxiv. 18. —In imitation of the ancient Jewish custom, Galbanum is a component of the incense used in the Irvingite chapels in London.

[8] Χαλβάνη—Theophr. *Hist. Plant.* ix. c. 1.

[9] Vincent, *Commerce of the Ancients*, ii. (1807 692.

of Galbanum which cost 16*s*., 1 lb. of Sagapenum (*Serapin*) at the same time costing only 2*s*.[1] In common with other products of the East, these drugs used to reach England by way of Venice, and are mentioned among the exports of that city to London in 1503.[2]

An edict of Henry III. of France promulgated in 1581, gives the prices per lb. of the gum resins of the *Umbelliferæ* as follows :—Opopanax, 32 sols, Sagapenum 22 sols, Asafœtida 15 sols, Galbanum 10 sols, Ammoniacum 6 sols 6 deniers.[3]

Description—Galbanum is met with in drops or tears, adhering *inter se* into a mass, usually compact and hard, but sometimes found so soft as to be fluid The tears are of the size of a lentil to that of a hazel-nut, translucent, and of various shades of light brown, yellowish or faintly greenish. The drug has a peculiar, not unpleasant, aromatic odour, and a disagreeable, bitter, alliaceous taste.

In one variety, the tears are dull and waxy, of a light yellowish tint when fresh, but becoming of an orange brown by keeping; they are but little disposed to run together, and are sometimes quite dry and loose, with an odour that somewhat reminds one of savine. In recent importations of this form of galbanum, we have noticed a considerable admixture of thin transverse slices of the root of the plant, an inch or more in diameter.

Chemical Composition—Galbanum contains volatile oil, resin and mucilage. The first, of which 7 per cent. may be obtained by distillation with water, is a colourless or slightly yellowish liquid, partly consisting of a hydrocarbon, $C^{10}H^{16}$, boiling at from 170° to 180°. This oil affords easily crystals of terpin, $C^{10}H^{16}+3\,OH^2$, if it is treated as mentioned in the article Oleum Cajuputi; it also affords the crystallized compound $C^{10}H^{16}+HCl$. But the prevailing part of oil of galbanum consists of hydrocarbons of a much higher boiling point. The crude oil has a mild aromatic taste, and deviates the ray of polarized light to the right.

The resin, which we find to constitute about 60 per cent. of the drug, is very soft, and dissolves in ether or in alkaline liquids, even in milk of lime, but only partially in bisulphide of carbon. When heated for some time at 100° C. with hydrochloric acid, it yields *Umbelliferone*, $C^9H^6O^3$, which may be dissolved from the acid liquid by means of ether or chloroform; it is obtained on evaporation in colourless acicular crystals. Umbelliferone is soluble in hot water; its solution exhibits, especially on addition of an alkali, a brilliant blue fluorescence which is destroyed by an acid. If a small fragment of galbanum is immersed in water, the fluorescence is immediately produced by a drop of ammonia.[4] The same phenomenon takes place with asafœtida, not at all with ammoniacum; it is probably due to traces of umbelliferone pre-existing in the former drugs. By boiling the umbel-

[1] Douët d'Arcq, *Comptes de l'Argenterie des Rois de France* (1851) 236.—The prices must be multiplied by 3 to give a notion of present value.

[2] Pasi, *Tariffa de Pesi e Misure*, Venet. 1521. 204 (1st edition, 1503).

[3] Fontanon, *Edicts et Ordonnances des Rois de France*, ii. (1585) 388.

[4] This property of umbelliferone may be beautifully shown by dipping some bibulous paper into water which has stood for an hour or two on lumps of galbanum, and drying it. A strip of this paper placed in a test tube of water with a drop of ammonia, will give a superb blue solution, instantly losing its colour on the addition of a drop of hydrochloric acid.

liferone with concentrated caustic lye, it splits up into resorcin, carbonic acid and formic acid.

Umbelliferone is also produced from many other aromatic umbelliferous plants, as *Angelica, Levisticum* and *Meum*, when their respective resins are submitted to dry distillation. According to Zwenger (1860) it may be likewise obtained from the resin of *Daphne Mezereum* L. The yield is always small; it is highest in galbanum, but even in this does not much exceed 0·8 per cent. reckoned on the crude drug.

By submitting galbanum-resin to dry distillation, there will be obtained a thick oil of an intense and brilliant blue,[1] which was noticed as early as about the year 1730 by Caspar Neumann of Berlin. It is a liquid having an aromatic odour and a bitter acrid taste; in cold it deposits crystals of umbelliferone, which can be extracted by repeatedly shaking the oil with boiling water. A small amount of fatty acids is also removed at the same time. Submitted to rectification the crude oil at first yields a greenish portion and then the superb blue oil. Kachler (1871) found that it could be resolved by fractional distillation into a colourless oil having the formula $C^{10}H^{16}$, and a blue oil to which he assigned the composition $C^{10}H^{16}O$, boiling at 289° C. As to the hydrocarbon, it boils at 240° C., and therefore differs from the essential oil obtained when galbanum is distilled with water. The blue oil, after due purification, agrees, according to Kachler, with the blue oil of the flowers of *Matricaria Chamomilla* L. Each may be transformed by means of potassium into a colourless hydrocarbon, $C^{10}H^{16}$; or by anhydride of phosphoric acid into another product, $C^{10}H^{14}$, likewise colourless. The latter, as well as the former hydrocarbon, if diluted with ether, and bromine be added, assumes for a moment a fine blue tint; the colourless oil as afforded by the drug on distillation with water assumes also the same coloration with bromine.

By fusing galbanum-resin with potash, Hlasiwetz and Barth (1864) obtained crystals (about 6 per cent.) of *Resorcin* or *Meta-Dioxybenzol*, together with acetic and volatile fatty acids. The name of this remarkable substance alludes to Orcin, which had been extracted in 1829 by Robiquet from lichens. The formula of Resorcin, $C^6H^4(OH)^2$, shows at once its relations to Orcin, $C^6H^3CH^3(OH)^2$. Resorcin has been ascertained to be frequently produced by melting other resins with potash; it has also been prepared on a large scale for the manufacture of the brilliant colouring matter called *Eosin*. Galbanum-resin treated with nitric acid yields Trinitroresorcin $C^6H(NO^2)^3(OH)^2$, the so-called *Styphnic Acid*.

If galbanum, or still better its resin, is very moderately warmed with concentrated hydrochloric acid, a red hue is developed, which turns violet or bluish if spirit of wine is slowly added. Asafœtida treated in the same way assumes a dingy greenish colour, and *ammoniacum is not altered* at all. This test probably depends upon the formation of resorcin, which in itself is not coloured by hydrochloric acid, but assumes a red or blue colour if sugar or mucilage or certain other substances are present. It is remarkable that ammoniacum, though likewise yielding resorcin when fused with potash, assumes no

[1] We have found it best to mix the galbanum-resin with coarsely powdered pumice-stone; the oil is then easily and abundantly obtainable.

red colour when warmed with hydrochloric acid. The mucilage of galbanum has not been minutely examined.

Commerce—Galbanum is, we believe, brought into commerce chiefly from Eastern Europe. It is stated that considerable quantities reach Russia by way of Astrachan and Orenburg.

Uses—Galbanum is administered internally as a stimulating expectorant, and is occasionally applied in the form of plaster to indolent swellings.

Allied Substances.

Sagapenum—This is a gum-resin which, when pure, forms a tough softish mass of closely agglutinated tears. It differs from asafœtida in forming brownish (not milk-white) tears, which when broken do not acquire a pink tint; also in not having an alliaceous odour. A good specimen presented to us by Professor Dymock of Bombay (1878) reminds in that and other respects rather of galbanum. We find this sagapenum to be devoid of sulphur but containing umbelliferone; it is extremely remarkable for the intense and permanent purely blue colour it acquires in cold when the smallest fragment of the drug is immersed in hydrochloric acid 1·13 sp. gr.

Sagapenum, which in mediæval pharmacy was often called *Serapinum*, is so frequently mentioned by the older writers that it must have been a plentiful substance. At the present day it can scarcely be procured genuine even at Bombay, whither it is sometimes brought from Persia. The botanical origin of the drug is unknown.

AMMONIACUM.

Gummi-resina Ammoniacum; Ammoniacum or Gum Ammoniacum; F. *Gomme-résine Ammoniaque;* G. *Ammoniak-gummiharz.*

Botanical Origin.—*Dorema Ammoniacum*, Don, a perennial plant,[1] with a stout, erect, leafless flower-stem, 6 to 8 feet high, dividing towards its upper part into numerous ascending branches, along which are disposed on thick short stalks, ball-like simple umbels, scarcely half an inch across, of very small flowers. The aspect of the full-grown plant is therefore very unlike that of *Ferula*. The *Dorema* has large compound leaves with broad lobes. The whole plant in its young state is covered with a tomentum of soft, stellate hairs, which give it a greyish look, but which disappear as it ripens its fruits. The withered stems long remain erect, and occurring in immense abundance and overtopping the other vegetation of the arid desert, having a striking appearance.[2] The root is described in the article on Sumbul, p. 313.

The plant occurs over a wide area of the barren regions of which Persia is the centre. According to Bunge and Bienert, its north-western limit appears to be Shahrud (S.E. of Asterabad), whence it extends eastwards to the deserts south of the Sea of Aral and the Sir-Daria. The most southern point at which the plant has been observed is Basiran, a village of Southern Khorassan in N. lat. 32°, E. long. 59°.

[1] Fig. in Bentley and Trimen, *Medic. Plants*, part 33 (1878).

[2] Fraser, *Journey into Khorasân*, 1825. 118; Polak, *Persien, das Land und seine Leute*, ii. (1865) 282.

Of the three or four other species of *Dorema*, *D. Aucheri* Boiss.[1] affords very good ammoniacum, as we know by an ample specimen of the gum deposited together with the plant in the British Museum by Mr. W. K. Loftus, who in 1751 collected both at Kirrind in Western Persia, where the plant is called in Kurdish *Zuh*. Boissier[2] includes as *D. Aucheri* another plant, called by Loftus *D. robustum*, the gum of which is certainly different from ammoniacum. Of the plant itself there are only *fruits* in the British Museum.

History—The first writer to mention ammoniacum is Dioscorides, who states it to be the juice of a *Narthex* growing about Cyrene in Libya, and that it is produced in the neighbourhood of the temple of Ammon. He says it is of two sorts, the one like frankincense in pure, solid tears, the other massive, and contaminated with earthy impurities. Pliny gives essentially the same account.

The succeeding Greek and Latin authors on medicine throw but little light on the drug, which however is mentioned by most of them as used in fumigation. Hence we find such terms as *Ammoniacum thymiama*,[3] *Ammoniacum suffimen*, *Thus Libycum*.

The African origin assigned to the drug by Dioscorides, has long perplexed pharmacologists; but it is now well ascertained that in Morocco a large species of *Ferula* yields a gum-resin having some resemblance to ammoniacum, and still an object of traffic with Egypt and Arabia, where it is employed, like the ancient drug, *in fumigations*. There can be but little doubt we think, that the ammoniacum of Morocco is identical with the ammoniacum of the ancients; it may well have been imported by way of Cyrene from regions lying further westward.[4]

Persian ammoniacum or the ammoniacum of European commerce may also have been known in very remote times, though we are unable to trace it back earlier than the 10th century, at which period it is mentioned by Isaac Judæus[5] and by the Persian physician Alhervi.[6] Both these writers designate it *Ushak*, a name which it bears in Persia to the present day.

Collection—The stem of the plant abounds in a milky juice which flows out on the slightest puncture. The agent which occasions the exudation is a beetle, multitudes of which pierce the stem. The gum, the drops of which speedily harden, partly remains adherent to the stem and partly falls to the ground; it is gathered about the end of July by the peasants, who sell it to dealers for conveyance to Ispahan or the coast.[7]

Young roots 3 to 4 years old are, according to Borszczow, extremely rich in milky juice which sometimes exudes into the surrounding soil in large drops; there is also an exudation from the fibrous crown of the root of a dark inferior sort of ammoniacum. The gum-resin appears to be collected in quantity only in Persia. One of the chief localities

[1] Fig. in Bentley and Trimen, part 4.

[2] *Flora Orientalis*, ii. (1872) 1009.

[3] Alexander Trallianus in *Puschmann's* edition (see appendix) 581. 588.

[4] Hanbury, *Pharm. Journ.* March 22, 1873. 741; or *Science Papers*, 375.

[5] *Opera Omnia*, Lugd. 1515, lib. ii. Practices c. 44.

[6] Seligmann, *Liber Fundamentorum Pharmacologiæ*, Vindob. 1830. 35.

[7] Johnson, *Journey from India to England through Persia*, etc., 1818. 93. 94; Hart, quoted by Don, *Linn. Trans.* xvi. (1833) 605.

for it are the desert plains about Yezdikhast, between Ispahan and Shiraz.

Description—Ammoniacum occurs in dry grains or tears of roundish form, from the size of a small pea to that of a cherry, or in nodular lumps. They are externally of a pale creamy yellow, opaque and milky-white within. By long keeping, the outer colour darkens to a cinnamon-brown. Ammoniacum is brittle, showing when broken a dull waxy lustre, but it easily softens with warmth. It has a bitter acrid taste, and a peculiar, characteristic, non-alliaceous odour. It readily forms a white emulsion when triturated with water. It is coloured yellow by caustic potash. Hypochlorites, as common bleaching powder, give it a bright orange hue, while they do not affect the Morocco drug.

Ammoniacum is obtained from the mature plant, the ripe mericarps of which, ⅜ of an inch in length, are often found sticking to the tears. By pressure the tears agglutinate into a compact mass, which is the *Lump Ammoniacum* of the druggists. It is generally less pure than the detached grains, and fetches a lower price.

Chemical Composition—Ammoniacum is a mixture of volatile oil with resin and gum. We obtained only ⅓ per cent. of oil which we find to be dextrogyrate; we failed in obtaining terpin (see Galbanum, p. 322) from it. The oil has the precise odour of the drug, contains, according to our experiments, no sulphur; a similar observation was made by Przeciszewski.[1] Vigier[2] asserts that it blackens silver, and that after oxidation with nitric acid, he detected in it sulphuric acid. He states that, with hydrochloric acid, the oil acquires a fine violet tint passing by all shades to black; we failed in obtaining this coloration. By diluting the oil with bisulphide of carbon, and then adding mineral acids, we observed only yellow colorations. The oil diluted with alcohol acquires a reddish hue by ferric chloride.

The resin ammoniacum usually amounts to about 70 per cent. Przeciszewski asserts that the indifferent resin when heated yields sulphuretted hydrogen. Our own experiments failed to show the presence of sulphur in the *crude* drug; and the same negative result has been more recently obtained in some careful experiments by Moss.[3] Water when boiled with the resin acquires a yellow hue and slightly acid reaction; the liquid assumes an intense red coloration on addition of ferric chloride.

Unlike the gum resin of allied plants, ammoniacum yields no umbelliferone. When melted with caustic potash it affords a little resorcin.

The mucilaginous matter of the drug consists of a gum readily soluble in water and a smaller quantity of about ¼ of an insoluble part, no doubt identical with that occurring in asafœtida and galbanum. The aqueous solution of the gum of ammoniacum is very slightly levogyre.

Commerce—Ammoniacum is shipped to Europe from the Persian Gulf by way of Bombay. The exports from the latter place in the year 1871–72 were 453 cwt., all shipped to the United Kingdom. The

[1] *Pharmakologische Untersuchungen über Ammoniacum, Sagapenum und Opopanax*, Dorpat, 1861.

[2] *Gommes-résines des Ombellifères* (Thèse), Paris, 1869. 93.

[3] *Pharm. Journ.* March 29, 1873. 761.

quantity imported into Bombay in 1872–73 was 1671 cwt., all from the Persian Gulf.[1]

Uses—The drug is administered as an expectorant and is also used in certain plasters.

Allied Gum-resins.

African Ammoniacum.—This is according to Lindley[2] the product of *Ferula tingitana* L., a species growing over all northern Africa as far as Syria, Rhodus and Chios. It is called *Kelth* in Morocco, its product, *Fasay*, being shipped occasionally at Mazagan (el Bridja) or also at Mogador. This gum-resin is in large, compact, dark masses, formed of agglutinated tears having a whitish or pale greenish, or a fawn colour. But there are also seen very impure masses. The weak odour of the Moroccan drug is not suggestive of true ammoniacum. Moss (1873) found in a specimen of the former 9 per cent. of gum and 67 per cent. of resin. It yielded umbelliferone to Hirschsohn (1875), and by melting it with potash Goldschmiedt (1878) obtained Resorcin and a peculiar acid, $C^{10}H^{10}O^6$, which he failed to obtain from true ammoniacum.

Opopanax.—A gum-resin occurring in hard, nodular, brittle, earthy-looking lumps of a bright orange-brown hue, and penetrating offensive odour, reminding one of crushed ivy-leaves. It is commonly attributed to *Opopanax Chironium* Koch, a native of Mediterranean Europe. We have never seen a specimen known to have been obtained from this plant; but can say that the gum-resin of the nearly allied *Opopanax persicum* Boiss., as collected by Loftus at Kirrind in Western Persia in 1851, has neither the appearance nor the characteristic odour of officinal opopanax. Powell,[3] who endeavoured to trace the origin of the drug, regards it as a product of Persia.

Opopanax was very common in old pharmacy, but has fallen out of use, and is now both rare and expensive.[4]

FRUCTUS ANETHI.

Semen Anethi; Dill Fruits, Dill Seeds; F. *Fruits d'Aneth;* G. *Dillfrüchte.*

Botanical Origin—*Anethum graveolens* L., (*Peucedanum*[5] *graveolens* Hiern) an erect, glaucous annual plant, with finely striated stems, usually to 1 to 1½ feet high, pinnate leaves with setaceous linear segments, and yellow flowers.

It is indigenous to the Mediterranean region, Southern Russia and the Caucasian provinces, but is found as a cornfield weed in many

[1] *Statement of the Trade and Navigation of the Presidency of Bombay*, 1871-72, and 1872-73.

[2] As stated by Pereira, *Mat. Medica*, ii. part 2 (1857) p. 186. See also Hanbury, *Science Papers*, 1876. 376.

[3] *Economic Products of the Punjab*, i. (1868) 402.

[4] Further particulars regarding Opopanax and Sagapenum, may be found in the theses of Przeciszewski (1861) and Vigier (1869), noticed in our article on Ammoniacum, and Dragendorff's *Jahresbericht*, 1875. 119. 120.

[5] Bentham and Hooker (*Gen. Plant.* 919) suppress the genus *Anethum*, uniting its one solitary species with *Peucedanum*.

other countries, and is frequently cultivated in gardens. It succeeds in Norway as far north as Throndhjem.

Dill, under the Hindustani name of *Suvā* or *Sōyah*, is largely grown in various ports of India, where the plant though of but a few months' duration, grows to a height of 2 to 3 feet. On account of a slight peculiarity in the fruit, the Indian plant was regarded by Roxburgh and De Candolle as a distinct species, and called *Anethum Sowa*, but it possesses no botanical characters to warrant its separation from *A. graveolens*.

History—Dill is commonly regarded to be the Ἄνηθον of Dioscorides, the *Anethum* of Palladius and other ancient writers, as well as of the New Testament.[1] In Greece the name Ἄνηθον is at present applied[2] to a plant of very similar appearance, *Carum Ridolfia* Benth. et Hook (*Anethum segetum* L.). By the later Greeks, the term Ἀνηθον was also used for dill.[3]

Dill, as well as coriander, fennel, cumin, and ammi, was in frequent requisition in Britain in Anglo-Saxon times.[4] The name is derived according to Prior[5] from the old Norse word *dilla, to lull*, in allusion to the reputed carminative properties of the drug. However this may be, we find the word occurring in the 10th century in the Vocabulary of Alfric, archbishop of Canterbury.[6] The words *dill* and *till*, undoubtedly meaning this drug, were also used in Germany and Switzerland as early as A.D. 1000.

Description—The fruit, which has the characters usual to *Umbelliferæ*, is of ovoid form, much compressed dorsally, surrounded with a broad flattened margin. The mericarps about $\frac{1}{10}$ of an inch wide, are mostly separate; they are provided with 5 equidistant, filiform ridges, of which the two lateral lose themselves in the paler, broad, thin margin. The three others are sharply keeled; the darkest space between them is occupied by a vitta and two occur on the commissure. In the Indian drug, the mericarps are narrower and more convex, the ridges more distinct and pale, and the border less winged. In other respects it accords with that of Europe. The odour and taste of dill are agreeably aromatic.

Microscopic Characters—The pericarp is formed of a small number of flattened cells, which in the inner layer are of a brown colour; the ridges consist as usual of a strong fibro-vascular bundle. The vittæ in a transverse section present an elliptic outline $\frac{1}{150}$ of an inch or less in diameter. The margin of the mericarp is built up of porous, parenchymatous tissue. The albumen as in the seeds of all umbellifers, consists of thick-walled, angular cells, loaded with fatty oil, and globular grains of albuminous matters which present a dark cross when examined by polarized light.

Chemical Composition—Dill fruit yields from 3 to 4 per cent. of

[1] Matt. xxiii. 23,—where it has been rendered *anise* by the English translators from Wicklif (1380) downwards. But in other versions, the word is correctly translated.

[2] Heldreich, *Nutzpflanzen Griechenlands* (1862) 40.

[3] Langkavel, *Botanik d. späteren Griechen*, Berlin, 1866. 39.

[4] *Leechdoms, &c.*, edited by Cockayne, 1864–66,—see especially *Herbarium Apuleii*, dating about A.D. 1050, in vol. i. pp. 219. 235. 237. 281. 293.

[5] *Popular Names of British Plants*, 1870.

[6] *Volume of Vocabularies*, edited by Wright, 1857. 30.

an essential oil, the largest proportion of which was found by Gladstone (1864-1872) to be a hydrocarbon, $C^{10}H^{16}$, to which he gave the name *Anethene*. This substance has a lemon-like odour, sp. gr. ·846, and boils at 172° C. It deviates a ray of polarized light strongly to the right. Nietzki (1874) ascertained that there is, moreover, present another hydrocarbon, $C^{10}H^{16}$, in a very small proportion, which boils at 155–160°. A third constituent of oil of dill is in all probability identical with carvol (see page 307); we prepared from the former immediately the crystals $(C^{10}H^{14}O)^2SH^2$.

Uses—The distilled water of dill is stomachic and carminative, and frequently prescribed as a vehicle for more active medicines. The seeds are much used for culinary and medicinal purposes by the people of India, but are little employed in Continental Europe.

FRUCTUS CORIANDRI.

Semen Coriandri; Coriander Fruits, Coriander Seeds, Corianders; F. *Fruits de Coriandre;* G. *Koriander.*

Botanical Origin—*Coriandrum sativum* L., a small glabrous, annual plant, apparently indigenous to the Mediterranean and Caucasian regions, not known growing wild, but now found as a cornfield weed throughout the temperate parts of the Old World. It is cultivated in many countries, and has thus found its way even to Paraguay. In England the cultivation of coriander has long been carried on, but only to a very limited extent.

History—Coriander appears to occur in the famous Egyptian papyrus Ebers; it is also mentioned, under the name of Kustumburu, in early Sanskrit authors, and is also met with in the Scriptures.[1]

The plant owes its names Κόριον, Κορίαννον, and Κοριάνδρον, or also in the middle ages, Κολιάνδρον, to the offensive odour it exhales when handled, and which reminds one of bugs,—in Greek Κόρις. This character caused it to be regarded in the middle ages as having poisonous properties.[2] The ripe fruits which are entirely free from the fœtid smell of the growing plant, were used as a spice by the Jews and the Romans, and in medicine from a very early period. Cato, who wrote on agriculture in the 3rd century B.C., notices the cultivation of coriander. Pliny states that the best is that of Egypt. It is of frequent occurrence in the book "De opsoniis et condimentis" of Apicius Cœlius, about the 3rd century of our era. Coriander is also included in the list of Charlemagne, alluded to pages 92, 98, etc.

Coriander was well known in Britain prior to the Norman Conquest, and often employed in ancient Welsh and English medicine and cookery.

Cultivation—Coriander, called by the farmers *Col*, is cultivated in the eastern counties of England, especially in Essex. It is sometimes sown with caraway, and being an annual is gathered and harvested the first year, the caraway remaining in the ground. The seedling plants are hoed so as to leave those that are to remain in rows 10 to 12 inches

[1] Exod. xvi. 31; Num. xi. 7.

[2] Petrus de Abbano, *Tract. de Venenis*, Venetiis, 1473. capp. 25. 46.

apart. The plant is cut with sickles, and when dry the seed is thrashed out on a cloth in the centre of the field. On the best land, 15 cwt. per acre is reckoned an average crop.[1]

Description—The fruit of coriander consists of a pair of hemispherical mericarps, firmly joined so as to form an almost regular globe, measuring on an average about $\frac{1}{8}$ of an inch in diameter, crowned by the stylopodium and calycinal teeth, and sometimes by the slender diverging styles. The pericarp bears on each half, 4 perfectly straight sharpish ridges, regarded as secondary (*juga secundaria*); two other ridges, often of darker colour, belonging to the mericarps in common, the separation of which takes place in a rather sinuous line. The shallow depression between each pair of these straight ridges is occupied by a zig-zag raised line (*jugum primarium*), of which there are therefore 5 in each mericarp. It will thus be seen that each mericarp has 5 (zig-zag) so-called *primary ridges*, and 4 (keeled and more prominent) *secondary*, besides the lateral ridges which mark the suture or line of separation. There are no vittæ on the outer surface of the pericarp. Of the 5 teeth of the calyx, 2 often grow into long, pointed, persistent lobes; they proceed from the outer flowers of the umbel.

Though the two mericarps are closely united, they adhere only by the thin pericarp, enclosing when ripe a lenticular cavity. On each side of this cavity, the skin of the fruit separates from that of the seed, displaying the two brown vittæ of each mericarp. In transverse section, the albumen appears crescent-shaped, the concave side being towards the cavity. The carpophore stands in the middle of the latter as a column, connected with the pericarp only at top and bottom.

Corianders are smooth and rather hard, in colour buff or light brown. They have a very mild aromatic taste, and, when crushed, a peculiar fragrant smell. When unripe, their odour, like that of the fresh plant, is offensive. The nature of the chemical change that occasions this alteration in odour has not been made out.

The Indian corianders shipped from Bombay are of large size and of elongated form.

Microscopic Structure—The structural peculiarities of coriander fruit chiefly refer to the pericarp. Its middle layer is made up of thick walled ligneous prosenchyme, traversed by a few fibro-vascular bundles which in the zig-zag ridges vary exceedingly in position.

Chemical Composition—The essential oil of coriander has a composition indicated by the formula $C^{10}H^{18}O$, and is therefore isomeric with borneol. If the elements of water are abstracted by phosphoric anhydride, it is converted, according to Kawalier (1852), into an oil of offensive odour, $C^{10}H^{16}$.

The fruits yield of volatile oil from 0·7 to 1·1 per cent.; as the vittæ are well protected by the woody pericarp, corianders should be bruised before being submitted to distillation. Trommsdorff (1835) found the fruits to afford 13 per cent. of fixed oil.

The fresh herb distilled in July when the fruits were far from ripe, yielded to one of us (F.) from 0·57 to 1·1 per mille of an essential oil possessing in a high degree the disagreeable odour already alluded to. This oil was found to deviate the ray of polarized light 1·1° to the right

[1] R. Baker, in Morton's *Cyclopædia of Agriculture*, i. (1855) 545.

when examined in a column 50 mm. long. The oil distilled by us from ripe commercial fruit deviated 5·1° to the right.

Production and Commerce—Coriander is cultivated in various parts of Continental Europe, and, as already stated, to a small extent in England. It is also produced in Northern Africa and in India. In 1872–73, the export of coriander from the province of Sind[1] was 948 cwt.; from Bombay[2] in the same year 619 cwt. From Calcutta[3] there were shipped in 1870–71, 16,347 cwt.

Uses—Coriander fruits are reputed stimulant and carminative, yet are but little employed in medicine. They are however used in veterinary practice, and by the distillers of gin, also in some countries in cookery.

FRUCTUS CUMINI.

Fructus vel Semen Cymini; Cumin or Cummin[4] *Fruits, Cummin Seeds;* F. *Graines de Cumin;* G. *Mutterkümmel, Kreuzkümmel, Langer oder Römischer Kümmel, Mohrenkümmel.*

Botanical Origin.—*Cuminum Cyminum* L., a small annual plant, indigenous to the upper regions of the Nile, but carried at an early period by cultivation to Arabia, India and China, as well as to the countries bordering the Mediterranean. The fruits of the plant ripen as far north as Southern Norway; but in Europe, Sicily and Malta alone produce them in quantity.

History—Cumin was well known to the ancients; it is alluded to by the Hebrew prophet Isaiah,[5] and is mentioned in the gospel of Matthew[6] as one of the minor titheable productions of the Holy Land. Under the name Κύμινον, it is commended for its agreeable taste by Dioscorides, in whose day it was produced on the coasts of Asia Minor and Southern Italy. It is named as *Cuminum* by Horace and Persius; Scribonius Largus, in the first century of our era, mentions Cuminum æthiopicum, silvaticum and thebaicum.

During the middle ages, cumin was one of the spices in most common use. Thus in A.D. 716, an annual provision of 150 ℔. of cumin for the monastery of Corbie in Normandy, was not thought too large a supply.[7] Edrisi mentioned cumin as a product of Morocco (see article Fructus Carui, p. 305), Algeria and Tunisia. It was in frequent use in England, its average price between 1264 and 1400 being a little over 2*d.* per ℔.[8] Cumin is enumerated in the *Liber albus*[9] of the city of London, compiled in 1419, among the merchandize on which the king levied the impost called *scavage.* It is mentioned[10] in 1453 as one of the articles

[1] *Statement of the Trade and Navigation of Sind for the year* 1872–73, Karachi, 1873. 36.

[2] Ditto for Bombay, 1872–73. ii. 90.

[3] *Annual Volume of Trade, etc. for the Bengal Presidency,* 1870–71. 121.

[4] *Comyne* in Wicklif's Bible (1380), *Commen* in Tyndale's (1534), *Commyn* in Cranmer's (1539), *Cummine* in the Authorised Version (1611), *Cumin* in Gerarde's *Herbal* (1636) and Paris's *Pharmacologia* (1822), *Cummin*, Ray (1693) and in modern trade-lists and price-currents.

[5] Ch. xxviii. 25–27.

[6] Ch. xxiii. 23.

[7] Pardessus, *Diplomata*, etc., Paris, 1849. ii. 309.

[8] Rogers, *Hist. of Agriculture and Prices in England*, 1876. i. 631, ii. 543–547.

[9] *Munimenta Gildhallæ Londoniensis*, edited by Riley, i. (1859) 224.

[10] Herbert, *Hist. of the Great Livery Companies of London*, 1834. 114.

of which the Grocers' Company had the weighing and oversight, and was classed in 1484 in the same way in the German warehouse in Venice.[1]

Description—The fruit, the colour of which is brown, has the usual structure of the order; it is of an elongated ovoid form, tapering towards each end, and somewhat laterally compressed. The mericarps, which do not readily separate from the carpophore, are about $\frac{1}{4}$ of an inch in length and $\frac{1}{10}$ of an inch in greatest breadth. Each has 5 primary ridges which are filiform, and scabrous or muriculate, and 4 secondary covered with rough hairs. Between the primary ridges is a single elongated vitta, and 2 vittæ occur on the commissural surface. A transverse section of the seed shows a reniform outline. There is a form of *C. Cyminum* in cultivation, the fruit of which is perfectly glabrous.

Cumin has a strong aromatic taste and smell, far less agreeable than that of caraway.

Microscopic Structure—The hairs are rather brittle, sometimes $\frac{1}{2}$ mm. in length, formed of cells springing from the epidermis. The larger consists of groups of cells, vertically or laterally combined, and enclosed by a common envelope; the smaller of but a single cell ending in a rounded point. The whole pericarp is rich in tannic matter, striking with salts of iron a dark greenish colour.

The tissue of the seed is loaded with colourless drops of a fatty oil; the vittæ with a yellowish-brown essential oil. But the most striking contents of the parenchyme of the albumen consist of transparent, colourless, spherical grains, 7 to 5 mkm. in diameter, several of which are enclosed in each cell. Under a high magnifying power, they show a central cavity with a series of concentric layers around it, frequently traversed by radial clefts. Examined in polarized light, these grains display exactly the same cross as is seen in granules of starch, although their behaviour with chemical tests at once proves that they are by no means that substance; in fact iodine does not render them blue, but intensely brown. Grains of the same character, assuming sometimes a crystalloid form, occur in most umbelliferous fruits, and in many seeds of other orders. All these bodies are composed of albuminous and fatty matters; the more crystalloid form as met with in the seeds of *Ricinus* and in the fruit of parsley, is the body called by Hartig *Aleuron.*

Chemical Composition—Cumin fruits yielded to Bley (1829) 7 per cent. of fat oil, 13 per cent. of resin (?), 8 of mucilage and gum, 15 of albuminous matter, and a large amount of malates. Their peculiar, strong, aromatic smell and taste, depend on the essential oil of which they afford as much as 4 per cent. It contains about 56 per cent. of *Cuminol* (or *Cuminaldehyde*), $C^6H^4\left\{\begin{matrix}CHO\\C^3H^7\end{matrix}\right.$, a liquid of sp. gr. 0·972, boiling point 237° C. It has also been met with, in 1858, by Trapp in the oil of Cicuta virosa. By boiling cuminol with potash in alcoholic solution, cuminalcohol, $C^6H^4\left\{\begin{matrix}CH^2OH\\C^3H^7\end{matrix}\right.$, as well as the potassium salt of cuminic acid, $C^6H^4\left\{\begin{matrix}COOH\\C^3H^7\end{matrix}\right.$, are formed.

[1] Thomas, *Fontego dei Todeschi in Venezia*, 1874. 252.

The oil of cumin, secondly, contains a mixture of hydrocarbons. That which constitutes about one half of the crude oil has been first obtained in 1841 by Gerhardt and Cahours, just from the oil under notice, and therefore called *Cymene* (or also *Cymol*). It is a liquid of 0·873 sp. gr. at 0° (32° F.), boiling at 175°; neither cymene nor cuminol have the same odour and taste as the crude oil. Many other plants have been noticed as containing cymene among the constituents of their essential oils. Thus for instance *Cicuta virosa* L., *Carum Ajowan* (page 304), *Thymus vulgaris* (see art. Folia Thymi), *Eucalyptus globulus* Labill.

Cymene, $C^6H^4\left\{\begin{matrix}CH^3\\C^3H^7\end{matrix}\right.$ (Propylmethyl-benzol), may also be artificially obtained from a large number of essential oils having the composition $C^{10}H^{16}$, or $C^{10}H^{14}O$, or $C^{10}H^{16}O$, or $C^{10}H^{18}O$. It differs very remarkably from the oils of the formula $C^{10}H^{16}$, inasmuch as cymene yields the crystallizable cymensulphonic acids when it is warmed with concentrated sulphuric acid.

Lastly, there is present in the oil of cumin a small amount of a terpene, $C^{10}H^{16}$, boiling at 155·8° C., as stated in 1865 by C. M. Warren, and in 1873 by Beilstein and Kupffer.

The dextrogyrate power of cuminol is a little less strong than that of cymene; artificial cymene is optically inert.

Commerce—Cumin is shipped to England from Mogador, Malta and Sicily. In Malta there were in 1863, 140 acres under cultivation with this crop; in 1865, 730 acres, producing 2766 cwt.[1]

The export of cumin from Morocco[2] in 1872 was 1657 cwt.; that from Bombay in the year 1872–73 was 6766 cwt.;[3] and 20,040 cwt. from Calcutta[4] in the year 1870-71.

Uses—Cumin is sold by druggists as an ingredient of curry powders, but to a much larger extent for use in veterinary medicine.

CAPRIFOLIACEÆ.

FLORES SAMBUCI.

Elder Flowers; F. *Fleurs de Sureau*; G. *Holunderblüthe, Fliederblumen.*

Botanical Origin—*Sambucus nigra* L.—a large deciduous shrub or small tree, indigenous to Southern and Central Europe (not in Russia), Western Asia, the Crimea, the regions of the Caucasus and Southern Siberia. It is believed to be a native of England and Ireland, but not to be truly wild in Scotland. In other northern parts of Europe, as Norway and Sweden, the elder appears only as a plant introduced there during the middle ages by the monks.[5]

History—The Romans, as we learn from Pliny, made use in

[1] *Statistical Tables relating to the Colonial and other possessions of the United Kingdom*, xi. 618. 619.

[2] *Consular Reports*, Aug. 1873, 917; in 1876 only 380 cwt.

[3] *Statement of the Trade and Navigation of the Presidency of Bombay for* 1872-73. pt. ii. 90.

[4] *Annual Volume of Trade, etc. for the Bengal Presidency for* 1870-71. 121.

[5] Schübeler, *Pflanzenwelt Norwegens* (1873-75) 286.

medicine of the plant under notice as well as of the *Dwarf Elder* (*S. Ebulus* L.) Both kinds were employed in Britain by the ancient English[1] and Welsh[2] leeches, and in Italy in the medicine of the school of Salernum.

Description—The elder produces in the early summer, conspicuous, many-flowered cymes, 4 to 5 inches in diameter, of which the long peduncle divides into 5 branches, which subdivide once or several times by threes or fives, ultimately separating by repeated forking into slender, furrowed pedicels about ¼ of an inch long, each bearing a single flower. In the second or third furcations, the middle flower remains short-stalked or sessile, and opens sooner than the rest. In like manner, on the outermost small forks only one of the florets is usually long-stalked. The whole of this inflorescence forms a flattish umbelliform cyme, perfectly glabrous and destitute of bracts.

The calyx is combined with the ovary and bordered with 4 or 5 small teeth. The corolla, which is of a creamy white, is monopetalous with a very short tube and 5 spreading ovate lobes. The stamens which are about as long as the divisions of the corolla and alternate with them, are inserted in the tube of the latter. The yellow pollen which thickly powders the flowers, appears under the microscope 3-pored. The projecting ovary is crowned by a 2- or 3-lobed sessile stigma.

For use in pharmacy, the part of the flower most desirable is the corolla, to obtain a good proportion of which the gathered cymes are left for a few hours in a large heap; the mass slightly heats, the corollas detach themselves, and are separated from the green stalks by shaking, rubbing, and sifting; they require to be then rapidly dried. This done, they become much shrivelled and assume a dull yellow tint. When fresh, they have a sweet faint smell, which becomes stronger and somewhat different by drying, and is quite unlike the repulsive odour of the fresh leaves and bark. Dried elder flowers have a bitterish, slightly gummy flavour. On the Continent they are sold with the stalks, *i.e.* in entire cymes.

Chemical Composition—Elder flowers yield a very small percentage of a butter-like essential oil, lighter than water, and smelling strongly of the flowers; it is easily altered by exposure to the air.[3] The oil is accompanied by traces of volatile acids.

Uses—Elder flowers are only employed in British medicine for making an aromatic distilled water, and for communicating a pleasant odour to lard (*Unguentum Sambuci*). The flowers of *Sambucus canadensis* L.[4] indigenous in the United States, which are extremely similar to those of our species, appear to be more fragrant. The *leaves* of the latter are sometimes used for giving a fine green tint to oil or fat, as in the *Oleum viride* and *Unguentum Sambuci*

[1] *Leechdoms, etc. of Early England* edited by Cockayne, iii. (1866) 324.347. According to the Rev. Edward Gillett (p. xxxii.), *S. Ebulus* is believed to have been brought to England by the Danes and planted on the battlefield and graves of their countrymen. In Norfolk it still bears the name of *Danewort* and *blood hilder* (blood elder).

[2] The Physicians of Myddfai (see Appendix) used sage, rue, mallow, and *elder flowers* as ingredients of a gargle. *Meddygon Myddvai*, 219. 403.

[3] For further information, see Gmelin, *Chemistry*, xiv. (1860) 368.

[4] Fig. in Bentley and Trimen, *Med. Plants*, part 21 (1877).

foliorum of the shops. The bark, once much employed, is now obsolete.

RUBIACEÆ.

GAMBIER.

Catechu pallidum, Extractum Uncariæ; Gambier, Pale Catechu, Gambier Catechu, Terra Japonica; F. *Gambir, Cachou jaune;* G. *Gambir.*

Botanical Origin—1. *Uncaria Gambier* Roxb. (*Nauclea Gambir* Hunter) a stout climbing shrub, supporting itself by means of its flower-stalks which are developed into strong recurved hooks.[1] It is a native of the countries bordering the Straits of Malacca, and especially of the numerous islands at their eastern end; but according to Crawfurd[2] it does not seem indigenous to any of the islands of the volcanic band. It also grows in Ceylon, where however no use is made of it.

2. *U. acida* Roxb.,[3] probably a mere variety of the preceding, and growing in the Malayan islands, appears to be used in exactly the same manner.

History—Gambier is one of the substances to which the name of *Catechu* or *Terra Japonica* is often applied; the other is *Cutch*, which has been already described (p. 243). By druggists and pharmaceutists the two articles are frequently confounded, but in the great world of commerce they are reckoned as quite distinct. In many price-currents and trade-lists, *Catechu* is not found under that name, but only appears under the terms *Cutch* and *Gambier*.

Crawfurd asserts that gambier has been exported from time immemorial to Java from the Malacca Straits. This statement appears highly questionable. Rumphius, who resided in Amboyna during the second half of the 17th century, was a merchant, consul and naturalist; and in these capacities became thoroughly conversant with the products of the Malay Archipelago and adjacent regions, as the six folio volumes of his *Herbarium Amboinense*, illustrated by 587 plates, amply prove.

Among other plants, he figures[4] *Uncaria Gambier*, which he terms *Funis uncatus*, and states to exist under two varieties, the one with broad, and the other with narrow leaves. The first form, he says, is called in Malay *Daun Gatta Gambir*, on account of the bitter taste of its leaves, which is perceptible in the lozenges (*trochisci*) called *Gatta Gambir*, so much so that one might suppose they were made from these leaves, which however is not the case. He further asserts that the leaves have a detergent, drying quality by reason of their bitterness, which is nevertheless not intense but quite bearable in the mouth: that they are masticated instead of *Pinang* [Betel nut] with *Siri* [leaf of *Piper Betle*] and lime: that the people of Java and Bali plant the first variety near their houses for the sake of its fragrant flowers; but

[1] Fig. in Bentley and Trimen, *Med. Plants*, part 7 (1876).

[2] *Dictionary of the Indian Islands*, 1865.

[3] Beautifully figured in Berg und Schmidt, *Offizinelle Gewächse*, xxx. c. 1863.

[4] *Herb. Amb.* v. 63. tab. 34.

though they chew its leaves instead of *Pinang*, it must not be supposed that it is this plant from which the lozenges *Gatta* are compounded, for that indeed is quite different.

Thus, if we may credit Rumphius, it would seem that the important manufacture of gambier had no existence at the commencement of the last century. As to "*Gatta Gambir*," his statements are scarcely in accord with those of more recent writers. We may however remark that that name is very like the Tamil *Katta Kāmbu*, signifying *Catechu*, which drug is sometimes made into little round cakes, and was certainly a large export from India to Malacca and China as early as the 16th century (p. 241).

That gambier was unknown to Europeans long after the time of Rumphius, is evident from other facts. Stevens, a merchant of Bombay, in his *Compleat Guide to the East India Trade*, published in 1766, quotes the prices of goods at Malacca, but makes no allusion to gambier. Nor is there any reference to it in Savary's *Dictionnaire de Commerce* (ed. of 1750), in which Malacca is mentioned as the great entrepôt of the trade of India with that of China and Japan.

The first account of gambier known to us, was communicated to the Batavian Society of Arts and Sciences in 1780, by a Dutch trader named Couperus. This person narrates[1] how the plant was introduced into Malacca from Pontjan in 1758, and how gambier is made from its leaves; and names several sorts of the drug and their prices.

In 1807, a description of "the drug called *Gutta Gambeer*," and of the tree from which it is made, was presented to the Linnean Society of London.[2] The writer, William Hunter, well known for scientific observations in connection with India, states that the substance is made chiefly at Malacca, Siak and Rhio, that it is in the form of small squares, or little round cakes almost perfectly white, and that the finer sorts are used for chewing with betel leaf in the same manner as catechu, while the coarser are shipped to Batavia and China for use in tanning and dyeing.

Manufacture—The gambier plant is cultivated in plantations. These were commenced in 1819 in Singapore, where there were at one time 800 plantations; but owing to scarcity of fuel, without an abundant supply of which the manufacture is impossible, and dearness of labour, gambier-planting was in 1866 fast disappearing from the island.[3] The official Blue Book, printed at Singapore in 1872, reports it as "*much increased*." It is largely pursued on the mainland (Johore), and in the islands of the Rhio-Lingga Archipelago, lying south-east of Singapore. On the island of Bintang, the most northerly of the group, there were about 1,250 gambier-plantations in 1854.

The plantations are often formed in clearings of the jungle, where they last for a few years and are then abandoned,[4] owing to the impoverishment of the soil and the irrepressible growth of the *lalang* grass (*Imperata Kœnigii* P. de B.), which is more difficult to eradicate than even primæval jungle. It has been found profitable to combine

[1] *Verhandelingen van het Bataviaasch Genootschap*, ii. (derde druk) 217-234.

[2] *Linn. Trans.* ix. (1808) 218-224.

[3] Collingwood, *Journ. of Linn. Soc.*, Bot., x. (1869) 52.

[4] This abuse of land has been repressed in Singapore.

with the cultivation of gambier that of pepper, for which the boiled leaves of the gambier form an excellent manure.

The gambier plants are allowed to grow 8 to 10 feet high, and as their foliage is always in season, each plant is stripped 3 or 4 times in the year. The apparatus and all that belongs to the manufacture of the extract are of the most primitive description.[1] A shallow cast-iron pan about 3 feet across is built into an earthen fireplace. Water is poured into the pan, a fire is kindled, and the leaves and young shoots, freshly plucked, are scattered in, and boiled for about an hour. At the end of this time they are thrown on to a capacious sloping trough, the lower end of which projects into the pan, and squeezed with the hand so that the absorbed liquor may run back into the boiler. The decoction is then evaporated to the consistence of a thin syrup, and baled out into buckets. When sufficiently cool it is subjected to a curious treatment:—instead of simply stirring it round, the workman pushes a stick of soft wood in a sloping direction into each bucket; and placing two such buckets before him, he works a stick up and down in each. The liquid thickens round the stick, and the thickened portion being constantly rubbed off, while at the same the whole is in motion, it gradually sets into a mass, a result which the workman affirms would never be produced by simple stirring round. Though we are not prepared to concur in the workman's opinion, it is reasonable to suppose that his manner of treating the liquor favours the crystallization of the catechin in a more concrete form than it might otherwise assume. The thickened mass, which is said by another writer to resemble soft yellowish clay, is now placed in shallow square boxes, and when somewhat hardened is cut into cubes and dried in the shade. The leaves are boiled a second time, and finally washed in water, which water is saved for another operation.

From informations obtained in 1878 it would appear that now the prevailing part of gambier is made by means of pressure into blocks.

A plantation with five labourers contains on an average 70,000 to 80,000 shrubs, and yields 40 to 50 catties (1 catty = $1\frac{1}{3}$ lb. = 604·8 grammes) of gambier daily.

Description—Gambier is an earthy-looking substance of light brown hue, consisting of cubes about an inch each side, more or less agglutinated, or it is in the form of entirely compact masses. The cubes are externally of a reddish brown and compact, internally of a pale cinnamon hue, dry, porous, friable, devoid of odour, but with a bitterish astringent taste, becoming subsequently sweetish. Under the microscope, the cubes of gambier are seen to consist of very small acicular crystals.

Chemical Composition—In a chemical point of view, gambier agrees with cutch, especially with the pale variety made in Northern India (p. 242). Both substances consist mainly of *Catechin*,[2] which may be obtained in the hydrated state as slender colourless needles, by exhausting gambier with cold water, and crystallizing the residue from 3 or 4 parts of hot water, which on cooling deposits nearly all the catechin. Ferric chloride strikes with the solution of catechin, even

[1] We borrow the following account, which is the best we have met with, from Jagor's *Singapore, Malacca, und Java*, Berlin, 1866. 64.

[2] Gautier (1877) suggests that it is not identical with catechin from Acacia Catechin (p. 244).

when much diluted, a green tint. If it is shaken with ferrous sulphate and an extremely small quantity of bicarbonate of sodium, a violet colour makes its appearance. The same reactions are produced by various substances of the tannic class.

The yellowish colouring matter of gambier was determined by Hlasiwetz (1867) and Löwe (1873) to be *Quercetin*, which is also a constituent of cutch. Quercetin is but very sparingly soluble in water, yet it is nevertheless found, in small quantity, in the aqueous extract of cutch, from which it may be removed by means of ether. As many species of *Nauclea* contain, according to De Vry,[1] *Quinovic Acid*, it is probable that that substance may be detected in gambier.

Some fine gambier in regular cubes which we incinerated left 2·6 per cent. of ash, consisting mainly of carbonates of calcium and magnesium.

Commerce—Singapore, which is the great emporium for gambier, exported in 1871 no less than 34,248 tons, of which quantity 19,550 tons had been imported into the colony chiefly from Rhio and the Malayan Peninsula.[2] In 1876 the export had increased to more than 50,000 tons of pressed block gambier and 2,700 tons of cubes. In 1877 it diminished to 39,117 tons, owing to difficulties which had arisen between the Chinese dealers, who supplied the drug in a rather wet state, and the European exporters. Of the above quantity 21,607 tons were shipped for London, 7,572 for Liverpool, 2,345 for Marseilles. Gambier usually fetches a lower price[3] in the London market than cutch.

The quantity imported into the United Kingdom in 1872 was 21,155 tons, value £451,737, almost the whole being from the Straits Settlements.

Uses—Gambier, under the name of *Catechu*, is used medicinally as an astringent, but the quantity thus consumed is as nothing in comparison with that employed for tanning and dyeing.

CORTEX CINCHONÆ.

Cortex Peruvianus, Cortex Chinæ; Cinchona Bark, Peruvian Bark; F. *Ecorce de Quinquina*; G. *Chinarinde*.

Botanical Origin—The genus *Cinchona* constitutes together with *Cascarilla* (including *Buena* and *Cosmibuena*), *Remijia*, *Ladenbergia*, *Macrocnemum*, and about 30 other nearly allied genera, the well-characterized tribe *Cinchoneæ* of the order *Rubiaceæ*. This tribe consists of shrubs or trees with opposite leaves, 2-celled ovary, capsular fruit, and numerous minute, vertical or ascending, peltate, winged, albuminous seeds.

(**A.**) *Remarks on the genus.*—The genus *Cinchona* is distinguished by deciduous stipules, flowers in terminal panicles, 5-toothed superior calyx, tubular corolla expanding into 5 lobes fringed at the margin. The corolla is of an agreeable weak odour, and of a rosy or purplish hue or white.

[1] *Pharm. Journ.* vi. (1865) 18.

[2] *Blue Book of the Colony of the Straits Settlements for* 1871.

[3] 17*s.* per cwt., March 1879; see Catechu, page 242, note 3.

The fruit is a capsule of ovoid or subcylindrical form, dehiscing from the base (the fruitstalk also splitting) into two valves, which are held together at the apex by the thick permanent calyx. The seeds, 30 to 40 in number, are imbricated vertically; they are flat, winged all round by a broad membrane, which is very irregularly toothed or lacerated at the edge.

The Cinchonas are evergreen, with finely-veined leaves, traversed by a strong midrib. The thick leafstalk, often of a fine red, is sometimes a sixth the length of the whole leaf, but usually shorter. The leaves are ovate, obovate, or nearly circular; in some species lanceolate, rarely cordate, always entire, glabrous or more rarely hirsute, often variable as to size and form in the same species.

Among the valuable species, several are distinguished by small pits called *scrobiculi*, situated on the under side of the leaf, in the axils of the veins which proceed from the midrib. These pits sometimes exude an astringent juice. In some species they are replaced by tufts of hair. The young leaves are sometimes purplish on the under side; in several species the full-grown foliage assumes before falling, rich tints of crimson or orange.

The species of Cinchona are so much alike that their definition is a matter of the utmost difficulty, and only to be accomplished by resorting to a number of characters which taken singly are of no great importance. Individual species are moreover frequently connected together by well-marked and permanent intermediate forms, so that according to the expression of Howard, the whole form a continuous series, the terminal members of which are scarcely more sharply separated from the allied genera, than from plants of their own series.

As to the number and value of the species known, there is some diversity of view. Weddell, in 1870, enumerated 33 species and 18 sub-species, besides numerous varieties and sub-varieties. Bentham and Hooker, in 1873, estimated the species as about 36.

Kuntze, in the book quoted at the end of the present article, proposed to reduce all the species to the four following:

1. *Cinchona Weddelliana* O. Kuntze, nearly answering to *C. Calisaya* Weddell.
2. *C. Pavoniana* O. Kuntze, including *C. micrantha* Ruiz and *Pavon* and several allied plants.
3. *C. Howardiana* O. Kuntze, constituted of *C. succirubra* Pavon and a few other species of former authors.
4. *C. Pahudiana* Howard.

Kuntze, who has examined the living Cinchonæ as cultivated in India, is of the opinion that all the numerous forms hitherto observed, both in the wild plants and in cultivation, are merely either belonging to the above four species or deriving from them chiefly by hybridation. Though much in favour of a reduction of the species, we are not yet prepared to accept Kuntze's arrangement.

(B.) *Area, Climate and Soil.*—The Cinchonas are natives of South America, where they occur exclusively on the western side of the continent between 10° N. lat. and 22° S. lat., an area which includes portions of Venezuela, New Granada, Ecuador, Peru, and Bolivia.

The plants are found in the mountain regions, no species whatever being known to inhabit the low alluvial plains. In Peru and Bolivia, the region of the Cinchona forms a belt, 1300 miles in length, occupying the eastern slope of the Cordillera of the Andes.[1] In Ecuador and New Granada, the tree is not strictly limited to the eastern slopes, but occurs on other of the Andine ranges.

The average altitude of the cinchoniferous region is given by Weddell as 5,000 to 8,000 feet above the sea-level. The highest limit, as noted by Karsten, is 11,000 feet. One valuable species, *C. succirubra*, occurs exceptionally as low as 2,600 feet. Generally, it may be said that the altitude of the Cinchona zone decreases in proportion as it recedes from the equator, and that the most valuable sorts are not found lower than 5,000 feet.

The climate of the tropical mountain regions in which the Cinchonas flourish, is extremely variable,—sunshine, showers, storms, and thick mist, alternating in rapid succession, yet with no very great range of temperature. A transient depression of the thermometer even to the freezing point, and not unfrequent hail-showers, may be borne without detriment by the more hardy species. Yet the mean temperature most favourable for the generality of species, appears to be 12 to 20° C. (54 to 68° F.)

Climatic agencies appear to influence the growth of Cinchona far more than the composition of the soil. Though the tree occurs in a great variety of geological formations, there is no distinct evidence that these conditions control in any marked manner either the development of the tree or the chemical constitution of its bark. Manure on the other hand, though not increasing perceptibly luxuriance of growth, has a decided effect in augmenting the richness of the bark in alkaloids.[2]

(C.) *Species yielding officinal barks.*—The Cinchona Barks of commerce are produced by about a dozen species; of these barks the greater number are consumed solely in the manufacture of quinine. Those admitted for pharmaceutical use are afforded by the following species:—

1. *Cinchona officinalis* Hooker[3]—A native of Ecuador and Peru, existing under several varieties. It forms a large tree, having lanceolate or ovate leaves, usually pointed, glabrous, and shining on the upper surface, and scrobiculate on the under. The flowers are small, pubescent and in short lax panicles, and are succeeded by oblong or lanceolate capsules, ½ an inch or more in length.

2. *C. Calisaya* Weddell—Discovered by Weddell in 1847,[4] although its bark had been an object of commerce since the latter half of the previous century.

The tree inhabits the warmest woods of the declivities which border the valleys of Bolivia and South-eastern Peru, at an altitude of 5000 to 6000 feet above the sea-level. More precisely, the chief localities for the tree are the Bolivian provinces of Enquisivi, Yungas de la Paz, Larecaja or Sorata, Caupolican or Apolobamba, and Muñecas: thence it

[1] That is to say the *eastern* Cordillera, the western and lower range being called the *Cordillera of the Coast*; no Cinchonas grow on the latter.

[2] Broughton, in *Pharm. Journ.* Jan. 4, 1873. 521.

[3] Figured in *Bot. Magazine*, vol. 89 (1863) tab. 5364, including *C. Condaminea* Humb. et Bonpl. and *C. Uritusinga* Pavon.

[4] *Ann. des Sciences nat.*, Bot. x. (1848) 6, and *Hist. nat. des Quinquinas*, 1849, tab. 3, figured in *Botanical Magazine*, 1873. 6052, and 1879. 6434.

passes northward into the Peruvian province of Carabaya, suddenly ceasing on the confines of the valley of Sandia, although, as Weddell observed, the adjacent valleys are to all appearance precisely similar.

When well grown, *C. Calisaya* has a trunk often twice as thick as a man's body, and a magnificent crown of foliage overtopping all other trees of the forest. It has ovate capsules of about the same length (½ an inch) as the elegant pinkish flowers, which are in large pyramidal panicles. The leaves are 3 to 6 inches long, of very variable form, but usually oblong and obtuse, rarely acute.

A variety named after Joseph de Jussieu who first noticed it, *β. Josephiana*, but known in the country as *Ichu-Cascarilla* or *Cascarilla del Pajonal*, differs from the preceding in that it is a shrub, 6 to 10 feet high, growing on the borders of mountain meadows and of thickets in the same regions as the larger form.

Other forms known in Bolivia as *Calisaya zamba, morada, verde* or *alta*, and *blanca*, have been distinguished by Weddell as varieties of *C. Calisaya*.

Towards the middle of the year 1865, *Charles Ledger*, an English traveller, obtained seeds of a superior Cinchona, which had been collected near Pelechuco, eastwards of the lake Titicaca, about 68° W. long. and 15° S. lat., in the Bolivian province of Caupolican. In the same year the seeds arrived in England, but were subsequently sold to the Dutch government, and raised with admirable success in Java, and a little later also in private plantations in British India. The bark of "*Cinchona Ledgeriana*" has since proved by far the most productive in quinine of all Cinchona Barks. The tree is a mere form of C. Calisaya.[1]

3. *C. succirubra* Pavon,[2]—a magnificent tree, 50 to 80 feet high, formerly growing in all the valleys of the Andes which debouch in the plain of Guayaquil. The tree is now almost entirely confined to the forests of Guaranda on the western declivities of Chimborazo, at 2,000 to 5,000 feet above the level of the sea.

The bark appears to have been appreciated in its native country at an early period, if we may conclude that the *Red Bark* mentioned by La Condamine in 1737 was that under notice. It would seem, however, to have scarcely reached Europe earlier than the second half of the last century.[3] The tree has broadly oval leaves, attaining about a foot in length, nearly glabrous above, pubescent beneath, large terminal panicles of rosy flowers, succeeded by oblong capsules 1 to 1¼ inches long.

The other species of *Cinchona*, the bark of which is principally consumed by the manufacturers of quinine, will be found briefly noticed, together with the foregoing, in the conspectus at page 355.

History—The early native history of Cinchona is lost in obscurity. No undoubted proofs have been handed down, to show that the aborigines of South America had any acquaintance with the medicinal properties of the bark. But traditions are not wanting.

[1] Ledger's Calisaya is beautifully figured and exactly described in Howard's *Quinology of the East Indian Plantations*, parts ii. and iii.

[2] Figured in Howard's *Nueva Quinologia*, art. *Chinchona succirubra*.

[3] Howard, *l.c.* p. 9.

William Arrot,[1] a Scotch surgeon who visited Peru in the early part of the last century, states that the opinion then current at Loxa was that the qualities and use of the barks of Cinchona were known to the Indians before any Spaniard came among them. Condamine, as well as Jussieu, heard the same statements, which appear to have been generally prevalent at the close of the 17th century.

It is noteworthy, on the other hand, that though the Peruvians tenaciously adhere to their traditional customs, they make no use at the present day of Cinchona bark, but actually regard its employment with repugnance.

Humboldt[2] declares that at Loxa the natives would rather die than have recourse to what they consider so dangerous a remedy. Pöppig[3] (1830) found a strong prejudice to prevail among the people of Huanuco against Cinchona as a remedy for fevers, and the same fact was observed farther north by Spruce[4] in 1861. The latter traveller narrates, that it was impossible to convince the *cascarilleros* of Ecuador that their *Red Bark* could be wanted for any other purpose than dyeing cloth; and that even at Guayaquil there was a general dislike to the use of quinine.

Markham[5] notices the curious fact that the wallets of the native itinerant doctors, who from father to son have plied their art since the days of the Incas, never contain cinchona bark.

Although Peru was discovered in 1513, and submitted to the Spanish yoke by the middle of the century, no mention has been found of the febrifuge bark with which the name of the country is connected, earlier than the commencement of the 17th century.

Joseph de Jussieu,[6] who visited Loxa in 1739, relates that the use of the remedy was first made known to a Jesuit missionary, who being attacked by intermittent fever, was cured by the bark administered to him by an Indian cacique at Malacotas, a village near Loxa. The date of this event is not given. The same story is related of the Spanish corregidor of Loxa, Don Juan Lopez Canizares, who is said to have been cured of fever in 1630.

Eight years later, the wife of the viceroy of Peru, Luis Geronimo Fernandez de Cabrera y Bobadilla, fourth count of Chinchon, having been attacked with fever, the same corregidor of Loxa sent a packet of powdered bark to her physician Juan de Vega, assuring him of its efficacy in the treatment of "*tertiana.*" The drug fully bore out its reputation, and the countess Ana was cured.[7] Upon her recovery, she caused to be collected large quantities of the bark, which she used to give away to those sick of fever, so that the medicine came to be called *Polvo de la Condesa*, i.e. *The Countess' Powder*. It was certainly

[1] *Phil. Trans.* xl. for 1737–38. 81.

[2] *Der Gesellsch. naturf. Freunde zu Berlin Magaz.* i. (1807) 60.

[3] *Reise in Chile, Peru,* etc. ii. (1836) 222.

[4] Blue Book — *East India Chinchona Plant*, 1863. 74. 75.

[5] *Travels in Peru and India*, 1862. 2.

[6] Quoted by Weddell in his *Hist. des Quinquinas*, p. 15, from De Jussieu's unpublished MS.—The town of Loxa or Loja was founded by the Spaniards in 1546.

[7] The circumstances are fully narrated by La Condamine (*Mém. de l'Acad. royale des Sciences*, année 1738). But the cure of the countess was known in Europe much before this, for it is mentioned by Sebastiano Bado in his *Anastasis, Corticis Peruviæ, seu Chinæ Chinæ defensio* published at Genoa in 1663. When Bado wrote, it was a debated question whether the bark was introduced to Europe by the count of Chinchon or by the Jesuit Fathers.

known in Spain the following year (1639), when it was first tried at Alcala de Henares near Madrid.[1]

The introduction of Peruvian Bark into Europe is described by Chifflet, physician to the archduke Leopold of Austria, viceroy of the Netherlands and Burgundy, in his *Pulvis Febrifugus Orbis Americani ventilatus*, published at Brussels in 1653 (or 1651 ?). He says that among the wonders of the day, many reckon the tree growing in the kingdom of Peru, which the Spaniards call *Palo de Calenturas*, i.e. *Lignum febrium*. Its virtues reside chiefly in the bark, which is known as *China febris*, and which taken in powder drives off the febrile paroxysms. He further states, that during the last few years the bark has been imported into Spain, and thence sent to the Jesuit Cardinal Joannes de Lugo at Rome.[2] Chifflet adds, that it has been carried from Italy to Belgium by the Jesuit Fathers going to the election of a general, but that it was also brought thither direct from Peru by Michael Belga, who had resided some years at Lima.

Chifflet, though candidly admitting the efficacy of the new drug when properly used, was not a strong advocate for it; and his publication started an acrimonious controversy, in which Honoratius Faber, a Jesuit (1655), Fonseca, physician to Pope Innocent X., Sebastiano Bado[3] of Genoa (1656 and 1663), and Sturm (1659) appeared in defence of the febrifuge; while Plempius (1655), Glantz, an imperial physician of Ratisbon (1653), Godoy, physician to the king of Spain (1653), René Moreau (1655), Arbinet and others contended in an opposite sense.

From one of these disputants, Roland Sturm, a doctor of Louvain, who wrote in 1659,[4] we learn that four years previously, some of the new febrifuge had been sent by the archduke Leopold to the Spanish ambassador at the Hague, and that he (Sturm) had been required to report upon it. He further states, that the medicine was known in Brussels and Antwerp as *Pulvis Jesuiticus*, because the Jesuit Fathers were in the habit of administering it gratis to indigent persons suffering from quartan fever; but that it was more commonly called *Pulvis Peruanus* or *Peruvianam Febrifugum*. At Rome it bore the name of *Pulvis eminentissimi Cardinalis de Lugo*, or *Pulvis patrum;* the Jesuits at Rome received it from the establishments of their order in Peru, and used to give it away to the poor in Cardinal de Lugo's palace. In 1658 Sturm saw 20 doses sent to Paris which cost 60 florins. He gives a copy of the handbill[5] of 1651 which the apothecaries of Rome used to distribute with the costly powder.

[1] Villerobal, quoted by Bado, *op. cit.* 202.

[2] The cardinal belonged to a family of Seville, which town had the monopoly of the trade with America.

[3] Bado in his *Anastasis*, lib. 3, quotes the opinion of many persons as coinciding with his own.

[4] *Febrifugi Peruviani Vindiciarum pars prior—Pulveris Historiam complectens ejusque vires et proprietates . . . exhibens*, Delphis, 1659. 12°.

[5] It is in these words:—*Modo di adoprare la Corteccia chiamata della Febre.*—Questa Corteccia si porta dal Regno di Peru, e si chiama China, o vero China della febre, laquale si adopra per la febre quartana, e terzana, che venga con freddo: s'adropra in questo modo, cioè:

Se ne piglia dramme due, e si pista fina, con passarla per setaccio; e tre hore prima incirca, che debba venir la febre si mette in infusione in un bicchiero di vino bianco gagliardissimo, e quando il freddo commincia à venire, ò si sente qualche minimo principio, si prende tutta la presa preparata, e si mette il patiente in letto.

Avertasi, si potrà dare detta Corteccia nel modo sudetto nella febre terzana, quando

The drug began to be known in England about 1655.[1] The *Mercurius Politicus*, one of the earliest English newspapers, contains in several of its numbers for 1658,[2] a year remarkable for the prevalence in England of an epidemic remittent fever, advertisements offering for sale—"*the excellent powder known by the name of the Jesuit's Powder*"—brought over by James Thomson, merchant of Antwerp.

Brady, professor of physic at Cambridge, prescribed bark about this time; and in 1660, Willis, a physician of great eminence, reported it as coming into daily use. This is also evidenced, with regard to the continent, by the pharmaceutical tariffs of the cities of Leipzig and Frankfurt of the year 1669, where "*China Chinæ*" has a place. ⅛ of an ounce (a "quint") is quoted in the latter at 50 kreuzers (about 1s. 6d.), whereas the same quantity of opium is valued at 4 kreuzers,[3] camphor 2 kreuzers, balsam of Peru 8 kreuzers.

Among those who contributed powerfully to the diffusion of the new medicine, was Robert Talbor *alias* Tabor. In his "Pyretologia" (see Appendix, T.) he by no means intimates that his method of cure depends on the use of bark. On the contrary, he cautions his readers against the dangerous effects of Jesuits' Powder when administered by unskilful persons, yet admits that, properly given, it is a "noble and safe medicine."

Talbor's reputation increasing, he was appointed in 1678 physician in ordinary to Charles II., and in 1679, the king being ill of tertian fever at Windsor, Talbor cured him by his secret remedy.[4] He acquired similar favour in France, and upon Talbor's death (1681), Louis XIV. ordered the publication of his method of cure, which accordingly appeared by Nicolas de Blegny, surgeon to the king.[5] This was immediately translated into English, under the title of *The English Remedy: or, Talbor's Wonderful Secret for Cureing of Agues and Feavers.—Sold by the Author Sir Robert Talbor to the most Christian King, and since his Death, ordered by his Majesty to be published in French, for the benefit of his subjects, and now translated into English for Publick Good* (Lond. 1682).

Cinchona bark was now accepted into the domain of regular medicine, though its efficacy was by no means universally acknowledged. It first appeared in the London Pharmacopœia in 1677, under the name of *Cortex Peruanus.*

quella sia fermata in stato di molti giorni.

L'esperienza continua, hà liberata quasi tutti quelli, che l'hanno presa, purgato prima bene il corpo, e per quattro giorni doppo non pigliar niuna sorte di medicamento, ma auvertasi di non darla se non con licenza delli Sig. Medici, acciò giudicano se sia in tempo à proposito di pigliarla.

[1] So says Sir G. Baker, who has traced the introduction of Cinchona in a very able paper published in the *Medical Transactions* of the College of Physicians of London, iii. (1785) 141–216.

[2] Namely No. 422. June 24–July 1; No. 426. July 22–29; No. 439. Oct. 21–28. No. 545. Dec. 9–16.—We have examined the copy at the British Museum.

[3] Ph. Journ. vi. (1876) 1022.

[4] In the *Recueil* for 1680, p. 275 (see appendix, Talbor) the king is said to have had another attack of fever at Windsor, for which he took "*du Quinquina préparé*," which again cured him.

[5] *Le Remède anglois pour la guérison des fièvres, publié par ordre du Roy, avec les observations de Monsieur le premier Médecin de sa Majesté, sur la composition, les vertus, et l'usage de ce remède*, par Nicolas de Blegny, Chirurgien ordinaire du corps de Monsieur, et Directeur de l'Académie des nouvelles découvertes de Médecine, Paris. 1682. 12°.

For the first accurate information on the botany of Cinchona, science is indebted to the French.[1]

Charles-Marie de la Condamine, while occupied in common with Bouguer and Godin, as an astronomer from 1736 to 1743, in measuring the arc of a degree near Quito, availed himself of the opportunity to investigate the origin of the famous Peruvian Bark. On the 3rd and 4th of February, 1737, he visited the Sierra de Cajanuma, 2½ leagues from Loxa, and there collected specimens of the tree now known as *Cinchona officinalis* var. *α. Condaminea*. At that period the very large trees had already become rare, but there were still specimens having trunks thicker than a man's body. Cajanuma was the home of the first cinchona bark brought to Europe; and in early times it enjoyed such a reputation, that certificates drawn up before a notary were provided as proof that parcels of bark were the produce of that favoured locality.

Joseph de Jussieu, botanist to the French expedition with which La Condamine was connected, gathered, near Loxa in 1739, a second *Cinchona* subsequently named by Vahl *C. pubescens*, a species of no medicinal value.

In 1742 Linnæus established the genus *Cinchona*,[2] and in 1753 first described the species *C. officinalis*, recently restored and exactly characterized by Hooker, aided by specimens supplied to him by Mr. Howard.

The cinchona trees were believed to be confined to the region around Loxa, until 1752 when Miguel de Santisteban, superintendent of the mint at Santa Fé, discovered some species in the neighbourhood of Popayan and Pasto.

In 1761 José Celestino Mutis, physician to the Marquis de la Vega, viceroy of New Granada, arrived at Carthagena from Cadiz, and immediately set about collecting materials for writing a *Flora* of the country. This undertaking he carried on with untiring energy, especially from the year 1782 until the end of his life in 1808,—first for seven years at Real del Sapo and Mariquita at the foot of the Cordillera de Quindiu, and subsequently at Santa Fé de Bogotá. Mutis gave up his medical appointment in 1772, for the purpose of entering a religious order, and ten years later was entrusted by the Government with the establishment and direction of a large museum of natural history, first at Mariquita, afterwards at Santa Fé.

A position similar to that of Mutis in New Granada had also been conferred in 1777 on the botanists Hipolito Ruiz and José Pavon with regard to southern Peru, whence originated the well-known *Flora Peruviana et Chilensis*,[3] as well as most important direct contributions to our knowledge on the subject of Cinchona.

About the same time (1776), Renquizo (Renquifo or Renjifo) found cinchona trees in the neighbourhood of Huanuco, in the central tract

[1] *Sur l'arbre de Quinquina* par M. de la Condamine—*Mém. de l'Académie royale des Sciences pour l'année* 1738. pp. 226–243, with two plates.

[2] Markham has vigorously contended that the name *Cinchona* should be altered to *Chinchona* as better commemorating the countess of Chinchon. But the inconvenience of changing so well-established a name and its many derivatives, has outweighed these considerations.—See list of works relating to Cinchona at the end of the present article.

[3] Published at Madrid, 1798-1802, in 4 volumes folio, with 425 plates.

of Peru, whereby the monopoly of the district of Loxa was soon broken up.

Numerous and important quinological discoveries were subsequently made by Mutis, or rather by his pupils Caldas, Zea, and Restrepo,[1] as well as on the other hand by Ruiz and Pavon, and their successors Tafalla and Manzanilla. Mutis did not bring his labours to any definite conclusion, and his extensive botanical collections and 5,000 coloured drawings, were sent to Madrid only in 1817, and there remained in a lamentable state of neglect.

Some of his observations first appeared in print in 1793-94, under the title of *El Arcano de la Quina* in the *Diario*, a local paper of Santa Fé, and were reprinted at Madrid in 1828 by Don Manuel Hernandez de Gregorio. The botanical descriptions of the cinchonas of New Granada, forming the fourth part of the *Arcano*, remained forgotten and lost to science until rescued by Markham and published in 1867.[2] The drawings belonging to the descriptions were photographed and engraved a little later, and form part of Triana's *Nouvelles Etudes sur les Quinquinas*, which appeared in 1870.

The two Peruvian botanists succeeded somewhat better in securing their results. Ruiz in 1792, in his *Quinologia*,[3] and in 1801 conjointly with Pavon in a supplement thereto, brought together a portion of their important labours relating to cinchona. But an essential part called *Nueva Quinologia*, written between 1821 and 1826, remained unpublished; and after an oblivion of over thirty years, it came by purchase into the hands of Mr. John Eliot Howard, who published it, and with rare liberality enriched it with 27 magnificent coloured plates, mostly taken from the very specimens of Pavon lying in the herbarium of Madrid.

Between the pupils of Mutis on the one hand, and those of Ruiz and Pavon on the other, there arose an acrimonious controversy regarding their respective discoveries, which has been equitably summarized by Triana in the work just mentioned.

Production—The hardships of bark-collecting in the primeval forests of South America are of the severest kind, and undergone only by the half-civilized Indians and people of mixed race, in the pay of speculators or companies located in the towns. Those who are engaged in the business, especially the collectors themselves, are called *Cascarilleros* or *Cascadores*, from the Spanish word *Cascara*, bark. A majordomo at the head of the collectors directs the proceedings of the several bands in the forest itself, where provisions and afterwards the produce are stowed away in huts of slight construction.

Arrot in 1736, and Weddell and Karsten in our own day, have given from personal observation a striking picture of these operations.

The cascarillero having found his tree, has usually to free its stem from the luxuriant climbing and parasitic plants with which it is en-

[1] ". . Mutis n'avait qu'une notion inexacte et confuse du genre *Cinchona* et de ses véritables caractères ; c'est en définitive qu'aucune de ses espèces, dans le sens strict du mot, n'a été reconnue ni découverte par lui."—Triana, *Nouv. Etudes*, p. 8.

[2] Markham, *Chinchona Species of New Granada*, Lond. 1867.

[3] *Quinologia, ó tratado de árbol de la Quina, ó Cascarilla*, Madrid, 1792. 4°. pp. 103.

[4] *Supplemento á la Quinologia*, Madrid, 1801. 4°. pp. 154.

circled. This done, he begins in most cases at once to remove, after a previous beating, the sapless layer of outer bark. In order to detach the valuable inner bark, longitudinal and transverse incisions are made as high as can be reached on the stem. The tree is then felled, and the peeling completed. In most cases, but especially if previously beaten, the bark separates easily from the wood. In many localities it has to be dried by a fire made on the floor of a hut, the bark being placed on hurdles above,—a most imperfect arrangement. In Southern Peru and Bolivia however, according to Weddell, even the thickest Calisaya bark is dried in the sun without requiring the aid of the fire.

The thinner bark as it dries rolls up into tubes or quills called *canutos* or *canutillos*, while the pieces stripped from the trunks are made to dry flat by being placed one upon another and loaded with weights, and are then known as *plancha* or *tabla*. The bark of the root was formerly neglected, but is now in several instances brought into the market.

After drying, the barks are either assorted, chiefly according to size, or all are packed without distinction in sacks or bales. In some places, as at Popayan, the bark is even *stamped*, in order to reduce its bulk as much as possible. The dealers in the export towns enclose the bark in *serons*[1] of raw bullock-hide, which, contracting as it dries, tightly compresses the contents (100 lb. or more) of the package. In many places however wooden chests are used for the packing of bark.

Conveyance to the Coast and Commercial Statistics—The ports to which bark is conveyed for shipment to Europe are not very numerous.

Guayaquil on the Pacific coast is the most important for produce of Ecuador. The quantity shipped thence in 1871 was 7,859 quintals.[2] Pitayo bark is largely exported from Buenaventura in the Bay of Choco further north.

Payta, the most northerly port of Peru, and Callao, the port of Lima, likewise export bark, the latter being the natural outlet for the barks of Central Peru from Huanuco to Cusco.

Islay, and more particularly Arica, receive the valuable barks of Carabaya and of the high valleys of Bolivia. In 1877 the export of Arica was equal to 5100 cwt.

The barks of Peru and Bolivia find an exceptional outlet also by the Amazon and its tributaries, and are shipped to Europe from port of Brazil. Howard[3] has given an interesting account of one of the first attempts to utilize this eastern route, made by Senr. Pedro Rada in 1868.

There is a large export of the barks of New Granada, principally from Santa Marta, whence the shipments[4] in 1871 were 3,415,149 lb.; and in 1872, 2,758,991 lb. From the neighbouring port of Savanilla, which represents the city of Barranquilla, the sea-terminus of the navigation of the Magdalena, the export of bark in 1871 was 1,043,835 lb., value £38,715;[5] it amounted to 2 millions of kilogrammes in 1877. All Columbia is stated, in 1877, to have shipped 3½ millions of kilo-

[1] From *zurrón*, the Spanish name for a pouch or game-bag.

[2] *Consular Reports*, presented to Parliament, July 1872.

[3] Seemann's *Journ. of Bot.* vi. (1868) 323.

[4] *Consular Reports*, August 1873. 743.

[5] *Ibid.* August 1872.

grammes of bark; yet a good deal of the excellent barks of the Columbian State of Santander, especially those of the neighbourhood of Bucaramanga, find their way to Maracaibo, taking the name of that place.

Some Cinchona bark is also shipped from Venezuela by way of Puerto Cabello.

The quantity of bark appearing in the *Annual Statement of Trade* as "Peruvian Bark" imported into the United Kingdom in 1872, was 28,451 cwt., valued £285,620; of which 11,843 cwt. was shipped from New Granada, 4,668 cwt. from Ecuador, and 5,829 cwt. from Peru, the remainder being entered as from the ports of Chili, Brazil, Central America and other countries. The imports into the United Kingdom in 1876 were 26,021 cwt., valued at £272,154.

Cultivation—The reckless system of bark-cutting in the forests of South America, which has resulted in the utter extermination of the tree from many localities, has aroused the attention of the Old World, and has at length prompted serious efforts to cultivate the tree on a large scale in other countries.

The idea of cultivating Cinchonas out of their native regions was advanced by Ruiz in 1792, and by Fée of Strassburg in 1824.[1] Royle[2] pointed out in 1839 that suitable localities for the purpose might be found in the Neilgherry Hills and probably in many other parts of India, and argued indefatigably in favour of the introduction of the tree.

The subject was also urged in reference to Java in 1837 by Fritze, director of medical affairs in that island; in 1846 by Miquel, and subsequently by other Dutch botanists and chemists.[3]

Living Cinchonas had been taken to Algeria as early as 1849, by the intervention of the Jesuits of Cusco, but their cultivation met with no success.

Weddell in 1848 brought cinchona seeds from South America to France, and strenuously insisted on the importance of cultivating the plant. His seeds, especially those of *C. Calisaya*, germinated at the Jardin des Plantes in Paris, and in June 1850, living seedlings were sent to Algeria; and in April 1852, through the Dutch Government, to Java.

The first important attempts at cinchona-cultivation were made by the Dutch. Under the auspices of the Colonial Minister Pahud, afterwards Governor-General of the Dutch East Indies, the botanist Hasskarl was despatched to Peru for the purpose of obtaining seeds and plants. His mission was so far successful, that a collection of plants contained in 21 Wardian cases, was shipped in August 1854 from Callao, in a frigate sent expressly to receive them. Notwithstanding every care, the plants did not reach Java in good condition; and when Hasskarl resigned his appointment in 1856, he bequeathed to his successor Junghuhn only 167 young cinchonas, though 400 specimens had been shipped from South America.

An impulse to the project of cinchona-planting was given in 1852

[1] *Cours d'Hist. nat. pharmaceutique*, ii. (1828) 252.

[2] *Illustrations of the Bot. of the Himalayan Mountains*, i. (1839) 240.

[3] According to K. W. van Gorkom, suggestions to the same end were made to the Dutch Government as early as 1829 by Reinwardt.

by Royle, in a report addressed to the East India Company, in which he pointed out that the Government of India were then spending more than £7,000 a year for Cinchona bark, in addition to about £25,000 for quinine.[1]

After some unsatisfactory endeavours on the part of the British Government to obtain plants and seeds through the intervention of H. M. Consuls in South America, Mr. Markham offered his services, which were accepted. Markham, though not a professed botanist, was well qualified for the task by a previous acquaintance with the country and people of Peru and Bolivia, and by a knowledge of the Spanish and Quichua languages,—and even more so by a rare amount of zeal, intelligence, and forethought. Being fully aware of the difficulties of the undertaking, he earnestly insisted that nothing should be neglected which could ensure success; and in particular made repeated demands for a steam-vessel to convey the young plants across the Pacific to India, which unfortunately were not complied with. He further urged the desirableness of not confining operations to a single district, but of endeavouring to procure by different collectors all the more valuable species.

The prudence of this latter suggestion was evident, and Markham was enabled to engage the services of Richard Spruce, the distinguished botanist, then resident in Ecuador, who expressed his readiness to undertake a search for the Red Bark trees (*C. succirubra*) in the forests of Chimborazo. He also secured the co-operation of G. J. Pritchett for the neighbourhood of Huanuco, and of two skilful gardeners, John Weir and Robert Cross. The last-named was employed in 1861 to procure seeds of *C. officinalis* from the Sierra de Cajanuma near Loxa, and in 1863-64 those of *C. pitayensis* from the province of Pitayo in Ecuador.[2]

Markham reserved for himself the border-lands of Peru and Bolivia, in order to obtain *C. Calisaya*; and for this purpose started from Islay in March 1860. Arriving in the middle of April by way of Arequipa and Puno, at Curcero, the capital of the province of Carabaya, he made his way to the village of Sandia, near which he met with the first specimens of *Cinchona* in the form of the shrubby variety of *C. Calisaya*, termed *Josephiana*. He afterwards found the better variety *a. vera*, and also *C. ovata* R. et P., *C. micrantha* R. et P., and *C. pubescens* Vahl. Of these sorts, but chiefly of the first three, 456 plants were shipped at Islay in June 1860.

In consequence of the hostile attitude of the people, and the jealousy of the Bolivian Government, lest an important monopoly should be broken up, added to the difficulties arising from insalubrious climate and the want of roads, the obstacles encountered by Markham were very great, and no attempt could be made to wait for the ripening of the seeds of the Calisaya, which takes place in the month of August.[3]

[1] In 1870, the Indian Government purchased no less than 81,600 ounces of sulphate of quinine, besides 8,832 ounces of the sulphates of cinchonine, cinchonidine and quinidine. The quantities bought in subsequent years have been much smaller until the present year (1874).

[2] *Report on the Expedition to procure seeds of C. Condaminea* [1862]; also *Report to the Under Secretary of State for India on the Pitayo Chinchona*, by Robt. Cross, 1865.

[3] Great difficulty was at first experienced in successfully conveying living Cinchona plants to India, even in Wardian cases

The expedition of Spruce was successful, but was also attended with much difficulty and danger, of which there are vivid pictures in the interesting narratives by himself and by Cross, published in the Parliamentary Returns of 1863 and 1866.[1]

The service entrusted to Pritchett was also efficiently performed; and he succeeded in bringing to Southampton six cases containing plants of *C. micrantha* and *C. nitida*, besides a large supply of seeds.

Some important supplies of plants and seed for British India have likewise been obtained from the Dutch plantations in Java. Seeds of *C. lancifolia*, the tree affording the valuable bark of New Granada, were procured through Dr. Karsten.

Previously to the arrival in India of the first consignment of plants, careful inquiries were instituted from a meteorological and geological point of view, as to the localities most adapted for the cultivation. This resulted in the selection for the first trial of certain spots among the Neilgherry (or Nilgiri) Hills on the south-west coast of India and in the Madras Presidency. Of this district, the chief town is Ootocamund (or Utakamand), situated about 60 miles south of Mysore and the same distance from the Indian Ocean. Here the first plantation was established in a woody ravine, 7,000 feet above the sea-level, a spot pronounced by Mr. Markham to be exceedingly analogous, as respects vegetation and climate, to the Cinchona valleys of Carabaya. Other plantations were formed in the same neighbourhood, and so rapid was the propagation, that in September 1866, there were more than 1½ millions of Cinchona plants on the Neilgherry Hills alone.[2] The species that grows best there is *C. officinalis*.

The number was stated to be in 1872, 2,639,285, not counting the trees of private planters. The largest are about 30 feet high, with trunks over 3 feet in girth. The area of the Government plantations on the Neilgherry Hills is 950 acres.[3]

Plantations have also been made in the coffee-producing districts of Wynaad, and in Coorg, Travancore and Tinnevelly, in all instances, we believe, as private speculations.

Cinchona plantations have been established by the Government of India in the valleys of the Himalaya in British Sikkim,[4] and some have been started in the same region by private enterprise. In the former there were on the 31st March 1870, more than 1½ millions of plants permanently placed, the species growing best being *C. succirubra* and *C. Calisaya*. The Cinchona plantation of Rungbi near Darjiling (British Sikkim) covered in 1872 2,000 acres. In the Kangra valley of the Western Himalaya, plantations have been commenced, as well as in the Bombay Presidency, and in British Burma.

and the collections formed by Hasskarl, Markham, and Pritchett almost all perished after reaching their destination (Markham's letter, 26 Feb. 1861). But the propagation by seed has proved very rapid.

[1] *Correspondence relating to the introduction of the Chinchona Plant into India*, ordered by the House of Commons to be printed 20 March 1863 and 18 June 1866.

[2] Blue Book (Chinchona Cultivation, 1870. p. 30).—A name that must always be remembered in connection with the Neilgherry plantations, is that of William Graham McIvor, who by his rare practical skill and sagacity in the cultivation and management of the tree, has rendered most signal services in its propagation in India.

[3] *Moral and material progress and condition of India during* 1871–72, presented to Parliament 1873. p. 33.

[4] The first annual Report dates from 1862 to 1863; I am indebted to Dr. King for that of 1876–1877.—F. A. F.

Ceylon offers favourable spots for the cultivation of Cinchona, in the mountain region which occupies the centre of the island, as at Hakgalle, near Neuera-Ellia, 5,000 feet above the sea, where a plantation was formed by Government in 1861. The production of bark has been taken up with spirit by the coffee-planters of Ceylon.

The Government of India has acted with the greatest liberality in distributing plants and seeds of Cinchona, and in promoting the cultivation of the tree among the people of India; and it has freely granted supplies of seed to other countries.

The plantations of Java commenced by Hasskarl, increased under Junghuhn's management to such an extent, that in December 1862 there were 1,360,000 seedlings and young trees, among which however the more valuable species, as *C. Calisaya*, *C. lancifolia*, *C. micrantha* and *C. succirubra*, were by far the least numerous, whereas *C. Pahudiana*, of which the utility was by no means well established, amounted to over a million. The disproportionate multiplication of this last was chiefly due to its quickly yielding an abundance of seeds, and to its rapid and vigorous growth. Another defect in the early Dutch system of cultivation arose from the notion that the Cinchona requires to be grown in the shade of other trees, and to a less successful plan of multiplying by cuttings and layers.

These and other matters were the source of animated and often bitter discussions, which terminated on the one hand by the death of Junghuhn in 1864, and on the other by the skilful investigations of De Vry. This eminent chemist was despatched by the Government of Holland in 1857 to Java, that he might devote his chemical knowledge to the investigation of the natural productions of the island, including the then newly introduced Cinchona. It was March 16th, 1859, when Dr. de Vry laid before the governor-general, Mr. Pahud, the first crystals of sulphate of quinine he had prepared from bark grown in that island.

Under K. W. van Gorkom, who was appointed superintendent in 1864, the Dutch plantations have assumed a very prosperous state. J. C. Bernelot Moens,[1] the present director, stated that at the end of 1878 the leading species was Calisaya in its various forms, including more than 400,000 plants of Ledger's Calisaya. Numerous analyses of Bernelot Moens show a percentage of from 4½ to 10·6 of quinine in the latter variety. Some of them, however, in December 1878, afforded not more than 0·64 per cent. of quinine and 1·26 of cinchonidine.

The regular shipments of the barks from Java to the Amsterdam market are going on, and the barks are sold there with regard to the results of the government chemist's analyses.

Cinchona Bark from the Indian plantations began to be brought into the London market in 1867,[2] and now arrives in constantly increasing quantities.

The history of the transplantation of the Cinchona down to the year 1867 has been made the subject of the report of Soubeiran and Delondre mentioned at the end of the present article.

[1] I am indebted to the Dutch administration for their interesting statistical documents relating to Cinchona.—F. A. F.

[2] When I was in London, in August 1867, I went to Finsbury Place, to meet Mr. Spruce, and was happy enough to find there also Mr. Howard, who presented Mr. S. and myself with market samples of the *first* importation of *C. succirubra*, from Denison plantation, Ootacamund.—F. A. F.

Description—(A.) *Of Cinchona Barks generally*—In the development of their bark, the various species of Cinchona exhibit considerable diversity. Many are distinguished from an early stage by an abundant exfoliation of the outer surface, while in others this takes place to a smaller degree, or only as the bark becomes old. The external appearance of the bark varies therefore very much, by reason of the greater or less development of the suberous coat. The barks of young stems and branches have a greyish tint more or less intense, while the outer bark of old wood displays the more characteristic shades of brown or red, especially after removal of the corky layers.

In the living bark, these colours are very pale, and only acquire their final hue by exposure to the air, and drying. Some of them however are characteristic of individual species, or at least of certain groups, so that the distinctions originated by the bark-collectors of *pale, yellow, red,* etc.[1] and adopted by druggists, are not without reason.

In texture, the barks vary in an important manner by reason of diversity in anatomical structure. Their fracture especially depends upon the number, size, and arrangement of the liber fibres, as will be shown in our description of their microscopic characters.

The taste in all species is bitter and disagreeable, and in some there is in addition a decided astringency. Most species have no marked odour, at least in the dried state. But this is not the case in that of *C. officinalis*, the smell of which is characteristic.

(B.) *Of the Barks used in pharmacy*—For pharmaceutical preparations as distinguished from the pure alkaloids and their salts, the Cinchona barks employed are chiefly of three kinds.

1. *Pale Cinchona Bark, Loxa Bark, Crown Bark*[2]—This bark, which previous to the use of Quinine and for long afterwards, was the ordinary *Peruvian Bark* of English medicine, is only found in the form of quills, which are occasionally as much as a foot in length, but are more often only a few inches or are reduced to still smaller fragments. The quills are from $\frac{3}{4}$ down to an $\frac{1}{8}$ of an inch in diameter, often double, and variously twisted and shrunken. The thinnest bark is scarcely stouter than writing paper; the thickest may be $\frac{1}{10}$ of an inch or more.[3] The pieces have a blackish brown or dark greyish external surface, variously blotched with silver-grey, and often beset with large and beautiful lichens. The surface of some of the quills is longitudinally wrinkled and moderately smooth; but in the majority it is distinctly marked by transverse cracks, and is rough and harsh to the touch. The inner side is closely striated and of a bright yellowish brown.

The bark breaks easily with a fracture which exhibits very short fibres on the inner side. It has a well-marked odour *sui generis*, and an astringent bitter taste. Though chiefly afforded by *C. officinalis*, some other species occasionally contribute to furnish the Loxa Bark of commerce as shown in the conspectus at p. 355.

[1] The following are common terms in reference to the barks of Peru:—*Amarilla* (yellow), *blanca* (white), *colorado* or *roja* (red), *naranjada* (orange), *negrilla* (*brown*).

[2] *Cortex Cinchonæ pallidæ*; F. *Quinquina Loxa*; G. *Loxachina*. The term *Crown Bark* was originally restricted to a superior sort of Loxa Bark, shipped for the use of the royal family of Spain.

[3] In the old collections of the Royal College of Physicians, there are specimens of very thick Loxa Bark, of a quality quite unknown there at the present day. They are doubtless the produce of ancient trees, such as were noticed by La Condamine.

2. *Calisaya Bark, Yellow Cinchona Bark.*[1]—This bark, which is the most important of those commonly used in medicine, is found in flat pieces (α.), and in quills (β.), both afforded by *C. Calisaya* Wedd., though usually imported separated.

α. *Flat Calisaya*—is in irregular flat pieces, a foot or more in length by 3 to 4 inches wide, but usually smaller, and $\frac{2}{10}$ to $\frac{4}{10}$ of an inch in thickness; devoid of suberous layers and consisting almost solely of liber, of uniform texture, compact and ponderous. Its colour is a rusty orange-brown, with darker stains on the outer surface. The latter is roughened with shallow longitudinal depressions, sometimes called *digital furrows.*[2] The inner side has a wavy, close, fibrous texture. The bark breaks transversely with a fibrous fracture; the fibres of the broken ends are very short, easily detached, and with a lens are seen to be many of them faintly yellowish and translucent.

A well-marked variety, known as *Bolivian Calisaya*, is distinguished for its greater thinness, closer texture, and for containing numerous laticiferous ducts which are wanting in common flat Calisaya bark.

β. *Quill Calisaya*—is found in tubes $\frac{3}{4}$ to $1\frac{1}{2}$ inch thick, often rolled up at both edges, thus forming double quills. They are always coated with a thick, rugged, corky layer, marked with deep longitudinal and transverse cracks, the edges of which are somewhat elevated. This suberous coat, which is silvery white or greyish, is easily detached, leaving its impression on the cinnamon-brown middle layer. The inner side is dark brown and finely fibrous. The transverse fracture is fibrous but very short. The same bark also occurs in quills of very small size, and is then not distinguishable with certainty from Loxa bark.

3. *Red Cinchona Bark.*—Though still retaining a place in the British Pharmacopœia, this is by far the least important of the Cinchona barks employed in pharmacy. But as the tree yielding it (*C. succirubra*) is now being cultivated on a large scale in India, the bark may probably come more freely into use.

Red Bark of large stems, which is the most esteemed kind, occurs in the form of flat or channelled pieces, sometimes as much as $\frac{1}{2}$ an inch in thickness, coated with their suberous envelope which is rugged and warty. Its outermost layer in the young bark has a silvery appearance. The inner surface is close and fibrous and of a brick-red hue. The bark breaks with a short fibrous fracture.[3]

(C.) *Of the Barks not used in pharmacy*—Among the non-officinal barks, the most important are afforded by *Cinchona lancifolia* Mutis and *C. pitayensis* Wedd., natives of the Cordilleras of Columbia.

These barks are largely imported and used for making quinine, the former under the name of *Columbian, Carthagena*, or *Caqueta bark.* It varies much in appearance, but is generally of an orange-brown; the corky coat, which scales off easily, is shining and whitish. The barks of *C. lancifolia* often occur in fine large quills or thick flattish pieces. Their anatomical structure agrees in all varieties which we have examined, in the remarkable number of thick-walled and

[1] *Cortex Cinchonæ flavæ, Cortex Chinæ regius; F. Quinquina Calisaya;* G. *Königschina.*

[2] From the notion that they resemble the marks left by drawing the fingers over wet clay.

[3] Thick Red Bark that happens to have a very deep and brilliant tint is eagerly bought at a high price for the Paris market.

tangentially extended cells of the middle cortical layer and the medullary rays. In percentage of alkaloids, Carthagena barks are liable to great variation.

The *Pitayo Barks* are restricted to the south-western districts of Columbia,[1] and are usually imported in short flattish fragments, or broken quills, of brownish rather than orange colour, mostly covered with a dull greyish or internally reddish cork. The middle cortical layer exhibits but few thick-walled cells; the liber is traversed by very wide medullary rays, and is provided with but a small number of widely scattered liber fibres, which are rather thinner than in most other Cinchona barks. The Pitayo barks are usually rich in alkaloids, quinine prevailing. *Cinchona pitayensis* is one of the hardiest species of the valuable Cinchonas, and is therefore particularly suitable for cultivation, which however has not yet been carried out as largely as that of either *C. officinalis* or *C. succirubra.*

In the Conspectus on the next page, we have arranged the principal species of *Cinchona,* with short indications of the barks which some of them afford.[2]

Microscopic Structure—The first examination of the minute structure of Cinchona barks is due to Weddell, whose observations have been recorded in one of his beautiful plates published in 1849.[3] Since that time numerous other observers have laboured in the same field of research.

General Characters.—These barks, as contrasted with those of other trees, do not exhibit any great peculiarities of structure; and their features may be comprehended in the following statements. The *epidermis,* in the anatomical sense, occurs only in the youngest barks, which are not found in commerce. The *corky layer,* which replaces the epidermis, is constructed of the usual tabular cells. In some species as *C. Calisaya,* it separates easily, at least in the older bark, whereas in others as *C. succirubra,* the bark even of trunks is always coated with it. In several species the corky tissue is not only found on the surface, but strips of it occur also in the inner substance of the bark. In this case the portions of tissue external to the inner corky layers or bands are thrown off as *bork-scales* (*periderm* of Weddell). This peculiar form of suberous tissue[4] was first examined (not in cinchona) in 1845 by H. von Mohl, who called it *rhytidoma* (*Borke* of the Germans). In *C. Calisaya* it is of constant occurrence, but not so usually in *C. succirubra* and some others; the rhytidoma therefore affords a good means of distinguishing several barks.

The inner portion of the bark exhibits a *middle* or *primary layer* (*mesophlœum*),[5] made up of parenchyme; and a second inner layer or *liber* (*endophlœum*)[6] displaying a much more complicated structure. The primary layer disappears if rhytidoma is formed: barks in which

[1] Pitayo is an Indian village eastward of Popayan; see map of the country btween Pasto and Bogotá in Blue Book (East India Chinchona Plant) 1866. 257.

[2] Two species included by Weddell in his *Notes sur les Quinquinas,* namely *C. Chomeliana* Wedd. and *C. barbacoensis* Karst., have been omitted, as not in our opinion belonging to the genus.

[3] *Hist. nat. des Quinquinas,* tab. ii.

[4] Flückiger, *Grundlagen,* Berlin, 1872. 61. fig. 48.

[5] *Enveloppe ou tunique cellulaire* of Weddell; *Mittelrinde* of the Germans.

[6] In German *Bast,* or *Phloëm* of modern German botany.

CONSPECTUS OF THE PRINCIPAL SPECIES OF CINCHONA.

SPECIES (EXCLUDING SUB-SPECIES AND VARIETIES) ACCORDING TO WEDDELL.	WHERE FIGURED.	NATIVE COUNTRY.	WHERE CULTIVATED.	PRODUCT.
I. Stirps Cinchonæ officinalis				
1. Cinchona officinalis Hook	Bot. Mag. 5364	Ecuador (Loxa)	India, Ceylon, Java.	Loxa or Crown Bark, Pale Bark.
2. „ macrocalyx Pav.	Howard N. Q.	Peru	- - -	Ashy Crown Bark. The sub-species *C. Palton* affords an important sort called *Palton Bark* much used in the manufacture of quinine.
3. „ lucumæfolia Pav.	Do.	Ecuador, Peru.		
4. „ lanceolata R. et P. (?)	Do.	Peru	- - -	Carthagena Bark, confounded with Palton Bark, but is not so good.
5. „ lancifolia Mutis	Karsten tab. 11. 12.	New Granada	India	Columbian Bark. Imported in large quantities for manufacture of quinine. The soft Columbian Bark is produced by Howard's var. *oblonga*.
6. „ amygdalifolia Wedd.	Wedd. tab. 6.	Peru, Bolivia	- - -	A poor bark, but not now imported.
II. Stirps Cinchonæ rugosæ				
7. Cinchona pitayensis Wedd.	Karst. tab. 22. (*C. Trianæ*)	New Granada (Popayan)	India	Pitayo Bark. Very valuable; used by makers of quinine; it is the chief source of quinidine.
8. „ rugosa Pav.	Howard N. Q.	Peru	- - -	Bark unknown, probably valueless.
9. „ Mutisii Lamb.	Do.	Ecuador	- - -	Bark not in commerce, contains only aricine.
10. „ hirsuta R. et P.	Wedd. tab. 21.	Peru.	- - -	
11. „ carabayensis Wedd.	Wedd. tab. 19.	Peru, Bolivia	- - -	Bark not collected.
12. „ Pahudiana How.	Howard N. Q.	Peru	India, Java	A poor bark, yet of handsome appearance; propagation of tree discontinued.
13. „ asperifolia Wedd.	Wedd. tab. 20.	Bolivia	- - -	Bark not collected.
14. „ umbellulifera Pav.	Howard N. Q.	Peru	- - -	Bark not known as a distinct sort.
15. „ glandulifera R. et P.	Do.	Peru	- - -	Do.
16. „ Humboldtiana Lamb.	Do.	Peru	- - -	False Loxa Bark, Jaen Bark. A very bad bark.
III. Stirps Cinchonæ micranthæ				
17. Cinchona australis Wedd.	Wedd. tab. 8.	South Bolivia	- - -	An inferior bark, mixed with Calisaya.
18. „ scrobiculata H. et B.	Do.	Peru	- - -	Bark formerly known as *Red Cusco Bark* or *Santa Ana Bark*.
19. „ peruviana How.	Howard N. Q.	Peru	India	Grey Bark, Huanuco or Lima Bark. Chiefly consumed on the Continent.
20. „ nitida R. et P.	Do.	Peru	India	
21. „ micrantha R. et P.	Do.	Peru	India	
IV. Stirps Cinchonæ Calisayæ				
22. Cinchona Calisaya Wedd.	Wedd. tab. 9.	Peru, Bolivia	India, Ceylon, Java, Jamaica, Mexico,	Calisaya Bark, Bolivian Bark, Yellow Bark. The tree exists under many varieties, bark also very variable.
23. „ elliptica Wedd.	- - -	Peru (Carabaya)	- - -	Carabaya Bark. Bark scarcely now imported. *C. euneura* Miq. (flower and fruit unknown) may perhaps be this species.
V. Stirps Cinchonæ ovatæ				
24. Cinchona purpurea R. et P.	Howard N. Q.	Peru (Huamalies)	- - -	Huamalies Bark. Not now imported.
25. „ rufinervis Wedd.	Do.	Peru, Bolivia	- - -	Bark, a kind of light Calisaya.
26. „ succirubra Pav.	Do.	Ecuador	India, Ceylon, Java, Jamaica.	Red Bark. Largely cultivated in British India.
27. „ ovata R. et P.	Do.	Peru, Bolivia	India (?), Java (?)	Inferior Brown and Grey Barks.
28. „ cordifolia Mutis	Karsten tab. 8.	New Granada, Peru	- - -	Columbian Bark (in part). Tree exists under many varieties; bark of some used in manufacture of quinine.
29. „ tucujensis Karst.	Karsten tab. 9.	Venezuela	- - -	Maracaibo Bark.
30. „ pubescens Vahl	Wedd. tab. 16.	Ecuador, Peru, Bolivia	- - -	Arica Bark (Cusco Bark from var. *Pelletieriana*). Some of the varieties contain aricine. *C. calyptera* Miq. is probably a var. of this species.
31. „ purpurascens Wedd.	Wedd. tab. 18	Bolivia	- - -	Bark unknown in commerce.

this is the case are therefore at last exclusively composed of liber, of which Flat Calisaya Bark is a good example.

The liber is traversed by *medullary rays*, which in cinchona are mostly very obvious, and project more or less distinctly into the middle cortical tissue. The liber is separated by the medullary rays into wedges,[1] which are constituted of a parenchymatous part and of yellow or orange fibres. The number, colour, shape, and size, but chiefly the arrangement of these fibres, confer a certain character common to all the barks of the group under consideration.

The liber-fibres[2] are elongated and bluntly pointed at their ends, but never branched, mostly spindle-shaped, straight or slightly curved, and not exceeding in length 3 millimetres. They are consequently of a simpler structure than the analogous cells of most other officinal barks. They are about $\frac{1}{4}$ to $\frac{1}{3}$ mm. thick, their transverse section exhibiting a quadrangular rather than a circular outline. Their walls are strongly thickened by numerous secondary deposits, the cavity being reduced to a narrow cleft, a structure which explains the brittleness of the fibres. The liber-fibres are either irregularly scattered in the liber-rays, or they form radial lines transversely intersected by narrow strips of parenchyme, or they are densely packed in short bundles. It is a peculiarity of cinchona barks that these bundles consist always of a few fibres (3 to 5 or 7), whereas in many other barks (as cinnamon) analogous bundles are made up of a large number of fibres. Barks provided with long bundles of the latter kind acquire therefrom a very fibrous fracture, whilst cinchona barks from their short and simple fibres exhibit a short fracture. It is rather granular in Calisaya bark, in which the fibres are almost isolated by parenchymatous tissue. In the bark of *C. scrobiculata*, a somewhat short fibrous fracture[3] is due to the arrangement of the fibres in radial rows. In *C. pubescens*, the fibres are in short bundles and produce a rather woody fracture.

Besides the liber-fibres, there are some other cells contributing to the peculiarity of individual cinchona barks. This applies chiefly to the *laticiferous ducts* or *vessels*[4] which are found in many sorts; they are scattered through the tissue intervening between the middle cortical layer and the liber, and consist of soft, elongated, unbranched cells, mostly exceeding in diameter the neighbouring parenchymatous cells.

As to the *contents of the tissue* of cinchona barks, crystallized alkaloids are not visible. Howard has published figures representing minute rounded aggregations of crystalline matter in the cells, which he supposes to be kinovates of the alkaloids; and also distinct acicular crystals which he holds to be of the same nature. These remarkable appearances are easily observable, yet only after sections of the bark have been boiled for a minute in weak caustic alkali and then washed with water; it may well be doubted whether they are strictly natural. The liquids which are capable of dissolving the alkaloids in the free state do not afford any if they are applied to the barks. The alkaloids being contained in the bark in the form of salts, the latter are decom-

[1] *Baststrahlen* or *Phloëmstrahlen* of the Germans.

[2] *Fibres corticales* of Weddell; *Baströhren* or *Bastzellen* in German.

[3] *Fracture filandreuse*, Weddel; *fädiger Bruch* of the Germans.

[4] *Vaisseaux laticifères* of Weddell; *Milchsaftschläuche* in German.

posed by caustic lye, and the alkaloids set at liberty assume the crystallized state. This is in our opinion the origin of the crystals under notice.

The greater number of the parenchymatous cells are loaded with small starch granules, or in young and fresh barks with chlorophyll. In several barks, as in that of *C. lancifolia* Mutis, numerous cells of the middle cortical layer and even of the medullary rays, are provided with somewhat thick walls, and contain either a soft brown mass or crystalline oxalate of calcium. These cells have therefore been called *resin-cells* and *crystal-cells*; they are mostly isolated, not forming extensive groups or zones, and their walls are not strongly thickened as in true sclerenchymatous tissue. If thin sections of the barks are moistened with dilute alcoholic perchloride of iron, the walls of the cells, except the fibres and the cork, assume a blackish-green due to cinchotannic acid; this applies even to the starch granules.

Characters of particular sorts.—The modifications of general structure just described, are sufficient to impart a special character to the bark of many species of Cinchona, provided the bark is examined at its full development, the structural peculiarities being far from well-marked in young barks.

Thus it is not possible to point out any distinctive features for the *Loxa Bark* of commerce, because it is mostly taken from young wood. We may say of it, that neither resin-cells nor crystal-cells occur in its middle layer, that its laticiferous vessels become soon obliterated, and have indeed disappeared in the older quills; and that the liber-fibres form interrupted, not very regular, radial rows.

The quills of *C. Calisaya* display large laticiferous ducts, which are wanting in the flat bark. There is a peculiar sort of the latter called *Bolivian Calisaya* (already mentioned at p. 353), the flat pieces of which still possess very obvious laticiferous vessels. As to the liber-fibres of Calisaya bark, they are, as before stated (p. 356), scattered throughout the parenchymatous tissue or endophlœum. In the bark of *C. scrobiculata*, which might at first sight be confounded with Calisaya bark, the liber-fibres form radial, less interrupted rows. The microscope affords therefore the means of distinguishing these two barks.

The barks of *C. succirubra* are particularly rich in laticiferous ducts, mostly of considerable diameter, in which the formation of new parenchyme may not unfrequently be observed. The orange liber-fibres occurring in this bark are less numerous, more scattered, and of smaller size than in Calisaya. The fracture of Red Bark, especially the flat sort, is therefore more finely granular and not so coarse as that of Calisaya.

The structural characters of Cinchona barks may lastly be fully appreciated by examining barks of the allied genera *Buena*, *Cascarilla* and *Ladenbergia*, which were formerly known under the name of *False Cinchona Barks*. The microscope shows that the liber-fibres of the latter are soft, branched and long, densely packed into large bundles, imparting therefore a well-marked fibrous structure. The external appearance of these barks is widely different from that of true cinchona barks; none of them it would appear is now collected for the purpose of adulteration.

Chemical Composition—The most important and at the same time peculiar principles of Cinchona bark are the *Alkaloids*,—enumerated in the following table:—[1]

Cinchonine	$C^{20}H^{24}N^2O$.
or, as proposed by Skraup (1878)	$C^{19}H^{22}N^2O$
Cinchonidine (*Quinidine* of many writers) .	same formula.
Quinine	$C^{20}H^{24}N^2O^2$.
Quinidine (*Conquinine* of Hesse) . . .	same formula.
Quinamine	$C^{19}H^{24}N^2O^2$.
Conquinamine (*Conchinamine*) . . .	same formula.

B. A. Gomes[2] of Lisbon (1810) first succeeded in obtaining active principles of cinchona, by treating an alcoholic extract of the bark with water, adding to the solution caustic potash, and crystallizing the precipitate from alcohol. The basic properties of the substance thus obtained, which Gomes called *Cinchonino*, were observed in the laboratory of Thénard by Houtou-Labillardière, and communicated to Pelletier and Caventou.[3] Shortly before that time, Sertürner had asserted the existence of organic alkalis: and the French chemists, guided by that brilliant discovery, were enabled to show that the *Cinchonino* of Gomes belonged to the same class of substances. Pelletier and Caventou, however, speedily pointed out that it consisted of two distinct alkaloids, one of which they named *Quinine*, the other *Cinchonine*. In 1827 the Institut de France awarded to the two chemists for their discovery the Montyon prize of 10,000 francs (see page 57, note 4).

Cinchonidine (thus called by Pasteur in 1853) was first obtained and characterized under the name of *Quinidine* in 1847, by F. L. Winckler of Darmstadt, from Maracaibo Bark (*C. tucujensis* Karst.); and in 1852 it was more closely studied by Leers, still under the name of *quinidine*.

Cinchovatine, formerly stated to be a peculiar alkaloid, has been shown by Hesse in 1876 to agree with cinchonidine.

Quinidine is the name applied by Henry and Delondre to an alkaloid they obtained in 1833; its peculiar nature was not clearly proved until 1853, when Pasteur examined it, and 1857 when De Vry showed its identity with the *Beta-quinine* extracted in 1849 by Van Heijningnen from commercial quinoidin. The name *quinidine* having been since applied to different basic substances more or less pure, Hesse (1865) has proposed to replace it by that of *Conquinine* (Conchinin in German). The alkaloid is especially characteristic of the Pitayo barks, and also occurs in the Calisaya barks from Java.

Quinamine was discovered in 1872 by Hesse, in bark of *C. succirubra* cultivated at Darjiling in British Sikkim; it is also of common occurrence in the barks collected in Java. *Conquinamine* was extracted in 1873 by Hesse from old barks from British India.

Paricine is another basic substance discovered in 1845 by Winckler, in the bark of *Buena hexandra* Pohl. Hesse detected it along with

[1] Hesse, in 1877, pointed out the existence of a series of new alkaloids existing in Cinchona. We refrain from repeating his statements, which will be found abstracted in the *Yearbook of Pharm.* 1878. 63.

[2] Ensaio sobre o Cinchonino, e sobre sua influencia na virtude da quina e d'outras cascas.—*Mem. da Acad. R. das Sciencias de Lisboa*, iii. (1812) 202-217.

[3] *Ann. de Chim. et de Phys.* xv. (1820) 292.

quinamine in the bark of *C. succirubra;* its composition is not yet known.

Aricine, $C^{23}H^{26}N^2O^4$, and *Cusconine*, $C^{23}H^{26}N^2O^4 + 2\ OH^2$, occur in the so-called false Cinchona barks of not ascertained botanic origin. These alkaloids differ in many respects from those of true Cinchona barks.[1]

Pitoyine was pointed out by Peretti (1837), but Hesse has shown (1873) that the bark called *China bicolorata Tecamez*[2] or *Pitoya Bark* from which it was obtained, is altogether destitute of alkaloid.

Lastly may be mentioned *Paytine*, $C^{21}H^{24}N^2O + OH^2$, a crystallizable alkaloid discovered in 1870 by Hesse in a white bark of uncertain origin.[3] It is allied to quinamine and quinidine, but has not been met with in any known cinchona bark.

By heating for a length of time solutions of the cinchona alkaloids with an excess of some mineral acid, Pasteur (1753) obtained amorphous modifications of the natural bases. Quinine thus afforded *Quinicine*, having the same composition; cinchonine and cinchonidine furnished *Cinchonicine*, likewise agreeing in composition with the alkaloids from which it originates. These amorphous products may also be obtained by heating the natural bases in glycerin at 200° C., when a red substance is also formed. In quinine manufactories, amorphous alkaloids are constantly met with, being partly produced in the course of the manipulations to which the materials are subjected. Yet cinchona barks also afford *amorphous alkaloids* at the very outset of analysis, whence we must infer their existence in the living plant.

The name *Quinoidine* (or rather "*Chinioïdin*") was applied by Sertürner (1829) to an uncrystallizable basic substance, which he prepared from cinchona barks, and found to be a peculiar alkaloid. The term has subsequently been bestowed upon a preparation which has found its way into commerce and medical practice, in the form of a dark brown brittle extractiform mass, softening below 100° C., and having usually a slight alkaline reaction. It is obtained in quinine factories by precipitating the brown mother-liquors with ammonia, and contains the amorphous alkaloids naturally occurring in the barks. Quinoidin should not be used unless, when previously dried at 100°, it proves to afford at least 70 per cent. of alkaloids soluble in ether.

Quinine and the allied alkaloids have not been met with in any appreciable amount in other parts of the cinchonas than the bark, nor has their presence been ascertained in other plants than those of the tribe *Cinchoneæ*.

Characters of the Cinchona Alkaloids.

1. *Quinine*.—It is obtained from alcoholic solutions, in prisms of the composition $C^{20}H^{24}N^2O^2 + 3\ OH^2$, fusing at 57° C. The crystals may be deprived of water by warming or exposure over oil of vitriol, and they

[1] *Yearbook of Pharm.* 1878. 59.

[2] So called from Tecamez or Tacames, a small port of Ecuador in about lat. 1° N. The bark which was first noticed in Lambert's *Description of the Genus Cinchona*, 1797. 30. tab. ii., is of unknown botanical origin. In its external appearance, as well as in its structure, this bark is widely different from any Cinchona bark.—See also Vogl, in the second pamphlet quoted at page 391. 10; Oberlin and Schlagdenhauffen, *Journ. de Pharm.* 28. (1878) 252.

[3] Flückiger in Wiggers and Husemann, *Jahresbericht* for 1872. 132.

fuse at 177° C. The anhydrous alkaloid is likewise crystallizable; it requires about 21 parts of ether for solution, but dissolves more readily in chloroform or absolute alcohol. These solutions deviate the ray of polarized light to the left, and so do likewise solutions of the salts of quinine. Yet one and the same quantity of alkaloid exhibits a very different rotatory power according to the solvent used, though the volume of the solution remain the same. Even the common sulphate differs in this respect from the two other sulphates of quinine. The same remark applies to the optical power of the other alkaloids.

If ten volumes of a solution of quinine, or of one of its salts, are mixed in a test tube with one volume of chlorine water, and a drop of ammonia is added, a brilliant green colour makes its appearance. In solutions rich in quinine, a green precipitate, *Thalleioquin* or *Dalleiochine* is produced; in solutions containing less than $\frac{1}{1000}$ of quinine, no precipitate is formed, but the fluid assumes a green even more beautiful than in a stronger solution. The test succeeds with a solution containing only one part of quinine in 5,000, and in a solution containing not more than $\frac{1}{20000}$ of quinine, if bromine is used instead of chlorine.[1]

The bitter taste of quinine is not appreciable in solutions containing less than one part in 100,000. The blue fluorescence displayed by a solution of quinine in dilute sulphuric acid is observable in solutions containing much less than one part in 200,000 of water; yet it is not apparent in very strong solutions.

Besides the *common medicinal* sulphate, $2\,C^{20}H^{24}N^2O^2 + SO^4H^2 + 8\,OH^2$, quinine forms two other crystallizable sulphates, namely the sulphate, $C^{20}H^{24}N^2O^2 + SO^4H^2 + 7\,OH^2$, and a third having the composition $C^{20}H^{24}N^2O^2 + 2\,SO^4H^2 + 7\,OH^2$.

Herapath, at Bristol, showed in 1852 that quinine forms with sulphuric acid and iodine a peculiar compound, *Iodo-sulphate of Quinine*, having the composition $(C^{20}H^{24}N^2O^2)^4 + 3\,(SO^4H^2) + 2\,HI + 4\,I + 3\,OH^2$. As this substance possesses optical properties analogous to those of tourmaline, it was called by Haidinger, *Herapathite*. It may be easily obtained by dissolving sulphate of quinine in 10 parts of weak spirit of wine containing 5 per cent. of sulphuric acid, and adding an alcoholic solution of iodine until a black precipitate is no longer formed. This precipitate is collected on a filter and washed with alcohol; then dissolved in boiling spirit of wine and allowed to crystallize. The tabular crystals thus obtained are extremely remarkable on account of their dichroism and polarizing power, as well as for the sparing solubility, since they require 1000 parts of boiling water for solution; their sparing solubility in cold alcohol may be utilized for separating quinine from the other cinchona alkaloids and estimating its quantity.

2. *Quinidine* or *Conquinine*—forms crystals having the composition, $C^{20}H^{24}N^2O^2 + 2\,OH^2$; the anhydrous alkaloid melts at 168° C., and requires about 30 parts of ether for solution. Its solutions are strongly dextrogyre; it agrees with quinine as regards bitterness, fluorescence and the thalleioquin test, and forms a neutral and an acid sulphate. The most striking character of quinidine is afforded by its hydriodate, the crystals of which require for solution at 15° C., 1250 parts of water or 110 parts of alcohol sp. gr. ·834. Quinidine may therefore be sepa-

[1] *Pharm. Journ.*, May 11, 1872. 901.

rated from the other alkaloids of bark by a solution of iodide of potassium which will precipitate the hydriodate. According to Hesse (1873), quinidine is further characterized by the fact that its sulphate is soluble in 20 parts of chloroform at 15° C., the sulphates of the other cinchona-alkaloids being far less soluble in that liquid. The common medicinal sulphate of quinine, *e.g.*, requires for solution 1000 parts of chloroform.

3. *Cinchonine.*—This alkaloid forms crystals which are always anhydrous; they fuse at 257° C., and require about 400 parts of ether and 120 of spirit of wine for solution. Cinchonine further differs from quinine by its dextrogyre power, its want of fluorescence, and its non-susceptibility to the thalleioquin test. Its hydriodate is readily soluble in water, and still more so in alcohol whether dilute or strong.

4. *Cinchonidine*—forms anhydrous crystals melting at 206° C., soluble in 76 parts of ether, or 20 of spirit of wine, then affording levogyre liquids, devoid of fluorescence, and not acquiring a green colour (thalleioquin) by means of chlorine water and ammonia. Hydrochlorate of cinchonidine forms pyramidal crystals of the monoclinic system, very different from the hydrochlorates of the allied alkaloids.

5. *Quinamine.*—The crystals are anhydrous, fuse at 172° C., and form at a temp. of 20°, with 32 parts of ether or 100 parts of spirit of wine, a dextrogyre solution. Quinamine is even to some extent soluble in boiling water, and abundantly in boiling ether, benzol, or petroleum ether. The solutions of quinamine do not stand the thalleioquin test, nor do they display fluorescence; in acid solution, the alkaloid is liable to be transformed into an amorphous state. Quinamine moistened with concentrated nitric acid, assumes like paytine a yellow coloration. Its hydriodate is readily soluble in boiling water, but very sparingly in cold water, especially in presence of iodide of potassium, in which respect it is allied to quinidine as well as to paytine.

The more important properties of the Cinchona-alkaloids may be summarized as follows:—

a. *Hydrated* crystals are formed by . . .	Quinine, Quinidine, (or Conquinine).
No hydrated crystals by	Cinchonine, Cinchonidine, Quinamine.
b. *Abundantly* soluble in ether	Quinine, Quinidine, Quinamine, and the amorphous alkaloids.
Sparingly soluble in ether	Cinchonidine.
Almost insoluble in ether	Cinchonine.
c. *Levogyre* solutions afforded by . . .	Quinine, Cinchonidine.
Dextrogyre solutions by	Cinchonine, Quinidine, Quinamine, Conquinamine, and the amorphous alkaloids.
d. Thalleioquin is formed by	Quinine, Quinidine, and also by Quinicine.
Thalleioquin cannot be obtained from	Cinchonine, Cinchonidine, Quinamine, nor from Cinchonicine.
e. Fluorescence is displayed by solutions of	Quinine, Quinidine.
No fluorescence in solutions of pure . .	Cinchonine, Cinchonidine, Quinamine.

Proportion of Alkaloids in Cinchona Barks—This is liable to very great variation. We know from the experiments of Hesse (1871), that the bark of *C. pubescens* Vahl is sometimes devoid of alkaloid.[1] Similar observations made near Bogota upon *C. pitayensis* Wedd., *C.*

[1] *Berichte der Deutschen Chem. Gesellschaft zu Berlin*, 1871. 818.

corymbosa Karst., and *C. lancifolia* Mutis, are due to Karsten. He ascertained[1] that barks of one district were sometimes devoid of quinine, while those of the same species from a neighbouring locality yielded 3½ to 4½ per cent. of sulphate of quinine.

Another striking example is furnished by De Vry[2] in his examination of quills of *C. officinalis* grown at Ootacamund, which he found to vary in percentage of alkaloids, from 11·96 (of which 9·1 per cent. was quinine) down to less than 1 per cent. An extremely remarkable variation has also been displayed, as already alluded to at p. 351, by Ledger's Calisaya.

Among the innumerable published analyses of cinchona bark, there are a great number showing but a very small percentage of the useful principles, of which quinine, the most valuable of all, is not seldom altogether wanting. The highest yield on the other hand hitherto observed, was obtained by Broughton[3] from a bark grown at Ootacamund. This bark afforded not less than 13½ per cent. of alkaloids, among which quinine was predominant. In Java too, Cinchona Ledgeriana (see pp. 341, 351) has proved since to afford much more alkaloid than any American barks; as much as 13·25 per cent. of quinine have been observed in its bark.

The few facts just mentioned show that it is impossible to state even approximately any constant percentage of alkaloids in any given bark. We may however say that good *Flat Calisaya Bark*, as offered in the drug trade for pharmaceutical preparations, contains at least 5 to 6 per cent. of quinine.

As to *Crown* or *Loxa Bark*, the *Cortex Cinchonæ pallidæ* of pharmacy, its merits are, to say the least, very uncertain. On its first introduction in the 17th century, when it was taken from the trunks and large branches of full-grown trees, it was doubtless an excellent medicinal bark; but the same cannot be said of much of that now found in commerce, which is to a large extent collected from very young wood.[4] Some of the Crown Bark produced in India is however of extraordinary excellence, as shown by the recent experiments of De Vry.[5]

As to *Red Bark*, the thick flat sort contains only 3 to 4 per cent. of alkaloids, but a large amount of colouring matter. The quill Red Bark of the Indian plantations is a much better drug, some of it yielding 5 to 10 per cent. of alkaloids, less than a third of which is quinine and a fourth cinchonidine, the remainder being cinchonine and sometimes also traces of quinidine (conquinine).

The variations in the amount of alkaloids relates not merely to their total percentage, but also to the proportion which one bears to another. Quinine and cinchonine are of the most frequent occurrence; cinchonidine is less usual, while quinidine is still less frequently met with and never in large amount. The experiments performed in India[6] have already shown that external influences contribute in an important

[1] *Die medicinischen Chinarinden Neu-Granada's*, 17. 20. 39.

[2] *Pharm. Journ.* Sept. 6, 1873. 181.

[3] Blue Book—"*East India Chinchona Plant*," 1870. 282; *Yearbook of Pharmacy*, 1871. 85.

[4] See Howard's analyses and observations, *Pharm. Journ.* xiv. (1855) 61–63.

[5] *Pharm. Journ.* Sept. 6, 1873. 184.

[6] Blue Book, 1870. 116. 188. 205.

manner to the formation of this or that alkaloid; and it may even be hoped that the cultivators of cinchona will discover methods of promoting the formation of quinine and of reducing, if not of excluding, that of the less valuable alkaloids.

Most salts of the alkaloids of cinchona afford a beautiful purple tar when they are heated in a test tube, and the same is also produced with the powdered bark, provided alkaloids be present. No other bark, as far as we know, yields a similar product of the dry distillation. It is not observed even in using true Cinchona barks, which are devoid of alkaloids. This method for ascertaining the presence of alkaloids in Cinchona barks has been proposed in 1858 by Grahe of Kasan. Hesse has improved Grahe's test in the following way: he extracts the powdered bark with slightly acidulated water and dries up the liquid with a little of the powder. *Grahe's test* at once shows whether a given bark contains Cinchona alkaloids or not.

Acid principles of Cinchona Barks—Count Claude de la Garaye[1] observed (1746) a crystalline salt deposited in extract of cinchona bark, which salt was known for some time in France as *Sel essential de la Garaye*. Hermbstädt at Berlin (1785) showed it to be a salt of calcium, the peculiarity of whose acid was pointed out in 1790 by C. A. Hoffmann,[2] an apothecary of Leer in Hanover, who termed it *Chinasäure*. The composition of this substance, which is the *Kinic Acid* of English chemists, was ascertained by Liebig in 1830 to be $C^7H^{12}O^6$, or now $C^6H^7(OH)^4COOH$. The acid forms large monoclinic prisms, fusible at 162° C., of a strong and pure acid taste, soluble in two parts of water, also in spirit of wine, but hardly in ether. The solutions are levogyre. Kinic acid appears to be present in every species, and also to occur in barks of allied genera; and in fact to be of somewhat wide distribution in the vegetable kingdom. By heating it or a kinate, interesting derivatives are obtained; thus, by means of peroxide of manganese and sulphuric acid, we get yellow crystals of *Kinone* or *Quinone*, $C^6H^4O^2$,—a reaction which may be used for ascertaining the presence of kinic acid. Kinic acid is devoid of any noteworthy physiological action.

Cincho-tannic Acid—is precipitated from a decoction of bark by acetate of lead, after the decoction has been freed from cinchona-red by means of magnesia. Dr. de Vry informed us that the Indian barks are usually richer in cincho-tannic acid; their cold infusion becomes turbid on addition of hydrochloric acid, which forms an insoluble compound with the former.

The cincho-tannate of lead decomposed by sulphuretted hydrogen, and the solution cautiously evaporated *in vacuo*, yields the acid as an amorphous, hygroscopic substance, readily soluble in water, alcohol, or ether. The solutions, especially in presence of an alkali, are quickly decomposed, a red flocculent matter, *Cinchona-red*, being produced. Solutions of cincho-tannic acid assume a greenish colour on addition of a ferric salt. By destructive distillation, cincho-tannic acid affords pyrocatechin.

Quinovic (or *Chinovic*) *Acid*, $C^{24}H^{38}O^4$, crystallizes in hexagonal scales which are sparingly soluble in cold alcohol, more readily in boiling alcohol, but not dissolved by water, ether, or chloroform. It

[1] *Chimie hydraulique*, Paris, 1746. 114. [2] Crell's *Chem. Annalen*, 1790, ii. 314-317.

occurs in cinchona barks, and has been met with by **Rembold** (1868) in the rhizome of *Potentilla Tormentilla* Sibth.

Other Constituents of Cinchona Barks—Quinovic acid is accompanied by *Quinovin* (or *Chinovin*), $C^{30}H^{48}O^{8}$, an amorphous bitter substance, first obtained (1821) by Pelletier and Caventou under the name of *Kinovic Acid*, from *China nova*,[1] in which it occurs combined with lime. Quinovin in alcoholic solution was shown in 1859 by Hlasiwetz to be resolved by means of hydrochloric gas into quinovic acid, $C^{24}H^{38}O^{4}$, and an uncrystallizable sugar, *Mannitan*, $C^{6}H^{12}O^{5}$, with subtraction of $H^{2}O$. The formation of quinovic acid takes place more easily, if quinovin is placed in contact with sodium amalgam and spirit of wine, when, after 12 hours, mannitan and quinovate of sodium are formed (Rochleder, 1867).

Quinovin, although an indifferent substance, may be removed from cinchona barks by weak caustic soda, from which it is precipitable by hydrochloric acid, together with quinovic acid and cinchona-red. Milk of lime then dissolves quinovin and quinovic acid, but not the red substance. Quinovic acid and quinovin again precipitated by an acid, may be separated by chloroform in which the latter only is soluble, or also by cold dilute alcohol sp. gr. about 0·926, quinovin being readily removed by this liquid.

Quinovin dissolves in boiling water; its solutions, as well as those of quinovic acid, are dextrogyre. Quinovin seems to be a constituent of almost every part of the cinchonas and the allied *Cinchoneæ*, although the amount of it in barks does not apparently exceed 2 per cent. It is accompanied by quinovic acid: both substances are stated to have tonic properties.

Cinchona-red, an amorphous substance to which the red hue of cinchona barks is due, is produced as shown by Rembold (1867), when cincho-tannic acid is boiled with dilute sulphuric acid, sugar being formed at the same time. By fusing cinchona-red with potash, protocatechuic acid, $C^{7}H^{6}O^{4}$, is produced. Cinchona-red is sparingly soluble in alcohol, abundantly in alkaline solutions, but neither in water nor in ether. Thick Red Bark in which it is abundant, affords it to the extent of over 10 per cent.

The Cinchona barks yield but a scanty percentage of ash, not exceeding 3 per cent., a fact well according with the small amount they contain of oxalate and kinate of calcium.

Estimation of the Alkaloids in Cinchona Bark—The microscope will enable us, as already shown, to ascertain whether a given bark is derived from *Cinchona*, but it can furnish no exact information as to the actual value of such bark as a drug.

Yet there is a very simple test by which the presence of a cinchona-alkaloid may be demonstrated. These alkaloids heated in a glass tube in the presence of a volatile acid or of substances capable of producing a volatile acid, evolve heavy vapours of a beautiful crimson colour, as mentioned p. 363.

[1] The bark of *Buena magnifolia* Wedd., a tree with fragrant flowers and magnificent foliage, figured in Howard's "*Nueva Quinologia of Pavon*" as Cinchona magnifolia. Its bark is destitute of alkaloids; it also used to appear occasionally in the London market since about the year 1820.—See also our article on *Cortex Cascarillæ*.

But to ascertain the real value of a cinchona bark, a quantitative estimation of the alkaloids is necessary. A good process for this operation has been given by De Vry.[1] It is as follows :—Mix 20 grammes of powdered bark, dried at 100° C., with milk of lime (5 grm. slaked lime to 50 grm. water), dry the mixture slowly ; by stirring it frequently, the cincho-tannic acid loses its solubility, being gradually transformed into cinchona-red. Then boil the dry powder with 200 cubic centimetres of alcohol 0·830 sp. gr. Pour the liquid on to a small filter, and afterwards the residual bark and lime mixed with 100 cub. cent. more alcohol. Wash the powder on the filter with 100 cub. cent. of spirit. From the mixed liquids, about 370 cub. cent., separate the calcium by a few drops of weak sulphuric acid. Filter, distill off the spirit and pour into a capsule the residual liquid,—to which add a small quantity of spirit and water with which the distilling apparatus has been rinsed out. Let the capsule be now heated on a water-bath until all the spirit shall have been expelled; and let the remaining liquor which contains all the alkaloids in the form of acid sulphates be filtered. There will remain on the filter quinovic acid and fatty substances, which must be washed with slightly acidulated water. The filtrate and washings reduced to about 50 cub. cent., should be treated while still warm with caustic soda in excess. After cooling, this is decanted off from the precipitate, and then water added to it before throwing it on to a filter. It is then to be washed with the smallest quantity of water pressed between folds of blotting paper, removed therefrom and dried. The weight multiplied by 5 will indicate the percentage of *mixed* alkaloids in the bark.

To separate the alkaloids from each other, treat the powdered mass with ten times its weight of ether. This will resolve it into two portions—(a) *insoluble in ether*, (b) *soluble in ether*.

(a.) This should be converted into neutral acetates, and to the solution there should be added iodide of potassium, which will possibly separate a little *quinidine*. After removal of the latter (if present), add solution of tartrate of potassium and sodium, which will throw down in a crystalline form tartrate of *cinchonidine;* from the mother-liquor, *cinchonine* may be precipitated by caustic soda.

(b.) The ether having been evaporated, the residue is to be dried at 100° C. and weighed. It may in many cases practically be considered as consisting of quinine only. If however the estimation of quinidine (conquinine) and quinamine is required, the residue, or a determined portion of it, should be dissolved in acetic acid just as much as will be necessary for affording a neutral solution. From this the hydroiodate of quinidine is precipitated by means of an alcoholic solution of iodide of potassium. In the filtrate quinine may be precipitated by adding a few drops of dilute sulphuric acid and an alcoholic tincture of iodine. The herapathite thus formed (see p. 360) is collected after a day, dried at 100° and weighed; it then contains 55 per cent. of quinine.

After adding a few drops of sulphurous acid, the alcohol should now be evaporated from the fluid from which the crystals of herapathite have

[1] *Pharm. Journ.* iv. (1873) 241, and Dr. de Vry's papers mentioned at the end of the present article, p. 369; also private communications.

been removed, and caustic lye added, by which the amorphous alkaloids will be precipitated, including *quinamine* if present.

Uses—Cinchona bark enjoys the reputation of being a most valuable remedy in fevers. But the uncertainty of its composition and its inconvenient bulk render it a far less eligible form of medicine than the alkaloids themselves. It is nevertheless much used as a general tonic in various pharmaceutical preparations.

As to the alkaloids, the only one which is in general use is *quinine*. The neglect of the others is a regrettable waste, which the result of recent investigations ought to obviate. In the year 1866 the Madras Government appointed a Medical Commission to test the respective efficacy in the treatment of fever, of Quinine, Quinidine, Cinchonine and Cinchonidine. Of the sulphates of these alkaloids, a due supply, specially prepared under Mr. Howard's superintendence, was placed at the disposal of the Commission. From the report[1] it appears that the number of cases of paroxysmal malarious fevers treated was 2472,—namely 846 with Quinine, 664 with Quinidine, 569 with Cinchonine, and 403 with Cinchonidine. Of these 2472 cases, 2445 were cured, and 27 failed. The difference in remedial value of the four alkaloids, as deduced from these experiments, may be thus stated:—

Quinidine—ratio of failure	per 1000 cases treated		6
Quinine	,,	,,	7
Cinchonidine	,,	,,	10
Cinchonine	,,	,,	23

The Indian Government, acting on the recommendation of Mr. Howard, has officially advised (Dec. 16, 1873) the more free use in India of cinchona alkaloids other than quinine, and especially of *sulphate of cinchonidine*, which is procurable in abundance from Red Bark.[2] Quinidine on the other hand, which has proved the most valuable of all, is only obtainable from a few barks and in very limited amount.

Dr. de Vry since 1876 advocates the use of what he calls *Quinetum*. This preparation is obtained by exhausting the barks with slightly acidulated water, and precipitating the whole amount of alkaloids by caustic soda. In India the remedy is known as "the Febrifuge."[3]

Adulteration—There is not now any frequent importation of *spurious* cinchona barks, but the substitution of bad varieties for good is sufficiently common. To discriminate these in a positive manner by ascertaining the percentage of quinine, which is the chief criterion of value, recourse must be had to chemical analysis, a method of performing which has been described. Entirely worthless barks may be easily recognized by means of Grahe's test (p. 363).

Modern Works relating to Cinchona.

The following enumeration has been drawn up for the sake of those desiring more ample information than is contained in the foregoing

[1] Blue Book—*East India Cinchona Cultivation*, 1870. pp. 156-172.—The report contains very interesting and important medical details. See also Dougal in *Edin. Med. Journ.* Sept. 1873.

[2] We heard that the Government has purchased (April 1874) by tender between 300 and 400 lb. of cinchonidine.

[3] *Pharm. Journ.* viii. (1878) 1060.

pages, but it has no pretension to be a complete list of all publications that have lately appeared on the subject.

Berg (Otto) *Chinarinden der pharmakognostischen Sammlung zu Berlin.* Berlin, 1865, 4°. 48 pages and 10 plates showing the microscopic structure of barks.

Bergen (Heinrich von), *Monographie der China.* Hamburg, 1826, 4°. 348 pages and 7 coloured plates representing the following barks:—China rubra, Huanuco, Calisaya, flava, Huamalies, Loxa, Jaen. An exhaustive work for its period in every direction.

Blue-books—*East India* (*Chinchona Plant*). Folio.

a. *Copy of Correspondence relating to the introduction of the Chinchona Plant into India, and to proceedings connected with its cultivation from March* 1852 *to March* 1863. Ordered by the House of Commons to be printed, 20 March 1863. 272 pages.

Contains Correspondence of Royle, Markham, Spruce, Pritchett, Cross, McIvor, Anderson and others, illustrated by 5 maps.

b. *Copy of further Correspondence relating to the introduction of the Chinchona Plant into India, and to proceedings connected with its cultivation, from April* 1863 *to April* 1866. Ordered by the House of Commons to be printed, 18 June 1866. 379 pages.

Contains Monthly Reports of the plantations on the Neilgherry Hills; Annual Reports for 1863–64, 1864–65, with details of method of propagation and cultivation, barking, mossing, attacks of insects, illustrated by woodcuts and 4 plates; report of Cross's journey to Pitayo, with map; Cinchona cultivation in Wynaad, Coorg, the Pulney Hills and Travancore, with map; in British Sikkim, the Kangra Valley (Punjab), the Bombay Presidency, and Ceylon.

c. *Copy of all Correspondence between the Secretary of State for India and the Governor-General, and the Governors of Madras and Bombay, relating to the cultivation of Chinchona Plants, from April* 1866 *to April* 1870. Ordered by the House of Commons to be printed, 9 August 1870. 285 pages.

Contains reports on the Neilgherry and other plantations, with map; appointment of Mr. Broughton as analytical chemist, his reports and analyses; reports on the relative efficacy of the several cinchona alkaloids, on cinchona cultivation at Darjiling and in British Burma.

d. *Copies of the Chinchona Correspondence* (*in continuation of return of* 1870), *from August* 1870 *to July* 1875. Ordered by the House of Commons to be printed, 21 June 1877. 190 pages.

Contain also reports on the alkaloid manufactory in India, collection and shipment of barks, and analyses of barks.

Delondre (Augustin Pierre) et Bouchardat (Apollinaire), *Quinologie,* Paris, 1854, 4°. 48 pages, and 23 good coloured plates exhibiting all the barks then met with in commerce.

Delondre (Augustin), see Soubeiran.

Gorkom (K. W. van), *Die Chinacultur auf Java,* Leipzig, 1869, 61 pages. An account of the management of the Dutch plantation.

Hesse (Oswald). This chemist has summarized his elaborate researches on Cinchona in the German Dictionary of Chemistry, articles Chinin, Cinchonin, etc. 1876–1877.

Howard (John Eliot), *Illustrations of the Nueva Quinologia of Pavon.* London, 1862, folio, 163 pages and 30 beautiful coloured plates.—Figures of Cinchona mostly taken from Pavon's specimens in the herbarium of Madrid, and three plates representing the structure of several barks.

Howard (J. E.), *Quinology of the East India Plantations.* London, 1869, folio x. and 43 pages, with 3 coloured plates exhibiting structural peculiarities of the barks of cultivated *Cinchonæ.*

Howard (J. E.) The same, parts ii. and iii., Lond. 1876, folio xiv. and 74 p., with 2 views, 2 black plates and 13 coloured figures of *Cinchona Calisaya* (*Ledgeriana*), *C. officinalis, C. pitayensis,* and others.

Karsten (Hermann), *Die medicinischen Chinarinden Neu-Granada's.* Berlin, 1858, 8°. 71 pages, and 2 plates showing microscopic structure of a few barks. An English translation prepared under the supervision of Mr. Markham, has been printed by the India Office under the title of *Notes on the Medicinal Cinchona Barks of New Granada by H. Karsten,* 1861. The plates have not been reproduced.

Karsten (Hermann), *Floræ Columbiæ terrarumque adjacentium specimina selecta.* Berolini, 1858, folio. Beautiful coloured figures of various plants including Cinchona, under which name are several species usually referred to other genera. Only three parts have been published.

King (George), *A Manual of Cinchona cultivation in India.* Calcutta, 1876, 80 pages, small folio.

Kuntze (Otto), *Cinchona. Arten, Hybriden and Cultur der Chininbäume.* Leipzig, 1878. 124 pages and 3 plates. A review of this book will be found in the *Archiv der Pharmacie, 213,* (1878) 473–480.

McIvor (W. G.) *Notes on the propagation and cultivation of the medicinal Cinchonas or Peruvian bark trees.* Madras, 1867, 33 pages, 9 plates. The author explains the "motsing system" alluded to p. 362.

McIvor (William Graham), *A letter on the cultivation of Chinchona on the Nilgiris.* Ootacamund, 1876, 27 pages.

Markham (Clements Robert), *The Chinchona Species of New Granada, containing the botanical descriptions of the species examined by Drs. Mutis and Karsten; with some account of those botanists, and of the results of their labours.* London, 1867, 8°. 139 pages and 5 plates. The plates are not coloured, yet are good reduced copies of those contained in Karsten's *Floræ Columbiæ;* they represent the following:—*Cinchona corymbosa, C. Trianæ, C. lancifolia, C. cordifolia, C. tucujensis.*

Markham. *A Memoir of the Lady Ana de Osorio, Countess of Chinchon, vice-queen of Peru* (A.D. 1629-1639), *with a plea for the correct spelling of the Chinchona genus.* London, 1874, 4°. 99 pages, with a map, heraldic figures and views.

See also Hanbury, *Science Papers,* 1876, p. 475.

Miquel (Friedrich Anton Wilhelm), *De Cinchonæ speciebus quibusdam, adjectis iis quæ in Java coluntur. Commentatio ex Annalibus Musei Botanici Lugduno-Batavi exscripta.* Amstelodami, 1869, 4°. 20 pages.

Oudemans (Anthony Cornelis), *Sur le pouvoir rotatoire spécifique des principaux alcaloïdes du quinquina. Archives néerlandaises*, x. (1875), 193-268, and xii. (1877).

Phoebus (Philipp), *Die Delondre-Bouchardat'schen China-Rinden.* Giessien, 1864, 8°. 75 pages and a table. The author gives a description without figures, of the microscopic structure of the type-specimens figured in Delondre and Bouchardat's *Quinologie.*

Planchon (Gustave), *Des Quinquinas.* Paris et Montpellier, 1864, 8° 150 pages. A description of the cinchonas and their barks. An English translation has been issued under the superintendence of Mr. Markham by the India Office, under the title of *Peruvian Barks by Gustave Planchon.* London, printed by Eyre and Spottiswoode, 1866.

Soubeiran (J. Léon) et Delondre (Augustin), *De l'introduction et de l'acclimation des Cinchonas dans les Indes néerlandaises et dans les Indes britanniques.* Paris, 1868, 8°. 165 pages.

Triana (Josè) *Nouvelles études sur les Quinquinas.* Paris, 1870, folio, 80 pages, and 33 plates. An interesting account of the labours of Mutis, illustrated by uncoloured copies of some of the drawings prepared by him in illustration of his unpublished *Quinologia de Bogotá*, especially of the several varieties of *Cinchona lancifolia;* also an enumeration and short descriptions of all the species of *Cinchona*, and of New Granadian plants (chiefly *Cascarilla*) formerly placed in that genus.

An abstract of the book will be found in Just's *Botanischer Jahresbericht* für 1873, 484-494.

Vogl (August), *Chinarinden des Wiener Grosshandels und der Wiener Sammlungen.* Wien, 1867, 8°. 134 pages, no figures. A very exhaustive description of the microscopic structure of the barks occurring in the Vienna market, or preserved in the museums of that city.

Vogl (A.), *Beiträge zur Kenntniss der sogenannten falschen Chinarinden.* Wien, 1876, 4°. 26 pages, 7 microscopic sections.

Vrij (John Eliza de) *Kinologische studiën.* More than 30 papers published since 1868 in the *Nieuw Tijdschrift voor de Pharmacie in Nederland.* They are chiefly devoted to the chemistry of the barks from Java and British India.

Weddell (Hugh Algernon), *Histoire naturelle des Quinquinas, ou monographie du genre Cinchona, suivie d'une description du genre Cascarilla et de quelques autres plantes de la même tribu.* Paris, 1849, folio, 108 pages, 33 plates, and map. Excellent uncoloured figures of Cinchona and some allied genera, and beautiful coloured drawings of the officinal barks. Plate I. exhibits the anatomical structure of the plant; Plate II. that of the bark.

Weddell (H. A.), *Notes sur les Quinquinas, Extrait des Annales des Sciences naturelles*, 5° série, tomes xi. et xii. Paris, 1870, 8°. 75 pages. A systematic arrangement of the genus *Cinchona*, and description of its (33) species, accompanied by useful remarks on their barks. An English translation has been printed by the India Office with the title—*Notes on the Quinquinas by H. A. Weddell*, London, 1871, 8°. 64 pages. A German edition by Dr. F. A. Flückiger has also appeared under the title *Uebersicht der Cinchonen von H. A. Weddell.* Schaffhausen and Berlin, 1871, 8°. 43 pages, with additions and indexes.

RADIX IPECACUANHÆ.

Ipecacuanha Root, Ipecacuan; F. *Racine d'Ipécacuanha annelee;* G. *Brechwurzel.*

Botanical Orgin—*Cephaëlis*[1] *Ipecacuanha* A. Richard—This is a small shrub, 8 to 16 inches high, with an ascending, afterwards erect, simple stem, and somewhat creeping root, growing socially in moist and shady forests of South America, lying between 8° and 22° S. lat., especially in the Brazilian provinces of Pará, Maranhão, Pernambuco, Bahia, Espiritu Santo, Minas, Rio de Janeiro, and São Paulo. Within the last half century, it has been discovered in the vast interior province of Matto Grosso, chiefly in that part of it which forms the valley of the Rio Paraguay. From information given to Weddell,[2] it would seem probable that the plant extends beyond the frontiers of Brazil to the Bolivian province of Chiquitos.

The root which is brought into commerce is furnished chiefly by the region lying between the towns of Cuyabá, Villa Bella, Villa Maria, and Diamantina in the province of Matto Grosso; but to some extent also by the woods in the neighbourhood of the German colony of Philadelphia on the Rio Todos os Santos, a tributary of the Mucury, north of Rio de Janeiro.

Prof. Balfour of Edinburgh, who has paid much attention to the propagation of ipecacuanha, finds that the plant exists under two varieties, of which he has published figures;[3] they may be thus distinguished:

a. Stem woody, leaves of firm texture, elliptic or oval, wavy at the edges, with but few hairs on surface and margin. Long in cultivation: origin unknown.

b. Stem herbaceous, leaves less firm in texture, more hairy on margin, not wavy. Grows in the neighbourhood of Rio de Janeiro.

The plant cultivated in India seems disposed to run into several varieties, but according to the experience gained in Edinburgh, the diversity of form apparent in young plants tends to disappear with age.

History—In an account of Brazil, written by a Portuguese friar, who, it would seem, had resided in that country from about 1570 to 1600, and published by Purchas,[4] mention is made of three remedies for the bloody flux, one of which is called *Igpecaya* or *Pigaya;* the drug here spoken of is probably that under notice.

[1] I am informed by my friend Professor Müller of Geneva that in describing the Rubiaceæ for the *Flora Brasiliensis* he will include Cephaëlis Ipecacuanha in the genus *Mapouria.*—F.A.F. March 1879.

[2] *Ann. des Sciences nat.* Bot. xi. (1849) 193-202.

[3] *Trans. of Roy. Soc. of Edinb.* xxvi. (1872) 781. plates 31-32.—Fig. in Bentley and Trimen, *Med. Plants.* part 15 (1876).

[4] Purchas, *His Pilgrimes,* Lond. iv. (1625),—a treatise of Brasill, written by a Portugall which had long lived there, p. 1311.

Piso and Marcgraf[1] in their scientific exploration of Brazil met with two kinds of ipecacuanha; the one provided with a brown root is Cephaëlis Ipecacuanha, which they figured. The root of the other variety, which they called *Ipecacuanha blanca*, is that of Richardsonia scabra (see page 376 below). Piso and Marcgraf described the virtues of these roots, apparently supposing them to be much the same as to their action. Although in common use in Brazil, ipecacuanha was not employed in Europe prior to the year 1672. At that date, a traveller named Legras brought from South America a quantity of the root to Paris, some of which came into the possession of the "maître appoticaire" Claquenelle.[2] It would appear that the root was prescribed from the latter by Legras (said to have been himself acquainted with the practice of medicine[3]), and also by Jean Adrien Helvetius, a young Dutch physician, then living in Paris. Yet no success at first was obtained, the drug being administered in too large doses. In 1680, a merchant of Paris named Garnier became possessed of 150 lb. of ipecacuanha, the valuable properties of which in dysentery he vaunted to his medical attendant Afforty, and to Helvetius. Garnier on his convalescence[4] made a present of some of the new drug to Afforty, who attached to it but little importance. Helvetius, on the other hand, was induced to prescribe the root in cases of dysentery, which he did with the utmost success. It is stated by Eloy that Helvetius even caused placards to be affixed to the corners of the streets (about the year 1686), announcing his successful treatment with the new drug, supplies of which he obtained through Garnier from Spain, and sold as a secret medicine. The fame of the cures effected by Helvetius reached the French Court, and caused some trials of the drug to be made at the Hôtel Dieu. These having been fully successful, Louis XIV. accorded to Helvetius the sole right of vending his remedy.[5] Subsequently several great personages, including the Dauphin of France, having experienced its benefit, the king consulted his physician, Antoine d'Aquin, and the well-known Jesuit Père François de Lachaise, who had become the King's confessor in 1675. Through them was chiefly negotiated the purchase from Helvetius of his secret, for 1000 louis-d'or, and made public in 1688. The right of Helvetius to this payment was disputed in law by Garnier, but maintained by a decision of the Châtelet of Paris.[6]

The botanical source of ipecacuanha was the subject of much dispute until finally settled by Antonio Bernardino Gomez, a physician of the Portuguese navy, who brought authentic specimens from Brazil to Lisbon in the year 1800.[7]

[1] *Hist. nat. Brasil.* 1648. Piso, p. 101, Marcgraf, p. 17.

[2] Pomet, *Histoire générale des Drogues*, i. (1694) 47.

[3] Mérat and De Lens, *Dict. de Mat. Méd.* iii. (1831) 644, call Legras a physician, and say that Garnier brought himself the 150 lb. from abroad.

[4] Eloy, *Histoire générale de la Médecine*. Mons. ii. (1778) 485, mentions a *sick druggist*, who presented Helvetius with the ipecacuanha. Garnier, according to Eloy, was a "Marchand chapelier."—Leibnitz, in *Ephemerid. Academ. Cæsareo-Leopold*, 1696, Appendix, p. 6, miscalled the merchant Grenier.

[5] An abstract of the royal patent is given by Leibnitz, *l.c.* 20 (date not added).

[6] On the history of ipecacuanha, consult also Sprengel, *Geschichte der Arzneykunde*, iv. (1827) 542.—We have not seen the pamphlet quoted by Haller, *Bibl. bot.* ii. 17: Helvetius, *Usage de l'Hipecacoanha*. 4° (no date).

[7] *Trans. of Linn. Soc.* vi. (1801) 137.

Collection[1]—The ipecacuanha plant, *Poaya* of the Brazilians, grows in valleys, yet prefers spots which are rather too much raised to be inundated or swampy. Here it is found under the thick shade of ancient trees growing mostly in clumps. In collecting the root, the *poayero*, for so the collector of *poaya* is called, grasps in one handful if he can, all the stems of a clump, pushing under it obliquely into the soil a pointed stick to which he gives a see-saw motion. A lump of earth enclosing the roots is thus raised; and, if the operation has been well performed, those of the whole clump are got up almost unbroken. The *poayero* shakes off adhering soil, places the roots in a large bag which he carries with him, and goes on to seek other clumps. A good collector may thus get as much as 30 lb. of roots in the day; but generally a daily gathering does not exceed 10 or 12 lb., and there are many who scarcely get 6 or 8 lb. In the rainy season, the ground being lighter, the roots are removed more easily than in dry weather. The *poayeros*, who work in a sort of partnership, assemble in the evening, unite their gatherings, which having been weighed, are spread out to dry. Rapid drying is advantageous; the root is therefore exposed to sunshine as much as possible, and if the weather is favourable, it becomes dry in two or three days. But it has always to be placed under cover at night on account of the dew. When quite dry, it is broken into fragments, and shaken in a sieve in order to separate adherent sand and earth, and finally it is packed in bales for transport.

The harvest goes on all the year round, but is relaxed a little during the rains, on account of the difficulty of drying the produce. As fragments of the root grow most readily, complete extirpation of the plant in any one locality does not seem probable. The more intelligent *poayeros* of Matto Grosso are indeed wise enough intentionally to leave small bits of root in the place whence a clump has been dug, and even to close over the opening in the soil.

Cultivation—The importance in India of ipecacuanha as a remedy for dysentery, and the increasing costliness of the drug,[2] have occasioned active measures to be taken for attempting its cultivation in that country. Though known for several years as a denizen of botanical gardens, the ipecacuanha plant has always been rare, owing to its slow growth and the difficulty attending its propagation.

It was discovered in 1869 by M'Nab, curator of the Botanical Garden of Edinburgh, that if the annulated part of the root of a growing ipecacuanha plant be cut into short pieces even only $\frac{1}{16}$ of an inch thick, and placed in suitable soil, each piece will throw out a leaf-bud and become a separate plant. Lindsay, a gardener of the same establishment, further proved that the petiole of the leaf is capable of producing roots and buds, a discovery which has been utilized in the propagation of the plant at the Rungbi Cinchona plantation in Sikkim.

In 1871, well-formed fruits were obtained from the ipecacuanha plants growing in the Edinburgh Botanical Garden: this was promoted

[1] Abstracted from the interesting eye-witness account of Weddell, *l.c.*

[2] The following are the average prices at which the drug was purchased wholesale, in London during three periods of ten years each:—

10 years ending	1850,	average price	2*s*. 9½*d*. per lb.
10 ,,	1860,	,,	6*s*. 11½*d*. ,,
10 ,,	1870,	,,	8*s*. 8½*d*. ,,

by artificial fertilization, especially when the flowers of a plant producing *long styles* were fertilized with the pollen of one having *short* styles,—for *Cephaëlis* like *Cinchona* has dimorphic flowers.

With regard to the acclimatization of the plant in India, much difficulty has been encountered, and successful results are still problematical. The first plant was taken to Calcutta by Dr. King in 1866, and by 1868 had been increased to nine; but in 1870–71, it was reported that, notwithstanding every care, the plants could not be made to thrive. Three plants which had been sent to the Rungbi plantation in 1868, grew rather better; and by adopting the method of root propagation, they were increased by August 1871, to 300. Three consignments of plants, numbering in all 370, were received from Scotland in 1871–72, besides a smaller number from the Royal Gardens, Kew. From these various collections, the propagation has been so extensive, that on 31 March 1873, there were 6,719 young plants in Sikkim, in addition to about 500 in Calcutta, and much more in 1874.

The ipecacuanha plant in India has been tried under a variety of conditions as regards sun and shade, but thus far with only a moderate amount of success. The best results are those that have been obtained at Rungbi, 3000 feet above the sea, where the plants, placed in glazed frames, were reported in May 1873 as in the most healthy condition.[1]

Description—The stem creeps a little below the surface of the soil, emitting a small number of slightly branching contorted roots, a few inches long. These roots when young are very slender and thread-like, but grow gradually knotty and become by degrees invested with a very thick bark, transversely corrugated or ringed. Close examination of the dry root shows that the bark is raised in narrow warty ridges, which sometimes run entirely round the root, sometimes encircle only half its circumference. The whole surface is moreover minutely wrinkled longitudinally. The rings or corrugations of a full sized root number about 20 in an inch; not unfrequently they are deep enough to penetrate to the wood.

The root attains a maximum diameter of about $\frac{2}{10}$ of an inch; but as imported, a large proportion of it is much smaller. The woody central part is scarcely $\frac{1}{20}$ of an inch in diameter, sub-cylindrical, sometimes striated, and devoid of pith.

Ipecacuanha is of a dusky grey hue, occasionally of a dull ferruginous brown. The root is hard, breaks short and granular (not fibrous), exhibiting a resinous, waxy, or farinaceous interior, white or greyish. The bark, which constitutes 75 to 80 per cent. of the entire root, may be easily separated from the less brittle wood. It has a bitterish taste and faint, musty smell; when freshly dried it is probably much more odorous. The wood is almost tasteless. In the drug of commerce the roots are always much broken, and there is often a considerable separation of bark from wood; portions of the non-annulated, woody, subterraneous stem are always present.

During the last few years there has been imported into London a variety of ipecacuanha, distinguished as *Carthagena* or *New Granada*

[1] *Annual Report of the Royal Botanical Gardens*, Calcutta, 31 May 1873—from which we have abstracted many of the foregoing particulars. The report for 1876-1877 is by no means favourable to the prospects of Cephaëlis in India.

Ipecacuanha, and differing from the Brazilian drug chiefly in being of larger size. Thus, while the maximum diameter of the annulated roots of Brazilian ipecacuanha is about $\frac{2}{10}$ of an inch, corresponding roots of the New Granada variety attain nearly $\frac{3}{10}$. The latter, moreover, has a distinct radiate arrangement of the wood, due to a greater developement of the medullary rays, and is rather less conspicuously annulated. Lefort (1869) has shown that the New Granada drug is a little less rich in emetine than the ipecacuanha of Brazil.

Mr. R. B. White, of Medellin in the valley of the Cauca, New Granada, near which place the drug has been collected, has been good enough to send us herbarium specimens of the plant with roots attached; they agree entirely with *Cephaëlis Ipecacuanha*.

Microscopic Structure—The root is coated with a thin layer of brown cork cells; the interior cortical tissue is made up of a uniform parenchyme, in which medullary rays cannot be distinguished. In the woody column they are obvious; the prevailing tissue consists of short pitted vessels. The cortical parenchyme and the medullary rays are loaded with small starch granules. Some cells of the interior part of the bark contain however only bundles of acicular crystals of oxalate of calcium.

Chemical Composition—The peculiar principles of ipecacuanha are *Emetine* and *Ipecacuanhic Acid*, together with a minute proportion of a fœtid volatile oil. The activity of the drug appears to be due solely to the alkaloid, which taken internally is a potent emetic.

Emetine, discovered in 1817 by Pelletier and Magendie, is a bitter substance with distinct alkaline reaction, amorphous in the free state as well as in most of its salts; we have succeeded in preparing a crystallized hydrochlorate.

The root yields of the alkaloid less than 1 per cent.; the numerous higher estimates that have been given relate to impure emetine, or have been arrived at by some defective methods of analysis.[1]

The formula assigned to emetine by Reich (1863) was $C^{27}H^{30}N^2O^5$, that given by Glénard (1875) $C^{15}H^{22}NO^2$, and lastly that found in 1877 by Lefort and F. Würtz, $C^{28}H^{40}N^2O^5$.

The alkaloid may be obtained by drying the powdered bark of the root with a little milk of lime, and exhausting the mixture with boiling chloroform, petroleum-benzin or ether. It is a white powder turning brown on exposure to light and softening at 70° C. Emetine assumes an intense and permanent yellow colour with solution of chlorinated lime and a little acetic acid, as shown by Power (1877). A solution containing but $\frac{1}{5000}$ of emetine still displays that reaction. We found the alkaloid to be destitute of rotatory power, at least in the chloroform solution.

The above reactions may be easily shown thus:—Take 10 grains of powdered ipecacuanha, and mix them with 3 grains of quick-lime and a few drops of water. Dry the mixture in the water bath and transfer it to a vial containing 2 fluid drachms of chloroform: agitate frequently, then filter into a capsule containing a minute quantity of acetic acid,

[1] See the results obtained by Richard and Barruel, by Magendie and Pelletier, and by Attfield, as recorded by the last-named chemist in *Proceedings of the British Pharmaceutical Conference* for 1869. 37-39.

and allow the chloroform to evaporate. Two drops of water now added will afford a nearly colourless solution of emetine, which, placed in a watch-glass, will readily give amorphous precipitates upon addition of a saturated solution of nitrate of potassium, or of tannic acid, or of a solution of mercuric iodide in iodide of potassium. To the nitrate Power's test may be further applied.

If the *wood* separated as exactly as possible from the bark is used, and the experiment performed in the same way, the solution will reveal only traces of emetine. By addition of nitrate of potassium, no precipitate is then produced, but tannic acid or the potassico-mercuric iodate afford a slight turbidity. This experiment confirms the observation that the bark is the seat of the alkaloid, as might indeed be inferred from the fact that the wood is nearly tasteless.

Ipecacuanhic Acid, regarded by Pelletier as gallic acid, but recognised in 1850 as a peculiar substance by Willigk,[1] is reddish-brown, amorphous, bitter, and very hygroscopic. It is related to caffetannic and kinic acids; Reich has shown it to be a glucoside.

Ipecacuanha contains also, according to Reich, small proportions of resin, fat, albumin, and fermentable and crystallizable sugar; also gum and a large quantity of pectin. The bark yielded about 30 per cent., and the wood more than 7 per cent. of starch.

Commerce—The imports of ipecacuanha into the United Kingdom in 1870 amounted to 62,952 lb., valued at £16,639.[2]

Uses—Ipecacuanha is given as an emetic, but much more often in small doses as an expectorant and diaphoretic. In India it has proved of late a most important remedy for dysentery. Since the year 1858 when the administration of ipecacuanha in large (30 grains) doses began to be adopted, the mortality in the cases treated for this complaint has greatly diminished.[3]

Adulteration and Substitutes—It can hardly be said that ipecacuanha as at present imported is ever adulterated. Although it may contain an undue proportion of the woody stems of the plant, it is not fraudulently admixed with other roots. But it very often arrives much deteriorated by damp: we have the authority of an experienced druggist for saying that at least three packages out of every four offered in the London drug sales, have either been damaged by sea-water or by damp during their transit to the coast.

Several roots have been described as *False Ipecacuanha*, but we know not one that would not be readily distinguished at first sight by any druggist of average knowledge and experience.

In Brazil the word *Poaya* is applied to emetic roots of plants of at least six genera, belonging to the orders *Rubiaceæ*, *Violarieæ*, and *Polygaleæ*; while in the same country, the name *Ipecacuanha* is used for various species of *Ionidium*[4] as well as for *Cephaëlis*.

[1] Gmelin, *Chemistry*, xv. (1862) 523.

[2] *Annual Statement of the Trade and Navigation of the U.K. for* 1870.—The more recent issues of this return have been simplified to such an extent that drugs are for the greater part included under one head.

[3] In the Madras Presidency, the death-rate from dysentery was 71 per 1000 cases treated: under the new method of treatment, it has been reduced to 13·5. In Bengal it has fallen from 88·2 to 28·8 per 1000.—*Supplement to the Gazette of India*, January 23, 1869.

[4] As *Ionidium Ipecacuanha* Vent., *I. Poaya* St. Hil., *I. parviflorum* Vent., the first of which affords the *Poaya branca* or

Some of these roots, which are occasionally brought to Europe under the notion that they may find a market, have been described and figured by pharmacologists. We shall notice only the following :—

1. *Large Striated Ipecacuanha*—This is the root of *Psychotria emetica* Mutis (*Rubiaceæ*), a native of New Granada. It is considerably stouter than true ipecacuanha, but consists like the latter of a woody column covered with a thick brownish bark. The latter, though marked here and there with constrictions and fissures, is not annulated like ipecacuanha, but has very evident longitudinal furrows. But its most remarkable character is that it remains *soft and moist, tough to the knife*, even after many years; and the cut surface has a dull violet hue. The root has a sweetish taste and abounds in sugar;[1] its decoction is not rendered blue by iodine, nor is any starch to be detected by means of the microscope. The drug occasionally appears in the London market.

2. *Small Striated Ipecacuanha*—This drug in outward appearance closely resembles the preceding, but is usually of smaller size,—sometimes much smaller and in short pieces tapering towards either end. It also differs in being brittle, abounding in starch, and having its woody column provided with numerous pores, easily visible under a lens. Prof. Planchon[2] of Paris, who has particularly examined both varieties of Striated Ipecacuanha, is of opinion that the drug under notice may be derived from some species of *Richardsonia.*

3. *Undulated Ipecacuanha* — The root thus called is that of *Richardia scabra* L. (*Richardsonia scabra* St. Hilaire), a plant of the same order as *Cephaëlis*, very common in Brazil, where it grows in cultivated ground and sandy places, or by roadsides, and even in the less frequented streets of Rio de Janeiro. Authentic specimens have been forwarded to us by Mr. Glaziou of Rio de Janeiro, and Mr. J. Correa de Méllo of Campinas; and we have also had ample supplies of the plant cultivated by us near London and at Strassburg, where Richardsonia succeeds in the open air.

The root in the fresh state is pure white, but by drying becomes of a deep iron-grey. In the Brazilian specimens, there is a short crown emitting as many as a dozen prostrate stems; below this there is generally, as in true ipecacuanha, a naked woody portion, which extends downwards into a thicker root, $\frac{2}{10}$ of an inch in diameter, and six or more inches long. This part of the root is marked by deep fissures on alternate sides, which give it a knotty, sinuous, or undulating outline. It has a brittle, very thick bark, white and farinaceous within, surrounding a strong flexible slender woody column. The root has an earthy odour not altogether unlike that of ipecacuanha, and a slightly sweet taste. It affords no evidence of emetine when tested in the manners described at p. 374, and can therefore easily be distinguished from the true drug.

White Ipecacuanha of the Brazilians.—See C. F. P. von Martius, *Specimen Mat. Med. Bras.* 1824; A. de St. Hilaire, *Plantes usuelles des Brésiliens*, 1827-28.

[1] Attfield in *Pharm. Journ.* xi. (1870) 140.

[2] *Journ. de Pharm.* xvi. (1872) 405: xvii. 19.

VALERIANACEÆ.

RADIX VALERIANÆ.

Valerian Root; F. Racine de Valériane; G. Baldrianwurzel.

Botanical Origin—*Valeriana officinalis* L., an herbaceous perennial plant, growing throughout Europe from Spain to Iceland, the North Cape and the Crimea, and extending over Northern Asia to the coasts of Manchuria. The plant is found in plains and uplands, ascending even in Sweden to 1200 feet above the sea-level.

In England, valerian is cultivated in many villages[1] near Chesterfield in Derbyshire, the wild plant which occurs in the neighbourhood not being sufficiently plentiful to supply the demand.

In Vermont, New Hampshire and New York, as well as in Holland, the plant is grown to some extent, but by far the largest supply would appear to be grown in the environs of the German town Cölleda, not far from Leipzig.

Valerian is propagated by separating the young plants which are developed at the end of runners emitted from the rootstock.

The wild plant, according to the situation it inhabits, exhibits several divergent forms. Among eight or more varieties noticed by botanists,[2] we may especially distinguish α. *major* with a comparatively tall stem and all the leaves toothed, β. *minor* (*V. angustifolia* Tausch) with entire or slightly dentate leaves, and also *V. sambucifolia* Mikan, having only 4 or 5 pairs of leaflets.

History—The plant which the Greeks and Romans called Φοῦ or *Phu*, and which Dioscorides and Pliny describe as a sort of wild nard, is usually held to be some species of valerian.[3]

The word *Valeriana* is not found in the classical authors. We first meet with it in the 9th or 10th century, at which period and for long afterwards, it was used as synonymous with *Phu* or *Fu*.

Thus in the writings of Isaac Judæus[4] occurs the following:—"*Fu id est valeriana, melior rubea et tenuis et quæ venit de Armenia et est diversa in sua complexione. . . .*"

Constantinus Africanus[5]—"*Fu, id est valeriana. Naturam habet sicut spica nardi. . . .*"

The word *Valeriane* occurs in the recipes of the Anglo-Saxon leeches written as early as the 11th century.[6] *Valeriana, Amantilla* and *Fu* are used as synonymous in the *Alphita*, a mediæval vocabulary of the school of Salernum.[7]

Saladinus[8] of Ascoli directs (*circa* A.D. 1450) the collection in the month of August of "*radices fu id est valerianæ.*"

[1] Namely Ashover, Woolley Moor, Morton, Stretton, Higham, Shirland, Pilsley, North and South Wingfield, and Brackenfield. From the produce of these villages, one wholesale dealer in Chesterfield obtained in 1872 about 6 tons (13,440 lb.) of root.

[2] Regel, *Tentamen Floræ Ussuriensis*, 1862 (*Mém. de l'Académie de St. Pétersbourg*).

[3] *V. officinalis* L. and nine other species occur in Asia Minor (Tchihatcheff).

[4] *Opera Omnia*, Lugd. 1515, cap. 45.—It must be remembered that this is a translation from the Arabic. How the word in question stands in the original we have no means of knowing.

[5] *De omnibus medico cognitu necessariis*, Basil. 1539. 348.

[6] *Leechdoms, Wortcunning and Starcraft of early England*, iii. (1866) 6. 136.

[7] S. de Renzi, *Collectio Salernitana*, iii. (1854) 271-322.

[8] *Compendium Aromatariorum*, Bonc 1488.

Valerian was anciently called in English *Setwall*, a name properly applied to *Zedoary;* and the root was so much valued for its medicinal virtues, that as Gerarde[1] (1567) remarks, the poorer classes in the north of England esteemed "*no broths, pottage, or physicall meats*" to be worth anything without it. Its odour, now considered intolerable, was not so regarded in the 16th century, when it was absolutely the custom to lay the root among clothes as a perfume[2] in the same way as those of *Valeriana celtica* L. and the Himalayan valerians are still used in the East.

Some of the names applied to valerian in Northern and Central Europe are remarkable. Thus in Scandinavia we find *Velandsrot, Velamsrot, Vandelrot* (Swedish); *Vendelród, Venderód, Vendingeród* (Norwegian); and *Velandsurt* (Danish)—names all signifying *Vandels' root.*[3] Valerian is also called in Danish *Danmarks græs.* Among the German-speaking population of Switzerland, a similar word to the last, namely *Tannmark*, is applied to valerian. The *Denemarcha* mentioned by St. Hildegard,[4] about A.D. 1160, is the same. These names seem to point to some connexion with Northern Europe which we are wholly unable to explain.

Pentz, a pharmaceutical assistant at Pyrmont, was the first, in 1829, to draw attention to the acid reaction of the distilled water of valerian. Another German assistant, Grote, at Verden, showed in 1831 that the acidity was by no means due to acetic acid, but to a peculiar kind of acid. The latter was identified in 1843 by Dumas with the acid artificially obtained from amylic alcohol and that extracted in 1817 by Chevreul from the fat of dolphins.

Description—The valerian root of the shops consists of an upright rhizome of the thickness of the little finger, emitting a few short horizontal branches, besides numerous slender rootlets.[5] The rhizome is naturally very short, and is rendered still more so by the practice of cutting it in order to facilitate drying. The rootlets, which are generally 3 to 4 inches long, attain $\frac{1}{10}$ of an inch in diameter, tapering and dividing into slender fibres towards their extremities. They are shrivelled, very brittle, and, as well as the rhizome, of a dull, earthy brown. When broken transversely, they display a dark epidermis, forming part of a thick white bark which surrounds a slender woody column. The interior of the rhizome is compact, firm and horny, but when old becomes hollow, a portion of the tissue remaining however in the form of transverse septa.

The drug has a peculiar, somewhat terebinthinous and camphor-like odour, and a bitterish, aromatic taste. The root when just taken from the ground has no distinctive smell, but acquires its characteristic odour as it dries.

Microscopic Structure[6]—In the rhizome as well as in the rootlets, the cortical part is separated from the central column by a dark cambial

[1] *Herball*, 1636. 1078.

[2] Turner's *Herball*, part 3 (1568) 76; Langham, *Garden of Health*, 1633. 598.

[3] H. Jenssen-Tusch, *Nordiske Plantenavne*, Kjöbenhavn, 1867. 258.

[4] *Physica*, Argent. 1533. 62.

[5] The morphological peculiarities of valerian root are well explained in Irmisch, *Beitrag zur Naturgeschichte der einheimischen Valeriana-Arten*, Halle, 1854, 44 pages, 4°, 4 plates.

[6] The structure of the rhizomes and root of the different species of valerian has been discussed by Joannes Chatin in his *Études*

zone; the medullary rays are not distinctly obvious. In old rootstocks, sclerenchymatous cells are met with in the cortical tissue.

The parenchyme of the drug is loaded with small starch granules, brownish grains of tannic matter and drops of essential oil. Numerous oil ducts are met with in the outer layer of the tissue.

Chemical Composition—Volatile oil is contained in the dry root to the extent of ½ to 2 per cent., yet on an average appears scarcely to exceed ¾ per cent. This variation in quantity is partly explained by the influence of locality, a dry, stony soil yielding a root richer in oil than one that is moist and fertile. In the latter the plant may be distinguished as the variety *sambucifolia*, which has a less vigorous root, devoid of runners.

Schoonbroodt[1] has shown that the most important influence is the recent condition of the root. He states that if the root is submitted to distillation when perfectly fresh, it yields a neutral water and a large quantity of essential oil. The latter has but a very faint odour, but by exposure to the air it slowly acidifies, especially if a little alkali is added, and acquires a strong smell. *Valerianic Acid* which is thus formed amounts to 6 per mille of the fresh root. The dried root yields a distillate of decided valerian odour, containing valerianic acid, but in proportion not exceeding 4 per mille of the root calculated as fresh.

The oil of valerian is of a very peculiar yellowish or brownish, sometimes even almost a little greenish hue, and possessing the characteristic odour of the drug. We found it to deviate the plane of polarization from 11° to 13° to the left when examined by Wild's Polaristrobometer in a column of 50 millimetres. By submitting it to fractional distillation we noticed[2] that it affords a magnificent blue fraction. A superb violet or blue colour is produced if one drop of the *crude oil* dissolved in about 20 drops of bisulphide of carbon is mixed with 1 drop of nitric acid 1·20 sp. gr. Other colorations are produced if bromine or concentrated sulphuric acid are used;[3] even the tincture of valerian displays similar reactions.

Bruylants (1878) has isolated from oil of valerian—1st. A hydrocarbon, $C^{10}H^{16}$, boiling at 157° C., yielding a crystallized compound with HCl. 2nd. The liquid compound $C^{10}H^{18}O$, which by means of chromic acid affords common camphor and formic, acetic and valerianic acids, which are met with in old valerian root, owing no doubt to the slow oxidation of the compound $C^{10}H^{18}O$. 3rd. There is also present a crystallizable compound of the same composition, which is probably identical with the camphor of Dryobalanops aromatica (see our article on Camphora). It would appear that this substance is of alcoholic nature, being combined in the root with the 3 organic acids mentioned under 2nd. On distilling, these compound ethers are resolved partly into the alcohol $C^{10}H^{18}O$ (borneol) and the acids. This decomposition is fully performed, if the root is macerated with alkaline water, and then, on distilling, a slight excess of sulphuric acid is added. 4th. At

sur les Valérianées, Paris, 1872, illustrated by 14 beautiful plates.

[1] *Journ. de Médecine de Bruxelles*, 1867 and 1868; *Jahresbericht* of Wiggers and Husemann, 1869. 17.

[2] *Archiv der Pharmacie*, 209 (1876).

[3] *Jahresbericht* of Wiggers and Husemann, 1871. 462.

about 300° a greenish portion is coming over, which can be obtained colourless by again rectifying it. This oil assumes intense colorations if it is shaken with concentrated mineral acids; it becomes blue by distilling it over potash.

Valerianic acid as afforded by the root is not agreeing with normal valerianic acid. It is, more exactly, *isovalerianic acid*, or isopropyl-acetic acid: $(CH^3)^2CH.CH^2COOH$, which is produced by Valeriana as well as by Archangelica officinalis and Viburnum Opulus. The same acid also may be obtained from the fat of Dolphinus globiceps.

After the root has been submitted to the distillation of the oil, there is found a strongly acid residue containing malic acid, resin, and sugar,—the last capable, according to Schoonbroodt, of reducing cupric oxide.

Uses—Valerian is employed as a stimulant and antispasmodic.

Substitutes—In the London market there has been offered "*Kesso*," the root of *Patrinia scabiosaefolia* Link,[1] a Japanese herb of the order Valerianaceæ. This drug consists of a very short rootstock giving off a large number of rootlets about 5 inches long and $\frac{1}{10}$ of an inch in diameter. By the absence of a well-marked upright rhizome in this *Japanese Valerian* it is widely differing from our Valerian, although at first sight it agrees to some extent with it. As to the odour and taste we find Kesso almost identical with true Valerian.

The less aromatic and now disused root of *Valeriana Phu* L. consists of a thicker rhizome which lies in the earth obliquely; it is less closely annulated and rooted at the bottom only. It resembles by no means true Valerian.

COMPOSITÆ.

RADIX INULÆ.

Radix Enulæ, Radix Helenii; Elecampane;[2] F. *Racine d'Aunée;* G. *Alantwurzel.*

Botanical Origin—*Inula Helenium* L.—This stately perennial plant is very widely distributed, occurring scattered throughout the whole of central and southern Europe, and extending eastward to the Caucasus, Southern Siberia and the Himalaya. It is found here and there apparently wild in the south of England and Ireland, as well as in Southern Norway and in Finland (Schübeler).

Elecampane was formerly cultivated in gardens as a medicinal and culinary plant, and in this manner has wandered to North America. In Holland and some parts of England and Switzerland, it is cultivated on a somewhat larger scale, most largely probably near Cölleda (see p. 377).

History—The plant was known to the ancient writers on agriculture and natural history, and even the Roman poets were acquainted with it, and mention Inula as affording a root used both as a medicine and a condiment. Vegetius Renatus, about the beginning of the 5th century, calls it Inula Campana, and St. Isidore in the beginning of the 7th names it as *Inula*, adding—"quam *Alam* rustici vocant." It is frequently mentioned in the Anglo-Saxon writings on medicine current in England prior to the Norman Conquest; it is also the "marchalan"

[1] According to Holmes, *Ph. J.* x. (1879) 22.

[2] A corruption of *Enula Campana*, the latter word referring to the growth of the plant in Campania (Italy).

of the Welsh Physicians[1] of the 13th century and was generally well known during the middle ages. Not only was its root much employed as a medicine, but it was also candied and eaten as a sweetmeat.

Description—For pharmaceutical use, the root is taken from plants two or three years old; when more advanced, it becomes too woody. The principle mass of the root is a very thick short crown, dividing below into several fleshy branches of which the larger are an inch or two in diameter, covered with a pale yellow bark, internally whitish, and juicy. The smaller roots are dried entire; the larger are variously sliced, which occasions them to curl up irregularly. When dried, they are of a light grey, brittle, horny, smooth-fractured. Cut transversely the young root exhibits an indistinct radiate structure, with a somewhat darker cambial zone separating the thick bark from the woody nucleus. The pith is not sharply defined, and is often porous and hollow. In the older roots the bark is relatively much thinner, and the internal substance is nearly uniform. Elecampane root has a weak aromatic odour suggestive of orris and camphor, and a slightly bitter, not unpleasant, aromatic taste.

Microscopic Structure—The medullary rays, both of the woody column and the inner part of the bark (*endophlœum*), exhibit large balsam-ducts. In the fresh root they contain an aromatic liquid, which as it dries deposits crystals of helenin, probably derived from the essential oil. The parenchymatous cells of the drug are loaded with inulin in the form of splinter-like fragments, devoid of any peculiar structure.

Chemical Composition—It was observed by Le Febvre, as early as 1660, that when the root of elecampane is subjected to distillation with water a crystallizable substance collects in the head of the receiver from which it speedily passes on as the operation proceeds. Similar crystals may also be observed after carefully heating a thin slice of the root, and are even found as a natural efflorescence on the surface of root that has been long kept. They can be extracted from the root by means of alcohol and precipitated with water. Kallen (1874, 1876) showed that the crystals chiefly consist of the *anhydride*, $C^{15}H^{20}O^{2}$, of *alantic acid*, melting at 66° C. The anhydride, which is very little aromatic, can easily be sublimed, although it begins to boil only at 275°, yet not without decomposition. Alantic anhydride dissolves in caustic lye, but on saturating the solution with an acid, alantic acid, $C^{15}H^{22}O^{3}$, separates. It is not present in the root.

The anhydride is accompanied by a small quantity of *Helenin*, $C^{6}H^{8}O$, and *Alantcamphor* (i.e. Elecampane-camphor). The crystals of helenin have a slightly (?) bitterish taste, but no odour, and melt at 110°. The camphor, occurring in but very small amount, has not yet been analyzed; it agrees probably with the formula $C^{10}H^{16}O$; it melts at 64° C., and in taste and smell is suggestive of peppermint. It is very difficult entirely to remove helenin from alantcamphor, these substances being soluble to nearly the same extent in alcohol or ether. By distilling the second of them with pentasulphide of phosphorus, *Cymene*, $C^{10}H^{14}$, was obtained.

By distilling the root under notice with water, the alantic anhydride is chiefly obtained, but impregnated with *Alantol*, $C^{10}H^{16}O$ (probably).

[1] *Meddygon Myddfai*, p. 61. 284. 311 (see Appendix).

The latter can be removed from the crystals by pressing them between folds of bibulous paper. On submitting this again to distillation, alantol is obtained as an aromatic liquid, boiling at 200°.

The substance most abundantly contained in elecampane root is *Inulin*, discovered in it by Valentine Rose at Berlin in 1804. It has the same composition as starch, $C^6H^{10}O^5$, but stands to a certain extent in opposition to that substance, which it replaces in the root-system of *Compositæ*. In living plants, inulin is dissolved in the watery juice, and on drying is deposited within the cells in amorphous masses, which in polarized light are inactive, and are not coloured by iodine. There are various other characters, by which inulin differs from starch. Thus for instance, inulin readily dissolves in about 3 parts of boiling water; the solution is perfectly clear and fluid, not paste-like; but on cooling deposits nearly all the inulin. The solution is levogyre and is easily transformed into uncrystallizable sugar. With nitric acid, inulin affords no explosive compound as starch does.

Sachs showed in 1864 that by immersing the roots of elecampane, or *Dahlia variabilis* or of many other perennial *Compositæ*, in alcohol or glycerin, inulin may be precipitated in a crystalline form. Its globular aggregates of needle-shaped crystals ("sphæro-crystals") then exhibit under the polarizing microscope a cross similar to that displayed by starch grains.

The amount of inulin varies according to the season, but is most abundant in the autumn. Of the various sources for it, the richest appears to be elecampane. Dragendorff, who has made it the subject of a very exhaustive treatise,[1] obtained from the root in October not less than 44 per cent., but in spring only 19 per cent.

In the roots of the *Compositæ* inulin is accompanied, according to Popp,[2] by two closely allied substances, *Synanthrose*, $C^{12}H^{22}O^{11}+H^2O$, and *Inuloïd*, $C^6H^{10}O^5+H^2O$. Synanthrose is soluble in dilute alcohol, devoid of any rotatory power, and deliquescent. Inuloïd is much more readily soluble in water than inulin. Both these substances are probably present in elecampane.

Inulin is widely distributed in the perennial roots of compositæ, and has also been met with in the natural orders Campanulaceæ, Goodenovieæ (or Goodeniaceæ), Lobeliaceæ, Stylidieæ, and lastly by Kraus (1879) in the root of *Ionidium Ipecacuanha* St. Hilaire, Violaceæ; the formerly so-called *Ipecacuanha alba lignosa* (see p. 375, note 4).

Uses—Elecampane is an aromatic tonic, but as a medicine is now obsolete. It is chiefly sold for veterinary practice. In France and Switzerland (Neuchâtel), it is employed in the distillation of *Absinthe*.

Substitutes—Dioscorides in speaking of *Costus* root states that it is often mixed with that of elecampane of Kommagene (north-western Syria). The former, derived from *Aplotaxis*[3] *auriculata* DC. (*A. Lappa* Decaisne, *Aucklandia Costus* Falconer), is remarkably similar to elecampane both in external appearance and structure. Costus is an important spice, incense and medicine in the east from the antiquity down to

[1] *Materialien zu einer Monographie des Inulins*, St. Petersburg, 1870. 141 pages—See also *Prantl's* paper on Inulin, as abstracted in *Pharm. Journ.* Sept. 1871. 262.

[2] Wiggers and Husemann, *Jahresbericht* for 1870. 68.

[3] Bentham and Hooker unite this plant with *Saussurea*.

the present day;[1] it would be of great interest to examine it chemically with regard to elecampane.

RADIX PYRETHRI.

Pellitory Root, Pellitory of Spain; F. *Pyrèthre salivaire;* G. *Bertramwurzel.*

Botanical Origin—*Anacylus Pyrethrum* DC. (*Anthemis Pyrethrum* L.), a low perennial plant with small, much divided leaves, and a radiate flower resembling a large daisy. It is a native of northern Africa, especially Algeria, growing on the high plateaux that intervene between the fertile coast regions and the desert.

History—The πύρεθρον of Dioscorides was an umbelliferous plant, the determination of which must be left to conjecture. The pellitory of modern times was familiar to the Arabian writers on medicine, one of whom, Ibn Baytar, describes it very correctly from specimens gathered by himself near the city of Constantine in Algeria. The plant, says he, called by the Berbers *sandasab*, is found nowhere but in Western Africa, from which region it is carried to other countries.[2]

Pellitory root is a favourite remedy in the East, and has long been an article of export by way of Egypt to India. An Arabic name for it is *Aāqarqarhā* or *Akulkara*[3], a word which, under slight variations, is found in the principal languages of India. In Germany, pellitory was known as early as the 12th century; it is named in the oldest printed works on materia medica. In the 13th century "pellitory of *Spain*" (Pelydr ysbain) was a proved "remedy for the toothache" with the Welsh physicians.[4]

Description—The root as found in the shops is simple, 3 to 4 inches long by $\frac{3}{8}$ to $\frac{4}{8}$ of an inch thick, cylindrical, or tapering, sometimes terminated at top by the bristly remains of leaves, and having only a few hair-like rootlets. It has a brown, rough, shrivelled surface, is compact and brittle, the fractured surface being radiate and destitute of pith. The bark, at most $\frac{1}{25}$ of an inch thick, adheres closely to the wood, a narrow zone of cambium intervening. The woody column is traversed by large medullary rays in which, as in the bark, numerous dark resin-ducts are scattered. The root has a slight aromatic smell, and a persistent, pungent taste, exciting a singular tingling sensation, and a remarkable flow of saliva. The drug is very liable to the attacks of insects.

Microscopic Structure—The cortical part of this root is remarkable on account of its suberous layer, which is partly made up of sclerenchyme (thick-walled cells). Balsam-ducts (oil-cells) occur as well in the middle cortical layer as in the medullary rays. Most of the parenchymatous cells are loaded with lumps of inulin; pellitory in fact is one of those roots most abounding in that substance.

Chemical Composition—Pellitory has been analysed by several

[1] See Cooke, *Pharm. Journ.* viii. (1877) 41; Flückiger, *ibid.* 121.

[2] Sontheimer's translation, ii. (1842) 179.

[3] *Haq'rcarcha;* see Steinschneider, in Rohlfs' Archiv für Geschichte der Medicin (1879) 342.

[4] *Meddygon Myddfai* (see Appendix) 184. 292. 374.

chemists, whose labours have shown that its pungent taste is due in great part to a resin, not yet fully examined. The root also contains a little volatile oil besides, sugar, gum, and a trace of tannic acid. The so-called *Pyrethrin* is a mixed substance.

Commerce—The root is collected chiefly in Algeria and is exported from Oran and to a smaller extent from Algiers. But from the information we have received from Colonel Playfair, British Consul-General for Algeria, and from Mr. Wood, British Consul at Tunis, it appears that the greater part is shipped from Tunis to Leghorn and Egypt. Mr. Wood was informed that the drug is imported from the frontier town of Tebessa in Algeria into the regency of Tunis, to the extent of 500 *cantars* (50,000 lb.) per annum.

Bombay imported in the year 1871–72, 740 cwt. of this drug, of which more than half was shipped to other ports of India.[1]

Uses—Chiefly employed as a sialogogue for the relief of toothache, occasionally in the form of tincture as a stimulant and rubefacient.

Substitute—In Germany, Russia and Scandinavia, African pellitory is replaced by the root of *Anacyclus officinarum* Hayne, an annual herb long cultivated in Prussia and Saxony.[2] Its root of a light grey is only half as thick as that of *A. Pyrethrum*, and is always abundantly provided with adherent remains of stalks and leaves. It is quite as pungent as that of the perennial species.

FLORES ANTHEMIDIS.

Chamomile Flowers; F. *Fleurs de Camomille Romaine;* G. *Römische Kamillen.*

Botanical Origin—*Anthemis nobilis* L., the Common or Roman Chamomile, a small creeping perennial plant, throwing up in the latter part of the summer solitary flower-heads.

It is abundant on the commons in the neighbourhood of London, and generally throughout the south of England; and extends to Ireland, but is not a native of Scotland, except the islands of Bute and Cumbrae, where Anthemis is stated to grow wild. It is plentiful in the west and centre of France, Spain, Portugal, Italy, and Dalmatia; and occurs as a doubtful native in Southern and Central Russia.

History—The identification of the chamomile in the classical and other ancient authors seems to be impossible, on account of the large number of allied plants having similar inflorescence.

The chamomile has been cultivated for centuries in English gardens, the flowers being a common domestic medicine. The double variety was well known in the 16th century.

The plant was introduced, according to Gesner, into Germany from Spain about the close of the middle ages. Tragus first designated it *Chamomilla nobilis*,[3] and Joachim Camerarius (1598), who had ob-

[1] *Statement of the Trade and Navigation of the Presidency of Bombay* in 1871-72, pt. ii. 19. 98.

[2] For further information on the medicinal species of *Anacyclus*, see a paper by Dr. P. Ascherson in *Bonplandia*, 15 April 1858.

[3] *De Stirpium* . . ., 1552. 149.—In Germany the epithet *edel* (= *nobilis*) is frequently used in popular botany to designate useful or remarkable plants. Tragus may have been induced to bestow it on the species under notice, on account of its superiority to *Matricaria Camomilla*, the so-called *Common Chamomile* of the Germans.

served its abundance near Rome, gave it the name of *Roman Chamomile*.

Porta, about the year 1604,[1] states that 100 pounds of *Flores Chamæmeli* yielded 2 drachmæ of a green volatile oil; we suppose he distilled the flowers under notice.

Production—The camomile is cultivated at Mitcham, near London, the land applied to this purpose being in 1864 about 55 acres, and the yield reckoned at about 4 cwt. per acre. The flowers are carefully gathered, and dried by artificial heat; and fetch a high price in the market.[2]

The plant is grown on a large scale at Kieritzsch, between Leipzig and Altenburg, and near Zeiz and Borna, all in Saxony; and likewise to some extent in Belgium and France.

Description—The chamomile flowers found in commerce are never those of the wild plant, but are produced by a variety in which the tubular florets have all, or for the greater part been converted into ligulate florets. In the flowers of some localities this conversion has been less complete, and such flowers having a somewhat yellow centre, are called by druggists *Single Chamomiles;* while those in which all the florets are ligulate and white, are known as *Double Chamomiles.*

Chamomile flowers have the general structure found in the order *Compositæ.* They are ½ to ¾ of an inch across, and consist of a hemispherical involucre about ⅜ of an inch in diameter, composed of a number of nearly equal bracts, scarious at the margin. The receptacle is solid, conical, about ¼ of an inch in height, beset with thin, concave, blunt, narrow, chaffy scales, from the bases of which grow the numerous florets. In the wild plant, the outer of these, to the number of 12 or more, are white, narrow, strap-shaped, and slightly toothed at the apex. The central or disc florets are yellow and tubular, with a somewhat bell-shaped summit from which project the two reflexed stigmas. In the cultivated plant, the ligulate florets predominate, or replace entirely the tubular. The florets which are wholly destitute of pappus are reflexed, so that the capitulum when dried has the aspect of a little white ball. Minute oil-glands are sparingly scattered over the tubular portion of the florets of either kind. The flowers of chamomile, as well as the green parts of the plant, have a strong aroma, and a very bitter taste.

In trade, dried chamomile flowers are esteemed in proportion as they are of large size, very double, and of a good white—the last named quality being due in great measure to fine dry weather during the flowering period. Flowers that are buff or brownish, or only partially double, command a lower price.

Chemical Composition—Chamomile flowers yield from 0·6 to 0·8 per cent. of essential oil,[3] which is at first of a pale blue, but becomes yellowish-brown in the course of a few months.

At Mitcham, oil of chamomile is usually distilled from the *entire plant*, after the best flowers have been gathered. The oil has a shade

[1] *De distillatione*, Romæ, 1608. 83.

[2] About £9 per cwt., Foreign Chamomiles being worth from £3 to £4.

[3] Information obligingly given by Messrs. Schimmel & Co., Leipzig. The oil distilled by them was examined in Prof. Fittig's laboratory, Strassburg.

of green, to remove which it is exposed to sunlight; it thus acquires a brownish-yellow colour, at the same time throwing down a considerable deposit.

The investigations of several chemists, performed in 1878-79 in Fittig's laboratory, have shown the oil to contain the following constituents:—At 147-148° C. *isobutylic ethers* and hydrocarbons are distilling, at 177° *angelicate* of *isobutyl*, at 200°-201° *angelicate* of *isamyl*, at 204°-205° *tiglinate* of *isamyl* (both these compound ethers answering to the formula $C^5H^7O.OC^5H^{11}$). In the residual portion hexylic alcohol, $C^6H^{13}OH$, and an alcohol of the formula $C^{10}H^{16}O$, are met with, both probably occurring in the form of compound ethers. By decomposing the angelicates and the tiglinate above named with potash, angelic acid, $C^5H^8O^2$, and tiglinic (or methylcrotonic) acid, isomeric to the former, are obtained to the extent of about 30 or more per cent. of the crude oil. In the oil examined by Fittig, angelic acid was prevailing; from another specimen E. Schmidt (1879) obtained but very little of it, tiglinic acid was by far prevailing (see also article Oleum Crotonis).

We have performed some experiments in order to isolate the *bitter principle*, but have not succeeded in obtaining it in a satisfactory state of purity; it forms a brown extract, apparently a glucoside. We can also confirm the statement that no alkaloid is present.

Uses—An infusion or an extract of chamomile is often used as a bitter stomachic and tonic.

Adulteration and Substitution—The flower-heads of *Matricaria Chamomilla* L., designated in Germany *Common Chamomiles* (*gemeine Kamillen*), are sometimes asked for in this country. In aspect as well as in odour, they are very different from the chamomiles of English pharmacy; they are quite single, not bitter, and have the receptacle devoid of scales and hollow.

A cultivated variety of *Chrysanthemum Parthenium* Pers., or Feverfew, with the florets all ligulate, and some scales on the receptacle (not having the receptacle *naked*, as in the wild form), common in gardens,[1] has flower-heads exceedingly like double chamomiles. But they may be distinguished from the latter by their *convex* or *nearly flat* receptacle, with the scales lanceolate and acute, and less membranous.

The chamomiles of the Indian bazaars which are brought from Persia and known as *Bābūnah*, are (as we infer from the statement of Royle) the flowers of *Matricaria suaveolens* L., a slender form of *M. Chamomilla*, growing in Southern Russia, Persia, Southern Siberia, also in North America.

The fresh wild plant of *Anthemis nobilis* L., pulled up from the ground, is sold in London for making extract, a proceeding highly reprehensible supposing the extract to be sold for medicinal use.

[1] Is not this plant the *Anthemis ? parthenioides* Bernh., of which De Candolle says (*Prod.* vi. 7)—". . . simillima *Mat. Parthenio*, sed paleis inter flores instructa. Ferè semper plena in hortis occurrit, et forte ideo paleæ receptaculi ex luxuriante statu ortæ ut in *Chrysanthemi indico et sinensi* . . ."?

SANTONICA.

Flores Cinæ, Semen Cinæ,[1] *Semen Santonicæ, Semen Zedoariæ, Semen Contra, Semen Sanctum; Wormseed;* F. *Semen-contra, Semencine, Barbotine;* G. *Wurmsamen, Zitwersamen.*

Botanical Origin—*Artemisia maritima*, var. *a. Stechmanniana* Besser[2] (*A. Lercheana* Karel. et Kiril, in Herbb. Kew, et Mus. Brit.; *A. maritima* var. *a. pauciflora* Weber, quoad Ledebour, *Flor. Ross.* ii. 570).

Artemisiæ of the section *Seriphidium* assume great diversity of form:[3] they have been the object of attentive study on the part of the Russian botanists Besser (1834-35) and Ledebour (1844-46), whose researches have resulted in the union of many supposed species, under the head of the Linnæan *Artemisia maritima*. This plant has an extremely wide distribution in the northern hemisphere of the old world, occurring mostly in saltish soils. It is found in the salt marshes of the British Islands, on the coasts of the Baltic, of France and the Mediterranean, and on saline soils in Hungary and Podolia; thence it extends eastward, covering immense tracts in Southern Russia, the regions of the Caspian, and Central Siberia, to Chinese Mongolia.

The particular variety which furnishes at least the chief part of the drug, is a low, shrubby, aromatic plant, distinguished by its very small, erect, ovoid flowerheads, having oblong, obtuse, involucral scales, the interior scales being scarious. The stem in its upper half is a fastigiate, thyrsoid panicle, crowned with flowerheads. The localities for the plant are the neighbourhood of the Don, the regions of the lower Volga near Sarepta and Zaritzyn, and the Kirghiz deserts.

The drug, which consists of the minute, unopened flowerheads, is collected in large quantities, as we are informed by Björklund (1867), on the vast plains or steppes of the Kirghiz, in the northern part of Turkestan. It was formerly gathered about Sarepta, a German colony in the Government of Saratov, but from direct information we have (1872) received, it appears to be obtained there no longer.

The emporium for worm-seed is the great fair of Nishnei-Novgorod (July 15th to Aug. 27th), whence the drug is conveyed to Moscow, St. Petersburg, and Western Europe.

Wormseed is found in the Indian bazaars. A specimen received by us from Bombay does not materially differ in form from the Russian drug, but is slightly shaggy and mixed with tomentose stalks. It is probably brought from Afghanistan and Cabul.[4]

Wilkomm[5] has described, as mother-plant of wormseed, an

[1] From the Italian *semenzina*, the diminutive of *semenza* (seed).

[2] W. S. Besser in *Bulletin de la Soc. imp. des Naturalistes de Moscou*, vii. (1834) 31.—A specimen of the plant in question labelled in Besser's handwriting, with a memorandum that it is collected for medicinal use, is in the Herbarium of the Royal Gardens, Kew. It completely agrees with the *Semen Cinæ* of Russian and German commerce. This remark also applies to a specimen of *A. Lercheana* Karel. et Kiril. in the same herbarium.

[3] "Si aliæ Artemisiæ multùm variant, Seriphidia inconstantiâ formarum omnes superant. . . ."—Besser.

[4] *Artemisia* No. 3201, Herb. Griffith, Afghanistan, in the Kew Herbarium has capitules precisely agreeing with this Bombay drug.

[5] *Bot. Zeitung*, 1 März 1872. 130; *Pharm. Journ.* 23 March 1872. 772 (abstract).

Artemisia which he calls *A. Cina.* It was obtained in Turkestan by Prof. Petzholdt, who received it from the people gathering the drug. The specimen kindly communicated to us by Prof. Willkomm has flowerheads which do not entirely resemble the wormseed of trade, in that they have fewer scales, but their number may be somewhat varying.

History—Several species of *Absinthium* are mentioned by Dioscorides, one of which called Ἀψίνθιον θαλάσσιον or Σέριφον, having very small seeds (capitules), and growing in Cappadocia, he states to be taken in honey as a remedy for ascarides and lumbrici: one can hardly doubt but that this is the modern wormseed. Another species is described by the same author as being called Σαντόνιον, from its growing in the country of the Santones in Gaul (the modern Saintonge); he asserts it to resemble σέριφον in its properties.

In an epistle on intestinal worms attributed to Alexander Trallianus,[1] who practised medicine with great success at Rome in the 6th century, the use is recommended of a decoction of *Absinthium marinum* (θαλασσία ἀψίνθη) as a cure for ascarides and round worms.

Semen sanctum vel Alexandrinum is mentioned as a vermifuge for children by Saladinus about A.D. 1450, and by Ruellius, Dodonæus, the Bauhins, and other naturalists of the 16th century. Tragus[2] mentions that it is imported by way of Genoa. Its ancient reputation has been fully maintained in modern times, and in the form partly of *Santonin*, the drug is still extensively employed.

Description—Good samples of the drug consist almost exclusively of entire, unopened flowerheads or capitules, which are so minute that it requires about 90 to make up the weight of one grain. In samples less pure, there is an admixture of stalks, and portions of a small pinnate leaf. The flowerheads are of an elliptic or oblong form, about $\frac{1}{16}$ of an inch long, greenish yellow when new, brown if long kept; they grow singly, less frequently in pairs, on short stalks, and are formed of about 18 oblong, obtuse, concave scales, closely imbricated. This involucre is much narrowed at the base in consequence of the lowermost scales being considerably shorter than the rest. The capitule is sometimes associated with a few of the upper leaves of the stem, which are short, narrow, and simple. Notwithstanding its compactness, the capitule is somewhat ridged and angular,[3] from the involuclar scales having a strong, central nerve or keel. The middle portion of each scale is covered with minute, yellow, sessile glands, which are wanting on the transparent scarious edge. The latter is marked with extremely fine striæ and is quite glabrous; in the young state the keel bears a few woolly colourless hairs, but at maturity the whole flowerhead is shining and nearly glabrous.[4] The florets number from 3 to 5; they have (in the bud) an ovoid corolla, glandular in its lower portion, a little longer than the ovary, which is destitude of pappus.

[1] Contained in a work by Hieronymus Mercurialis, entitled *Variarum Lectionum libri quatuor*, Venet. 1570; also in Puschmann's edition of *Alexander* (see Appendix), i. 238. 240.

[2] In Brunfels (*De vera herbarum cognitione*), Argentorati, 1531. 196.

[3] Maceration in water, which restores the natural shape of the flowerheads, shows that this shrunken, angular form is not found in the growing plant.

[4] Yet too much stress must not be laid on this character, for as Besser remarks—"*periclinii squamæ in uno loco tomento brevi plus minusve canæ, in aliis nudæ, imo nitidæ.*"

Wormseed when rubbed in the hand exhales a powerful and agreeable odour, resembling cajuput oil and camphor; it has a bitter aromatic taste.

Chemical Composition—Wormseed yields from 1 to 2 per cent. of essential oil, having its characteristic smell and taste. The oil is slightly levogyrate and chiefly consists of the liquid $C^{10}H^{18}O$, accompanied by a small amount of hydrocarbon. The former has the odour of the drug, yet rather more agreeable; sp. gr. 0·913 at 20° C. It boils without decomposition at 173°–174°, but in presence of P^2O^5 or P^2S^5 abundantly yields cymol (see p. 333). The latter had already been observed by Völckel (1854) under the name of *cinene* or *cynene*, yet he assigned to it the formula $C^{12}H^9$; Hirzel (1854) called it cinæbene.

The water which distills over carries with it volatile acids of the fatty series, also *angelic acid* (see pp. 313, 386).

The substance to which the remarkable action of wormseed on the human body[1] is due is *Santonin*, $C^{15}H^{18}O^3$. It was discovered in 1830 by Kahler, an apothecary of Düsseldorf, who gave a very brief notice of it in the *Archiv der Pharmacie* of Brandes (xxxiv. 318). Immediately afterwards Augustus Alms, a druggist's assistant at Penzlin in the grand duchy of Mecklenburg-Schwerin, knowing nothing of Kahler's discovery, obtained the same substance and named it *Santonin*. Alms recommended it to the medical profession, pointing out that it is the anthelminthic principle of wormseed.[2] Santonin constitutes from 1½ to 2 per cent. of the drug, but appears to diminish in quantity very considerably as the flowers open. It is easily extracted by milk of lime, for, though not an acid and but sparingly soluble in water even at a boiling heat, it is capable of combining with bases. With lime it forms then santoninate of calcium, which is readily soluble in water. On addition of hydrochloric acid, santoninic acid, $C^{15}H^{20}O^4$, separates, but parts with OH^2, santonin being thus immediately reproduced. Similar facts have been recorded with regard to alantic acid (see p. 381).

Santonin forms crystals of the orthorhombic system, melting at 170°, which are inodorous, but have a bitter taste, especially when dissolved in chloroform or alcohol.[3] They are colourless, but when exposed to daylight, or to the blue or violet rays, but not to the other colours of the spectrum, they assume a yellow hue, and split into irregular fragments. This change, which takes place even under water, alcohol or ether, is not accompanied by any chemical alteration. This behaviour of santonin when exposed to light, resembles that of erythrocentaurin, $C^{27}H^{24}O^8$. The latter has been obtained by means of ether, from the alcoholic extract of *Erythræa Centaurium*, and of some other *Gentianaceæ*. Méhu (1866) has shown that the colourless crystals of that substance when exposed to sunlight, assume a brilliant red colour, *without* undergoing any chemical alteration. The *colourless* solutions of this body in chloro-

[1] As the affected vision, so that objects appear as if seen through a yellow medium. Other effects are recorded by Stillé (*Therapeutics and Mat. Med.* ii. 641).

[2] The paper of Alms being contained in the very same periodical (p. 319) as that of Kahler (and further in vol. xxxix. 190), affords additional evidence of the independence of the discovery.

[3] Its ready solubility in 3 or 4 parts of chloroform renders its estimation easy when mixed with sugar, as in a santonin lozenge.

form or alcohol yield the original substance. Yet as to santonin, Sestini and Cannizzaro (1876) have shown, that its dilute alcoholic solution, on long exposure to sunlight, affords a compound ether of photosantonic acid, namely $C^{15}H^{18}O^{4}(C^{2}H^{5})^{2}$.

Wormseed contains, in addition to the above described bodies, resin, sugar, waxy fat, salts of calcium and potassium, and malic acid; when carefully selected and dried, it yielded us 6·5 per cent. of ash, rich in silica.

Commerce—Ludwig of St. Petersburg has stated that the imports of wormseed into that city were about as follows:—In 1862, 7400 cwt.; in 1863, 10,500 cwt.; in 1864, 11,400 cwt. The drug was brought from the Kirghiz steppes by Semipalatinsk and by Orenburg.

Uses—The drug is employed exclusively for its anthelminthic properties, partly in the form of santonin. It proves of special efficacy for the dislodgement of *Ascaris lumbricoides*.

RADIX ARNICÆ.

Rhizoma Arnicæ, Arnica Root; F. *Racine d'Arnica;* G. *Arnicawurzel.*

Botanical Origin—*Arnica montana* L., a perennial plant growing in meadows throughout the northern and central regions of the northern hemisphere, but not reaching the British Islands. In western and central Europe it is an inhabitant of the mountains, but in colder countries it grows in the plains.

In high latitudes, as in Arctic Asia and America, a peculiar form of the plant distinguished by narrow, almost linear leaves has been named *A. angustifolia* Vahl; but numerous transitional forms prove its identity with the ordinary *A. montana* of Europe.

History—The older botanists as Matthiolus, Gesner, Camerarius, Tabernæmontanus, and Clusius were acquainted with Arnica and had some knowledge of its medicinal powers, which appear to have been expressly recommended, towards the end of the 16th century, by Franz Joël, professor of Greifswald, Germany.[1] All parts of the plant were no doubt popular remedies in Germany at an early period, but Arnica was only introduced into regular medicine on the recommendation of Johann Michael Fehr of Schweinfurt and of several other physicians.[2] But for enthusiastic laudation of the new remedy, all these writers fall far short of Collin of Vienna, who imagined that in Arnica he had found a European plant possessing all the virtues of Peruvian Bark.[3] In his hands fevers and agues gave way under its use, and more than 1000 patients in the Pazman Hospital were alleged to have been cured of intermittents by an electuary of the flowers, between 1771 and 1774. Such happy results were not obtained by other physicians.

Arnica (*herba, flos, radix*) had a place in the London Pharmacopœia

[1] Sprengel, *Geschichte der Arzneykunde*, iv. (1827) 546.

[2] Fehr, *De Arnica lapsorum panacea*, in *Ephemerid. nat. cur.* Dec. 1, (1678. 1679) No. 2. p. 22 ("usus est in *radice, foliis* et *floribus*").—G. A. de la Marche, *Dissertatio*, Halæ Magdeburg, 1744.

[3] Heinrich Joseph Collin, *Heilkräfte des Wolverley*, Breslau, 1777 (translation); also *Arnicæ, in febribus et aliis morbis putridis vires*,—in the *Anni Medici* of Störck and Collin, ed. nov., Amstel., iii. (1779) 133.

of 1788, but it soon fell out of notice, so that Woodville writing in 1790, remarks that he had been unable to procure the plant from any of the London druggists. Of late years it has gained some popular notoriety as an application in the form of tincture, for preventing the blackness of bruises, but in England it is rarely prescribed internally.

Description—The arnic root of pharmacy consists of a slender, contorted, dark-brown rootstock, an inch or two long, emitting from its under side an abundance of wiry simple roots, 3, 4 or more inches in length; it usually bears the remains of the rosette of characteristic, ovate, coriaceous leaves, which are 3- to 5-nerved, ciliated at the margin, and slightly pubescent on their upper surface. It has a faintly aromatic, herby smell, and a rather acrid taste.

Microscopic Structure—On a transverse section, the rootstock exhibits a large pith surrounded by a strong woody ring. In the innermost part of the cortical layer, large oil-ducts are found corresponding to the fibro-vascular bundles. Neither starch granules, inulin, or oxalate of calcium are visible in the tissue. The rootlets are of a different structural character, but also contain oil-ducts.

Chemical Composition—Several chemists have occupied themselves in endeavouring to isolate the active principle of arnica. Bastick described (1851) a substance which he obtained in minute quantity from the flowers and named *Arnicine*. He states it to possess alkaline properties, to be non-volatile, slightly soluble in water, more so in alcohol or ether; when neutralized with hydrochloric acid, it forms a crystalline salt.

The *Arnicin* extracted by Walz (1861) both from the root and flowers of arnica is a different substance; it is an amorphous yellow mass of acrid taste, slightly soluble in water, freely in alcohol or ether, and dissolving also in alkaline solutions. It is precipitable from its alcoholic solution by tannic acid or by water. Walz assigns to arnicin the formula $C^{20}H^{30}O^{4}$; other chemists that of $C^{35}H^{54}O^{7}$. Arnicin has not yet been proved a glucoside, although it is decomposed by dilute acids.

Sigel (1873) obtained from dried arnica root about ½ per cent. of essential oil, and 1 per cent. from the fresh; the oil of the latter had a sp. gr. of 0·999 at 18° C. The oil was found to be a mixture of various bodies, the principle being *dimethylic ether of thymohydroquinone* $C^{10}H^{12}\left\{\begin{matrix}OCH^{3}\\OCH^{3}\end{matrix}\right.$, boiling at about 235°. The water from which the oil separates contains *isobutyric acid*, probably also a little *angelic* and *formic acid*; but neither capronic nor caprylic acid, which had been pointed out by Walz.

Arnica root contains *inulin*, which Dragendorff extracted from it to the extent of about 10 per cent.

Uses—Arnica is used chiefly in the form of tincture as a popular application to bruises and chilblains; internally it is occasionally prescribed as a stimulant and diaphoretic.

Adulteration—Arnica root has been met with[1] adulterated with the root of *Geum urbanum* L., a common herbaceous plant of the order

[1] Holmes in *Pharm. Journ.*, April 11, 1874. 810.

Rosaceæ. The latter is thicker than the rhizome of arnica, being $\frac{3}{10}$ to $\frac{4}{10}$ of an inch in diameter; it is a true *root*, furnished on all sides with rootlets, and has an *astringent* taste. The leaves of *Geum* are pinnate and quite unlike those of arnica.

FLORES ARNICÆ.

Botanical Origin—See preceding article.

History—The flowers probably in the first line attracted the attention of popular medicine in Germany, as we pointed out, page 390.

Description—*Arnica montana* produces large, handsome, orange-yellow flowers, solitary at the summit of the stem or branches. The involucral scales of the capitulum (20 to 24) are of equal length, but are imbricated, forming a double row. They are very hairy, the shorter hairs being tipped with viscid glands. The receptacle is chaffy, $\frac{1}{4}$ of an inch in diameter, with about 20 ligulate florets, and of tubular a much larger number. The ligulate florets, an inch in length, are oblong, toothed at the apex, and traversed by about 10 parallel veins. The achenes are brown and hairy, crowned by pappus consisting of a single row of whitish barbed hairs.

The receptacle is usually inhabited by a fly, *Trypeta arnicivora* Löw[1]; the Pharmacopœia Germania (1872) therefore ordered the florets to be deprived of the involucre and receptacle—"flosculi a peranthodio liberati." From a chemical point of view the usefulness of this direction may be doubted.

Arnica flowers have a weak, not unpleasant odour; they were formerly used in making the tincture, but as the British Pharmacopœia now directs that preparation to be made with the root, they have almost gone out of use in Great Britain.

Chemical Composition—The flowers appear to be rather richer in arnicin than the root, and are said to be equal if not superior to it in medicinal powers; yet the essential oil they contain is not the same. It is obtained in but extremely small amount and has a greenish or blue coloration. Hesse (1864) has proved that the flowers are devoid of a peculiar volatile alkaloid which had been supposed to be present in them.

RADIX TARAXACI.

Dandelion Root, Taraxacum Root; F. Pissenlit; G. Löwenzahnwurzel.

Botanical Origin—*Taraxacum officinale* Wiggers (*T. Dens-leonis* Desf., *Leontodon Taraxacum* L.), a plant of the northern hemisphere, found over the whole of Europe, Central and Northern Asia, and North America, extending to the Arctic regions. It varies under a considerable number of forms, several of which have been regarded as distinct species. In many districts it is a troublesome weed.

History—Though the common Dandelion is a plant which must have been well known to the ancients, no indubitable reference to it can be traced in the classical authors of Greece and Italy; it is thought

[1] Figured in Nees von Esenbeck's *Plantæ medicinales*, Düsseldorf, ii. (1833) fol. 39.

that ἀθάκη of Theophrast and others means it. The word *Taraxacum* is however usually regarded as of Greek origin;[1] we have first met with as *Tarakhshagun* in the works of the Arabian physicians, who speak of it as a sort of *Wild Endive*. It is thus mentioned by Rhazes in the 10th, and by Avicenna in the 11th century.

The name *Dens Leonis*, an equivalent of which is found in nearly all the languages of Europe, is stated in the herbal of Johann von Cube[2] to have been bestowed on this plant by one Wilhelm, a surgeon, who held it in great esteem; but of this personage and of the period during which he lived we have sought information in vain, and we may remember that Dens Leonis ("Dant y Llew") is already met with in the Welsh medicine of the 13th century.[3]

Dandelion was also much valued as medicine in the time of Gerarde and Parkinson, and is still extensively employed.

Collection—In England, taraxacum root is considered to be in perfection for extract in the month of November, the juice at that period affording an ampler and better product than at any other. Bentley contends that it is more bitter in March, and most of all in July, and that at the former period at least it should be preferred.

Description—The root is perennial, and tapering, simple, or slightly branched, attaining in a good soil a length of a foot or more, and half an inch to an inch in diameter. Old roots divide at the crown into several heads. The root is fleshy and brittle; externally of a pale brown, internally white, and abounding in an inodorous milky juice of bitter taste. It shrinks very much in drying, losing in weight about 76 per cent.[4]

Dried dandelion root is half an inch or less in thickness, dark brown, shrivelled with wrinkles running lengthwise often in a spiral direction; when quite dry, it breaks easily with a short corky fracture, showing a very thick white bark, surrounding a woody column. The latter is yellowish, very porous, without pith or rays. A rather broad but indistinct cambium-zone separates the wood from the bark, which latter exhibits numerous well-defined concentric layers. The root has a bitterish taste.

Microscopic Structure—On the longitudinal section, especially in a tangential direction, the brownish zones are seen to contain laticiferous vessels, only about 2 mkm. in diameter. These traverse their zones in a vertical direction, giving off numerous lateral branches, which however remain always confined to their zone. Within each of these zones, the lacticiferous vessels form consequently an anastomosing net. We may say that the root is thus vertically traversed by about 10 to 20 concentric rings of lacticiferous vessels.[5] They may be made beautifully evident by means of anilin-blue, with which a thin longitudinal section

[1] Perhaps from τράζυνον or τρόξυνον signifying *Wild Lettuce*; according to some, from τάραξιν, a disease of the eye which the plant was used to cure, or from the verb *ταράσσω, I disturb*.

[2] *Herbarius zu teutsch und von aller handt kreuteren*, Augspurg, 1488. cap. cliii.

[3] The *Physicians of Myddvai*, 284 (see Appendix).

[4] Thus 5496 lb. of the washed root afforded of dry only 1277 lb., or 23·2 per cent. — Information communicated by Messrs. Allen and Hanburys, London.

[5] For further particulars about them, see Vogl, *Sitzungsber. der Wiener Akademie*, vi. (1863) 668 with plate; Hanstein, *Milchsaftgefässe und verwandte Organe der Rinde* Berlin, 1864. 72. 73. pl. ix.

of the fresh root may be moistened. The root must be allowed to partially dry, but only till the milky juice coagulates; the thin slice then energetically absorbs the colouring matter.[1]

The tissue of the dried root is loaded with inulin, which does not occur in the solid form in the living plant. The woody part of taraxacum root is made up of large scalariform vessels accompanied by parenchymatous tissue, the former much prevailing.

Chemical Composition—The fresh milky juice of dandelion is bitter and neutral, but it soon acquires an acid reaction and reddish brown tint, at the same time coagulating with separation of masses of what has been called by Kromayer (1861), *Leontodonium*. This chemist, by treating this substance with hot water, obtained a bitter solution yielding an active (?) principle to animal charcoal, from which it was removed by means of boiling spirit of wine. After the evaporation of the alcohol, Kromayer purified the liquid by addition of basic acetate of lead, saturation of the filtered solution with sulphuretted hydrogen and evaporation to dryness. The residue then yielded to ether an acrid resin, and left a colourless amorphous mass of intensely bitter taste, named by Kromayer *Taraxacin*. Polex (1839) obtained apparently the same principle in warty crystals; he simply boiled the milky juice with water and allowed the concentrated decoction to evaporate.

The portion of the "*Leontodonium*," not dissolved by water, yields to alcohol a crystalline substance, Kromayer's *Taraxacerin*, $C^8H^{16}O$. It resembles lactucerin and has in alcoholic solution an acrid taste. How far the medicinal value of dandelion is dependent on the substances thus extracted, is not yet known.

Dragendorff (1870) obtained from the root gathered near Dorpat in October and dried at 100° C., 24 per cent. of *Inulin* and some sugar. The root collected in March from the same place yielded only 1·74 per cent. of inulin, 17 of uncrystallizable sugar and 18·7 of *Levulin*. The last-named substance, discovered by Dragendorff, has the same composition as inulin, but dissolves in cold water; the solution tastes sweetish, and is devoid of any rotatory power. Inulin is often to be seen as a glistening powder when extract of taraxacum is dissolved in water.

T. and H. Smith of Edinburgh (1849) have shown that the juice of the root by a short exposure to the air undergoes a sort of fermentation which results in the abundant formation of *Mannite*, not a trace of which is obtainable from the perfectly fresh root. Sugar which readily underwent the vinous fermentation was found by the same chemists in considerable quantity.

The leaves and stalks of dandelion (but not the roots) were found by Marmé (1864) to afford the *Inosite*, $C^6H^{12}O^6 + 2\,OH^2$.

The root collected in the meadows near Bern immediately before flowering, carefully washed and dried at 100° C., yielded us 5·24 per cent. of ash, which we found to consist of carbonates, phosphates, sulphates, and in smaller quantity also of chlorides.

Uses—Taraxacum is much employed as a mild laxative and tonic, especially in hepatic disorders.

Adulteration—The roots of *Leontodon hispidus* L. (Common Hawk-

[1] The reader who is not familiar with this process may refer to a paper by Pocklington in *Pharm. Journ.* April 13, 1872. 822.

bit) have occasionally been supplied by fraudulent herb-gatherers in place of dandelion. Both plants have runcinate leaves, but those of hawkbit are hairy, while those of dandelion are smooth. The (fresh) root of the former is tough, breaking with difficulty and rarely exuding any milky juice.[1]

The dried root of dandelion is exceedingly liable to the attacks of maggots, and should not be kept beyond one season.

HERBA LACTUCÆ VIROSÆ.

Prickly Lettuce; F. *Laitue vireuse;* G. *Giftlattich.*

Botanical Origin—*Lactuca virosa* L.,[2] a tall herb occurring on stony ground, banks and roadsides, throughout Western, Central and Southern Europe. It is abundant in the Spanish Peninsula and in France, but in Britain is only thinly scattered, reaching its northern limit in the south-eastern Highlands of Scotland.

History—The introduction of this lettuce into modern medicine is due to Collin (the celebrated physician of Vienna, mentioned in our article on Rad. Arnicæ, p. 390), who about the year 1771 recommended the inspissated juice in the treatment of dropsy. In long-standing cases, this extract was given to the extent of half an ounce a day.

The College of Physicians of Edinburgh inserted *Lactuca virosa* L. in their pharmacopœia of 1792, while in England its place was taken by the Garden Lettuce, *L. sativa* L. The Authors of the *British Pharmacopœia* of 1867 have discarded the latter, and directed that *Extractum Lactucæ* shall be prepared by inspissating the juice of *L. virosa.*

Description—The plant is biennial, producing in its first year depressed obovate undivided leaves, and in its second a solitary upright stem, 3 to 5 feet high, bearing a pinacle of small, pale yellow flowers, resembling those of the Garden Lettuce. The stem, which is cylindrical and a little prickly below, has scattered leaves growing horizontally; they are of a glaucous green, ovate-oblong, often somewhat lobed, auricled, clasping, with the margin provided with irregular spinescent teeth, and midrib white and prickly. The whole plant abounds in a bitter, milky juice of strong, unpleasant, opiate smell.

Chemical Composition—We are not aware of any modern chemical examination having been made of *Lactuca virosa.* The more important constituents of the plant are those found in *Lactucarium,* to the article on which the reader is referred.

Uses—The inspissated expressed juice of the fresh plant is reputed narcotic and diuretic, but is probably nearly inert.

[1] Giles, *Pharm. Journ.* xi. (1851) 107.

[2] Bentham unites this plant with *L. Scariola* L., but in most works on botany they are maintained as distinct species.

LACTUCARIUM.

Lactucarium, Lettuce Opium, Thridace;[1] F. and G. *Lactucarium.*

Botanical Origin—The species of *Lactuca* from which lactucarium is obtained, are three or four in number, namely—

1. *Lactuca virosa* L., described in the foregoing article.

2. *L. Scariola* L., a plant very nearly allied to the preceding and perhaps a variety of it, but having the foliage less abundant, more glaucous, leaves more sharply lobed, much more erect and almost parallel with the stem. It has the same geographical range as *L. virosa.*

3. *L. altissima* Bieb., a native of the Caucasus, now cultivated in Auvergne in France for yielding lactucarium. It is a gigantic herb, having when cultivated a height of 9 feet and a stem 1½ inches in diameter. Prof. G. Planchon believes it to be a mere variety of *L. Scariola* L.

4. *L. sativa* L., the common Garden Lettuce.[2]

History—Dr. Coxe of Philadelphia was the first to suggest that the juice of the lettuce, collected in the same manner as opium is collected from the poppy, might be usefully employed in medicine. The result of his experiments on the juice which he thus obtained from the garden lettuce (*L. sativa* L.), and called *Lettuce Opium*, was published in 1799.[3]

The experiments of Coxe were continued some years later by Duncan, Young, Anderson, Scudamore and others in Scotland, and by Bidault de Villiers and numerous observers in France. The production of lactucarium in Auvergne was commenced[4] by Aubergier, pharmacien of Clermont-Ferrand, about 1841.

Secretion—All the green parts of the plant are traversed by a system of vessels, which when wounded, especially during the period of flowering, instantly exude a white milky juice. The stem, at first solid and fleshy but subsequently hollow, owes its rigidity to a circle of about 30 fibro-vascular bundles, each of which includes a cylinder of cambium. At the boundary between this tissue and the primary cortical parenchyme, is situated the system of milk-vessels, exhibiting on transverse section a single or double circle of thin-walled tubes, the cavities of which contain dark brown masses of coagulated juice. In longitudinal section, they appear branched and transversely bound together, as in the milk-vessels of taraxacum. The larger of these tubes, 35 mkm. in diameter, correspond pretty regularly in position with the vascular bundles. Each of the latter is also separated from the pith by a band or arch of cambium, in the circumference of which isolated smaller milk-vessels occur.

The system of milk-vessels[5] is therefore double, belonging to the

[1] The term Thridace is also applied to *Extract of Lettuce.*

[2] The authors of the French *Codex* of 1866 name as the source of lactucarium that form of the garden lettuce which has been called by De Candolle *Lactuca capitata.* Maisch has obtained lactucarium from *L. elongata* Mühl. (*Am. Journ. of Pharm.* 1869. 148).

[3] Inquiry into the comparative effects of the *Opium officinarum*, extracted from the *Papaver somniferum* or *White Poppy* of Linnæus, and that procured from the *Lactuca sativa* or *Common cultivated Lettuce* of the same author.—*Transact. of the American Philosophical Society*, iv. (1799) 387.

[4] *Comptes Rendus*, xv. (1842) 923.

[5] Beautifully delineated by Hanstein in the work referred to at p. 352, note 2; see also Trécul, *Ann. des Sciences nat. Bot.* v.

pith on the one side, and to the bark on the other, the two being separated by juiceless wood. The milk vessels of the bark are covered by only 2 to 6 rows of parenchyme cells of the middle bark, rapidly decreasing in size from within outwards, and these are protected by a not very thick-walled epidermis. Hence it is easy to understand how the slightest puncture or incision may reach the very richest milk-cells.

The drops of milky juice, when exposed to the air, quickly harden to small yellowish-brown masses, whitish within.

Collection and Description—Lactucarium has been especially collected since about the year 1845, in the neighbourhood of the small town of Zell on the Mosel between Coblenz and Trèves in Rhenish Prussia. The introduction of this industry is due to Mr. Goeris, apothecary of that place, to whom we are indebted for the following information, and for some further particulars, to Mr. Meurer of Zell.

The plant is grown in gardens, where it produces a stem only in its second year. In May just before it flowers, its stem is cut off at about a foot below the top, after which a transverse slice is taken off daily until September. The juice, which is pure white but readily becomes brown on the surface, is collected from the wounded top by the finger, and transferred to hemispherical earthen cups, in which it quickly hardens so that it can be turned out. It is then dried in the sunshine until it can be cut into four pieces, when the drying is completed by exposure to the air for some weeks on frames.

At Zell, 300 to 400 kilogrammes (661 to 882 ℔.) of lactucarium are annually produced; the whole district furnishes at best but 20 quintals annually. The price the drug fetches on the spot varies from 4 to 10 thalers per kilogramme (about 6s. to 14s. per ℔.) In the Eifel district, where lactucarium was formerly collected, none is now produced.

As found in trade, German lactucarium consists of angular pieces formed as already described, but rendered more or less shrunken and irregular by loss of moisture and by fracture. Externally they are of a dull reddish brown, internally opaque and wax-like, and when recent, of a creamy white. By exposure to the air, this white becomes yellow and then brown. Lactucarium has a strong unpleasant odour, suggestive of opium, and a very bitter taste.

The lactucarium produced by Aubergier of Clermont-Ferrand is of excellent quality, but does not appear to differ from that obtained on the Mosel, except that it is in circular cakes about 1½ inches in diameter, instead of in angular lumps.

Scotch lactucarium, which was formerly the only sort found in the market, is still (1872) met with. Mr. Fairgrieve, who produces it in the neighbourhood of Edinburgh, collects the juice into little tin vessels, in which it quickly thickens; it is then turned out and dried with a gentle heat, the drug being broken up as the process of drying goes on. It is thus obtained in irregular earthy-looking lumps of a deep brown hue, of which the larger may be about an inch in length. In smell, it exactly resembles the drug collected on the Continent.[1]

We have also before us Austrian lactucarium, prepared at Waidhofen

(1866) 69; Dippel, *Entstehung der Milchsaftgefässe*, Rotterdam, 1865. tab. 1. fig. 17.

[1] We are indebted to Mr. H. C. Baildon for a specimen of Scotch lactucarium collected about the year 1844, and to Messrs. T. and H. Smith for a sample of Mr. Fairgrieve's article.

on the Thaya, where about 35 kilogrammes are annually produced. It is in fine tears of vigorous smell.

We are unacquainted with Russian lactucarium, which has been quoted at a very high price in some continental lists.

Chemical Composition—Lactucarium is a mixture of very different organic substances, together with 8 to 10 per cent. of inorganic matter. It is not completely taken up by any solvent, and when heated merely softens but does not melt. Nearly half the weight of lactucarium consists of a substance called *Lactucerin* or *Lactucon*, which in our opinion is closely allied to if not identical with similar substances occurring in numerous milky juices. Lactucerin as afforded by the drug under examination is probably a mixture of several bodies. It may be obtained by exhausting lactucarium with boiling alcohol sp. gr. 0·830; it is deposited in crystals, which when duly purified have the form of slender colourless, microscopic needles. Lactucerin is an inodorous, tasteless substance, insoluble in water, but dissolving in ether and in oils both fixed and volatile, not quite so readily either in benzol, or in bisulphide of carbon. We found it to melt at 232° C. and to agree with the formula $C^{19}H^{30}O$; Franchimont (1879) assigns to it the formula $C^{14}H^{24}O$, melting point 296°.

Euphorbon (see Euphorbium), echicerin (see Cortex Alstoniæ), taraxacerin (p. 394), the cynanchol, $C^{15}H^{24}O$, extracted in 1875 by Buttleroff from *Cynanchum acutum* L., are remarkably analogous to lactucerin.

In the lactucarium of Zell, we further met with a large amount of a substance which is readily soluble in bisulphide of carbon. It is an amorphous mass, melting below 100°, separating from alcohol as a syrupy mass.

Cold alcohol, as well as boiling water, takes out of lactucarium about 0·3 per cent. of a crystallizable bitter substance, *Lactucin*, $C^{11}H^{12}O^{3}H^{2}O$, which although it reduces alkaline cupric tartrate, is not a glucoside. It may be best obtained by means of dialyse. Lactucin forms white pearly scales, readily soluble in acetic acid, but insoluble in ether. It loses its bitterness when treated with an alkali.

From the mother-liquors that have yielded lactucin, Ludwig, in 1847, obtained *Lactucic Acid*, as an amorphous light yellow mass, becoming crystalline after long standing. Lastly lactucarium has further afforded in small quantity an amorphous substance named *Lactucopicrin*, $C^{44}H^{64}O^{21}$, apparently produced from lactucin by oxidation; it is stated by Kromayer (1862) to be soluble in water or alcohol, and to be very bitter.

Of the widely diffused constituents of plants, lactucarium contains caoutchouc (40–50 per cent.), gum, oxalic, citric, malic and succinic acids, sugar, mannite, and asparagin, together with potassium, calcium and magnesium salts of nitric and phosphoric acids. We obtained crystals of nitrate of potassium by concentrating the aqueous decoction of lactucarium. On distillation with water, a volatile oil having the odour of lactucarium passes over in very small quantity.

Uses—The soporific powers universally ascribed in ancient times to the lettuce are supposed to exist in a concentrated form in lactucarium. Yet numerous experiments have failed to show that this substance possesses more than very slight sedative properties, if indeed it is not absolutely inert.[1]

LOBELIACEÆ.

HERBA LOBELIÆ.

Lobelia, Indian Tobacco ; F. *Lobelie enflée ;* G. *Lobeliakraut.*

Botanical Origin—*Lobelia inflata* L., an annual herb, 9 to 18 inches high, with an angular upright stem, simple or more frequently branching near the top, widely diffused throughout the eastern part of North America from Canada to the Mississippi, growing in neglected fields, along roadsides, and on the edges of woods, and thriving well in European gardens.

History—*Lobelia inflata* was described and figured by Linnæus[2] from specimens cultivated by him at Upsala about 1741, but he does not attribute to the plant any medicinal virtues.

The aborigines of North America made use of the herb, which from this circumstance and its acrid taste, came to be called *Indian Tobacco.* In Europe it was noticed by Schöpf,[3] but with little appreciation of its powers. In America it has long been in the hands of quack doctors, but its value in asthma was set forth by Cutler in 1813. It was not employed in England until about 1829, when, with several other remedies, it was introduced to the medical profession by Reece.[4]

Description—The leaves are 1 to 3 inches long, scattered, sessile, ovate-lanceolate, rather acute, obscurely toothed, somewhat pubescent. The edge of the leaf bears small whitish glands, and between them isolated hairs which are more frequent on the under than on the upper surface. They are usually in greater abundance on the lower and middle portions of the stem.

The stem of the growing plant exudes when wounded a small quantity of acrid milky juice, contained in laticiferous vessels running also into the leaves. The inconspicuous blossoms are arranged in a many-flowered, terminal, leafy raceme. The five-cleft, bilabiate corolla is bluish with a yellow spot on the under lip, its tube being as long as the somewhat divergent limb of the calyx.

The capsule is ovoid, inflated, ten-ribbed, crowned by five elongated sepals which are half as long as the ripe fruit. The latter is two-celled, and contains a large number of ovate-oblong seeds about $\frac{1}{50}$ of an inch in length, having a reticulated, pitted surface.

The herb found in commerce is in the form of rectangular cakes, 1 to $1\frac{3}{4}$ inches thick, consisting of the yellowish-green chopped herb, compressed as it would seem while still moist, and afterwards neatly

[1] Stillé, *Therapeutics and Mat. Med.* i. (1868) 756. Garrod (*Med. Times and Gazette*, 26 March, 1864), gave lactucarium in drachm doses, repeated 3 or 4 times a day, without being able to perceive that it had any effect either as an anodyne or hypnotic.

[2] *Acta Soc. Reg. Scient. Upsal.* 1746. 23.

[3] *Mat. Med. Americana*, Erlangæ, 1787. 128.

[4] *Treatise on the Bladder-podded Lobelia*, Lond. 1829.

trimmed. The cakes arrive wrapped in paper, sealed up and bearing the label of some American druggist or herb-grower.

Lobelia has a herby smell and, after being chewed, a burning acrid taste resembling that of tobacco.

Chemical Composition—Lobelia has been examined by Procter, Pereira (1842), Reinsch (1843), Bastick (1851), also by F. F. Mayer.[1] The first-named chemist[2] traced the activity of the plant to an alkaloid which he termed *Lobelina*, and his observations were confirmed by the independent experiments of Bastick.[3] Lewis (1878) obtained it by mixing the drug with charcoal and exhausting the powder with water containing a little acetic acid. The liquid is cautiously evaporated to the consistency of an extract and triturated with magnesia, from the excess of which the aqueous solution of lobeline is separated by filtration. It is agitated with amylic alcohol (or ether), which by spontaneous evaporation affords the alkaloid. The latter is again dissolved in water and filtered through animal charcoal; from the dried powder lobeline is to be removed by ether.

Lobeline is an oily, yellowish fluid with a strong alkaline reaction, especially when in solution. In the pure state it smells slightly of the plant, but more strongly when mixed with ammonia. Its taste is pungent and tobacco-like, and when taken in minute doses, it exercises in a potent manner the poisonous action of the drug. Lobeline is to some extent volatile, but its decomposition begins when it is heated to 100° C. either pure or in presence of dilute acids or caustic alkalis. Lobeline dissolves in water, but more readily in alcohol or ether, the latter of which is capable of removing it from its aqueous solution. It neutralizes acids, forming with some of them crystallizable salts, soluble in water or alcohol.

The herb likewise contains traces of essential oil (the *Lobelianin* of Pereira?), resin and gum. The seeds afforded Procter about 30 per cent. of fixed oil, sp. gr. 0·940, which was found to dry very rapidly. The *Lobeliin* of Reinsch appears to be an indefinite compound.

In 1871 Enders at our request performed some researches on Lobelia in order to isolate the acrid substance to which the herb owes its taste. He exhausted the drug with spirit of wine and distilled the liquid in presence of charcoal, which then retained the acrid principle. The charcoal was washed with water, and then treated with boiling alcohol. This on evaporation yielded a green extract, which was further purified by means of chloroform. Warty tufts were thus finally obtained, yet always of a brownish colour. The tufts are readily soluble in ether and chloroform, but only slightly in water; they possess the acrid taste of lobelia. This substance, which we may term *Lobelacrin*, is decomposed if merely boiled with water; by the influence of alkalis or acids it is resolved into sugar and *Lobelic Acid*. The latter is soluble in ether, water, and alcohol, and is non-volatile; it yields a soluble salt with baryum oxide, whereas its plumbic salt is insoluble in water.

Lewis suggests that lobelacrin is nothing else than *lobeliate of lobeline*, which he believes to exist ready formed in the plant. From a

[1] *American Journ. of Pharm.* xxxvii. (1866) 209; also *Jahresbericht* of Wiggers and Husemann, 1866. 252.

[2] *Am. Journ. of Pharm*, iii. (1838) 98; vii. (1841) 1; *Pharm. Journ.* x. (1851) 456.

[3] *Pharm. Journ.* x. (1851) 270.

decoction of the drug, on addition of sulphate of copper, lobeliate of copper is precipitated. By decomposing the latter with sulphuretted hydrogen, concentrating the solution and shaking it with warm ether, Lewis obtained a yellow solution affording on evaporation a crystalline mass of lobelic acid.

Uses—Lobelia is a powerful nauseating emetic; in large doses an acro-narcotic poison. It is prescribed in spasmodic asthma.

ERICACEÆ.

FOLIA UVÆ URSI.

Bearberry Leaves; F. *Feuilles de Busserole*; G. *Bärentraubenblätter*.

Botanical Origin—*Arctostaphylos Uva-ursi* Sprengel (*A. officinalis* Wimmer et Grabowsky, *Arbutus Uva-ursi* L.), a small, procumbent, evergreen shrub, distributed over the greater part of the northern hemisphere. It occurs in North America, Iceland, Northern Europe, and Russian Asia, and on the chief mountain chains of Central and Southern Europe. In Britain it is confined to Scotland, the north of England, and Ireland.

History—The bearberry was used in the 13th century by the Welsh "Physicians of Myddfai," described by Clusius in 1601, and recommended for medicinal use in 1763 by Gerhard of Berlin and others.[1] It had a place in the London Pharmacopœia for the first time in 1788.

Description—The leaves are dark green, $\frac{3}{4}$ to 1 inch in length by $\frac{2}{8}$ to $\frac{3}{8}$ of an inch in breadth, obovate, rounded at the end, gradually narrowed into a short petiole. They are entire, with the margin a little reflexed, and in the young state slightly pubescent, otherwise the whole leaf is smooth, glabrous, and coriaceous; the upper surface shining, deeply impressed with a network of veins; the under minutely reticulated with dark veins.[2] The leaves have a very astringent taste, and when powdered a tea-like smell.

Chemical Composition—Kawalier (1852) has shown that a decoction of bearberry treated with basic acetate of lead yields a gallate of that metal, thus proving that gallic acid exists ready-formed in the leaves. When the filtrate, freed from lead by sulphuretted hydrogen, is properly concentrated, it deposits acicular crystals of *Arbutin*, a bitter neutral substance, easily soluble in hot water, less so in cold, dissolving in alcohol, but sparingly in ether.

By contact for some days with emulsin, or by boiling with dilute sulphuric acid, arbutin is resolved, according to Hlasiwetz and Habermann (1875), as follows:—

$$\underset{\text{Arbutin.}}{C^{25}H^{34}O^{14}} + 2\,OH^2 = \underset{\text{Glucose.}}{C^6H^{12}O^6} \;.\; \underset{\text{Hydrokinone.}}{C^6H^4(OH)^2} \;.\; \underset{\text{Methyl-hydrokinone.}}{C^6H^4(OH.OCH^3)}$$

Yet possibly arbutin is a mixture of the glucoside compounds of both hydrokinone and methyl-hydrokinone.

[1] Murray, *Apparatus Medicaminum*, ii. (1794) 64–81.

[2] Microscopic structure of the leaves, see Pocklington, *Pharm. Journ.* v. (1874) 301.

By heating arbutin with peroxide of manganese and dilute sulphuric acid, on the other hand, *Kinone*, $C^6H^4O^2$, and formic acid are produced. If a concentrated decoction of the leaves is allowed to stand for some months, a decomposition of the arbutin takes place, and a certain quantity of hydrokinone can be isolated by shaking the liquid with ether.

Arbutin is apparently widely distributed among the plants belonging to the order Ericaceæ. Maisch in 1874 showed it to occur in *Arctostaphylos glauca* Swindley, *Gaultheria procumbens* L. (Wintergreen) and several other allied American plants. Kennedy (1875) isolated arbutin from *Kalmia latifolia* L. (Spoonwood), where it occurs in smaller quantity than in bearberry leaves.

Kinic acid (see p. 363) is probably absent in all these plants containing arbutin.

Uloth (1859) had already noticed pyrocatechin (p. 244) and hydrokinone among the products of the distillation of an aqueous extract of bearberry leaves. Arbutin itself also yields hydrokinone by means of dry distillation. Hydrokinone forms colourless crystals, melting at 169° C.

In the mother liquor from which the arbutin has crystallized, there remains a small quantity of the very bitter substance called *Ericolin*, occurring in greater abundance in Calluna, Ledum, Rhododendron, and other *Ericaceæ*. *Ericolin* is an amorphous yellowish mass, softening at 100° C. and resolved, when heated with dilute sulphuric acid, into sugar and *Ericinol*, a colourless, quickly resinifying oil of a peculiar, not disagreeable odour; its composition[1] agrees with the formula $C^{10}H^{16}O$. The same, or $C^{20}H^{32}O^2$, is to be assigned to *Ursone*, which H. Trommsdorff, in 1854, obtained from bearberry leaves by exhausting them with ether (in which however it is but slightly soluble). Ursone is a colourless and tasteless crystallizable substance. It melts at 200° C., and sublimes apparently unchanged. Tonner (1866) met with it in the leaves of an Australian *Epacris*, a plant of the same order as the bearberry.

Lastly, tannic acid is present in the leaves under notice; their aqueous infusion is nearly colourless, but assumes a violet hue on addition of ferrous sulphate. After a short time a reddish precipitate is produced, which quickly turns blue. By using ferric chloride, a bluish black precipitate immediately separates.

Adulteration—The leaves of *Vaccinium Vitis-idæa* L., called *Red Whortleberry* or *Cowberry*, have been confounded with those of bearberry, which in form they much resemble. But they are easily distinguished by being somewhat crenate towards the apex, dotted and reticulate on the under surface and more revolate at the margin.

Uses—An astringent tonic used chiefly in affections of the bladder.

[1] Gmelin, *Chemistry*, xvi. (1864) 28.

EBENACEÆ.

FRUCTUS DIOSPYRI.

Indian Persimmon.

Botanical Origin—*Diospyros Embryopteris* Pers. (*Embryopteris glutinifera* Roxb.), a middle-sized or large evergreen tree, native of the western coast of India, Ceylon, Bengal, Burma, Siam, and also Java.[1]

History—The tree, which is mentioned in the earliest epic poems of the Sanskrit literature under the name of *tinduka*,[2] was also known about the year 1680 to Rheede, and was figured in his *Hortus Malabaricus*.[3] The circumstance that the unripe fruit abounds in an astringent viscid juice which is used by the natives of India for daubing the bottoms of boats, was communicated by Sir William Jones to Roxburgh in 1791. The introduction of the fruit into medicine, which is due to O'Shaughnessy,[4] has been followed by its admission to the *Pharmacopœia of India*, 1868.

Description—The fruit is usually solitary, subsessile or pedunculate, globular or ovoid, 1½ to 2 inches long, and as much as 1½ inch in diameter, surrounded at the base by a large and deeply 4-lobed calyx. It is of a yellowish colour, covered with a rusty tomentum; internally it is pulpy, 6- to 10-celled, with thin flat solitary seeds. The fruit is used only in the unripe and fresh state; the pulp is then excessively astringent. At maturity, in the month of April near Bombay, the fruit becomes eatable, but is very little appreciated.

Chemical Composition—No analysis has been made of this fruit, but there can be no doubt that in common with that of other species of *Diospyros*, it is, when immature, rich in tannic acid. Charropin (1873),[5] who has examined the fruit of the American *D. virginiana* L., found it to contain a tannic acid which he considered identical with that of nutgalls, besides an abundance of pectin, glucose, and a yellow colouring matter insoluble in water but dissolving freely in ether.

Uses—The inspissated juice has been recommended as an astringent in diarrhœa and chronic dysentery.

STYRACEÆ.

RESINA BENZOË.

Benzoïnum; Benzoin, Gum Benjamin; F. *Benjoin;* G. *Benzoëharz.*[6]

Botanical Origin—*Styrax Benzoin* Dryander, a tree of moderate height, with stem as thick as a man's body and beautiful crown of

[1] Fig. in Bentley and Trimen, *Med. Plants*, part 18 (1877).

[2] As we learn from Dr. Rice.—Prof. Dymock (1876) gives *Timbooree* as the Bombay name.

[3] Tom. iii. tab. 41.

[4] *Bengal Dispensatory*, Calcutta, 1842. 428.

[5] *Etude sur le Plaqueminier* (*Diospyros*), thèse, Paris, 1873. 28–30.

[6] *Benzoin* in Malay and Javanese is termed *Kamâñan*, *Kamiñan*, and *Kamayan*, abbreviated to *mâñan* and *miñan* (Crawfurd); it is called in Siamese *kom-yan* or *kan-yan*; in Chinese *ngán-si-hiáng*.

The name *Benzoin* is also applied to the beautiful prisms $C^{14}H^{12}O^{2}$ obtained by treating Bitter Almond Oil with an alcoholic solution of potash.

foliage, indigenous to Sumatra and Java, in the first of which islands benzoin is produced.

The tree yielding the superior benzoin of Siam, though commonly referred to this species, has never been examined botanically, and is actually unknown. The French expedition for the exploration of the Mekong and Cochin China (1866–68), reported the drug to be produced in the cassia-yielding forests on the eastern bank of the river in question in about N. lat. 19°. Whether any benzoin is obtained from *S. Finlaysoniana* Wall, as conjectured by Royle, we know not.

History—There is no evidence that the Greeks and Romans,[1] or even the earlier Arabian physicians, had any acquaintance with benzoin; nor is the drug to be recognized among the commodities which were conveyed to China by the Arab and Persian traders between the 10th and 13th centuries, though the camphor of Sumatra is expressly named.

The first mention of benzoin known to us (disregarding the word kalanusari, which in the St. Petersburg Dictionary is given as the old Sanskrit name of benzoin) occurs in the travels of Ibn Batuta,[2] who having visited Sumatra during his journey through the East, A.D. 1325–49, notes that the island produces *Java Frankincense* and camphor. The word *Java* was at that period a designation of Sumatra, or was even used by the Arabs to signify the islands and productions of the Archipelago generally.[3] Hence came the Arabic name *Lubán Jáwí*, i.e. *Java Frankincense*, corrupted into *Banjawi*, *Benjui*, *Benzui*, *Benzoë* and *Benzoïn*, and into the still more vulgar English *Benjamin*.

We have no further information about the drug until the latter half of the following century, when we find a record that in 1461 the sultan of Egypt, Melech Elmaydi, sent to Pasquale Malipiero, doge of Venice, a present of 30 *rotoli* of *Benzoi*, 20 *rotoli* of Aloes Wood, two pairs of Carpets, a small flask of balsam (of Mecca), 15 little boxes of Theriaka, 42 loaves of Sugar, 5 boxes of Sugar Candy, a horn of Civet, and 20 pieces of Porcelain.[4] Agostino Barberigo, another doge of Venice, was presented in a similar manner in 1490 by the sultan of Egypt with 35 *rotoli* of Aloes Wood, the same quantity of *Benzui* and 100 loaves of Sugar.[5]

Among the precious spices sent from Egypt in 1476 to Caterina Cornaro, queen of Cyprus, were 10 ℔. of Aloes Wood and 15 ℔. of *Benzui*.[6] These notices indicate the high value set upon the drug when first brought to Europe.

The occurrence of benzoin in Siam is noticed in the journal of the voyage of Vasco da Gama,[7] where, in enumerating the kingdoms of India, it is stated that Xarnaux (Siam[8]) yields much benzoin worth 3 *cruzados*, and aloes worth 25 *cruzados* per *farazola*. According to the

[1] Crawfurd suggests that the *Malabathrum* of the ancients is possibly *benzoin*.—*Dict. of Indian Islands*, 1856. 50.

[2] *Voyages d'Ibn Batoutah*, traduit par Defrémery et Sanguinetti, Paris, 1853–59. iv. 228. 240.

[3] Yule, *Book of Ser Marco Polo*, ii. (1871) 228.

[4] Muratori, *Rerum Italicarum Scriptores*, xxii. (1733) 1170.—100 *rotoli* = 175 lb. avoirdupois.

[5] L. de Mas Latrie, *Hist. de l'île de Chypre*, etc. iii. (1861) 483.

[6] *Ibid.* iii. 406.

[7] *Roteiro da Viagem de Vasco da Gama em* 1497, par Herculano e o Barão Castello de Paiva, segunda edição, Lisboa, 1861. 109.

The Roteiro is also found in Flückiger, *Documente zur Geschichte der Pharmacie*, Halle, 1876. 13.

[8] Yule, *op. cit.* ii. 222.

same record, the price of benzoin (*beijoim*) in Alexandria was 1 *cruzado* per *arratel*, half the value of aloes wood.

The Portuguese traveller Barbosa[1] visited in 1511 Calicut on the Malabar Coast, and found *Benzui* to be one of the more valuable items of export, one *farazola* (22 ℔. 6 oz.) costing 65 to 70 *fanoes;* camphor fetched nearly the same price, and mace only 25 to 30 *fanoes.* From other sources we gather that benzoin was an article of Venetian trade in the beginning of the 16th century.

Garcia de Orta, writing at Goa (1563), was the first to give a lucid and intelligent account of benzoin, detailing the method of collection, and distinguishing the drug of Siam and Martaban from that produced in Java and Sumatra.

It began then to be regularly imported into Europe,[2] being frequently called *Asa dulcis.* The chemists of that time submitted it, like many other substances, to dry distillation. Benzoic acid occasionally separating from the oily products ("*oleum Benzoës*") was noticed already by Nostredame,[3] Rosello,[4] Liebaut,[5] Blaise de Vigenère,[6] and others. It was a common pharmaceutical preparation, under the name of *Flores Benzoës,* since the 17th century.[7]

In the early part of the 17th century, there was direct commercial intercourse between England and both Siam and Sumatra, an English factory existing at Ayuthia (Siam) until 1623; and benzoin was doubtless one of the commodities imported. The import duties levied upon it in England in 1635 amounted to 10*s.* per lb.[8]

Production—Benzoin is collected in Northern and Eastern Sumatra, especially in the Batta country, lying southward of the state of Achin.[9] The tree grows in plenty also in the highlands of Palembang in the south and its resin is collected. It is chiefly on the coast regions that considerable plantations are found. Teysmann saw the cultivation in the tracts of the river Batang Leko, the trees being planted about 15 feet apart. The benzoin from the interior is mostly from wild trees, which occur at the foot of the mountains at an elevation of 300 to 1000 feet.

The trees, which are of quick growth, are raised from seeds grown on the [edges of?] rice-fields; they require no particular attention beyond being kept clear of other plants, until about 6 or 7 years old, when they have trunks 6 to 8 inches in diameter, and

[1] Flückiger, *l.c.*, page 14.

[2] Cardanus, *Les livres de la subtilité,* Paris, 1556 (first edition, 1550), page 160 *b.* states: "belzoi est de vil prix pour l'abondance."

[3] *Excellent et moult utile opuscule à touts necessaire qui desirent avoir cognoissance de plusieurs exquises receptes,* 1556.

[4] Alexii Pedemontani (or Hieron. Rosello), *De secretis libri vi.,* Basil, 1560, page 107.

[5] *Quatre livres de secrets de medecine et de la philosophie chimique,* Paris, 1579, page 146.

[6] *Traicté du feu et du sel,* Paris, 1622, page 99.—Vigenère speaks distinctly of "filamens ou aiguilles," i.e. crystals.—He died in 1596.

[7] Flückiger, *Pharm. Journ.* vi. (1876) 1022.

[8] *The Rates of Marchandizes,* London, 1635.

[9] Miquel, *Prodromus Floræ Sumatranæ,* 1860. 72; Marsden, *Hist. of Sumatra,* London, 1783. 123.—The latter author resided at Bencoolen, as an official of the English Government.

The statement of Crawfurd, *l.c.*, that benzoin is collected in Borneo "*on the northern coast in the territory of Brunai*" is to us inexplicable. Mr. St. John, British Consul in Borneo, in an official report on the trade of Brunai, dated from that place 29 January 1858, enumerates the various productions of the district, but does not name benzoin.

are capable of yielding the resin. Incisions are then made in their stems, from which there exudes a thick, whitish, resinous juice, which soon hardens by exposure to the air, and is carefully scraped off with a knife.

The trees continue to yield at the rate of about three pounds per annum for 10 or 12 years, after which period they are cut down. The resin which exudes during the first three years is said to be fuller of white tears, and therefore of finer quality, than that which issues subsequently, and is termed by the Malays *Head Benzoin*. That which flows during the next 7 or 8 years, is browner in colour and less valuable, and is known as *Belly Benzoin;* while a third sort, called *Foot*, is obtained by splitting the tree and scraping the wood; this last is mixed with much bark and refuse.[1]

Benzoin is brought for sale to the ports of Sumatra in large cakes called *Tampangs*, wrapped in matting. These have to be broken, and softened either by the heat of the sun or by that of boiling water, and then packed into square cases which the resin is made to fill.

The only account of the collection of *Siam Benzoin* is that given by Sir R. H. Schomburgk, for some years British Consul at Bangkok.[2] He represents that the bark is gashed all over, and that the resin which exudes, collects and hardens between it and the wood, the former of which is then stripped off. This account is confirmed by the aspect of some of the Siam benzoin of commerce as well as by that of pieces of bark in our possession; but it is also evident that *all* the Siam drug is not thus obtained. Schomburgk adds, that the resin is much injured and broken during its conveyance in small baskets on bullocks' backs to the navigable parts of the Menam, whence it is brought down to Bangkok.[3]

Whether benzoin owes its original fluidity to a volatile oil holding the resin in solution, and its solidification to the volatilization of this oil, or whether the resin itself hardens by oxidation,—what occasions the remarkable diversity of aspect between the opaque and milk-like, and the completely transparent resin, are questions to be investigated by some future observer.

Description—Benzoin (always termed in English commerce *Gum Benjamin*) is distinguished as of two kinds, *Siam* and *Sumatra*. Each sort occurs in various degrees of purity, and under considerable differences of appearance.

1. *Siam Benzoin*—The most esteemed sort is that which consists entirely of flattened tears or drops, an inch or two long, of an opaque, milk-like, white resin, loosely agglutinated into a mass. More frequently the mass is quite compact, consisting of a certain proportion of white tears of the size of an almond downwards, imbedded in a deep, rich amber-brown, translucent resin. Occasionally the translucent resin preponderates, and the white tears are almost wanting. In some packages, the tears of white resin are very small, and the whole mass

[1] The terms *Head*, *Belly* and *Foot*, equivalent to our words *superior*, *medium* and *inferior*, are used in the East to distinguish the qualities of many other commodities, as Borneo Camphor, Esculent Birds'-nests, Cardamoms, Galbanum, &c.

[2] This account must have been derived from others, for Sir R. H. Schomburgk never visited the region producing benzoin.

[3] *Pharm. Journ.* iii. (1862) 126.

has the aspect of a reddish-brown granite. There is always a certain admixture of bits of wood, bark, and other accidental impurities.

The white tears when broken, display a stratified structure with layers of greater or less translucency. By keeping, the white milky resin becomes brown and transparent on the surface.

Siam benzoin is very brittle, the opaque tears showing a slightly waxy, the transparent a glassy fracture. It easily softens in the mouth and may be kneaded with the teeth like mastich. It has a delicate balsamic, vanilla-like, fragrance, but very little taste. When heated it evolves a more powerful fragrance, together with the irritating fumes of benzoic acid; its fusing point is 75° C. The presence of benzoic acid may be shown by the microscopical examination of splinters of the resin under oil of turpentine.

Siam benzoin is imported in cubic blocks, which takes their form from the wooden cases in which they are packed while the resin is still soft.

2. *Sumatra Benzoin*—Prior to the renewal of direct commercial intercourse with Siam in 1853, this was the sort of benzoin most commonly found in commerce.

It is imported in cubic blocks exactly like the preceding, from which it differs in its generally greyer tint. The mass however, when the drug is of good quality, contains numerous opaque tears, set in a translucent, greyish-brown resin, mixed with bits of wood and bark. When less good, the white tears are wanting, and the proportion of impurities is greater. We have even seen samples consisting almost wholly of bark. In odour, Sumatra benzoin is both weaker and less agreeable than the Siam drug, and generally falls short of it in purity[1] and handsome appearance, and hence commands a much lower price. The greyish-brown portion melts at 95°, the tears at 85° C.

A variety of Sumatra benzoin is distinguished by the London drug-brokers as *Penang Benjamin* or *Storax-smelling Benjamin*. We have seen it of very fine quality, full of white tears (some of them two inches long), the intervening resin being greyish.[2] The odour is very agreeable, and perceptibly different from that of Siam benzoin, or the usual Sumatra sort. Whether this drug is produced in Sumatra and by *Styrax Benzoin* we know not; but it is worthy of note that *S. subdenticulata* Miq., occurring in Western Sumatra, has the same native name (*Kajoe Kĕminjan*) as *S. Benzoin*, and that Miquel remarks of it—"*An etiam benzoiferum?*"[3]

Chemical Composition—Benzoin consists mainly of amorphous resins perfectly soluble in alcohol and in potash, having slightly acid properties, and differing in their behaviour to solvents. If two parts of the drug are boiled with one part of caustic lime and 20 parts of water, benzoin acid is removed. From the residue the excess of lime is dissolved by hydrochloric acid, and the remaining resins washed and dried. About one-third of them will be found readily soluble in ether, the prevailing portion dissolves in alcohol, and a small amount remains undissolved.

[1] In the *Public Ledger*, May 2, 1874, the prices are quoted thus:—Siam Gum Benjamin, 1st and 2nd qualities, £10 to £28 per cwt.; Sumatra, 1st and 2nd, £7 10s. to £12.

[2] There were 8 cases of this drug offered at Public Sale, 13 April 1871.

[3] *Prod. Floræ Sumatranæ*, 1860. 474.

By distilling the resin of benzoin with ten times its weight of zinc dust, Ciamician (1878) chiefly obtained toluol, $C^6H^5(CH^3)$.

Subjected to dry distillation, benzoin affords as chief product *Benzoic Acid*, $C^7H^6O^2$, together with empyreumatic products, among which Berthelot has proved the presence (in Siam benzoin) of *Styrol* (p. 274). The latter has been obtained in 1874 by Theegarten from Sumatra benzoë by distilling it with water. When the resin is fused with potash, it is partly decomposed and then, according to Hlasiwetz and Barth (1866), yields among other products, protocatechuic acid (more than 5 per cent.), $C^6H^3(OH)^2COOH$, para-oxybenzoic acid, $C^6H^4(OH)COOH$, and pyrocatechin, $C^6H^4(OH)^2$.

Benzoic acid exists ready-formed in the drug to the extent of 14 to 18 per cent.[1] Although the acid dissolves in 12 parts of boiling water, the resin in which it is imbedded precludes its complete extraction by this means. It is however easily accomplished by the aid of an alkali, most advantageously by milk of lime, which does not combine with the amorphous resins.

Benzoin is not manifestly acted on by bisulphide of carbon, but if kept in contact with it for a month or two, very large colourless crystals of benzoic acid make their appearance. Brought into a warm room, the crystals quickly dissolve, but are easily reproduced by exposure to cold.

Most pharmacopœias require not the inodorous acid obtained by a wet process, but that afforded by sublimation, which contains a small amount of fragrant empyreumatic products. The resin, when repeatedly subjected to sublimation, affords as much as 14 per cent. of benzoic acid. It has long been known that the opaque white tears of benzoin are less rich in benzoic acid than the transparent brown resin in which they lie. From the latter, S. W. Brown (1833) extracted 13 per cent. of impure acid, but from the former scarcely 8½ per cent. We are by no means sure that such difference is constant.

Bitter almond oil, which by oxidation yields benzoic acid, is wanting in benzoin. Very little volatile oil is in fact to be got; half a pound of the best Penang benzoin yielded us by distillation with water only a few drops of an extremely fragrant oil (*styrol?*).

Ferric chloride imparts to an alcoholic solution of benzoin a dark brownish green, which is not acquired under the same circumstances by the aqueous decoction of the powdered resin. Benzoin dissolves in cold oil of vitriol, forming a solution of splendid carmine hue, from which water separates crystals of benzoic acid.

Kolbe and Lautemann in 1860 discovered in Siam and Penang benzoin together with benzoic acid, an acid of different constitution, which in 1861 they recognized as *Cinnamic Acid*, $C^9H^8O^2$. Aschoff (1861) found in a sample of Sumatra benzoin, cinnamic acid only, of which he got 11 per cent; and in amygdaloid Siam and Penang benzoin only benzoic acid. In some samples of the latter, one of us (F.) has likewise met with cinnamic acid. On triturating this sort with peroxide of lead and boiling the mixture with water, the odour of bitter-almond oil, due to the oxidation of cinnamic acid, is evolved.

The simultaneous occurrence of benzoic and cinnamic acids, or the

[1] Löwe (1870) and Rump (1878) attempted to prove that the acid is partly present in the form of a compound, but they have not shown with which substance it is combined in the drug.

absence of one or other of them in benzoin, is due to circumstances at present unexplained. Rump is of the opinion that the last-named acid exclusively is present in the Penang (or Sumatra) benzoin and that no variety of the drug contains both those acids.

Rump (1878) treated Siam benzoic with caustic lime (see p. 407), precipitated the benzoic acid with hydrochloric acid, and agitated the liquid with ether. The latter on evaporating afforded a mixture of benzoic acid and *Vanillin* (see article Vanilla).

Commerce—The statistics of Singapore,[1] the great emporium of the commerce of the Indian Archipelago, show the imports of Gum Benjamin in 1871 as 7442 cwt., of which quantity 6185 cwt. had been shipped from Sumatra and 405 cwt. from Siam. In 1877 only 1871 peculs (2227 cwts.) were exported from Singapore. Penang, which is also a mart for this drug was stated in 1871 to have received from Sumatra for trans-shipment, 4959 cwt. of Gum Benjamin.

Padang in Sumatra exported in 1870, 4303 peculs (5122 cwt.); and in 1871, 4064 peculs (4838 cwt.) of benzoin.[2]

The imports of Gum Benjamin into Bombay in the year 1871-72 were no less than 5975 cwt., and the exports 1043 cwt.[3]

Uses—Benzoin appears to be nearly devoid of medicinal properties, and is but little employed. It is chiefly imported for use as incense in the service of the Greek Church.

OLEACEÆ.

MANNA.

Manna; F. *Manne*; G. *Manna*.

Botanical Origin—*Fraxinus Ornus* L. (*Ornus europæa* Pers.), the Manna-ash, is a small tree found in Italy, whence it extends northwards as far as the Canton of Tessin in Switzerland and the Southern Tyrol. It also occurs in Hungary (Buda) and the eastern coasts of the Adriatic, in Greece, Turkey (Constantinople), in Asia Minor about Smyrna and at Adalia on the south coast. It grows in the islands of Sicily, Sardinia and Corsica, and is found in Spain at Moxente in Valencia.[4] As an ornamental tree it has been introduced into Central Europe, where it is often seen of greater dimensions, sometimes acquiring a height of about 30 feet. It blossoms in early summer, producing numerous feathery panicles of dull white flowers which give it a pleasing appearance. The foliage exhibits great variation in shape of leaflets, even where the tree is uncultivated; and the fruits also are very diverse in form.

In some districts of Sicily, a little manna is obtained from the Common Ash, *F. excelsior* L.

History—The name *Manna*, though originally applied to the aliment miraculously provided for the sustenance of the ancient Israelites

[1] *Blue Book* for the Colony of the Straits Settlements, Singapore, 1872.

[2] *Consular Reports*, August 1873. 953.

[3] *Statement of the Trade and Navigation of the Presidency of Bombay for* 1871–72, pt. ii. 26. 79.

[4] *Fraxinus Bungeana* DC., a tree of Northern China, appears to be hardly distinct from *F. Ornus*.

during their journey to the Holy Land, has been used to designate other substances of distinct nature and origin. Of these, the best known and most important is the saccharine exudation of *Fraxinus Ornus* L., which constitutes the *Manna* of European medicine.

It appears evident[1] that previous to the 15th century, the manna in Europe was imported from the East and was not that of the ash. Raffaele Maffei, called also Volaterranus, a writer who flourished in the second half of the 15th century, states that manna began to be gathered in Calabria in his time, but that it was inferior to the oriental.[2] At this period the manna collected was that which exuded spontaneously from the leaves of the tree, and was termed *Manna di foglia* or *Manna di fronda:* that which flowed from the stem bore the name of *Manna di corpo* and was less esteemed. All such manna was very dear.

About the middle of the 16th century, the plan of making incisions in the trunk and branches was resorted to, and although it was strenuously opposed even by legislative enactment, the more copious supplies which it enabled the collectors to obtain led it to being generally adopted. The Ricettario Fiorentino of the year 1573[3] states that the manna "fatta con arte," *i.e.* obtained by incisions, came from Cosenza in Calabria and differed not little from Syrian "manna mastichina."[4]

Manna di foglia became in fact utterly unknown, so that Cirillo of Naples, writing in 1770, expresses doubt whether it ever had any existence.[5]

With regard to the history of manna-production in Sicily, there is this curious fact, that near Cefalù there exists an eminence in the Madonia range, called *Gebelman* or *Gibelmanna*, which in Arabic signifies *manna-mountain*. This name is not of modern origin, but is found in a diploma of the year 1082, concerning the foundation of the bishopric of Messina; and it has been held to indicate that manna was there collected during the Saracenic occupation of Sicily, A.D. 827 to 1070. We have not been successful in finding any evidence whether this supposition is well founded. On the other hand, it is remarkable that no writer, so far as we know, mentions manna as a production of Sicily, before Paolo Boccone of Palermo, who, after naming many localities for the drug in continental Italy, states that it is also obtained in Sicily.[6]

Manna was also produced until recently in the Tuscan Maremma, but neither from that locality, nor from the States of the Church, where it was collected in the time of Boccone, is any supply now brought into commerce, though the name of Tolfa, a town near Civita Vecchia, is still used to designate an inferior sort of the drug.

The collection of manna in Calabria, which was imported up to the end of last century, has now almost entirely ceased.[7]

[1] Hanbury, *Historical Notes on Manna*, *Pharm. Journ.* xi. (1870) 326; or *Science Papers*, 355.

[2] *Commentarii Urbani*, Paris, 1515. lib. 38. f. 413.

[3] P. 46; we have not seen the edition of 1498.

[4] Mastichina alludes probably to the granular form of that manna—perhaps it was that of Alhagi, which we shall mention further on, p. 414.

[5] *Phil. Trans.* lx. (1771) 233.

[6] *Museo di Fisica*, Venet. 1697. Obs. xiv.–xv.

[7] Hanbury in *Giornale Botanico Italiano*, Ottobre 1872. 267; *Pharm. Journ.* Nov. 30. 1872. 421; *Science Papers*, 365.

Production—The manna of commerce is collected at the present day exclusively in Sicily. The principal localities producing the drug are the districts around Capaci, Carini, Cinisi, and Favarota, small towns 20 to 25 miles west of Palermo near the shores of the bay of Castellamare; also the townships of Geraci, Castelbuono, and other places in the district of Cefalù, 50 to 70 miles eastward of Palermo.

The manna-ash, in the districts whence the best manna is obtained, does not at the present day form natural woods, but is cultivated in regular plantations called *frassinetti*. The trees, which attain a height of from 10 to 20 feet, are planted in rows and stand about 7 feet apart, the soil between being at times loosened, kept free from weeds, and enriched by manure. After a tree is 8 years old and when its stem is at least 3 inches in thickness, the gathering of manna may begin; and may continue for 10 or 12 years, when the stem is usually cut down, and a young one brought up from the same root takes its place. The same stump thus has often two or three stems rising from it.

To obtan manna, transverse cuts from 1½ to 2 inches long and 1 inch apart, are made in the bark, just reaching to the wood. One cut is made daily, beginning at the bottom of the tree, the second directly above the first, and so on while dry weather lasts. In the following year, cuts are made in the untouched part of the stem, and in the same way in succeeding seasons. When after some years the tree has been cut all round and is exhausted, it is felled. Pieces of sticks or straws are inserted in the incisions, and become encrusted with the very superior manna, called *Manna a cannolo*, which however is unknown in commerce as a special sort. The fine manna ordinarily seen appears to have hardened on the stem of the tree. The manna which flows from the lower incisions, and is often collected on tiles or on a cup-shaped piece of the stem of the prickly pear (*Opuntia*), is less crystalline, and more gummy and glutinous, and is regarded of inferior quality.

The best time for notching the stems is in July and August, when the trees have ceased to push forth more leaves. Dry and warm weather is essential for a good harvest. The manna after removal from the tree, is laid upon shelves in order that it may dry and harden before it is packed. The masses left adhering to the stem after the finer pieces have been gathered, are scraped off and form part of the *Small Manna* of commerce.[1]

Secretion—We have examined microscopically the bark of stems of *Fraxinus Ornus* that had been incised for manna at Capaci. It exhibits no peculiarity explaining the formation of manna, or any evidence that the saccharine exudation is due to an alteration of the cell-walls as in the case of tragacanth. The bark is poor in tannic matter; it contains starch, and imparts to water a splendid fluorescence due to the presence of *Fraxin*.

Description—Various terms have been used by pharmacological writers to designate the different qualities of manna, but in English

[1] Our account of the production of manna has been derived from the observations of Stettner, who visited Sicily in the summer of 1847 (*Archiv der Pharm.* iii. 194; also Wiggers' *Jahresbericht*, 1848. 35; *Hooker's Journ. of Bot.* i. 1849. 124), from those of Cleghorn (*Trans. of the Bot. Soc. of Edinburgh*, x. 1868-69. 132), and from personal investigations made by one of us in the neighbourhood of Palermo in May 1872. See Hanbury, *Science Papers*, 367.

commerce they are not now employed; and the better kinds of the drug are called simply *Flake Manna*, while the smaller pieces, usually loosely agglutinated and sold separately, are termed *Small Manna* or *Tolfa Manna*.

Owing to the gradual exudation of the juice and the deposition of one layer over another, manna has a stalactitic aspect. The finest pieces are mostly in the form of three-edged sticks, sometimes as much as 6 to 8 inches long and an inch or more wide, grooved on the inner side, which is generally soiled by contact with the bark ; of a porous, crystalline, friable structure and of a pale brownish yellow tint, becoming nearly pure white in those parts which have been most distant from the bark of the tree. The pieces which are of deeper colour, and of an unctuous or gummy appearance, are less esteemed. Good manna is crisp and brittle, and melts in the mouth with an agreeable, honey-like sweetness, not entirely devoid of traces of bitterness and acridity. Its odour may be compared to that of honey or moist sugar.

Manna of the best quality dissolves at ordinary temperatures in about six parts of water, forming a clear, neutral liquid. It contains besides mannite, a small proportion of sugar and gum.

The manna which exudes from the older stems and from the lower parts of even young trees, contains more or less considerable quantities of gum and fermentable sugar, as well as extraneous impurities. The less favourable weather of the later summer and autumn promotes an alteration in the composition of the juice, and impairs its property of concreting into a crystalline mass.

Chemical Composition—The predominant constituent of manna, at least of the better sorts, is *Manna-sugar* or *Mannite*, $C^6H^8(OH)^6$ which likewise occurs, though in much smaller quantity, in many other plants besides *Fraxinus*. Artificially, it is produced by treating glucose, $C^6H^{12}O^6$, with sodium-amalgam, and indirectly in the fermentation of glucose or of cane-sugar. It is isomeric with dulcite or melampyrin; crystallizes in shining prisms or tables, belonging to the rhombic system ; melts at 166° C., and in very small quantity may by careful heating be sublimed and decomposed. It dissolves in 6·5 parts of water at 16° C., less freely in aqueous alcohol, very sparingly in absolute alcohol, and not in ether. The solution has an extremely weak rotatory power, and is not altered by boiling with dilute acids or alkalis, or with alkaline cupric tartrate.

Berthelot has shown that mannite is susceptible of fermentation, though not so easily as sugars belonging to the group of carbo-hydrates. The quantity of mannite in the best manna varies from 70 to 80 per cent.

When a solution of manna is mixed with alkaline cupric tartrate, rapid reduction to cuprous hydrate takes place even in the cold. This effect is due to the presence of a sugar which, according to Backhaus (1860), consists of ordinary dextro-glucose. It may amount to as much as 16 per cent., and is found in the best flake manna, but most abundantly in the unctuous varieties. Buignet[1] has pointed out that the rotatory power of this sugar being inconsiderable, it probably consists

[1] *Journ. de Pharm.* vii. (1867) 401 ; viii. (1868) 5.

of a mixture of *Cane-sugar* and *Levulose.* He found however that an aqueous solution of manna deviates powerfully to the right, a fact which he considers due to the presence of a large proportion of *Dextrin.* The best kinds of manna, according to Buignet, contain about 20 per cent. of dextrin; the inferior much more.

In our experiments we have not succeeded in isolating either dextrin or cane-sugar. There is present, even in the finest manna, a small amount of a dextrogyre mucilage, which is precipitated by neutral acetate of lead, and yields mucic acid when boiled with concentrated nitric acid.

Ether extracts from an aqueous solution of manna a very small quantity of red-brown resin, having an offensive odour and sub-acrid taste; together with traces of an acid which reduces silver-salts and appears to be easily resinified. The quantity of water in the inferior kinds of manna often amounts to 10 or 15 per cent. The finest manna affords about 3·6 per cent. of ash.

The greenish colour of certain pieces of manna was formerly attributed to the presence of copper, till Gmelin, on account of the fluorescence of the solution, ascribed it to *Æsculin.* It is in reality produced by a body much resembling æsculin, namely *Fraxin*, $C^{16}H^{18}O^{10}$, occurring in the bark of the manna-ash and of the common ash, and together with æsculin, in that of the horse-chestnut. Fraxin crystallizes in colourless prisms, easily soluble in hot water and in alcohol, and having a faintly astringent and bitter taste. By dilute acids, it is resolved into *Fraxetin*, $C^{10}H^{8}O^{5}$, and *Glucose*, $C^{6}H^{12}O^{6}$. The presence of fraxin in manna, especially in the inferior sorts, is made apparent by the faint fluorescence of the alcoholic manna solution. The smallest fragment of the bark of the ash or the manna ash immersed in water displays the same fluorescence.

Commerce—The exports of manna from Sicily[1] (chiefly from Palermo) have been as follows:—

1869	1870	1871
2546 cwt., val. £15,972.	1564 cwt., val. £10,220.	3038 cwt., val. £19,528.

About half the quantity is sent to France. Italian commercial statistics[2] represent the export of manna in 1870 thus:—*in canelli* 58,691 kilo. (1155 cwt.), *in sorte* 186,664 kilo. (3676 cwt.). The United Kingdom imported in the year 1870, 230 cwt. of manna, valued at £4447.[3]

In 1877 the exports of "canelli" from Messina were 4273 kilogrammes, and of the drug "in sorte" 52,874 kilogr.; total value, 127,145 lire.

Adulteration—It can hardly be said that manna is subject to adulteration, though attempts to introduce a spurious manna made of glucose have been recorded. But considerable skill and ingenuity have been expended in converting the inferior sorts of manna into what has the aspect of fine natural Flake Manna, the manufacturers admitting however the factitiousness of their product. The artificial Flake Manna has the closest superficial resemblance to very fine pieces of the natural

[1] *Report by Consul Dennis on the Commerce and Navigation of Sicily* in 1869, 1870 *and* 1871.

[2] Direzione generale delle Gabelle—*Movimento commerciale del regno d'Italia nel* 1870, Milano, 1871.

[3] *Annual Statement of the Trade and Navigation of the U.K. for* 1870, p. 102

drug, but differs in its more uniform colour, and in being uncontaminated with the slight impurities, from which natural manna is never wholly free. It differs also in that when broken, no crystals of mannite are to be seen in the interstices of the pieces, and it wants the peculiar odour and slightly bitter flavour of natural manna. If one part of it is boiled with four of alcohol (0·838), a viscid honey-like residue will be obtained, whereas natural manna leaves undissolved a hard substance. Histed [1] found it to afford about 40 per cent. of mannite, while fine manna similarly treated yielded 70 per cent.

Uses—A gentle laxative, much less frequently employed in this country than formerly, but still largely consumed in South America. Mannite, which possesses similar properties, is often prescribed in Italy.

Other sorts of Manna.

Various plants besides *Fraxinus* afford, under certain conditions, saccharine exudations, some of which constituted the *Oriental Manna* used in Europe in early times. So far as is known, they differ from officinal manna in containing no mannite.

Alhagi Manna; Turunjabín (Arabic); is afforded by *Alhagi Camelorum* Fisch. (Hedysarum Alhagi Pallas, non L.), a small spiny plant of the order *Leguminosæ* found in Persia, Afghanistan and Beluchistan. It had already been noticed by Isztachri.[2] Excellent specimens of the manna, kindly obtained for us in the north-west of India by Dr. E. Burton Brown and Mr. T. W. H. Tolbort, show it as a substance in little roundish, hard, dry tears, varying from the size of a mustard seed to that of a hemp-seed, of a light brown colour, agreeable saccharine taste, and senna-like smell. The leaflets, spines and pods of the plant, mixed with the grains of this manna, are characteristic and easily recognizable.

Villiers (1877) showed this manna to contain cane-sugar, a dextrogyrate glucose, and *melezitose* (see further on: Briançon manna, page 416). Ludwig[3] had also found some dextrin and mucilage.

Alhagi Manna is collected near Kandahar and Herat, where it is found on the plants at the time of flowering. It is imported into India from Kabul and Kandahar to the extent of about 25 *maunds* (2000 lb.) annually; its value is reckoned at 30 rupees per *secr*, = 30*s*. per lb.[4]

Gaz-anjabin (Arabic); *Tamarisk Manna* (in part)—In the months of June and July, the shrubs of tamarisk (*Tamarix gallica* var. *mannifera* Ehrenb.) growing in the valleys of the peninsula of Sinai, especially in the Wady es Sheikh, exude from their slender branches, in consequence of the puncture of an insect (*Coccus manniparus* Ehrenb.) little honey-like drops, which in the coolness of early morning are found in a solid state. This substance is *Tamarisk Manna*: it is collected by the Arabs, and by them sold to the monks of St. Katharine, who dispose of it to the pilgrims visiting the convent.

[1] *On artificial Flake Manna*, in *Pharm. Journ.* xi. (1870) 629.

[2] Tchihatcheff, *l'Asie mineure*, ii. (1856) 355.

[3] *Archiv der Pharmacie*, 193 (1870) 32–52.

[4] Stewart, *Punjab Plants*, Lahore (1869) p. 57; Davies, *Report on the trade and resources of the countries on the N. W. boundary of British India*, Lahore, 1862.

Tamarisk Manna is also produced (but is perhaps no longer collected ?) in Persia, where it is called *Gaz-angabín*;[1] and probably likewise in the Punjab,[2] from which regions it may have been brought to Europe in ancient times.

A specimen of tamarisk manna brought from Sinai, examined in 1861 by Berthelot, had the appearance of a thick yellowish syrup, contaminated with vegetable remains. It was found to consist of cane-sugar, inverted sugar (lævulose and glucose), dextrin and water, the last constituting one-fifth of the whole.[3]

Although the name *Gaz-angabín* signifies *tamarisk-honey*, it is used according to Haussknecht[4] at the present time in Persia, to designate certain round cakes, common in all the bazaars, of which the chief constituent is a manna collected in the mountain districts of Chahar-Mahal and Faraidan, and especially about the town of Khonsar, south-west of Ispahan, from *Astragalus florulentus* Boiss. et Haussk. and *A. adscendens* Boiss. et Haussk. The best sorts of this manna, which are termed *Gaz Alefi* or *Gaz Khonsari*, are obtained in August by shaking it from the branches, the little drops finally sticking together and forming a dirty, greyish-white, tough mass. The commoner sort got by scraping the stem, is still more impure. The specimen of it brought by Haussknecht yielded to Ludwig[5] dextrin, uncrystallizable sugar and organic acids.

Shir-khist—Ancient writers on materia medica as Garcia d'Orta (1563) mention a sort of manna known by this name. The substance is still found in the bazaars of North-western India, being imported in small quantity from Afghanistan and Turkistan.[6] Haussknecht in his paper on Oriental Manna already quoted, states that it is the exudation of *Cotoneaster nummularia* Fisch. et Mey. (*Rosaceæ*), also of *Atraphaxis spinosa* L. (*Polygonaceæ*), and that it is brought chiefly from Herat. We have to thank Dr. E. Burton Brown of Lahore, and Mr. Tolbort for specimens of this manna, which, from fragments it contains, is without doubt derived from a *Cotoneaster*. It is in irregular roundish tears, from about ¼ up to ¾ of an inch in greatest length, of an opaque dull white, slightly clammy, and easily kneaded in the fingers. It has a manna-like smell, a pure sweet taste and crystalline fracture. With water, it forms a syrupy solution with an abundant residue of starch granules.

Shír-khist was found by Ludwig to consist of an exudation analogous to tragacanth, but containing at the same time two kinds of gum, an amorphous levogyre sugar, besides starch and cellulose.

Oak Manna—The occurrence of a saccharine substance on the oak is noticed by both Ovid and Virgil, and it is also mentioned by the Arabian physicians, as Ibn Baytar[7] and Elluchasem Elimithar.[8] The last named, who died A.D. 1052, states that the exudation appears upon the oaks in the region of Diarbekir. At the present day, it is the object of some industry among the wandering tribes of Kurdistan, who,

[1] Angelus, *Pharm. Persica* (see appendix) p. 359.

[2] Stewart, *op. cit.* p. 92.

[3] *Comptes Rendus*, liii. (1861) 583; *Pharm. Journ.* iii. (1862) 274.

[4] *Archiv d. Pharmacie*, 192 (1870) 246.

[5] *Loc. cit.*

[6] Davies in the work quoted at page 414, note 4.

[7] Ed. Sontheimer, i. (1840) 375.

[8] *Tacuini Sanitatis*, Argentorati (1531) 24.

according to Haussknecht, collect it from *Quercus Vallonea* Kotschy and *Q. persica* Jaub. et Spach. These trees are visited in the month of August by immense numbers of a small white *Coccus*, from the puncture of which a saccharine fluid exudes, and solidifies in little grains. The people go out before sunrise, and shake the grains of manna from the branches on to linen cloths, spread out beneath the trees. The exudation is also collected by dipping the small branches on which it is formed, into vessels of hot water, and evaporating the saccharine solution to a syrupy consistence, which in this state is used for sweetening food, or is mixed with flour to form a sort of cake.

A fine specimen of the Oak Manna of Diarbekir was sent to the London International Exhibition of 1862. It constituted a moist soft mass of agglutinated tears, much resembling an inferior sort of ash-manna, and had an agreeable saccharine taste.

A less pure form of this manna occurs as a compact, greyish, saccharine mass, sometimes hard enough to be broken with a hammer. It consists of sugary matter, mixed with abundance of small fragments of green leaves, and has a herby smell and pleasant sweet taste. A sample of it brought from Diarbekir, examined by one of us, yielded 90 per cent. of dextrogyre sugar, which could not be obtained in a crystalline state, though it exists in such condition in the crude drug. Starch and dextrine were entirely wanting.[1]

A specimen furnished to Ludwig[2] by Haussknecht afforded much mucilage, a small amount of starch, about 48 per cent. of dextrogyre grape sugar, with traces of tannic acid and chlorophyll.

Briançon Manna—This is a white saccharine substance which, in the height of summer and in the early part of the day, is found adhering in some abundance to the leaves of the larch (*Pinus Larix* L.), growing on the mountains about Briançon in Dauphiny. It was formerly collected for use in medicine, but only to a very limited extent, for it was rare in Paris in the time of Geoffroy (1709–1731), and at the present day has quite disappeared from trade, though still gathered by the peasants. A specimen collected for one of us near Briançon in 1854, consists of small, detached, opaque, white tears, many of them oblong and channelled, and encrusting the needle-like leaf of the larch; they have a sweet taste and slight odour.[3] Under the microscope they exhibit indistinct crystals.

Briançon manna has been examined in 1858 by Berthelot, who detected in it a peculiar sugar termed *Melezitose*, answering to the formula $C^{12}H^{22}O^{11} + OH^{2}$.

Several other saccharine exudations have been observed by travellers and naturalists; we shall simply enumerate the more remarkable, referring the reader for further information to the original notices.

Pirus glabra Boiss. affords in Luristan a substance which, according to Haussknecht, is collected by the inhabitants, and is extremely like Oak Manna. It is stated by the same traveller that *Salix fragilis* L., and *Scrophularia frigida* Boiss., likewise yield in Persia saccharine exudations. A kind of manna was anciently collected from the cedar, *Pinus Cedrus* L.[4] Manna is yielded in Spain by *Cistus ladaniferus*

[1] Further particulars, see Flückiger, *Ueber die Eichenmanna von Kurdistan*, in *Archiv der Pharmacie*, 200 (1872) 159.

[2] *Loc. cit.* p. 35.

[3] Hanbury, *Science Papers*, p. 438.

[4] Geoffroy, *Mat. Med.* ii. (1741) 584.

L.[1] *Australian Manna*, which is in small rounded, opaque, white, dry masses, is found on the leaves of *Eucalyptus viminalis* Labill. It contains a kind of sugar called *Melitose*,[2] has a sweet thistle, is devoid of medicinal properties and is not collected for use.[3]

The substance named *Tigala* (corrupted into *Trehala*), from which a peculiar sugar has been obtained,[4] is the coccoon of a beetle, and not properly a saccharine exudation.[5]

The *Lerp Manna* of Australia is also of animal origin.[6] It consists of water 14, white threadlike portion 33, sugar 53 parts. The threads possess some of the characteristic properties of starch, from which they differ entirely by their form and unalterability even in boiling water. Yet in sealed tubes, they dissolve in 30 parts of water at 135° C. The sugar is dextrogyre; it impregnates the threads as a soft brown amorphous mass. In the purified state it does not crystallize, even after a long time. By means of dilute sulphuric acid, the threads are converted into crystalline grape-sugar.

OLEUM OLIVÆ.

Olive Oil; Salad Oil; F. *Huile d'Olives;* G. *Olivenöl; Baumöl; Provencer Oel.*

Botanical Origin—*Olea europæa* L., an evergreen tree,[7] seldom exceeding 40 feet in height, yet attaining extreme old age, abundantly cultivated in the countries bordering the Mediterranean, up to an elevation of about 2000 feet above the sea-level.[8] *Olea ferruginea* Royle (*O. cuspidata* Wallich), a tree abundant in Afghanistan, Beluchistan and Western Sind, has been supposed to be a wild form of *O. europæa*, but is regarded by Brandis[9] as a distinct species. It is not known to have been ever cultivated, yet its fruit, which is of a small size and but sparingly produced, is capable of affording a good oil.

History—In ancient Egypt the olive was known by the term *bāk;* it can be traced as far as the 17th century before our era.[10]

According to the elaborate investigations of Ritter[11] and of A. De Candolle,[12] the olive tree is a native of Palestine, and perhaps of Asia Minor and Greece. Its original area also extends over north-eastern

[1] Dillon, *Travels through Spain* (1780) p. 127.

[2] Gmelin, *Chemistry*, xv. 296.

[3] *Pharm. Journ.* iv. (1863) 108.

[4] *Comptes Rendus*, xlvi. (1858) 1276; Gmelin, *Chemistry*, xv. 299.

[5] Belon, *Singularitez* (1554) l. 2. cap. 91; Guibourt, *Comptes Rendus* (1858) 1213; Hanbury, *Journ. Linn. Soc.*, Zoology, iii. (1859) 178; also *Science Papers*, 158.

[6] Dobson, *Proceedings of Royal Society of Van Diemen's Land*, i. (1851) 234; *Pharm. Journ.* iv. (1863) 108; Flückiger, *Wittstein's Vierteljahresschrift*, xvii. (1868) 161; *Archiv der Pharmacie*, 196 (1871) 7; abstracted in the *Yearbook of Pharmacy*, 1871. 188.

[7] Readers desiring full information about the olive tree, its oil, its history, etc., should refer to the extremely exhaustive work of Coutance, *l'Olivier*, Paris, 1877, 456 pages, 120 figures.

[8] Grisebach states the elevation above the sea of olive-cultivation thus:—Portugal (Algarve) 1400 feet; Sierra Nevada 3000; do., southern slope 4200; Nice 2400; Etna 2200; Macedonia 1200; Cilicia 2000.—*Die Vegetation der Erde nach ihrer klimatologischen Anordnung*, i. (1872) 262. 283. 342.

[9] *Forest Flora of North-western and Central India*, 1874, 307.

[10] Brugsch-Bey, *Reise nach der grossen Oase Kargeh*, Leipzig, 1878. 80. etc.—See also *Journ. of Botany*, 1879. 52.

[11] *Erdkunde von Asien*, vii. (part 2. 1844) 516–537.

[12] *Géographique Botanique* (1855) 912.

Africa; Schweinfurth[1] regards it as undoubtedly wild on the mountains of Elbe and Soturba in lat. 22 N. on the western shores of the Red Sea, a locality which he visited in 1868. The olive tree has also been met with as far eastward as the country of the Gallas, where it is much appreciated as affording excellent timber.[2] It is also stated by Theophrastus, that in his time the tree was plentiful in the Cyrenaica, the modern Barca, in northern Africa.

The olive would appear to have been introduced at a very remote period into north-western Africa and Spain. Willkomm (1876) is of the opinion that it was originally a native of the whole Mediterranean region.

At the present day it is largely cultivated in Algeria, Spain, Portugal, Southern France, Italy, the Greek Peninsula and Asia Minor. In the Crimea the tree grows well, but does not afford good fruit. It was carried to Lima in Peru about 1560 and still flourishes there, and in great plenty in the coast valleys further south as far as Santiago in Chili.[3]

Olive oil is mentioned in the Bible so frequently that it must have been an important object with the ancient Hebrews. It held an equally prominent place among the Greeks and Romans,[4] whose writers on agriculture and natural history treat of it in the most circumstantial manner. Olive fruits preserved in brine were used by the Romans as an article of food,[5] and were an object of commerce with Northern Europe as early as the 8th century.[6]

Production—In common with many important cultivated plants, the olive occurs under several varieties differing more or less from the wild form, the finer of which are propagated by grafting. It is also increased by the suckers which old trees throw up from their naked roots, and which are easily made to develope into separate plants.[7] The fruit, an oval drupe, half an inch to an inch or more in length, and of a deep purple, is remarkable for the large amount of fat oil contained in its pulpy portion (sarcocarp). The latter is most rich in oil when ripe, containing then nearly 70 per cent., besides 25 per cent. of water. The unripe fruit, as well as other parts of the plant, abounds in mannite, which disappears in proportion as the oil increases. The ripe olive contains no mannite, it having probably been transformed into fatty oil.[8]

The process for extracting olive oil varies slightly in different countries, but consists essentially in subjecting the crushed pulp of the ripe fruit to moderate pressure. The olives, which are gathered from the trees, or collected from the ground, in November, or during the whole winter and early spring, are crushed under a millstone to a pulpy mass. This is then put into coarse bags, which, piled upon one another, are

[1] *Bot. Zeitung*, 1868. 860.

[2] Arnoux, *Revue des Deux Mondes*, Janvier 1879. 381.

[3] Perez-Rosales, *Essai sur le Chili*, Hambourg, 1857. 133.

[4] Hehn, *Kulturpflanzen und Hausthiere in ihrem Uebergange aus Asien nach Griechenland und Italien*, Berlin, 1877. 88–142, —an interesting account of the importance of the olive in ancient times.

[5] Specimens may be seen among the antiquities found at Pompei.

[6] Diploma of Chilperic, A.D. 716.—Pardessus, *Diplomata, Chartæ*, etc., Paris, ii. (1849) 309.

[7] Winter, in *Pharm. Journ.* Sept. 7, 1872.

[8] De Luca in *Journ. de Pharm.* xlv. (1864) 65.—Some further researches by Harz on the formation of olive oil may be found in the *Jahresbericht* of Wiggers and Husemann (1870) 392.

subjected to moderate pressure in a screw press. The oil thus obtained is conducted into tubs or cisterns containing water, from the surface of which it is skimmed with ladles. This is called *Virgin Oil.* After it has ceased to flow, the contents of the bags are shovelled out, mixed with boiling water, and submitted to stronger pressure than before, by which a second quality of oil is got. If the fruit is left for a considerable time in heaps it undergoes decomposition, yielding by pressure a very inferior quality of oil called in French *Huile fermentée.* The worst oil of all, obtained from the residues, has the name of *Huile tournante* or *Huile d'enfer.*

It is said that in some districts the millstones are so mounted as to crush the pulp without breaking the olive-stones, and that thus the oil of the pulp is obtained unmixed with that of the kernels.[1] We have made many inquiries in Italy and France as to this method of oil-making, but cannot find that it is anywhere followed.

The fixed oil of the kernels of ripe olives has been extracted and examined by one of us (F.) Though the kernels have a bitterish taste, the oil they yield is quite bland; by exposure to the vapour of hyponitric acid, it concretes like that of the pulp. If the whole of it were extracted in making olive oil, it would only be about as 1 part of oil of the *kernel,* to 40 parts of oil of the *pulp.*

Description—Olive Oil is a pale yellow or greenish yellow, somewhat viscid liquid, of a faint agreeable smell and of a bland oleaginous taste, leaving in the throat a slight sense of acridity.[2] Its specific gravity on an average is 0·916 at 17°·5 C. In cold weather, olive oil loses its transparency by the separation of a crystalline fatty body. The deposition takes place at a few degrees above the freezing point of water, and in some oils even at 10° C. (50° F.) If the oil is allowed to congeal perfectly, and is then submitted to strong pressure, about one-third of its weight of solid fat may be separated. After repeated crystallizations, this fat melts at 20 to 28° C. The fluid part or *Olein,* continues fluid at − 4° to − 10° C. Olive oil belongs to the class of the less alterable, non-drying oils.

The foregoing description does not apply to the inferior sorts of oil, which congeal more easily, are more or less deep-coloured, have a disagreeable odour and taste, and quickly turn rancid. These inferior oils have their special applications in the arts.

Chemical Composition—The chief constituent of olive oil is *Olein* or more correctly *Triolein,* $C^3H^5(O.C^{18}H^{33}O)^3$, identical so far as at present ascertained with the fluid part of all oils of the non-drying class. The proportion of olein in olive oil, as well as in other oils, is liable to variation, the result partly of natural circumstances and partly of the processes of manufacture. The best oils are rich in olein.

As to the solid part of olive oil, Chevreul believed it to be constituted of *Margarin,* which he first examined in 1820. But Heintz (1852 and later) showed margarin to be a mixture of palmitin with other compounds of glycerin and fatty acids. Collett in 1854 isolated *Palmitic Acid,*

[1] *The Grocer,* April 25, 1868, supplement; Pereira, *Elem. of Mat. Med.* ii. (1850) 1505.

[2] This according to our experience is the case even with oil as it runs from the pulp and therefore in the freshest condition; but the acrid after-taste is more perceptible in oil which has been long kept.

$C^{16}H^{32}O^2$, from olive oil; and Heintz and Krug (1857) further proved that *Tripalmitin* is the chief of the solid constituents of olive oil. They also met with an acid melting at 71°·4 C., which they regarded as *Arachic Acid* (p. 187). As to stearic acid, Heintz and Krug did not fully succeed in evidencing its presence in olive oil.

Lastly, Benecke discovered in olive oil a small quantity of *Cholesterin*, $C^{26}H^{44}O$. It may be removed by means of glacial acetic acid or alcohol, which dissolve but very little of the oil.

Commerce—Various sorts of olive oil are distinguished in the English market, as Florence, Gallipoli, Gioja, Spanish (Malaga and Seville), Sicily, Myteline, Corfu and Mogador.

Olive oil was imported into the United Kingdom in the year 1872 to the value of £1,193,064. Nearly half the quantity was shipped from Italy, one-fifth from Spain, and the remainder from other Mediterranean countries.

The average annual production in Italy is estimated at about 3 millions of hectolitres (66 million gallons), but the quantity exported does not reach half that amount.

The statistics of the French Government indicate the annual production of olive oil in France to be not more than 250,000 hectolitres, equivalent in value to 30 millions of francs (£1,200,000).[1]

Uses—The uses of olive oil in medicine and its immense consumption in the warmer parts of Europe as an article of food, are too well known to require more than a passing allusion.

Adulteration—Olive Oil is the subject of various fraudulent admixtures with less costly oils, the means of detecting which has engaged much attention. Of the various methods by which chemists have endeavoured to ascertain the purity of olive oil, the following are the more noteworthy:—

a. Drying oils (such as the oils of poppy and walnut) may be distinguished by their not being converted into solid crystallizable elaidin by hyponitric acid or concentrated solution of nitrate of protoxide of mercury. Olive oil which contains any considerable proportion of one of these oils, no longer solidifies if exposed for a moment to one of the above-mentioned reagents. This test however is not of sufficient delicacy for small amounts of drying oils.

b. Olive oil being one of the lighter oils, the specific gravity may to some degree indicate admixture with a heavier oil. To make use of this fact, Gobley and other chemists have invented an instrument called an *elaiometer*, for taking the specific gravity of oils.

c. Observation of the Cohesion-figure.—This test, proposed by Tomlinson in 1864,[2] depends on the forces of cohesion, adhesion, and diffusion. Thus, if a drop of any oil hanging from the end of a glass rod is gently deposited upon the surface of chemically clean water, contained in a clean glass, a contest takes place between the

[1] Exposition de 1867 à Paris, *Rapports du Jury International*, xi. 108.—In the work of Coutance, quoted p. 417, note 7, nearly 400,000 hectolitres are calculated for the year 1866.

[2] *Pharm. Journ.* v. (1864) 387. 495, with figures.

forces in question the moment the drop flattens down by its gravity upon the surface of the water. The adhesion of the liquid surface tends to spread out the drop into a film, the cohesive force of the particles of the drop strives to prevent that extension, and the resultant of these forces is a figure which Mr. Tomlinson believes to be definite for every independent liquid. The figure thus produced is named the *cohesion-figure.*

So far as our experience goes, the processes hitherto recommended for testing olive oil (and there are several that we have not mentioned) are only available in cases where the adulteration is considerable, and are quite insufficient for discovering a small admixture of other oils. How little they are appreciated, may be inferred from the fact that the Chamber of Commerce of Nice[1] offered a reward of 15,000 francs (£600) for a simple and easy process for making evident an admixture with olive oil of 5 per cent. at least of any seed-oil.

APOCYNEÆ.

CORTEX ALSTONIÆ.

Cortex Alstoniæ scholaris ; Dita Bark ;[2] *Alstonia Bark.*

Botanical Origin—*Alstonia*[3] *scholaris* R. Brown (*Echites scholaris* L.), a handsome forest tree, 50 to 90 feet in height, common throughout the Indian Peninsula from the sub-Himalayan region to Ceylon and Burma; found also in the Philippines, Java, Timor and Eastern Australia, likewise in Tropical Africa. It has oblong obovate leaves, in whorls of 5 to 7, and slender pendulous pods a foot or more in length.

History—Saptachhada and saptaparna (literally seven-leaf), occurring in early Sanskrit epic poetry and also in Susruta, are ancient names of Alstonia (Dr. Rice). Rheede[4] in 1678 and Rumphius[5] in 1741 described and figured the tree, and mentioned the use made of its bark by the native practitioners. Rumphius also explained the trivial name *scholaris* as referring to slabs of the close-grained wood which are used as school-slates, the letters being traced upon them in sand. The tonic properties of the bark were favourably spoken of by Graham in his *Catalogue of Bombay Plants* (1839), and further recommended by Dr. Alexander Gibson in 1853.[6] The drug has a place in the *Pharmacopœia of India,* 1868.

Description—The drug, as presented to one of us by the late Dr. Gibson and by Mr. Broughton of Ootacamund, consists of irregular fragments of bark, $\frac{1}{8}$ to $\frac{1}{2}$ an inch thick, of a spongy texture, easily breaking with a short, coarse fracture. The external surface is very uneven and rough, dark grey or brownish, sometimes with blackish

1 *Annales de Chimie et de Physique,* March, 1869. 309.

2 From *Dita,* the name of the tree in the island of Luzon.

3 So named in honour of Charles Alston, Professor of Botany and Materia Medica (1740-1760) in the University of Edinburgh.—The plant is figured in Bentley and Trimen, *Med. Pl.* part 25 (1877).

4 *Hortus Malabaricus,* i. tab. 45.

5 *Herb. Amboin.* ii. tab. 82.

6 *Pharm. Journ.* xii. (1853) 422.

spots; the interior substance and inner surface (liber) is of a bright buff. A transverse section shows the liber to be finely marked by numerous small medullary rays. The bark is almost inodorous; its taste is purely bitter and neither aromatic nor acrid.

Microscopic Structure—The cortical tissue is covered with a thin suberous coat; the middle layer of the bark is built up of a thin walled parenchyme, through which enormous, hard, thick-walled cells are scattered in great numbers and are visible to the naked eye, as they form large irregular groups of a bright yellow colour. Towards the inner part these stone-cells disappear, the tissue being traversed by undulated medullary rays, loaded with very small starch grains; many of the other parenchymatous cells of the liber contain crystals of calcium oxalate. The longitudinal section of the liber exhibits large but not very numerous laticiferous vessels, containing a brownish mass, the concrete milk-juice in which all parts of the tree abound.

Chemical Composition—The first attempts to isolate the active principles of this bark were made by two apothecaries, Scharlée at Batavia[1] (1862) and Gruppe at Manila[2] (1872).

In 1875 Jobst and Hesse exhausted the powdered bark with petroleum ether, and then extracted, by boiling alcohol, the salt of an alkaloid, which they called *Ditamine.* After the evaporation of the alcohol, it is precipitated by carbonate of sodium and dissolved by ether, from which it is removed by shaking it with acetic acid. Ditamine as again isolated from the acetate forms an amorphous and somewhat crystalline, bitterish powder of decidedly alkaline character; the barks yields about 0·02 per cent. of it.

From the substances extracted by means of petroleum ether, as above stated, Jobst and Hesse further isolated (1) *Echicaoutchin,* $C_{25}H_{40}O_2$, an amorphous yellowish mass; (2) *Echicerin,* $C_{30}H_{48}O_2$, forming acicular crystals, melting at 157° C.; (3) *Echitin,* $C_{32}H_{52}O_2$, crystallized scales, melting at 170°; (4) *Echiteïn,* $C_{42}H_{70}O_2$, which forms rhombic prisms, melting at 195°; (5) *Echiretin,* $C_{35}H_{56}O_2$, an amorphous substance melting at 52° C.

Echicaoutchin may be written thus: $(C_5H_8)_5O_2$, echicerin $(C_5H_8)_6O_2$, echiretin $(C_5H_8)_7O_2$; these formulæ at once point out how nearly the three last named substances are allied. They are probably constituents of the milky-juice of the tree.

Lastly, Jobst and Hesse pointed out the existence of another alkaloid in Dita bark.

Harnack (1877) on the other hand is of the opinion that it contains only one alkaloid, which he terms *Ditaïne.* He used the alcoholic extract of the bark which he treated with ether to which he added a little ammonia. By this process ditamine of Jobst and Hesse would have been removed, but Harnack suggests that only a little ditaïne is dissolved by ether. He then mixed the extract with potash and exhausted it with alcohol, which afforded crystals of ditaïne, answering to the formula $C_{22}H_{30}N_2O_4$; its physiological action is nearly the same as that of curare. Ditaïne is but sparingly soluble in ether or petro-

[1] Geneesk, *Tijdschr. Nederl. Indië,* x. (1863) 209; also *Archiv der Pharmacie,* 212 (1878) 439.

[2] *Jahresbericht* of Wiggers and Husemann, 1873. 51.

leum ether, but dissolves readily in water, alcohol, or chloroform; it has a decidedly alkaline reaction. It would appear that it is a glucoside.

Dita bark is stated[1] to yield 5 per cent. of "ditaïne"; but this probably refers not to the pure alkaloid.

Uses—The bark has been recommended as a tonic and antiperiodic, being extravagantly praised as a substitute for quinine.

ASCLEPIADEÆ.

RADIX HEMIDESMI.

Hemidesmus Root, Nunnari Root, Indian Sarsaparilla.

Botanical Origin—*Hemidesmus indicus* R. Brown (*Periploca indica* Willd., *Asclepias Pseudo-sarsa* Roxb.), a twining shrub, growing throughout the Indian Peninsula and in Ceylon. The leaves are very diverse, being narrow and lanceolate in the lower part of the plant, and broadly ovate in the upper branches.[2]

History—In the ancient Sanskrit literature the plant occurs frequently under the name *Sārivā*, and its root under the name of *Nannāri* or *Ananta-mūl* (*i.e.* endless root) has long been employed in medicine in the southern parts of India.[3] Ashburner in 1831 was the first to call the attention of the profession in Europe to its medicinal value.[4] In 1864 it was admitted to a place in the *British Pharmacopœia*, but its efficiency is by no means generally acknowledged.

Description[5]—The root is in pieces of 6 inches or more in length; it is cylindrical, tortuous, longitudinally furrowed, from $\frac{2}{10}$ to $\frac{1}{10}$ of an inch in thickness, mostly simple or provided with a few thin rootlets emitting slender, branching woody aerial stems, $\frac{3}{10}$ of an inch or less thick. Externally it is dark brown, sometimes with a slight violet-grey hue, which is particularly obvious in the sunshine. The transverse section of the hard root shows a white mealy or brownish or somewhat violet cortical layer, not exceding $\frac{1}{10}$ of an inch in thickness, and a yellowish woody column, separated by a narrow dark undulated cambial line. Neither the wood nor the cortical tissue present a radiate structure in the stout pieces; in the thinner roots, medullary rays are obvious in the woody part. The extremely thin corky layer easily separates from the bark, which latter is frequently marked transversely by large cracks. The root, whether fresh or dried, has an agreeable odour resembling tonka bean or melilot. The dried root has a sweetish taste with a very slight acidity. The stems are almost tasteless and inodorous. The root found in the English market is often of very bad quality.

[1] *Yearbook of Pharm.* 1878. 624, from *Proc. of the American Pharm. Association*, 1877.

[2] Fig. in Bentley and Trimen, *Med. Plants*, part 6 (1876).

[3] There is an Indian root figured as *Palo de Culebra* by Acosta (*Tractado de las Drogas . . . de las Indias Orientales*, 1578, cap. lv.) which is astonishingly like the drug in question. He describes it moreover as having a sweet smell of melilot. The plant he says is called in Canarese *Duda sali.* The figure is reproduced in Antoine Colin's translation, but not in that of Clusius.

[4] *Lond. Med. and Phys. Journ.* lxv. 189.

[5] Taken from excellent specimens obligingly sent to us from India by Dr. L. W. Stewart and Mr. Broughton.

Microscopic Structure—All the proper cortical tissue shows a uniform parenchyme, not distinctly separated into liber, medullary rays and mesophlœum. On making a longitudinal section however, one can observe some elongated laticiferous vessels filled with the colourless concrete milky juice. In a transverse section, they are seen to be irregularly scattered through the bark, chiefly in its inner layers, yet even here in not very considerable number. They are frequently 30 mkm. in diameter and not branched.

The wood is traversed by small medullary rays, which are obvious only in the longitudinal section. The parenchymatous tissue of the root is loaded with large, ovoid starch granules. Tannic matters do not occur to any considerable amount, except in the outermost suberous layer.

Chemical Composition—The root has not been submitted to any adequate chemical examination. Its taste and smell appear not to depend on the presence of essential oil, so far as may be inferred from microscopic examination; and it is probable the aroma is due to a body of the cumarin class. According to Scott,[1] the root yields by simple distillation with water a steroptene, which is probably the substance obtained by Garden in 1837, and supposed to be a volatile acid.

Uses—The drug is reputed to be alterative, tonic, diuretic and diaphoretic, but is rarely employed, at least in England.

CORTEX MUDAR.

Cortex Calotropidis; Mudar; F. *Ecorce de racine de Mudar.*

Botanical Origin—The drug under notice is furnished by two nearly allied species of *Calotropis*, occupying somewhat distinct geographical areas, but not distinguished from each other in the native languages of India. These plants are:—

1. *Calotropis procera* R. Brown (*C. Hamiltonii* Wight), a large shrub, 6 or more feet high, with dark green, oval leaves, downy beneath, abounding in acrid milky juice.

It is a native of the drier parts of India, as the Deccan, the Upper Provinces of Bengal, the Punjab and Sind, but is quite unknown in the southern provinces; it also extends to Persia, Palestine, the Sinaitic Peninsula, Arabia, Egypt, to the oasis Dachel, and other oases of the Sahara, to Nubia, Abyssinia, the lake Tsad and through the Sudan. Lastly it has been naturalized in the West Indies.

2. *C. gigantea* R. Brown (*Asclepias gigantea* Willd.), a large erect shrub, 6 to 10 feet high, with stem as thick as a man's leg,[2] much resembling preceding, indigenous to Lower Bengal and the southern parts of India, Ceylon, the Malayan Peninsula, and the Moluccas.

Both species are extremely common in waste ground over their respective areas.[3]

[1] *Pharm. of India*, 457; also *Chem. Gazette*, 1843. 378.

[2] Hence the specific name *gigantea*.

[3] The botanical distinctions between the two species may be stated thus:—

C. procera, corolla cup-shaped, petals somewhat erect, flowerbuds spherical, appendages of corona with a blunt upward point. See Fig. in Bentley and Trimen, *Med. Plants*, part 25 (1877).

C. gigantea, corolla opening flat, flowerbuds bluntly conical or oblong, appendages of corona rounded.

History—The ancient name of the plant, which occurs already in the Vedic literature, was *Arka* (wedge), alluding to the form of the leaves which were used in sacrificial rites. From one of the Sanskrit names of this plant, namely *Mandāra,* Mudār is a corruption;[1] the latter is frequently mentioned in the writings of Susruta.

The plant was likewise well known to the Arabian physicians.[2]

C. procera was observed in Egypt by Prosper Alpinus (1580-84), and upon his return to Italy was figured, and some account given of its medicinal properties.[3] It is also the "Apocynum syriacum" figured by Clusius.[4]

C. gigantea was figured by Rheede[5] in 1679, and in our own day by Wight.[6]

The medicinal virtues of mudar, though so long esteemed by the natives of India, were not investigated experimentally by Europeans until the present century, when Playfair recommended the drug in elephantiasis, and its good effects were afterwards noticed by Vos (1826), Cumin (1827), and Duncan (1829). The last-named physician also performed a chemical examination of the root-bark, the activity of which he referred to an extractive matter which he termed *Mudarine.*[7]

Description—The root-bark of *C. procera,* as we have received it,[8] consists of short, arched, bent, or nearly flat fragments, ⅛ to ⅕ of an inch thick. They have outwardly a thickish, yellowish-grey, spongy cork, more or less fissured lengthwise, frequently separating from the middle cortical layer; the latter consists of a white mealy tissue, traversed by narrow brown liber-rays. The bark is brittle and easily powdered; it has a mucilaginous, bitter, acrid taste, but no distinctive odour. The light-yellow, fibrous wood is still attached to many of the pieces.

The roots of *C. gigantea* are clothed with a bark which seems to be undistinguishable from that of *C. procera* just described. The wood of the root consists of a porous, pale-yellow tissue, exhibiting large vascular bundles, and very numerous small medullary rays, consisting of 1 to 3 rows of the usual cells.[9]

Microscopic Structure—In the root-bark of *C. procera,* the suberous coat is made up of large, thin-walled, polyhedral, or almost cubic cells; the middle cortical layer, of a uniform parenchyme, loaded with large starch granules, or here and there containing some thick-walled cells (sclerenchyme) and tufts of oxalate of calcium. The large medullary rays are built up of the usual cells, having porous walls and containing starch and oxalate. In a longitudinal section, the tissue, chiefly of the middle cortical layer, is found to be traversed by numerous laticiferous

[1] Information for which we are indebted to Dr. Rice.

[2] Ibn Baytar, translated by Sontheimer, ii. (1842) 193.

[3] *De Plantis Ægypti,* Venet. 1592. cap. xxv.

[4] *Rarior. plantar. hist.* ii. (1601) lxxxvii.

[5] *Hortus Malabaricus,* ii. tab. 31.

[6] *Illustrations of Indian Botany,* Madras, ii. (1850) tab. 155.—*C. procera* is figured by the same author in his *Icones Plantarum Indiæ Orientalis,* iv. tab. 1278.

[7] *Edinb. Med. and Surg. Journ.* xxxii. (1829) 60.

[8] We are indebted for an authentic specimen to Dr. E. Burton Brown of Lahore.

[9] Roots of *C. gigantea* kindly supplied to us by Dr. Bidie of Madras consist of light, woody truncheons, ½ to 2¼ inches in diameter.

vessels, containing the dry milk juice[1] as a brownish granular substance not soluble in potash.

The microscopic characters of the root-bark of *C. gigantea* agree with those here detailed of *C. procera*. The stems of *Calotropis* are distinguished by strong liber fibres, which are not met with in the roots.

Chemical Composition—By following the process of Duncan above alluded to, 200 grammes of the powered bark of *C. gigantea* yielded us nothing like his *Mudarine*, but 2·4 grammes of an acrid *resin*, soluble in ether as well as in alcohol. The latter solution reddens litmus; the former on evaporation yields the resin as an almost colourless mass. If the aqueous liquid is separated from the crude resin, and much absolute alcohol added, an abundant precipitate of mucilage is obtained. The liquid now contains a bitter principle, which after due concentration may be separated by means of tannic acid.

We obtained similar results by exhausting the bark of *C. procera* with dilute alcohol. The tannic compound of the bitter principle was mixed with carbonate of lead, dried and boiled with spirit of wine. This after evaporation furnished an amorphous, very bitter mass, not soluble in water, but readily so in absolute alcohol. The solution is *not* precipitated by an alcoholic solution of acetate of lead. By purifying the bitter principle with chloroform or ether, it is at last obtained colourless. This bitter matter is probably the active principle of *Calotropis;* we ascertained by means of the usual tests that no alkaloid occurs in the drug. The large juicy stem, especially that of *C. gigantea*, ought to be submitted to an accurate chemical and therapeutical examination.[2]

Uses—Mudar is an alterative, tonic and diaphoretic,—in large doses emetic. By the natives of India, who employ it in venereal and skin complaints, almost all parts of the plant are used. According to Moodeen Sheriff,[3] the bark of the root and the dried milky juice are the most efficient; the latter is however somewhat irregular and unsafe in its action. The same writer remarks that he has found that the older the plant, the more active is the bark in its effects. He recommends that the corky outer coat, which is tasteless and inert, should be scraped off before the bark is powdered for use: of a powder so prepared, 40 to 50 grains suffice as an emetic.

The stems of *C. gigantea* afford a very valuable fibre which can be spun into the finest thread for sewing or weaving.[4]

[1] It is evidently with a view to the retention of this juice, that the *Pharmacopœia of India* orders the bark to be stripped from the roots when the latter are half-dried. Moodeen Sheriff remarks of *C. gigantea*, that although it is frequently used in medicine, no part of it is sold in the bazaars,—no doubt from the circumstance that the plant is everywhere found wild and can be collected as required.

[2] List's *Asclepione* (Gmelin's *Chemistry*, xvii. 368) might then be sought for.

[3] *Supplement to the Pharmacopœia of India*, Madras, 1869. 364; for further information on the therapeutic uses of mudar, see also *Pharm. of India*, 458.

[4] Drury, *Useful Plants of India*, 2nd ed. 1873. 101.

FOLIA TYLOPHORÆ.

Country or Indian Ipecacuanha.

Botanical Origin—*Tylophora asthmatica* Wight et Arnott (*Asclepias asthmatica* Roxb.), a twining perennial plant, common in sandy soils throughout the Indian Peninsula and naturalized in Mauritius. It may be distinguished from some of its congeners by its reddish or dull pink flowers, with the scale of the staminal corona abruptly contracted into a long sharp tooth.[1]

History—The employment of this plant in medicine is well known to the Hindus, who call it *Antamul* and use it with considerable success in dysentery, but we have not succeeded in tracing it in the ancient Indian literature. During the last century it attracted the attention of Roxburgh[2] who made many observations on the administration of the root, while physician to the General Hospital of Madras from 1776 to 1778. It was also used very successfully in the place of ipecacuanha by Anderson, Physician-General to the Madras army.[3] In more recent times, the plant has been prescribed by O'Shaughnessy, who pronounced the root an excellent substitute for ipecacuanha if given in rather larger doses.[4] Kirkpatrick[5] administered the drug in at least a thousand cases, and found it of the greatest value; he prescribed the *dried leaf*, not only because superior to the root in certainty of action, but also as being obtainable without destruction of the plant. The drug has been largely given by many other practitioners in India. *Tylophora* is also employed in Mauritius, where it is known as *Ipéca sauvage* or *Ipéca du pays*. It has a place in the *Bengal Pharmacopœia* of 1844, and in the *Pharmacopœia of India* of 1868.

Description[6]—The leaves are opposite, entire, from 2 to 5 inches long, ¾ to 2¼ inches broad, somewhat variable in outline, ovate or subrotund, usually cordate at the base, abruptly acuminate or almost mucronate, rather leathery, glabrous above, more or less downy beneath with soft simple hairs. The pedicel, which is channelled, is ⅛ to ¾ of an inch in length. In the dry state the leaves are rather thick and harsh, of a pale yellowish green; they have a not unpleasant herbaceous smell, with but very little taste.[7]

Chemical Composition—A concentrated infusion of the leaves has a slightly acrid taste. It is abundantly precipitated by tannic acid, by neutral acetate of lead or caustic potash, and is turned greenish-black by perchloride of iron. Broughton of Ootacamund (India) has informed us (1872) that from a large quantity of the leaves he obtained a small

[1] Fig. in Bentley and Trimen, *Med. Plants*, part 29 (1878).

[2] *Flora Indica*, ed. Carey, ii. (1832) 33.

[3] Fleming, *Catalogue of Indian Plants and Drugs*, Calcutta, 1810. 8.

[4] *Bengal Dispensatory* (1842) 455.

[5] *Catalogue of Madras Exhibition of* 1855, —list of Mysore drugs; also *Pharm. of India*, 458.

[6] Drawn up from an ample specimen kindly presented to us, together with one of the root, by Mr. Moodeen Sheriff of Madras.

[7] A figure of the leaves may be found in a paper on *Unto-mool* by M. C. Cooke, *Pharm. Journ.* Aug. 6, 1870. 105; and one of the whole plant in Wight's *Icones Plantarum Indiæ Orientalis*, iv. (1850) tab. 1277.

amount of crystals,—insufficient for analysis. Dissolved and injected into a small dog, they occasioned purging and vomiting.

Uses—Employed in India, as already mentioned, as a substitute for ipecacuanha, chiefly in the treatment of dysentery. The dose of the powdered leaves as an *emetic* is 25 to 30 grains, as a diaphoretic and expectorant 3 to 5 grains.

Radix Tylophoræ—This root is met with in the Indian bazaars, and has been employed, as before stated, as much or more than the leaf. It consists of a short, knotty, descending rootstock, about $\frac{1}{8}$ of an inch in thickness, emitting 2 to 3 aerial stems, and a considerable number of wiry roots. These roots are often 6 inches or more in length by $\frac{1}{2}$ a line in diameter, and are very brittle. The whole drug is of a pale yellowish brown; it has no considerable odour, but a sweetish and subsequently acrid taste. In general appearance it is suggestive of valerian, but is somewhat stouter and larger.

Examined microscopically, the parenchymatous envelope of the rootlets is seen to consist of two layers, the inner forming a small nucleus sheath. The outer portion is built up of large cells, loaded with starch granules and tufted crystals of oxalate of calcium. Salts of iron do not alter the tissue.

LOGANIACEÆ.

NUX VOMICA.

Semen Nucis Vomicæ; Nux Vomica; F. *Noix vomique;* G. *Brechnuss.*

Botanical Origin—*Strychnos Nux-vomica* L., a moderate sized tree with short, thick, often crooked stem, and small, greenish-white, tubular flowers ranged in terminal corymbs. It is indigenous to most parts of India, especially the coast districts, and is found in Burmah, Siam, Cochin China and Northern Australia.

The ovary of *S. Nux-vomica* is bi-locular, but as it advances in growth the dissepiment becomes fleshy and disappears. The fruit, which is an indehiscent berry of the size and shape of a small orange, is filled with a bitter, gelatinous white pulp, in which the seeds, 1 to 5 in number, are placed vertically in an irregular manner. The epicarp forms a thin, smooth, somewhat hard shell, which at first is greenish, but when mature, of a rich orange-yellow. The pulp of the fruit contains strychnine,[1] yet it is said to be eaten in India by birds.[2] The wood, which is hard and durable, is very bitter.

[1] Roxburgh's assertion that the pulp "*seems perfectly innocent,*" induced us to examine it chemically, which we were enabled to do through the kindness of Dr. Thwaites, of the Royal Botanical Gardens, Ceylon. The *inspissated pulp* received from Dr. T., diluted with water, formed a very consistent jelly having a slightly acid reaction and very bitter taste. Some of it was mixed with slaked lime, dried, and then exhausted by boiling chloroform. The liquid left on evaporation a yellowish resinoid mass, which was warmed with acetic acid. The colourless solution yielded a perfectly white, crystalline residue, which was dissolved in water, and precipitated with bichromate of potassium. The crystallized precipitate dried, and moistened with strong sulphuric acid, exhibited the violet hue characteristic of strychnine.

To confirm this experiment, we obtained through the obliging assistance of Dr. Bidie of Madras, some of the white pulp taken with a spoon from the interior of the ripe fruit, and at once immersed *per se* in spirit of wine. The alcoholic fluid gave abundant evidence of the presence of strychnine.

[2] According to Cleghorn by the hornbill

History—Nux Vomica, which was unknown to the ancients, is thought to have been introduced into medicine by the Arabians. But the notices in their writings which have been supposed to refer to it, are far from clear and satisfactory. We have no evidence moreover that it was used in India at an early period. Garcia de Orta, an observer thoroughly acquainted with the drugs of the west coast of India in the middle of the 16th century, is entirely silent as to nux vomica. Fleming,[1] writing at the begining of the present century, remarks that nux vomica is seldom, if ever, employed in medicine by the Hindus, but this statement does not hold good now.

The drug was however certainly made known in Germany in the 16th century. Valerius Cordus[2] wrote a description of it about the year 1540, which is remarkable for its accuracy. Fuchs, Bauhin and others noticed it as *Nux Metella*, a name taken from the *Methel* of Avicenna and other Arabian authors.[3]

It was found in the English shops in the time of Parkinson (1640), who remarks that its chief use is for poisoning dogs, cats, crows, and ravens, and that it is rarely given as a medicine.

Description—Nux Vomica is the *seed*, removed from the pulp and shell. It is disc-like, or rather irregularly orbicular, a little less than an inch in diameter, by about a quarter of an inch in thickness, slightly concave on the dorsal, convex on the ventral surface, or nearly flat on either side, often furnished with a broad, thickened margin so that the central portion of the seed appears depressed. The outside edge is rounded or tapers into a keel-like ridge. Each seed has on its edge a small protuberance, from which is a faintly projecting line (raphe) passing to a central scar, which is the hilum or umbilicus; a slight depression marks the opposite side of the seed. The seeds are of a light greyish hue, occasionally greenish, and have a satiny or glistening aspect, by reason of their being thickly covered with adpressed, radiating hairs. Nux vomica is extremely compact and horny, and has a very bitter taste.

After having been softened by digestion in water, the seed is easily cut along its outer edge, then displaying a mass of translucent, cartilaginous albumen, divided into two parts by a fissure in which lies the embryo. This latter is about $\frac{3}{10}$ of an inch long, having a pair of delicate 5- to 7-nerved, heart-shaped cotyledons, with a club-shaped radicle, the position of which is indicated on the exterior of the seed by the small protuberance already named.

Microscopic Structure—The hairs of nux vomica are of remarkable structure. They are formed as usual of the elongated cells of the epidermis, and have their walls thickened by secondary deposits, which are interrupted by longitudinally extended pores; they are a striking

(*Buceros malabaricus*); according to Roxburgh by "many sorts of bird." Beddome (*Flora Sylvatica*, Madras, 1872. 243) says the pulp is quite harmless, and the favourite food of many birds.

In Garnier, *Exploration en Indo-China* ii. (Paris, 1873) 488, allusion is made to a tree similar to that under notice having fruits which are devoid of poison *before maturity*.

[1] *Catalogue of Indian Med. Plants. and Drugs*, Calcutta, 1810. 37.

[2] *Hist. Stirpium*, edited by C. Gesner, Argentorat. 1561. lib. iv. c. 21.

[3] Clusius and others held the opinion that the *Nux methel* of the Arabs was the fruit of a *Datura*, and an Indian species was accordingly named by Linnæus *D. Metel*.

object in polarized light. The albumen is made up of large cells, loaded with albuminoid matters and oily drops, but devoid of starch. In water the thick walls of this parenchyme swell up and yield some mucilage; the cotyledons are built up of a narrow, much more delicate tissue, traversed by small fibro-vascular bundles.

The alkaloids are not directly recognizable by the microscope; but if very thin slices of nux vomica are kept for some length of time in glycerin, they develope feathery crystals, doubtless consisting of these bases.

Chemical Composition—The bitter taste and highly poisonous action of nux vomica are chiefly due to the presence of *Strychnine* and *Brucine*. Strychnine, $C^{21}H^{22}N^2O^2$, was first met with in 1818 by Pelletier and Caventou in St. Ignatius' Beans, and immediately afterwards in nux vomica. It crystallizes from an alcoholic solution in large anhydrous prisms of the orthorhombic system. It requires for solution about 6700 parts of cold or 2500 of boiling water; the solution is of decidedly alkaline reaction, and an intensely bitter taste which may be distinctly perceived though it contain no more than $\frac{1}{600000}$ of the alkaloid. The best solvents for strychnine are spirit of wine or chloroform; it is but very sparingly soluble in absolute alcohol, benzol, amylic alcohol, or ether. The alcoholic solution deviates the ray of polarized light to the left.

Strychnine is not restricted to the fruit of the plant under notice, but also occurs in the wood and bark.[1] It is moreover found in the wood of the root of *Strychnos colubrina* L., and in the bark of the root of *Strychnos Tieute* Lesch., both species indigenous to the Indian Archipelago.

The discovery of *Brucine* was made in 1819 by the same chemists, in nux vomica bark, then supposed to be derived from *Brucea ferruginea* Héritier (*B. antidysenterica* Miller), an Abyssinian shrub of the order Simarubeæ. The presence of brucine in nux vomica and St. Ignatius' Bean was pointed out by them in 1824. Brucine, dried over sulphuric acid, has the formula $C^{23}H^{26}N^2O^4$, but it crystallizes from its alcoholic solution with $4\,OH^2$. In bitterness and poisonous properties, as well as in rotatory power, it closely resembles strychnine, differing however in the following particulars:—it is soluble in about 150 parts of boiling water, melts without alteration a little above 130° C. In common with its salts, it acquires a dark red colour when moistened with concentrated nitric acid.

The proportion of strychnine in nux vomica appears to vary from $\frac{1}{4}$ to $\frac{1}{2}$ per cent. That of brucine is variously stated to be 0·12 (Merck), 0·5 (Wittstein), 1·01 (Mayer) per cent.

A third crystallizable base, called *Igasurine*, was stated in 1853 by Desnoix to occur in the liquors from which strychnine and brucine had been precipitated by lime. Schützenberger's investigations (1858) are far from proving the existence of "igasurine."[2]

In nux vomica, as well as in St. Ignatius' Beans, the alkaloids,

[1] It is remarkable that parasitic plants of the order *Loranthaceæ* growing on *Strychnos Nux-vomica* acquire the poisonous properties of the latter.—*Pharm. of India*, 1868. 108.

[2] For further information on igasurine, consult Gmelin, *Chemistry*, xvii. (1866) 589; Watts, *Dictionary of Chemistry*, iii. (1865) 243; *Pharm. Journ.* xviii. (1859) 432.

according to their discoverers, are combined with *Strychnic* or *Igasuric Acid*; Ludwig (1873), who prepared this body from the latter drug, describes it as a yellowish-brown amorphous mass, having a strongly acid reaction and a sour astringent taste, and striking a dark green with ferric salts. We have ascertained the correctness of Ludwig's observations.

Nux vomica dried at 100° C. yielded us when burnt with soda-lime 1·822 per cent. of nitrogen, indicating about 11·3 per cent. of protein substances. By boiling ether, we removed from the seeds 4·14 per cent. of fat; Meyer[1] found it to yield butyric, capronic, caprylic, caprinic and other acids of the series of the common fatty acids, and also one acid richer in carbon than stearic acid. Nux vomica also contains mucilage and sugar. The latter, which according to Rebling (1855) exists to the extent of 6 per cent., reduces cupric oxide without the aid of heat. When macerated in water, the seeds easily undergo lactic fermentation, not however attended with decomposition of the alkaloids. The stability of strychnine is remarkable, even after ten years of contact with putrescent animal substances.

Commerce—Large quantities of nux vomica are brought into the London market from British India.[2] The export from Bombay in the year 1871–72 was 3341 cwt., all shipped to the United Kingdom.[3] Madras in 1869–70 exported 4805 cwt.; and Calcutta in 1865–66, 2801 cwt. The quantity imported into the United Kingdom in 1870[4] was 5534 cwt.

Nux vomica is stated by Garnier (*l. c.* page 429, note) to be largely exported from Cambodja to China.

Uses—Tincture and extract of nux vomica, and the alkaloid strychnine, are frequently administered as tonic remedies in a variety of disorders.

SEMEN IGNATII.

Faba Sancti Ignatii; St. Ignatius' Beans; F. *Fèves de Saint-Ignace, Noix Igasur;* G. *Ignatiusbohnen.*[5]

Botanical Origin—*Strychnos Ignatii* Bergius[6] (*S. philippensis* Blanco, *Ignatiana philippinica* Loureiro), a large climbing shrub, growing in Bohol, Samar, and Çebu, islands of the Bisaya group of the Philippines, and according to Loureiro in Cochin China, where it has been introduced. The inflorescence and foliage are known to botanists only

[1] *Jahresbericht der Chemie*, 1875. 856.

[2] We have seen 1136 packages offered in a single drug-sale (30 March 1871).

[3] *Statement of the Trade and Navigation of Bombay for* 1871-72, pt. ii. 62.

[4] No later returns are accessible.

[5] The plant and seeds are known in the Bisaya language by the names of *pangaguason, aguason, canlara, mananaog, dancagay, catalonga* or *igasur*; in the islands of Bohol and Çebu, where the seeds are produced, by that of *coyacoy*, and by the Spaniards of the Philippines as *Pepita de Bisaya* or *Pepita de Catbalogan* (Clain, *Remedios Faciles*, Manila, 1857. p. 610). The name *St. Ignatius' Bean* applied to them in Europe, is employed in South America to designate the seeds of several medicinal *Cucurbitaceæ*, as those of *Feuillea trilobata* L., *Hypanthera Guapeva* Manso and *Anisosperma Passiflora* Manso.

[6] *Materia Medica*, Stockholm, 1778. i. 146.—We omit citing the Linnean *Ignatia amara*, as it has been shown by Bentham that the plant so named by the younger Linnæus is *Posoqueria longiflora* Aubl. of the order *Rubiaceæ*, a native of Guiana.

from the descriptions given by Loureiro[1] and Blanco.[2] The fruit is spherical, or sometimes ovoid, 4½ inches in diameter by 6¾ long, as shown by Ray and Petiver's figure. It has a smooth brittle shell enclosing seeds to the number of about 24. G. Bennett,[3] who saw the fruits at Manila sold in the bazaar, says they contain from 1 to 12 seeds, imbedded in a glutinous blackish pulp.[4] According to Jagor[5] the shrub is abundant near Basey, in the south-western part of the island of Samar, on the straits of San Juanico; its seeds are met with as a medicine in many houses in the Philippines.

History—It is stated by Murray[6] and later writers that this seed was introduced into Europe from the Philippines by the Jesuits, who, on account of its virtues, bestowed upon it the name of Ignatius, the founder of their order. However this may be, the earliest account of the drug appears to be that communicated by Camelli, Jesuit missionary at Manila, to Ray and Petiver, and by them laid before the Royal Society of London in 1699.[7] Camelli proclaimed the seed to be the *Nux Vomica legitima* of the Arabian physician Serapion, who flourished in the 9th century; but in our opinion there is no warrant whatever for supposing it to have been known at so remote a period.[8] Camelli states that the seed, which he calls *Nux Pepita seu Faba Sancti Ignatii*, is much esteemed as a remedy in various disorders, though he was well aware of its poisonous properties when too freely administered. In Germany, St. Ignatius' Bean was made known about the same period by Bohn of Leipzig.[9]

The drug is found in the Indian bazaars under a name which is evidently corrupted from the Spanish *pepita*. It is met with in the drugshops of China as *Leu-sung-kwo*, i.e. *Luzon fruit*.

Description—St. Ignatius' Beans are about an inch in length; their form is ovoid, yet by mutual pressure it is rendered very irregular, and they are 3-, 4-, or 5-sided, bluntly angular, or flattish, with a conspicuous hilum at one end. In the fresh state, they are covered with silvery adpressed hairs: portions of a shaggy brown epidermis are here and there perceptible on those found in commerce, but in the majority the seed shows the dull grey, granular surface of the albumen itself.

Notwithstanding the different outward appearance, the structure of St. Ignatius' Beans accords with that of nux vomica. The radicle however is longer, thicker, and frequently somewhat bent, and the cotyledons are more pointed. The horny brownish albumen is translucent,

[1] *Flora Cochinchinensis*, ed. Willd. i. (1793) 155.

[2] *Flora de Filipinas*, ed. 2. 1845. 61.

[3] *London Med. and Phys. Journ.* January 1832.

[4] The only specimen of the fruit I have seen was in the possession of my late friend Mr. Morson. It measured exactly 4 inches in diameter, and when opened (15 January 1872) was found to contain 17 mature, well-formed seeds, with remnants of dried pulp.—D. H. I have seen another one in the Jardin des Plantes, Paris.—F. A. F.

[5] *Reisen in den Philippinen*, Berlin, 1873. 213.

[6] *Apparatus Medicaminum*, vi. (1792) 26.

[7] *Phil. Trans*, xxi. (1699) 44. 87; Ray, *Hist. Plant.* iii. lib. 31. 118.

[8] The Philippines were unknown to the Europeans of the Middle Ages. They were discovered by Magellan in 1521, but their conquest by the Spaniards was not effectually commenced until 1565. Previous to the Spanish occupation, they were governed by petty chiefs, and were frequented for the purposes of commerce by Japanese, Chinese, and Malays.

[9] Martiny, *Encyklopädie der Rohwaarenkunde*, i. (1843) 576.

very hard, and difficult to split. The whole seed swells considerably by prolonged digestion in warm water, and has then a heavy, earthy smell. The beans are intensely bitter and highly poisonous.

Microscopic Structure—The hairs of the epidermis are of an analogous structure, but more simple than in nux vomica. The albumen and cotyledons agree in structural features with those of the same parts in nux vomica.

Chemical Composition—Strychnine exists to the extent of about 1·5 per cent.; the seeds also contain 0·5 per cent. of brucine. Dried over sulphuric acid and burnt with soda-lime, it yielded us an average of 1·78 per cent. of nitrogen, which would answer to about 10 per cent. of albuminoid matter.

Commerce—We have no information as to the collection of the drug. The seeds are met with irregularly in English trade, being sometimes very abundant, at others scarcely obtainable.

Uses—The same as those of nux vomica. When procurable at a moderate price, the seeds are valued for the manufacture of strychnine.

RADIX SPIGELIÆ.

Radix Spigeliæ Marilandicæ; Indian Pink Root, Carolina Pink Root, Spigelia.[1]

Botanical Origin—*Spigelia marilandica* L., an herbaceous plant about a foot high, indigenous in the woods of North America, from Pennsylvania to Wisconsin and southward. According to Wood and Bache, it is collected chiefly in the Western and South-western States.

History—The anthelminthic properties of the root, discovered by the Indians, were brought to notice in Europe about the year 1754 by Linning, Garden, and Chalmers, physicians of Charleston, South Carolina. The drug was admitted to the London Pharmacopœia in 1788.

Description—Pink root has a near resemblance to serpentary, consisting of a short, knotty, dark brown rhizome emitting slender wiry roots. It is quite wanting in the peculiar odour of the latter drug, or indeed in any aroma; in taste it is slightly bitter and acrid. Sometimes the entire plant with its quadrangular stems a foot high is imported. It has opposite leaves about 3 inches long, sessile, ovate-lanceolate, acuminate, smooth or pubescent.

Microscopic Structure—The transverse section of the rhizome, about $\frac{2}{10}$ of an inch in diameter, shows a small woody zone enclosing a large pith of elliptic outline, consisting of thin-walled cells. Usually the central tissue is decayed. In the roots, the middle cortical layer predominates; it swells in water, after which its large cells display fine spiral markings. The nucleus-sheath observable in serpentary is wanting in spigelia.

Chemical Composition—Not satisfactorily known: the vessels of the wood contain resin, the parenchyme starch; in the cortical part of the rhizome some tannic matters occur, but not in the roots. Feneulle

[1] *Pink Root* is sometimes erroneously latinized in price-lists, "*Radix caryophylli.*"

(1823) asserts that the drug yields a little essential oil. The experiments of Bureau[1] show that spigelia acts on rabbits and other animals as a narcotico-acrid poison.

Uses—Spigelia has long been reputed a most efficient medicine for the expulsion of *Ascaris lumbricoides*, but according to Stillé,[2] its real value for this purpose has probably been over-estimated. This author speaks of it as possessing alterative and tonic properties. In England, it is rarely prescribed by the regular practitioner, but is used as a household medicine in some districts. It is much employed in the United States.

GENTIANEÆ.

RADIX GENTIANÆ.

Gentian Root; F. Racine de Gentiane; G. Enzianwurzel.

Botanical Origin—*Gentiana lutea* L., a handsome perennial herb, growing 3 feet high, indigenous to open grassy places on the mountains of Middle and Southern Europe. It occurs in Portugal, Spain, the Pyrenees, in the islands of Sardinia and Corsica, in the Apennines, the mountains of Auvergne, the Jura, the Vosges, the Black Forest, and throughout the chain of the Alps as far as Bosnia and the Danubian Principalities. Among the mountains of Germany, it is found on the Suabian Alps near Würzburg, and here and there in Thuringia, but not further north, nor does it occur in the British Islands.

History—The name *Gentiana* is said to be derived from Gentius, a king of the Illyrians, living B.C. 180–167, by whom, according to both Pliny and Dioscorides, the plant was noticed. Whether the species thus named was *Gentiana lutea* is doubtful. During the middle ages, gentian was commonly employed for the cure of disease, and as an antidote to poison. Tragus in 1552 mentions it as a means of diluting wounds, an application which has been resorted to in modern medical practice.

Description—The plant has a cylindrical, fleshy, simple root, of pale colour, occasionally almost as much as 4 feet in length by 1½ inches in thickness, producing 1 to 4 aerial stems.

The dried root of commerce is in irregular, contorted pieces, several inches in length, and ½ to 1 inch in thickness; the pieces are much wrinkled longitudinally, and marked transversely, especially in their upper portion, with numerous rings. Very often they are split to facilitate drying. They are of a yellowish brown; internally of a more orange tint, spongy, with a peculiar, disagreeable, heavy odour, and intensely bitter taste. The crown of the root, which is somewhat thickened, is clothed with the scaly bases of leaves. The root is tough and flexible,—brittle only immediately after drying. We found it to lose in weight about 18 per cent. by complete drying in a water-bath; it regained 16 per cent. by being afterwards exposed to the air.

[1] *De la famille des Loganiacées*, 1856. 130.

[2] *Therapeutics and Materia Medica*, Philadelphia, ii. (1868) 651.

Microscopic Structure—A transverse section shows the bark separated by a dark cambial zone from the central column; the radial arrangement of the tissues is only obvious in the latter part. In the bark, liber fibres are wanting; and in the centre there is no distinct pith. The fibro-vascular bundles are devoid of thick-walled ligneous prosenchyme; this may explain the consistence, and the short even fracture of the root. It is moreover remarkable on account of the absence both of starch and oxalate of calcium; the cells appear to contain chiefly sugar and a little fat oil.

Chemical Composition—The bitter taste of gentian is due to a substance called *Gentiopicrin* or *Gentian-bitter*, $C^{20}H^{30}O^{12}$. Several chemists, as Henry, Caventou, Trommsdorff, Leconte and Dulk have described the bitter principle of gentian in an impure state, under the name of *Gentianin*, but Kromayer in 1862 first obtained it in a state of purity. Gentiopicrin is a neutral body crystallizing in colourless needles, which readily dissolve in water. It is soluble in spirit of wine, but in absolute alcohol only when aided by heat; it does not dissolve in ether. A solution of caustic potash or soda forms with it a yellow solution. Under the influence of a dilute mineral acid, gentiopicrin is resolved into glucose, and an amorphous, yellowish-brown, neutral substance, named *Gentiogenin*. Fresh gentian roots yield somewhat more than $\frac{1}{10}$ per cent. of gentiopicrin; from the dried root it could not be obtained in a crystallized state. The medicinal Tincture of Gentian, mixed with solution of caustic potash, loses its bitterness in a few days, probably in consequence of the destruction of the gentiopicrin.

Another constituent of gentian root is *Gentianin* or *gentisin* $C^{14}H^{10}O^5$ or $(OH)^2C^6H^3.CO.C^6H^2\left\{\begin{matrix}CH^3\\O\\O\end{matrix}\right.\!>$. It forms tasteless yellowish prisms, sparingly soluble in alcohol, requiring about 5000 parts of water for solution. With alkalis it yields intensely yellow crystallizable compounds, which, however, are easily decomposed already by carbonic acid. Gentianin may be sublimed if carefully heated at 250° C. By melting it with caustic potash, acetic acid, phloroglucin, $C^6H^3(OH)^3$, and oxysalicylic acid, $C^6H^3(OH)^2COOH$, are produced, as shown in 1875 by Hlasiwetz and Habermann. The name of *gentianic acid* or *gentisinic acid* had been applied to the oxysalicylic acid obtained by the above decomposition before it was identified with oxysalicylic acid from other sources.

Gentian root abounds in pectin; it also contains, to the extent of 12 to 15 per cent., an uncrystallizable sugar, of which advantage is taken in Southern Bavaria and Switzerland for the manufacture by fermentation and distillation of a potable spirit.[1] This use of gentian and its consumption in medicine have led to the plant being almost extirpated in some parts of Switzerland where it formerly abounded.

The experiments of Maisch (1876) and Ville (1877) have shown tannic matters to be absent from the root.

Commerce—Gentian root finds its way into English commerce through the German houses; and some is shipped from Marseilles. The quantity imported into the United Kingom in 1870 was 1100 cwt.

[1] Th. Martius, *Pharm. Journ.* xii. (1853) 371.

Uses—Gentian is much used in medicine as a bitter tonic. Ground to powder, the root is an ingredient in some of the compositions sold for feeding cattle.

Substitutes—It can hardly be said that gentian is adulterated, yet the roots of several other species possessing similar properties are occasionally collected; of these we may name the following:—

1. *Gentiana purpurea* L.—This species is found in Alpine meadows of the Apennines, Savoy and Switzerland, in Transylvania, and in South-western Norway; a variety also in Kamtchatka.[1] The root is frequently collected;[2] it attains at most 18 inches in length and a diameter of about 1 inch at the summit, from which arise 8 to 10 aerial stems, clothed below with many scaly remains of leaves. The top of the root has thus a peculiar branched appearance, never found in the root of *G. lutea*, with which in all other respects that of *G. purpurea* agrees. The latter is perhaps even more intensely bitter.

2. *G. punctata* L.—Nearly the same description applies to this species, which is a native of the Alps of South-Eastern France, Savoy, the southern parts of Switzerland, extending eastward to Austria, Hungary and Roumelia.

3. *G. pannonica* Scop.—a plant of the mountains of Austria, unknown in the Swiss Alps, has a root which does not attain the length or the thickness of the root of *G. purpurea*, with which it agrees in other respects. It is officinal in the Austrian Pharmacopœia.

4. *G. Catesbæi* Walter (*G. Saponaria* L.)—indigenous in the United States. Its root, usually not exceeding 3 inches in length by ⅓ inch in diameter, has a very thin woody column within a spongy whitish cortical tissue and a bright yellow epidermis. This root is less bitter than the above enumerated drugs; the same remark applies also to those European Gentianae which like *G. Catesbæi* are provided with blue flowers.

HERBA CHIRATÆ.

Herba Chirettæ vel Chiraytæ; Chiretta or Chirayta.

Botanical Origin—*Ophelia*[3] *Chirata* Grisebach (*Gentiana Chirayita* Roxb.), an annual herb of the mountainous regions of Northern India from Simla through Kumaon to the Murung district in South-eastern Nepal.

History—Chiretta has long been held in high esteem by the Hindus, and is frequently mentioned in the writings of Susruta. It is called in Sanscrit *Kirāta-tikta*, which means the *bitter plant of the Kirātas*, the Kirātas being an outcast race of mountaineers in the north of India. In England, it began to attract some attention about

[1] Grisebach (*Die Vegetation der Erde*, i. 1872. 223) gives very interesting particulars relating to the area of growth of *Gentiana purpurea*, *G. punctata* and *G. pannonica*. He is decidedly of the opinion that they are distinct species.

[2] In Norway it is, strange to say, called sweetroot, "*Sötrot*," according to Schübeler, *Pflanzenwelt Norwegens*, 1873-1875, p. 259.

[3] Ὀφέλλειν, to bless, in allusion to the medical virtues of the herb.—Fig. in Bentley and Trimen, *Med. Plants*, part 7 (1876).

the year 1829; and in 1839 was introduced into the Edinburgh Pharmacopœia. The plant was first described by Roxburgh in 1814.

Chiretta was regarded by Guibourt as the *Calamus aromaticus* of the ancients, but the improbability of this being correct was well pointed out by Fée[1] and by Royle, and is now generally admitted.

Description—The entire plant is collected when in flower, or more commonly when the capsules are fully formed, and tied up with a slip of bamboo into flattish bundles of about 3 feet long,[2] each weighing when dry from $1\frac{1}{2}$ to 2 lb. The stem, $\frac{2}{10}$ to $\frac{3}{10}$ of an inch in thickness, is of an orange-brown, sometimes of a dark purplish colour; the tapering simple root, often much exceeding the stem in thickness, is 2 to 4 inches long and up to $\frac{1}{2}$ an inch thick. It is less frequently branched, but always provided with some rootlets. In stronger specimens, the root is somewhat oblique or geniculate; perhaps the stem is in this case the product of a second year's growth and the plant not strictly annual. Each plant usually consists of a single stem, yet occasionally two or more spring from a single root. The stem rises to a height of 2 to 3 feet, and is *cylindrical in its lower and middle portion*, but bluntly quadrangular in its upper, the four edges being each marked with a prominent decurrent line, as in *Erythræa Centaurium* and many other plants of the order. The decussate ramification resembles that of other gentians; its stems are jointed at intervals of $1\frac{1}{2}$ to 3 or 4 inches, bearing opposite semi-amplexicaul leaves on their cicatrices. The stem consists in its lower portion of a large woody column, coated with a very thin rind, and enclosing a comparatively large pith. The upper parts of the stem and branches contain a broad ring of thick-walled woody parenchyme. The numerous slender axillary and opposite branches are elongated, and thus constitute a dense umbellate panicle. They are smooth and glabrous, of a greenish or brownish grey colour.

The leaves are ovate-acuminate, cordate at the base, entire, sessile, the largest 1 inch or more in length, 3- to 5- or 7-nerved, the midrib being strongest. At each division of the panicle there are two small bracts. The yellow corolla is rotate, 4-lobed, with glandular pits above the base; the calyx is one-third the length of the petals, which are about half an inch long. The one-celled, bivalved capsule contains numerous seeds.

The flowers share the intense bitterness of the whole drug. The wood of stronger stems is devoid of the bitter principles.

Chemical Composition—A chemical examination of chiretta has been made at our request under the direction of Professor Ludwig of Jena, by his assistant Mr. Höhn. The chief results of this careful and elaborate investigation may be thus described.[3]

Among the bitter principles of the drug, *Ophelic Acid*, $C^{13}H^{20}O^{10}$, occurs in the largest proportion. It is an amorphous, viscid, yellow substance, of an acidulous, persistently bitter taste, and a faint gentian-like odour. With basic acetate of lead, it produces an abundant yellow precipitate. Ophelic acid does not form an insoluble compound with tannin; it dissolves in water, alcohol and ether. The first solution

[1] *Cours d'Histoire nat. pharmaceutique*, ii. (1828) 395.

[2] The other kinds of chiretta to be named presently are usually much shorter.

[3] For full details, see *Archiv der Pharmacie*, 189 (1869) 229.

causes the separation of protoxide of copper from an alkaline tartrate of that metal.

A second bitter principle, *Chiratin*, $C^{26}H^{48}O^{15}$, may be removed by means of tannic acid, with which it forms an insoluble compound. Chiratin is a neutral, not distinctly crystalline, light yellow, hygroscopic powder, soluble in alcohol, ether and in warm water. By boiling hydrochloric acid, it is decomposed into *Chiratogenin*, $C^{13}H^{24}O^{3}$, and ophelic acid. Chiratogenin is a brownish, amorphous substance, soluble in alcohol but not in water, nor yielding a tannic compound. No sugar is formed in this decomposition.

These results exhibit no analogy to those obtained in the analysis of the European gentians. Finally, Höhn remarked in chiretta a crystallizable, tasteless, yellow substance, but its quantity was so minute that no investigation of it could be made.

The leaves of chiretta, dried at 100° C., afforded 7·5 per cent. of ash; the stems 3·7; salts of potassium and calcium prevailing in both.

Uses.—Chiretta is a pure bitter tonic, devoid of aroma and astringency. In intense bitterness it exceeds gentian, *Erythræa* and other European plants of the same order. It is much valued in India, but is not very extensively used in England, and not at all on the Continent. It is said to be employed when cheap, in place of gentian, to impart flavour to the compositions now sold as *Cattle Foods*.

Substitutes and Adulteration—Some other species of *Ophelia*, namely, *O. angustifolia* Don, *O. densifolia* Griseb., *O. elegans* Wight, *O. pulchella* Don, and *O. multiflora* Dalz, two or three species of *Exacum*, besides *Andrographis paniculata* Wall., are more or less known in the Indian bazaars by the name of *Chiretta*[1] and possess to a greater or less degree the bitter tonic properties of that drug. Another *Gentianacea*, *Slevogtia orientalis* Griseb., is called *Chota Chiretta*, i.e. *small chiretta*. It would exceed due limits were we to describe each of these plants: we have therefore given a somewhat detailed description of the true chiretta, which will suffice for its identification. We have frequently examined the chiretta found in the English market, but have never met with any other than the legitimate sort.[2] Bentley noticed in 1874 the substitution of *Ophelia angustofolia*, which he found to be by far less bitter than true chiretta.

CONVOLVULACEÆ.

SCAMMONIUM.

Scammony; F. *Scammonée*; G. *Scammonium*.

Botanical Origin—*Convolvulus Scammonia* L., a twining plant much resembling the common *C. arvensis* of Europe, but differing from it in being of larger size, and having a stout tap-root. It occurs

[1] Moodeen Sheriff, *Suppl. to the Pharmacopœia of India*, 1869. pp. 138. 189.—Consult also *Pharmacopœia of India*, 1868. pp. 148-9.

[2] Mr. E. A. Webb has pointed out a case of false-packing in which the roots of *Rubia cordifolia* L. (*Munjit*) had been enclosed in the bundles of chiretta.

in waste bushy places in Syria, Asia Minor, Greece, the Greek Islands, extending northward to the Crimea and Southern Russia, but appears to be wanting in Northern Africa, Italy, and in all the western parts of the Mediterranean basin.

History—The dried milky juice of the scammony plant has been known as a medicine from very ancient times. Theophrastus in the 3rd century B.C. was acquainted with it; it was likewise familiar to Dioscorides, Pliny, Celsus, and Rufus of Ephesus, each of whom has given some account of the manner in which it was collected. Scammony used then also to be called *Diagrydion*, from the Greek word δάκρυ, tear. The mediæval Arabian physicians also knew scammony and the plant from which it is derived. The drug was used in Britain in the 10th and 11th centuries, and would appear to be one of the medicines recommended to King Alfred the Great, by Helias, patriarch of Jerusalem.[1] It is repeatedly named in the medical writings in use prior to the Norman conquest (A.D. 1066), in one of which directions are given for recognizing the goodness of the drug by the white emulsion it produces when wetted.

The botanists of the 16th and 17th centuries, as Brunfels, Gesner, Matthiolus, Dodonæus, and the Bauhins, described and figured the plant partly under the name of *Scammonia syriaca*. The collecting of the drug was well described by Russell, an English physician of Aleppo (1752), whose account[2] is accompanied by an excellent figure representing the plant and the means of obtaining its juice.

Scammony was formerly distinguished by the names *Aleppo* and *Smyrna*, the former sort being twice or thrice as costly as the latter; at the present day Aleppo scammony has quite lost its pre-eminence.

Localities producing the drug—Scammony is collected in Asia Minor, from Brussa and Boli in the north, to Macri and Adalia in the south, and eastward as far as Angora. But the most productive localities within this area are the valley of the Mendereh, south of Smyrna: and the districts of Kirkagach and Demirjik, north of that town. The neighbourhood of Aleppo likewise affords the drug. A little is obtained further south in Syria, from the woody hills and valleys about the lake of Tiberias and Mount Carmel.

Production—The scammony plant has a long woody root, which throws off downwards a few lateral branches, and produces from its knotty summit numerous twining stems which are persistent and woody at the base. In plants of three or four years old, the root may be an inch or more in diameter; in older specimens it sometimes acquires a diameter of three or four inches. In length, it is from two to three feet, according to the depth of soil in which it grows. When the root is wounded, there exudes a milky juice which dries up to a

[1] Such is the opinion expressed by the Rev. O. Cockayne. The letter of Helias to Alfred is imperfect, and mentions only balsam, petroleum, theriaka, and a white stone used as a charm. But from the reference to these four articles in another part of the MS., in connection with scammony, ammoniacum, tragacanth, and galbanum, there is ground for believing that the latter (Syrian and Persian) drugs were included in the lost part of the patriarch's letter. —See *Leechdoms, Wortcunning and Starcraft of Early England*, edited by Cockayne (Master of the Rolls Series), vol. ii. pages xxiv. 289. 175, also 273. 281.

[2] *Medical Observations and Inquiries*, i. (1757) 12.

golden-brown, transparent, gummy-looking substance:—this is *pure scammony.*[1]

The method followed in collecting scammony for use appears to be nearly the same in all localities. It has been thus described to us by two eye-witnesses, both long resident in the East.[2] Operations commence by clearing away the bushes among which the plant is commonly found; the soil around the latter is then removed, so as to leave 4 or 5 inches of the root exposed. This is then cut off in a slanting direction at 2 to 4 inches below the crown, and a mussel-shell is stuck into it just beneath the lowest edge, so as to receive the milky-sap which instantly flows out. The shells are usually left till evening, when they are collected, and the cut part of the root scraped with a knife, so as to remove any partially dried drops of juice. These latter are called by the Smyrna peasants, *kaimak* or cream, the softer contents of the shell being called *gala* or milk.

Sometimes the scammony is allowed to dry in the shell, and such must be regarded as representing the drug in its utmost perfection. But scammony in shells is not brought into commerce, though a little of it is reserved by the peasants for their own use.

The contents of the shells and the scraped-off drops are next emptied into a covered copper pot or a leathern bag, carried home, made homogenous by mixing with a knife, and at once allowed to dry. In this way a form of scammony is obtained closely approaching that dried in the shell. But it is a quality of exceptional goodness. Usually the peasant does not dry off the juice promptly, but allows his daily gatherings to accumulate; and when he has collected a pound or two, he places it in the sunshine to soften, and then kneads it, sometimes with the addition of a little water, into a plastic mass, which he lastly allows to dry. By this long exposure to heat, and retention in a liquid state, the scammony juice undergoes fermentation, acquires a strong cheesy odour and dark colour, and when finally dried, exhibits a more or less porous or bubbly structure, never observable in shell scammony.

Scammony is very extensively adulterated. The adulteration is often performed by the peasants, who mix foreign substances into the drug while it is yet soft; and it is also effected by the dealers, some of whom purchase it of the peasants in a half-dried state. The substances used for sophistication are numerous, the commonest and most easily detected being, according to our experience, carbonate of lime and flour. Woodashes, earth (not always calcareous), gum arabic, and tragacanth are also employed; more rarely, wax, yolk of egg, pounded scammony roots, rosin, or black-lead.

Description.—The pure juice of the root, simply dried by exposure to the sun and air, is an amorphous, transparent, brittle substance, of resinous aspect, a yellowish-brown colour, and glossy fracture. Scammony possessing these characters is occasionally met with in the form of flattish irregular masses, about ½ to ¾ of an inch in thickness, very brittle by reason of internal fissures, yet with but few air-cavities. In

[1] Named probably from Σκάμμα, a *trench* or *pit*, in allusion to the excavation made around the root.

[2] The one was the late Mr. S. H. Maltass of Smyrna, whose interesting paper may be found in *Pharm. Journ.* xiii. (1854) 264; the other is Mr. Edward T. Rogers, formerly of Caiffa, now (1874) British Consul at Cairo.

mass, it is of a chesnut-brown, but in small fragments it is seen to be very pale yellowish-brown and transparent, with the freshly fractured surface vitreous and shining. When powdered it is of a very light buff. Rubbed with the moistened finger it forms a white emulsion. Treated with ether it yields 88 to 90 per cent. of soluble matter, and a nearly colourless residuum. This scammony, as well as the pure juice in the shell, is very liable to become mouldy; but besides this, it throws out, if long kept, a white, mammillated, crystalline efflorescence, the nature of which we have not been able to determine. But if scammony is kept quite dry, neither mouldiness nor efflorescence makes its appearance.

The ordinary fine scammony of commerce, known as *Virgin Scammony*, is also in large flat pieces or irregular flattened lumps and fragments, which in mass have a dark-grey or blackish hue. Viewed in thin fragments, it is seen to be translucent and of a yellowish-brown. It is very easily broken, exhibits a shining fracture, gives an ashy grey powder, and has a peculiar cheesy odour. Some of the pieces have a porous, bubbly structure, indicative of fermentation; the more solid often show the efflorescence already mentioned. Scammony has not much taste, but leaves an acrid sensation in the throat.

Chemical Composition—Scammony owes its active properties as a medicine to a resin shown (1860) by Spirgatis to be identical with that found in the root of the Mexican *Ipomœa orizabensis*, known in commerce as *Male Jalap:* this resin called *Jalapin* will be described in the next article. The other constituents of pure scammony are not well known. One of them is the substance which, as already stated, makes its appearance as small masses of cauliflower crystals on the surface of pure scammony, when the latter is kept in air not perfectly dry.

Whether the odour observable in commercial scammony is due to a volatile fatty acid developed by fermentation, is a question still to be investigated.

Commerce—The export of scammony from Smyrna amounted in 1871 to 278 cases, valued at £8320; in 1872 to 185 cases, value £6100. According to a report of Consul Skene on the trade of Northern Syria,[1] 737 cases of scammony were exported from the province of Aleppo in 1872,—six-sevenths of the quantity being for England. In 1873 Aleppo exported by way of Alexandretta to England 46,500 kilogrammes of scammony root and 900 kilogrammes of the resin, the latter being valued at 36,000 francs (£1444).

An establishment at Brussa, founded by Della Sudda, of Constantinople, is stated to export since 1870 a very good scammony resin extracted by alcohol.[2]

Uses—Employed as an active cathartic, often in combination with colocynth and calomel.

Adulteration—Scammony is very often imported in an adulterated state, but the adulteration is so clumsily effected, and is so easily discoverable by simple tests, or even by ocular examination, that druggists have but little excuse for accepting a bad article.

We have already named the substances used in the sophistication of

[1] Presented to Parliament, July 1873.

[2] Dragendorff's *Jahresbericht*, 1876. 158.

scammony: of these, the most frequent are carbonate of lime and farinaceous matter. The first may generally be recognized by examining the fractured surface of the drug with a good lens, when the white particles of the carbonate will be perceived. If the surface is then touched (while still *sub lente*) with hydrochloric acid, effervescence will prove the presence of a carbonate. Other earthly adulterants can be discovered by incineration, or by examining the residue of the drug after treatment with ether. Starchy substances, the presence of which may be surmised by the scammony being difficult to break, are detectable by the microscope or by solution of iodine, a cold decoction of scammony not being affected by that reagent. Scammony that is ponderous, dull and clayey, not easily broken in the fingers, or which when broken does not exhibit a clean, glossy surface, or which does not afford at least 80 per cent. of matter soluble in ether, should be rejected. That which is made up in the form of hard, dark, circular cakes is widely different from pure scammony.

Scammony may be distinguished from *Resin of Scammony* by its property of forming an emulsion when wetted. The resin is also more glossy and almost entirely soluble in ether.

Radix Scammoniæ.

The frauds commonly practised on the scammony of commerce have given rise to various schemes for obtaining the drug in a purer form, as well as at a more moderate price.[1]

So far back as 1839, the Edinburgh College prescribed a *Resina Scammonii*, which was prepared by exhausting scammony with a spirit of wine, distilling off the spirit, and washing the residue with water. Such an extract was manufactured by the late Mr. Maltass of Smyrna, and occasionally shipped to London.

In consequence of a suggestion made by Mr. Clark, manufacturer of liquorice at Sochia near Scala Nuova, south of Smyrna, a patent was taken out (1856) by Prof. A. W. Williamson of London, for preparing this resin directly from the dried root by means of alcohol. The same chemist shortly afterwards devised an improved process, which consists in boiling the roots first with water and then with dilute acid, so as to deprive them of all matters soluble in those menstrua, and afterwards extracting the resin by alcohol.

Resin of Scammony, obtained either from scammony or from the dried root, is ordered in the *British Pharmacopœia* of 1867, and is manufactured by a few houses. It is a brown, translucent, brittle substance of resinous fracture, entirely soluble in ether, and not forming an emulsion when wetted with water.

Scammony root is occasionally brought into the London market, sometimes in rather large quantity,[2] but it is not generally kept by druggists, nor do we find it quoted in price-currents. Its collection is even opposed in some parts of Turkey by the local authorities.[3]

[1] Scammony was quoted in a London price-current, April 1874, at 8s. to 36s. per lb., Resin of Scammony at 14s. per lb.

[2] Thus 100 bales were offered in a drug sale, 3 July 1873.

[3] Such was the case at Aleppo, as we know by a private letter from Mr. Consul Skene.—D. H.

The root consists of stout, woody, cylindrical pieces, often spirally twisted, 2 to 3 inches in diameter, covered with a rough, furrowed, greyish-brown bark. They are internally pale brown, tough and resinous, with a faint odour and taste resembling jalap. A good sample yielded us 5½ per cent. of resin; Kingzett and Farries (1877) showed the root to be devoid of an alkaloid.

RADIX JALAPÆ.

Tuber Jalapæ; Jalap, Vera Cruz Jalap; F. *Racine de Jalap;* G. *Jalape.*

Botanical Origin—*Ipomœa Purga* Hayne (*Convolvulus Purga* Wenderoth, *Exogonium Purga* Bentham), a tuberous-rooted plant, throwing out herbaceous, twining stems, clothed with cordate-acuminate sharply auricled leaves, and bearing elegant salver-shaped, deep pink flowers. It grows naturally on the eastern declivities of the Mexican Andes, at an elevation above the sea of 5000 to 8000 feet, especially about Chiconquiaco and the adjacent villages, and also around San Salvador on the eastern slope of the Cofre de Perote. In these localities where rain falls almost daily, and where the diurnal temperature varies from 15° to 24° C. (60° to 75° F.), the plant occurs in shady woods, flourishing in a deep rich vegetable soil.

The jalap grows freely in the south of England, if planted in a sheltered border, but its flowers are produced so late in autumn that they rarely expand, and the tubers, which develope in some abundance, are liable to be destroyed in winter unless protected from frost.

The plant has been introduced on the Neilgherry Hills in the south of India; it succeeds there remarkably well,[1] and might be extensively propagated if there were any adequate inducement.

History—The use as a purgative of the tuber of a convolvulaceous plant of Mexico, was made known by the early Spanish voyagers; and so highly was the new drug esteemed that large quantities of it reached Europe during the 16th century.

Monardes, writing in 1565, says the new drug was called *Ruybarbo de las Indias* or *Ruybarbo de Mechoacan*, the latter name being given in allusion to the province of Michoacan whence the supplies were derived. Some writers have advanced the opinion that mechoacan root was the modern jalap, but in this we do not concur, for the description given of mechoacan and the place of its production do not apply well to jalap. Both drugs were moreover well known about 1610; they were perfectly distinguished by Colin, an apothecary of Lyons (1619), who mentions jalap ("*racine de Ialap*") as then newly brought to France.[2] They were however often confounded, or at least only distinguished by their difference of tint. Thus jalap, which at that period used to be imported cut into transverse slices,[3] was termed, from its darker colour, *Black*

[1] Thus at Ootacamund, Mr. Broughton, in a letter to one of us (15 January 1870), speaks of receiving "a cluster of tubers" weighing over 9 lb., and remarks that the plant grows as easily as yam.

[2] Monardes, *Hist. des Medicamens*, trad. par Colin, ed. 2. 16.—The first edition of this work seems to be unknown.

[3] Hill, *History of the Mat. Med.* Lond. 1751. 549.

Mechoacan; and on the other hand, the paler mechoacan was in later times known as *White Jalap.*

Mechoacan root is now known to consist (at least in part) of the large thick tuber of *Ipomœa Jalapa* Pursh (*Batatas Jalapa* Choisy), a plant of the Southern United States and Mexico. As a drug it has been long obsolete in Europe, having given place to jalap, which is a more active and efficient purgative.

The botanical source of jalap was not definitely ascertained until about the year 1829, when Dr. Coxe of Philadelphia published a description and coloured figure, taken from living plants sent to him two years previously from Mexico.[1]

Manner of Growth—Though we have cultivated the jalap plant for many years, we have had no opportunity of examining the seedling, but judging from analogy suppose that it has at first a small tap-root which gradually thickens after the manner of a radish. A root of jalap, called by some *tuber* and by others *tubercule*, throws out in addition to aerial stems, slender, prostrate, underground shoots which emit roots at intervals. These roots while but an inch or two long become thickened and carrot-shaped, gradually enlarging into napiform tuber-like bodies, which emit a few rootlets from their surface and taper off below in long, slender ramifications. The thickened roots have no trace of leaf-organs; the aerial stems grows from the shoot from which they originated.

Fresh jalap roots (tubers) are externally rough and dark brown, internally white and fleshy.

Collection—Jalap is said to be dug up in Mexico during the whole year.[2] The smaller roots are dried entire; the larger are cut transversely, or are gashed so that they may dry more easily. As drying by sun-heat would be almost impracticable owing to the wetness of the climate, the roots are placed in a net, and suspended over the almost constantly burning hearth of the Indian's hut, where they gradually dry, and at the same time often contract a smoky smell. Much of the jalap that has of late arrived has been more freely sliced than usual, and has obviously been dried with less difficulty.

According to Schiede, whose account was written in 1829,[3] the Indians of Chiconquiaco were at that period commencing the cultivation of jalap in their gardens.

Description—The jalap of commerce consists of irregular, ovoid roots, varying from the size of an egg to that of a hazel-nut, but occasionally as large as a man's fist. They are usually pointed at the lower end, deeply wrinkled, contorted and furrowed, and of a dark-brown hue, dotted over with numerous little, elongated, lighter coloured scars, running transversely. The large roots are incised lengthwise, or cut into halves or quarters, but the smaller are usually entire. Some of the small roots are spindle-shaped or cylindrical; others can be found which are nearly globular, smooth and pitchy-looking, but these latter are seldom solid. Good jalap is ponderous, tough, hard and often horny, becoming brittle when long kept, and breaking with a resinous non-

[1] *American Journal of Med. Sciences*, v. (1829) 300. pl. 1–2.

[2] It is plain that such a proceeding is irrational. The roots should be dug up when the aerial stems have died down.

[3] *Linnæa*, iii. (1830) 473; *Pharm. Journ.* viii. (1867) 652.—We are not aware of any more recent account.

fibrous fracture; internally it is of a pale dingy brown or dirty white. It has a faint smoky, rather coffee-like odour, and a mawkish taste, followed by acridity.

Microscopic Structure—Seen in transverse section, jalap exhibits no radiate structure, but numerous small concentric rings, which in many pieces are very regularly arranged. They are due to the laticiferous cells, differing from the surrounding parenchyme only by their contents and rather large size. These laticiferous cells traverse the tissue in a vertical direction, constituting vertical bands, as may be observed on a longitudinal section; the single cells are simply placed one on the other, and do not form elongated ducts as in *Lactuca* or *Taraxacum*.

The fibro-vascular bundles of jalap are neither numerous nor large; they are accompanied by thin-walled cells, so that firm woody rays do not occur. Parenchymatous cells are abundant, and, on a longitudinal fracture especially, if subsequently moistened, are seen to constitute concentric layers. The laticiferous cells are always found in the outer part of each layer. The suberous coat with which the drug is covered is made up of the usual tabular cells.

The parenchyme of jalap is loaded with starch grains; in the pieces which have been submitted to heat in order to dry them, the starch appears as an amorphous mass, and the drug then exhihits a horny consistence and greyish fracture, instead of being mealy. Crystals of calcium oxalate are frequently met with. The laticiferous cells contain the resin of jalap in a semi-fluid state, even in the dry drug; drops of the resinous emulsion flow out of the cells, if thin slices are moistened by any watery liquid.

Chemical Composition—Jalap owes its medicinal efficacy to a resin, which is extractable by exhausting the drug with spirit of wine, concentrating the alcoholic solution to a small bulk, and pouring it into water. The resin precipitated in this manner is then washed and dried; it is contained in jalap to the extent of 12 to 18 per cent.[1]

From this crude resin, which is the *Resina jalapæ* of the pharmacopœias, ether or chloroform extracts 5 to 7 (12, Umney) per cent. of a resin which, according to Kayser,[2] partially solidifies when in contact with water in crystalline needles. We can by no means confirm Kayser's statement. The residue (insoluble in ether) is one of the substances to which the name *Jalapin* has been applied.[3] W. Mayer, 1852–1855, who designated it *Convolvulin*,[4] found it to have the composition $C^{31}H^{50}O^{16}$. When purified, it is colourless; it dissolves easily in ammonia as well as in the fixed alkalis, and is not re-precipitated by acids, having been converted by assumption of water into amorphous *Convolvulic Acid*, which is readily soluble in water. Both convolvulin and convolvulic acid are resolved by moderate heating with dilute acids, or with emulsin, into crystallizable

[1] Guibourt obtained of it 17 per cent., Umney 21·5, Squibb 11 to 16, T. and H. Smith "not more than 15," D. Hanbury 11 to 15·8. Jalap grown in Bonn afforded to Marquart 12 per cent.; a root cultivated at Munich gave Widnmann 22 per cent.; from plants produced in Dublin W. G. Smith got 9 to 12 per cent.; and fine tubers from Ootacamund in India yielded to one of us 18 per cent. of resin. Broughton is of opinion that exposure of the sliced tuber to the air in the process of drying, favours the formation of resin, by the oxidation of a hydrocarbon.

[2] Gmelin, *Chemistry*, xvi. (1864) 159.

[3] As by Pereira, *Elem. of Mat. Med.* ii. (1850) 1463.

[4] Gmelin, *op. cit.* xvi. 154.

Convolvulinol, $C^{26}H^{50}O^{7}$, and sugar. Convolvulinol in contact with aqueous alkalis is converted into *Convolvulinolic Acid*, $C^{26}H^{48}O^{6}$, which is slightly soluble in water and crystallizable.

When convolvulin or its derivatives is treated with nitric acid, it yields several acids, one of which is the *Sebacic Acid*, $C^{8}H^{16}\begin{cases}COOH\\COOH\end{cases}$, which is to be obtained by treating castor oil or other fatty substances in the same manner. Sebacic acid forms crystalline scales, soluble in boiling water, melting at 128°. That from jalap was first thought to be a peculiar acid, and therefore termed *ipomic* or *ipomæic acid*. Its identification is due to Neison and Bayne (1874).

Convolvulin (dry) melts at 150° C., but a small amount of water renders it fusible below 100° C. It is insoluble in oil of turpentine and in ammonia. It dissolves in dilute nitric acid without becoming coloured or evolving gas. Convolvulin possesses in a high degree the purgative property of jalap, but this is not the case with convolvulinol.

The other constituents of jalap include starch, uncrystallizable sugar, gum, and colouring matter. The sugar, according to Guibourt, exists to the extent of 19 per cent.

Commerce—We have no means of knowing to what extent jalap is produced in Mexico. The imports of the drug into the United Kingdom amounted in 1870 to 169,951 lb. Very considerable quantities have of late (1873) appeared in the London drug-sales.

Uses—Jalap is employed as a brisk cathartic.

Other kinds of Jalap.

Besides true jalap, the roots of certain other *Convolvulaceæ* of Mexico have been employed in Europe, either in the form of jalapin, or as adulterants of the more costly, legitimate drug. The two following have been extensively imported and have been traced to their botanical source; but there are others, of more occasional occurrence, the origin of which has not been ascertained.[1]

1. *Light, Fusiform*, or *Woody Jalap, Male Jalap, Orizaba Root, Jalap Tops* or *Stalks, Purgo macho* of the Mexicans.

This drug is derived from *Ipomœa orizabensis* Ledanois,[2] a plant of Orizaba, which is but imperfectly known. It is described as a pubescent climber, having a spindle-shaped root about two feet long of woody and fibrous texture. The drug occurs in irregular rectangular or block-like pieces, evidently portions of a very large root, divided transversely and longitudinally. Sometimes it is more like true jalap, being in entire roots, of smaller size, spindle-shaped, not spherical. It has a somewhat lighter colour than jalap, and much deeper longitudinal wrinkles. The larger pieces often exhibit deep cuts from an axe or knife; transverse slices are of rare occurrence. Although generally less ponderous than jalap, the Orizaba drug is nevertheless of a compact and often horny texture. From jalap it is easily distinguished by its radiated transverse section, and the numerous thick bundles of vessels which project as woody fibres from the fractured surface.

[1] For information about some of these, consult Guibourt, *Histoire des Drogues*, ii. (1869) 523.

[2] *Journ. de Chimie méd.* x. (1834) 1–22. pl. 1. 2. (with unsatisfactory figures).

In chemical constitution Orizaba root is closely parallel to jalap. The resin was named by Mayer *Jalapin;* it is the *Jalapin* of Gmelin's *Chemistry* (xvi. 405), and perhaps the jalapin of English pharmacy.[1]

In the pure state it is a colourless amorphous translucent resin, *dissolving perfectly in ether*,[2] thus differing from convolvulin the corresponding resin of jalap. We find that it is readily soluble also in acetone, amylic alcohol, benzol and phenol, not in bisulphide of carbon. It has the composition of $C^{34}H^{56}O^{16}$, so that it is homologous with convolvulin; the decomposition-products of jalapin obtained by similar treatment, namely jalapic acid, jalapinol, and jalapinolic acid, are likewise homologous with the corresponding substances obtained from convolvulin. All these bodies when treated with nitric acid yield ipomœic acid. Jalapin has the same fusing point as convolvulin, and behaves in the same manner with alkalis.

The root afforded us 11·8 per cent. of resin dried at 100° C. When perfectly washed, decolorized and dissolved in two parts of alcohol, this resin turned the plane of polarization of a ray of light 9·8° to the left, in a column of 50 mm. long. Convolvulin under the same conditions turned it only 5·8°. The resin of Orizaba root is held by chemists to be identical with that of scammony, of which it has the drastic action.

2. *Tampico Jalap,—Purga de Sierra Gorda* of the Mexicans.—The plant which affords this drug has been described by one of us (1869) under the name of *Ipomœa simulans*.[3] It is closely related to *I. Purga* Hayne, from which by its foliage it cannot be distinguished, but it has a *bell-shaped corolla* and *pendulous flowerbuds*, which are very different. *I. simulans* Hanbury grows in Mexico along the mountain range of the Sierra Gorda in the neighbourhood of San Luis de la Paz, from which town and the adjacent villages its roots are carried down to Tampico. It has also been found on the lofty Cordillera near Oaxaca, but whether there collected we know not.

The drug, to which in trade the name *Tampico Jalap* is commonly applied, has been imported during the last few years in considerable quantities. In appearance it closely approaches true jalap, but the roots are generally smaller, more elongated or finger-like, more shrivelled and corky-looking, wanting in the little transverse scars that are plentifully scattered over the roots of true jalap. Many pieces occur however which it is impossible to distinguish by the eye from true jalap, with which it agrees also in odour and taste.

Tampico jalap yielded to one of us 10 per cent. of *purified* resin, entirely soluble in ether. Umney[4] obtained 12 to 15 per cent. of resin almost wholly soluble in ether; Evans got 13 per cent., but found only about half of this to be soluble in ether.[5] According to Andouard[6] the resin of Tampico jalap is not deficient in purgative powers.

[1] The name is ill-chosen and misleading, but having been adopted in standard works, it might occasion greater confusion to attempt to supersede it, and its several derivatives.

[2] It is at least a fact, that of numerous samples of jalapin that we have examined (1871), every one is *completely soluble in ether*.

[3] Hanbury, On a species of *Ipomœa*, affording Tampico Jalap, *Journ. of Linn. Soc.*, Bot. xi. (1871) 279, tab. 2; *Pharm. Journ.* xi. (1870) 848; *American Journ. of Pharm*, xviii. (1870) 330; *Science Papers*, 1876. 349.

[4] *Pharm. Journ.* ix. (1868) 282.

[5] *Ibid.* ix. (1868) 330.

[6] *Etude sur les Convolvulacées purgatives* (thèse) Paris, 1864. 31.

SEMEN KALADANÆ.

Semen Pharbitidis; Kaladana.

Botanical Origin—*Ipomœa Nil*[1] Roth (*Pharbitis Nil* Choisy, *Convolvulus Nil* L.), a twining annual plant, with a large blue corolla, much resembling the Major Convolvulus (*Pharbitis hispida* Choisy) of English gardens, but having three-lobed leaves.[2] It is found throughout the tropical regions of both hemispheres, and is common in India, ascending the mountains to a height of 5000 feet.

History—The seeds of this plant were employed in medicine by the Arabian physicians under the name *Habbun-nil;* and they have probably been long in use among the natives of Hindustan. In recent times they have been recommended by O'Shaughnessy, Kirkpatrick, Bidie, Waring[3] and many other European practitioners in India as a safe and efficient cathartic.

Description—The shape of the seeds is that which would result if a nearly spherical body were divided perpendicularly around its axis into 6 or 8 almost equal segments, only that the back is less regularly vaulted. The seeds are ¼ of an inch high and nearly as much broad; 100 of them weigh on an average about 6 grammes. There is a smaller variety imported from Calcutta, of which 100 seeds weigh but little over 3 grammes; in every other respect the two sorts are identical. Both are of a dull black, excepting at the umbilicus, which is brown and somewhat hairy. The adjacent parts of the thin shell (testa) crack in various directions, if the seed is kept for a short time in cold water. If it is removed from the upper part of the vaulted back, the radicle becomes visible, surrounded by the undulated folds of the cotyledons, which join perpendicularly, but cannot be easily unfolded by reason of the thin seminal integument. Cut transversely, the cotyledons show the same curled structure. Throughout their tissue, small bright glands in considerable number are observable, even without a lens. The kernel, which is devoid of albumen, has at first a nutty taste, with subsequently a disagreeable persistent acridity. When bruised in a mortar, the seeds evolve a heavy earthy smell.

Microscopic Structure—The seed is covered with a dark blackish cuticle, formed of a densely packed tissue, the cells of which show zigzag outlines. The dark brown epidermis is composed of very close cylindrical cells, about 70 mkm. in length and 5 to 7 mkm. in diameter; they require to be treated with chromic acid in order that their structure may be distinctly seen.

The tissue of the kernels is made up of thick-walled cells. Between this tissue and the shell there is a colourless layer, about 70 mkm. thick, of thin-walled corky parenchyme. The cotyledons contain in their narrow tissue numerous granules of albuminous matter, mucilage, a little tannic acid, crystals of oxalate of calcium, and a few starch granules. The glands or hollows, before alluded to as occurring through-

[1] In Hindustani *Nil* signifies *blue*, and *Kala-dana*, black seed.

[2] Fig. in Bentley and Trimen, *Med. Plants*, part 22 (1877).

[3] *Pharm. Journ.* vii. (1866) 496.

out the tissue of the cotyledons, are about 70 mkm. in diameter, and contain an oily liquid.

Chemical Composition—By exhausting the seeds dried at 100° C. with boiling ether, we obtained a thick light-brownish oil having an acrid taste and concreting below 18° C. The powdered seeds yielded of this oil 14·4 per cent. Water removes from the seeds a considerable amount of mucilage, some albuminous matter and a little tannic acid. The first is soluble to some extent in dilute spirit of wine, and may be precipitated therefrom by an alcoholic solution of acetate of lead.

The active principle of kaladana is a *resin*, soluble in alcohol, but neither in benzol nor in ether. From the residue of the seeds after exhaustion by ether, treatment with absolute alcohol removed a pale yellowish resin in quantity equivalent to 8·2 per cent. of the seed.

Kaladana resin, which has been introduced into medical practice in India under the name of *Pharbitisin*,[1] has a nauseous acrid taste and an unpleasant odour, especially when heated. It melts about 160° C. The following liquids dissolve it more or less freely, namely, spirit of wine, absolute alcohol, acetic acid, glacial acetic acid, acetone, acetic ether, methylic and amylic alcohol, and alkaline solutions. It is on the other hand insoluble in ether, benzol, chloroform, and sulphide of carbon. With concentrated sulphuric acid, it forms a brownish yellow solution, quickly assuming a violet hue. This reaction however requires a very small quantity of the powdered resin. If a solution of the resin in ammonia, after having been kept a short time, is acidulated, no precipitate is formed; but the solution is now capable of separating protoxide of copper from an alkaline solution of the tartrate, which originally it did not alter. Heated with nitric acid, the resin affords *sebacic acid* (see p. 446).

From these reactions of kaladana resin, we are entitled to infer that it agrees with the resin of jalap or *Convolvulin*. To prepare it in quantity, it would probably be best to treat the seeds with common acetic acid, and to precipitate it by neutralizing the solution. We have ascertained that the resin is not decomposed when digested with glacial acetic acid at 100° C., even for a week.

We have had the opportunity of examining a sample of kaladana resin manufactured by Messrs. Rogers and Co., chemists of Bombay and Poona, which we found to agree with that prepared by ourselves. It is a light yellowish friable mass, resembling purified jalap resin, and like it, capable of being perfectly decolorized by treatment with animal charcoal.

Uses—Kaladana seeds have cathartic powers like jalap. Besides the resin, an extract, tincture and compound powder have been introduced into the *Pharmacopœia of India*. In many parts of India the natives take the roasted seeds as a purgative.

[1] *Pharmacopœia of India*, 1868, 156.

SOLANACEÆ.

STIPES DULCAMARÆ.

Caules Dulcamaræ ; Bitter-sweet, Dulcamara, Woody Nightshade ; F. *Douce amère, Morelle grimpante ;* G. *Bittersüss.*

Botanical Origin—*Solanum Dulcamara* L., a perennial shrubby plant, having small purple flowers and red berries, occurring throughout Europe, except in the extreme north. It is also found in Northern Africa, and in Asia Minor, and has become naturalized in North America. It is common in moist, shady hedges and thickets.[1]

History—Bitter nightshade, "manyglog," was an ingredient, together with wild sage and betony, of a drink which the Welsh "Physicians of Myddfai" in the 13th century prepared for the bite of a mad dog.[2] The stalks of bitter-sweet were also used in the medical practice by the German physicians and botanists of the 16th century, one of whom, Tragus (1552), has figured and described it, under the name of *Dulcis amara* or *Dulcamarum.*

Description—The older stems are woody; the upper and younger are soft and green, long and straggling, attaining by the support of other plants a height of 6 feet or more, and dying back in the winter. For medicinal use, the shoots of a year or two old should be gathered, either late in the year, or early in the spring before the leaves come out. These shoots are several feet long, by about $\frac{1}{8}$ of an inch thick, of a light greenish-brown, sometimes cylindrical, at others indistinctly 4- or 5-sided, slightly furrowed longitudinally, or somewhat warty.

The thin, shining cork-bark easily exfoliates, showing beneath it the mesophlœum which is rich in chlorophyll. The stalks are mostly hollow, and partially filled with a whitish pith. The wood when dried is about half or one-third as broad as the hollow centre, and the green bark considerably narrower than the wood; the latter has a radiate structure, and in older stems exhibits two or three sharply-defined annual rings. The stems are usually cut into short lengths before being dried for use.

The odour, which is rather fœtid and unpleasant, is to a great extent dissipated by drying. The taste, at first slightly bitter, is afterwards sweetish. The bitter appears to be more predominant in the spring than in the autumn.

Microscopic Structure—The epidermis of younger shoots consists of tabular thick-walled cells, many of them being elevated from the surface as short blunt hairs. The older stems are covered with the usual suberous envelope. The boundary between the mesophlœum and the endophlœum is marked by a ring of strong liber fibres, some of which also occur in the pith. The woody part is rich in large vessels. In the parenchymatous tissue of bitter-sweet, small crystals of oxalate of

[1] *Solanum nigrum* L. which slightly resembles dulcamara, is a low-growing annual or biennial, with *herbaceous* stems, and berries usually *black.*

[2] *Meddygon Myddvai* (see Appendix) 185. 293. 375.

calcium, not of a well-defined outline, and minute starch granules are deposited.

Chemical Composition—The taste of bitter-sweet appears due, according to Schoonbroodt (1867), to a bitter principle yielding by decomposition, sugar and *Solanine*,—the latter in very small amount. Solanine is an alkaloid; it was first prepared in 1820 by Desfosses, a pharmacien at Besançon, from the berries of *Solanum nigrum* L., and was subsequently detected by the same chemist in the leaves and stalks of *S. Dulcamara*, and by Peschier in the berries. Winckler (1841) observed that the alkaloid of dulcamara stems can be obtained only in an amorphous state, and that it behaves to platinic and mercuric chlorides differently from the solanine of potatoes. Moitessier (1856) confirmed this observation, and obtained only amorphous salts of the solanine of bitter-sweet.

Zwenger and Kind on the one hand, and O. Gmelin on the other (1859 and 1858), found that solanine, $C^{43}H^{69}NO^{16}$ (or $C^{42}H^{87}NO^{15}$, according to Hilger, 1879), is a conjugated compound of sugar and a peculiar crystallizable alkaloid, *Solanidine*, $C^{26}H^{39}NO$ (or $C^{26}H^{41}NO^{2}$?). The latter, under the influence of strong hydrochloric acid, gives up water, and is converted into the amorphous and likewise basic compound, *Solanicine*.

Wittstein (1852) stated another alkaloid, dulcamarine, to be present in the stems of bitter-sweet. But Geissler (1875) proved that this substance, when perfectly pure, contains no nitrogen, and is not an alkaloid. Geissler obtained his *Dulcamarin* by warming an aqueous decoction of the drug with charcoal, which he dried and exhausted with boiling alcohol. This on evaporation afforded a yellowish amorphous matter, which was dissolved in water and mixed with a very little ammonia; a substance containing nitrogen then separated. The liquid was evaporated, the residue again dissolved in alcohol, and the alcohol distilled. Dulcamarin thus obtained is a yellowish powder of at first bitter and subsequently permanently sweet taste. It dissolves in water or alcohol, not in ether, chloroform, bisulphide of carbon, By boiling dulcamarin with dilute acids it splits up according to the following equation:—

$$\underset{\text{Dulcamarin.}}{C^{22}H^{34}O^{10}} + 2\ OH^{2} = \underset{\text{Sugar.}}{C^{6}H^{12}O^{6}} \ . \ \underset{\text{Dulcamaretin.}}{C^{16}H^{26}O^{6}}.$$

Dulcamaretin, a dark-brown, tasteless mass, is soluble in alcohol, not in water or ether.

Uses—Dulcamara is occasionally given in the form of decoction, in rheumatic or cutaneous affections; but its real action, according to Garrod, is unknown. This physician remarks[1] that it does not dilate the pupil or produce dryness of the throat like belladonna, henbane or stramonium. He has given to a patient 3 pints of the decoction *per diem* without any marked action, and has also administered as much as half a pound of the fresh berries with no ill effect.

[1] *Essentials of Materia Medica*, 1855. 196.

FRUCTUS CAPSICI.

Pod Pepper, Red Pepper, Guinea Pepper, Chillies, Capsicum; F. *Piment ou Corail des Jardins, Poivre d'Inde ou de Guinée;* G. *Spanischer Pfeffer.*

Botanical Origin—The plants, the fruits of which are known as *Pod Pepper*, have for a long period been cultivated in tropical countries, and are now found in such numerous varieties that an exact determination of the original species is a point of great difficulty. Of several species having pungent fruits, the two following are those which supply the spice found in British commerce:—

1. *Capsicum fastigiatum* Blume,[1] a small ramous shrub, with 4-sided, fastigiate, diverging branches; fruit-bearing peduncles sub-geminate, slender, erect; fruit very small, subcylindrical, oblong, straight, with calyx obconical and truncate. It occurs apparently wild in Southern India, and is extensively cultivated in Tropical Africa and America.

Roxburgh, who describes this plant under the name *C. minimum*, terms it *East Indian Bird Chilly* or *Cayenne Pepper Capsicum*. Wight says that it is consumed by the natives of India, but that it is not the sort preferred. It is this species that the authors of the British Pharmacopœia have cited as the source of the *Fructus Capsici* to be used in medicine, and it certainly furnishes the greater part of the Pod Pepper now found in the London market.

2. *C. annuum* L., an herbaceous (sometimes shrubby?) plant, with fruit extremely variable in size, form, and colour, in some varieties erect, in others pendulous. According to Naudin, in whose opinion we concur, *C. longum* DC.[2] and *C. grossum* Willd. are not specifically distinct from this plant. It furnishes the larger kinds of Pod Pepper and, as we believe, much of the Cayenne Pepper which is imported in the state of powder.

History—All species of *Capsicum* appear to be of American origin; no ancient Sanskrit or Chinese name for the genus is known, and the Latin and Greek names that have been referred to it are extremely doubtful.[3]

The earliest reference to the fruit as a condiment that we have met with, occurs in a letter written in 1494 to the Chapter of Seville by Chanca, physician to the fleet of Columbus in his second voyage to the West Indies. The writer in noticing the productions of Hispaniola, remarks that the natives live on a root called *Age*, which they season with a spice they term *Agi*, also eaten with fish and meat.[4] The first of these words signifies *yam*, the second is the designation of Red Pepper, and still the common name for it in Spanish. Capsicum and

[1] Wight, *Icones Plant. Indiæ Orient.* iv. (1850) tab. 1617; *Capsicum minimum* Roxb. *Flor. Ind.* i. (1832) 574. Farre has ascertained that this is the *Capsicum frutescens* of the *Species Plantarum* of Linnæus, but not that of the *Hortus Cliffortianus* of the same botanist, to which latter the name *C. frutescens* is usually applied.

[2] The chief distinction between *C. annuum* and *C. longum* is that the former has an *erect*, the latter a *pendulous* fruit.

[3] Dunal in De Cand. *Prodromus*, xiii. i. 412.

[4] *Letters of Christopher Columbus*, translated by Major (Hakluyt Society), 1870. 68.

its uses are more particularly described by Fernandez, who reached Tropical America from Spain in A.D. 1514.[1]

In the *Historia Stirpium* of Leonhard Fuchs, published at Basle in 1542, fol. 733, may be found the first and excellent figures of *Capsicum longum* DC. under the name of *Siliquastrum* or *Calicut Pepper*; the author states that the plant has been introduced into Germany from India a few years previously. From this might be inferred an Indian origin; but on the other hand, Clusius asserts that the plant was brought from Pernambuco by the Portuguese, whose commercial intercourse with India would easily explain it being carried thither at an early period. He further states, that the American capsicum had been generally introduced into the gardens at Castille, and that it was used all the year round, green or dried, as a condiment and as pepper. He also saw it cultivated in abundance at Brünn in Moravia in 1585.[2]

Capsicum longum DC. was grown in England by Gerarde (1597 *et antea*), who speaks of the pods as well known, and sold "in the shops at Billingsgate by the name of Ginnie Pepper."

Description—As already indicated, the Pod Pepper of commerce is of two kinds, namely:—

1. Fruits of *Capsicum fastigiatum*—These are $\frac{1}{2}$ to $\frac{3}{4}$ of an inch in length, by about $\frac{2}{10}$ of an inch in diameter, of an elongated, subconical form, tapering to a blunt point, and slightly contracted towards the base. The calyx, which is not always present, is cup-shaped, 5-toothed, 5-sided, supported on a slender, straight pedicel, $\frac{3}{4}$ to 1 inch long. The fruits, which are somewhat compressed and shrivelled by drying, and also brittle when old, have a leathery, smooth, shining translucent, thin, dry pericarp, of a dull orange-red, enclosing about 18 seeds, attached in two cells to a thin central partition. The seeds have the form of roundish or ovate discs, about $\frac{1}{8}$ of an inch in diameter, somewhat thickened at the edges; the embryo is curved, almost into a ring. The taste of the pericarp, and likewise of the seeds, is extremely pungent and fiery. The dried fruit has an odour by no means feeble, which we cannot compare to that of any other substance.

2. Fruits of *Capsicum annuum* of the commonest variéty resemble those of *C. fastigiatum*, except that they are of longer size, being from 2 to 3 or more inches in length, often rather more tapering towards the extremity. The seeds scarcely surpass in size those of *C. fastigiatum*.

Microscopic Structure—The pericarp consists of two layers, the outer being composed of yellow thick-walled cells. The inner layer is twice as broad and exhibits a soft shrunken parenchyme, traversed by thin fibro-vascular bundles. The cells of the outer layer especially are the seat of the fine granular colouring matter. If it is removed by an alcoholic solution of potash, a cell-nucleus and drops of fat oil make their appearance. The structural details of this fruit afford interesting subjects for microscopical investigation.

Chemical Composition—Bucholz in 1816, and about the same time Braconnot, traced the acridity of capsicum to a substance called

[1] *Historia de las Indias*, Madrid, i. (1851) 275.

[2] Caroli Clusii *Curæ posteriores*, Antverp., 1611. 95.

Capsicin. It is obtained by treating the alcoholic extract of ether, and is a thick yellowish red liquid, but slightly soluble in water. When gently heated, it becomes very fluid, and at a higher temperature is dissipated in fumes which are extremely irritating to respiration. It is evidently a mixed substance, consisting of resinous and fatty matters.

Felletár in 1869 exhausted capsicum fruits with dilute sulphuric acid, and distilled the decoction with potash. The distillate, which was strongly alkaline and smelt like conine, was saturated with sulphuric acid, evaporated to dryness, and exhausted with absolute alcohol. The solution, after evaporation of the alcohol, was treated with potash, and yielded by distillation a volatile alkaloid having the odour of conine.

From experiments made by one of us (F.) we can fully confirm the observations of Felletár. We have obtained the volatile base in question, and find it to have the smell of conine. It occurs both in the pericarp and in the seeds, but in so small proportion that we were unsuccessful in isolating it in sufficient quantity to allow of accurate examination.

Dragendorff states (1871) that petroleum ether is the best solvent for the alkaloid of capsicum; he obtained crystals of its hydrochlorate, the aqueous solution of which was precipitated by most of the usual tests, but not by tannic acid.

The colouring matter of capsicum fruits is sparingly soluble in alcohol, but readily in chloroform. After evaporation, an intensely red soft mass is obtained, which is not much altered by potash; it turns first blue, then black with concentrated sulphuric acid, like many other yellow colouring substances. By alcohol chiefly *palmitic* acid is extracted from the fruit, as shown by Thresh in 1877.

The fruits of *Capsicum fastigiatum* have a somewhat strong odour; on distilling consecutively two quantities, each of 50 ℔., we obtained a scanty amount of flocculent fatty matter, which possesses an odour suggestive of parsley. Both this matter, as well as the distilled water, were neutral to litmus paper, and the water tasteless. We separated the latter, and exposed the remaining greasy mass to a temperature of about 50° C., when it for the most part melted. The clear liquid on cooling solidified, and now consisted of tufted crystals, which we further purified by recrystallization from alcohol. Thus about 2 centigrammes were obtained of a neutral white stearoptene, having a decidedly aromatic, not very persistent taste, by *no means acrid*, but rather like that of the essential oil of parsley. The crystals melted at 38° C. On keeping them for some days at the temperature of the water-bath, covered with a watch-glass, some drops of essential oil were volatilized, which had the same taste and did not solidify; the crystals were consequently accompanied by a liquid oil. When kept for some days more in that condition, the crystals themselves began to be volatilized, and the part remaining behind acquired a brownish hue. This no doubt points out another impurity, as we ascertained by the following experiment. With boiling solution of potash, the stearoptene produces a kind of soap, which on cooling yields a transparent jelly. If this is dissolved and diluted, it becomes turbid by addition of an acid. This probably depends upon the presence of a little fatty matter, a suggestion which is confirmed by the somewhat offensive smell given off by our stearoptene if it is heated in a glass tube.

Buchheim's "Capsicol"[1] is in our opinion a doubtful substance.

Thresh (1876-1877) succeeded in isolating a well defined, highly active principle, the *Capsaicin*, from the extract which he obtained by exhausting Cayenne pepper with petroleum. From the red liquor dilute caustic lye removes capsaicin, which is to be precipitated in minute crystals by passing carbonic acid through the alkaline solution. They may be purified by recrystallizing them from either alcohol, ether, benzine, glacial acetic acid, or hot bisulphide of carbon; in petroleum capsaicin is but very sparingly soluble, yet dissolves abundantly on addition of fatty oil. The latter being present in the pericarp is the cause why capsaicin can be extracted by the above process.

The crystals of capsaicin are colourless and answer to the formula $C^9H^{14}O^2$; they melt at 59° C. and begin to volatilize at 115° C., but decomposition can only be avoided by great care. The vapours of capsaicin are of the most *dreadful acridity*, and even the ordinary manipulation of that substance requires much precaution. Capsaicin is not a glucoside; it is a powerful rubefacient, and taken internally produces very violent burning in the stomach.

Commerce—Chillies or Pod Pepper are shipped from Zanzibar, Western Africa and Natal, but no general statistics of the quantity imported into Great Britain are accessible.

The exports from Sierra Leone in 1871 reached 7258 lb.[2] The colony of Natal, which produces Cayenne Pepper in the county of Victoria, where sugar-cane and coffee are also grown, shipped in the same year 9072 lb.[3]

Official returns[4] show that in 1871 Singapore imported 1071 cwt. (119,952 lb.) of chillies, chiefly from Penang and Pegu. The spice is largely consumed by the Chinese.

Bombay imported of dried chillies in the year 1872-3, 5567 cwt. (623,504 lb.) principally from the Madras Presidency, and exported 3323 cwt.[5]

Uses—Capsicum on account of its pungent properties is often administered as a local stimulant in the form of gargle, and occasionally as a liniment; and internally to promote digestion. In all warm countries it is much employed as a condiment.

RADIX BELLADONNÆ.

Belladonna Root; F. *Racine de Belladone*; G. *Belladonnawurzel.*

Botanical Origin—*Atropa Belladonna* L., a tall, glabrous or slightly downy herb, with a perennial stock, native of central and Southern Europe, where it grows in the clearings of woods. The plant extends eastward to the Crimea, Caucasia and Northern Asia Minor.

[1] *Jahresbericht* of Wiggers and Husemann, 1873. 567; also *Yearbook of Pharm.* 1876. 251.

[2] *Blue Book* of the Colony of Sierra Leone for 1871.

[3] Do. of Natal for 1871.

[4] Do. of the Straits Settlements for 1871.

[5] *Statement of the Trade and Navigation of Bombay for* 1872-73, pt. ii. 58. 91.

In Britain it is chiefly found in the southern counties, but even of these it is a doubtful native.

In a few localities in England and France, as well as in North America, the plant is cultivated for medicinal use.

History—Although a plant so striking as belladonna can hardly have been unknown to the classical authors, it cannot with certainty be identified in their writings.

Saladinus of Ascoli,[1] who wrote an enumeration of medicinal plants about A.D. 1450, names the leaves of both *Solatrum furiale* and *Solatrum minus*, the former of which is probably *Belladonna*. However this may be, the first indubitable notice of it that we have met with, is in the *Grand Herbier* printed at Paris, probably about 1504.[2] The plant is also mentioned about this period as *Solatrum mortale* or *Dolwurtz*, in the writings of Hieronymus Brunschwyg.[3]

In 1542 belladonna was well figured as *Solanum somniferum* or *Dollkraut* by the German botanist Leonhard Fuchs, who fully recognized its poisonous properties.[4] Yet it was confounded by other writers of this period as Tragus,[5] who reproduced Fuchs' figure as "*Solanum hortense!*" *Strygium* and *Strychnon* were other names not unfrequently applied to Atropa during the 16th and 17th centuries.

Matthiolus, who terms the plant *Solatrum majus*, states[6] that it is commonly called by the Venetians *Herba Bella donna*, from the circumstance of the Italian ladies using a distilled water of the plant as a cosmetic. Gesner[7] was also familiar with the name Belladonna. The introduction of the root of belladonna into British medicine is of recent date, and is due to Mr. Peter Squire of London, who recommended it as the basis of a useful anodyne liniment, about the year 1860.

Description—Belladonna has a large, fleshy, tapering root, 1 to 2 inches thick, and a foot or more in length, from which diverge stout branches. Externally the fresh roots are of an earthy brown, rough with cracks and transverse ridges. The bark is thick and juicy, and as well as the more fibrous central portion, is internally of a dull creamy white. A transverse section of the main root shows a distinct radiate structure. The root has an earthy smell with but very little taste at first, but a powerfully acrid after-taste is soon developed.

Dried root of Belladonna is sold in rough irregular pieces of a dirty greyish colour, whitish internally, breaking easily with a short fracture, and having an earthy smell not unlike that of liquorice root. The bark being probably the chief seat of the alkaloid, roots not exceeding the thickness of the finger should be preferred. The drug is for the most part imported from Germany, and is often of doubtful quality. English-grown root purchased in a fresh state (the large and old being rejected), then washed, cut into transverse segments and dried by a gentle heat, furnishes a more reliable and satisfactory article.

[1] *Compendium Aromatariorum*, 1488.

[2] *Le Grant Herbier en francoys, contenãt les qualitez, vertus et proprietez des herbes* etc., Paris (no date) 4°. cap. *De Solastro rustico.*

[3] *Das destillier Buch* (sub voce *Nachtschet Wasser*). Strassburg, 1521, fol. 93 *b*. The figure probably refers to Atropa, but that given in the edition of the same work of the year 1500 shows *Solanum nigrum*.

[4] *Historia Stirpium*, Basil. 1542. 689.

[5] *De Stirpium .... historia*, Argentorati, 1552. 301.

[6] *Comment. in lib. vi. Dioscoridis*, Venetiis, 1558. 533.

[7] *De hortis Germaniæ*, Argentorat. 1561, fol. 282.

Microscopic Structure—There is a considerable structural difference between the main root and its branches, the former alone containing a distinct pith. This pith is included in a woody circle, traversed by narrow medullary rays. In the outer part of the woody circle, parenchymatous tissue is more prevalent than vascular bundles. The transverse section of the branches of the root exhibits a central vascular bundle instead of a medullary column. The outer vascular bundles show no regular arrangement; and medullary rays are not clearly obvious in the transverse section.

The woody parts, both of the main root and its branches, contain very large dotted vessels accompanied by a prosenchymatous tissue. The cells of the latter, however, are always thin-walled; the absence of proper so-called ligneous tissue explains the easy fracture of the root. Sometimes the prosenchyme in which the vessels are imbedded assumes a brownish hue and a waxy appearance, and such parts exhibit a very irregular structure.

In the cortical portion of belladonna root, many of the cells of the middle layer, and likewise some of the central parts of the root, are loaded with extremely small octahedric crystals of calcium oxalate. But most of the parenchymatous cells are filled up with small starch granules.

Chemical Composition—In 1833 Mein prepared from the root, and Geiger and Hesse from the herb, the crystallizable alkaloid *Atropine*. The researches of Lefort (1872) have proved that the roots contain it in very variable proportions, the young being much richer in alkaloid than the old.[1] The maximum proportion obtained was 0·6 per cent.; this was from root of the thickness of the finger. Large old roots, 7 or 8 years of age, afford from 0·25 to 0·31 per cent. They have besides a smaller proportion of bark than young roots, and it is chiefly in the bark that the alkaloid appears to reside. Manufacturers of atropine employ exclusively the root.

Ludwig and Pfeiffer (1861), by decomposing atropine with potassium chromate and sulphuric acid, obtained benzoic acid and propylamine. Other products are formed when atropine is treated with strong hydrochloric acid, baryta water or caustic soda, thus—*Atropine*, $C^{17}H^{23}NO^{3}$ + $H^{2}O$ = *Tropic Acid*, $C^{9}H^{10}O^{3}$ + *Tropine*, $C^{8}H^{15}NO$.

Tropic acid, $C^{6}H^{5}C\,(OH)\left\{\begin{matrix}CH^{3}\\ COOH\end{matrix}\right.$, being further boiled with the same agents is converted into atropic acid, $C^{6}H^{5}C\left\{\begin{matrix}CH^{2}\\ COOH\end{matrix}\right.$, which, especially by using hydrochloric acid, is gradually transformed into isotropic acid. Both these acids are isomeric to cinnamic acid, $C^{9}H^{8}O^{2}$, but otherwise remarkably dissimilar.

Tropine is a strongly alkaline body, readily soluble both in water and alcohol, and furnishing tabular crystals by the evaporation of its solution in ether. Neither tropine nor tropic acid, it is stated by Kraut (1863), is present in the leaves and root of belladonna.

Hübschmann (1858) detected in belladonna root a second but uncrystallizable alkaloid, called *Belladonnine*; it has a resinous aspect, is distinctly alkaline, and when heated emits, like atropine, a peculiar odour.

[1] For Lefort's process for estimating atropine, see p. 458.

The root further contains, according to Richter (1837) and Hübschmann, a fluorescent substance, as well as a red colouring matter called *Atrosin*.[1] The latter occurs in greatest abundance in the fruit, and would probably repay further investigation.

Uses—Belladonna root is chiefly used for the preparation of atropine, which is employed for dilating the pupil of the eye. A liniment made with belladonna root is used for the relief of neuralgic pains.

Adulteration—We may point out that the roots of *Mandragora microcarpa, M. officinarum,* and *M. vernalis* Bertoloni are very nearly allied to the root under notice, both in external appearance and in their structure. They are not likely to be confounded with Belladonna root, their mother plants being indigenous in the South of Europe.

FOLIA BELLADONNÆ.

Belladonna Leaves; F. *Feuilles de Belladone;* G. *Tollkraut.*

Botanical Origin—*Atropa Belladonna* L. (p. 455).

History—Belladonna Leaves and the extract prepared from them were introduced into the London Pharmacopœia of 1809. For further particulars regarding the history of belladonna, see the preceding article.

Description—Belladonna or Deadly Nightshade produces thick, smooth herbaceous stems, which attain a height of 4 to 5 feet. They are simple in their lower parts, then usually 3-forked, and afterwards 2-forked, producing in their upper branches an abundance of bright green leaves, arranged in unequal pairs, from the bases of which spring the solitary, pendulous, purplish, bell-shaped flowers, and large shining black berries.

The leaves are 3 to 6 inches long, stalked, broadly ovate, acuminate, attenuated at the base, soft and juicy; those of barren roots are alternate and solitary. The young shoots are clothed with a soft, short pubescence, which on the calyx is somewhat more persistent, assuming the character of viscid, glandular hairs. If bruised, the leaves emit a somewhat offensive, herbaceous odour which is destroyed by drying. When dried, they are thin and friable, of a brownish green on the upper surface and greyish beneath, with a disagreeable, faintly bitter taste. Of fresh leaves 100 lb. yield 16 lb. of dried (Squire).

Chemical Composition—The important constituent of belladonna leaves is *Atropine*. Lefort (1872)[2] estimated its amount by exhausting the leaves previously dried at 100° C. by means of dilute alcohol, concentrating the tincture, and throwing down the alkaloid with a solution of iodo-hydrargyrate of potassium. The precipitate thus obtained was calculated to contain 33·25 per cent. of atropine. Lefort examined leaves from plants both cultivated and growing wild in the environs of Paris, and gathered either before or after flowering. He found cultivation not to affect the percentage of alkaloid,—that the leaves of the young plant were rather less rich than those taken at the period of full

[1] Gmelin, *Chemistry*, xvii. (1866) 1.

[2] *Journ. de Pharm.* xv. (1872) 269. 341.

inflorescence,—and that the latter (dried) yielded 0·44 to 0·48 per cent. of atropine.

Larger percentages are recorded by Dragendorff;[1] as much as 0·95 per cent. of atropine as obtained from the dried unripe fruits, 0·83 from the dried leaves, 0·21 from the root. The estimation was performed in nearly the same way as that followed by Lefort.

Belladonna herb yields *Asparagin*, which according to Biltz (1839) crystallizes out of the extract after long keeping. The crystals found in the extract by Attfield (1862) were however chloride and nitrate of potassium. The same chemist obtained by dialysis of the juice of belladonna, nitrate of potassium, and square prisms of a salt of magnesium containing some organic acid; the juice likewise affords ammonia.[2] The dried leaves yielded us 14·5 per cent. of ash consisting mainly of calcareous and alkaline carbonates.

Uses—The fresh leaves are used for making *Extractum Belladonnæ*, and the dried for preparing a tincture. They should be gathered while the plant is well in flower.

HERBA STRAMONII.

Stramonium, Thornapple; F. Herbe de Stramoine; G. *Stechapfelblätter.*

Botanical Origin—*Datura*[3] *Stramonium* L., a large, quick-growing, upright annual, with white flowers like a convolvulus, and ovoid spiny fruits. It is now found as a weed of cultivation in almost all the temperate and warmer regions of the globe. In the south of England it is often met with in rich waste ground, chiefly near gardens or habitations.

History—The question of the native country and early distribution of *D. Stramonium* has been much discussed by botanical writers. Alphonse De Candolle,[4] who has ably reviewed the arguments advanced in favour of the plant being a native respectively of Europe and America or Asia, enounces his opinion thus:—that *D. Stramonium* L. appears to be indigenous to the Old World, probably the borders of the Caspian Sea or adjacent regions, but certainly not of India; that it is very doubtful if it existed in Europe in the time of the ancient Roman Empire, but that it appears to have spread itself between that period and the discovery of America.

Stramonium was cultivated in London towards the close of the 16th century by Gerarde, who received the seed from Constantinople and freely propagated the plant, of the medicinal value of which he had a high opinion. The use of the herb in more recent times is due to the experiments of Störck.[5]

Description—Stramonium produces a stout, upright, herbaceous

[1] *Werthbestimmung stark wirkender Droguen*, Petersburg, 1876. 28.

[2] The fresh juice kept for a few days has been known to evolve *red vapours* (nitrous acid?) when the vessel containing it was opened.—H. S. Evans in *Pharm. Journ.* ix. (1850) 260.

[3] *Datura* from the Sanskrit name *D'hustúra*, applied to *D. fastuosa* L. The origin of the word *Stramonium* is not known to us.

[4] *Géographie Botanique*, ii. (1855) 731.

[5] Libellus quo demonstratur *Stramonium*, Hyoscyamum, Aconitum . . esse remedia, Vindob. 1762.

green stem, which at a short distance from the ground, throws out spreading forked branches, in the axil of each fork of which arises a solitary white flower, succeeded by an erect, spiny, ovoid capsule. At each furcation and directed outwards is a large leaf. This arrangement of parts is repeated, and as the plant grows vigorously, it often becomes much branched and acquires in the course of the summer a considerable size.

The leaves of stramonium have long petioles, are unequal at the base, oval, acuminate, sinuate-dentate with large irregular pointed teeth or lobes, downy when young, glabrous at maturity. When fresh they are somewhat firm and juicy, emitting when handled a disagreeable fœtid smell. The larger leaves of plants of moderate growth attain a length of 6 to 8 or more inches.

For medicinal purposes, the entire plants are pulled up, the leaves and younger shoots are stripped off, quickly dried, and then broken and cut into short lengths, so as to be conveniently smoked in a pipe, that being the method in which the drug is chiefly consumed in England. The offensive smell of the fresh plant is lost by drying, being replaced by a rather agreeable tea-like odour. The dried herb has a bitterish saline taste.

Chemical Composition—The leaves of stramonium contain, in common with the seeds, the alkaloid *Daturine* (see p. 461), but in extremely small proportion, not exceeding in fact $\frac{2}{10}$ to $\frac{3}{10}$ per mille. They are rich in saline and earthy constituents; selected leaves dried at 100° C. yielded us 17·4 per cent. of ash.

Uses—Scarcely employed in any other way than in smoking like tobacco for the relief of asthma.—Col. Grant (1871) found the herb to be smoked in pipes by the Nubians for chest-complaint.

Substitute—*Datura Tatula* L.—This plant is closely allied to *D. Stramonium* L., propagating itself on rich cultivated ground with nearly the same facility; but it is not so generally diffused.

De Candolle is of opinion that it is indigenous to the warmer parts of America, whence it was imported into Europe in the 16th century, and naturalized first in Italy, and then in South-Western Europe. By many botanists it has been united to *D. Stramonium*, but Naudin,[1] who has studied both plants with the greatest attention, especially with reference to their hybrids, is decidedly in favour of considering them distinct. *D. Tatula* differs from *D. Stramonium* in having stem, petiole, and nerves of leaves *purplish* instead of *green;* and corolla and anthers of a *violet* colour instead of *white,*—characters which, it must be admitted, are of very small botanical value.

D. Tatula has been recommended for smoking in cases of asthma, on the ground of its being *stronger* than *D. Stramonium ;* but we are not aware of any authority as to the comparative strength of the two species.

[1] *Comptes Rendus*, lv. (1862) 321.

SEMEN STRAMONII.

Stramonium Seeds; F. *Semences de Stramoine*; G. *Stechapfelsamen.*

Botanical Origin—*Datura Stramonium* L., see preceding article.

Description—The spiny, ovoid capsule of stramonium opens at the summit in four regular valves. It is bilocular, with each cell incompletely divided into two, and contains a large number (about 400) of flattened, kidney-shaped seeds. The seeds are blackish or dark brown, about 2 lines long and ½ a line thick, thinning off towards the hilum which is on the straighter side. The surface of the seed is finely pitted and also marked with a much coarser series of shallow reticulations or rugosities. A section parallel to the faces of the seed exhibits the long, contorted embryo, following the outline of the testa, and bedded in the oily white albumen. The cylindrical form of the embryo is seen in a transverse section of the seed.

The seeds have a bitterish taste, and when bruised a disagreeable odour. When the entire seeds are immersed in dilute alcohol, they afford a tincture displaying a beautiful green fluorescence, turning yellow on addition of ammonia.

Microscopic Structure—The testa is formed of a row of radially extended, thick-walled cells. They are not of a simply cylindrical form, but their walls are sinuously bent in and out in the direction of their length. Viewed in a direction tangential to the surface, the cells appear as if indented one into the other. Towards the surface of the seed the cell-walls are elevated as dark brown tubercles and folds, giving to the seed its reticulated and pitted surface. The albumen and embryo exhibit the usual contents, namely fatty oil and albuminoid substances.[1]

Chemical Composition—The active constituent of stramonium seeds is the highly poisonous alkaloid *Daturine*, of which they afford only about $\frac{1}{10}$ per cent., while the leaves and roots contain it in still smaller proportion.[2] Daturine was discovered in 1833 by Geiger and Hesse, and regarded as identical with atropine by A. von Planta (1850), who found it to have the same composition as that alkaloid. The two bodies exhibit the same relations as to solubility and fusing point (88–90° C.); and they also agree in crystallizing easily. The experiments of Schroff (1852), tending to show that although daturine and atropine act in the same manner, the latter has twice the poisonous energy of the former, raised a further question as to the identity of the two alkaloids. Poehl (1876) also stated solutions of daturine to be levogyrate, those of atropine being devoid of rotatory power. From the observations of Erhard (1866), it would appear that the crystalline form of some of the salts of atropine and daturine is different. In stramonium seeds daturine appears to be combined with malic acid. The seeds yielded to Cloëz (1865) 2·9 per cent. of ash and 25 per cent. of fixed oil.

Uses—Stramonium seeds are prescribed in the form of extract or tincture as a sedative or narcotic.

[1] We have not seen W. G. Mann, *Onderzoek van het zaad van Datura Stramonium*, Enschede, 1875.

[2] Günther in Wiggers and Husemann's *Jahresbericht* for 1869. 54.

SEMEN ET FOLIA DATURÆ ALBÆ.

Seeds and Leaves of the Indian or White-flowered Datura.

Botanical Origin—*Datura alba* Nees, a large, spreading annual plant, 2 to 6 feet high, bearing handsome, tubular, white flowers 5 to 6 inches long. The capsules are pendulous, of depressed globular form, rather broader than high, covered with sharp tubercles or thick short spines. They do not open by regular valves as in *D. Stramonium*, but split in different directions and break up into irregular fragments.

D. alba appears to be scarcely distinct from *D. fastuosa* L. Both are common in India, and are grown in gardens in the south of Europe.[1]

History—The mediæval Arabian physicians were familiar with *Datura alba*, which is well described by Ibn Baytar[2] under precisely the same Arabic name (*Jouz-masal*) that it bears at the present day; they were also fully aware of its poisonous properties.

Garcia de Orta[3] (1563) observed the plant in India, and has narrated that its flowers or seeds are put into food to intoxicate persons it was designed to rob. It was also described by Christoval Acosta, who in his book on Indian drugs[4] mentions two other varieties, one of them with yellow flowers, the seeds of either being very poisonous, and often administered with criminal intent, as well as for the cure of disease. Graham[5] says of the plant that it possesses very strong narcotic properties, and has on several occasions been fatally used by Bombay thieves, who have administered it in order to deprive their victims of the power of resistance.

The seeds and fresh leaves have a place in the *Pharmacopœia of India*, 1868.

Description—The seeds of *D. alba* are very different in appearance from those of *D. Stramonium*, being of a light yellowish-brown, rather larger size, irregular in shape and somewhat shrivelled. Their form has been likened to the human ear; they are in fact obscurely triangular or flattened-pearshaped, the rounded end being thickened into a sinuous, convoluted, triple ridge, while the centre of the seed is somewhat depressed. The hilum runs from the pointed end nearly half-way up the length of the seed. The testa is marked with minute rugosities, but is not so distinctly pitted as in the seed of the *D. Stramonium*; it is also more developed, exhibiting in section large intercellular spaces to which are due its spongy texture. The seeds of the two species agree in internal structure as well as in taste; but those of *D. alba* do not give a fluorescent tincture.

The leaves, which are only employed in a fresh state, are 6 to 10 inches in length, with long stalks, ovate, often unequal at the base,

[1] Seeds of *D. alba* sent to us from Madras by Dr. Bidie, were sown by our friend M. Naudin of Collioure (Pyrénées Orientales), and produced the plant under three forms, viz.:—1. The true *D. alba* as figured in Wight's *Icones*.—2. Plants with flowers, violet without and nearly white within (*D. fastuosa*).—3. Plants with double corollas of large size and of a yellow colour.

[2] Sontheimer's translation, i. 269.

[3] *Aromatum historia*, 1574, lib. 2. c. 24.

[4] *Tractado de las Drogas . . . de las Indias Orientales*, Burgos, 1578. 85.

[5] *Catalogue of Bombay Plants*, 1839. 141.

acuminate, coarsely dentate with a few spreading teeth. They evolve an offensive odour when handled.

Microscopic Structure—The testa is built up of the same tissues as in *D. Stramonium*, but the thick-walled cells constituting the spongy part are far larger, and distinctly show numerous secondary deposits, making a fine object for the microscope.

Chemical Composition—Neither the seeds nor the leaves of *D. alba* have yet been examined chemically, but there can scarcely be any doubt that their very active properties are due to *Daturine*, for the preparation of which the former would probably be the best source.

Uses—The seeds in the form of tincture or extract have been employed in India as a sedative and narcotic, and the fresh leaves, bruised and made into a poultice with flour, as an anodyne application.

FOLIA HYOSCYAMI.

Henbane Leaves; F. *Feuilles de Jusquiame;* G. *Bilsenkraut.*

Botanical Origin—*Hyoscyamus niger* L., a coarse, erect herb, with soft, viscid, hairy foliage of unpleasant odour, pale yellowish flowers elegantly marked with purple veins, and 5-toothed bottle-shaped calyx. It is found throughout Europe from Portugal and Greece to Central Norway and Finland, in Egypt, Asia Minor, the Caucasus, Persia, Siberia and Northern India. As a weed of cultivation it now grows also in North America[1] and Brazil. In Britain it occurs wild, chiefly in waste places near buildings; and is cultivated for medicinal use.

Henbane exists under two varieties, known as *annual* and *biennial*, but scarcely presenting any other distinctive character.

Biennial Henbane (*Hyoscyamus niger* var. *a. biennis*) is most esteemed for pharmaceutical preparations. It is raised by seed, the plant producing the first year only a rosette of luxuriant stalked leaves, 12 or more inches in length. In the second, it throws up a flower stem of 2 to 3 feet in height, and the whole plant dies as the fruit matures.

Annual Henbane (*H. niger* var. *β. annua*, vel *agrestis*) is a smaller plant, coming to perfection in a single season. It is the usual wild form, but it is also grown by the herbalists.[2]

History—Hyoscyamus, under which name it is probable the nearly allied South European species, *H. albus* L., was generally intended, was medicinal among the ancients, and particularly commended by Dioscorides.

In Europe, henbane has been employed from remote times. Benedictus Crispus, archbishop of Milan, in a work written shortly before A.D. 681, notices it under the name of *Hyoscyamus* and *Symphoniaca*.[3] In the 10th century, its virtues were particularly recorded by Macer Floridus[4] who called it *Jusquiamus*.

[1] It had become naturalized in North America prior to 1672, as we find it mentioned by Josselyn in his *New England's Rarities discovered* (Lond. 1672) among the plants "sprung up since the English planted and kept cattle in New England."

[2] *Pharm. Journ.* i. (1860) 414.

[3] S. de Renzi, *Collectio Salernitana*, Napoli, i. (1852) 74. 84.

[4] *De Viribus Herbarum*, edited by Choulant, Lips. 1832. 108.

Frequent mention is made of it in the Anglo-Saxon works on medicine of the 11th century,[1] in which it is called *Henbell*, and sometimes *Belene*, the latter word perhaps traceable in *βιλινουντία*, which Dioscorides[2] gives as the Gallic designation of the plant. In the 13th century henbane was also used by the Welsh "Physicians of Myddvai."

The word *Hennibone*, with the Latin and French synonyms *Jusquiamus* and *Chenille*, occurs in a vocabulary of the 13th century; and *Hennebane* in a Latin and English vocabulary of the 15th century.[3] In the *Arbolayre*, a printed French herbal of the 15th century,[4] we find the plant described as *Hanibane* or *Hanebane* with the following explanation—"Elle est aultrement appeler cassilago et aultrement simphoniaca. La semence proprement a nom jusquiame ou hanebane, et herbe a nom cassilago. . . ." Both *Hyoscyamus* and *Jusquiamus* are from the Greek Ὑοσκύαμος, i.e. *Hog-bean*.

Though a remedy undeniably potent, henbane in the first half of the last century had fallen into disuse. It was omitted from the London pharmacopœias of 1746 and 1788, and restored only in 1809. Its re-introduction into medicine was chiefly due to the experiments and recommendations of Störck.[5]

During the middle ages the seeds and roots of henbane were also much used.

Description—The stems of henbane, whether of the annual or biennial form, are clothed with soft, viscid, hairy leaves, of which the upper constitute the large, sessile, coarsely-toothed bracts of the unilateral flower-spike. The middle leaves are more toothed and subamplexicaul. The lower leaves are stalked, ovate-oblong, coarsely dentate, and of large size. The stems, leaves, and calyces of henbane are thickly beset with long, soft, jointed hairs; the last joint of many of these hairs exudes a viscid substance occasioning the fresh plant to feel clammy to the touch. In the cultivated plant, the hairiness diminishes.

After drying, the broad light-coloured midrib becomes very conspicuous, while the rest of the leaf shrinks much and acquires a greyish green hue. The drug derived from the flowering plant as found in commerce is usually much broken. The fœtid, narcotic odour of the fresh leaves is greatly diminished by drying. The fresh plant has but little taste.

Dried henbane is sold under three forms, which are not however generally distinguished by druggists. These are 1. *Annual plant*, foliage and Green tops. 2. *Biennial plant*, leaves of the first year. 3. *Biennial plant*, foliage and green tops. The third form is always regarded as the best, but no attempt has been made to determine with accuracy the relative merits of the three sorts.

Chemical Composition—*Hyoscyamine*, the most important among the constituents of henbane, was obtained in an impure state by Geiger and Hesse in 1833. Höhn in 1871 first isolated it from the seeds.

[1] *Leechdoms etc. of Early England*, iii. (1866) 313.

[2] Lib. iv. c. 69. (ed. Sprengel).

[3] Wright, *Volume of Vocabularies*, 1857. 141. 265.

[4] See p. 148, note 3, also Brunet, *Manuel du Libraire*, i. (1860) 377.

[5] See p. 459, note 5.

which are far richer in it than the leaves.[1] The seeds are deprived of the fatty oil (26 per cent.) and treated with spirit of wine containing sulphuric acid, which takes out the hyoscyamine in the form of sulphate. The alcohol is then evaporated and tannic acid added; the precipitate thus obtained is mixed with lime and exhausted with alcohol. The hyoscyamine is again converted into a sulphate, the aqueous solution of which is then precipitated with carbonate of sodium, and the alkaloid dissolved by means of ether. After the evaporation of the ether, hyoscyamine remains as an oily liquid which after some time concretes into wart-like tufted crystals, soluble in benzol, chloroform, ether, as well as in water. Höhn and Reichardt assign to hyoscyamine the formula $C^{15}H^{23}O^{3}$. The seeds yield of it only 0·05 per cent.

Hyoscyamine is easily decomposed by caustic alkalis. By boiling with baryta in aqueous solution, it is split into *Hyoscine*, $C^{6}H^{13}N$, and *Hyoscinic Acid*, $C^{9}H^{10}O^{3}$. The former is a volatile oily liquid of a narcotic odour and alkaline reaction. By keeping it over sulphuric acid it crystallizes and also yields crystallized salts; hyoscine may be closely allied to conine, $C^{8}H^{15}N$. Hyoscinic acid, a crystallizable substance having an odour resembling that of empyreumatic benzoic acid.[2] It melts, according to Höhn, at 105°; tropic acid (see p. 457), melting at 118°, agrees so very nearly with hyoscinic acid that further researches will probably prove these acids to be identical.

Another process for extracting hyoscyamine is due (1875) to Thibaut. He removes by bisulphide of carbon the fatty oil from the powdered seeds, and exhausts them with alcohol slightly acidulated by tartaric acid. The alcohol being distilled off, the author precipitates the alkaloid by means of a solution containing 6 per cent. of iodide of potassium and 3 per cent. iodine. By decomposing the precipitate with sulphurous acid, hydroiodic acid and sulphate of hyoscyamine are formed. The latter is dried up at 35° with magnesia and the hyoscyamine extracted by alcohol or chloroform. The crystals melt at 90°. Thibaut found the alkaloid thus prepared from seeds differing from that yielded by the leaves, the latter having a somewhat strong odour.

Attfield[3] has pointed out that extract of henbane is rich in nitrate of potassium and other inorganic salts. In the leaves, the amount of nitrate is, according to Thorey,[4] largest before flowering, and the same observation applies to hyoscyamine.

Uses—Henbane in the form of tincture or extract is administered as a sedative, anodyne or hypnotic. The impropriety of giving it in conjunction with free potash or soda, which render it perfectly inert, has been demonstrated by the experiments of Garrod.[5] Hyoscyamine, like atropine, powerfully dilates the pupil of the eye.

Substitutes—*Hyoscyamus albus* L., a more slender plant than *H.*

[1] From the experiments of Schoonbroodt (1868), there is reason to believe that the active principle of henbane can be more easily extracted from the *fresh* than from the *dried* plant.

[2] I have had the opportunity of examining the above substances as prepared by the said chemists.—F. A. F. July 1871.

[3] *Pharm. Journ.* iii. (1862) 447.

[4] Wiggers and Husemann, *Jahresbericht*, 1869. 56.

[5] *Pharm. Journ.* xvii. (1858) 462; xviii. (1859) 174.

niger L., with stalked leaves and bracts, a native of the Mediterranean region, is sometimes used in the south of Europe as medicinal henbane. *H. insanus* Stocks, a plant of Beluchistan, is mentioned in the *Pharmacopœia of India* as of considerable virulence, and sometimes used for smoking.

FOLIA TABACI.

Herba Nicotianæ; Tobacco; F. *Tabac;* G. *Tabakblätter.*

Botanical Origin—*Nicotiana Tabacum* L.—The common Tobacco plant is a native of the New World, though not now known in a wild state. Its cultivation is carried on in most temperate and sub-tropical countries.

History—It is stated by C. Ph. von Martius[1] that the practice of smoking tobacco has been widely diffused from time immemorial among the natives of South America, as well as among the inhabitants of the valley of the Mississippi as far north as the plant can be cultivated.

The Spaniards became acquainted with tobacco when they landed in Cuba in 1492, and on their return introduced it into Europe for the sake of its medicinal properties. The custom of inhaling the smoke of the herb was learnt from the Indians, and by the end of the 16th century had become generally known throughout Spain and Portugal, whence it passed into the rest of Europe, and into Turkey, Egypt, and India, notwithstanding that it was opposed by the severest enactments both of Christian and Mahommedan governments. It is commonly believed that the practice of smoking tobacco was much promoted in England, as well as in the north of Europe generally, by the example of Sir Walter Raleigh and his companions.

Tobacco was introduced into China, probably by way of Japan or Manila, during the 16th or 17th century, but its use was prohibited by the emperors both of the Ming and Tsing dynasties. It is now cultivated in most of the provinces, and is universally employed.[2]

The first tolerably exact description of the tobacco plant is that given by Gonzalo Fernandez de Oviedo y Valdés, governor of St. Domingo, in his *Historia general de las Indias*,[3] printed at Seville in 1535. In this work, the plant is said to be smoked through a branched tube of the shape of the letter Y, which the natives call *Tabaco*.

It was not until the middle of the 16th century that growing tobacco was seen in Europe,—first at Lisbon, whence the French ambassador, Jean Nicot, sent seeds to France in 1560 as those of a valuable medicinal plant, which was even then diffused throughout Portugal.[4]

Monardes,[5] writing in 1571, speaks of tobacco as brought to Spain a few years previously, and valued for its beauty and for its medicinal

[1] *Beiträge zur Ethnographie und Sprachenkunde Americas, zumal Brasiliens*, i. (1867) 719.

[2] Mayers in *Hong Kong Notes and Queries*, May, 1867; F. P. Smith, *Mat. Med. and Nat. Hist. of China*, 1871. 219.

[3] Lib. v. c. 2.

[4] Nicot, *Thrésor de la langue Françoyse*, Paris, 1606. 429.

[5] *Segunda parte del libro de las cosas que se traen de nuestras Indias occidentales, que sirven al uso de medicina.* Do se trata del Tabaco . . . . , Sevilla, 1571, 3.

virtues. Of the latter he gives a long account, noticing also the methods of smoking and chewing the herb prevalent among the Indians. He also supplies a small woodcut representing the plant, which he states to have white flowers, red in the centre.

Jacques Gohory,[1] who cultivated the plant in Paris at least as early as 1572, describes its flowers as shaded with red, and enumerates various medicinal preparations made from it.

In the *Maison Rustique* of Charles Estienne, edition of 1583, the author gives a "*Discours sur la Nicotiane ou Petum masclе,*" in which he claims for the plant the first place among medicinal herbs, on account of its singular and almost divine virtues.

The cultivation of tobacco in England, except on a very small scale in a physic garden, has been prohibited by law[2] since 1660.

Description—Amongst the various species of *Nicotiana* cultivated for the manufacturing of smoking tobacco and snuff, *N. Tabacum* is by far the most frequent, and is almost the only one named in the pharmacopœias as medicinal. Its simple stem, bearing at the summit a panicle of tubular pink flowers, and growing to the height of a man, has oblong, lanceolate simple leaves, with the margin entire. The lower leaves, more broadly lanceolate, and about 2 feet long by 6 inches wide, are shortly stalked. The stem-leaves are semi-amplexicaul, and decurrent at the base. Cultivation sometimes produces cordate-ovate forms of leaf, or a margin more or less uneven, or nearly revolute.

All the herbaceous parts of the plant are clothed with long soft hairs, made up of broad, ribbon-like, striated cells, the points of which exude a glutinous liquid. Small sessile glands are situated here and there on the surface of the leaf.[3] The lateral veins proceed from the thick midrib in straight lines, at angles of 40° to 75°, gently curving upwards only near the edge. In drying, the leaves become brittle and as thin as paper, and always acquire a brown colour. Even by the most careful treatment of a single leaf, it is not possible to preserve the green hue.

The smell of the fresh plant is narcotic; its taste bitter and nauseous. The characteristic odour of dried tobacco is developed during the process of curing.

Chemical Composition—The active principle of tobacco, first isolated in 1828 by Posselt and Reimann, is a volatile, highly poisonous alkaloid termed *Nicotine*, $C^{10}H^{14}N^2$. It is easily extracted from tobacco by means of alcohol or water, as a malate, from which the alkaloid can be separated by shaking it with caustic lye and ether. The ether is then expelled by warming the liquid, which finally has to be mixed with slaked lime and distilled in a stream of hydrogen, when the nicotine begins to come over at about 200° C.

Nicotine is a colourless oily liquid, of sp. gr. 1·027 at 15° C., deviating the plane of polarization to the left; it boils at 247° and

[1] *Instruction sur l'herbe Petum ditte en France l'herbe de la Royne ou Médicée* . . . Paris, 1572.

[2] 12 Car. II. c. 34; 15 Car. II. c. 7.—For further information on the history of tobacco, see Tiedemann, *Geschichte des Tabaks*, Frankfurt, 1854.—We have not consulted Fairholt, *Tobacco, its History*, Lond. 1859.

[3] Microscopic structure of tobacco leaves. See Pocklington, *Pharm. Journal*, v. (1874) 301.

does not concrete even at – 10° C. It has a strongly alkaline reaction, an unpleasant odour, and a burning taste. It quickly assumes a brown colour on exposure to air and light; and appears even to undergo an alteration by repeated distillation in an atmosphere deprived of oxygen. Nicotine dissolves in water, but separates on addition of caustic potash; it occurs in the dried leaves to the extent of about 6 per cent., but is subject to great variation. The seeds of tobacco are stated by Kosutany[1] as grown in Hungary to contain from 0·28 to 0·67 per cent. of the alkaloid.

It has not been met with in tobacco-smoke by Vohl and Eulenberg (1871), though other chemists assert its occurrence. The vapours were found by the former to contain numerous basic substances of the picolinic series, and ceded to caustic potash, hydrocyanic acid,[2] sulphuretted hydrogen, several volatile fatty acids, phenol and creasote. There was further observed in the imperfect combustion of tobacco the formation of laminæ fusible at 94° C., and having a composition $C^{19}H^{18}$. Oxide of carbon is also largely met with.

Tobacco leaves, whether fresh or dried, yield when distilled with water a turbid distillate in which, as observed by Hermbstädt in 1823, there are formed, after some days, crystals of *Nicotianin* or *Tobacco Camphor*. According to J. A. Barral, nicotianin contains 7·12 per cent. of nitrogen (?). By submitting 4 kilogrammes of good tobacco of the previous year to distillation with much water, we obtained nicotianin, floating on the surface of the distillate, in the form of minute acicular crystals, which we found to be devoid of action on polarized light. The crystals have no peculiar taste, at least in the small quantity we tried; they have a tobacco-like smell, perhaps simply due to the water adhering to them. When an attempt was made to separate them by a filter, they entirely disappeared, being probably dissolved by an accompanying trace of essential oil. The clear water showed an alkaline reaction partly due to *nicotine;* this was proved by adding a solution of tannic acid, which caused a well-marked turbidity. Nicotianine is in our opinion a fatty acid contaminated with a little volatile oil as in the case of Capsicum (see page 454), or Iris (see article Rhizome Iridis).

Among the ordinary constituents of leaves, tobacco contains albumin, resin and gum. In smoking, these substances, as well as the cellulose of the thick midrib, would yield products not agreeable to the consumer. The manufacturer therefore discards the midrib, and endeavours by further preparation to ensure at least the partial destruction of these unwelcome constituents, as well as the formation of certain products of fermentation (ferment-oils), which may perhaps contribute to the aroma of tobacco, especially when saccharine substances, liquorice, or alcohol, are added in the maceration to which tobacco is subjected.

Tobacco leaves are remarkably rich in inorganic constituents, the proportion varying from 16 to 27 per cent. According to Boussingault, they contain when dry about 1 per cent. of phosphoric acid, and from 3 to 5 per cent. of potash, together with 2½ to 4½ per cent. of nitrogen partly in the form of nitrate, so that to enable the tobacco plant to flourish, it must have a rich soil or continual manuring.[3]

[1] Dragendorff's *Jahresbericht*, 1874. 98.

[2] Poggiale and Marty (1870) stated hydrocyanic acid to be absent.

[3] For further particulars on the chemistry of tobacco cultivation see Boussingault, *Ann. de Chim. et de Phys.* ix. (1866) 50.

The lime, amounting to between a quarter and a half of the entire quantity of ash, is in the leaf combined with organic acids, especially malic, perhaps also citric. The proportion of potash varies greatly, but may amount to about 30 per cent. of the ash.

Commerce—There were imported into the United Kingdom in the year 1872, 45,549,700 lb. of unmanufactured tobacco, rather more than half of which was derived from the United States of America. The total value of the commodity thus imported was £1,563,382; and the duty levied upon the quantity retained for home consumption amounted to £6,694,037. In 1876 the consumption of tobacco had increased to 47,000,000 lb., *i. e.* 1½ lb. per head of the population.

In the United States 559,049 acres of land being in 1875 under cultivation with tobacco yielded a crop of 367,000,000 lb.

Uses—Tobacco has some reputation in the removal of alvine obstructions, but it is a medicine of great potency and is very rarely used.

Substitutes—Of the other species of *Nicotiana* cultivated as *Tobacco, N. rustica* L. is probably the most extensively grown. It is easily distinguished by its greenish yellow flowers, and its stalked ovate leaves. In spite of their coarser texture, the leaves dry more easily than those of *N. Tabacum,* and with some care may even be made to retain their green colour. *N. rustica* furnishes *East Indian Tobacco,* also the kinds known as *Latakia* and *Turkish Tobacco.*

N. persica Lindl. yields the tobacco of Shiraz. *N. quadrivalvis* Pursh, *N. multivalvis* Lindl. and *N. repanda* Willd. are also cultivated plants, the last named, a plant of Havana, being used in the manufacture of a much valued kind of cigar.

SCROPHULARIACEÆ.

FOLIA DIGITALIS.

Foxglove Leaves; F. *Feuilles de Digitale;* G. *Fingerhutblätter.*

Botanical Origin—*Digitalis purpurea* L., an elegant and stately plant, common throughout the greater part of Europe, but preferring siliceous soils and generally absent from limestone districts. It is found on the edges of woods and thickets, on bushy ground and commons, becoming a mountain plant in the warm parts of Europe. It occurs in the island of Madeira, in Portugal, Central and Southern Spain, Northern Italy, France, Germany, the British Isles and Southern Sweden, and in Norway as far as 63° N. lat.; it is however very unequally distributed, and is altogether wanting in the Swiss Alps and the Jura.[1] As a garden plant it is well known.

History—The Welsh "Physicians of Myddvai" appear to have frequently made use of foxglove for the preparation of external medicines.[2] Fuchs[3] and Tragus[4] figured the plant; the former gave it the

[1] Dr. R. Cunningham found (1868) *Digitalis purpurea* completely naturalized about San Carlos in the Island of Chiloe in Southern Chili.

[2] *Meddygon Myddfai* (see Appendix) in many places.

[3] *De Hist. Stirpium,* 1542. 892.

[4] *De Stirpium . . . nomenclaturis,* etc. 1552—"*Campanula sylvestris seu Digitalis.*"

name of *Digitalis*, remarking that up to the time at which he wrote, there was none for the plant in either Greek or Latin. At that period it was regarded as a violent medicine. Parkinson recommended it in 1640 in the "Theatrum botanicum," and it had a place in the London Pharmacopœia of 1650 and in several subsequent editions. The investigation of its therapeutic powers (1776–9) and its introduction into modern practice are chiefly due to Withering, a well-known English botanist and physician.[1]

The word *fox-glove* is said to be derived from the Anglo-Saxon *Foxes-glew*, i.e. *fox-music*, in allusion to an ancient musical instrument consisting of bells hung on an arched support.[2] In the Scandinavian idioms the plant bears likewise the name of *foxes bell*.

Description—Foxglove is a biennial or perennial, the leaves of which ought to be taken from the plant while in full flower. The lower leaves are ovate with the lamina running down into a long stalk; those of the stem become gradually narrower, passing into ovate-lanceolate with a short broadly-winged stalk, or are sessile. All have the margin crenate, crenate-dentate, or sub-serrate, are more or less softly pubescent or nearly glabrous on the upper side, much paler and densely pubescent on the under, which is marked with a prominent network of veins. The principal veins diverge at a very acute angle from the midrib, which is thick and fleshy. The lower leaves are often a foot or more long, by 5 to 6 inches broad; those of the stem are smaller.

When magnified, the tip of each crenature or serrature of the leaf is seen to be provided with a small, shining, wart-like gland. The hairs of the lower surface are simple, and composed of jointed cells which flatten in drying; those of the upper surface are shorter.

In preparing foxglove for medicinal use, it is the custom of some druggists to remove the whole of the petiole and the thicker part of the midrib, retaining only the thin lamina, which is dried with a gentle heat.[3] The fresh leaf has when bruised an unpleasant herbaceous smell, which in drying becomes agreeable and tea-like. The dried leaf has a very bitter taste.

Chemical Composition—Since the beginning of the present century, numerous attempts have been made to prepare the active principle of foxglove, and the name *Digitalin* has been successively bestowed on widely different substances.

Among the investigators engaged in these researches, we may point out Walz (1846-1858), Kosmann (1845-46, 1860), Homolle partly with Quévenne (1845-61), Nativelle (1872), and especially Schmiedeberg (1874).[4] The latter has prepared a new, well-defined, crystallizable principle, *Digitoxin*, from Digitalis. He exhausted with water the leaves previously dried and powdered, and then extracted them repeatedly with dilute alcohol, 50 per cent.; the

[1] Withering (William), *Account of the Fox-glove*, Birmingham, 1785. 8°.

[2] Prior, *Popular Names of British Plants*, ed. 2. 1870. 84.

[3] This method of preparing the leaf was directed in the London Pharmacopœia of 1851, but it had long been in use. No particular directions are given in the British Pharmacopœia.

[4] For further particulars on Schmiedeberg's very elaborate researches, the reader may consult my abstract of them in *Pharm. Journ.* v. (1875) 741.—F.A.F.

tincture thus obtained was then mixed with basic acetate of lead as long as it produced a precipitate. The latter being separated, the filtered liquid was concentrated and the deposit now formed, after some days, removed from the aqueous liquid. It was then washed with a dilute solution of carbonate of sodium, by which a yellow matter (*chrysophan?*) was partly removed. The substance was then dried, and yielded to chloroform a brownish mass, which after the chloroform had been driven off, was purified by benzin. This liquid dissolved the remainder of the yellow or orange matter, and a little fat, leaving crude digitoxin, which is to be purified by recrystallization from warm alcohol, 80 per cent., adding a little charcoal. This purification still yields yellowish crystals, which ought to be washed again with carbonate of sodium, ether or benzin, and then recrystallized from warm absolute alcohol, containing a little chloroform. This process, however, will only afford colourless crystals provided it be so performed as to cause the separation of digitoxin on account of the cooling of the solution, not by the evaporation of the solvent. If the liquid is instead allowed to evaporate it will soon assume a darker coloration. In the way just pointed out, perfectly colourless scales or needle-shaped crystals of pure digitoxin are at length formed, the yield being not more considerable than about *one* part from 10,000 of dried leaves.

Digitoxin is insoluble in water, to which it does not even impart its intensely bitter taste as displayed in the alcoholic solution. It is likewise insoluble in benzin or bisulphide of carbon, very sparingly soluble in ether, more abundantly so in chloroform, the latter liquid however acting but very slowly on digitoxin. Its best solvent is alcohol, either cold or warm. The composition of digitoxin answers to the formula, $C^{21}H^{32}O^{7}$.

Digitoxin warmed with concentrated hydrochloric acid assumes a yellow or greenish hue, the same which is commonly attributed to commercial "digitalin." Digitoxin is not a saccharogenous matter; in alcoholic solution it is decomposed by dilute acids, and then affords *Toxiresin*, an uncrystallizable, yellowish substance, which may easily be separated on account of its ready solubility in ether; it appears to be produced also if digitoxin is maintained for some time in the state of fusion at about 240° C. Toxiresin proved to be a very powerful poison, acting energetically on the heart and muscles of frogs. The very specific action of foxglove is due—*not* exclusively—to digitoxin; it is so highly poisonous that Schmiedeberg thinks it not at all fit for medicinal use, which might rather be confined to other constituents of foxglove, as, for instance, to those obtained from the seeds under the names of digitalin and digitaléin. The latter, however, are of more difficult extraction than digitoxin.

The preparation of digitoxin is similar to that of *Nativelle's* crystallized "digitalin;" the former as well as paradigitogenin[1] are largely found in Nativelle's digitalin.

The *Digitalin of Nativelle*—The researches on digitalis of this chemist, for which the Orfila prize of 6000 francs was awarded in 1872, have resulted in the extraction of a crystallized preparation

[1] A derivative of *digitoxin* as extracted by Schmiedeberg from the seeds of foxglove.

possessing active medicinal properties. It may be obtained by the following process:—

The leaves, previously exhausted by water, are extracted by means of alcohol, sp. gr. ·930. The tincture is concentrated until its weight is equal to that of the leaves used, and then diluted by adding thrice its weight of water. A pitch-like deposit is then formed; *digitaléin* and other substances remaining in solution. The deposit dried on blotting paper is boiled with double its weight of alcohol, sp. gr. ·907; on cooling, crystals are slowly deposited during some days. They should be washed with a little diluted alcohol (·958) and dried: to purify them, they should be first recrystallized from chloroform, and subsequently from boiling alcohol sp. gr. ·828, some charcoal being used at the same time. Digitalin is thus obtained in *colourless needle-shaped crystals*. It assumes an intense emerald green colour when moistened with hydrochloric acid, and has an extremely bitter taste. On the animal economy, it displays all the peculiar effects of digitalis, the dose of a milligramme taken by an adult person once or twice a day occasioning somewhat alarming symptoms, but smaller doses exhibiting the sedative power of the herb.

Another body occurring in foxglove is the crystallizable sugar called *Inosite*, which was detected by Marmé in the leaves, as well as in those of dandelion (p. 394). Pectic matters are also present in foxglove leaves.

Uses—Foxglove is a very potent drug, having the effect of reducing the frequency and force of the heart's action, and hence is given in special cases as a sedative; it is also employed as a diuretic.

Adulteration—The dried leaves of some other plants have occasionally been supplied for those of foxglove. Such are the leaves of *Verbascum*, which are easily recognized by their thick coat of branched stellate hairs; of *Inula Conyza* DC. and *I. Helenium* L., which have the margin almost entire, and in the latter plant the veins diverging nearly at a right angle from the midrib; in both plants the under side of the leaf is less strongly reticulated than in foxglove. But to avoid all chance of mistake, it is desirable that druggists should purchase the *fresh flowering plant*, which cannot be confounded with any other, and strip and dry the leaves for themselves.

ACANTHACEÆ.

HERBA ANDROGRAPHIDIS.

Kariyát or Creyat.

Botanical Origin—*Andrographis*[1] *paniculata* Nees ab E. (*Justicia* Burm.), an annual herb, 1 to 2 feet high, common throughout India, growing under the shade of trees. It is found likewise in Ceylon and Java, and has been introduced into the West Indies. In some districts of India it is cultivated.

[1] *Andrographis* from ἀνήρ and γραφίς, in allusion to the brush-like anther and filament.—Fig. in Bentley and Trimen's *Med. Plants*, part 23 (1877).

History—It is probable that in ancient Hindu medicine this plant was administered indiscriminately with chiretta, which, with several other species of *Ophelia*, is known in India by nearly the same vernacular names. Ainslie asserts that it was a component of a famous bitter tincture called by the Portuguese of India *Droga amara;* but on consulting the authority he quotes[1] we find that the bitter employed in that medicine was *Calumba*. *Andrographis* is known in Bengal as *Mahā-tīta*, literally *king of bitters*, from the Sanskrit tikta, "bitter," a title of which it has been thought so far deserving that it has been admitted to a place in the *Pharmacopœia of India*.

Description—The straight, knotty branch stems are obtusely quadrangular, about ¼ of an inch thick at the base, of a dark green colour and longitudinally furrowed. The leaves are opposite, petiolate, lanceolate, entire, the largest ½ an inch or more wide and 3 inches long. Their upper surface is dark green, the under somewhat lighter, and as seen under a lens finely granular. The leaves are very thin, brittle, and, like the stems, entirely glabrous.

In the well-dried specimen before us, for which we are indebted to Dr. G. Bidie of Madras, flowers are wanting and only a few roots are present. The latter are tapering and simple, emitting numerous thin rootlets, greyish externally, woody and whitish within. The plant is inodorous and has a persistent pure bitter taste.

Chemical Composition—The aqueous infusion of the herb exhibits a slight acid reaction, and has an intensely bitter taste, which appears due to an indifferent, non-basic principle, for the usual reagents do not indicate the presence of an alkaloid. Tannic acid on the other hand produces an abundant precipitate, a compound of itself with the bitter principle. The infusion is but little altered by the salts of iron; it contains a considerable quantity of chloride of sodium.

Uses—Employed as a pure bitter tonic like quassia, gentian, or chiretta, with the last of which it is sometimes confounded.

SESAMEÆ.

OLEUM SESAMI.

Sesamé Oil, Gingeli, Gingili or Jinjili Oil, Til or Teel Oil, Benné Oil; F. *Huile de Sésame;* G. *Sesamöl.*

Botanical Origin—*Sesamum indicum* DC., an erect, pubescent annual herb, 2 to 4 feet high,[2] indigenous to India, but propagated by cultivation throughout the warmer regions of the globe, and not now found anywhere in the wild state. In Europe, *Sesamum* is only grown in some districts of Turkey and Greece, and on a small scale in Sicily and in the islands of Malta and Gozo. It does not succeed well even in the South of France.

History—Sesamé is a plant which we find on the authority of the

[1] Paolino da San Bartolomeo, *Voyage to the East Indies* (1776-1789), translated from the German, Lond. 1800. pp. 14. 409.

[2] Fig. in Bentley and Trimen's *Med. Plants*, part 23 (1877).

most ancient documents of Egyptian, Hebrew,[1] Sanskrit, Greek, and Roman literature, has been used by mankind for the sake of its oily seeds from the earliest times. The Egyptian name *Semsemt* already occurring in the Papyrus Ebers, is still existing in the Coptic *Semsem*, the Arabic *Simsim*, and the modern *Sesamum*. The Indian languages have their own terms for it, the Hindustani *Til*, from the Sanskrit *Tila*, being one of the best known.[2] *Tila* already occurs in the Vedic literature. In the days of Pliny the oil was an export from Sind to Europe by way of the Red Sea, precisely as the seeds are at the present day.

During the middle ages the plant, then known as *Suseman* or *Sempsen*, was cultivated in Cyprus, Egypt and Sicily; the oil was an article of import from Alexandria to Venice. Joachim Camerarius gave a good figure of the plant in his "Hortus medicus et philosophicus" 1588 (tab. 44). In modern times sesamé oil gave way to that of olives, yet at present it is an article which, if not so renowned, is at least of far greater consumption.

Production—The plant comes to perfection within 3 or 4 months; its capsule contains numerous flat seeds, which are about $\frac{2}{10}$ of an inch long by $\frac{1}{20}$ thick, and weigh on an average $\frac{1}{18}$ of a grain. To collect them, the plant when mature is cut down, and stacked in heaps for a few days, after which it is exposed to the sun during the day, but collected again into heaps at night. By this process the capsules gradually ripen and burst, and the seeds fall out.[3]

The plant is found in several varieties affording respectively white, yellowish, reddish, brown or black seeds. The dark seeds may be deprived of a part of their colouring matter by washing, which is sometimes done with a view to obtain a paler oil.[4]

We obtained from yellowish seeds 56 per cent. of oil; on a large scale, the yield varies with the variety of seed employed and the process of pressing, from 45 to 50 per cent.

Description—The best kinds of sesamé oil have a mild agreeable taste, a light yellowish colour, and scarcely any odour; but in these respects the oil is liable to vary with the circumstances already mentioned. The white seeds produced in Sind are reputed to yield the finest oil.

We prepared some oil by means of ether, and found it to have a sp. gr. of 0·919 at 23° C.; it solidified at 5° C., becoming rather turbid at some degrees above this temperature. Yet sesamé oil is more fluid at ordinary temperatures than ground-nut oil, and is less prone to change by the influence of the air. It is in fact, when of fine quality, one of the less alterable oils.

Chemical Composition—The oil is a mixture of olein, stearin and

[1] Isaiah xxviii. 27.

[2] The word *Gingeli* (or *Gergelim*), which Roxburgh remarks was (as it is now) in common use among Europeans, derives from the Arabic *chulchulân*, denoting sesame seed in its husks before being reaped (Dr. Rice). The word *Benné* is, we believe, of West African origin, and has no connection with *Ben*, the name of *Moringa*.

[3] For further particulars see Buchanan, *Journey from Madras through Mysore, etc.* i. (1807) 95. and ii. 224.

[4] This curious process is described in the *Reports of Juries, Madras Exhibition*, 1856, p. 31.—That the colouring matter of the seeds is actually soluble in water is confirmed by Lépine of Pondicherry as we have learnt from his manuscript notes presented to the Musée des Produits des Colonies de France at Paris. The seeds may even be used as a dye.

other compounds of glycerin with acids of the fatty series. We prepared with it in the usual way a lead plaster, and treated the latter with ether in order to remove the oleate of lead. The solution was then decomposed by sulphuretted hydrogen, evaporated and exposed to hyponitric vapours. By this process we obtained 72·6 per cent. of *Elaïdic Acid.* The specimen of sesamé oil prepared by ourselves consequently contained 76·0 per cent. of olein, inasmuch as it must be supposed to be present in the form of triolein. In commercial oils the amount of olein is certainly not constant.

As to the solid part of the oil, we succeeded in removing fatty acids, freely melting, after repeated crystallizations, at 67° C., which may consist of stearic acid mixed with one or more of the allied homologous acids, as palmitic and myristic. By precipitating with acetate of magnesium, as proposed by Heintz, we finally isolated acids melting at 52·5 to 53°, 62 to 63°, and 69·2° C., which correspond to myristic, palmitic and stearic acids.

The small proportion of solid matter which separates from the oil on congelation cannot be removed by pressure, for even at many degrees below the freezing point it remains as a soft magma. In this respect sesamé oil differs from that of olive.

Sesamé oil contains an extremely small quantity of a substance, perhaps resinoid, which has not yet been isolated. It may be obtained in solution by repeatedly shaking 5 volumes of the oil with one of glacial acetic acid. If a cold mixture of equal weights of sulphuric and nitric acids is added in like volume, the acetic solution acquires a greenish yellow hue. The same experiment being made with spirit of wine substituted for acetic acid, the mixture assumes a blue colour, quickly changing to greenish yellow. The oil itself being gently shaken with sulphuric and nitric acids, takes a fine green hue, as shown in 1852 by Behrens, who at the same time pointed out that no other oil exhibits this reaction. It takes place even with the bleached and perfectly colourless oil. Sesamé oil added to other oils, if to a larger extent than 10 per cent., may be recognised by this test. The reaction ought to be observed with small quantities, say 1 gramme of the oil and 1 gramme of the acid mixture, previously cooled.

Commerce—The commercial importance of Sesamé may be at once illustrated by the fact that France imported in 1870, 83 millions; in 1871, 57½ millions; and 1872, 50 millions of kilogrammes (984,693 cwt.) of the seed.[1]

The quantity shipped from British India in the year 1871-72 was 565,854 cwt., of which France took no less than 495,414 cwt.[2] The imports of the seed into the United Kingdom in 1870 were to the value of only about £13,000.

Sesamé is extensively produced in Corea and in the Chinese island of Formosa, which in 1869 exported the exceptionally large quantity of 46,000 peculs[3] (1 pecul = 133 lb.). Zanzibar and Mozambique also furnish considerable quantities of sesamé, whilst on the West Coast of

[1] *Documents Statistiques réunis par l'Administration des Douanes sur le commerce de la France*, année 1872.

[2] *Statement of the Trade and Navigation of British India with Foreign Countries*, Calcutta, 1872. 62.

[3] *Reports on Trade at the Treaty Ports in China for* 1870, Shanghai, 1871. 81.

Africa the staple oil-seed is Ground-nut (*Arachis hypogæa* L. p. 186). The chief place for the manufacture of sesamé oil is Marseilles.

Uses—Good sesamé oil might be employed without disadvantage for all the purposes for which olive oil is used.[1] As its congealing point is some degrees below that of olive oil, it is even more fitted for cool climates. Sesamé seeds are largely consumed as food both in India and Tropical Africa. The foliage of the plant abounds in mucilage, and in the United States is sometimes used in the form of poultice.

LABIATÆ.

FLORES LAVANDULÆ.

Lavender Flowers; F. Fleurs de Lavande; G. Lavendelblumen.

Botanical Origin—*Lavandula vera* DC., a shrubby plant growing in the wild state from 1 to 2 feet high, but attaining 3 feet or more under cultivation. It is indigenous to the mountainous regions of the countries bordering the western half of the Mediterranean basin. Thus it occurs in Eastern Spain, Southern France (extending northward to Lyons and Dauphiny), in Upper Italy, Corsica, Calabria and Northern Africa,—on the outside of the olive region.[2] In cultivation it grows very well in the open air throughout the greater part of Germany and as far north as Norway and Livonia; the northern plant would even appear to be more fragrant, according to Schübeler.[3]

History—There has been much learned investigation in order to identify lavender in the writings of the classical authors, but the result has not been satisfactory, and no allusion has been found which unquestionably refers either to *L. vera* or to *L. Spica*,[4] whereas *L. Stœchas* was perfectly familiar to the ancients.

The earliest mention of lavender that we have observed, occurs in the writings of the abbess Hildegard,[5] who lived near Bingen on the Rhine during the 12th century, and who in a chapter *De Lavendula* alludes to the strong odour and many virtues of the plant. In a poem of the school of Salerno entitled *Flos Medicinæ*[6] occur the following lines:—

> "Salvia, castoreum, *lavendula*, primula veris,
> Nasturtium, athanas hæc sanant paralytica membra."

In 1387 cushions of satin were made for King Charles VI. of France, to be stuffed with "*lavende*."[7] Its use was also popular at an early period in the British isles, for we find "*Llafant*" or "*Llafanllys*" mentioned among the remedies of the "Physicians of Myddvai."[8] And

[1] For pharmaceutical uses, the larger proportion of olein and consequent lesser tendency to solidify, should be remembered.

[2] On Mont Ventoux near Avignon, the region of *Lavandula vera* is comprised, according to Martins, between 1500 and 4500 feet above the sea-level.—*Ann. des Sc. Nat.*, Bot. x. (1838) 145. 149.

[3] *Pflanzenwelt Norwegens*, Christiania (1873-1875) 260.

[4] F. de Gingins-Lassaraz, *Hist. des Lavandes*, Genève et Paris, 1826.

[5] *Opera Omnia*, accurante J. P. Migne, Paris, 1855. 1143.

[6] S. de Renzi, *Collectio Salernitana*, Napoli, i. 417-516.

[7] Douët d'Arcq, *Comptes de l'Argenterie des rois de France*, ii. (1874) 148.

[8] *Meddygon Myddfai* (see Appendix) 287.

in Walton's "Description of an inn," about the year 1680 to 1690, we find the walls stuck round with ballads, where the sheets smelt of *lavender*. . . .[1]

Lavender was well known to the botanist of the 16th century.

Description—The flowers of Common Lavender are produced in a lax terminal spike, supported on a long naked stalk. They are arranged in 6 to 10 whorls (verticillasters), the lowest being generally far remote from those above it. A whorl consists of two cymes, each having, when fully developed, about three flowers, below which is a rhomboidal acuminate bract, as well as several narrow smaller bracts belonging to the particular flowers. The calyx is tubular, contracted towards the mouth, marked with 13 nerves and 5-toothed, the posterior tooth much larger than the others. The corolla of a violet colour is tubular, two-lipped, the upper lip with two, the lower with three lobes. Both corolla and calyx, as well as the leaves and stalks, are clothed with a dense tomentum of stellate hairs, amongst which minute shining oil-glands can be seen by the aid of a lens.

The flowers emit when rubbed a delightful fragrance, and have a pleasant aromatic taste. The leaves of the plant are oblong linear, or lanceolate, revolute at the margin and very hoary when young.

For pharmaceutical use or as a perfume, lavender flowers are stripped from the stalks and dried by a gentle heat. They are but seldom kept in the shops, being grown almost entirely for the sake of their essential oil.

Production of Essential Oil—Lavender is cultivated in the parishes of Mitcham, Carshalton and Beddington and a few adjoining localities, all in Surrey, to the extent of about 300 acres. It is also grown at Market Deeping in Lincolnshire; also at Hitchin in Hertfordshire, where lavender was apparently cultivated as early as the year 1568.[2]

At the latter place there were in 1871 about 50 acres so cropped.

The plants which are of a small size, and grown in rows in dry open fields, flower in July and August. The flowers are usually cut with the stalks of full length, tied up in mats, and carried to the distillery there to await distillation. This is performed in the same large stills that are used for peppermint. The flowers are commonly distilled with the stalks as gathered, and either fresh, or in a more or less dry state. A few cultivators distill only the flowering heads, thereby obtaining a superior product. Still more rarely, the flowers are stripped from the stalks, and the latter rejected *in toto*.[3] According to the careful experiments of Bell,[4] the oil made in this last method is of exceedingly fine quality. The produce he obtained in 1846 was $26\frac{1}{2}$ ounces per 100 lb. of flowers, entirely freed from stalks; in 1847, $25\frac{1}{2}$ ounces; and in 1848, 20 ounces: the quantities of flowers used in the respective years were 417, 633, and 923 lb. Oil distilled from the stalks alone was found to have a peculiar rank odour. In the distillation of

[1] Macaulay, *Hist. of England*, i. ch. 3, Inns.

[2] Perhs, *Proc. American Pharm. Association*, 1876. 819.

[3] For more particulars see the interesting account of Holmes, *Pharm. Journ.* viii. (1877) 301. The author describes also the disease which is affecting the lavender since about the year 1860.

[4] *Pharm. Journ.* viii. (1849) 276.

lavender, it is said that the oil which comes over in the earlier part of the operation is of superior flavour.

We have no accurate data as to the produce of oil obtained in the ordinary way, but it is universally stated to vary extremely with the season. Warren[1] gives it as 10 to 12 lb., and in an exceptional case as much as 24 lb. from the acre of ground under cultivation. At Hitchin,[2] the yield would appear to approximate to the last-named quantity. The experiments performed in Bell's laboratory as detailed above, show that the flowers deprived of stalks afforded on an average exactly 1½ per cent. of essential oil.

Oil of *Lavandula vera* is distilled in Piedmont, and in the mountainous parts of the South of France, as in the villages about Mont Ventoux near Avignon, and in those some leagues west of Montpellier (St. Guilhen-le-désert, Montarnaud and St. Jean de Fos)—in all cases from the wild plant. This foreign oil is offered in commerce of several qualities, the highest of which commands scarcely one-sixth the price of the oil produced at Mitcham.[3] The cheaper sorts at least are obtained by distilling the *entire plant.*

Chemical Composition—The only constituent of lavender flowers that has attracted the attention of chemists is the essential oil (*Oleum Lavandulæ*). It is a pale yellow, mobile liquid, varying in sp. gr. from 0·87 to 0·94 (Zeller), having a very agreeable odour of the flowers and a strong aromatic taste. The oil distilled at Mitcham (1871) we find to rotate the plane of polarization 4·2° to the left, in a column of 50 mm.

Oil of lavender seems to be a mixture in variable proportions of oxygenated oils and stearoptene, the latter being identical, according to Dumas, with common camphor. In some samples it is said to exist to the extent of one-half, and to be sometimes deposited from the oil in cold weather; we have not however been able to ascertain this fact. The oil according to Lallemand (1859) appears also to contain compound ethers.

Commerce—Dried lavender flowers are the object of some trade in the south of Europe. According to the official *Tableau général du Commerce de la France,* Lavender and Orange Flowers (which are not separated) were exported in 1870 to the extent of 110,958 kilo. (244,741 lb.),—chiefly to the Barbary States, Turkey and America. There are no data to show the amount of oil of lavender imported into England.

Uses—Lavender flowers are not prescribed in modern English medicine. The volatile oil has the stimulant properties common to bodies of the same class and is much used as a perfume.

Other Species of Lavender.

1. *Lavandula Spica* DC. is a plant having a very close resemblance to *L. vera,* of which Linnæus considered it a variety, though its distinctness is now admitted. It occurs over much of the area of *L. vera,* but does not extend so far north, nor is it found in such elevated situa-

[1] *Pharm. Journ.* vi. (1865) 257.

[2] *Ibid.* i. (1860) 278. The statement is that an acre of land yields "*about 6 Winchester quarts*" of oil.—One Winchester quart = 282 litres.

[3] The Mitcham oil fetches 30s. to 60s. per lb., according to the season.

tions, or beyond the limit of the olive. It is in fact a more southern plant and more susceptible to cold, so that it cannot be cultivated in the open soil in Britain except in sheltered positions. In Languedoc and Provence, it is the common species from the sea-level up to about 2000 feet, where it is met by the more hardy *L. vera*.[1]

Lavandula Spica is distilled in the south of France, the flowering wild plant in its entire state being used. The essential oil, which is termed in French *Essence d'Aspic*, is known to English druggists as *Oleum Lavandulæ spicæ*, *Oleum Spicæ*, or *Oil of Spike*. It resembles true oil of lavender, but compared with that distilled in England it has a much less delicate fragrance. This however may depend upon the frequent adulteration, for we find that flowers of the two plants (*L. vera* and *L. Spica*) grown side by side in an English garden, are hardly distinguishable in fragrance. Porta already even, in speaking of the oil of lavender flowers, stated:[2] "e *spica fragrantior* excipitur, ut illud quod ex Gallia provenit . . . ."—Lallemand (1859) isolated from oil of spike a camphor which he believes to be identical with common camphor.

Oil of Spike is used in porcelain painting and in veterinary medicine.

2. ***Lavandula Stœchas*** L.—This plant was well known to the ancients; Dioscorides remarks that it gives a name to the Stœchades, the modern isles of Hières near Toulon, where the plant still abounds. It has a wider range than the two species of *Lavandula* already described, for it is found in the Canaries and in Portugal, and eastward throughout the Mediterranean region to Constantinople and Asia Minor. It may at once be known from the other lavenders by its flower-spike being on a *short* stalk, and terminating in 2 or 3 conspicuous purple bracts.

The flowers, called *Flores Stœchados* or *Stœchas arabica*,[3] were formerly kept in the shops, and had a place in the London Pharmacopœia down to 1746. We are not aware that they are, or ever were distilled for essential oil, though they are stated to be the source of *True Oil of Spike*.[4]

HERBA MENTHÆ VIRIDIS.

Spearmint.

Botanical Origin—*Mentha viridis* L. is a fragrant perennial plant, chiefly known in Europe, Asia and North America, as the Common Mint of gardens, and only found apparently wild in countries where it has long been cultivated. It occurs occasionally in Britain under such circumstances.[5]

[1] On the high land between Nice and Turbia, I have observed the two species growing together, and that *L. vera* is in flower two or three weeks earlier than *L. Spica*.—D. H.

[2] *De distillatione*, Romæ, 1608. 87.

[3] The incorrectness of the term *Arabica* is noticed by Pomet. How it came to be applied we know not.

[4] Pereira, *Elem. of Mat. Med.* ii. (1850) 1368.—Nor do we know if *L. lanata* Boiss., a very fragrant species closely allied to *L. Spica* DC., and a native of Spain, is distilled in that country.

[5] Bentham, *Handbook of the British Flora*, 1858. 413.—Parkinson (1640) remarks of *Speare Mint* that it is "onely found planted in gardens with us."

Mentha viridis is regarded by Bentham as not improbably a variety of *M. silvestris* L., perpetuated through its ready propagation by suckers. J. G. Baker remarks, that while these two plants are sufficiently distinct as found in England, yet continental forms occur which bridge over their differences.[1]

History—Mint is mentioned in all early mediæval lists of plants, and was certainly cultivated in the convent gardens of the 9th century. Turner, who has been called "the father of English botany," states in his *Herball*[2] that the garden mint of his time was also called "*Spere Mynte*." We find spearmint also described by Gerarde who terms it *Mentha Romana* vel *Sarracenica*, or *Common Garden Mint*, but his statement that the leaves are *white*, *soft*, and *hairy* does not well apply to the plant as now found in cultivation.

Description—Spearmint has a perennial root-stock which throws out long runners. Its stem 2 to 3 feet high is erect, when luxuriant branched below with short erecto-patent branches, firm, quadrangular, naked or slightly hairy beneath the nodes, often brightly tinged with purple. Leaves sessile or the lower slightly stalked, lanceolate or ovate-lanceolate, rounded or even cordate at the base, dark green and glabrous above, paler and prominently veined with green or purple beneath, rather thickly glandular, but either quite naked or hairy only on the midrib and principal veins, the point narrowed out and acute, the teeth sharp but neither very close nor deep, the lowest leaves measuring about 1 inch across by 3 or 4 inches long. Inflorescence a panicled arrangement of spikes, of which the main one is 3 or 4 inches long by $\frac{3}{8}$ inch wide, the lowest whorls sometimes $\frac{1}{2}$ an inch from each other and the lowest bracts leafy. Bracteoles linear-subulate, equalling or exceeding the expanded flowers, smooth or slightly ciliated. Pedicels about $\frac{3}{4}$ line long, purplish glandular, but never hairy. Calyx also often purplish, the tube campanulato-cylindrical, $\frac{3}{8}$ line long, the teeth lanceolate-subulate, equalling the tube, the flower part of which is naked, but the teeth and often the upper part clothed more or less densely with erecto-patent hairs. Corolla reddish-purple, about twice as long as the calyx, naked both within and without. Not smooth.

The plant varies slightly in the shape of its leaves, elongation of spike and hairiness of calyx. The entire plant emits a most fragrant odour when rubbed, and has a pungent aromatic taste.

Production—Spearmint is grown in kitchen gardens, and more largely in market gardens. A few acres are under cultivation with it at Mitcham, chiefly for the sake of the herb, which is sold mostly in a dried state.

The cultivation of spearmint is carried on in the United States in precisely the same manner as that of peppermint, but on a much smaller scale. Mr. H. G. Hotchkiss of Lyons, Wayne County, State of New York, has informed us that his manufacture of the essential oil amounted in 1870 to 1162 lb. The plant he employs appears from the specimen with which he has favoured us, to be identical with the spearmint of English gardens, and is not the Curled Mint (*Mentha crispa*) of Germany.

[1] Seemann's *Journal of Botany*, Aug. 1865. p. 239. We borrow Mr. Baker's careful description of *Mentha viridis*.

[2] Part 2. (1568) 54.

Chemical Composition—Spearmint yields an essential oil (*Oleum Menthæ viridis*) in which reside the medicinal virtues of the plant. Kane,[1] who examined it, gives its sp. gr. as 0·914, and its boiling point as 160° C. The oil yielded him a considerable amount of stearoptene. Gladstone[2] found spearmint oil to contain a hydrocarbon almost identical with oil of turpentine in odour and other physical properties, mixed with an oxidized oil to which is due the peculiar smell of the plant. The latter oil boils at 225° C.; its sp. gr. is 0·951, and it was found to be isomeric with carvol, $C^{10}H^{14}O$. According to our experiments the oil, distilled from Curled Mint grown in Germany, deviates the plane of polarization 37°·4 to the left when examined in a column of 100 millimetres. We prepared from it the crystallized compound $(C^{10}H^{14}O)^2SH^2$, and isolated from it the liquid $C^{10}H^{14}O$, which differs from carvol (see Fructus Carui, page 306) by its levogyrate power.[3]

Uses—Spearmint is used in the form of essential oil and distilled water, precisely in the same manner as peppermint. In the United States the oil is also employed by confectioners and the manufacturers of perfumed soap.

Substitutes—Oil of spearmint is now rarely distilled in England, its high cost[4] causing it to be nearly unsaleable. The cheaper foreign oil is offered in price-currents as of two kinds, namely *American* and *German*. Of the first we have already spoken: the second, termed in German *Krauseminzöl*, is the produce of *Mentha aquatica* L. var. γ *crispa* Bentham, a plant cultivated in Northern Germany. Its oil seems to agree with the oil of spearmint.

HERBA MENTHÆ PIPERITÆ.

Peppermint; F. Menthe poivrée; G. Pfefferminze.

Botanical Origin—*Mentha piperita* Hudson (non Linn.), an erect usually glabrous perennial, much resembling the Common Spearmint of the gardens, but differing from it in having the leaves all stalked, the flowers larger, the upper whorls of flowers somewhat crowded together, and the lower separate. In the opinion of Bentham it is possibly a mere variety of *M. hirsuta* L., with which it can be connected by numerous intermediate forms.

Peppermint rapidly propagates itself by runners, and is now found in wet places in several parts of England, as well as on the Continent. It is cultivated on the large scale in England, France, Germany, and North America.

History—*Mentha piperita* was first observed in Hertfordshire by Dr. Eales, and communicated to Ray, who in the second edition of his *Synopsis Stirpium Britannicarum*, 1696, noticed it under the name of *Mentha spicis brevioribus et habitioribus, foliis Menthæ fuscæ, sapore fervido piperis*; and in his *Historia Plantarum*[5] as "*Mentha palustris*

[1] *Philosophical Magazine*, xiii. (1838) 444.

[2] *Journ. of Chemical Society*, ii. (1854) 11.

[3] Flückiger, *Pharm. Journ.* vii. (1876) 75.

[4] Price from 1824 to 1839, 40*s*. to 48*s*. per lb.

[5] Tomus iii. (1704) 284.

. . . *Peper-Mint*."[1] Dale, who found the plant in the adjoining county of Essex, states[2] that it is esteemed a specific in renal and vesical calculus; and Ray, in the third edition of his *Synopsis*, declares it superior to all other mints as a remedy for weakness of the stomach and for diarrhœa. Peppermint was admitted to the London Pharmacopœia in 1721, under the designation of *Mentha piperitis sapore*.

The cultivation of peppermint at Mitcham in Surrey dates from about 1750,[3] at which period only a few acres of ground were there devoted to medicinal plants. At the end of the last century, above 100 acres were cropped with peppermint. But so late as 1805 there were no stills at Mitcham, and the herb had to be carried to London for the extraction of the oil. Of late years the cultivation has diminished in extent, by reason of the increased value of land and the competition of foreign oil of peppermint.

On the Continent Mentha Piperitis was grown as early as 1771 at Utrecht; Gaubius[4] appears to have been the first to notice "*Camphora Europæa Menthæ Piperitidis*," i.e. Menthol (see page 483).

In Germany peppermint became practically known in the latter half of the last century, especially through the recommendation of Knigge.[5]

Description—The rootstock of peppermint is perennial, throwing out runners. The stem is erect, 3 to 4 feet high, when luxuriant somewhat branched below with erecto-patent branches, firm, quadrangular, slightly hairy, often tinged with purple. Leaves all stalked, the stalks of the lower ½ to ¾ of an inch long, naked or nearly so, the leaf lanceolate, narrowed or rather rounded towards the base, the point narrowed out and acute, the lowest 2 to 3 inches long by about ¾ of an inch broad, naked and dull green above, paler and glandular all over, but only slightly hairy upon the veins beneath; the teeth sharp, fine, and erecto-patent. Inflorescence in a loose lanceolate or acutely conical spike, 2 to 3 inches long by about ¾ of an inch broad at the base, the lowest whorls separate, and usually the lowest bracts leaf-like. Bracteoles lanceolate acuminate, about equalling the expanded flowers, slightly ciliated. Pedicels 1 to 1½ lines long, purplish, glandular but not hairy. Calyx often purplish, the tube about 1 line long and the teeth ½ a line, the tube campanulate-cylindrical, purplish, not hairy, but dotted over with prominent glands; the teeth lanceolate subulate, furnished with short erecto-patent hairs. Corolla reddish purple about twice as long as the calyx, naked both within and without. Nut smooth[6] (*rugose*, according to our observation). The odour and taste are strongly aromatic.

In var. 2. *vulgaris* of Sole, *M. piperita β*. Smith, the plant is more hairy, with the spikes broader and shorter, or even bluntly capitate.

Chemical Composition—The constituent for the sake of which peppermint is cultivated is the essential oil, *Oleum Menthæ piperitæ*, a

[1] I have examined the original specimen still preserved among Ray's plants in the British Museum and find it to agree perfectly with the plant now in cultivation.—D. H.

[2] *Pharmacologiæ Supplementum*, Lond. 1705. 117.

[3] Lysons, *Environs of London*, i. (1800) 254.

[4] *Adversariorum varii argumenti liber unus*, Leidæ, 1771. 99.

[5] *De Menthâ Piperitide Commentatio*, Erlangæ, 1780.

[6] This description is borrowed from Mr. Baker's paper on the English Mints, referred to at page 480, note 1.

colourless, pale yellow, or greenish liquid, of sp. gr. varying from 0·84 to 0·92. We learn from information kindly supplied by Messrs. Schimmel and Co., Leipzig, that the best peppermint grown in Germany, carefully dried, affords from 1 to 1·25 per cent. of oil. It has a strong and agreeable odour, with a powerful aromatic taste, followed by a sensation of cold when air is drawn into the mouth. We find that the Mitcham oil examined by polarized light in a column 50 mm. long, deviates from 14°·2 to 10°·7 to the left, American oil 4°·3.

When oil of peppermint is cooled to –4° C., it sometimes deposits colourless hexagonal crystals of *Peppermint Camphor*, $C^{10}H^{19}OH$, called also *Menthol*. We have never observed it, nor are we aware that menthol has been noticed in America. but it is largely afforded by eastern mints, and found in commerce under the name of *Chinese* or *Japanese Oil of Peppermint*,[1] either liquid, and easily depositing the camphor, or also forming a crystalline mass impregnated with the liquid oil.

Pure menthol has the exquisite odour and taste of peppermint; it forms hexagonal crystals, melting at 42° C., and boiling at 212° C. By distilling menthol with P^2O^5 it yields menthene, $C^{10}H^{18}$, a levogyrate liquid, boiling at 163°, the peculiar odour of which reminds of peppermint.[2] The Chinese crystallized oil of peppermint has sometimes a bitterish after-taste and an odour similar to that of spearmint, but by recrystallization it assumes the pure flavour.

The liquid part of the oil of peppermint has not yet been thoroughly investigated; it appears to consist chiefly of the compound $C^{10}H^{18}O$. Upon the liquid portions depend the remarkable colorations which the oil of peppermint is capable of assuming. If 50 to 70 drops of the crude oil are shaken with one drop of nitric acid, sp. gr. about 1·2, the mixture changes from faintly yellowish to brownish, and, after an hour or two, exhibits a bluish, violet or greenish colour; in reflected light, it appears reddish and not transparent. The colour thus produced lasts a fortnight. We have thus examined the various samples of peppermint oil at our command, and may state that the finest among them assume the most beautiful coloration and fluorescence, which, however, shows very appreciable differences. An inferior oil of American origin was not coloured; and a very old sample of an originally excellent English oil was likewise not coloured by the test. Menthol is not altered when similarly treated.[3] The nitric acid test is not capable of revealing adulterations of peppermint oil, for the coloration takes place with an oil to which a considerable quantity of oil of turpentine has been added.

Remarkable colorations of a different hue are also displayed by the various kinds of oil of peppermint if other chemical agents are mixed with it. Thus green or brownish tints are produced by means of *anhydrous* chloral; the oil becomes bluish or greenish or rose-coloured

[1] The Chinese oil is distilled at Canton, and was exported from Canton in 1872 to the extent of 800 lbs.; it was valued at about 30*s*. per lb.—See also Flückiger in *Pharm. Journ.* Oct. 14, 1871. 321. As to Japan we are informed that there are large plantations of peppermint; the oil "Hakano Abura" is exported from Hiogo and Osaka, but frequently adulterated. Mr. Holmes informed me (1879) that he found the mother plant coming nearest to *Mentha canadensis*.—F. A. F.

[2] On Japanese Peppermint Camphor see Beckett and Alder Wright, *Yearbook of Pharm.* 1875. 605.

[3] *Pharm. Journ.* Feb. 25, 1871. 682.

if shaken with a concentrated solution of bisulphite of sodium. It is worthy of note that oils of different origin, which cannot be distinguished by means of nitric acid, exhibit totally different colorations if mixed with either of the liquids just named, or with vapour of bromine. This behaviour may be of some use in the examination of commercial sorts of peppermint oil.

As to bisulphite of sodium, it yields a solid compound with certain kinds of peppermint oil, which we have not yet examined.

Production and Commerce—In several parts of Europe, as well as in the United States, peppermint is cultivated on the large scale as a medicinal plant.

In England the culture is carried on in the neighbourhood of Mitcham in Surrey, near Wisebeach in Cambridgeshire, Market Deeping in Lincolnshire, and Hitchin in Hertfordshire.

At Mitcham in 1850 there were about 500 acres under cultivation; in 1864 only about 219 acres.[1] At Market Deeping there were in 1871 about 150 acres cropped with peppermint. The usual produce in oil may be reckoned at 8 to 12 lb. per acre. The fields of peppermint at Mitcham are level, with a rich, friable soil, well manured and naturally retentive of moisture. The ground is kept free from weeds, and in other respects is carefully tilled. The crop is cut in August, and the herb is usually allowed to dry on the ground before it is consigned to the stills. These are of large size, holding 1000 to 2000 gallons, and heated by coal; each still is furnished with a condensing worm of the usual character, which passes out into a small iron cage secured by a padlock, in which stands the oil separator. The distillation is conducted at the lowest possible temperature. The water that comes over with the oil is not distilled with another lot of herb, but is for the most part allowed to run away, a very little only being reserved as a perquisite of the workmen. The produce is very variable, and no facilities exist for estimating it with accuracy.[2] It is however stated that a ton of dried peppermint yields from 2½ to 3½ pounds of oil, which equals 0·11 to 0·15 per cent. But we have been assured by a grower at Mitcham that the yield is as much as 6 pounds from a ton, or 0·26 per cent.

At Mitcham and its neighbourhood two varieties of peppermint are at present recognized, the one being known as *White Mint*, the other as *Black Mint*, but the differences between the two are very slight. The Black Mint has *purple* stems; the White Mint, *green* stems, and as we have observed, leaves rather more coarsely serrated than those of the Black. The Black Mint is more prolific in essential oil than the White, and hence more generally cultivated; but the oil of the latter is superior in delicacy of odour and commands a higher price. White Mint is said to be principally grown for drying in bundles, or as it is termed "*bunching*."

Peppermint is grown on a vastly larger scale in America, the localities where the cultivation is carried on being Southern Michigan, Western

[1] *Pharm. Journ.* x. (1851) 297. 340; also Warren in *Pharm. Journ.* vi. (1865) 257. To these papers and to personal inquiries we are indebted for most of the particulars relating to peppermint culture at Mitcham.

[2] Only the larger growers have stills. These they let to smaller cultivators who pay so much for distilling a charge, *i.e.* whatever the still can be made to contain, without reference to weight. Hence the dried herb is preferred to the fresh, as a larger quantity can be distilled at one time.

New York, and Ohio. In Michigan where the plant was introduced in 1855, there were in 1858 about 2100 acres devoted to its growth, all with the exception of about 100 acres being in the county of St. Joseph, where there are about 100 distilleries. The average produce of this district was estimated in 1858 at 15,000 lb; but the yield fluctuates enormously, and in the exceptionally fine season of 1855 it was reckoned at 30,000 lb. We must suppose that it is sometimes much larger, for we have been informed by Mr. H. G. Hotchkiss, of Lyons, Wayne County, State of New York, one of the most well-known dealers, in a letter under date Oct. 10, 1871, that the quantity sent out by him in the previous year reached the enormous amount of 57,365 lb. It is further stated by the official statistics of Hamburg for the year 1876 that this port received 25,840 lb. of peppermint oil from the United States and 14,890 lb. from Great Britain.

From the statistics quoted by Stearns[1] it would appear that the produce of oil per acre is somewhat higher in America than in England, but from various causes information on this head cannot be very reliable.

Peppermint is cultivated at Sens in the department of the Yonne in France[2] and in Germany in the environs of Leipzig, where the little town of Cölleda produces annually as much as 40,000 cwts. of the herb.

The annual crop of the world is supposed to yield 90,000 lb. of peppermint oil.[3]

Peppermint oil varies greatly in commercial value, that of Mitcham commanding twice or three times as high a price as the finest American. Even the oil of Mitcham is by no means uniform in quality, certain plots of ground affording a product of superior fragrance. A damp situation or badly drained ground is well known to be unfavourable to the quantity and quality of oil.

The presence of weeds among the peppermint is an important cause of deterioration to the oil, and at Mitcham some growers give a gratuity to their labours to induce them to be careful in throwing out other plants when cutting the herb for distillation. One grower of peppermint known to us was compelled to abandon the cultivation, owing to the enormous increase of *Mentha arvensis* L. which could not be separated, and which when distilled with the peppermint ruined the flavour of the latter. In America great detriment is occasioned by the growth of *Erigeron canadensis* L. Newly cleared ground planted with peppermint is liable to the intrusion of another plant of the order *Compositæ*, *Erechtites hieracifolia* Raf., which is also highly injurious to the quality of the oil.[4]

Uses—A watery or spirituous solution of oil of peppermint is a grateful stimulant, and is a frequent adjunct to other medicines. Oil of peppermint is extensively consumed for flavouring sweatmeats and cordials.

[1] To whose paper *On the Peppermint Plantations of Michigan* in the *Proceedings of the Americ. Pharm. Assoc.* for 1858, we owe the few particulars for which we can here afford space.—To be further consulted, same *Proceedings*, 1876. 828.

[2] *Journ. de Pharm.* viii. (1868) 130.—Abstract from Roze, *La Menthe poivrée, sa culture en France, ses produits, falsifications de l'essence et moyens de les reconnaître*, Paris, 1868. 43 pages.

[3] Todd, *Proceedings Am. Ph. Ass.* 1876, 828.

[4] Maisch *American Journ. of Pharm.* March 1870. 120.

HERBA PULEGII.

Pennyroyal[1]; F. *Menthe pouliot, Pouliot vulgaire*; G. *Polei.*

Botanical Origin—*Mentha Pulegium* L., a small perennial aromatic plant, common throughout the south of Europe and extending northward to Sweden, Denmark, England and Ireland, eastward to Asia Minor and Persia, and southward to Abyssinia, Algeria, Madeira and Teneriffe. It has been introduced into North[2] and South America. For medicinal use it is cultivated on a small scale.

History—Pennyroyal was in high repute among the ancients. Both Dioscorides and Pliny describe its numerous virtues. In Northern Europe it was also much esteemed, as may be inferred from the frequent reference to it in the Anglo-Saxon and Welsh works on medicine.

Gerarde considered the plant to be "so exceedingly well known to all our English nation" that it needed no description. In his time (*circa* 1590), it used to be collected on the commons round London, whence it was brought in plenty to the London markets. At the present day pennyroyal has fallen into neglect, and is not named in the British Pharmacopœia of 1867.

Description—The plant has a low, decumbent, branching stem, which in flowering rises to a height of about 6 inches. Its leaves, scarcely an inch in length and often much less, are petiolate, ovate, blunt, crenate at the margin, dotted with oil-glands above and below. The flowers are arranged in a series of dense, globose whorls, extending for a considerable distance up the stem. The whole plant is more or less hairy. It has a strong fragrant odour, less agreeable to most persons than that of peppermint or spearmint. Its taste, well perceived in the distilled water, is highly aromatic.

Chemical Composition—The most important constituent of pennyroyal is the essential oil, known in pharmacy as *Oleum Pulegii*, to which is due the odour of the plant. It has been examined by Kane,[3] according to whom it has a sp. gr. of 0·927. Its boiling was found to fluctuate between 183° and 188° C. The formula assigned to it by this chemist is $C^{10}H^{16}O$. We ascertained that it contains no carvol (see page 481.)

Production—Pennyroyal is cultivated at Mitcham and is mostly sold dried; occasionally the herb is distilled for essential oil. The oil found in commerce is however chiefly French or German, and far less costly than that produced in England.

Uses—The distilled water of pennyroyal is carminative and antispasmodic, and is used in the same manner as peppermint water.

[1] *Pennyroyal*, in old herbals *Puloil royal* is derived from *Puleium regium*, an old Latin name given from the supposed efficacy of the plant in destroying fleas (Prior).

[2] The native Pennyroyal is however a different plant, namely *Hedeoma pulegioides* Pers., figured in part 21 (1877) of Bentley and Trimen's *Med. Plant.*

[3] *Phil. Mag.* xiii. (1838) 442.

HERBA THYMI VULGARIS.

Garden Thyme ; F. Thym vulgaire ; G. Thymiankraut.

Botanical Origin—*Thymus vulgaris* L., a small, erect, woody shrub reaching 8 to 10 inches in height, gregarious on sterile uncultivated ground in Portugal, Spain, Southern France and Italy, and in the mountainous parts of Greece. On Mont Ventoux near Avignon, it reaches an elevation above the sea of 3700 ft. (Martins). It is commonly cultivated in English kitchens as a sweet herb,[1] and succeeds as an annual even in Iceland.

History—We are not aware that thyme had any reputation in the antiquity, nor do we know at what period it was first introduced in northern countries. Garden thyme was commonly cultivated in England in the 16th century, and was well figured and described by Gerarde. It is even said to have been formerly grown on a large scale for medicinal use in the neighbourhood of Deal and Sandwich in Kent.[2] *Camphor of Thyme* was noticed by Neumann, apothecary to the Court at Berlin in 1725;[3] it was called *Thymol*, and carefully examined in 1853 by Lallemand, and recommended instead of phenol (carbolic acid) in 1868 by Bouilhon, apothecary, and Paquet, M.D. of Lille.

Description—The plant produces thin, woody, branching stems, bearing sessile, linear-lanceolate, or ovate-lanceolate leaves. These are about ¼ of an inch long, revolute at the margin, more or less hoary, especially on the under side, and dotted with shining oil-glands. The small purple flowers are borne on round terminal heads, with sometimes a few lower whorls. The entire wild plant has a greyish tint by reason of a short white pubescence, yet as seen in gardens the plant is more luxuriant, greener and far less tomentose. It is extremely fragrant when rubbed, and has a pungent aromatic taste.

Production of Essential Oil—Though cultivated in gardens for culinary use, common thyme is not grown in England on a large scale. Its essential oil (*Oleum Thymi*), for which alone it is of interest to the druggist, is distilled in the south of France. In the neighbourhood of Nîmes, where we have observed the process, the entire plant is used, and the distillation is carried on at two periods of the year, namely in May and June when the plant is in flower, and again late in the autumn. The oil has a deep, reddish-brown colour, but becomes colourless though rather less fragrant by re-distillation. The two sorts of oil, termed respectively *Huile rouge de Thym* and *Huile blanche de Thym*, are found in commerce. The yield is about 1 per cent.

Oil of thyme is frequently termed in English shops *Oil of Origanum*, which it in no respect resembles, and which was never, so far as we know, found in commerce.[4]

[1] In many of the references to thyme, *Wild Thyme* (*Thymus Serpyllum* L.) is to be understood, and not the present species.

[2] Booth in *Treasury of Botany*, ii. (1866) 1149.

[3] *Phil. Trans.* No. 389.

[4] For a note on *True Oil of Origanum*, see Hanbury, *Pharm. Journ.* x. (1851) 324, also *Science Papers*, 1876, p. 46.

Chemical Composition—The only constituent of the herb that has attracted any attention is the above-named essential oil. This liquid by fractional distillation is resolved into two portions: the first, more volatile and boiling below 180° C., is a mixture of two hydrocarbons, *Cymene*, $C^{10}H^{14}$ (see page 333), and *Thymene*, $C^{10}H^{16}$, the latter boiling at 165° C.

The second, named *Thymol*, $C^{10}H^{14}O$, which may also be extracted from the crude oil by means of caustic lye, has been described in our article *Fructus Ajowan*, at page 303. Commercial oil of thyme is said to be sometimes fraudulently deprived of thymol by that treatment.

Uses—Oil of thyme is an efficient external stimulant, and is sometimes employed as a liniment. Its chief consumption is in veterinary medicine. Thymol has been proposed as a disinfectant in the place of carbolic acid, in cases in which the odour of the latter is objectionable. The herb is not used in modern English medicine, but is often employed on the Continent.

HERBA ROSMARINI.

Herba Anthos; Rosemary; F. *Romarin;* G. *Rosmarin.*

Botanical Origin—*Rosmarinus officinalis* L., an evergreen shrub, attaining a height of 4 feet or more, abundant on dry rocky hills of the Mediterranean region, from the Spanish peninsula[1] to Greece and Asia Minor. It generally prefers the neighbourhood of the sea, but occurs even in the Sahara, where it is collected and conveyed by caravans to Central Africa.[2] It does not succeed well in Germany.

History—Rosemary[3] is mentioned by Pliny, who ascribes to it numerous virtues. It was also familiar to the Arab physicians of Spain, one of whom, Ibn Baytar (13th cent.), states it to be an object of trade among the vendors of aromatics.[4] In the middle ages rosemary was doubtless much esteemed, as may be inferred from the fact that it was one of the plants which Charlemagne ordered to be grown on the imperial farms.

It was probably in cultivation in Britain prior to the Norman Conquest, as it is recommended for use in an Anglo-Saxon herbal of the 11th century.[5] In the "Physicians of Myddvai" a curious chapter[6] is devoted to the virtues of Rosemary, called "Ysbwynwydd, and Rosa Marina in Latin." The essential oil was distilled by Raymundus Lullus[7] about A.D. 1330. John Philip de Lignamine,[8] a writer of the 15th century, describes Rosemary as the usual condiment of salted meats.

[1] From Galicia in Spain, stems of Rosmarinus having 2½ inches in diameter were to be seen at the Paris Exhibition, 1878.

[2] Duveyrier, *Les Touaregs du Nord*, 1864. 187.

[3] From *ros* and *marinus*,—literally *marine dew*. Various opinions have been held as to the allusion conveyed by the name.

[4] Sontheimer's translation, i. 73.

[5] *Herbarium Apuleii—Leechdoms etc. of Early England*, i. (1864) 185.

[6] *Meddygon Myddfai* (see Appendix) p. 261. 292. 440.

[7] Manget, *Bibliotheca chemica curiosa*, Genevæ, i. (1702) 829.

[8] *Conservatorium Sanitatis* (or also, according to Haller, *Biblioth. botanica*, i. 237, *De conservatione sanitatis*, Bononiæ, 1475) cap. 81.

Description—Rosemary has sessile, linear, entire, opposite leaves about an inch in length, revolute at the margin; they are of coriaceous texture, green and glabrous above, densely tomentose and white beneath. Examined under a lens, the tomentum both of the leaves and young shoots is seen to consist of white stellate hairs; in that of the shoots which is less dense, minute oil-glands are discernible. These glands are of two kinds, large and small, and probably do not yield one and the same oil. The flowers have a campanulate 2-lipped calyx, and a pale blue and white corolla, the upper lip of which is emarginate and erect, the lower 3-lobed with the central lobe concave and pendulous. The whole plant has a very agreeable smell and a strong aromatic taste. It flowers in the early spring.

Production of Essential Oil—Rosemary is cultivated on a very small scale in English herb-gardens, and though a little oil has been occasionally distilled from it, English oil of rosemary is an article practically unknown in commerce. That with which the market is supplied is produced in the south of France and on the contiguous coasts of Italy. The plant, which is plentifully found wild, is gathered in summer (not while in flower) and distilled, the operator being sometimes an itinerant herbalist who carries his copper alembic from place to place, erecting it where herbs are plentiful, and where a stream of water enables him to cool a condenser of primitive construction.

Oil of rosemary is also produced on a somewhat large scale in the island of Lesina, south of Spalato in Dalmatia, whence it is exported by way of Trieste, even to France and Italy, to the extent of 300 to 350 quintals annually.[1]

Some of the French manufacturers of essences offer oil of rosemary at a superior price as drawn *from the flowers*, by which we presume is meant the *flowering tops*, for the separation of the actual flowers would be impracticable on a large scale. The great bulk of the oil found in commerce is however that distilled from the entire plant.

Chemical Composition—The peculiar odour of rosemary depends on the essential oil, which is the only constituent of the plant that has afforded matter for chemical research.

Lallemand (1859) by fractional distillation, resolved oil of rosemary into two liquids,—the one a mobile hydrocarbon boiling at 165° C. and turning the plane of polarization to the left; the other, boiling between 200° and 210° C., deposits when exposed to a low temperature a large quantity of camphor. Gladstone (1864) found the oil to consist almost wholly of a hydrocarbon, $C^{10}H^{16}$. This, according to our experiments, constitutes about $\frac{4}{5}$ of the oil; it deviates the plane of polarization to the left, whereas a fraction boiling at 200° to 210° C. deviates to the right. By warming the latter with nitric acid, we observed the odour of common camphor, and may therefore infer that a compound, $C^{10}H^{18}O$, is present in the oil under examination.

From Montgolfier's investigations (1876) it would appear that the stearoptene or camphor above alluded to is a mixture of a dextrogyrate and a lævogyrate substance.

[1] Unger, *Der Rosmarin und seine Verwendung in Dalmatien—Sitzungsberichte der Wiener Akademie*, lvi. (1867) 587; abstracted, with a few additions, in *Pharm. Journ.* ix. (1879) 618.

Uses—The flowering tops and dried leaves are kept by the herbalists, but are not used in regular medicine. The volatile oil is employed as an external stimulant in liniments, and also as a perfume. Rosemary is popularly supposed to promote the growth of the hair.

PLANTAGINEÆ.

SEMEN ISPAGHULÆ.

Ispaghúl Seeds, Spogel Seeds.

Botanical Origin—*Plantago decumbens* Forsk. (*P. Ispaghula* Roxb.),[1] a plant of variable aspect, from an inch to a foot in height, erect or decumbent, with linear lanceolate leaves which may be nearly glabrous, or covered with shaggy hairs. The flower-spikes differ according to the luxuriance of the plant, being in some specimens cylindrical and 1½ inches long, in others reduced to a globular head. The plant has a wide range, occurring in the Canary Islands, Egypt, Arabia, Beluchistan, Afghanistan, and North-western India. Stewart[2] says it is common in the Peshawar valley and Trans-Indus generally up to 2000 feet; also on the plains and lower hills of the Punjab, but that he has never seen it cultivated in the latter region. It is said to be cultivated at Multan and Lahore, also in Bengal and Mysore.

History—The seeds which are found in all the bazaars of India and are held in great esteem, are generally designated by the Persian word *Ispaghúl*; but they also bear the Arabic name *Bazre-qatúná*, under which we find them mentioned by the Persian physician Alhervi[3] in the 10th century, and about the same period or a little later by Avicenna.[4] Several other Oriental writers are quoted by Ibn Baytar[5] as referring to a drug of the same name, which may possibly have included the seeds of other species, as *Plantago Psyllium* L. and *P. Cynops*, having similar properties, and known to have been used from an early period.

J. H. Linck, whom we mentioned in our article on Oleum Cajuputi (p. 278), described in 1719 the seed under notice, yet without knowing its name; it further attracted the notice of Europeans towards the close of the last century,[6] and has been often prescribed as a demulcent in dysentery and diarrhœa. It was admitted to the *Pharmacopœia of India* of 1868.

Description—The seeds, like those of other species of *Plantago*, are of boat-shaped form, the albumen being deeply furrowed on one side and vaulted on the other. They are a little over $\frac{1}{10}$ of an inch in length and nearly half as broad, and so light that 100 weigh scarcely three

[1] After the examination of numerous specimens, we adopt the course taken by Dr. Aitchison (*Catalogue of the Plants of the Punjab and Sindh*, Lond. 1869) of uniting *P. Ispaghula* to *P. decumbens*. The union of species in this group may probably be carried still further.—For a fig. see Bentley and Trimen, *Med. Plants*, part 21 (1877).

[2] *Punjab Plants*, Lahore 1869. 174—also MS. note attached to specimens in Herb. Kew.

[3] *Liber Fundamentorum Pharmacologiæ*, ed. Seligmann, Vindobonæ, 1830. 40.

[4] Lib. ii. tract. 2. c. 541. (Valgrisi edition, 1564. i. 357.)

[5] Sontheimer's transl. i. (1840) 132.

[6] Fleming, *Catal. of Indian Med. Plants and Drugs*, Calcutta, 1810. 31.

grains. Their colour is a light pinkish grey with an elongated brown spot on the vaulted back, due to the embryo, which at this point is in close contact with the translucent testa. From this brown spot the thick radicle runs to the top of the seed. The hollow side of the seed is also brown and partially covered with a thin white membrane.

The seeds are highly mucilaginous in the mouth, but have neither taste nor odour. Those of the allied *P. Psyllium* have nearly the same form, but are shining and of a dark brown hue.

Microscopic Structure—This can be best investigated by immersing the seed in benzol, as in this medium the mucilage is insoluble. When thus examined, the whole surface is seen to consist of polyhedral cells, separated by a very thin brown layer from the albumen, which on the back of the seed is only 70 mkm. thick. The albumen is made up of thick-walled cells, loaded with granules of matter which acquire an orange hue on addition of iodine. The two cotyledons adhere in a direction perpendicular to the bottom of the furrow; their tissue is composed of thin-walled smaller cells, containing also albuminous granules and drops of fatty oil.

If the seed is immersed in water, the cells composing the epidermis instantly swell and elongate, and soon burst, leaving only fragments of their walls. When examined under glycerin, the change is more gradual, and the outer walls of the cells yielding the mucilage display a series of thin layers, which slowly swell and disappear by the action of water. The mucilage is consequently not contained within the cells, but is formed of the secondary deposits on their walls, as in linseed and quince pips.

Chemical Composition—Mucilage is so abundantly yielded by these seeds, that one part of them with 20 parts of water forms a thick tasteless jelly. On addition of a larger quantity of water and filtering, but little mucilage passes, the greater part of it adhering to the seeds. The mucilage separated by straining with pressure does not redden litmus, is not affected by iodine, nor precipitated by borax, alcohol or ferric chloride. The fat oil and albuminous matter of the seed have not been examined.

Uses—A decoction of the seeds (1 p. to 70 p. of water) is employed in India as a cooling, demulcent drink. The seeds powdered and mixed with sugar, or made gelatinous with water, are sometimes given in chronic diarrhœa.

POLYGONACEÆ.

RADIX RHEI.

Rhubarb; F. *Rhubarbe*; G. *Rhabarber*.

Botanical Origin—No competent observer, as far as we know, has ever ascertained as an eye-witness the species of Rheum which affords the commercial rhubarb. Rheum officinale, from which it seems, at least partly, derived is the only species yielding a rootstock which agrees with the drug.

Rheum officinale Baillon is a perennial noble plant resembling the Common Garden Rhubarb, but of larger size. It differs from the latter in several particulars: the leaves spring from a distinct crown rising some inches above the surface of the ground; they have a sub-cylindrical petiole, which as well as the veins of the under side of the lamina is covered with a pubescence of short erect hairs. The lamina, the outline of which is orbicular, cordate at the base, is shortly 5- to 7-lobed, with the lobes coarsely and irregularly dentate; it attains 4 to 4½ feet in length and rather more in breadth. The first leaves in spring display before expanding the peculiar metallic red hue of copper.

The plant was discovered in South-eastern Tibet, where it is said to be often cultivated for the sake of its medicinal root; but it is supposed to grow in various parts of Western and North-western China, whence the supplies of rhubarb are derived. It was obtained by the French missionaries about the year 1867 for Dabry, French Consul at Hankow, who transmitted specimens to Dr. Soubeiran of Paris. From one of these which flowered at Montmorency in 1871, a botanical description was drawn up by Baillon.[1]

To what extent the rhubarb of commerce is derived from this plant is not known. But that the latter may be a true source of the drug is supported by the fact, that there is at least no important discrepancy between it and the accounts and figures, scanty and imperfect though they are, given by Chinese authors and the old Jesuit missionaries; and still more by the agreement in structure which exists between its root and the Asiatic rhubarb of commerce.

We have engaged in 1873 Mr. Rufus Usher at Bodicott (see below, p. 500) to cultivate Rheum officinale, which is there admirably succeeding; but it must be granted that as yet the root, notwithstanding the most careful preparation in drying it, is far from displaying the rich yellow of the commercial drug. It is most obviously marked on the other hand with the characteristic ring of stellate markings, which we have constantly observed in many roots of Rheum officinale cultivated by us at Clapham Common near London, as well as at Strassburg or, by other observers, at Paris.

Rheum palmatum L., a species known as long as 1750, has always been supposed to yield also rhubarb, and this has again been asserted by the Russian Colonel Przewalski, who observed in 1872 and 1873 that plant in the Alpine parts of Tangut round the Lake Kuku-nor, in the Chinese province of Kansu, in 36°–38° North Lat.—Rheum palmatum has been frequently cultivated in Russian Asia and in many parts of Europe since the last century, but without producing a root agreeing with Chinese rhubarb. Now, Przewalski states that from this species the drug under notice is largely collected along the river Tetung-gol (or Datung-ho), a tributary of the upper Hoang-ho, northward of the Kuku-nor. Specimens of that root were largely brought to St. Petersburg by Przewalski, but Dragendorff expressly points out in his *Jahresbericht* for 1877 (p. 78) that it is *dissimilar* to true rhubarb.

[1] *Adansonia*, x. 246; *Association Française pour l'avancement de la Science*, Comptes Rendus de la 1re Session, 1872. 514-529. pl. x.—The figure which is reproduced in Lanessan's French translation of the *Pharmacographia*, ii. (Paris, 1878) 210, gives a good idea of the highly ornamental character of Rheum officinale.

History[1]—The Chinese appear to have been acquainted with the properties of rhubarb from a period long anterior to the Christian era, for the drug is treated of in the herbal called *Pen-king*, which is attributed to the Emperor Shen-nung, the father of Chinese agriculture and medicine, who reigned about 2700 B.C. The drug is named there *Huang-liang*, yellow, excellent, and *Ta-huang*, the great yellow.[2] The latter name also occurs in the great Geography of China, where it is stated that rhubarb was a tribute of the province Si-ning-fu, eastward of Lake Kuku Nor,[3] from about the 7th to the 10th centuries of our era.

As regards Western Asia and Europe, we find a root called *ῥᾶ* or *ῥῆον*, mentioned by Dioscorides as brought from beyond the Bosphorus. The same drug is alluded to in the fourth century by Ammianus Marcellinus,[4] who states that it takes its name from the river Rha (the modern Volga), on whose banks it grows. Pliny describes a root termed *Rhacoma*, which when pounded yielded a colour like that of wine but inclining to saffron, and was brought from beyond Pontus.

The drug thus described is usually regarded as rhubarb, or at least as the root of some species of *Rheum*, but whether produced in the regions of the Euxine (Pontus), or merely received thence from remoter countries, is a question that cannot be solved.

It is however certain that the name *Radix pontica* or *Rha ponticum*, used by Scribonius Largus[5] and Celsus,[6] was applied in allusion to the region whence the drug was received. Lassen has shown that trading caravans from Shensi in Northern China arrived at Bokhara as early as the year 114 B.C. Goods thus transported might reach Europe either by way of the Black Sea, or by conveyance down the Indus to the ancient port of Barbarike. Vincent suggests[7] that the *rha* imported by the first route would naturally be termed *rha-ponticum*, while that brought by the second might be called *rha-barbarum*.

We are not prepared to accept this plausible hypothesis. It receives no support from the author of the Periplus of the Erythrean Sea (*circa* A.D. 64), whose list of the exports of Barbarike[8] does not include rhubarb; nor is rhubarb named among the articles on which duty was levied at the Roman custom-house of Alexandria (A.D. 176-180).[9]

The terms *Rheum barbarum* vel *barbaricum* or *Reu barbarum* occur in the writings of Alexander Trallianus[10] about the middle of the 6th century, and in those of Benedictus Crispus,[11] archbishop of Milan, and Isidore[12] of Seville, who both flourished in the 7th century. Among the Arabian writers on medicine, the younger Mesue, in the early part of the 11th century, mentions the rhubarb of China as superior to the

[1] For further particulars see Flückiger, *Pharm. J.* vi. (1876) 861; also *Proc. Americ. Pharm. Assoc.* 1876. 130, with fig. showing Rheum officinale grown in a poor soil.

[2] Bretschneider, *Chinese Botanical Works*, Foochow, 1870. 2.

[3] Flückiger, *l.c.*

[4] *Scriptores Historiæ Romanæ latini veteres*, ii. (1743) 511 (Amm. Marc. xxii. c. 8.)

[5] *De Compositione Medicamentorum*, c. 167.

[6] *De Medicinâ*. lib. v. c. 23.

[7] Vincent, *Commerce and Navigation of the Ancients*, ii. (1807) 389.

[8] *Ibid., op. cit.* ii. 390.

[9] *Ibid., op. cit.* ii. 686.

[10] Lib. viii. c. 3 (Haller's edition).

[11] Migne, *Patrologiæ Cursus*, lxxxix. 374.

[12] Migne. *op. cit.*, lxxxii. 628. The explanation given by Isidore is this:—"*Reubarbarum*, sive *Reuponticum*: illud quod trans Danubium in solo barbarico; istud quod circa Pontum colligitur, nominatum est. *Reu* autem *radix* dicitur. *Reubarbarum* ergo, quasi *radix barbara*. *Reuponticum* quasi *radix pontica*." But Isidore was fond of such derivations.

Barbaric or Turkish.[1] Constantinus Africanus[2] about the same period speaks of Indian and Pontic *Rheum*, the former of which he declares to be preferable. In 1154 the celebrated Arabian geographer Edrisi[3] mentions rhubarb as a product of China, growing in the mountains of Buthink—probably the environs of north-eastern Tibet near Lake Tengri Nor (or Bathang in Western Szechuen ?).

Rhubarb in the 12th century was probably imported from India, as we may infer from the tariff of duties levied at the port of Acon in Syria, in which document[4] it is enumerated along with many Indian drugs. A similar list of A.D. 1271, relating to Barcelona, mentions *Ruibarbo*.[5] In a statute of the city of Pisa called the *Breve Fundacariorum*, dating 1305, rhubarb (*ribarbari*) is classified with commodities of the Levant and India.[6]

The first and almost the only European who has visited the rhubarb-yielding countries of China is the famous Venetian traveller, Marco Polo,[7] who speaking of the province of Tangut says—". . et par toutes les montagnes de ces provinces se treuve le *reobarbe* en grant habondance. Et illec l'achatent les marchans et le portent par le monde."

A sketch of the history of rhubarb would be incomplete without some reference to the various routes by which the drug has been conveyed to Europe from the western provinces of the Chinese Empire, and which have given rise to the familiar designations of *Russian*, *Turkey* and *China Rhubarb*.[8]

The *first* route is that over the barren steppes of Central Asia by Yarkand, Kashgar, Turkestan, and the Caspian to Russia; the *second* by the Indus or the Persian Gulf to the Red Sea and Alexandria, or by Persia to Syria and Asia Minor; and the *third* by way of Canton, the only port of the Chinese Empire which, previous to the year 1842, held direct communication with Europe.

In 1653 China first permitted Russia to trade on her actual frontiers. The traffic in Chinese goods was thereupon diverted from the line of the Caspian and Black Sea further north, taking its way from Tangut across the steppes of the high Gobi, and through Siberia by Tobolsk to Moscow. Thus it is mentioned in 1719 that Urga on the north edge of the Gobi desert was the principal depôt for rhubarb. From the earliest times, Bucharian merchants appear to have been agents on this traffic, the producers of the drug never concerning themselves about its export.

Consequent on the rectification of frontier in 1728, a line of custom-houses was established by treaty between Russia and China, whereby the commerce, previously unrestricted, was limited to the government caravans which passed the frontier only at Kiachta and at Zuruchaitu, south of Nerchinsk. The latter place always remained unimportant,

[1] *Ravedsceni, Raved barbarum*, and *Raved Turchicum* are the terms used in the Latin translations we have consulted.

[2] *De omnibus medico cognitu necessariis*, Basil. 1539. 354.

[3] Translation of Jaubert, i. (Paris, 1836) 494.

[4] *Assises de Jérusalem* contained in the *Recueil des Historiens des Croisades, Lois*, ii. (1843) 176.

[5] Capmany, *Memorias de . . . Barcelona*, i. (1779) 44.

[6] Bonaini, *Statuti inediti della città di Pisa dal xii al xiv secolo*, iii. (Firenze, 1857) 106. 115.

[7] Pauthier, *Le Livre de Marco Polo . . . rédigé en français sous sa dictée en 1298 par Rusticien de Pise*, i. (1865) 165. ii. 490.

[8] For further particulars, see my paper mentioned at page 493, note 1.—F. A. F.

while Kiachta and the opposite Chinese town of Maimatchin became the staple depôts of rhubarb.

The root was subjected to special control as early as 1687-1697 by the Russian Government, who finally monopolized the trade about 1704. Caravans fitted out by the Crown alone brought the drug to Moscow, until 1762, when the caravan-trade was for a while thrown open. It was not until this period that the export of rhubarb became considerable, although the stringent regulations, established in 1736, were still maintained. The surveillance of rhubarb was exercised at Kiachta in a special court or office called the *Brake*,[1] under instructions from the Russian Minister of War, by an apothecary appointed for six years, the object being to remove from the rhubarb brought for inspection all inferior or spurious pieces, and to improve the selected drug by trimming, paring and boring. It was then carefully dried, and packed in chests, which were sown up in linen, and rendered impervious to wet by being pitched and then covered with hide. The drug was despatched, but only in quantities of 1000 *puds* (40,000 lb.), once a year by way of Lake Baikal and Irkutsk to Moscow, whence it was transmitted to St. Petersburg, to be there delivered to the Crown apothecaries and in part to be sold to druggists.

We are indebted for these accounts chiefly to Calau,[2] an apothecary appointed to supervise the examination of rhubarb, and who resided a long time at Kiachta. An exact account of the remarkable policy of the Russian Government in relation to that drug was also given by Von Schröders[3] in 1864.

So long as China kept all her ports closed to foreign commerce except Canton in the extreme south, a large supply of fine rhubarb found its way to Europe by way of Russia. But the unpleasant accompaniments of the Russian supervision, which was exercised with unsparing severity,[4] and the extreme tediousness of the land-transport, made the Chinese very ready to accept an easier outlet for their goods. Accordingly we find that the opening of a number of ports in the north of China exerted a very depressing influence on the trade of Kiachta, which was augmented by the rebellion that raged in the interior of China for some years from 1852.

On these accounts Russia in 1855 removed certain restrictions on the trade, though without abandoning the Rhubarb Office. She withdrew in 1860 the custom-house to Irkutsk, and declared Kiachta a free port, while by the treaty with China of November 1860, she insisted on that country abandoning all restrictions on trade.

But the over-land rhubarb trade had already been destroyed: the Chinese, tempted by the increased demand occasioned by the new trading-ports, became less careful in the collection and curing of the root, while the Russians insisted with the greatest strictness on the drug being of the accustomed quality. Hence it happened that from 1860 hardly any rhubarb was delivered at Kiachta, either for the

[1] From the German word *Bracke*, the name applied to persons appointed for the examination of merchandize brought to the ports of the Baltic.

[2] Ganger's *Rep. für Pharm. und Chemie*, 1842. 452–457; *Pharm. Journ.* ii. (1843) 658.

[3] Canstatt's *Jahresbericht* for 1864. i. 35–42.

[4] Thus in 1860 the Russians compelled the Chinese to burn 6000 lb. of rhubarb, on the pretext that it was *too small!*

government use or to private traders; and in 1863 the Rhubarb Office was abolished.

Thus the so-called *Russian* or *Muscovitic* or *Crown Rhubarb*, familiarly known in England as *Turkey Rhubarb*, a drug which for its uniformly good quality long enjoyed the highest reputation, has become a thing of the past, which can only now be found in museum collections. It began to appear in English commerce at the commencement of the last century. Alston,[1] who lectured on botany and materia medica at Edinburgh in 1720, speaks of rhubarb as brought from Turkey and the East Indies,—"and of late, likewise from Muscovy."

It has been shown (p. 494) that rhubarb was shipped from Syria in the 12th century. Vasco da Gama[2] mentions it in 1497 among the exports of Alexandria. In fact, the drug was carried from the far east to Persia, whence it was brought by caravans to Aleppo, Tripoli, Alexandria, and even to Smyrna. From these Levant ports it reached Europe, and was distributed as *Turkey Rhubarb*; while that which was shipped direct from China, or by way of India, became known as *China*, *Canton*, or *East India Rhubarb*. The latter was already the more common sort in England as early as 1640.[3]

As the rhubarb of the Levant disappeared from trade, that of Russia took not only its place but likewise its name, until the term "*Turkey Rhubarb*" came to be the accepted designation of the drug imported from Russia. This strange confusion of terms was not however prevalent on the Continent, but was chiefly limited to British trade.

The risk and expense of the enormous land-transport over almost the whole breadth of Asia, caused rhubarb in ancient times to be one of the very costly drugs. Thus at Alexandria in 1497, it was valued at twelve times the price of benzoin. In France in 1542,[4] it was worth ten times as much as cinnamon, or more than four times the price of saffron. At Ulm in 1596,[5] it was more costly than opium. A German price-list of the magistrate of Schweinfurt, of 1614, shows *Radix Rha Barbari* to be six times as dear as fine myrrh, and more than twice the price of opium. An official English list[6] giving the price of drugs in 1657, quotes opium as 6*s*. per lb., scammony 12*s*., and rhubarb 16*s*.

Production and Commerce—The districts of the Chinese Empire which produce rhubarb extend over a vast area. They are comprised in the four northern provinces of China Proper, known as Chihli, Shansi, Shensi,[7] and Honan; the immense north-western province of Kansuh, formerly partly included in Shensi, but now extending across the desert of Gobi and to the frontiers of Tibet; the province of Tsing-hai inhabited by Mongols, which includes the great salt lake of Koko-nor and the districts of Tangut, Sifan, and Turfan; and lastly the mountains of the western province of Szechuen. The plant is found on the pasturages

[1] *Lectures on the Mat. Med.* i. (1770) 502.

[2] *Roteiro da viagem de Vasco da Gama*, por A. Herculano e o Barão de Castello de Paiva, ed. 2. Lisboa, 1861. 115.—For an abstract of the "Roteiro," see Flückiger, *Documente zur Geschichte der Pharm.* 1876. 13.

[3] Parkinson, *Theatrum Botanicum*, 1640. 155.

[4] Leber, *Appréciation de la fortune privée au moyen âge*, éd. 2. 1847. 308-9.

[5] Reichard, *Beiträge zur Geschichte der Apotheken*, Ulm, 1825. 208.

[6] *Book of the Values of Merchandize imported, according to which Excize is to be paid by the First Buyer*, Lond. 1657.

[7] According to Consul Hughes of Hankow, San-yuan in Shensi (north of Singanfu) is one of the principal marts for rhubarb.

of the high plateaux, growing particularly well on spots that have been enriched by encampments.

What little we know regarding the production of rhubarb and its preparation for the market, from Catholic missionaries,[1] is of a rather meagre and unsatisfactory character. The root is dug up at the beginning of autumn when the vegetation of the plant is on the decline, and the operation is probably continued for a few months, or in some districts for the whole winter. It is cleaned, its cortical part sliced off, and the root cut into pieces for drying. This is performed either by the aid of fire heat, or by simple exposure to sun and air, or the pieces are first partially dried on a hot stone, and then strung on a cord and suspended until the desiccation is complete.

According to F. von Richthofen[2] the best rhubarb is collected exclusively from plants growing wild in the high alps of western Szechuen, especially in the Bayankara range, between the sources of the Hoangho and the rivers Ya-lung-Kiang and Min-Kiang. This variety is chiefly known under the name Shensi rhubarb, although the inhabitants of the province of Szechuen pretend the superiority of the drug of their own country. The important places for the commodity are Sining-fu in the province of Kansu, and Kwan-hien in Szechuen. In the plain of Tshing-tu-fu, according to Richthofen, rhubarb is cultivated in fields, but its product is stated to be much inferior to that of the true plant which is said not to succeed under culture.

Rhubarb is now purchased for the European market chiefly at Hankow on the upper Yangtsze, whither it is brought from the provinces of Shensi, Kansu, and Szechuen. From Hankow it is sent down to Shanghai, and there shipped for Europe. The exports from Hankow are stated in official documents[3] to have amounted to the following numbers of peculs (one pecul = $133\frac{1}{3}$ lb. = 60·479 kilogrammes):

1866	1867	1868	1869	1870	1871	1872
2985	3425	2866	3398	3370	3859	3167

In 1877 there were exported by way of Hankow 2096 peculs from Shensi and 3385 peculs from Szechuen.—From all the Chinese ports, 5124 peculs of rhubarb were shipped in 1874.

Much smaller quantities (554 peculs in 1872, 1055 peculs in 1874) are shipped from Tientsin; and there are occasional exportations from Canton, Amoy, Foochow, and Ningpo. The imports of rhubarb into the United Kingdom in 1870 amounted to 343,306 lb., the estimated value of which was £62,716.[4]

We have no information about the rhubarb which is stated by Bellew[5] to grow on the hills near Kayn or Ghayn in eastern Persia (about $32\frac{1}{2}$° N. lat.).

Description—China Rhubarb as imported into Europe[6] consists of

[1] Chauveau, Vicar Apostolic of Tibet (1870), and Biet, a French missionary, both quoted by Collin in his thesis *Des Rhubarbes*, Paris, 1871. 22. 24.

[2] *Petermann's Geograph. Mittheilungen*, viii. (1873) 302.

[3] *Reports on Trade at the Treaty Ports of China for* 1870; *Commercial Reports* from Her Majesty's Consuls in China, 1872. No. 3. p. 57, and 1874 (1875) No. 5.

[4] *Annual Statement of the Trade and Navigation of the United Kingdom for* 1870. 79.

[5] *From the Indus to the Tigris*, London, 1874. 321.

[6] It is now often trimmed by wholesale druggists to simulate the old Russian rhubarb.

portions of a massive root which display considerable diversity of form, arising from the various operations of paring, slicing and trimming, to which they have been subjected. Thus some pieces are cylindrical or rather barrel-shaped, others conical, while a large proportion are plano-convex, and others again are of no regular shape. These forms are not all found in the same package, the drug being usually sorted into *round* and *flat rhubarb*. In dimensions we find 3 to 4 inches the commonest length, though an occasional piece 6 inches long or more may be met with. The width may be stated at 2 to 3 inches. The outer surface of the root is somewhat shrivelled, often exhibiting portions of a dark bark that have not been pared away. Many pieces are pierced with a hole, in which may be found the remains of a cord used to suspend the root while drying. The drug is dusted over with a bright brownish-yellow powder, on removal of which the outer side of the root is seen to have a rusty-brown hue, or viewed with a lens to be marked by the medullary rays, which appear as an infinity of short broken lines of deep brown, traversing a white ground.

The character which most readily distinguishes the rhubarb of China is that well-developed pieces, broken transversely, display these dark lines arranged as an internal ring of *star-like spots*. Although this character is by no means obvious in every piece of Chinese rhubarb, it is of some utility from the fact that in European rhubarb, such spots are generally wholly wanting, or at most occur only sparingly and in an isolated manner.

In judging of rhubarb, great stress is laid upon the appearance of the root when broken, and the circumstance of the fractured surface presenting no symptoms of decay, discoloration, or sponginess.[1] In good rhubarb, the interior is found to be compact, and beautifully veined with reddish-brown and white, sometimes not unmixed with iron-grey. The root when chewed tastes gritty, by reason of the crystals it contains of oxalate of calcium; but it is besides bitter, astringent and nauseous. The odour is peculiar, and except by the druggist, is mostly regarded as very disagreeable.

Microscopic Structure.—The tissue of rhubarb is made up of a white parenchyme, brown medullary rays and a few irregularly scattered very large fibro-vascular bundles, which are devoid of ligneous cells.

On a transverse fracture of specimens, which are not too much peeled, a narrow dark cambial zone may be distinguished. In that part of the root, only the medullary rays display the usual radial arrangement, and in the interior of the root no regular structure is met with. There is no well-marked pith, but the central portion of the tissue shows a mixture of white parenchyme and brown medullary rays running in every direction. In full-grown roots, the central part is separated from the cambial zone by the band of stellate patches[2] already mentioned.

[1] The quality and appearance of rhubarb are far more regarded in England than on the Continent. To ensure a fine powder of brilliant hue, the drug is most carefully prepared, each root being split open, and any dark or decayed portion removed with a chisel or file, while the operator is not allowed to handle the drug except with leather gloves.

[2] Their formation has been investigated by Schmitz, Proceedings of the "*Naturforschende Gesellschaft zu Halle*"; the author also shows that the drug is chiefly afforded by the rhizome.—An abstract of the paper will be found in Just's *Botanischer Jahresbericht*, 1874. 461.

As to the contents of the white cells, they are loaded either with starch or tufted crystals of oxalate of calcium, the amount of the latter being especially liable to variation. Scheele, after having discovered the oxalic acid, pointed out in 1784 that the crystals under notice consist of that acid in combination with lime; he was the first to point out the true composition of those crystals which are of so wide a distribution throughout the vegetable kingdom. The medullary rays contain the substances peculiar to rhubarb, but none of them occur in a crystalline state.

Chemical Composition.—The active constituent of the root has long been supposed to reside in the yellowish red contents of the medullary rays. Schrader as early as 1807 prepared a *Rhubarb-Bitter*, to which he attributed the medicinal powers of the drug. Since then several substances of the same kind have been separated by various methods, and described under different names: such are the *Rhabarberstoff* of Trommsdorff, the *Rheumin* of Hornemann, the *Rhabarberin* of Buchner and Herberger, the *Rhubarb-Yellow* or *Rheïn*, and the *Rhabarbaric Acid* of Brandes.

Schlossberger and Döpping in 1844 first recognized among the abovenamed substances a definite chemical body named *Chrysophan* or *Chrysophanic Acid*, $C^{14}H^{5}\left\{\begin{matrix}CH^{3}\\(OH)^{2}\end{matrix}\right.O^{2}$, which had been found in 1843 by Rochleder and Heldt in the yellow lichen, *Parmelia parietina*. It partly forms the yellow contents of the medullary rays of rhubarb, and when isolated crystallizes in golden yellow needles or in plates. It dissolves in ether, alcohol, or benzol; though scarcely soluble in water, it is nevertheless extracted from the root to some extent by that solvent, probably by reason of some accompanying substance. Alkalis dissolve it, forming fine dark red solutions. Chrysophan, $C^{15}H^{10}O^{4}$, is a derivative of anthracene, $C^{14}H^{10}$, and closely allied to alizarin, $C^{14}H^{8}O^{4}$.

By precipitating alcoholic solutions of extract of rhubarb with ether, Schlossberger and Döpping obtained, together with chrysophan, resinous bodies which they named *Aporetin*, *Phæoretin* and *Erythroretin*.

De la Rue and Müller (1857) extracted from rhubarb, in addition to chrysophan, an allied substance, *Emodin*, which crystallizes in orange-coloured prisms, sometimes as much as two inches long. Its constitution was subsequently found to agree with the formula $C^{14}H^{4}\left\{\begin{matrix}CH^{3}\\(OH)^{3}\end{matrix}\right.O^{2}$.

Kubly (1867) has obtained from rhubarb the following constituents:—

1. *Rheo-tannic Acid*, $C^{26}H^{26}O^{14}$, a yellowish powder abundantly present in rhubarb, soluble in water or alcohol, not in ether. Its solutions produce blackish green precipitates with persalts of iron, and greyish ones slowly turning blue, with protosalts of the same.

2. *Rheumic Acid* (*Rheumsäure*), $C^{20}H^{16}O^{9}$, obtained as a reddish-brown powder, by boiling rheo-tannic acid with a dilute mineral acid, a fermentable sugar being developed at the same time. Rheumic acid exhibits nearly the same reactions as rheo-tannic acid, but is very sparingly soluble in cold water. It partly pre-exists in rhubarb.

3. Neutral *colourless* substance, sparingly soluble in hot water, and separating from the latter in prismatic *crystals* of the formula $C^{10}H^{12}O^{4}$;

no name has yet been given to it. A "white crystalline resin" (and a dark brown crystalline resin) has been isolated in 1878 by Dragendorff.

4. *Phæoretin*, $C^{16}H^{16}O^{7}$, agreeing with the substance thus named by Schlossberger and Döpping. It is a brown powder, soluble in alcohol or in acetic acid, but not in ether, chloroform or water.

5. *Chrysophan*, described above.

According to Dragendorff (1878) *mucilaginous matters* occur in the different varieties of rhubarb to the amount of from 11 to 17 per cent. He states them to consist of mucilage (properly so called), arabic acid, metarabic acid and pararabin, and moreover enumerates also *pectose* among the constituents of the drug.

Small quantities of albuminoid substances, malic acid, fat and sugar have also been met with in rhubarb. As to its mineral constituents, their amount is exceedingly variable. Two samples of good China Rhubarb dried at 100° C. and incinerated, yielded us respectively 12·9 and 13·87 per cent. of ash. Another sample, which we had particularly selected on account of its pale tint, afforded no less than 43·27 per cent. of ash. The ash consists of carbonates of calcium and potassium. English rhubarb from Banbury (portions of a large specimen) left after incineration 10·90 per cent of ash.

From a practical point of view the chemical history of rhubarb is far from satisfactory, for we are still ignorant to what principle the drug owes its therapeutic value, or what are the pharmaceutical preparations in which the active matter may be most appropriately exhibited. Chrysophan is said to act as a purgative, but less powerfully than rhubarb itself.

Uses—Rhubarb is one of the commonest and most valuable purgatives; it is also taken as a stomachic and tonic.

Substitutes—These are found in the roots of the various species of *Rheum* cultivated in Europe. In most countries, the cultivation of rhubarb for medicinal use has at some time been attempted. Yet in but few instances has it been persistently carried on; and though the drug produced has often been of good appearance, it has failed to gain the confidence of medical men, and to acquire much importance in the drug-market. The European rhubarb most interesting from our point of view is

English Rhubarb—So early as 1535, Andrew Boorde, an English Carthusian monk and practitioner of medicine, obtained seeds of rhubarb, which he sent as "*a grett tresure*" to Sir Thomas Cromwell, Secretary of State to Henry VIII.; but as he says they "*come owtt of barbary*," we must be allowed to hold their genuineness as doubtful.[1]

In the following century, namely about the year 1608, Prosper Alpinus of Padua cultivated as the True Rhubarb a plant which is now known as *Rheum Rhaponticum* L., a native of Southern Siberia and the regions of the Volga.[2] From this stock, Sir Matthew Lister, physician to Charles I., procured seeds when in Italy, and gave them to Parkinson,[3] who raised plants from them.

[1] Boorde's *Introduction and Dyetary*, reprinted by the Early English Text Society, 1870. 56.

[2] Prosper Alpinus, *De Rhapontico*, Lugd. Bat. 1718.

[3] *Theatrum Botanicum*, 1640. 157.

Collinson obtained rhubarb plants from seeds procured in Tartary, and sent to him in 1742 by Professor Siegesbeck of St. Petersburg.[1]

About 1777 Hayward, an apothecary of Banbury in Oxfordshire, commenced the cultivation of rhubarb with plants of *Rh. Rhaponticum*, raised from seeds sent from Russia in 1762. The drug he produced was so good that the Society of Arts awarded him in 1789 a silver medal, and in 1794 a gold medal.[2] The Society also awarded medals about the same time (1789-1793) to growers of rhubarb in Somersetshire, Yorkshire, and Middlesex, some of whom, it appears, cultivated *Rh. palmatum*. On the death of Hayward in 1811, his rhubarb plants came into the possession of Mr. P. Usher, by whose descendants, Mr. R. Usher and sons, they are still cultivated at Bodicott, a village near Banbury.

The authors of this book had the pleasure of inspecting the rhubarb fields of Messrs. Usher on Sept. 4, 1872, and of seeing the whole process of preparing the root for the market.[3] The land under cultivation is about 17 acres, the soil being a rich friable loam. The roots are taken from the ground during the autumn up to the month of November. It is considered advantageous that they should be 6 or 7 years old, but they are seldom allowed to attain more than 3 or 4 years. The clumps of root as removed from the field to the yard, where the trimming takes place, are of huge size, weighing with the earth attached to them as much as 60 or 70 lb. They are partially cleaned, the smaller roots are cut off, and the large central portion is rapidly trimmed into a short, cylindrical mass the size of a child's head. This latter subsequently undergoes a still further paring, and is finally sliced longitudinally; the other and less valuable roots are also pared, trimmed, and assorted according to size. The fresh roots are fleshy, easily cut, and of a beautiful deep yellow. All are dried in buildings constructed for the purpose, and heated by flues. The drying occupies several weeks. The root after drying has a shrivelled, unsightly appearance, which may be remedied by paring and filing. The finished drug has to be stored in a warm dry place.

When well prepared, Banbury rhubarb is of excellent appearance. The finest pieces, which are semi-cylindrical, are quite equal in size to the drug of China. The colour is as good, and the fractured surface exhibits pink markings not less distinct and brilliant. Even the smaller roots, which are dried as sticks, have internally a good colour, and afford a fine powder. But the odour is somewhat different from that of Chinese rhubarb; the taste is less bitter but more mucilaginous and astringent, and the root is of a more spongy, soft, and brittle texture. The structure is the same as that of the Chinese rhubarb, except that, as already stated, the star-like spots, if present, are isolated, and not arranged in a regular zone.

The drug commands but a low price, and is chiefly sold, it is said, for exportation in the state of powder. It is not easily purchased in London.

French and German Rhubarb—The cultivation of rhubarb was

[1] Dillwyn, *Hortus Collinsonianus*, 1843. 45.

[2] *Trans. of Soc. of Arts*, viii. (1790) 75; xii. (1794) 225.

[3] No use is made of the leaves.—Some further particulars are given by Holmes, *Pharm. Journal*, vii. (1877) 1017.

commenced in France in the latter half of the last century, and has been pursued with some enthusiasm in various localities. The species grown were *Rheum palmatum* L., *Rh. undulatum* L., *Rh. compactum* L., and *Rh. Rhaponticum* L. The first was thought by Guibourt[1] to afford a root more nearly approaching than any other the rhubarb of China; but it is that which is cultivated the least readily, the central root being liable to premature decay. Both this plant and *Rh. undulatum* were formerly cultivated by order of the Russian Government on a large scale at Kolywan and Krasnojarsk in Southern Siberia, but the culture has, we believe, been long abandoned.[2]

As to France, it appears from inquiries we have lately made (1873), that except in the neighbourhood of Avignon and in a few other scattered localities, the cultivation has now ceased.

Rheum Rhaponticum is the source of the rhubarb which is produced at Austerlitz and Auspitz in Moravia, and at Ilmitz, Kremnitz and Frauenkirchen in Hungary. Some rhubarb is also produced in Silesia from *Rh. Emodi* Wall. (*Rh. australe* Don.).

MYRISTICEÆ.

MYRISTICA.

Nuclei Myristicæ, Semen Myristicæ, Nux moschata; Nutmeg; F. *Muscade, Noix de Muscade;* G. *Muskatnuss.*

Botanical Origin—*Myristica fragrans* Houttuyn (*M. moschata* Thunb., *M. officinalis* Linn. f.), a handsome, bushy, evergreen tree,[3] with dark shining leaves, growing in its native islands to a height of 40 to 50 feet. It is found wild in the very small volcanic group of Banda, from Damma to Amboina, in Ceram, Bouro, Jilolo (Halmahera), the western peninsula of New Guinea, and in many of the adjacent islands, but it is not indigenous to any of the islands westward of these, or to the Philippines (Crawfurd).

The nutmeg tree has been introduced into Bencoolen on the west coast of Sumatra, Malacca, Bengal, the islands of Singapore and Penang, as well as Brazil and the West Indies; but it is only in a very few localities that the cultivation has been attended with success.

In its native countries the tree comes into bearing in its ninth year, and is said to continue fruitful until 60 or even 80 years old, yielding annually as many as 2000 fruits. It is diœcious, and one male tree furnishes pollen sufficient for twenty female.

History—It has been generally believed that neither the nutmeg nor mace was known to the ancients. C. F. Ph. von Martius[4] however maintains that mace was alluded to in the comedies of Plautus,[5] written about two centuries before the Christian era.

[1] *Histoire des Drogues*, ii. (1849) 398.

[2] Twelve chests of this rhubarb, said to be of the crop of 1793, which had been lying in the Russian Government warehouses, were offered for sale in London, Dec. 1, 1853. Samples of the drug now 80 years old are in our possession, and still sound and good.

[3] Most beautifully figured by Blume, "Rumphia" i. (1835) tab. 55; *Myristica fatua*, ii. 59.

[4] *Flora Brasiliensis*, fasc. 11–12. 133; also in Buchner's *Repertorium für Pharmacie*, ix. (1860) 529–538.

[5] *Pseudolus*, act. iii. scena 2.

The words *Macer*, *Macar*, *Machir* or *Macir*, occurring in the writings of Scribonius Largus, Dioscorides, Galen, and Pliny are thought by Martius to refer in each instance to mace. But that the substance designated by these names was not mace, but the bark of a tree growing in Malabar, was pointed out by Acosta nearly three centuries ago, and by many subsequent writers, and, as we think, with perfect correctness.[1]

Nutmegs and mace were imported from India at an early date by the Arabians, and thus passed into western countries. Aëtius, who was resident at the court of Constantinople about the year 540, appears to have been acquainted with the nutmeg, if that at least is intended by the term *Nuces Indicæ*, prescribed together with cloves, spikenard, costus, calamus aromaticus and sandal wood, as an ingredient of the *Suffumigium moschatum*.[2]

Masudi,[3] who appears to have visited India in A.D. 916–920, pointed out that the nutmeg, like cloves, areca nut and sandal wood, was a product of the eastern islands of the Indian Archipelago. The Arabian geographer Edrisi, who wrote in the middle of the 12th century, mentions both nutmegs and mace as articles of import into Aden;[4] and again "*Nois mouscades*" are among the spices on which duty was levied at Acre in Palestine, *circa* A.D. 1180.[5] About a century later, another Arabian author, Kazwini,[6] expressly named the Moluccas as the native country of the spices under notice.

The Sanskrit name of the nutmeg-tree most commonly in use, also with Susruta, is Jātī (Dr. Rice).

One of the earliest references to the use of nutmegs in Europe occurs in a poem written about 1195, by Petrus D'Ebulo,[7] describing the entry into Rome of the Emperor Henry VI., prior to his coronation in April 1191. On this occasion the streets were fumigated with aromatics, which are enumerated in the following line:—

"Balsama, thus, aloë, *myristica*, cynnama, nardus."

By the end of the 12th century, both nutmegs and mace were found in Northern Europe,—even in Denmark, as may be inferred from the allusion to them in the writings of Harpestreng.[8] In England, mace, though well known, was a very costly spice, its value between A.D. 1284 and 1377 being about 4*s*. 7*d*. per lb., while the average price of a sheep during the same period was but 1*s*. 5*d*., and of a cow 9*s*. 5*d*.[9] It was also dear in France, for in the *Compte de l'exécution* of the will of Jeanne d'Evreux, queen of France, in 1372, six ounces of mace are

[1] Mérat et De Lens, *Dict. de Mat. Méd.* iv. (1832) 173.—The tree is, we think, *Ailantus malabarica* DC., order of the Simarubeæ.

[2] Aëtius, tetrabiblos iv. serm. 4. c. 122. —It must however be admitted that *Nux Indica* in mediæval authors usually signifies the Coco-nut, but also sometimes *Nux vomica* or even *Areca nut*. For particulars see Flückiger, *Documente zur Geschichte der Pharm.* 1876. 18.

[3] *Les prairies d'or*, i. (1861) 341.

[4] *Géographie*, i. (1836) 51.

[5] In the work quoted at p. 282, note 3.

[6] *Kosmographie*, übersetzt von Ethé, i. (1869) 227.

[7] *Carmen de motibus siculis*, Basil., 1746. 23.—A new edition of this work, by Prof. Winkelmann, was published in 1874.

[8] *Danske Laegebog*, quoted by Meyer, *Geschichte der Botanik*, iii. (1856) 537.

[9] Rogers, *Hist. of Agriculture and Prices in England*, i. (1866) 361–362. 628.—It is remarkable that *nutmegs* are not mentioned, though *mace* is named repeatedly.

appraised per ounce at 3 sols 8 deniers, equal to about 8*s.* 3*d.* of our present money.[1]

The use of these spices was diffused throughout Europe long before the Portuguese in 1512 had discovered the mother-plant in the isles of Banda. The Portuguese held the trade of the Spice Islands for about a century, when it was wrested from them by the Dutch, who pursued the same policy of exclusiveness that they had followed in the case of cloves and cinnamon. In order to secure their monopoly, they endeavoured to limit the trees to Banda and Amboyna, and to exterminate them elsewhere, which in fact they did at Ceram and the small neighbouring islands of Kelang and Nila. So completely was the spice trade in their hands, that the crops of sixteen years were said to be at one time in their warehouses, those of recent years being never thrown on the market. Thus the crop of 1744 was being sold in 1760, in which year an immense quantity of nutmegs and cloves was burned at Amsterdam lest the price should fall too low.[2]

During the occupation of the Spice Islands by the English from 1796 to 1802, the culture of the nutmeg was introduced into Bencoolen and Penang,[3] and many years afterwards into Singapore. Extensive plantations of nutmeg-trees were formed in the two islands last named, and by a laborious and costly system of cultivation were for many years highly productive.[4] In 1860 the trees were visited by a destructive blight, which the cultivators were powerless to arrest, and which ultimately led to the ruin of the plantations, so that in 1867 there was no such thing as nutmeg cultivation either in Penang or Singapore.[5]

Though so long valued in Europe and Asia, neither nutmegs nor mace seem to have been employed in former times as a condiment in the islands where they are indigenous.[6]

Collection and Preparation—Almost the whole surface of the Banda Isles, observes Mr. Wallace,[7] is planted with nutmeg-trees, which thrive under the shade of the lofty *Canarium commune.* The light volcanic soil, the shade, and the excessive moisture of these islands, where it rains more or less every month in the year, seem exactly to suit the nutmeg-tree, which requires no manure and scarcely any attention.

In Bencoolen[8] the trees bear all the year round, but the chief harvest takes place in the later months of the year, and a smaller one in April,

[1] Leber, *Appréciation de la fortune privée au moyen âge*, éd. 2, 1847. 95.

[2] Valmont de Bomare, *Dict. d'Histoire Nat.* iv. (1775) 297.—This author writes as an eye-witness of the destruction he has recorded:—"Le 10 Juin 1760, j'en ai vu à Amsterdam, près de l'Amirauté, un feu dont l'aliment étoit estimé huit millions argent de France: on devoit en brûler autant le lendemain. Les pieds des spectateurs baignoient dans l'huile essentielle de ces substances . . ."

[3] How tempting the cultivation must have appeared, may be judged from the price of mace, which we find quoted on the 3rd January 1806, in the *London Price Current* (which gives only *import prices*), as 85*s.* to 90*s.* per lb.;—to these rates must be added the duty of 7*s.* 1*d.* per lb.

[4] Seemann, *Hooker's Journ. of Bot.* iv. (1852) 83.

[5] Collingwood in *Journ. of Linnean Society*, Bot., x. (1869) 45.

[6] Crawfurd, *Dictionary of the Indian Islands*, 1856. 304.—Much additional information will be found in this work.

[7] *The Malay Archipelago*, i. (1869) 452. —See also Bickmore, *Travels in the East Indian Archipelago*, 1868. 225.

[8] Lumsdaine, *Pharm. Journ.* xi. (1852) 516. For further information on the management of nutmeg plantations in Sumatra, consult the original paper.

May and June. The fruit as it splits is gathered by means of a hook attached to a long stick, the pericarp removed, and the mace carefully stripped off, The nuts are then taken to the drying house (a brick building), placed on frames, and exposed to the gentle heat of a smouldering fire, with arrangements for a proper circulation of air. This drying operation lasts for two months, during which time the nutmegs are turned every second or third day. At the end of this period, the kernels are found to rattle in the shell, an indication that the drying is complete. The shells are then broken with a wooden mallot, the nutmegs picked out and sorted, and finally rubbed over with dry sifted lime. In Banda the smaller and less sightly nutmegs are reserved for the preparation of the expressed oil.

The old commercial policy of the Dutch originated the singular practice of breaking the shell, and immersing the kernel of the artificially dried seed in milk of lime,—sometimes for a period of three months. This was done with a view to render impossible the germination of any nutmegs sent into the market. The folly of such a procedure was demonstrated by Teijsmann, who proved that mere exposure to the sun for a week is sufficient to destroy the vitality of the seed. By immersion in milk of lime many nutmegs are spoiled and the necessity is incurred of a second drying. Lumsdaine has also shown that even the *dry* liming process is, to say the least, entirely needless. Nutmegs are well preserved in their natural shell, in which state the Chinese have the good sense to prefer them.

The process of liming nutmegs is however still largely followed; and the prejudice in favour of the spice thus prepared is so strong in certain countries, that nutmegs not limed abroad have sometimes to be limed in London to fit them for exportation. Penang nutmegs are always imported in the natural state,—that is, *un-limed*.

Description—The fruit of *Myristica fragrans* is a pendulous, globose drupe, about 2 inches in diameter, and not unlike a small round pear. It is marked by a furrow which passes round it, and by which at maturity its thick fleshy pericarp splits into two pieces, exhibiting in its interior a single seed, enveloped in a fleshy foliaceous mantle or arillus, of fine crimson hue, which is *mace*. The dark brown, shining, ovate seed is marked with impressions corresponding to the lobes of the arillus; and on one side, which is of paler hue and slightly flattened, a line indicating the raphe may be observed.

The bony testa does not find its way into European commerce, the so-called *nutmeg* being merely the kernel or nucleus of the seed. Nutmegs exhibit nearly the form of their outer shell with a corresponding diminution in size. The London dealers esteem them in proportion to their size, the largest, which are about one inch long by $\frac{8}{10}$ of an inch broad, and four of which will weigh an ounce, fetching the highest price. If not dressed with lime, they are of a greyish brown, smooth yet coarsely furrowed and veined longitudinally, marked on the flatter side with a shallow groove. A transverse section shows that the inner seed coat (*endopleura*) penetrates into the albumen in long narrow brown strips, reaching the centre of the seed, thereby imparting the peculiar marbled appearance familiar in a cut nutmeg.

At the base of the albumen and close to the hilum, is the embryo, formed of a short radicle with cup-shaped cotyledons, whose slit and curled edges penetrate into the albumen. The tissue of the seed can be cut with equal facility in any direction. It is extremely oily, and has a delicious aromatic fragrance, with a spicy rather acrid taste.

Microscopic Structure—The testa consists mainly of long, thin, radially arranged, rigid cells, which are closely interlaced and do not exhibit any distinct cavities. The endopleura which forms the adhering coat of the kernel and penetrates into it, consists of soft-walled, red-brown tissue, with small scattered bundles of vessels. In the outer layers the endopleura exhibits small collapsed cells; but the tissue which fills the folds that dip into the interior consists of much larger cells. The tissue of the albumen is formed of soft-walled parenchyme, which is densely filled with conspicuous starch-grains, and with fat, partly crystallized. Among the prismatic crystals of fat, large thick rhombic or six-sided tables may often be observed. With these are associated grains of albuminoid matter, partly crystallized.

Chemical Composition—After starch and albuminoid matter, the principal constituent of nutmeg is the *fat*, which makes up about a fourth of its weight, and is known in commerce by the incorrect name of *Oil of Mace* (see p. 507).

The volatile oil, to which the smell and taste of nutmegs are chiefly due, amounts to between 3 and 8 per cent.,[1] and consists, according to Cloëz (1864), almost entirely of a hydrocarbon, $C^{10}H^{16}$, boiling at 165° C., which Gladstone (1872), who assigns it the same composition, calls *Myristicene*. The latter chemist found in the crude oil an oxygenated oil, *Myristicol*, of very difficult purification and possibly subject to change during the process of rectifying. It has a high boiling point (about 220° C. ?) and the characteristic odour of nutmeg; unlike carvol with which it is isomeric, it does not form a crystalline compound with hydrosulphuric acid.

Oil of nutmegs, distilled in London by Messrs. Herring and Co., examined in column 200 mm. long, we found to deviate the ray of polarized light, 15°·3 to the right; that of the Long Nutmeg (*Myristica fatua* Houtt.), furnished to us by the same firm, deviated 28°·7 to the right.

From the facts recorded by Gmelin,[2] it would appear that oil of nutmeg sometimes deposits a stearoptene called *Myristicin*. We are not acquainted with such a deposit; yet we have been kindly furnished by Messrs. Herrings with a crystalline substance which they obtained during the latter part of the process of distilling both common and long nutmegs. It is a greyish greasy mass, which by repeated crystallizations from spirit of wine, we obtained in the form of brilliant, colourless scales, fusible at 54° C., and still possessing the odour of nutmeg. The crystals are readily soluble in benzol, bisulphide of carbon or chloroform, sparingly in petroleum ether; their solution in spirit of wine has a decidedly acid reaction, and is devoid of rotatory power. By boiling them with alcohol, sp. gr. 0·843, and anhydrous carbonate of

[1] Messrs. Herrings & Co. of London have informed us, that 2874 lb. of nutmegs distilled in their laboratory afforded 67 lb. of essential oil, *i.e.* 2·33 per cent. But Messrs. Schimmel & Co., Leipzig, state (1878) that they obtain as much as from 6 to 8 per cent.

[2] *Chemistry*, xiv. (1860) 389.

sodium, we obtained a solution which, after removal of the alcohol, left a residuum perfectly soluble in boiling water, forming a jelly on cooling. By adding hydrochloric acid to the warm aqueous solution, the original crystallizable substance again made its appearance, yet almost devoid of odour. It is in fact nothing else than *Myristic Acid* (see page 508).[1]

Production and Commerce—The nutmegs and mace now brought into the market are to a large extent the produce of the Banda Islands,[2] of which however only three, namely Lontar or the Great Banda, Pulo Ai, and Pulo Nera, have what are termed *Nutmeg Parks*. According to official statements of the Dutch, the first-named island possessed in 1864 about 266,000 fruit-bearing trees; Ternate on the western coast of Jilolo, 46,000; Menado in the island of Celebes, 35,000; and Amboyna, only 31,000. The nutmegs of the Banda Islands are shipped to Batavia. The quantity exported from Java in 1871 (all, we believe, from Batavia, and therefore the produce of the Banda Islands) is stated as 8107 peculs (1,080,933 lb.), of which 2300 peculs (306,666 lb.) were shipped to the United States, and a rather large quantity to Singapore.[3] The last-named port also shipped in the same year a very large quantity (310,576 lb.) of nutmegs to North America,[4] and in 1877 the total export of nutmegs and mace from Singapore was 5323 peculs (709,733 lb.).

Nutmegs were exported from Padang in Sumatra in the year 1871, to the extent of 2766 peculs (368,800 lb.), chiefly to America and Singapore. The quantity annually imported into the United Kingdom ranges from 500,000 to 800,000 lb.

Uses—Nutmeg is a grateful aromatic stimulant, chiefly employed for flavouring other medicines. It is also in constant use as a condiment, though less appreciated than formerly.

Oleum Myristicæ expressum.

Oleum Macidis, Balsamum vel Oleum Nucistæ; Expressed Oil of Nutmegs, Nutmeg Butter, Oil of Mace; F. *Beurre de Muscade;* G. *Muskatbutter, Muskatnussöl.*

This article reaches England chiefly from Singapore, in oblong, rectangular blocks, about 10 inches long by 2½ inches square, enveloped in a wrapper of palm leaves. It is a solid unctuous substance of an orange-brown colour, varying in intensity of shade, and presenting a mottled aspect. It has a very agreeable odour and a fatty aromatic taste.

In operating on 2 lb. of nutmegs, first powdered and heated in a waterbath and pressed while still hot, we obtained 9 ounces of solid oil, equivalent to 28 per cent. This oil, which in colour, odour and consistence does not differ from that which is imported, melts at about

[1] *Yearbook of Pharmacy*, 1874, 490.

[2] Some idea of the extremely small area of these famous islands may be gathered from the fact that the Great Banda, the largest of them, is but about 7 miles long by 2 miles broad; while the entire group occupies no more than 17·6 geographical square miles.

[3] *Consular Reports*, Aug. 1873. 952–3. In 1875, 8990 peculs were exported from Java.

[4] *Blue Books for the Colony of the Straits Settlements for* 1871, Singapore, 1872.

45° C.; and dissolves perfectly in two parts of warm ether or in four of warm alcohol sp. gr. ·800.

Nutmeg butter contains the volatile oil already described, to the extent of about six per cent., besides several fatty bodies. One of the latter, termed *Myristin* $C^3H^5(O.C^{14}H^{27}O)^3$, may be obtained by means of benzol, or by dissolving in ether that part of the butter of nutmeg which is insoluble in cold spirit of wine. The crystals of myristin melt at 31° C. By saponification they furnish glycerin, and *Myristic Acid*, $C^{14}H^{28}O^2$, the latter fusing at 53°·8 C. Playfair in 1841 was the first to isolate (in Liebig's laboratory at Giessen) myristic acid. Myristin also occurs in spermaceti, coco-nuts, as well as, according to Mulder, in small quantity, in the fixed oils of linseed and poppy seed. Nutmegs according to Comar (1859) yield 10 to 12 per cent. of myristin.

That part of nutmeg butter, which is more readily soluble in spirit of wine or benzol, contains another fat, which however has not yet been investigated. It is accompanied by a reddish colouring matter.

MACIS.

Mace; F. Macis; G. Macis, Muskatblüthe.

Botanical Origin—*Myristica fragrans* Houttuyn (see p. 502). The seed which, deprived of its hard outer shell or testa, is known as the *nutmeg*, is enclosed when fresh in a fleshy net-like envelope, somewhat resembling the husk of a filbert. This organ, which is united, though not very closely, at the base of the stony shell both with the hilum and the contiguous portion of the raphe, of which parts it is an expansion, is termed *arillus*,[1] and when separated and dried constitutes the mace of the shops. In the fresh state it is fleshy, and of a beautiful crimson; it envelopes the seed completely only at the base, afterwards dividing itself into broad flat lobes; which branch into narrower strips overlapping one another towards the summit.

History—Included in that of the nutmeg (see preceding article).

Description—The mace, separated from the seed by hand, is dried in the sun, thereby losing its brilliant red hue and acquiring an orange-brown colour. It has a dull fatty lustre, exudes oil when pressed with the nail, and is horny, brittle, and translucent. Steeped in water it swells rather considerably. The entire arillus, compressed and crumpled by packing, is about 1$\frac{3}{4}$ inches long with a general thickness of about $\frac{1}{20}$ of an inch or even at $\frac{1}{10}$ the base. Mace has an agreeable aromatic smell nearly resembling that of nutmeg, and a pungent, spicy, rather acrid taste.

Microscopic Structure—The uniform, small-celled, angular parenchyme is interrupted by numerous brown oil-cells of larger size. The inner part of the tissue contains also thin brown vascular bundles. The cells of the epidermis on either side are colourless, thick-walled, longitudinally extended, and covered with a peculiar cuticle of broad,

[1] On the nature and origin of this organ, see Baillon, *Histoire des Plantes*, ii. (1870) 499; also *Dictionnaire de Botanique*.

flat, riband-like cells, which cannot however be removed as a continuous film. The parenchyme is loaded with small granules, to which a red colour is imparted by Millon's test (solution of mercurous nitrate) and an orange hue by iodine. The granules consequently consist of albuminous matter, and starch is altogether wanting.

Chemical Composition—The nature of the chemical constituents of mace may be inferred from the following experiments performed by one of us:—17 grammes of finely powdered mace were entirely exhausted by boiling ether, and the latter allowed to evaporate. It left behind 5·57 grm., which after drying at 100° C. were diminished to 4·17. The difference, 1·40 grammes, answers to the amount of *essential oil*, of which consequently 8·2 per cent. had been present.

The residue, amounting to 24·5 per cent., was a thickish aromatic *balsam*, in which we have not been able to ascertain the presence of *fat*; it consisted of resin and semi-resinified essential oil. Alcohol further removed 1·4 per cent. of an uncrystallizable sugar, which reduced cupric oxide.

The drug having been thus treated with ether and with alcohol, yielded almost nothing to cold water, but by means of boiling water 1·8 per cent. of a mucilage was obtained, which turned blue by addition of iodine, or reddish violet if previously dried. This substance is not soluble in an ammoniacal solution of cupric oxide; it appears rather to be an intermediate body between mucilage and starch.[1] The composition of mace is therefore very different from that of nutmeg.

As to the *volatile oil*, of which several observers have obtained from 7 to 9 per cent.,[2] it is a fragrant colourless liquid which we found, when examined in a column 200 mm. long, deviated the ray 18°·8 to the right. Its greater portion consists according to Schacht (1862) of *Macene*, $C^{10}H^{16}$, boiling at 160° C., and distinguished from oil of turpentine by not forming a crystalline hydrate when mixed with alcohol and nitric acid. Koller (1865) states that macene is identical with the hydrocarbon of oil of nutmeg (myristicene), yet the latter is said by Cloëz to yield no solid compound when treated with hydrochloric gas. Macene on the other hand furnishes crystals of $C^{10}H^{16}$,HCl. Crude oil of mace contains, like that of nutmeg, an oxygenated oil, the properties of which have not yet been investigated.

Commerce—Mace, mostly the produce as it would appear of the Banda Islands, was shipped from Java in 1871 to the extent of 2101 peculs (282,133 lb.); and from Padang in Sumatra (excluding shipments to Java) to the amount of 457 peculs (60,933 lb.).[3] The spice is exported principally to Holland, Singapore, and the United States; Great Britain receives about 60,000 to 80,000 lb. annually.

Uses—Mace is but rarely employed in medicine. It is chiefly consumed as a condiment.

[1] See my paper: *Ueber Stärke und Cellulose* in *Archiv der Pharm.* 196 (1871) 31. —F. A. F.

[2] In an actual experiment (1868) in the laboratory of Messrs. Herrings & Co., London, 23 lb. of mace yielded 23 oz. of volatile oil, which is equivalent to 6¼ per cent.; but Messrs. Schimmel & Co., Leipzig, obligingly inform us (1878) that they observed a percentage of from 11 to 17.

[3] *Consular Reports*, August 1873. 952-3.

LAURACEÆ.

CAMPHORA.

Camphor,[1] *Common Camphor, Laurel Camphor;* **F.** *Camphre;* **G.** *Campher.*

Botanical Origin—*Cinnamomum Camphora* Fr. Nees et Ebermaier (*Laurus Camphora* L., *Camphora officinarum* C. Bauh.), the Camphor tree or Camphor Laurel is widely diffused, being found throughout Central China and in the Japanese Islands. In China it abounds principally in the eastern and central provinces, as in Chekiang, Fokien and Kiangsi; but it is wanting, according to Garnier (1868), in Yünnan and Szechuen. It is plentiful, on the other hand, in the island of Formosa, where it covers the whole line of mountains from north to south, up to an elevation of 2000 feet above the level of the sea. It flourishes in tropical and subtropical countries, and forms a large and handsome tree in sheltered spots in Italy as far north as the Lago Maggiore. The leaves are small, shining, and glaucous beneath, and have long petioles; the stem affords excellent timber, much prized on account of its odour for making clothes' chests and drawers of cabinets.

Dryobalanops aromatica, the camphor tree of Borneo and Sumatra, yields a peculiar camphor, which we shall describe further on.

History—The two kinds of Camphor afforded by the two trees just named have always been regarded by the Chinese as perfectly distinct substances, and in considering the history of camphor this fact must be borne in mind.

On perusing the accounts of Laurel Camphor given by Chinese writers,[2] the remarkable fact becomes apparent, that although the tree was evidently well known in the 6th century, and probably even earlier, and is specially noticed on account of its valuable timber, no mention is made in connexion with it of any such substance as *camphor*.

Le-she-chin, the author of the celebrated herbal *Pun-tsao-kang-muh*, written in the middle of the 16th century, was well acquainted with the two sorts of camphor,—the one produced by the camphor laurel of his own country, the other imported from the Malay islands; and he narrates how the former was prepared by boiling the wood, and refined by repeated dry sublimations.

Marco Polo, towards the end of the 13th century, saw the forests of Fokien in South-eastern China, in which, says he, are many of the trees which give camphor.[3] It would thus appear that Laurel Camphor was known as early as the time of Marco Polo, yet it is certain that the more ancient notices which we shall now quote have reference to

[1] The word *Camphor*, generally written by old Latin authors *Caphura*, and by English *Camphire*, is derived from the Arabic *Káfúr*, which in turn is supposed to come from the Sanskrit *Karpūra*, signifying *white*.

[2] Passages from several have been translated and kindly placed at our disposal by Mr. A. Wylie. Dr. Bretschneider of Pekin and Mr. Pauthier of Paris (see p. 494, note 7,) have also been good enough to aid us in the same manner.

[3] Yule, *Book of Ser Marco Polo*, ii. (1871) 185.

the much valued Malay Camphor, which remains up to the present day one of the most precious substances of its class.

There is no evidence that camphor reached Europe during the classical period of Greece and Rome. The first mention of it known to us occurs in one of the most ancient monuments of the Arabic language, the poems of Imru-l-Kais,[1] a prince of the Kindah dynasty, who lived in Hadramaut in the beginning of the 6th century. Nearly at the same period, Aëtius of Amida (the modern Diarbekir) used camphor medicinally, but from the manner in which he speaks of it, it was evidently a substance of some rarity.[2]

In fact, for many centuries subsequent to this period, camphor was regarded as one of the most rare and precious of perfumes. Thus, it is mentioned in A.D. 636, with musk, ambergris, and sandal wood, among the treasures of Chosroes II., of the Sassanian dynasty of kings of Persia, in the palace at Madain on the Tigris, north of Babylon.[3]

Among the immense mass of valuables dispersed at Cairo on the downfall of the Fatimite Khalif Mostanser in the 11th century, the Arabian historians[4] enumerate with astonishment, besides vast quantities of musk, aloes wood, sandal wood, amber, large stores of *Camphor of Kaisur*, and hundreds of figures of *melons in camphor*, adorned with gold and jewels, which were contained in precious vessels of gold and porcelain. One grain (crystal ?) of camphor is mentioned as weighing 5 mithkals, one melon of the weight of 70 mithkals, was contained in a golden box weighing no less than 3,000 mithkals (1 mithkal = 71·49 gr. Troy = 4·63 grammes). It is also on record that about A.D. 642, Indian princes sent camphor as tribute or a gift to the Chinese Emperors;[5]—further, that in the Teenpaou period (A.D. 742-755), the Cochinchinese brought to the Chinese court a tribute of Barus camphor, said by the envoy to be found in the trunks of old trees, the like of which for fragrance was never seen again.[6] Masudi,[7] four centuries later, mentions a similar present from an Indian to a Chinese potentate, when 1,000 *menn*[8] of aloes-wood were accompanied by 10 *menn* of camphor, the choice quality of the latter being indicated by the remark that it was in pieces as large or larger than a pistachio-nut.

Again, between A.D. 1342 and 1352, an embassy left Pekin bearing a letter from the Great Khan to Pope Benedict XII., accompanied by presents of silk, precious stones, *camphor*, musk, and spices.[9]

Ibn Batuta, the celebrated traveller, relates that after having visited the King of Sumatra, he was presented on leaving (A.D. 1347) with aloes-wood, *camphor*, cloves, and sandal-wood, besides provisions.

Ishâk ibn Amrân, an Arabian physician living towards the end of

[1] In the description of Arabia by Ibn Hagik el Hamdany, fol. 170 of the MS. at Aden (Prof. Sprenger).

[2] He directs two ounces of camphor to be added to a certain preparation, provided camphor is sufficiently abundant.—Tetr. iv. sermo 4. c. 114.

[3] G. Weil, *Geschichte der Chalifen*, i. (Mannheim, 1846) 75.

[4] Quatremère, *Mém. sur l'Egypte*, ii. (1811) 366–375.—It is interesting to find that *Káfúre-kaisúri*, i.e., *Kaisur Camphor*, is a term still known in the Indian bazaars.

[5] Käuffer, *Geschichte von Ostasien*, ii. (1859) 491.

[6] Translation from the Chinese communicated by Mr. A. Wylie.

[7] *Les Prairies d'or*, i. (Paris, 1861) 200.

[8] The Arabian *mená* or *menn* is equal to 2½ pounds Troy, or 933 grammes.

[9] Yule, *Cathay and the way thither*, ii. 357.

the 9th century, and Ibn Khurdádbah, a geographer of the same period, were among the first to point out that camphor is an export of the Malayan Archipelago; and their statements are repeated by the Arabian writers of the middle ages, who all assert that the best camphor is produced in Fansúr. This place, also called Kansúr or Kaisúr, was visited in the 13th century by Marco Polo, who speaks of its camphor as selling for its weight in gold; Yule[1] believes it to be the same spot as Barus, a town on the western coast of Sumatra, still giving a name to the camphor produced in that island.

From all these facts and many others that might be adduced,[2] it undoubtedly follows that the camphor first in use was that found native in the trunk of the Sumatran *Dryobalanops aromatica*, and not that of the Camphor Laurel. At what period and at whose instigation the Chinese began to manufacture camphor from the latter tree is not known.

Camphor was known in Europe as a medicine as early as the 12th century, as is evident from the mention of it by the abbess Hildegard[3] (who calls it *ganphora*), Otho of Cremona,[4] and the Danish canon Harpestreng (*ob.* A.D. 1244).

Garcia de Orta states (1563) that it is the camphor of China which alone is exported to Europe, that of Borneo and Sumatra being a hundred times more costly, and all consumed by eastern nations. They partly devoted the latter to ritual purposes, as for instance embalming, partly to "eating," *i.e.* for the preparation of the betel-leaves for chewing. Neuhof[5] states that the other ingredients used in China for that purpose are: Areca nuts (see article Semen Arecæ) and lime or Lycium (see page 35), *Caphur de Burneo*, aloë (*i.e.* Aloë-wood, see Aloë), and musk. Kämpfer,[6] who resided in Japan in 1690–92, and who figured the Japanese camphor tree under the name *Laurus camphorifera*, expressly declares the latter to be entirely different from the camphor tree of the Indian Archipelago. He further states that the camphor of Borneo was among the more profitable commodities imported into Japan by the Dutch, whose homeward cargoes included Japanese camphor to the extent of 6,000 to 12,000 ℔ annually.[7] This camphor was refined in Holland by a process long kept secret, and was then introduced into the market. In Pomet's time (1694 and earlier), crude camphor was common in France, but it had to be sent to Holland for purification.

It is doubtful whether at that period, or even much later, any camphor was obtained from Formosa. Du Halde[8] makes no allusion to it as a production of that island; nor does he mention it among the commodities of Emouy (Amoy), which was the Chinese port then in most active communication with Formosa.

Production—The camphor of European commerce is produced in

[1] *The Book of Ser Marco Polo*, ii. (1874) 282, 285.

[2] For further historical details, compare my paper in the *Schweizerische Wochenschrift für Pharmacie*, 27 Sept., 4 and 11 Oct. 1867, or in Buchner's *Repertorium f. Pharmacie*, xvii. (1868) 28.—F. A. F.

[3] S. Hildegardis *Opera Omnia*, accurante J. P. Migne, Paris, 1855. 1145.

[4] Choulant, *Macer Floridus*, Lips. 1832. 161.

[5] *Gesantschaft, etc.* Amsterdam, 1666. 363.

[6] *Amœnitates exoticæ* (1712) 770.

[7] *Hist. of Japan*, translated by Scheuchzer, i. (1727) 353. 370.

[8] *Description de la Chine*, i. (1735) 161.

the island of Formosa and in Japan. We have no evidence that any is manufactured at the present day in China, although very large trees, often from 8 to 9 feet in diameter, are common, for instance in Kiangsi, and camphor wood is an important timber of the Hankow market.

In Formosa, the camphor-producing districts lie in the narrow belt of debateable ground, which separates the border Chinese settlements from the territory still occupied by the aboriginal tribes. The camphor is prepared from the wood, which is cut into small chips from the trees, by means of a gouge with a long handle. In this process there is great waste, many trees being cut and then left with a large portion of valuable timber to perish. The next operation is to expose the wood to the vapour of boiling water, and to collect the camphor which volatilizes with the steam. For this purpose, stills are constructed thus:—a long wooden trough, frequently a hollowed trunk, is fixed over a furnace and protected by a coating of clay. Water is poured into it, and a board perforated with numerous small holes is luted over it. Above these holes the chips are placed and covered with earthen pots. A fire having been lighted in the furnace, the water becomes heated, and the steam passing through the chips, carries with it the camphor, which condenses in minute white crystals in the upper part of the pots. From these it is scraped out every few days, and is then very pure and clean. Four stills, each having ten pots placed in a row over one trough, are generally arranged under one shed. These stills are moved from time to time, according as the gradual exhaustion of timber in the locality renders such transfer desirable. A considerable quantity of camphor is however manufactured in the towns, the chips being conveyed thither from the country. A model of a much better still, which was contributed from Formosa to the Paris Exhibition in 1878, is perhaps referring to a town manufacture.

Camphor is brought from the interior to Tamsui, the chief port of Formosa, the baskets holding about half a pecul each (1 pecul = 133⅓ lbs.), lined and covered with large leaves. Upon arrival, it is stored in vats holding from 50 to 60 peculs each, or it is packed at once in the tubs, or lead-lined boxes, in which it is exported. From the vats or tubs there drains out a yellowish essential oil known as *Camphor Oil*, which is used by the Chinese in rheumatism.[1] In 1877 hydraulic pressure has been established for the separation of the oil and moisture; the raw camphor loses about 20 per cent. of these admixtures.

Kämpfer in his account[2] of the manufacture of camphor in the Japanese province of Satzuma and in the islands of Gotho, describes the boiling of the chips in an iron pot covered with an earthen head containing straw in which the camphor collects. In the province of Tosa, island of Sikok, there is now a still in use, which is quite conveniently combined with a cooling apparatus consisting of a wooden trough, over which cold water is flowing.[3]

[1] The foregoing particulars are chiefly extracted from the *Trade Report of Tamsui* by E. C. Taintor, Acting Commissioner of Customs, published in the *Reports on Trade at the Treaty Ports in China* for 1869, Shanghai, 1870, and from James Morrison's *Description of the island of Formosa*, in the *Geogr. Magazine*, 1877, 263 and 319.

[2] *Op. cit.* p. 772.

[3] Both of the above mentioned stills from Sikok and Formosa are figured in my "*Account of the Paris Exhibition*," *Archiv der Pharmacie*, 214 (1879) 12.—F.A.F.

Purification—Camphor as it is exported from Japan and Formosa requires to be purified by sublimation. The crude drug consists of small crystalline grains, which cohere into irregular friable masses, of a greyish white or pinkish hue. Dissolved in spirit of wine, it leaves from 2 to 10 per cent. of impurities consisting of gypsum, common salt, sulphur, or vegetable fragments.

In Europe, crude camphor is sublimed from a little charcoal or sand, iron filings or quick-lime, and sent into the market as *Refined Camphor* in the form of large bowls or concave cakes, about 10 inches in diameter, 3 inches in thickness, and weighing from 9 to 12 lb.[1] Each bowl has a large round hole at the bottom, corresponding to the aperture of the vessel in which the sublimation has been conducted. This operation is performed in peculiar glass flasks termed *bomboloes*, in the upper half of which the pure camphor concretes. These flasks having been charged and placed in a sand-bath, are rapidly heated to about 120°–190° C. in order to remove the water. Afterwards the temperature is slowly increased to about 204° C., and maintained during 24 hours. The flasks are finally broken.

As camphor is a neutral substance, the addition of lime probably serves merely to retain traces of resin or empyreumatic oil. Iron would keep back sulphur were any present.

In the United States the refiners use iron vessels; their product is in flat disks, about 16 inches in diameter by one inch in thickness.

The refining of camphor is carried on to a large extent in England, Holland, Hamburg, Paris, Bohemia (Aussig), in New York and Philadelphia. It is a process requiring great care on account of the inflammability of the product. The temperature must also be nicely regulated, so that the sublimate may be deposited not merely in loose crystals, but in compact cakes. In India where the consumption of camphor is very large, the natives effect the sublimation in a copper vessel, the charge of which is 1½ maunds (42 lb.): fire is applied to the lower part, the upper being kept cool.[2]

Description—Purified Camphor forms a colourless crystalline, translucent mass, traversed by numerous fissures, so that notwithstanding a certain toughness, a mass can readily be broken by repeated blows. By spontaneous and extremely slow evaporation at ordinary temperatures, camphor sublimes in lustrous hexagonal plates or prisms, having but little hardness. If triturated in a mortar, camphor adheres to the pestle, so that it cannot be powdered *per se*. But if moistened with spirit of wine, ether, chloroform, methylic alcohol, glycerin, or an essential or fatty oil, pulverization is effected without difficulty. By keeping a short time, the powder acquires a crystalline form. With an equal weight of sugar, camphor may also be easily powdered.

Camphor melts at 175° C., boils at 204°, and volatilizes somewhat rapidly even at ordinary temperatures. To this latter property, combined with slight solubility, must be attributed the curious rotatory motion which small lumps of camphor (as well as barium butyrate, stannic bromide, chloral hydrate, and a few other substances) exhibit when thrown on to water.

[1] These are the dimensions of the cakes manufactured in the laboratory of Messrs. Howards of Stratford, but it is obvious that they may vary with different makers.

[2] Mattheson, *England to Delhi*, Lond. 1870, 474.

The solubility of camphor in water is very small, 1300 parts dissolving about one; but even this small quantity is partially separated on addition of some alkaline or earthy salt, as sulphate of magnesium. Alcohols, ethers, chloroform, carbon bisulphide, volatile and fixed oils and liquid hydrocarbons, dissolve camphor abundantly.

The sp. gr. of camphor at 0° C. and up to 6° is the same as that of water; yet at a somewhat higher temperature, camphor expands more quickly, so that at 10° to 12° C. its sp. gr. is only 0·992.

In concentrated solution or in a state of fusion, camphor turns the plane of polarization strongly to the right. Officinal solution of camphor (*Spiritus Camphoræ*) is too weak, and does not deviate the ray of light to a considerable amount.[1] Crystals of camphor are devoid of rotatory power.

The taste and odour of camphor are *sui generis*, or at least are common only to a group of nearly allied substances. Camphor is not altered by exposure to air or light. It burns easily, affording a brilliant smoky flame.

Chemical Composition.—Camphor, $C^{10}H^{16}O$, by treatment with various reagents, yields a number of interesting products: thus when repeatedly distilled with chloride of zinc or anhydrous phosphoric acid, it is converted into *Cymene* or *Cymol*, $C^{10}H^{14}$, a body contained in many essential oils, or obtainable therefrom.

Camphor, and also camphor oil, when subjected to powerful oxidizing agents, absorbs oxygen, passing gradually into crystallized *Camphoric Acid*, $C^{10}H^{16}O^4$ or $C^8H^{14}(COOH)^2$, water and carbonic acid being at the same time eliminated. Many essential oils, resins and gum-resins likewise yield these acids when similarly treated.

By means of less energetic oxidizers, camphor may be converted into *Oxy-Camphor*, $C^{10}H^{16}O^2$, still retaining its original odour and taste (Wheeler, 1868).

Commerce—Two kinds of crude camphor are known in the English market, namely:

1. *Formosa* or *China Camphor*, imported in chests lined with lead or tinned iron, and weighing about 1 cwt. each; it is of a light brown, small in grain, and always wet, as the merchants cause water to be poured into the cases before shipment, with a view, it is pretended, of lessening the loss by evaporation. The exports of this camphor from Tamsui in Formosa[2] were in peculs (one pecul = 13·33 lb. avdp. = 60·479 kilogrammes) as follows:

1870	1871	1872	1875	1876	1877
14,481	9691	10,281	7139	8794	13,178

The shipments of camphor from Takow, the other open port of Formosa, are of insignificant amount. Planks of camphor wood are now exported in some quantity from Tamsui.

2. *Japan Camphor* is lighter in colour and occasionally of a pinkish tint; it is also in larger grains. It arrives in double tubs (one within the other) without metal lining, and hence is drier than the previous sort; the tubs hold about 1 cwt. It fetches a somewhat higher price than the Formosa camphor.

[1] *Pharm. Journ.* 18 April 1874. 830.

[2] *Returns of Trade at the Treaty Ports in China for* 1872, part. 2, p. 124.

Hiogo and Osaka exported in 1871, 7089 peculs (945,200 lb.), and Nagasaki 745 peculs (99,333 lb.), the total value being 116,718 dollars.[1] In 1877 the value of camphor exported from Japan was stated to be equal to 240,000 dollars. The imports of *Unrefined Camphor* into the United Kingdom amounted in 1870 to 12,368 cwt. (1,385,216 lb.); of *Refined Camphor* in the same year to 2361 cwt.[2]

Camphor is largely consumed by the natives of India; the quantity of the crude drug imported into Bombay in the year 1872-73 was 3801 cwt.[3]

Uses—Camphor has stimulant properties and is frequently used in medicine both internally and externally. It is largely consumed in India.

Other kinds of Camphor; Camphor Oils.

Camphor, as stated above at page 512, was the name originally applied to the product of Dryobalanops; it was then also given to that of Camphor Laurel, and in 1725 Caspar Neumann, of Berlin, first pointed out that many essential oils afford crystals ("stearoptenes" of later chemists), for which he proposed the general name of camphor. Many of them are agreeing with the formula $C^{10}H^{16}O$, and there are also numerous liquids of the same composition. It would appear, however, that no stearoptene of any other plant is absolutely identical with common camphor; Lallemand's statement (see p. 479), that oil of spike affords the latter, requires further examination.

Many other liquid and solid constituents of essential oils, or substances afforded by treating them with alcoholic potash, answer to the formula $C^{10}H^{17}(OH)$. Among them we may point out the two following: they are the only substances of the class of "camphors," besides common camphor, which are of some practical importance.

Barus Camphor, Borneo Camphor, Malayan Camphor, Dryobalanops Camphor—This, as already explained, is the substance to which the earliest notices of camphor refer. The tree which affords it is *Dryobalanops aromatica* Gärtn. (*D. Camphora* Colebrooke), of the order *Dipterocarpeæ*, one of the most majestic objects of the vegetable kingdom.[4] The trunk is very tall, round, and straight, furnished near the base with huge buttresses; it rises 100 to 150 feet without a branch, then producing a dense crown of shining foliage, 50 to 70 feet in diameter, on which are scattered beautiful white flowers of delicious fragrance. The tree is indigenous to the Dutch Residencies on the north-west coast of Sumatra, between 0° and 3° N. lat., from Ayer Bangis to Barus and Singkel, and to the northern part of Borneo, and the small British island of Labuan.

The camphor is obtained from the trunk, in longitudinal fissures of which it is found in a solid crystalline state, and extracted by laboriously splitting the wood. It can only be got by the destruc-

[1] *Commercial Reports from H. M. Consuls in Japan*, No. 1, 1872.—The returns for Hiogo and Osaka are upon the authority of the Chamber of Commerce.

[2] *Statement of the Trade and Navigation of the United Kingdom* for 1870. p. 61—no later returns accessible.

[3] *Statement of the Trade and Navigation of Bombay for* 1872-73. ii. 27.

[4] For a full account and figure of it, see W. H. de Vriese's excellent *Mémoire sur le Camphrier de Sumatra et de Bornéo*, Leide, 1857. 23 p. 4°. and 2 plates.

tion of the entire tree;—in fact, many trees afford none, so that to avoid the toil of useless felling, it is now customary to try them by cutting a hole in the side of the trunk, but the observation so made is often fallacious. Spenser St. John, British Consul in Borneo, was told that trees in a state of decay often contain the finest camphor.[1] The camphor when collected is carefully picked over, washed and cleaned, and then separated into three qualities, the best being formed of the largest and purest crystals, while the lowest is greyish and pulverulent.

Dryobalanops attaining more than 150 feet in height, the quantity of camphor which it yields must necessarily be greatly variable. The statements are from about 3 to 11 lb.

A good proportion of the small quantity produced is consumed in the funeral rites of the Batta princes, whose families are often ruined by the lavish expense of providing the camphor and buffaloes which the custom of their obsequies requires. The camphor which is exported is eagerly bought for the China market, but some is also sent to Japan, Laos, Cochin China, Cambodia, and Siam.

The quantity annually shipped from Borneo was reckoned by Motley in 1851 to be about 7 peculs (933 lbs.). The export from Sumatra was estimated by De Vriese at 10 to 15 quintals per annum.[2] The quantity imported into Canton in 1872 was returned as $23\frac{7}{10}$ peculs (3,159 lb.), value 42,326 taels, equivalent to about 80*s.* per lb.[3] In the *Annual Statement of the Trade of Bombay* for the year 1872-3, 2 cwt. of *Malayan Camphor* is stated to have been imported; it was valued at 9,141 Rs. (£914). In the "Indian tariff," 1875, the duty is fixed *per cwt.* at 40 rupees for crude camphor, 65 rupees for refined camphor, and 80 rupees *per pound* for Baros camphor ("Bhemsaini camphor"). The price in Borneo in 1851 of camphor of fine quality was 30 dollars per catty, or about 95*s.* per lb.: consequently the drug never finds its way into European commerce.

Borneo Camphor, also termed by chemists *Borneol* or *Camphyl Alcohol*, is somewhat harder than common camphor, also a little heavier so that it sinks in water. It is less volatile, and does not crystallize on the interior of the bottle in which it is kept; and it requires for fusion a higher temperature, namely 198° C. It has a somewhat different odour, resembling that of common camphor with the addition of patchouli or ambergris. The composition of borneol is represented by the formula $C^{10}H^{17}(OH)$. It may be converted by the action of nitric acid into common camphor, which it nearly resembles in most of its physical properties. Conversely, borneol may also be prepared from common camphor. By continued oxydation borneol yields camphoric acid.

Camphor Oil of Borneo—Besides camphor, the *Dryobalanops* furnishes another product, a liquid termed *Camphor Oil*, which must not be confounded with the camphor oil that drains out of crude laurel camphor. This Bornean or Sumatran *Camphor Oil* is obtained by tapping the trees, or in felling them (see also p. 229). In the latter way,

[1] *Life in the Forests of the Far East*, ii. (1862) 272.

[2] In Milburn's time (*Oriental Commerce*, ii. 1813. 308), Sumatra was reckoned to export 50 peculs, and Borneo 30 peculs a year. Rondot's statement (see Cassia Buds) that China imports of Barus camphor about 800 peculs annually is plainly erroneous.

[3] *Returns of Trade at the Treaty Ports in China for* 1872, p. 30.

Motley in cutting down a tree in Labuan in May, 1851, pierced a reservoir in the trunk from which about five gallons of camphor oil were obtained, though much could not be caught.[1] The liquid was a volatile oil holding in solution a resin, which after a few days' exposure to the air, was left in a syrupy state. This camphor oil, which is termed *Borneene*, is isomeric with oil of turpentine, $C^{10}H^{16}$, yet in the crude state holding in solution borneol and resin. By fractional distillation, it may be separated into two portions, the one more volatile than the other but not differing in composition.

Camphor Oil of Formosa, which has been already referred to as draining out of the crude camphor of *Cinnamomum Camphora*, is a brown liquid holding in solution an abundance of common camphor, which it speedily deposits in crystals when the temperature is slightly reduced. From Borneo Camphor Oil it may be distinguished by its *odour of sassafras*. We find no optical difference in the rotatory power of the oils; both are dextrogyre to the same extent, which is still the case if the camphor from the lauraceous camphor oil is separated by cooling. Borneo camphor oil, for a sample of which we are indebted to Prof. de Vriese, deposits no camphor even when kept at −15° C.

Ngai Camphor, *Blumea Camphor*—It has been known for many years that the Chinese are in the habit of using a third variety of camphor, having a pecuniary value intermediate between that of common camphor and of Borneo camphor. This substance is manufactured at Canton and in the island of Hainan, the plant from which it is obtained being *Blumea balsamifera* DC., a tall herbaceous *Composita*, of the tribe *Inuloideæ*, called in Chinese *Ngai*, abundant in Tropical Eastern Asia.

The drug has been supplied to us[2] in two forms,—crude and pure,—the first being in crystalline grains of a dirty white, contaminated with vegetable remains; the second in colourless crystals as much as an inch in length. By sublimation the substance may be obtained in distinct, brilliant crystals, agreeing precisely with those of Borneo camphor, which they also resemble in odour and hardness, as well as in being a little heavier than water and not so volatile as common camphor.

The chemical examination of Ngai camphor, performed by Plowman,[3] under the direction of Prof. Attfield, has proved that it has the composition $C^{10}H^{18}O$, like Borneo camphor. But the two substances differ in optical properties,[4] an alcoholic solution of Ngai camphor being *levogyre* in about the same degree that one of Borneo camphor is *dextrogye*. By boiling nitric acid, Borneo camphor is transformed into common (*dextrogyre*) camphor, whereas Ngai camphor affords a similar yet *levogyre* camphor, in all probability identical with the stearoptene of *Chrysanthemum Parthenium* Pers.

As Ngai camphor is about ten times the price of Formosa camphor, it never finds its way to Europe as an article of trade. In China it is consumed partly in medicine and partly in perfuming the fine kinds of

[1] Ibn Khurdádbah in the 9th century mentions it as being obtained in this way.

[2] Through the courtesy of Mr. F. H. Ewer, of the Imperial Maritime Customs, Canton.—Hanbury, *Science Papers*, 189. 393.

[3] *Pharm. Journ.* March 7, 1874. 710.

[4] Flückiger in *Pharm. Journ.* April 18, 1874. 829.

Chinese ink. The export of this camphor by sea from Canton is valued at about £3,000 a year; it is also exported from Kiungchow, in the island of Hainan.

CORTEX CINNAMOMI.

Cortex Cinnamomi Zeylanici; Cinnamon; F. *Cannelle de Ceylan;* G. *Zimmt, Ceylon Zimmt, Kaneel.*

Botanical Origin—*Cinnamomum zeylanicum* Breyne,—a small evergreen tree, richly clothed with beautiful, shining leaves usually somewhat glaucous beneath, and having panicles of greenish flowers of disagreeable odour.

It is a native of Ceylon, where, according to Thwaites, it is generally distributed through the forests up to an elevation of 3,000 feet, and one variety even to 8,000 feet. It is exceedingly variable in stature, and in the outline, size and consistence of the leaf; and several of the extreme forms are very unlike one another and have received specific names. But there are also numerous intermediate forms; and in a large suite of specimens, many occur of which it is impossible to determine whether they should be referred to this species or to that. Thwaites[1] is of opinion that some still admitted species, as *C. obtusifolium* Nees and *C. iners* Reinw., will prove on further investigation to be mere forms of *C. zeylanicum.*

Beddome,[2] Conservator of Forests in Madras, remarks that in the moist forests of South-western India there are 7 or 8 well-marked varieties which might easily be regarded as so many distinct species, but for the fact that they are so connected *inter se* by intermediate forms, that it is impossible to find constant characters worthy of specific distinction. They grow from the sea level up to the highest elevations, and, as Beddome thinks, owe their differences chiefly to local circumstances, so that he is disposed to class them simply as forms of *C. zeylanicum.*

History—(For that of the essential oil of cinnamon see page 526). Cinnamon was held in high esteem in the most remote times of history. In the words of the learned Dr. Vincent, Dean of Westminster,[3] it seems to have been the first spice sought after in all oriental voyages. Both cinnamon and cassia are mentioned as precious odoriferous substances in the Mosaic writings and in the Biblical books of Psalms, Proverbs, Canticles, Ezekiel and Revelations, also by Theophrastus, Herodotus, Galen, Dioscorides, Pliny, Strabo and many other writers of antiquity: and from the accounts which have thus come down to us, there appears reason for believing that the spices referred to were nearly the same as those of the present day. That cinnamon and cassia were extremely analogous, is proved by the remark of Galen, that the finest cassia differs so little from the lowest quality of cinnamon, that the first may be substituted for the second, provided a double weight of it be used.

[1] *Enumeratio Plantarum Zeylaniæ*, 1864. 252.—Consult also Meissner in De Cand. *Prod.* xv. sect. i. 10.

[2] *Flora Sylvatica for Southern India*, 1872. 262.

[3] *Commerce and Navigation of the Ancients in the Indian Ocean*, ii. (1807) 512.

It is also evident that both were regarded as among the most costly of aromatics, for the offering made by Seleucus II. Callinicus, king of Syria, and his brother Antiochus Hierax, to the temple of Apollo at Miletus, B.C. 243, consisting chiefly of vessels of gold and silver, and olibanum, myrrh (σμύρνη), costus (page 382), included also two pounds of *Cassia* (κασία), and the same quantity of *Cinnamon* (κιννάμωμον).[1]

In connexion with this subject there is one remarkable fact to be noticed, which is that none of the cinnamon of the ancients was obtained from Ceylon. "In the pages of no author," says Tennent,[2] "European or Asiatic, from the earliest ages to the close of the thirteenth century, is there the remotest allusion to cinnamon as an indigenous production, or even as an article of commerce in Ceylon." Nor do the annuals of the Chinese, between whom and the inhabitants of Ceylon, from the 4th to the 8th centuries, there was frequent intercourse and exchange of commodities, name *Cinnamon* as one of the productions of the island. The Sacred Books and other ancient records of the Singhalese are also completely silent on this point.

Cassia, under the name of *Kwei*, is mentioned in the earliest Chinese herbal,—that of the emperor Shen-nung, who reigned about 2700 B.C., in the ancient Chinese[3] Classics, and in the *Rh-ya*, a herbal dating from 1200 B.C. In the *Hai-yao-pên-ts'ao*, written in the 8th century, mention is made of *Tien-chu kwei*. Tien-chu is the ancient name for India: perhaps the allusion may be to the cassia bark of Malabar.

In connexion with these extremely early references to the spice, it may be stated that a bark supposed to be *cassia* is mentioned as imported into Egypt together with gold, ivory, frankincense, precious woods, and apes, in the 17th century B.C.[4]

The accounts given by Dioscorides, Ptolemy and the author of the Periplus of the Erythrean Sea, indicate that cinnamon and cassia were obtained from Arabia and Eastern Africa; and we further know that the importers were Phœnicians, who traded by Egypt and the Red Sea with Arabia. Whether the spice under notice was really a production of Arabia or Africa, or whether it was imported thither from Southern China (the present source of the best sort of cassia), is a question which has excited no small amount of discussion.

We are in favour of the second alternative,—firstly, because no substance of the nature of cinnamon is known to be produced in Arabia or Africa; and secondly, because the commercial intercourse which was undoubtedly carried on by China with India and Arabia, and which also existed between Arabia, India and Africa, is amply sufficient to explain the importation of Chinese produce.[5] That the spice was a

[1] Chishull, *Antiquities Asiaticæ*, 1728. 65-72.

[2] *Ceylon*, i. (1859) 575.

[3] We are indebted to Dr. Bretschneider of Pekin for these references to Chinese literature. For information about some of the works quoted, see his pamphlet *On the Study and Value of Chinese Botanical Works*, Foochow, 1870.

[4] Dümichen, *Fleet of an Egyptian Queen*, Leipzig, 1868, p. 1.

[5] "... That there was an ulterior commerce beyond Ceylon is indubitable; for at Ceylon the trade from Malacca and the Golden Chersonese met the merchants from Arabia, Persia and Egypt. This might possibly have been in the hands of the Malays or even the Chinese, who seem to have been navigators in all ages as universally as the Arabians. ...." Vincent, *op. cit.* ii. 284. 285.—In the time of Marco Polo, the trade of China westward met the trade of the Red Sea, no longer in Ceylon, but on the coast of Malabar,

production of the far East is moreover implied by the name *Darchini* (from *dar*, wood or bark, and *Chini*, Chinese) given to it by the Arabians and Persians.

If this view of the case is admissible, we must regard the ancient cinnamon to have been the substance now known as *Chinese Cassia lignea* or *Chinese Cinnamon*, and cassia as one of the thicker and perhaps less aromatic barks of the same group, such in fact as are still found in commerce.

Of the circumstances which led to the collection of cinnamon in Ceylon, and of the period at which it was commenced, nothing is known. That the Chinese were concerned in the discovery is not an unreasonable supposition, seeing that they traded to Ceylon, and were in all probability acquainted with the cassia-yielding species of *Cinnamomum* of Southern China, a tree extremely like the cinnamon tree of Ceylon.

Whatever may be the facts, the early notices of cinnamon as a production of Ceylon are not prior to the 13th century. The very first, according to Yule,[1] is a mention of the spice by Kazwini, an Arab writer of about A.D. 1275, very soon after which period it is noticed by the historian of the Egyptian Sultan Kelaoun, A.D. 1283. The prince of Ceylon is stated to have sent an ambassador, Al-Hadj-Abu-Othman, to the Sultan's court. It was mentioned that Ceylon produced elephants, Bakam (the wood of *Cæsalpinia Sapan* L.—see page 216), pearls and also *cinnamon*.[2]

A still more positive evidence is due to the Minorite friar, John of Montecorvino, a missionary who visited India. This man, in a letter under date December 20th, 1292 or 1293, written at "Mabar, città dell' India di sopra," and still extant in the Medicean library at Florence, says that the cinnamon tree is of medium bulk, and in trunk, bark and foliage, like a laurel, and that great store of its bark is carried forth from the island which is near by Malabar.[3]

Again, it is mentioned by the Mahomedan traveller Ibn Batuta about A.D. 1340,[4] and a century later by the Venetian merchant Nicolo di Conti, whose description of the tree is very correct.[5]

The circumnavigation of the Cape of Good Hope led to the real discovery of Ceylon by the Portuguese in 1505, and to their permanent occupation of the island in 1536, chiefly for the sake of the cinnamon. It is from the first of these dates that more exact accounts of the spice began to reach Europe. Thus in 1511 Barbosa distinguished the fine cinnamon of Ceylon from the inferior *Canella trista* of Malabar. Garcia de Orta, about the middle of the same century, stated that Ceylon cinnamon was forty times as dear as that of Malabar. Clusius, the translator

apparently at Calicut, where the Portuguese found it on their first arrival. Here, says Marco, the ships from Aden obtained their lading from the East, and carried it into the Red Sea for Alexandria, whence it passed into Europe by means of the Venetians.—See also Yule, *Book of Ser Marco Polo*, ii. (1871) 325. 327.

[1] *Marco Polo*, ii. 255.

[2] *Quatremère* (in the book quoted at page 511, note 4), ii. 284.

[3] Yule, *Cathay and the way thither*, i. 213, also Kunstmann, *Anzeigen der baierischen Akademie*, 24 and 25 December 1855. p. 163 and 169.

[4] *Travels of Ibn Batuta*, translated by Lee, Lond. 1829. 184.

[5] Ramusio, *Raccolta delle Navigationi et Viaggi*, i. (1563) 339; Kunstmann, *Kenntniss Indiens im fünfzehnten Jahrhundert*, 1864. 39.

of Garcia, saw branches of the cinnamon-tree as early as 1571 at Bristol and in Holland.

At this period cinnamon was cut from trees growing wild in the forests in the interior of Ceylon, the bark being exacted as tribute from the Singhalese kings by the Portuguese. A peculiar caste called *chalias*, who are said to have emigrated from India to Ceylon in the 13th century, and who in after-times became cinnamon-peelers, delivered the bark to the Portuguese. The cruel oppression of these *chalias* was not mitigated by the Dutch, who from the year 1656 were virtually masters of the whole seaboard, and conceded the cinnamon trade to their East India Company as a profitable monopoly, which the Company exercised with the greatest severity.[1] The bark previous to shipment was minutely examined by special officers, to guard against frauds on the part of the *chalias*.

About 1770 De Koke conceived the happy idea, in opposition to the universal prejudice in favour of wild-growing cinnamon, of attempting the cultivation of the tree. This project was carried out under Governors Falck and Van der Graff with extraordinary success, so that the Dutch were able, independently of the kingdom of Kandy, to furnish about 400,000 lb. of cinnamon annually, thereby supplying the entire European demand. In fact, they completely ruled the trade, and would even *burn* the cinnamon in Holland, lest its unusual abundance should reduce the price.

After Ceylon had been wrested from the Dutch by the English in 1796, the cinnamon trade became the monopoly of the English East India Company, who then obtained more cinnamon from the forests, especially after the year 1815, when the kingdom of Kandy fell under British rule. But though the *chalias* had much increased in numbers, the yearly production of cinnamon does not appear to have exceeded 500,000 lb. The condition of the unfortunate *chalias* was not ameliorated until 1833, when the monopoly granted to the Company was finally abolished, and Government, ceasing to be the sole exporters of cinnamon, permitted the merchants of Colombo and Galle to share in the trade.

Cinnamon however was still burdened with an export duty equal to a third or a half of its value; in consequence of which and of the competition with cinnamon raised in Java, and with cassia from China and other places, the cultivation in Ceylon began to suffer. This duty was not removed until 1853.

The earliest notice of cinnamon in connexion with Northern Europe that we have met with, is the diploma granted by Chilperic II., king of the Franks, to the monastery of Corbie in Normandy, A.D. 716, in which provision is made for a certain supply of spices and grocery, including 5 lb. of *Cinnamon*.[2]

The extraordinary value set on cinnamon at this period is remarkably illustrated by some letters written from Italy, in which mention is here and there incidentally made of presents of spices and incense.[3] Thus in A.D. 745, Gemmulus, a Roman deacon, sends to Boniface, archbishop of Mayence ("*cum magnâ reverentiâ*"), 4 ounces of *Cinnamon*, 4

[1] Tennent, *op. cit.* ii. 52.

[2] Pardessus, *Diplomata*, etc., Paris, 1849. ii. 309.

[3] Jaffé, *Bibliotheca Rerum Germanicarum*, Berlin, iii. (1866) 154. 199. 214. 216–8. 109.

ounces of Costus, and 2 pounds of Pepper. In A.D. 748, Theophilacias, a Roman archdeacon, presents to the same bishop similar spices and incense. Lullus, the successor of Boniface, sends to Eadburga, *abbatissa Thanetensis*,[1] *circa* A.D. 732–751—"*unum graphium argenteum et storacis et* cinnamomi *partem aliquam*"; and about the same date, another present of cinnamon to archbishop Boniface is recorded. Under date A.D. 732–742, a letter is extant of three persons to the abbess Cuneburga, to whom the writers offer—"*turis et piperis et* cinnamomi *permodica xenia, sed omni mentis affectione destinata*."

In the 9th century, *Cinnamon*, pepper, costus, cloves, and several indigenous aromatic plants were used in the monastery of St. Gall in Switzerland as ingredients for seasoning fish.[2]

Of the pecuniary value of this spice in England, there are many notices from the year 1264 downwards.[3] In the 16th century it was probably not plentiful, if we may judge from the fact that it figures among the New Year's gifts to Philip and Mary (1556-57), and to Queen Elizabeth (1561-62).[4]

Production and Commerce[5]—The best cinnamon is produced, according to Thwaites,[6] from a cultivated or selected form of the tree (var. *a.*), distinguished by large leaves of somewhat irregular shape. But the bark of all the forms possesses the odour of cinnamon in a greater or less degree. It is not however always possible to judge of the quality of the bark from the foliage, so that the peelers when collecting from uncultivated trees, are in the habit of tasting the bark before commencing operations, and pass over some trees as unfit for their purpose. The bark of varieties *β. multiflorum* and *γ. ovalifolium* is of very inferior quality, and said to be never collected unless for the purpose of adulteration.

The best variety appears to find the conditions most favourable to its culture, in the strip of country, 12 to 15 miles broad, on the south-west coast of Ceylon, between Negumbo, Colombo and Matura, where the tree is grown up to an elevation of 1500 feet. A very sandy clay soil, or fine white quartz, with a good sub-soil and free exposure to the sun and rain, are the circumstances best adapted for the cultivation. The management of the plantations resembles that of oak coppice in England. The system of pruning checks the plant from becoming a tree, and induces it to form a stool from which four or five shoots are allowed to grow; these are cut at the age of 1½ to 2 years, when the greyish-green epidermis begins to turn brown by reason of the formation of a corky layer. They are not all cut at the same time, but only as they arrive at the proper state of maturity; they are then 6 to 10 feet high and ½ to 2 inches thick. In some of the cinnamon gardens at Colombo, the stools are very large and old, dating back, it is supposed, from the time of the Dutch.

In consequence of the increased flow of sap which occurs after the

[1] Doubtless *Eadburh*, third abbess of Minster in the Isle of Thanet in Kent. She died A.D. 751.

[2] *Pharm. Journ.* viii. (1877) 121.

[3] Eden, *State of the Poor*, ii. (1797) appendix; Rogers, *Hist. of Agriculture and Prices in England*, ii. (1866) 543.

[4] Nicholls, *Progresses and Processions of Q. Elizabeth*, i. (1823) xxxiv. 118.

[5] Additional information may be found in two papers by Marshall, in Thomson's *Annals of Philosophy*, x. (1817) 241 and 346; see also Leschenault de la Tour, *Mém. du Musée d'Hist. nat.* viii. (1822) 436-446.

[6] *Op. cit.* 252-253.

heavy rains in May and June, and again in November and December, the bark at those seasons is easily separated from the wood, so that a principal harvest takes place in the spring, and a smaller one in the latter part of the year.

The shoots having been cut off by means of a long sickle-shaped hook called a *catty*, and stripped of their leaves, are slightly trimmed with a knife, the little pieces thus removed being reserved and sold as *Cinnamon Chips*. The bark is next cut through at distances of about a foot, and slit lengthwise, when it is easily and completely removed by the insertion of a peculiar knife termed a *mama*, the separation being assisted, if necessary, by strongly rubbing with the handle. The pieces of bark are now carefully put one into another, and the compound sticks firmly bound together into bundles. Thus they are left for 24 hours or more, during which a sort of "*fermentation*" (?) goes on which facilitates the subsequent removal part. This is accomplished by placing each quill on a stick of wood of suitable thickness, and carefully scraping off with a knife the outer and middle cortical layer. In a few hours after this operation, the peeler commences to place the smaller tubes within the larger, also inserting the small pieces so as to make up an almost solid stick, of about 40 inches in length. The cinnamon thus prepared is kept one day in the shade, and then placed on wicker trays in the sun to dry. When sufficiently dry, it is made into bundles of about 30 ℔. each.[1]

The cinnamon gardens of Ceylon were estimated in 1860–64 to occupy an area of about 14,400 acres; in the catalogue of the British Colonies, Paris Exhibition, 1878, about 2 millions of acres are stated to be under cultivation in the island, 26,000 acres with cinnamon.[2]

The exports of cinnamon from Ceylon have been as follows:—

1871	1872	1875
1,359,327 lb., value £67,966.	1,267,953 lb., value £64,747.	1,500,000 lb.

At present the cultivation of coffee is displacing that of cinnamon, the exports of the former in 1875 being 928,606 cwts. valued at $4\frac{1}{4}$ millions sterling. Of the crop of 1872 there were 1,179,516 ℔. of cinnamon shipped to the United Kingdom, 53,439 ℔. to the United States of North America, and 10,000 ℔. to Hamburg.

Besides the above-named exports of cinnamon, the official statistics[3] record the export of "*Cinnamon Bark*"—8846 ℔. in 1871—23,449 ℔. in 1872. This name includes two distinct articles, namely *Cinnamon Chips*, and a very thick bark derived from old stems. The *Cinnamon Chips* which, as explained on the previous page, are the first trimmings of the shoots, are very aromatic; they used to be considered worthless, and were thrown away. The second article, to which in the London drug sales the name "*Cinnamon Bark*" is restricted, is in flat or slightly channelled fragments, which are as much as $\frac{4}{10}$ of an inch in thickness, and remind one of New Granada cinchona

[1] Formerly called *fardela* or *fardello*, a name signifying in the Romance languages *bundle* or *package*. The word *fardel*, having the same meaning, is found in old English writers.

[2] Yet the cultivation was far more extensive in the earlier part of the century, as we may judge by the statement that the five principal cinnamon gardens around Negumbo, Colombo, Barberyn, Galle, and Matura, were *each from 15 to 20 miles in circumference* (Tennent's *Ceylon*, ii. 163).

[3] *Ceylon Blue Books* for 1871 and 1872, printed at Colombo.

bark. It is very deficient in aromatic qualities, and quite unfit for use in pharmacy.

In most other countries into which *Cinnamomum zeylanicum* has been transplanted, it has been found that, partly from its tendency to pass into new varieties and partly perhaps from want of careful cultivation and the absence of the skilled cinnamon-peeler, it yields a bark appreciably different from that of Ceylon. Of other cinnamon-producing districts, those of Southern India may be mentioned as affording the *Malabar* or *Tinnevelly*, and the *Tellicherry Cinnamon* of commerce, the latter being almost as good as the cinnamon of Ceylon.[1] The cultivation in Java commenced in 1825. The plant, according to Miquel, is a variety of *C. zeylanicum*, distinguished by its very large leaves which are frequently 8 inches long by 5 inches broad. The island exported in 1870, 1109 peculs (147,866 lb.); in 1871 only 446 peculs (59,466 lb.).[2]

Cinnamon is also grown in the French colony of Guyana and in Brazil, but on an insignificant scale. The samples of the bark from those countries which we have examined are quite unlike the cinnamon of Ceylon. That of Brazil in particular has evidently been taken from stems several years old.

The importations of cinnamon into the United Kingdom from Ceylon are shown by the following figures:—

1867	1869	1870	1871	1872	1876
859,034 lb.	2,611,473 lb.	2,148,405 lb.	1,430,518 lb.	1,015,461 lb.	1,339,060 lb.

During 1872, 56,000 lb. of cinnamon were imported from other countries.

Description—Ceylon cinnamon of the finest description is imported in the form of sticks, about 40 inches in length and $\frac{3}{8}$ of an inch in thickness, formed of tubular pieces of bark about a foot long, dexterously arranged one within the other, so as to form an even rod of considerable firmness and solidity. The quills of bark are not rolled up as simple tubes, but each side curls inwards so as to form a channel with in-curving sides, a circumstance that gives to the entire stick a somewhat flattened cylindrical form. The bark composing the stick is extremely thin, measuring often no more than $\frac{1}{100}$ of an inch in thickness. It has a light brown, dull surface, faintly marked with shining wavy lines, and bearing here and there scars or holes at the points of insertion of leaves or twigs. The inner surface of the bark is of a darker hue. The bark is brittle and splintery, with a fragrant odour, peculiar to itself and the allied barks of the same genus. Its taste is saccharine, pungent, and aromatic.

The bales of cinnamon which arrive in London are always re-packed in the dock warehouses, in doing which a certain amount of breakage occurs. The spice so injured is kept separate and sold as *Small Cinnamon*, and is very generally used for pharmaceutical purposes. It is often of excellent quality.

Microscopic Structure—By the peeling above described, Ceylon cinnamon is deprived of the suberous coat and the greater part of the middle cortical layer, so that it almost consists of the mere liber (*endo-*

[1] Some of it however is very thick, though neatly quilled.

[2] *Consular Reports*, Aug. 1873. 952.

phlœum). Three different layers are to be distinguished on a transverse section of this tissue :—

1. The external surface which is composed of one to three rows of large thick-walled cells, forming a coherent ring; it is only interrupted by bundles of liber-fibres, which are obvious even to the unaided eye; they compose in fact the wavy lines mentioned in the last page.

2. The middle layer is built up of about ten rows of parenchymatous thin-walled cells, interrupted by much larger cells containing deposits of mucilage, while other cells, not larger than those of the parenchyme itself, are loaded with essential oil.

3. The innermost layer exhibits the same thin-walled but smaller cells, yet intersected by narrow, somewhat darker, medullary rays, and likewise interrupted by cells containing either mucilage or essential oil.

Instead of bundles of liber-fibres, fibres mostly isolated are scattered through the two inner layers, the parenchyme of which abounds in small starch granules accompanied by tannic matter. On a longitudinal section, the length of the liber-fibres becomes more evident, as well as oil-ducts and gum-ducts.

Chemical Composition—The most interesting and noteworthy constituent of cinnamon is the essential oil, which the bark yields to the extent of ½ to 1 per cent., and which is distilled in Ceylon,—very seldom in England. It was prepared by Valerius Cordus, who stated,[1] somewhat before 1544, that the oils of *cinnamon* and *cloves* belong to the small number of essential oils which are heavier than water, "fundum petunt." About 1571 the essential oils of *cinnamon*, mace, *cloves*, *pepper*, nutmegs and several others, were also distilled by Guintherus of Andernach,[2] and again, about the year 1589, by Porta.[3]

In the latter part of the last century, it used to be brought to Europe by the Dutch. During the five years from 1775 to 1779 inclusive, the average quantity *annually* disposed of at the sales of the Dutch East India Company was 176 ounces. The wholesale price in London between 1776 and 1782 was 21*s.* per ounce; but from 1785 to 1789, the oil fetched 63*s.* to 68*s.*, the increase in value being doubtless occasioned by the war with Holland commenced in 1782. The oil is now largely produced in Ceylon, from which island the quantity exported in 1871 was 14,796 ounces; and in 1872, 39,100 ounces.[4] The oil is shipped chiefly to England.

Oil of cinnamon is a golden-yellow liquid, having a sp. gr. of 1·035, a powerful cinnamon odour, and a sweet and aromatic but burning taste. It deviates a ray of polarized light a very little to the left. The oil consists chiefly of *Cinnamic Aldehyde*, $C^6H^5(CH)^2COH$, together with a variable proportion of hydrocarbons. At a low temperature it becomes turbid by the deposit of a camphor, which we have not examined. The oil easily absorbs oxygen, becoming thereby contaminated with resin and cinnamic acid, $C^6H^5(CH)^2COOH$.

Cinnamon contains sugar, mannite, starch, mucilage, and tannic

[1] In his book "De artificiosis extractionibus," published by Gesner, Argentorati, 1561, fol. 226.

[2] *De medicina veteri et nova*, Basileæ, 1571. 630–635.

[3] *Magiæ Naturalis libri xx.* Neapoli 1589. 184.

[4] *Ceylon Blue Books* for 1871 and 1872.

acid. The *Cinnamomin* of Martin (1868) has been shown by Wittstein to be very probably mere mannite. The effect of iodine on a decoction of cinnamon will be noticed under the head of Cassia Lignea. Cinnamon afforded to Schätzler (1862) 5 per cent. of ash consisting chiefly of the carbonates of calcium and potassium.

Uses—Cinnamon is used in medicine as a cordial and stimulant, but is much more largely consumed as a spice.

Adulteration—Cassia lignea being much cheaper than cinnamon, is very commonly substituted for it. So long as the bark is entire, there is no difficulty in its recognition, but if it should have been reduced to powder, the case is widely different. We have found the following tests of some service, when the spice to be examined is in powder:—Make a decoction of powdered cinnamon of known genuineness; and one of similar strength of the suspected powder. When cool and strained, test a fluid ounce of each with one or two drops of tincture of iodine. A decoction of cinnamon is but little affected, but in that of cassia a deep blue-black tint is immediately produced (see further on, Cort. Cassiæ). The cheap kinds of cassia, known as *Cassia vera*, may be distinguished from the more valuable *Chinese Cassia*, as well as from cinnamon, by their richness in mucilage. This can be extracted by cold water as a thick glairy liquid, giving dense ropy precipitates with corrosive sublimate or neutral acetate of lead, but not with alcohol.

Other products of the Cinnamon Tree.

Essential Oil of Cinnamon Leaf (*Oleum Cinnamomi foliorum*)—This is a brown, viscid, essential oil, of clove-like odour, which is sometimes exported from Ceylon. It has been examined by Stenhouse (1854), who found it to have a sp. gr. of 1·053, and to consist of a mixture of *Eugenol* (p. 284) with a neutral hydrocarbon having the formula $C^{10}H^{16}$. It also contains a small quantity of benzoic acid.

Essential Oil of Cinnamon Root (*Oleum Cinnamoni radicis*)—A yellow liquid, lighter than water, having a mixed odour of camphor and cinnamon, and a strong camphoraceous taste. Both this oil and that of the leaf were described by Kämpfer (1712) and by Seba in 1731,[1] and perhaps by Garcia de Orta so early as 1563. Solid camphor may also be obtained from the root. A water distilled from the flowers, and a fatty oil expressed from the fruits are likewise noticed by old writers, but are unknown to us.

CORTEX CASSIÆ LIGNEÆ.

Cassia Lignea, Cassia Bark.

Botanical Origin—Various species of *Cinnamomum* occurring in the warm countries of Asia from India eastward, afford what is termed in commerce *Cassia Bark*. The trees are extremely variable in foliage, inflorescences and aromatic properties, and the distinctness of several of the species laid down even in recent works is still uncertain.

[1] *Phil. Trans.* xxxvi. (1731) 107.

The bark which bears *par excellence* the name of *Cassia* or *Cassia lignea*, and which is distinguished on the Continent as *Chinese Cinnamon*, is a production of the provinces of Kwangtung, Kwangsi and Kweichau in Southern China. The French expedition of Lieut. Garnier for the exploration of the Mekong and of Cochin China (1866–68) found cassia growing in about N. lat. 19° in the forests of the valley of the Se Ngum, one of the affluents on the left bank of the Mekong near the frontiers of Annam. A part of this cassia is carried by land into China, while another part is conveyed to Bangkok.[1] Although it is customary to refer it without hesitation to a tree named *Cinnamomum Cassia*, we find no warrant for such reference: no competent observer has visited and described the cassia-yielding districts of China proper, and brought therefrom the specimens requisite for ascertaining the botanical origin of the bark.[2]

Cassia lignea is also produced in the Khasya mountains in Eastern Bengal, whence it is brought down to Calcutta for shipment.[3] In this region there are three species of *Cinnamomum*, growing at 1000 to 4000 feet above the sea-level, and all have bark with the flavour of cinnamon, more or less pure: they are *C. obtusifolium* Nees, *C. pauciflorum* Nees, and *C. Tamala* Fr. Nees et Eberm.

Cinnamomum iners Reinw., a very variable species occurring in Continental India, Ceylon, Tavoy, Java, Sumatra and other islands of the Indian Archipelago, and possibly in the opinion of Thwaites a mere variety of *C. zeylanicum*, but according to Meissner well distinguished by its paler, thinner leaves, its nervation, and the character of its aroma, would appear to yield the cassia bark or wild cinnamon of Southern India.[4]

C. Tamala Fr. Nees et Eberm., which besides growing in Khasya is found in the contiguous regions of Silhet, Sikkim, Nepal, and Kumaon, and even reaches Australia, probably affords some cassia bark in Northern India.

Large quantities of a thick sort of cassia have at times been imported from Singapore and Batavia, much of which is produced in Sumatra. In the absence of any very reliable information as to its botanical sources, we may suggest as probable mother-plants, *C. Cassia* Bl. and *C. Burmanni* Bl., var. *α. chinense*, both stated by Teijsmann and Binnendijk to be cultivated in Java.[5] The latter species, growing also in the Philippines, most probably affords the cassia bark which is shipped from Manila.

History—In the preceding article we have indicated (p. 520) the remote period at which cassia bark appears to have been known to the Chinese; and have stated the reasons that led us to believe the cin-

[1] Thorel, *Notes médicales du Voyage d'Exploration du Mékong et de Cochinchine*, Paris, 1870. 30.—Garnier, *Voyage en Indo-Chine*, ii. (Paris, 1873) 438.

[2] The greatest market in China for cassia and cinnamon according to Dr. F. Porter Smith, is Taiwu in Ping-nan hien (Sin-chau fu), in Kwangsi province.—*Mat. Med. and Nat. Hist. of China*, 1871. 52.—The capital of Kwangsi is Kweilin fu, literally *Cassia-Forest*.

[3] Hooker, *Himalayan Journals*, ed. 2. ii. (1855) 303.

[4] A specimen of the stem-bark of *C. iners* from Travancore, presented to us by Dr. Waring, has a delightful odour, but is quite devoid of the taste of cinnamon.

[5] *Catalogues Plantarum quæ in Horto Botanico Bogoriensi coluntur*, Batavia, 1866. 92.

namon of the ancients was that substance. It must, however, be observed that Theophrastus, Dioscorides, Pliny, Strabo and others, as well as the remarkable inscription on the temple of Apollo at Miletus, represent cinnamon and cassia as distinct, but nearly allied substances. While, on the other hand, the author of the Periplus of the Erythrean Sea, in enumerating the products shipped from the various commercial ports of Eastern Africa[1] in the first century, mentions *Cassia* (*κασία* or *κασσία*) of various kinds, but never employs the word *Cinnamon* (*κινναμώμον*).

In the list of productions of India on which duty was levied at the Roman custom house at Alexandria, *circa* A.D. 176–180, *Cinnamomum* is mentioned as well as *Cassia turiana*, *Xylocassia* and *Xylocinnamomum*.[2] Of the distinction here drawn between cinnamon and cassia we can give no explanation; but it is worthy of note that *twigs* and *branches* of a *Cinnamomum* are sold in the Chinese drug shops, and may not improbably be the *xylocassia* or *xylocinnamon* of the ancients.[3] The name *Cassia lignea* would seem to have been originally bestowed on some such substance, rather than as at present on a mere bark. The spice was also undoubtedly called *Cassia syrinx* and *Cassia fistularis* (p. 221),—names which evidently refer to a bark which had the form of a tube. In fact there may well have been a diversity of qualities, some perhaps very costly. It is remarkable that such is still the case in China, and that the wealthy Chinese employ a thick variety of cassia, the price of which is as much as 18 dollars per catty, or about 56*s*. per lb.[4]

Whether the *Aromata Cassiæ*, which were presented to the Church at Rome under St. Silvester, A.D. 314–335, was the modern cassia bark, is rather doubtful. The largest donation, 200 lb., which was accompanied by pepper, saffron, storax, cloves, and balsam, would appear to have arrived from Egypt.[5] Cassia seems to have been known in Western Europe as early as the 7th century, for it is mentioned with cinnamon by St. Isidore, archbishop of Seville.[6] Cassia is named in one of the Leech-books in use in England prior to the Norman conquest.[7] The spice was then sold in London as *Canel* in 1264, at 10*d*. per lb., sugar being at the same time 12*d*., cumin 2*d*., and ginger 18*d*.[8] In the *Boke of Nurture*,[9] written in the 15th century by John Russell, chamberlain to Humphry, duke of Gloucester, cassia is spoken of as

[1] Vincent, *Commerce and Navigation of the Ancients in the Indian Ocean*, ii. (1807) 130. 134. 149. 150. 157.—That the ancients should confound the different kinds of cassia is really no matter for surprise, when we moderns, whether botanists, pharmacologists, or spice-dealers, are unable to point out characters by which to distinguish the barks of this group, or even to give definite names to those found in our warehouses.

[2] Vincent, *op. cit.* ii. 701–716.

[3] See further on, Allied Products, *Cassia twigs*, page 533.

[4] Very fine specimens of this costly bark have been kindly supplied to us by Dr. H. F. Hance, British Vice-Consul at Whampoa.

[5] Vignolius, *Liber Pontificalis*, Romæ, i. (1724) 94. 95.

[6] Migne, *Patrologiæ Cursus*, lxxxii. (1850) 622.—St. Isidore evidently quotes Galen, but his remarks imply that both spices were know at the period when he wrote.

[7] Cockayne, *Leechdoms, etc., of Early England*, ii. (1865) 143.

[8] Rogers, *Hist. of Agriculture and Prices in England*, ii. (1866) 543.

[9] The book has been reprinted for the Early English Text Society, 1868.—Russell says:—"Looke that your stikkes of *synamome* be thyñ, bretille and fayre in colewr . . . . for *canelle* is not so good in this crafte and cure."—And in his directions "*how to make Ypocras*," he prescribes *synamome* in that "*for lordes*," but "*canelle*" in that for "*commyn peple*."

resembling cinnamon, but cheaper and commoner, exactly as at the present day.

Production—We have no information whether the tree which affords the cassia bark of Southern China is cultivated, or whether it is exclusively found wild.

The Calcutta cassia bark collected in the Khasya mountains and brought to Calcutta is afforded by wild trees of small size. Dr. Hooker who visited the district with Dr. Thomson in 1850, observes that the trade in the bark is of recent introduction.[1] The bark which varies much in thickness, has been scraped of its outer layer.

Cassia is extensively produced in Sumatra, as may be inferred from the fact that Padang in that island, exported of the bark in 1871, 6127 peculs (817,066 lb.), a large proportion of which was shipped to America.[2] Regarding the collection of cassia on the Malabar coast, in Java and in the Philippines, no particular account has, so far as we know, been published. Spain imported from the Philippines by way of Cadiz in 1871, 93,000 lb. of cassia.[3]

Description — *Chinese Cassia lignea*, otherwise called *Chinese Cinnamon*, which of all the varieties is that most esteemed, and approaching most nearly to Ceylon cinnamon, arrives in small bundles about a foot in length and a pound in weight, the pieces of bark being held together with bands of bamboo.

The bark has a general resemblance to cinnamon, but is in simple quills, not inserted one within the other. The quills moreover are less straight, even and regular, and are of a darker brown; and though some of the bark is extremely thin, other pieces are much stouter than fine cinnamon,—in fact, it is much less uniform. The outer coat has been removed with less care than that of Ceylon cinnamon, and pieces can easily be found with the corky layer untouched by the knife.

Cassia bark breaks with a short fracture. The thicker bark cut transversely shows a faint white line in the centre running parallel with the surface. Good cassia in taste resembles cinnamon, than which it is not less sweet and aromatic, though it is often described as less fine and delicate in flavour.

An unusual kind of cassia lignea is imported since 1870 from China and offered in the London market as *China Cinnamon*,[4] though it is not the bark that bears this name in continental trade. The new drug is in *unscraped* quills, which are mostly of about the thickness of ordinary Chinese cassia lignea; it has a very saccharine taste and pungent cinnamon flavour.

The less esteemed kinds of cassia bark, which of late years have been poured into the market in vast quantity, are known in commerce as *Cassia lignea, Cassia vera* or *Wild Cassia*, and are further distinguished by the names of the localities whence shipped, as Calcutta, Java, Timor, etc.

The barks thus met with vary exceedingly in colour, thickness and aroma, so that it is vain to attempt any general classification. Some

[1] Hooker, *op. cit.*

[2] *Consular Reports*, August 1873. 953.

[3] Consul Reade, *Report on the Trade, etc., of Cadiz for* 1871, where the spice is called "*cinnamon.*"

[4] Flückiger in Wiggers and Husemann's *Jahresbericht* for 1872. 52.

have a pale cinnamon hue, but most are of a deep rich brown. They present all variations in thickness, from that of cardboard to more than a quarter of an inch thick. The flavour is more or less that of cinnamon, often with some unpleasant addition suggestive of insects of the genus *Cimex*. Many, besides being aromatic, are highly mucilaginous, the mucilage being freely imparted to cold water. Finally, we have met with some thick cassia bark of good appearance that was distinguished by astringency and the almost entire absence of aroma.

Microscopic Structure—A transverse section of such pieces of *Chinese Cassia lignea* as still bear the suberous envelope, exhibits the following characters. The external surface is made up of several rows of the usual cork-cells, loaded with brown colouring matter. In pieces from which the cork-cells have been entirely scraped, the surface is formed of the mesophlœum, yet by far the largest part of the bark belongs to the liber or endophlœum. Isolated liber-fibres and thick-walled cells (stone-cells) are scattered even through the outer layers of a transverse section. In the middle zone they are numerous, but do not form a coherent sclerenchymatous ring as in cinnamon (p. 526). The innermost part of the liber shares the structural character of cinnamon with differences due to age, as for instance the greater development of the medullary rays. Oil-cells and gum-ducts are likewise distributed in the parenchyme of the former.

The "*China Cinnamon*" of 1870 (p. 530) comes still nearer to Ceylon cinnamon, except that it is coated. A transverse section of a quill, not thicker than one millimetre, exhibits the three layers described as characterizing that bark. The sclerenchymatous ring is covered by a parenchyme rich in oil-ducts, so that it is obvious that the flavour of this drug could not be improved by scraping. The corky layer is composed of the usual tabular cells. The liber of this drug in fact agrees with that of Ceylon cinnamon.

In *Cassia Barks of considerable thickness*, the same arrangement of tissues is met with, but their strong development causes a certain dissimilarity. Thus the thick-walled cells are more and more separated one from another, so as to form only small groups. The same applies also to the liber-fibres, which in thick barks are surrounded by a parenchyme, loaded with considerable crystals of oxalate of calcium. The gum-ducts are not larger, but are more numerous in these barks, which swell considerably in cold water.

Chemical Composition—Cassia bark owes its aromatic properties to an essential oil, which, in a chemical point of view, agrees with that of Ceylon cinnamon. The flavour of cassia oil is somewhat less agreeable, and as it exists in the less valuable sorts of cassia, decidedly different in aroma from that of cinnamon. We find the sp. gr. of a Chinese cassia oil to be 1·066, and its rotatory power in a column 50 mm. long, only 0°·1 to the right, differing consequently in this respect from that of cinnamon oil (p. 526).

Oil of cassia sometimes deposits a stearoptene, which when purified is a colourless, inodorous substance, crystallizing in shining brittle prisms.[1] We have never met with it.

[1] Rochleder and Schwarz (1850) in Gmelin's *Chemistry*, xvii. 395.

If thin sections of cassia bark are moistened with a dilute solution of perchloride of iron, the contents of the parenchymatous part of the whole tissue assume a dingy brown colour; in the outer layers the starch granules even are coloured. *Tannic matter* is consequently one of the chief constituents of the bark; the very cell-walls are also imbued with it. A decoction of the bark is turned blackish green by a persalt of iron.

If cassia bark (or Ceylon cinnamon) is exhausted by *cold water*, the clear liquid becomes turbid on addition of iodine; the same occurs if a concentrated solution of iodide of potassium is added. An abundant precipitate is produced by addition of iodine dissolved in the potassium salt. The colour of iodine then disappears. There is consequently a substance present which unites with iodine; and in fact, if to a *decoction* of cassia or cinnamon the said solution of iodine is added, it strikes a bright blue coloration, due to starch. But the colour quickly disappears, and becomes permanent only after much of the test has been added. We have not ascertained the nature of the substance that thus modifies the action of iodine: it can hardly be tannic matter, as we have found the reaction to be the same when we used bark that had been previously repeatedly treated with spirit of wine and then several times with boiling ether.

The mucilage contained in the gum-cells of the thinner quills of cassia is easily dissolved by cold water, and may be precipitated together with tannin by neutral acetate of lead, but not by alcohol. In the thicker barks it appears less soluble, merely swelling into a slimy jelly.

Commerce—Cassia lignea is exported from Canton in enormous and increasing quantities. The shipments which in 1864 amounted to 13,800 peculs, reached 40,600 in 1869,[1] 61,220 in 1871, and 76,464 peculs (10,195,200 lb.) value £267,703, in 1872.[2] In 1874 the exports were 54,268 peculs (1 pecul = 133⅓ lb.) and 58,313 peculs in 1878; from the other ports of China cassia is not shipped to any extent. England usually receives no more than about 1,000,000 lb. of cassia, of which only 40,000 lb. appear to be consumed in the country. Hamburg imports about 2,000,000 lb. annually immediately from China. Yet in 1878 the quantity imported into London was 26,744 peculs (3,500,000 lb.), that received at Hamburg 13,548 peculs.

Cassia lignea is exported in chests containing 2 peculs each.

Oil of cassia was shipped from the south of China to the United Kingdom, to the extent in 1869 of 47,517 lb.; in 1870, of 28,389 lb.[3] Hamburg is also a very important place for this oil; in the official statistics of that port for 1875 the imports from China are stated to have amounted to 30,000 lb., besides 10,000 lb. imported from Great Britain; in 1876 Hamburg imported 5,900 lb. from China and 17,000 lb. from England.

Uses—The same as those of cinnamon.

[1] *Canton Trade Report* for 1869.

[2] *Commercial Reports from H. M. Consuls in China*, presented to Parliament 1873,—(Consul Robertson).

[3] *Annual Statement of the Trade and Navigation of the United Kingdom for* 1870. 290.—66,650 were exported in 1877 from Pakhoi.

Allied Products.

Cassia Twigs.—The branches of the cassia trees, alluded to at page 529, would appear to be collected from the same trees which yield the cassia lignea. Garnier (*l.c.* at p. 528) says that the youngest branches are made into fagots, adding that they have the odour of bugs.

Cassia twigs are not as yet exported to Europe, but they constitute a very important article of the trade of the interior of China. In 1872 no less than 456,533 lb. of this *Wood of Cassia* or *Cassia Twigs* were shipped from Canton, for the most part to other Chinese ports.—The imports of Hankow, in 1874, of these twigs were 1925 peculs (259,667 lb.) valued at 5677 taels (1 tael about equal to 5*s.* 11*d.*).[1]

In the Paris Exhibition of 1878 we had the opportunity of examining some bundles of cassia twigs from western Kwangtung. The branches were as much as 2 feet in length and of the thickness of a finger. We found their bark to possess the usual flavour of cassia lignea.

Cassia Buds, Flores Cassiæ—These are the *immature fruits* of the tree yielding Chinese cassia lignea, and have been used in Europe since the middle ages. In the journal of expenses (A.D. 1359-60) of John, king of France, when a prisoner at Somerton Castle in England, there are several entries for the spice under the name of *Flor de Canelle;* it was very expensive, costing from 8*s.* to 13*s.* per lb., or more than double the price of mace or cloves. On one occasion two pounds of it had to be obtained for the king's use from Bruges.[2] From the *Form of Cury*[3] written in 1390, it appears that cassia buds ("*Flō de queynel*") were used in preparing the spiced wine called *Hippocras.*

Cassia buds are shipped from Canton, but the exports have much declined. Rondot, writing in 1848,[4] estimated them as averaging 400 peculs (53,333 lb.) a year. In 1866 there were shipped from Canton only 233 peculs (31,066 lb.); in 1867, 165 peculs (22,000 lb.)[5] The quantity of cassia buds imported into the United Kingdom in 1870 was 29,321 lb.;[6] the spice is sold chiefly by grocers. The great market for this drug is Hamburg, where in 1876, according to the official statistics, 1324 cwt. of cassia buds were imported.

In Southern India, the more mature fruits of one of the varieties of *Cinnamomum iners* Reinw. are collected for use, but are very inferior to the Chinese cassia buds.

Folia Malabathri or *Folia Indi*—is the name given to the dried, aromatic leaves of certain Indian species of *Cinnamomum,* formerly employed[7] in European medicine, but now obsolete. Under the name *Taj-pat,* the leaves are still used in India; they are collected in Mysore from wild trees.

Ishpingo—This is the designation in Quito of the calyx of a tree of the laurel tribe, used in Ecuador and Peru in the place of cinnamon. Though but little known in Europe, it has a remarkable history.

[1] *Returns of Trade at the Treaty Ports in China for* 1872, p. 34; for 1874, p. 7.

[2] Douet d'Arcq, *Comptes de l'Argenterie des Rois de France,* 1851. 206. 218. 222. 239. etc.

[3] See p. 245, note 3.

[4] *Commerce d'exportation de la Chine,* 45.

[5] *Reports on Trade at the Treaty Ports in China for* 1867, Shanghai, 1868. 49.

[6] *Annual Statement of the Trade and Navigation of the U.K. for* 1870. 101.

[7] For further information consult Heyd, *Levantehandel,* ii. (1879) 663.

The existence of a spice-yielding region in South America, having come to the ears of the Spanish conquerors, was regarded as a matter of interest. It would appear that cinnamon was enumerated in the earliest accounts among the precious products of the New World.[1] Such high importance was attached to it that in Ecuador an expedition was fitted out. The direction of the enterprise was confided to Gonzalo Pizarro, who with 340 soldiers, and more than 4000 Indians, laden with supplies, quitted the city of Quito on Christmas Day, 1539. The expedition, which lasted two years, resulted in the most lamentable failure, only 130 Spaniards surviving the hardships of the journey. In the account of it given by Garcilasso de la Vega, the cinnamon tree is described as having large leaves like those of a laurel, with fruits resembling acorns growing in clusters.[2] Fernandez de Oviedo[3] has also given some particulars regarding the spice, together with a figure fairly representing its remarkable form; and the subject has been noticed by several other Spanish writers, including Monardes.[4]

Notwithstanding the celebrity thus conferred on the spice, and the fact that the latter gives its name to a large tract of country,[5] and is still the object of a considerable traffic, the tree itself is all but unknown to science. Meissner places it doubtfully under the genus *Nectandra*, with the specific name *cinnamomoides*, but confesses that its flowers and fruits are alike unknown.[6]

The spice, for an ample specimen of which we have to thank Dr. Destruge, of Guayaquil, consists of the enlarged and matured woody calyx, 1½ to 2 inches in diameter, having the shape of a shallow funnel, the open part of which is a smooth cup (like the cup of an acorn), surrounded by a broad, irregular margin, usually recurved. The outer surface is rough and veiny, and the whole calyx is dark brown, and has a strong, sweet, aromatic taste, like cinnamon, for which in Ecuador it is the common substitute.

Dr. Destruge has also furnished us with a specimen of the *bark*, which is in very small uncoated quills, exactly simulating true cinnamon. We are not aware whether the bark is thus prepared in quantity.

[1] Account of Petrus Martyr d'Angleria to Cardinal Ascanio Sforza, in Michael Herr's *Die new Welt*, etc., Strassburg, 1534. fol. 175.

[2] *Travels of Pedro de Cieza de Leon*, A.D. 1532-50, translated by Markham (Hakluyt Society) Lond. 1864. chap. 39-40; also *Expedition of Gonzalo Pizarro to the Land of Cinnamon*, by Garcilasso Inca de la Vega, forming part of the same volume.

[3] *Historia de las Indias*, Madrid, i. (1851) 357. (lib. ix. c. 31).

[4] *De la Canela de nuestras Indias.—Historia de las cosas que se traen de nuestras Indias occidentales*, Sevilla, 1574. 98.

[5] The village of San José de Canelos, which may be considered as the centre of the cinnamon region, was determined by Mr. Spruce to be in lat. 1° 20 S., long. 77° 45 W., and at an altitude above the sea of 1590 feet. The forest of canelos, he tells us, has no definite boundaries; but the term is popularly assigned to all the upper region of the Pastasa and its tributaries, from a height of 4000 to 7000 feet on the slopes of the Andes, down to the Amazonian plain, and the confluence of the Bombonasa and Pastasa.

[6] De Candolle, *Prodromus*, xv. sect. i. 167.

CORTEX BIBIRU.

Cortex Nectandræ ; Greenheart Bark, Bibiru or Bebeeru Bark.

Botanical Origin—*Nectandra Rodiæi* Schomburgk—The Bibiru or Greenheart is a large forest tree,[1] growing on rocky soils in British Guiana, twenty to fifty miles inland. It is found in abundance on the hill sides which skirt the rivers Essequibo, Cuyuni, Demerara, Pomeroon and Berbice. The tree attains a height of 80 to 90 feet, with an undivided erect trunk, furnishing an excellent timber which is ranked in England as one of the eight first-class woods for shipbuilding, and is to be had in beams of from 60 to 70 feet long.

History—In 1769 Bancroft, in his *History of Guiana,* called attention to the excellent timber afforded by the *Greenheart* or *Sipeira.* About the year 1835 it became known that Hugh Rodie, a navy surgeon who had settled in Demerara some twenty years previously, had discovered an alkaloid of considerable efficacy as a febrifuge, in the bark of this tree.[2] In 1843 this alkaloid, to which Rodie had given the name *Bebeerine,* was examined by Dr. Douglas Maclagan ; and the following year the tree was described by Schomburgk under the name of *Nectandra Rodiæi.*[3]

Description—Greenheart bark occurs in long heavy flat pieces, not unfrequently 4 inches broad and $\frac{3}{10}$ of an inch thick, externally of a light greyish brown, with the inner surface of a more uniform cinnamon hue and with strong longitudinal striæ. It is hard and brittle ; the fracture coarse-grained, slightly foliaceous, and only fibrous in the inner layer. The grey suberous coat is always thin, often forming small warts, and leaving when removed longitudinal depressions analogous to the *digital furrows* of Flat Calisaya Bark (p. 353), but mostly longer. Greenheart bark has a strong bitter taste, but is not aromatic. Its watery infusion is of a very pale cinnamon brown.

Microscopic Structure—The general features of this bark are very uniform, almost the whole tissue having been changed into thick-walled cells. Even the cells of the corky layer show secondary deposits ; the primary envelope has entirely disappeared, and no transition from the suberous coat to liber is obvious.

The prevalent forms of the tissue are the stone-cells and very short liber-fibres, intersected by small medullary rays and crossed transversely by parenchyme or small prosenchyme cells with walls a little less thickened, so as to appear in a transverse section as irregular squares or groups. The only cells of a peculiar character are the sharp-pointed fibres of the inner liber, which are curiously saw-shaped, being provided with numerous protuberances and sinuosities.

The very small lumen of the thick-walled cells contains a dark brown mass which is coloured greenish-black by sulphate of iron ; the same coloration takes place throughout the less dense tissue surround-

[1] Fig. in Bentley and Trimen's *Medic. Plants*, part 26 (1877).

[2] Halliday, *On the Bebeeru tree of British Guiana, and Sulphate of Bebeerine, the former a substitute for Cinchona, the latter for Sulphate of Quinine.—Edinburgh Med. and Surg. Journ.* vol xl. 1835.

[3] *Hooker's Journ. of Bot.* 1844. 624.

ing the groups of stone-cells, and may in each case be due to tannic matter.

Chemical Composition—Greenheart bark contains an alkaloid which has long been regarded as peculiar, under the name of *Bibirine* or *Bebirine*. It was however shown by Walz in 1860 to be apparently identical with *Buxine*, a substance discovered as early as 1830 in the bark and leaves of the Common Box, *Buxus sempervirens* L. In 1869 the observation of Walz was to some extent confirmed by one of us,[1] who further demonstrated that *Pelosine*, an alkaloid occurring in the stems and roots of *Cissampelos Pareira* L. and *Chondodendron tomentosum* Ruiz et Pavon (p. 28), is undistinguishable from the alkaloids of greenheart and box.

The alkaloid of bibiru bark, which may be conveniently prepared from the crude sulphate used in medicine under the name of *Sulphate of Bibirine*, is a colourless amorphous substance, the composition of which is indicated by the formula $C^{18}H^{21}NO^{3}$. It is soluble in 5 parts of absolute alcohol, in 13 of ether, and in 1400 (1800, Walz) of boiling water, the solution in each case having a decidedly alkaline reaction on litmus. It dissolves readily in bisulphide of carbon, as well as in dilute acids. The salts hitherto known are uncrystallizable. The solution of a neutral acetate affords an abundant white precipitate on the addition of an alkaline phosphate, nitrate or iodide, of iodo-hydrargyrate or platino-cyanide of potassium, perchloride of mercury, or of nitric or iodic acid.

Maclagan, one of the earliest investigators of greenheart, has obtained in co-operation with Gamgee[2] certain alkaloids from the *wood* of the tree, to one of which these chemists have assigned the formula $C^{20}H^{23}NO^{4}$ and the name *Nectandria*. Two other alkaloids, the characters of which have not yet been fully investigated, are stated to have been obtained from the same source.

Bibiric Acid, which Maclagan obtained from the *seeds*, is described as a colourless, crystalline, deliquescent substance, fusing at 150° C. and volatile at 200° C., then forming needle-shaped groups.

Commerce—The supplies of greenheart bark are extremely uncertain, and the drug is scarcely to be found in the market. It has been imported in barrels containing 80 to 84 lb. each, or in bags holding ½ to ¾ cwt.

Uses—The bark has been recommended as a bitter tonic and febrifuge, but is hardly ever employed except in the form of what is called *Sulphate of Bibirine*, which, as we have said, is *crude Sulphate of Buxine*.[3] It is a dark amorphous substance which, having while in a syrupy state been spread out on glazed plates, is obtained in thin translucent laminæ. We find it to yield scarcely one-third of its weight of the pure alkaloid.

[1] Flückiger, *Neues Jahrbuch für Pharmacie*, xxxi. (1869) 257 ; *Pharm. Journ.* xi. (1870) 192.

[2] *Pharm. Journ.* xi. (1870) 19.

[3] Mr. W. H. Campbell, of Georgetown, Demerara, has assured me that neither the bark nor its alkaloid is held in esteem in the colony.—D.H.

RADIX SASSAFRAS.

Sassafras Root ; F. *Bois de Sassafras, Lignum Sassafras ;* G. *Sassafrasholz.*

Botanical Origin—*Sassafras officinalis* Nees (*Laurus Sassafras* L.), a tree growing in North America, from Canada, southward to Florida and Missouri. In the north it is only a shrub, or a small tree 20 to 30 feet high, but in the Middle and Southern United States, and especially in Virginia and Carolina, it attains a height of 40 to 100 feet. The leaves are of different forms, some being ovate and entire, and others two- or three-lobed, the former, it is said, appearing earlier than the latter.

History—Monardes relates that the French during their expedition to Florida (1562–1564) cured their sick with the wood and root of a tree called *Sassafras*, the use of which they had learnt from the Indians.[1] Laudonnière, who was a member of that expedition, and diligently set forth the wonders of Florida, observes that, among forest trees, the most remarkable for its timber and especially for its fragrant bark, is that called by the savages *Pavame* and by the French *Sassafras*.[2]

The drug was known in Germany, at least since 1582, under the above names or also by that of *Lignum Floridum* or *Fennel-wood, Xylomarathrum*.[3]

The sassafras tree had been introduced into England in the time of Gerarde (*circa* 1597), who speaks of a specimen growing at Bow. At that period the wood and bark of the root were used chiefly in the treatment of ague.

In 1610, a paper of instructions from the Government of England to that of the new colony of Virginia, mentions among commodities to be sent home, "*Small sassafras Rootes*," which are "to be drawen in the winter and dryed and none to be medled with in the somer ;—and yet is worthe £50 and better per tonne."[4] The shipments were afterwards much overdone, for in 1622 complaint is made that other things than *tobacco* and *sassafras*[5] were neglected to be shipped.

Angelus Sala, an Italian chemist living in Germany about the year 1610-1630, in distilling sassafras noticed that the oil was heavier than water ;[6] it was quoted in 1683 in the tariff of the apothecary of the elector of Saxony, at Dresden.[7] John Maud in 1738 obtained crystals of safrol as long as 4 inches ;[8] in 1844 they were examined by Saint-Evre.

Description—Sassafras is imported in large branching logs, which often include the lower portion of the stem, 6 to 12 inches in diameter.[9]

[1] *Historia medicinal de las cosas que se traen de nuestras Indias occidentales*, (Sevilla, 1574) 51.

[2] De Laet, *Novus Orbis*, 1633. 215.—René de Laudonnière, *Histoire notable de la Floride*. 1586.

[3] *Pharm. Journ.* v. (1876) 1023.

[4] *Colonial Papers*, vol. i. No. 23 (MS. in the Record Office, London).

[5] *Colonial Papers*, vol. ii. No. 4.

[6] *Opera medico-chymica*, Francofurti, 1682, p. 83.

[7] Flückiger, *Documente* (quoted at p. 404, note 7) 70.

[8] *Phil. Trans. R. Soc. of London*, viii. (1809) 243.

[9] The sassafras logs met with in English trade often include a considerable portion of trunk-wood, which, as well as the bark that covers it, is inert, and should be sawn off and rejected before the wood is rasped.

The roots proper, which diminish in size down to the thickness of a quill, are covered with a dull, rough, spongy bark. This bark has an inert, soft corky layer, beneath which is a firmer inner bark of brighter hue, rich in essential oil. The wood of the root is light and easily cut, in colour of a dull reddish brown, and with a fragrant odour and spicy taste similar to that of the bark but less strong. It is usually sold in the shops rasped into shavings.

The *bark of the root* (*Cortex sassafras*) is a separate article of commerce, but not much used in England. It consists of channelled, flattish, or curled, irregular fragments seldom exceeding 4 inches long by 3 inches broad and generally much smaller, and from $\frac{1}{16}$ to $\frac{1}{4}$ of an inch in thickness. The inert outer layer has been carefully removed, leaving a scarred, exfoliating surface. The inner surface is finely striated and exhibits very minute shining crystals. The bark has a short, corky fracture, and in colour is a bright cinnamon brown of various shades. It has a strong and agreeable smell, with an astringent, aromatic, bitterish taste.

Microscopic Structure—The wood of the root exhibits, in transverse section, concentric rings transversed by narrow medullary rays. Each ring contains a number of large vessels in its inner part, and more densely packed cells in its outer. The prevailing part of the wood consists of prosenchyme cells. Globular cells, loaded with yellow essential oil, are distributed among the woody prosenchyme. The latter as well as the medullary rays abounds in starch.

The *bark* is rich in oil-cells and also contains cells filled with mucilage; it owes its spongy appearance and exfoliation to the formation of secondary cork bands (*rhytidoma*) within the mesophlœum and even in the liber. The cortical tissue abounds in red colouring matter, and further contains starch and, less abundantly, oxalate of calcium.

Chemical Composition—The wood of the root yields 1 to 2 per cent. of volatile oil,[1] and the root-bark twice as much. The stem and leaves of the tree contain but a very small quantity. The oil, which as found in commerce is all manufactured in America, has the specific odour of sassafras, and is colourless, yellow, or reddish-brown, according, as the distillers assert, to the character of the root employed. As the colour of the oil does not affect its flavour and market value, no effort is made to keep separate the different varieties of root.

Oil of Sassafras has a sp. gr. of 1·087 to 1·094, increasing somewhat by age (Procter). When cooled, it deposits crystals of *Safrol* or *Sassafras Camphor*. This body, which we obtained in the form of hard, four- or six-sided prisms with the odour of sassafras, often attaining more than 4 inches in length and 1 inch in diameter, belongs to the monosymmetric system, as shown by Arzruni.[2] Safrol, $C^{10}H^{10}O^2$, liquefies at 8°·5 C. (47° F.), having at 12° C. a sp. gr. of 1·11; it boils at 232° C., and is devoid of rotatory power, nor is it soluble in alkalis. The researches of Grimaux and Ruotte (1869) show the oil to contain nine-tenths of its weight of *Safrol* which they observed only in the liquid state.

[1] According to information obtained by Procter, 11 bushels of chips (the charge of a still) yields from 1 to 5 lb. of oil, the amount varying with the quality of the root and the proportion of bark it may contain.—Procter, *Essay on Sassafras* in the *Proceedings of the American Pharm. Association*, 1866. 217.

[2] Poggendorff's *Annalen*, clviii. (1876) 249, with figures of the crystals.

Another constituent of sassafras oil has been termed by Grimaux and Ruotte *Safrene;* it boils at 155° to 157° C., has a sp. gr. of 0·834 and the formula $C^{10}H^{16}$. It has the same odour as safrol, but deviates the plane of polarization to the right.

It was further found by the same observers that the crude oil contains an extremely small quantity of a substance of the phenol class, which can be removed by caustic lye and separated by an acid.

We succeeded in obtaining this substance by using that portion of the crude oil from which the safrol had separated. The phenol remains in the mother-liquor after it has again been cooled and has afforded a new crystallization of safrol. The phenol thus obtained assumes a beautiful greenish blue hue on addition of an alcoholic solution of perchloride of iron.

The *Sassarubin* and *Sassafrin* of Hare (1837) are impure products of the decomposition of sassafras oil by means of sulphuric acid.

The *bark* and also to some extent the *wood,* in both cases of the root, contain tannic acid which produces a blue colour with persalts of iron. By oxidation, we must suppose, it is converted into the red colouring matter deposited in the bark and, in smaller quantity, in the heart-wood of old trees. The young wood is nearly white. The said red substance probably agrees with that to which Reinsch in 1845 and 1846 gave the name of *Sassafrid,* and is doubtless analogous to cinchona-red and ratanhia-red. Reinsch obtained it to the extent of 9·2 per cent.

Production and Commerce—Baltimore is the chief mart for sassafras root, bark and oil, which are brought thither from within a circuit of 300 miles. The roots are extracted from the ground by the help of levers, partly barked and partly sent untouched to the market, or are cut up into chips for distillation on the spot. Of the bark as much as 100,000 lb. were received in Baltimore in 1866. The quantity of oil annually produced previous to the war is estimated at 15,000 to 20,000 lb. There are isolated small distillers in Pennsylvania and West New Jersey, who are allowed by the owners of a "*sassafras wilderness*" to remove from the ground the roots and stumps without charge. Sassafras root is not medicinal in the United States, the more aromatic root-bark being reasonably preferred.[1]

Uses—Sassafras is reputed to be sudorific and stimulant, but in British practice it is only given in combination with sarsaparilla and guaiacum. Shavings of the wood are sold to make *Sassafras Tea.*

In America the essential oil is used to give a pleasant flavour to effervescing drinks, tobacco and toilet soaps.[2]

Substitutes—The odour of sassafras is common to several plants of the order *Lauraceæ.* Thus the bark of *Mesphilodaphne Sassafras* Meissn., a tree of Brazil, resembles in odour true sassafras. We have seen a very thick sassafras bark brought from India, the same we suppose as that which Mason[3] describes as abundantly produced in Burma.

The bark of *Atherosperma moschatum* Labillardière, an Australian tree, is occasionally exported from Australia under the name of Sassafras

[1] Besides this, *the pith of sassafras* is also there used as a popular remedy; it is entirely devoid of odour and taste, and is very slightly mucilaginous.

[2] *American Journ. of Pharm.* 1871. 470.

[3] *Burmah, its people and natural productions,* 1860. 497.

bark. It has the odour of the true drug, but differs from it by its grey colour.

The large separate cotyledons of two lauraceous trees of the Rio Negro, doubtfully referred by Meissner to the genus *Nectandra*, furnish the so-called *Sassafras Nuts* or *Puchury* or *Pilchurim Beans* of Brazil, occasionally to be met with in old drug warehouses.

On the Orinoko and in Guiana an oleo-resin, called *Sassafras Oil* or *Laurel Oil*, is obtained by boring into the stem of *Oreodaphne opifera* Nees, which sometimes contains a cavity holding a large quantity of this fluid.[1] A similar oil (*Aceite de Sassafras*) is afforded on the Rio Negro by *Nectandra Cymbarum* Nees.[2]

THYMELEÆ.

CORTEX MEZEREI.

Mezereon Bark; F. *Ecorce de Mézéréon, Bois gentil.;* G. *Seidelbast-Rinde.*

Botanical Origin—*Daphne Mezereum* L., an erect shrub, 1 to 3 feet high, the branches of which are crowded with purple flowers in the early spring, before the full expansion of the oblong, lanceolate, deciduous leaves. The flowers are succeeded by red berries. It is a native of the hilly parts of almost the whole of Europe, from Italy to the Arctic regions, and extends eastward to Siberia. In Britain it occurs here and there in a few of the southern and midland counties, and even reaches Yorkshire and Westmoreland, but there is reason to think it is not truly indigenous. Gerarde, who was well acquainted with it, did not regard it as a British plant.

History—The Arabian physicians used a plant called *Mázariyún*, the effects of which they compared to those of euphorbium; it was probably a species of *Daphne*. The word *mázariyún* is, we are told by competent Arabic scholars, not of Arabic origin, but in all probability derived from the Greek idiom, in which however we are unable to trace its origin. *D. Mezereum* was known to the early botanists of Europe, as *Daphnoides Chamælæa, Thymelæa, Chamædaphne.* Tragus described it and figured it in 1546 under the name of *Mezereum Germanicum.* The bark had a place in the German pharmacy of the 17th century under the name of cortex *Coccognidii* s. *Mezerei;* the berries were the *Cocca gnidia* s. *knidia* of the old pharmacy.

Description—Mezereon has a very tough and fibrous bark easily removed in long strips which curl inwards as they dry; it is collected in winter and made up into rolls or bundles. The bark, which rarely exceeds $\frac{1}{20}$ of an inch in thickness, has an internal greyish or reddish-brown corky coat which is easily separable from a green inner layer, white and satiny on the side next the wood. That of younger branches is marked with prominent leaf-scars. The bark is too tough to be broken, but easily tears into fibrous strips. When fresh, it has an

[1] *Brit. Guiana* at the Paris Exhibition, 1878, Sect. C. p. 7.

[2] Spruce in *Hooker's Journ. of Bot.* vii. (1855) 278.

unpleasant odour which is lost in drying; its taste is persistently burning and acrid. Applied in a moist state to the skin, it occasions, after some hours, redness and even vesication.

Microscopic Structure—The cambial zone is formed of about ten rows of delicate unequal cells. The libre consists chiefly of simple fibres alternating with parenchymatous bundles, and traversed by medullary rays. The fibres are very long,—frequently more than 3 mm., and from 5 to 10 mkm. in diameter, their walls being always but little thickened. In the outer part of the liber there occur bundles of thick-walled bast-tubes, while chlorophyll and starch granules appear generally throughout the middle cortical layer. The suberous coat is made up of about 30 dense rows of thin-walled tabular cells, which examined in a tangential section, have an hexagonal outline. Small quantities of tannic matter are deposited in the cambial and suberous zones.

Chemical Composition—The acrid principle of mezereon is a resinoid substance contained in the inner bark; it has not yet been examined. The fruits were found by Martius (1862) to contain more than 40 per cent. of a fatty, vesicating oil, which appears to be likewise present in the bark.

The name *Daphnin* has been given to a crystallizable substance obtained by Vauquelin in 1808 from *Daphne alpina*, and afterwards found by C. G. Gmelin and Baer in the bark of *D. Mezereum*. Zwenger in 1860 ascertained it to be a glucoside of bitter taste, having the composition $C^{15}H^{16}O^{9} + 2\,OH^{2}$, the same as that of Æsculin, the fluorescing principle occurring in the bark of *Æsculus Hippocastanum* and the root-bark of *Gelsemium nitidum* Michaux (*G. sempervirens* Aiton).—*Coccognin*, isolated in 1870 by Casselmann from the fruits of *D. Mezereum*, appears to be closely allied to if not identical with daphnin.

When daphnin is boiled with dilute hydrochloric or sulphuric acid, it furnishes *Daphnetin*, $C^{9}H^{6}O^{4} + OH^{2}$, described by Zwenger as crystallizing in colourless prisms. By dry distillation of an alcoholic extract of mezereon bark, the same chemist obtained *Umbelliferone* (p. 322).

Uses—Mezereon taken internally is supposed to be alterative and sudorific, and useful in venereal, rheumatic and scrofulous complaints; but in English medicine it is never now given except as an ingredient of the Compound Decoction of Sarsaparilla. An ethereal extract of the bark has been introduced (1867) as an ingredient of a powerful stimulating liniment. On the Continent, the bark itself, soaked in vinegar and water, is applied with a bandage as a vesicant.

Substitutes—Owing to the difficulty of procuring the bark of the root of *D. Mezereum*, the herbalists who supply the London druggists have been long in the habit of substituting that of *D. Laureola* L., an evergreen species, not uncommon in woods and hedge-sides in several parts of England. The *British Pharmacopœia* (1864 and 1867) permits *Cortex Mezerei* to be obtained indiscriminately from either of these species, and does not follow the London College in insisting on the *bark of the root* alone. That of the stem of *D. Laureola* corresponds in structure with the bark of the true mezereon, but wants the prominent leaf-scars that mark the upper branches of the latter; it is reputed to be somewhat less acrid than mezereon bark. The mezereon bark of English trade is now mostly imported from Germany, and seems to be derived from *D. Mezereum*.

In France, use is made of the stem-bark of *D. Gnidium* L., a shrub growing throughout the whole Mediterranean region as far as Morocco. The bark is dark grey or brown, marked with numerous whitish leaf-scars, which display a very regular spiral arrangement. The leaves themselves, some of which are occasionally met with in the drug, are sharply mucronate and very narrow. As to structural peculiarities, the bark of *D. Gnidium* has the medullary rays more obvious and more loaded with tannic matters than those of *D. Mezereum;* but the middle cortical layer is less developed. The bark, which is called *Ecorce de Gaoru*, is employed as an epispastic.

ARTOCARPACEÆ.

CARICÆ.

Fructus Caricæ, Fici; Figs; F. *Figues;* G. *Feigen.*

Botanical Origin—*Ficus Carica* L., a deciduous tree, 15 to 20 feet in height, with large rough leaves, forming a handsome mass of foliage.

The native country of the fig stretches from the steppes of the Eastern Aral, along the south and south-west coast of the Caspian Sea (Ghilan, Mazanderan, and the Caucasus), through Kurdistan, to Asia Minor and Syria. In these countries the fig-tree ascends into the mountain region, growing undoubtedly wild in the Taurus at an elevation of 4,800 feet.[1]

The fig-tree is repeatedly mentioned in the Scriptures, where with the vine it often stands as the symbol of peace and plenty. The fig was not known in Greece, the Archipelago, and the neighbouring coasts of Asia Minor during the Homeric age, though both were very common in the time of Plato. The fig-tree was early introduced into Italy, whence it reached Spain and Gaul. In the opinion of palæontologists the fig-tree was originally indigenous to the last-named Mediterranean regions.

Charlemagne, A.D. 812, ordered its cultivation in Central Europe. It was brought to England in the reign of Henry VIII. by Cardinal Pole, whose trees still exist in the garden of Lambeth Palace. But it had certainly been in cultivation at a much earlier period, for the historian Matthew Paris relates[2] that the year 1257 was so inclement that apples and pears were scarce in England, and that *figs*, cherries, and plums totally failed to ripen.

At the present day the fig-tree is found cultivated in most of the temperate countries both of the Old and New World.[3] It is met with in the plains of north-western India, and in the outer hills of the north-western Himalaya as high as 5,000 feet; also in the Dekkan, and in Beluchistan and Afghanistan.

[1] Ritter, *Erdkunde von Asien*, vii. (1844) 2. 544.

[2] *Eng. Hist.*, Bohn's ed., iii. (1854) 255.

[3] Introduced into Mexico by Cortez about A.D. 1560.

History—Figs were a valued article of food among the ancient Hebrews[1] and Greeks, as they are to the present day in the warmer countries bordering the Mediterranean.[2] In the time of Pliny many varieties were in cultivation The Latin word *Carica* was first used to designate the dried fig of Caria, a strip of country in Asia Minor opposite Rhodes, an esteemed variety of the fruit corresponding to the Smyrna fig of modern times.

In a diploma granted by Chilperic II., king of the Franks, to the monastery of Corbie, A.D. 716, mention is made of "*Karigas*" in connection with dates, almonds and olives, by which we think dried figs *(Caricæ)* were intended.[3] Dried figs were a regular article of trade during the middle ages, from the southern to the northern parts of Europe. In 1380 the citizens of Bruges, in regulating the duties which the "Lombards," *i.e.* Italians, had to pay for their imports, quoted also figs from Cyprus and from Marbella, a place south-west of Malaga.[4]

In England the average price between A.D. 1264 and 1398 was about 1¾*d.* per lb., raisins and currants being 2¾*d.*[5]

Description—A fig consists of a thick, fleshy, hollow receptacle of a pear-shaped form, on the inner face of which grow a multitude of minute fruits.[6] This receptacle, which is provided with an orifice at the top, is at first green, tough and leathery, exuding when pricked a milky juice. The orifice is surrounded, and almost closed by a number of thick, fleshy scales, near which and within the fig, the male flowers are situated, but they are often wanting or are not fully developed. The female flowers stand further within the receptacle, in the body of which they are closely packed; they are stalked, have a 5-leafed perianth and a bipartite stigma. The ovary, which is generally one-celled, becomes when ripe a minute, dry, hard nut, popularly regarded as a seed.

As the fig advances to maturity, the receptacle enlarges, becomes softer and more juicy, a saccharine fluid replacing the acrid milky sap. It also acquires a reddish hue, while its exterior becomes purple, brown, or yellow, though in some varieties it continues green. The fresh fig has an agreeable and extremely saccharine taste, but it wants the juiciness and refreshing acidity that characterize many other fruits.

If a fig is not gathered its stalk loses its firmness, the fruit hangs pendulous from the branch, begins to shrivel and become more and more saccharine by loss of water, and ultimately, if the climate is favourable, it assumes the condition of a *dried fig*. On the large scale however, figs are not dried on the tree, but are gathered and exposed to the sun and air in light trays till they acquire the proper degree of dryness. They

[1] See in particular 1 Sam. xxv. 18 and 1 Chron. xii. 40; where we read of large supplies of dried figs being provided for the use of fighting men. Also Num. xx. 5; Jer. xxiv. 2; 2 Reg. xx. 7.

[2] On the Riviera of Genoa dried figs eaten with bread are a common winter food of the peasantry.

[3] Pardessus, *Diplomata, Chartæ*, etc., ii. (1849) 309

[4] *Recesse und andere Akten der Hansetage*, ii. (Leipzig, 1872) 235.

[5] Rogers, *Hist. of Agriculture and Prices in England*, i. (1866) 632.

[6] Albertus Magnus, in allusion to the peculiar growth of the fig, remarks that the tree "fructum autem profert sine flore." Page 386 of the work quoted in the Appendix.

can only be preserved in those regions where the summer and autumn are very warm and dry.

Dried figs are termed by the dealers either *natural* or *pulled*. The first are those which have not been compressed in the packing, and still retain their original shape.[1] The second are those which after drying have been made supple by squeezing and kneading, and in that state packed with pressure into drums and boxes.

Smyrna figs, which are the most esteemed sort, are of the latter kind. They are of irregular, flattened form, tough, translucent, covered with a saccharine efflorescence; they have a pleasant fruity smell and luscious taste. Figs of inferior quality, as those called in the market *Greek Figs*, differ chiefly in being smaller and less pulpy.

Microscopic Structure—The outer layer of a dried fig is made up of small, thick-walled and densely packed cells, so as to form a kind of skin. The inner lax parenchyme consists of larger thin-walled cells, traversed by vascular bundles and large, slightly branched, laticiferous vessels. The latter contain a granular substance not soluble in water. In the parenchyme, stellate crystals of oxalate of calcium occur, but in no considerable number.

Chemical Composition—The chemical changes which take place in the fig during maturation are important, but no researches have yet been made for their elucidation. The chief chemical substance in the ripe fig is grape sugar, which constitutes from 60 to 70 per cent. of the dried fruit. Gum and fatty matter appear to be present only in very small quantity. We have observed that unripe figs are rich in starch.

Production and Commerce—Dried figs were imported into the United Kingdom in 1872 to the amount of 141,847 cwt., of which 91,721 cwt. were shipped from Asiatic Turkey, the remainder being from Portugal, Spain, the Austrian territories and other countries. In 1876 the imports were 163,763 cwt., valued at £318,717.

Kalamata, in the Gulf of Messenia, Greece, and Cosenza in the Italian province of Calabria citeriore, are also particularly known as supplying figs to some parts of continental Europe. In 1876 the exports of Kalamata to Trieste were 9½ millions of kilogrammes.

Uses—Dried figs are thought to be slightly laxative, and as such are occasionally recommended in habitual constipation. They enter into the composition of *Confectio Sennæ*.

MORACEÆ.

FRUCTUS MORI.

Baccæ Mori, Mora; Mulberries; F. *Mûres;* G. *Maulbeeren.*

Botanical Origin—*Morus nigra* L., a handsome bushy tree, about 30 feet in height, growing wild in Northern Asia Minor, Armenia, and the southern Caucasian regions as far as Persia. In Italy, it was em-

[1] The word *Eleme* applied in the London shops to dried figs of superior quality ("Eleme Figs") is probably a corruption of the Turkish *ellémé*, signifying *hand-picked*.

ployed for feeding the silkworm until about the year 1434, when *M. alba* L. was introduced from the Levant,[1] and has ever since been commonly preferred. Yet in Greece, in many of the Greek islands, Calabria and Corsica, the species planted for the silkworm is still *M. nigra*.

The mulberry tree is now cultivated throughout Europe, yet, excepting in the regions named, by no means abundantly. It ripens its fruit in England, as well as in Southern Sweden and Gottland, and in Christiania (Schübeler).

History—The mulberry tree is mentioned in the Old Testament,[2] and by most of the early Greek and Roman writers. Among the large number of useful plants ordered by Charlemagne (A.D. 812) to be cultivated on the imperial farms, the mulberry tree (*Morarius*) did not escape notice.[3] We meet with it also in a plan sketched A.D. 820, for the gardens of the monastery of St. Gall in Switzerland.[4] The cultivation of the mulberry in Spain is implied by a reference to the preparation of *Syrup of Mulberries* in the Calendar of Cordova,[5] which dates from the year 961.

A curious reference to mulberries, proving them to have been far more esteemed in ancient times than at present, occurs in the statutes of the abbey of Corbie of Normandy, in which we find a *Brevis de Melle*, showing how much *honey* the tenants of the monastic lands were required to pay annually, followed by a statement of the quantity of *Mulberries* which each farm was expected to supply.[6]

Description—The tree bears unisexual catkins; the female, of an ovoid form, consists of numerous flowers with green four-lobed perianths and two linear stigmas. The lobes of the perianth overlapping each other become fleshy, and by their lateral aggregation form the spurious berry, which is shortly stalked, oblong, an inch in length, and, when ripe, of an intense purple. By detaching a single fruit, the lobes of the former perianth may be still discerned. Each fruit encloses a hard lenticular nucule, covering a pendulous seed with curved embryo and fleshy albumen.

Mulberries are extremely juicy and have a refreshing, subacid, saccharine taste; but they are devoid of the fine aroma that distinguishes many fruits of the order *Rosaceæ*.

Chemical Composition—In an analysis made by H. van Hees (1857) 100 parts of mulberries yielded the following constituents:—

Glucose and uncrystallizable sugar	9·19
Free acid (supposed to be *malic*)	1·86
Albuminous matter	0·39
Pectic matter, fat, salts, and gum	2·03
Ash	0·57
Insoluble matters (the seeds, pectose, cellulose, &c.)	1·25
Water	84·71

[1] A. De Candolle, *Géogr. botanique*, ii. (1855) 856.

[2] 2 Sam. v. 23, 24.

[3] Pertz, *Monumenta Germaniæ historica*, Leges, iii. (1835) 181.—Consult also Hehn, *Kulturpflanzen*, 1877.

[4] F. Keller, *Bauriss des Kolsters S. Gallen*, facsimile, Zürich, 1844.

[5] *Le Calendrier de Cordoue de l'année* 961, publié par R. Dozy, Leyde, 1873. 67.

[6] Guérard, *Polyptique de l'Abbé Irminon*, Paris, ii. 335.

With regard to the results of researches on other edible fruits, made about the same time in the laboratory of Fresenius, it would appear that the mulberry is one of the most saccharine, being only surpassed by the cherry (10·79 of sugar) and grape (10·6 to 19·0).[1] It is richer in sugar than the following, namely :—

Raspberries, yielding	4	per cent. of sugar and	1·48	of (malic) acid.
Strawberries ,,	5·7	,, ,,	1·31	,, ,,
Whortleberries ,,	5·8	,, ,,	1·34	,, ,,
Currants ,,	6·1	,, ,,	2·04	,, ,,

The amount of free acid in the mulberry is not small, nor is it excessive. The small proportion of insoluble matters is worthy of notice in comparison, for instance with the whortleberry, which contains no less than 13 per cent. The colouring matter of the mulberry has not been examined. The acid is probably not simply malic, but in part tartaric.

Uses—The sole use in medicine of mulberries is for the preparation of a syrup employed to flavour or colour any other medicines. In Greece, the fruit is submitted to fermentation, thereby furnishing an inebriating beverage.

CANNABINEÆ.

HERBA CANNABIS.

Cannabis Indica; Indian Hemp; F. *Chanvre Indien;* G. *Hanfkraut.*

Botanical Origin—*Cannabis sativa* L., Common Hemp, an annual diœcious plant, native of Western and Central Asia, cultivated in temperate as well as in tropical countries.

It grows wild luxuriantly on the banks of the lower Ural and Volga near the Caspian Sea, extending thence to Persia, the Altai range, and Northern and Western China. It is found in Kashmir and on the Himalaya, growing 10 to 12 feet high, and thriving vigorously at an elevation of 6000 to 10,000 feet. It likewise occurs in Tropical Africa, on the eastern and western coasts as well as in the central tracts watered by the Congo and Zambesi, but whether truly indigenous is doubtful. It has been naturalized in Brazil, north of Rio de Janeiro, the seeds having been brought thither by the negroes from Western Africa. The cultivation of hemp is carried on in many parts of continental Europe, but especially in Central and Southern Russia.

The hemp plant grown in India exhibits certain differences as contrasted with that cultivated in Europe, which were noticed by Rumphius in the 17th century, and which (about A.D. 1790), induced Lamarck to claim for the former plant the rank of a distinct species, under the name of *Cannabis indica.* But the variations observed in the two plants are of so little botanical importance and are so inconstant, that the maintenance of *C. indica* as distinct from *C. sativa* has been abandoned by general consent.

[1] The fig excepted, which is much more saccharine than any.

In a medicinal point of view, there is a wide dissimilarity between hemp grown in India and that produced in Europe, the former being vastly more potent. Yet even in India there is much variation, for, according to Jameson, the plant grown at altitudes of 6000 to 8000 feet affords the resin known as *Charas*, which cannot be obtained from that cultivated on the plains.[1]

History—Hemp has been propagated on account of its textile fibre and oily seeds from a remote period.

The ancient Chinese herbal called *Rh-ya*, written about the 5th century B.C., notices the fact that the hemp plant is of two kinds, the one producing seeds, the other flowers only.[2] In Susruta, Charaka and other early works on Hindu medicine, hemp (*B'hanga*) is mentioned as a remedy. Herodotus states that hemp grows in Scythia both wild and cultivated, and that the Thracians made garments from it which can hardly be distinguished from linen. He also describes how the Scythians expose themselves as in a bath to the vapour of the seeds thrown on hot coals.[3]

The Greeks and Romans appear to have been unacquainted with the medicinal powers of hemp, unless indeed the care-destroying Νηπενθές should, as Royle has supposed, be referred to this plant. According to Stanislas Julien,[4] anaesthetic powers were ascribed by the Chinese to preparations of hemp as early as the commencement of the 3rd century.

The employment of hemp both medical and dietetic appears to have spread slowly through India and Persia to the Arabians, amongst whom the plant was used in the early middle ages. The famous heretical sect of Mahomedans, whose murderous deeds struck terror into the hearts of the Crusaders during the 11th and 12th centuries, derived their name of *Hashishin*, or, as it is commonly written, *assassins*, from *hashísh* the Arabic for *hemp*,[5] which in certain of their rites they used as an intoxicant.[6] In 1286 of our era, the Sultan of Egypt, Bibars al Bondokdary, prohibited the sale of hashish, the monopoly of which had been leased before.[7]

The use of hemp (*bhang*) in India was particularly noticed by Garcia de Orta[8] (1563), and the plant was subsequently figured by Rheede, who described the drug as largely used on the Malabar coast. It would seem about this time to have been imported into Europe, at least occasionally, for Berlu in his *Treasury of Drugs*, 1690, describes it as coming from Bantam in the East Indies, and "*of an infatuating quality and pernicious use.*"

It was Napoleon's expedition to Egypt that was the means of again

[1] *Journ. of the Agric. and Hortic. Soc. of India*, viii. 167.

[2] Bretschneider, *On Chinese Botanical Works*, 1870. 5. 10. Part of the *Rh-ya* was written in the 12th cent. B.C.

[3] Rawlinson's translation, iii. (1859) book 4, chap. 74-5.

[4] *Comptes Rendus*, xxviii. (1849) 195.

[5] Hence the words *assassin* and *assassinate*. Weil, however, is of opinion that the word *assassin* is more probably derived from *sikkin*, a dagger.—*Geschichte der Chalifen*, iv. (1860) 101.

[6] The miscreant who assassinated Justice Norman at Calcutta, 20 Sept. 1871, is said to have acted under the influence of *hashish*. Bellew (*Indus to the Tigris*, 1874. 218) states that the Afghan chief who murdered Dr. Forbes in 1842, had for some days previously been more or less intoxicated with *Charas* or *Bhang*.

[7] *Quatremère, Memoires sur l'Egypte* ii. (1811) 504, according to Makrisi.

[8] *Colloquios dos simples e drogas e cousas medicinaes da India*, ed. 2 Lisboa, 1872, 27.

calling attention to the peculiar properties of hemp, by the accounts of De Sacy (1809) and Rouger (1810). But the introduction of the Indian drug into European medicine is of still more recent date, and is chiefly due to the experiments made in Calcutta by O'Shaughnessy in 1838-39.[1] Although the astonishing effects produced in India by the administration of preparations of hemp are seldom witnessed in the cooler climate of Britain, the powers of the drug are sufficiently manifest to give it an established place in the pharmacopœia.

Production—Though hemp is grown in many parts of India, yet as a drug it is chiefly produced in a limited area in the districts of Bogra and Rājshāhi, north of Calcutta, where the plant is cultivated for the purpose in a systematic manner. The retail sale, like that of opium and spirits, is restricted by a license, which in 1871-2 produced to the Government of Bengal about £120,000, while upon opium (chiefly consumed in Assam) the amount raised was £310,000.[2] Bhang is one of the principal commodities imported into India from Turkestan.

Description—The leaves of hemp have long stalks with small stipules at their bases, and are composed of 5 to 7 lanceolate-acuminate leaflets, sharply serrate at the margin. The loose panicles of male flowers, and the short spikes of female flowers, are produced on separate plants, from the axils of the leaves. The fruits, called *Hemp-seeds*, are small grey nuts or achenes, each containing a single oily seed. In common with other plants of the order, hemp abounds in silica which gives a roughness to its leaves and stems. In European medicine, the only hemp employed is that grown in India, which occurs in two principal forms, namely:—

1. *Bhang*, *Siddhī* or *Sabzī* (Hindustani); *Hashīsh* or *Qinnaq* (Arabic). This consists of the dried leaves and small stalks, which are of a dark green colour, coarsely broken, and mixed with here and there a few fruits. It has a peculiar but not unpleasant odour, and scarcely any taste. In India, it is smoked either with or without tobacco, but more commonly it is made up with flour and various additions into a sweetmeat or *majun*,[3] of a green colour. Another form of taking it is that of an infusion, made by immersing the pounded leaves in cold water.

2. *Ganja* (Hindustani); *Qinnab* (Arabic); *Guaza*[4] of the London drug-brokers. These are the flowering or fruiting shoots of the female plant, and consist in some samples of straight, stiff, woody stems some inches long, surrounded by the upward branching flower-stalks; in others of more succulent and much shorter shoots, 2 to 3 inches long, and of less regular form. In either case, the shoots have a compressed and glutinous appearance, are very brittle, and of a brownish-green hue. In odour and in the absence of taste *ganja* resembles *bhang*. It is said that after the leaves which constitute *bhang* have been gathered,

[1] For a notice of them, see O'Shaughnessy, *On the preparation of the Indian Hemp or Gunjah*, Calcutta, 1839; also *Bengal Dispensatory*, Calcutta, 1842. 579–604. An immense number of references to writers who have touched on the medicinal properties of hemp, will be found in the elaborate essay entitled *Studien über den Hanf*, by Dr. G. Martius (Erlangen, 1855).

[2] Blue Book quoted at p. 52, note 1.

[3] Magi-oun is the Persian name for electuaries, of which more than 70 are found, for instance, in the *Pharmacopœia Persica* (see Appendix, Angelus), p. 291 to 321.

[4] This name is not used in India, but seems to be a corruption of *ganja*.

little shoots sprout from the stem, and that these picked off and dried form what is called *ganja*.[1]

Chemical Composition—The most interesting constituents of hemp, from a medical point of view, are the *resin* and *volatile oil*.

The former was first obtained in a state of comparative purity by T. and H. Smith in 1846.[2] It is a brown amorphous solid, burning with a bright white flame and leaving no ash. It has a very potent action when taken internally, two-thirds of a grain acting as a powerful narcotic, and one grain producing complete intoxication. From the experiments of Messrs. Smith, it seems to us impossible to doubt that to this resin the energetic effects of cannabis are mainly due.

When water is repeatedly distilled from considerable quantities of hemp, fresh lots of the latter being used for each operation, a volatile oil lighter than water is obtained, together with ammonia. This oil, according to the observations of Personne (1857), is amber-coloured, and has an oppressive hemp-like smell. It sometimes deposits an abundance of small crystals. With due precautions it may be separated into two bodies, the one of which, named by Personne *Cannabene*,[3] is liquid and colourless, with the formula $C^{18}H^{20}$; the other, which is called *Hydride of Cannabene*, is a solid, separating from alcohol in platy crystals to which Personne assigns the formula $C^{18}H^{22}$. He asserts that cannabene has indubitably a physiological action, and even claims it as the sole active principle of hemp. Its vapour he states to produce when breathed a singular sensation of shuddering, a desire of locomotion, followed by prostration and sometimes by syncope.[4] Bohlig in 1840 observed similar effects from the oil, which he obtained from the fresh herb, just after flowering, to the extent of 0·3 per cent.

It remains to be proved whether an *alkaloid* is present in hemp, as suggested by Preobraschensky.

The other constituents of hemp are those commonly occurring in other plants. The leaves yield nearly 20 per cent. of ash.

As to the resin of Indian hemp, Bolas and Francis in treating it with nitric acid, converted it into *Oxycannabin*, $C^{20}H^{20}N^{2}O^{7}$. This interesting substance may, they say, be obtained in large prisms from a solution in methylic alcohol. It melts at 176° C. and then evaporates without decomposition; it is neutral.[6] One of us (F.) has endeavoured to obtain it from the purified resin of charas, but without success.

Uses—Hemp is employed as a soporific, anodyne, antispasmodic, and as a nervous stimulant. It is used in the form of alcoholic extract, administered either in a solid or liquid form. In the East it is consumed to an enormous extent by Hindus and Mahomedans, who either

[1] Powell, *Economic Products of the Punjab*, Roorkee, i. (1868) 293.

[2] *Pharm. Journ.* vi. (1847) 171.

[3] *Journ. de Pharm.* xxxix. (1857) 48; Canstatt's *Jahresbericht* for 1857, i. 28.

[4] Personne, though he admits the activity of the resin prepared by Smith's process, contends that it is a mixed body, and that further purification deprives it of all volatile matter and renders it inert. This is not astonishing when one finds that the "purification" was effected by treatment with caustic lime or soda lime, and exposure to a temperature of 300° C. (572° F.)! That the resin of the Edinburgh chemists does not owe its activity to volatile matter, is proved by their own experiment of exposing a small quantity in a very thin layer to 82° C. for 8 hours: the medicinal action of the resin so treated was found to be unimpaired.

[5] Dragendorff's *Jahresbericht*, 1876. 98.

[6] *Chemical News*, xxiv. (1871) 77.

smoke it with tobacco, or swallow it in combination with other substances.[1]

Charas.

No account of hemp as a drug would be complete without some notice of this substance, which is regarded as of great importance by Asiatic nations.

Charas or *Churrus* is the resin which exudes in minute drops from the yellow glands, with which the plant is provided in increasing number according to the elevated temperature (and altitude ?) of the country where it grows. The varieties of hemp richest in resin, at least in the Laos country in the Malayan Peninsula, scarcely attain the height of 3 feet, and show densely curled leaves.[2] Charas is collected in several ways:—one is by rubbing the tops of the plants in the hands when the seeds are ripe, and scraping from the fingers the adhering resin. Another is thus performed:—men clothed in leather garments walk about among growing hemp, in doing which the resin of the plant attaches itself to the leather, whence it is from time to time scraped off. A third method consists in collecting, with many precautions to avoid its poisonous effects, the dust which is caused when heaps of dry *bhang* are stirred about.[3]

By whichever of these processes obtained, charas is of necessity a foul and crude drug, the use of which is properly excluded from civilized medicine. As before remarked (p. 547) it is not obtainable from hemp grown indiscriminately in any situation even in India, but is only to be got from plants produced at a certain elevation on the hills.

The best charas, which is that brought from Yarkand, is a brown, earthy-looking substance, forming compact yet friable, irregular masses of considerable size. Examined under a strong pocket lens, it appears to be made up of minute, transparent grains of brown resin, agglutinated with short hairs of the plant. It has a hemp-like odour, with but little taste even in alcoholic solution. A second and a third quality of Yarkand charas represent the substance in a less pure state. Charas viewed under the microscope exhibits a crystalline structure, due to inorganic matter. It yields from ½ to ⅓ of its weight of an amorphous resin, which is readily dissolved by bisulphide of carbon or spirit of wine. The resin does not redden litmus, nor is it soluble in caustic potash. It has a dark brown colour, which we have not succeeded in removing by animal charcoal. The residual part of charas yields to water a little chloride of sodium, and consists in large proportion of carbonate of calcium and peroxide of iron. These results have been obtained in examining samples from Yarkand.[4] Other specimens which we have also examined, have the aspect of a compact dark resin.

Charas is exported from Yarkand[5] and Kashgar, the first of which

[1] For further information, consult Cooke's *Seven Sisters of Sleep*, Lond., chap. xv.—xvii; also *Jahresbericht* of Wiggers and Husemann, 1872. 600.

[2] Garnier, *Voyage d'Exploration en Indo-Chine*, ii. (1873) 410.

[3] Powell, *Economic Products of the Punjab*, Roorkee, 1868. 293.

[4] Obtained by Colonel H. Strachey, and now in the Kew Museum. It is by no means evident by what process they were collected.

[5] Forsyth, *Correspondence on Mission to Yarkand*, ordered by the House of Commons to be printed, Feb. 28, 1871; also Henderson and Hume, *Lahore to Yarkand*, Lond. 1873. 334.

places exported during 1867, 1830 *maunds* (146,400 lb.) to Lê, whence the commodity is carried to the Punjab and Kashmir. Smaller quantities are annually imported from Kandahar and Samarkand;[1] some charas appears also (1876) to be exported from Mandshuria to China. The drug is mostly consumed by smoking with tobacco; it is not found in European commerce.

STROBILI HUMULI.

Humulus vel Lupulus; Hops; F. *Houblon;* G. *Hopfen.*

Botanical Origin—*Humulus Lupulus* L.,—a diœcious perennial plant, producing long annual twining stems which climb freely over trees and bushes. It is found wild, especially in thickets on the banks of rivers, throughout all Europe, from Spain, Sicily and Greece to Scandinavia; and extends also to the Caucasus, the South Caspian region, and through Central and Southern Siberia to the Altai mountains. It has been introduced into North America, Brazil (Rio Grande do Sul), and Australia.

History—Hops have been used from a remote period in the brewing of beer, of which they are now regarded as an indispensable ingredient. Hop gardens, under the name *humularia* or *humuleta*, are mentioned as existing in France and Germany in the 8th and 9th centuries; and Bohemian and Bavarian hops have been known as an esteemed kind since the 11th century. A grant alleged to have been made by William the Conqueror in 1069, of hops and hop-lands in the county of Salop,[2] would indicate, were it free from doubt, a very early cultivation of the hop in England.

As to the use made of hops in these early times, it would appear that they were regarded in somewhat of a medicinal aspect. In the *Herbarium of Apuleius*,[3] an English manuscript written about A.D. 1050, it is said of the hop (*hymele*) that its good qualities are such that men put it in their usual drinks; and St. Hildegard,[4] a century later, states that the hop (*hoppho*) is added to beverages, partly for its wholesome bitterness, and partly because it makes them keep.

Hops for brewing were among the produce which the tenants of the abbey of St Germain in Paris[5] had to furnish to the monastery in the beginning of the 9th century; yet in the middle of the 14th century, beer without such addition was still brewed in Paris.

The brewsters, bakers and millers of London were the subject of a mandate of Edward I. in A.D. 1298; but there is no reason for inferring that the manufacture of malt liquor at this period involved the use of hops. It is plain indeed that somewhat later, hops were *not* generally used, for in the 4th year of Henry VI. (1425-26), an information was laid against a person for putting into beer "an unwholesome weed called

[1] Stewart, *Punjab Plants*, Lahore, 1869. 216.

[2] Blount, *Tenures of Land and Customs of Manors*, edited by Hazlitt, 1874. 165.

[3] *Leechdoms, Wortcunning and Starcraft of Early England*, edited by Cockayne, i. (1864) 173; ii. (1865) ix.

[4] *Opera Omnia*, accurante J. P. Migne, Paris, 1855. 1153.

[5] Guérard, *Polyptique de l'abbé Irminon*, i. (1844) 714. 896.

an hopp;"[1] and in the same reign, Parliament was petitioned against "that wicked weed called *hops*."

But it is evident that hops were soon found to possess good qualities, and that though their use was denounced, it was not suppressed. Thus in the regulations for the household of Henry VIII. (1530-31), there is an injunction that the brewer is "not to put any hops or brimstone into the ale";[2] while in the very same year (1530), hundreds of pounds of Flemish hops were purchased for the use of the noble family of L'Estranges of Hunstanton.[3]

In 1552 the cultivation of hops in England was distinctly sanctioned by the 5th and 6th of Edward VI. c.5, which directs that land formerly in tillage should again be so cultivated, excepting it should have been set with *hops* or saffron. Notwithstanding these facts, hops were for a long period hardly regarded an essential in brewing, as may be gathered from the remark of Gerarde (*ob.* A.D. 1607), who speaks of them as used "to season" beer or ale, explaining that notwithstanding their manifold virtues, they "rather make it a physical drinke to keepe the body in health, than an ordinary drinke for the quenching of our thirst." In reality, other herbs were for a long period employed to impart to malt liquor a bitter or aromatic taste, as Ground Ivy (*Nepeta Glechoma* Benth.); anciently called Ale-hoof or Gill; Alecost (*Balsamita vulgaris* L.); Sweet Gale (*Myrica Gale* L.); and Sage (*Salvia officinalis* L.). Even Long Pepper and Bay Berries were used for the same purpose,[4] but in addition to hops.

Though English hops were esteemed superior to foreign, and were extensively grown as early as 1603, as shown by an act of James I.,[5] Flemish hops continued to be imported in considerable quantities down to 1693.

Structure—The inflorescence of the male plant constitutes a large panicle; that of the female is less conspicuous, consisting of stalked catkins which by their growth develope large leafy imbricating bracts, ultimately forming an ovoid cone or strobile, which is the officinal part. This catkin consists of a short central zigzag stalk, bearing overlapping rudimentary leaflets, each represented by a pair of stipules. Between them are 4 female florets, each supported by a bract. After flowering, the stipules as well as the bracts are much enlarged, and then form the persistent, yellowish-green, pendulous strobile. At maturity, each bract infolds at its base a small lenticular closed fruit or nut, $\frac{1}{10}$ of an inch in diameter. The nut is surrounded by a membranous, one-leafed perigone, and contains within its fragile, brown shell an exalbuminous seed. These fruits, as well as the axis and the base of all the leaf-like organs, are beset with numerous shining, translucent glands, to which the aromatic smell and taste of hops are due.

Description—Hops as found in commerce consist entirely of the fully developed strobiles or cones, more or less compressed. They have a greenish yellow colour, an agreeable and peculiar aroma, and a bitter aromatic burning taste. When rubbed in the hand they feel clammy, and emit a more powerful odour. By keeping, hops lose their greenish

[1] The authority for this statement is an isolated memorandum in a MS. volume (No. 980) by Thomas Gybbons, preserved in the Harleian collection in the British Museum.

[2] *Archæologia*, iii. (1786) 157.

[3] *Ibid.* xxv. (1834) 505.

[4] Holinshed, *Chronicles*, vol. i. book 2. cap. 6.

[5] 1 James I. (anno 1603) cap. 18.

colour and become brown, at the same time acquiring an unpleasant odour, by reason of the formation of a little valerianic acid. Exposure to the vapour of sulphurous acid retards or prevents this alteration. For medicinal use, hops smelling of sulphurous acid should be avoided, though in reality the acid speedily becomes innocuous. Liebig has refuted the objections raised by brewers to the sulphuring of hops.

Chemical Composition—Besides the constituents of the glands which are described in the next article, hops contain according to Etti's elaborate investigations (1876, 1878) *humulotannic acid* and *phlobaphene*. The former is a whitish amorphous mass, soluble in alcohol, hot water or acetic ether, not in ether. By heating the humulotannic acid at 130° C., or by boiling its aqueous or alcoholic solutions, it gives off water, and is transformed into phlobaphene, a dark red amorphous substance,

$$\underset{\text{humulotannic acid.}}{(C^{25}H^{24}O^{13})^2} = OH^2 \ . \ \underset{\text{phlobaphene.}}{C^{50}H^{46}O^{25}}.$$

The latter substance, on boiling it with dilute mineral acids, again loses water and furnishes glucose.

From raw phlobaphene ether removes the *bitter principles* of hops, a colourless crystallizable and a brown amorphous *resin*, besides chlorophyll and essential oil.

By distilling hops with water, 0·9 per cent. of *essential oil* are obtained. Personne (1854) stated it to contain *Valerol*,[1] $C^6H^{10}O$, which passes into valerianic acid; the latter in fact occurs in the glands, yet according to Méhu[2] only to the extent of 0·1 to 0·17 per cent. When distilled from the fresh strobiles the oil has a greenish colour, but a reddish-brown when old hops have been employed. We find it to be devoid of rotatory power, neutral to litmus paper, and not striking any remarkable coloration with concentrated sulphuric acid.

Griessmayer (1874) has shown that hops contain *Trimethylamine*, and in small proportion a liquid volatile alkaloid not yet analysed, which he terms *Lupuline*. The latter is stated to have the odour of conine, and to assume a violet hue when treated with chromate of potassium and sulphuric acid.

Lastly, Etti also found arabic (pectic) acid, phosphates, nitrates, malates, citrates, and also sulphates, chiefly of potassium, to occur in hops. The amount of ash afforded by hops dried at 100° C. would appear to be on an average about 6–7 per cent.

Production and Commerce—England was estimated as having in 1873, 63,276 acres under hops. The chief district for the cultivation is the county of Kent, where in that year 39,040 acres were devoted to this plant. Hops are grown to a much smaller extent in Sussex, and in still diminished quantity in Herefordshire, Hampshire, Worcestershire and Surrey. The other counties of England and the principality of Wales produce but a trifling amount, and Scotland none at all.

In continental Europe, hops are most largely produced in Bavaria and Würtemberg, Belgium and France, but in each on a smaller scale than in England. France in 1872 is stated to have 9223 acres under hops.[3]

[1] A substance with which we are not acquainted.

[2] *Thèse*, Montpellier, 1867.

[3] *Agricultural Returns of Great Britain*, &c., 1873, presented to Parliament, 48. 49. 70. 71.

Notwithstanding the extensive production of hops in England, there is a large importation from other countries. The importation in 1872 was 135,965 cwt., valued at £679,276: of this quantity, Belgium supplied 66,630 cwt., Germany 36,612 cwt., Holland 16,675 cwt., the United States 10,414 cwt., France 5328 cwt. During the same period hops were exported from the United Kingdom to the extent of 31,215 cwt.[1]

Uses—Hops are administered medicinally as a tonic and sedative, chiefly in the form of tincture, infusion or extract.

GLANDULÆ HUMULI.

Lupulina; Lupulin, Lupulinic Grains; F. *Lupuline;* G. *Hopfendrüsen, Hopfenstaub.*

Botanical Origin—*Humulus Lupulus* L. (see preceding article). The minute, shining, translucent glands of the strobile constitute when detached therefrom the substance called *Lupulin.*

History—The glands of hop were separated and chemically examined by L. A. Planche, a pharmacien of Paris, whose observations were first briefly described by Loiseleur-Deslongchamps in 1819.[2] In the following year, Dr. A. W. Ives of New York[3] published an account of his experiments upon hops and their glands, to which latter he applied the name of *Lupulin.* Payen and Chevallier, Planche and others, made further experiments on the same subject, endorsing the recommendation of Ives that lupulin (or, as they preferred to call it, *Lupuline*) might be advantageously used in medicine in place of hops.

Production—Lupulin is obtained by stripping off the bracts of hops, and shaking and rubbing them; and then separating the powder by a sieve. The powder thus detached ought to be washed by decantation, so as to remove from it the sand or earth with which it is always contaminated; finally it should be dried, and stored in well-closed bottles. From the dried strobiles, 8 to 12 per cent. of lupulin may be obtained.

Description—Lupulin seen in quantity appears as a yellowish-brown granular powder, having an agreeable odour of hops and a bitter aromatic taste. It is gradually wetted by water, instantly by alcohol or ether, but not by potash or sulphuric acid. By trituration in a mortar the cells are ruptured so that it may be worked into a plastic mass. Thrown into the air and then ignited, it burns with a brilliant flame like lycopodium.

Microscopic Structure—The lupulinic gland or grain, like the generality of analogous organs, is formed by an intumescence of the cuticle of the nuculæ and bracts of hop (see p. 552). Each grain is originally attached by a very short stalk, which is no longer perceptible in the drug. The gland, exhausted by ether and macerated in water, is a globular or ovoid thin-walled sac, measuring from 140 to 240 mkm. It consists of two distinct, nearly hemispherical parts; that originally

[1] *Annual Statement of the Trade of the United Kingdom* for 1872. 49. 93.

[2] *Manuel des Plantes usuelles et indigènes,* 1819. ii. 503.

[3] Silliman's *Journ. of Science,* ii. (1820) 302.

provided with the stalk is built up of tabular polyhedric cells, whilst the upper hemisphere shows a continuous delicate membrane. This part therefore easily collapses, and thus exhibits a variety of form, the greater also as the grains turn pole or equator to the observer.[1]

The hop gland is filled with a thick, dark brown or yellowish liquid, which in the drug is contracted into one mass occupying the centre of the gland. It may be expelled in minute drops when the wall is made to burst by warming the grain in glycerin. The colouring matter, to which the wall owes its fine yellow colour, adheres more obstinately to the thinner hemisphere, and is more easily extracted from the thicker part by means of ether.

Chemical Composition—The odour of lupulinic grains resides in the essential oil, described in the previous article. The bitter principle formerly called *Lupulin* or *Lupulite* was first isolated by Lermer (1863) who called it the *bitter acid of hops* (*Hopfenbittersäure*). It crystallizes in large brittle rhombic prisms, and possesses in a high degree the peculiar bitter taste of beer, in which however it can be present only in very small proportion, it being nearly insoluble in water, though easily dissolved by many other liquids. The composition of this acid, $C^{32}H^{50}O^{7}$, appears to approximate it to absinthiin; it is contained in the glands in but small proportion. Still smaller is the amount of another crystallizable constituent, regarded by Lermer as an alkaloid.

The main contents of the hop gland consist of wax (*Myricylic palmitate*, according to Lermer), and resins, one of which is crystalline and unites with bases.

A good specimen of German lupulin, dried over sulphuric acid, yielded us 7·3 per cent. of ash. The same drug exhausted by boiling ether, afforded 76·8 per cent. of an extremely aromatic extract, which on exposure to the steam bath for a week, lost 3·03 per cent., this loss corresponding to the volatile oil and acids. The residual part was soluble in glacial acetic acid and could therefore contain but very little fatty matter.

Uses—The drug has the properties of hops, but with less of astringency. It is not often prescribed.

Adulteration—Lupulin is apt to contain sand, and on incineration often leaves a large amount of ash. Other extraneous matters which are not unfrequent may be easily recognized by means of a lens. As the essential oil in lupulin is soon resinified, the latter should be preferred fresh, and should be kept excluded from the air.

[1] For a full account of the formation of the glands, see Trécul, *Annales des Sciences Nat.*, Bot., i. (1854) 299. An abstract may be found in Méhu's *Etude du Houblon et du Lupulin*, Montpellier, 1867.

ULMACEÆ.

CORTEX ULMI.

Elm Bark; F. Ecorce d'Orme; G. Ulmenrinde, Rüsterrinde.

Botanical Origin—*Ulmus campestris* Smith, the Common Elm, a stately tree, widely diffused over Central, Southern and Eastern Europe, southward to Northern Africa and Asia Minor, and eastward as far as Amurland, Northern China, and Japan. It is probably not truly indigenous to Great Britain; but the Wych Elm, *U. montana* With., is certainly wild in the northern and western counties;[1] the latter is, according to Schübeler, the only species indigenous to Norway.

History—The classical writers, and especially Dioscorides, were familiar with the astringent properties of the bark of πτελέα, by which name *Ulmus campestris* is understood. Imaginary virtues are ascribed by Pliny to the bark and leaves of *Ulmus*. Elm bark is frequently prescribed in the English Leech Books of the 11th century, at which period a great many plants of Southern Europe had already been introduced into Britain.[2] Its use is also noticed in Turner's *Herbal* (1568) and in Parkinson's *Theater of Plants* (1640), the author of the latter remarking that "all the parts of the Elme are of much use in Physicke."

In the Scandinavian antiquity the fibrous bark of *Ulmus montana* used to be made up into ropes.[3]

Description—Elm bark for use in medicine should be removed from the tree in early spring, deprived of its rough corky outer coat, and then dried. Thus prepared, it is found in the shops in the form of broad flattish pieces, of a rusty yellowish colour, and striated surface especially on the inner side. It is tough and fibrous, nearly inodorous, and has a woody, slightly astringent taste.

Microscopic Structure—The liber, which is the only officinal part, consists of thick-walled, tangentially extended parenchyme, in which there are some large cells filled with mucilage, while the rest contain a red-brown colouring matter. The mucilage forms a stratified deposit within the cell. Large bast-bundles, arranged in irregular rows, alternate with the parenchyme, and are intersected by narrow, reddish, medullary rays consisting of 2 or 3 rows of cells. The bast-bundles contain numerous long tubes about 30 mkm. thick, with narrow cavities; and besides these, somewhat larger tubes with porous transverse walls (cribriform vessels). Each cubic cell of the neighbouring bast-parenchyme encloses a large crystal, seldom well defined, of oxalate of calcium.

[1] On the word *elm*, Dr. Prior remarks that it is nearly identical in all the Germanic and Scandinavian dialects, yet does not find its root in any of them, but is an adaptation of the Latin *Ulmus*.—*Popular Names of British Plants*, ed. 2. 1870. 71.

[2] *Leechdoms, Wortcunning and Starcraft of Early England*, edited by Rev. O. Cockayne, ii. (1865) pp. 53. 67. 79. 99. 127 and p. xii.—In the Anglo-Saxon recipes, both *Elm* and *Wych Elm* are named in the Welsh "*Meddygon Myddfai*" (see Appendix). Elmwydd or Ilwyf and "Ulmus romanus," Ilwyf Rhufain, are met with.

[3] Schübeler, *Pflanzenwelt Norwegens*, 1873–75, p. 216.

Chemistry—The chief soluble constituent of elm bark is mucilage with a small proportion of tannic acid, the latter, according to Johanson (1875), probably agreeing with that of oak bark and bark of willows. The concentrated infusion of elm bark yields a brown precipitate with perchloride of iron; the dilute assumes a green coloration with that test. Starch is wanting, or only occurs in the middle cortical layer, which is usually rejected.

Elms in summer-time frequently exude a gum which, by contact with the air, is converted into a brown insoluble mass, called *Ulmin*. This name has been extended to various decomposition-products of organic bodies, the nature and affinities of which are but little known.[1]

Uses—Elm bark is prescribed in decoction as a weak mucilaginous astringent, but is almost obsolete.

CORTEX ULMI FULVÆ.

Slippery Elm Bark.

Botanical Origin—*Ulmus fulva* Michaux, the Red or Slippery Elm, a small or middle-sized tree,[2] seldom more than 30 to 40 feet high, growing on the banks of streams in the central and northern United States from Western New England to Wisconsin and Kentucky, and found also in Canada.

History—The Indians of North America attributed medicinal virtues to the bark of the Slippery Elm, which they used as a healing application to wounds, and in decoction as a wash for skin diseases. It is the "Salve Bark" or "Cortex unguentarius" of Schöpf.[3] Bigelow, writing in 1824, remarks that the mucilaginous qualities of the inner bark are well known.

Description—The Slippery Elm Bark used in medicine consists of the liber only. It forms large flat pieces, often 2 to 3 feet long by several inches broad, and usually $\frac{1}{20}$ to $\frac{3}{20}$ of an inch thick, of an extremely tough and fibrous texture. It has a light reddish-brown colour, an odour resembling that of fenugreek (which is common to the leaves also), and a simply mucilaginous taste.

In collecting the bark the tree is destroyed, and no effort is made to replace it, the wood being nearly valueless. Thus the supply is diminishing year by year, and the collectors who formerly obtained large quantities of the bark in New York and other eastern states have now to go westward for supplies.[4]

Microscopic Structure—The transverse section shows a series of undulating layers of large yellowish bundles of soft liber fibres, alternating with small brown parenchymatous bands. The whole tissue is traversed by numerous narrow medullary rays, and interrupted by large intercellular mucilage-ducts. In order to examine the latter, longitudinal sections ought to be moistened with benzol, aqueous liquids causing great alteration. In a longitudinal section, the mucilage-ducts are seen

[1] Gmelin, *Chemistry*, xvii. (1866) 458.

[2] Fig. in Bentley and Trimen's *Med. Plants*, part 34 (1878).

[3] *Mat. Med. Americ.*, Erlangæ, 1787. 32.

[4] *Proceedings of the American Pharmaceutical Association for* 1873, xxi. 435.

to be 70 to 100 mkm. long, and to contain colourless masses of mucilage, distinctly showing a series of layers. Crystals of calcium oxalate, as well as small starch grains, are very plentiful throughout the surrounding parenchyme.

Chemical Composition—The most interesting constituent of the bark is mucilage, which is imparted to either cold or hot water, but does not form a true solution. The bark moistened with 20 parts of water swells considerably, and becomes enveloped by a thick neutral mucilage, which is not altered either by iodine or perchloride of iron. This mucilage when diluted, even with a triple volume of water, will yield only a few drops when thrown on a paper filter. The liquid which drains out is precipitable by neutral acetate of lead. By addition of absolute alcohol, the concentrated mucilage is not rendered turbid, but forms a colourless transparent fluid deposit.

Adulteration—Farinaceous substances admixed to the powdered drug may be detected by means of the microscope.

Uses—Slippery Elm Bark is a demulcent like althæa or linseed. The powder is much used in America for making poultices; it is said to preserve lard from rancidity, if the latter is melted with it and kept in contact for a short time.

EUPHORBIACEÆ.

EUPHORBIUM.

Euphorbium, Gum Euphorbium; F. *Gomme-résine d'Euphorbe;* G. *Euphorbium.*

Botanical Origin—*Euphorbia resinifera* Berg, a leafless, glaucous, perennial plant resembling a cactus, and attaining 6 or more feet in height. Its stems are ascending, fleshy and quadrangular, each side measuring about an inch. The angles of the stem are furnished at intervals with pairs of divergent, horizontal, straight spines about $\frac{1}{4}$ of an inch long, and confluent at the base into ovate, subtriangular discs. These spines represent stipules: above each pair of them is a depression, indicating a leaf-bud. The inflorescence is arranged at the summits of the branches, on stalks each bearing three flowers, the two outer of which are supported on pedicels. The fruit is tricoccous, $\frac{3}{10}$ of an inch wide, with each carpel slightly compressed and keeled.[1]

The plant is a native of Morocco, growing on the lower slopes of the Atlas in the southern province of Suse. Dr. Hooker and his fellow-travellers met with it in 1870 at Netifa and Imsfuia,[2] south-east of the city of Morocco, which appears to be its westward limit.

History—Euphorbium was known to the ancients. Dioscorides[3] and Pliny[4] both describe its collection on Mount Atlas in Africa, and notice its extreme acridity. According to the latter writer, the drug received

[1] Fig. in Bentley and Trimen's *Med. Plants*, part 24 (1877).

[2] Or Mesfioua, according to Ball, who also quotes the province Demenet.—*Journ. of the Linnean Soc.* Bot. xvi. (1878) 662.

[3] Lib. iii. c. 86.

[4] Lib. v. c. 1; lib. xxv. c. 38.

its name in honour of Euphorbus, physician to Juba II., king of Mauritania. This monarch, who after a long reign died about A.D. 18, was distinguished for his literary attainments, and was the author of several books[1] which included treatises on opium and euphorbium. The latter work was apparently extant in the time of Pliny.

Euphorbium is mentioned by numerous other early writers on medicine, as Rufus Ephesius, who probably flourished during the reign of Trajan, by Galen in the 2nd century, and by Vindicianus and Oribasius in the 4th. Aëtius and Paulus Ægineta, who lived respectively in the 6th and 7th centuries, were likewise acquainted with it; and it was also known to the Arabian school of medicine. In describing the route from Aghmat to Fez, El-Bekri[2] of Granada, in 1068, mentioned the numerous plants "El-forbioun" growing in the country of the Beni Ouareth, a tribe of the Sanhadja; the author noticed the spiny herbaceous stems of the shrub abounding in the purgative milky juice.

Höst[3] (1760-1768) stated that the plant, which he also correctly compared with Opuntia, is growing near Agader, south of Mogador.

The plant yielding euphorbium was further described at the beginning of the present century by an English merchant named Jackson, who had resided many years in Morocco. From the figures he published,[4] the species was doubtfully identified with *Euphorbia canariensis* L., a large cactus-like shrub, with quadrangular or hexagonal stems, abounding on scorched and arid rocks in the Canary Islands.

In the year 1749 it was pointed out in the (*Admiralty*) *Manual of Scientific Enquiry*, that the stems of which fragrants are found in commercial euphorbium, do not agree with those of *E. canariensis*. Berg carried the comparison further, and finally from the fragments in question drew up a botanical description, which with an excellent figure he published[5] as *Euphorbia resinifera*. The correctness of his observations has been fully justified by specimens[6] which were transmitted to the Royal Gardens, Kew, in 1870, and now form flourishing plants.

The drug has a place in all the early printed pharmacopœias.

Collection—Euphorbium is obtained by making incisions in the green fleshy branches of the plant. These incisions occasion an abundant exudation of milky juice which hardens by exposure to the air, encrusting the stems down which it flows; it is finally collected in the latter part of the summer. So great is the acridity of the exudation, that the collector is obliged to tie a cloth over his mouth and nostrils, to prevent the entrance of the irritating dust. The drug is said to be collected in districts lying east and south-east of the city of Morocco.

Description—The drug consists of irregular pieces, seldom more than an inch across and mostly smaller, of a dull yellow or brown waxy-

[1] Smith, *Dict. of Greek and Roman Biography*, ii. (1846) 636.

[2] *Description de l'Afrique septentrionale*, traduite par M. de Slane, *Journal asiatique*, xiii. (Paris, 1859) 413.

[3] *Nachrichten von Marokos und Fes*, Kopenhagen, 1781. 308.

[4] *Account of the Empire of Morocco and the district of Suse*, Lond. 1809. 81. pl. 7.—The plate represents an entire plant, and also what purports to be a portion of a branch of the natural size. The latter is really the figure of a different species,—apparently that which has been recently named by Cosson *Euphorbia Beaumierana*.

[5] Berg und Schmidt, *Offizinelle Gewächse*, iv. (1863) xxxiv. d.

[6] They were procured by Mr. William Grace, and forwarded to England by Mr. C. F. Carstensen, British Vice-Consul at Mogador.

looking substance, among which portions of the angular spiny stem of the plant may be met with. Many of the pieces encrust a tuft of spines or a flower-stalk or are hollow. The substance is brittle and translucent; splinters examined under the microscope exhibit no particular structure, even by the aid of polarized light; nor are starch granules visible.[1] The odour is slightly aromatic, especially if heat is applied; but 10 lb. of the drug which we subjected to distillation afforded no essential oil. Euphorbium has a persistent and extremely acrid taste; its dust excites violent sneezing, and if inhaled, as when the drug is powdered, occasions alarming symptoms.

Chemical Composition—Analysis of euphorbium performed by one of us[2] showed the composition of the drug to be as follows:—

Amorphous resin, $C^{10}H^{16}O^{2}$	38
Euphorbon, $C^{15}H^{22}O$	22
Mucilage	18
Malates, chiefly of calcium and sodium ...	12
Mineral compounds	10
	100

The amorphous resin is readily soluble in cold spirit of wine containing about 70 per cent. of alcohol. The solution has no acid reaction, but an extremely burning acrid taste: in fact it is to the amorphous indifferent resin that euphorbium owes its intense acridity. By evaporating the resin with alcoholic potash and neutralizing the residue with a dilute aqueous acid, a brown amorphous substance, the *Euphorbic Acid* of Buchheim,[3] is precipitated. It is devoid of the acridity of the resin from which it originated, but has a bitterish taste.

From the drug deprived of the amorphous resin as above stated, ether (ether or petroleum) takes up the *Euphorbon*, which may be obtained in colourless, although not very distinct crystals, which are at first not free from acrid taste. But by repeated crystallizations and finally boiling in a weak solution of permanganate of potassium, they may be so far purified as to be entirely tasteless. Euphorbon is insoluble in water; it requires about 60 parts of alcohol, sp. gr. 0·830, for solution at the ordinary temperature. In boiling alcohol euphorbon dissolves abundantly, also in ether, benzol, amylic alcohol, chloroform, acetone, or glacial acetic acid.

Euphorbon melts at 116° C. (113° to 114°, Hesse) without emitting any odour. By dry distillation a brownish oily liquid is obtained, which claims further examination. If euphorbon dissolved in alcohol is allowed to form a thin film in a porcelain capsule, and is then moistened with a little concentrated sulphuric acid, a fine violet hue is produced in contact with strong nitric acid slowly added by means of a glass rod. The same reaction is displayed by *Lactucerin* (see Lactucarium), to which in its general characters euphorbon is closely allied.

[1] By careful investigation a very few are found at last.

[2] Flückiger in Wittstein's *Vierteljahresschrift für prakt. Pharmacie*, xvii. (1868) 82–102.—The drug analysed consisted of selected fragrants, free from extraneous substances.

[3] Wiggers and Husemann, *Jahresbericht*, 1873. 559.

Hesse (1878) assigns to euphorbon the formula $C^{15}H^{24}O$, and points out that its solutions in chloroform or ether are dextrogyrate.

As to the mucilage of euphorbium, it may be obtained from that portion of the drug which has been exhausted by cold alcohol and by ether. Neutral acetate of lead, as well as silicate or borate of sodium, precipitate this mucilage, which therefore does not agree with gum arabic.

If an aqueous extract of euphorbium is mixed with spirit of wine, and the liquid evaporated, the residual matter assumes a somewhat crystalline appearance, and exhibits the reactions of *Malic Acid.* Subjected to dry distillation, white scales and acicular crystals of *Maleic* and *Fumaric Acids*, produced by the decomposition of the malic acid, are sublimed into the neck of the retort. A sublimate of the same kind may sometimes be obtained directly by heating fragments of euphorbium. Among the mineral constituents of the drug, chloride of sodium and calcium are noticeable; scarcely any salt of potassium is present.

Commerce—The drug is shipped from Mogador. The quantity imported into the United Kingdom in 1870 is given in the *Annual Statement of Trade* as 12 cwt.

Uses—Euphorbium was formerly employed as an emetic and purgative, but as an internal remedy it is completely obsolete. We have been told that it is now in some demand as an ingredient of a paint for the preservation of ships' bottoms.

CORTEX CASCARILLÆ.

Cortex Eleutheriæ; Cascarilla Bark, Sweet Wood Bark, Eleuthera[1] *Bark;* F. *Ecorce de Cascarille;* G. *Cascarill-Rinde.*

Botanical Origin—*Croton Eluteria* Bennett,[2] a shrub or small tree, exclusively native of the Bahama Islands.

History—It is not improbable that cascarilla bark was imported into Europe in the first half of the 17th century, as there was much intercourse subsequent to the year 1630 between England and the Bahamas.[3] These islands were occupied in 1641 by the Spaniards, who became at that time acquainted with the Peruvian bark or Cascarilla (see page 346), as we have shown at page 343. The external appearance of the bark of Eluteria being somewhat similar to that of Cinchona quills, the former began soon to be known under the name of *China nova.* This

[1] From Eleuthera, one of the Bahama Islands, so named from the Greek ἐλεύθερος, signifying *free* or *independent.*

[2] Bentley and Trimen's *Med. Plants*, part i. (1875).

[3] In that year a patent was granted by Charles I. for the incorporation of a Company for colonizing the Bahama Islands, and a complete record is extant of the proceedings of the Company for the first eleven years of its existence. In some of the documents, particular mention is made of the introduction, actual or attempted, of useful plants, as cotton, tobacco, fig, pepper, pomegranate, palma Christi, mulberry, flax, indigo, madder, and jalap; and there is also frequent allusion to the importation of the produce of the islands, but no mention of *Cascarilla.* See *Calendar of State Papers.* Colonial Series, 1574–1660, edited by Sainsbury, Lond. 1860. pp. 146. 148. 149. 164. 168. 185. etc.

drug occurs along with true Cinchona bark, *China de China*, in the tariff of the year 1691 of the pharmaceutical shops of the German town Minden, in Westphalia. There can be no doubt that the cheaper kind of "China," called China nova, was really the bark under examination, for in many other tariffs a few years later distinct mention is made of *Cortex Chinæ novæ seu Schacorillæ;* and Savary, in his "Dictionnaire de Commerce" (1723, 1750), confirms the fact, adding that it was first seen in the great fair of Brunswick.[1] Another early statement concerning Cascarilla bark likewise refers to the duchy of Brunswick. Stisser, a professor of anatomy, chemistry, and medicine in the University of Helmstedt in Brunswick, relates that he received the drug under the name of *Cortex Eleuterii* from a person who had returned from England, in which country, he was assured, it was customary to mix it with tobacco for the sake of correcting the smell of the latter when smoked. He also mentions that it had been confounded with Peruvian bark, from which however it was very distinct in odour, etc.[2] Eleutheria bark was then frequently prescribed as a febrifuge in the place of Cinchona bark, then a more expensive medicine. Hence the name *cascarilla*, signifying in Spanish *little bark,* which was the customary designation of Peruvian bark, was erroneously applied to the Bahama bark, until at last it quite superseded the original and more correct appellation. That of *China nova* was subsequently applied to a quite different bark (see page 364). The drug under notice was first introduced into the London Pharmacopœia in 1746 as *Eleutheriæ Cortex,* which was its common name among druggists down to the end of the last century. In the Bahamas the name *cascarilla* is still hardly known, the bark being there called either *Sweet Wood Bark* or *Eleuthera Bark.*

The plant affording cascarilla has been the subject of much discussion, arising chiefly from the circumstance that several nearly allied West Indian species of *Croton* yield aromatic barks resembling more or less the officinal drug. Catesby in 1754 figured a Bahama plant, *Croton Cascarilla* Bennett, from which the original *Eleuthera Bark* was probably derived, though it certainly affords none of the cascarilla of modern commerce. Woodville in 1794, and Lindley in 1838, both investigated the botany of the subject, the latter having the advantage of authentic specimens communicated by the Hon. J. C. Lees of New Providence, to whom one of us also is indebted for a similar favour. The question was not however finally set at rest until 1859, when J. J. Bennett by the aid of specimens collected in the Bahamas by Daniell in 1857-8, drew up lucid diagnoses of the several plants which had been confounded, and disentangled their intricate synonymy.[3]

Description—Cascarilla occurs in the form of tubular or channelled

[1] Flückiger, *Pharm. Journ.*, vi. (1876) 1022, and "Documente" quoted there, pp. 74-77, etc.

[2] Stisser (J. A.) *Actorum Laboratorii Chemici specimen secundum*, Helmestadi, 1693. c. ix. Stisser is said to have mentioned Cascarilla bark in his pamphlet "De machinis fumiductoriis," Hamburg, 1686, but we found this to be incorrect. Nor have we seen the paper of Vincent Garcia Salat, "Unica quæstiuncula, in qua examinatur pulvis de Burango, vulgo *Cascarilla*, in curatione tertianæ," Valentiæ. 1692. It is quoted by Haller, *Bibl. Bot.* ii. (1772) 688, and several later authors, but appears to be extremely rare.

[3] *Journal of Proceedings of Linn. Soc.* iv. (1860) Bot. 29.

pieces of a dull brown colour, somewhat rough and irregular, rarely exceeding 4 inches in length by ½ an inch in diameter. The chief bulk of that at present imported is in very small thin quills and fragments, often scarcely an inch in length, and evidently stripped from very young wood. The younger bark has a thin suberous coat easily detached, blotched or entirely covered with the silvery-white growth of a minute lichen (*Verrucaria albissima* Ach.), the perithecium of which appears as small black dots. The older bark is more rugose, irregularly tessellated by longitudinal cracks and less numerous transverse fissures. Beneath the corky envelope the bark is greyish-brown.

The bark breaks readily with a short fracture, the broken surface displaying a resinous appearance. It has a very fragrant odour, especially agreeable when several pounds of it are reduced to coarse powder and placed in a jar; it has a nauseous bitter taste. When burned it emits an aromatic smell, and hence is a common ingredient in fumigating pastilles.

Microscopic Characters—The suberous coat is made up of numerous rows of tabular cells, the outermost having their exterior walls much thickened. The mesophlœum exhibits the usual tissue, containing starch, chlorophyll, essential oil, crystals of oxalate of calcium, and a brown colouring matter. The latter assumes a dark bluish coloration on addition of a persalt of iron. In the inner portion of that layer ramified laticiferous vessels are also present. The liber consists of parenchyme and of fibrous bundles, intersected by small medullary rays. On the transverse section, the fibrous bundles show a wedge-shaped outline; they are for the most part built up, not of true liber-fibres, but of cylindrical cells having their transverse walls perforated sieve-like (*vasa cribriformia*). The contents of the parenchymatous part of the liber are the same as in the mesophlœum; as to the oxalate of calcium, the variety of its crystals is remarkable.[1]

Chemical Composition—Cascarilla contains a volatile oil, which it yields to the extent of 1·1 per cent. According to Völckel (1840), it is a mixture of at least two oils, the more volatile of which is probably free from oxygen. Gladstone (1872) assigns to the hydrocarbon of cascarilla oil the composition of oil of turpentine. By examining the oil optically we found it to have a weak rotatory power—some samples deviated to the right, some to the left. The resin, in which cascarilla is rich, has not yet been examined more exactly.

The bitter principle was isolated in 1845 by Duval, and called *Cascarillin*. C. and E. Mylius (1873) have obtained it from a deposit in the officinal extract, in microscopic prisms readily soluble in ether or hot alcohol, very sparingly in water, chloroform or spirit of wine. It melts at 205° C., is not volatile, nor a glucoside. Its composition answers to the formula $C^{12}H^{18}O^{4}$.

Commerce—The bark is shipped from Nassau, the chief town of New Providence (Bahamas), and is usually packed in sacks. The quantity imported into the United Kingdom in 1870 was 12,261 cwt.,

[1] For more particulars see Pocklington, *Pharm. Journ.* iii. (1873) 664.

valued at £16,482. The exports from the Bahamas were 676 cwt. in 1875, and 1,093 cwt. in 1876.

Uses—Cascarilla is prescribed as a tonic, usually in the form of a tincture or infusion.

Adulteration—A spurious cascarilla bark has lately been noticed in the London market; it was imported from the Bahamas mixed with the genuine, to which it bears a close similarity. The quills of it resemble the larger quills of cascarilla; though covered with a lichen, the latter has not the silvery whiteness of the *Verrucaria* of cascarilla. The spurious bark has a suberous coat that does not split off; its inner surface is pinkish-brown, and distinctly striated longitudinally. In microscopic structure the bark may be said to resemble cascarilla and still more copalchi. But it is at once distinguishable by its numerous *roundish groups* of sclerenchymatous cells, which become very evident when thin sections are moistened with ammonia, and then with solution of iodine in iodide of potassium. The bark has an astringent taste, without bitterness or aroma; its tincture is not rendered milky by addition of water, but is darkened by ferric chloride,—in these respects differing from a tincture of cascarilla. Mr. Holmes[1] suggests that this spurious cascarilla is probably the bark of *Croton lucidus* L.

Copalchi Bark; Quina blanca of the Mexicans.

This drug is derived from *Croton niveus*[2] Jacquin (*C. Pseudo-China* Schlechtendal), a shrub growing 10 feet high, native of the West Indian Islands, Mexico, Central America, New Granada and Venezuela. It has occasionally been imported into Europe, in quills a foot or two in length, much stouter and thicker than those of cascarilla, to which in odour and taste it nearly approximates. The bark has a thin, greyish, papery suberous layer, which when removed shows the surface marked with minute transverse pits, like the lines made by a file; it has a short fracture.[3]

Copalchi bark was examined by J. Eliot Howard,[4] and found to contain a minute proportion of a bitter alkaloid soluble in ether, which resembled quinine in yielding a deep green colour when treated with chlorine and ammonia, though it did not afford any characteristic compound with iodine. Mauch,[5] who also analysed the bark, could not obtain from it any organic base. He extracted by distillation the essential oil, which he found to consist of a hydrocarbon and an organic acid,—the latter not examined; he likewise got from the bark an uncrystallizable bitter principle, which proved to be not a glucoside.

[1] *Pharm. Journ.* iv. (1874) 810.

[2] De Candolle's *Prodromus*, xv. part 2. (1862) 518; beautifully figured in Hayne, *Arzneigewächse*, xiv. (1843) plate 2.

[3] For more particulars see Oberlin and Schlagdenhauffen, *Journ. de Pharm.* 28 (1878) 248.

[4] *Pharm Journ.* xiv. (1855) 319.

[5] Wittstein's *Vierteljahresschrift für prakt. Pharm.* xviii. (1869) 161.

SEMEN TIGLII.

Semen Crotonis; Croton Seeds; F. *Graines de Tilly ou des Moluques, Petits Pignons d'Inde;* G. *Purgirkörner, Granatill.*

Botanical Origin—*Croton Tiglium*[1] L. (*Tiglium officinale* Klotzsch), a small tree, 15 to 20 feet high, indigenous to the Malabar Coast and Tavoy, cultivated in gardens in many parts of the East, from Mauritius to the India Archipelago. The tree has small inconspicuous flowers, and brown, capsular, three-celled fruits, each cell containing one seed. The leaves have a disagreeable smell and nauseous taste.

History—In Europe, the seeds and wood of the tree were first described in 1578 by Christoval Acosta—the former, with a figure of the plant, appearing under the name of *Piñones de Maluco.*[2] The plant was also described and figured by Rheede (1679)[3] and Rumphius (1743).[4] The seeds, which were officinal in the 17th century, but had become obsolete, were recommended about 1812 by English medical officers in India,[5] and the expressed oil by Perry, Frost, Conwell and others about 1821–24. The oil then in use was imported from India, and was often of doubtful purity, so that some druggists felt it necessary to press the seeds for themselves.[6]

Description—Croton seeds are about half an inch long, by nearly $\frac{3}{8}$ of an inch broad, ovoid or bluntly oblong, divided longitudinally into two unequal parts, of which the more arched constitutes the dorsal and the flatter the ventral side. From the hilum, a fine raised line (raphe) passes to the other end of the seed, terminating in a darker point, indicating the chalaza. The surface of the seed is more or less covered with a bright cinnamon-brown coat, which when scraped shows the thin, brittle, black testa filled with a whitish, oily kernel, invested with a delicate seed-coat. The kernel is easily split into two halves consisting of oily albumen, between which lie the large, veined, leafy cotyledons and the radicle. The taste of the seed is at first merely oleaginous, but soon becomes unpleasantly and persistently acrid.

Microscopic Structure—The testa consists of an outer layer of radially arranged, much elongated and thick-walled cells; the inner parenchymatous layer contains small vascular bundles. The soft tissue of the albumen is loaded with drops of fatty oil. If this is removed by means of ether and weak potash lye, there remain small granules of albuminoid matter, the so-called *Aleuron,* and crystals of oxalate of calcium.

Chemical Composition—The principal constituent of croton seeds is the fatty oil, the *Oleum Crotonis* or *Oleum Tiglii* of pharmacy ot

[1] Fig. in Bentley and Trimen's *Medic. Plants,* part 1 (1875).

[2] *Tractado, etc.,* Burgos, 1578. c. 48.—After speaking of the virtues of the seeds, he adds—"tambien las buenas mugeres de aquellas partes, amigas de sus maridos, les dã hasta quatro destos por la boca, para embiar a los pobretos al otro mundo"!

[3] *Hortus Malabaricus,* ii. tab. 33.

[4] *Herbarium Amboinense,* iv. tab. 42.

[5] Ainslie, *Mat. Med. of Hindoostan,* 1813. 292.

[6] The oil was very expensive. I find by the books of Messrs. Allen and Hanburys, that the seeds cost in 1824, 10*s.*, and in 1827, 18*s.* per lb. The oil was purchased in 1826 by the same house at 8*s.* to 10*s.* per ounce.—D. H.

which the kernels afford from 50 to 60 per cent. That used in England is for the most part expressed in London, and justly regarded as more reliable than that imported from India, with which the market was formerly supplied. It is a transparent, sherry-coloured, viscid liquid, slightly fluorescent, and having a slight rancid smell and an oily, acrid taste. Its solubility in alcohol (·794) appears to depend in great measure on the age of the oil, and the greater or less freshness of the seeds from which it was expressed,—oxidized or resinified oil dissolving the most readily.[1] We found the oil which one of us had extracted by means of bisulphide of carbon to be levogyre.

Croton oil consists chiefly of the glycerinic ethers of the common fatty acids, such as stearic, palmitic, myristic and lauric acids. They partly separate in the cold; the acids also may partly be obtained by passing nitrous acid through croton oil. There are also present in the latter, in the form of glycerinic ethers, the more volatile acids, as formic, acetic, isobutyric and one of the valerianic acids.[2] The volatile part of the acids yielded by croton oil contains moreover an acid which was regarded by Schlippe (1858) as angelic acid, $C^5H^8O^2$. Yet in 1869 it was shown by Geuther and Frölich to be a peculiar acid, which they called *Tiglinic acid.* Its composition answers to the same formula, C^4H^7COOH, as that of angelic acid; but the melting points (angelic acid 45°, tiglinic 64° C.) and boiling points (angelic acid 185°, tiglinic 198°·5) are different. Both these acids have been mentioned in our article on Flores Anthemidis, at page 386. Tiglinic acid may also be obtained artificially; it is the methylcrotonic acid of Frankland and Duppa (1865).

Schlippe also stated croton oil to afford a peculiar liquid acid termed *Crotonic Acid,* $C^4H^6O^2$. According to Geuther and Frölich, however, an acid of this formula does not occur at all in croton oil. By synthetic methods three different acids of that composition are obtainable.

The *drastic principle* of croton oil has not yet been isolated. Buchheim[3] suggested that the action of the oil depends upon "*Crotonoleic acid,*" which however he failed in isolating satisfactorily. It is remarkable that the wood and leaves of *Croton Tiglium* appear to partake also of the drastic properties of the seeds.

Schlippe asserts that he has separated the *vesicating matter* of croton oil: if the oil be agitated with alcoholic soda, and afterwards with water, the supernatant liquor will be found free from acridity, while the alcoholic solution will yield, on addition of hydrochloric acid, a small quantity of a dark brown oil, called *Crotonol,* possessing vesicating properties. We have not succeeded in obtaining it, nor, so far as we know, has any other chemist except its discoverer.

The shells of the seeds (testa) yield upon incineration 2·6 per cent. of ash; the kernels dried at 100° C. 3·0 per cent.

Commerce—The shipments of croton seeds arrive chiefly from Cochin or Bombay, packed in cases, bales or robbins; but there are no statistics to show the extent of the trade.

[1] Warrington, *Pharm. Journ.* vi. (1865) 382-387.

[2] Schmidt and Berendes, 1878.

[3] In the *Jahresbericht* of Wiggers and Husemann, 1873. 560.

Uses—Croton seeds are not administered. The oil is given internally as a powerful cathartic, and is applied externally as a rubefacient.

Substitutes—The seeds of *Croton Pavanæ* Hamilton, a native of Ava and Camrup (Assam), and those of *C. oblongifolius* Roxb., a small tree common about Calcutta, are said to resemble those of *C. Tiglium* L., but we have not compared them. Those of *Baliospermum montanum* Müll. Arg. (*Croton polyandrus* Roxb.) partake of the nature of croton seeds, and according to Roxburgh are used by the natives of India as a purgative.

SEMEN RICINI.

Semen Cataputiæ majoris; Castor Oil Seeds, Palma Christi Seeds; F. *Semence de Ricin;* G. *Ricinussamen.*

Botanical Origin—*Ricinus communis* L., the castor oil plant, is a native of India where it bears several ancient Sanskrit names.[1] By cultivation, it has been distributed through all the tropical and many of the temperate countries of the globe. In the regions most favourable to its growth, it attains a height of 40 feet. In the Azores, and the warmer Mediterranean countries as Algeria, Egypt, Greece, and the Riviera, it becomes a small tree, 10 to 15 feet high; while in France, Germany, and the south of England, it is an annual herb of noble foliage, growing to a height of 4 or 5 feet. In good summers, it ripens seeds in England and even as far north as Christiania in Norway.

Ricinus communis exhibits a large number of varieties, several of which have been described and figured as distinct species. Müller, after a careful examination of the whole series, maintains them as a single species, of which he allows 16 forms, more or less well marked.[2]

History—The castor oil plant was known to Herodotus who calls it Κίκι, and states that it furnishes an oil much used by the Egyptians, in whose ancient tombs seeds of Ricinus are, in fact, met with.[3] At the period when Herodotus wrote, it would appear to have been already introduced into Greece, where it is cultivated to the present day under the same ancient name.[4] The *Kikajon* of the Book of Jonah, rendered by the translators of the English Bible *gourd*, is believed to be the same plant. Κίκι is also mentioned by Strabo as a production of Egypt, the oil from which is used for burning in lamps and for unguents.

Theophrastus and Nicander give the castor oil plant the name of Κρότων. Dioscorides, who calls it Κίκι or Κρότων, describes it as of the stature of a small fig-tree, with leaves like a plane, and seeds in a prickly pericarp, observing that the name Κρότων is applied to the seed on account of its resemblance to an insect [*Ixodes Ricinus* Latr.], known by that appellation. He also gives an account of the process for extracting castor oil (Κίκινον ἔλαιον), which he says is not fit for food, but is used externally in medicine; he represents the seeds as

[1] The most ancient and most usual is *Eranda*; this word has passed into several other Indian languages.

[2] De Candolle, *Prodr.*, xv. sect. 2. 1017.

[3] *Journ. of Botany*, 1879, 54.

[4] Heldreich, *Nutzpflanzen Griechenlands*, Athen, 1862. 58.

extremely purgative. There is a tolerably correct figure of *Ricinus* in the famous MS. Dioscorides which was executed for the Empress Juliana Anicia in A.D. 505, and is now preserved in the Imperial Library at Vienna.

The castor oil plant was cultivated by Albertus Magnus, Bishop of Ratisbon, in the middle of the 13th century.[1] It was well known as a garden plant in the time of Turner (1568), who mentions the oil as *Oleum cicinum vel ricininum.*[2] Gerarde, at the end of the same century, was familiar with it under the name of *Ricinus* or *Kik.* The oil he says is called *Oleum cicinum* or *Oleum de Cherua,*[3] and used externally in skin diseases.

After this period the oil seems to have fallen into complete neglect, and is not even noticed in the comprehensive and accurate *Pharmacologia* of Dale (1693). In the time of Hill (1751) and Lewis (1761) Palma Christi seeds were rarely found in the shops, and the oil from them was scarcely known.[4]

In 1764 Peter Canvane, a physician who had practised many years in the West Indies, published a "*Dissertation on the Oleum Palmæ Christi, sive Oleum Ricini; or (as it is commonly call'd) Castor Oil,*"[5] strongly recommending its use as a gentle purgative. This essay, which passed through two editions, and was translated into French, was followed by several others,[6] thus thoroughly drawing attention to the value of the oil. Accordingly we find that the seeds of *Ricinus* were admitted to the London Pharmacopœia of 1788, and directions given for preparing oil from them. Woodville in his *Medical Botany* (1790) speaks of the oil as having "*lately come into frequent use.*"

At this period and for several years subsequently, the small supplies of the seeds and oil required for European medicine were obtained from Jamaica.[7] This oil was gradually displaced in the market by that produced in the East Indies: the rapidity with which the consumption increased may be inferred from the following figures, representing the value of the Castor Oil shipped to Great Britain from Bengal in three several years, namely 1813–14, £610; 1815–16, £1269; 1819–20, £7102.[8]

Description—The fruit of *Ricinus* is a tricoccous capsule, usually provided with weak prickles, containing one seed in each of its three cells. The seeds attain a length of $\frac{3}{10}$ to $\frac{6}{10}$, and a maximum breadth of $\frac{4}{10}$ of an inch, and are of a compressed ellipsoid form. The apex of the seed is prolonged into a short beak, on the inner side of which is a

[1] *De Vegetabilibus*, ed. Jessen, 1867. 347.

[2] Turner's *Herbal*, pt. ii. 116.

[3] From the Arabic *khirva*, *i.e.* Palma Christi.

[4] Hill, *Hist. of the Mat. Med.*, Lond. 1751. 537.—Lewis, *Hist. of the Mat. Med.*, Lond. 1761. 468.

[5] The word *castor* in connection with the seeds and oil of *Ricinus* has come to us from Jamaica, in which island, by some strange mistake, the plant was once called *Agnus Castus*. The true Agnus Castus (*Vitex Agnus castus* L.) is a native of the Mediterranean countries and not of the West Indies.

[6] For a list of which consult Mérat et De Lens, *Dict. de Mat. Méd.* vi. (1834) 95.

[7] How small was the traffic in Castor Oil in those days, may be judged from the fact that the stock in 1777 of a London wholesale druggist (Joseph Gurney Bevan, predecessor of Allen and Hanburys) was 2 Bottles (1 Bottle = 18 to 20 ounces) valued at 8*s*. per bottle. The accounts of the same house show at stocktaking in 1782, 23 Bottles of the oil, which had cost 10*s*. per bottle. In 1799 Jamaica exported 236 Casks of Castor Oil and 10 Casks of seeds (Renny, *Hist. of Jamaica*, 1807. 235).

[8] H. H. Wilson, *Review of the External Commerce of Bengal from* 1813 *to* 1828, Calcutta, 1830, tables pp. 14–15.

large tumid caruncle: from this latter proceeds the raphe as far as the lower end of the ventral surface, where it forks, its point of disappearance through the testa being marked by a minute protuberance. If the caruncle is broken off, a black scar, formed of two little depressions, remains.

The shining grey epidermis is beautifully marked with brownish bands and spots, and in this respect exhibits a great variety of colours and markings. It cannot be rubbed off, but may after maceration be peeled off in leathery strips. The black testa, grey within, is not thicker than in croton seed, but is much more brittle. The kernel or nucleus fills the testa completely, and is easily separated, still covered by the soft white inner membrane.

The kernel in respect to structure and situation of the embryo, agrees exactly with that of *Croton Tiglium* (p. 565), excepting that the somewhat gaping cotyledons of *Ricinus* are proportionately broader, and have their thick midrib provided with 2 or 3 pairs of lateral veins. If not rancid, the kernel has a bland taste, with but very slight acridity.

Microscopic Structure—The thin epidermis consists of pentagonal or hexagonal porous tabular cells, the walls of which are penetrated in certain spots by brownish colouring matter, whence the singular markings on the seed. It is these cells only that become blackened when a thin tangential slice is saturated with a solution of ferric chloride in alcohol.

Beneath these tabular cells there is found in the unripe seed[1] a row of encrusted colourless cells, deposited in a radial direction on the testa. In the mature seed this layer of cells is not perceptible, and therefore appears to perish as the seed ripens. The testa itself is built up of cylindrical, densely packed cells, 300 to 320 mkm. long, and 6 to 10 mkm. in diameter. The kernel shares the structure of that of *C. Tiglium*, but is devoid of crystals of oxalate of calcium. If the endopleura of *Ricinus* is moistened with dilute sulphuric acid, acicular crystals of sulphate of calcium separate from it after a few hours.

When thin slices of the kernel are examined under concentrated glycerin, no drops of oil are visible, notwithstanding the abundance of this latter; and it becomes conspicuous only by addition of much water. Hence it is probable that the oil exists in the seed as a kind of compound with its albuminoid contents.[2] As to the latter, they partly form in the albumen of *Ricinus* beautiful octohedra or tetrahedra, which are also found in many other seeds.[3]

Chemical Composition—The most important constituent of the seed is the fixed oil, called *Castor Oil*, of which the peeled kernels afford at most half of their weight.

The oil, if most carefully prepared from peeled and winnowed seeds by pressure without heat, has but a slightly acrid taste, and contains only a very small proportion of the still unknown drastic constituent of the seeds. Hence the seeds themselves, or an emulsion prepared with

[1] Gris, *Annales des Sciences Nat.*, Bot., xv. (1861) 5–9.

[2] Sachs, *Lehrbuch der Botanik*, 1874. 54.

[3] For further particulars, see Trécul, *Ann. des Sc. Nat.*, Bot., x., (1858) 355; Radlkofer, *Krystalle proteinartiger Körper*, Leipzig, 1859. 61. and tab. 2 fig. 10; Pfeffer, *Proteinkörner* in Pringsheim's *Jahrbücher für wissenschaftliche Botanik*, viii. (1872) 429. 464.

them, act much more strongly than a corresponding quantity of oil. Castor oil, extracted by absolute alcohol or by bisulphide of carbon, likewise purges much more vehemently than the pressed oil.

The castor oil of commerce has a sp. gr. of about 0·96, usually a pale yellow tint, a viscid consistence, and a very slight yet rather mawkish odour and taste. Exposed to cold, it does not in general entirely solidify until the temperature reaches – 18° C. In thin layers it dries up to varnish-like film.

Castor oil is distinguished by its power of mixing in all proportions with glacial acetic acid or absolute alcohol. It is even soluble in four parts of spirit of wine (·838) at 15° C., and mixes without turbidity with an equal weight of the same solvent at 25° C. The commercial varieties of the oil however differ considerably in these as well as in some other respects.

The optical properties of the oil demand further investigation, as we have found that some samples deviate the ray of polarized light to the right and others to the left.

By saponification castor oil yields several fatty acids, one of which appears to be *Palmitic Acid.* The prevailing acid (peculiar to the oil) is *Ricinoleic Acid,* $C^{18}H^{34}O^{3}$; it is solid below 0° C., does not solidify in contact with the air by absorption of oxygen, and is not homologous with oleic or linoleic acid, neither of which is found in castor oil. Castor oil is nevertheless thickened if 6 parts of it are warmed with 1 part of starch and 5 of nitric acid (sp. gr. 1·25), *Ricinelaïdin* being thus formed. From this *Ricinelaïdic Acid* may easily be obtained in brilliant crystals.

As to the albuminoid matter of the seed, Fleury (1865) obtained 3·23 per cent. of nitrogen which would answer to about 20 per cent. of such substances. The same chemist further extracted 46·6 per cent. of fixed oil, 2·2 of sugar and mucilage, besides 18 per cent. of cellulose.

Tuson in 1864, by exhausting castor oil seeds with boiling water, obtained from them an alkaloid which he named *Ricinine.* He states that it crystallizes in rectangular prisms and tables, which when heated fuse, and upon cooling solidify as a crystalline mass; the crystals may even be sublimed. Ricinine dissolves readily in water or alcohol, less freely in ether or benzol. With mercuric chloride, it combines to form tufts of silky crystals, soluble in water or alcohol. Werner (1869) on repeating Tuson's process on 30 lb. of Italian castor oil seeds, also obtained a crop of crystals, which in appearance and solubility had many of the characters ascribed to ricinine, but differed in the essential point that when incinerated they left a residuum of magnesia. Werner regarded them as the magnesium salt of a new acid. Tuson[1] repudiates the suspicion that ricinine may be identical with Werner's magnesium compound. E. S. Wayne of Cincinnati (1874) found in the leaves of *Ricinus* a substance apparently identical with Tuson's ricinine; but he considers that it has no claim to be called an alkaloid.

The testa of castor oil seeds afforded us 10·7 per cent. of ash, one tenth of which we found to consist of silica. The ash of the kernel previously dried at 100 C. amounts to only 3·5 per cent.

Production and Commerce—Castor oil is most extensively pro-

[1] *Chemical News,* xxii. (1870) 229.

duced in India, where two varieties of the seeds, the large and the small, are distinguished, the latter being considered to yield the better product. In manufacturing the oil, the seeds are gently crushed between rollers, and freed by hand from husks and unsound grains. At Calcutta, 100 parts of seed yield on an average 70 parts of cleaned kernels, which by the hydraulic press afford 46 to 51 per cent. of their weight of oil; the oil is afterwards subjected to a very imperfect process of purification by heating it with water.[1]

The exports of castor oil from Calcutta[2] in the year 1870–71 amounted to 654,917 gallons, of which 214,959 gallons were shipped to the United Kingdom. The total imports of castor oil into the United Kingdom[3] in the year 1870 were returned as 36,986 cwt. (about 416,000 gallons), valued at £82,490. Of this quantity, British India (chiefly Bengal) furnished about two-thirds; and Italy 11,856 cwt. (about 133,000 gallons), while a small remainder is entered as from "other parts." In 1876 the imports were 79,677 cwt., valued at £133,838.

Italian Castor Oil, which has of late risen into some celebrity, is pressed from the seed of plants grown chiefly about Verona and Legnago, in the north of Italy. The manufactory of Mr. Bellino Valeri at the latter town produced in the year 1873, 1200 quintals of castor oil, entirely from Italian seed. Two varieties of *Ricinus* are cultivated in these localities, the black-seeded Egyptian and the red-seeded American; the latter yields the larger percentage, but the oil is not so pale in colour. The seeds are very carefully deprived of their integuments, and having been crushed, are submitted to pressure in powerful hydraulic presses, placed in a room which in winter is heated to about 21° C. The outflow of oil is further promoted by plates of iron warmed to 32–38° C. being placed between the press-bags. The peeled seeds yield about 40 per cent. of oil.[4]

All the castor oil pressed in Italy is not pressed from Italian seed. By an official return[5] it appears that in the year 1872–73 there were exported from Bombay to Genoa 1350 cwt. of castor oil seeds, besides 2452 gallons of castor oil. There are no data to show what was exported from the other presidencies of India in that year.

Uses—Castor oil is much valued as a mild and safe purgative; while the commoner qualities are used in soap-making, and in India for burning in lamps. The seeds are not now administered. The *leaves* of the plant applied in decoction to the breasts of women are said to promote or even to occasion the secretion of milk. This property, which has long been known to the inhabitants of the Cape Verd Islands,[6] was particularly observed by Dr. M'William about the year 1850. It has even been found that the galactagogue powers of the plant are exerted when the leaves are administered internally.

[1] *Madras Exhibition of Raw Products, etc. of Southern India*,—Reports by the Juries, Madras, 1856. 28.

[2] *Annual Volume of Trade and Navigation for the Bengal Presidency for* 1870-71, Calcutta, 1871. 119.

[3] *Annual Statement of the Trade, etc. of the U.K. for* 1870.—No later returns.

[4] H. Groves, *Pharm. Journ.* viii. (1867) 250.

[5] *Annual Statement of the Trade and Navigation of the Presidency of Bombay for* 1872-73, part ii. 87. 88.

[6] Frezier, *Voyage to the South Seas*, Lond. 1717. p. 13.—Turner in his Herbal (1568) gives the plant an opposite character, for the bruised leaves, says he, "swage the brestes or pappes swellinge wyth to muche plenty of milke."

KAMALA.

Kamela, Glandulæ Rottleræ.

Botanical Origin—*Mallotus philippinensis*[1] Müller Arg. (*Croton philippensis* Lam., *Rottlera tinctoria* Roxb., *Echinus philippinensis* Baillon), a large shrub, or small tree, attaining 20 or 45 feet in height, of very wide distribution. It grows in Abyssinia and Southern Arabia, throughout the Indian peninsulas, ascending the mountains to 5000 feet above the sea-level, in Ceylon, the Malay Archipelago, the Philippines, the Loo-choo islands, Formosa, Eastern China and in North Australia, Queensland and New South Wales.

The tricoccous fruits of many of the *Euphorbiaceæ* are clothed with prickles, stellate hairs, or easily removed glands. This is especially the case in the several species of *Mallotus*, most of which have the capsules covered with stellate hairs, together with small glands. In that under notice, the capsule is closely beset with ruby-like glands which, when removed by brushing and rubbing, constitute the powder known by the Bengali name of *Kamala*. These glands are not confined to the capsule, but are scattered over other parts of the plant, especially among the dense tomentum with which the under side of the leaf is covered.

History—In India the glands of Mallotus have been long known, for they have several ancient Sanskrit names: one of these is *Kapila*, which as well as the Telugu *Kapila-podi*, is sometimes used by Europeans, though not so frequently as the word *Kāmalā* or *Kamela*, which belongs to the Hindustani, Bengali and Guzratti languages. The Sanskrit word *Kapila* signifies tawny or dusky red, the Tamil *Podi* means the pollen of a flower or dust in general.

It does not appear that as a drug the glandular powder of *Mallotus*, or as it is more conveniently called, *Kamala*, attracted any particular notice in Europe until a very recent period, though it is named by Ainslie, Roxburgh, Royle and Buchanan, the last of whom gives an interesting account of its collection and uses.[2] In 1852, specimens of it as found in the bazaar of Aden, under the old Arabic name of *Wars*, were sent to one of us by Port-Surgeon Vaughan, with information as to its properties as a dye for a silk and as a remedy in cutaneous diseases.[3] But the real introduction of the drug as a useful medicine is due to Mackinnon, surgeon in the Bengal Medical Establishment, who administered it successively in numerous cases of tapeworm. Anderson of Calcutta, C. A. Gordon, and Corbyn in India, and Leared in London, confirmed the observations of Mackinnon, and fully established the fact that kamala is an efficient tænifuge.[4] It was introduced into the *British Pharmacopœia* in 1864.

[1] Fig. in Bentley and Trimen's *Med. Plants*, part i. (1875.)—A beautiful figure in Roxburgh, *Plants of the Coast of Coromandel*, ii. (1798) tab. 168.

[2] *Journey through Mysore, Canara, etc.*, (Lond. 1807) i. 168. 204. 211, ii. 343.

[3] Hanbury, *Pharm. Journ.* xii. (1853) 386. 589; or *Science Papers*, 73.

[4] *Ibid.* xvii. (1858) 408; *Science Papers*, 75.

An analogous drug is mentioned by Paulus Aegineta[1] in the 7th century as well as by the Arabian physicians[2] as early as the 10th century, under the name of *Kanbil* or *Wars*. Ibn Khurdádbah, an Arab geographer, living A.D. 869–885, states that from Yemen come striped silks, ambergris, *wars*, and gum.[3] It is described to be a reddish yellow powder like sand, which falls on the ground in the valleys of Yemen, and is a good remedy for tapeworm and cutaneous diseases. One writer compares it to powdered saffron; another speaks of two kinds,—an Abyssinian which is *black* (or violet), and an Indian which is *red*. Masudi,[4] in the first half of the 10th century speaks of *qinbil*, which he says consists of sandy fruits of red hue. They are useful as an anthelminthic and for cutaneous diseases. A similar explanation of the qinbil is found in Qamus, a dictionary writer in the 13th century in Yemen. About the year 1216, a learned traveller, Abul Abbas Ahmad Annabati,[5] (Annabati=the botanist) or Abul Abbas el-Nebáti, who was a native of Seville, remarks that the drug is known in the Hejaz and brought from Yemen, but that it is unknown in Andalusia and does not grow there.

Kazwini,[6] nearly at the same period, was also acquainted with *wars*, a plant *sown* in Yemen and resembling Sesam; Constantinus Africanus likewise mentioned "*huars*." Wars, Wors, Wurrus or Warras in Arabia properly signifies saffron.

In modern times, we find Niebuhr[7] speaks of the same substance (as "*wars*"), stating it to be a dye-stuff, of which quantities are conveyed from Mokha to Oman.

Production—Kamala is one of the minor products of the Government forests in the Madras Presidency, but is also collected in many other parts of India. The following particulars have been communicated to us by a correspondent[8] in the North-west Provinces:—

". . . Enormous quantities of *Rottlera tinctoria* are found growing at the foot of these hills, and every season numbers of people, chiefly women and children, are engaged in collecting the powder for exportation to the plains. They gather the berries in large quantities and throw them into a great basket in which they roll them about, rubbing them with their hands so as to divest them of the powder, which falls through the basket as through a sieve, and is received below on a cloth spread for the purpose. This powder forms the *Kamala* of commerce, and is in great repute as an anthelminthic, but is most extensively used as a dye. The adulterations are chiefly the powdered leaves, and the fruit-stalks with a little earthy matter, but the percentage is not large. The operations of picking the fruit and rubbing off the powder commence here in the beginning of March and last about a month. . . . ."

A similar powder is collected in Southern Arabia, whence it is shipped to the Persian Gulf and Bombay. It is also brought, under the name of *Wars*, from Hurrur, a town in Eastern Africa, which is a

[1] Adams' translat. iii. 457.

[2] Quoted by Ibn Baytar,—see Sontheimer's translation, ii. (1842) 326. 585.

[3] Ibn Khordadbeh, *Livre des routes etc.*—*Journ. Asiatique*, v. (1865) 295.

[4] *Les Prairies d'or*, i. (Paris, 1861) 367.

[5] Quoted by Ibn Baytar.

[6] Ed. Lichtenfels, i. (Göttingen, 1849).

[7] *Description de l'Arabie*, 1774. 133.

[8] F. E. G. Matthews, Esq., of Nainee Tal.

great trading station between the Galla countries and Berbera.[1] Yet the Arabian and African drug consists in most cases not of kamala, but of those dark glands which we describe further on, at p. 575.

Description—Kamala is a fine, granular, mobile powder, consisting of transparent, crimson granules, the bright colour of which is mostly somewhat deadened by the admixture of grey stellate hairs, minute fragments of leaves and similar foreign matter. It is nearly destitute of taste and smell, but an alcoholic solution poured into water emits a melon-like odour. Kamala is scarcely acted on by water, even at a boiling heat; on the other hand, alcohol, ether, chloroform or benzol extract from it a splendid red resin. Neither sulphuric nor nitric acid acts upon it in the cold, nor does oil of turpentine become coloured by it unless warmed. It floats on water, but sinks in oil of turpentine. When sprinkled over a flame, it ignites after the manner of lycopodium. Heated alone, it emits a slight aromatic odour; if pure, it leaves after incineration about 1·37 per cent. of a grey ash.

Microscopic Structure—The granules of kamala are irregular spherical glands, 50 to 60 mkm. in diameter; they have a wavy surface, are somewhat flattened or depressed on one side, and enclose within their delicate yellowish membrane a structureless yellow mass in which are imbedded numerous, simple, club-shaped cells containing a homogeneous, transparent, red substance. These cells are grouped in a radiate manner around the centre of the flattened side, so that on the side next the observer, 10 to 30 of them may easily be counted, while the entire gland may contain 40 to 60. In a few cases, a very short stalk-cell is also seen at the centre of the base.

When the glands are exhausted by alcohol and potash, and broken by pressure between flat pieces of glass, they separate into individual cells which swell up slightly, while the membranous envelope is completely detached, and appears as a simple coherent film. After this treatment the cells, but not their membranous envelope, acquire by prolonged contact with strong sulphuric acid and iodine water a more or less brown or blue colour: the wllas of the cells alone correspond therefore to cellulose. Vogl (1864) supposes that a cell of the epidermis of the fruit first developes a young cellule, which by partition is resolved into the stalk-cell and the true mother-cell of the small clavate resin-cellules. At first, the contents of the latter do not differ from the mass in which they are imbedded, and perhaps pass gradually into resin by metamorphosis of the cellular substance.

The glands of kamala are always accompanied by colourless or brownish, thick-walled, stellate hairs, two or three times as long as the glands, often containing air, which do not exhibit any peculiarity of form, but resemble the hairs of other plants, as *Verbascum* or *Althæa*.

Chemical Composition—Kamala has been analysed by Anderson of Glasgow (1855) and by Leube (1860). From the labours of these chemists, it appears that the powder yields to alcohol or ether nearly 80 per cent. of resin. We find it to be soluble also in glacial acetic acid or in bisulphide of carbon, not in petroleum ether. By treatment of the resin extracted by ether with cold alcohol, Leube resolved it into

[1] Burton, *Journ. of R. Geogr. Society*, xxv. (1855) 146. Haggenmacher, *Reise in das Somaliland*, in Petermann's *Geogr. Mittheilungen*, Ergänzungsheft, xlvii. (1874) 39.

two brittle reddish yellow resins, of which the one is more easily soluble and fuses at 80° C., and the other dissolves less readily and fuses at 191°. Both dissolve in alkaline solutions, and can be precipitated by acids without apparent change.

Anderson found that a concentrated ethereal solution of kamala allowed to stand for a few days, solidified into a mass of granular crystals, which by repeated solution and crystallization in ether were obtained in a state of purity. This substance, named by Anderson *Rottlerin*,[1] forms minute, platy, yellow crystals of a fine satiny lustre, readily soluble in ether, sparingly in cold alcohol, more so in hot, and insoluble in water. The mean of four analyses gave the composition of rottlerin as $C^{22}H^{20}O^{6}$.

We have been able to confirm the foregoing observations so far as that we have obtained an abundance of minute acicular crystals, by allowing an ethereal solution of kamala to evaporate spontaneously to a syrupy state. But the purification of these crystals, which was also attempted by our friend Mr. T. B. Groves,[2] was unsuccessful, for when freed from the protecting mother-liquor, they underwent a change and assumed an amorphous form. We have, on the other hand, succeeded in isolating the crystals from the "*Kamalin,*" as sold by E. Merck of Darmstadt. By fusing them with caustic potash we obtained paraoxybenzoic acid (see page 408).

Uses—The drug is administered for the expulsion of tapeworm; it has also been used as an external application in *herpes circinnatus*. In India it is employed for dyeing silk a rich orange-brown.

Adulteration—Kamala is very liable to adulteration with earthy substances, even to the extent of 60 per cent. This contamination may easily be known by the grittiness of the drug, and by a portion of it sinking when it is stirred up with water, but in the most decisive manner by incineration. Sometimes kamala contains an undue proportion of foreign vegetable matter, as remains of the capsules, leaves, etc., which can partly be separated by a lawn sieve. We have met with a large quantity of very impure Kamala in the London market (1878), which was offered for cleaning polished metallic surfaces.

Substitute—A very remarkable form of so-called kamala was imported in 1867 from Aden by Messrs. Allen and Hanburys, druggists, of London.[3] It arrived neatly packed in oblong, white calico bags, of three sizes, each inscribed with Arabic characters, indicating with the name of the vendor or collector, a native of Hurrur, the net weight, which was either 100, 50, or 25 Turkish ounces. No more than two supplies, in all 136 lb., could be obtained.

The drug was in coarser particles than kamala, of a deep purple, and had a distinct odour resembling that which is produced when a tincture of kamala is poured into water. It had been carefully collected and was free from earthy admixture, yet it left upon incineration 12 per cent. of ash. Under the microscope it presented still greater differences, the grains being cylindrical or subconical, 170 to 200 mkm. long, by 70 to 100 mkm. broad, with *oblong* resin-cells,

[1] See *Science Papers*, 78.

[2] *Yearbook of Pharmacy*, 1872. 599.

[3] It has been particularly described by one of us in *Pharm. Journ.* ix. (1868) 279, with wood-cuts.

arranged perpendicularly in three or four storeys; mixed with the grains were a few long, simple hairs. Another fact of some interest is, that at a temperature of 93° to 100° C., this drug becomes quite black, while kamala undergoes no change of colour.

In 1878 our friend Professor Schär was informed by a Swiss firm, Messrs. Furrer and Escher of Aden, that Kanbil, Qinbil or Kamala are unknown there. But they sent under the name of *Vars* a powder, which Prof. Schär as well as one of us (F.) find identical with the drug which had been imported by Messrs. Allen and Hanbury. Prof. Schär was also informed that Vars is used chiefly in the coast districts of Mascat (Oman) and Hadramaut, in skin diseases, for expelling the tape worm and as a dye.

Thus the appellation Wurrus or Waras is to be restricted to the dark purple or violet glands occurring in eastern Africa and Yemen, although the Waras sent to one of us[1] by Vaughan was kamala.

As to the mother-plant of Waras[2] we have no information to offer; we attempted in vain to ascertain its origin. It is evident that it is the "black Abyssinian" powder already alluded to at page 573.

PIPERACEÆ.

FRUCTUS PIPERIS NIGRI.

Piper nigrum; Black Pepper; F. *Poivre noir;* G. *Schwarzer Pfeffer.*

Botanical Origin—*Piper nigrum* L.—The pepper plant is a perennial climbing shrub, with jointed stems branching dichotomously, and broadly ovate, 5- to 7-nerved, stalked leaves. The slender flower-spikes are opposite the leaves, stalked, and from 3 to 6 inches long; and the fruits are sessile and fleshy.

Piper nigrum is indigenous to the forests of Travancore and Malabar, whence it has been introduced into Sumatra, Java, Borneo, the Malay Peninsula, Siam, the Philippines and the West Indies.

History—Pepper[3] is one of the spices earliest used by mankind, and although now a commodity of but small importance in comparison with sugar, coffee, and cotton, it was for many ages the staple article of trade between Europe and India. It would require in fact a volume to give a full idea of the prominent importance of pepper during the middle ages.

In the 4th century B.C., Theophrastus noticed the existence of two kinds of pepper (πέπερι), probably the *Black Pepper* and *Long Pepper* of modern times. Dioscorides stated pepper to be a production of India, and was acquainted with *White Pepper* (λευκὸν πέπερι). Pliny's information on the same subject is curious; he tells us that in his time a pound of long pepper was worth 15, of white 7, and of black pepper 4 *denarii;* and expresses his astonishment that mankind should so

[1] Hanbury, *Science Papers*, 73.

[2] Some information will be met with in Capt. Hunter's *Account of Aden*, 1877. p. 107. In 1875–1876 there were exported from Aden 42,975 lb. of Waras.

[3] The word *pepper*, which with slight varieties has passed into almost all languages, comes from the Sanskrit name for *Long Pepper*, *pippali*, the change of the *l* into *r* having been made by the Persians, in whose ancient language the *l* is wanting.

highly esteem pepper, which was neither a sweet taste nor attractive appearance, or any desirable quality besides a certain pungency.

In the Periplus of the Erythrean Sea, written about A.D. 64, it is stated that pepper is exported from Baraké, the shipping place of Nelkunda, in which region, and there only, it grows in great quantity. These have been identified with places on the Malabar Coast between Mangalore and Calicut.[1]

Long pepper and Black pepper are among the Indian spices on which the Romans levied duty at Alexandria about A.D. 176.[2]

Cosmas Indicopleustes,[3] a merchant, and in later life a monk, who wrote about A.D. 540, appears to have visited the Malabar Coast, or at all events had some information about the pepper-plant from an eye-witness. It is he who furnishes the first particulars about it, stating that it is a climbing plant, sticking close to high trees like a vine. Its native country he calls *Male*.[4] The Arabian authors of the middle ages, as Ibn Khurdádbah (*circa* A.D. 869-885), Edrisi in the middle of the 12th, and Ibn Batuta in the 14th century, furnished nearly similar accounts.

Among Europeans who described the pepper plant with some exactness, one of the first was Benjamin of Tudela, who visited the Malabar Coast in A.D. 1166. Another was the Catalan friar, Jordanus,[5] about 1330; he described the plant as something like ivy, climbing trees and forming fruit, like that of the wild vine. "This fruit," he says, "is at first green, then, when it comes to maturity, black." Nearly the same statements are repeated by Nicolo Conti, a Venetian, who at the beginning of the 15th century, spent twenty-five years in the East. He observed the plant in Sumatra, and also described it as resembling ivy.[6]

In Europe, pepper during the middle ages was the most esteemed and important of all spices, and the very symbol of the spice trade, to which Venice,[7] Genoa, and the commercial cities of Central Europe were indebted for a large part of their wealth; and its importance as a means of promoting commercial activity during the middle ages, and the civilizing intercourse of nation with nation, can scarcely be overrated.

Tribute was levied in pepper,[8] and donations were made of this spice, which was often used as a medium of exchange when money was scarce. During the siege of Rome by Alaric, king of the Goths, A.D. 408, the ransom demanded from the city included among other things 5000 pounds of gold, 30,000 pounds of silver, and 3000 pounds

[1] Vincent, *Commerce and Navigation of the Ancients*, ii. (1807) 458.

[2] Vincent, *op. cit.* ii. 754; also Meyer, *Geschichte der Botanik*, ii. (1865) 167.

[3] Migne, *Patrologiæ Cursus*, series Græca, lxxxviii. (1860) 443. 446.

[4] *Bar* (as in *Malabar*) merely signifies in Arabic, *coast*.

[5] *Mirabilia descripta* by Friar Jordanus, translated by Col. Yule. London, Hakluyt Society, 1863. 27.

[6] "Piperis arbor persimilis est ederæ, grana ejus viridia ad formam grani juniperi, quæ modico cinere aspersa torrentur ad solem."—Kunstmann, *Kenntniss Indiens im xv. Jahrhundert*, München (1863) 40.

[7] In the beginning of the 15th century the great emporium of the trade in pepper appears to have been the vicinity of the Church S. Giacomo de Rialto at Venice. In the "capitolare dei Visdomini del fontego dei Todeschi (German court) in Venezia," edit. of Thomas, Berlin, 1874, the chapter 228, page 116, is devoted to "*La mercadantia del pevere.*"

[8] For some examples of this, see *Histoire de la vie privée des Français*, par le Grand d'Aussy, nouvelle éd., ii. (1815) 182.

of *pepper.*[1] After the conquest of Cæsarea in Palestine, A.D. 1101, by the Genoese, each of them received two pounds of pepper and 48 soldi for his part of the booty.[2] Facts of this nature, of which a great number might be enumerated, sufficiently illustrate the part played by this spice in mediæval times.

The general prevalence during the middle ages of *pepper-rents*, which consisted in an obligation imposed upon a tenant to supply his lord with a certain quantity of pepper, generally a pound, at stated times, shows how acceptable was this favourite condiment, and how great the desire of the wealthier classes to secure a supply of it when the market was not always certain.[3]

The earliest reference to a trade in pepper in England that we have met with, is in the Statutes of Ethelred, A.D. 978-1016,[4] where it is enacted that the Easterlings coming with their ships to Billingsgate should pay at Christmas and Easter for the privilege of trading with London, a small tribute of cloth, five pairs of gloves, *ten pounds of pepper,*[5] and two barrels of vinegar.

The merchants who trafficked in spices were called *Piperarii,*—in English *Pepperers,* in French *Poivriers* or *Pebriers.* As a fraternity or guild, they are mentioned as existing in London in the Reign of Henry II. (A.D. 1154–1189). They were subsequently incorporated as the Grocers' Company, and had the oversight and control of the trade in spices, drugs, dye-stuffs, and even metals.[6]

The price of pepper during the middle ages was always exorbitantly high, for the rulers of Egypt extorted a large revenue from all those who were engaged in the trade in it and other spices.[7] Thus in England between A.D. 1263 and 1399, it averaged 1s. per lb., equivalent to about 8s. of our present money. It was however about 2s. per lb. (= 16s.) between 1350 and 1360.[8] In 1370 we find pepper in France valued 7 sous 6 deniers per lb. (= fr. 21. c. 30):—in 1542 at a price equal to fr. 11 per lb.[9]

The high cost of this important condiment contributed to incite the Portuguese to seek for a sea-passage to India. It was some time after the discovery of this passage (A.D. 1498) that the price of pepper first experienced a considerable fall; while about the same period the cultivation of the plant was extended to the western islands of the Malay Archipelago. The trade in pepper continued to be a monopoly of the Crown of Portugal as late as the 18th century.

The Venetians used every effort to retain the valued traffic in their own hands, but in vain; and it was a fact of general interest when on the 21st of January 1522 a Portuguese ship brought for the first time

[1] Zosimus, *Historia* (Lips. 1784) lib. v. c. 41.

[2] Belgrano, *Vita privata dei Genovesi* 1875. 152.

[3] Rogers, *Agriculture and Prices in England*, i. (1866) 626. The term *peppercorn rent*, which has survived to our times, now only signifies a nominal payment.

[4] *Ancient Laws and Institutes of England*, published by the Record Commission, i. (1840) 301.

[5] A striking contrast to the announcement in a commercial paper, 27 Feb. 1874, that the stock of pepper in the public warehouses of London the previous week was 6035 tons!

[6] Herbert, *Hist. of the twelve great Livery Companies of London*, Lond. 1834. 303, 310.

[7] Reinaud, *Nouveau Journal asiatique*, 1829, Juillet, 22–51.

[8] Rogers, *op. cit.* i. 641.

[9] Leber, *Appréciation de la fortune privée au moyen-âge*, éd. 2, Paris, 1847. 95. 305.

the spices of India direct to the city of Antwerp. Strange to say, they were received with great mistrust!

Pepper was heavily taxed in England. In 1623 the imposts levied on it amounted to 5*s* per lb.; and even down to 1823 it was subject to a duty of 2*s*. 6*d*. per lb.

Production—In the south-west of India, the plant, or *Pepper Vine* as it is called, grows on the sides of the narrow valleys where the soil is rich and moist, producing lofty trees by which a constant, favourable coolness is maintained. In such places the pepper-vine runs along the ground and propagates itself by striking out roots into the soil. The natives tie up the end of the vines lying on the ground to the nearest tree, on the bark of which the stems put out roots so far as they have been tied, the shoots above that hanging down. The plant is capable of growing to a height of 20 or 30 feet, but for the sake of convenience it is usually kept low, and is often trained on poles. In places where no vines occur naturally, the plant is propagated by planting slips near the roots of the trees on which it is to climb.

The pepper plants if grown on a rich soil begin to bear even in the first year, and continue to increase in productiveness till about the fifth, when they yield 8 to 10 lb. of berries per plant, which is about the average produce up to the age of 15 to 20 years; after this they begin to decline.

When one or two berries at the base of the spike begin to turn red, the whole spike is pinched off. Next day the berries are rubbed off with the hands and picked clean; then dried for three days on mats, or on smooth hard ground, or on bamboo baskets near a gentle fire.

In Malabar the pepper-vine flowers in May and June, and the fruits become fit for gathering at the commencement of the following year.[1]

The largest quantities of pepper are produced in the island of Rhio, near Singapore, in Djohor (in the south-eastern coast of the Malayan Peninsula), and in Penang. The latter island affords on an average about one-half of the total crop.

Description—The small, round, berry-like fruits grow somewhat loosely to the number of 20 to 30, on a common pendulous fruit-stalk. They are at first green, then become red, and if allowed to ripen, yellow; but they are gathered before complete maturity, and by drying in that state turn blackish grey or brown. If left until quite ripe they lose some of their pungency, and gradually fall off.

The berries after drying are spherical, about $\frac{1}{5}$ inch in diameter, wrinkled on the surface, indistinctly pointed below by the remains of the very short pedicel, and crowned still more indistinctly by the 3- or 4-lobed stigma. The thin pericarp tightly encloses a single seed, the embryo of which in consequence of premature gathering is undeveloped, and merely replaced by a cavity situated below the apex. The seed itself contains within the thin red-brown testa a shining albumen, grey and horny without, and mealy within. The pungent taste and peculiar smell of pepper are familiar to all.

Microscopic Structure—The transverse section of a grain of

[1] For a full account of the cultivation of pepper, see Buchanan, *Journey from Madras through Mysore, Canara, and Malabar*, ii. (1807) 455–520; iii. 158.

black pepper exhibits a soft yellowish epidermis, covering the outer pericarp. This is formed of a closely-packed yellow layer of large, mostly radially arranged, thick-walled cells, each containing in its small cavity a mass of dark-brown resin. The middle layer of the pericarp consists of soft, tangentially-extended parenchyme, containing an abundance of extremely small starch granules and drops of oil. The shrinking of this loose middle layer is the chief cause of the deep wrinkles on the surface of the berry. The next inner layer of the pericarp exhibits towards its circumference tangentially-arranged, soft parenchyme, the cells of which possess either spiral striation or spiral fibres, but towards the interior loose parenchyme, free from starch, and containing very large oil-cells.

The testa is formed in the first place of a row of small yellow thick-walled cells. Next to them follows the true testa, as a dense, dark-brown layer of lignified cells, the individual outlines of which are undistinguishable.

The albumen of the seeds consists of angular, radially-arranged, large-celled parenchyme. Most of its cells are colourless and loaded with starch; others contain a soft yellow amorphous mass. If thin slices are kept under glycerin for some time, these masses are slowly transformed into needle-shaped crystals of piperin.

Chemical Composition—Pepper contains resin and essential oil, to the former of which its sharp pungent taste is due. The essential oil has more of the smell than of the taste of pepper.[1] The drug yields from 1·6 to 2·2 per cent. of this volatile oil, which agrees with oil of turpentine in composition as well as in specific gravity and boiling point. We find it, in a column 50 mm. long, to deviate the ray of polarized light 1°·2 to 3°·4 to the left.

The most interesting constituent of pepper, *Piperin*, which pepper yields to the extent of 2 to 8 per cent., agrees in composition with the formula $C^{17}H^{19}NO^{3}$, like morphine. Piperin has no action on litmus paper; it is not capable of combining directly with an acid, yet unites with hydrochloric acid in the presence of mercuric and other metallic chlorides, forming crystallizable compounds. It is insoluble in water; when perfectly pure, its crystals are devoid of colour, taste and smell. Its alcoholic solution is without action on polarized light. Piperin may be resolved, as found by Anderson in 1850, into *Piperic Acid*, $C^{12}H^{10}O^{4}$, and *Piperidine*, $C^{5}H^{11}N$. The latter is a liquid colourless alkaloid, boiling at 106° C., having the odour of pepper and ammonia, and directly yielding crystallizable salts.

Besides these constituents, pepper also contains some fatty oil in the mesocarp. Of inorganic matter, it yields upon incineration from 4·1 to 5·7 per cent.

Commerce—Singapore is the great emporium for pepper, of which 197,478 peculs (26⅓ million lb.) were imported there in 1877. The largest part of it finds its way to England. The import of pepper into the United Kingdom during 1872, was 27,576,710 lb. valued at £753,970.

[1] As noticed by Rheede in 1688: "... oleum ex pipere destillatum levem piperis odorem spirans, saporis parum acris."—*Hort. Malab.* vii. 24.—The oil was however obtained long before by Valerius Cordus, Guintherus Andernacensis and Porta (see our article Cortex Cinnamomi, page 526).

Of this quantity, the Straits Settlements supplied 25,000,000 lb., and British India 256,000 lb. Of the quantity of 25,917,070 lb., imported in 1876 into Great Britain, the home consumption was 9 million lb.

The exports of pepper from the United Kingdom in 1872 amounted to 17,891,620 lb., the largest quantity being taken by Germany (5,201,574 lb.) Then follows Italy (2,288,647 lb.); and Russia, Holland and Spain, each of which took more than a million pounds.[1]

The varieties of pepper quoted in price-currents are *Malabar, Aleppee and Cochin, Penang, Singapore, Siam.*

A large quantity is also shipped from Singapore to China, the imports of that country in 1877 of both black and white pepper, being 53,844 peculs (7,179,200 lb.)

Uses—Pepper is not of much importance as a medicine, and is rarely if ever prescribed, except indirectly as an ingredient of some preparation.

Adulteration—Whole pepper is not, we believe, liable in Europe to adulteration;[2] but the case is widely different as regards the pulverized spice. Notwithstanding the enormous penalty of £100, to which the manufacturer, possessor, or seller of adulterated pepper is liable,[3] and the low cost of the article, ground pepper has hitherto been frequently sophisticated by the addition of the starches of cereals and potatoes, of sago, mustard husks, linseed and capsicum. The admixture of these substances may for the most part be readily detected, after some practice, by the microscope.[4]

White Pepper.

This form of the spice is prepared from black pepper by removing its dark outer layer of pericarp, and thereby depriving it of a portion of its pungency. It is mentioned by Dioscorides, yet was evidently very little known in Europe even during the middle ages. In the time of Platearius,[5] white pepper was supposed to be derived from a plant different from Piper nigrum.

Buchanan,[6] referring to Travancore, remarks that white pepper is made by allowing the berries to ripen; the bunches are then gathered, and having been kept for three days in the house, are washed and bruised in a basket with the hand till all the stalks and pulp are removed.

The finest white pepper is obtained from Tellicherry, on the Malabar Coast, but only in small quantity. The more important places for its preparation are the Straits Settlements, chiefly Rhio. The export of white pepper from Singapore in 1877 was 48,460 peculs. Most of the spice finds its way to China, where it is highly esteemed. In Europe, pepper in its natural state is with good reason preferred.

[1] *Annual Statement of the Trade of the U.K. for* 1872. 59. 125.

[2] According to Moodeen Sheriff (*Suppl. to Pharm. of India*, 134) the berries of *Embelia* (Samara) *Ribes*, order *Myrsineæ*, are said to be sometimes used for adulterating black pepper in the Indian bazaars.

[3] By the 59 George III. c. 53 § 22 (1819).

[4] Consult, Hassall, *Food and its Adulterations*, Lond. 1855. 42; Evans, *Pharm. Journ.* i. (1860) 605.

[5] *Glossæ in antidotarium Nicolai.* ccxlvi. verso.

[6] In the work quoted, page 579, ii. 465, 533, and iii. 224.

The grains of white pepper are of rather larger size than those of black, and of a warm greyish tint. They are nearly spherical or a little flattened. At the base the skin of the fruit is thickened into a blunt prominence, whence about 12 light stripes run meridian-like towards the depressed summit. If the skin is scraped off, the dark-brown testa is seen enclosing the hard translucent albumen. In anatomical structure, as well as in taste and smell, white pepper agrees with black, which in fact it represents in a rather more fully-grown state.

White pepper appears to afford on an average not more than 1·9 per cent. of essential oil, but to be richer in piperin, of which Cazeneuve and Caillol (1877) extracted as much as 9 per cent. The amount of ash yielded by white pepper is 1·1 per cent. on an average, that is to say, considerably less than by black pepper.

FRUCTUS PIPERIS LONGI.

Piper longum; Long Pepper; F. *Poivre long;* G. *Langer Pfeffer.*

Botanical Origin—*Piper officinarum* C. DC. (*Chavica*[1] *officinarum* Miq.), a diœcious shrubby plant, with ovate-oblong acuminate leaves, attenuated at the base, and having pinnate nerves. It is a native of the Indian Archipelago, as Java, Sumatra, Celebes and Timor. Long pepper is the fruit spike, collected and dried shortly before it reaches maturity.

Piper longum L.[2] (*Chavica Roxburghii* Miq.), a shrub indigenous to Malabar, Ceylon, Eastern Bengal, Timor and the Philippines, also yields long pepper, for the sake of which it is cultivated along the eastern and western coasts of India. It may be distinguished from the previous species by its 5-nerved leaves, cordate at the base.[3]

History—A drug termed Πέπερι μακρὸν, *Piper longum*, was known to the ancient Greeks and Romans, and may have been the same as the *Long Pepper* of modern times.

In the Latin verses bearing the name of Macer Floridus,[4] which were probably written in the 10th century, mention is made of Black, White, and Long Pepper. The last-named spice, or *Macropiper*, is named by Simon of Genoa,[5] who was physician to Pope Nicolas IV. and chaplain to Boniface VIII. (A.D. 1288-1303), and travelled in the East for the study of plants. Piper longum is also met with in the list of drugs on which (A.D. 1305) duty was levied at Pisa.[6] Nicolo Conti of Venice, who lived in India from 1419 to 1444, noticed Long Pepper.[7] Saladinus[8] in the middle of the 15th century enumerates long pepper among the drugs necessary to be kept by apothecaries, and it has had a place in the pharmacopœias to the present time.

[1] The genus *Chavica* separated from *Piper* by Miquel, has been re-united to it by Casimir de Candolle (*Prod.* xvi. s. 1). The latter genus is now composed of not fewer than 620 species!

[2] Fig. in Bentley and Trimen's *Med. Plants*, part 18 (1877).

[3] For good figures of the two plants, see Hayne's *Arzney-Gewächse*, xiv. (1843) tab. 20. 21.

[4] Choulant, *Macer Floridus de Viribus Herbarum*, Lipsiæ, 1832. 114.

[5] *Clavis Sanationis*, Venet. 1510.

[6] Bonaini, *Statuti inediti della città di Pisa*, iii. (1857) 492.

[7] Kunstmann, *Kenntniss Indiens im 15ten Jahrhundert*, München, 1863. 40.

[8] See Appendix.

Production—In Bengal the plants are cultivated by suckers, and require to be grown on a rich, high and dry soil; they should be set about five feet asunder. An English acre will yield in the first year about three maunds (1 maund = 80 lbs.) of the pepper, in the second twelve, and in the third eighteen; after which, as the plant becomes less and less productive, the roots are grubbed up, dried, and sold as *Pipli-múl*, of which there is a large consumption in India as a medicine. The pepper is gathered in the month of January, when full grown, and exposed to the sun until perfectly dry. After the fruit has been collected, the stem and branches die down to the ground.[1]

Description—Long pepper consists of a multitude of minute baccate fruits, closely packed around a common axis, the whole forming a spike of 1½ inch long and ¼ of an inch thick. The spike is supported on a stalk ½ an inch long; it is rounded above and below, and tapers slightly towards its upper end. The fruits are ovoid, $\frac{1}{10}$ of an inch long, crowned with a nipple-like point (the remains of the stigma), and arranged spirally with a small peltate bract beneath each. A transverse section of a spike exhibits 8 to 10 separate fruits, disposed radially with their narrower end pointed towards the axis. Beneath the pericarp, the thin brown testa encloses a colourless albumen, of which the obtuser end is occupied by the small embryo.

The long pepper of the shops is greyish-white, and appears as if it had been rolled in some earthy powder. When washed, the spikes acquire their proper colour,—a deep reddish-brown. The drug has a burning aromatic taste, and an agreeable but not powerful odour.

The foregoing description applies to the long pepper of English commerce, which is now obtained chiefly from Java (see next page), where *P. officinarum* is the common species. In fact the fruits of this latter, as presented to us by Mr. Binnendyk, of the Botanical Garden, Buitenzorg, near Batavia, offer no characters by which we can distinguish them from the article found in the London shops. Those of *P. Betle* L. var. *γ. densum* are extremely similar, but we do not know that they are collected for use.

Microscopic Structure—The structure of the individual fruits resembles that of black pepper, exhibiting however some characteristic differences. The epicarp has on the outside, tangentially-extended, thick-walled, narrow cells, containing gum; the middle layer consists of wider, thin-walled, obviously porous parenchyme containing starch and drops of oil. In the outer and middle layers of the fruit numerous large thick-walled cells are scattered, as in the external pericarp of *Piper nigrum;* in long pepper, however, they do not form a close circle. The inner pericarp is formed of a row of large, cubic or elongated, radially-arranged cells, filled with volatile oil. A row of smaller tangentially-extended cells separates these oil-cells from the compact brown-red testa, which consists of lignified cells like the inner layer of the testa of black pepper, but without the thick-walled cells peculiar to the latter. The albumen of long pepper is distinguished from that of black pepper by the absence of volatile oil.

Chemical Constituents—The constituents of long pepper appear to be the same as those of black pepper. We ascertained the presence

[1] Roxburgh, *Flora Indica*, i. (1832) 155.

of piperin; 8 pounds of the drug were not sufficient to afford us an appreciable quantity of the volatile oil. The resin and volatile oil reside exclusively in the pericarp. Long pepper, according to Blyth (1874), yields 8½ per cent of ash.

Commerce—Long pepper is at present exported from Penang and Singapore, whither it is brought chiefly from Java, and to a much smaller extent from Rhio. The quantity exported from Singapore in 1871 amounted to 3,366 cwt., of which only 447 cwt. were shipped to the United Kingdom, the remainder being sent chiefly to British India.[1] The export from Penang is from 2,000 to 3,000 peculs annually. There is also a considerable export of long pepper from Calcutta.

Uses—Long pepper is scarcely used as a medicine, black pepper having been substituted in the few preparations in which it was formerly ordered, but it is employed as a spice and in veterinary medicine.

The aromatic root of *Piper longum*, called in Sanskrit *Pippali-mula*[2] (whence the modern name *pipli-múl*), is a favourite remedy of the Hindus and also known to the Persians and Arabs.

CUBEBÆ.

Fructus vel Baccæ vel Piper Cubebæ[3]; *Cubebs;* F. *Cubèbes;* G. *Cubeben.*

Botanical Origin—*Piper Cubeba* Linn. f. (*Cubeba officinalis* Miq.), a climbing, woody, diœcious shrub, indigenous to Java, Southern Borneo and Sumatra.[4]

History—Cubebs have been introduced into medicine by the Arabian physicians of the middle ages, who describe them as having the form, colour, and properties of pepper. Masudi[5] in the 10th century stated them to be a production of Java. Edrisi,[6] the geographer, in A.D. 1153 enumerated them among the imports of Aden.

Among European writers, Constantinus Africanus of Salerno was acquainted with this drug as early as the 11th century; and in the beginning of the 13th its virtues were noticed in the writings of the Abbess Hildegard in Germany, and even in those of Henrik Harpestreng in Denmark.[7]

Cubebs are mentioned as a production of Java ("*grant isle de Javva*") by Marco Polo; and by Odoric, an Italian friar, who visited the island about forty years later. In the 13th century the drug was an article of European trade, and would appear to have already been regularly imported into London.[8] Duty was levied upon them as *Cubebas silvestres* at Barcelona in 1271.[9] They are mentioned about this period as sold in the fairs of Champagne in France, the price being 4 *sous* per lb.[10] They were also sold in England: in accounts under date 1284

[1] *Blue Book of the Straits Settlements* for 1871.

[2] Already in the Rāmāyana.

[3] *Cubeba* from the Arabic *Kabábah.*

[4] Fig. in Bentley and Trimen's *Med. Plants*, part 27 (1877).

[5] *Les Prairies d'or*, i. 341.

[6] *Géographie*, trad. par Jaubert, i. 51. 89.

[7] Meyer, *Geschichte der Botanik*, iii. 537.

[8] *Munimenta Gildhallæ Londoniensis; Liber albus*, i. (1859, State papers) 230.

[9] Capmany, *Memorias sobre la Marina, etc., de Barcelona*, i. (Madrid, 1779) 44.

[10] Bourquelot, *Études sur les foires de la Champagne*, *Mémoires etc. de l'Institut*, v. (1865) 288.

they are enumerated with almonds, saffron, raisins, white pepper, grains [of paradise], mace, galangal, and gingerbread, and entered as costing 2*s*. per lb. In 1285—2*s*. 6*d*. to 3*s*. per lb.; while in 1307, 1 lb. purchased for the King's Wardrobe cost 9*s*.[1]

From the journal of expenses of John, king of France, while in England during 1359–60, it is evident that cubebs were in frequent use as a spice. Among those who could command such luxuries, they were eaten in powder with meat, or they were candied whole. A patent of pontage granted in 1305 by Edward I., to aid in repairing and sustaining the Bridge of London, and authorizing toll on various articles, mentions among groceries and spices, cubebs as liable to impost.[2] Cubebs occur in the German lists of medicines of Frankfort and Nördlingen, about 1450 and 1480;[3] they are also mentioned in the *Confectbuch* of Hans Folcz of Nuremberg, dating about 1480.[4]

It cannot however be said that cubebs were a common spice, at all comparable with pepper or ginger, or even in such frequent use as grains of paradise or galangal. Garcia de Orta (1563) speaks of them as but seldom used in Europe; yet they are named by Saladinus as necessary to be kept in every *apotheca*.[5] In a list of drugs to be sold in the apothecaries' shops of the city of Ulm, A.D. 1596, cubebs are mentioned as *Fructus carpesiorum vel cubebarum*, the price for half an ounce being quoted as 8 *kreuzers*, the same as that of opium, best manna, and amber, while black and white pepper are priced at 2 *kreuzers*.[6]

Although it was always well known that the cubebs were a product of Java and that island is stated to have exported in 1775 as much as 10,000 lb. of this spice,[7] its mother plant was made known only in 1781 by the younger Linnaeus.

The action of cubebs on the urino-genital organs was known to the old Arabian physicians. Yet modern writers on materia medica even at the commencement of the present century, mentioned the drug simply as an aromatic stimulant resembling pepper, but inferior to that spice and rarely employed,[8]—in fact it had so far fallen into disuse that it was omitted from the London Pharmacopœia of 1809. According to Crawfurd, its importation into Europe, which had long been discontinued, recommenced in 1815, in consequence of its medicinal virtues having been brought to the knowledge of the English medical officers serving in Java, by their Hindu servants.[9]

Cultivation and Production[10]—Cubebs are cultivated in small

[1] Rogers, *Hist. of Agriculture and Prices in England*, i. 627–8, ii. 544.—To get some idea of the relative value of commodities then and now, multiply the ancient prices by 8.

[2] *Liber niger Scaccarii*, Lond. 1771, i. *478.—A translation may be found in the *Chronicles of London Bridge*, 1827, 155.

[3] *Archiv der Pharmacie*, 201 (1872) 441 and 211 (1877) 101.

[4] Choulant, *Macer Floridus*, etc., Lips. 1832, 188.

[5] *Compendium aromatariorum*, Bonon., 1488.

[6] Richard, *Beiträge zur Geschichte der Apotheken*, 1825. 124.

[7] Miquel, *Commentarii phytographici*, i. (Lugd. Bat., 1839).

[8] In Duncan's *Edinburgh New Dispensatory*, ed. 2. 1804, *Piper Cubeba* is very briefly described, but with no allusion to its possessing any special medicinal properties. In the 6th edition of the same work (1811) it was altogether omitted. See also Murray's *System of Mat. Med. and Pharm.* i. (1810) 266.

[9] *Dictionary of the Indian Islands*, 1856. 117.—Mr. Crawfurd himself communicated to the *Edinburgh Medical and Surgical Journal* of 1818 (xiv. 32) a paper making known the "wonderful success" with which cubebs had been used in gonorrhœa.

[10] We are indebted for some particulars under this head to our friends Mr. Binnendyk, of the Buitenzorg Botanical Garden near Batavia, and Dr. De Vry.

special plantations and also in coffee plantations, in the district of Banjoemas in the south of Java. The fruits are bought by Chinese who carry them to Batavia. They are likewise produced in Eastern Java and about Bantam and Soebang in the north-west; and extensively in the Lampong country in Sumatra. There has of late been a large distribution of plants among the European coffee planters.

The cultivation of cubebs is easy. In the coffee estates certain trees are required for shade: against these *Piper Cubeba* is planted, and climbing to a height of 18 to 20 feet, forms a large bush.

Description—The cubebs of commerce consist of the dry globose fruits, gathered when full grown, but before they have arrived at maturity. The fruit is about ¼ of an inch in diameter, when very young sessile, but subsequently elevated on a straight thin stalk, a little longer or even twice as long as itself. By this stalk the fruit is attached in considerable numbers (sometimes more than 50) to a common thickened stalk or rachis, about 1½ inch long.

Commercial cubebs are spherical, sometimes depressed at the base, very slightly pointed at the apex, strongly wrinkled by the shrinking of the fleshy pericarp; they are of a greyish-brown or blackish hue, frequently covered with an ashy-grey bloom. The stalk is the elongated base of the fruit, and remains permanently attached. The common axis or rachis, which is almost devoid of essential oil, is also frequently mixed with the drug.

The skin of the fruit covers a hard, smooth brown shell containing the seed, which latter when developed has a compressed spherical form, a smooth surface, and adheres to the péricarp only at the base; its apex either projects slightly or is pressed inwards. The albumen is solid, whitish, oily, and encloses a small embryo below the apex. In the cubebs of the shops, the seed is mostly undeveloped and shrunken, and the pericarp nearly empty.

Cubebs have a strong, aromatic, persistent taste, with some bitterness and acridity. Their smell is highly aromatic and by no means disagreeable.

Microscopic Structure—This exhibits some peculiarities. The skin of the fruit below the epidermis, is made up of small, cubic, thick-walled cells, forming an interrupted row, and only half as large as in black pepper. The broad middle layer consists of small cubic thick-walled cells, forming an interrupted row, and only half as large as in black pepper. The broad middle layer consists of small-celled undeveloped tissue containing drops of oil, granules of starch, and crystalline groups of cubebin, probably also fat. This middle layer is interrupted by very large oil-cells, which frequently enclose needle-shaped crystals of cubebin, united in concentric groups. The much narrower inner layer consists of about four rows of somewhat larger tangentially-extended soft cells, holding essential oil. Next to these comes the light-yellow brittle shell, formed of a densely packed row of encrusted, radially-arranged, elongated thick-walled cells. Lastly, the embryo is covered with a thin brown membrane, and exhibits the structure and contents as that of *Piper nigrum*, excepting that in *P. Cubeba* the cells are rounder, and the crystals consist of cubebin and not of piperin.

Chemical Composition—The most obvious constituent of cubebs is the volatile oil, the proportion of which yielded by the drug varies from 4 to 13 per cent. The causes of this great variation may be found in the constitution of the drug itself, as well as in the alterability of the oil, and the fact that its prevailing constituents begin not to boil below 264° C. It is, as shown in 1875 by Oglialoro, a mixture of an oil $C^{10}H^{16}$, boiling at 158°–163°, which is present to a very small amount, and two oils of the formula $C^{15}H^{24}$, boiling at 262°–265° C. One of the latter deviates the place of polarization strongly to the left, and yields the crystallized compound $C^{15}H^{24}$ 2 HCl, melting at 118° C. The other hydrocarbon is less lævogyrate and cannot be combined with HCl.

One part of oil of cubebs, diluted with about 20 parts of bisulphide of carbon, assumes at first a greenish, and afterwards a blue coloration, if one drop of a mixture of concentrated sulphuric and nitric acids (equal weight of each acid) is shaken with the solution.

The oil distilled from old cubebs on cooling at length deposits large, transparent, inodorous octohedra of *camphor of cubebs*, $C^{30}H^{48} + 2\ OH^{2}$, belonging to the rhombic system. They melt at 65° and may be sublimed at 148°. We have not succeeded in obtaining them by keeping the oil of fresh cubebs for two years in contact with water, to which a little alcohol and nitric acid was added.

Another constituent of cubebs is *Cubebin*, crystals of which may sometimes be seen in the pericarp even with a common lens. It was discovered by Soubeiran and Capitaine in 1839; it is an inodorous substance, crystallizing in small needles or scales, melting at 125°, having a bitter taste in alcoholic solution; it dissolves freely in boiling alcohol, but is mostly deposited upon cooling; it requires 30 parts of cold ether for solution, and is also abundantly soluble in chloroform. We found this solution to be slightly lævogyre; it turns red on addition of concentrated sulphuric acid. If the solution of cubebin in chloroform is shaken with dry pentoxide of phosphorus, it turns *blue* and gradually becomes red by the influence of moisture. Cubebin is nearly insoluble in cold, but slightly soluble in hot water. Bernatzik (1866) obtained from cubebs 0·40 per cent. of cubebin, Schmidt (1870) 2·5 per cent. The crystals, which are deposited in an alcoholic or ethereal extract of cubebs, consist of cubebin in an impure state. Cubebin is devoid of any remarkable therapeutic action. Its composition, according to Weidel (1877) answers to the formula $C^{10}H^{10}O^{3}$; by melting it with caustic potash, cubebin is resolved as follows:—

$$C^{10}H^{10}O^{3}\ .\ 5\ O = CO^{2}\ .\ \underset{\text{Acetic Acid.}}{C^{2}H^{4}O^{2}}\ .\ \underset{\text{Protocatechuic Acid.}}{C^{6}H^{3}(OH)^{2}COOH.}$$

The resin extracted from cubebs consists of an indifferent portion, nearly 3 per cent., and of *Cubebic Acid*, amounting to about 1 per cent. of the drug. Both are amorphous, and so, according to Schmidt, are the salts of cubebic acid. Bernatzic however, found some of them, as that of barium, to be crystallizable. Schulze (1873) prepared cubebic acid from the crystallized sodium-salt, but was unable to get it other than amorphous. The resins, the indifferent as well as the acid, possess the therapeutic properties of the drug.

Schmidt further pointed out the presence in cubebs, of gum (8 per cent.), fatty oil, and malates of magnesium and calcium.

Commerce—Cubebs were imported into Singapore in 1872 to the extent of 3062 cwt., of which amount 2348 cwt. were entered as from Netherlands India. The drug was re-shipped during the same year to the amount of 2766 cwt., the quantity exported to the United Kingdom being 1180 cwt., to the United States of America 1244 cwt., and to British India 104 cwt.[1] In the previous year, a larger quantity was shipped to India than to Great Britain.

Uses—Cubebs are much employed in the treatment of gonorrhœa. The drug is usually administered in powder; less frequently in the form of ethereal or alcoholic extract, or essential oil.

Bernatzik and Schmidt, whose chemical and therapeutical experiments have thrown much light on the subject, have shown that the efficacy of cubebs being dependent on the indifferent resin and cubebic acid, preparations which contain the utmost amount of these bodies and exclude other constituents of the drug, are to be preferred. They would reject the essential oil, as they find its administration devoid of therapeutic effects.

The preparations which consequently are to be recommended, are the berries deprived of their essential oil and constituents soluble in water, and then dried and powdered; an alcoholic extract prepared from the same, or the purified resins.

Adulteration—Cubebs are not much subject to adulteration, though it is by no means rare that the imported drug contains an undue proportion of the inert stalks (rachis)[2] that require to be picked out before the berries are ground. Dealers judge of cubebs by the oiliness and strong characteristic smell of the berries when crushed. Those which have a large proportion of the pale, smooth, ripe berries, which look *dry* when broken, are to be avoided.

We have occasionally found in the commercial drug a small, smooth two-celled fruit, of the size, shape, and colour of cubebs, but wanting the long pedicel. A slight examination suffices to recognize it as not being cubebs. We have also met with some cubebs of larger size than the ordinary sort, much shrivelled, with a stouter and flattened pedicel, one and a half times to twice as long as the berry. The drug has an agreeable odour different from that of common cubebs, and a very bitter taste. From a comparison with herbarium specimens, we judge that it may possibly be derived from *Piper crassipes* Korthals (*Cubeba crassipes* Miq.), a Sumatran species.

The fruits of *Piper Lowong* Bl. (*Cubeba Lowong* Miq.), a native of Java, and those of *P. ribesioides* Wall. (*Cubeba Wallichii* Miq.) are extremely cubeb-like.[3] Those of *Piper caninum* A. Dietr. (*Cubeba canina* Miq.), a plant of wide distribution throughout the Malay Archipelago as far as Borneo, for a specimen of which we have to thank Mr. Binnendyk of Buitenzorg, are smaller than true cubebs, and have stalks only half the diameter of the berry.

In the south of China the fruits of *Laurus Cubeba* Lour. have been

[1] *Straits Settlements Blue Book for* 1872. 294. 338.—There are no statistics for showing the *total import* of cubebs into the United Kingdom.

[2] They yielded to Schmidt 1·7 per cent. of oil and 3 per cent of resin.

[3] Figured in Nees von Esenbeck, *Plantæ medicinales*, Düsseldorf, i. (1828), tab. 22. A different figure is given by Miquel, *Comment. phytogr.* (1839), tab. 3.

frequently mistaken by Europeans for cubebs. The tree which affords them is unknown to modern botanists; Meissner refers it doubtfully to the genus *Tetranthera*.[1]

Ashantee Pepper, African Cubebs, or West African Black Pepper.

This spice is the fruit of *Piper Clusii* Cas. DC. (*Cubeba Clusii* Miq.), a species of wide distribution in tropical Africa, most abundantly occurring in the country of the Niamniam, about 4° to 5° N. lat., and 28° to 29° E. long. Its splendid red fruit bunches are spoken of with admiration by Schweinfurth,[2] who states that *Piper Clusii* is one of the characteristic and most conspicuous plants of those regions. The dried fruit is a round berry having a general resemblance to common cubebs but somewhat smaller, less rugose, attenuated into a slender pedicel once or twice as long as the berry and usually curved. The berries are crowded around a common stalk or rachis; they are of an ashy grey tint, and have a hot taste and the odour of pepper. According to Stenhouse, they contain piperin and not cubebin.[3]

The fruit of *Piper Clusii* was known as early as 1364 to the merchants of Rouen and Dieppe, who imported it from the Grain Coast, now Liberia,[4] under the name of pepper. The Portuguese likewise exported it from Benin as far back as 1485, as *Pimienta de rabo*, i.e. *tailed pepper*, and attempted in vain to sell it in Flanders.[5] Clusius received from London a specimen of this drug, of which he has left a good figure in his *Exotica*.[6] He says that its importation was forbidden by the King of Portugal for fear it should depreciate the pepper of India. The spice was also known to Gerarde and Parkinson; in our times it has been afresh brought to notice by the late Dr. Daniell.[7] In tropical Western Africa it is used as a condiment, and might easily be collected in large quantities, provided it should prove a good substitute for pepper.[8]

HERBA MATICO.

Matico.

Botanical Origin—*Piper angustifolium*[9] Ruiz et Pavon (*Artanthe elongata* Miq.), a shrub growing in the moist woods of Bolivia, Peru, Brazil, New Granada and Venezuela, also cultivated in some localities. A slightly different, somewhat stouter form of the plant with leaves 7 to 8 inches long (var. *α. cordulatum* Cas. DC.), occurs in the Brazilian provinces of Bahia, Minas Geraes and Ceará, as well as in Peru and the northern parts of South America.

[1] De Candolle, *Prod.* xv. sect. i. 199; Hanbury in *Pharm. Journ.* iii. (1862) 205, with figure; also *Science Papers*, 247.

[2] *Im Herzen Africas*, i. (1874) 507; ii. 399.

[3] *Pharm. Journ.* xiv. (1855) 363.

[4] Margry, *Les navigations françaises et la révolution maritime du XIVe au XVIe siècle*, 1867. 26.

[5] Giovanni di Barros, *l'Asia*, i. (Venet. 1561) 80.

[6] Lib. i. c. 22, p. 184 (1605).

[7] *Pharm. Journ.* xiv. (1855) 198.

[8] One cask of it was offered for sale in London as "*Cubebs*," 11 Feb. 1858.

[9] Fig. in Bentley and Trimen's *Med. Plants*, part 18 (1877).

History—The styptic properties of this plant are said to have been discovered by a Spanish soldier named Matico,[1] who having applied some of the leaves to his wounds, observed that the bleeding was thereby arrested; hence the plant came to be called *Yerba* or *Palo del Soldado* (soldier's herb or tree). The story is not very probable, but it is current in many parts of South America, and its allusion is not confined to the plant under notice.

The hæmostatic powers of matico, which are not noticed in the works of Ruiz and Pavon, were first recognized in Europe by Jeffreys,[2] a physician of Liverpool, in 1839, but they had already attracted attention in North America as early as 1827.

Description—Matico, as it arrives in commerce, consists of a compressed, coherent, brittle mass of leaves and stems, of a light green hue and pleasant herby odour. More closely examined, it is seen to be made up of jointed stems bearing lanceolate, acuminate leaves, cordate and unequal at the base, and having very short stalks. The leaves are rather thick, with their whole upper surface traversed by a system of minute sunk veins, which divide it into squares and give it a tessellated appearance. On the under side, these squares form a corresponding series of depressions which are clothed with shaggy hairs. The leaves attain a length of about 6 inches by 1½ inches broad. The flower and fruit spikes which are often 4 to 5 inches long, are slender and cylindrical with the flowers or fruits densely packed. The leaves of matico have a bitterish aromatic taste; their tissue shows numerous cells, filled with essential oil.[3]

Chemical Composition—The leaves yield on an average 2·7 per cent.[4] of essential oil, which we find slightly[5] dextrogyre; a large proportion of it distills at 180° to 200° C., the remainder becoming thickish. Both portions are lighter than water; but another specimen of the oil of matico which we had kept for some years, sinks in water. We have observed that in winter the oil deposits remarkable crystals of a camphor, more than half an inch in length, fusible at 103° C; they belong to the hexagonal system, and have the odour and taste of the oil from which they separate.

Matico further affords, according to Marcotte (1864),[6] a crystallizable acid, named *Artanthic Acid*, besides some tannin. The latter is made evident by the dark brown colour which the infusion assumes on addition of ferric chloride. The leaves likewise contain resin, but as shown by Stell in 1858, neither piperin, cubebin, nor any analogous principle such as the so-called *Maticin* formerly supposed to exist in them.

Commerce—The drug is imported in bales and serons by way of Panama. Among the exports of the Peruvian port of Arica in 1877, we noticed 195 quintales (19,773 lb) of Matico.

Uses—Matico leaves, previously softened in water, or in a state of

[1] Matico is the diminutive of *Mateo*, the Spanish for *Matthew*.

[2] *Remarks on the efficacy of Matico as a styptic and astringent*, 3rd ed., Lond. 1845.

[3] Microscopic examination of the leaves, Pocklington, *Pharm. Journ.* v. (1874) 301.

[4] As Messrs. Schimmel & Co., Leipzig, kindly informed me.—F. A. F.

[5] Deviating only 0°.7 in a column 50 mm. long.

[6] Guibourt (et Planchon), *Hist. des Drogues*, ii. (1869) 278.—We are not acquainted with "artanthic acid."

powder, are sometimes employed to arrest the bleeding of a wound. The infusion is taken for the cure of internal hæmorrhage.

Substitutes—Several plants have at times been brought into the market under the name of *matico*. One of these is *Piper aduncum* L.[1] (*Artanthe adunca* Miq.), of which a quantity was imported into London from Central America in 1863, and first recognized by Bentley (1864). In colour, odour, and shape of leaf it nearly agrees with ordinary matico; but differs in that the leaves are marked beneath by much more prominent ascending parallel nerves, the spaces between which are not rugose but comparatively smooth and nearly glabrous. In chemical characters, the leaves of *P. aduncum* appear to accord with those of *P. angustifolium*.

Piper aduncum is a plant of wide distribution throughout Tropical America. Under the name of *Nhandi* or *Piper longum* it was mentioned by Piso in 1648[2] on account of the stimulant action of its leaves and roots,—a property which causes it to be still used in Brazil, where however no particular styptic virtues seem to be ascribed to it.[3] The fruits are there employed in the place of cubebs. Sloane's figure[4] of "Piper longum, arbor folio latissimo" also shows *Piper aduncum*.

According to Triana, *Piper lanceæfolium* HBK. (*Artanthe* Miq.), and another species not recognized, yield matico in New Granada.[5] *Waltheria glomerata* Presl (*Sterculiaceæ*) is called *Palo del Soldado* at Panama and its leaves are used as a vulnerary.[6] In Riobamba and Quito, *Eupatorium glutinosum* Lamarck, is also called Chusalonga or *Matico*.[7]

ARISTOLOCHIACEÆ.

RADIX SERPENTARIÆ.

Radix Serpentariæ Virginianæ; Virginian Snake-root, Serpentary Root; F. *Serpentaire de Virginie;* G. *Schlangenwurzel.*

Botanical Origin—*Aristolochia Serpentaria* L., a perennial herb, commonly under a foot high, with simple or slightly branched, flexuose stems, producing small, solitary, dull purple flowers, close to the ground. It grows in shady woods in the United States, from Missouri and Indiana to Florida and Virginia,—abundantly in the Alleghanies and in the Cumberland Mountains, less frequently in New York, Michigan and the other Northern States. The plant varies exceedingly in the shape of its leaves.

History—The botanists of the 16th century, being fond of appellations alluding to the animal kingdom, gave the names of *Serpentaria*

[1] For a good figure, see Jacquin, *Icones* II. (1781-1793) tab. 210.

[2] *De Medicinâ Brasiliensi*, lib. 4. c. 57.

[3] Langgaard, *Diccionario de Medicina domestica e popular*, Rio de Janeiro, ii. (1865) 44.

[4] *Voyage to Jamaica* I. (1707) 135, and tab. 88.

[5] Exposition de 1867—Catalogue de M. José Triana, p. 14.

[6] Seemann, *Botany of the Herald*, 1852-57. 85.

[7] Bentham, *Plantae Hartwegianæ*, Lon. 1839. 198.

or Colubrina, *i.e.* snake-root, to the rhizome of *Polygonum Bistorta*, L. In America it was not the appearance, but the application of the drug under notice to which it owes the name snake-root.

The earliest account of *Virginian* snake-root is that of Thomas Johnson, an apothecary of London who published an edition of Gerarde's Herbal in 1636. It is evident however that Johnson confounded a species of *Aristolochia* from Crete with what he calls "that snake-weed that was brought from Virginia and grew with Mr. John Tradescant at South Lambeth, anno 1632." It was very briefly noticed by Cornuti in his *Canadensium Plantarum Historia* (1635), and in a much more intelligent manner by Parkinson in 1640. These authors, as well as Dale (1693) and Geoffroy (1741), extol the virtues of the root as a remedy for the bite of the rattlesnake, or of a rabid dog. Serpentary was introduced into the London Pharmacopœia in 1650.

Description—The snake-root of commerce includes the rhizome, which is knotty, contorted, scarcely 1 inch in length by ⅛ of an inch in thickness, bearing on its upper side the short bases of the stems of previous years, and throwing off from the under, numerous, slender, matted, branching roots, 2 to 4 inches long. The rhizome is often still attached to portions of the weak, herbaceous stem, which sometimes bears the fruit,—more rarely flowers and leaves. The drug has a dull brown hue, an aromatic odour resembling valerian but less unpleasant, and a bitterish aromatic taste, calling to mind camphor, valerian and turpentine.

Microscopic Structure—In the rhizome, the outer layer of the bark consists of a single row of cuboid cells; the middle cortical portion (*mesophlœum*) of about six layers of larger cells. In the liber, which is built up of numerous layers of smaller cells, those belonging to the medullary rays are nearly cuboid with distinctly porous walls, those of the liber bundles being smaller and arranged in a somewhat crescent-shaped manner. Groups of short, reticulated or punctuated vessels alternate in the woody rays with long, porous, ligneous cells; those close to the pith having thick walls. The largest cells of all are those composing the pith; the latter, seen in transverse section, occupies not the very centre of the rootstock, but is found nearer to its upper side. The rootlets exhibit a central fibro-vascular bundle, surrounded by a nucleus sheath. In the mesophlœum both of the rootstock and the rootlets, there occur a few cells containing a yellow essential oil. The other cells are loaded with starch.

Chemical Composition—Essential oil exists in the drug to the extent of of about ½ per cent.; and resin in nearly the same proportion. The outer cortical layer, as well as the zone of the nucleus-sheath, contains a little tannin, and a watery infusion of the drug is coloured greenish by perchloride of iron. Neutral acetate of lead precipitates some mucilage as well as the bitter principle, which latter may also be obtained by means of tannic acid. It is an amorphous, bitter substance, which deserves further investigation. By an alkaline solution of tartrate of copper the presence in serpentary of sugar is made evident.

Commerce—Virginian snake-root is imported from New York and Boston, in bales, casks or bags.

Uses—The drug is employed in the form of an infusion or tincture as a stimulating tonic and diaphoretic; it is more often prescribed in combination with cinchona bark than by itself. Its ancient reputation for the cure of snake-bites is now disregarded.

Adulteration and Substitution—Virginian snake-root is said to be sometimes adulterated with the root of *Spigelia marilandica* L., which has neither its smell nor taste (see p. 433); or with that of *Cypripedium pubescens* L., which it scarcely at all resembles. It is not uncommon to find here and there in the serpentary of commerce, a root of *Panax quinquefolium* L. accidentally collected, but never added for the purpose of adulteration.

The root of *Aristolochia reticulata* Nutt., a plant of Louisiana and Arkansas, has been brought into commerce in considerable quantity as *Texan* or *Red River Snake-root*.[1] We are indebted for an authentic specimen from the Cherokee country to Mr. Merrell, a large dealer in herbs at St. Louis, Missouri, who states that all the serpentary grown south-west of the Rocky Mountains is the produce of that species. The late Prof. Parrish of Philadelphia was kind enough to supply us with specimens of the same drug, as well as with reliable samples of true *Virginian* or *Middle States Snake-root.*

The Texan snake-root is somewhat thicker and less matted than that derived from *A. Serpentaria*, but has the odour and taste of the latter; some say it is less aromatic. The plant, portions of which are often present, may be easily distinguished by its leaves being *coriaceous, sessile* and *strongly reticulated* on their under surface.

CUPULIFERÆ.

CORTEX QUERCUS.

Oak Bark; F. *Ecorce de Chêne*; G. *Eichenrinde.*

Botanical Origin—*Quercus Robur* L., a tree, native of almost the whole of Europe, from Portugal and the Greek Peninsula as far north as 58° N. lat. in Scotland, 62° in Norway, and 56° in the Ural Mountains.

There are two remarkable forms of this tree which are regarded by many botanists as distinct species, but which are classed by De Candolle[2] as sub-species.

Sub-species I. *pedunculata*—with leaves sessile or shortly stalked, and acorns borne on a long peduncle, and acorns either sessile or growing on a short peduncle.

Sub-species II. *sessiliflora*—with leaf-stalks more or less elongated.

Both forms occur in Britain. The first is the common oak of the greater part of England and the lowlands of Scotland. The second is frequently scattered in woods in which the first variety prevails, but it rarely constitutes the mass of the oak woods in the south of England. In North Wales however, in the hilly parts of the north of England, and in Scotland, it is the commoner of the two forms (Bentham).

[1] Wiegand in *American Journ. of Pharm.* x. (1845) 10; also *Proceedings of the Am. Pharm. Association*, xxi. (1873) 441.

[2] *Prodromus*, xvi. (1864) sect. 2. fasc. 1.)

History—The astringent properties of all parts of the oak[1] were well known to Discorides, who recommends a decoction of the inner bark in colic, dysentery and spitting of blood. Yet oak bark seems at no time to have been held in great esteem as a medicine, probably on account of its commonness; and it is now almost superseded by other astringents. For tanning leather it has always been largely employed.

Description—For medicinal use the bark of the younger stems or branches is collected in the early spring. It varies somewhat in appearance according to the age of the wood from which it has been taken: that usually supplied to English druggists is in channelled pieces of variable length and a tenth of an inch or less in thickness, smooth, of a shining silvery grey, variegated with brown, dotted over with little scars. The inner surface is light rusty-brown, longitudinally striated. The fracture is tough and fibrous. A transverse section shows a thin, greenish cork-layer, within which is the brown parenchyme, marked with numerous rows of translucent colourless spots. The smell of dry oak bark is very faint; but when the bark is moistened the odour of tan becomes evident. The taste is astringent and in old barks slightly bitter.

Microscopic Structure—The outer layer of young oak bark consists of small flat cork-cells; the middle layer of larger thick-walled cells slightly extended in a tangential direction, and containing brown grains and chlorophyll. This tissue passes gradually into the softer narrower parenchyme of the inner bark, which is irregularly traversed by narrow medullary rays. It exhibits moreover a ring, but slightly interrupted, of thick-walled cells (sclerenchyme) and isolated shining bundles of liber fibres.

Groups of crystals of calcium oxalate are frequent in the middle and inner bark, but the chief constituents of the cells are brown granules of colouring matter and tannin. As the thickness of the bark increases the liber is pushed more to the outside, the middle cortical layer being partly thrown off by secondary cork-formation (rhytidoma, see pp. 354 and 538). Hence the younger barks, which alone are medicinal, are widely different from the older in structure and appearance.

Chemical Composition—The most interesting constituent is a peculiar kind of tannin. Stenhouse pointed out in 1843 that the tannic acid of oak bark is not identical with that of nutgalls; and such many years afterwards was proved to be the case.

The first-named substance, now called *Querci-tannic Acid*, yields by destructive distillation pyrocatechin, and according to Johanson (1875) very little pyrogallol. By boiling it with dilute sulphuric acid querci-tannic acid is split up into a red derivative and sugar. A solution of gelatine is precipitated by querci-tannic acid as well as by gallo-tannic acid; yet the compound formed with the latter is very liable to putrefaction, whereas the tannin of oak bark, which is accompanied by a large amount of extractive matter, furnishes a stable compound, and is capable of forming good leather.

As querci-tannic acid has not yet been isolated in a pure state, the exact estimation of the strength of the tanning principle in oak bark has not been accomplished, although it is important from an economic as well as from a scientific point of view. The method of Neubauer

[1] Probably not *Q. Robur* L.

(1873) depends upon the amount of permanganate of potassium decomposable by the extract of a given weight of oak bark. Neubauer found in the bark of young stems, as grown for tanning purposes, from 7 to 10 per cent. of querci-tannic acid, soluble in cold water.

Braconnot (1849) extracted from the seeds of the oaks under notice a crystallized sugar, which was shown in 1851 by Dessaignes to be a peculiar substance, which he termed *Quercite*. Prunier proved (1877–1878) that it agrees with the formula $C^6H^7(OH)^5 + 4\,OH^2$, and is closely allied to kinic acid, $C^6H^7(OH)^4COOH$ (see page 363). Quercite gives off water at 100°, melts at 225° C., and again losing water yields a crystallized anhydride. In the oak bark extremely small quantities of querite appear also to be present, as pointed out by Johanson.

A colourless, crystallizable, bitter substance, soluble in water, but not in absolute alcohol or ether, was extracted from oak bark in 1843 by Gerber, and named *Quercin*. It requires further examination: Eckert (1864) could not detect its existence in young oak bark.

Uses—Occasionally employed as an astringent, chiefly for external application.

GALLÆ HALEPENSES.

Gallæ Turcicæ; Galls, Nutgalls, Oak Galls, Aleppo or Turkey Galls; F. *Noix de Galle, Galle d'Alep;* G. *Levantische oder Aleppische Gallen, Galläpfel.*

Botanical Origin—*Quercus lusitanica* Webb, var. *infectoria* (*Q. infectoria* Oliv.),[1] a shrub or rarely a tree, found in Greece, Asia Minor, Cyprus and Syria. It is probable that other varieties of this oak, as well as allied species, contribute to furnish the Aleppo galls of commerce.

History—Oak galls are named by Theophrastus, and were well known to other ancient writers. Alexander Trallianus prescribed them as a remedy in diarrhœa.[2]

The earliest accurate descriptions and figures of the oak and the insect producing the galls are due to Olivier.[3] Pliny[4] mentions the interesting fact that paper saturated with an infusion of galls may be used as a test for discovering sulphate of iron, when added as an adulteration to the more costly verdigris: this, according to Kopp, is the earliest instance of the scientific application of a chemical reaction.[5] For tanning and dyeing, galls have been used from the earliest times, during the middle ages however they were not precisely an article of great importance, being then, no doubt, for a large part replaced by sumach.

Nutgalls have long been an object of commerce between Western Asia and China. Barbosa in his *Description of the East Indies*[6] written in 1514 calls them *Magican*,[7] and says they are brought from the Levant

[1] De Candolle, *Prodromus*, xvi. sect. 2. fasc. i. 17.

[2] Puschmann's edition, quoted in the Appendix, i. 237.

[3] *Voyage dans l'Empire Othoman*, ii. (1801), pl. 14–15.

[4] Lib. 34. c. 26.

[5] *Geschichte der Chemie*, ii. (1844) 51.

[6] Published by the Hakluyt Society, Lond. 1866. 191.

[7] Nearly the same name is still used in the Tamil, Telugu, Malayalim and Canarese languages.

to Cambay by way of Mekka, and that they are worth a great deal in China and Java. From the statements of Porter Smith[1] we learn that they are still prized by the Chinese.

Formation—Many plants are punctured by insects for the sake of depositing their eggs, which operation gives rise to those excrescences which bear the general name of *gall*.[2]

Oaks are specially liable to be visited for this purpose by insects of the order *Hymenoptera* and the genus *Cynips*, one species of which, *Cynips Gallæ tinctoriæ* Olivier (*Diplolepis Gallæ tinctoriæ* Latreille), occasions the galls under notice.

The female of this little creature is furnished with a delicate borer or ovipositor, which she is able to protrude from the extremity of the abdomen; by means of it she pierces the tender shoot of the oak, and deposits therein one or more eggs. This minute operation occasions an abnormal affluence to the spot of the juices of the plant, the result of which is the growth of an excrescence often of great magnitude, in the centre of which (but not as it appears until the gall has become full-grown) the larva is hatched and undergoes its transformations.

When the larva has assumed its final development and become a winged insect, which requires a period of five to six months, the latter bores itself a cylindrical passage from the centre of the gall to its surface, and escapes.

In the best kind of gall found in commerce, this stage has not yet arrived, the gall having been gathered while the insect is still in the larval state. In splitting a number of galls, it is not difficult to find specimens in all stages, from those containing the scarcely distinguishable remains of the minute larva, to those which show the perfect insect to have perished when in the very act of escaping from its prison.

Description—Aleppo galls[3] are spherical, and have a diameter of $\frac{4}{10}$ to $\frac{8}{10}$ of an inch. They have a smooth and rather shining surface, marked in the upper half of the gall by small pointed knobs and ridges, arranged very irregularly and wide apart; the lower half is more frequently smooth. The aperture by which the insect escapes is always near the middle. When not perforated, the galls are of a dark olive green, and comparatively heavy; but after the fly has bored its way out, they become of a yellowish brown hue, and lighter in weight. Hence the distinction in commerce of *Blue* or *Green Galls*, and *White Galls*.

Aleppo galls are hard and brittle, splitting under the hammer; they have an acidulous, very astringent taste followed by a slight sweetness, but have no marked odour. Their fractured surface is sometimes close-grained, with a waxy or resinous lustre; sometimes (especially towards the kernel-like centre) loosely granular, or sometimes again it exhibits a crystalline-looking radiated structure or is full of clefts. The colour of the interior varies from pale brown to a deep greenish yellow. The

[1] *Mat. Med. and Nat. Hist. of China*, 1871. 100.

[2] French writers, as Moquin-Tandon, distinguish the thick-walled galls of *Cynips* from the thin, capsular galls formed by *Aphis*, terming the former *galles* and the latter *coques* (shells).

[3] There are many other varieties of oak gall, for descriptions of some of which, see Guibourt, *Hist. des Drogues*, ii. (1869) 292; and for information on the various gall-insects of the family *Cynipsidæ* and the excrescences they produce, consult a paper by Abl in Wittstein's *Vierteljahresschrift für prakt. Pharm.* vi. (1857) 343-361.

central cavity, sometimes nearly $\frac{1}{4}$ of an inch in diameter, which served as a dwelling for the insect, is lined with a thin hard shell. If the insect has perished while still very young, the central cavity and the aperture contain a mass of loose starchy cellular tissue, or its pulverulent remains: if the insect has not been developed at all, the centre of the gall is entirely composed of this tissue.

Microscopic Structure—The cellular tissue of the gall is formed in the middle layer of large spherical cells with rather thick porous walls, becoming considerably smaller towards the circumference. The outermost rows are built up of cells having but a very small lumen and comparatively thick walls, so that they form a sort of rind. Here and there throughout the entire tissue, there occur isolated bundles of vessels which pass through the stalk into the gall. Towards the kernel, the parenchyme gradually passes into radially-extended, wider, thin-walled cells, the walls of which are marked with spiral striæ. The hard shell of the chamber[1] is composed of larger, radially-extended, thick-walled cells, with beautifully stratified porous walls. On the inner side of this shell there are found, after the escape of the insect, the remains of the starchy tissue already mentioned, which originally filled the chamber and had been consumed by the insect as nourishment.

The parenchyme-cells outside the shell contain chlorophyll and tannin; the latter is in transparent, colourless, sharp-edged masses, insoluble in benzol, but dissolving slowly in water, quickly in alcohol. Thin slices soaked in glycerin appear after some time covered with beautiful crystals of gallic acid. The thick-walled cells (stone-cells) and the neighbouring striated cells, are rich in octahedra of calcium oxalate. The tissue of the gall situated within the shell of thick-walled cells contains starch in large, compressed, mostly spherical granules; also isolated masses of brown resin. Besides these, there appears to be in this part of the tissue an albuminoid compound.

Chemical Composition—The rough taste of galls is due to their chief constituent, *Tannic* or *Gallo-tannic Acid*, $C^{14}H^{10}O^{9}$, or $\left.\begin{matrix} C^6H^2(OH)^2COOH \\ C^6H^2(OH)^3CO \end{matrix}\right\} O$, the type of a numerous family of substances to which vegetables owe their astringent properties. Tannic matter was long supposed to be of one kind, namely that found in the oak gall, but the researches of later years have proved the tannin of different plants to possess distinctive characters: hence the term *gallo-tannic* acid to distinguish that of galls, from which it is principally derived. It was however shown by Stenhouse as far back as the year 1843, again in 1861, as well as by still more recent unpublished experiments, that the tannic acid found in Sicilian sumach, the leaves of *Rhus Coriaria* L., is identical with that of oak galls. Löwe in 1873 came to the same conclusion. The best oak galls yield of this acid, from 60 to 70 per cent.

Gallic Acid is also contained in galls ready-formed to the extent of about 3 per cent. Free sugar, resin, protein-substances, have also been found. Neither gum nor dextrin is present.

Commerce—The introduction into dyeing of new chemical sub-

[1] *Couche protectrice* of Lacaze-Duthiers—*Recherches pour servir à l'histoire des galles.* —*Ann. des Sciences Nat.*, Bot. xix. (1853) 273-354.

stances, and the increased employment of sumach and myrobalans, have caused the trade in nutgalls to decline considerably during the last few years. The province of Aleppo which used to export annually 10,000 to 12,000 quintals, exported in 1871 only 3000 quintals.[1] A staple market for the galls which are collected in the mountains of Kurdistan is Diarbekir, whence they are sent to Trebizond for shipment. Galls are also shipped in some quantity at Bussorah, Bagdad, Bushire, and Smyrna.

There were imported into the United Kingdom from ports of Turkey and Persia during 1872, 6349 cwt. of galls, valued at £18,581.

Uses—Oak galls in their crude state are seldom used in medicine unless it be externally; but the tannic and gallic acids extracted from them are often administered.

Other kinds of Gall.

Chinese or Japanese Galls—The only kind of galls, besides those of the oak, which are of commercial importance. They are described at page 167.

Pistacia Galls—The genus *Pistacia*, which belongs to the same order as *Rhus*, is very liable to the attacks of *Aphis*, which produce upon its leaves and branches excrescences of exactly the same nature as Chinese galls. In the south of Europe, horn-like follicles, often several inches long,[2] are frequently met with on the branches of *Pistacia Terebinthus* (page 165). These *Gallæ vel Folliculi Pistacinæ*, in Italian *Carobbe di Giudea*, were formerly used in medicine and in dyeing.[3] They were noticed in 1555 by Belon, but already well known as early as the time of Theophrastus.

Another much smaller gall of different shape is formed (by the same insect ?) on the ribs of the leaves of *Pistacia Terebinthus; P. Lentiscus* (page 161) affords also a similar small excrescence.

Again, another growth of the same character constitutes the small and very astringent galls known in the Indian bazaars by the names of *Bazghanj* and *Gule-pistah*, the latter signifying *flower of pistachio;* they have been termed in Europe *Bokhara Galls*. They were imported by sea into Bombay in the year 1872-73, to the extent of 184 cwt., chiefly from Sind;[4] and are also carried into North-western India by way of Peshawar and by the Bolan Pass. Occasionally a package finds its way into a London drug sale.

Tamarisk Galls—These are roundish knotty excrescences of the size of a pea up to ½ an inch in diameter, found in North-western India on the branches of *Tamarix orientalis* L., a large, quick-growing tree, common on saline soils. The galls are used in India in the place of oak galls, and are mentioned as "non-officinal" in the *Pharmacopœia of India*, 1867 We are not aware that they have been the subject of any particular chemical research; their microscopic structure has been investigated by Vogl.[5]

[1] Consul Skene—*Reports of H.M. Consuls*, No. 1. 1872. 270.

[2] For a figure, see *Pharm. Journ.* iii. (1844) 387. For the structure see Marchand, in the paper quoted at page 166, note 4, plate iii.

[3] Analysis by Martius may be found in Liebig's *Ann. d. Pharm.* xxi. (1837) 179.

[4] From the returns quoted at page 333, note 3.

[5] *Zeitschrift des Oesterreichischen Apothekervereines*, 1877. 14.

SANTALACEÆ.

LIGNUM SANTALI.

Lignum Santalinum album vel citrinum; Sandal Wood; F. *Bois de Santal citrin;* G. *Weisses oder Gelbes Sandelholz.*

Botanical Origin—*Santalum album*[1] L., a small tree, 20 to 30 feet high, with a trunk 18 to 35 inches in girth, a native of the mountainous parts of the Indian peninsula, but especially of Mysore and parts of Coimbatore and North Canara, in the Madras Presidency; it grows in dry and open places, often in hedge-rows, not in forests. The same tree is also found in the islands of the Eastern Archipelago, notably of Sumba (otherwise called Chandane or Sandal-wood Island), and Timur.

In later times, sandal wood has been extensively collected in the Hawaiian or Sandwich Islands, where its existence was first pointed out about the year 1778, from *Santalum Freycinetianum* Gaud. and *S. pyrularium* A. Gray;[2] in the Viti or Fiji Islands from *S. Yasi* Seem.; in New Caledonia from *S. austro-caledonicum*, Vieill[3]; and in Western Australia from *Fusanus spicatus* Br. (*Santalum spicatum* DC., *S. cygnorum* Miq.).[4] The mother plants of *Japanese* and *West Indian* sandal wood are not known to us.

In India the sandal-wood tree is protected by Government, and is the source of a profitable commerce. In other countries it has been left to itself, and has usually been extirpated, at least from all accessible places, within a few years of its discovery.

History—Sandal wood, the Sanskrit name for which, *Chandana*, has passed into many of the languages of India, is mentioned in the *Nirukta* or writings of Yaska, the oldest Vedic commentary extant, written not later than the 5th century B.C. The wood is also referred to in the ancient Sanskrit epic poems, the *Ramayana* and *Mahabharata*, parts of which may be of nearly as early date.

The author of the *Periplus of the Erythrean Sea*, written about the middle of the 1st century, enumerates sandal wood (Ξύλα σαγαλίνα) among the Indian commodities imported into Omana in the Persian Gulf.[5]

The Τζανδάνα mentioned towards the middle of the 6th century by Cosmas Indicopleustes,[6] as brought to Taprobane (Ceylon) from China and other emporia, was probably the wood under consideration. In Ceylon its essential oil was used as early as the 9th century in embalming the corpses of the princes.

[1] Fig. in Bentley and Trimen's *Medic. Plants*, part 18 (1877).

[2] Seemann, *Flora Vitiensis*, 1865–73. 210–215.

[3] The natural woods having been nearly exhausted, the tree is now under culture in the island. *Catalogue des produits des colonies françaises, Exposition de 1878.* p. 332; they state there that the island of Nossi-bé, on the north-western coast of Madagascar, also supplies some sandal wood.

[4] Whether *Santalum lanceolatum* Br., a tree found throughout N. and E. Australia, and called *sandal wood* by the colonists, is an object of trade, we know not.

[5] Vincent, *Commerce and Navigation of the Ancients*, ii. (1807) 378.

[6] Migne, *Patrologiæ Cursus*, series Græca, tom. 88. 446.

Sandal wood is named by Masudi[1] as one of the costly aromatics of the Eastern Archipelago. In India it was used in the most sacred buildings, of which a memorable example still exists in the famous gates of Somnath, supposed to be 1000 years old.[2]

In the 11th century sandal wood was found among the treasures of the Egyptian khalifs, as stated in our article on camphor at page 511.

Among European writers, Constantinus Africanus, who flourished at Salerno in the 11th century, was one of the earliest to mention Sandalum.[3] Ebn Serabi, called Serapion the Younger, who lived about the same period, was acquainted with *white*, *yellow*, and *red* sandal wood.[4] All three kinds of sandal wood also occur in a list of drugs[5] in use at Frankfort, *circa* A.D. 1450; and in the *Compendium Aromatariorum* of Saladinus, published in 1488, we find mentioned as proper to be kept by the Italian apothecary,—"*Sandali trium generum, scilicet albi, rubii et citrini.*"

Whether the *red* sandal here coupled with *white* and *yellow* was the inodorous wood of *Pterocarpus santalinus*, now called *Lignum santalinum rubrum* or *Red Sanders* (see p. 199), is extremely doubtful. It may have meant real sandal wood, of which three shades, designated *white*, *red*, and *yellow*, are still recognized by the Indian traders.[6]

On the other hand, we learn from Barbosa[7] that about 1511 *white* and *yellow* sandal wood were worth at Calicut on the Malabar Coast from eight to ten times as much as the *red*, which would show that in his day the red was not a mere variety of the other two, but something far cheaper, like the Red Sanders Wood of modern commerce.

In 1635 the subsidy levied on sandal wood imported into England was 1s. per lb. on the *white*, and 2s. per lb. on the *yellow*.[8]

The first figure and satisfactory description of *Santalum album* occur in the *Herbarium Amboinense* of Rumphius (ii. tab. 11).

Production—The dry tracts producing this valuable wood occupy patches of a strip of country lying chiefly in Mysore and Coimbatore, about 250 miles long, north and north-west of the Neilgherry Hills, and having Coorg and Canara between it and the Indian Ocean; also a piece of country further eastward in the districts of Salem and North Arcot, where the tree grows from the sea-level up to an elevation of 3000 feet. In Mysore, where sandal wood is most extensively produced, the trees all belong to Government, and can only be felled by the proper officers. This privilege was conferred on the East India Company by a treaty with Hyder Ali, made 8 August 1770, and the

[1] I. 222 in the work quoted in the Appendix.

[2] They are 11 feet high and 9 feet wide, and richly carved out of sandal wood; they were constructed for the temple of Somnath in Guzerat, once esteemed the holiest temple in India. On its destruction in A.D. 1025, the gates were carried off to Ghuzni in Afghanistan, where they remained until the capture of that city by the English in 1842, when they were taken back to India. They are now preserved in the citadel of Agra. For a representation of the gates, see *Archæologia*, xxx. (1844) pl. 14.

[3] *Opera*, Basil. 1536–39, *Lib. de Gradibus*, 369.

[4] *Liber Serapionis aggregatus in medicinis simplicibus*, 1473.

[5] Flückiger, *Die Frankfurter Liste*, Halle, 1873. 11.

[6] Thus Milburn in his *Oriental Commerce* (1813) says—" . . . the deeper the colour, the higher is the perfume; and hence the merchants sometimes divide sandal into *red*, *yellow*, and *white*, but these are all different shades of the same colour, and do not arise from any difference in the species of the tree."—(i. 291.)

[7] Ramusio, *Navigationi et Viaggi*, etc., Venet. 1554. fol. 357 b., *Libro di Odoardo Barbosa Portoghese*.

[8] *The Rates of Marchandizes*, Lond. 1635.

monopoly has been maintained to the present day. The Mysore annual exports of sandal wood are about 700 tons, valued at £27,000.[1] They are shipped from Mangalore.

A similar monopoly existed in the Madras Presidency until a few years ago, when it was abandoned. But sandal wood is still a source of revenue to the Madras Government, which by the systematic management of the Forest Department has of late years been regularly increasing. The quantity of sandal wood felled in the Reserved Forests during the year 1872-3 was returned as 15,329 maunds (547½ tons).[2]

The sandal-wood tree, which is indigenous to the regions just mentioned, used to be reproduced by seeds sown spontaneously or by birds; but it is now being raised in regular plantations, the seeds being sown two or three in a hole with a chili (*Capsicum*) seed, the latter producing a quick-growing seedling which shades the sandal while young.[3] It is probable that the nurse-plant affords *sustenance*, for it has been shown[4] that *Santalum* is parasitic, its roots attaching themselves by tuber-like processes to those of many other plants; and it is also said that young sandal plants thrive best when grass is allowed to grow up in the seed-beds.

The trees attain their prime in 20 to 30 years, and have then trunks as much as a foot in diameter. A tree having been felled, the branches are lopped off, and the trunk allowed to lie on the ground for several months, during which time the white ants eat away the greater part of the inodorous sapwood. The trunk is then roughly trimmed, sawn into billets 2 to 2½ feet long, and taken to the forest depots. There the wood is weighed, subjected to a second and more careful trimming, and classified according to quality. In some parts it is customary not to fell but to dig the tree up; in others the root is dug up after the trunk has been cut down,—the root affording valuable wood, which with the chips and sawdust are preserved for distillation, or for burning in the native temples. The sap wood and branches are worthless.[5]

In 1863 a sort of sandal wood afforded by *Fusanus spicatus* (p. 599) was one of the chief exports of Western Australia, whence it was shipped to China. A trifling payment for permission to cut growing timber of any kind was the only barrier placed on the felling of the trees. The farmers employed their teams during the dull season in bringing to Perth or Guildford the logs of sandal which had been felled and trimmed in the bush; and there was a flourishing trade so long as trees of a fair size could be obtained within 100 or even 150 miles of the towns, where the commodity was worth £6 to £6 10s. per ton. But the ill-regulated and improvident destruction of the trees in the more easily accessible districts has so reduced their numbers that the trade

[1] B. H. Baden Powell, *Report on the Administration of the Forest Department in the several provinces under the Government of India*, 1872–73, Calcutta, 1874. vol. i. 27.

[2] *Report of the Administration of the Madras Presidency during the year* 1872–73, Madras, 1874. 18. 143.

[3] Beddome, *Flora Sylvatica for Southern India*, 1872. 256.

[4] Scott in *Journ. of Agricult. and Horticult. Soc. of India*, Calcutta, vol. ii. part 1 (1871) 287.

[5] Elliot, *Experiences of a Planter in the Jungles of Mysore*, ii. (1871) 237; also verbal information communicated by Capt. Campbell Walker, Deputy Conservator of Forests, Madras.

in that part of Australia soon came to an end.[1] Australian sandal wood appears however to be still an article of commerce, if one may draw such an inference from the fact that 47,904 cwt. of sandal wood were imported into Singapore from Australia in the year 1872. It was mostly re-shipped to China.[2]

Description—Sandal wood is not much known in English commerce, and is by no means always to be found even in London. That which we have examined, and which we believe was Indian, was in cylindrical logs, mostly about 6 inches in diameter (the largest 8 inches—smallest 3 inches) and 3 to 4 feet long, extremely ponderous; the bark had been removed. A transverse section of sandal wood exhibits it of a pale brown, marked with rather darker concentric zones and (when seen under a lens) numerous open pores. The tissue is traversed by medullary rays, also perceptible by the aid of a lens. The wood splits easily, emitting when comminuted an agreeable odour which is remarkably persistent; it has a strongish aromatic taste.

The varieties of sandal wood are not classified by the few persons who deal in the article in London, and we are unable to point out characters by which they may be distinguished. In the price-currents of commercial houses in China three sorts of sandal wood are enumerated, namely, *South Sea Island, Timor,* and *Malabar*;. the last fetches three or four times as high a price as either of the others. Even the Indian sandal wood may vary in an important manner. Beddome,[3] conservator of forests in Madras, and an excellent observer, remarks that the finest sandal wood is that which has grown slowly on rocky, dry and poor land; and that the trees found in a rich alluvial soil, though of very fine growth, produce no heart-wood and are consequently valueless. A variety of the tree with more lanceolate leaves (var. β *myrtifolium* DC.), native of the eastern mountains of the Madras Presidency, affords a sandal wood which is nearly inodorous.

Microscopic Structure—The woody rays or wedges show a breadth varying from 35 to 420 mkm., the primary being frequently divided by secondary medullary rays. These latter rays consist of one, often of two, rows of cells of the usual form. The woody tissue which they enclose is chiefly made up of small ligneous fibres with pointed ends, some larger parenchymatous cells, and thick-walled vessels. The resin and essential oil reside chiefly in the medullary rays, as shown by the darker colour of these latter.

Chemical Composition—The most important constituent is the essential oil, which the wood yields to the extent of from 2 to 5 per cent.[4] In India, with imperfect stills, 2·5 per cent. of the oil are obtained; the roots yield the largest amount and the finest quality of it.[5] It is a light yellow, thick liquid, possessing the characteristic odour of sandal; that which we examined had a sp. gr. of 0·963. We did not succeed in finding a fixed boiling point of the oil; it began to boil at 214° C., but

[1] Millett, *An Australian Parsonage*, Lond., 1872, 43. 95. 382.

[2] *Straits Settlements Blue Book for* 1872, Singapore, 1873. 298. 347.—It is possible that the sandal wood in question may have been the produce of the South Sea Islands, shipped from an Australian port.

[3] *Op. cit.*

[4] Information obligingly communicated by Messrs. Schimmel and Co., Leipzig (1878).

[5] Dr. Bidie, in *Pharmacopœia of India*, 1868, p. 461.

the temperature quickly rose to 255°, the oil acquiring a darker hue. Oil of sandal wood varies much in the strength and character of its aroma, according to the sort of wood from which it is produced.

The oil as largely prepared by Messrs. Schimmel & Co., in a column 100 millimetres long, deviates the plane of polarization 18·6° to the *left*. Oil of Venezuela sandal wood, from the same distillers, examined in the same manner, deviates 6°·75 to the *right*.

From the wood, treated with boiling alcohol, we obtained about 7 per cent. of a blackish extract, from which a tannate was precipitated by alcoholic solution of acetate of lead. Decomposed by sulphuretted hydrogen, the tannate yielded a tannic acid having but little colour, and striking a greenish hue with a ferric salt. The extract also contained a dark resin.

Commerce—The greatest trade in sandal wood is in China, which country in the year 1866 imported at the fourteen treaty ports then open 87,321 peculs, equivalent to 5,197 tons; of this vast quantity the city of Hankow on the river Yangtsze, received no less than 61,414 peculs, or more than seven times as much as any other port.[1] The imports into Hankow have recently been much smaller, namely, 14,989 peculs in 1871 and 12,798 peculs in 1872.[2] On the other hand, Shanghai lying near the mouth of the same great river, imported in 1872, 59,485 peculs of sandal wood, the estimated value of which was about £100,000. In 1877 the imports of all China were 72,934 peculs.

A considerable trade in sandal wood is done in Bombay, the quantity imported thither annually being about 650 tons, and the annual export about 400 tons.[3]

Oil of sandal wood is largely manfactured on the ghats between Mangalore and Mysore, where fuel for the stills is abundant. Official returns[4] represent the quantity of the oil imported into Bombay in the year 1872–73 as 10,348 lbs., value £8,374; 4,500 lbs. were re-exported by sea.

Uses—The essential oil has of late been prescribed as a substitute for copaiba, otherwise sandal wood has hardly any uses in modern European medicine. It is employed as a perfume and for the fabrication of small articles of ornament. Among the natives of India it is largely consumed in the celebration of sepulchral rites, wealthy Hindus showing their respect for a departed relative by adding sticks of sandal wood to the funereal pile. The powder of the wood made into a paste with water is used for making the caste mark, and also for medicinal purposes. The consumption of sandal wood in China appears to be principally for the incense used in the temples.

[1] *Reports on Trade at the ports in China open to foreign trade for* 1866, published by order of the Inspector-General of Customs, Shanghai, 1867. 120. 121.—One pecul = 133⅓ lb.

[2] *Commercial Reports of H.M. Consuls in China for* 1871 (p. 50) *and* 1872 (pp. 62. 159).

[3] From the official document quoted at p. 601, note 1.

[4] See p. 333, note 3.

Gymnosperms.

CONIFERÆ.

TEREBINTHINA VULGARIS.

Crude or Common Turpentine; F. Térebenthine commune; G. Gemeiner Terpenthin.

Botanical Origin—The trees which yield Common Turpentine may be considered in two groups, namely, European and American.

1. *European*—In Finland and Russia Proper, the Scotch Pine, *Pinus silvestris* L.; in Austria and Corsica, *P. Laricio* Poiret; and in South-western France, *P. Pinaster* Solander (*P. maritima* Poiret), extensively cultivated as the *Pin maritime*, yield turpentine in their respective countries.

2. *American*—In the United States, the conifers most important for terebinthinous products are the Swamp Pine, *Pinus australis* Michaux (*P. palustris* Mill.), and the Loblolly Pine, *P. Tæda* L.

History—The resin of pines and firs was well known to the ancients, who obtained it in much the same manner as that practised at the present day. The turpentine used in this country has for many years past been derived from North America. Up to the last century, both it and the substance called *Common Frankincense* were imported from France. The late civil war in the United States and the blockade of the Southern ports, occasioned a great scarcity of American turpentine; and terebinthinous substances from all other countries were poured into the London market. The actual supplies, however, were mainly furnished by France.

Kopp[1] quotes a passage showing that the essential oil of turpentine was known to Marcus Græcus, who termed it *Aqua ardens*. This almost unknown personage is the reputed inventor of *Greek Fire*, a dreaded engine of destruction in mediæval warfare.

Secretion—The primary formation of resin-ducts in the bark of coniferous trees has been explained by Dippel,[2] Müller,[3] and Frank.[4] The subsequent diffusion of the resinous juice through the heart-wood, sap-wood, and bark, has been elaborately investigated by Hugo von Mohl.[5] From the various forms under which this diffusion exists in the

[1] *Geschichte der Chemie*, iv. (1847) 392.
[2] *Botanische Zeitung*, 1863.
[3] Pringsheim. *Jahrb. für wissenschaftl. Botanik.* 1866.
[4] *Beiträge zur Pflanzenphysiologie*, Leipzig, 1868. 119.
[5] *Botanische Zeitung*, 1859. 329.

different species have arisen the diverse methods of obtaining the terebinthinous resins.

Thus in the wood of the Silver Fir (*Pinus Picea* L.) resin-ducts are altogether wanting;—and led by experience, the Alpine peasant collects the turpentine of this tree by simply puncturing the little cavities which form under its bark. In the Scotch Pine (*P. silvestris* L.), they are more abundant in the wood than in the bark, a fact which might be anticipated by observing how rarely this tree exudes resin spontaneously.

Oil of turpentine, like volatile oils in general, undergoes on exposure to the air certain alterations giving rise to what is called *resinification*. The formic acid which is produced in small quantity during this change characterizes it as one of oxidation; the chief products however are not exactly known, and not one of them has been proved identical with any natural resin. The common assumption that resins are produced from volatile oils by simple oxidation, is consequently not yet entirely justified.

Extraction—In the United States[1] turpentine is obtained to the largest extent from *Pinus australis*, of which tree there are vast forests, the piny woods or pine-barrens, extending from Virginia to the Mexican Gulf, especially through North and South Carolina, Georgia and Alabama. But it is in North Carolina that the extraction of turpentine is principally carried on.

In the winter, *i.e.* from November to March, the negroes in a *Turpentine Orchard*, as the district of forest to be worked is called, are occupied in making in the trunks of the trees, cavities which are technically known as *boxes*. For this purpose a long narrow axe is used, and some skill is required to wield it properly. The boxes are made from 6 to 12 inches above the ground, and are shaped like a distended waistcoat-pocket, the bottom being about 4 inches below the lower lip, and 8 or 10 below the upper. On a tree of medium size, a box should be made to hold a quart. The less the axe approaches the centre of the tree the better, as vitality is the less endangered. An expert workman will make a box in less than 10 minutes. From one to four boxes are made in each tree, a few inches of bark being left between them. The greater number of trees from which turpentine is now obtained, are from 12 to 18 inches in diameter, and have three boxes each.

The boxes having been made, the bark and a little of the wood immediately beneath it, which are above the box, are *hacked;* and from this excoriation, the sap begins to flow about the middle of March, gradually filling the box. Each tree requires to be freshly hacked every 8 or 10 days, a very slight wound above the last being all that is needed. The hacking is carried on year after year, until it reaches 12 to 15 feet or more, ladders being used. The turpentine, which is called *dip*, is removed from the boxes by a spoon or ladle of peculiar form, and collected into barrels, which are made on the spot and are of very rude construction. The first year's flow of a new tree, having but a small surface to traverse before it reaches the box, is of special goodness and is termed *Virgin dip*.

[1] The account here given is taken from F. L. Olmsted's *Journey in the Seaboard Slave States*, New York, 1856, p. 338, etc.

The turpentine which concretes upon the trunk is occasionally scraped off and barrelled by itself, and is known in the market as *scrape*, or by English druggists as *Common Frankincense* or *Gum thus*.

Although a large amount of turpentine is shipped to the northern ports for distillation, a still larger is distilled in the neighbourhood of the turpentine orchards. Copper stills are used, capable of containing 5 to 20 barrels of turpentine. The turpentine is distilled without water, the volatile oil as it flows from the worm being received in the barrel in which it is afterwards sent to market. When all the oil that can be profitably drawn off has been obtained, a spigot is removed from an opening in the bottom of the still, and the residual *Rosin*, appearing as a viscid fluid-like molasses, is allowed to flow out. Only the first qualities of rosin, as that obtained from *Virgin dip*, are generally considered worth saving, the less pure sorts being simply allowed to run to waste. When it is intended to save the rosin, the latter is drawn off into a vat of water, which separates the chips and other rubbish, and the rosin is then placed in barrels for the market. A North Carolina turpentine orchard will remain productive under ordinary treatment for fifty years.

The collection of turpentine in the departments of the Landes and Gironde in the south-west of France, is performed in a more rational manner than in America, inasmuch as the plan of making deep cavities in the tree for the purpose of receiving the resin, is avoided by the simple expedient of placing a suitable vessel beneath the lowest incision.[1] The turpentine which concretes upon the stem is termed in France *Galipot* or *Barras*.

Description—Common turpentine is chiefly of two varieties, namely, *American* and *Bordeaux;* the first alone is commonly found in the English market.

American Turpentine—A viscid honey-like fluid, of yellowish colour, somewhat opaque, but becoming transparent by exposure to the air; it has an agreeable odour and warm bitterish taste. When long kept in a bottle, it is seen to separate into two layers, the upper clear and faintly fluorescent, the lower somewhat turbid or granular. When the latter portion is examined under the microscope, it is found to consist mainly of minute crystals of peculiar curved or bluntly elliptic form. These crystals are abietic acid; when the turpentine is warmed, the crystals are speedily dissolved.

Bordeaux Turpentine—in all essential particulars agrees with American Turpentine; it appears to separate rather more readily than the latter into two layers,—a transparent and an opaque or crystalline.

Chemical Composition—The turpentines are mixtures of resin and essential oil. The latter, which amounts to from 15 to 30 per cent., consists for the greater part of various hydrocarbons, corresponding to the formula $C^{10}H^{16}$. Many of the crude turpentine oils, and some of them even after rectification, are energetically acted on by metallic

[1] For further particulars, see Guibourt, *Hist. des drog.* ii. (1869) 259, also Curie, *Produits résineux du Pin maritime.* Paris 1874. 24 pages, 1 plate; Matthieu, *Flore forestière* 1860, p. 353.

sodium. This re-action proves the presence of a certain quantity of oxygenated oils, not one of which has thus far been isolated.

The turpentine oils, although agreeing in composition, exhibit a series of physical differences according to their origin. One and the same tree, indeed, yields from its several organs oils of different properties. The boiling point varies between 152° and 172° C. The sp. gr. at mean temperatures ranges from 0·856 to 0·870. Greater differences are exhibited in the optical properties, some varieties of the oil turning the plane of polarization to the right, others to the left. This rotatory power differs in many cases from that of the turpentine from which the oil was derived.[1] The odour of oil of turpentine varies with the species from which it has been obtained.

When crude turpentine is distilled with water, nearly the whole of the oil passes over, while the resin remains. This resin is called *Colophony* or *Rosin*. When it still contains a little water, it is distinguished in English trade as *Yellow Rosin ;* when fully deprived of water, it becomes what is called *Transparent Rosin*. That of deeper colour acquired by a still longer application of heat, bears the name of *Black Rosin*.

Colophony softens at 80° C., and melts completely at 100° into a clear liquid. At about 150° it forms a somewhat darker liquid, but without undergoing a loss in weight; at higher temperatures, it gradually decomposes. Pure colophony has a sp. gr. of 1·07, and is homogeneous, transparent, amorphous, and very brittle. At temperatures between 15° and 20° C., it requires for solution 8 parts of dilute alcohol (0·883). On addition of a caustic alkali, it dissolves in spirit much more freely. It is plentifully soluble in acetone or benzol.

The composition of colophony agrees with the formula $C^{44}H^{62}O^{4}$. By shaking coarsely powdered colophony with warm dilute alcohol, it is converted into a crystalline body, *Abietic Acid*, $C^{44}H^{64}O^{5}$,—a result due simply to hydration. Under such treatment, colophony yields 80 to 90 per cent. of abietic acid,[2] and therefore consists chiefly of the anhydride of that acid. This is probably the case with the resins of other conifers. The living tree contains only the anhydride, for the fresh resinous juice is clear and amorphous after the expulsion of the oil; and when exposed to the air it loses oil, takes up water and solidifies as the crystalline acid, —a change which may easily be traced by the aid of the microscope, in drops taken direct from the trunk. Amorphous colophony retains its transparency even in a moist atmosphere, and appears to be capable of passing into the state of abietic acid, only when the assumption of the needful molecule of water is aided, in nature by the presence of the essential oil, or artificially by that of alcohol.

Colophony when boiled with alkaline solutions forms greasy salts of abietic acid, the so-callen *resin-soaps*, which are used as additions to other soaps.

Siewert's *Silvic Acid* is regarded by Maly (1864) as a product of the decomposition of abietic acid; and the *Pimaric*, *Pinic* and *Silvic Acids* of former investigators, as impure abietic acid. Pimaric acid however, which is the chief constituent of *Galipot*, appears to be decidedly

[1] For some particulars, see my notice in the *Jahresbericht* of Wiggers and Husemann for 1869, p. 36.—F. A. F.

[2] Flückiger in *loc. cit.* 1867. 36.—Most chemists assign to this acid the formula $C^{20}H^{30}O^{2}$, and call it *silvic acid*.

different, so far as we can judge from the experiments of Duvernoy (1865) and of one of ourselves (F.)

Abietic acid, as well as the unaltered coniferous resins, deviate the ray of polarized light, whereas American colophony, dissolved in acetone, is devoid of optical power.

Commerce—The supplies of turpentine are chiefly derived from the United States, but the trade has undergone a great change, as shown by the following figures, which represent the quantities imported in the several years:—

1869	1870	1871	1872
60,468 cwt.	51,257 cwt.	2,231 cwt.	1,000 cwt.

This greatly diminished importation of the crude article is partially explained by a larger importation of Oil of Turpentine and Rosin; but the increase is by no means sufficient to account for the vast diminution indicated by the above figures. The quantities of these latter articles imported into the United Kingdom during the year 1872 were as follows:—*Oil of Turpentine*, 220,292 cwt., value £470,085, six-sevenths being furnished by the United States of America and the remainder chiefly by France. *Rosin*, 919,494 cwt., value £492,246; of this quantity, the United States supplied nine-tenths, and France the larger part of the remainder.[1]

Uses—Turpentine, Common Frankincense and Colophony are ingredients of certain plasters and ointments. Oil of turpentine is occasionally administered internally as a vermifuge or diuretic, and applied externally as a stimulant. But these substances are immeasurably less important in medicine than in the arts.

Thus Americanum vel vulgare.

This substance, known among druggists as *Common Frankincense* or *Gum Thus*, is the resin which, as explained at p. 605, concretes upon the stems of the pines in the American turpentine orchards, and is there called *Scrape*. It corresponds to the *Galipot* or *Barras* of the French, which in old times supplied its place.

It is a semi-opaque, softish resin, of a pale yellow colour, smelling of turpentine; it is generally mixed with pine leaves, bits of wood and other impurities, so that it requires straining before it is used. By keeping, it becomes dry and brittle, of deeper colour and milder odour. Under the microscope, it exhibits a crystalline structure due to *Abietic Acid*, of which it chiefly consists. It is imported from America in barrels, but in insignificant quantities and only for the druggist's use. Sometimes, however, it is distilled as common turpentine.

Dry pine resin, of which Common Frankincense is the type, evolves when heated an agreeable smell; hence in ancient times it was commonly used in English churches in place of the more costly olibanum. At present it is scarcely employed except in a few plasters.

[1] *Annual Statement of the Trade of the U.K. for* 1872. pp. 53. 56. 60. 210.

TEREBINTHINA VENETA.

Terebinthina Laricina; Venice Turpentine, Larch Turpentine; F. *Térébenthine de Venise ou de Briançon, Térébenthine du mélèze;* G. *Venetianischer Terpenthin, Lärchen-Terpenthin.*

Botanical Origin—*Pinus Larix* L. (*Larix europæa* DC.), a tall forest tree of the mountains of Southern Central Europe, from Dauphiny through the Alps to Styria and the Carpathians, ascending to an elevation of 3000 to 5500 feet above the sea-level. It is largely grown in plantations in England and also, since 1738, in Scotland.

History—The turpentine of the larch was known to Dioscorides as imported from the Alpine regions of Gaul.[1] Pliny also was acquainted with it, for he correctly remarks that it does not harden. Galen in the 2nd century also mentions it, admitting that it may well be substituted for Chian turpentine (see p. 165), the true, legitimate *Terebinthina.* Yet even in the beginning of the 17th century many pharmacologists complained of such a substitution. Mattioli[2] gave an account of the method of collecting it about Trent in the Tirol, by boring the trees to the centre, which is true to the present day. It used formerly to be exported from Venice, then the great emporium for drugs of all kinds; the turpentine may even at times have been collected in the territories of the Venetian republic. We find it expressly called *Terebinthina Veneta* by Guintherus of Andernach.[3]

The name *larch* seems to belong to the turpentine rather than to the tree. Dioscorides says the resin is called by the natives *λάρικα,* and a similar name is mentioned by Galen. In Pasi's *Tariffa de pesi e misure,* 1521 (see Appendix), we find "*Termentina sive Larga,*"—and *larga* is still an Italian name for larch turpentine. The peasants of the Southern Tirol call it *Lerget,* and in Switzerland the common name in German is *Lörtsch.*

Extraction—Larch turpentine is collected in the Tirol, chiefly about Mals, Meran, Botzen and Trent. A very small amount is obtained occasionally in the Valais in Switzerland, and in localities in Piedmont and France where the larch is found. The resin is obtained from the heart-wood, by making in the spring a narrow cavity reaching to the centre of the stem at about a foot from the ground. This is then stopped up until the autumn of the same or of the following year, when it is opened and the resin taken out with an iron spoon. If only one hole is thus made, the tree yields about half a pound yearly without appreciable detriment. But if on the other hand a number of wide holes are made, and especially if they are left open, as was formerly the practice in the Piedmontese and French Alps, a larger product amounting to as much as 8 lb. is obtained annually, but the tree ceases to yield after some years, and its wood is much impaired in value.

Mohl, who witnessed the collection of this turpentine in the Southern

[1] Lib. i. cap. 92.

[2] *Comment. in libr. i. Dioscoridis,* Venetiis, 1565. 106.

[3] *De medicina veteri et nova etc.,* Basileae, 1571. 183.

Tirol,[1] observed that when a growing larch stem was sawn through, the resin flowed most abundantly from the heart-wood, and in smaller quantity, though somewhat more quickly, from the sap-wood, and that the bark contained but few resin-ducts. The practice of closing the cavities is adopted, not only for the sake of preserving the wood and for the greater convenience of removing the turpentine, but also because it tends to maintain the transparency and purity of the latter.

Description—Venice turpentine is a thick, honey-like fluid, slightly turbid, yet not granular and crystalline; it has a pale-yellowish colour and exhibits a slight fluorescence. Its odour resembles that of common turpentine, but is less powerful; its taste is bitter and aromatic. When exposed to the air, it thickens but slowly to a clear varnish, and hardens but very slowly when mixed with magnesia. Larch turpentine, though common on the Continent, is seldom imported into England,[2] and the article sold for it is almost always spurious.

Chemical Composition—Larch turpentine dissolves in spirit of wine, forming a clear liquid which reddens litmus; hot water agitated with it also acquires a faint acid reaction, due to formic and probably also to succinic acid. Glacial acetic acid, amylic alcohol, and acetone mix with it perfectly. By distillation it yields on an average 15 per cent. of essential oil of the composition, $C^{10}H^{16}$, which boils at 157° C., and when saturated with dry hydrochloric acid gas, easily produces crystals of the compound $C^{10}H^{16} + HCl$. The residual resin is soluble in two parts of warm alcohol of 75 per cent., and more copiously in concentrated alcohol.

Two parts of the turpentine diluted with one of benzol or acetone deviate the ray of polarized light 9·5° to the *right*. The essential oil deviates 6·4° to the *left;* the resin perfectly freed from volatile oil and dissolved in half its weight of acetone, deviates 12·6° to the *right* in a column 50 mm. long.

We have not succeeded in preparing a crystallized acid from the resin of Venice turpentine, although its composition according to *Maly* (1864) is the same as that of American colophony, which is easily transformed into crystallized abietic acid.

Uses—Venice turpentine appears to possess no medicinal properties that are not equally found in other substances of the same class, and as a medicine it has fallen into disuse. But in name at least it is in frequent requisition for horse and cattle medicines.

Adulteration—Alston (1740–60) said of Venice turpentine[3] that it is seldom found in the shops,—a remark equally true at the present day, for but few druggists trouble themselves to procure it genuine. The Venice turpentine usually sold is an artificial mixture of common resin and oil of turpentine, which may be easily distinguished from the product of the larch by the facility with which it dries when spread on a piece of paper,[4] and by its stronger turpentine smell.

[1] *Botanische Zeitung,* xvii. (1859) 329, abstracted in the *Jahresbericht* of Wiggers, 1859. 18.

[2] On one occasion I observed Venice Turpentine in a public drug sale in London, 21 barrels imported from Trieste being offered, 14 July, 1864.—D. H.

[3] *Lectures on the Materia Medica,* Lond. ii. (1770) 398.

[4] Thus if a thin layer of true Venice tur-

CORTEX LARICIS.

Larch Bark.

Botanical Origin—*Pinus Larix* L.—see p. 609.

History—The bark of the larch has long been known to possess astringent properties; hence it has been used in tanning. Gerarde,[1] who wrote near the close of the 16th century, likened it to that of the pine, which he described to be of a binding nature; but there is no evidence that it was an officinal drug.

About the year 1858 larch bark was recommended by Dr. Frizell of Dublin, and afterwards by other physicians, as a stimulating astringent and expectorant. In consequence of the favourable effects which have resulted from its use it has been included in the *Additions to the Pharmacopœia of* 1867.

Description—The bark that we have seen is in flattish pieces or large quills, externally reddish-brown. In those taken from older wood there is a large amount of an exfoliating corky coat, displaying as it is removed bright rosy tints, while the liber is of a different texture, slightly fibrous and whitish. The inner surface is smooth and of a pinkish-brown, or pale yellow. The bark breaks with a short fracture, exhaling an agreeable balsamic terebinthinous odour; it has a well-marked astringent taste. For medicinal use the inner bark is to be preferred.

Microscopic Structure—A transverse section exhibits resin-ducts, but far less numerous than in the bark of many allied trees. The medullary rays are not very distinct. Throughout the middle layer of the bark large isolated thick-walled cells of very irregular shape are scattered.

Chemical Composition—Larch bark has been examined by Stenhouse,[2] who finds it to contain a considerable amount of a peculiar tannin, yielding olive-green precipitates with salts of iron. The same chemist also discovered[3] in larch bark an interesting crystallizable substance called *Larixin* or *Larixinic Acid*, which has the composition $C^{10}H^{10}O^{5}$. It may be obtained by digesting the bark in water in 80° C. and evaporating the infusion to a syrupy consistence. From this, by still further cautious heating in a retort, the larixin may be distilled, during which operation some of it crystallizes on the inner surface of the receiver, the remainder being dissolved in the distilled liquor. From the latter it may be obtained in crystals by evaporation. The substance forms colourless crystals, sometimes as much as an inch long; it volatilizes even at 93° C., and melts at 153°. It requires about 88 parts of water for solution at 15° C., but more freely dissolves in boiling water or in alcohol. From ether, in which it is but sparingly soluble, it separates in brilliant crystals. The solutions have a bitterish astrin-

pentine and another of common turpentine be spread on two sheets of paper it will be found after the lapse of some weeks that the former cannot be touched without adhering to the fingers, while the latter will have become a dry, hard varnish.

[1] *Herball, enlarged by Johnson*, Lond. 1636. 1366.

[2] *Proceedings of the Royal Society*, xi. (1862) 404.

[3] *Phil. Trans.*, vol. 152 (1862) 53.—We write the name *Larixin* instead of *Larixine*, with the concurrence of Dr. Stenhouse.

gent taste and a slightly acid reaction, and assume a purple hue on addition of ferric chloride. When a solution of baryta is added to a concentrated solution of larixin, the latter being in excess, a bulky gelatinous precipitate falls; it is readily soluble in boiling water and is deposited again on cooling. Stenhouse failed to obtain it either from the bark of *Pinus Abies* L., or from that of *P. silvestris* L.

Uses—Larch bark, chiefly in the form of tincture, has been prescribed to check profuse expectoration in cases of chronic bronchitis; it has also been found useful in arresting internal hæmorrhage.

TEREBINTHINA CANADENSIS.

Balsamum Canadense; Canada Balsam, Canadian Turpentine; F. *Térébenthine ou Baume de Canada;* G. *Canada-Balsam.*

Botanical Origin—*Pinus balsamea* L. (*Abies balsamea* Marshall), the Balsam Fir or Balm of Gilead Fir, a handsome tree, 20 to 40 feet high, with a trunk 6 to 12 inches in diameter, sometimes attaining still larger dimensions, growing in profusion in the Northern and Western United States of America, Nova Scotia and Canada, but not observed beyond 62° N. lat. It resembles the Silver Fir of Europe (*Pinus Picea* L.), but has the bracts short-pointed and the cones more acute at each end.

Canada balsam is also furnished by *Pinus Fraseri* Pursh, the Small-fruited or Double Balsam Fir, a tree found on the mountains of Pennsylvania, Virginia, and southward on the highest of the Alleghanies.[1]

Pinus canadensis L. (*Abies canadensis* Michx.), the Hemlock Spruce or Pérusse, a large tree abundant in the same countries as *P. balsamea*, and extending throughout British America to Alaska, is said to yield a similar turpentine, which however has not yet been sufficiently examined. The Hemlock Spruce is of considerable importance on account of the resin collected from its trunk, and the essential oil distilled from its foliage, the latter operation being performed on a large scale in Madison County, New York. The inner bark of the tree is a valuable material for tanning.

History—The French, in whose possession Canada remained until the year 1763, were probably acquainted with Canada balsam long before this period. Yet no mention of it is found in Pomet's work, but in 1759 it was at Strassburg a current article of the pharmacy.[2] As to England, Lewis, in his *History of the Materia Medica* published in 1761, says that "*an elegant balsam,*" obtained from the Canada Fir, is sometimes brought into Europe under the name of *Balsamum Canadense.* Canada balsam was first introduced into the London Pharmacopœia in 1788. From the books of a London druggist, J. Gurney Bevan, we find that its wholesale price in 1776 was 4*s*., in 1788, 5*s*. per ℔.

Description—Canada balsam is a transparent resin of honey-like

[1] Asa Gray, *Botany of the Northern United States*, New York, 1866. 422.

[2] Flückiger, *Pharm. Journ.* vi. (1876). 1021.

consistence, and of a light straw-colour with a greenish tint. By keeping, it slowly becomes thicker and of a somewhat darker hue, but always retains its transparency. When carefully examined in direct sunlight, it exhibits a slight greenish fluorescence in the same degree as other turpentines or as copaiba; this optical power appears to increase if the balsam is exposed to a heat of about 200° C.

Canada balsam has a pleasant aromatic odour and bitterish, feebly acrid, not disagreeable taste. On account of its flavour it is sometimes called *Balm of Gilead*, but erroneously, as this latter is derived from a tree of the genus *Balsamodendron* growing in Arabia. We found a good commercial balsam to have a sp. gr. of 0·998 at 14·5° C., water at the same temperature being 1·000. Four parts, mixed with one of benzol and examined in a column of 50 mm. in length, deviated a ray of polarized light 2° to the right. The balsam is perfectly soluble in any proportion in chloroform, benzol, ether, or warm amylic alcohol; and the solution in each case reddens litmus. With sulphate of carbon it mixes readily, but the mixture is somewhat turbid. Glacial acetic acid, acetone or absolute alcohol dissolve the balsam partially, leaving, after ebullition and cooling, a considerable amount of amorphous residue. Colophony and Venice turpentine are completely dissolved by the liquids in question, as well as by spirit of wine containing 70 to 75 per cent. of alcohol.

Chemical Composition—Like all analogous exudations of the *Coniferæ*, Canada turpentine is a mixture of resins with an essential oil. If the latter is allowed to evaporate, the former are left as a transparent, somewhat tough and elastic mass. The proportion of the components is within certain limits, variable in different samples. The specimen beforementioned lost after an exposure in a steam-bath during several days, no less than 20 per cent of volatile oil, or even 24 per cent. if the experiment was made on a very small scale, as with 20 grammes or less in a thin layer.

By distillation with water, it is not easy to obtain more than 17 to 18 per cent. of essential oil. The resin in this case is a tough, elastic, non-transparent mass, retaining obstinately a large proportion of water, which can only be removed by keeping it for some time at a temperature of 100°–176° C.

The oil as obtained by distillation with water is colourless, and has the odour of common oil of turpentine rather than the agreeable smell of the balsam; it consists of an oil, $C^{10}H^{16}$, mixed with an insignificant proportion of an oxygenated oil, the presence of which may be proved by the slight evolution of hydrogen on addition of metallic sodium, after the oil has been freed from water by contact with fused chloride of calcium. After this treatment, a small proportion begins to distil at about 160°, but by far the larger part boils at 167° C., a small portion only distilling at last at 170° and above. The oil obtained at 167°, examined under the conditions already mentioned, has a sp. gr. of 0·863, and the power of rotating a ray of polarized light 5·6° to the left. The portion distilling at 160° does not differ in this respect; but that passing over at 170°, deviates the ray 7·2° to the left. The oil readily dissolves a large proportion of glacial acetic acid; an equal weight of each mixes perfectly at about 54° C., but some acetic acid separates on cooling.

The essential oil of Canada balsam, saturated with dry hydrochloric acid, does not yield a solid crystallizable compound; but this is easily obtained on addition of fuming nitric acid and gently heating, when the inside of the retort becomes covered by sublimed crystals of $C^{10}H^{16}+HCl$.

Thus this oil in its general characters bears a close resemblance to the essential oils of the cones of *Pinus Picea* L., and of the leaves of *P. Pumilio* Hänke, and to most of the French varieties of oil of turpentine, rather than to the American turpentine oils, which rotate to the right, and combine immediately with HCl to form a solid crystalline compound.

On the other hand, the resin of Canada balsam is dextrogyre: two parts of it, entirely deprived of essential oil and dissolved in one of benzol, deviating the ray 8·5° to the right. The optical powers of the two components (oil and resin) are therefore antagonistic.

The resin of Canada balsam consists however of two different bodies, 78·7 per cent. of it being soluble in boiling absolute alcohol, and 21·3 (in our specimen) remaining as an amorphous mass, readily soluble in ether. Neither the alcoholic nor the ethereal solution yields a crystalline residue if allowed to evaporate. They redden litmus, but we did not succeed in obtaining any crystallized resinous acid, crystals of which are formed if common turpentine or colophony is digested with dilute alcohol. Glacial acetic acid acts upon the resins like absolute alcohol. Caustic alkalis do not dissolve either the balsam or the resin; the former however is considerably thickened by incorporation with $\frac{1}{6}$ of its weight of recently calcined magnesia. If the mixture, moistened with dilute alcohol, is kept at 93° C. for some days and frequently stirred, a mass of hard consistence, finally translucent, results. Caustic ammonia heated with the balsam in a closed bottle, forms a thick milky jelly, which does not afterwards separate.

Hence, according to our investigations, 100 parts of Canada turpentine consist of

Essential oil, $C^{10}H^{16}$, with a very small proportion of an oxygenated oil	24
Resin soluble in boiling alcohol	60
Resin soluble only in ether	16

The result of Wirzen's examination of Canada balsam[1] are not in complete accordance with those here stated. He found 16 per cent. of oil and three different amorphous resins, one of which had the composition of abietic acid.

Production and Commerce—Canada balsam is obtained either by puncturing the vesicles which form under the suberous envelope of the trunk and branches, and collecting their fluid contents in a bottle, or by making incisions. It is obtained principally in Lower Canada, and is shipped from Montreal and Quebec, in kegs or large barrels. In the neighbourhood of Quebec, about 2000 gallons (20,000 lb.) used to be collected annually; but in 1868, owing to distress among the farmers, the quantity obtained was unusually large, and it was estimated that nearly 7000 gallons would be exported to England and the United

[1] *De balsamis et præsertim de Balsamo Canadense*, Helsingforsiæ, 1849,—abstracted in the *Jahresbericht* of Wiggers for 1849. 38.

States.[1] During a recent scarcity (1872–73) a sort of balsam from Oregon has been substituted in the American market for true Canada balsam.[2]

Uses—The medicinal properties of Canada balsam resemble those of copaiba and other terebinthinous oleo-resins, yet it is now rarely employed as a remedy. The balsam is much valued for mounting objects for the microscope, as it remains constantly transparent and uncrystalline. It is also used for making varnish.

TEREBINTHINA ARGENTORATENSIS.

Strassburg Turpentine; F. Térébenthine d'Alsace ou de Strasbourg, Térébenthine du sapin; G. Strassburger Terpenthin.

Botanical Origin—*Pinus Picea* L. (*Abies pectinata* DC.), the Silver Fir,[3] a large handsome tree, growing in the mountainous parts of Middle and Southern Europe from the Pyrenees to the Caucasus, and extending under a slightly different form (var. *β. cephalonica*) into continental Greece and the islands of Eubœa and Cephalonia.

History—Belon in his treatise *De Arboribus coniferis* (1553) described this turpentine, which is also briefly yet accurately noticed by Samuel Dale,[4] a learned apothecary of London and the friend of Sloane and Ray. It had a place in the London Pharmacopœia until 1788, when it was omitted from the materia medica.

Extraction—The oleo-resin of *P. Picea*, like that of *P. balsamea*, is contained in little swellings of the bark[5] of young stems, and is extracted by the tedious process of puncturing them and receiving in a suitable vessel the one or two drops which exude from each. It is still collected near Mutzig and Barr, in the Vosges (1878), though only to a very small extent.

Description—An authentic sample collected for one of us by the Surveyor of Forests in the Bernese Jura, Switzerland, resembles very closely Canada balsam, but is devoid of any distinct fluorescence. It has a light yellow colour, a very fragrant odour,[6] more agreeable than that of Canada balsam, and is devoid of the acrid bitterish taste of the latter.

We found our specimen to have sp. gr. of distilled water. It deviates a ray of polarized light 3° to the left, if examined either pure or diluted with a fourth of its weight of benzol, in the manner described at p. 610. Our drug is soluble in the same liquids as the Canadian, yet is miscible with glacial acetic acid, absolute alcohol and acetone, without leaving any considerable flocculent residue. It is even soluble in spirit of wine, the solution being but very little turbid. The solutions have an acid reaction.

[1] From information obligingly communicated by Mr. N. Mercer of Montreal and Mr. H. Sugden Evans of London.—See also *Proc. Am. Pharm. Assoc.*, 1877, page 337, abstracted in *Ph. Jour.* viii. (1878) 813.

[2] *Proceedings of the American Pharmaceutical Association*, Philadelphia, 1873. 119—also 1874. 433.

[3] *Sapin* in French; *Weisstanne* or *Edeltanne* in German.

[4] *Pharmacologia*, Lond. 1693. 395.

[5] See Morel, *Ph. Jour.* viii. (1877) 21.

[6] Hence it is sometimes called in French *Térébenthine au citron.*

Chemical Composition—After the complete desiccation of a small quantity, there remained 72·4 per cent. of a brittle, transparent resin, soluble in glacial acetic acid, but not entirely in absolute alcohol or in acetone. By submitting half a pound of the turpentine to distillation with water, we obtained 24 per cent. of essential oil, the remaining resin being when cold perfectly friable. The fresh oil, purified by sodium, deviates the ray of polarized light to the left, whereas the remaining resin, dissolved in half its weight of benzol, shows a weak dextrogyre rotation. The oil boils at 163° C. After having kept it for two years and a half in a well-stopped bottle, we find that it has become considerably thicker and now deviates to the right. If saturated with dry hydrochloric acid, the oil does not yield a solid compound.

This oil has nearly the same agreeable odour as the crude oleo-resin, yet the essential oil of the *cones* of the same tree is still more fragrant. The latter is one of the most powerfully deviating oils, the rotation being 51° to the left, and it is consequently extremely different from the oil obtained from the turpentine of the stem, though its composition is represented by the same formula, $C^{10}H^{16}$.

A peculiar sugar called *Abietite*, nearly related to mannite but having the composition $C^{12}H^{16}O^{6}$, has been detected by Rochleder[1] in the leaves of the Silver Fir.

Uses—Strassburg turpentine possesses the properties of common turpentine, with the advantage of a very agreeable odour. It was formerly held in great esteem, but has now become nearly forgotten.

PIX BURGUNDICA.

Pix abietina; Burgundy Pitch; F. *Poix de Bourgogne ou des Vosges, Poix jaune;* G. *Fichtenharz, Tannenharz.*

Botanical Origin—*Pinus Abies* L. (*Abies excelsa* DC.), the Norway Spruce Fir,[2] a noble tree attaining an elevation of 100–160 feet, widely distributed throughout Northern and the mountainous parts of Central Europe, but not indigenous to Great Britain, though extensively planted. In Russian Lapland it reaches at 68° N. lat. almost the extreme limit of tree-vegetation, while southward it extends to the Spanish Pyrenees. In the Alps it ascends to 6,000 feet above the level of the sea.

History—In accordance with the definition of the London Pharcopœias and the custom of English druggists the name *Burgundy Pitch* is restricted to the product of the above-named species. The pharmacologists of France use an equivalent term with the same limitations; but in other parts of the Continent *Pix Burgundica* has a wider meaning, and is allowed to include the turpentines of other *Coniferæ*. We here employ it in the English sense.

Parkinson, an apothecary of London and herbarist to King Charles I., speaks of "*Burgony Pitch*" as a thing well known in his time.[3] Dale in his *Pharmacologia* (1693) mentions *Pix Burgundica* as being imported into England from Germany, and it is also noticed by Salmon

[1] Wiggers and Husemann, *Jahresbericht*, 1868. 53.

[2] *Pesse* or *Epicéa* of the French; *Fichte* or *Rothtanne* of the Germans.

[3] *Theater of Plants*, 1640. 1542.

(1693), who says "it is brought to us out of Burgundy, Germany and other places near Strasburgh."[1]

Pomet, writing in Paris about the same period, discards the prefix *Burgundy* as a fiction, remarking that the best *Poix grasse* comes from Holland and Strassburg.[2]

Whether this resin ever was collected in Burgundy we are unable to determine. It may probably have acquired the name through having been brought into commerce from Switzerland and Alsace by way of Franche Comté, otherwise called Comté de Bourgogne or Haute Bourgogne.[3]

Burgundy pitch is enumerated among the materia medica of the London Pharmacopœia of 1677, and in every subsequent edition. In that of 1809 it was defined under the name of *Pix arida*, as the *prepared resin of Pinus Abies*.

Production—Burgundy pitch is produced in Finland, in the Black Forest in the Grand Duchy of Baden, Austria and Switzerland. On the estate of Baron Linder at Svarta near Helsingfors, it is obtained by melting the crude resin in contact with the vapour of water, and straining. The quantity annually produced there was stated in 1867 to be 35,000 kilogr. (689 cwt.);[4] that afforded by an establishment at Ilm in the same country amounted to 80,000 kilogr. (1,575 cwt.).[5]

In the neighbourhood of Oppenau and on the Kniebis mountain in the Grand Duchy of Baden the stems of the firs are wounded at equal distances by making perpendicular channels, 1½ inches wide and the same in depth. The resin which exudes from these channels is scraped off with an iron instrument made for the purpose, and purified by being melted in hot water and strained. This is performed in three or four small establishments at Oppenau and the neighbouring village of Löcherberg. In this state the resin, which is opaque and contains much moisture, is called *Wasserharz*. By further training and evaporating a portion of the water its quality is improved.

The manufacture in that part of Germany is on the decline, partly in consequence of the timber being injured by the wounding of the trees, so that the collecting of resin is not permitted in the large forests belonging to the governments of Baden and Würtemberg. We have had the opportunity of observing[6] that in the establishments in question French turpentine or *galipot*, imported from Bordeaux, as well as American rosin or colophony, are used in quantities certainly exceeding that of the resin grown on the spot.

In the middle of the last century some Burgundy pitch was produced, according to Duhamel,[7] in the present canton of Neuchâtel, but no such branch of industry is now pursued there, at least on a large scale. On the other hand, in the districts of Moutier and Delémont in the Bernese Jura this resin is still collected, though it is not known as *Burgundy Pitch*, but is termed simply *Poix blanche* (White Pitch).

[1] *Compleat English Physician*, 1693. 1031.

[2] *Hist. des Drogues*, Paris, 1694. part i. 287.

[3] Chabræus in his *Stirpium Sciagraphia* (1666) remarks that he had seen the *Pesse* [*P. Abies* L.] in great plenty "*in Burgundicis montibus*," yet makes no particular allusion to its yielding resin.

[4] *Pharm. Journ.* ix. (1876) 164; also in Hanbury's *Science Papers*, pp. 46 to 53.

[5] *Oesterreichischer Ausstellungs-Bericht*, x. (Wien, 1868) 471.

[6] I spent several days in the localities in 1873.—F. A. F.

[7] *Traité des Arbres*, etc. i. (1775) 12.

The surveyor of the forests of this district, which is one of the richest in *Pinus Abies*, has informed one of us that from 790 to 850 quintals are collected and exported to Basle, Zürich, Aarau and Vaud. The pitch is worth *in loco* (1868) 100 to 110 francs (£4 to £4 8*s.*) the *bosse* of 6 quintals. The quantities collected in other parts of Switzerland are even less considerable.

Description—Pure Burgundy pitch, of which we have numerous authentic specimens, is a rather opaque, yellowish-brown substance, hard and brittle when cold, yet gradually taking the form of the vessel in which it is kept. It is strongly adhesive, breaks with a clear conchoidal fracture, and has a very agreeable, aromatic odour, especially when heated. It does not exhibit a crystalline structure, although, as we have frequently observed, the resin on the stem of the tree is distinctly crystalline.

Burgundy pitch is readily soluble in glacial acetic acid, acetone, absolute alcohol, and even in alcohol of 75 per cent (sp. gr. 0·860), yet its solubility in these liquids is considerably altered by the presence of water or essential oil; and still more by the formation of abietic acid in the resin itself. The same influences also affect the melting point.

The crude resin of *Pinus Abies*,[1] deprived of essential oil and dissolved in one part of absolute alcohol, was found to deviate a ray of polarized light 3° to the left, in a column of 50 mm.; the essential oil deviated 8·5° to the same direction. The oil contains a small amount of an oxygenated oil. After treatment with sodium the oil which remains does not form a solid compound if saturated with hydrochloric acid.

Chemical Composition—The investigations of Maly mentioned at p. 607 afford a satisfactory elucidation of the chemical properties of the pinic resinous exudations. They all, according to that chemist, are mixtures of the same amorphous resin, $C^{44}H^{62}O^{4}$, with essential oils of the composition $C^{10}H^{16}$. These terebinthinous juices are collected and sold either in their natural state as *turpentine*, or deprived more or less completely of their volatile oil, in which condition they are represented by *Burgundy Pitch*, and finally by *rosin* or *colophony*.

The turpentines flowing down the stems of the trees gradually lose their transparency if allowed to dry slowly in the air, becoming at the same time harder and somewhat granular. This alteration is due to the incorporation of water, which at last is not only mixed with the components of the resinous juice, but to some extent combines chemically with the resin so as to transform it into a crystalline body having the characters of an acid. The fact is easily observed if clear drops of the turpentine of *Pinus silvestris*, *P. Abies* or *P. Picea* are collected in vials and kept perfectly dry. Thus treated these turpentines remain transparent, but the addition of water causes after a short time the formation of microscopic crystals of abietic acid, rendering them more or less opaque.

If turpentines are collected before they lose their essential oil by evaporation and oxidation, and before they have become crystalline, they can be retained perfectly transparent by distilling off the volatile oil without water. The distillation being most commonly carried on *with water*, the remaining resin is opaque.

[1] Collected by myself.—F. A. F.

Maly is of opinion that the same amorphous resin occurs in all the *Coniferæ*, and that it yields by hydration the same acid, namely *Abietic*, which has been described by former chemists as *Pinic, Silvic*, and *Pimaric* acids, all of which indeed are admitted to have the same composition. We must however remember that several sorts of turpentine, as Canada Balsam, appear incapable, according to our experiments, of yielding any crystalline resinoid compound whatever; and that their amorphous resin being but partially soluble is certainly not a homogeneous substance.

The crystals as formed naturally in the common turpentines do not exhibit precisely the same forms as those obtained artificially when the resins are agitated with warm diluted alcohol, as in the preparation of abietic acid. As to *Pimaric Acid*, we have prepared it in quantity from *galipot*, the resin of *Pinus Pinaster*, but have always found its crystalline character entirely different from that of abietic acid.[1]

We are inclined, therefore, to think that the composition of the resins of *Coniferæ* is not so uniform as Maly suggests. The remarkable variety of their essential oils is a fact which seems in favour of our view.

Uses—Burgundy pitch is prescribed as an ingredient of plasters, and thus employed is useful as a mild stimulant. In Germany it has some economic applications, one of which is the lining of beer casks, for which purpose a composition is used called *Brauerpech* (brewers' pitch), made by mixing it with colophony or *galipot*.

Adulteration—No drug is the subject of more adulteration than Burgundy pitch, so much so that the very name is understood by some pharmacologists to be that of a manufactured compound. The substance commonly sold in England is made by melting together colophony with palm oil or some other fat, water being stirred in to render the mixture opaque. In appearance it is very variable, different samples presenting different shades of bright or dull yellow or yellowish-brown. Many when broken exhibit numerous cavities containing air or water; all are more or less opaque, becoming in time transparent on the surface by the loss of water. Artificial Burgundy pitch is offered for sale in bladders; it has a weak terebinthinous odour, and is devoid of the peculiar fragrance of the genuine. The presence of a fatty oil is easily discovered by treatment with double its weight of glacial acetic acid, which forms a turbid mixture, separating by repose into two layers, the upper being oily.

PIX LIQUIDA.

Wood Tar; F. *Goudron végétal, Poix liquide;* G. *Holztheer, Fichtentheer.*

Botanical Origin—Tar is obtained by submitting the wood of the stems and roots of coniferous trees to dry or destructive distillation. That found in commerce is produced in Northern Europe, chiefly from two species, namely *Pinus silvestris* L. and *P. Ledebourii* Endl. (*Larix sibirica* Ledeb.). These trees constitute the vast forests of Arctic Europe and Asia.

[1] *Jahresbericht* of Wiggers and Husemann for 1867. 37.

History—Theophrastus gives a circumstantial description of the preparation of tar, which applies with considerable accuracy to the processes still practised in those districts where no improved methods of manufacture have yet been introduced.

Production—The great bulk of the vegetable tar used in Europe, and known in commerce as *Archangel* or *Stockholm Tar*, is prepared in Finland, Central and Northern Russia, and Sweden.

The process is conducted in the following manner:—vast stacks of pine wood consisting chiefly of the roots and lower portions of the trunks (the more valuable parts of the trees being used as timber), and containing as much as 30,000 to 70,000 cubic feet, are carefully packed together, and then covered with a thick layer of turf, moss, and earth, beaten down with heavy stampers. The whole stack of billets is constructed over a conical or funnel-like cavity made in the ground, if possible on the side of a hill, this arrangement being adopted for the purpose of carrying on a downward distillation. Fire being applied the combustion of the mass of wood has to be carried on very slowly and without flame in order to obtain the due amount of tar and a charcoal of good quality. During its progress the products, chiefly tar, collect in the funnel-like cavity, from which they are discharged by a tube into a cast-iron pan placed beneath the stack, or simply into hollow tree trunks. The time required for combustion varies from one to four weeks, according to the size of the stack.

During the last few years this rude process has been improved and accelerated by the introduction of rationally constructed wrought-iron stills, furnished with refrigerating condensers, as proposed in Russia by Hessel in 1861. By this mode of manufacture the yield in tar of pine wood is about 14 per cent. from stems, dried by exposure to the open air; and 16 to 20 per cent. from roots. Large quantities of pyroligneous acid and oil of turpentine are at the same time secured. The wood of the beech and of other non-coniferous trees appears not to afford more than 10 per cent. of tar, while turf yields only from 3 to 9 per cent.

Description—The numerous empyreumatic products which result from the destructive distillation of pine wood, and which we call *tar*, constitute a dark brown or blackish semi-liquid substance, of peculiar odour and sharp taste. When deprived of water and seen in thin layers, tar is perfectly transparent. The magnifying glass shows some of the varieties to contain colourless crystals of *Pyrocatechin*, scattered throughout the dark viscid substance, and to these tar owes its occasionally granular, honey-like consistence.[1] A gentle heat causes them to melt and mix with the other constituents.

True vegetable tar has always a decidedly acid reaction. It is readily miscible with alcohol, glacial acetic acid, ether, fixed and volatile oils, chloroform, benzol, amylic alcohol or acetone. It is soluble in caustic alkaline solutions, but not in pure water or watery liquids. The sp. gr. of tar from the roots of conifers is about 1·06 (Hessel) yet at a somewhat elevated temperature, it becomes lighter than warm water.

Water agitated with tar acquires a light yellowish tint, and the taste and odour of tar, as well as an acid reaction. On evaporation the

[1] The crystals are a pretty object for the microscope, when examined by polarized light.

solution becomes brown, and at last microscopic crystals are obtained with a brown residue like tar itself, which is no longer soluble in water. A microscopical examination of tar which has been exhausted with water, shows that all crystals have disappeared.

Chemical Composition—Dry wood may be heated to about 150° C. without decomposition; but at a more elevated temperature, it commences to undergo a change, yielding a large number of products, the nature and comparative quantity of which depend upon circumstances. If the process is carried on in a closed vessel, a residue will be got which has more or less resemblance to coal. By heating fir-wood enclosed with some water to 400° C., Daubrée (1857) obtained a coal-like substance, which yielded by a subsequent increase of temperature scarcely any volatile products.

The results are widely different if a process is followed which permits the formation of volatile bodies; and these substances are formed in largest proportion, if the heat acts quickly and intensely. At lower degrees of heat, more charcoal results and more water is evolved.

Among the volatile products of destructive distillation, those alone which are condensed at the ordinary temperature of the air are of pharmaceutical interest; and of these, chiefly the portion not soluble in water, or that which is called *Tar* or *Liquid Pitch*. The aqueous portion of the products consist principally of empyreumatic acetic acid, to which tar owes its acid reaction.

The tissue of wood is chiefly formed of cellulose, intimately combined with a saccharine substance, which may be separated if the wood is boiled with dilute acids. The remaining cellulose is however not yet pure, but is still united to a substance which, as shown by Erdmann,[1] is capable of yielding pyrocatechin.

It is well known that sugar subjected to an elevated temperature, yields a series of pyrogenous products; and the same fact is observed if purified cellulose is heated in similar manner. But for tar-making, wood is preferred which is impregnated with resins and essential oils, and these latter furnish another series of empyreumatic products. From these circumstances, the components of wood-tar are of an extremely complicated character, which is still more the case when other woods than those of conifers form part of the material submitted to distillation. In the case of beech-wood, *Creasote* is formed, which is obtained only in very small quantity from the *Coniferæ*. Volatile alkaloids and carbolic acid, which are largely produced in the destructive distillation of coal, appear not to be present in wood-tar.

The components of the latter may be considered under two heads:—first, the *lighter aqueous portion*, which separates from the other products of distillation, forming what is called *Impure Pyroligneous Acid*. This contains chiefly acetic acid and *Methyl Alcohol* or *Wood Naphtha*, CH^4O; *Acetone*, C^3H^6O; besides other liquid products abundantly soluble in water and acetic acid. In this portion, some pyrocatechin also occurs.

The second class of pyrogenous products of wood consists of a homologous series of liquid hydrocarbons, sparingly soluble in water, and which therefore are chiefly retained in the heavy layer below the pyroligneous acid, forming the proper wood-tar. The liquid in question

[1] Liebig, *Annalen der Chemie u. Pharmacie*, Suppl. v. (1867) 229.

furnishes *Toluol* or *Toluene*, C^7O^8 (boiling point 114° C.), *Xylole* C^8H^{10}, and several other analogous substances.

If tar is redistilled, an elevated temperature being used towards the end of the process, some crystallizable solid bodies are obtained, the most important of which is that called *Paraffin*, having the formula C^nH^{2n+2}, *n* varying from 20 to 24.

The crystals already mentioned as occurring in tar are *Pyrocatechin*. They are easily sublimed at some degrees above their fusing point (104° C.), or removed by acetic acid, in which as well as in water they are readily soluble. Hence in some sorts of tar this substance does not occur, it having probably been removed by water.

Pyrocatechin, $C^6H^4(OH)^2$, can be obtained by the destructive distillation of many other substances, as catechu, kino, the extracts of rhatany and bearberry leaves, and other extracts rich in that form of tannin which produces *greenish* (not *blue-black*) precipitates in salts of iron. It is extracted from the granular sorts of wood-tar, by exposing them at a proper temperature to a current of heated dry air, or by exhausting them with water. Ether when shaken with the concentrated aqueous solution and left to evaporate, leaves colourless crystals of pyrocatechin which after purification are devoid of acid reaction. They have a peculiar burning persistent taste, and are very pungent and irritating when allowed to evaporate. A solution of pyrocatechin yields with perchloride of iron a dark green coloration changing to black after a few moments, and becoming red on the addition of potash. This mixture finally acquires a magnificent violet hue, like a solution of alkaline permanganate. No alteration is produced in a solution of pyrocatechin by protosalts of iron.

Among the few medicinal preparations of tar, is *Tar Water*, called *Aqua vel Liquor Picis*, made by agitating wood-tar with water. The presence in it of pyrocatechin is easily proved by the above-mentioned reactions, or by a few drops of red chromate of potassium, which produces a brownish black colouration. It may hence be inferred that pyrocatechin is perhaps the active ingredient in tar-water, and that for making this liquid the granular, crystalline sorts of tar should be preferred.[1]

Commerce—Tar as well as pitch is manufactured in Finland, and shipped from various ports in the Gulf of Bothnia, as Uleaborg, Gamla Carleby, Jacobstad, Ny Carleby and Christinestad ; also from Archangel and Onega on the White Sea. Some tar is also produced in Volhynia, and finds its way by the Dnieper to the Black Sea.

The North of Sweden likewise produces tar, chiefly about Umea and Lulea, the distillation being now performed in well-constructed apparatus of iron.

The pine forests of North America afford tar and pitch. Wilmington in North Carolina exported in 1871, 25,260 barrels of tar, and 3788 barrels of pitch.[2]

The imports of tar into the United Kingdom in 1872, were 189,291

[1] We may suppose that the authors of the French *Codex* were not of this opinion, inasmuch as in making *Eau de Goudron*, they order that the liquid obtained by the first maceration of the tar, shall be thrown away.

[2] Consul Walker, *Report on the Trade of North and South Carolina—Consular Reports* presented to Parliament, May, 1872.

barrels, valued at £218,339. Of this quantity 145,483 barrels were shipped from the northern ports of Russia.

The barrels in which tar arrives hold about 30 gallons. Smaller sized vessels termed *half-barrels* are also used, though less frequently.

Uses—In medicine of no great importance: an ointment of tar is a common remedy in cutaneous diseases, and tar water is sometimes taken internally. The consumption of tar in ship-building and for the preservation of fences, sufficiently explains the large importations.

Other Varieties of Tar.

Juniper Tar, *Pyroleum Oxycedri, Oleum Juniperi empyreumaticum, Oleum Cadinum, Huile de Cade*.—This is a tar originally obtained by the destructive distillation of the wood of the *Cade, Juniperus Oxycedrus* L., a shrub or small tree, native of the countries bordering the Mediterranean. It was for centuries used in the South of France as an external remedy, chiefly for domestic animals, but had fallen into complete oblivion until ten years ago, when it began to be prescribed in skin complaints.

The *Huile de Cade* now in use, is transparent and devoid of crystals. It is somewhat thinner than Swedish tar, but closely agrees with it in other respects. It is imported from the Continent, but where made and from what wood we know not. *Huile de Cade* is mentioned by Olivier de Serres,[1] a celebrated French writer on agriculture of the 16th century; it is named by Parkinson[2] in 1640; also by Pomet,[3] in whose time (1694) it was rarely genuine, common tar being sold in its place.

Beech Tar—Tar is also manufactured from the wood of the beech, *Fagus silvatica* L., and has a place in some pharmacopœias as the best source of creasote.

Birch Tar—is made to a small extent in Russia, where it is called *Dagget*, from the wood of *Betula alba* L. It contains an abundance of pyrocatechin, and is esteemed on account of its peculiar odour well known in the Russia leather. A purified oil of birch tar is sold by the Leipzig distillers.

PIX NIGRA.

Pix sicca vel solida vel navalis; Pitch, Black Pitch; F. *Poix noire;* G. *Schiffspech, Schusterpech, Schwarzes Pech.*

Botanical Origin—see *Pix liquida.*

Production—When the crude products of the dry distillation of pine wood, as described in the previous article, are submitted to re-distillation, the following results are obtained. The first 10 to 15 per cent. of volatile matter consists chiefly of methylic alcohol and acetone. A higher temperature causes the vaporization of the acetic acid, while the still retains the tar. This last, subjected to a further distillation, may be separated into a liquid portion called *Oil of Tar* (*Oleum Picis liquidæ*), and a residuum which, on cooling, hardens and forms the

[1] *Théâtre d'Agriculture*, Paris, 1600. 941.

[2] *Theatrum Botanicum*, 1033.

[3] *Hist. des Drogues*, Paris, 1694. part i. chap. xii. xiv.

product under notice, namely *Black Pitch*. Again heated to a very elevated temperature, it is capable of yielding paraffin, anthracene and naphthalene.

Description—Pitch is an opaque-looking, black substance, breaking with a shining conchoidal fracture, the fragments showing at the thin translucent edges a brownish colour. No trace of distinct crystallization is observable when very thin fragments are examined, even by polarized light. Pitch has a peculiar disagreeable odour, rather different from that of tar. Its alcoholic solution has a feeble taste somewhat like that of tar, but pitch itself when masticated is almost tasteless. It softens by the warmth of the hand, and may then be kneaded. It readily dissolves in those liquids which are solvents of tar. Alcohol of 75 per cent. acts freely on it, leaving behind in small proportion a dark viscid residue. The brown solution reddens litmus paper, and yields a dingy brownish precipitate with perchloride of iron, and whitish precipitates with alcoholic solution of neutral acetate of lead, or with pure water. Pitch dissolves in solution of caustic potash, evolving an offensive odour.

Chemical Composition—From the method in which pitch is prepared, we may infer that it contains some of the less volatile and less crystallizable compounds found in tar. Ekstrand (1875) extracted from it *Retene*, $C^{18}H^{18}$, a colourless, inodorous crystalline substance, melting at 90° C.

The pitch of beechwood boiled with a caustic alkali, yields a fœtid volatile oil; when this solution is acidulated, fatty volatile acids are evolved. These principles however have not yet been isolated either from the pitch of pine or beech. The whitish compound formed by acetate of lead in an alcoholic solution of pitch deserves investigation, and perhaps might be the starting point for acquiring a better knowledge of the chemistry of this substance.

Commerce—The same countries that produce tar produce also pitch. The quantity of the latter imported into the United Kingdom during 1872 was 35,482 cwt., four-fifths of which were supplied by Russia. Pitch is also manufactured from tar in Great Britain.

Uses—Pitch is occasionally administered in the form of pills, or externally as an ointment; but its medicinal properties are, to say the least, very questionable.

FRUCTUS JUNIPERI.

Baccæ Galbuli Juniperi; Juniper Berries; F. *Baies de Genièvre;* G. *Wacholderbeeren, Kaddigbeeren.*

Botanical Origin—*Juniperis communis* L., a diœcious evergreen, occurring in Europe from the Mediterranean to the Arctic regions, throughout Russian Asia as far as Sachalin, and in the north-western Himalaya, where it is ascending in Kashmir at 5400 feet, in Lahoul to 12,500, on the upper Bias and in Gurhwal to 14,000 feet. It abounds in the islands of Newfoundland, Saint Pierre, and Miquelon, and is also found in Continental North America. Dispersed over this vast area the Common Juniper presents several varieties. In England and in the greater part of Europe it forms a bushy shrub from 2 to 6 feet high, but in the interior of Norway and Sweden it becomes a small forest tree of 30 to 36 feet, often attaining an age of hundreds of years.[1] In high mountain regions of temperate Europe and in Arctic countries it assumes a decumbent habit (*Juniperus nana* Willd.), rising only a few inches above the soil.

History—The fruits of juniper, though by no means exclusively those of *J. communis*, were commonly used in medicine by the Greek and Roman as well as by the Arabian physicians; they had a place among the drugs of the Welsh "physicians of Myddvai" (see Appendix), and are mentioned in some of the earliest printed herbals. The oil was distilled by Schnellenberg[2] as early as 1546.

Popular uses were formerly assigned in various parts of Europe to juniper berries. They were employed as a spice to food;[3] and a spirit, of which wormwood was an ingredient, was obtained from them by fermentation and distillation. The spirit called in French *Genièvre* became known in English as *Geneva*, a name subsequently contracted into *Gin*.[4]

Description—The flowers form minute axillary catkins; those of the female plant consist of 3 to 5 whorls of imbricated bracts. Of these the uppermost three soon become fleshy and scale-like, and alternate with three upright ovules having an open pore at the apex. After the flowers have faded these three fleshy bracts grow together to form a berry-like fruit termed a *galbulus*, which encloses three seeds. The three points and sutures of the fruit-scales are conspicuous in the upper part of the young fruit; but after maturity the sutures alone are visible, forming a depressed mark at its summit. A small point, surrounded by two or three trios of minute bracts, indicates the base of the fruit.

This fruit or pseudo-berry remains ovate and green during its first year, and it is not until the second autumn that it becomes ripe. It is then spherical, $\frac{3}{10}$ to $\frac{4}{10}$ of an inch in diameter, of a deep purplish colour, with a blue-grey bloom. Its internal structure may be thus described:—beneath the thin epicarp there is a loose yellowish-brown sarcocarp, enclosing large cavities, the oil-ducts; the three hard seeds lying close together, triangular and sharp-edged at the top, are attached to the sarcocarp at their outer sides, and only as far as the lower half. The upper half, which is free, is covered by a thin membrane. In the longitudinal furrows of the hard testa towards the lower half of the seed are small prominent sacs growing out into the sarcocarp. Each seed bears on its inner side 1 or 2, and on its convex outer surface 4 to 8 of these sacs, which in old fruits contain the resinified oil in an amorphous colourless state.

Juniper berries when crushed have an aromatic odour, and a spicy, sweetish, terebinthinous taste.

Microscopic Structure—The outer layer of the fruit consists of a colourless transparent cuticle, which covers a few rows of large cubic

[1] Schübeler, *Culturpflanzen Norwegens*, Christiania, 1873–1875. 140, with fig.

[2] *Artzneybuch*, Königsberg, 1556. 35.

[3] Valmont de Bomare, *Dict. d'Hist. nat.* ii. (1775) 45.

[4] The gin distilled in Holland is flavoured with juniper berries, yet, as we are told, but very slightly, only 2 lb. being used to 100 gallons.

or tabular cells having thick, brown, porous walls. These cells contain a dark granular substance and masses of resin. The sarcocarp, which in the ripe state consists of large, elliptic, thin-walled, loosely coherent cells, contains chlorophyll, drops of essential oil, and a crystalline substance soluble in alcohol,—no doubt a stearoptene. Before maturity it likewise contains starch granules and large oil-cells. This tissue is traversed by very small vascular bundles containing annulated and dotted vessels.

Chemical Composition—The most important constituent of juniper berries is the volatile oil, obtainable to the extent of 0·4 to 1·2 per cent. The latter amount is obtained from Hungarian, 0·7 per cent. from German fruits.[1] It is a mixture of levogyre oils, the one of which having the composition $C^{10}H^{16}$ boils at 155° C.; the prevailing portion of the oil, boiling at about 200°, consists of hydrocarbons, which are polymeric with terpene, $C^{10}H^{16}$. The crude oil as distilled by us deviated 3°·5 to the left in a column of 50 mm.

By passing nitrosyl chloride gas, NOCl, into it, Tilden (1877) obtained from the portion boiling below 160° the crystallized compound $C^{10}H^{16}$ (NOCl), which is yielded by all the terpenes.

Another important constituent of juniper berries is the glucose, of which Trommsdorff (1822) obtained 33 per cent., while Donath (1873) found 41·9, and Ritthausen (1877) not more than 16 per cent. in the berries deprived of water. Of albuminoid substances about 5 per cent. are present, of inorganic matters 3 to 4 per cent. The fruit, moreover, contains also according to Donath small amounts of formic, acetic, and malic acids, besides resin.

Collection and Commerce—Juniper berries are largely collected in Savoy, and in the departments of the Doubs and Jura in France, whence they find their way to the hands of the Geneva druggists. They are also gathered in Austria, the South of France and Italy. In Hamburg price-currents they are quoted as *German* and *Italian*. The largest supplies are apparently furnished by Hungaria.

Uses—The berries and the essential oil obtained from them are reputed diuretic, yet are not often prescribed in English medicine.

HERBA SABINÆ.

Cacumina vel Summitates Sabinæ; Savin or Savine; F. *Sabine;* G. *Sevenkraut.*

Botanical Origin—*Juniperus Sabina* L., a woody evergreen shrub, usually of small size and low-growing, spreading habit, but in some localities erect and arborescent.

It occurs in the Southern Alps of Austria (Tirol) and Switzerland (Visp or Vièges and Stalden in the Valais, also in Grisons and Vaud), and in the adjacent mountains of France and Piedmont, ascending to elevations of 4,000 to 5,000 feet. It is also found in the Pyrenees, Central Spain, Italy and the Crimea; likewise in the Caucasus, where it reaches 12,000 feet above the sea level. Eastward it extends to the Elburs range, south of the Caspian, and throughout Southern Siberia, where it

[1] According to Messrs. Schimmel & Co. (see p. 306, note 2.)

ascends in the Balkhasch and Alatau mountains to 8,600 feet. In North America it has been gathered on the banks of the river Saskatchewan, at Lake Huron, in Newfoundland, and in Saint Pierre and Miquelon. There are, however, a few very closely allied species which may occasionally have been confounded with savin.

History—Savin is mentioned as a veterinary drug by Marcus Porcius Cato,[1] a Roman writer on husbandry who flourished in the second century B.C.; and it was well known to Dioscorides (under the name of βράθυ) and Pliny. The plant, which is frequently named in the early English leech-books written before the Norman Conquest,[2] may probably have been introduced into Britain by the Romans. Charlemagne, A.D. 812, ordered that it should be cultivated on the imperial farms of Central Europe. Its virtues as a stimulating application to wounds and ulcers are noticed in the verses of Macer Floridus,[3] composed in the 10th century.

Description—The medicinal part of savin is the young and tender green shoots, stripped from the more woody twigs and branches. These are clothed with minute scale-like rhomboid leaves, arranged alternately in opposite pairs. On the younger twigs they are closely adpressed, thick, concave, rounded on the back, in the middle of which is a conspicuous depressed oil gland. As the shoots grow older the leaves become more pointed and divergent from the stem. Savin evolves, when rubbed or bruised, a strong and not disagreeable odour. The blackish fruit or *galbulus* resembling a small berry, $\frac{2}{10}$ of an inch in diameter, grows on a short recurved stalk, and is covered with a blue bloom. It is globular, dry, but abounding in essential oil, and contains 1 to 4 little bony nuts.

To mycologists, *Juniperus Sabina*, at least in the cultivated state, is interesting on account of the parasitic fungus *Podisoma fuscum* Duby, the mycelium of which produces, on the leaves of the pear-trees, the so-called *Roestelia cancellata* Rebentisch.

Chemistry—The odour of savin is due to an essential oil, of which the fresh tops afford 2 to 4 per cent., and the berries about 10 per cent. Examined in a column 50 millimetres long it was found to deviate the ray of polarized light 27° to the right, the oil used having been distilled by one of us in London from the fresh plant cultivated at Mitcham. The same result was obtained from the oil abstracted ten years previously from savin collected wild on the Alps of the Canton de Vaud, Switzerland. We find that, by the prolonged action of the air, if the oil is kept in a vessel not carefully closed, the rotatory power after the lapse of years is greatly reduced. Savin oil, according to Tilden (1877), yields a small amount of an oil boiling at 160°, which answers to the formula $C^{10}H^{16}O$. The greater part of the oil was found by that chemist to boil above 200° C. Tilden asserts that no terpene is present in the oil of savin; we have not been able to obtain from it a crystallized hydrochloride. Savin tops contain traces of tannic matter.

[1] Cap. lxx. (*Bubus medicamentum*).

[2] Cockayne, *Leechdoms, etc., of Early England*, ii. (1865) xii.

[3] Choulant, *Macer Floridus de viribus herbarum*, Lipsiæ, 1832. 48. . . . "Duplum si desunt *cinnama* poni In medicamentis iubet *Oribasius* auctor."

Uses—Savin is a powerful uterine stimulant, producing in overdoses very serious effects. It is but rarely administered internally. An ointment of savin, which from the chlorophyll it contains is of a fine green colour, is used as a stimulating dressing for blisters.

Substitutes—There are several species of juniper which have a considerable resemblance to savin; and one of them, commonly grown in gardens and shrubberies, is sometimes mistaken for it. This is *Juniperus virginiana* L., the *Red Cedar* or *Savin* of North America. In its native country it is a tree, attaining a height of 50 feet or more, but in Britain it is seldom more than a large shrub, of loose spreading growth, very different from the low, compact habit of savin.[1] The foliage is of two sorts, consisting either of minute, scale-like, rhomboid leaves like those of savin, more rarely of elongated, sharp, divergent leaves a quarter of an inch in length, resembling those of common Juniper. Both forms often occur on the same branch. The plant is much less rich in essential oil than true savin,[2] for which it is sometimes substituted in the United States.

The foliage of *Juniperus phœnicea* L., a Mediterranean species, has some resemblance to savin for which it is said to be sometimes substituted,[3] but it is quite destitute of the peculiar odour of the latter. The specific name of the former alludes to its *red* fruit, from φοινίκιος, purple.

[1] We have examined numerous herbarium specimens (wild) of *J. virginiana* and *J. Sabina*, but except difference of stature and habit, can observe scarcely any characters for separating them as species. The fruit stalk in *J. virginiana* is often pendulous as in *J. Sabina*. Each plant has two forms,—arboreous and fruticose.

[2] This we ascertained by distilling under precisely similar conditions 6 lbs. 6 oz. of the fresh shoots of each of the two plants, *Juniperus Sabina* and *J. virginiana*: the first gave 9 drachms of essential oil, the second only ½ a drachm. The latter was of a distinct and more feeble odour, and a different dextrogyre power. In America the oil of *J. virginiana* is known as "*Cedar Oil*," and used as a taenifuge. It contains a crystallizable oxygenated portion. This oil however is afforded by the wood. Red Cedar wood from Florida is stated by Messrs. Schimmel & Co. (see p. 306) to afford as much as 4 to 5 per cent. of that oil.

[3] *Bonplandia*, x. (1862) 55.

Monocotyledons.

CANNACEÆ.

AMYLUM MARANTÆ.

Arrowroot.

Botanical Origin—*Maranta arundinacea*,[1] L.—An herbaceous branching plant, 4 to 6 feet high, with ovate lanceolate, puberulous or nearly glabrous leaves, and small white flowers, solitary or in lax racemes. It is a native of the tropical parts of America from Mexico to Brazil, and of the West Indian Islands; and under the slightly different form known as *M. indica* Tussac, it occurs in Bengal, Java and the Philippines. This Asiatic variety is now found in the West Indies and Tropical America, but apparently as an introduced plant.[2]

History—The history of arrowroot is comparatively recent. Passing over some early references of French writers on the West Indies to an *Herbe aux flèches*, which plant it is impossible to identify with *Maranta*, we find in Sloane's catalogue of Jamaica plants (1696), *Canna Indica radice alba alexipharmaca*. This plant, discovered in Dominica, was sent thence to Barbadoes and subsequently to Jamaica, it being, says Sloane, "*very much esteemed for its alexipharmack qualities.*" It was observed, he adds, that the native Indians used the root of the plant with success against the poison of their arrows, "*by only mashing and applying it to the poison'd wounds*": and further, that it cures the poison of the manchineel (*Hippomane Mancinella* L.), of the wasps of Guadaloupe, and even stops "*a begun gangreen.*"[3]

Patrick Browne (1756) notices the reputed alexipharmic virtues of *Maranta*, which was then cultivated in many gardens in Jamaica, and

[1] Fig. in Bentley and Trimen's *Med. Plants*, part 23 (1877).

[2] We accept the opinion of Körnicke (*Monographiæ Marantaccarum Prodromus, Bull. de la Soc. imp. des Naturalistes de Moscou*, xxxv. 1862, i.) that *Maranta arundinacea* L. and *M. indica* Tuss. are one and the same species. Grisebach maintains them as distinct (*Flora of the British West Indian Islands*, 1864, 605), allowing both to be natives of Tropical America; but he fails to point out any important character by which they may be distinguished from each other. According to Miquel (*Linnæa*, xviii. 1844. 71) the plant in the herbarium of Linnæus labelled *M. arundinacea*, is *M. indica*. We have ourselves made arrowroot from the fresh rhizomes of *M. arundinacea*, in order to compare it with an authentic specimen obtained in Java from *M. indica*: no difference could be found between them.

[3] Sloane, *Catal. plant. quæ in ins. Jamaica sponte proveniunt, vel vulgò coluntur*, Lond. 1696. 122; also *Hist. of Jamaica*, i. (1707) 253.

says that the root "*washed, pounded fine and bleached, makes a fine flour and starch*,"—sometimes used as food when provisions are scarce.[1]

Hughes, when writing of Barbadoes in 1750, describes arrowroot as a very useful plant, the juice mixed with water and drunk being regarded as "*a preservative against any poison of an hot nature*"; while from the root the finest starch is made, far excelling that of wheat.[2] The properties of *Maranta arundinacea* as a counter-poison are insisted upon at some length by Lunan,[3] who concludes his notice of the plant by detailing the process for extracting starch from the rhizome.

Arrowroot came into use in England about the commencement of the present century, the supplies being obtained, as it would appear, from Jamaica.[4]

The statements of Sloane, which are confirmed by Browne and Lunan, plainly indicate the origin and meaning of the word *arrowroot*, and disprove the notion of the learned C. F. Ph. von Martius (1867) that the name is derived from that of the Arnac or Aroaquis Indians of South America, who call the finest sort of fecula they obtain from the Mandioc *Aru-aru*. It is true that *Maranta arundinacea* is known at the present day in Brazil as *Araruta*, but the name is certainly a corruption of the English word *arrowroot*, the plant according to general report having been introduced.[5]

Manufacture—For the production of arrowroot, the rhizomes are dug up after the plant has attained its complete maturity, which in Georgia is at the beginning of winter. The scales which cover them are removed and the rhizomes washed; the latter are then ground in a mill, and the pulp is washed on sieves, or in washing machines constructed for the purpose, in order to remove from it the starch. This is allowed to settle down in pure water, is then drained and finally dried with a gentle heat. Instead of being crushed in a mill, the rhizomes are sometimes grated to a pulp by a rasping machine.

In all stages of the process for making arrowroot, nice precautions have to be taken to avoid contamination with dust, iron mould, insects, or anything which can impart colour or taste to the product. The rhizome contains about 68 per cent. of water, and yields about a fifth of its weight of starch.[6]

Description—Arrowroot is a brilliant white, insipid, inodorous, powder, more or less aggregated into lumps which seldom exceed a pea in size; when pressed it emits a slight crackling sound. It exhibits the general properties of starch, consisting entirely of granules which are subspherical, or broadly and irregularly egg-shaped; when seen in water they show a distinct stratification in the form of fine concentric rings around a small star-like hilum. They have a diameter of 5 to 7 mkm. when observed in the air or under benzol. If the water in which they

[1] *Civil and Natural History of Jamaica*, 1756. 112. 113.

[2] *Natural History of Barbados*, 1750. 221.

[3] *Hortus Jamaicensis*, i. (1814) 30.

[4] Thus in 1799 there were exported from Jamaica 24 casks and boxes of "*Indian Arrow-root*."—Renny, *Hist. of Jamaica*, 235.

[5] Since the above was written, the following lines bearing on this question have been received from Mr. Spruce:—". . I know not Martius' derivation of '*arrowroot*.' On the Amazon it is called '*ararúta*'—plainly a corruption of the English name, and explained by the fact that it was first cultivated, as I was told, from tubers obtained in the East Indies."

[6] This was in the German colony of Blumenau in Southern Brazil—Eberhard, *Arch. der Pharm.* 134 (1868) 257.

lie be cautiously heated on the object-stage of the microscope, the tumefaction of the granules will be found to begin exactly at 70° C. Heated to 100° C. with 20 parts of distilled water, arrowroot yields a semitransparent jelly of somewhat earthy taste and smell. By hydrochloric acid of sp. gr. 1·06, arrowroot is but imperfectly dissolved at 40° C.

The specific gravity of all varieties of starch is affected by the water which they retain at the ordinary temperature of the air. Arrowroot after prolonged exposure to an atmosphere of average moisture, and then kept at 100° C. till its weight was constant, was found to have lost 13·3 per cent. of water. On subsequent exposure to the air, it regained its former proportion of water.

Weighed in any liquid which is entirely devoid of action on starch, as petroleum or benzol, the sp. gr. of arrowroot was found by one of us to be 1·504; but 1·565 when the powder had been previously dried at 100° C.

Microscopic Structure of Arrowroot and of Starch in general.—The granules are built up of layers,—a structure which may be rendered evident by the gradual action of chloride of calcium, chromic acid, or an ammoniacal solution of cupric oxide. When one of these liquids in a proper state of dilution is made to act upon starch, or when for that purpose a liquid is chosen which does not act upon it energetically, such as diastase, bile, pepsin, or saliva, it is easy to obtain a residue, which according to Nägeli, is no longer capable of swelling up in boiling water, nor is immediately turned blue by iodine, except on the addition of sulphuric acid; but which is dissolved by ammoniacal cupric oxide. These are the essential properties of cellulose; and this residue has been regarded as such by Nägeli, while the dissolved portion has been distinguished as *Granulose* (Maschke, 1852).

C. Nägeli in his important monograph on starch[1] has described the action of saliva when digested with starch for a day, at a temperature of 40° to 47° C.; he says that the residue is a skeleton, corresponding in form to the original grain but somewhat smaller, light, and very mobile in water. He concludes that its interstitial spaces must have been previously filled with granulose.

This experiment, which has been repeated by one of us (F.), does not in our opinion warrant all the inferences that Nägeli has drawn from it: it is true that many separate parts of the grain are dissolved by the saliva, while others have disappeared down to a mere film, and others again have been attacked in a very irregular manner. But we cannot agree with the statement that anything comparable to a skeleton of the grain has been left. After longer action at a higher temperature, which however must not exceed 65° C., a more copious dissolution of the starch, either by saliva or by bile, takes place; but in no case is it complete.[2]

Chemistry of Starch—Its composition answers to the formula $(C^6H^{10}O^5)^2+3\ OH^2$, or when dried at 100° C., $C^6H^{10}O^5$. Musculus however showed, in 1861, that by the action of dilute acids or of *Diastase*,

[1] *Die Stärkekörner*, Zürich, 1858. 4°, also W. Nägeli, *Stärkegruppe, etc.*, Leipzig, 1874.

[2] Further particulars on this question may be found in my paper *Ueber Stärke und Cellulose—Archiv der Pharmacie*, 196 (1871) 7.—F. A. F.

starch is resolved into *Dextrin*, $C^{12}H^{20}O^{10}$, and *Dextrose*, $C^{6}H^{12}O^{6}$, with which decomposition, the formula, $C^{18}H^{32}O^{16}$, would be more in accord. Sachsse (1877) on the other hand advocates the formula $C^{36}H^{62}O^{31}$ + 12 OH^{2}.

Cold water is not without action on starch; if the latter be continuously triturated with it, the filtrate, in which no particles can be detected by the microscope, will assume a blue colour on addition of iodine, without the formation of a precipitate. The proportion of starch thus brought into solution is infinitely small, and always at the expense of the integrity of the grains. It is even probable that the solution in this case is due to the minute amount of heat, which must of necessity be developed by the trituration.

Certain reagents capable of attacking starch act upon it in very different ways. The action in the cold of concentrated aqueous solutions of easily soluble neutral salts or of chloral hydrate is remarkable. Potassium bromide or iodide, or calcium chloride for instance, cause the grains to swell, and render them soluble in cold water. At a certain degree of dilution a perfectly clear liquid is formed, which at first contains neither dextrin nor sugar; it is coloured blue, but is not precipitated by iodine water; and starch can be thrown down from it by alcohol. This precipitate, though entirely devoid of the structural peculiarity of starch, still exhibits some of the leading properties of that substance; it is coloured in the same manner by iodine, does not dissolve even when fresh in ammoniacal cupric oxide, and after drying is insoluble in water, whether cold or boiling. The progress of the solvent is most easily traced when calcium chloride is used, as this salt acts more slowly than the others we have mentioned. It leaves scarcely any perceptible residue. This fact in our opinion militates against the notion that starch is composed of a peculiar amylaceous substance, deposited within a skeleton of cellulose.

The remarkable action of iodine upon starch was discovered in 1814 by Colin and Gaultier de Claubry. It is extremely different in degree, according to the peculiar kind of starch, the proportion of iodine, and the nature of the substance the grains are impregnated with, before or after their treatment with iodine. The action is even entirely arrested (no blue colour being produced) by the presence in certain proportion of quinine, tannin, *Aqua Picis*, and of other bodies.

The combination of iodine with starch does not take place in equivalent proportions, and is moreover easily overcome by heat. The iodine combined with starch amounts at the utmost to 7·5 per cent. The compound is most readily formed in the presence of water, and then produces a deep indigo blue. Almost all other substances capable of penetrating starch grains, weaken the colour of the iodine compound to violet, reddish yellow, yellow, or greenish blue. These different shades, the production of which has been described by Nägeli with great diffuseness, are merely the colours which belong to iodine itself in the solid, liquid, or gaseous form. They must be referred to the fact that the particles of iodine diffuse themselves in a peculiar but hitherto unexplained manner within the grain or in the swollen and dissolved starch.

Commerce of Arrowroot—The chief kinds of arrowroot found in commerce are known as *Bermuda*, *St. Vincent*, and *Natal;* but that of

Jamaica and other West India Islands, of Brazil, Sierra Leone, and the East Indies, are quoted in price-currents, at least occasionally. Of these the Bermuda enjoys the highest reputation and commands by far the highest price; but its good quality is shared by the arrowroot of other localities, from which, when equally pure, it can in nowise be distinguished. Greenish,[1] however, points out that in Natal arrowroot the layers (or laminæ) are more obvious than in other varieties, although it appears that the former is also produced by Maranta.

The importations of arrowroot into the United Kingdom during the year 1870 amounted to 21,770 cwt., value £33,063. Of this quantity the island of St. Vincent in the West Indies furnished nearly 17,000 cwt., and the colony of Natal about 3000 cwt. The exports from St. Vincent in 1874 were 2,608,100 ℔., those of the Bermudas in 1876 only 45,520 ℔.[2] The shipments from the colony of Natal during the years 1866 to 1876 varied from 1,076 cwt. in 1873 to 4,305 cwt. in 1867.[3]

Uses—Arrowroot boiled with water or milk is a much-valued food in the sick-room. It is also an agreeable article of diet in the form of pudding or blancmange.

Adulteration—Other starches than that of *Maranta* are occasionally sold under the name of *Arrowroot*. Their recognition is only possible by the aid of the microscope.

Substitutes for Arrowroot.

Potato Starch—This substance, known in trade as *Farina* or *Potato Flour*, is made from the tubers of the potato (*Solanum tuberosum* L.) by a process analogous to that followed in the preparation of arrowroot. It has the following characters:—examined under the microscope, the granules are seen to be chiefly of two sorts, the first small and spherical, the second of much larger size, often 100 mkm. in length, having an irregularly circular, oval or egg-shaped outline, finely marked with concentric rings round a minute inconspicuous hilum. When heated in water, the grains swell considerably even at 60° C. Hydrochloric acid, sp. gr. 1·06, dissolves them at 40° quickly and almost completely, the granules being no longer deposited, as in the case of arrowroot similarly treated. The mixture of arrowroot and hydrochloric acid is inodorous, but that of potato starch has a peculiar though not powerful odour.

Canna Starch, Tous-les-Mois,[4] Toulema, Tolomane—A species of *Canna* is cultivated in the West India Islands, especially St. Kitts, for the sake of a peculiar starch which, since about the year 1836, has been extracted from its rhizomes by a process similar to that adopted in making arrowroot. The specific name of the plant is still undeter-

[1] *Yearbook of Pharm.* (1875) 529.

[2] Papers relating to H.M. Colonial Possessions. Reports for 1875-76. Presented to both Houses of Parliament, July 1877. 54. 4.

[3] Statist. Abstr. for the several Colonial and other Possessions of the United Kingdom, 14th number, 1878. p. 60.

[4] It is commonly stated that the name *Tous-les-mois* was given in consequence of the plant flowering *all the year round*. But this explanation appears improbable: no such name is mentioned by Rochefort, Aublet, or Descourtilz, who all describe the *Balisier* or *Canna*. It seems more likely that the term is the result of an attempt to confer a meaning on an ancient name—perhaps *Touloula*, which is one of the Carib designations for *Canna* and *Calathea*.

mined; it is said to agree with *Canna edulis* Ker (*C. indica* Ruiz et Pavon).[1]

The starch, which bears the same name as the plant, is a dull white powder, having a peculiar satiny or lustrous aspect, by reason of the extraordinary magnitude of the starch granules of which it is composed. These granules examined under the microscope are seen to be flattened and of irregular form, as circular, oval, oblong, or oval-truncate. The centre of the numerous concentric rings with which each granule is marked, is usually at one end rather than in the centre of a granule. The hilum is inconspicuous. The granules though far larger than those of the potato, are of the same density as the smaller forms of that starch, and, like them, float perfectly on chloroform. When heated, they begin to burst at 72° C. Dilute hydrochloric acid acts upon them as it does on arrowroot.

Canna starch boiled with 20 times its weight of water affords a jelly less clear and more tenacious than that of arrowroot, yet applicable to exactly the same purposes. The starch is but little known and not much esteemed in Europe; it was exported in 1876 from St. Kitts to the amount of 51,873 lb, besides 5,300 lb arrowroot starch.[2]

Curcuma Starch, Tikor, Tikhar.—The pendulous, colourless tubers of some species of *Curcuma*, but especially of *C. angustifolia* Roxb. and *C. leucorrhiza* Roxb., have long been utilized in Southern India for the preparation of a sort of arrowroot, known by the Hindustani name of *Tikor*, or *Tikhur*, and sometimes called by Europeans *East Indian Arrowroot.*[3] The granules of this substance much resemble those of *Maranta*, but they are neither spherical nor egg-shaped. On the contrary, they are rather to be described as flat discs, 5 to 7 mkm. thick, of elliptic or ovoid outline, sometimes truncate; many attain a length of 60 to 70 mkm. They are always beautifully stratified both on the face and on the edge. The hilum is generally situated at the narrower end. We have observed that when heated in water, the tumefaction of the grains commences at 72° C.

Curcuma starch, which in its general properties agrees with common arrowroot, is rather extensively manufactured in Travancore, Cochin and Canara on the south-western coast of India, but in a very rude manner. Drury[4] states that it is a favourite article of diet among the natives, and that it is exported from Travancore and Madras; we can add that it is not known as a special kind in the English market, and that the article we have seen offered in the London drug sales as *East Indian Arrowroot* was the starch of *Maranta*.

[1] Fig. in Bentley and Trimen's *Medic. Plants*, part 8 (1876).

[2] Page 102 of the Reports quoted at p. 633, note 2.

[3] Living roots of the plant used for making this arrowroot at Cochin, have been kindly forwarded to us by A. F. Sealy, Esq. of that place.

[4] *Useful Plants of India*, ed. 2. 1873. 168.

ZINGIBERACEÆ.

RHIZOMA ZINGIBERIS.

Radix Zingiberis; Ginger; F. *Gingembre;* G. *Ingwer.*

Botanical Origin—*Zingiber officinale* Roscoe (*Amomum Zingiber* L.), a reed-like plant, with annual leafy stems, 3 to 4 feet high, and flowers in cone-shaped spikes borne on other stems thrown up from the rhizome. It is a native of Asia, in the warmer countries of which it is universally cultivated,[1] but not known in a wild state. It has been introduced into most tropical countries, and is now found in the West Indies, South America, Tropical Western Africa, and Queensland in Australia.

History—Ginger is known in India under the old name of *Sringavera*, derived possibly from the Greek Ζιγγίβερι As a spice it was used among the Greeks and Romans, who appear to have received it by way of the Red Sea, inasmuch as they considered it to be a production of Southern Arabia.

In the list of imports from the Red Sea into Alexandria, which in the second century of our era were there liable to the Roman fiscal duty (*vectigal*), *Zingiber* occurs among other Indian spices.[2] During the middle ages it is frequently mentioned in similar lists, and evidently constituted an important item in the commercial relations between Europe and the East. Ginger thus appears in the tariff of duties levied at Acre in Palestine about A.D. 1173;[3] in that of Barcelona[4] in 1221; Marseilles[5] in 1228; and Paris[6] in 1296. The *Tarif des Péages*, or customs tariff, of the Counts of Provence in the middle of the 13th century, provides for the levying of duty at the towns of Aix, Digne, Valensole, Tarascon, Avignon, Orgon, Arles, &c., on various commodities imported from the East. These included spices, as pepper, *ginger*, cloves, zedoary, galangal, cubebs, saffron, canella, cumin, anise; dye stuffs, such as lac, indigo, Brazil wood, and especially alum from Castilia and Volcano; and groceries, as racalicia (liquorice), sugar and dates.[7]

In England ginger must have been tolerably well known even prior to the Norman Conquest, for it is frequently named in the Anglo-Saxon leech-books of the 11th century, as well as in the Welsh "Physicians of Myddvai" (see Appendix). During the 13th and 14th centuries it was, next to pepper, the commonest of spices, costing on an average nearly 1*s.* 7*d.* per lb., or about the price of a sheep.[8]

[1] The mode of cultivation is described by Buchanan, *Journey from Madras through Mysore, etc.* ii. (1807) 469.—Fig. of the plant in Bentley and Trimen's *Medic. Plants*, part 32 (1878).

[2] Vincent, *Commerce and Navigation of the Ancients*, ii. (1807) 695.

[3] *Recueil des Historiens des Croisades; Lois*, ii. (1843) 176.

[4] Capmany, *Memorias sobre la Marina, etc. de Barcelona*, Madrid, ii. (1779) 3.

[5] Méry et Guindon, *Hist. des Actes . . . de la Municipalité de Marseille*, i. (1841) 372.

[6] *Revue archéologique*, ix. (1852) 213.

[7] *Collection de Cartulaires de France*, Paris, viii. (1857) pp. lxxiii–xci., Abbaye de St. Victor, Marseilles.

[8] Rogers, *Hist. of Agriculture and Prices in England*, i. (1866) 629.

The merchants of Italy, about the middle of the 14th century, knew three kinds of ginger, called respectively *Belledi*, *Colombino*, and *Micchino*. These terms may be explained thus:—*Belledi* or *Baladi* is an Arabic word, which, as applied to ginger, would signify *country* or *wild*, i.e. *common ginger*. *Colombino* refers to Columbum, Kolam or Quilon, a port in Travancore frequently mentioned in the middle ages. Ginger termed *Micchino* denotes that the spice had been brought from or by way of Mecca.[1]

Ginger preserved in syrup, and sometimes called *Green Ginger*, was also imported during the middle ages, and regarded as a delicacy of the choicest kind.

The plant affording ginger must have been known to Marco Polo (*circa* 1280–90), who speaks of observing it both in China and India. John of Montecorvino, who visited India about 1292 (see p. 521), describes ginger as a plant like a flag, the root of which can be dug up and transported. Nicolo Conti also gave some description of the plant and of the collection of the root, as witnessed by him in India.[2]

The Venetians received ginger by way of Egypt; yet some of the superior kinds were conveyed from India overland by the Black Sea, as stated by Marino Sanudo[3] about 1306.

Ginger was introduced into America by Francisco de Mendoça, who took it from the East Indies to New Spain.[4] It was shipped for commercial purposes from the Island of St. Domingo as early at least as 1585; and from Barbados in 1654.[5] According to Renny,[6] 22,053 cwt. were exported from the West Indies to Spain in 1547.

Description—Ginger is known in two forms, namely the rhizome dried with its epidermis, in which case it is called *coated*; or deprived of epidermis, and then termed *scraped* or *uncoated*. The pieces, which are called by the spice-dealers *races* or *hands*, rarely exceed 4 inches in length, and have a somewhat palmate form, being made up of a series of short, laterally compressed, lobe-like shoots or knobs, the summit of each of which is marked by a depression indicating the former attachment of the leafy stem.

To produce the *uncoated ginger*, which is that preferred for medicinal use, the fresh rhizome is scraped, washed, and then dried in the sun.

Thus prepared, it has a pale buff hue, and a striated, somewhat fibrous surface. It breaks easily, exhibiting a short and farinaceous fracture with numerous bristle-like fibres. When cut with a knife the younger or terminal portion of the rhizome appears pale yellow, soft and amylaceous, while the older part is flinty, hard and resinous.

Coated ginger, or that which has been dried without the removal of the epidermis, is covered with a wrinkled, striated brown integument, which imparts to it a somewhat coarse and crude appearance, which is usually remarkably less developed on the flat parts of the rhizome. Internally, it is usually of a less bright and delicate hue than ginger

[1] Yule, *Book of Ser Marco Polo*, ii. (1871) 316.—See, however, Heyd, *Levantehandel*, II. (1879) 601.

[2] See Appendix.

[3] Marinus Sanutus, *Liber secretorum fidelium crucis*, Hanoviæ (1611) 22.

[4] Monardes, *Historia de las cosas que se traen de nuestras Indias occidentales*, Sevilla, (1574) 99.

[5] *Calendar of State Papers, Colonial Series*, 1574–1660, Lond. 1860, p. 4; see also pp. 414, 434.

[6] Renny, *Hist. of Jamaica*, Lond. 1807. 154.

from which the cortical part has been removed. Much of it indeed is dark, horny and resinous.

Ginger has an agreeable aromatic odour with a strong pungent taste.

Varieties—Those at present found in the London market are distinguished as *Jamaica, Cochin, Bengal,* and *African*. The first three are *scraped* gingers; the last-named is a *coated* ginger, that is to say, it still retains its epidermis. Jamaica Ginger is the sort most esteemed; and next to it the Cochin. But of each kind there are several qualities, presenting considerable variation *inter se*.

Scraped or decorticated ginger is often bleached, either by being subjected to the fumes of burning sulphur, or by immersion for a short time in solution of chlorinated lime. Much of that seen in the grocers' shops looks as if it had been whitewashed, and in fact is slightly coated with calcareous matter,—either sulphate or carbonate of calcium.[1]

Microscopic Structure—A transverse section of coated ginger exhibits a brown, horny external layer, about one millimètre broad, separated by a fine line from the whitish mealy interior portion, through the tissue of which numerous vascular bundles and resin-cells are irregularly scattered. The external tissue consists of a loose outer layer, and an inner composed of tabular cells: these are followed by peculiar short prosenchymatous cells, the walls of which are sinuous on transverse section and partially thickened, imparting a horny appearance. This delicate felted tissue forms the striated surface of *scraped ginger*, and is the principal seat of the resin and volatile oil, which here till large spaces. The large-celled parenchyme which succeeds is loaded with starch, and likewise contains numerous masses of resin and drops of oil. The starch granules are irregularly spherical, attaining at the utmost 40 mkm. Certain varieties of ginger, owing to the starch having been rendered gelatinous by scalding, are throughout horny and translucent. The circle of vascular bundles which separates the outer layers and the central portion is narrow, and has the structure of the corresponding circle or nucleus sheath in turmeric.

Chemical Composition—Ginger contains a volatile oil which is the only constituent of the drug that has hitherto been investigated. By distilling 112 ℔. of Jamaica ginger with water in the usual way, we obtained 4½ ounces of this oil, or about ¼ per cent. It is a pale yellow liquid of sp. gr. 0·878, having the peculiar odour of ginger, but not its pungent taste. It dissolves but sparingly in alcohol (0·83); and deviates the ray of polarized light 21°.6 to the left, when examined in a column 50 mm. long. We learn from kind information given us (1878) by Messrs. Schimmel & Co. at Leipzig, that they obtain as much as 2·2 per cent. of oil from good ginger.

The burning taste of ginger is due to a resin which we have not examined, but which well deserves careful analysis. Protocatechuic acid, which is so commonly afforded by resins (see page 243), is also produced by melting the resin of ginger with caustic potash, as shown in 1877 by Stenhouse and Groves.

[1] Mr. Garside (*Pharm. Journ.* April 18, 1874) found both. We have not observed the carbonate to be used.

Commerce—Great Britain imported of ginger as follows:—

1868	1869	1870	1871	1872
52,194 cwt.	34,535 cwt.	33,854 cwt.	32,723 cwt.	32,174 cwt.

In 1876 the imports were 62,164 cwt., valued at £169,252.

The drug was received in 1872 thus:—

From Egypt	4,923 cwt.
,, Sierra Leone	6,167 ,,
,, British India	13,310 ,,
,, British West Indies	7,543 ,,
,, other countries	231 ,,
Total	32,174

The shipments from Jamaica during the years 1866 to 1876 varied from 599,786 ℔. in 1872 to 1,728,075 in 1867. In 1876 there were exported 1,603,764 ℔., valued at £28,882.[1]

Uses—Ginger is an agreeable aromatic and stomachic, and as such is often a valuable addition to other medicines. It is much more largely employed as a condiment than as a drug.

RHIZOMA CURCUMÆ.

Radix Curcumæ;[2] *Turmeric*; F. *Curcuma*; G. *Gelbwurzel, Kurkuma.*

Botanical Origin—*Curcuma longa*[3] L.—Turmeric is indigenous to Southern Asia, and is there largely cultivated both on the continent and in the islands.

History—Dioscorides mentions an Indian plant as a kind of *Cyperus* (Κύπειρος) resembling ginger, but having when chewed a yellow colour and bitter taste: probably turmeric was intended. Garcia de Orta (1563), as well as Fragoso (1572), describe turmeric as *Crocus indicus.* A list of drugs sold in the city of Frankfort about the year 1450, names *Curcuma* along with zedoary and ginger.[4]

In its native countries, it has from remote times been highly esteemed both as a condiment and a dye-stuff; in Europe, it has always been less appreciated than the allied spices of the ginger tribe. In an inventory of the effects of a Yorkshire tradesman, dated 20th Sept., 1578, we find enumerated—"*x. owncis of turmeracke, x d.*"[5]

Description—The base of the scrape thickens in the first year into an ovate root-stock; this afterwards throws out shoots, forming lateral or secondary rhizomes, each emitting roots, which branch into fibres or are sometimes enlarged as colourless spindle-shaped tubers, rich in starch. The lateral rhizomes are doubtless in a condition to develope themselves as independent plants when separated from the parent. The central rhizomes formerly known as *Curcuma rotunda*, and the

[1] Statist. Abstract (as quoted p. 633, note 3), p. 71.

[2] *Curcuma* from the Persian *kurkum*, a name applied also to saffron. The origin of the word *Turmeric* is not known to us; *Terra merita* seems to be a corruption of it.

[3] Fig. in Bentley and Trimen's *Med. Plants*, part 9. (1876).

[4] Flückiger, *Die Frankfurter Liste*, Halle, 1873. 11.

[5] Raine, *Wills and Inventories of the Archdeaconry of Richmond* (Surtees Society), 1853. 277.

elongated lateral ones as *Curcuma longa*, were regarded by Linnæus as the production of distinct species.

The radical tubers of some species of *Curcuma*, as *C. angustifolia* Roxb., are used for making a sort of arrowroot (p. 637). Sometimes they are dried, and constitute the peculiar kind of turmeric which the Chinese call *Yuh-kin*.[1]

The turmeric of commerce consists of the two sorts of rhizome just mentioned, namely, the *central* or *round* and the *lateral* or *long*. The former are ovate, pyriform or subspherical, sometimes pointed at the upper end and crowned with the remains of leaves, while the sides are beset with those of roots and marked with concentric ridges. The diameter is very variable, but is seldom less than ¾ of an inch, and is frequently much more. They are often cut and usually scalded in order to destroy their vitality and facilitate drying.

The lateral rhizomes are subcylindrical, attenuated towards either end, generally curved, covered with a rugose skin, and marked more or less plainly with transverse rings. Sometimes one, two or more short knobs or shoots grow out on one side. The rhizomes, whether round or long, are very hard and firm, exhibiting when broken a dull, waxy, resinous surface, of an orange or orange-brown hue, more or less brilliant. They have a peculiar aromatic odour and taste.

Several varieties of turmeric distinguished by the names of the countries or districts in which they are produced, are found in the English market: but although they present differences which are sufficiently appreciable to the eye of the experienced dealer, the characters of each sort are scarcely so marked or so constant as to be recognizable by mere verbal description. The principal sorts now in commerce are known as *China*, *Madras*, *Bengal*, *Java*, and *Cochin*. Of these the first named is the most esteemed, but it is seldom to be met with in the European market.[2]

Madras Turmeric is a fine sort in large, bold pieces. Sometimes packages of it contain exclusively round rhizomes, while others are made up entirely of the long or lateral.

Bengal Turmeric differs from the other varieties chiefly in its deeper tint, and hence is the sort preferred for dyeing purposes.

Java Turmeric presents no very distinctive features; it is dusted with its own powder, and does not show when broken a very brilliant colour. Judging by the low price at which it is quoted it is not in great esteem. It is the produce of *Curcuma longa* var. *β. minor*[3] Hassk.

Microscopic Structure—The suberous coat is made up of 8 to 10 rows of tabular cells; the parenchyme of the middle cortical layer of large roundish polyhedral cells. Towards the centre the transverse section exhibits a coherent ring of fibro-vascular bundles representing a kind of medullary sheath. The parenchyme enclosed by this ring is traversed by scattered bundles of vessels, and in most of its cells contains starch in amorphous, angular, or roundish masses, which are

[1] Hanbury, *Pharm. Journ.* iii. (1862) 206; also *Science Papers*, 254, fig. 11.—It is not wholly devoid of yellow colouring matter.

[2] A good deal is exported from Takow in Formosa, but mostly to Chinese ports.—*Returns of Trade at the Treaty Ports of China for* 1872. p. 106.

[3] From information communicated by Mr. Binnendyk, of the Botanical Garden, Buitenzorg, Java.

so far disorganized that they no longer exhibit the usual appearance in polarized light, but are nevertheless turned blue by iodine. The starch has been reduced to this condition by scalding.

Resin likewise occurs in separate cells, forming dark yellowish-red particles. The entire tissue is penetrated with yellow colouring matter, and shows numerous drops of essential oil, which in the fresh rhizome is no doubt contained in peculiar cells.

Chemical Composition—The drug yielded us (1876) one per cent. of a yellow essential oil, which contains a portion boiling at 250° C., answering to the formula $C^{19}H^{14}O$; this liquid differs from carvol (p. 306) by being unable to combine with SH^2. The other constituents of curcuma oil boil at temperatures much above 250°; we found the crude oil and its different portions slightly dextrogyrate.

The aqueous extract of the drug tastes bitter, and is precipitated by tannic acid.

The colouring matter, *Curcumin*, $C^{10}H^{10}O^3$, may be obtained to the amount of ⅓ per cent. by depriving first the drug of fat and essential oil. The powder, after that treatment with bisulphide of carbon, is gradually exhausted, according to Daube (1871), with warm petroleum (boiling point 80° – 90° C.). On cooling chiefly the last portions of petroleum deposit the crystalline curcumin. Its alcoholic solution is purified by mixing it cautiously with basic acetate of lead, not allowing the liquid to assume a decidedly acid reaction. The red precipitate thus formed is collected, washed with alcohol, immersed in water, and decomposed with sulphuretted hydrogen. From the dried mixture of sulphide of lead and curcumin the latter is lastly removed by boiling alcohol.

By Ivanow-Gajewsky (1873) the best produce of curcumin is stated to be obtained by washing an ethereal extract of turmeric with weak ammonia, dissolving the residue in boiling concentrated ammonia, and passing into the solution carbonic acid, by which the curcumin is precipitated in flakes.

After due recrystallization from alcohol curcumin forms yellow crystals, having an odour of vanilla, and exhibiting a fine blue in reflected light. They melt at 165° C. Curcumin is scarcely soluble, even in boiling water, but dissolves readily on addition of an alkali either caustic or carbonate. On acidulating these solutions, a yellow powder of curcumin is precipitated. Curcumin is not abundantly dissolved by ether, very sparingly by benzol or bisulphide of carbon. It is not volatile; heated with zinc dust it yields an oil boiling at 290°; fused with caustic potash, curcumin affords protocatechuic acid (page 243).

Paper tinged with an alcoholic solution of curcumin displays on addition of an alkali a brownish-red coloration, becoming violet on drying. Boracic acid produces an orange tint, turning blue by addition of an alkaline solution.[1] This behaviour of (impure) curcumin was

[1] The following is a striking experiment, showing some of these changes of colour:—Place a little crushed turmeric or the powder on blotting paper, and moisten it repeatedly with chloroform, allowing the latter to evaporate. There will thus be formed on the paper a yellow stain, which on addition of a slightly acidulated solution of borax and drying assumes a purple hue. If the paper is now sprinkled with dilute ammonia it will acquire a transient blue. This reaction enables one to recognize the presence of turmeric in powdered rhubarb or mustard.

pointed out by Vogel as early as 1815, and has since that time been utilized as a chemical test.

Borax added to an alcoholic solution of curcumin gives rise to a crystallizable substance, which Ivanow-Gajewsky (1870) isolated by heating an alcoholic extract of turmeric with boracic and sulphuric acids. It forms a purple crystalline powder with a metallic green lustre, insoluble in water, but soluble in alcohol. Its solution is coloured dark blue by an alkali.

According to the same chemist there also exists in curcuma an alkaloid in very small quantity. Kachler (1870) found in the aqueous decoction an abundance of *bioxalate of potassium*.

Commerce—In the year 1869 there were imported into the United Kingdom 64,280 cwt. of turmeric; in 1870, 44,900 cwt.,—a very large proportion being furnished by Bengal and Pegu. The export from Calcutta[1] in the year 1870-71 was 59,352 cwt.

Bombay exported in the year 1871-72, 29,780 cwt., of which the greater portion was shipped to Sind and the Persian Gulf, and only 910 cwt. to Europe.[2]

Uses—Turmeric is employed as a condiment in the shape of curry powder, and as such is often sold by druggists; but as a medicine it is obsolete. It is largely consumed in dyeing.

Substitute—*Cochin Turmeric* is the produce of some other species of *Curcuma* than *C. longa*. It consists exclusively of a bulb-shaped rhizome of large dimensions, cut transversely or longitudinally into slices or segments. The cortical part is dull brown; the inner substance is horny and of a deep orange-brown, or when in thin shavings of a brilliant yellow. Mr. A. Forbes Sealy of Cochin has been good enough to send us (1873) living rhizomes of this *Curcuma*, which he states is mostly grown at Alwaye, north-east of Cochin, and is never used in the country as *turmeric*, though its starchy tubers are employed for making arrowroot. The rhizomes sent are thick, short, conical, and of enormous size, some attaining as much as 2½ inches in diameter. Internally they are of a bright orange-yellow.

The beautiful figures of Roscoe[3] show several species of Curcuma and Zingiber provided with yellow tubers or rhizomes, all probably containing curcumin.

RHIZOMA GALANGÆ.

Radix Galangæ[4] *minoris; Galangal;* F. *Racine de Galanga;* G. *Galgant.*

Botanical Origin—*Alpinia officinarum* Hance,[5] a flag-like plant,

[1] Returns quoted at p. 571, note 2.

[2] *Statement of the Trade and Navigation of Bombay for* 1871-72, pt. ii. 95.

[3] *Monandrous Plants of the order Scitamineæ*, Liverpool, 1828, especially *Zingiber Cassumunar*.

[4] *Galanga* appears to be derived from the Arabic name *Khulanjan*, which in turn comes from the Chinese *Kau-liang Kiang*, signifying, as Dr. F. Porter Smith has informed us, *Kau-liang ginger*. Kau-liang is the ancient name of a district in the province of Kwangtung.

[5] *Journ. of Linnean Society*, Botany, xiii. (1871) 1; also Trimen's *Journ. of Bot.*, ii. (1873) 175; Bentley and Trimen's *Med. Plants*, part 31 (1878).—Dr. Thwaites of Ceylon, who has the plant in cultivation, has been good enough to send us a fine coloured drawing of it in flower.

with stems about 4 feet high, clothed with narrow lanceolate leaves, and terminating in short and simple racemes of elegant white flowers, shaded and veined with dull red. It grows cultivated in the island of Hainan in the south of China, and, as is supposed, in some of the southern provinces of the Chinese Empire.

History—The earliest reference to galangal we have met with occurs in the writings of the Arabian geographer Ibn Khurdádbah[1] about A.D. 869–885, who in enumerating the productions of a country called Sila, names galangal together with musk, aloes, camphor, silk, and cassia. Edrisi,[2] three hundred years later, is more explicit, for he mentions it with many other productions of the far East, as brought from India and China to Aden, then a great emporium of the trade of Asia with Egypt and Europe. The physician Alkindi,[3] who lived at Bassora and Bagdad in the second half of the 9th century, and somewhat later Rhazes and Avicenna, notice galangal, the use of which was introduced into Europe[4] through the medical system promulgated by them and other writers of the same school. As to Great Britain, galingal, as it was frequently spelt, also occurs in the Welsh "Meddygon Myddfai" (see Appendix).

Many notices exist showing that galangal was imported with pepper, ginger, cloves, nutmegs, cardamoms and zedoary; and that during the middle ages it was used in common with these substances as a culinary spice, which it is still held to be in certain parts of Europe.[5] The plant affording the drug was unknown until the year 1870, when a description of it was communicated to the Linnean Society of London by Dr. H. F. Hance, from specimens collected by Mr. E. C. Taintor, near Hoihow in the north of Hainan.

Description—The drug consists of a cylindrical rhizome, having a maximum diameter of about ¾ of an inch, but for the most part considerably smaller. This rhizome has been cut while fresh into short pieces, 1½ to 3 inches in length, which are often branched, and are marked transversely at short intervals by narrow raised sinuous rings, indicating the former attachment of leaves or scales. The pieces are hard, tough and shrivelled, externally of a dark reddish-brown, displaying when cut transversely an internal substance of rather paler hue (but never white), with a darker central column. The drug exhales when comminuted an agreeable aroma, and has a strongly pungent, spicy taste.

Microscopic Structure—The central portion of the rhizome is separated from the outer tissue by the nucleus sheath, which appears as a well-defined darker line. Yet the central tissue does not differ much from that surrounding it, both being composed of uniform parenchyme cells, traversed by scattered vascular bundles. There also occur throughout the whole tissue isolated cells loaded with essential oil or resin. But the larger number of cells abound in large starch granules of an unusual club-shaped form. Some cells contain a brown substance, dif-

[1] Work quoted in the Appendix—tome v. 294.

[2] *Géographie*, i. (1836) 51.

[3] *De Rerum gradibus*, Argentorati, 1531. 162.

[4] Macer Floridus (see p. 627), cap. 70, was already acquainted with it.

[5] Hanbury, *Historical Notes on the Radix Galangæ of pharmacy*—*Journ. of Linnean Society*, Bot. xiii. (1871) 20; *Pharm. Journ.* Sept. 23, 1871. 248; *Science Papers*, 370.

fering from resin in being insoluble in alcohol. The corky layer is remarkable from its cells having undulated walls.

Chemical Composition—The odour of galangal is due to an essential oil, which the rhizoma yields to the extent of only 0·7 per cent., and which we found to be very slightly deviating the plane of polarization to the left.

Brandes[1] extracted from Galangal, by means of ether, an inodorous, tasteless, crystalline body called *Kämpferid*, which is worthy of further examination.

The pungent principle of the drug, which is probably analogous to that of ginger, has not been studied.

Commerce—Galangal is shipped from Canton to other ports of China, to India and Europe, but there are no general statistics to give an idea of the total production. From official returns quoted by Hance, the export of the year 1869, which seems to have been exceptionally large, amounted to 370,800 ℔. From Kiung-chow, island of Hainan, 2,113 peculs (281,733 ℔.) were exported in 1877.

Uses—The drug is an aromatic stimulant of the nature of ginger, now nearly obsolete in British medicine. It is still a popular remedy and spice in Livonia, Esthonia and central Russia, and by the Tartars is taken with tea. It is also in some requisition in Russia among brewers, and the manufacturers of vinegar and cordials, and finally as a cattle medicine.

Substitute—The rhizoma of *Alpina Galanga* Willd., a plant of Java, constitutes the drug known as *Radix Galangæ majoris* or *Greater Galangal*, packages of which occasionally appear in the London drug sales. It may be at once distinguished from the Chinese drug by its much larger size and the pale buff hue of its internal substance, the latter in strong contrast with the orange-brown outer skin.

FRUCTUS CARDAMOMI.

Semina Cardamomi minoris; Cardamoms, Malabar Cardumoms; F. Cardamomes; G. Cardamomen.

Botanical Origin—*Elettaria*[2] *Cardamomum* Maton (*Alpinia Cardamomum* Roxb.), a flag-like perennial plant, 6 to 12 feet high, with large lanceolate leaves on long sheathing stalks, and flowers in lax flexuose horizontal scapes, 6 to 18 inches in length, which are thrown out to the number of 3 or 4, close to the ground. The fruit is ovoid, three-sided, plump and smooth, with a fleshy green pericarp.

The Cardamom plant grows abundantly, both wild and under cultivation, in the moist shady mountain forests of North Canara, Coorg and Wynaad on the Malabar Coast; at an elevation of 2500 to 5000 feet above the sea. It is truly wild in Canara and in the Anamalai, Cochin and Travancore forests.[3] The cardamom region has a mean temperature of 22 C. (72° F.), and a mean rainfall of 121 inches.

[1] *Archiv der Pharm.* xix. (1839) 52.

[2] From *Elettari*, the Mallyalim name of the plant.—Fig. in Bentley and Trimen's *Med. Plants*, part 24 (1877).

[3] The small "*Cardamom*" island in the Laccadive group, west of Malabar, is inhabited by Moplahs, known (as we are informed by Dr. King, Calcutta) in the south of India as dealers in cardamoms.

A well-marked variety, differing chiefly in the elongated form and large size of its fruits, is found wild in the forests of the central and southern provinces of Ceylon. It was formerly regarded as a distinct species under the name of *Elettaria major*, but careful observation of growing specimens has shown that it possesses no characters to warrant it being considered more than a variety of the typical plant, and it is therefore now called *E. Cardamomum* var. *β*. It is only known to occur in Ceylon, where the ordinary cardamom of Malabar is not found except as a cultivated plant.[1]

History—Cardamoms, *Elā*, are mentioned in the writings of Susruta, and hence may have been used in India from a remote period. It is not unlikely that in common with ginger and pepper they reached Europe in classical times, although it is not possible from the descriptions that have come down to determine exactly what was the Καρδάμωμον of Theophrastus and Dioscorides, or the Ἄμωμον of the last-named writer. The *Amomum*, *Amomis* and *Cardamomum* of Pliny are also doubtful, the description he gives of the last being unintelligible as applied to anything now known by that name.

In the list of Indian spices liable to duty at Alexandria, *circa* A.D. 176–180 (see Appendix, A), *Amomum* as well as *Cardamomum* is mentioned. St. Jerome names *Amomum* together with musk, as perfumes in use among the voluptuous ecclesiastics of the 4th century.[2]

Cardamoms are named by Edrisi[3] about A.D. 1154 as a production of Ceylon, and also as an article of trade from China to Aden; and in the same century they are mentioned together with cinnamon and cloves (p. 282) as an import in Palestine by way of Acre, then a trading city of the Levant.[4]

The first writer who definitely and correctly states the country of the cardamom appears to be the Portuguese navigator Barbosa[5] (1514), who frequently names it as a production of the Malabar coast. Garcia de Orta[6] mentions the shipment of the drug to Europe; he also ascertained that the larger sort was produced in Ceylon. The Malabar cardamon plant was figured by Rheede under its indigenous name of *Elettari*.[7]

The essential oil of cardamoms was distilled before 1544 by Valerius Cordus (see p. 526, note 1).

Cultivation and Production—Although the cardamom plant grows wild in the forests of Southern India, where it is commonly called *Ilāchi*, its fruits are largely obtained from cultivated plants. The methods of cultivation, which vary in the different districts, may be thus described:—

1. Previous to the commencement of the rains the cultivators ascend the mountain sides, and seek in the shady evergreen forests a spot where some cardamom plants are growing. Here they make small clearings, in

[1] Thwaites, *Enumeratio Plantarum Zeylaniæ*, 1864. 318.

[2] *S. Hieronymi Opera Omnia*, ed. Migne, ii. (1845) 297, in *Patrologiæ cursus completus*, vol. xxii.

[3] In the work quoted in the Appendix, i. (1836) 73, 51.—It is questionable whether *Elettaria* is intended at p. 51.

[4] A *long* and *curious article* on *cardamoms*, by a pharmacist of Cairo, 13th century, named *Abul Mena*, is quoted by Leclerc, *Histoire de la Médecine arabe*, ii. (Paris, 1876) 215.

[5] *Description of the Coasts of East Africa and Malabar*, Hakluyt Society, 1866. 59. 64, 147. 154. etc.

[6] In the work quoted at p. 547, note 8.

[7] *Hortus Malabaricus*, xi. (1692) tab. 4–5.

which the admission of light occasions the plant to develope in abundance. The cardamom plants attain 2 to 3 feet in height during the following monsoon, after which the ground is again cleared of weeds, protected with a fence, and left to itself for a year. About two years after the first clearing the plants begin to flower, and five months later ripen some fruits, but a full crop is not got till at least a year after. The plants continue productive six or seven years. A garden, 484 square yards in area, four of which may be made in an acre of forest, will give on an average an annual crop of 12¼ lbs. of garbled cardamoms.[1] Ludlow, an Assistant Conservator of Forests, reckons that not more than 28 lbs. can be got from an acre of forest. From what he says, it further appears that the plants which come up on clearings of the Coorg forests are mainly *seedlings*, which make their appearance in the same *quasi*-spontaneous manner as certain plants in the clearings of a wood in Europe. He says they commence to bear in about 3½ years after their first appearance.[2] The plan of cultivation above described is that pursued in the forests of Travancore, Coorg and Wynaad.

2. On the lower range of the Pulney Hills, near Dindigul, at an elevation of about 5,000 feet above the sea, the cardamom plant is cultivated in the shade. The natives burn down the underwood, and clear away the small trees of the dense moist forests called *sholas*, which are damp all the year round. The cardamoms are then sown, and when a few inches high are planted out, either singly or in twos, under the shade of the large trees. They take five years before they bear fruit; "in October," remarks our informant,[3] "I saw the plants in full flower and also in fruit,—the latter not however ripe."

3. In North Canara and Western Mysore the cardamom is cultivated in the betel-nut plantations. The plants, which are raised from seed, are planted between the palms, from which and from plantains they derive a certain amount of shade. They are said to produce fruit in their third year.

Cardamoms begin to ripen in October, and the gathering continues during dry weather for two or three months. All the fruits on a scape do not become ripe at the same time, yet too generally the whole scape is gathered at once and dried,—to the manifest detriment of the drug. This is done partly to save the fruit from being eaten by snakes, frogs and squirrels, and partly to avoid the capsules splitting, which they do when quite mature. In some plantations however the cardamoms are gathered in a more reasonable fashion. As they are collected the fruits are carried to the houses, laid out for a few days on mats, then stripped from their scapes, and the drying completed by a gentle fire-heat. In Coorg the fruit is stripped from the scape before drying, and the drying is sometimes effected wholly by sun-heat.

In the native states of Cochin and Travancore cardamoms are a monopoly of the respective governments. The rajah of the latter state requires that all the produce shall be sold to his officials, who forward

[1] *Report on the Administration of Coorg for the year* 1872–73, Bangalore, 1873. 44.

[2] Elliot, *Experiences of a Planter in the Jungles of Mysore*, Lond. ii. (1871) 201, 209.

[3] Col. Beddome, Conservator of Forests, Madras. We have likewise to acknowledge information on this head from Dr. Brandis, Inspector-General of Forests in India, and Dr. King, Director of the Botanic Garden, Calcutta.

it to the main depôt at Alapalli or Aleppi, a port in Travancore, where his commercial agent resides. The rajah is tenacious of his rights, and inserts a clause in the leases he grants to European coffee-planters, of whom a great many have settled in his territory, requiring that cardamoms shall not be grown.

The cardamoms at Aleppi are sold by auction, and bought chiefly by Moplah merchants for transport to different parts of India, and also, through third parties, to England. All the lower qualities are consumed in India, and the finer alone shipped to Europe.

In the forests belonging to the British Government cardamoms are mostly reckoned among the miscellaneous items of produce; but in Coorg, the cardamom forests are now let at a rental of £3,000 per annum under a lease which will expire in 1878.[1]

Dr. Cleghorn, late Conservator of Forests in the Madras Presidency, observes in a letter to one of us, that the rapid extension of coffee culture along the slopes of the Malabar mountains has tended to lessen the production of cardamoms, and has encroached considerably upon the area of their indigenous growth. A recent writer[2] has shown from his own experience that the cultivation of the cardomom is a branch of industry worth the attention of Europeans, and has given many valuable details for insuring successful results.

Description—The fruit of the Malabar cardamom as found in commerce is an ovoid or oblong, three-sided, three-valved capsule, containing numerous seeds arranged in three cells. It is rounded at the base, and often retains a small stalk; towards the apex it is more or less contracted, and terminates in a short beak. The longitudinally-striated, inodorous, tasteless pericarp is of a pale greyish-yellow, or buff, or brown when fully ripe, of a thin papery consistence, splitting lengthwise into three valves. From the middle of the inner side of each valve a thin partition projects towards the axis, thereby producing three cells, each of which encloses 5 to 7 dark brown, aromatic seeds, arranged in two rows and attached in the central angle.

The seeds, which are about two lines long, are irregularly angular, transversely rugose, and have a depressed hilum and a deeply channelled raphe. Each seed is enclosed in a thin colourless aril.

Cardamoms vary in size, shape, colour and flavour: those which are shortly ovoid or nearly globular, and $\frac{4}{10}$ to $\frac{6}{10}$ of an inch in length, are termed in trade language *shorts;* while those of a more elongated form, pointed at each end, and $\frac{7}{10}$ to $\frac{9}{10}$ of an inch long, are called *short-longs*. They are further distinguished by the names of localities, as Malabar (or Mangalore), Aleppi, and Madras. The *Malabar Cardamoms*, which are the most esteemed, are of full colour, and occur of both forms, namely *shorts* and *short-longs;* they are brought to Europe *viâ* Bombay. Those terms *Aleppi* are generally *shorts*, plump, beaked and of a peculiar greenish tint; they are imported from Calicut, and sometimes from Aleppi. The *Madras* are chiefly of elongated form (*short-longs*) and of a more pallid hue; they are shipped at Madras and Pondicherry.

Cardamoms are esteemed in proportion to their plumpness and heaviness, and the sound and mature condition of the seeds they

[1] Report quoted at p. 645, note 1.

[2] Elliot, *op. cit.*, chap. 12.

contain. Good samples afford about three-fourths of their weight of seeds.[1]

The fruits of the second form (var. β) of *Elettaria Cardamomum*, known in trade as *Ceylon Cardamoms*, are from 1 to 2 inches in length, and $\frac{3}{10}$ to $\frac{4}{10}$ of an inch in breadth, distinctly three-sided, often arched, and always of a dark greyish-brown. The seeds are larger and more numerous than those of the Malabar plant, and somewhat different in odour and taste.

Microscopic Structure—The testa of the seed consists of three distinct layers, namely an exterior of thick-walled, spirally-striated cells, somewhat longitudinally extended, and exhibiting on transverse section, square, not very large, cavities; then a row of large cells with thin transverse walls; and finally, an internal layer of deep brown, radially-arranged cells, the walls of which have so thick a deposit that at the most only small cavities remain.

The granular, colourless, sac-shaped albumen encloses a horny endosperm, in which the embryo is inserted the projecting radicle being directed towards the hilum. The cells of the albumen have the form of elongated polyhedra, almost entirely filled with very small starch granules. Besides them, there occur in most of the cells, somewhat larger masses of albuminoid matter having a rhombohedric form, distinctly observable when thin slices of the seed are examined under almond oil in polarized light. These remarkable crystalloid bodies resemble those occurring in the seeds of cumin (p. 332).

Chemical Composition—The parenchyme of the albumen and embryo is loaded with fatty oil and essential oil, the former existing in the seed to the extent of about 10 per cent.

The percentage of essential oil is stated by Messrs. Schimmel & Co., Leipzig, to be equal to 5 in the Madras Cardamoms, and to 3·5 in the Ceylon. We found the latter to be dextrogyrate; the same gentlemen presented us (1876) with a crystallized deposit from the latter oil, which appears to be *identical with common camphor*. Its alcoholic solution deviates the plane of polarization to the right, apparently to the same amount as that of common camphor (see also oil of spike, p. 479).

Dumas and Péligot (1834) state to have obtained from the essential oil of cardamoms (inodorous?) crystals of terpin, $C^{10}H^{16} + 3\,OH^2$. The ash of cardamoms, in common with that of several other plants of the same order, is remarkably rich in manganese.[2]

Commerce—There are no statistics to show the production of cardamoms in the south of India or even the quantity exported. The shipments in the year 1872-73 from Bombay, to which port the drug is largely sent from the Madras Presidency, amounted to 1,650 cwt., of which 1,055 cwt. were exported to the United Kingdom.[3]

Cardamoms, the produce of Ceylon and therefore of the *large* variety, were exported from that island in 1872 to the extent of 9,273 lb.—the whole quantity being shipped to the United Kingdom.[4]

[1] Thus 202 lb. shelled at various times during 10 years, afforded 154½ lb. of seeds. (Information from the laboratory accounts of Messrs. Allen and Hanburys, Plough Court, Lombard Str.)

[2] *Pharm. Journ.* iii. (1872) 208.

[3] *Statement of the Trade, etc. of Bombay for* 1872-73. ii. 58. 90.

[4] *Ceylon Blue Book for* 1872, Colombo 1873. 543.

Uses—Cardamoms are an agreeable aromatic, often administered in conjunction with other medicines. As an ingredient in curry powder, they have also some use as a condiment. But the consumption in England is small in comparison with what it is in Russia, Sweden, Norway and parts of Germany, where they are constantly employed as a spice for the flavouring of cakes. In these countries Ceylon cardamoms are also used, but exclusively for the manufacture of liqueurs. In India, cardamoms, besides being used in medicine, are employed as a condiment and for chewing with betel.

Other sorts of Cardamom.

The fruits of several other plants of the order *Zingiberaceæ* have at various times been employed in pharmacy under the common name of *Cardamom*. We shall here notice only those which have some importance in European or Indian commerce.[1]

Round or Cluster Cardamom—*Amomum Cardamomum* L., the mother-plant of this drug, is a native of Cambodia, Siam, Sumatra and Java.

During the intercourse with Siam, which was frequent in the early part of the 17th century, this drug, which is there in common use, occasionally found its way into Europe. Clusius received a specimen of it in 1605 as the true *Amomum* of the ancients, and figured it as a great rarity.[2] As *Amomum verum* it had a place in the pharmacopœias of this period. Parkinson (1640), who figures it as *Amomum genuinum*, says that "of late days it hath been sent to Venice from the East Indies." Dale (1693) and Pomet (1694) both regarded it as a rare drug; the latter says it is brought from Holland, and that it is the only thing that ought to be used when *Amomum* is ordered. In 1751 it was so scarce that in making the *Theriaca Andromachi* some other drug had always to be substituted for it.[3]

Thus it had completely disappeared, when about the year 1853 commercial relations were re-opened with Siam; and among the commodities poured into the market were *Round Cardamoms*. They were not appreciated, and the importations becoming unprofitable, soon ceased.[4] They are nevertheless an article of considerable traffic in Eastern Asia.

Round Cardamoms are produced in small compact bunches.[5] Each fruit is globular, $\frac{6}{10}$ to $\frac{7}{10}$ of an inch in diameter, marked with longitudinal furrows, and sometimes distinctly three-lobed. The pericarp is thin, fragile, somewhat hairy, of a buff colour, enclosing a three-lobed mass of seeds, which are mostly shrivelled as if the fruit had been gathered unripe. The seeds, which have a general resemblance to those of the Malabar cardamom, have a strong camphoraceous, aromatic taste.

There is a large export from Siam of cardamoms of this and the following sort. The shipments from Bangkok in 1871 amounted to

[1] For additional information on the various sorts of Cardamom, consult Guibourt, *Hist. des Drog.* ii. (1869) 215–227; Pereira, *Elements of Mat. Med.* ii., part i. (1855) 243–263; Hanbury in *Pharm. Journ.* xiv. (1855) 352. 416; *Science Papers*, 93–15.

[2] *Exoticorum Libri*, 377. Yet it already occurs in the *Dispensatorium* of Valerius Cordus.

[3] Hill, *Hist. of the Mat. Med.*, Lond. (1751) 472.

[4] Thus 43 bags, imported direct from Bangkok, were offered for sale in London, 26 March, 1857, and bought in at 1*s.* 6*d.* per lb.

[5] Fig. in Guibourt, *l. c.* 215.

4,678 peculs (623,733 lbs.), and were all to Singapore and China.[1] In 1875 we noticed the export from Bangkok of 267 peculs of "true" cardamoms, valued at 45,140 dollars, and 3,267 peculs of "bastard" cardamoms, value 92,865 dollars; the latter no doubt refer to the following kind:[2]—

Xanthioid Cardamom; Wild or Bastard Cardamom of Siam—This is afforded by *Amomum xanthioides* Wallich, a native of Tenasserim and Siam. During the past thirty years the seeds of this plant, deprived of their capsules, have often been imported into the London market, and they are now also common in the bazaars of India.[3] They closely resemble the seeds of the Malabar cardamom, differing chiefly in flavour and in being rather more finely rugose. Occasionally they are imported still cohering in ovoid, three-lobed masses, as packed in the pericarp. Sometimes they are distinguished as *Bastard* or *Wild*, but are more generally termed simply *Cardamom Seeds*. They are a considerable article of trade in Siam.

The fruits of this species grow in round clusters and are remarkable for having the pericarp thickly beset with weak fleshy spines,[4] which gives them some resemblance to the fruits of a *Xanthium*, and has suggested the specific name.

Bengal Cardamom—This drug, which with the next two has been hitherto confounded under one name,[5] is afforded by *Amomum subulatum* Roxb.,[6] a native of the Morung mountains, to the S.S.W. of Darjiling, in about 26°·30′ N. lat. The fruit is known by the name of *Winged Bengal Cardamom, Morung Elachi* or *Buro Elachi*. They average about an inch in length, and are of ovoid or slightly obconic form, and obscurely 3-sided; the lower end is rounded and usually devoid of stalk. The upper part of the fruit is provided with 9 narrow jagged wings or ridges, which become apparent after maceration; and the summit terminates in a truncate bristly nipple,—never protracted into a long tube. The pericarp is coarsely striated, and of a deep brown. It easily splits into 3 valves, inclosing a 3-lobed mass of seeds, 60 to 80 in number, agglutinated by a viscid saccharine pulp, due to the aril with which each seed is surrounded. The seeds are of roundish form, rendered angular by mutual pressure, and about ⅛ of an inch long; they have a highly aromatic, camphoraceous taste.

Nepal Cardamom—The description of the Bengal cardamom applies in many points to this drug, to which it has a singularly close resemblance. The fruit is of the same size and form, and is also crowned in its upper part with thin jagged ridges, and marked in a similar manner with longitudinal striæ; and lastly, the seeds have the same shape and flavour. But it differs, firstly, in bearing on its summit a tubular calyx, which is as long or longer than the fruit itself; and, secondly, in the fruit being often attached to a short stalk. The fruits are borne on an ovoid scape, 3 to 4 inches long, densely crowded with

[1] *Commercial Report of H. M. Consul-General in Siam for* 1871.

[2] *Science Papers*, 102–103.

[3] Moodeen Sheriff, *Supplement to Pharmacopœia of India*, Madras, 1869. 44. 270.

[4] See figures in *Pharm. Journ.* xiv. (1855) 418; also *Science Papers*, 1876, p. 101–103.

[5] As by Pereira, *Elem. of Mat. Med.* ii. (1850) 1135.

[6] According to Dr. King, in Sir Joseph Hooker's *Report on the Royal Gardens at Kew*, 1877. 27.

overlapping bracts, which are remarkably broad and truncate with a sharp central claw,—very distinct from the much narrower ovate bracts of *A. aromaticum*, as shown in Roxburgh's unpublished drawing of that plant.

The plant, which is unquestionably a species of *Amomum*, has not yet been identified with any published description. We have to thank Colonel Richard C. Lawrence, British Resident at Katmandu, for sending us a fruit-scape in alcohol, some dried leaves, and also the drug itself,—the last agreeing perfectly with specimens obtained through other channels.

The Nepal cardamom, the first account of which is due to Hamilton,[1] is cultivated on the frontiers of Nepal, near Darjiling. The plant is stated by Col. Lawrence to attain 3 to 6 feet in height, and to be grown on well-watered slopes of the hills, under the shelter of trees. The fruit is exported to other parts of India.

Java Cardamom—A well-marked fruit, produced by *Amomum maximum* Roxb., a plant of Java. The fruits are arranged to the number of 30 to 40 on a short thick scape, and form a globose group, 4 inches in diameter. They are stalked, and of a conical or ovoid form, in the fresh state as much as 1½ inches long by 1 inch broad. Each fruit is provided with 9 to 10 prominent wings, ⅛ of an inch high, running from base to apex, and coarsely toothed except in their lowest part. The summit is crowned by a short, withered, calycinal tube.

Mr. Binnendyk, of the Botanical garden of Buitenzorg, in Java, who has kindly supplied us with fine specimens of *A. maximum*, as well as with an admirable coloured drawing, states that the plant is cultivated, and that its fruits are sold for the sake of their agreeable edible pulp. We do not know whether the dried fruits or the seeds are ever exported. Pereira confounded them with Bengal and Nepal cardamoms.

Korarima Cardamom—The Arab Physicians were acquainted with a sort of cardamom called *Heil*, which was later known in Europe, and is mentioned in the most ancient printed pharmacopœias as *Cardamomum majus*,[2] a name occurring also in Valerius Cordus and Mattiolus. Like some other Eastern drugs, it gradually disappeared from European commerce, and its name came to be transferred to *Grains of Paradise*, which to the present day are known in the shops as *Semina Cardamomi majoris*.

The true *Cardamomum majus* is a conical fruit,[3] in size and shape not unlike a small fig reversed, containing roundish angular seeds, of an agreeable aromatic flavour, much resembling that of the Malabar cardamom, and quite devoid of the burning taste of grains of paradise. Each fruit is perforated, having been strung on a cord to dry; such strings of cardamoms are sometimes used by the Arabs as rosaries. The fruit in question is called in the Galla language *Korarima*, but it is also known as *Gurágí* spice, and by its Arabic names of *Heil* and

[1] *Account of the Kingdom of Nepal*, Edin. 1819. 74-75.

[2] As the *Tesaurus Aromatariorum*, printed at Milan in 1496, in which it is called *Heil* or *Gardamomum majus*.

[3] Figured in Pereira, *Materia Medica* ii. part i. (1855) 250, and already in Mattioli's *Commentar. in Dioscorid.* lib. i. (1558) 27.

Habhal-habashi.[1] According to Beke,[2] it is conveyed to the market of Báso (10° N. lat.), in Southern Abyssinia, from Tumhé, a region lying in about 9° N. lat. and 35° E. long.; thence it is carried to Massowah, on the Red Sea, and shipped for India and Arabia. Von Heuglin[3] speaks of it as brought from the Galla country. It is not improbable that it is the same fruit which Speke[4] saw growing in 1862 at Uganda, in lat. 0°, and which he says is strung like a necklace by the Wagonda people. Under the name of *Heel Habashee*, Korarima cardamoms were contributed in 1873 from Shoa to the Vienna exhibition; we have also been presented, in 1877, with an excellent specimen of them, recently imported, by Messrs. Schimmel & Co., Leipzig.

Pereira proposed for the plant the name of *Amomum Korarima*, but it has never been botanically described. It would appear from the above statements that it must be indigenous to the whole mountainous region of Eastern Africa, from the Victoria Nyanza lake (Uganda) to the countries of Tumhé, Guragne, and Shoa, south and south-eastward of Abyssinia.

GRANA PARADISI.

Semina Cardamomi majoris, Piper Melegueta; Grains of Paradise, Guinea Grains, Melegueta Pepper; F. *Grains de Paradis, Maniguette;* G. *Paradieskörner.*

Botanical Origin—*Amomum Melegueta* Roscoe—an herbaceous, reed-like plant, 3 to 5 feet high, producing on a scape rising scarcely an inch above the ground, a delicate, wax-like, pale purple flower, which is succeeded by a smooth, scarlet, ovoid fruit, 3 to 4 inches in length, rising out of sheathing bracts.[5]

It varies considerably in the dimensions of all its parts, according to more or less favourable circumstances of soil and climate. In Demerara, where the plant grows luxuriously in cultivation, the fruit is as large as a fine pear, measuring with its tubular part as much as 5 inches in length by 2 inches in diameter; on the other hand, in some parts of West Africa it scarcely exceeds in size a large filbert. It has a thick fleshy pericarp, enclosing a colourless acid pulp of pleasant taste, in which are imbedded the numerous seeds.

A. Melegueta is widely distributed in tropical West Africa, occurring along the coast region from Sierra Leone to Congo. The littoral region, termed, in allusion to its producing grains of paradise, the *Grain Coast, Pepper Coast,* or *Melegueta Coast,* lies between Liberia and Cape Palmas; or, more exactly, between Capes Mesurado (Montserrado) and St. Andrews. The Gold Coast, whence the seeds are now principally exported, is in the Gulf of Guinea, further eastward.

Of the distribution of the plant in the interior we have no exact information. Yet the name Melegueta refers to the ancient empire of

[1] So named by Forskal in 1775 (*Materia Medica Kahirina,* 151. n. 41) who says "*frequens in re culinariâ et medicâ, loco piperis.*"

[2] *Letters on the commerce of Abyssinia, etc.,* addressed to the Foreign Office, 1852: 4. 16. 20.

[3] *Reise nach Abessinien,* Jena, 1868. 223.

[4] *Journal of the discovery of the source of the Nile,* 1863. 648.

[5] Fig. in Bentley and Trimen's *Medical Plants,* part 30 (1878).

Melle (Meli or Melly), formerly extending over the upper Niger region, about in 4° E. long., and then inhabited by the Mandingos, now by the Fulbe or Fullăn. Messena is their most considerable place. In that region *Amomum Melegueta* may be indigenous, or the spice, being formerly exported from the coast by way of Melle, took its commercial name in allusion to the latter.

History—There is no evidence that the ancients were acquainted with the seeds called *Grains of Paradise;* nor can we find any reference to them earlier than an incidental mention under their African name, in the account[1] of a curious festival held at Treviso in A.D. **1214**: it was a sort of tournament, during which a sham fortress, held by twelve noble ladies and their attendants, was besieged and stormed by assailants armed with flowers, fruits, sweetmeats, perfumes, and spices, amongst which last figure—*Melegetæ!*

After this period there are many notices, showing the seeds to have been in general use. Nicolas Myrepsus,[2] physician at the court of the Emperor John III. at Nicœa, in the 13th century, prescribed Μενεγέται; and his contemporary, Simon of Genoa,[3] at Rome, names the same drug as *Melegete* or *Melegette*. *Grana Paradisi* are enumerated among spices sold at Lyons[4] in 1245, and were used about the same time by the Welsh Physicians of Myddvai under the name *Grawn Paris*.[5] They also occur as *Greyn Paradijs* in a tariff of duties levied at Dordrecht in Holland[6] in 1358. And again among the spices used by John, king of France, when in England, A.D. 1359–60, *Grainne de Paradis* is repeatedly mentioned.[7]

In the earliest times the drug was conveyed by the long land journey from the Mandingo country through the desert to the Mediterranean port, Monte di Barca (Mundibarca), on the coast of Tripoli. There the spice was shipped by the Italians, and being the produce of an unknown region and held in great esteem, it acquired the name of *Grains of Paradise*,[8] or also, as already stated at page 650, that of *Semina Cardamomi Majoris*. That they came from Melli is expressly stated also by Leonhard Fuchs.[9] Small quantities of the drug still reach Tripoli in the same way.

Towards the middle of the 14th century, there began to be direct commercial intercourse with tropical Western Africa. Margry[10] relates that ships were sent thither from Dieppe in 1364, and took cargoes of ivory and *malaguette* from near the mouth of the river Cestos, now Sestros. A century later the coast was visited by the Portuguese, who termed it *Terra de malaguet*. The celebrated Columbus also, who traded to the coast of Guinea, called it *Costa di Maniguetta*. Soon after this period the spice became a monopoly of the kings of Portugal.

[1] Rolandini Patavini *Chronica*—Pertz, *Monumenta Germaniæ historica; scriptores*, xix. (1866) 45–46.—Yet *qâfala*, occurring in Edrisi, probably means grains of paradise.

[2] *De Compositione Medicamentorum; de antidotis*, cap. xxii.

[3] *Clavis Sanationis*, Venet. 1510. 19. 42.

[4] *Bibliothek d. lit. Vereins*, Stuttgart, xvi. p. xxiii.

[5] *Meddygon Myddfai* (see Appendix) 283. 286.

[6] Sartorius und Lappenberg, *Geschichte der Deutschen Hansa*, ii. 448.

[7] Douet d'Arcq, 219, 266—see p. 533, note 2.

[8] G. di Barros, *Asia*, Venet. 1561. 33 (65).

[9] *De componendorum miscendorumque medicamentorum ratione*, libr. iv. Lugduni, 1556. 50.

[10] Quoted at p. 589, note 4.

English voyagers visited the Gold Coast in the 16th century, bringing thence in exchanging for European goods, gold, ivory, pepper, and *Grains of Paradise*.[1] The pepper was doubtless that of *Piper Clusii* (p. 589).

Grains of paradise, often called simply *grains*, were anciently used as a condiment like pepper. They were also employed with cinnamon and ginger in making the spiced wine called *hippocras*, in vogue during the 14th and 15th centuries.

In the Portuguese and Spanish idioms, the name *Melegueta*, spelt in various ways, as *Melegette, Melligetta, Mallaguetta, Manigete, Maniguette*, was subsequently also applied to other substitutes of pepper, and even to that spice itself.

In the hands of modern botanists, the plant affording grains of paradise has been the subject of a complication of errors which it is needless to discuss. Suffice it to say, that *Amomum Granum Paradisi* as described by Linnæus cannot be identified;—that in 1817, Afzelius, a Swedish botanist, who resided some years at Sierra Leone, published a description of "*Amomum Granum Paradisi?* Linn.,"[2] but that the specimen of it alleged to have been received from him, and now preserved in the herbarium of Sir J. E. Smith, belongs to another species. Under these circumstances, the name given to the grains of paradise plant by Roscoe, *A. Melegueta*, has been accepted as quite free from doubt.[3]

Description—The seeds are about $\frac{1}{10}$ of an inch in diameter, rather variable in form, being roundish, bluntly angular or somewhat pyramidal. They are hard, with a shining, reddish-brown, shagreen-like surface. The hilum is beak-shaped and of paler colour. The seeds when crushed are feebly aromatic, but have a most pungent and burning taste.

Microscopic Structure—In structure, grains of paradise agree in most respects with cardamom seeds. Yet in the former, the cells of the albumen have very thin, delicate walls which are much more elongated. Of the testa, only the innermost layer agrees with the corresponding part of cardamom; whilst the middle layer has the cell walls so much thickened that only a few cavities, widely distant from one another, remain open. The outer layer of the testa consists of thick-walled cells, the cavities of which appear, on transverse section, radially extended. The albumen is loaded with starch granules of 2 to 5 mkm. diameter, the whole amount in each cell being agglutinated, so as to form a coherent mass.

Chemical Composition—Grains of paradise contain a small proportion of essential oil; 53 lb. yielded us only 2½ oz., equivalent to nearly 0·30 per cent.[4] The oil is faintly yellowish, neutral, of an agreeable odour reminding one of the seeds, and of an aromatic, not acrid taste. It has a sp. gr. at 15·5° C., of 0·825. It is but sparingly soluble in absolute alcohol or in spirit of wine; but mixes clearly with

[1] Hakluyt, *Principal Navigations*, ii. pt. 2.—First Voiage of the *Primerose* and *Lion* to Guinea and Benin, A.D. 1553.

[2] *Remedia Guineensia*, Upsaliæ, p. 71.

[3] I have repeatedly raised *Amomum Melegueta* from commercial Grains of Paradise, and have cultivated the plant for some years, obtaining not only flowers, but large well-ripened fruits containing fertile seeds. —D. H.

[4] This oil was obtained and tried in medicine in the beginning of the 17th century.—Porta, *De Distillatione*, Romæ, 1608, lib. iv. c. 4.

bisulphide of carbon; it dissolves iodine without explosion. When saturated with dry hydrochloric gas, no solid compound is formed.

The oil begins to boil at about 236° C., and the chief bulk of it distills at 257°–258°: the residual part is a thick brownish liquid. Examined in a column of 50 mm. long, the crude oil deviates 1·9° to the left. The portion passing over at 257°–258° deviates 1·2°, the residue 2° to the left. The optical behaviour is consequently in favour of the supposition that the oil is homogeneous. This is corroborated by the results of three elementary analyses which lead to the formula $C^{20}H^{32}O$.

In order to ascertain whether the seed contains a fatty oil, 10 grammes, powdered with quartz, were exhausted with boiling ether. This gave upon evaporation 0·583 grm. of a brown viscid residue, almost devoid of odour, but of intense pungency. As it was entirely soluble in glacial acetic acid or in spirit of wine, we may consider it a *resin*, and not to contain any fatty matter.

The seeds, dried at 100° C., afforded us 2·15 per cent. of ash, which, owing to the presence of manganese, had a green hue.

Commerce—Grains of paradise are chiefly shipped from the settlements on the Gold Coast, of which Cape Coast Castle and Accra are the more important. Official returns[1] show that the exports in 1871 from this district were as follows:—to Great Britain 85,502 lb., the United States 35,630 lb., Germany 28,501 lb., France 27,125 lb., Holland 14,250 lb.—total, 191,011 lb. (1705 cwt.) In 1872 the total shipments amounted to the enormous quantity of 620,191 lb., valued at £10,303: in 1875 only 151,783 lb., valued at £912, were exported.

Uses—The seeds are used in cattle medicines, occasionally as a condiment, but chiefly, we believe, to give a fiery pungency to cordials.

ORCHIDACEÆ.

SALEP.

Radix Salep, Radix Satyrii; *Salep*; F. *Salep*; G. *Salepknollen*.

Botanical Origin—Most, if not all, species of *Orchis* found in Europe and Northern Asia are provided with tubers which, when duly prepared, are capable of furnishing salep. Of those actually so used, the following are the more important, namely—*Orchis mascula* L., *O. Morio* L., *O. militaris* L., *O. ustulata* L., *O. pyramidalis* L., *O. coriophora* L., and *O. longicruris* Link. These species which have the tubers *entire* are natives of the greater part of Central and Southern Europe, Turkey, the Caucasus and Asia Minor.[2]

The following species with *palmate* or *lobed* tubers have a geographical area no less extensive, namely *O. maculata* L., *O. saccifera* Brongn., *O. conopsea* L., and *O. latifolia* L. The last-named reaches North-Western India and Tibet; and *O. conopsea* occurs in Amurland in the extreme east of Asia.

[1] *Blue Book for the Colony of the Gold Coast in* 1871.

[2] Tchihatcheff enumerates 36 species of *Orchis* as occurring in Asia Minor.—*Asie Mineure*, Bot. ii. 1860.

The salep of the Indian bazaars, known as *Sālib misri*, for fine qualities of which the most extravagant prices are paid by wealthy orientals, is derived from certain species of *Eulophia*, as *E. campestris* Lindl., *E. herbacea* Lindl., and probably others.[1]

History—Under the superstitious influence of the so-called *doctrine of signatures*,[2] salep[3] has had for ages a reputation in Eastern countries as a stimulant of the generative powers; and many Europeans who have lived in India, although not prepared to admit the extravagant virtues ascribed to it by Hindus and Mahommedans, yet regard it as a valuable nutrient in the sick room.

The drug was known to Dioscorides and the Arabians, as well as to the herbalists and physicians of the middle ages, by whom it was mostly prescribed in the fresh state. Gerarde (1636) has given excellent figures of the various orchids whose tubers, says he, "*our age useth.*"

Geoffroy[4] having recognized the salep imported from the Levant to be the tubers of an orchis, pointed out in 1740 how it might be prepared from the species indigenous to France.

Collection—The tubers are dug up after the plant has flowered, and the shrivelled ones having been thrown aside, those which are plump are washed, strung on threads and scalded. By this process their vitality is destroyed, and the drying is easily effected by exposure to the sun or to a gentle artificial heat. Though white and juicy when fresh, they become by drying hard and horny, and lose their bitterish taste and peculiar odour.

Salep is largely collected near Melassa (Milas) and Mughla (or Moola), south-east of Smyrna, and also brought there from Mersina, opposite the north-eastern cape (Andrea) of Cyprus. The drug found in English trade is mostly imported from Smyrna. That sold in Germany is partly obtained from plants growing wild in the Taunus mountains, Westerwald, Rhön, the Odenwald, and in Franconia. Salep is also collected in Greece, and used in that country and Turkey in the form of decoction, which is sweetened with honey and taken as an early morning drink.[5] The salep of India is produced on the hills of Afghanistan, Beluchistan, Kabul and Bokhara;[6] the Neilgherry Hills in the south, and even Ceylon are said likewise to afford it.

Description—Levant salep, such as is found in the English market, consists of tubers half an inch to an inch in length, of ovoid or oblong form, often pointed at the lower end, and rounded at the upper where is a depressed scar left by the stem; palmate tubers are unfrequent. They are generally shrunken and contorted, covered with a roughly granular skin, pale brown, translucent, very hard and horny, with but little odour and a slight not unpleasant taste. After maceration in water for several hours, they regain their original form and volume.

[1] The Indian species of *Eulophia* have been reviewed by Lindley in *Journ. of Linn. Soc.* Bot. iii. (1859) 23.

[2] See Appendix, Porta.

[3] *Salep* is the Arabic for *fox*, and the drug is called in that language *Khus yatu's salab*, i.e. *fox's testicle*; or *Khus yatu'l kalb*, i.e. *dog's testicle*. The word *Orchis*, and the old English names *Dogstones*, *Foxstones*, *Harestones* and *Goatstones* have all been given in allusion to the form of the tubers.

[4] *Mém. de l'Acad. des Sciences* for 1740. 99.

[5] Heldreich, *Nutzpflanzen Griechenlands*, Athen, 1862. 9.

[6] Powell, *Economic Products of the Punjab*, Roorkee, i. (1868) 261; Stewart, *Punjab Plants*, Lahore, 1869. 236.

German salep is more translucent and gummy-looking, and has the aspect of being more trimmed and prepared.

Microscopic Structure—The fresh tuber exhibits on transverse section a few outer rows of thin-walled cells rich in starch. These are followed by parenchyme of elongated colourless cells likewise containing starch, and isolated bundles of acicular crystals of oxalate of calcium. In this parenchyme, there are numerous larger cells filled with homogenous mucilage. Small vascular bundles are irregularly scattered throughout the tuber. In *Orchis mascula* and *O. latifolia* the starch grains are nearly globular, and about 25 mkm. in diameter. In dried salep the cell-walls are distorted and the starch grains agglomerated.

Chemical Composition—The most important constituent of salep is a sort of mucilage, the proportions of which according to Dragendorff (1865) amounts to 48 per cent.; but it is doubtless subject to great variation. Salep yields this mucilage to cold water, forming a solution which is turned blue by iodine, and mixes clearly with neutral acetate of lead like gum arabic. On addition of ammonia, an abundant precipitate is formed. Mucilage of salep precipitated by alcohol and then dried, is coloured violet or blue, if moistened with a solution of iodine in iodide of potassium. The dry mucilage is readily soluble in ammoniacal solution of oxide of copper; when boiled with nitric acid, oxalic, but not mucic acid is produced. In these two respects, the mucilage of salep agrees with cellulose, rather than with gum arabic. In the large cells in which it is contained, it does not exhibit any stratification, so that its formation does not appear due to a metamorphosis of the cell-wall itself. Mucilage of salep contains some nitrogen and inorganic matter, of which it is with difficulty deprived by repeated precipitation by alcohol.

It is to the mucilage just described that salep chiefly owes its power of forming with even 40 parts of water a thick jelly, which becomes still thicker on addition of magnesia or borax. The starch however assists in the formation of this jelly; yet its amount is very small, or even *nil* in the tuber bearing the flowering stem, whereas the young lateral tuber abounds in it. The starch so deposited is evidently consumed in the subsequent period of vegetation, thus explaining the fact that tubers are found, the decoction of which is not rendered blue by iodine. Salep contains also sugar and albumin, and when fresh, a trace of volatile oil. Dried at 110° C., it yields 2 per cent. of ash, consisting chiefly of phosphates and chlorides of potassium and calcium (Dragendorff).

Commerce—The shipments of salep from Smyrna are about 5000 okkas (one okka equal to 283·2 lb. avdp. = 128·5 kilogrammes) annually.

Uses—Salep possesses no medicinal powers; but from its property of forming a jelly with a large proportion of water, it has come to be regarded as highly nutritious,—a popular notion in which we do not concur. A decoction flavoured with sugar and spice, or wine, is an agreeable drink for invalids, but is not much used in England.[1]

[1] As powdered salep is difficult to mix with water, many persons fail in preparing this decoction; but it may be easily managed by first stirring the salep with a little spirit of wine, then adding the water *suddenly* and boiling the mixture. The proportions are powdered salep 1 drachm, spirit 1½ fluid drachms, water ½ a pint.

VANILLA.

Vanilla;[1] F. *and* G. *Vanille.*

Botanical Origin—*Vanilla planifolia* Andrews—Indigenous to the hot regions (*tierra caliente*) of Eastern Mexico, diffused by cultivation through other tropical countries. The plant, which is rather fleshy and has large greenish inodorous flowers,[2] grows in moist, shady forests, climbing the trees by means of its aërial roots.

History—The Spaniards found vanilla in use in Mexico as a condiment to chocolate, and by them it was brought to Europe; but it must have long remained very scarce, for Clusius, who received a specimen in 1602 from Morgan, apothecary to Queen Elizabeth, described it as *Lobus oblongus aromaticus*, without being in the least aware of its native country or uses.[3] In the *Thesaurus* of Hernandez there is a figure and account of the plant under the name of *Araco aromatico*.[4]

In the time of Pomet (1694) vanilla was imported by way of Spain, and was much used in France for flavouring chocolate and scenting tobacco. It had a place in the materia medica of the London Pharmacopœia of 1721, and was well known to the druggists of the first half of the 18th century, after which it seems to have gradually disappeared from the shops. Of late times it has been imported in great abundance, and is now plentifully used, not only by the chocolate manufacturer, but also by the cook and confectioner.

Cultivation—The culture of vanilla is very simple. Shoots about three feet long having been fastened to trees, and scarcely touching the ground, soon strike roots on to the bark, and form plants which commence to produce fruit in three years, and remain productive for thirty to forty.

The fertilization of the flower is naturally brought about by insect agency. This was practised as early as 1830 by Neumann in the Jardin des Plantes at Paris, and in 1837 by Morren,[5] the director of the Botanical Garden of Liège, since which the production of the pods has been successfully carried on in all tropical countries[6] without the aid of insects. Even in European forcing houses the plant produces fruits of full size, which for aroma bear comparison with those of Mexico.

In vanilla plantations the pods are not allowed to arrive at complete maturity, but are gathered when their green colour begins to change. According to the statements of De Vriese,[7] they are dried by a rather circuitous process, namely by exposing them to heat alternately uncovered, and wrapped in woollen cloths, whereby they are artificially

[1] Diminutive of the Spanish *vaina*, a pod or capsule.

[2] Beautifully figured in Berg and Schmidt's *Offizinelle Gewächse*, xxxiii. tab. *a* and *b* (1862).

[3] *Exotica* (1605) lib. iii. c. 18. 72.

[4] *Rerum Medicarum Novæ Hispaniæ Thesaurus*, Romæ, 1651. p. 38.—The original drawing was one of a series of 1200, executed at great cost in Mexico by order of the King of Spain during the previous century.

[5] *Ann. of Nat. Hist.* iii. (1839) 1.

[6] In Réunion it was introduced in 1839 by Perrottet, the well-known botanist. See Delteil, *Etude sur la Vanille*, Paris, 1874. 54 pages, 2 plates.

[7] *De Vanielje*, Leyden, 1856. 22, with figures.

ripened, and acquire their ultimate aroma and dark hue. They are then tied together into small bundles.

In Réunion the drying of the pods is performed since 1857 by dipping them previously in boiling water.

Description—The fruit when fresh is of the thickness of the little finger, obscurely triquetrous, opening longitudinally by two unequal valves. It is fleshy, firm, smooth, and plump; when cut transversely it exudes an inodorous slimy juice, abounding in spiculæ of oxalate of calcium.[1] It is one-celled, with a three-sided cavity, from each wall of which projects a two-branched placenta, each branch subdividing into two backward-curling lobes. There are thus in all 12 ridges, which traverse the fruit lengthwise, and bear the seeds. Fine hair-like papillæ line as a thick fringe the three angles of the cavity, and secrete the odorous matter, which after drying is diffused through the whole pod. The papillæ likewise contain drops of oil, which is freely absorbed by the paper in which a pod is wrapped. That the odorous matter is not resident in the fleshy exterior mass we have ascertained by slicing off this portion of a fresh fruit and drying it separately; the interior alone proved to be fragrant.

The vanilla of commerce occurs in the form of fleshy, flexible, stick-like pods, 3 to 8 inches long, and $\frac{3}{10}$ to $\frac{4}{10}$ of an inch wide, of a compressed cylindrical form, attenuated and hooked at the stalk end. The surface is finely furrowed lengthwise, shining, unctuous, and often beset with an efflorescence of minute colourless crystals. The pod splits lengthwise into two unequal valves, revealing a multitude of minute, shining, hard, black seeds of lenticular form, imbedded in a viscid aromatic juice.

The finest vanilla is the Mexican. *Bourbon Vanilla*, which is the more plentiful, is generally shorter and less intense in colour, and commands a lower price.

Microscopic Structure—The inner half of the pericarp contains about 20 vascular bundles, arranged in a diffuse ring. The epidermis is formed of a row of tabular thick-walled cells, containing a granular brown substance. The middle layer of the pericarp is composed of large thin-walled cells, the outer of which are axially extended, while those towards the centre have a cubic or spherical form. All contain drops of yellowish fat and brown granular masses, which do not decidedly exhibit the reaction of tannin. The tissue further encloses needles of oxalate of calcium and prisms of vanillin.

On the walls of the outer cells of the pericarp[2] are deposited spiral fibres, which occur still more conspicuously in the aërial roots and in the parenchyme of the leaves of other orchids. The placentæ are coated with delicate, thin-walled cells.

Chemical Composition—Vanilla owes the fragrance for which it is remarkable to *Vanillin*, which is found in a crystalline state in the interior or on the surface of the fruit, or dissolved in the viscid oily

[1] This juice like that of the squill has an irritating effect on the skin, a fact of which the cultivators in Mauritius are well aware.

[2] Vanilla grown in Europe is devoid of such cells. We can fully corroborate this statement (first made by Berg) from the examination of very aromatic pods produced in 1871 at Hillfield House, Reigate. We have even failed in finding those cells in any vanilla of recent importation (1878).

liquid surrounding the seeds. It was formerly regarded as cinnamic or benzoic acid, and then as cumarin, until Gobley (1858) demonstrated its peculiar nature.

The admirable researches of Tiemann and Haarmann performed in Hofmann's laboratory at Berlin (1874–1876) have shown that vanillin is constituted according to the formula $C^6H^3\begin{cases}OCH^3\\OH\\CHO\end{cases}$. It is the aldehyde of methyl-protocatechuic acid, and like other aldehydes yields a crystallized compound with the bisulphites of alkalis. This is obtained by shaking an ethereal extract (*e*) of vanilla, with a saturated solution of bisulphite of sodium. The vanillin compound remaining in aqueous solution is mixed with sulphuric acid and ether; the latter on evaporation affords crystals of vanillin. They melt at 81°, and may be sublimed by cautiously heating them. Vanillin is but sparingly soluble in cold water, and requires about 11 parts of it at 100° C. for solution; it strikes a fine dark violet with perchloride of iron.

The said chemists have further demonstrated that vanillin may be formed artificially. In the sapwood of pines there occurs a substance called *Coniferin*, $C^{16}H^{22}O^8 + 2\,H^2O$, first observed in 1861 by Hartig. By means of emulsin coniferin taking up H^2O, can be resolved into sugar and another crystallizable substance:—$C^{16}H^{22}O^8 + H^2O = C^6H^{12}O^6 + C^{10}H^{12}O^3$. The second substance thus derived may be collected by means of ether, which dissolves neither coniferin nor sugar. By oxidizing it, or coniferin itself, by bichromate of potassium and sulphuric acid, *Vanillin* is obtained. The latter has been for sometime manufactured in that way by Tiemann, but now eugenol (see p. 285) is used for that purpose. Another source for vanillin is benzoin (p. 409).

The amount of vanillin was stated by Haarmann and Tiemann to be 1·69 per cent. in Mexican vanillin, from 1·9 to 2·48 in the Bourbon variety, and 2·75 in that from Java. The so-called *Vanillon* affords only 0·4 to 0·7 per cent. of vanillin.

From the above-mentioned ethereal solution (*e*), after it has been deprived of vanillin, vanillate of sodium may be removed by a dilute solution of carbonate of sodium. On acidulating the aqueous solution crystals of *vanillic acid*, $C^6H^3\begin{cases}OCH^3\\OH\\COOH\end{cases}$ are precipitated. If the ether of the solution (*e*), after it has been treated with carbonate of sodium, is allowed to evaporate, a mixture of fatty substances and a resin are obtained. The latter has a peculiar odour, somewhat suggestive of castoreum; vanillic acid is almost inodorous.

Leutner (1872) also found in vanilla fatty and waxy matter 11·8, resin 4·0, gum and sugar 16·5 per cent.; and obtained by incineration of the drug 4·6 per cent. of ash.

Production and Commerce—The chief seats of vanilla-production in Mexico are the slopes of the Cordilleras, north-west of Vera Cruz, the centre of the culture being Jicaltepec, in the vicinity of Nautla.[1] The finest specimens were contributed in 1878 to the Paris Exhibition

[1] *Culture du vanillier au Mexique*, in the *Revue Coloniale*, ii. (1849) 383–390; also J. W. von Müller, *Reisen in . . . Mexico*, ii. (Leipzig, 1864) 284–290.

from Agapito, Fonticilla, Misantla, Papantla, also from Teziutlan, province of Puebla. There are likewise "*Baynillales*," plantations of vanilla, on the western declivity of the Cordilleras in the State of Oaxaca, and in lesser quantity in those of Tabasco, Chiapas, and Yucatan. The eastern parts of Mexico exported in 1864, by way of Vera Cruz and Tampico, about 20,000 kilo. of vanilla, chiefly to Bordeaux. Since then the production seems to have much declined, the importation into France having been only 6,896 kilo. in 1871, and 1,938 in 1872.[1]

The cultivation of vanilla in the small French colony of Réunion or Bourbon (40 miles long by 27 miles broad), introduced by Marchant in 1817 from Mauritius, has of late been very successful, notwithstanding many difficulties occasioned by the severe cyclones which sweep periodically over the island, and by microscopic fungi which greatly injured the plant. In 1849 the export of vanilla from Réunion was 3 kilogrammes, in 1877 it reached 30,973 kilogrammes. The neighbouring island of Mauritius also produces vanilla, of which it shipped in 1872 7,139 lbs., in 1877 the quantity was 20,481 lbs. There is likewise a very extensive cultivation of vanilla in Java.

Vanilla comes into the market chiefly by way of France, which country, according to the official statistics, imported in 1871, 29,914 kilo. (65,981 lbs.); in 1872, 26,587 (58,643 lbs.); in 1874 that quantity amounted to 34,906 kilo.

Uses—Vanilla has long ceased to be used in medicine, at least in this country, but is often sold by druggists for flavouring chocolate, ices, creams, and confectionery.

IRIDACEÆ.

RHIZOMA IRIDIS.

Radix Iridis Florentinæ; Orris Root; F. *Racine d'Iris;* G. *Veilchenwurzel.*

Botanical Origin—This drug is derived from three species of *Iris*, namely:—

1. *Iris germanica* L., a perennial plant with beautiful large deep blue flowers, common about Florence and Lucca, ascending to the region of the chestnut. It is also found dispersed throughout Central and Southern Europe, and in Northern India and Morocco; and is one of the commonest plants of the gardens round London, where it is known as the *Blue Flag*.

1. *I. pallida* Lam., a plant differing from the preceding by flowers of a delicate pale blue, growing wild in stony places in Istria. It is abundant about Florence and Lucca in the region of the olive, but is a doubtful native.

3. *I. florentina* L., closely allied to *I. pallida*, yet bearing large white flowers, is indigenous to the coast region of Macedonia and the south-western shores of the Black Sea, Hersek, in the Gulf of Ismid, and about Adalia in Asia Minor. It also occurs in the neighbourhood

[1] *Documents Statistiques réunis par l'Administration des Douanes sur le Commerce de la France*, année 1872, p. 64.

of Florence and Lucca, but in our opinion only as a naturalized plant.[1]

These three species, but especially *I. germanica* and *I. pallida*, are cultivated for the production of orris root in the neighbourhood of Florence. They are planted on the edges of terraces and on waste, stony places contiguous to cultivated ground. *I. florentina* is seldom found beyond the precincts of villas, and is far less common than the other two.

History—In ancient Greece and Rome, orris root was largely used in perfumery; and Macedonia, Elis, and Corinth were famous for their unguents of iris.[2] Theophrastus and Dioscorides were well acquainted with orris root; the latter, as well as Pliny, remarks that the best comes from Illyricum, the next from Macedonia, and a sort still inferior from Libya; and that the root is used as a perfume and medicine. Visiani[3] considers that *Iris germanica* is the Illyrian iris of the ancients, which is highly probable, seeing that throughout Dalmatia (the ancient Illyricum) that species is plentiful, and *I. florentina* and *I. pallida* do not occur. At what period the two latter were introduced into Northern Italy we have no direct evidence, but it was probably in the early middle ages. The ancient arms of Florence, a white lily or iris on a red shield,[4] seem to indicate that that city was famed for the growth of these plants. Petrus de Crescentiis[5] of Bologna, who flourished in the 13th century, mentions the cultivation of the *white* as well as of the purple iris, and states at what season the root should be collected for medicinal use.

But the true Illyrian drug was held to be the best; and Valerius Cordus[6] laments that it was being displaced by the Florentine, though it might easily be obtained through the Venetians.

Orris root mixed with anise was used in England as a perfume for linen as early as 1480 (p. 311), under which date it is mentioned in the *Wardrobe Accounts* of Edward IV.

All the species of iris we have named were in cultivation in England in the time of Gerarde,—that is, the latter end of the 16th century. The starch of the rhizome was formerly reckoned medicinal, and directions for its preparation are to be found in the *Traicté de la Chymie* of Le Febvre, i. (1660) 310.

Production—The above-mentioned species of iris are known to the Tuscan peasantry by the one name of *Giaggiolo*. The rhizomes are collected indiscriminately, the chief quantity being doubtless furnished by the two more plentiful species, *I. germanica* and *I. pallida*. They are dug up in August, are then peeled, trimmed, and laid out in the

[1] From observations made at Florence in the spring of 1872, I am led to regard the three spices here named as quite distinct. The following comparative characters are perhaps worth recording :—

I. germanica — flower-stem scarcely 1½ times as tall as leaves; flowers more crowded than in *I. pallida*, varying in depth of colour but never pale blue.

I. pallida — bracts brown and scariose; flower-stem twice as high as leaves.

I. florentina — bracts green and fleshy; flower-stem short as in *I. germanica;* is a more tender plant than the other two, and blossoms a little later.—D.H.

[2] For further information, consult Blümner, *Die gewerbliche Thätigkeit der Völker des klassischen Alterthums*, 1869. 57. 76. 83.

[3] *Flora Dalmatica*, i. (1842) 116.

[4] Dante, *Divina commedia*, cant. xvi.

[5] *De omnibus agriculturæ partibus*, Basil. 1548. 219.

[6] *Dispensatorium*, Norimb. 1529. 288.

sunshine to dry, the larger bits cut off being reserved for replanting. At the establishment of Count Strozzi, founded in 1806 at Pontasieve near Florence, which lies in the midst of the orris district, the rhizomes, collected from the peasants by itinerant dealers, are separated into different qualities, as *selected* (*scelti*) and *sorts* (*in sorte*), and are ultimately offered in trade either entire, or in small bits (*frantumi*), parings (*raspature*), powder (*polvere di giaggiolo o d' ireos*), or manufactured into orris peas.

The growing of orris is only a small branch of industry, the crops being a sort of side-product, but it is nevertheless shared between the tenant and landowner as is usual on the Tuscan system of husbandry.[1]

In the mountainous neighbourhood of Verona, the rhizomes of *Giglio celeste* or *Giglio selvatico, i.e.*, Iris germanica, are collected and chiefly brought to the small places of Tregnano and Illasi, north-east of Verona. The peasants distinguish the selected long roots (*radice dritta*), the knotty roots (*radice groppo*) which are used for the issue-peas, and the fragments (*scarto*) employed in perfumery.

Some orris root is also exported from Botzen in southern Tyrol.

Description.—The rootstock is fleshy, jointed and branching, creeping horizontally near the surface of the ground. It is formed in old plants of the annual joints of five or six successive years, the oldest of which are evidently in a state of decay. These joints are mostly dichotomous, subcylindrical, a little compressed vertically, gradually becoming obconical, and obtaining a maximum size when about three years old. They are 3 to 4 inches long and sometimes more than 2 inches thick. Those only of the current year emit leaves from their extremities. The rhizome is externally yellowish-brown, internally white and juicy, with an earthy smell and acrid taste. By drying, it gradually acquires its pleasant violet odour, but it is said not to attain its maximum of fragrance until it has been kept for two years.

We have carefully compared with each other the fresh rhizomes of the three species under notice, but are not able to point out any definite character for distinguishing them apart.

Dried orris root as found in the shops occurs in pieces of 2 to 4 inches long, and often as much as 1¼ inches wide. A full-sized piece is seen to consist of an elongated, irregularly subconical portion emitting at its broader end one or two (rarely three) branches which, having been cut short in the process of trimming, have the form of short, broad cones, attached by their apices to the parent rootstock. The rootstock is flattened, somewhat arched, often contorted, shrunken and furrowed. The lower side is marked with small circular scars, indicating the point of insertion of rootlets. The brown outer bark has been usually entirely removed by peeling and paring; and the dried rhizome is of a dull, opaque white, ponderous, firm and compact. It has an agreeable and delicate odour of violets, and a bitterish, rather aromatic taste, with subsequent acridity.

A sort of orris root which has been dried without the removal of the outer peel, is found under the name of *Irisa* in the Indian bazaars, and now and then in the London market. It is, we suppose, the

[1] Groves, *Pharm. Journ.* iii. (1872) 229.—We have also to thank him for information communicated personally.

produce of *Iris germanica* L. (*I. nepalensis* Wall.), which, according to Hooker, is cultivated in Kashmír. Orris root of rather low quality is now often imported from Morocco; it is obtained, we believe, exclusively from *I. germanica*.

Microscopic Structure—On transverse section, the white bark about 2 mm. broad, is seen to be separated by a fine brown line from the faintly yellowish woody tissue. The latter is traversed by numerous vascular bundles, in diffuse and irregular rings, and exhibits here and there small shining crystals of oxalate of calcium. It is made up uniformly of large thick-walled spherical porous cells, loaded with starch granules, which are oval, rather large and very numerous; prisms of calcium oxalate are also visible. The latter were noticed already by one of the earliest microscopic observers, Anton van Leeuwenhoek, about the year 1716. The spiral vessels are small and run in very various directions. The foregoing description is applicable to any one of the three species we have named.

Chemical Composition—When orris root is distilled with water, a crystalline substance, called *Orris Camphor*, is found floating on the aqueous distillate. This substance, which we first obtained from the laboratory of Messrs. Herrings & Co. of London, is yielded, as we learn from Mr. Umney, to the extent of 0·12 per cent.—that is to say, 3 cwt. 3 qrs. 23 ℔. of rhizome afforded of it 8½ ounces.[1] Messrs. Schimmel & Co. of Leipzig also presented us with the same substance, of which they obtain usually 0·60 to 0·80 per cent. Orris camphor has the exquisite and persistent fragrance of the drug; we have proved[2] that this presumed stearoptene or camphor of orris root consists of *myristic acid*, $C^{14}H^{28}O^{2}$ (see page 508), impregnated with the minute quantity of essential oil occurring in the drug. The oil itself would appear not to preexist in the living root, but to be formed on drying it.

By exhausting orris root with spirit of wine, a soft brownish resin is obtained, together with a little tannic matter. The resin has a slightly acrid taste; the tannin strikes a green colour with persalts of iron.

Commerce—Orris root is shipped from Leghorn, Trieste and Mogador,—from the last-named port to the extent in 1876 of 834 cwt.[3] There are no data to show the total imports into Great Britain. France imported in the year 1870 about 50 tons of orris root.

Uses—Frequently employed as an ingredient in tooth-powders, and in France for making issue-peas; but the chief application is as a perfume.

CROCUS.

Croci stigmata; Saffron[4]; F. *and* G. *Saffran.*

Botanical Origin—*Crocus sativus* L., a small plant with a fleshy bulb-like corm and grassy leaves, much resembling the common Spring

[1] The produce of some previous operations, in which 23 cwt. of orris was distilled, afforded but little over one-tenth per cent.

[2] *Pharm. Journ.* vii. (1876) 130.

[3] *Consular Reports*, 1876. 1416.

[4] The word *Saffron* is derived from the Arabic *Asfar*, yellow.

Crocus of the gardens, but blossoming in the autumn. It has an elegant purple flower, with a large orange-red stigma, the three pendulous divisions of which are protruded beyond the perianth.

The Saffron Crocus is supposed to be indigenous to Greece, Asia Minor, and perhaps Persia, but it has been so long under cultivation in the East that its primitive home is somewhat doubtful.[1]

History—Saffron, either as a medicine, condiment, perfume, or dye, has been highly prized by mankind from a remote period, and has played an important part in the history of commerce.

Under the Hebrew name *Carcôm*, which is supposed to be the root of the word *Crocus*, the plant is alluded to by Solomon;[2] and as Κρόκος, by Homer, Hippocrates, Theophrastus, and Theocritus. Virgil and Columella mention the saffron of Mount Tmolus; the latter also names that of Corycus in Cilicia, and of Sicily, both which localities are alluded to as celebrated for the drug by Dioscorides and Pliny.

Saffron was an article of traffic on the Red Sea in the first century; and the author of the Periplus remarks that Κρόκος is exported from Egypt to Southern Arabia, and from Barygaza in the gulf of Cambay.[3] It was well known under the name *kunkuma* to the earlier Hindu writers.

It was cultivated at Derbend and Ispahan in Persia, and in Transoxania in the 10th century,[4] whence it is not improbable the plant was carried to China, for according to the Chinese it came thither from the country of the Mahomedans. Chinese writers have recorded that under the Yuen dynasty (A.D. 1280–1368), it became the custom to mix *Sa-fa-lang* (Saffron) with food.[5]

There is evidence to show that saffron was a cultivated production of Spain[6] as early as A.D. 961; yet it is not so mentioned, but only as an eastern drug, by St. Isidore, archbishop of Seville in the 7th century. As to France, Italy, and Germany, it is commonly said that the saffron crocus was introdued into these countries by the Crusaders. Porchaires, a French nobleman, is stated to have brought some bulbs to Avignon towards the end of the 14th century, and to have commenced the cultivation in the Comtat Venaissin, where it existed down to recent times. About the same time, the growing of saffron is said to have been introduced by the same person into the district of Gâtinais, south of Paris.[7] At that period, saffron was one of the productions of Cyprus,[8] with which island France was then, through the princes of Lusignan, particularly related.

During the middle ages, the saffron cultivated at San Gemignano in Tuscany was an important article of exportation to Genoa.[9] That of

[1] Chappellier has pointed out that *Crocus sativus* L. is unknown in a wild state, and that it hardly ever produces seed even though artificially fertilized; and has argued from these facts that it is probably a hybrid.—*Bulletin de la Soc. bot. de France*, xx. (1853) 191.

[2] *Canticles*, ch. iv. 14.

[3] Lassen, *Indische Alterthumskunde*, iii. (1857) 52.

[4] Istachri, *Buch der Länder*, übersetzt von Mordtmann, 87. 93. 124. 126; Edrisi, *Géographie*, trad. par Jaubert, 168. 192.

[5] Bretschneider, *Chinese Botanical Works*, Foochow, 1870. 15.

[6] *Le Calendrier de Cordoue de l'année 961*, Leyde, 1873. 33. 109.

[7] Conrad et Waldmann, *Traité du Safran du Gâtinais*, Paris, 1846. (23 pages;—no authority quoted).

[8] De Mas Latrie, *Hist. de l'île de Chypre*, iii. 498.

[9] Bourquelot, *Foires de la Champagne*, Mém. de l'Acad. des inscript. et belles-lettres de l'Institut, v. (1865) 286.

Aquila in the Abruzzi was also famous, and used to be distinguished in price-lists till the beginning of the present century; the culture of saffron is still going on there to a small extent.[1] The growing of saffron in Sicily, which was noticed even by Columella, is carried on to the present day, but the quantity produced is insufficient even for home consumption.[2] In Germany and Switzerland, where a more rigorous climate must have increased the difficulties of cultivation, the production of saffron was an object of industry in many localities.[3]

The saffron crocus is said to have been introduced into England during the reign of Edward III. (A.D. 1327–1377).[4] Two centuries later English saffron was even exported to the Continent, for in a priced list of the spices sold by the apothecaries of the north of France, A.D. 1565–70, mention is made of three sorts of saffron, of which "*Safren d'Engleterre*" is the most valuable.[5] It was evidently produced in considerable quantities, for in 1682 we find in the tariff of the "Apotheke" of Celle, Hanover, crocus austriacus optimus, and *Crocus communis anglicus*.[6]

In the beginning of the last century (1723–28), the cultivation of saffron was carried on in what is described by a contemporary writer[7] as—"all that large tract of ground that lies between Saffron Walden and Cambridge, in a circle of about 10 miles diameter." The same writer remarks that saffron was formerly grown in several other counties of England. The cultivation of the crocus about Saffron Walden, which was in full activity when Norden[8] wrote in 1594, had ceased in 1768, and about Cambridge at nearly the same time.[9] Yet the culture must have lingered in a few localities, for in the early part of the present century a little English saffron was still brought every year from Cambridgeshire to London, and sold as a choice drug to those who were willing to pay a high price for it.

Saffron was employed in ancient times to a far greater extent than at the present day. It entered into all sorts of medicines, both internal and external; and it was in common use as a colouring and flavouring ingredient of various dishes for the table. The drug, from its inevitable costliness, has been liable to sophistication from the earliest times. Both Dioscorides and Pliny refer to the frauds practised on it, the latter remarking—"*adulteratur nihil æquè*."

During the middle ages the severest enactments were not only made, but were actually carried into effect, against those who were guilty of sophisticating saffron, or even of possessing the article in an adulterated state. Thus at Pisa, in A.D. 1305, the *fundacarii*, or keepers of the public warehouses, were required by oath and heavy penalties to denounce the owners of any falsified saffron consigned to their custody.[10]

[1] Groves, *Pharm. Journ.* vi. (1875) 215.

[2] Inzenga, in *Annali d' Agricoltura Siciliana*, i. (1851) 51.

[3] Tragus, *De Stirpium*, etc. 1552, p. 763; Ochs, *Geschichte der Stadt und Landschaft Basel*, iii. (1819) 189.

[4] Morant, *Hist. and Antiq. of Essex*, ii. (1768) 545.

[5] The other sorts are "*Safren Calulome*" and "*Safren Noort*."—*Archives générales du Pas de Calais*, quoted by Dorvault, *Revue pharmaceutique de* 1858. p. 58.

[6] *Pharm. Journ.* vi. (1876) 1023.

[7] Douglass, *Phil. Trans.* Nov. 1728.566.

[8] *Description of Essex*, Camden Society, 1840. 8.

[9] Morant, *op. cit.*; Lysons, *Magna Britannia*, vol. ii. pt. i. (1808) 36. Lysons records that at Fulbourn, a village near Cambridge, there had been no *tithe of saffron* since 1774.

[10] Bonaini, *Statuti inediti della città di Pisa dal xii. al xiv. secolo*, iii. (1857) 101.

The Pepperers of London about the same period were also held responsible to check dishonest tampering with saffron.[1]

In France, an edict of Henry II., of 18th March, 1550, recites the advantages derived from the cultivation of saffron in many parts of the kingdom, and enacts the confiscation and burning of the drug when falsified, and corporal punishment of offenders.[2]

The authorities in Germany were far more severe. A *Safranschau* (Saffron inspection) was established at Nuremberg in 1441, in which year 13 lb. of saffron was publicly burnt at the Schönen Brunnen in that city. In 1444, Jobst Findeker was burnt together with his adulterated saffron! And in 1456, Hans Kölbele, Lienhart Frey, and a woman, implicated in falsifying saffron, were buried alive. The *Safranschau* was still in vigour as late as 1591: but new regulations for the inspection of saffron were passed in 1613.[3] There was also in the same city a *Gewürzschau*, or Spice-inspection, from 1441 to 1797. Similar inspections were established in most German towns during the middle ages.

Description—The flower of the saffron crocus has a style 3 to 4 inches long, which in its lower portion is colourless, and included within the tube of the perianth. In its upper part it becomes yellow, and divides into three tubular, filiform, orange-red stigmas, each about an inch in length. The stigmas expand towards their ends, and the tube of which they consist is toothed at the edge and slit on its inner side. The stigma is the only part officinal, and alone is rich in colouring matter.

Commercial saffron (*Hay Saffron* of the druggists) is a loose mass of thread-like stigmas, which when unbroken are united in threes at the upper extremity of the yellow style. It is unctuous to the touch, tough and flexible; of a deep orange-red, peculiar aromatic smell, and bitter and rather pungent taste. It is hygroscopic and not easily pulverized; it loses by drying at 100° C. about 12 per cent. of moisture, which it quickly reabsorbs.[4]

The colouring power of saffron is very remarkable: we have found that a single grain rubbed to fine powder with a little sugar will impart a distinct tint of yellow to 700,000 grains (10 gallons) of water.

Microscopic Structure—The tissue of the stigma consists of very thin, sinuous, closely-felted, thread-shaped cells, and small spiral vessels. The yellow colouring matter penetrates the whole, and is partly deposited in granules. The microscope likewise exhibits oil-drops, and small lumps, probably of a solid fat. Large isolated pollen grains are also present.

Chemical Composition—The splendid colouring matter of saffron has long been known as *Polychroit;* but in 1851 Quadrat, who instituted some fresh researches on the drug, gave it the name of *Crocin*, which was

[1] Riley, *Memorials of London and London Life in the 13th, 14th, and 15th centuries*, 1868. 120.

[2] De la Mare, *Traité de la Police*, Paris, iii. (1719) 428.

[3] J. F. Roth, *Geschichte des Nürnbergischen Handels*, 1800–1802, iv. 221.

[4] Eight lots of saffron weighing *in toto* 61 lb., dried at various times during the course of nine years, lost 7 lb. 2¼ oz., i.e. 11·7 per cent.—(Laboratory records of Messrs. Allen & Hanburys, Plough Court, Lombard Street.)

also adopted in 1858 by Rochleder. Weiss in 1867[1] has shown that it is a glucoside, for which he retains the name of *Polychroit*, while the new colouring matter which results from its decomposition he terms *Crocin*. It agrees with the *Crocetin* of Rochleder.

Polychroit was prepared by Weiss in the following manner: saffron was treated with ether, by which fat, wax, and essential oil were removed; and it was then exhausted with water. From the aqueous solution, gummy matters and some inorganic salts were precipitated by strong alcohol. After the separation of these substances, polychroit was precipitated by addition of ether. Thus obtained, it is an orange-red, viscid, deliquescent substance, which, dried over sulphuric acid, becomes brittle and of a fine ruby colour. It has a sweetish taste, but is devoid of odour, readily soluble in spirit of wine or water, and sparingly in absolute alcohol. By dilute acids, it is decomposed into *Crocin*, sugar, and an aromatic volatile oil having the smell of saffron. Weiss gives the following formula for this decomposition:—

$$\underset{\text{polychroit}}{C^{48}H^{60}O^{18}} + H^2O = \underset{\text{crocin}}{2(C^{16}H^{18}O^6)} \;.\; \underset{\text{essential oil}}{C^{10}H^{14}O} \;.\; \underset{\text{sugar}}{C^6H^{12}O^6}.$$

Crocin is a red powder, insoluble in ether, easily soluble in alcohol, and precipitable from this solution on addition of ether. It is only slightly soluble in water, but freely in an alkaline solution, from which an acid precipitates it in purple-red flocks. Strong sulphuric and nitric acids occasion the same colours as with polychroit; the former producing deep blue, changing to violet and brown, and the latter green, yellow, and finally brown. It is remarkable that hydrocarbons of the benzol class do not dissolve the colouring matter of saffron.

The oil obtained by decomposing crocin is heavier than water; it boils at about 209° C., and is easily altered,—even by water. It is probably identical with the volatile oil obtainable to the extent of one per cent. from the drug itself, and to which its odour is due.

Saffron contains sugar (glucose?), besides that obtained by the decomposition of polychroit. The drug leaves after incineration 5 to 6 per cent. of ash.

Production and Commerce—In France the cultivation is carried on by small peasant proprietors; the flowers are collected at the end of September or in the beginning of October. The stigmas are quickly taken out, and immediately dried on sieves over a gentle fire, to which they are exposed for only half an hour. According to Dumesnil[2] 7,000 to 8,000 flowers are required for yielding 500 grammes (17½ oz.) of fresh saffron, which by drying is reduced to 100 grammes.

Notwithstanding the high price of saffron, its cultivation is by no means always profitable, from the many difficulties by which it is attended. Besides occasional injury from weather, the bulbs are often damaged by parasitic fungi as stated by Duhamel in 1728[3] and again by Montagne in 1848.[4]

The most considerable quantity of saffron is now produced in Spain, namely in Lower Arragon, in Novelda near Alicante, in the province

[1] Wiggers and Husemann, *Jahresbericht* for 1868. 35.

[2] *Bulletin de la Société impériale d'acclimatation*, Avril, 1869.

[3] *Mém. de l'Acad. des Sciences*, 1728. p. 100.

[4] *Étude micrographique de la maladie du Safran, connue sous le nom de tacon.*

Albacete (Northern Murcia), in La Mancha, near Huelva, and also near Palma in the island of Mallorca. It is brought into commerce as *Alicante* and *Valencia Saffron*. The quantity of saffron exported from Spain in 1864 was valued at £190,062; in 1865, £135,316; in 1866, £47,083. The drug was chiefly exported to France.[1]

French saffron, which enjoys a better reputation for purity than the Spanish, is cultivated in the arrondissement of Pithiviers-en-Gâtinais, in the department of the Loiret, which district annually furnishes a quantity valued at 1,500,000 (£60,000) to 1,800,000 francs.[2] The exports of France in 1875 were 97,021 kilogrammes, 84,337 of which being imported from Spain.

In Austria, Maissau, north-east of Krems on the Danube, still produces excellent saffron, though only to a very small extent; the district was formerly celebrated for the drug. Saffron is produced in considerable quantity in Ghayn, an elevated mountain region separating Western Afghanistan from Persia.[3] A very little of inferior quality is collected at Pampur in Kashmír, under heavy imposts of the Maharaja.[4] Saffron is also cultivated in some districts of China. Finally, the cultivation has been introduced into the United States, and a little saffron is collected by the German inhabitants of Lancaster County, Pennsylvania.[5] But in almost all countries the cultivation of saffron is on the decline, and in very many districts has altogether ceased.

The imports of saffron into the United Kingdom amounted in 1870 to 43,950 lb., valued at £95,690. The article is largely exported to India, but there are no general statistics to show the amount. Bombay imported in the year 1872-73, 21,994 lb., value £35,115.[6] It is a curious fact that now Spanish saffron finds regularly its way to India.

Uses—Saffron is of no value for any medicinal effects, and retains a place in the pharmacopœia solely on the ground of its utility as a colouring agent. A peculiar preference for it as a condiment exists in various countries, but especially in Austria, Germany and some districts of Switzerland. This predilection prevails even in England—at least in Cornwall, where the use of saffron for colouring cakes is still common. Saffron is largely used by the natives of India in religious rites, in medicine and for the colouring and flavouring of food.

As a dye-stuff saffron is no longer employed, at least in this country, its use having been superseded by less costly substances.

Adulteration—Saffron is often adulterated, but the frauds practised on it are not difficult of detection. Sometimes the falsification consists in the addition of florets of *Calendula* dyed with logwood, or of safflower, or the *stamens* of the saffron crocus, any of which may be detected if a small pinch of the drug be dropped on the surface of warm water, when the peculiar form of the saffron stigma will at once become evident.

[1] *Statistical Tables relating to Foreign Countries* (Blue Book) 1870. 286. 289.

[2] Dumesnil, *l. c.*

[3] Bellew, *From the Indus to the Tigris*, Lond. 1874. 304.

[4] Hügel, *Kaschmir*, ii. (1840) 274.—Powell, *Punjab Products*, i. (1868) 449.—*Pharm. Journ.* vi. (1875) 279.

[5] *Proc. of the American Pharm. Assoc.* 1866. 254.

[6] *Annual Statement of the Trade and Navigation of the Presidency of Bombay for* 1872–73. pt. ii. 30.

Another adulteration of late much practised, and not always easy to detect by the eye, consists in coating genuine saffron with carbonate of lime, previously tinged orange-red. If a few shreds of such saffron be placed on the surface of water in a wineglass and gently stirred, the water will *immediately* become turbid, and the carbonate of lime will detach itself as a white powder and subside. Saffron thus adulterated will *freely effervesce* when dilute hydrochloric acid is dropped upon it. We have examined Alicante Saffron, the weight of which had been increased more than 20 per cent. by this fraudulent admixture. The earthy matter employed in sophisticating saffron is said to be sometimes emery powder, rendered adherent by honey. We have found that adulterated with carbonate of lime to leave from 12 to 28 per cent. of ash.[1]

PALMÆ.

SEMEN ARECÆ.

Nuces Arecæ vel Betel; Areca Nuts, Betel Nuts; F. *Semence ou Noix d'Arec;* G. *Arekanüsse, Betelnüsse.*

Botanical Origin—*Areca Catechu* L., a most elegant palm,[2] with a straight smooth trunk, 40 to 50 feet high and about 20 inches in circumference. The inflorescence is arranged on a branching spadix, with the male flowers on its upper portion and the female near its base. The tree is cultivated in the Malayan Archipelago, the warmer parts of the Indian Peninsula, Ceylon, Indo-China and the Phillippines. It is probably indigenous to the first-named region.

History—The Areca palm is mentioned in the Sanskrit writings as *Guvāca.* It is called in Chinese *Pin-lang,* a name apparently derived from *Pinang,* a designation for the tree in the Malay Islands, whence the Chinese anciently derived their supply of the seeds. The oldest Chinese work to mention the *pin-lang* is the *San-fu-huang-tu,* a description of Chang-an, the capital of the Emperor Wu-ti, B.C. 140–86. It is there stated that after the conquest of Yunnan, B.C. 111, some remarkable trees and plants of the south were taken to the capital, and among them more than 100 *pin-lang,* which were planted in the imperial gardens. Bretschneider,[3] to whose researches we are indebted for this information, cites several other Chinese works, from the first century downwards, showing that areca nuts were brought from the then unsubdued provinces of Southern China, the Malayan Archipelago and India. The custom of presenting areca nut to a guest is alluded to in a work of the 4th century.

The Arabian writers, as for instance Ibn Batuta, were well acquainted with the areca nut, which they called *Fófal,* and with the Indian custom of masticating it with lime.

Areca nut, though held in great estimation among Asiatics as a masticatory, and supposed to strengthen the gums, sweeten the breath and

[1] *Science Papers,* 368.

[2] Bentley and Trimen, *Medic. Plants,* part 21 (1877).

[3] *On the study of Chinese botanical works,* Foochow, 1870. 27.

improve digestion, has not until recently been regarded as possessing any particular medicinal powers beyond those of a mild astringent.[1] It has often been administered as a vermifuge to dogs, and in India and China is given with the same intent to the human subject. Some successful trials recently made of it for the expulsion of tapeworm have led to it being included in the *Additions to the British Pharmacopœia of 1867*, published in 1874.

Description—The areca palm produces a smooth ovoid fruit, of the size of a small hen's egg, slightly pointed at its upper end, and crowned with the remains of the stigmas. Its exterior consists of a thick pericarp, at first fleshy, but, when quite mature, composed of fine stringy fibres running lengthwise, with much coarser ones below them. This fibrous coat is consolidated into a thin crustaceous shell or endocarp, which surrounds the solitary seed. The latter has the shape of a very short rounded cone, scarcely an inch in height; it is depressed at the centre of the base, and has frequently a tuft of fibres on one side of the depression, indicating its connexion with the pericarp. The testa, which seems to be partially adherent to the endocarp, is obscurely defined, and inseparable from the nucleus. Its surface is conspicuously marked with a network of veins, running chiefly from the hilum. When a seed is split open, it is seen that these veins extend downwards into the white albumen, reaching almost to its centre, thus giving the seed a strong resemblance both in structure and appearance to a nutmeg. The embryo, which is small and conical, is seated at the base of the seed. Areca nuts are dense and ponderous, and very difficult to break or cut. They have when freshly broken a weak cheesy odour, and taste slightly astringent.

Microscopic Structure—The white horny albumen is made up of large thick-walled cells, loaded with an albuminoid matter, which on addition of iodine assumes a brown hue. The cell-walls display large pores, the structure of which, after boiling in caustic ley, becomes clearly evident in polarized light. The brown tissue which runs into the albumen is of loose texture, and resembles the corresponding structure in a nutmeg. The thin walls of its cells are marked with fine spiral striations, and in this tissue, as well as on the brown surface of the seed, delicate spiral vessels are scattered. All the brown cells assume a rich red if moistened with caustic ley, and a dingy green with ferric chloride.

Chemical Composition—We have exhausted the powder of the seeds, previously dried at 100° C., with ether; and thereby obtained a *colourless* solution, which after evaporation left an oily liquid, concreting on cooling. This fatty matter, representing 14 per cent. of the seed, was thoroughly crystalline and melted at 39° C. By saponification we obtained from it a crystalline fatty acid fusing at 41° C., which may consequently be a mixture of lauric and myristic acids. Some of the fatty matter was boiled with water: the water on evaporation afforded an extremely small trace of tannin but no crystals, which had catechin been present should have been left.

[1] J. J. Berlu, *The Treasury of Drugs Unlocked*, London, 1724, no doubt had before him the areca nuts in speaking of "*Nuces indicæ* (see also p. 503, note 2), like a nutmeg in shape, in chewing turns red; it is said they will make one drunk . . . . but I could never find it."

The powdered seeds which had been treated with ether were then exhausted by cold spirit of wine (·832), which afforded 14·77 per cent. (reckoned on the original seeds) of a red amorphous *tannic matter*, which after drying, proved to be but little soluble in water, whether cold or boiling. Submitting to destructive distillation, it afforded *Pyrocatechin*. Its aqueous solution is not altered by ferrous sulphate, unless an alkali is added, when it assumes a violet hue, with separation of a copious dark purplish precipitate. On addition of a ferric salt in minute quantity to the aqueous solution of the tannic matter, a fine green tint is produced, quickly turning brown by a further addition of the test, and violet by an alkali. An abundant dark precipitate is also formed.

The seeds having been exhausted by both ether and spirit of wine, were treated with water, which removed from them chiefly mucilage precipitable by alcohol. The alcohol thus used afforded on filtration traces of an acid, the examination of which was not pursued. After exhaustion with ether, spirit of wine and water, a dark brown solution is got by digesting the residue in ammonia: from this solution, an acid throws down an abundant brown precipitate, not soluble even in boiling alcohol. We have not been able to obtain crystals from an aqueous decoction of the seeds, nor by exhausting them directly with boiling spirit of wine. We have come therefore to the conclusion that *Catechin* (p. 243) is not a constituent of areca nuts, and that any extract, if ever made from them, must be essentially different to the *Catechu* of *Acacia* or of *Nauclea*, and rather to be considered a kind of tannic matter of the nature of *Ratanhia-red* or *Cinchona-red*.

By incinerating the powdered seeds, 2·26 per cent. were obtained of a brown ash, which, besides peroxide of iron, contained phosphate of magnesium.

Commerce—Areca nuts are sold in India both in the husk (pericarp) and without it, and the two sorts are enumerated in the Customs Returns under distinct heads. Their widespread consumption in the East gives rise to an enormous trade, of which some notion may be formed by a consideration of the few statistics bearing upon it which are accessible.

Thus, Ceylon exported of areca nuts in the year 1871, 66,543 cwt., value £62,593; in 1872, 71,715 cwt.,—the latter quantity entirely to India; in 1875 of the total export of 94,567 cwt. 86,446 were shipped to India.[1]

The Madras Presidency largely trades in the same commodity. In the year 1872–1873 there were shipped thence to Bombay 43,958 cwt., besides about two millions of the entire fruit.[2] An extensive traffic in areca nuts is carried on at Singapore and especially in Sumatra.

Uses—Powdered areca nut may be given for the expulsion of tapeworm in the dose of 4 to 6 drachms, taken in milk. The remedy should be administered to the patient after a fast of about twelve hours; some recommend the previous exhibition of a purgative. It is said to be efficacious against *lumbricus* as well as *tænia*.

The charcoal afforded by burning areca nuts in a close vessel is sold as a tooth powder; but except greater density, it possesses no advantage over the charcoal from ordinary wood.

[1] Ceylon Blue Books. [2] From the returns quoted at p. 571, note 5.

As a masticatory areca nut is chewed with a little lime and a leaf of the Betel Pepper, *Piper Betle* L. The nut for this purpose is used in a young and tender state, or is prepared by boiling in water; it is sometimes combined with aromatics, as camphor or cardamom.

SANGUIS DRACONIS.

Resina Draconis; Dragon's Blood; F. *Sang-dragon;* G. *Drachenblut.*

Botanical Origin—*Calamus Draco*[1] Willd. (*Dæmonorhops Draco* Mart.)—This is one of the Rotang or Rattan Palms, remarkable for their very long flexible stems, which climb among the branches of trees by means of spines on the leafstalk. The species under notice, called in Malay *Rotang Jernang,* grows in swampy forests of the Residency of Palembang and in the territory of Jambi, in Eastern Sumatra, and in Southern Borneo, which regions furnish the dragon's blood of commerce. It is said to occur also in Penang and in various islands of the Sunda chain.

History—The substance which is mentioned by Dioscorides under the name of Κιννάβαρι, as a costly pigment and medicine brought from Africa, and which is also described by Pliny who distinguished it from minium, was certainly the resin called *Dragon's Blood.* It was not however that of the Rotang Palm, *Calamus Draco,* or even of any tree of the Indian Archipelago, but was on the contrary a production of the island of Socotra (see p. 675).

Dragon's blood is, we believe, not named by any of the earlier voyagers to the India islands. Ibn Batuta, who visited both Java and Sumatra between A.D. 1325 and 1349, and notices their producing benzoin (see p. 404), cloves, camphor, and aloes-wood, is silent about dragon's blood. Barbosa, whose intelligent narrative (A.D. 1514) of the East Indies[2] is full of reference to the trade and productions of the different localities he visited, states that aloes and *dragon's blood* are produced in Socotra, but makes no mention of the latter commodity as found at Malacca, Java, Sumatra, or Borneo.

The fact we wish to prove is corroborated by the accounts of early commercial intercourse between the Chinese and Arabs recently published by Bretschneider.[3] From the 10th to the 15th century there was carried on between these nations a trade, the objects of which were not only the productions of the Arabian Gulf and countries further north, but also those of the Indian Archipelago. One of the islands with which the Arabs and Persians carried on a great commerce was Sumatra, whence they obtained the precious camphor so much valued by the Chinese, but not, so far as it appears, the resin dragon's blood. As to the productions brought from Arabia they are enumerated as Ostriches, Olibanum, Liquid Storax, Myrrh, and *Dragon's Blood,* besides a few other articles not yet determined. It is worthy of remark that the Chinese are still the principal consumers of dragon's blood, though like

[1] Beautifully figured by Blume, *Rumphia,* ii. (1836) tab. 131–132.

[2] *Description of the Coasts of East Africa and Malabar* (Hakluyt Society), 1866. 30. 191–197.

[3] *Knowledge possessed by the Chinese of the Arabs, etc.,* 1871.

the rest of mankind they have to content themselves with the plentiful drug of Sumatra and Borneo, instead of the more ancient sort produced in Socotra.

The first clear account of the production of the resin in India is that given by Rumphius, who in his *Herbarium Amboinense*[1] describes the process by which it is collected at Palembang.

Production—The fruit of *Calamus Draco*, which is produced in panicles in great profusion, is globose and of the size of a large cherry, clothed with smoothed downward-overlapping scales. These scales are sub-quadrangular, thick and shell-like, marked with a longitudinal furrow; the largest, which are found towards the middle of the fruit, are 2 lines long by 3 broad. At maturity the fruit is covered with an exudation of red resin, which encrusts it so abundantly that the form of the scales can hardly be seen.

The resin, which is naturally friable, is collected by gathering the fruits, and shaking or beating them in a sack, by which process it is soon separated. It is then sifted to remove from it scales and other portions of the fruit. By exposure to the heat of the sun or in a covered vessel to that of boiling water, the resin is so far softened that it can be moulded into sticks or balls, which are forthwith wrapped in a piece of palm leaf. It is thus that the best dragon's blood, or *jernang*, is obtained. An inferior quality is got by boiling the pounded fruits in water, and making the resin into a mass, frequently with the addition of other substances by way of adulteration. The foregoing is the account of the manufacture of the drug given by Blume.[2]

Description—Dragon's Blood is found in commerce chiefly in two forms, known respectively as *Reed* and *Lump*.

1. *Reed Dragon's Blood* (Dragon's Blood in sticks, *Sanguis draconis in baculis*). Some of fine quality purchased in London in 1842 is in sticks 13 to 14 inches in length, and ¾ to 1 inch in diameter, neatly wrapped in palm-leaf, secured by 8 or 9 transverse bands of some flexible grass. The average weight of each stick, including the enveloping leaf, is five ounces. The resin has evidently been wrapt up while soft, as the sticks are furrowed longitudinally by pressure of the surrounding leaf. The smooth surface is of an intense blackish-brown; when seen in thin splinters the resin appears transparent, and of a pure and brilliant crimson. The fractured surface looks resinous and rough, is a little porous, and contains numerous particles of the scales of the fruit. Rubbed on paper it leaves a red mark of not very splendid tint. Heated with alcohol it left 20 per cent. of pulverulent residue consisting chiefly of vegetable matter. Sticks of smaller size are more common.

2. *Lump Dragon's Blood* (*Sanguis draconis in massis*) is imported in large rectangular blocks or irregular masses. From the fine *Reed Dragon's Blood*, just described, it differs in containing a larger proportion of remains of the fruit, including numerous entire scales. Hence it has a coarser fracture, and the fractured surface is less intense in tint. Its taste is slightly acrid. Exhausted with alcohol it leaves a residue amounting in the specimen we tested to 27 per cent.

[1] Pars. v. (1747) 114–115. tab. 58.

[2] *Rumphia*, iii. (1847) 9. tab. 131. 132.

Dragon's blood is abundantly soluble in the usual solvents of resins, namely, the alcohols (even in dilute spirit of wine), benzol, chloroform, bisulphide of carbon, and the oxygenated essential oils, as that of cloves. The residue left after the evaporation of these liquids is amorphous and of the original fine red colour. The drug is likewise dissolved by glacial acetic acid as well as by caustic soda; the latter solution on addition of an excess of acid yields a dingy brown, jelly-like precipitate, which on drying turns dark red like the original drug. In ether dragon's blood is sparingly soluble, and still less so in oil of turpentine; but in the most volatile portions of petroleum, the so-called petroleum, ether we find it to be entirely insoluble. It has a slightly sweetish and somewhat acrid taste; melts at about 120° C., evolving the aromatic but irritating fumes of benzoic acid; boiled with water the resin becomes soft and partially liquid.

Chemical Composition—Dragon's blood is a peculiar resin, which according to Johnston[1] answers to the formula $C^{20}H^{20}O^{4}$. By heating it and condensing the vapour an aqueous acid liquid is obtained, together with a heavy oily portion of a pungent burning taste and crystals of benzoic acid. The composition of these products has not yet been thoroughly ascertained, but the presence of acetone, *Toluol*, $C^6H^5(CH^3)$, *Dracyl* of Glénard and Boudault (1844), and *Styrol*, C^8H^8 (*Draconyl*), has been pointed out,[2] the latter perhaps due to the existence in the drug of metastyrol (p. 274), as suggested by Kovalewsky.[3] Both these hydrocarbons are *lighter* than water; yet we find that the above oily portion yielded by dry distillation sinks in water, a circumstance possibly occasioned by the presence of benzoic alcohol, $C^6H^5(CH^2OH)$.

As benzoic acid is freely soluble in petroleum ether it ought to be removed from the drug by that solvent: on making the experiment we got traces of an amorphous red matter, a little of an oily liquid, but nothing crystalline. Cinnamic acid, on the other hand, is always present, according to Hirschsohn (1877). As to the watery liquid, it assumes a blue colour on addition of perchloride of iron, whence it would appear to contain phenol or pyrogallol rather than pyrocatechin (p. 196).

By boiling dragon's blood with nitric acid, benzoic, nitro-benzoic, and oxalic acids are chiefly obtained, and only very little picric acid. *Hlasiwetz* and *Barth* melted the drug with caustic potash, and found among the products thus formed phloroglucin (p. 243), para-oxybenzoic, protocatechuic, and oxalic acids, as well as several acids of the fatty series. Benzoin yields similar products.

Commerce—Dragon's blood is shipped from Singapore and Batavia. Large quantities are annually exported from Banjarmasin in Borneo to these places and to China.[4]

Uses.—In medicine, only as the colouring agent of plasters and tooth powders; in the arts, for varnish.

Adulteration—Dragon's blood varies exceedingly in quality,[5] of

[1] *Phil. Trans.* 1839. 134; 1840. 384.

[2] Gmelin, *Chemistry*, xvii. (1866) 387.

[3] Gmelin, *Chemistry*, xvii. 388; also *Annalen der Chemie*, cxx. (1861) 68.

[4] Low, *Sarawak, its inhabitants and productions*, 1848. 43.

[5] The present price, £3 to £11 per cwt., sufficiently indicates this.

which the principal criterion regarded by the dealers is *colour*. Some of the inferior sorts make only a dull brick-red mark when rubbed on paper, and have an earthy-looking fracture. The sticks moreover do not take the impression of the enveloping leaf as when they are more purely resinous. A sample of inferior Reed Dragon's Blood afforded us 40 per cent. of matter, insoluble in spirit of wine.

Other sorts of Dragon's Blood.

Dragon's Blood of Socotra—We have already stated (p. 672) that the *Cinnabar* mentioned by Dioscorides was brought from Africa. That the term really designated dragon's blood seems evident from the fact that the author of the Periplus of the Erythrean Sea,[1] written *circa* A.D. 54–68, names it (Κιννάβαρι) as a production of the island of Dioscorida, the ancient name of Socotra.

The Arabians, as Abu Hanifa and Ibn Baytar,[2] describe dragon's blood as brought from Socotra, giving to the drug the very name by which it is known to the Arabs at the present day, namely, *Dam-ul-akh-wain*. Barbosa (1514) as well as Giovanni di Barros[3] mention it as a production of the island; and in our own times it has been noticed by Wellstead,[4] Vaughan,[5] and A. von Kremer.[6] It is now but little collected. Vaughan states, as well as Von Wrede, that the tree is found in Hadramaut and on the east coast of Africa. The latter statement is also made in letters (1877, 1878), with which we were favoured by Captain Hunter of Aden and Hildebrandt of Berlin (see pages 140 and 141), by the latter of whom we were presented with a photographic sketch of the tree growing in the Somali country, at elevations of from 2500 to 5500 feet, and called there Moli. It is *Dracæna schizantha* Baker,[7] a tree attaining 8 metres in height. The resin has an acidulous taste, and is, according to Hildebrandt, not exported, but occasionally eaten by the Somalis. The tree from which dragon's blood is collected in Socotra is, according to Capt. Hunter, *Dracæna Ombet* Kotschy.

The *Drop Dragon's Blood*, of which small parcels imported from Bombay or Zanzibar occasionally appear in the London market, is however this drug. It is in small tears and fragments, seldom exceeding an inch in length, has a clean glassy fracture, and in thin pieces is transparent and of a splendid ruby colour. From Sumatran dragon's blood it may be distinguished by not containing the little shell-like scales constantly present in that drug, and by not evolving when heated on the point of a knife the irritating fumes of benzoic acid.

Dragon's Blood of the Canary Islands—This substance is afforded by *Dracæna Draco* L., a liliaceous tree[8] resembling a *Yucca*, of which the famous specimen at Orotava in Teneriffe has often been described on account of its gigantic dimensions and venerable age.[9]

[1] *Voyage of Nearchus and Periplus of the Erythrean Sea*, translated by Vincent, Oxford, 1809. 90.

[2] Sontheimer's ed. i. 104. 426. ii. 117.

[3] *L'Asia*, sec. deca. Venet. 1561. p. 10. a.

[4] *Travels in Arabia*, Lond. 1838. ii. 449.

[5] *Pharm. Journ.* xii. (1853) 385.

[6] *Aegypten*, Leipzig, 1863.

[7] On Hildebrandt's East African Plants, *Journ. of Bot.* xv. (1877) 71.

[8] Histological observations on the structure of the stem, accompanied by excellent figures, will be found in a memoir by Rauwenhoff (*Bijdrage tot de kennis van Dracæna Draco*, pp. 55. tabb. 5) in the *Verhand d. Kon. Acad. v. Wetensch., afd. Natuurk.* x. 1863.

[9] It was destroyed in 1867 by a hurricane.

On the exploration of Madeira and Porto Santo in the 15th century, dragon's blood was one of the valued productions collected by the voyagers, and is named as such by Alvise da ca da Mosto in 1454.[1] It is also mentioned by the German physician Hieronymus Münzer, who visited Lisbon about 1494.[2]

The tree yields the resin after incisions are made in its stem; but so far as we know the exudation has never formed a regular and ordinary article of commerce with Europe. It has been found in the sepulchral caves of the aboriginal inhabitants.

The name *Dragon's Blood* has also been applied to an exudation obtained from the West Indian *Pterocarpus Draco* L., and to that of *Croton Draco* Schlecht.; but the latter appears to be of the nature of kino, and neither substance is met with in European commerce.

AROIDEÆ.

RHIZOMA CALAMI AROMATICI.

Radix Calami aromatici, Radix Acori; Sweet Flag Root; F. *Acore odorant ou vrai, Roseau aromatique;* G. *Kalmus.*

Botanical Origin—*Acorus Calamus* L., an aromatic, flag-like plant, growing on the margins of streams, swamps, and lakes, from the coasts of the Black Sea, through Southern Siberia, Central Asia, and India, as far as Amurland, Northern China, and Japan; indigenous also to North America. It is now established as a wild plant in the greater part of Europe, reaching from Sicily as far north as Scotland, Scandinavia, and Northern Russia; and is cultivated to a small extent in Burma and Ceylon.

Regarding the introduction of *Acorus Calamus* into Western Europe, it is believed in Poland to have been introduced there in the 13th century by the Tartars, yet it seems not to have attracted then any attention. The well-informed botanist, Bock (Tragus), mentioning the use of the preserved rhizome by wealthy persons, states[3] that he had never seen the plant growing in Germany. Clusius[4] relates that he first received a living plant in 1574, sent from the lake Apollonia near Brussa in Asia Minor. Camerarius,[5] writing in 1588, speaks of it as introduced some years previously, and then plentiful in Germany, which seems to show a rapid propagation. Gerarde at the close of the century looked upon *Acorus* as an Eastern plant, which he says is grown in many English gardens, and might hence be fitly called the "*Sweet Garden Flag.*" Berlu,[6] in 1724, observes of the root that—"*it is brought in quantities from Germany:*" hence we may infer that it was not then collected in England, as we know it was at a later period.[7]

[1] Ramusio, *Raccolta delle Navigationi et Viaggi*, Venet. i. 97.

[2] Kunstmann, *Abhandlungen der Baierischen Akademie der Wissenschaften*, vii. (1855) 342. et seq.

[3] *Teutsche Speiskammer*, Strassburg, 1550. ciiii.

[4] *Rariorum Stirpium Historia*, Antv. 1576. 520.

[5] *Hortus medicus et philosophicus*, Francof. 1588. 5.

[6] *Treasury of Drugs*, ed. ii. 1724. 115.

[7] See also Trimen in *Journ. of Botany*, ix. (1871) 163.

History—Sweet Flag root has been from the earliest times a favourite medicine of the natives of India, in which country it is sold in every bazaar. Ainslie[1] asserts that it is reckoned so valuable in the bowel complaints of children that there is a penalty incurred by any druggist who will not open his door in the middle of the night to sell it, if demanded!

The descriptions of *Acoron*, a plant of Colchis, Galatia, Pontus, and Crete, given by Dioscorides and Pliny, certainly refer to this drug. We think that the Κάλαμος ἀρωματικός of Dioscorides, which he states to grow in India, is the same, though Royle regards it as an *Andropogon*. The Κάλαμος of Theophrastus and the *Calamus* of the English Bible[2] are considered by some authors to refer to the Sweet Flag.

Celsus in the first century mentioned *Calamus Alexandrinus*, the drug being probably then brought from India by way of the Red Sea. We know by the testimony of Amatus Lusitanus[3] that in the 16th century it used to be so imported into Venice. Rheede,[4] moreover, described and figured *Acorus Calamus* as an Indian plant under the name *Vacha*, which it still bears on the Malabar Coast. But in the pharmaceutical tariff of the German town of Halberstadt of the year 1697, "*Calamus aromaticus verus, Indianischer Calmus*," and "*Calamus aromaticus nostras*," *common Calmus*, are quoted at exactly the same price,[5] and Murray[6] states expressly that in his time (1790) Asiatic calamus was still met with in the pharmacies of Continental Europe, but that it had mostly been replaced by the home-grown drug. At the present time the *Calamus aromaticus* of commerce is European; in all essential characters it agrees with that of India, a package of which is now and then offered in the London drug sales.

Collection—The London market is supplied from Germany, whither the drug is brought, we believe, from Southern Russia. It is no longer collected in England,—at least in quantity, though it used to be gathered some years ago in Norfolk.

Description—The rootstock of sweet flag occurs in somewhat tortuous, subcylindrical or flattened pieces, a few inches long, and from ½ to 1 inch in greatest diameter. Each piece is obscurely marked on the upper surface with the scars, often hairy, of leaves, and on the under with a zigzag line of little, elevated, dot-like rings,—the scars of roots. The rootstock is usually rough and shrunken, varying in colour from dark brown to orange-brown, breaking easily with a short corky fracture, and exhibiting a pale brown spongy interior. The odour is aromatic and agreeable; the taste, bitterish and pungent.

The fresh rootstock is brownish-red or greenish, white or reddish within, and of a spongy texture. Its transverse section is tolerably uniform; a fine line (medullary sheath) separates the outer tissue from the lighter central part, the diameter of which is twice or three times the width of the former.

Microscopic Structure—The outermost layer is made up of

[1] *Mat. Med. of Hindoostan*, Madras, 1813. 54.

[2] Exod. xxx. 23; Cant. iv. 14; Ezek. xxvii. 19.—See also page 715, footnote 2.

[3] *In Diosc. de Mat. Med. Enarrationes*, Argent. 1554. 33.

[4] *Hortus Malabar*. xi. (1692) tab. 48. 49.

[5] Flückiger, *Documente* (quoted page 562), 78.

[6] *Apparatus Medicaminum*, v. 40.

extended epiblema-cells or of a brown corky tissue, the latter occurring in the parts free from leaf-scars. The prevailing tissue, both of the outer and the central part, consists of uniform nearly globular cells, traversed by numerous vascular bundles, especially at the boundary line (medullary sheath). Besides them, the rootstock like that of many fresh-water plants, exhibits a large number of intercellular holes. These air-holes, or more correctly water-holes, are somewhat longitudinally extended, so as to form a kind of net-work, imparting a spongy consistence[1] to the fresh rootstock. At certain places, where the series of cells cross one another, especially in the outer part, there are single cells filled with essential oil,[2] which may be made very conspicuous by adding to sections dilute potash or perchloride of iron. The other cells are loaded with small starch granules; a little mucilage and tannic matter is met with in the exterior coat.

Chemical Composition—The dried rhizome yielded us 1·3 per cent. of a yellowish neutral essential oil of agreeable odour, which in a column of 50 mm. long, deviates 13·8° to the right. By working on a large scale, Messrs. Schimmel & Co., Leipzig, obtain 2·4 to 2·6 per cent.

According to Kurbatow (1873), this oil contains a hydrocarbon, $C^{10}H^{16}$, boiling at 159° C., and forming a crystalline compound with HCl, and another hydrocarbon boiling at 255–258° C., affording no crystallizable hydrochloric compound. By submitting the oil to fractional distillation, we noticed, above 250°, a blue portion, which may be decolorized by sodium. The crude oil acquires a dark brownish colour on addition of perchloride of iron, but is not at all soluble in concentrated potash solution.

The bitter principle *Acorin* was extracted by Faust in 1867, as a semifluid, brownish glucoside, containing nitrogen, soluble both in ether and in alcohol, but neither in benzol nor in water. In order to obtain this substance, we precipitated the decoction of 10 lb. of the drug by means of tannic acid, and followed the method commonly practised in the preparation of bitter principles. By finally exhausting the residue with chloroform, we succeeded in obtaining a very bitter, perfectly crystalline body, but in so minute a quantity, that we were unable to investigate its nature.

Uses—Sweet Flag is an aromatic stimulant and tonic, now rarely used in regular medicine. It is sold by the herbalist for flavouring beer, and for masticating to clear the voice. It is said to be also used by snuff manufacturers.

Adulteration—The rhizome of the Yellow Flag, *Iris Pseudacorus* L., is occasionally mixed with that of the Sweet Flag, from which it may be distinguished by its want of aroma, astringent taste, dark colour, and dissimilar structure.

[1] This was possibly alluded to by Albertus Magnus (A.D. 1193-1280), who says:—(Calamus aromaticus)—nascitur in India et Ethiopia sub cancro, et habet interius ex parte concava "pellem subtilem, *sicut telæ sunt aranearum*."—*De Vegetabilibus*, Jessen's ed. 1867. 376. We suppose the drug under notice was intended.

[2] Hence the practice of *peeling* the rhizome which prevails in some parts of the Continent ought to be abandoned.

LILIACEÆ.

ALOË.

Aloes; F. Aloès ou Suc d'Aloès; G. Aloë.

Botanical Origin—Several species of *Aloë*[1] furnish a bitter juice which when inspissated forms this drug. These plants are natives of arid, sunny places in Southern and Eastern Africa, whence a few species have been introduced into Northern Africa, Spain,[2] and the East and West Indies.

The aloes are succulent plants of liliaceous habit with persistent fleshy leaves, usually prickly at the margin, and erect spikes of yellow or red flowers. Many are stemless; others produce stems some feet in height, which are woody and branching. In the remote districts of Namaqua Land and Damara Land in Western South Africa, and in the Transkei Territory and Northern Natal to the eastern, aloes have been discovered which attain 30 to 60 feet in height, with stems as much as 12 feet in circumference.[3] The following species may be named with more or less of certainty as yielding the drug.[4]

Aloë socotrina Lam. (*A. vera* Miller), native of the southern shores of the Red Sea and Indian Ocean, Socotra, and Zanzibar (?). It is the source of the *Socotrine* and *Moka Aloes*. *A. officinalis* Forsk. and *A. rubescens* DC. are considered to be varieties of this plant. *A. abyssinica* Lam. may probably contribute to the aloes shipped from the Red Sea.

A. vulgaris Lam. (*A. perfoliata*, var. *π. vera* Linn., *A. barbadensis* Mill), a plant of India and of Eastern and Northern Africa, now found also on the shores of Southern Spain, Sicily, Greece, and the Canaries; introduced in the beginning of the 16th century (or earlier) into the West Indies. It affords *Barbados* and *Curaçao Aloes*. *A. indica* Royle, a plant of the North-west Provinces of India, common in Indian gardens, appears to be a slight variety of *A. vulgaris* Lam. *A. litoralis* König, said to grow in abundance at Cape Comorin, is unknown to us. Dr. Bidie suggests that it is a form of the preceding, stunted by a poor saline soil and exposure to the sea breeze. Both *A. indica* and *A. litoralis* are named in the *Pharmacopœia of India*.

Aloë ferox L., and hybrids obtained by crossing it with *A. africana* Mill. and *A. spicata* Thunberg, *A. perfoliata* Linn. (*quoad* Roxb.) and *A. linguæformis* are reputed to yield the best *Cape Aloes*.

A. africana Mill. and its varieties, and *A. plicatilis* Mill. afford an extract which Pappe[5] says is thought to be less powerful.

A. arborescens Mill., *A. Commelini* Willd. and *A. purpurascens*

[1] From the Syriac *Alwai*.

[2] *Aloë arborescens*, *A. purpurascens*, and *A. vulgaris* may be seen luxuriantly growing in Valencia, Granada, Gibraltar.

[3] Dyer in *Gardeners' Chronicle*, May 2, 1874, with figures.

[4] Good figures of *Aloë africana*, *A. arborescens*, *A. ferox*, *A. purpurascens*, *A. socotrina*, and *A. vulgaris* will be found in the work *Monographia generis Aloës et Mesembryanthemi*, auctore Jos. Principe de Salm-Reifferscheid-Dyck, Bonnae, 1836-1863. fol.

[5] *Floræ Capensis Medicæ Prodromus*, ed. 2, 1857. 41.

Haworth are stated to produce a portion of the *Cape Aloes* of commerce.[1]

Various species of *Agave*, especially *A. americana* L., are largely grown, since the first half of the 16th century, in the south of Europe, and popularly called *Aloë*. All of them are plants of Mexico, while the true aloes are natives of the old world. Botanically the genus *Agave* differs from *Aloë*, in that the former has the ovary *inferior*, while in the latter it is *superior*. From a chemical point of view there is also no analogy at all between Aloë and Agave.

History—Aloes was known to the Greeks as a production of the island of Socotra as early as the 4th century B.C., if we might credit a remarkable legend thus given in the writings of the Arabian geographer Edrisi.[2] When Alexander had conquered the king of the Persians and his fleets had vanquished the islands of India, and he had killed Pour, king of the Indies, his master Aristotle recommended him to seek the island that produces *Aloes*. So when he had finished his conquests in India, he returned by way of the Indian Sea into that of Oman, conquered the isles therein, and arrived at last at Socotra, of which he admired the fertility and the climate. And from the advice which Aristotle gave him he determined to remove the original inhabitants and to put Greeks in their place, enjoining the latter to preserve carefully the plant yielding aloes, on account of its utility, and because that without it certain sovereign remedies could not be compounded. He thought also that the trade in and use of this noble drug would be a great advantage for all people. So he took away the original people of the island of Socotra, and established in their stead a colony of Ionians, who remained under his protection and that of his successors, and acquired great riches, until the period when the religion of the Messiah appeared, which religion they embraced. They then became Christians, and so their descendants have remained up to the present time (*circa* A.D. 1154).

This curious account, which Yule[3] says is doubtless a fable, but invented to account for facts, is alluded to by the Mahomedan travellers of the 9th century[4] and in the 10th by Masudi,[5] who says that in his time aloes was produced only in the island of Socotra, where its manufacture had been *improved* by Greeks sent thither by Alexander the Great.

Aloes is not mentioned by Theophrastus, but appears to have been well known to Celsus, Dioscorides, Pliny and the author of the Periplus of the Erythrean Sea, as well as to the later Greek[6] and the Arabian physicians. From the notices of it in the Anglo-Saxon leech-books and a reference to it as one of the drugs recommended to Alfred the Great by the Patriarch of Jerusalem, we may infer that its use was not unknown in Britain as early as the 10th century.[7]

[1] In the above revision of the medicinal species of *Aloë* we have made free use of the observations on the same subject mentioned in the *Dictionnaire de Botanique*. We have also had the advantage of consulting W. Wilson Saunders, Esq., F.R.S., whose long familiarity with these plants in cultivation impart great weight to his opinion.

[2] *Géographie d'Edrisi*, i. (1836) 47.

[3] *Marco Polo*, ii. 343.

[4] *Anciennes Relations des Indes et de la Chine de deux Voyageurs Mahométans, qui y allèrent dans le neuvième siècle*, traduites de l'Arabe, Paris, 1718. 113.

[5] Tome iii. 36.—See Appendix.

[6] Alexander Trallianus, in Puschmann's edition (quoted in the Appendix), i. 578, speaks of Ἀλόης ἡπατίτιδος—*Aloë hepatica*.

[7] See p. 439. note 1.

At this period and for long afterwards the drug was imported into Europe by way of the Red Sea and Alexandria. After the discovery of a route to India by the Cape of Good Hope the old line of commerce probably began to change.

Pires, an apothecary at Cochin, in a letter on Eastern drugs[1] addressed to Manuel, king of Portugal, in 1516, reports that aloes grows in the island of Çacotora, Aden, Cambaya, Valencia of Arragon, and in other parts,—the most esteemed being that of Çacotora, and next it that of Spain; while the drug of Aden and Cambaya is so bad as to be worthless.

In the early part of the 17th century there was a direct trade in aloes between England and Socotra; and in the records of the East India Company there are many notices of the drug being bought of the "King of Socotra." Frequently the king's whole stock of aloes is mentioned as having been purchased.[2]

Wellstead, who travelled in Socotra in 1833,[3] says that in old times the aloë was far more largely grown there than at present, and that the walls which enclosed the plantations may still be seen. He adds that the produce was a monopoly of the Sultan of the island. At the present day the few productions of Socotra that are exported are carried by the Arab coasting vessels, coming annually from the Persian Gulf to Zanzibar, at which place they are transhipped for Indian and other ports. Dr. Kirk, who has resided at Zanzibar from 1866 to 1873, informs us that aloes from Socotra arrives in a very soft state packed in goatskins. From these it is transferred to wooden boxes, in which it concretes, and is shipped to Europe and America. To avoid loss the skins have to be washed; and the aloetic liquor evaporated.

Ligon,[4] who visited the island of Barbados in 1647–50, that is about twenty years after the arrival of the first settlers, speaks of the aloë as if it were indigenous, mentioning also the useful plants which had been introduced. At that period the settlers knew how to prepare the juice for medicinal use, but had not begun to export it. Barbados aloes was in the drug warehouses of London in 1693.[5]

The manufacture of aloes in the Cape Colony of South Africa was observed by Thunberg in 1773 on the farm of a boer named Peter de Wett, who was the first to prepare the drug in that country.[6] Cape Aloes is enumerated in the stock of a London druggist in 1780, its cost being set down as £10 per cwt. (1*s*. 9½*d*. per lb.).

A new and distinct sort of aloes, manufactured in the colony of Natal, appeared in English commerce in 1870. It will be described further on.

Lignum Aloes—It is important to bear in mind that the word *Aloes* or *Lign Aloës*, in Latin *Lignum Aloës*, is used in the Bible and in many ancient writings to designate a substance totally distinct from the modern *Aloes*, namely the resinous wood of *Aquilaria Agallocha* Roxburgh, a large tree[7] of the order Thymeleaceæ, growing in the

[1] See Appendix.

[2] *Calendar of State Papers*, Colonial Series, East Indies, China and Japan, 1513–1616, Lond. 1862.

[3] *Journ. of the Roy. Geograph. Soc.* v. (1835) 129–229.

[4] *History of Barbadoes*, Lond. 1673. 98.

[5] Dale's *Pharmacologia* (1693) 361.

[6] Thunberg, *Travels in Asia, Europe and Africa*, ii. 49. 50.

[7] Fig. in Royle, *Illustr. of the Himalayan Bot. etc.* (1839) tab. 36. See also *Dictionnaire de Botanique*.

Malayan Peninsula. Its wood constituted a drug[1] which was, down to the beginning of the present century, generally valued for use as incense, but now esteemed only in the East.

Structure of the Leaf—The stout fleshy leaves of an aloë have a strong cuticle and thick-walled epidermis. Their interior substance is formed of very loose, large-celled, colourless pulp, traversed by vascular bundles, which, on transverse section, are seen to be accompanied by a group of large thin-walled cells[2] containing the bitter juice which constitutes the drug under notice. These cells, on a longitudinal section, are seen to be considerably elongated, adjoining a single row of smaller, prismatic, truncated cells,[3] by which the former are separated from the cortical layer. The prismatic cells contain a yellow juice, apparently different from that which yields aloes. The cortical tissue is filled with granules of chlorophyll, and exhibits between the cells groups of needles of calcium oxalate. Similar crystals are also found sparingly in the pulp.

The transparent pulp-tissue[4] is rich in mucilage, which after dilution with water is precipitated by neutral acetate of lead, but is not coagulated by boiling.

The amount of bitter principles in the leaf probably varies with the age of the latter and with the season of the year. Haaxman mentions that, in Curaçao, the maximum is found when the leaves are changing from green to brown.

Cultivation and Manufacture—In Barbados,[5] where *Aloë vulgaris* is systematically cultivated for the production of the drug, the plants are set 6 inches apart, in rows which are 1 to 1½ foot asunder, the ground having been carefully prepared and manured. They are kept free from grass and weeds, but yams or pulse are frequently grown between them, The plants are always dwarf, never in the least degree arborescent; almost all of those above a year old bear flowers, which being bright yellow, have a beautiful effect. The leaves are 1–2 feet long; they are cut annually, but this does not destroy the plant, which, under good cultivation, lasts for several years.

The cutting takes place in March and April, and is performed in the heat of the day. The leaves are cut off close to the plant, and placed *very quickly*, the cut end downwards, in a V-shaped wooden trough, about 4 feet long and 12 to 18 inches deep. This is set on a sharp incline, so that the juice which trickles from the leaves very rapidly flows down its sides, and finally escapes by a hole at its lower end into a vessel placed beneath. No pressure of any sort is applied to the leaves. It takes about a quarter of an hour to cut leaves enough to fill a trough. The troughs are so distributed as to be easily accessible to the cutters. Their number is generally five; and by the time the fifth

[1] Hanbury, *Science Papers*, 1876. 263; also Flückiger, *Die Frankfurter Liste*, Halle, 1873. 37. (*Archiv der Pharm.* cci. 511).—For full historical information see Heyd, *Levantehandel*, ii. (1879), 559.

[2] The cells lettered *e* in Berg's figure C, plate iv. *f.* of his "*Offizinelle Gewächse.*"

[3] The cells *d*, in Berg's figure.

[4] This central pulpy tissue is *quite tasteless*, and is actually used as food in times of scarcity in some parts of India.—Stewart, *Punjab Plants*, 1869. 232.

[5] For the particulars we here give respecting Barbados aloes, we have cordially to thank Sir R. Bowcher Clarke, Chief Justice of Barbados, and also Major-General Munro, stationed (1874) at Barbados in command of troops.

is filled, the cutters return to the first and throw out the leaves, which they regard as exhausted. The leaves are neither infused nor boiled, nor is any use afterwards made of them except for manure.

When the vessels receiving the juice become filled, the latter is removed to a cask and reserved for evaporation. This may be done at once, or it may be delayed for weeks or even months, the juice, it is said, not fermenting or spoiling. The evaporation is generally conducted in a copper vessel; at the bottom of this is a large ladle, into which the impurities sink, and are from time to time removed as the boiling goes on. As soon as the inspissation has reached the proper point, which is determined solely by the experienced eye of the workman, the thickened juice is poured into large gourds or into boxes, and allowed to harden.

The drug is not always readily saleable in the island, but is usually bought up by speculators who keep it till there is a demand for it in England. The cultivators are small proprietors, but little capable as to mind or means of making experiments to improve the manufacture of the drug. It is said, however, that occasionally a little aloes of very superior kind is made for some special purpose by exposing the juice in a shallow vessel to solar heat till completely dry. But such a drug is stated to cost too much time and trouble to be profitable.[1] The manufacture of aloes in the Dutch West Indian island of Curaçao is conducted in the same manner.[2]

The manufacture of aloes in the Cape Colony has been thus described to us in a letter[3] from Mr. Peter MacOwan of Gill College, Somerset East:—The operator scratches a shallow dish-shaped hollow in the dry ground, spreads therein a goatskin, and then proceeds to arrange around the margin a radial series of aloë leaves, the cut ends projecting inwards. Upon this, a second series is piled, and then a third—care being taken that the ends of each series overhang sufficiently, to drop clear into the central hollow. When these preparations have been made, the operator either "loafs about" after wild honey, or, more likely, lies down to sleep. The skin being nearly filled, four skewers run in and out at the edge square-fashion, give the means of lifting this primitive saucer from the ground, and emptying its contents into a cast-iron pot. The liquid is then boiled, an operation conducted with the utmost carelessness. Fresh juice is added to that which has nearly acquired the finished consistence; the fire is slackened or urged just as it happens, and the boiling is often interrupted for many hours, if neglect be more convenient than attention. In fact, the process is thoroughly barbarous, conducted without industry or reflection; it is mostly carried on by Bastaards and Hottentots, but not by Kaffirs. "The only aloë I have seen used," says Mr. MacOwan, "is the very large one with di- or tri-chotomous inflorescence,—*A. ferox*, I believe." Backhouse[4] also names "*Aloë ferox?*" as the species he saw used near Port Elizabeth in 1838.

From another correspondent, we learn that the making of aloes in

[1] Some extremely fine Barbados aloes in the London market in 1842 was said to have been manufactured in a vacuum-pan.

[2] Oudemans, *Handleiding tot de Pharmacognosie*, 1865. 316.

[3] Under date May 7, 1871, addressed to myself.—D. H.

[4] *Visit to Mauritius and South Africa*, 1844. 157, also 121.

the Cape Colony is not carried on by preference, but is resorted to when more profitable work is scarce. The drug is sold by the farmers to the merchants of the towns on the coast, some of whom have exerted themselves to obtain a better commodity, and have even imported living aloe-plants from Barbados.

Nothing is known of the manufacture of the so-called *Socotrine* or *Zanzibar Aloes,* or even with certainty in what precise localities it is carried on.

General Description—The differences in the several kinds of commercial aloes are due to various causes, such as the species of *Aloë* employed and the method of extracting the juice. The drug varies exceedingly: some is perfectly transparent and amorphous, with a glassy conchoidal fracture; some is opaque and dark with a dull waxy fracture, or opaque and pallid; or it may be of a light orange-brown and highly crystalline. It varies in consistence in every degree, from dry and brittle to pasty, and even entirely fluid and syrup-like.

These diverse conditions are partially explained by an examination of the very fluid aloes that has been imported of recent years from Bombay. If some of this aloes is allowed to repose, it gradually separates into two portions,—the upper a transparent, black liquid,—the lower, an orange-brown crystalline sediment. If the whole be allowed to evaporate spontaneously, we get aloes of two sorts in the same mass; the one from the upper portion being dark, transparent and amorphous, the other rather opaque and highly crystalline. Should the two layers become mixed, an intermediate form of the drug results.

The *Hepatic Aloes* of the old writers[1] was doubtless this rather opaque form of Socotrine Aloes; but the term has come to be used somewhat vaguely for any sort of liver-coloured aloes, and appears to us unworthy to be retained. Much of the opaque, so-called *Hepatic Aloes* does not however owe its opacity to crystals, but to a feculent matter the nature of which is doubtful.

The odour of aloes is a character which is much depended on by dealers for distinguishing the different varieties, but it can only be appreciated by experience, and certainly cannot be described.[2]

Varieties—The principal varieties of aloes found in English commerce are the following:—

1. *Socotrine Aloes*—also called *Bombay, East Indian*, or *Zanzibar Aloes*, and when opaque and liver-coloured, *Hepatic Aloes*. It is imported in kegs and tin-lined boxes from Bombay, whither it has been carried by the Arab traders from the African coast, the Red Sea ports, or by way of Zanzibar, from Socotra. When of fine quality, it is of a dark reddish-brown, of a peculiar, rather agreeable odour, comparable to myrrh or saffron. In thin fragments, it is seen to be of an orange-brown; its powder is of a tawny reddish-brown. When moistened with spirit of wine, and examined in a thin stratum under the microscope, good

[1] As Macer Floridus in the 10th century, who writes:—

"Sunt Aloës species geminæ, quæ subrubet estque
Intus sicut hepar cum frangitur, hæc *epatita*
Dicitur et magnas habet in medicamine vires,
Utilior picco quæ fracta colore videtur."

[2] Thus the pale, liver-coloured aloes of Natal is invariably associated with the transparent Cape Aloes, simply from the fact that the two drugs have a similar smell. Again, the aloes of Curaçao is at once recognized by its odour, which an experienced druggist pronounces to be quite different from that of the aloes produced in Barbados.

Socotrine Aloes is seen to contain an abundance of crystals. As imported, it is usually soft, at least in the interior of the mass, but it speedily dries and hardens by keeping.[1] It is occasionally imported in a completely fluid state (*Liquid Socotrine Aloes, Aloë Juice*), and is not unfrequently somewhat sour and deteriorated.

Some fine aloes from Zanzibar, of which a very small quantity was offered for sale in 1867, was contained in a skin, and composed of two layers, the one amorphous, the other a granular translucent substance of light colour, which when softened and examined with a lens, was seen to be a mass of crystals. A very bad, dark, fœtid sort of aloes is brought to Aden from the interior. It seems to be the *Moka Aloes* of some writers.

The quantity of aloes imported into Bombay in the year 1871–72 was 892 cwt., of which 736 cwt. are reported as shipped from the Red Sea ports and Aden.[2]

2. ***Barbados Aloes***—Characteristic samples show it as a hard dry substance of a deep chocolate-brown, with a clean, dull, waxy fracture. In small fragments it is seen to be translucent and of an orange-brown hue. When breathed upon, it exhales an odour analogous to, but easily distinguishable from, that of Socotrine aloes. It is imported in boxes and gourds. The gourds, into which the aloes has been poured in a melted state through a square hole, over which a bit of calico is afterwards nailed, contain from 10 to 40 lb. or more. Of late years, Barbados aloes having a smooth and glassy fracture has been imported; it is known to the London drug-brokers as "*Capey Barbados.*" By keeping, it passes into the usual variety having a dull fracture.

The export of aloes from Barbados in 1871, as shown by the *Blue Book* for that colony, was 1046 cwt., of which 954 cwt. were shipped to the United Kingdom.

Curaçao Aloes—manufactured in the Dutch West Indian islands of Curaçao, Bonaire, and Aruba, is imported into this country by way of Holland, packed in boxes of 15 to 28 lb. each. In appearance it resembles Barbados aloes, but has a distinctive odour.

4. ***Cape Aloes***—The special features of this sort of aloes are its brilliant conchoidal fracture and peculiar odour. Small splinters seen by transmitted light are highly transparent and of an amber colour; the powder is of a pale tawny yellow. When the drug is moistened and examined under the microscope, no crystals can be detected, even after the lapse of some days. Cape aloes has the odour of other kinds of aloes, with a certain sourish smell which easily distinguishes it. Several qualities are recognized, chiefly by the greater or lesser brilliancy of fracture, and by the tint of the powder.

From the *Blue Book* for the Colony of the Cape of Good Hope, published at Cape Town in 1873, it appears that the export of aloes in 1872 was 484,532 lb. (4326 cwt.); and that the average market value during the year was 3¾*d.*, the lowest price, 1½*d.*, being at Riversdale and

[1] The average loss as estimated in the drying of 560 lb., upon several occasions, was about 14 per cent.—Laboratory statistics, communicated by Messrs. Allen and Hanburys, London.

[2] *Statement of the Trade and Navigation of the Presidency of Bombay for* 1871-72, pt. ii. 19.

Mossel Bay, and the highest, 11*d*., at Swellendam. The drug is shipped from Cape Town, Mossel Bay and Algoa Bay.

5. *Natal Aloes*—Aloes is also imported from Natal, and since 1870 in considerable quantity. Most of it is of an hepatic kind and completely unlike the ordinary Cape aloes, inasmuch as it is of a greyish-brown and very opaque. Moreover it contains a crystalline principle which has been found in no other sort of aloes.

The drug is manufactured in the upper districts of Natal, between Pietermaritzburg and the Quathlamba mountains, especially in the Umvoti and Mooi River Counties, at an elevation of 2000 to 4000 feet above the sea. The plant used is a large aloë which has not yet been botanically identified. The people who make the drug are British and Dutch settlers, employing Kaffir labourers. The process is not very different from that followed in making Cape aloes, but is conducted with more intelligence. The leaves are cut obliquely into slices, and allowed to exude their juice in the hot sunshine. The juice is then boiled down in iron pots, some care being taken to prevent burning, by stirring the liquid as it becomes thick. The drug while still hot, is poured into wooden cases, in which it is shipped to Europe.[1] The exports from the colony have been as follows:—[2]

1868	1869	1870	1871	1872
none	38 cwt.	646 cwt.	372 cwt.	501 cwt.

Chemical Composition—All kinds of aloes have an odour of the same character and a bitter disagreeable taste. The odour which is often not unpleasant, especially in Socotrine aloes, is due to a *volatile oil*, which the drug contains only in minute proportion. T. and H. Smith of Edinburgh, who contributed a specimen of it to the Vienna Exhibition of 1873, inform us that they obtained it by subjecting to distillation with water 400 lb. of aloes, which quantity they estimate to have yielded about an ounce. The oil is stated in a letter we have received from them, to be a mobile pale yellow liquid, of sp. gr. 0·863, with a boiling point of 266–271° C.

Pure aloes dissolves easily in spirit of wine with the exception of a few flocculi; it is insoluble in chloroform and bisulphide of carbon, as well as in the so-called petroleum ether, the most volatile portion of American petroleum. The sp. gr. of fine transparent fragments of aloes, dried at 100° C., and weighed in the last-named fluid at 16° C., was found by one of us (F.) to be 1·364; showing that aloes is much more ponderous than most of the resins, which seldom have a higher sp. gr. than 1·00 to 1·10. In water aloes dissolves completely only when heated. On cooling, the aqueous solution, whether concentrated or dilute, becomes turbid by the separation of resinous drops, which unite into a brown mass,—the so-called *Resin of Aloes.*[3] The clear solution, after separation of this substance, has a slightly acid reaction; it is coloured dark brown by alkalis, black by ferric chloride, and is precipitated yellowish-grey by neutral lead acetate. Cold water dissolves about

[1] We have to thank J. W. Akerman, Esq., of Pietermaritzburg, for the foregoing information as to the manufacture of this drug.

[2] *Blue Books for the Colony of Natal for* 1868, 1869, 1870, 1871, 1872.

[3] The average yield of aqueous extract made by the pharmacopœia process from commercial Socotrine aloes containing about 14 per cent. of water, was found from the record of five experiments, in which 179 lb. were used, to be 62·7 per cent. Barbadoes aloes, which is always much drier, afforded on an average 80 per cent.

half its weight of aloes, forming an acid liquid which exhibits similar reactions. The solution of aloes in potash or ammonia is precipitated by acids, but not by water.

The most interesting constituents of aloes are the substances known as *Aloïn*. This name was originally applied to an aloïn which, as it appears to be found exclusively in Barbados aloes, is now termed *Barbaloïn*, in order to distinguish it from allied substances occurring in Natal and Socotrine aloes.

Barbaloïn was discovered by T. and H. Smith of Edinburgh in 1851,[1] and was described (1851) by Stenhouse. From good qualities of the drug it can be obtained, according to Tilden,[2] as a crystalline mass, to the extent of 20 to 25 per cent., but in others it appears to occur partly amorphous or in a chemically altered state. Barbaloïn is a neutral substance, crystallizing in tufts of small yellow prisms. These crystals represent *hydrated* aloïn, and part with one molecule of water (=2·69 per cent.) by desiccation *in vacuo*, or by the prolonged heat of a water-bath. Barbaloïn, $C^{34}H^{36}O^{14} + H^2O$, dissolves sparingly in water or alcohol but very freely if either liquid be even slightly warmed; it is insoluble in ether.

The solutions alter quickly if made a little alkaline, but if neutral or slightly acid, are by no means very prone to decomposition. By oxidation with nitric acid, barbaloïn yields, as Tilden (1872) has shown, about a third of its weight of chrysammic acid, besides aloëtic, oxalic, and picric acids. It easily combines with bromine to form yellow needles of *Bromaloïn*, $C^{34}H^{30}Br^6O^{14}$; *Chloraloïn*, $C^{34}H^{30}Cl^6O^{14} + 6H^2O$, crystallizing in prisms, has likewise been obtained.

In examining Natal aloes in 1871, we observed it to contain a distinct crystalline body, much less soluble than the ordinary aloïn of Barbados aloes. We have accordingly named it *Nataloïn*.

Nataloïn exists naturally in Natal aloes, from which it can be easily prepared in the crude state, if the drug is triturated with an equal weight of alcohol at a temperature not exceeding 48° C. This will dissolve the amorphous portion, from which the crystals should be separated by a filter, and washed with a small quantity of cold spirit. From 16 to 25 per cent. of crude nataloïn in pale yellow crystals may be thus extracted. When purified by crystallization from methylic alcohol or spirit of wine, it forms thin, brittle, rectangular scales, often with one or more of their angles truncated. The formula assigned to nataloïn by Tilden, which is supported by the composition of the acetyl derivative he has succeeded in obtaining, is $C^{25}H^{28}O^{11}$.

At 15·5° C., 60 parts of alcohol, 35 of methylic alcohol,[3] 50 of acetic ether, 1236 of ether, and 230 of absolute alcohol, dissolve respectively one part of nataloïn. It is scarcely more soluble in warm than in cold spirit of wine, so that to obtain crystals it is best to allow the solution to evaporate spontaneously. Water hot or cold dissolves it very sparingly. Nataloïn gives off no water when exposed over oil of vitriol, or to a temperature of 100° C. By the action of nitric acid, it affords both oxalic and picric acids, but no chrysammic acid. It appears not

[1] Most beautiful specimens have been presented to each of us by these gentlemen.

[2] *Pharm. Journ.* April 28, 1872. 845.—See also Nov. 5, 1870. 375.

[3] The best crystals can be got by this solvent.

to combine with chlorine or bromine, and we have failed in obtaining from it any such body as bromaloïn.

Liquid Socotrine aloes, imported into London about 1852, was noticed by Pereira to abound in minute crystals, which he termed the *Aloïn of Socotrine Aloes*, and regarded as probably identical with that of Barbados aloes. Some fine dry aloes from Zanzibar of very pale hue, in our possession, is in reality a perfectly crystalline mass.

Histed was the first to assert that the crystalline matter of Socotrine or Zanzibar aloes is a peculiar substance, according neither with barbaloïn nor with nataloïn. This observation was fully corroborated by our own experiments,[1] made chiefly on the Zanzibar aloes just described, and we shall call the substance thus discovered *Socaloïn*. In this drug, the crystals are prisms of comparatively large size, such as we have never observed in Natal aloes. They cannot be so easily isolated as nataloïn, since they are nearly as soluble as the amorphous matter surrounding them. Histed recommends treating the powdered crude drug with a little alcohol, sp. gr. 0·960, and strongly pressing the pasty mass between several thicknesses of calico; then dissolving the yellow crystalline cake in warm weak alcohol, and collecting the crystals which are formed by cooling and repose.

Socaloïn forms tufted acicular prisms, which by solution in methylic alcohol may be got 2 to 3 millimetres long. It is much more soluble than nataloïn. At ordinary temperatures, 30 parts of alcohol, 9 of acetic ether, 380 of ether, 90 of water are capable of dissolving respectively one part of socaloïn; while in methylic alcohol, it is most abundantly soluble. Socaloïn is a hydrate, losing when dried over oil of vitriol 11 to 12 per cent. of water, but slowly regaining it if afterwards exposed to the air. Its elementary composition according to the analysis made by one of us (F.) is $C^{34}H^{38}O^{15}+5\,H^2O$. We have not succeded in obtaining any well-defined bromine compound of socaloïn.

The three aloïns, *Barbaloïn, Nataloïn,* and *Socaloïn,* are easily distinguished by the following beautiful reaction first noticed by Histed:—a drop of nitric acid on a porcelain slab gives with a few particles of barbaloïn or nataloïn, a vivid crimson,[2] but produces little effect with socaloïn. To distinguish barbaloïn from nataloïn, test each by adding a minute quantity to a drop or two of oil of vitriol, then allowing the *vapour* from a rod touched with nitric acid to pass over the surface. Barbaloïn (and socaloïn) will undergo no change, but nataloïn will assume a fine blue.[3]

The researches of E. von Sommaruga and Egger in Vienna (1874) have been directed in particular to the aloïn of Socotrine aloes. The melting point of this aloïn was found to be between 118° and 120° C., that of barbaloïn being much higher. The authors conclude that the three form an homologous series, that their composition may probably be represented thus:—

Barbaloïn	$C^{17}H^{20}O^7$
Nataloïn	$C^{16}H^{18}O^7$
Socaloïn	$C^{15}H^{16}O^7$

[1] Flückiger, *Crystalline Principles in Aloes,—Pharm. Journ.* September 2, 1871. 195.

[2] Rapidly fading in the case of barbaloïn, but permanent with nataloïn unless heat be applied.

[3] These reactions may be sometimes got even with the crude drugs.

They derive in all probability from anthracene, $C^{14}H^{10}$.

The portion of aloes insoluble in cold water was formerly distinguished as *Resin of Aloes*, from the soluble portion which was called *Bitter of aloes* or *Aloëtin*. From the labours of Kossmann (1863), these portions appear to have nearly the same composition. The soluble portions treated with dilute sulphuric acid, is said to yield *Aloëresic* and *Aloëretic Acids*, both crystallizable, besides the indifferent substance *Aloëretin*. These observations have not to our knowledge been confirmed.

It has been shown by Tilden and Rammell[1] that the *Resin of Aloes* may by prolonged treatment with boiling water be separated into two bodies, which they distinguish as *Soluble Resin A.* and *Insoluble Resin B.* With the first it is possible to form a brominated compound, which though non-crystalline is apparently of definite composition. In the view of these chemists the *Resin A.* is a kind of anhydride of barbaloïn—Barbaloïn, $2(C^{34}H^{36}O^{14})$ less H^2O = Aloe Resin A., $C^{68}H^{70}O^{27}$. The resin boiled with nitric acid yields a large amount of chrysammic acid, together with picric and oxalic acids, and carbonic anhydride. *Insoluble Resin B.* was found to have nearly the same composition as *Resin A.*

Aloes treated with various reagents affords a number of remarkable products. Thus, according to Rochleder and Czumpelick (1861) it yields, when boiled with soda-lye, colourless crystals an inch long, which appear to consist of a salt of *Paracumaric Acid*, together with small quantities of fragrant essential oils and volatile fatty acids.

When boiled with dilute sulphuric acid, aloes yields paracumaric acid, from which by fusion with caustic potash, as also directly from aloes, Hlasiwetz (1865) obtained *Para-oxybenzoic Acid* (p. 408). Weselsky (1872-73) has shown that accompanying the last two products, there is a peculiar, crystallizable acid, $C^9H^{10}O^3$, which he has named *Alorcinic Acid*.

By distillation with quick-lime, E. Robiquet (1846) obtained *Aloïsol*, a yellowish oil, which Rembold (1866) proved to be a mixture of dimethylated phenol (*Xylenol*) $C^6H^3 \left\{ \begin{matrix} (CH^3)^2 \\ OH \end{matrix} \right.$, with acetone and hydrocarbons.

Nitric acid forms with Barbadoes aloes, but still better, as Tilden has shown, with barbaloïn, *Aloëtic Acid*, $C^{14}H^4(NO^2)^4O^2$, *Chrysammic Acid*, $C^{14}H^4(NO^2)^4O^4$, and finally *Picric Acid*, together with *Oxalic Acid*. The first two of these acids are distinguished by the splendid tints of their salts, which might be utilized in dyeing.

Chlorine, passed into an aqueous solution of aloes, forms a variety of substitution-products, and finally *Chloranil*, $C^6Cl^4O^2$.

When somewhat strongly heated, aloes swells up considerably, and after ignition leaves a light, slow-burning charcoal, almost free from inorganic constituents. Ordinary Cape aloes, for example, dried at 100° C., leaves only 1 per cent. of ash.

Commerce—There were imported into the United Kingdom in the year 1870, 6264 cwt. of aloes. Of this quantity, South Africa shipped

[1] *Pharm. Journ.* Sept. 21, 1872. 235.

4811 cwt.; and Barbados 970 cwt. The remainder was probably furnished by Eastern Africa.

The commercial value of the varieties of aloes is very different. In 1874, *Barbados Aloes* was quoted in price-currents at £3 5*s.* to £9 10*s.* per cwt.; *Socotrine* at £5 to £13; while *Cape Aloes* was offered at £1 10*s.* to £2. In England, the first two alone are allowed for pharmaceutical preparations. Even the *Veterinary Pharmacopœia*[1] names only *Aloë Barbadensis.* Cape Aloes is esteemed on the Continent, and chiefly consumed there.

Use—Aloes is a valuable purgative in very common use, it is generally given combined with other drugs.

Adulteration—The physical characters of aloes, such as colour of the powder, odour, consistence and freedom from obvious impurity, coupled with its solubility in weak alcohol, usually suffice for determining its goodness.

BULBUS SCILLÆ.

Radix Scillæ; Squill; F. *Bulbe ou squames de Scille, Ognon marin;* G. *Meerzwiebel.*

Botanical Origin—*Urginea maritima* Baker[2] (*Scilla maritima* L., *Urginea Scilla* Steinheil). It is found generally in the regions bordering the Mediterranean, as in Southern France, Italy, Dalmatia, Greece, Asia Minor, Syria, North Africa and the Mediterranean islands. In Sicily, where it grows most abundantly, Urginea ascends to elevations of 3000 feet. It is also very common throughout the South of Spain, where it is by no means confined to the coast; it occurs also in Portugal. In the Riviera of Genoa the peasants like to see it growing under the fig trees.

Two varieties of squill, termed respectively *white* and *red*, are distinguished by druggists. In the first, the bulb-scales are colourless; in the second they are of a roseate hue. No other difference in the plants can be pointed out, nor have the two varieties distinct areas of growth.

History—Squill is one of the most ancient of medicines. Epimenides, a Greek who lived in the 30th Olympiad, is said to have made much use of it, from which circumstance it came to be called *Epimenidea.*[3] It is also mentioned by Theophrastus, and was probably well known to all the ancient Greek physicians. Pliny was not only acquainted with it, but had noticed its two varieties. Dioscorides describes the method of making vinegar of squills; and a similar preparation, as well as compounds of squill with honey, were administered by the Arabian physicians, and still remain in use. The medical school of Salerno preferred the red variety of the drug, which on the whole is not frequently met with in mediæval literature.

Description—The bulb of squill is pear-shaped, and of the size of a

[1] By R. V. Tuson, London, 1869.

[2] *Journ. of Linn. Soc.*, Bot., xiii. (1872) 221.—The genus *Urginea* has flat, discoid seeds, while in *Scilla* proper they are triquetrous. The name *Urginea* was given in allusion to the Algerian tribe Ben *Urgin*, near Bona, where Steinheil (1834) examined this plant.

[3] Haller, *Bibliotheca botanica*, i. 12.

man's fist or larger, often weighing more than four pounds. It has the usual structure of a tunicated bulb; its outer scales are reddish-brown, dry, scarious, and marked with parallel veins. The inner are fleshy and juicy, colourless or of a pale rose tint, thick towards the middle, very thin and delicate at the edges, smooth and shining on the surface. The fresh bulb has a mucilaginous, bitter, acrid taste, but not much odour.

For medicinal use, squill is mostly imported ready dried. The bulbs are collected in the month of August, at which period they are leafless, freed from their dry outer scales, cut transversely into thin slices, and dried in the sun. Thus prepared, the drug appears in the form of narrow, flattish or four-sided curved strips, 1 to 2 inches long, and $\frac{3}{8}$ to $\frac{5}{8}$ of an inch wide, flexible, translucent, of a pale dull yellowish colour, or when derived from the red variety, of a decided roseate hue. When thoroughly dried, they become brittle and pulverizable, but readily absorb water to the extent of about 11 per cent. Powdered squill by the absorption of water from the air, readily cakes together into a hard mass.

Microscopic Structure—The officinal portion of the plant being simply modified leaves, has the histological characters proper to many of those organs. The tissue is made up of polyhedral cells, covered on both sides of the scales by an epidermis provided with stomata. It is traversed by numerous vascular bundles, and also exhibits smaller bundles of laticiferous vessels. If thin slices of squill be moistened with dilute alcohol, most of the parenchymatous cells are seen to be loaded with *mucilage*, which contracts into a jelly on the addition of alcohol. In the interior of this jelly, crystalline particles are met with consisting of oxalate of calcium. This salt is largely deposited in cells, forming either bundles of needle-shaped crystals, or large solitary square prisms, frequently a millimetre long. In either case they are enveloped by the mucilaginous matter already mentioned. Oxalate of calcium as occurring in other plants has been shown in many instances to originate in the midst of mucilaginous matter. The fact is remarkably evident in *Scilla*, especially when examined in polarized light.

On shaking thin slices of the bulb with water, the crystals are deposited in sufficient quantity to become visible to the naked eye, though their weight is actually very small. Direct estimation of the oxalic acid (by titration with chamæleon solution) gave us only 3·07 per cent. of $C^2CaO^4,3H^2O$ from white squill dried at 100° C., which moreover yielded only 2 to 5 per cent. of ash. It is these extremely sharp brittle crystals which occasion the itching and redness, and sometimes even vesication, which result from rubbing a slice of fresh squill on the skin. These effects, which have long been known, were attributed to a volatile acrid principle, until their true cause was recognized by Schroff.[1]

The mucilage also contains albuminous matters, hence the orange colour it assumes on addition of iodine. The vascular bundles are accompanied by some rows of longitudinally extended cells, containing a small number of starch granules. In the red squill the colouring matter is contained in many of the parenchymatous cells, others being entirely devoid of it. It turns blackish-green if a persalt of iron be added.

[1] We have found that the slimy juice of the leaves of *Agapanthus umbellatus* Hérit., which is very rich in spicular crystals, also occasions when rubbed on the skin both itching and redness, lasting for several hours.

Chemical Composition—The most abundant among the constituents of squill are mucilaginous and saccharine matters. Mucilage may be precipitated by means of neutral and basic acetate of lead, yet there remains in solution another substance of the same class, called *Sinistrin*. It was discovered in 1879 by Schmiedeberg, who obtained it by mixing the powder of squill, either red or white, with a solution of basic acetate of lead in slight excess. The gummy matters thus forming insoluble lead compounds being removed, the liquid is deprived of the lead and mixed with slaked lime. An insoluble compound of sinistrin and calcium separates and yields the former on decomposing the well washed precipitate with carbonic acid. The small amount of calcium remaining in the filtrate is to be removed by adding cautiously to the warm solution the small quantity just required of oxalic acid. Lastly, sinistrin is thrown down by alcohol. It is a white amorphous powder, on exposure to air soon forming transparent brittle lumps. The composition of sinistrin is that of dextrin = $C^6H^{10}O^5$, both these substances being very closely allied, yet the aqueous solution of sinistrin deviates the plane of polarization to the left. The rotatory power appears not to be much influenced by the concentration or the temperature of the solution of sinistrin.

An alkaline solution of tartrate of copper is not acted upon by sinistrin. It is transformed into sugar by boiling it for half an hour with water containing 1 per cent. of sulphuric acid. The sugar thus produced is stated by Schmiedeberg to consist of lævulose[1] and another sugar, which in all probability, when perfectly pure, must prove devoid of rotatory power.

The name sinistrin[2] has also been applied to a mucilaginous matter extracted from barley (see Hordeum decorticatum); it remains to be proved that the latter is identical with the sinistrin of squill.

We have obtained a considerable amount of an uncrystallizable levogyre sugar by exhausting squill with dilute alcohol.[3] Alcohol added to an aqueous infusion of squill causes the separation of the mucilage, together with albuminoid matter. If the alcohol is evaporated and a solution of tannic acid is added, the latter will combine with the *bitter principle* of squill, which has not yet been isolated, although several chemists have devoted to it their investigations, and applied to it the names of *Scillitin* or *Skuleïn*. Schroff, to whom we are indebted for a valuable monograph on Squill,[4] infers from his physiological experiments the presence of a non-volatile acrid principle (*Skulein?*), together with scillitin, which latter he supposes to be a glucoside.

Merck of Darmstadt has isolated *Scillipicrin*, soluble in water; *Scillitoxin*, likewise a bitter principle, insoluble in water, but readily dissolving in alcohol; and *Scillin*, a crystalline substance, abundantly soluble in boiling ether. The physiological action of these substances and of *Scillaïn* has been examined (1878) by Moeller, and by Jarmersted (1879); that of scillitoxin and scillaïn was found to be analogous to that of Digitalis.

[1] This is the name applied to the lævogyrate uncrystallizable glucose produced, together with crystallizable dextro-glucose, by decomposing cane sugar by means of dilute acids.

[2] In 1834 first proposed, by Marquart, for inulin.

[3] In Greece they have even attempted to manufacture alcohol by fermenting and distilling squill bulbs.—Heldreich, *Nutzpflanzen Griechenlands*, 1862. 7.

[4] Reprinted from the *Zeitschrift der Gesellschaft der Aerzte zu Wien*, No. 42 (1864). Abstracted also in Canstatt's *Jahresbericht* 1864. 19, and 1865. 238.

Commerce—Dried squill, usually packed in casks, is imported into England from Malta.

Use—Commonly employed as a diuretic and expectorant.

Substitutes—There are several plants of which the bulbs are used in the place of the officinal squill, but which, owing to the abundance and low price of the latter, never appear in the European market.

1. ***Urginea altissima*** Baker (*Ornithogalum altissimum* L.), a South African species, very closely related to the common squill, and having, as it would appear, exactly the same properties.[1]

2. ***U. indica*** Kth. (*Scilla indica* Roxb.), a widely diffused plant, occurring in Northern India, the Coromandel Coast, Abyssinia, Nubia, and Senegambia. It is known by the same Arabic and Persian names as *U. maritima*, and its bulb is used for similar purposes. But according to Moodeen Sheriff[2] it is a poor substitute for the latter, having little or no action when it is old and large.

3. ***Scilla indica*** Baker[3] (non Roxb.), (*Ledebouria hyacinthina* Roth), native of India and Abyssinia, has a bulb which is often confused in the Indian bazaars with the preceding, but is easily distinguishable when entire by being *scaly* not tunicated); it is said to be a better representative of the European squill.[4]

4. ***Drimia ciliaris*** Jacq., a plant of the Cape of Good Hope, of the order *Liliaceæ*. Its bulb much resembles the officinal squill, but has a juice so irritating if it comes in contact with the skin, that the plant is called by the colonists *Jeukbol*, i.e. *Itch-bulb*. It is used medicinally as an emetic, expectorant, and diuretic.[5]

5. ***Crinum asiaticum*** var. ***toxicarium*** Herbert (*C. toxicarium* Roxb.), a large plant, with handsome white flowers and noble foliage, cultivated in Indian gardens, and also found wild in low humid spots in various parts of India and the Moluccas, and on the sea-coast of Ceylon. The bulb has been admitted to the *Pharmacopœia of India* (1868), chiefly on the recommendation of O'Shaughnessy, who considers it a valuable emetic. We have not been able to examine a specimen, and cannot learn that the drug has been the subject of any chemical investigation.

MELANTHACEÆ.

RHIZOMA VERATRI ALBI.

Radix Veratri, Radix Hellebori albi; White Hellebore; F. *Racine d'Ellébore blanc;* G. *Weisse Nieswurzel, Germer.*

Botanical Origin—*Veratrum album* L.—This plant occurs in moist grassy places in the mountain regions of Middle and Southern Europe,

[1] Pappe, *Floræ Medicæ Capensis Prodromus*, ed. 2, 1857. 41.

[2] *Supplement to the Pharmacopœia of India*, Madras, 1869. 250.

[3] Saunders, *Refugium Botanicum*, iii. (1870) appendix, p. 12.

[4] *Suppl. to the Pharm. of India*, 250.

[5] Pappe, *op. cit.* 42.

as Auvergne, the Pyrenees, Spain, Switzerland, and Austria. In Norway it reaches, according to Schübeler (*l. c.* p. 556), the latitude of 71°. It also grows throughout European and Asiatic Russia as far as 61° N. lat., in Amurland, the island of Saghalin, Northern China, and Japan.

History—The confusion that existed among the ancients between *Melampodium, Helleborus,* and *Veratrum,* makes the identification of the plant under notice extremely unsatisfactory.[1] It was perfectly described or figured by Brunfels, Tragus, and other botanists of the 16th century, and likewise well known to Gerarde (*circa* A.D. 1600). Under the names of *Elleborus* (or *Helleborus albus* and *Veratrum,* it has had a place in all the London Pharmacopœias. In the British Pharmacopœia (1867) it has been replaced by the nearly allied American species, *Veratrum viride* Aiton.

Description—White Hellebore has a cylindrical, fleshy, perennial rootstock, 2 to 3 inches in length, and ¾ to 1 inch in diameter, beset with long stout roots. When fresh it has an alliaceous smell. In the dried state, as it occurs in commerce, it is cylindrical or subconical, of a dull earthy black, very rough in its lower half with the pits and scars of old roots; more or less beset above with the remains of recent roots. The top is crowned with the bases of the leaves, the outer of which are coarsely fibrous. The plant has generally been cut off close to the summit of the rhizome, which latter is seldom quite entire, being often broken at its lower end, or cut transversely to facilitate drying. Internally it is nearly colourless; a transverse section shows a broad white ring surrounding a spongy pale buff central portion.

The drug has a sweetish, bitterish acrid taste, leaving on the tongue a sensation of numbness and tingling. In the state of powder, it occasions violent sneezing.

Microscopic Structure—When cut transversely, the rhizome shows at a distance of 2–4 mm. from the thin dark outer bark, a fine brown zigzag line (medullary sheath) surrounding the central part, which exhibits a pith not well defined. The zone between the outer bark and the medullary sheath is pure white, with the exception of some isolated cells containing resin or colouring matter, and those places where the rootlets pass from the interior. The latter is sprinkled as it were, with short, thin somewhat lighter bundles of vessels which run irregularly out in all directions. The parenchyme of the centre rhizome is filled with starch, and contains numerous needles of calcium oxalate. The rootlets, which the collectors usually remove, are living and juicy only in the upper half of the rhizome, the lower part of which is rather woody and porous.

Chemical Composition—In 1819 Pelletier and Caventou detected in the rhizome of *Veratrum* a substance which they regarded as identical with veratrine, the existence of which had just been discovered by Meissner in cebadilla seeds. But according to the observations of Maisch (1870) and Dragendorff,[2] the veratrine of cebadilla cannot be found either in *Veratrum album* or *V. viride.*

Simon (1837) found in the root the alkaloid *Jervine,* Tobien (1877)

[1] Those who wish to study the question, can consult Murray's *Apparatus Medicaminum.* vol. v. (1790) 142–146.

[2] *Beitr. zur gerichtl. Chemie,* St Petersb., 1872. 95.

the *Veratroïdine*, discovered by Bullock (1876) in *Veratrum viride*. Tobien assigns to jervine the formula $C^{27}H^{47}N^2O^3$; that of veratroïdine is not yet settled. The latter is to some extent soluble in water.

Weppen (1872) has isolated from this drug *Veratramarin*, an amorphous, deliquescent, bitter principle. It occurs in minute quantity only, and is resolvable into sugar and other products. Veratramarin dissolves in water or spirit of wine, not in ether or in chloroform. The same observer has also isolated, to the extent of ½ per mille, *Jervic Acid* in hard crystals of considerable size,[1] of the composition $C^{14}H^{10}O^{12} + 2\ H^2O$. The acid requires 100 parts of water for solution at the ordinary temperature, and a little less of boiling alcohol. It is decidedly acid, and forms well-defined crystallizable salts, containing 4 atoms of the monovalent metals.

By exhausting the entire rhizome (roots included) with ether and anhydrous alcohol, we obtained 25·8 per cent. of soft resin, which deserves further examination. Pectic matter to the amount of 10 per cent. was pointed out by Wiegand in 1841.

According to Schroff (1860), in the rootlets the active principle resides in the cortical part, the woody central portion being inert. He also asserts that the rhizome acts less strongly than the rootlets, and in a somewhat different manner.

Commerce—The drug is imported from Germany in bales. The price-currents distinguish *Swiss* and *Austrian*, and generally name the drug as "*without fibre*."

Uses—Veratrum is an emetic and drastic purgative, rarely used internally. It is occasionally employed in the form of ointment in scabies. Its principal consumption is in veterinary medicine.

Substitutes—The rhizome of the Austrian *Veratrum nigrum* L. is said to be sometimes collected instead of White Hellebore; it is of much smaller size, and, according to Schroff, less potent. That of the Mexican *Helonias frigida* Lindley (*Veratrum frigidum* Schl.) appears to exactly resemble that of *Veratrum album*.

RHIZOMA VERATRI VIRIDIS.

American White Hellebore,[2] *Indian Poke.*

Botanical Origin—*Veratrum viride* Aiton, a plant in every respect closely resembling *V. album*, of which it is one of the numerous forms. In fact, the green-coloured variety of the latter (*V. Lobelianum* Bernh.), a plant not uncommon in the mountain meadows of the Alps, comes so near to the American *V. viride* that we are unable to point out any important character by which the two can be separated.[3]

[1] For good specimens of which I am indebted to Dr. Weppen.—F. A. F.

[2] The name *Green Hellebore* is sometimes applied to this drug, but it properly belongs to *Helleborus viridis* L., which is medicinal in some parts of Europe.

[3] Sims in contrasting *Veratrum viride* with *V. album* observes that the flowers of the former are "more inclined to a yellow green," the petals broader and more erect, with the margins, especially about the claw, thickened and covered with a white mealiness. *Bot. Mag.* xxvii. (1808) tab. 1096.—Regel has described four varieties of *Veratrum album* L., as occurring in the region of the Lower Ussuri and Amurland, one of which, var. γ., he has identified with the American *V. viride*.—*Tentamen Floræ Ussuriensis*, St. Petersb. 1761. 153.

The American *Veratrum* is common in swamps and low grounds from Canada to Georgia.

History—The aborigines of North America were acquainted with the active properties of this plant before their intercourse with Europeans, using it according to Josselyn,[1] who visited the country in 1638-1671, as a vomit in a sort of ordeal. He calls it *White Hellebore*, and states that it is employed by the colonists as a purgative, antiscorbutic and insecticide.

Kalm (1749) states[2] that the early settlers used a decoction of the roots to render their seed-maize poisonous to birds, which were made "delirious" by eating the grain, but not killed; and this custom was still practised in New England in 1835 (Osgood).

The effects of the drug have been repeatedly tried in the United States during the present century; and about 1862, in consequence of the strong recommendations of Drs. Osgood, Norwood, Cutter, and others, it began to be prescribed in this country.

Description—In form, internal structure, odour and taste, the rhizome and roots accord with those of *Veratrum album*; yet owing to the method of drying and preparing for the market, the American veratrum is immediately distinguishable from the White Hellebore of European commerce. We have met with it in three forms:—

1. The rhizome with roots attached, usually cut lengthwise into quarters, sometimes transversely also, densely beset with the pale brown roots, which towards their extremities are clothed with slender fibrous rootlets.

2. Rhizome and roots compressed into solid rectangular cakes, an inch in thickness.

3. The rhizome *per se*, sliced transversely and dried. It forms whitish, buff, or brownish discs, ½ to 1 inch or more in diameter, much shrunken and curled by drying. This is the form in which the drug is required by the United States Pharmacopœia.

Chemical Composition—No chemical difference between *Veratrum viride* and *V. album* has yet been ascertained. The presence of veratrine, suspected by previous chemists, was asserted by Worthington[3] in 1839, J. G. Richardson of Philadelphia in 1857, and S. R. Percy in 1864. Scattergood[4] obtained from the American drug 0·4 per cent. of this alkaloid, which however, in consequence of some observations of Dragendorff (p. 694), we must hold to be not identical with that of cebadilla. As stated in a previous page jervine and veratroïdine are present as in the White Hellebore of Europe. Robbins[5] further isolated *Veratridine*, a crystallized alkaloid possessed of a similar physiological action to that of veratrine, though in a less degree. Veratridine is readily soluble in ether; its solution in concentrated sulphuric acid is at first yellow, changing quickly to a pink-red, and, after several hours' standing, assumes a clear indigo-blue colour, much the same as that displayed by veratrine *if mixed with sugar* (Weppen's test, 1874). The resin of the

[1] *New Englands Rarities discovered*, Lond. 1672. 43; also *Account of two Voyages to New England*, Lond., 1674, 60. 76.

[2] *Travels in North America*, vol. ii. (1771) 91.

[3] *Am. Journ. of Pharm.* iv. (1839) 89.

[4] *Proc. of Am. Pharm. Assoc.* 1862. 226.

[5] *Ibid*, 1877. 439. 523.

drug may be prepared by exhausting it with alcohol and precipitating with boiling acidulated water, repeating the process in order to entirely eliminate the alkaloids. It is a dark brown mass, yielding about a fourth of its weight to ether. Scattergood obtained it to the extent of 4½ per cent. By exhausting the drug successively with ether, absolute alcohol and spirit of wine, we extracted from it not less than 31 per cent. of a soft resinoid mass. Worthington pointed out the presence of gallic acid and of sugar.

Uses—*Veratrum viride* has of late been much recommended as a cardiac, arteral and nervous sedative. It is stated to lower the pulse, the respiration and heat of the body, not to be narcotic, and rarely to occasion purging;[1] but to what principle these effects are due has not yet been ascertained. By some observers, as Bigelow,[2] Fée,[3] Schroff,[4] and Oulmont,[5] it is alleged to have the same medicinal powers as the European *Veratrum album*.

SEMEN SABADILLÆ.

Fructus Sabadillæ; Cebadilla, Cevadilla; F. *Cévadille;* G. *Sabadillsamen, Läusesamen.*

Botanical Origin—*Asagræa officinalis* Lindley (*Veratrum officinale* Schlecht., *Sabadilla officinarum* Brandt, *Schœnocaulon officinale* A. Gray).—A bulbous plant, growing in Mexico, in grassy places on the eastern declivities of the volcanic range of the Cofre de Perote, and Orizaba, near Teosolo, Huatusco and Zacuapan, down to the sea-shore, also in Guatemala. Cebadilla is (or was) cultivated near Vera Cruz, Alvarado and Tlacatalpan in the Gulf of Mexico.

Another form of *Asagræa*, first noticed by Berg,[6] but of late more particularly by Ernst of Caracas, who thinks it may constitute a distinct species, is found in plenty on grassy slopes, 3,500 to 4,000 feet above the sea-level, in the neighbourhood of Caracas, and southward in the hilly regions bordering the valley of the Tuy.[7] It differs chiefly in having broader and more carinate leaves.[8] Of late years it has furnished large quantities of seed, which, freed from their capsules, have been shipped from La Guaira to Hamburg.

History—Cebadilla was first described in 1517 by Monardes, who states that it is used by the Indians of New Spain as a caustic and

[1] Cutter, *Lancet*, Jan. 4, Aug. 16, 1862; *Pharm. Journ.* iv. (1863) 134.

[2] *American Medical Botany*, ii. (1819) 121-136.

[3] *Cours d'Hist. Nat. Pharm.* i. (1828) 319.

[4] *Medizinische Jahrbücher*, xix. (Vienna, 1863) 129-148.

[5] Buchner's *Repertorium für Pharmacie*, xviii. (1868) 50; also Wiggers and Husemann's *Jahresbericht*, xviii. 1868. 505.

[6] Berg u. Schmidt, *Offiz. Gewächse*, i. (1858) tab. ix. e. "*Sabadilla officinarum.*"

[7] Ernst, communication to the Linnean Society of London, 15 Dec., 1870.

[8] *Veratrum Sabadilla* Retzius is stated by Lindley (*Flora Medica*, p. 586) to be a native of Mexico and the West Indian Islands, and to furnish a portion of the cebadilla seeds of commerce. The plant is unknown to us: we have searched for it in vain in the herbaria of Kew and the British Museum. It is not mentioned as West Indian by Grisebach (*Flor. of Brit. W. I. Islands*, 1864; *Cat. Plant. Cubensium*, 1866). The figure by Descourtilz (*Flor. méd. des Antilles*, iii. 1827. t. 1859) who had the plant growing at St. Domingo, shows it to resemble *Veratrum album* L., and therefore to be very different from *Asagræa*.

corrosive application to wounds; but it does not seem to have been brought into European commerce, for neither Parkinson who described it in 1640 as the *Indian Causticke Barley*, nor Ray (1693) did more than copy from Monardes. It was regarded in Germany a rare drug even in 1726, but in the latter half of the last century it begun to be recommended in France and Germany for the destruction of pediculi. A famous composition for this purpose was the *Poudre des Capucins*, consisting of a mixture of stavesacre, tobacco, and cebadilla, which was applied either dry or made into an ointment with lard.[1] Cebadilla was also administered combined into a pill with gamboge and valerian,[2] for the destruction of intestinal worms, but its virulent action made it hazardous.

Upon the introduction of veratrine into medicine about 1824 cebadilla attracted some notice, and was occasionally prescribed in the form of tincture and extract; but it subsequently fell into disuse, and is now only employed for the manufacture of veratrine.

Description—Each fruit consists of three oblong pointed follicles, about ½ an inch in length, surrounded below by the remains of the 6-partite calyx, and attached to a short pedicel. The follicles are united at the base, spread somewhat towards the apex, and open by their ventral suture. They are of a light brown colour and papery substance. Each usually contains two pointed narrow black seeds, $\frac{3}{16}$ of an inch in length, which are shining, rugose, and angular or concave by mutual pressure. The compact testa encloses an oily albumen, at the base of which, opposite to the beaked apex, lies the small embryo. The seed is inodorous and has a bitter acrid taste; when powdered, it produces violent sneezing.

Microscopic Structure—A transverse section shows the horny concentrically radiated albumen, closely attached to the testa. The latter consists of an outer layer of cuboid cells, and three rows of smaller, thin-walled, tangentially-extended cells, all of which have brown walls. The tissue of the albumen is made up of large porous cells, containing drops of oil, granules of albuminoid matter, and mucilage. Traces of tannic acid occur only in the outer layers of the seed.

Chemical Composition—Meissner, an apothecary of Halle, Prussia, in 1819 discovered in cebadilla a basic substance, which he termed *Sabadilline;* in publishing, in 1821, the description of it the word "*alkaloid*" was introduced by Meissner at that occasion. The name *Veratrine*[3] was applied likewise in 1819 by Pelletier and Caventou to a similar preparation. For many years this substance was known only as an amorphus powder, in which state it frequently contained a considerable proportion of resin; but in 1855 it was obtained by G. Merck in large rhombic prisms. Cebadilla yields only about 3 per mille of veratrine. The alkaloid is easily soluble in spirit of wine, ether or chloroform; these solutions, as well as the watery solutions of its salts, are devoid of rotatory power. Veratrine, like the drug from which it is derived, occasions, if inhaled, prolonged sternutation.

[1] Murray, *Apparatus Medicaminum*, v. (1790) 171; Mérat and De Lens, *Dict. Mat. Méd.* vi. (1834) 862.

[2] Peyrilhe, *Cours. d'Hist. Nat. Méd.* ii. (1804) 490.

[3] So called from Schlechtendal's name for the plant, *Veratrum officinale*.

Again, in 1834, Conerbe described an alkaloid from cebadilla under the name of *Sabadilline*, and *Weigelin* (1871) another called *Sabatrine*.

From the investigations of Wright and Luff (1878) it appears that the above-mentioned statements must be resumed thus:—There are in cebadilla three alkaloids, namely *Veratrine*, $C^{37}H^{53}NO^{11}$, *Cevadine*, $C^{32}H^{49}NO^{9}$, and *Cevadilline*, $C^{34}H^{53}NO^{8}$, the second only being crystallizable.

Veratrin may be decomposed by means of caustic lye into a new alkaloid, verine, and dimethyl-protocatechuic acid, $C^6H^3 \left\{ \begin{matrix} (OCH^3)^2 \\ COOH \end{matrix} \right.$. By the same treatment, cevadine yields an acid which appears to be identical with tiglinic acid (page 566), and an alkaloid called cevine.

Cebadilla yielded to Pelletier and Caventou a volatile fatty acid, *Sabadillic* or *Cevadic Acid*, the needle-shaped crystals of which fuse at 20° C. Lastly, E. Merck (1839) found a second peculiar acid termed *Veratric Acid*, affording quadrangular prisms, which can be sublimed without decomposition. It is yielded by cebadilla to the extent of but ⅛ per mille. It has been shown in 1876 by Körner to be identical with dimethyl-protocatechuic acid just mentioned (see also our article *Tubera Aconiti*, p. 9).

Commerce—The quantity of cebadilla (*seeds* only) shipped in 1876 from La Guaira, the port of Caracas, was 35,033 kilos., of which 25,966 went to Germany. No other sort is now imported.

Uses—Cebadilla is at present, we believe, only used as the source of veratrine. In Mexico, the bulb of the plant is employed as an anthelminthic, under the name of *Cebolleja*, but it is said to be very dangerous in its action.

CORMUS COLCHICI.

Tuber vel Bulbus vel Radix Colchici; Meadow Saffron Root; F. *Bulbe de Colchique;* G. *Zeitlosenknollen.*

Botanical Origin—*Colchicum autumnale* L.—This plant grows in meadows and pastures over the greater part of Northern Africa, Middle and Southern Europe, and is plentiful in many localities in England and Ireland. In the Swiss Alps, it ascends to an elevation of 5500 feet above the sea level.

History—Dioscorides drew attention to the poisonous properties of Κολχικὸν, which he stated to be a plant growing in Messenia and Colchis.[1]

This character for deleterious qualities seems to have prevented the use of colchicum both in classical and mediæval times. Thus Tragus (1552) warns his readers against its use in gout, for which it is recommended in the writings of the Arabians. Jacques Grévin, a physician of Paris, author of *Deux Livres des Venins*, dedicated to Queen Elizabeth of England, and printed at Antwerp in 1568, observes—"ce poison est ennemy de la nature de l'homme en tout et par tout." Dodoens

[1] His description is exact, except that he declares the corm to have a *sweet* taste, which seems not true for *Colchicum autumnale*, but may be so for some other species

calls it *perniciosum Colchicum*; and Lyte in his translation of this author (1578) says—"Medow or Wilde Saffron is corrupt and venemous, therefore not used in medicine." Gerarde declares the roots of "*Mede Saffron*" to be "very hurtfull to the stomacke."

Wedel published in 1718, at Jena, an essay *De Colchico veneno et alexipharmaco*, in which, to show the great disfavour in which this plant had been held, he remarks,—"hactenus . . . velut infame habitum et damnatum fuit colchicum, indignum habitum inter herbas medicas vel officinales . . ." He further states that, in the 17th century, the corms were worn by the peasants in some parts of Germany as a charm against the plague.

In the face of these severe denunciations, it is strange to find that in the London Pharmacopœia of 1618 (the second edition), "*Radix Colchici*," as well as *Hermodactylus*, is enumerated among the simple drugs; and again in the editions of 1627, 1632 and 1639. It is omitted in that of 1650, and does not reappear in subsequent editions until 1788, when owing to the investigations of Störck (1763), Kratochwill (1764), De Berge (1765) Ehrmann (1772), and others, the possibility of employing it usefully in medicine had been made evident.

Development of the Corm[1]—At the period of flowering, the corm is surrounded with a brown, closed double membrane or tunic, which is prolonged upwards into a sheath around the flowering-stem; at the base of the corm is a tuft of simple roots. On removing the membranes, we find a large, ovoid, fleshy body (Corm No. 1), marked at its apex by a depressed scar, the point of attachment of the flower-stem of the previous year; it is on one side flattened, and traversed by a shallow longitudinal furrow, from the upper part of which arises a much smaller and rudimentary corm (No. 2), bearing a flower-stem. After the production of the flower in the autumn, Corm No. 2 increases in size, throwing up as spring advances its fruit-stem and leaves, and acquires, after these latter have come to maturity, its full development. Corm No. 1 on the other hand, having performed its functions, shrivels and diminishes in size, in proportion as No. 2 advances to maturity, and ultimately decays, leaving a rounded cicatrix, showing its point of attachment to its successor.

Collection—In England the corms are usually dug up and brought to market in July, at the period between the decay of the foliage and the production of the flower, or even after the latter has appeared. For some preparations, they are used in the fresh state. If to be dried, it is customary to slice them across thinly and evenly with a knife, and to dry the slices quickly in a stove with a gentle heat; the membranes are afterwards removed by sifting or winnowing.

Schroff has stated, as the result of his experiments,[2] that the corms possess the greatest medicinal activity when collected in the autumn during or after inflorescence; that they ought to be dried *entire*, by exposure to the sun and air; and that if thus preserved, they lose none of their strength, even if kept for several years.

[1] The term *corm* is applied by English writers to the short, fleshy, bulb-shaped base of an annual stem, either lateral as in *Colchicum*, or terminal as in *Crocus*. By many continental botanists, the corm of *Colchicum* is regarded either as a form of tuber, or of bulb.

[2] *Oesterreichische Zeitschrift für praktische Heilkunde*, 1856, Nos. 22–24; also Wiggers, *Jahresbericht der Pharm*. 1856. 15.

Description—The fresh corm is conical or inversely pear-shaped, about 2 inches long by an inch or more wide, rounded on one side, flattish on the other, covered by a bright brown, membranous skin, within which is a second of paler colour. When cut transversely, it appears white, firm, fleshy and homogeneous, abounding in a bitter, starchy juice, of disagreeable odour. The dried slices are inodorous, and have a bitterish taste. They should be of a good white, clean, crisp and brittle,—not mouldy or stained.

Microscopic Structure—The outer membrane is formed of tangentially-extended cells, with thick brownish walls; the main body of the corm, of large thin-walled, more or less regularly globular cells, loaded with starch, and interrupted by vascular bundles containing spiral vessels. The original form of the starch granules is globular or egg-shaped, but from mutual pressure and agglutination, many are angular or truncated. A large proportion are more or less compound, consisting of several granules united into one. In all, the hilum is very distinct, appearing in some as a mere point, but in most as a line or star.

Chemical Composition—The corms contain *Colchicin* (see next article), starch, sugar, gum, resin, tannin, and fat. When sliced and dried, they lose about 70 per cent. of water.[1] By drying, the (probably) volatile body upon which the odour of the fresh corm depends, is lost.

Uses—Colchicum is much prescribed in cases of gout, rheumatism, dropsy, and cutaneous maladies.

Other medicinal species of Colchicum.

Under the name *Hermodactylus*,[2] the corms of other species of *Colchicum* of Eastern origin anciently enjoyed great reputation in medicine. These corms are in structure precisely like those of ordinary colchicum; they are entire, but deprived of membranous envelopes, of a flattened, heart-shaped form, not wrinkled on the surface, and often very small in size. The starch grains they contain are similar to those of *C. autumnale*, but in some specimens twice as large.

There is a great uncertainty as to the species of *Colchicum* which furnish hermodactyls. Prof. J. E. Planchon, who has written an elaborate article on the subject,[3] is in favour of *C. variegatum* L., a native of the Levant. But one can hardly suppose this plant to be the source of the hermodactyls (*Sūrinjān*) of the Indian bazaars, which are stated to be brought from Kashmir.

[1] This is the average obtained during ten years in drying 16 cwt., in the laboratory of Messrs. Allen and Hanburys, London.

[2] The *Bitter Hermodactyl* of Royle is not in our opinion the produce of a *Colchicum* at all; see also Cooke in *Pharm. Journ.* April 1, 1871.

[3] *Ann. des Sciences Nat.*, Bot., iv. (1855) 132; abstract in *Pharm. Journ.* xv. (1856) 465.

SEMEN COLCHICI.

Colchicum Seed; F. Semence de Colchique; G. Zeitlosensamen.

Botanical Origin—*Colchicum autumnale* L., see page 699. The inflated capsule, which grows up in the spring after the disappearance of the flower in the autumn, is three-celled, dehiscent towards the apex by its ventral sutures, and contains, attached to the inner angle of the carpels, numerous globular seeds, which arrive at maturity in the latter part of the summer.

History—Colchicum seeds were introduced into medical practice by Dr. W. H. Williams, of Ipswich, about 1820, on the ground of their being more certain in action than the corm.[1] They were admitted to the London Pharmacopœia in 1824.

Description—The seeds are of globose form, about $\frac{1}{10}$ of an inch in diameter, somewhat pointed by a strophiole, which when dry is not very evident. They are rather rough and dull; when recent of a pale brown, but become darker by drying, and at the same time exude a sort of saccharine matter. They are inodorous even when fresh, but have a bitter acrid taste; they are very hard and difficult to powder.

Microscopic Structure—The reticulated, brown coat of the seed consists of a few rows of large, thin-walled tangentially-extended cells, considerably smaller towards the interior, the outermost containing starch grains in small number. The thin testa is closely adherent to the horny greyish albumen. The cells of the latter are remarkable for their thick walls, showing wide pores; they contain granular plasma and oil-drops. The very small leafless embryo may be observed on transverse section close beneath the testa on the side opposite the strophiole.

Chemical Composition—The active principle of colchicum seed is termed *Colchicin*, but the chemists who have made it the subject of investigation are not agreed as to its properties. Thus Oberlin (1856) showed it to contain nitrogen, but without possessing basic properties. By treatment with acids, the amorphous colchicin yields a crystallizable body, *Colchiceïn*. Hübler (1864) prepared colchicin in the same way by which the so-called "bitter principles," like dulcamarin (p. 451) are obtainable. He assigned to colchiceïn acid qualities and, strangely enough, the same formula he gave for colchicin itself, namely $C^{17}H^{19}NO^5$. Maisch[2] as well as Diehl[3] again obtained discrepant results. *Colchicin* of definite composition has not yet been isolated.

It would appear that in an aqueous or alcoholic extract of the seed an extremely small amount of an alkaloid is present, but that a basic substance is immediately formed on addition of mineral acids, or also oxalic acid. This suggestion is to some extent supported by the following facts:—

By adding the usual test solution for alkaloids, *i.e.* iodohydrogyrate of potassium (50 grammes of iodide of potassium, 13·5 of perchloride of mercury in one litre), to an aqueous solution of an alcoholic extract of

[1] *London Medical Repository*, Aug. 1, 1820.

[2] *Pharm. Journ.* ix. (1867) 249.

[3] *Proc. Americ. Pharm. Assoc.* 1867. 363.

the seeds, a very slight turbidity, or an insignificant precipitate is observed. Yet on addition of sulphuric, or nitric, or hydrochloric acid, an abundant precipitate of a beautiful yellow is at once produced. This experiment succeeds with a few seeds, either entire or powdered; it may be conveniently applied for the detection of colchicum in any preparation. We have ascertained that the yellow precipitate can be obtained also with the other parts of the plant. If the yellow compound is decomposed by sulphuretted hydrogen, the filtrate, after due concentration, now precipitates immediately on addition of the iodohydrorgyrate, yet still more abundantly in presence of a mineral acid.

The seeds contain traces of gallic acid, much sugar and fatty oil. Of the last we obtained 6·6 per cent. by exhausting the dried seed with ether. The oil concreted at —8° C. Rosenwasser (1877) obtained 8·4 per cent. of the oil.

Uses—The same as those of the corm.

SMILACEÆ.

RADIX SARSAPARILLÆ.

Radix Sarzæ vel Sarsæ ; Sarsaparilla ; F. *Racine de Salsepareille ;* G. *Sarsaparillwurzel.*

Botanical Orgin—Sarsaparilla is afforded by several plants of the genus *Smilax*, indigenous to the northern half of South America, and the whole of Central America as far as the southern and western coast-lands of Mexico.

These plants are woody climbers, often ascending lofty trees by the strong tendrils which spring from the petiole of the leaf. Their stems are usually angular, armed with stout prickles, and thrown up from a large woody rhizome. The medicinal species inhabit swampy tropical forests, which are extremely deleterious to the health of Europeans, and can only be explored amid great difficulties. This circumstance taken in connexion with the facts that the plants are diœcious, that their scandent habit often renders their flowers and fruits (produced at different seasons) inaccessible, and that their leaves vary exceedingly in form,[1] explains why we are but very imperfectly acquainted with the botanical sources of sarsaparilla.

It is not too much to assert that the sarsaparilla plant of no district in Tropical America is scientifically well known. The species moreover, to which the drug is assigned, have for the most part been founded upon characters that are totally insufficient, so that after an attentive study of herbarium specimens, we are obliged to regard as still doubtful several of the plants that have been named by previous writers.

Having made these preliminary remarks, we will enumerate the plants to which the sarsaparilla of commerce has been ascribed.

[1] The common *Smilax aspera* L., of Southern Europe, is a plant which presents such diversity of foliage, that if like its congeners of Tropical America, it were known only by a few leafy scraps preserved in herbaria, it would assuredly have been referred to several species.

1. *Smilax officinalis* H.B.K.—This plant was obtained in the year 1805, by Humboldt, at Bajorque, a village since swept away by the stream, about in 7° N. lat., on the Magdalena in New Granada. The specimens, comprising only a few imperfect leaves, which we have examined in the National Herbarium of Paris, are the materials upon which Kunth founded the species. Humboldt[1] states, that quantities of the root are shipped by way of Mompox and Cartagena to Jamaica and Cadiz.

In 1853 this plant was again gathered at Bajorque by the late De Warszewicz, who sent to one of us (H.) leaves and stems, accompanied by the root, which latter agrees with the *Jamaica Sarsaparilla* of commerce. But at Bajorque the root is no longer collected for exportation.

The same botanical collector, at the request of one of us, obtained in the year 1851, on the volcano and Cordillera of Chiriqui in Costa Rica, fruits, leaves, stems, and roots, of the plant there collected by the Indians as *Sarsa peluda* or *Sarson*. These specimens agree, so far as comparison is possible, with those of the Bajorque plant, while the root is undistinguishable from the Jamaica sarsaparilla of the shops. Other specimens of the same plant, gathered by the same collector in 1853, were forwarded to England with a living root, which latter however could not be made to grow.

Finally, in 1869, Mr. R. B. White obligingly communicated to us leaves and roots of a sarsaparilla collected at Patia in New Granada, which apparently belongs to the same species.

In the island of Jamaica, there has been cultivated for many years, and of late with a view to medicinal use, a sarsaparilla plant which appears to be *Smilax officinalis*. The specimens transmitted to us[2] include neither flowers nor fruits; but the leaves and square stem accord exactly with those of the plant collected at Bajorque. The root is of a light cinnamon-brown, and far more amylaceous than the so-called *Jamaica Sarsaparilla* of commerce (see p. 710).

2. *Smilax medica* Schl. et Cham.—This species,[3] which was discovered in Mexico by Schiede in 1820, is without doubt the source of the sarsaparilla shipped from Vera Cruz. According to our observations, it has a flexuose (or zigzag) stem, and much smaller foliage than *S. officinalis;* the leaves, though very variable, often assume an auriculate form, with broad, obtuse, basal lobes.

It grows on the eastern slopes of the Mexican Andes, and is the only species of that region of which the roots are collected. These, according to Schiede, are dug up all the year round, dried in the sun and made into bundles.

[1] Kunth, *Synopsis Plant.* i. (1822) 278.—*Smilax officinalis* is a large, strong climber, attaining a height of 40 to 50 feet, with a perfectly square stem armed with prickles at the angles. The leaves are often a foot in length, of variable form, being triangular, ovate-oblong, or oblong-lanceolate, either gradually narrowing towards the apex or rounded and apiculate, and at the base either attenuated into the petiole, or truncate, or cordate. They are usually 5-nerved, the 3 inner nerves being prominent and enclosing an elliptic area. The flowers are in stalked umbels. A fine specimen of the plant is most luxuriantly growing since many years in the Royal Gardens, Kew, but has not flowered.

[2] We owe them to the kindness of H. J. Kemble, Esq., who procured them, with specimens of the root, from the Government garden at Castleton.

[3] Figured in Nees von Esenbeck's *Plantæ Medicinales*, suppl. tab. 7.

Doubt and confusion hang over the other species of *Smilax* which have been quoted as the sources of sarsaparilla. *S. syphilitica* H.B.K., with flowers in a raceme of umbels, discovered on the Cassiquiare in New Granada, and well figured by Berg and Schmidt from an authentic specimen, appears from Pöppig's statements to yield some of the sarsaparilla shipped at Pará. But Kunth states that Pöppig's plant, gathered near Ega, is not that of Humboldt and Bonpland. Spruce, who collected *S. syphilitica* (herb. No. 3779) in descending the Rio Negro in 1854, has informed us that the Indians in various places in the Amazon valley always strenuously asserted it to be a species worthless for "*Salsa.*"

S. papyracea, described by Poiret[1] in 1804, and figured by Martius,[2] is but very imperfectly known. It has foliage resembling that of *S. officinalis*, but, judging from Spruce's specimens (No. 1871) collected on the Rio Negro, a *multangular* stem. It is probably the source of the *Pará Sarsaparilla.*

S. cordato-ovata Rich. is a doubtful plant, perhaps identical with *S. Schomburgkiana* Knth., a Panama species. Pöppig alleges that its root is mixed with that of the plant which he calls *S. syphilitica.*

S. Purhampuy Ruiz, a Peruvian species, said to afford a valuable sort of sarsaparilla, is practically unknown, and is not admitted by Kunth.[3]

No new information on the several above mentioned species of Smilax is found in the review of this genus by A. and C. De Candolle,[4] where 105 American species are enumerated

History—Monardes[5] has recorded that sarsaparilla was first introduced to Seville about the year 1536 or 1545, from New Spain; and a better variety soon afterwards from Honduras. He further narrates that a drug of excellent quality was subsequently imported from the province of Quito, that it was collected in the neighbourhood of Guayaquil, and was of a dark hue, and larger and thicker than that of Honduras.

Pedro de Ciezo de Leon, in his Chronicle of Peru,[6] which contains the observations made by him in South America between 1532 and 1550, gives a particular account of the sarsaparilla which grows in the province of Guayaquil and the adjacent island of Puna, and recommends the sudorific treatment of syphilis, exactly as pursued at the present time.

These statements are confirmed by the testimony of other writers. Thus, João Rodriguez de Castello Branco, commonly known as Amatus Lusitanus, a Portuguese physician of Jewish origin, who practised chiefly in Italy, has left a work recording his medical experiences and narrating cases of successful treatment.[7] One of the latter concerns a patient suffering from acute rheumatism, for whom he finally prescribed

[1] Lamarck, *Encyclopédie méthodique*, Bot., vi. 1804. 468.

[2] *Flor. Bras.* i. (1842-71) tab. 1.

[3] It must not be supposed that *all* species of *Smilax* are capable of furnishing the drug. There are many, even South American, which like the *S. aspera* of Europe, have *thin, wiry* roots, which would never pass for medicinal sarsaparilla.

[4] *Monographiæ phanerogamarum*, i. (1878) 6–199.

[5] Pages 18 and 88 of the work quoted in the Appendix.

[6] *Parte primera de la Chronica del Peru*, Sevilla, 1553, folio lxix.—a translation for the Hakluyt Society in 1864, by Markham, who observes that Cieza de Leon never himself visited Guayaquil.

[7] *Curationum medicinalium centuriæ quatuor*, Basileæ. 1556. 365.

Sarsaparilla. This drug, he explains, has of late years been brought from the newly found country of Peru, that it is in long whip-like roots, growing from the stock of a sort of bramble resembling a vine, that the Spaniards call it *Zarza parrilla,* and that it is an excellent medicine.

About the same period, sarsaparilla was described by Auger Ferrier,[1] a physician of Toulouse, who states that in the treatment of syphilis, which he calls *Lues Hispanica,* it is believed to be better than either *China root* or *Lignum sanctum.* Girolamo Cardano of Milan, in a little work called *De radice Cina et Sarza Parilia judicium,*[2] expresses similar opinions. After so strong recommendations, the drug soon found its way to the pharmaceutical stores; we find it quoted for instance in 1563, in the tariff of the "Apotheke" of the little town of Annaberg in Saxony.[3] We have also noticed "Sarsaparilla" in the *Ricettario Fiorentino* of the year 1573.[4] Gerarde,[5] who wrote about the close of the century, states that the sarsaparilla of Peru is imported into England in abundance.

Collection of the Root—Mr. Richard Spruce, the enterprising botanical explorer of the Amazon valley, has communicated to us the following particulars on this subject, which we give in his own graphic words:—

"When I was at Santarem on the Amazon in 1849–50, where considerable quantities of sarsaparilla are brought in from the upper regions of the river Tapajóz, and again when on the Upper Rio Negro and Uaupés in 1851–53, I often interrogated the traders about their criteria of the good kinds of sarsaparilla. Some of them had bought their stock of Indians of the forest, and had themselves no certain test of its genuineness or of its excellence, beyond the size of the roots, the thickest fetching the best price at Pará. Those who had gathered sarsaparilla for themselves were guided by the following characters:— 1. Many stems from a root. 2. Prickles closely set. 3. Leaves thin.— The first character was (to them) alone essential, for in the species of *Smilax* that have solitary stems, or not more than two or three, the roots are so few as not to be worth grubbing up; whereas the multicaul species have numerous long roots,—three at least to each stem,— extending horizontally on all sides.

"In 1851, when I was at the falls of the Rio Negro, which are crossed by the equator, nine men started from the village of St. Gabriel to gather *Salsa,* as they called it, at the head of the river Cauaburís. During their absence I made the acquaintance of an old Indian, who told me that four years ago he had brought stools of *Salsa* from the Cauaburís and had planted them in a *tabocál,*—a clump of bamboos, indicating the site of an ancient Indian village,—on the other side of the falls, whither he invited me to go and witness the gathering of his first crop of roots. On the 23rd March, I visited the *tabocál,* and found some half-dozen plants of a *Smilax* with very prickly stems, but

[1] *De Pudendagra lue Hispanica, libri duo,* first published at Toulouse in 1553, and many times reprinted. We have consulted the Antwerp edition of 1564, with which Cardano's work is printed. The latter is said to have first appeared in 1559.

[2] Basileæ, 1559, fol.

[3] Flückiger, *Documente* (quoted at p. 404, note 7) 24.

[4] See Appendix.

[5] *Herball,* enlarged by Johnson, 1636. 859.

no flowers or fruit. At my request the Indian operated on the finest plant first. It had five stems from the crown, and numerous roots about 9 feet long, radiating horizontally on all sides. The thin covering of earth was first scraped away from the roots by hand, aided by a pointed stick; and had the *salsa* been the only plant occupying the ground, the task would have been easy. But the roots of the *salsa* were often difficult to trace among those of bamboo and other plants, which had to be cut through with a knive whenever they came in the way. The roots being at length all laid bare—(in this case it was the work of half a day, but with large plants it sometimes takes up a whole day or even more)—they were cut off near the crown, a few slender ones being allowed to remain, to aid the plant in renewing its growth. The stems also were shortened down to near the ground, and a little earth and dead leaves heaped over the crown, which would soon shoot out new stems

"The yield of this plant, of four years' growth, was 16 lb.—half a Portuguese *arroba*—of roots; but a well-grown plant will afford at the first cutting from one to two arrobas. In a couple of years, a plant may be cut again, but the yield will be much smaller and the roots more slender and less starchy."

General Description—The medicinal species of *Smilax* have a thick, short, knotty rhizome, called by the druggists *chump*, from which grow in a horizontal direction long fleshy roots, from about the thickness of a quill to that of the little finger. These roots are mostly simple, forked only towards their extremities, beset with thread-like branching rootlets of nearly uniform size, which however are not emitted to any great extent from the more slender part of the root near the stock. When fresh the root is plump,[1] but as found in commerce in the dried state it is more or less furrowed longitudinally, at least in the vicinity of the rhizome. When examined with a good lens both roots and rootlets may be seen in some specimens to be clothed with short velvety or shaggy hairs.

The presence or absence in greater or less abundance of starch in the bark of the root is regarded as an important criterion in estimating the good quality of sarsaparilla. In England the non-amylaceous or non-mealy roots are preferred, they alone being suitable for the manufacture of the dark fluid-extract that is valued by the public. On the Continent, and especially in Italy, sarsaparilla, which when cut exhibits a thick bark, pure white within, is the esteemed kind.

The more or less plentiful occurrence of starch in the roots of *Smilax* is a character which has no botanical significance, and appears, indeed, to vary in the same species. If one examines Jamaica sarsaparilla by shaving off a little of the bark, one finds a large majority of roots to be non-amylaceous in their entire length; but others can be picked out which, though non-amylaceous for some distance from the rhizome, acquire a starchy bark, which is *white* internally in their middle and lower portions;—and there are still others which are slightly starchy even as they start from the parent rhizome, becoming

[1] We have been kindly permitted to examine the fresh root of the large plant of *Smilax officinalis* in the Royal Gardens, Kew; and have found that it agrees in appearance and in structure with Jamaica sarsaparilla.

still more as they advance. In Guatemala sarsaparilla, which is considered a very mealy sort, it is easy to perceive that the bark is hardly amylaceous in the vicinity of the rhizome, but that it acquires an enormous deposit of fecula as it proceeds in its growth.

Sarsaparilla varies greatly in the abundance of rootlets, technically called *beard*, with which the roots are clothed. This character depends partly on natural circumstances, and partly on the practice of the collectors who remove or retain the rootlets at will. Dr. Rhys of Belize has stated that the proportion of rootlets depends much on the nature of the soil, their development being most favoured by moist situations.

Dry sarsaparilla has not much smell, yet when large quantities are boiled, or when a decoction is evaporated, a peculiar and very perceptible odour is emitted. The taste of the root is earthy, and not well marked, and even a decoction has no very distinctive flavour.

Microscopic Structure[1]—On a *tranverse section* of the root, its fibro-vascular bundles are seen to be restricted to the central part, being all enclosed by a brown ring. Within this ring the bundles are densely packed so as to form a ligneous zone. The very centre of the section consists of white medullary tissue, through which sometimes a certain number of fibro-vascular bundles are scattered. A similar medullary parenchyme is met with between the brown ring or nucleus sheath or the epidermis. On a *longitudinal section* the latter exhibits several rows of elongated cells, having their outer brown walls thickened by secondary deposits. The brown nucleus sheath, on the other hand, consists of only one row of prismatic cells, their inner and lateral walls alone having secondary deposits. The vascular bundles contain large scalariform vessels and lignified prosenchymatous cells.

The parenchymatous cells, if not devoid of solid contents, are loaded with large compound starch granules; some cells also exhibit bundles of acicular crystals of calcium oxalate. In non-mealy sarsaparilla the vessels and ligneous cells sometimes contain a yellow resin.

The various sorts of sarsaparilla differ, not only in being mealy or non-mealy, but also as regards the thickness of the ligneous zone, which in some of them is many times thinner than the diameter of the central medullary tissue. In other kinds this diameter is very much smaller. Yet the nucleus sheath affords still better means for distinguishing the sorts of this drug, if we examine its single cells in a transverse section. The outline of such a cell may be of a square or somewhat rounded shape, or it may be more or less extended. In this case it may be extended in the direction of a radius, or in the direction of a tangent. The secondary deposits may vary in thickness.

Sorts of Sarsaparilla—In the present state of our knowledge no botanical classification of the different kinds of sarsaparilla being possible, we shall resort to the arrangement adopted by Pereira and

[1] For more particulars consult Vandercolme, *Histoire bot. et thérapeut. des Salsepareilles*, Paris, 1870, 127 pp., 3 plates; and Otten, in Dragendorff's *Jahresbericht*, 1876. 74.

place them in two groups,—the *mealy*, or those of which starch is a prevalent constituent, and the *non-mealy*, or those in which starch exists to a comparatively small extent.

(A.) *Mealy Sarsaparillas.*

1. ***Honduras Sarsaparilla***—This drug is exported from Belize. It is made up in hanks or rolls about 30 inches long and 2½ to 4 inches or more in diameter, closely wound round with a long root so as to form a neat bundle. The hanks are united into bales by large pieces of hide, placed at top and bottom, and held together with thongs of the same, further strengthened with iron hoops.

The roots are deeply furrowed, or sometimes plump and smooth, more or less provided with *beard* or rootlets. In a very large proportion of their length they exhibit when cut a thick bark loaded with starch ; yet in those parts which are near the rhizome the bark is brown, resinous, and non-amylaceous. They are of a pale brown, sometimes verging into orange. But the drug is subject to great variation, so that it is impossible to lay down absolutely distinctive characters.

The annual imports into the United Kingdom of sarsaparilla from British Honduras during the five years ending with 1870 averaged about 52,000 lb.

2. ***Guatemala Sarsaparilla***—This sort of sarsaparilla, which first appeared in commerce about 1852, resembles the Honduras kind in many of its characters, and is packed in a similar manner. But it has a more decided *orange hue;* the roots as they start from the rhizome are lean, shrunken, and but little starchy, but they become gradually stouter ($\frac{3}{16}$ inch diam.), and acquire a thick bark, which is internally very white and mealy. There is a tendency in the bark of this sarsaparilla to crack and split off, so that bare spaces showing the central woody column are not unfrequent.

According to Bentley,[1] who examined specimens of the plant, this drug is derived from *Smilax papyracea;* we are not prepared to agree in this opinion.

3. ***Brazilian, Para or Lisbon Sarsaparilla***—Though formerly held in high esteem Brazilian sarsaparilla is not now appreciated in England, and is rarely seen in the London market.[2] It is packed in a very distinctive manner, the roots being tightly compressed into a cylindrical bundle, 3 feet or more in length and about 6 inches in diameter, firmly held together by the flexible stem of a bignoniaceous plant, closely wound round them, the ends being neatly shaved off.

(B.) *Non-mealy Sarsaparillas.*

4. ***Jamaica Sarsaparilla***—To the English druggist this is the most important variety ; it is that which appears to have the greatest claim to possess some medicinal activity, and it is the only sort admitted to the *British Pharmacopœia.* Although constantly called *Jamaica sarsaparilla*, it is well known that it only bears the name of Jamaica through

[1] *Pharm. Journ.* xii. (1853) 470, with figure.

[2] We noticed 66 rolls of it from Pará, offered for sale 15 Dec. 1853.—D. H.

having been formerly shipped from Central America by way of that island.[1] At the commencement of the last century, Jamaica was an emporium for sarsaparilla, great quantities of which, according to Sloane,[2] were brought thither from Honduras, New Spain and Peru. Its actual place of growth, according to De Warszewicz (1851), is the mountain range known as the Cordillera of Chiriqui, in that part of the isthmus of Panama adjoining the republic of Costa Rica: here the plant grows at an elevation of 4000 to 8000 feet above the level of the sea. The root is brought by the natives to Boca del Toro on the Atlantic coast for shipment.

The drug consists of roots, 6 feet or more in length, bent repeatedly so as to form bundles of 18 inches long, and 4 in diameter, which are secured by being twined round (but less trimly and closely than the Honduras sort) with a long root of the same drug. The rhizome is entirely absent, but the fibre or beard is preserved, and is reckoned a valuable portion of the drug. The roots are deeply furrowed, shrunken, and generally more slender than in the Honduras kind; the bark when shaved off with a penknife is seen to be brown, hard and non-mealy throughout. Yet it is by no means uncommon to find roots which have a smooth bark rich in starch. In colour, Jamaica sarsaparilla varies from a pale earthy brown to a deeper more ferruginous hue, the latter tint being the most esteemed.

The sarsaparilla referred to at p. 704 as grown in the island of Jamaica, is a well prepared drug, yet so pale in colour and so amylaceous, that it finds but little favour in the English market. There were exported of it from Jamaica in 1870, 1747 lb.;[3] in 1871, 1290 lb.

5. *Mexican Sarsaparilla*—The roots of this variety are not made into bundles, but are packed in straight lengths of about 3 feet into bales, the chump and portion of an angular (but not *square*) thorny stem being frequently retained. The roots are of a pale, dull brown, lean, shrivelled, and with but few fibres. When thick and large, they have a somewhat starchy bark, but when thin and near the rhizome, they are non-amylaceous.

6. *Guayaquil Sarsaparilla*—An esteemed kind of sarsaparilla has long been exported from Guayaquil (p. 705). Mr. Spruce has informed us that it is obtained in most of the valleys that debouch into the plain on the western side of the Equatorial Andes, but chiefly in the valley of Alausi, where, in 1859, he saw plants of it at the junction of the small river Puma-cocha with the Yaguachi. The plant appears to be very productive, an instance being on record of as much as 75 lb. of fresh roots having been obtained from a single stock.[4]

Guayaquil sarsaparilla differs considerably from the sorts previously noticed. It is rudely packed in large bales, and is not generally made into separate hanks. The rhizome (chump) and a portion of the stem

[1] The connexion between Jamaica and Central America dates back from the time of Charles II., during whose reign (1661–85), the king of the Mosquito Territory, a district never conquered by the Spaniards, applied to the governor of Jamaica for protection, which was accorded. The protectorate lasted until 1860, when Mosquitia was ceded to the government of Nicaragua.

[2] *Nat. Hist. of Jamaica*, i. (1707), introduction, p. lxxxvi.

[3] *Blue Books—Island of Jamaica* for 1870 and 1871.

[4] *Journ. of Linn. Soc.*, Bot., iv. (1860) 185.

are often present, the latter being *round* and not prickly. The root is dark, large and coarse-looking, with a good deal of fibre. The bark is furrowed, rather thick, and not mealy in the slenderer portions of the root which is near the rootstock; but as the root becomes stout, so its bark becomes smoother, thicker and amylaceous, exhibiting when cut a fawn-coloured or pale yellow interior.

The quantity exported from Guayaquil in 1871 was 1017 quintals, value £3814.[1]

Chemical Composition—Galileo Pallotta, at Naples, in 1824, first attempted to obtain from sarsaparilla a peculiar principle, which he believed to be an alkaloid, and termed *Pariglina*, or as now written *Parillin*. He exhausted the crude drug with boiling water and mixed the decoction with milk of lime, whereby a greyish precipitate was produced. This was dried, and treated with hot alcohol which extracted the parillin. Pallotta says the substance slightly reddens litmus, but does not explicitly state whether he got it in crystals or not. Berzelius in 1826 replaced the name pariglina by *Smilacin*. The same substance was obtained, more or less pure, by Thubeuf in 1831 and called *Salseparin*; Batka in 1833 termed it *Parillinic acid*. We have isolated parillin[2] by exhausting Mexican sarsaparilla with boiling alcohol, 0·835 sp. gr., and evaporating the tincture to $\frac{1}{8}$ of the weight of the root. By diluting 2 parts of the residue with 3 parts of cold water, a yellowish deposit of crude parillin is formed and may be separated after a few days by decantation. The deposit is then mixed with about half a volume of strong alcohol, now filtered and washed with dilute alcohol, about 0·965 sp. gr. It may further be purified by repeated re-crystallization from dilute alcohol and the use of a little charcoal. The yield is about 0·19 per cent. of perfectly white crystallized parillin; a little more may be removed from the washings, but with much difficulty. These liquids and the mother liquors may be concentrated and boiled with a little sulphuric acid in order to afford parigenin.

Parillin forms brilliant scales, or can be obtained in thin prisms from boiling alcohol 0·965 sp. gr. Parillin is almost insoluble in cold water, but dissolves in 20 parts of boiling water. On cooling, the latter solution affords no crystals; an abundance of them are however produced on addition of alcohol. Parillin is also soluble in 25 parts of alcohol, 0·814 sp. gr., at 25° C., and much more abundantly in boiling alcohol, from which it partly separates in crystals on cooling. In both absolute alcohol or water, parillin is less soluble than in dilute alcohol. Hence aqueous solutions are precipitated by absolute alcohol, and parillin, on the other hand, separates from alcoholic solutions on addition of cold water. With chloroform, parillin yields a viscid solution which affords no crystals.

The alcoholic solutions of parillin have a somewhat acrid taste, and are devoid of rotatory power.

By dilute mineral acids, parillin is resolved into *Parigenin* and sugar; the liquid gradually acquires a dingy brown or greenish hue and fluorescence, which is most obvious if parillin dissolved in chloroform is decomposed by hydrochloric gas. Parigenin is easily isolated;

[1] Vice-Consul Smith on the commerce of Ecuador—*Consular Reports*, presented to Parliament, July, 1872.

[2] *Yearbook of Pharm.* 1878. 136.

it is insoluble even in boiling water, but crystallizes in white scales from alcohol.

The composition of parillin and parigenin is not settled; the former belongs to the class of saponin. Yet parillin differs from saponin as contained in Saponaria or Quillaja[1] by not being sternutatory; its solutions froth when shaken.

The presence in sarsaparilla of starch, resin, and calcium oxalate, as revealed by the microscope, has been already pointed out. Pereira[2] examined the *essential oil*, which is heavier than water and has the odour and taste of the drug; 140 lb. of Jamaica sarsaparilla afforded of it only a few drops.

The nature of the dark extractive matter which water removes from the root in abundance, and the proportion of which is considered by druggists a criterion of goodness, has not been studied.

Commerce—The importation of sarsaparilla into the United Kingdom in 1870 (later than which year we have no returns) amounted to 345,907 lb., valued at £26,564.

Uses—Sarsaparilla is regarded by many as a valuable alterative and tonic, but by others as possessing little if any remedial powers. It is still much employed, though by no means so extensively as a few years ago. The preparations most in use are those obtained by a prolonged boiling of the root in water.

TUBER CHINÆ.

Radix Chinæ; China Root; F. *Squine*; G. *Chinawurzel*.

Botanical Origin—*Smilax China* L., a woody, thorny, climbing shrub, is commonly said to afford this drug. The plant is a native of Japan, the Loochoo islands, Formosa, China, Cochinchina, also of Eastern India, as Kasia, Assam, Sikkim, Nepal. The chief authority for attributing the China root to this plant is Kämpfer, who saw the latter in Japan and figured it.[3]

S. glabra Roxb. and *S. lanceæfolia* Roxb., natives of India and Southern China, have tubers which, according to Roxburgh, cannot be distinguished from the China root of medicine, though the plants are perfectly distinct in appearance from *S. China*. Dr. Hance,[4] of Whampoa, received a living specimen of China root, which proved to be that of *S. glabra*. The three above-named species all grow in the island of Hongkong.

History—The use of this drug as a remedy for syphilis was made known to the Portuguese at Goa by Chinese traders about A.D. 1535. Garcia de Orta, who makes this statement, further narrates that so

[1] See Christophson, in Dragendorff's *Jahresbericht*, 1874. 155.

[2] *Elements of Mat. Med.* ii. (1850) 1168.

[3] "*Sankira*," p. 783 in the first work quoted in the Appendix; another fig. will be found in Nees von Esenbeck's *Plantæ medicinales*, Düsseldorf, 1828.

[4] Trimen's *Journ. of Bot.* i. (1872) 102.—*S. glabra* and *S. lanceæfolia* have been figured by Seemann in his *Botany of the Herald*, 1852–57, tabb. 99–100. *S. China* is well represented in the Kew Herbarium, where we have examined specimens from Nagasaki, Hakodadi, and Yokohama; from Loochoo, Corea, Formosa, Ningpo; and Indian ones from Khasia, Assam, and Nepal.

great was the reputation of the new drug, that the small quantities first brought to Malacca were sold at the rate of 10 crowns per *ganta*, a weight of 24 ounces.

Possibly the drug found its way to Europe even before that year, for we find a careful description of it in the posthumous works[1] of Valerius Cordus and Walther Ryff[2] states in 1548 that the root was brought a few years ago to Venice.

The reported good effects of China root on the Emperor Charles V. who was suffering from gout, acquired for the drug a great celebrity in Europe, and several works[3] were written in praise of its virtues. But though its powers were soon found to have been greatly over-rated, it still retained some reputation as a sudorific and alterative, and was much used at the end of the 17th century in the same way as sarsaparilla. It still retains a place in some modern pharmacopœias.

Description—The plant produces stout fibrous roots, here and there thickened into large tubers, which when dried become the drug China root. These tubers, as found in the market, are of irregularly cylindrical form, usually a little flattened, sometimes producing short knobby branches. They are from about 4 to 6 or more inches in length, and 1 to 2 inches in thickness, covered with a rusty-coloured, rather shining bark, which in some specimens is smooth and in others more or less wrinkled. They have no distinct traces of rudimentary leaves, which however are perceptible on those of some allied species. Some still retain portions of the cord-like woody runners on which they grew; the bases of a few roots can also be observed. The tubers mostly show marks of having been trimmed with a knife.

China root is inodorous and almost insipid. A transverse section exhibits the interior as a dense granular substance of a pale fawn colour.

Microscopic Structure—The outermost cortical layer is made up of brown, thick-walled cells, tangentially extended. They enclose numerous tufts of needle-shaped crystals of calcium oxalate, and reddish brown masses of resin. The bark is at once succeeded by the inner parenchyme which contrasts strongly with it, consisting of large, thin-walled, porous cells which are completely gorged with starch, but here and there contain colouring matter and bundles of crystals. The starch granules are large (up to 50 mkm.), spherical, often flattened and angular from mutual pressure. Like those of colchicum, they exhibit a radiate hilum: very frequently they have burst and run together, probably in consequence of the tubers having been scalded. The vascular bundles scattered through the parenchyme, contain usually two large scalariform or reticulated vessels, a string of delicate thin-walled parenchyme, and elegant wood-cells with distinct incrusting layers and linear pores.

Chemical Composition—The drug is not known to contain any substance to which its supposed medicinal virtues can be referred. We

[1] Edit. by Conrad Gesner, fol. 212 of the work quoted in the Appendix.

[2] .... *Bericht der Natur .... der Wurtzel China*, Würzburg, 1548. 4°.

[3] The earliest of which is by Andreas Vesalius, *Epistola rationem, modumque propinandi radicis* Chymae [sic !] *decocti, quo nuper invictissimus Carolus V. imperator usus est*, Venet, 1546.

have endeavoured to obtain from it *Parillin*, the crystalline principle of sarsaparilla, but without success.

Commerce—China root is imported into Europe from the South of China—usually from Canton. The quantity shipped from that port in 1872, was only 384 peculs (51,200 lb.); while the same year there was shipped from Hankow, the great trading city of the Yangtsze, no less than 10,258 peculs (1,367,733 lb.), all to Chinese ports. For the year 1874, these figures were: Hankow 9393 peculs, valued at 53,194 taels (one tael about 5*s.* 10*d.*), Kewkiang 3627 peculs, Ningpo 2905 peculs,[1] and for 1877 Hankow 12,075 peculs, Kewkiang 3942 peculs.

Uses—Notwithstanding the high opinion formerly entertained of the virtues of China root, it has in England fallen into complete disuse. In China and India it is still held in great esteem for the relief of rheumatic and syphilitic complaints, and as an aphrodisiac and demulcent. Polak asserts that the tubers of *Smilax* are consumed as food by Turcomans and Mongols.[2]

Substitutes—Several American species of *Smilax* furnish a nearly allied drug, which at various times has been brought into commerce as *Radix Chinæ occidentalis*. It was already known to the authors of the 16th century; we met with it in 1872, and before, in the London market, as an importation from Puntas Arenas, the port of Costa Rica on the Pacific coast.

Of the exact species it is difficult to speak with certainty: but *S. Pseudo-China* L. and *S. tamnoides* L. growing in the United States from New Jersey southwards; *S. Balbisiana* Knth., a plant common in all the West Indian Islands; and *S. Japicanga* Griseb., *S. syringoides* Griseb. and *S. Brasiliensis* Spreng., are reputed to afford large tuberous rhizomes which in their several localities replace the China root of Asia, and are employed in a similar manner.[3]

GRAMINEÆ.

SACCHARUM.

Sugar, Cane Sugar, Sucrose; F. *Sucre, Sucre de canne;* G. *Zucker, Rohrzucker.*

Botanical Origin—*Saccharum officinarum* L., the Sugar Cane. The jointed stem is from 6 to 12 feet high, solid, hard, dense, internally juicy, and hollow only in the flowering tops. Several varieties are cultivated, as the *Country Cane*, the original form of the species; the *Ribbon Cane*, with purple or yellow stripes along the stem; the *Bourbon* or *Tahiti Cane*, a more elongated, stronger, more hairy and very pro-

[1] *Returns of Trade at the Treaty Ports in China for* 1872, pp. 34, 154, and the same for 1874.

[2] See p. 324, note 2.—We quote this statement with reserve, knowing that both Chinese and Europeans sometimes confound China root with the singular fungoid production termed *Pachyma Cocos*. The first is called in Chinese *Tu-fuh-ling*,—the second *Fuh-ling* or *Pe-fuh-ling*.—See Hanbury, *Pharm. Journ.* iii. (1862) 421; and *Science Papers*, 202. 267.—F. Porter Smith, *Mat. Med. and Nat. Hist. of China*, 1871. 198; Dragendorff, *Volksmedicin Turkestans* in Buchner's *Repertorium*, xxii. (1873) 135.

[3] De Candolle's monograph, quoted at p. 705, note 4, may be consulted on the above species.

ductive variety. *Saccharum violaceum* Tussac, the *Batavian Cane*, is also considered to be a variety; but the large *S. chinense* Roxb. introduced from Canton in 1796 into the Botanic Gardens of Calcutta, may be a distinct species; it has a long, slender, erect panicle, while that of *S. officinarum* is hairy and spreading, with the ramifications alternate and more compound, not to mention other differences in the leaves and flowers.

The sugar cane is cultivated from cuttings, the small seeds very seldom ripening. It succeeds in almost all tropical and subtropical countries, reaching in South America and Mexico an elevation above the sea of 5000–6000 feet. It is cultivated in most parts of India and China up to 30–31° N. lat., the mountainous regions excepted.

From the elaborate investigations of Ritter,[1] it appears that *Saccharum officinarum* was originally a native of Bengal, and of the Indo-Chinese countries, as well as of Borneo, Java, Bali, Celebes, and other islands of the Malay Archipelago. But there is no evidence that it is now found anywhere in a wild state.

History[2]—The sugar cane was doubtless known in India from time immemorial, and grown for food as it still is at the present day, chiefly in those regions which are unsuited for the manufacture of sugar.[3]

Herodotus, Theophrastus, Seneca, Strabo, and other early writers had some knowledge of raw sugar, which they speak of as the *Honey of Canes* or *Honey made by human hands*, not that of bees; but it was not until the commencement of the Christian era, that the ancients manifested an undoubted acquaintance with sugar, under the name of *Saccharon*.

Thus Dioscorides[4] about A.D. 77 mentions the concreted honey called *Σάκχαρον* found upon canes (*ἐπὶ τῶν καλάμων*) in India and Arabia Felix, and which in substance and brittleness resemble salt. Pliny evidently knew the same thing under the name *Saccharum;* and the author of the Periplus of the Erythrean Sea, A.D. 54–68, states that honey from canes, called *σάκχαρι*, is exported from Barygaza, in the Gulf of Cambay, to the ports of the Red Sea, west of the *Promontorium Aromatum*, that is to say to the coast opposite Aden. Whether at that period sugar was produced in Western India, or was brought thither from the Ganges, is a point still doubtful.

Bengal is probably the country of the earliest manufacture of sugar; hence its names in all the languages of Western-Asiatic and European nations are derived from the Sanskrit *Sharkarā*, signifying a substance in the shape of small grains or stones. It is strange that this word contains no allusion to the *taste* of the substance.

Candy, as sugar in large crystals is called, is derived from the Arabic *Kand* or *Kandat*, a name of the same signification. An old Sanskrit name of Central Bengal is *Gura*, whence is derived the word *Gula*, meaning *raw sugar*, a term for sugar universally employed in

[1] *Erdkunde von Asien*, ix. West-Asien, Berlin, 1840. pp. 230-291.

[2] The learned investigations of Heyd, *Levantehandel*, ii. (1879) 665–667, afford exhaustive information about the medicinal history of sugar.

[3] The production which the English translators of the Bible have rendered *Sweet Cane*, and which is alluded to by the prophets Isaiah (ch. xliii. 24) and Jeremiah (ch. vi. 20) as a commodity imported from a distant country, has been the subject of much discussion. Some have supposed it to be the sugar cane; others, an aromatic grass (*Andropogon*). In our opinion, there is more reason to conclude that it was *Cassia Bark*.

[4] Lib. ii. c. 104.

the Malayan Archipelago, where on the other hand they have their own names for the sugar cane, although not for sugar. This fact again speaks in favour of Ritter's opinion, that the preparation of sugar in a dry crystalline state is due to the inhabitants of Bengal. Sugar under the name of *Shi-mi*, i.e. *Stone-honey*, is frequently mentioned in the ancient Chinese annals among the productions of India and Persia; and it is recorded that the Emperor Tai-tsung, A.D. 627–650, sent an envoy to the kingdom of Magadha in India, the modern Bahar, to learn the method of manufacturing sugar.[1] The Chinese, in fact, acknowledge that the Indians between A.D. 766 and 780 were their first teachers in the art of refining sugar, for which they had no particular ancient written character.

An Arabian writer, Abu Zayd al Hasan,[2] informs us that about A.D. 850 the sugar cane was growing on the north-eastern shore of the Persian Gulf; and in the following century, the traveller Ali Istakhri[3] found sugar abundantly produced in the Persian province of Kuzistan, the ancient Susiana. About the same time (A.D. 950), Moses of Chorene, an Armenian, also stated that the manufacture of sugar was flourishing near the celebrated school of medicine at Jondisabur in the same province, and remains of this industry in the shape of millstones, &c., still exist near Ahwas.

Persian physicians of the 10th and 11th centuries, as Rhazes, Haly Abbas, and Avicenna, introduced sugar into medicine. The Arabs cultivated the sugar cane in many of their Mediterranean settlements, as Cyprus, Sicily, Italy, Northern Africa, and Spain. The Calendar of Cordova[4] shows that as early as A.D. 961 the cultivation was well understood in Spain, which is now the only country in Europe where sugar mills still exist.[5]

William II., King of Sicily, presented in A.D. 1176 to the convent of Monreale mills for grinding cane, the culture of which still lingers at Avola near Syracuse, though only for the sake of making rum. In 1767, the sugar plantations and sugar houses at this spot were described by a traveller[6] as "worth seeing."

During the middle ages England, in common with the rest of Northern Europe, was supplied with sugar from the Mediterranean countries, especially Egypt and Cyprus. It was imported from Alexandria as early as the end of the 10th century by the Venetians, with whom it long remained an important article of trade. Thus we find[7] that in A.D. 1319, a merchant in Venice, Tommaso Loredano, shipped to London 100,000 lb. of sugar, the proceeds of which were to be returned in *wool*, which at that period constituted the great wealth of England. Sugar was then very dear: thus from 1259 to 1350, the average price in England was about 1*s.* per lb., and from 1351 to 1400, 1*s.* 7*d.*[8] In France during the same period it must have been largely obtainable, though doubtless expensive. King John II. ordered in 1353 that the apothecaries of Paris should not use honey in making those confections

[1] Bretschneider, *Chinese Botanical Works*, 1870. 46.

[2] Ritter, *l.c.* 286.

[3] P. 57 of the book quoted in the Appendix.

[4] *Le Calendrier de Cordoue de l'année* 961, par R. Dozy, Leyde, 1873. 25. 41. 91.

[5] There are several in the neighbourhood of Malaga.

[6] Riedesel, *Travels through Sicily*, Lond. 1773. 67.

[7] Marin, *Commercio de' Veneziani*, v. 306.

[8] Rogers, *Hist. of Agriculture and Prices in England*, i. (1866) 633. 641.

which ought to be prepared with the good white sugar called *cafetin*,[1] a name alluding to the peculiar shape of the loaf which was not uncommon at that time.[2]

The importance of the sugar manufacture in the East was witnessed in the latter half of the 13th century by Marco Polo;[3] and in 1510 by Barbosa and other European travellers; and the trading nations of Europe rapidly spread the cultivation of the cane over all the countries, of which the climate was suitable. Thus its introduction into Madeira goes back as far as A.D. 1420; it reached St. Domingo in 1494,[4] the Canary Islands in 1503, Brazil in the beginning of the 16th century, Mexico about 1520, Guiana about 1600, Guadaloupe in 1644, Martinique in 1650,[5] Mauritius towards 1750, Natal[6] and New South Wales, about 1852, while from a very early period the sugar cane had been propagated from the Indian Archipelago over all the islands of the Pacific Ocean.

The ancient cultivation in Egypt, probably never quite extinct, has been revived on an extensive scale by the Khedive Ismail Pasha. There were 13 sugar factories, making raw sugar, belonging to the Egyptian Government at work in 1872, and about 100,000 acres of land devoted to sugar cane. The export of sugar from Egypt in 1872 reached 2 millions of *kantars*, or about 89,200 tons.[8]

The imperfection of organic chemistry previous to the middle of the 18th century, permitted no exact investigations into the chemical nature of sugar. Marggraf of Berlin[9] proved in 1747 that sugar occurs in many vegetables, and succeeded in obtaining it in a pure crystallized state from the juice of beet-root. The enormous practical importance of this discovery did not escape him, and he caused serious attempts to be made for rendering it available, which were so far successful that the first manufactory of beet-sugar was established in 1796 by Achard at Kunern in Silesia.

This new branch of industry[10] was greatly promoted by the prohibitive measures, whereby Napoleon excluded colonial sugar from almost the whole Continent; and it is now carried forward on such a scale that 640,000 to 680,000 tons of beet-root sugar are annually produced in Europe, the entire production of cane sugar being estimated at 1,260,000 to 1,413,000 tons.[11]

Among the British colonies, Mauritius,[12] British Guiana,[13] Trinidad,[14]

[1] *Ordonnances des rois de France*, ii. (1729) 535.

[2] Several other varieties of sugar occurring in the mediæval literature are explained in the *Documente* (quoted at page 404, footnote 7) p. 32.

[3] Yule, *Book of Ser Marco Polo*, ii. (1871) 79. 171. 180. &c.

[4] *Letters of Christ. Columbus* (Hakluyt Society) 1870. 81–84.

[5] De Candolle, *Géogr. botanique*, 836.

[6] The value of the sugar exported from Natal in 1871 reached the astonishing amount of £180,496 and £135,201 in 1876.

[7] Yet owing to the gold discoveries, the propagation of the cane in Australia was little thought of until about 1866 or 1867, when small lots of sugar were made.

[8] Consul Rogers, *Report on the Trade of Cairo for* 1872, presented to Parliament.

[9] *Expériences chymiques faites dans le dessein de tirer un véritable sucre de diverses plantes qui croissent dans nos contrées*, par Mr. Marggraf, traduit du latin—*Hist. de l'Académie royale des sciences et belles lettres*, année 1747 (Berlin 1749) 79–90.

[10] And also that of *milk sugar*, which was then much used on the Continent to *adulterate* cane sugar.

[11] *Produce Markets Review*, March 28, 1868.

[12] 2,255,249 quintals (one quintal = 108 lb. avdp.) in 1876.

[13] 120,030 hhds (one hogshead = 1,792 lb.) in 1876.

[14] 114,968,384 lb. in 1876.

Barbados,[1] and Jamaica,[2] produce at present the largest quantity of sugar.

Production—No crystals are found in the parenchyme of the cane, the sugar existing as an aqueous solution, chiefly within the cells of the centre of the stem. The transverse section of the cane exhibits numerous fibro-vascular bundles, scattered through the tissue, as in other monocotyledonous stems; yet these bundles are most abundant towards the exterior, where they form a dense ring covered with a thin epidermis, which is very hard by reason of the silica which is deposited in it.[3] In the centre of the stem the vascular bundles are few in number; the parenchyme is far more abundant, and contains in its thin-walled cells an almost clear solution of sugar, with a few small starch granules and a little soluble albuminous matter. This last is met with in larger quantity in the cambial portion of the vascular bundles. Pectic principles are combined with the walls of the medullary cells, which however do not swell much in water (Wiesner).

From these glances at the microscopical structure of the cane, the process to be followed for obtaining the largest possible quantity of sugar becomes evident. This would consist in simply macerating thin slices of the cane in water, which would at once penetrate the parenchyme loaded with sugar, without much attacking the fibro-vascular bundles containing more of albuminous than of saccharine matter. By this method, the epidermal layer of the cane would not become saturated with sugar, nor would it impede its extraction,—results which necessarily follow when the cane is crushed and pressed.[4]

The process hitherto generally practised in the colonies,—that of extracting the juice of the cane by crushing and pressing,—has been elaborately described and criticised by Dr. Icery of Mauritius.[5] In that island, the cane, six varieties of which are cultivated, is when mature composed of *Cellulose*, 8 to 12 per cent.; *Sugar*, 18 to 21; *Water*, including albuminous matter and salts, 67 to 73. Of the entire quantity of juice in the cane, from 70 to 84 per cent. is extracted for evaporation, and yields in a crystalline state about three-fifths of the sugar which the cane originally contained. This juice, called in French *vesou*, has on an average the following composition:—

Albuminous matters	0·03
Granular matter (starch ?)	0·10
Mucilage containing nitrogen	0·22
Salts, mostly of organic acids[6]	0·29
Sugar	18·36
Water	81·00
	100·00

[1] 38,013 hhds. in 1876.

[2] 29,074 hhds. in 1876.

[3] Stems of American sugar cane, dried at 100° C., yielded 4 per cent of ash, nearly half of which was silica.—Popp, in Wiggers' *Jahresbericht*, 1870. 35.

[4] The plan of obtaining a syrup by macerating the sliced fresh cane, has been tried in Guadaloupe, but abandoned owing to some practical difficulties in exhausting the cane and in carrying on the evaporation of the liquors with sufficient rapidity. Experiments for extracting a pure syrup by means of cold water from the *sliced and dried* cane, seem to promise good results.—See a paper by Dr. H. S. Mitchell in *Journ. of Soc. of Arts*, Oct. 23, 1868.

[5] *Annales de Chimie et de Physique*, v. (1865) 350–410.—See also, for Cuba, Alvaro Reynoso *Ensayo sobre el cultivo de la caña de Azúcar*, Madrid, 1865. 359.—For British Guiana, *Catal. of Contributions from Brit. Guiana to Paris Exhib.* 1867. pp. xxxviii.-xli.

[6] *Aconitic Acid* (p. 11) has been met with by Behr (1877) in West Indian molasses.

There is also present in the juice a very small amount of a slightly aromatic substance (essential oil?) to which the *crude* cane sugar owes a peculiar odour which is not observed in sugar from other sources. The first two classes of the above enumerated substances render the juice turbid, and greatly promote its fermentation, but they easily separate by boiling, and the juice may then be kept a short time without undergoing change. In many colonies the yield is said to be far inferior to what it should be; yet the juice is obtained in a state allowing of easier purification, when its extraction is not carried to the furthest limit.

In beet root as well as in the sugar cane, cane sugar only was said to be present; Icery however has proved that in the cane some uncrystallizable (inverted) sugar is always present. Its quantity varies much, according to the places where the cane grows, and its age. The tops of quick-growing young canes yielded a *vesou* containing 2·4 per cent. of uncrystallizable sugar; 3·6 of cane sugar; and 94 of water. Moist and shady situations greatly promote the formation of the former kind of sugar, which also prevails in the tops, chiefly when immature. Hence that observer concludes that at first the uncrystallizable variety of sugar is formed, and subsequently transformed into cane sugar by the force of vegetation, and especially by the influence of light. Perfectly ripened canes contain only $\frac{1}{75}$ to $\frac{1}{50}$ of all their sugar in the uncrystallizable state.

Description and Chemical Composition—Cane sugar is the type of a numerous class of well-defined organic compounds, of frequent occurrence throughout the vegetable and animal kingdoms, or artificially obtained by decomposing certain other substances; in the latter case, however, glucose or some other sugar than cane sugar is obtained. Cane sugar, $C^{12}H^{22}O^{11}$, or $C^{12}H^{14}(OH)^{8}O^{3}$, melts, without change of composition, at 160° C., several other kinds of sugar giving off water, with which they form crystallized compounds at the ordinary temperature.

Cane sugar forms hard crystals of the oblique rhombic system, having a sp. gr. of 1·59. Two parts are dissolved at 15° C. by one part of water,[1] and by much less at an elevated temperature; a slight depression of the thermometer is observable in the former case. One part of sugar dissolved in one of water, forms a liquid of sp. gr. 1·23; two of sugar in one of water, a liquid of sp. gr. 1·33. Sugar requires 65 parts of spirit of wine (sp. gr. 0·84) or 80 parts of anhydrous alcohol for solution; ether does not act upon it.

A ray of polarized light is deviated by an aqueous solution of cane sugar to the *right*, but by some other kinds of sugar to the *left*, as first shown by Biot. These optical powers are highly important, both in the practical estimation of solutions of sugar, and in scientific studies connected with sugar or saccharogenous substances. The optical as well as chemical properties of sugar are altered by many circumstances, as the action of dilute acids or alkalis, or by the influence of minute fungi. Yeast occasions sugar to undergo alcoholic fermentation. Other ferments set up an action by which butyric, lactic or propionic acid are produced.

Cane sugar is of a purer and sweeter taste than most other sugars. Though it does not alter litmus paper, yet with alkalis it forms com-

[1] It is commonly stated that *three* parts can be dissolved in one of cold water; but this is not the fact.

pounds some of which are crystallizable. From an alkaline solution of tartrate of copper, cane sugar throws down no protoxide, unless after boiling.

If sugar is kept a short time in a state of fusion at 160° C., it is converted into one molecule of *Grape Sugar* and one of *Levulosan;* the former can be either isolated by crystallization or destroyed by fermentation, the latter being incapable of crystallizing or of undergoing fermentation.

Cane sugar which has been melted at 160° C. is deliquescent and readily soluble in anhydrous alcohol, and its rotatory power is diminished or entirely destroyed. It is no longer crystallizable, and its fusing point has become reduced to about 93° C. Yet before undergoing these evident alterations, it assumes an amorphous condition if allowed to melt with a third of its weight of water, becoming always a little coloured by pyrogenous products. In the course of time, however, this amorphous sugar loses its transparency and reassumes the crystalline form. Like sulphur and arsenious acid, it is capable of existing either in a crystallized or an amorphous state.

If sugar is heated to about 190° C. water is evolved, and we obtain the dark brown products commonly called *Caramel* or *Burnt Sugar.* They are of a peculiar sharp flavour, of a bitter taste, incapable of fermenting and deliquescent. One of the constituents of caramel, *Caramelane,* $C^{12}H^{18}O^{9}$, has been obtained by Gélis (1862) perfectly colourless. When the heat is augmented, the sugar at last suffers a decomposition resembling that which produces tar (see p. 621), its pyrogenous products being the same or very analogous to those of the dry distillation of wood.

Varieties of Cane Sugar—The experiments of Marggraf referred to at p. 717, note 9, showed that cane sugar is by no means confined to the sugar cane; and it is in fact extracted on an extensive scale from several other plants, of which the following deserve mention:—

Beet Root—The manufacture of cane sugar from the fleshy root of a cultivated variety of *Beta maritima* L., is now largely carried on in Continental Europe and in America, and with admirable results.

Of fresh beet root, 100 parts contain on an average 80 per cent. of water, 11 to 13 of cane sugar, and about 7 per cent. of pectic and albuminous matters, cellulose and salts. Of the total amount of juice which the root contains, eight-ninths are extracted; and by the best process now in practice, 8 to 9 parts of sugar from every 100 parts of fresh root. The yield of crystalline sugar is still on the increase, owing to continual improvements in the mechanical and chemical parts of the process.

Palm—Several species are of great utility for the production of the sugar called by Europeans *Jaggery.*[1] This substance is obtained by the natives of India in the following manner:—The young growing spadix, or flowering shoot, of the palm is cut off near its apex; and an earthen vessel is tied on to the stump to receive the juice that flows out. This vessel is emptied daily; while to promote a continuous flow of sap, a thin slice is cut from the wounded end. The juice thus collected, if at once boiled down, yields the crude brown sugar known as *jaggery.* If allowed to ferment, it becomes the inebriating drink called *Toddy* or

[1] A word of Sanskrit origin, corrupted from the Canarese *sharkari.*

palm wine; or it may be converted into vinegar. The spirit distilled from toddy is *Arrack*.

Of the sugar-yielding palms of Asia, *Phœnix silvestris* Roxb., which is supposed to be the wild form of the date palm, is one of the more important. The coco-nut palm, *Cocos nucifera* L.; the magnificent Palmyra palm, *Borassus flabelliformis* L.; and the Bastard Sago, *Caryota urens* L., also furnish important quantities of sugar. In the Indian Archipelago, sugar is obtained from the sap of *Arenga saccharifera* Mart., which grows there in abundance as well as in the Philippines and the Indo-Chinese countries. It is also got from *Nipa fruticans* Thunb., a tree of the low coast regions, extensively cultivated in Tavoy.

De Vry[1] has advocated the manufacture of sugar from the palm as the most philosophical, seeing that its juice is a nearly pure aqueous solution of sugar: that as no mineral constituents are removed from the soil in this juice, the costly manuring, as well as the laborious and destructive processes required to eliminate the juice from such plants as the sugar cane and beet root, are avoided. And finally, that palms are perennial, and can many of them be cultivated on a soil unsuitable for any cereal.

Maple—In America, considerable quantities of sugar identical with that of the cane are obtained in the woods of the Northern United States and of Canada, by evaporating the juice of maples. The species chiefly employed are *Acer saccharinum* Wangenh., the Common Sugar Maple, and its variety (var. *nigrum*) the Black Sugar Maple. *A. Pennsylvanicum* L., *A. Negundo* L. (*Negundo aceroides* Moench.) and *A. dasycarpum* Ehrh. are also used; the sap of the last is said to be the least saccharine.

As the juice of these trees yields not more than about 2 per cent. of sugar, it requires for its solidification a large expenditure of fuel. The manufacture of maple sugar can therefore be advantageously carried on only in countries remote from markets whence ordinary sugar can be procured, or in regions where fuel is extremely plentiful. In North America it flourishes only between 40° and 43° N. lat. We are not aware of any estimate of the total production of maple sugar. The Census of Pennsylvania of 1870 gave the following figures as referring to its manufacture in that State:—

1850	1860	1870
2,326,525 lb.	2,768,965 lb.	1,545,917 lb.[2]

Sorghum—Another plant of the same order as *Saccharum* is *Sorghum saccharatum* Pers. (*Holcus saccharatus* L.) a native of Northern China,[3] which has of late been much tried as a sugar-yielding plant both in Europe and North America; yet without any great success, as the purification of the sugar is accomplished with peculiar difficulty. As in the sugar cane, there are in sorghum crystallizable and uncrystallizable sugars, the former being at its maximum amount when the grain reaches maturity. The importance of the plant however is rapidly increasing on account of the value of its leaves and grain as food for

[1] *Journ. de Pharm.* i. (1865) 270.

[2] Consul Kortright, in *Consular Reports* presented to Parliament, July 1872. p. 988.

[3] Introduced into Europe in 1850, by M. de Montigny, French Consul at Shanghai.—Sicard, *Monographie de la Canne à sucre de la Chine, dite* Sorgho à sucre, Marseille, 1856; Joulie, *Journ. de Pharm.* i. (1865) 188.

horses and cattle, and of its stems which can be employed in the manufacture of paper and of alcohol.

Commerce—The value of the sugar imported into the United Kingdom is constantly increasing, as shown by the following figures:—

	1868	1870	1872
Unrefined . .	£13,339,758	£14,440,502	£18,044,898
Refined . . .	£1,156,188	£2,744,366	£3,142,703

The quantity of *Unrefined Sugar* imported in 1872 was 13,776,696 cwt., of which about 3,000,000 cwt. were furnished by the Spanish West India Islands, 2,700,000 cwt. by the British West India Islands, 1,800,000 cwt. by Brazil, 1,100,000 cwt. by France, and 960,000 cwt. by Mauritius.

Of *Refined Sugar* the imports from France and Belgium into the United Kingdom were—

1874	1875	1876
133,800	102,300	92,044 tons.

Uses—Refined sugar is employed in pharmacy for making syrups, electuaries and lozenges, and is useful not merely for the sake of covering the unpleasant taste of other drugs, but also on account of a preservative influence which it exerts over their active constituents.

Muscovado or Raw Sugar is not used in medicine. The dark uncrystallizable syrup, known in England as *Molasses, Golden Syrup*, and *Treacle*,[1] and in foreign pharmacy as *Syrupus Hollandicus vel communis*, which is formed in the preparation of pure sugar by the influence of heat, alkaline bodies, microscopic vegetation, and the oxygen of the air, is sometimes employed for making pill masses. The treacle of colonial sugar alone is adapted for this purpose, that of beet root having a disagreeable taste, and containing from 19 to 21 per cent. of oxalate, tartrate and malate of potassium, and only 56 to 64 of sugar.[2] The treacle of colonial sugar usually contains 5 to 7 per cent. of salts.

HORDEUM DECORTICATUM.

Hordeum perlatum, Fructus vel Semen Hordei; Pearl Barley; F. *Orge mondé ou perlé;* G. *Gerollte Gerste, Gerstegraupen.*

Botanical Origin—*Hordeum distichum* L.,—the Common or Long-eared Barley is probably indigenous to western temperate Asia, but has been cultivated for ages throughout the northern hemisphere. In Sweden its cultivation extends as far as 68° 38′ N. lat.; on the Norwegian coast up to the Altenfjord in 70° N. lat.; even in Lapland, it succeeds as high as 900 to 1350 feet above the level of the sea. In several of the southern Swiss Alpine valleys, barley ripens at 5000 feet, and in the Himalaya at 11,000 feet. In the Equatorial Andes, where it is extensively grown, it thrives up to at least 11,000 feet above the sea. No other cereal can be cultivated under so great a variety of climate.

[1] How the word *Treacle* came to be transferred from its application to an opiate medicine to become a name for *molasses*, we know not. In the description of sugar-making given by Salmon in his *English Physician or Druggist's Shop opened*, Lond. 1663, treacle is never mentioned, but only "*melussas*."

[2] Landolt, *Zeitschr. für analyt. Chem.* vii. (1868) 1–29.

According to Bretschneider,[1] barley is included among the five cereals which it is related in Chinese history were sowed by the Emperor Shen-nung, who reigned about 2700 B.C.; but it is not one of the five sorts of grain which are used at the ceremony of ploughing and sowing as now annually performed by the emperors of China.

Theophrastus was acquainted with several sorts of barley (Κριθή), and among them, with the six-rowed kind or *hexastichon*, which is the species that is represented on the coins struck at Metapontum[2] in Lucania, between the 6th and 2nd centuries B.C.

Strabo and Dioscorides in the 1st century allude to drinks made from barley, which according to Tacitus were even then familiar to the German tribes, as they are known to have been still earlier to the Greeks and Egyptians.

Barley is mentioned in the Bible as a plant of cultivation in Egypt and Syria, and must have been, among the ancient Hebrews, an important article of food, judging from the quantity allowed by Solomon to the servants of Hiram, king of Tyre (B.C. 1015). The tribute of barley paid to King Jotham by the Ammonites (B.C. 741) is also exactly recorded. The ancients were frequently in the practice of removing the hard integuments of barley by roasting it, and using the torrefied grain as food.

Manufacture—For use in medicine and as food for the sick, barley is not employed in its crude state, but only when deprived more or less completely of its husk. The process by which this is effected is carried on in mills constructed for the purpose, and consists essentially in passing the grain between horizontal millstones, placed so far apart as to rub off its integuments without crushing it. Barley partially deprived of its husk is known as *Scotch, hulled* or *Pot Barley*. When by longer and closer grinding the whole of the integuments have been removed, and the grain has become completely rounded, it is termed *Pearl Barley*. In the *British Pharmacopœia* it is this sort alone which is ordered to be used.

Description—Pearl Barley is in subspherical or somewhat ovoid grains about 2 lines in diameter, of white farinaceous aspect, often partly yellowish from remains of the adhering husk, which is present on the surface, as well as in the deep longitudinal furrow with which each grain is indented. It has the farinaceous taste and odour which are common to most of the cereal grains.

Microscopic Structure—The albumen which constitutes the main portion of the grain is composed of large thin-walled parenchyme, the cells of which on transverse section are seen to radiate from the furrow, and to be lengthened in that direction rather than longitudinally. In the vicinity of the furrow alone the tissue of the albumen is narrower. Its predominating large cells show a polygonal or oval outline, whilst the outer layer is built up of two, three or four rows of thick-walled, coherent, nearly cubic gluten-cells. This layer, about 70 mkm. thick, is coated with an extremely thin brown tegument, to which succeeds a layer about 30 mkm. thick, of densely packed, tabular, greyish or yellowish

[1] *On Chinese Botanical Works*, etc., Foochow, 1870. 7. 8.

[2] Metapontum lay in the plain between the rivers Bradano and Basento in the gulf of Taranto.

cells of very small size; this proper coat of the fruit in the furrow is of rather spongy appearance.

In some varieties of barley the fruit is constituted of the above tissues alone and the shell, but in most the paleæ are likewise present. They consist chiefly of long fibrous, thick-walled cells, two or four rows deep, constituting a very hard layer. On tranverse section, this layer forms a coherent envelope about 35 mkm. thick; its cells when examined in longitudinal section show but a small lumen of peculiar undulated outline from secondary deposits.

The gluten-cells varying considerably in the different cereal grains, afford characters enough to distinguish them with certainty. In wheat, for instance, the gluten-cells are in a single row, in rice they form a double or single row, but its cells are transversely lengthened.

The inner tissue of the albumen in barley is filled up with large irregularly lenticular, and with extremely small globular starch granules, the first being 20 to 35 mkm., the latter 1, 2 to 3 mkm. in diameter, with no considerable number of intermediate size. The concentric layers constituting the large granules may be made conspicuous by moistening with chromic acid.

The layer alluded to as being composed of *gluten-cells* is loaded with extremely small granules of albuminous matters (gluten), which on addition of iodine are coloured intensely yellow. These granules, which, considering barley as an article of food, are of prominent value, are not confined to the gluten-cells, but the neighbouring starch-cells also contain a small amount of them: and in the narrow zone of denser tissue projecting from the furrow into the albumen, protein principles are equally deposited, as shown by the yellow coloration which iodine produces.

The gluten-cells, the *membrane embroynnaire* of Mège-Mouriès, contain also, according to the researches on bread[1] made by this chemist (1856), *Cerealin*, an albuminous principle soluble in water, which causes the transformation of starch into dextrin, sugar, and lactic acid. In the husks (*épiderme*, *épicarpe* and *endocarpe*) of wheat, Mège-Mouriès found some volatile oil and a yellow extractive matter, to which, together with the cerealin, is due the acidity of bread made with the flour containing the bran.

Chemical Composition—Barley has been submitted to careful analyses by many chemists, more especially by Lermer.[2] The grains contain usually 13 to 15 per cent. of water; after drying, they yield to ether 3 per cent. of fat oil, with insignificant proportions of tannic and bitter principles, residing chiefly in the husks. Lermer further found in the whole grains, 63 per cent. of starch, 7 of cellulose, 6·6 of dextrin, 2·5 of nitrogen, a small amount of lactic acid, and 2·4 of ash.

The analysis of Poggiale (1856) gave nearly the same composition, namely, water 15, oil 2·4, starch 60, cellulose 8·8, albuminous principles 10·7, ash 2·6.

The protein, or albuminous matter consists of different principles, chiefly insoluble in cold water. The soluble portion is partly coagulated on boiling, partly retained in solution: 2·5 per cent. of nitrogen, as

[1] He actually examined *wheat*, not barley; we assume the chemical constitution of the two grains to be similar.

[2] Wittstein, *Vierteljahresschr. für prakt. Pharm.* xii. (1863) 4–23.

above, would answer to about 16 per cent. of albuminous matters. Their soluble part seems to be deposited in the starch-cells, next to the gluten-cells, which latter contain the insoluble portion.

The ash, according to Lermer, contains 29 per cent. of silicic acid, 32·6 of phosphoric acid, 22·7 of potash, and only 3·7 of lime. In the opinion of Salm-Horstmar, fluorine and lithia are indispensable constituents of barley.

The fixed oil of barley, as proved in 1863 by Hanamann, is a compound of glycerin with either a mixture of palmitic and lauric acids, or less probably with a peculiar fatty acid. Beckmann's *Hordeinic Acid* obtained in 1855 by distilling barley with sulphuric acid, is probably lauric acid. Lintner (1868) has shown barley to contain also a little *Cholesterin* (p. 420).

Lastly, Kühnemann (1875) extracted from barley a crystallized dextrogyrate sugar, and (1876) an amorphous lævogyrate mucilaginous substance *Sinistrin* (see p. 692); according to that chemist, dextrin is altogether wanting in barley.

Barley when malted loses 7 per cent.; it then contains 10 to 12 per cent. of sugar, produced at the expense of the starch; before malting, no sugar is to be found.

Uses—Barley as a medicine is unimportant. A decoction is sometimes prescribed as a demulcent or as a diluent of active remedies. An aqueous extract of malt has been employed.

OLEUM ANDROPOGONIS.

Oleum Graminis Indici; Indian Grass Oil.

Botanical Origin—Among the numerous species of *Andropogon*[1] which have foliage abounding in essential oil, the following furnish the fragrant *Grass Oils* of commerce:—

1. *Andropogon Nardus* L.,[2]—a noble-looking plant, rising when in flower to a height of 6 or more feet, extensively cultivated in Ceylon and Singapore for the production of *Citronella Oil.*

2. *A. citratus* D.C.,[3] Lemon Grass,—a large coarse glaucous grass, known only in a cultivated state, and very rarely producing flowers. It is grown in Ceylon and Singapore for the sake of its essential oil, which is called *Lemon Grass Oil, Oil of Verbena* or *Indian Melissa Oil;* it is also commonly met with in gardens throughout India and is not unfrequent in English hothouses. In Java it is called *Sireh.*

3. *A. Schœnanthus* L.,[4] a grass of Northern and Central India, having

[1] Major-General Munro has at our request investigated the botanical characters of the fragrant species of *Andropogon*, and examined a numerous suite of specimens in our possession. The synonyms in foot-notes are given upon his authority.

[2] *A. Martini* Thwaites, *Enum. Plantarum Zeylaniæ* nec aliorum.—Fig. in Bentley and Trimen's *Med. Plants*, part 28 (1878).

[3] *A. citratum* A. P. De Candolle, *Catalogus Plantarum Horti Botanici Monspeliensis*, 1813; *A. Schœnanthus* Wallich, *Plant. Asiat. rariores*, iii. (1832) tab. 280; Roxburgh, *Flora Indica*, i. (1820) 278, quoad observationes, sed non quoad diagnosis.

[4] Ventenat, *Jardin de Cels*, 1803. tab. 89; *A. Martini* Roxb. *Flor. Ind.* i. (1820) 280; *A. pachnodes* Trinius, *Species Graminum*, iii. (1836) tab. 327; *A. Calamus aromaticus* Royle, *Illustrations of Bot. of Himalayan Mountains*, 1839. tab. 97.

leaves rounded or slightly cordate at the base, yielding by distillation the oil known as *Rúsa Oil, Oil of Ginger Grass* or *of Geranium*.

History—The aromatic properties of certain species of *Andropogon* were well known to Rheede, Rumphius, and other early writers on Indian natural history; and an oil distilled from the *Sireh* grass in Amboyna was known as a curiosity as early as 1717.[1]

But it is only in very recent times that the volatile oils of these plants have become objects of commerce with Europe. Lemon grass oil is mentioned by Roxburgh in 1820 as being distilled in the Moluccas; and it was first imported into London about the year 1832. Citronella oil is of much more recent introduction. Ginger grass oil, called in Hindustani *Rúsa ka tel*, is stated by Waring[2] to have been first brought to notice by Dr. N. Maxwell in 1825.

Production—Citronella and Lemon grass are cultivated about Galle and at Singapore, the same estate often producing both. The grasses are distilled separately, the essential oils being regarded as entirely distinct, and having different market values. In Ceylon they are cut for distillation at any time of year, but mostly in December and January.

On the Perseverance Estate at Gaylang, Singapore, belonging to Mr. John Fisher, an area of 950 acres is cultivated with aromatic grasses and other plants, for the production of essential oils. The manufacture was tried on a small scale in 1865, and has been so successful that an aggregate of 200 lb. of various essential oils is now produced *daily*. These oils are stated to be Citronella, Lemon Grass, Patchouly, Nutmeg, Mace, Pepper, and Oman (p. 302): and mint is now being cultivated.[3]

Ginger grass oil is distilled in the collectorate of Khandesh in the Bombay Presidency. That produced in the district of Namár in the valley of the Nerbudda, is sometimes called *Grass Oil of Namar*. We have no particulars of the distillation, which however must be carried on extensively.

Description—The Indian grass oils are lighter than water, devoid of rotatory power when examined by polarized light, and do not alter litmus paper. They are all extremely fragrant, having an odour like a mixture of lemon and rose. Lemon grass, which in colour is a deep golden brown, has an odour resembling that of the sweet-scented verbena of the gardens, *Lippia citriodora* H.B.K. Ginger grass oil, the colour of which varies from pale greenish yellow to yellowish-brown, has the odour of *Pelargonium Radula* Aiton. The colour of citronella oil is a light greenish-yellow. The manufacture of Winter of Ceylon, and of Fisher of Singapore, have a reputation for excellence, and are generally indicated by name in drug sale catalogues.

Chemical Composition—Stenhouse[4] examined in 1844 oil of ginger grass given to him by Christison as *Oil of Namur* (or *Nimar*). The sample was of deep yellow, and apparently old, for when mixed with water and subjected to distillation, it left nearly one half its bulk of a fluid resin, the oil which passed over being colourless. After rectification from chloride of calcium, it was shown to consist of a hydrocarbon mixed with a small proportion of an oxygenated oil. The latter having

[1] *Ephemerides Naturæ Curiosorum*, cent. v.-vi. (1717), appendix 157.

[2] *Pharmacopœia of India*, 1868. 465.

[3] *Straits Settlements Blue Book for* 1872, Singapore, 1873. 465.

[4] *Mem. of Chem. Soc.* ii. (1845) 122.

been decomposed by sodium, and the oil again rectified, a second analysis was made which proved it isomeric with oil of turpentine.

A genuine grass oil from Khandesh, derived as we suppose from the same species, which was examined by one of us (F.), yielded nothing crystalline when saturated with dry hydrochloric acid; but when the liquid was afterwards treated with fuming nitric acid, crystals of the compound, $C^{10}H^{16}$, HCl, sublimed into the upper part of the vessel. We have observed that the oils both of lemon grass and citronella yield solid compounds, if shaken with a saturated solution of bisulphite of sodium.

Citronella oil was found by Gladstone (1872) to be composed chiefly of an oxidized oil, which he called *Citronellol*, and which he separated by fractional distillation into two portions, the one boiling at 202–205° C., the other 199–202° C. The composition of each portion is indicated by the formula $C^{10}H^{16}O$.

Wright's researches (1874) tend rather to show the prevailing part of citronella oil to consist of the liquid $C^{10}H^{18}O$, boiling near 210°, which he calls *Citronellol*. It unites with bromine, and the resulting compound, upon heating, breaks up according to the following equation:—

$$C^{10}H^{18}OBr^2 = OH^2 \ . \ 2\,HBr \quad \underset{\text{Cymene.}}{C^{10}H^{14}}.$$

Commerce—The growing trade in grass oil is exemplified in a striking manner by the following statistics. The export of *Citronella Oil* from Ceylon in 1864 was 622,000 ounces, valued at £8230. In the *Ceylon Blue Book*, the exports for 1872 are returned thus:—

To the United Kingdom	1,163,074 ounces	1,595,257 ounces.[1]
British India	5,713 ,,	
United States of North America . .	426,470 ,,	

In 1875 the oil shipped from Ceylon to the United Kingdom was valued at 42,871 rupees, that sent to other foreign countries at 45,871 rupees, to British possessions 660 rupees (one rupee equal to about 2*s*).

Oil of Lemon Grass, which is a more costly article and less extensively produced, was exported from Ceylon during the same year to the extent of 13,515 ounces, more than half of which quantity was shipped to the United States. There are no analogous statistics for these two oils from Singapore, where, as stated at p. 726, they are now largely manufactured.

By the official *Report on the External Commerce of Bombay*, published in 1867, we find that during the year ending 31 March, 1867, *Grass Oil* [i.e. *Ginger-grass or Rusa Oil*] was exported thence to the amount of 41,643 lb. This oil is shipped to England and to the ports of the Red Sea.

Uses—Grass oils are much esteemed in India as an external application in rheumatism. Rúsa oil is said to stimulate the growth of the hair. Internally, grass oil is sometimes administered as a carminative in colic; and an infusion of the leaves of lemon grass is prescribed as a diaphoretic and stimulant. In Europe and America the oils are used almost exclusively by the soapmakers and perfumers.[2]

[1] In addition to which, there were "842 *dozens and* 33 *packages*" of the same oil shipped to the United States. One ounce equal to 31·1 grammes.

[2] The foliage of the large odoriferous species of *Andropogon* is used in India for thatching. It is eaten voraciously by cattle, whose flesh and milk become flavoured with its strong aroma.

But the most remarkable use made of any grass oil is that for adulterating *Attar of Rose* in European Turkey. The oil thus employed is that of *Andropogon Schœnanthus* L. (see p. 725); and it is a curious fact that its Hindustani name is closely similar in sound to the word *rose.* Thus under the designation *Rusa, Rowsah, Rosa, Rosé, Roshé,*[1] it is exported in large quantities from Bombay to the ports of Arabia, probably chiefly to Jidda, whence it is carried to Turkey by the Mahommedan pilgrims. In Arabia and Turkey, it appears under the name *Idris yaghi,* while in the attar-producing districts of the Balkan it is known, at least to Europeans, as *Geranium Oil* or *Palmarosa Oil.* Before being mixed with attar, the oil is subjected to a certain preparation, which is accomplished by shaking it with water acidulated with lemon juice, and then exposing it to the sun and air. By this process, described by Baur,[2] the oil loses a penetrating after-smell, and acquires a pale straw colour. The optical and chemical differences between grass oil thus refined and attar of rose are slight and do not indicate a small admixture of the former. If grass oil is added largely to attar, it will prevent its congealing.

Adulteration—The grass oil prepared by the natives of India is not unfrequently contaminated with fatty oil.

Other Products of the genus Andropogon.

Herba Schœnanthi vel Squinanthi, *Juncus odoratus, Fœnum Camelorum.*

The drug bearing these names has had a place in pharmacy from the days of Dioscorides down to the middle of the last century, and is still met with in the East. The plant which affords it, formerly confounded with other species, is now known to be *Andropogon laniger* Desf., a grass of wide distribution, growing in hot dry regions in Northern Africa (Algeria), Arabia, and North-western India, reaching Thibet, where it is found up to an elevation of 11,000 feet. Mr. Tolbort has sent us specimens under the name of *Khávi,* gathered by himself in 1869 between Multán and Kot Sultán, and quite agreeing with the drug of pharmacy. The grass has an aromatic pungent taste, which is retained in very old specimens. We are not aware that it is distilled for essential oil.

Cuscus or Vetti-ver[3]—This is the long fibrous root of *Andropogon muricatus* Retz, a large grass found abundantly in rich moist ground in Southern India and Bengal. Inscriptions on copper-plates lately discovered in the district of Etawah, south-east of Agra, and dating from A.D. 1103 and 1174, record grants of villages to Brahmins by the kings of Kanauj, and enumerate the imposts that were to be levied. These include taxes on mines, salt pits and the trade in precious metals, also on mahwah (*Bassia*) and mango trees, and on *Cuscus Grass.*[4]

Cuscus, which appears occasionally in the London drug sales, is used in England for laying in drawers as a perfume. In India it serves for

[1] 50 cases, containing about 2250 lb., imported from Bombay, were offered as "*Rose Oil*" at public sale, by a London drugbroker, 31 July, 1873.

[2] See p. 267.

[3] *Cuscus,* otherwise written *Khus-khus,* a name adopted by the English in India, is probably from the Persian *Khas. Vetti-ver* is the Malyalim name of the plant.

[4] *Proc. of Asiat. Soc. of Bengal,* Aug. 1873. 161.

making *tatties* or screens, which are placed in windows and doorways, and when wetted, diffuse an agreeable odour and coolness. It is also used for making ornamental baskets and many small articles, and has some reputation as a medicine.

RHIZOMA GRAMINIS.

Radix Graminis; Couch Grass, Quitch Grass, Dog's Grass; F. *Chiendent commun ou Petit Chiendent;* G. *Queckenwurzel, Graswurzel.*

Botanical Origin—*Agropyrum repens* P. Beauv. (*Triticum repens* L.), a widely diffused weed, growing in fields and waste places in all parts of Europe, in Northern Asia down to the region south of the Caspian, also in North America; and in South America to Patagonia and Tierra del Fuego.

History—The ancients were familiar with a grass termed Ἄγρωστις and *Gramen*, having a creeping rootstock like that under notice. It is impossible to determine to what species the plant is referable, though it is probable that the grass *Cynodon Dactylon* Pers., as well as *Agropyrum repens*, was included under these names.

Dioscorides asserts that its root taken in the form of decoction, is a useful remedy in suppression of urine and vesical calculus. The same statements are made by Pliny; and again occur in the writings of Oribasius[1] and Marcellus Empiricus[2] in the 4th, and of Aëtius[3] in the 6th century, and are repeated in the mediæval herbals,[4] where also figures of the plant may be found, as for instance in Dodonæus. The drug is also met with in the German pharmaceutical tariffs of the 16th century. Turner[5] and Gerarde both ascribe to a decoction of grass root diuretic and lithontriptic virtues. The drug is still a domestic remedy in great repute in France, being taken as a demulcent and sudorific in the form of *tisane*.

Description—Couch-grass has a long, stiff, pale yellow, smooth rhizome, $\frac{1}{10}$ of an inch in diameter, creeping close under the surface of the ground, occasionally branching, marked at intervals of about an inch by nodes, which bear slender branching roots and the remains of sheathing rudimentary leaves.

As found in the shops, the rhizome is always free from rootlets, cut into short lengths of $\frac{1}{8}$ to $\frac{1}{4}$ of an inch, and dried. It is thus in the form of little, shining, straw-coloured, many-edged, tubular pieces, which are without odour, but have a slightly sweet taste.

Microscopic Structure—A transverse section of this rhizome shows two different portions of tissue, separated by the so-called nucleus-sheath. The latter consists of an unbroken ring of prismatic cells, analogous to those occurring in sarsaparilla. In *Rhizoma Graminis*, the outer part of the tissue exhibits a diffuse circle of about 20 liber bundles, and the interior part about the same number of fibro-vascular bundles more

[1] *De virtute simplicium*, cap. i. (Agrostis).
[2] *De medicamentis*, cap. xxvi.
[3] Tetrabibli primæ, sermo i.
[4] As in the *Herbarius Patavie* printed in 1485, in which it is said of *Gramen*—"aqua decoctionis ejus . . . valet contra dissuriam . . . et frangit lapidem et curat vulnera vesicæ et provocat urinam . . . ."
[5] *Herball*, part 2, 1568. 13.

densely packed. The pith is reduced to a few rows of cells, the rhizome being always hollow, except at the nodes. No solid contents are to be met with in the tissue.

Chemical Composition—The constituents of couch-grass include no substance to which medicinal powers can be ascribed. The juice of the rhizome afforded to H. Müller[1] about 3 per cent. of sugar, and 7 to 8 per cent. of *Triticin*, $C^{12}H^{22}O^{11}$, a tasteless, amorphous, gummy substance, easily transformed into sugar if its concentrated solution is kept for a short time at 110° C. When treated with nitric acid, it yields oxalic acid. The rhizome affords also another gummy matter containing nitrogen, and quickly undergoing decomposition; the drug moreover is somewhat rich in acid malates. Mannite is probably occasionally present as in taraxacum (p. 394), for such is the inference we draw from the opposite results obtained by Stenhouse and by Völcker. Starch, pectin and resin are wanting. The rhizome leaves 4½ per cent. of ash.

Uses—A decoction of the rhizome has of late been recommended in mucous discharge from the bladder.

Substitutes—*Agropyrum acutum* R. et S., *A. pungens* R. et S., and *A. junceum* P. Beauv., by some botanists regarded as mere maritime varieties of *A. repens*, have rootstocks perfectly similar to this latter.

Cynodon Dactylon Pers., a grass very common in the South of Europe and the warmer parts of Western Europe, also indigenous to Northern Africa as far as Sennaar and Abyssinia, affords the *Gros Chiendent* or *Chiendent pied-de-poule* of the French. It is a rhizome differing from that of couch-grass in being a little stouter. Under the microscope it displays an entirely different structure, inasmuch as it contains a large number of much stronger fibro-vascular bundles, and a cellular tissue loaded with starch, and is therefore in appearance much more woody. It thus approximates to the rhizome of *Carex arenaria* L., which is as much used in Germany as that of *Cynodon* in Southern Europe. The latter appears to contain *Asparagin* (the *Cynodin* of Semmola[2]), or a substance similar to it.

[1] *Archiv der Pharm.* 203. (1873) 17.

[2] Della *Cinodina*, nuovo prodotto organico, trovato nella gramigna officinale, *Cynodon Dactylon.*—*Opere minori di Giovanni Semmola*, Napoli, 1841.—Abstracted in the *Jahresbericht* of Berzelius, Tübingen, 1845. 535.

II.—CRYPTOGAMOUS OR FLOWERLESS PLANTS.

Vascular Cryptogams.

LYCOPODIACEÆ.

SPORÆ LYCOPODII.

Lycopodium; Semen vel Sporulæ Lycopodii; F. *Lycopode;* G. *Bärlappsamen, Hexenmehl.*

Botanical Origin—*Lycopodium clavatum* L.—This plant, the Common Clubmoss, is almost cosmopolitan. It is found on hilly pastures and heaths throughout Central and Northern Europe from the Alps and Pyrenees to the Arctic reunions, in the mountains of the east and centre of Spain, throughout Russian Asia to Amurland and Japan, in North and South America, the Falkland Isles, Australia and the Cape of Good Hope. It occurs throughout Great Britain, but is most plentiful on the moors of the northern counties.

The part of the plant employed in pharmacy is the minute spores, which, as a yellow powder, are shaken out of the kidney-shaped capsules or sporangia, growing on the inner side of the bracts covering the fruit-spike.

The manner in which those sporæ are able to reproduce the mother plant is not yet satisfactorily ascertained.[1]

History—The Common Clubmoss was well known as *Muscus terrestris* or *Muscus clavatus*, to the older botanists, as Tragus, Dodonæus, Tabernæmontanus, Bauhin, Parkinson and Ray, by most of whom its supposed virtues as a herb have been commemorated. Though the powder (spores) was officinal in Germany, and used as an application to wounds in the middle of the 17th century,[2] it does not appear to have been known in the English shops until a comparatively recent period. It is not included by Dale[3] in the list of drugs sold by London druggists in 1692, nor enumerated in English drug lists of the last century; and it never had a place in the London Pharmacopœia.

[1] The few particulars may be found in the excellent description of Lycopodium in Luerssen's "*Medicinisch-pharmaceutische Botanik*," i. (Leipsig, 1878) 635, with figures.

[2] Schröder, *Pharmacopœia Medico-chymica*, ed. 4, Lugd. 1656. 538.—Flückiger, "*Documente*" (quoted p. 404) 63. 68.

[3] *Pharmacologia*, Lond. 1693.

Description—Lycopodium is a fine, mobile, inodorous, tasteless powder of pale yellow hue, having at 16° C. a sp. gr. of 1·062. It floats on water and is wetted with difficulty, yet sinks in that fluid after boiling. By strong titration it coheres, assumes a grey tint, and leaves an oily stain on paper; it may then be mixed with water. It is immediately moistened by oily and alcoholic liquids, chloroform, or ether. It loses only 4 per cent. of moisture when dried at 100° C. When slowly heated, it burns away quietly, but when projected into flame, it ignites instantly and explosively, burning with much light, an effect exhibited by some other pulverulent bodies having a peculiar structure, as fern spores and kamala.

Microscopic Structure—Under the microscope lycopodium is seen to be composed of uniform cells or granules, 25 mkm. in diameter, each bounded by four faces, one of which (the base) is convex, while the others terminate in a triangular pyramid, the three furrowed edges of which do not reach quite to the base. These tetrahedral granules are marked by minute ridges, forming by their intersections, regular five- or six-sided meshes. At the points of intersection, small elevations are produced, which, under a low magnifying power, give the granules a speckled appearance. Below this network lies a yellow, coherent, thin, but compact membrane, which exhibits considerable power of resistance, not being ruptured either by boiling water or by potash lye. Oil of vitriol does not act upon it in the cold, even after several days; but it instantly penetrates the grains and renders them transparent, while at the same time numerous drops of oil make their appearance and quickly exude.

Chemical Composition—One of the most remarkable constituents of lycopodium spores is a fixed oil, which they contain to the astonishing amount of 47 per cent. Bucholz pointed out its existence in 1807, but obtained it only to the extent of 6 per cent. Yet if the spores are thoroughly comminuted by prolonged trituration with sand, and are then exhausted with chloroform or ether, we find that the larger proportion above mentioned can be obtained. The oil is a bland liquid, which does not solidify even at − 15° C.

By subjecting lypocodium or its extract to distillation with or without an alkali, Stenhouse obtained volatile bases, the presence of which we can fully confirm; but they occur in exceedingly small proportion. The ash of lycopodium amounts to 4 per cent.; it is not alkaline; it contains alumina, and one per cent. of phosphoric acid, constituents likewise found in the green parts of the plant.

Production and Commerce—To obtain lycopodium, the tops of the plant are cut as the spikes approach maturity, taken home, and the powder shaken out and separated by a sieve. It is collected chiefly in July and August, in Russia, Germany and Switzerland. The quantity obtained varies greatly by reason of frequent failures in the growth of the plant.

France imported in 1870, 7262 kilo. (16,017 lb.) of lycopodium, chiefly from Germany. The consumption in England is probably very much smaller, but there are no data to consult.

Uses—Lycopodium is not now regarded as possessing any medicinal virtues, and is only used externally for dusting excoriated surfaces and for placing in pill boxes to prevent the mutual adhesion of pills. It is also employed by the pyrotechnist.

Adulteration—The spores are so peculiar in structure, that they can be distinguished with certainty by the microscope from all other substances. It is only the species of clubmoss that are nearly related to *L. clavatum*,[1] that yield an analogous product, and this may be used with equal advantage.

The pollen of phænogamous plants, as of *Pinus silvestris*, looks at first sight much like lycopodium, but its structure is totally different and very easily recognized by the microscope.

Water, even on boiling, is unable to dissolve anything from lycopodium; slight traces of sulphate of calcium are not seldom met with in the filtrate. Yet an undue proportion of gypsum will be detected by the following methods:—

Starch and dextrin, which are sometimes fraudulently mixed with the spores, are easily recognized by the well-known tests. Inorganic admixtures, as gypsum or magnesia, may be detected by their sinking in bisulphide of carbon, whereas lycopodium rises to the surface; or by incineration, a good commercial drug leaving about 4 per cent. of ash.

FILICES.

RHIZOMA FILICIS.

Radix Filicis maris; Male Fern Rhizome, Male Fern Root; F. *Racine de Fougère mâle;* G. *Farnwurzel.*

Botanical Origin—*Aspidium Filix mas* Swartz (*Polypodium* L. *Nephrodium* Michaux). The male fern is one of the most widely distributed species, usually growing in abundance and, in temperate regions, ascending as high as the arborescent vegetation. It occurs all over Europe from Sicily to Iceland, in Greenland, throughout Central and Russian Asia to the Himalaya and Japan; is found throughout China, and again in Java and the Sandwich Islands, as well as in Africa from Algeria to the Cape Colony and Mauritius. In North America it is wanting in the Eastern United States, being principally replaced by the nearly allied *Aspidium marginale* Sw. and *A. Goldieanum* Hook.; but it is met with in Canada, California and Mexico, as well as in New Granada, Venezuela, Brazil, and Peru.

History—The use of the rhizome of ferns as a vermifuge was well known to the ancients,[2] as Theophrastus, Dioscorides and Pliny all giving curious descriptions of the plant. The remedy would appear to have been administered also during the middle ages, for it was again noticed by Valerius Cordus,[3] and had a place in German pharmaceutical tariffs of the sixteenth century as well as in Schröder's Dispensatory.[4]

[1] Especially *L. annotinum*, *L. complanatum* and *L. inundatum*.

[2] Murray, *Apparatus medicaminum*, v. (1790) 453–471.

[3] Lib. 4, cap. 156 of the work quoted in the Appendix.

[4] *Medicin-chymische Apotheke*, Nürnberg, 1656. 20.

Yet Tragus[1] remarks that, at least in Germany, the root was little used. It was in fact subsequently nearly forgotten until revived by the introduction of certain secret remedies for tapeworm, of which powdered male fern rhizome, combined with drastic purgatives, was a chief constituent.

A medicine of this kind was prepared by Daniel Mathieu, a native of Neuchâtel, born in 1741, who established himself as an apothecary in Berlin. His treatment for the parasite was so successful that it attracted the notice of Frederick the Great, who purchased his nostrum for an annuity of 200 *thalers* (£30), besides conferring upon him the dignity of Aulic Councillor.[2]

Great celebrity was also gained for the method of treating tapeworm practised by Madame Nuffler or Nuffer, the widow of a surgeon at Murten (Morat), likewise in Switzerland, who in 1775 obtained for the secret from Louis XIV., after an inquiry by *savans* of the period, the sum of 18,000 livres. Her method of treatment consisted in the administration of—1. Panada made of bread with a little butter. 2. A clyster of salt water and olive oil. 3. The "*spécifique*"—simply *powdered fern-root.* 4. A purgative bolus of calomel, gamboge, acammony, and *Confectio hyacinthidis,*—given in the foregoing order.[3]

J. Peschier,[4] a pharmacien of Geneva, recommended as a substitute for the bulky powder of the root, an ethereal extract, an efficient preparation, which though proposed in 1825, was scarcely used in England until about 1851; at present it is the only form in which male fern is employed. Peschier already observed a crystallized deposit in his extract.

Description—The fresh rhizome or caudex is short and massive, 2–3 inches in diameter, decumbent, or rising a few inches above the ground, and bearing on its summit a circular tuft of fronds, which in their lower part are thickly beset with brown chaffy scales. Below the growing fronds are the remains of those of previous seasons, which retain in their firm, fleshy bases, vitality and succulence for years after their upper portion has perished. From among these fleshy bases, spring the black, wiry, branching roots.[5] The rhizome is rather fleshy, and easily cut with a knife, internally of a bright pale yellowish green; it has very little odour and a sweetish astringent taste. For pharmaceutical use, it should be collected in the late autumn, winter or early spring, divested of the dead portions, split open, dried with a gentle heat, reduced to coarse powder, and at once exhausted with ether. Extract obtained in this way is more efficient than that which has been got from rhizome that has been kept some time.

Microscopic Structure—On transverse section of the rootstock, the tissue shows rounded, somewhat polyhedral cells with porous walls; the outer cells are brown and rather smaller, but do not exhibit

[1] P. 547 of the work quoted in the Appendix.

[2] Cornaz, *Les familles médicales de la ville de Neuchâtel*, 1864. 20.

[3] *Traitement contre le Ténia ou ver solitaire, pratiqué à Morat en Suisse, examiné et éprouvé à Paris.* Publié par ordre du Roi, 1775. 4°, pp. 30. 3 plates, one representing the plant, its rhizome and leaves.—Also English translation by Dr. Simmons, London, 1778. 8°.

[4] *Bibliothèque Universelle*, xxx. (1825) 205; xxx. (1826) 326.

[5] For a full account of the growth and structure of that rhizome see Luerssen, *Medicinisch-pharmaceutische Botanik*, i. (1878) 504. 561.

the regular flattened shape, usual in many suberous coats. Within this cortical layer, there is a circle of about 10 large vascular bundles, besides a large number of smaller ones scattered beyond the circle. The leaf-bases exhibit a somewhat different structure, their vascular bundles, usually 8, forming but one diffuse circle.

The cells of the parenchyme contain starch, greenish or brownish granules of tannic matter, and drops of oil. In the green, vigorously vegetating parts of the rootstock there are numerous smaller and larger intercellular spaces, into which a few stalked glands project, as shown by Prof. Schacht of Bonn in 1863. These globular glands originate from the cells bordering the intercellular spaces. After their complete development, and the appearance of starch in the adjacent parenchyme, they exude a greenish fluid, which when thin slices of the rhizome are kept some time in glycerin, solidifies in acicular crystals.[1] Such glands appear to be wanting in most of the allied ferns, such as *Aspidium Oreopteris* Sw. and *Asplenium Filix fœmina* Bernh. They have been observed by one of us (F.), in the small rhizome of *A. spinulosum* Sw. Similar glands, but not exuding a green liquid, occur between the paleæ below the vegetating cone of the rootstock.

Chemical Composition—Of the numerous examinations which have been made of this drug, those of Bock (1852), of Luck (1860), and of Kruse (1876), may be especially mentioned. Besides the universally distributed constituents of plants, there have been found in the rhizome 5 to 6 per cent. of a green fatty oil, traces of volatile oil, resin, tannin (Luck's *Tannaspidic* and *Pteritannic Acids*) and crystallizable sugar, which according to Bock is probably cane sugar.

The medicinal ethereal extract, of which the rhizome yields about 8 per cent., deposits a colourless, granular, crystalline substance, noticed by Peschier as early as 1826, and subsequently designated by Luck, *Filicic Acid*. Grabowski (1867) assigned it the formula $C^{14}H^{18}O^{5}$. We learn from Prof. Buchheim that he regards filicic acid as the source of the medicinal efficacy of the drug. By fusion with potash, filicic acid is converted into phloroglucin and butyric acid. The green liquid portion of the extract consists mainly of a glyceride called *Filixolin*, from which Luck obtained by saponification two acids, the one volatile, *Filosmylic Acid*, the other non-volatile, termed *Filixolic Acid*.

Malin (1867) showed that the tannic acid of male fern may be decomposed by boiling dilute acids into sugar and a red substance, *Filix-red*, $C^{26}H^{18}O^{12}$, analogous to Cinchona-red.

Schoonbroodt[2] performed some interesting experiments with *fresh* fern root, showing that it contains *volatile acids* of the fatty series, among which is probably *formic*; but also a fixed acid, accompanied by an oil of disagreeable odour. The liquid distilled from the dried root did not evolve a similar odour, nor did it contain any acid body. A small quantity of essential oil was obtained by means of ether from the alcoholic extract of the fresh but not of the dried rootstock. The rhizome of male fern yields 2 to 3 per cent. of ash, con-

[1] The chemical nature of this body remains to be ascertained. The crystals are probably *Filicic Acid*, accompanied by chlorophyl and essential oil.

[2] *Journal de Médecine de Bruxelles*, 1867 and 1868—also in the *Jahresbericht* of Wiggers and Husemann, 1869. 21.

sisting mainly of phosphates, carbonates, and sulphates of calcium and potassium, together with silica.

Uses—The ethereal extract has been prescribed for all kinds of intestinal worms; but recent experience goes to prove that its effects are chiefly exhibited in cases of tapeworm. It is equally and thoroughly efficacious in the three kinds respectively termed *Tænia solium, T. medio-cannellata* and *Bothriocephalus latus.*

Substitution—The rhizomes of *Asplenium Filix fœmina* Bernh., *Aspidium montanum* Vogl. (*A. Oreopteris* Sw.) and *A. spinulosum* Sw. may scarcely be mistaken for that of *A. Filix mas.* The best means of distinguishing them is afforded by transverse sections of the leaf-bases. In *Filix mas,* the section exhibits 8 vascular bundles,—in the other ferns named, only 2,—a difference easily ascertained by examination under a lens. Practically, no other indigenous fern than *A. Filix mas* affords a rhizome of sufficient bulk so as to be remunerative. We are not acquainted with that of the American *Aspidium marginale* Swartz, the section of which shows 6 vascular bundles; its extract is stated by Cressler (1878) to be perfectly active.

Thallogens.

LICHENES.

LICHEN ISLANDICUS.

Iceland Moss; F. Lichen ou Mousse d'Islande; G. Isländisches Moos.

Botanical Origin—*Cetraria islandica* Acharius.[1]—It is abundant in high northern latitudes, as Greenland, Spitzbergen, Siberia, Scandinavia and Iceland, where it grows even in the plains. It is found in the mountainous parts of Great Britain, France, Italy, and Spain, in Switzerland (in elevations of nearly 10,000 feet), and in the Southern Danubian countries. It also occurs in North America and in the Antarctic regions.

History—In the North of Europe, this lichen has long been used under the general name of *Mosi*, *Mossa* or *Mus*,[2] as an article of food. It is the *Muscus crispæ Lactucæ similis* of Valerius Cordus,[3] and was also mentioned by Ole Borrich, of Copenhagen (1671), who called it *Muscus catharticus*, under the notion that in early spring it possesses purgative properties.[4] The pharmaceutical tariff of the same city, of the year 1672, likewise quotes *Muscus catharticus islandicus*.[5] Its medicinal employment in pulmonary disorders was favourably spoken of by Hjärne in 1683,[6] but it is only since 1757 that it has come into general use as a medicine, chiefly on the recommendation of Linnæus and Scopoli.

Description[7]—The plant consists of an erect, foliaceous, branching thallus, about 4 inches high, curled, channelled or rolled into tubes, terminating in spreading truncate, flattened lobes, the edges of which are fringed with short thick prominences. The thallus is smooth, grey, or of a light olive-brown; the under surface is paler and irregularly beset with depressed white spots. The apothecia (fruits), which are not very common, appear at the apices of the thallus, as rounded boss-like bodies, $\frac{2}{10}$ to $\frac{3}{10}$ of an inch across, of a dark, rusty colour. The colour

[1] *Cetraria* from *cetra*, an ancient shield of hide, in allusion to the circular apothecia.

[2] These names are generally applied in Scandinavia and Iceland to the smaller cryptogams, as lichens, true mosses, lycopodium, etc.

[3] Hist. stirpium, quoted in the Appendix.

[4] Bergius, *Materia Medica*, Stockholm, ii. (1778) 856.

[5] Flückiger, *Documente*, quoted at page 404.

[6] Murray, *Apparatus Medicaminum*, v. (1790) 510.

[7] For an exhaustive account and figures see Luerssen (quoted at p. 734) p. 176.

and mode of division of the thallus vary greatly, so that many varieties of the plant have been distinguished.

In the dry state, Iceland moss is light, harsh and springy; it absorbs water in which it is placed to the extent of a third of its weight, becoming soft and cartilaginous; it ordinarily contains about 10 per cent. of hygroscopic water. It is inodorous, but when wetted has a slight seaweed-like smell; its taste is slightly bitter.

Microscopic Structure—A transverse section exhibits, when strongly magnified, a broad loose central layer of long, thick-walled branching walls of *hyphæ*, containing air, and enclosing wide hollow spaces. This middle layer encloses a certain number of larger cells called *gonidia*, coloured with chlorophyll. The gonidia are not destroyed either by strong sulphuric acid, or by boiling them with potash. They assume however a deep violet colour when treated with caustic potash and then left for 24 hours in a solution of iodine in potassium iodide.

The tissues on either side of this central layer consists of very thickly felted hyphæ, without intervening spaces, and does not appear to contain any particular substance. This compact and tenacious tissue passes into a thin cortical layer consisting of cells very closely bound together. Under the influence of reagents this layer becomes very evident: thus when moistened with strong sulphuric or hydrochloric acid, it separates from the rest of the tissue as a coherent membrane, and rolls itself backward. On boiling with water the inner tissue swells up, the cell-walls being partly dissolved. Thin slices of the lichen are coloured reddish or pale blue by iodine water,—more distinctly blue, if previously treated with sulphuric acid. The colour spreads uniformly over the inner tissue, but no starch granules can be detected; the cortical layer is merely coloured brown by iodine. The white spots on the outer surface of the thallus are resolved by pressure under a plate of glass into minute round transparent granules, not coloured by iodine, and thick branched cells like those of the central layer.

The short thick prominences on the edge of the thallus, frequently terminate in one or more sac-like cavities (*spermogonia*) containing a large number of simple bar-shaped cells (*spermatia*), only 6 mkm. long; they are enveloped in transparent mucus, and may be expelled by pressure under glass. It has been shown by Stahl (1874) that they represent the fertilizing corpuscles or seaweeds of the class *Florideæ*.

The observations of De Bary (1866) and Schwendener (1867–70) confirmed and much extended by the researches of Bornet[1] (1873–74), have shown that the gonidia of lichens are referable to some species of *Alga*, and are capable of an independent existence; that the relations of the hyphæ to the gonidia are of such a nature as to exclude the possibility of either of those bodies being produced by the other; and further that the theory of parasitism is the only one capable of explaining these relations in a satisfactory manner. Under this singular theory, lichens are compound organisms, formed of an alga, and of a fungus living upon it as a parasite.

Chemical Composition—Boiling water extracts from Iceland

[1] *Recherches sur les gonidies des Lichens.*—*Ann. des Sciences nat.* Bot. xvii. (1873) 45–110; 11 plates; also xix. (1874) 314–320.—For a complete abstract of these and all the more recent investigations on this subject, see Luerssen (*l.c.*) 186 *et seq.*

moss as much as 70 per cent. of the so-called *Lichenin* or *Lichen-starch*, a body which is perfectly devoid of structure. The decoction (1 : 20) gelatinizes on cooling, and assumes a reddish or bluish tint by solution of iodine. This property of lichenin is plainly seen, when the drug is first exhausted by boiling spirit of wine containing some carbonate of potassium ; and then boiled with 50 to 100 parts of water, and the decoction precipitated by means of alcohol. The lichenin thus obtained in a purer state, must be deprived of alcohol by cautiously washing it with water. Powdered iodine will now immediately impart to it while still moist an *intense blue*. Its composition, $C^{12}H^{20}O^{10}$, agrees with that of starch and cellulose; and it must be regarded as a modification of the latter, being likewise soluble in water and in ammoniacal solution of copper. Lichenin is not a kind of mucilage, because it yields but insignificant traces of mucic acid, if treated with concentrated nitric acid ; and also because it contains no inorganic constituents.[1] The very trifling proportion of mucic acid it furnishes may depend upon the presence, in small amount, of an independent mucilaginous body.

According to Th. Berg (1873), lichenin consists of what he continues to call so, and another constituent, the latter only being coloured by iodine, possessing (dextrogyre) rotatory power, and also being insoluble in ammoniacal solution of copper. Berg's lichenin is not soluble in cold water, but readily dissolves in hot water, and again separates on cooling. The other constituent on the contrary is abundantly soluble in cold, and very sparingly in hot water. The drug yielded to Berg 20 per cent. of "true" lichenin and 10 per cent. of the other substance.

The chlorophyll of the gonidia is not soluble in hydrochloric acid, and hence is distinguished by Knop and Schnedermann as *Thallochlor* ; its quantity is extremely small.

The bitter principle of Cetraria, called *Cetraric Acid* or *Cetrarin*, $C^{18}H^{16}O^{8}$, crystallizes in microscopic needles, is nearly insoluble in cold water, and forms with alkalis, yellow, easily soluble, bitter salts. The lichen also contains a little sugar, and about 1 per cent. of a peculiar body, *Licheno-stearic Acid*, $C^{14}H^{24}O^{3}$, the crystals of which melt at 120° C. The *Lichenic Acid* found by Pfaff in 1826 in Iceland moss, and formerly regarded as a peculiar compound, has been proved identical with fumaric acid.

In common with many lichens, cetraria contains *Oxalic Acid* and is said to yield also some tartaric acid. The ash, which amounts to 1–2 per cent., consists to the extent of two-fifths of silicic acid combined chiefly with potash and lime.

Collection and Commerce—Iceland moss is collected in many districts where the plant abounds at least for local use, as in Sweden, whence some is shipped to other countries. It is also gathered in Switzerland, especially on the mountains of the Canton of Lucerne, and in Spain.[2] None is exported from Iceland.

Uses—It is given in decoction as a mild tonic, combined with more active medicines. It is very little employed in Iceland, and only in seasons of scarcity, when it is sometimes ground and mixed with the

[1] The various mucilages and gums yield from 4 to 20 per cent. of ash, but lichenin yields *none*.

[2] *Cat. of Spanish Productions*,—London Exhibition, 1851.

flour used in making the *grout* or grain soup. Occasionally it is taken boiled in milk. It is not given, as has been asserted, to domestic animals.

An interesting application of Iceland moss has recently been tried in Sweden. Sten-Stenberg treats it with sulphuric or hydrochloric acid, when 72 per cent. of grape sugar are formed, which may be converted into alcohol.[1]

FUNGI.

SECALE CORNUTUM.

Ergota; Ergot of Rye,[2] *Spurred Rye;* F. *Seigle ergoté;* G. *Mutterkorn.*

Botanical Origin—*Claviceps purpurea* Tulasne, a fungus of the order *Pyrenomycetes*, of which ergot is an immature form, it being the *sclerotium* (termed in the British Pharmacopœia *compact mycelium* or *spawn*) developed within the paleæ of numerous plants of the order *Gramineæ*.

Ergot is obtained almost exclusively from rye, *Secale cereale* L.; but the same fungus is produced on grasses belonging to many other genera, as *Agropyrum, Alopecurus, Ammophila, Anthoxanthum, Arrhenatherum, Avena, Brachypodium, Calamagrostis, Dactylis, Glyceria, Hordeum, Lolium, Poa,* and *Triticum.* Other organisms of diverse form, but of doubtful specific distinctness, are developed in *Molinia, Oryza, Phragmites,* and other grasses. In the order *Cyperaceæ* (e.g., *Scirpus*), peculiar ergots are known.

History—Although it is hardly possible that so singular a production as ergot should be unnoticed in the writings of the classical authors, we believe no undoubted reference to it has been discovered.[3] The earliest date under which we find ergot mentioned on account of its obstetric virtues is towards the middle of the 16th century, by Adam Lonicer of Frankfort, who describes its appearance in the ears of rye, and adds that it is regarded by women to be of remarkable and certain efficacy.[4] It is also very clearly described in the writings of Johannes Thalius, who speaks of it as used "*ad sistendum sanguinem.*"[5] In the next century it was noticed by Caspar Bauhin, who termed it *Secale luxurians,*[6] and by the English botanist Ray,[7] with allusion to its medicinal properties.

Rathlaw, a Dutch accoucheur, employed ergot in 1747. Thirty years later Desgranges of Lyons prescribed it with success; but its peculiar and important properties were hardly allowed until the commencement of the present century, when Dr. Stearns of New York succeeded in gaining for them fuller recognition.[8] Ergot of rye was not, however, admitted into the London Pharmacopœia until 1836.[9]

[1] Dingler's *Polytechnisches Journal,* 197 (1870) 177; also *Chemisches Centralblatt,* 1870. 607.

[2] From the French *ergot,* anciently *argot,* a cock's spur.

[3] Consult Pliny's *Nat. Hist.* book 18. ch. 44.

[4] *Kreuterbuch,* ed. 1582. 285 (not in the edition of 1560).

[5] *Sylva Hercynia,* Francof. 1588. 47.

[6] *Pinax Theatri Botanici,* Basil. 1623. 23.

[7] *Hist. Plant.* ii. (1693) 1241.

[8] Stillé, *Therapeutics and Mat. Med.* ii. (1868) 609.

[9] From 1825 to 1828 the wholesale price of ergot of rye in London was from 36s. to 50s. per lb., that is to say, from twelve to fifteen times its present value.

The use of flour containing a considerable proportion of ergot, gives rise to a very formidable disease, distinguished in modern medicine as *Ergotism*, but known in early times by a variety of names, as *Morbus spasmodicus, convulsivus, malignus, epidemicus vel cerealis, Raphania, Convulsio raphania*[1] or *Ignis sancti Antonii.*

Some of the malignant epidemics which visited Europe after seasons of rain and scarcity during the middle ages have been referred with more or less of probability to ergot-disease.[2] The chronicles of the 6th and 8th centuries note the occurrence of maladies which may be suspected as due to ergotized grain. There is less of doubt regarding the epidemics that prevailed from the 10th century and were frequent in France, and in the 12th in Spain. In the year 1596 Hessen (Hessia) and the adjoining regions were ravaged by a frightful pestilence, which the Medical Faculty of Marburg attributed to the presence of ergot in the cereals consumed by the population. The same disease appeared in France in 1630, in Voigtland (Saxony) in the years 1648, 1649, and 1675; again in various parts of France, as Aquitaine and Sologne, in 1650, 1670, and 1674. Freiburg and the neighbouring region were visited by the same malady in 1702; other parts of Switzerland in 1715–16; Saxony and Lusatia in 1716; many other districts of Germany in 1717, 1722, 1736, and 1741–2.[3] The last epidemic in Europe occasioned by ergot appears to be that which, after the rainy season of 1816, visited Lorraine and Burgundy, and proved fatal to many people of the poorer class. Ergot disease is sometimes observed in Abyssinia at the present day,[4] and a few cases of it have even been lately recorded in Bavaria.[5]

Formation—The true nature of ergot has long been the source of a great diversity of opinion, not set at rest by the admirable researches of L. R. Tulasne, from whose *Mémoire sur l'Ergot des Glumacées,*[6] the following account is for the most part extracted.

The formation of ergot often affects only a few caryopsides in a single ear; sometimes, however, more than twenty. In the former case, the healthy development of the other caryopsides is not prevented, but if too many are attacked, the entire ear decays. The more isolated ergots generally grow larger, and attain their greatest size on rye which springs up here and there among other cereals.

The first symptoms of ergot-formation is the so-called *honey-dew of rye*, a yellowish mucus, having an intensely sweet taste, and the peculiar disagreeable odour frequently belonging to fungi. Drops of this mucus show themselves here and there on the ears in the neighbourhood of diseased grains, and attract ants and beetles of various kinds, especially

[1] Pereira, *Elem. of Mat. Med.* ii. (1850) 1007.

[2] Consult Häser, *Lehrbuch der Geschichte der Medicin und der Volkskrankheiten*, 1845. i. 256. 830, ii. 94; C. F. Heusinger, *Recherches de Pathologie comparée*, Cassel, i. (1853) 543–554; Mérat et De Lens, *Dict. Mat. Med.* iii. 131, vii. 268.

[3] Tissot of Lausanne, *Phil. Trans.* lv. (1766) 106.—See also Dodart, *Mém. de l'Acad. R. des Sciences*, x., années 1666–1699 (Paris, 1730) 561; *Hist. de la Soc. Roy. de Méd.*, année 1776. 345; and *Mém. de Méd. et de Phys. méd.* année 1776. 260–311. 417.

[4] Th. von Heuglin, *Reise nach Abessinien* etc. Jena, 1868. 180.

[5] Wiggers and Husemann, *Jahresbericht* for 1870. 582.

[6] *Ann. des Sciences nat.*, Bot., xx. (1853) 1–56 and 4 plates.—More recent observations will be found in St. Wilson's paper, *Trans. of the Bot. Society of Edinburgh*, xii. (1876) 418–434 with figures; and especially in Luerssen (quoted at p. 735) 156, *et seqq.*

the yellowish-red *Rhagonycha melanura* Fabr., but not bees. On this account the beetle in question has been supposed to be instrumental in the development of ergot, and it may possibly be so, but only by transporting the saccharine mucus from one plant to another.

The honey-dew of rye contains neither oil-drops nor starch. After dilution with water, it produces a rapid and abundant separation of cuprous oxide from an alkaline solution of cupric tartrate. Dried over sulphuric acid, it solidifies into a crystalline mass. After a few days the drops of honey-dew dry up and disappear from the ear. The grain at this period becomes completely disintegrated, and devoid of starch.

The ergotized soft ovaries are covered with, and penetrated by a white, spongy, felted tissue, the *mycelium* of the young fungus. It is made up of slender, threadlike cells, the *hyphæ,* the outer layer of which consists of radially-diverging cells, the *basidia.* The whole mycelium forms by its crevices and folds a number of cavities opening externally; from its outer layer, which is also called the *hymenium* or *spermatophorum,* an immense number of agglutinated, elongated granules, the *conidia,* are separated. These cells, the products of the basidia, are not more than four mkm. in length, and give the floral organs the appearance of being covered with a whitish dust. The honey-dew likewise contains an abundance of conidia, but it is only on dilution that they are precipitated and become easily perceptible; the formation of the honey-dew is intimately connected with that of the conidia themselves. Ergot in this primary or mycelium stage was regarded as an independent fungus by Léveillé (1827), who named it *Sphacelia segetum.* According to Kühn (1863), it may even be directly reproduced by germination of the conidia within the ears of rye.

The myçelium penetrates and envelops the caryopsis, with the exception of the apex, and thereby prevents its further growth, destroying especially the epicarp and the embryo. At the base of the caryopsis, there is formed by tumefaction and gradual transverse separation of the thread-cells of the mycelium, a more compact kernel-like body (the future ergot) violet-black without, white within, which gradually but largely increases in size, and ultimately separates from the mycelium as the loose tissue of the latter dries and shrinks up after the completion of its functions. By this growth, the remains of the caryopsis, still recognizable by their hairs and by the rudiments of the style, as well as by the surviving portions of the mycelium-tissue, become visible above the paleæ on the apex of the mature ergot, now projecting prominently from the ear. Very rarely the ergot is crowned by a fully developed seed; in the commercial drug, the apex is usually broken off.

It is evident that in the process of development just described, the very tissue of the caryopsis of the rye does not undergo a *transformation,* but that it is *simply destroyed.* Neither in external form, nor in anatomical structure does ergot exhibit any resemblance to a caryopsis or a seed, although its development takes place between the flowering time and that at which the rye begins to ripen. It has been regarded as a complete fungus, and as such was named by De Candolle (1816) *Sclerotium Clavus* and by Fries *Spermœdia Clavus.*

No further change in the ergot occurs while it remains in the ear; but laid on damp earth, interesting phenomena take place. At certain points, small orbicular patches of the rind fold themselves back, and gradually throw out little white heads. These increase in size, whilst the outer layers of the neighbouring tissue gradually lose their firmness and become soft and rather granular, at the same time that the cells, of which they are made up, become empty and extended. In the interior of the ergot, the cells retain their oil drops unaltered. The heads assume a greyish-yellow colour, changing to purple, and finally after some weeks stretch themselves towards the light on slender shining stalks of a pale violet colour. The stalks often attain an inch in length, with a thickness of about ½ a line. They consist of thin, parallel, closely felted cell-threads, devoid of fat oil. Ergot is susceptible of this further development only so long as it is fresh, that is to say, at most until the next flowering time of rye. Within this period however, even fragments are capable of development. There are sometimes also produced colourless threads of mould which belong to other fungi, as *Verticillium cylindrosporum* Corda, and which frequently overgrow the *Claviceps*.[1]

At the point where the stalk joins the spherical or somewhat flattened head, the latter is depressed and surrounds the stalk with an annular border. After a short time there appear on the surface of the head, which is $\frac{1}{10}$ of an inch in diameter, a number of brownish warts, in which are the openings of minute cavities, the *conceptacula* or *perithecia*. On transverse section, they appear arranged radially round the circumference of the head. In each cavity are a large number of delicate sacs, only 3-5 mkm. thick, and about 100 mkm. long, the *thecæ* or *asci*, each containing, as is usual in fungi, 8 spores. These are simple thread-shaped cells, filled with a homogeneous solid mass.

The thicker ends of the spore-sacs (*asci*) open while still within the perithecium; the spores issue united in a bundle, and are emitted from the aperture of the perithecium. In consequence of their somewhat glutinous consistence, they remain united even after their extrusion, and form white silky flocks; their number in the 20 or 30 heads sometimes produced from a single ergot, often exceeds a million. The heads themselves die in two or three weeks after they have begun to make their appearance. They represent the true fructification of the fungus. This state of the plant appears to have been first noticed in 1801 by Schumacher, who called it *Sphæria;* it was subsequently known as *Cordiceps, Cordyliceps, Kentrosporium,* etc., until Tulasne proved it to be the final stage of development of ergot.

The three different forms of this structure, namely, the mycelium, the ergot, and the fruit-bearing heads, are therefore merely successive states of one and the same biennial fungus, which have been appropriately united by Tulasne under the name of *Claviceps purpurea.* The middle stage forms the *sclerotium,* which occurs in a large number of the most various fungi, and is a special state of rest of these plants. The direct proof that the mycelium is produced from spores of the fruit-

[1] Ergot of rye collected by myself in August, placed upon earth in a garden-pot and left in the open air unprotected through the winter, began to develop the *Claviceps* on the 20th March, and on another occasion on the 20th April, at which date some sowed in February also began to start. Sharp frost appears to retard the vegetation; thus, after the cold winter of 1869–70, *Claviceps,* even in the greenhouse, did not make its appearance before the 11th May. The earliest instance of fully developed *ergots* which I ever observed, occurred on the 11th of June; more frequently they are seen only in the beginning of July.—F. A. F.

head sown on ears of rye, was supplied by Kühn in 1863. It has already been mentioned that the same organism is produced from conidia; whence it appears that a twofold formation of ergot is possible, as is frequently the case in other fungi.

Description—Spurred rye, as found in commerce, consists of fusiform grains, which it is convenient to term *ergots*. They are from ⅓ to 1½ inch in length, and ½ to 4 lines in diameter; their form is subcylindrical or obtusely prismatic, tapering towards the ends, generally arched, with a longitudinal furrow on each side. At the apex of each ergot, there is often a small whitish easily detached appendage, while the opposite extremity is somewhat rounded. The ergots are firm, horny, somewhat elastic, have a close fracture, are brittle when dry, yet difficult to pulverize. The whitish interior is frequently laid bare by deep transverse cracks. The tissue is but imperfectly penetrated by water, even the thinnest sections swelling but slightly in that fluid.

Ergot of rye has a peculiar offensive odour, and a mawkish, rancid taste. It is apt to become deteriorated by keeping, especially when pulverized, partly from oxidation of the oil, and partly from the attacks of a mite of the genus *Trombidium*. To assist its preservation, it should be thoroughly dried, and kept in closed bottles.

Microscopic Structure—In fully developed ergot, no organs can be distinguished. It consists of uniform, densely felted tissue of short, thread-like, somewhat thick-walled cells, which are irregularly packed, and so intimately matted together that it is only by prolonged boiling of thin slices with potash, and alternate treatment with acids and ether, that the individual cells can be made evident. Without such treatment, the cells even in the thinnest sections, show a somewhat rounded, nearly isodiametric outline. This pseudo-parenchyme of ergot exhibits therefore an aspect somewhat different from that of the loosely felted cells (*hyphæ*) of other fungi. Ergot nevertheless is not made up of cells differing from those of fungi generally. If thin longitudinal slices of the innermost tissue are allowed to remain in a solution of chromic acid containing about 1 per cent., they will distinctly show the *hyphæ,* which are however considerably shorter than those of other fungi. They contain numerous drops of fat oil, but neither starch nor crystals. It is remarkable that this nearly empty and not much thickened parenchyme should form so compact and solid a tissue.

The cell-walls of the tissue of ergot are not coloured blue, even after prolonged treatment with iodine in solution of potassium iodide; or when the tissue has been previously treated with sulphuric acid, or kept for days in contact with potash and absolute alcohol at 100° C. In this respect the cellulose of fungi differs from that of phanerogamic plants.

Of the outermost rows of cells in ergot, a few only are of a violet colour, but they are not otherwise distinguishable from the colourless tissue,—or at most by the somewhat greater thickness of their walls.

Chemical Composition—The composition of ergot has been elaborately investigated by Wiggers as early as 1830. The drug contains about 30 per cent. of a non-drying, yellowish oil, chiefly consisting of olein, palmitin, and small proportions of volatile fatty acids, especially acetic and butyric, combined with glycerin. The large amount of oil is remarkable; the fungi, dried at 100°, usually contain not more than 5 per cent. of fat, mostly much less; they are on the other hand much richer in albumin than ergot of rye. The oil of the latter, as extracted by bisulphide of carbon, is accompanied by small quantities of *resin* and *cholesterin* (see p. 420). It is erroneous to attribute to this oil the poisonous properties of ergot, although it has been shown by Ganser[1] to display irritating properties when taken in doses of about 6 grammes. But the effects observed appear dependent on the presence in it of resin.

According to Wenzell (1864), ergot of rye contains two peculiar alkaloids, which he designated *Ecboline* and *Ergotine*,[2] and claimed to be the active principles of the drug. They were, however, got merely as brownish amorphous substances.

The two bases of ergot are, according to Wenzell, combined with *Ergotic Acid*, the existence of which has been further admitted by Ganser. It is said to be a volatile body yielding crystallizable salts.

A crystallized colourless alkaloid, *Ergotinine*, $C^{35}H^{40}N^4O^6$, has been isolated (1877-1878) by Tanret, a pharmacien of Troyes. He obtained it to the amount of about 0·04 per cent., some amorphous ergotinine moreover being present. Tanret exhausts the powdered drug with boiling alcohol, which by evaporation affords a fluid resin and an aqueous solution, besides a fatty layer. Some ergotinine is removed from the resin by shaking it with ether, and mixed with the main liquid. This is acidulated and purified by means of ether. Lastly, the ergotinine is extracted by adding a slight excess of carbonate of potassium and shaking with ether, and recrystallizing from alcohol. The solutions of ergotinine turn very soon greenish and red; they are fluorescent. Sulphuric acid imparts to it a red, violet, and finally blue hue.

Dragendorff and several of his pupils, since 1875, have isolated the following *amorphous* principles of the drug under notice :—(1) *Sclerotic acid* (doubtful formula $C^{12}H^{19}NO^9$), said to be a very active substance, chiefly in subcutaneous injections. About 4 per cent of colourless acid may be obtained from good ergot of rye. (2) *Scleromucin*, a mucilaginous matter, which may be precipitated by alcohol from aqueous extracts of the drug. Scleromucin when dried is no longer soluble in water. (3) *Sclererythrin*, the red colouring matter, probably allied to anthrachinon and the colouring substances of madder, chiefly to purpurin. (4) *Sclerojodin*, a bluish black powder, soluble in alkalis. (5) *Fuscosclerotinic acid*. (6) *Picrosclerotine*, apparently a highly poisonous alkaloid. Lastly (7) *Scleroxanthin*, $C^7H^7O^3 + OH^2$; and (8) *Sclerocrystallin*, $C^7H^7O^3$, have been obtained in crystals; their alcoholic solution is but little coloured, yet assumes a violet hue on addition of ferric chloride.

Tanret also observed in ergot of rye a volatile *camphoraceous substance*.

Ergot, in common with other fungi,[3] contains a sugar termed *Mycose*,

[1] *Archiv der Pharm.* cxliv. (1870) 200.

[2] The name *Ergotine* has also been given to a medicinal extract of ergot, prepared after a method devised by Bonjean, a pharmacien of Chambéry, vide *Journ. de Pharm.* iv. (1843) 107; Pereira, *Elem. of Mat. Med.* ii. (1850) 1012.

[3] See Müntz in *Comptes Rendus*, lxxvi. (1873) 649.

closely allied to cane sugar, and probably identical with *Trehalose* (see p. 417). Mycose crystallizes in rhombic octohedra, having the composition $C^{12}H^{22}O^{11} + 2H^2O$. Mitscherlich obtained of it about one-tenth per cent. It appears that the sugar exuded in the first stage of growth of the fungus,—the so-called *rye honey-dew,*—is in its principal characters different from mycose. Instead of the latter, Mitscherlich, as well as Fiedler and Ludwig, sometimes obtained from ergot *Mannite.*

Schoonbroodt also found in ergot *Lactic Acid.* Several other chemists have further proved the presence of acetic and formic acids.

Starch is entirely wanting in ergot at all times. The drug yields about 3 per cent. of nitrogen, corresponding probably to a large amount of albuminoid matter. Ganser, however, obtained only 3·2 per cent. of albumin *soluble in water.*

When ergot or its alcoholic extract is treated with an alkali it yields, as products of the decomposition of the albuminoid matters, ammonia or ammonia-bases,—according to Ludwig and Stahl, *Methylamine,*—according to others, *Trimethylamine.* Manassewitz, as well as Wenzell, state that phosphate of trimethylamine is present in an aqueous extract of ergot, but Ganser ascertained that no such base *pre-exists* in ergot. We have found that the crystals which abound in the extract, after it has been kept for some time, are an acid phosphate of sodium and ammonium with a small proportion of sulphate.[1]

Production and Commerce—Ergot of rye is to be met with in all the countries producing cereals; we have seen it in the high valleys of the Alps, and Schübeler states that it grows in Norway, as far north as 60° N. lat.

The drug is chiefly imported into London from Vigo in Spain and from Teneriffe; it is also shipped from Hamburg and France. Dr. de Lanessan, writing to one of us from Vigo in 1872, remarks that vast quantities of rye are grown in Galicia, and that owing to the humidity of the climate the grain is extensively ergotized,—in fact the parasite is present in one ear out of every three. At the time of harvest the ergots are picked out, and the rye is thus rendered fit for food.

Southern and Central Russia furnish considerable supplies of the drug. In the central parts of Europe, ergot does not everywhere occur in sufficient abundance to be collected, and it greatly diminishes as the state of agriculture improves. We have noticed that ergot from Odessa was of a slaty hue and in much smaller grains than that from Spain.

Uses—Ergot is principally used on account of its specific action on the uterus in parturition.

Other Varieties of Ergot—*Ergot of Wheat* (Triticum vulgare), which is in shorter and thicker ergots than that of rye, is picked out by hand in some parts of Italy and France, from grain intended to be used for the manufacture of vermicelli and other pastes; and such ergot is sold to druggists. Carbonneaux Le Perdriel[2] has endeavoured to show

[1] The red colour of an alcoholic solution may serve for the detection of small quantities of ergot in flour. The reaction with potash, and evolution of the characteristic odour of herring brine may assist in the same object. Extraction of the fatty oil with carbon bisulphide may also be recommended as a test, inasmuch as good cereal grains contain but a very small percentage of fat.

[2] *De l'Ergot de Froment et de ses propriétés méd.* (thèse) Montpellier, 1862.

that it is less prone to become deteriorated by age than that of rye, and that it never produces the deleterious effects sometimes occasioned by the latter.

The same writer asserts that *Ergot of Oat* is sometimes collected and sold either *per se*, or mixed with that of rye. It differs from the latter in the ergots being considerably more slender.

Ergot of the North African grass *Arundo Ampelodesmos* Cirillo, known as *Diss*, has been collected for use, and according to Lallemant[1] is twice as active as that of rye. It is from 1 to 3 inches long by only about $\frac{1}{16}$ of an inch broad, generally arched, or in the large ergots twisted spirally. We find it to share the structural character of the ergot of rye; it is in all probability the same formation, yet remarkably modified.

ALGÆ (FLORIDEÆ).

CHONDRUS CRISPUS.

Fucus Hibernicus; Carrageen,[2] *Irish Moss;* F. *Mousse d'Irlande, Mousse perlée;* G. *Knorpeltang, Irländisches Moos, Perlmoos.*

Botanical Origin—*Chondrus crispus* Lyngbye (*Fucus crispus* L.), a sea weed of the class *Florideæ*, abundant on rocky sea-shores of Europe from the North Cape to Gibraltar; not frequent however in the Baltic, and altogether wanting in the Mediterranean, but largely met with on the eastern coasts of North America.

History—*Chondrus crispus* was figured in 1699 by Morison,[3] yet only Todhunter at Dublin introduced it to the notice of the medical profession in England in 1831, and shortly afterwards it attracted some attention in Germany. It was never admitted to the London or British pharmacopœia, and is but little esteemed in medicine.

Description—The entire plant is collected: in the fresh state it is soft and cartilaginous, varying in colour from yellowish-green to livid purple or purplish-brown, but becoming, after washing and exposure to the sun, white or yellowish, and when dry, shrunken, horny and translucent.

The base is a small flattened disc, from which springs a frond or thallus 4 to 6 inches or more in length, having a slender subcylindrical stem, expanding fan-like into wedge-shaped segments, of very variable breadth, flat or curled, and truncate, emarginate or bifid at the summit.

The fructification[4] consists of tetraspores or cystocarps, rising but slightly from the substance of the thallus, and appearing as little wart-like protuberances.

In cold water, carrageen swells up to its original bulk, and acquires a distinct seaweed-like smell. A quantity of water equal to 20 or 30

[1] *Etude sur l'Ergot du Diss*, Alger et Paris, 1863; *Journ. de Pharm.* i. (1865) 444.

[2] *Carrageen* in Irish signifies *moss of the rock*. We learn from an Irish scholar that it would be more correctly written *carraigeen*.

[3] *Plantar. hist. universal.* Oxon. iii. tab. 11.

[4] See Luerssen (quoted at p. 734) i. 124 *et seq.*

times its weight, boiled with it for ten minutes, solidifies on cooling to a pale mawkish jelly.

Microscopic Structure—The tissue of *Chondus crispus* is made up of globular or elongated, thick-walled cells. The superficial layers on both sides of the lobes constitute a kind of peel, easily separable in microscopic sections. The interior or medullary part exhibits a much less densely packed tissue formed of larger cells. The larger cavities of this tissue contain a granular mucilaginous matter, assuming a slight violet tinge on addition of iodine. In water however, the cell-walls swell up so as to form a gelatinous mass, in which separate cells can at last be scarcely distinguished.[1] In the fresh state, its cells also contain granules of chlorophyll imbued with a red matter, termed *Phycoerythrin*. But by washing and exposure to the air, these colouring substances are removed or greatly altered, and are no longer visible in the commercial drug.

Chemical Composition—The constituents of carrageen are those generally found in marine algæ, especially as regards the mucilage. This latter is insoluble in an ammoniacal solution of copper (Schweizer's test); by the action of fuming nitric acid, it yields, in common with gum, an abundance of mucic acid. The mucilage of carrageen, like many similar bodies, obstinately retains inorganic matter; after it had three times been dissolved in water, and as many times precipitated with alcohol, we found it still to yield the same quantity of ash as the raw drug itself, that is to say, more than 15 per cent. The mucilage, perfectly dried, is a tough horny substance, of a greyish colour; it quickly swells up in water, forming a jelly which is precipitable by neutral acetate of lead.

By boiling carrageen for a week with water containing 5 per cent. of sulphuric acid, Bente (1876) obtained crystals of *lævulinic acid*, $C^5H^8O^3$, and an amorphous sugar. The former is also afforded by cellulose of pine wood and by paper.

According to Blondeau,[2] the mucilage of carrageen contains 21 per cent. of nitrogen and 2·5 of sulphur, a statement which we are able to point out as erroneous. We find in it no sulphur, and only 0·88 per cent. of nitrogen. The drug itself yielded us not more than 1·012 per cent. of nitrogen.

When thin slices of the plant are treated with alcoholic potash, and then after washing left for 24 hours in contact with a solution of iodine in potassium iodide, they acquire a deep blue; yet, starch granules are not found in this seaweed. Lastly in connexion with carrageen may be mentioned *Fucusol*, an oily liquid isomeric with furfurol, obtained by boiling seaweeds with dilute sulphuric acid.

Commerce—The plant is collected on the west and north-west coast of Ireland: Sligo is said to be a great depôt for it. Carrageen of superior quality is sometimes imported from Hamburg.

The largest quantities of carrageen, sometimes half a million pounds a year, are gathered near Minot Ledge lighthouse, Scituate, Plymouth

[1] Alcohol, glycerin or a fatty oil are the liquids most suited for the microscopic examination of this drug.

[2] *Journ. de Pharm.* ii. (1865) 159.

county, on the coast of Massachusetts, where a systematic process of preparing it for the market is adopted.[1]

Uses—The mucilaginous decoction and jelly which carrageen affords are popular remedies in pulmonary and other complaints; but as nutriment such preparations are much over-estimated.[2]

Carrageen is sometimes used for feeding cows and calves; and under the name of *Alga marina*, for stuffing mattresses. It is largely used for industrial purposes, like other mucilaginous matter. Its mucilage serves for thickening the colours employed in calico-printing, and as size for paper and for cotton goods. In America it is used for fining beer.

Substitutes—*Gigartina mammillosa*[3] J. Agardh (*Chondrus mammillosus* Grev.) is collected indiscriminately with *Ch. crispus*. It is distinguished from the latter chiefly by having the flat portion of the thallus beset with elevated or stalked tubercles, bearing the cystocarps; but it has the same properties. *G. acicularis* Lamouroux, a species common on the coasts of France and Spain, and having slender cylindrical branches, is occasionally collected along with *Chondrus crispus*. Dalmon (1874) who has examined it, asserts it to be less soluble in boiling water than true carrageen. Small quantities of other seaweeds are often present through the negligence of the collectors.

FUCUS AMYLACEUS.

Alga Zeylanica; Ceylon Moss,[4] Jaffna Moss.

Botanical Origin—*Sphærococcus lichenoides* Agardh. (*Gracillaria lichenoides* Grev., *Plocaria candida* Nees), a light purple or greenish sea-weed, belonging to the class *Florideæ*, occurring on the coasts of Ceylon, Burma, and the Malay islands.[5]

History—Ceylon moss has long been in use among the inhabitants of the Indian Archipelago and the Chinese. It is probably one of the plants described by Rumphius[6] as *Alga coralloides*. In recent times it was brought to the notice of European physicians by O'Shaughnessy.[7]

Description—The plant, which as found in commerce is opaque and white, having been deprived of colour by drying in the sun and air, consists of cylindrical ramifying stems or filaments, $\frac{1}{10}$ of an inch in diameter and from 1 to 6 or more inches in length. The main stems bear numerous branches, simple or giving off slender secondary or tertiary ramifications, ending in a short point. When moistened, the plant increases a little in volume, becomes rather translucent, and

[1] Bates in *Amer. Journ. of Pharm.* 1868. 417; also *Pharm. Journ.* xi. (1869) and viii. (1877) 304.

[2] A person must eat a *pound* of stiff jelly made of the powdered sea-weed before he would have swallowed *half an ounce* of dry solid matter.

[3] Fig. in Luerssen (quoted at p. 734) 126.

[4] For convenience we accept the popular name of *moss*, though it is no longer in accordance with the signification of the word in modern science (see p. 737, note

[5] The *Pharmacopœia of India* (1868) names *Sphærococcus confervoides* Ag. (*Gracillaria* Grev.), a plant of the Atlantic Ocean and Mediterranean, not uncommon on the shores of Britain, as furnishing a portion of the drug under notice. Specimens which we have examined are widely different in structure from *S. lichenoides*, and are apparently devoid of starch.

[6] *Herb. Amboin.* vi. lib. xi. c. 56.

[7] *Indian Journ. of Med. Science*, Calcutta, March, 1834; *Bengal Dispensatory*, 1841. 668.

frequently exhibits whitish globular or mammiform fruits (cystocarps). It is somewhat friable, and after drying at 100° C. may easily be powdered. It is devoid of taste and smell, in this respect differing from most sea weeds.

Microscopic Structure—The transverse section shows a loose tissue made up of large empty cells, enclosed by a cortical zone 30 to 70 mkm. thick. This zone consists of small cells, loaded with globular starch-granules, from less than 1 up to 3 mkm. in diameter, so densely packed as to form what seems at first sight a single mass in each cell. In the larger cells the granules are attached to the walls; they do not display in polarized light the usual cross. The thick walls of the cells show a stratified structure, especially after having been moistened with chromic acid; on addition of a solution of iodine in an alkaline iodide, they assume a deep brown, but the starch-granules, which also abound in the cystocarps, display the usual blue tint.

Chemical Composition—The drug, as examined by O'Shaughnessy, yielded in 100 parts of vegetable jelly 54·5, starch 15·0, ligneous fibre (cellulose ?) 18·0, mucilage 4·0, inorganic salts 7·5.

Cold water removes the mucilage, which, after due concentration, may be precipitated by neutral acetate of lead. This mucilage, when boiled for some time with nitric acid, produces oxalic acid and microscopic crystals of mucic acid (beautifully seen by polarized light), soluble in boiling water and precipitating on cooling. With one part of the drug and 100 parts of boiling water a thick liquid is obtained which affords transparent precipitates with neutral acetate of lead or alcohol, in the same way as carrageen. With 50 parts of water, a transparent tasteless jelly, devoid of viscosity, is produced; in common with the mucilage, it furnishes mucic acid, if treated with nitric acid. Microchemical tests do not manifest albuminous matter in this plant.

Some chemists have regarded the jelly extracted by boiling water as identical with pectin, but the fact requires proof. Payen[1] called it *Gelose*, and found it composed of carbon 42·77, hydrogen 5·77, and oxygen 51·45 per cent. Gum Arabic contains carbon 42·12, hydrogen 6·41, and oxygen 51·47 = $C^{12}H^{22}O^{11}$. Payen's gelose imparts a gelatinous consistence to 500 parts of water; it is extracted by boiling water from the plant previously exhausted by cold water slightly acidulated.[2]

The inorganic salts of Ceylon moss consist, according to O'Shaughnessy, of sulphates, phosphates, and chlorides of sodium and calcium, with neither iodide nor bromide. Dried at 100° C., it yielded us 9·15 per cent of ash.

Uses.—A decoction of Ceylon moss made palatable by sugar and aromatics, has been recommended as a demulcent, and a light article of food for invalids. In the Indian Archipelago and in China, immense quantities of this and of some other species of seaweed[3] are used for making jelly and for other purposes.

[1] *Comptes Rendus*, xlix. (1859) 521; *Pharm. Journ.* i. (1860) 470. 508.

[2] Gelose even in the moist state is but little prone to change, and the jelly made by the Chinese as a sweetmeat which consists mainly of it, will keep good for years.

[3] Consult Martius, *Neues Jahrb. f. Pharm.* Bd. ix. März 1858; Cooke, *Pharm. Journ.* i. (1860) 504; Holmes, *Pharm. Journ.* ix. (1878) 45.

APPENDIX.

SHORT BIOGRAPHIC AND BIBLIOGRAPHIC NOTES,

Relating to Authors and Books quoted in the Pharmacographia. They may be completed by consulting especially the following works:—

CHOULANT, Geschichte und Literatur der älteren Medicin, Part I., Bücherkunde für die ältere Medicin. 1841.

KOPP, Geschichte der Chemie, 4 vols., 1843-1847.

MEYER, Geschichte der Botanik, 4 vols., 1854-1857.

PEREIRA, Tabular view of the history and literature of the Materia Medica, in the "Elements of Materia Medica," vol. ii. part ii. (1857) 836-869.

PRITZEL, Thesaurus literaturæ botanicæ. 1872.

Acosta, Christóbal, physician at Burgos; he travelled in the east and visited Mosambique and Cochin; died A.D. 1580.—*Tractado* de las Drogas y medicinas de las Indias Orientales con sus Plantas debuxadas al biuvo por Christoual Acosta medico y cirujano que las vio ocularmente. Burgos, 1578. Small 4°, 448 pages (and 38 pages indices). There are translations in Latin by *Clusius*, 1582; in Italian, 1585; in French by *Antoine Colin*, 1619, etc.
See pages 154. 423. 462. 503. 565.

Actuarius, Johannes, a physician to the court of Constantinople, towards the end of the 13th century, author of "*Methodus medendi*," and "*De medicamentorum compositione.*" Both these works were repeatedly printed during the 16th century; we are not aware of any recent editions.
See pages 222. 263.

Ægineta—See **Paulos.**

Aëtius of Amida, now Diarbekir, on the upper Tigris. He wrote, probably about A.D. 540-550, Aëtii medici græci ex veteribus medicinæ *Tetrabiblos.* Basileæ, 1542.
See pages 35. 175. 271. 511. 559.

Albertus Magnus (Count Albert von Bollstädt), 1193-1280, a Dominican monk, Bishop of Regensburg (Ratisbon).—Alberti Magni ex ordine Prædicatorum *De vegetabilibus* libri vii., historiæ naturalis pars xviii. Edit. E. Meyer and C. Jessen. 1867.
See pages 543. 568. 678.

Alexander Trallianus, of Tralles, now Aïdin-Güsilhissar, south-east of Smyrna, an eminent physician who wrote about the middle of the 6th century of our era, possibly at Rome.—Alexandri Tralliani medici libri xii. Edit. Joanne Guintero. Basileæ, 1556. 8vo.—An admirable German translation, together with the Greek original, has been published at Vienna, 2 vols., 1878-1879, by Puschmann.
See pages 6. 222. 281. 325. 388. 493. 529. 595. 680.

Alexandria, the Roman custom-house of.
In the Pandects of Justinian there is to be found a curious list of eastern drugs and other articles liable to duty at the Roman custom-house in Alexandria, from the time of Marcus Aurelius and Commodus, about A.D. 176-180. The complete list is reprinted in Vincent, Commerce of the Ancients, ii. (1807) 698; also in Meyer, Geschichte der Botanik, ii. (1855) 167.
See pages 222. 315. 321. 493. 577. 635. 644.

Alhervi. Abu Mansur Movafik ben Ali Alherui, a Persian physician of the 10th century. He compiled a work on medicines and food from Greek, Arabic, and Indian sources, which was published and partly translated by Seligmann: Liber *fundamentorum pharmacologiæ* . . . epitome codicis manuscripti persici bibl. caes. reg. Vienn. Vindobonae, 1830-1833.
See pages 12. 225. 325. 490.

Alkindi. Abu Jusuf Jakub ben Ishak ben Alsabah Alkindi. He wrote about A.D. 813-841 at Basra and Bagdad, about various subjects of natural philosophy, mathematics, medicine, music.
See page 642.

Alphita, a curious list of drugs and pharmaceutical preparations, probably compiled in the 13th century, and originally written in French (according to Häser, Geschichte der Medicin, i. 1875, 648 sqq.). Daremberg, La médecine, histoire et doctrine, 1865, attributes the Alphita to Maranchus.

The Alphita is contained in Salvatore de Renzi's *Collectio Salernitana; ossia documenti inediti* . . . . alla scuola medica Salernitana, iii. (Napoli, 1854) 270-322.

See page 377.

Alpinus, Prosper, 1553-1617, Professor of Botany and "Ostensore dei Semplici," *i.e.* teacher of drugs, in the University of Padua. He visited Egypt in 1580-1583. *De Plantis Ægypti* liber etc. Venetiis, 1592.

See pages 44. 94. 222. 425. 500.

Alrasis or **Arrasi**—See **Rhazes.**

Angelus a Sancto Josepho, originally Joseph Labrousse, of Toulouse, born 1636, died in 1697. He was at Ispahan as a Carmelite monk in 1664, and published in 1681 at Paris a Latin translation of what he called a *Pharmacopœa Persica.* Consult Lucien Leclerc, Histoire de la médecine arabe, ii. (Paris, 1876) 84.

See pages 12. 415. 548.

Anguillara, Luigi (born at Anguillara, died in 1570 at Ferrara), "Ostensor simplicium," *i.e.* professor of materia medica, in the University of Padova; author of *Semplici,* liquali in piu Pareri a diversi nobili huomini scritti apparono. Vinegia, 1561.

See page 303.

Arrianos Alexandrinos—See **Periplus.**

Avicenna. Abu Ali Alhosain Ben Sinâ Albochâri (of Bokhara), 980-1037. A learned philosopher, mathematician, student of medicine, minister, etc., the most celebrated among Arab physicians, their "doctor princeps." His "*Canon medicinæ*" was admired until the end of the 15th century as the most complete system of medicine, of which there are numerous editions, chiefly translations. We have particularly referred to "Avicennæ libri in re medica omnes, lat. redditi a J. P. *Mongio* et J. *Costæo,*" 2 vols. Venetiis, ap. Vinc. *Valgrisium,* 1564.

See pages 12. 31. 125. 161. 225. 393. 429. 490. 642. 716.

Ayurvedas—See **Susrutas.**

Baitar. Abu Mohammad Abdallah Ben Ahmad Almaliqî (of Malaga), called *Ibn Baitar.* He travelled from Spain to the east, lived about 1238–1248 as a physician to the court in Egypt, and died in 1248 at Damascus. His great work on Materia Medica—Liber magnæ collectionis simplicium alimentorum et medicamentorum—has been (very unsatisfactorily) translated into German by Joseph von Sontheimer, 2 vols. Stuttgart, 1840–1842.

See pages 4. 31. 115. 211. 305. 383. 415. 425. 462. 488. 490. 675.

Barbosa, Odoardo (Duarte Balbosa), a Portuguese who visited Malacca before 1511, and accompanied Magalhaes in his famous circumnavigation; killed in 1522 by the natives of the Philippines. Barbosa wrote in 1516 an excellent account of India, published in Ramusio's collection, Delle navigationi et viaggi, &c. Venetia, 1854. Libro di Odoardo Barbosa Portoghese, fol. 413–417. Also in "Coasts of East Africa and Malabar," published for the Hakluyt Society, London, 1866.—Barbosa quotes the prices of many drugs found in 1511–1516 at Calicut. An abstract of this interesting list will be found in Flückiger, Documente zur Geschichte der Pharmacie. Halle, 1876, 15.

See pages 43. 241. 405. 521. 595. 600. 644. 672. 675. 717.

Batutah. Abu Abdallah Mohammed . . . . Allawati Aththangi, called Ibn Batuta, of Tangier, in Morocco. 1303–1377. The greatest of the Arabic travellers; he visited the east as far as the Caspian regions, Delhi, Java, and Pekin, and also Northern Africa as far as Timbuktu.—*Voyages* d'Ibn

Batouta, texte arabe accompagné d'une traduction par C. Defrémerie et B. R Sanguinetti. 2 vols. Paris, 1853–1854.
See pages 404. 511. 521. 577. 669. 672.

Bauhin, Caspar, 1560–1624, professor of anatomy and botany in the University of Basel. See Hess, J. W. Kaspar Bauhin's Leben und Charakter. Basel, 1860. 72 pages.—*Pinax* theatri botanici. Basileæ, 1623.
See pages 31. 86. 388. 429. 439. 731. 740.

Belon, Pierre, 1517–1564, called Belon "du Mans," with reference to his native country near Le Mans, in the ancient province of Maine, France. He travelled in the Levant from 1546 to 1549, and wrote Les observations de plvsievrs *singvlaritez* et choses memorables, trouuées en Grèce, Asie, Iudée, Egypte, Arabie, et autres pays estranges. Paris, 1553.
See pages 175. 222. 254. 598. 615.

Benedictus Crispus (Benedetto Crespo), A.D. 681, Archbishop of Milan, died in 725 or 735.—*Commentarium* medicinale, ed. by Ullrich, 1835, a small pamphlet consisting of 241 verses, in which a few drugs are alluded to.
See pages 282. 463. 493.

Bock—See **Tragus.**

Brunfels, Otto, 1488–1534, originally a Carthusian friar, then a schoolmaster at Strassburg, author of several pamphlets against Catholicism; doctor of medicine, and lastly physician to the republic of Bern. His great work—Herbarum vivæ *eicones*, etc., 3 vol., Strassburg, 1530, 1531, 1536, containing 229 partly excellent woodcuts of plants occurring near Strassburg—is the earliest instance of good botanical figures.—See Flückiger, *Otto Brunfels*, in the Archiv der Pharmacie, vol. *212* (1878) 493–514.
See pages 170. 388. 439. 694.

Brunschwyg, Hieronymus, a surgeon living at Strassburg apparently towards the end of the 15th century. His "*Liber de arte distillandi* de simplicibus, Das buch der rechten kunst zu distilieren . . . ." Strassburg, 1500, with figures, was subsequently brought out in numerous editions and translations. In English: The noble handywork of surgery and of destillation. Southwark, 1525, fol., and The vertuose boke of distillacyon of the waters of all manner of herbes, translate out of duyche. London, 1527, fol.—See Choulant, Graphische Incunabeln für Naturgeschichte und Medicin, 1858–75.
See pages 170. 456.

Camellus or **Camelli**—See **Kamel.**

Camerarius, Joachim, 1534-1598, physician at Nürnberg. *Hortus medicus et philosophicus.* Francofurti, 1588. See *Irmisch*, Über einige Botaniker des 16ten Jahrhunderts. Sondershausen, 1862, 4°. p. 39.
See pages 384. 390. 474.

Cato, Marcus Porcius Cato Censorius, 234-149 B.C. In the book *De re rustica*, the earliest agricultural work in Roman literature, Cato treats of many useful plants, the complete list of which will be found in Meyer's Geschichte der Botanik, i. 342. We have usually referred to *Nisard's* edition in "Les Agronomes latins," Paris, 1877.
See pages 172. 245. 269. 289. 329. 627.

Celsus, Aulus Cornelius; about 25 B.C. to A.D. 50.—A. Cornelii Celsi de medicina libri octo, ed. C. Daremberg. Lipsiæ, 1859. The list of useful plants mentioned by him will be found in Meyer's Geschichte der Botanik, ii. 17.—See pages 35. 43. 179. 234. 291. 439. 493. 677. 680.

Charaka, *i.e.* book of health. An old Sanskrit work, analogous to Susruta's Ayurvedas (see Susruta), yet reputed in India to be older than the latter. Charaka is now being published, since 1868, at Calcutta, and also at Bombay, but is not yet translated in any modern idiom. There are Arabic versions of the end of the 8th century, as stated by Albirûnî in the 11th century, and by Ibn Baitar (see B.) For further particulars consult Roth, *Zeitschrift der Deutschen Morgenländischen Gesellschaft*, xxvi. (1872) 441 *sqq.*

Charlemagne, the great Emperor, 768-814. He ordered, in 812, by the "*Capitulare* de villis et cortis imperialibus," a considerable number of useful plants to be cultivated in the imperial farms. Several other plants are also mentioned, for similar purpose, in the Emperor's "*Breviarium* rerum fiscalium." A full account of both these remarkable documents will be found in Meyer's Geschichte der Botanik, iii. 401-412. See also B. Guérard, Explication du Capitulaire de Villis; Bibliothèque de l'Ecole des Chartes, IV. (1853) 201-247. 313-350. and 346-572.

See pages 92. 98. 172. 179. 245. 269, 308. 329. 488. 542. 545. 627.

Chordadbeh—See **Khurdadbah.**

Circa instans—See **Platearius.**

Clusius, Charles de l'Escluse, born at Arras, in the north of France, A.D. 1526; died A.D. 1609. He lived at Marburg, Wittenberg, Frankfurt, Strassburg, Lyons, Montpellier; travelled in Spain and Portugal; paid, in 1571, a visit to London, and again in a later year. Clusius was, from 1573 to 1587, the director of the imperial gardens at Vienna, and from 1593 to 1609 professor of botany in the University of Leiden. Among the works of this eminent man the most important, from a pharmaceutical point of view, are: 1. Aliquot *notæ* in Garciæ aromatum historiam. Antverpiæ, 1582. 2. *Rariorum plantarum historia.* Antv., 1601. 3. *Exoticorum libri decem.* Antv., 1605.—See Morren, Charles de l'Ecluse, sa vie et ses œuvres. Liége, Boverie, No. 1, 1875, 59 pp.

See pages 17. 21. 73. 83. 96. 202. 211. 254. 272. 287. 390, 401. 425. 429. 453. 521, 589. 648. 657.

Collectio Salernitana—See **Alphita.**

Columella, Lucius Junius Moderatus. Born at Cadiz; he wrote between A.D. 35 and 65 the most valuable agricultural work of the Roman literature: "*De re rustica* libri xii." It has been translated by *Nisard*, together with Columella's book, "*De arboribus*," for Firmin Didot's "Agronomes latins." Paris, 1877. The list of the numerous plants mentioned by Columella will be found in Meyer's Geschichte der Botanik ii., 68.

See pages 97. 245. 664.

Constantinus Africanus. Born at Carthage in the second half of the 10th century. A physician who spent his life in travels in the east and in studies in the medical school at Salerno (see S.), and in the famous Benedictine Abbey of Monte Cassino; died A.D. 1106. He transmitted the medical knowledge of the Arabs to the school of Salerno, of which he may be called the most distinguished fellow. See *Steinschneider* in *Virchow's* Archiv für patholog. Anatomie und Physiologie, *37* (1866) 351; and in *Rohlfs'* Archiv für Geschichte der Medicin, 1879, 1-22. Steinschneider shows that Constantin's work, De Gradibus, is chiefly based on that of *Ibn-al-Djazzâr*, who died about A.D. 1004.

See pages 130. 211. 377. 494. 573. 584. 600.

Conti, Niccolò dei. A Venetian merchant, who spent 25 years (from 1419 to 1444 ?) in India. His interesting accounts are by far the most valuable of that period. They have been published for the Hakluyt Society (ed.

by Major): India in the 15th century, Lond., 1857, 39 pp. A still more valuable edition and translation is due to Kunstmann: Kenntniss Indiens im 15ten Jahrhunderte. München, 1863. 66 pp.

See pages 282. 521. 577. 582, 636.

Cordus, Valerius. Born A.D. 1515 at Erfurt, professor of materia medica in the University of Wittenberg, then the most eminent man in that science. After his premature death, at Rome, in 1544, his works were published by *Conrad Gesner*, in a large volume printed in 1561 at Strassburg. It contains: (1) Valerii Cordi *Annotationes* in Dioscoridem; (2) *Historiæ stirpium* libri iv.; (3) De artificiosis *Extractionibus*, and several other papers of V. Cordus, besides the most remarkable book, *De Hortis Germaniæ*, by *Conrad Gesner* himself. A very careful biographic notice on *Cordus* is due to Irmisch, Einige Botaniker des 16 Jahrhunderts . . . Sondershausen, 1862. 4°. pp. 1-34.

See pages 31. 148. 170. 248. 260. 429. 526. 580. 644. 648. 650. 661. 713, 733. 737.

Cosmas—See **Kosmas**.

Crescenzi, Piero de', 1235-1320. He wrote, about A.D. 1304-1306, at Bologna, an esteemed book on agriculture, which was repeatedly printed towards the end of the 15th century, for instance, Opus *ruralium commodorum* Petri de Crescentiis, Argentine, 1486. There are numerous later translations and editions.

See pages 6. 157. 180. 661.

Dale, Samuel, a physician in London, 1659-1739. *Pharmacologia* seu manuductio ad Materiam medicam. Lond., 1693, 12mo.

See pages 592. 615. 616. 648. 681. 731.

Dioscorides, Pedanios, of Anazarba, in Cilicia, Asia Minor. He wrote, about A.D. 77 or 78, his great work on materia medica, the most valuable source of information on the botany of the ancients.

See pages 6. 35. 43. 92. 97. 147. 161. 166. 172. 175. 179. 183. 234. 262. 276. 291. 292. 305. 310. 321. 325. 328. 331. 377. 384. 388. 434. 439. 464. 486. 493. 503. 519. 529. 556. 558. 567. 568. 581. 594. 609. 627. 638. 644. 655. 661. 664. 672. 675. 677. 680. 690. 699. 715. 723. 728. 729. 733.

Dodonæus, Rembert Dodoens, 1517-1585, physician at Malines, Belgium.

See pages 303. 388. 439. 699. 729. 731.

Edrisi, or Alidrisi, an Arab nobleman, born about A.D. 1099 in Spain, living at King Roger's court, Palermo, where he compiled, in 1153, his remarkable geographical work. It summarizes all the earlier geographic literature of the Arabs, adding much valuable information gathered by the author from merchants and other travellers.—*Géographie* d'Edrisi, traduite en français, par P. Amedée Jaubert, 2 vols. Paris, 1836-1840. *Description* de l'Afrique et de l'Espagne, trad. par Dozy. Leyde, 1866.

See pages 115. 305. 316. 494. 503. 577. 584. 642. 644. 680.

Fernandez, latinized **Ferrandus.** Born at Madrid 1478. From 1514 to 1525 he was "veedor de las fundiciones do oro de Tierra-firma in America," *i.e.* superintendent of the foundries of gold in the American continent; died 1537 in Valladolid. *Historia general y natural de las Indias* islas y tierra firme del mar oceano por el Capitan *Gonzalo Fernandez de Oviedo y Valdés*, primer chronista del nuevo mundo. Publ. dal codice orig. y illustr. p. J. *Amador de los Rios.* This complete edition has been published in 4 vols., from 1853 to 1855, by the Academy of Madrid. We have not seen the earlier partial editions, viz. "*Summario* de la natural y general Historia de las Indias," Toledo, 1526, fol., "*Primera parte* de la Historia natural y general de las Indias," Sevilla, por *Cromberger*, 1535, fol.; nor "Cronica de las Indias," 1547. See also Colmeiro, La Botanica y los Botánicos de la peninsula Hispano-Lusitana, Madrid, 1858, 26, No. 220 (*Fernandez*) and 149; also *Haller*, Bibl. botanica, i. 272, who calls him *Gundisalvus* or *Gonsalvus Hernandez*. He is also quoted by others as *Oviedo*.

See pages 95. 101. 186. 213. 453, 466. 534.

Fuchs, Leonhard, 1501-1566, Professor of medicine in the University of Tübingen from 1535 to 1566, author of De *historia stirpium* commentarii insignes . . . . Basileæ, 1542, fol., a work equally remarkable for the excellent woodcuts and the careful descriptions.

See pages 170. 429. 453. 456. 469. 652.

Galenos, Claudius Galenus Pergamenus, A.D. 131-200, a most distinguished medical writer, imperial physician at Rome. Many drugs and officinal plants are mentioned in his numerous works, which were held in the highest reputation during the middle ages.

See pages 35. 222. 268. 503. 519. 559. 609.

Garcia—See **Orta**.

Gerarde, John, 1545-1607, London, surgeon.—The *Herball*, or generall historie of plantes, 1597.

See pages 31. 71. 170. 218. 254. 268. 453. 459. 480. 486. 487. 537. 552. 568. 589. 611. 655. 661. 694. 700. 729.

Gesner, Conrad, 1516-1565, Zürich, the most learned naturalist of his time (See also Cordus).

See pages 299. 384. 390. 439, 456.

Helvetius, Jean-Claude-Adrien, 1661-1727, physician at Paris.

See pages 26. 371.

Hernandez, Francisco, physician to King Philip II. of Spain; he lived about the years 1561-1577 in Mexico.—Quatro libros de la naturaleza y virtutes de las plantas y animales que estan recevidos en el uso de medicina en la Nueva España . . . . Mexico, 1615.—We have only referred to Antonio Reccho's translation: Nova plantarum, animalium et mineralium Mexicanorum Historia, rerum medicarum Novæ Hispaniæ *Thesaurus*. Romæ, 1651, fol. (first edition, 1628). Hernandez must not be confounded with *G. Fernandez de Oviedo* (See *Fernandez*).

See pages 202. 206. 657.

Hildegardis, 1099-1179, the abbess of the Benedictine monastery St. Ruprechtsberg, near Bingen ("Pinguia") on the Rhine. Her "*Physica*," one of the most interesting mediæval works of its kind, is contained in tom. cxcvii. (1855) 1117-1352 of *J. P. Migne's Patrologiæ cursus completus*, under the name "Subtilitatum diversarum naturarum creaturarum . . . . . Liber i. De Plantis.

See pages 305. 378. 476. 512. 551. 584.

Ibn Baitar—See **Baitar**.

Ibn Batuta—See **Batuta**.

Ibn Khordadbah—See **Khurdadbah**.

Idrisi—See **Edrisi**.

Isaac Judæus, or Abu Jaqûb Ishaq . . . . , an Egyptian Jew, living at Kâirowan, in Northern Africa, as a physician to the prince of the Aglabites; died about A.D. 932-941. See Choulant, *Bücherkunde für die ältere Medicin*, 1841, 347; also Meyer, Geschichte der Botanik, iii. 170.

See pages 217. 225. 325. 377.

Isidorus, Hispalensis, Bishop of Sevilla, about A.D. 595-636, author of a great cyclopœdia, *Etymologiarum* libri xx. We have referred to it in "Sancti Isidori Opera omnia," in the vol. lxxxii. (1859) of J. P. Migne's Patrologiæ cursus completus.
See pages 305. 380. 493. 529. 664.

Istachri, Abu Ishaq Alfarsi Alistachri (*i.e.* of Istachr, the ancient Persepolis, in the Persian province Fars). His geographical work has been translated (in the Transactions of the Academy of Ham) by Mordtmann: Das *Buch der Länder* von Schech Ebn Ishak el Farsi el Isztachri. Hamburg, 1845.
See pages 316. 414. 716.

Kamel (or **Camellus**), George Joseph, born at Brünn, Moravia, A.D. 1661, a member of the company of Jesus A.D. 1682. By permission of his superiors, he left in 1688 for the Marianne islands and the Philippines. After having acquired a certain knowledge of botany and pharmacy, he established, at Manila, a pharmaceutical shop with the view of supplying medicaments gratis to the poor; he died there in 1706. Kamel communicated his botanical investigations to *Ray* and *Petiver* (see R.); consult also A. de *Backer*, Bibliothèque des Ecrivains de la compagnie de Jésus, iv. (Liége, 1858) 89.
See pages 148. 432.

Kämpfer, Engelbert. Born in 1651 at Lemgo, Westphalia; travelled as a physician in Persia (1683-1685), India, Java, Siam (1690), Japan (1690-1692); graduated in 1694 at Leiden, and died in 1716 at Lemgo. His work, *Amœnitatum* exoticarum fasciculi v., Lemgo, 1712, was intended as a specimen of more elaborate accounts of the various observations of the well-informed and zealous author. But only a *History and description of Japan* was published in German in 1777, by Dohm at Lemgo. Kämpfer's unpublished manuscripts and collections were purchased, in 1753, by Sir Hans Sloane, for the British Museum.
See pages 20. 44. 167. 263. 272. 315. 512. 513. 527.

Kazwini, an Arabic geographer of the 13th century.—Ethé, Kazwini's *Kosmographie*. Leipzig, 1869.
See pages 503. 521. 573.

Khurdadbah or Ibn-Chordadbeh, engaged, towards the end of the 9th century, in the police and postal administration of Mesopotamia, and collecting informations about the products and tributes of the empire of the Khalifes. They are translated by Barbier du Meynard: Le *livre des routes et des provinces*, par Ibn Khordadbeh. Journal asiatique, v. (1865) 227-296 and 446-527.
See pages 282. 512. 518. 573. 577. 642.

Kosmas Alexandrinos Indikopleustes, a Greek merchant, a friend of Alexander Trallianus (p. 752), living in Egypt, travelling in India, and lastly, towards the middle of the 6th century, a monk. His monstrous work, *Christiana topographia*, contains, nevertheless, a small amount of valuable information. We referred to it as contained in Migne's Patrologiæ cursus completus, series græca, t. lxxxviii. (1850) 374.
See pages 281. 577. 599.

Lefebvre or Le Fèbre, Nicolas, 16..-1674, Paris (partly also London), "Apoticaire ordinaire du Roy, distillateur chymique de sa Majesté"—*Traité de la Chymie*, Paris, i. (1660) 375-377.
See pages 65. 381.

Liber pontificalis seu de gestis Romanorum pontificum. Romæ, 1724 (edition of *Vignolius*). A new edition will be brought out in the Monumenta Germaniæ.
See pages 137. 142. 281.

Macer Floridus, wrote, A.D. 1140, the book *De viribus herbarum*. The editio princeps was printed A.D. 1487 in Naples; the best edition is that of Choulant, Leipzig, 1832 (140 pages). Nothing exact is known about that author himself.
See pages 627. 642. 684.

Marcellus Empiricus, a high functionary of the two emperors Theodosius, towards the end of the 4th and in the beginning of the 5th centuries.—De *medicamentis* empiricis, physicis ac rationalibus liber. Basileæ, 1536.
See pages 183. 729.

Marcgraf, Georg, 1610-1644, astronomer and geographer to Count Johann Moriz von Nassau. See Piso.
See pages 187. 211. 228. 371.

Masudi, or Almasudi, Maçoudi. A.D. 900-958. Born at Bagdad, travelled in Arabia, India, and in the East of Africa. One of the distinguished geographic writers of the Arabs. His works are being published by the Société asiatique of Paris: *Les Prairies d'Or*, texte et traduction par Barbier de Meynard et Pavet de Courteille, 8 vols., 1869-1873 (in continuation).
See pages 503. 573. 584. 600. 680.

Mattioli, Pierandrea. Born in 1501 at Siena; living as a physician at Trento, Görz, Prag; died A.D. 1577. There are many editions of his chief work, *Commentarii* in sex libros Pedacii Dioscoridis Anazarbei de medica materia. The first, in Italian, was published in 1544 at Venice.
See pages 32. 147. 183. 390. 439. 456. 609. 650.

Meddygon Myddvai—See **Physicians.**

Mesuë, the younger. Jahjâ ben Mâsaweih ben Ahmed. . . . Born at Maredin, Kurdistan, physician to the Khalif Alhakem at Cairo; died A.D. 1015.
See pages 40. 225. 493.

Monardes, Nicolás, 1493-1588, physician at Sevilla.—Historia medicinal de las cosas que se traen de nuestras Indias occidentales, que sirven en medicina. Sevilla, 1569. Latin edition by Clusius, *De simplicibus medicamentis* ex occidentali India delatis, quorum in medicina usus est. Antverp. 1574. See Hanbury's appreciation of the book: Pharm. Journ. i. (1870) 298.
See pages 148. 202. 206. 443. 466. 534. 537. 697. 705.

Mutis, José Celestino, 1732-1808; 1760, physician to the viceroy of New Granada; 1782, in charge of an "expedicion real botanica" of that country. See Triana's work, quoted at page 369. Triana much reduces, apparently with good reason, the merits of Mutis, which would appear to have been overrated by Humboldt.
See pages 106. 345.

Nikandros Kolophonios, of Klaros, near Kolophon in Ionia, in the 2nd century B.C. Physician and poet.
See page 6.

Nostredame, Michel de. Born 1503 at Saint-Remi, Provence. Physician and astrologer at Aix and Lyons; died A.D. 1566 at Salon, Provence.
See page 405.

Oribasios Pergamenos, a friend and physician to the emperor Julianus Apostata, 4th century. We referred chiefly to *Bussemaker* et *Daremberg*, Oeuvres complètes d'*Oribasius*, 6 vols., 1851-1876.
See pages 35. 129. 175. 183. 222. 559. 729.

Orta, Garcia de, or Garcia ab Horto. (Years of birth and death unknown.)

He was a student of medicine and natural sciences in the Universities of Salamanca and Alcalá, and a teacher and physician in the University of Coimbra (or Lissabon ?). In 1534 Garcia accompanied Martim Affonso de Souza, grand admiral of the Indian fleet, to Goa, and lived there as a royal physician (Physico d'El Rey) to the hospital. Garcia appears to have been still living there in 1562, when he obtained the vice-regal privilege for his book "*Coloquios* dos simples e drogas he cousas mediçinais da India, e assi dalguãs frutas achadas nella ande se tratam. . . . Impresso em Goa, por Joannes de endem as × de Abril de 1563," 436 pp., 4°. (British Museum).—F. A. von Varnhagen has caused the Coloquios to be reprinted in 1872 at Lisbon. Garcia de Orta's Coloquios are, notwithstanding the utterly diffused style of the work, a precious source of information on eastern drugs. They had the good chance to be translated, as early as the year 1567, by Clusius, who omitted the insignificant parts of the book, re-arranged it conveniently, and added valuable notes. See Flückiger in Buchner's Repertorium für Pharmacie, xxv. (1876) 63-69.

See pages 43. 86. 130. 154. 200. 225. 241. 272. 405. 415. 429. 462. 512. 521. 527. 547. 585. 638. 644. 712.

Oviedo, Capitan Gonzalo Fernandez de Oviedo y Valdés—See **Fernandez.**

Palladius, Rutilius Taurus Aemilianus, an agricultural author of the 4th or 5th century of our era, living probably in northern Italy. We have chiefly referred to *Nisard's* edition of the fourteen books of Palladius "*De re rustica,*" which is contained in Firmin Didot's "Les Agronomes latins," Paris, 1877.

See page 328.

Parkinson, John, 1567-1629 (?), an apothecary of London, and director of the Royal Gardens at Hampton Court. *Theatrum botanicum,* or an herball of large extent. . . . . London, 1640. fol.

See pages 84. 189. 287. 429. 469. 470. 500. 556. 589. 616. 623. 648. 698. 731.

Paulus Ægineta (Paulos Aiginetes), a physician of the first half of the 7th century of our era, who appears to have lived for some time at Alexandria. Author of "seven books" on medicine, which have been first published, in Greek, in 1528 at Venice, and, in Latin, in 1532 at Paris, translated by Winter (Guinterus) of Andernach: *Compendii* medici libri septem. We have also referred to the translation of Adams.

See pages 3. 35. 175. 183. 271. 281. 559. 563.

Pavon, José, a Spanish botanist, who explored in common with Ruiz the flora of Peru. Biographic particulars about Pavon are wanting even in Colmeiro's La botánica y los botánicos de la peninsula Hispano-Lusitana, Madrid, 1858. 181.

See pages 345. 590.

Paxi or **Pasi,** Bartolomeo di; the author of a curious book giving practical information about the weights and measures in use in various countries. There are many editions, the first of which, as examined in 1876 by one of us (F.A.F.) in the library of San Marco, Venice, is found to bear the following title:—"Qui comincia la utilissima opera chiamata *Taripha,* la qvel tracta de ogni sorte de pexi e misure conrispondenti per tuto il mondo fata e composta per lo excelente e eximio Miser Bartholomeo di *Paxi* da Venezia. Stampado in uenezia per Albertin da lisona uercellese regnante l inclyto principe miser Leonardo Loredano. Anno domini 1503. A di 26 del mese de luio."

See pages 235. 609.

Peres—See Pires.

Periplus Maris Erythræi, a survey of the Red Sea and the Indian Ocean as far as the coast of Malabar. In his interesting account, written about between A.D. 54 and 68, the author, commonly called Arrian of Alexandria, gives a list of imports and exports of the various places which he had visited or of which he had good informations. See *Vincent*, Commerce and Navigation of the Ancients, etc. London, vol. i. (1800), ii. (1805); also C. *Müller*, Geographi græci minores, i. (Paris, 1855) 257-305. Anonymi (*Arriani* ut fertur) Periplus maris erythræi.

See pages 35. 142. 272. 493. 520. 529. 577. 599. 664. 675. 680. 715.

Physicians of Myddvai (Meddygon Myddfai). Rhys Gryg (*i.e.* the Hoarse), prince of South Wales (died in 1233 at Llandeilo Vawr), had his domestic physician, namely Rhiwallon, who was assisted by his three sons Cadwgan, Gruffydd, Einion, from a place called Myddvai, in the present county of Caermarthen. They made a collection of recipes, the original manuscript of which is in the British Museum. Another collection has been compiled, from the original sources, by Howel the Physician, son of Rhys, son of Llewelyn, son of Philip the Physician, a lineal descendant of Einion, the son of Rhiwallon. Both these compilations have been published at Llandovery in 1861, together with a translation, by John Pughe, under the above title (470 pp.)

See pages 6. 40. 65. 71. 141. 157. 161. 170. 180. 299. 305. 310. 316. 334. 380. 383. 393. 401. 450. 464. 469. 476. 488. 556. 625. 635. 642. 652.

Pires, Tomé (or Pyres, Pirez, as he also writes his name himself), a Portuguese apothecary. He was the first ambassador sent, probably in 1511, from Europe, or at least from Portugal, to China. Pires addressed, in 1512-1516, several letters from Cochin and Malacca to the Admiral Affonso d'Albuquerque and to King Manuel of Portugal. One of them, written January 27, 1516, from Cochin to the King, enumerates many drugs which were to be met with in that place—"dando l-lhe noticias das drogas da India," says the writer. This letter, still existing in the Real y Nacional Archivo da Torre do Tombo (corpo chronologico, part i. fasc. 19, No. 102), was communicated in 1838 by Bishop Condo Don Francisco de San Luiz to the Portuguese Pharmaceutical Society, and published in their "Jornal de Socied. Pharm. Lusit. ii. (1838) 36." It will also be found in the pamphlet[1] "Elogio historico e noticia completa de Thomé Pires, pharmaceutico e primeiro naturalista da India; e o primeiro embaixador europeo a China. Memoria publicada na Gazeta de Pharmacia por Pedro José da Silva." . . . Lisboa, 1866. 47 pp. ("y 22 fac simile de sua signatura"). We had, moreover, before us an authentic copy of the letter under notice, obligingly written 1st December, 1869, for one of us by Senhor Joaquim Urbano de Veiga, the Secretary of the Sociedad Pharmaceutica Lusitana. According to *Colmeiro*, La Botánica y los Botánicos de la Península Hispano-Lusitana, Madrid, 1858. 148, Peres was attached to the factory of Malacca as a "scribano" (secretary?) and "por tener conocimientos farmacéuticos," and was sent to China, with the character of an ambassador, in order to examine more freely the plants. He was imprisoned, says Colmeiro, at Pekin, and there died soon after 1521 in prison. Yet *Abel Rémusat*, in the 34th volume of the "Biographie universelle" (1823), p. 498, and also in his "Nouveaux mélanges asiatiques" ii. (1828) 203, states that Pires proceeded first to Canton, and reached Pekin in 1521. From this place he was sent to Canton and imprisoned for many years from political causes. He was still living in 1543.

See pages 43. 255. 681.

[1] Library of the Pharm. Soc. of Great Britain, London, among the "Pamphlets, No. 30" (Sept. 1878).

Piso, Willem. The Dutch, having conquered in 1630 from the Spanish the north-eastern part of the Brazilian coast, between Natal and Porto Calvo, Count *Johann Moriz von Nassau-Siegen* was appointed, in 1636, Governor-General of these possessions. He left them in 1644; the history of his reign is contained in the work of *Barlæus*, Rerum per Octoennium . . . gestarum . . . historia, Amstelodami, 1647. The Count had also instituted a scientific exploration of the environs of Pernambuco (or Recife), his residence, by his physician *Piso* and *Marcgraf*, the friend of the latter (see M.), who lived also at the Count's court. They devoted several years (from 1638 to 1641) zealously to their task. The results of their investigations are found in—(1) Historia naturalis Brasiliæ, published by Joh. de Laet, Lugd. Bat., 1643. (2) Pisonis de *medicina brasiliensi* libri iv., et G. Marcgravii *historiæ rerum naturalium Brasiliæ* libri viii. Lugd. Bat., 1648. (3) Pisonis de *utriusque Indiæ historia naturali* et *medica* libri xiv. Amstelodami, 1658.

See pages 27. 113. 114. 130. 152. 211. 228. 371. 591.

Platearius, Matthæus, one of the most distinguished writers of the famous medical school of Salerno, about the middle of the 12th century. He compiled the remarkable dictionary of drugs, "Liber de simplici medicina," which was extremely appreciated during the next centuries, and even reprinted as late as the beginning of the 17th century. The work begins with a definition of the signification of the term Simplex medicina; it is in these words: *Circa instans* negotium de simplicibus medicinis nostrum versatur propositum. Simplex autem medicina est, quae talis est, qualis a natura producitur: ut gariofilus, nux muscata et similia. . . . . The work of Platearius is therefore usually quoted under the name *Circa instans*. The list of the 273 drugs enumerated in "Circa instans" will be found in Choulant (*l.c.* at p. 751), p. 298. We have referred to "Circa instans" as contained in the volumes—Dispensarium magistri Nicolai præpositi ad aromatarios, Lugduni, 1517, or Practica Jo. Serapionis, Lugd. 1525.

See pages 225. 316. 581.

Plinius (Cajus Plinius Secundus), A.D. 23-79, the well-known author of the "*Naturalis historiæ* libri xxxvii." We have particularly used *Littré's* translation, "Histoire naturelle de Pline," published in 2 vols. by Firmin Didot, Paris, 1877.

See pages 6. 35. 43. 97. 147. 161. 179. 234. 276. 281. 291. 305. 310. 325. 329. 333. 377. 434. 439. 474. 486. 488. 493. 503. 519. 529. 543. 556. 558. 576. 595. 609. 627. 644. 661. 664. 672. 677. 680. 729. 733.

Plukenet, Leonard, 1642-1706, physician, director of the Royal gardens, London; collector of a large herbarium still existing in the British Museum.

See page 16.

Polo, Marco, a noble Venetian, the most famous among mediæval travellers. He spent 25 years, from 1271 to 1295, in Asia, chiefly in China. The account of his travels was written, in French, in 1298, by *Rusticiano* of Pisa, and published since in numerous translations and abstracts. We have chiefly referred to the two following excellent works: (1) *Pauthier*. Le livre de *Marco Polo*, publié pour la première fois d'après trois manuscrits inédits de la Bibliothèque impériale de Paris, 1865. (2) *Yule*. The book of Ser Marco Polo the Venetian, concerning the kingdom and marvels of the East, with notes and illustrations. 2 vols. London, 1871, second edition 1874.

See pages 200. 282. 494. 510. 512. 520. 584. 636. 717.

Pomet, Pierre, "marchand épicier et droguiste à Paris, ruë des Lombards, à la Barbe d'Or."—Histoire générale des drogues, 1694, fol. 528 pages, 400 engravings. There are later editions in 2 vols., 4°; that of 1735 by the author's son, an "apotiquaire" at St. Denis. See *Hanbury's* appreciation of the book, Pharm. Journ. i. (1870) 298.

See pages 21. 26. 73. 118. 126. 148. 260. 263. 479. 617. 623. 648. 657.

Porta, Giovanni Battista, 1539(?)-1615, a distinguished Napolitan nobleman. Of his remarkable works we have before us—*De distillatione*, lib. ix. Romæ 1608, 154 pp. It is partly contained also in Porta's Magiæ naturalis libri xx, 1589, yet not in the earlier editions of the Magia, the first of which appeared in 1558. Another work of the same author, the *Phytognomica*, Naples, 1583, may be mentioned as one of the chief works treating on the "Doctrine of Signatures." There are several editions of it, usually containing the curious figures of the tubers of orchids as especially connected with that superstitious doctrine.

See pages 118. 263. 385. 479. 526. 580. 653. 655.

Præpositus, Nicolaus, one of the eminent physicians of the school of Salerno (see S.) living in the first half of the 12th century. He gives in his *Antidotarium*, first edition, Venetiis 1471, the composition of about 150 medicines, which were much used, under his name, during the following centuries. They are enumerated in Choulant's book, mentioned p. 751 before.

Pun-tsao, a great Chinese herbal, written by *Le-she-chin*, in the middle of the 16th century. It consists of 40 thin octavo volumes, the first three of which contain about 1,100 woodcuts. For more exact information consult *Hanbury*, Science Papers, 212 et seq.

See pages 4. 76. 83. 167. 510. 520.

Ramusio, Giovanni Battista.—Terza editione delle navigationi e viaggi raccolti già da G. B. Ramusio, 3 vol. fol. Venetia, 1554. A valuable collection of accounts of mediæval travellers, chiefly Italian.

See page 4.

Ray (Wray, or Rajus) John, 1628-1705, a clergyman and distinguished botanist. His Herbarium is preserved in the British Museum. Historia plantarum, 3 vols., folio, London, 1686-1704.

See pages 254. 277. 481. 482. 615. 731. 740.

Redi, Francesco, a physician of Arezzo, who lived at Florence. *Esperienze* intorno a diverse cose naturali e particularmente a quelle che ci son portate dell' India. Firenze, 1671.

See pages 24. 111. 287.

Rhazes (Abu Bekr Muhammad ben Zakhariah Alrazi) from Raj, in the Persian province Chorassan, where he was a physician to the hospital and subsequently at Bagdad; died A.D. 923 or 932.

See pages 3. 271. 393. 642. 716.

Rheede tot Draakestein, Hendrik Adriaan van, 1636-1691, Dutch governor of Malabar. He ordered the most conspicuous plants of India to be figured and to be described, mostly by Jan Commelin, professor of botany at Amsterdam. This great and valuable work is the *Hortus indicus malabaricus*, 12 vols. folio, Amstelodami 1678-1703, with 794 plates.

See pages 130. 189. 211. 297. 403. 421. 425. 547. 565. 580. 644. 677. 726.

Ricettario Fiorentino; one of the earliest, if not the very first, printed Pharmacopœia published by authority. It bears title: Ricettario di dottori dell' arte, e di medicina del collegio Fiorentino all' instantia delli Signori Consoli della universita delli speciali. Firenze, 1498. Folio. We have referred to the edition of 1567, printed at "Fiorenza, Nella Stamperia dei Giunti 1574." There are other editions of that Florentine Pharmacopœia down to the year 1696.

See pages 40. 410. 706.

Roteiro. The account of the famous expedition of *Vasco da Gama* to the Cape (22nd November, 1497), due to one of his companions, *Alvaro Velho*. The author enumerates in his remarkable pamphlet (see title at page 496) several spices and drugs of India, stating their prices there and in Alexandria. See also *Heyd*, Geschichte des Levantehandels, ii. (1879) 507.
See pages 404. 496.

Ruel, or **Ruellius,** also **de la Rouelle,** Jean. 1474-1537. Physician at Soissons, lastly canon at Paris. De natura stirpium libri iii. Parisiis, 1536. Folio. (See also *Scribonius Largus.*)
See pages 31. 388.

Ruiz, Hipolito. 1754-1816. A Spanish botanist, in 1777 appointed director of the celebrated exploration of Peru and Chile. (See also Pavon.)
See pages 79. 345. 590.

Rumphius (Rumpf), Georg Eberhard, 1627-1702. Dutch governor of Amboina. He figured and described 715 plants of that island in the Herbarium amboinense, 7 vols., Amstelodami, 1741-1755, folio, 696 plates.
See pages 130. 189. 211. 278. 297. 336. 421. 565, 600. 673. 726. 749.

Saladinus, of Ascoli (probably Ascoli di Satiano in the Capitanata, Apulia), physician to one of the Princes of Tarentum (and apparently also to the grand constable of Naples, Prince Giovanni Antonio de Balzo Ursino). He is the author of the "*Compendium aromatariorum* Saladini, principis tarenti dignissimi medici, diligenter correctum et emendatum. Impressum in almo studio Bononiensi, 1488;" 4°. 58 pages. Further on, the author calls himself Dominus Saladinus de Esculo, Serenitatis Principis Tarenti phisicus principalis. At the end of his pamphlet he gives the list of drugs "communiter necessariis et usitatis in qualibet *aromataria* vel *apotheca.*" . . . . This book intended for the druggists, *aromatarii,* was written between A.D. 1442 and 1458, as shown by Hanbury, Science Papers, 358.
See pages 148. 183. 225. 377. 388. 456. 582. 585. 600.

Salerno, the school of medicine. During the middle ages, from about the 9th century, there were flourishing in the said Italian town a large number of distinguished medical practitioners and teachers. It is one of their merits to have transmitted the medical art and knowledge of the Arabs to mediæval Europe.—See also *Alphita, Constantinus Africanus, Platearius, Nicolaus Præpositus.* That once famous institution continued an obscure existence even down to the year 1811, when it was suppressed, November 29th, by order of Napoleon.—See pages 31. 225. 321. 334. 377. 690.

Sanudo, Marino, a well informed Venetian writer, author of (1) Vite de *duchi* di *Venezia,* in Muratori, Scriptores rerum italicarum xxii. (Mediolani, 1733) 954 et seq. (2) *Marinus Sanutus* dictus *Torsellus* Patricius Venetus, *Liber Secretorum* fidelium crucis super terræ sanctæ recuperatione et conservatione, in Orientalis Historiæ, tom ii. (Hanoviæ, 1611) 22; lib. i. part i. cap. 1. The latter work contains, at page 23, a classified list of eastern drugs; among the most valuable spices, Sanudo mentions cloves, cubebs, mace, nutmegs, spikenard; among those less costly, cinnamon, ginger, olibanum, pepper.
See pages 245. 636.

Scribonius Largus, a Roman physician of the first century of our era. He accompanied, in A.D. 43, the emperor Claudius when he attempted the definite conquest of the island of Britain. Scribonius is the author of the valuable book, *Compositiones Medicamentorum* seu Compositiones medicæ, the earliest edition of which is due to Ruel, Paris, 1529.
See pages 6. 35. 42. 147. 179. 219. 245. 331. 493. 503.

Simon Januensis—See pages 6. 44. 582. 652.

Sloane, Sir Hans, 1660-1753. In 1687 physician to the governor of Barbados and Jamaica. His library and large collections of natural history formed the nucleus of the British Museum. He wrote (1) *Catalogus* plantarum quæ in insula Jamaica sponte proveniunt vel vulgo coluntur . . . . . adjectis aliis quibusdam, quæ in insulis Maderæ, Barbados, Nieves et St. Christophori nascuntur, Londini, 1696. (2) A *voyage* to the islands Madera, Barbados, Nieves, St. Christophers and Jamaica. London, 1707-1725, fol.
See pages 18. 73. 188. 203. 288. 591. 615. 629. 710.

Susruta. The author of "*Ayurvedas*," *i.e.* the book of health, an old Sanskrit medical work in which a large number of eastern drugs are mentioned. It was first printed in the original language at Calcutta, 2 vols., 1835-1836, and afterwards translated under the name *Susrutas Ayurvedas*, id est medicinæ systema a venerabili *D'hanvantare* demonstratum, a Susruta discipulo compositum. Nunc primum ex Sanskrita in Latinum sermonem vertit . . . . Fr. Hessler, Erlangæ, 3 vols., 1844-1850. And by the same translator, Commentarii et annotationes in Susrutæ ayurvedam, 1852-1855. Susruta was once supposed to have written centuries before Christ, but chiefly the researches of Prof. Haas, London, in the *Zeitschrift der Deutschen Morgenländischen Gesellschaft*, xxx. (1876) 617 *sqq.* and xxxi. (1877) 647, make it not improbable that the Sanskrit "Susruta" might have been generated from the Greek Hippokrates by way of the intermediate form "Bukrat." The oldest testimony as to the time of Susruta (and Charaka, see before) is the statement of Ibn Abu Oseibiah, in the 13th century, that Susruta had been translated into Arabic about the end of the 8th century.
See pages 154. 188. 211. 225. 295. 315. 421. 425. 436. 503. 547. 572. 644.

Tabernæmontanus, Jacob Theodor, physician at Heidelberg; died A.D. 1590. A pupil of Tragus.—Neuw Kreuterbuch, Frankfurt, 1588, folio; second part, 1591, both with fig. Later editions, also in German, by Caspar Bauhin and Hieronymus Bauhin. Latin translation, Eicones plantarum seu stirpium . . . Francofurti, 1590, with 2225 engravings.
See pages 308. 390. 731.

Talbor, or also **Tabor,** Robert, 1642-1681. This singular personage having been apprenticed to Dear, an apothecary of Cambridge, settled in Essex, where he practised medicine with much success. He afterwards came to London, and in 1672 published a small book called Πυρετολογία, *a rational account of the cause and cure of agues* (London, 12°). As stated at page 344, he was appointed physician to the king, and on 27th July of the same year, received the honour of knighthood at Whitehall. But he was not a member of the College of Physicians; and to save him from attack, Charles II. caused a letter to be written restraining that body from interfering with him in his medical practice. (Baker, *l.c.* at page 344, note 1). The appointment as royal physician, made in consideration of "good and acceptable services performed," led to the issuing of a patent under the Privy Seal, dated 7th August, 1678, granting to Sir Robert Talbor an annuity of £100 per annum, together with the profits and privileges appertaining to a physician in ordinary to the sovereign. In 1679 Talbor visited France and Spain, as recorded in the *Recueil des nouvelles* etc. pendant l'année 1679 (Paris, 1780) 466 (this includes the *Gazette de France*, 23rd Sept., 1679). The journey to Spain he made in the suite of the young queen of Spain, Louise d'Orléans, niece of Louis XIV., of whom he is described as *premier médecin*. During Talbor's absence, his practice in London was carried on by his brother, Dr. John Talbor, as is proved by an advertisement in the *True News or Mercurius Anglicus*, January 7-10, 1679.

In France Talbor had the good fortune to cure the Dauphin of an attack of fever, and also treated with success other eminent persons. (See *Lettres de Madame de Sévigné,* nouv. ed. tome v., 1862, 559 ; also tome vi., letters of 15th and 29th Sept. and 6th Oct. 1679.) The physicians both in England and France were exceedingly jealous of the successes of an irregular practitioner like Talbor, and averse to admit the merits of his practice. Yet D'Aquin, first physician to Louis XIV., prescribed *Vin de Quinquina,* as well as powdered bark, for the king in 1686.—See J. A. Le Roi, J. *Journal de la santé du roi Louis XIV.*, Paris, 1862. 171. 431. But Talbor's happy results brought him into favour with Louis XIV., who induced him, in consideration of a sum of 2,000 louis d'or and an annual pension of 2,000 livres, to explain his mode of treatment, which proved to consist in the administration of considerable doses of cinchona bark infused in wine, as will be seen in the pamphlet : *Les admirables qualitez du Kinkina confirmées par plusieurs expériences,* Paris, 1689. 12°. Talbor did not long enjoy his prosperity, for he died in 1681, aged about 40 years. He was buried in Trinity Church, Cambridge, where a monumental inscription describes him as—"*Febrium malleus*" and physician to Charles II., Louis XIV., and the Dauphin of France. In Talbor's will, proved by his widow, Dame Elizabeth Talbor, alias Tabor, relict and executrix, 18th Nov. 1861, and preserved at Doctors' Commons, mention is made of an only son, Philip Louis.

See page 344.

Theophrastos Eresios, of Eresos, in the island of Lesbos, about 370-285 B.C. The earliest botanical author in Europe, having consigned in his works, written about the year 314 B.C. or later, an admirable amount of excellent observations, either of his own, or, as many suggest, originated from Aristotle. Among the numerous editions of Theophrast's works (printed as early as A.D. 1483) we may point out Wimmer's Latin translations, tom. i. *Historia plantarum,* tom. ii. *De Causis plantarum.* Leipzig, 1854 ; or the French edition of the same translator, Théophraste, Œuvres complètes. Paris, 1866, Firmin Didot.

See pages 42. 97. 136. 142. 146. 147. 161. 166. 175. 179. 234. 259. 292. 310. 321. 393. 418. 439. 519. 529. 567. 576. 595. 598. 620. 644. 661. 664. 677. 690. 715. 723. 733.

Tournefort, Joseph Pitton de, 1656-1708. Important as are his attempts to establish a scientific classification of plants, his merits as a careful observer (1700-1702) of eastern plants are of still more weight from a pharmaceutical standpoint. The latter is evidenced by his Relations d'un *voyage* du Levant. . . . . Paris, 1717, 2 vols.

See pages 163. 175.

Tragus (Bock), Hieronymus, 1498-1554. A friend and pupil of Brunfels (see B.), protestant clergyman at Hornbach, near Zweibrücken, Bavarian Palatinate. He gave remarkably good descriptions of the indigenous plants, with figures, in his "*Kreuterbuch,*" the best edition of which was published in German at Strassburg, A.D. 1551, and a translation in 1552: Hieronymi Tragi, de stirpium, maxime earum quae in Germania nostra nascuntur usitatis nomenclaturis, etc. libri tres.

See pages 170. 295. 384. 388. 434. 450. 456. 469. 540. 665. 676. 694. 699. 731. 734.

Turner, William, born at Morpeth, Northumberland (date not known), died 1568. In 1538 he was a student of theology and medicine in Pembroke College, Cambridge. Turner lived many years in Germany, and was an intimate friend of *Conrad Gesner.* The "New *Herball,* wherein are

contayned the names of herbes in Greeke, Latin, ... and in the potecaries and herbaries . . . . with the properties etc., by William Turner, London, 1551; the seconde parte, Collen (Cologne), 1562; the third parte, London, 1568," is the earliest scientific work on botany in the English literature. To its author is also due the foundation of the Kew Gardens.
See pages 292. 378. 480. 556. 568. 571. 729.

Vasco da Gama—See **Roteiro.**

Vegetius Renatus. A treatise on veterinary medicine, written apparently about the beginning of the 5th century of our era, is attributed to an author of the above name. See *Choulant*, p. 223 of the work quoted before (p. 751).
See pages 175. 380.

Vignolius—See **Liber pontificalis.**

Vindicianus, physician to the Emperor *Valentinianus* I., about A.D. 364-375. For further information see *Choulant's* work (quoted at p. 751), p. 215; also *Haller*, Bibl. bot. i. 151.
See page 559.

INDEX.

Natural Orders are printed in small capitals, as ACANTHACEÆ: headings of articles in thick type, as **Ammoniacum**.